Soldiers of the Cross

Blessed Francis Xavier Seelos and the Catholic Community in Annapolis During the Civil War

Soldiers of the Cross

Blessed Francis Xavier Seelos and the Catholic Community in Annapolis During the Civil War

Robert L. Worden

St. Mary's Parish
109 Duke of Gloucester Street
Annapolis, Maryland 21401–2528

Soldiers of the Cross: Blessed Francis Xavier Seelos and the Catholic Community in Annapolis During the Civil War

Printed by
Gatekeeper Press
7853 Gunn Hwy., Suite 209
Tampa, FL 33626
www.GatekeeperPress.com

First printing, 2024

Book design by Jerri Anne Hopkins

Library of Congress Control Number: 2022912351

ISBN: 9781662953101

On the cover: *Stained glass window in St. Mary's Church, dedicated to Father (now Blessed) Francis Xavier Seelos, St. Mary's Church, produced by Cathedral Stained Glass Studios of Cheltenham, Pennsylvania, and installed in 1979. Digital photo by Malcolm Dax, Signcraft, Annapolis, Maryland.*

In the name of the Father and the Son and the Holy Spirit. Amen.

Roman Catholics begin personal devotions, public worship, and even some temporal actions with this brief invocation. They did so in the past and will do so in the future. In traditional religious settings and ceremonies, especially in the days of the Latin-language Church, they more likely said . . .

In nomine Patris et Filii et Spiritu Sancti. Amen.

But in the multilingual Redemptorist and lay Catholic communities of Civil War-era Annapolis, one also might have heard the native language of the supplicant say . . .

Im Namen des Vaters und des Sohnes und des Heiligen Geistes. Amen.

among the Alsatian-, Austrian-, Bohemian-, German-, or Swiss-born; or perhaps . . .

In de Naam van de Vader en van de Zoon en van de Heilige Geest. Amen.

which was used by the Dutch priests, or the following may have been heard among the French and Belgian confreres, parishioners, or visitors:

Au nom du Père et du Fils et du Saint-Esprit. Amen.

In a rare instances, Irish forebears in Annapolis, who secretly maintained their Gaelic roots from the British overlords, might have begun their prayers with . . .

In ainm an Athar agus an Mhic agus an spioraid Naoimh. Áiméin.

And maybe, just maybe, men and women who in their hearts held memories of their African Catholic ancestors' native Swahili, may have quietly said:

Kwa jina la Baba na ya Mwana na ya Roho Mtakatifu. Amina

To all these prayerful persons—past, present, and future—this book is dedicated, as well as to all others seeking to learn of the works, joys, and travails of the tumultuous period of the American Civil War as it was experienced by the Catholic community in Annapolis and its environs.

Foreword

As pastor of St. Mary's, I am very grateful to Robert Worden for inviting me to write the foreword for this book. Since the earliest days of the Catholic missionary efforts to North America until the present, only fifteen men and women who served the Lord in America have been officially declared saints or been beatified. Two of these fifteen, Blessed Francis Seelos and St. John Neumann, are associated with St. Mary's. They were members of the Redemptorist Congregation founded by St. Alphonsus Liguori in 1732 in Naples, Italy. Blessed Francis Seelos considered St. John Neumann a spiritual a father to him. Both figure in this book.

In his previous book, *Saint Mary's Church in Annapolis, Maryland: A Sesquicentennial History, 1853–2003,* Dr. Worden, a parishioner since 1971 and an excellent historian, focused on the life and ongoing development of the parish during those 150 years. St. Mary's has been mother church to many parishes in Anne Arundel County and the Eastern Shore of Maryland and priests assigned here during the Civil War reached out with mission activities throughout the North and into Virginia and North Carolina. A particular area that brought Dr. Worden to his present writings was the fascinating account of Father Seelos going to Washington, D.C. in 1863 to meet with President Abraham Lincoln to speak about the Redemptorist seminarians, brothers, and priests confronted with the ongoing draft of Union soldiers during the Civil War. Throughout the war, it seemed that the seminarians, brothers, and priests at St. Mary's, including Father Seelos, might be drafted into the army.

The author's interest in the meeting between Father Seelos and President Lincoln led him into further studies of the Maryland, Anne Arundel County, Annapolis, and the United States Naval Academy, as well the Redemptorists of St. Mary's and its parishioners during the Civil War. Even before then there was a lingering movement of anti-Catholicism tinged with bigotry toward the waves of immigrants coming to America that had an impact on St. Mary's. When war came, Marylanders were deeply divided as to whether the state should join the Confederacy or remain in the Union. Although there was a large population of free African Americans, there were also enslaved people in Maryland. President Lincoln and the Federal government were determined to keep Maryland in the Union lest Washington be surrounded by Confederate states. The Naval Academy moved to Newport, Rhode Island, to avoid possible capture by southern forces. At times during the war, there were tens of thousands of Union soldiers in Annapolis and its surrounding areas. There was one instance in which the people of Annapolis believed that they were to be attacked by the Confederate army. Redemptorists and parishioners were involved in the preparations. Fortunately, this attack did not happen.

Before, during, and after the war, St. Mary's was the seminary for the Redemptorists and many generations of young men were trained here to be religious brothers and priests. At one point, there were more than eighty novices, seminarians, brothers, and priests living at St. Mary's. The priests taught the students, served local parishioners, and did heroic work caring for paroled, wounded, sick, and dying Union soldiers.

As I reflected upon the challenges Marylanders faced during the Civil War, I see our nation today is facing similar challenges. We Americans have strong divisions among ourselves over politics, the COVID-19 pandemic, racial equality, culture, crime, immigration, the power of secularism, and issues of the protection of life. In the time of the Civil War, many Catholics found strength in their families, in their neighbors, and in the faith. I believe that same reality is true for the parishioners of St. Mary's today as they continue to find comfort and grace in their parish community.

I have been a vowed Redemptorist for more than fifty years. As I read about the Redemptorists who went before me, and the zeal of these men, many of whom are buried in the Carroll Gardens cemetery overlooking Spa Creek, I take both inspiration and pride in these confreres. Among the many interesting vignettes the author shares is one of the great tragedies in our American Redemptorist history: the drowning of five Redemptorists in a boating accident in 1866.

As a Catholic, as a Redemptorist, as a man who loves American history, as a priest now serving in the city of Annapolis, Dr. Worden's excellent research brought alive to me the reality of what it was to live in Annapolis in the midst of the American Civil War. It was a trip I very much valued for my present reality of being a newly commissioned Annapolitan. Thank you, Robert.

Rev. Patrick Woods, C.Ss.R.
Pastor, St. Mary's Parish
109 Duke of Gloucester Street
Annapolis, Maryland 21401-2528

Contents

Introduction

This book is not about battles, victories, or defeats, nor about the generals or admirals who waged the war, although some of them are mentioned to provide context to story. Rather it is about a time of war and how a particular community coped with it. The book investigates how Roman Catholic clergy and residents of Annapolis and Anne Arundel County, Maryland, dealt with what the Civil War brought onto their doorsteps and into their daily lives. Union military forces occupied their city, county, and state. Residents had to survive four years of social and political upheaval, deal with economic opportunity and loss, and witness the end of the more than two-hundred-year-old culture of slavery. Day-to-day life continued despite battles waged nearby, in western Maryland and northern Virginia. Annapolis was not on the war front, but it was a massive staging and training ground for Union troops preparing for battle and the location of army hospitals and parole camps. A new cemetery was established just beyond the city limits for soldiers who did not survive their wounds or disease.

The central focus of this book is the local Catholic congregation. It included Black and White, free and enslaved, rich and poor, those in professional occupations and trades, enslavers, business owners, laborers, farmers, housewives, domestic servants, native and foreign born, soldiers and sailors and civilians, and Union and Confederate sympathizers. There also was a large community of men devoted to religious life. Life went on for this religious community and sacraments continued to be observed at St. Mary's, the only Catholic church in Anne Arundel County. Infants, children, and converted adults were baptized throughout the war. Youngsters and adults received First Communion, confessed their sins, and were confirmed. People of all ages attended Mass and other religious observances. Couples married and started families. Individuals, including soldiers, received the last rites of the church and were buried in the parish and military cemeteries. The parish—then and now—was administered by the Congregation of the Most Holy Redeemer (Congregatio Sanctissimi Redemptoris, or C.Ss.R.), commonly known as Redemptorists. Their principal occupation in Annapolis was running St. Mary's College, initially their American novitiate and then their seminary or house of advanced studies. During the war, hundreds of men entered, studied, taught, and worked in the college. Thirty-eight seminarians completed their theological studies and were ordained as priests during the war.

Although the men and women associated with St. Mary's during the Civil War were united in a common religious faith, many had opposing political beliefs and diverse economic, cultural, and racial backgrounds. Some members of this congregation are referred to as *residents* because not all were recognized as *citizens*. Some were of foreign birth and had not been naturalized through court action. The other non-citizens were people of color, both free and enslaved, whose rejected status had been confirmed in 1857 by the infamous Supreme Court *Dred Scott v. Sandford* decision. White women had the same civil rights as White men under the US Constitution, except they were not enfranchised. Black men and women held in bondage had no civil rights. Free Black men and women were only marginally better off in the eyes of the law. Mention is made of non-Catholic spouses and parents who are considered in this book as "associates" of the parish.

This book is the history of these lay men, women, and children and the Redemptorists in wartime and the decade preceding. It is a statement of facts, and some suppositions based on available evidence. It is in no way an espousal of racist statements quoted from the period local press or enunciated by officials. Their words are as they appeared in print, correspondence, diaries, and journals. The book gives readers an opportunity to consider the harmful implications of mid-nineteenth-century prejudices and the context in which they were displayed.

The idea for this book emerged after I completed *Saint Mary's Church in Annapolis, Maryland: A Sesquicentennial History, 1853–2003*. That book summarized the history of Catholicism in Maryland since its founding in 1634 and described Catholic developments in Anne Arundel County and Annapolis between 1695 and 1853, during which time the small Catholic community was served as a mission by itinerant Jesuits. Most of the book covered the period from 1853, with the arrival of the Redemptorists, to 2003, the one hundred and fiftieth anniversary of St. Mary's establishment as a formal parish. The Civil War years were briefly reviewed and, when the book was complete, a file folder of Civil War information was left for future possible use.

Research on this book began in 2008. Initially, I envisioned an article about the fifteen-month tenure (June 1862–September 1863) of Blessed Francis Xavier Seelos, rector of the Redemptorist community in Annapolis and pastor of St. Mary's. His life in Annapolis, his parochial ministry, and especially his face-to-face meeting with President Abraham Lincoln and other high officials in July 1863, piqued my interest. These activities alone are a story worth telling, as a measure of the man's leadership and spiritual development during wartime. But, while seeking information on Seelos, I found relevant information about other wartime Annapolis Redemptorists. Day-to-day life in Annapolis outside the Redemptorist seminary—involving the Catholic laity and their families—also came into focus. An account of St. Mary's laity, their involvement in parish life, and in their day-to-day lives in the larger community during wartime begged to be included. The Redemptorists also interacted with Catholics and potential converts in rural Anne Arundel County and well beyond. Thus I found four groups whose stories emerged and are worth telling: the Redemptorists operating within their religious community and college and serving as parish and missionary priests; local Catholic parishioners, some of whom had non-Catholic spouses; Catholics and potential converts in near and distant mission stations; and military men who were in Annapolis because of the war, as well as those who "went South." Some of these stories may be familiar; others have never been told in a historical work.

Although the Redemptorists were not officially commissioned as chaplains, they ministered to soldiers in local camps of instruction, hospitals, and parole camps during the war and more distantly in Virginia and North Carolina. Some years ago, a scholar developed a comprehensive list of 3,694 Civil War Catholic and Protestant chaplains; only two Redemptorists, both of whom served the Confederacy, were listed. Not being commissioned chaplains, none of the Annapolis Redemptorists were identified. A more recent effort is aimed at correcting that omission.[1]

Annapolis at the onset of the war was a town abandoned by the Naval Academy and occupied by the Union army. The city of slightly more than 4,500 residents grew to a transient population of tens of thousands of soldiers heading to the war front as well as those returning as wounded survivors of battles or paroled prisoners of war. With them came physicians, nurses, news correspondents, family members, sutlers, and other wartime camp followers. Some St. Mary's parishioners were pro-Union, others pro-secession. Some supported Maryland staying in the Union but were not opposed to the establishment of the Confederacy. Pro-South did not necessarily mean pro-slavery; some Unionists were enslavers and rejected abolition. And pro-South did not necessarily mean pro-Confederacy. Many were simply advocates of traditional Southern culture, including the baggage of slavery as protected by the United States Constitution. The Redemptorists were under strict orders to abstain from political discussions among themselves and with others. They did, however, take actions concerning their enrollment for the draft and possible military service as contrary to their conscientious scruples against bearing arms. Taking all this into consideration, there was a larger story to tell and the full concept for this book finally emerged.

This history is presented as both a chronological and subject-oriented narrative. Part One (chapters 1 and 2) is an antebellum prologue, reviewing the decade before the Civil War and discussing the local effects of the anti-Catholic, anti-foreigner Know Nothing era and the growth of the parish. Part Two (chapters 3 through 7) covers the war year-by-year and introduces numerous vignettes of situations confronting religious and laity alike. Part Three (chapters 8 and 9) is an epilogue that discusses the return to post-war normalcy and describes the legacy left by Civil War-era Catholics in Annapolis. Central to the entire story is the presence in Annapolis of the Redemptorists who served both parishioners and, as de facto chaplains, ministered to soldiers. The personal story of Blessed Francis Xavier Seelos, a man of great faith who is destined for formal sainthood, is woven throughout the chapters.

Research for this book included parish, city, county, state, and Federal government, and religious order records. A major resource was the *Chronica Domus C.Ss. Red. Annapoli*—the Redemptorists' Latin-language handwritten house chronicle that provides day-to-day on-site record of the seminary and, occasionally, parish activities. It is an invaluable and irreplaceable resource on the lives of the men at St. Mary's College and the parishioners during the Civil War. The *Chronica Domus* is supplemented with provincial annals, chronicles of other Redemptorist houses, individual personnel files, letters, newspapers, and other period sources. A review of modern-day scholarly literature provides the context of where St. Mary's and Annapolis fit into a larger picture.

No comprehensive list exists of men who were at St. Mary's College during the Civil War. The annual and sometimes semi-annual "Familia Domus" in the *Chronica Domus* and daily *Chronica Domus* entries were used to develop a list of the names of these men who came to Annapolis to enter the novitiate or continue their seminary studies, as well as those assigned as faculty and staff members of the college or who visited St. Mary's during the Civil War. Other Redemptorist archival sources, such as ledgers of investitures, professions, and ordinations, were consulted to verify a presence in Annapolis during the war.[2] Even if a man departed the novitiate before investiture or profession, he was listed as a Redemptorist community member in this inventory, which came to include the names of 293 men.

Similarly, no census of St. Mary's parishioners exists for the Civil War period. The first extant enumeration of St. Mary's parishioners dates to 1874 when the Archdiocese of Baltimore initiated its required annual "Notitiae."[3] So, I made a comprehensive review of the parish sacramental records for the years 1851–66 to determine who St. Mary's parishioners were during the Civil War. An infant baptized in the 1850s and still living during the war qualified as a child parishioner and was included. His or her parents were added to the list unless one or the other or both were noted as non-Catholic or one was a member of another denomination, in which case only the Catholic parent was listed. Godparents may or may not have been local residents and could have been out-of-town aunts, uncles, or friends. Sometimes the godparent's domicile was listed in the baptismal register, which helped determine whether or not they might have been a St. Mary's parishioner. Since there were no other Catholic parishes in Anne Arundel County at the time, anyone associated with St. Mary's and residing in Anne Arundel County was included in the list. Persons of African ancestry are almost always noted as "colored" or "Negro" and sometimes their enslaved (*servus* or *serva)* or free (*liberus* or *libera*) status was recorded. Scholars who have studied Southern sacramental registers report that some non-Catholic free Blacks had their children baptized in Catholic churches so they could obtain a written record of their "free" status as a safeguard against enslavement.[4] That also may have happened at St. Mary's. Although some Southern dioceses required separate registers for White and Black, St. Mary's kept only one set and recorded sacraments in chronological order while noting those who were Black.

Confirmation, marriage, and interment records also were valuable in list building because they indicated a person's presence in or around Annapolis. Individuals who did not appear in the sacramental registers but were discovered in 1850 and 1860 Federal census records as members of known local Catholic families were added to the list. Persons of more than five years of age enumerated in the 1870 census, or who were mentioned in contemporary documentation, also were added to the list. Some men in the sacramental records were Union soldiers who were in local army hospitals or camps and were baptized, confirmed, or married at St. Mary's, or buried in Annapolis after having received the last rites from a St. Mary's priest. There were other Catholic locals or soldiers who were not baptized, confirmed, married, or died during the period of consideration and whose names thus do not appear in the parish registers or any other St. Mary's context. Thus, an complete count would be much larger but impossible to make.

Other documentation consulted in compiling the parishioner list included historical newspapers and various government records. Several stories provided by current-day St. Mary's parishioners whose ancestors lived in Annapolis during the Civil War added key insights. Numerous other primary and secondary sources also were consulted and their information was collated into biographical data for 1,622 parishioners and associates. When combined with the biographic data developed for the 293 men identified at St. Mary's College between 1860 and 1866, numerous Civil War stories emerged from this wealth of disparate information.

During the fiftieth jubilee of St. Mary's Parish, Father Joseph Wissel, C.Ss.R., made an interesting observation about the Redemptorist college. He was the last surviving founder of the Redemptorist community in Annapolis in 1853. In 1903 Wissel addressed a church full of religious and laity on the many benefits the Redemptorists had received or given during those fifty years. In tracing this history, he recalled that:

> The Civil War began, battles were fought, soldiers marched over the length and breadth of the country north and south, but all this did not cause the slightest interruption to the religious training of the young men dwelling in that house.[5]

While I hesitate to quibble with this long-deceased eyewitness, the Redemptorists' own records from the Civil War era demonstrate that there were events that caused far more than "the slightest interruption." Furthermore, I was initially cautioned by other scholars that I might not find much new information on the Annapolis Redemptorists during the Civil War. This too turned out to not be true. Many previously untold facts emerged during the course of my research. What is related here, I hope, will leave the reader with an appreciation of the diversity, adversity, and opportunities faced by the Redemptorists and the Catholic laity of Annapolis and Anne Arundel County during the American Civil War. It is a story worth telling.

As a final introductory note, please be aware that words that were underlined in original documents and publications have been replaced here with italics to indicate when the writer used underlining for emphasis or foreign-language words. In some instances, especially in handwritten correspondence, it is unclear whether the sender or the recipient did the underlining. Such emphases have been left intact and rendered in italics. Correspondence received by government officials and official registers and letter books often have underlining in colored ink or pencil to draw attention to a personal or place name and for indexing purposes. Such underlining has been ignored. Unless generally accepted in English-language usage, foreign-language words have been italicized.

Readers of this book are encouraged to consult the endnotes. They include the source of information used and sometimes provide details that interrupted the flow of the text but are of potential value to readers and researchers.

Robert L. Worden
Annapolis, Maryland
March 1, 2023

Illustration credits, with the exception of the priest portraits on pages 232–33, are noted in the captions. The portraits on pages 232–33 are from the Redemptorist Archives of the Baltimore Province (RABP), except that of Father Wendelin Guhl on page 233. His portrait is from the *Brooklyn Daily Eagle,* May 30, 1898.

Prelude

A small figure bent over the granite stone set into the northeast corner of its foundation. His eyes glanced over the simple inscription: "1858." The master of ceremonies handed him the *aspergillum* to sprinkle holy water, and he proceeded, with appropriate prayers, to bless the cornerstone. The actions of the little man could hardly be seen by most of the observers. The assemblage of priests, novices, and numerous others surrounding him was obscured further by umbrellas held aloft to keep dry the Most Reverend John Nepomucene Neumann, bishop of Philadelphia. A Naval Academy observer reported that the day "commenced with rain and a stiff breeze from the S.E. Rain continued to fall until about 1 P.M." The local press reported that "the rain fell in torrents all the morning." And one of the participants in the event later recalled that "it rained terribly, very terribly. . . and all of us were thoroughly soaked" that Tuesday morning, May 11, 1858.[1]

The heavy rain cut short the cornerstone ceremony but the event was not without appropriate rites. Prior to Bishop Neumann's blessing, the rector of St. Mary's and the force behind building the new church, Father Michael Müller, C.Ss.R., celebrated a solemn High Mass in the old church some 130 yards to the west. He was assisted by Bishop Neumann's traveling companion, Redemptorist Father Aegidius Smulders, who served as deacon. Father John Henry Cornell, St. Mary's newly assigned young priest and music director, was subdeacon and Father Louis H. Claessens, a professor of philosophy at the Redemptorists' house of higher studies in Cumberland, Maryland, was master of ceremonies. Smulders gave a discourse "on the sublime dignity of the Holy Catholic Church." *The Maryland Republican*, a local weekly, reported that "a most able and instructing and eloquent discourse was delivered by Rev. F. Smulders, explanatory of the various forms and ceremonies on the occasion of the laying of a Corner Stone of a Catholic Church, which was listened to with marked attention."[2]

Bishop John Neumann, C.Ss.R. blessing the cornerstone of St. Mary's new church, May 11, 1858. Original art by Constance D. Robinson.

The same newspaper revealed that "a very long concourse of people had assembled" for the event and that they "marched with a band of music to the spot designated for the ceremonies." Although there is no record of who attended besides the principal clergy, it is likely that the entire Redemptorist community was present, including Jacob Engel, a not-too-shy Bavarian Redemptorist lay brother. Also probably attending was John Michael Himmelheber, a Bavarian-born engineer and stone mason who had accompanied the Redemptorists to Annapolis in 1853 and who most likely carved the cornerstone. Others who may have attended were Elihu Samuel Riley Sr., a trustee of the church and editor of the *Maryland Republican*; Dr. Edward Sparks, a Catholic physician, and his Episcopalian wife, Rosetta; Colonel John Walton, proprietor of the City Hotel and the wealthiest St. Mary's parishioner; Andrew Edward Denver, a Naval Academy watchman; Thomas G. Ford, assistant librarian of the Naval Academy; David Caldwell, a Calvert Street lumber merchant; Henry Holmes Treadway, a master carpenter, and his wife Emma; Alida Yates Leavenworth Roca McParlin, an Army surgeon's wife; housewife Anna Wells; Mary Anne Revell, whose son James had been the private secretary to Governor Thomas Watkins Ligon; John Mullan, a retired army sergeant from Fort Severn and his sister-in-law, Catherine Bright, a recent convert; Mary Seager, whose husband taught drawing at the Naval Academy; and Julia Ann Daley, wife of the county tax collector. All these people, and others, had donated money to purchase three new bells for the church that would be blessed by Bishop Neumann in 1859. And, perhaps, Mary Effine Lake, a free Black and owner of a popular fancy goods shop, and her husband Moses, a barber at the Naval Academy, or Rachel Teresa Smothers, a Catholic slave owned by a wealthy Episcopalian family, stood at the edge of the crowd, watching the momentous event. All of these people, and many more, played parts in the story of St. Mary's Parish during the soon-to-begin Civil War.[3]

Part One — Antebellum

Chapter 1: 1853–59 — Always Consecrated to Religion

Progress and Change in Maryland

Antebellum Maryland was a place of continuity and change. It was evolving from a largely agrarian Southern state with traces of its colonial heritage to a more heterogenous "border state" between North and South. Clipper ships, steamboats, railroads, canals, major roads, and telegraph lines connected the diverse parts of Maryland, from its Atlantic Ocean coast to Chesapeake Bay to the Appalachians. Manufacturing, extractive industries, and diversified farming had attracted both domestic and foreign migration to the northern and western parts of the state, which, in turn, brought further population growth and economic development. As one of the nation's major ports, Baltimore flourished in the first half of the nineteenth century. More westerly cities, such as Frederick, Hagerstown, and Cumberland, also became important centers of industry and population. Maryland's population grew by almost 50 percent between 1840 and 1860, some from natural increase but mostly from domestic and foreign migration. Pennsylvanians and others moved into the northern tier of Maryland, bringing additional labor, new investment, and less dependence on and inclination toward slavery. Political upheaval and famine in Europe sent legions of German and Irish immigrants flooding into Baltimore. Some remained, increasing the state's White population, while others moved westward.

In 1860 Maryland had 14,000 enslavers holding more than 87,000 men, women, and children in bondage. Maryland also had the largest free Black population in the United States—nearly 83,000 persons, 12 percent of the state's population—a situation that stimulated runaways, manumissions, and increasing freedom for Blacks as slavery declined in economic importance. Southern Maryland remained more static. Traditional tobacco farming, heavy with slave labor, was predominant in the southern counties (see map, "Anne Arundel County, 1860–65"). The Eastern Shore of Maryland, on the other side of Chesapeake Bay, also had large numbers of slaves, substantial old plantations, newer truck farms, and small towns that provided emerging urban amenities.[1]

Maryland political life also was changing. Old-line families and slave-owning southern and Eastern Shore counties had long controlled the politics of Maryland but the decline of the conservative Whig Party in the 1840s brought about political instability in Maryland. This instability, in turn, led to the enactment of a new reformist state constitution in 1851, which stimulated further change. It diminished the old disproportionate representation among the free White male voters in southern Maryland. Baltimore City and the western counties gained additional seats in the General Assembly. Curbs were put on the legislature's spending and many positions formerly appointed by the governor were made elective. The system of rotating the governorship and appointive offices among the northern, western, eastern, and southern regions came to an end. The Whig Party disintegrated, with some of its former adherents teaming with Democrats to support "fusion" candidates. The Democrats retained the Maryland governorship in 1851 (as they had for most of the 1840s) and carried the state in the presidential election of 1852, which Franklin Pierce won by a landslide.[2]

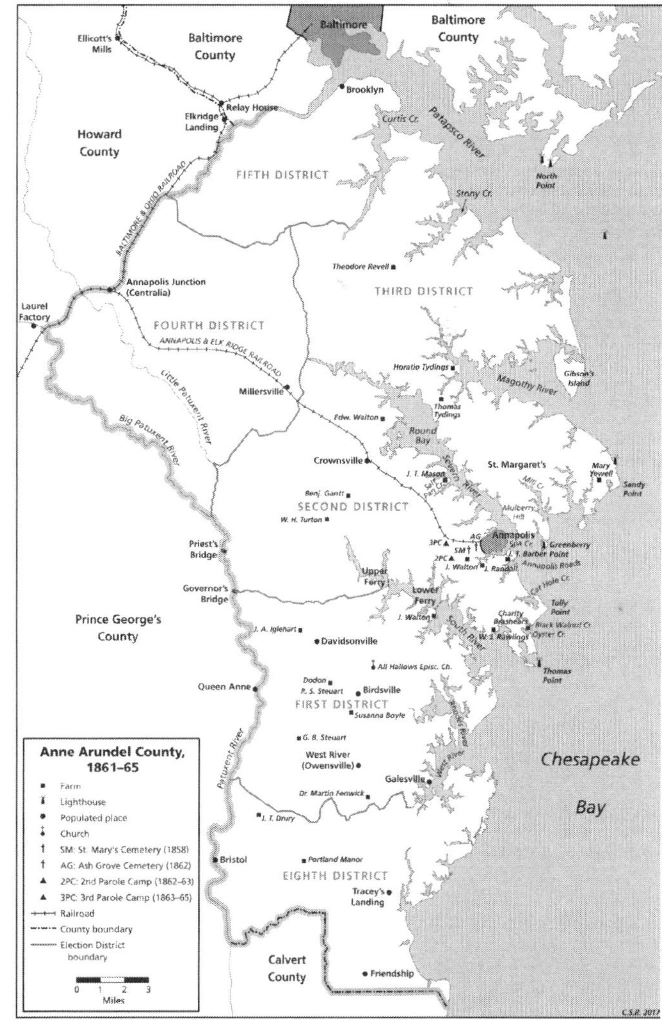

Discontent with evolving societal change had been occurring since the early nineteenth century. Many native-born Christians were uneasy with the growing Jewish population in Baltimore and very unhappy with the increasing European Catholic and other foreign migrations into Baltimore and throughout the state. They found sustenance in banding together against the dual threat to their way of life brought by "Romanists" and foreigners, who were usually seen as allied with the Democrats. As happened throughout the United States among like-minded nativists, Marylanders—many of whom were former Whigs—joined secret societies that avoided sharing information about themselves by saying they "knew nothing" about nativist schemes. They were called Know Nothings by their detractors but became powerful, eventually emerging politically as the American Party, which, by 1856, had become Maryland's leading political party. By 1858 the party gained control of Maryland's executive and legislative branches, an ominous development for Catholics and immigrants.[3]

From Mission to Parish

Annapolis in the 1850s was a small port city with a mostly Protestant population among both its White and Black, free and enslaved population. It was the seat of state and county governments and the location of a public liberal arts college, St. John's. Annapolis became even more cosmopolitan in 1845 with the establishment of the United States Naval Academy on the site of the US Army's Fort Severn. This was the setting into which a band of largely German-born Catholic religious men arrived in 1853. The property they took charge of was the gift to the Redemptorists in 1852.

Prior to 1853, Jesuit priests had been ministering to the Annapolis Catholic community since 1694/95, when the provincial capital relocated from St. Mary's City. They visited Annapolis on an occasional basis from southern Maryland and the Eastern Shore to celebrate Mass in the private chapel of Charles Carroll, "the Settler," the wealthy Irish-born but politically disenfranchised former provincial attorney general and staunch Catholic. By 1728 the Jesuits had a new establishment—White Marsh in Prince George's County—sixteen miles west of Annapolis. From there, on a monthly basis, they served the Carroll family chapel in Upper Marlborough, in Prince George's County, and the Darnall family chapel at Portland Manor near Bristol and the Carroll family chapel in Annapolis, both in Anne Arundel County.

Carroll's grandson, Charles Carroll of Carrollton, the only Catholic signer of the Declaration of Independence, was born in the family's Annapolis home in 1737 and lived most of his life there until he retired to Baltimore in 1821. He maintained a large waterfront property that archaeologist Elizabeth Kryder-Reid says "had been groomed as a showpiece of wealth and taste." With Carroll's departure, the family chapel was closed and a small church—St. Mary's—was built on an adjacent lot and run by the Jesuits from White Marsh. In 1851 Carroll's heirs offered the property to the Redemptorists. But around the same time, the Redemptorists were also offered a church, house, and thirty acres of land for a novitiate (a house of religious initiation) in Westminster, in Carroll County, Maryland. They declined the Annapolis offer, but when the Westminster plans failed to materialize, the Annapolis offer was renewed and accepted in 1852.[4]

The Jesuits would have preferred to keep their long-standing ties to Annapolis but had seldom provided a residential priest. They had been founded in Spain in 1540 during the Counter Reformation and had become a religious order emphasizing evangelization, education, and writing literature in defense of the Catholic Church. They had been a presence in Maryland since its founding in 1634. The Redemptorists had been founded in Italy in 1732 to serve the poor and abandoned people. The first Redemptorists arrived in the United States in

Saint John Nepomucene Neumann, C.Ss.R. (1811–60) as Third Bishop of Philadelphia. Engraving by Samuel Hollyer, 1891, Prints and Photographs Division, Library of Congress https://www.loc.gov/pictures/item/96508709/.

Father Bernard Hafkenscheid (1807–65). Source: Rev. Henry Borgmann, C.Ss.R., History of the Redemptorists at Annapolis, Md., from 1853 to 1903 *(Ilchester, Maryland: College Press, 1904), 13.*

1832 and over time became involved in preaching and missionary work, running parishes in various cities. By the early 1850s, they were looking for a permanent home for their novitiate.

The gift of the property to the Redemptorists was finalized on March 20, 1852, with a deed signed by Carroll's Caton granddaughters—Mary Ann, Marchioness of Wellesley; Elizabeth, Lady Stafford; Louisa, Duchess of Leeds; and Emily MacTavish of Baltimore. The property came at no cost to the Redemptorists and a settlement fee was paid by the Caton daughters to their trustee. The forty-acre Duke of Gloucester Street property was conveyed jointly to three priests: Bernard J. Hafkenscheid, the Redemptorist superior in the United States; and his two consultors, John Nepomucene Neumann and Gabriel Rumpler.[5] The deed mentioned nothing about religious uses of the property but, on May 1, 1852, a covenant between the donors and the recipients described the conditions of the gift:

> 1. The House, garden, and enclosure back and front, to be always consecrated to Religion. If the Redemptorist Fathers find it inconvenient to hold the property; they hereby pledge themselves to give it to some other order that will be useful to the Community generally. — The rest of the property to be also conveyed to the Religious order as an endowment.
>
> 2. One Mass to be said every Month for the Souls of Mr. Carroll of Carrollton and Mr. and Mrs. Caton.
>
> 3. One Mass to be offered up for the four Daughters of Mrs. Caton. – Lady Wellesley, Lady Stafford, Duchess of Leeds, Mrs. MacTavish and her descendants — Once in every Month.[6]

The Carrolls had owned the property since 1706 and five generations had lived in the large house. It now was in hands of a Catholic religious order. The property, however, had been described just four years earlier as exhibiting "the most utter desolation" and the house "fast going to ruin" with the garden walks "filled with rubbish, and the ornaments bestrewed upon the ground." Major work was needed to put the place in order for the Redemptorist novitiate.[7]

The property on which St. Mary's Church was located was conveyed by Colonel James Boyle to the Redemptorists in 1853. Boyle was a former mayor of Annapolis, former deputy attorney general of Maryland, and a convert to Catholicism. He also was trustee for the church property, a 0.9-acre parcel on the west side of the Carroll property. Carroll of Carrollton had conveyed it in 1823 to his granddaughter, Mary Ann Caton Patterson after she had overseen the funding and construction of the 150-person brick church. Nearly thirty years later,

The Carroll House, home of the Redemptorist novitiate 1853–60. Border detail from "Bird's Eye View of the City of Annapolis, Md." Edward Sachse, Baltimore, 1860. RABP.

Mary Ann, as an absentee owner of advancing age living in England as the widowed marchioness of Wellesley, executed a deed on March 29, 1851, making Boyle her trustee. The property was, in the words of the deed, "dedicated as a Roman Catholic Church of the Blessed Virgin Mary, for the sole purpose of religion, charity and education." Besides St. Mary's Church, the parcel included a small rectory, a burial ground, and several old residences. Boyle agreed—at his "election and discretion"—to convey the property to the Archbishop of Baltimore "for the time being and his successors," or "to the order of Jesus, or any other religious order acknowledged by the Church of Rome." So, when the Redemptorists were given the adjacent Carroll House property in 1852, Boyle complied with instructions received from England, and on February 4, 1853, conveyed the church property to Hafkenscheid, Neumann, and Rumpler.[8]

The first Redemptorists—Father Gabriel Rumpler, the Redemptorist novice master, and two lay brothers—and engineer and stone mason John Himmelheber, arrived in Annapolis from Baltimore on March 16, 1853, to make preparations for the arrival on April 1 of newly ordained Father Joseph Wissel, five professed students (those who had completed their novitiate and had professed vows of poverty, chastity, and obedience as well as a vow and oath of perseverance as a Redemptorist), ten novices (men taking the initial step toward formally entering the Redemptorist congregation by spending a year of self-discernment in hope of finding a vocation in religious life), two candidate novices (those waiting to be "invested" with the long black Redemptorist habit), and three lay brothers (men usually skilled in a trade who devoted themselves to a life of religious service). They established a novitiate officially known as "Hospitium ad S. Teresia" (Foundation of St. Teresa, sometimes also referred to as "Collegio S. Teresia"). It was named after St. Teresa of Ávila, the sixteenth-century contemplative nun whose theological writings influenced the Redemptorists' founder, St. Alphonsus Liguori. The Annapolis Redemptorists adopted St. Teresa as their patron. They lived, prayed, and studied in the refurbished Carroll House and took charge of St. Mary's Church, which now became home to a permanent parish.[9]

The move to Annapolis gave the Redemptorists the greater stability afforded by a permanent location for their college and novitiate. Previously, novices had been placed in a Redemptorist house (known as *collegium*) in Baltimore and later in Pittsburgh, and then again in Baltimore. After a year, successful novices professed vows and became seminarians and studied philosophy, theology, and standard academic subjects. Originally, the professed students had been shifted around in twos and threes to Redemptorist parishes in Pittsburgh, Rochester, Philadelphia, New York City, and Baltimore. In 1851, Hafkenscheid established a permanent seminary for the professed students at Sts. Peter and Paul Parish in Cumberland, but he knew it was also important to have a permanent home for the novitiate, thus the move to Annapolis in 1853. Having the two houses in smaller cities was also an advantage for the teaching priests who no longer also had to minister to large urban parishes and face the distractions of a fast-growing metropolis. It was important, too, as Wissel related many years later, "to have a retired place for the rearing of young members for the Order."[10]

Baltimore's population had reached 160,054 by 1850, more than doubling its size in twenty years, and had become an important industrial and transportation hub. It also was a destination for Irish and German immigrants and, coincident with this immigration, came a significant rise in rowdyism and crime, and resentment among some parts of the native population. By 1850 there were more than 19,000 Maryland residents born in Ireland and 26,000 born in German states. Nationwide an estimated 80 percent of the Irish immigrants and 30 percent of the German immigrants were Catholics. This inflow also brought increasing numbers of missionary priests to America and led to the growth of American seminaries to train clergy to minister to the growing population. Catholic immigrants and the Catholic Church in general became convenient scapegoats for what was seen as wrong in American society. Catholics were the subject of sometimes vehement anti-Catholic sermons by Baltimore's Protestant clergy who fomented against the growing secularism of their city. Despite the presence of Catholics in Maryland since its founding in 1634, the Catholic Church itself was seen by many critics as an alien institution, run by foreign-born priests and bishops who used an archaic foreign language in their liturgies and were led by an Italian pope. Priests speaking with foreign accents conducted elaborate and seemingly arcane rituals, and obeyed a centralized hierarchy in Rome. The Catholic Church seemed to some observers to lack the directness and simplicity characteristic of egalitarian "American" religion with its native-born clergy and Puritan ethic. Immigration and conversions brought about major growth in Catholic parishes in Baltimore and, much to the chagrin of Protestant clergy and public educators, the priests established parochial schools. By 1850 Maryland's Catholic population reportedly reached between 31,000 and 51,000 members, with sixty-five parishes statewide. The property these Catholics and their church owned was reportedly valued at more than any other religious denomination.[11]

Around this time, the secular press and Protestant leaders warned about the dangers of the substantial growth of the Catholic Church in America. The Catholic population in the United States had reached more than 1.5 million by 1850 and the number of Catholic churches in the United States increased by 885 percent since 1820. There were reportedly 158 convents, 1,664 nuns, and 91 academies for girls. Historian Jay Dolan, writing on Catholic revivalism, cites an 876 percent increase in the Catholic population of the United States between 1830 and 1860.[12]

Compared to the multiplicity of religious sects in the United States—and whose own denominations were increasingly divided over the issue of slavery—the growth of Catholicism seemed a monolithic threat. Catholic clergy were seen as meddlers despoiling the traditional American ways of life, a view that contributed to the growing nativism of the era. Ironically, many recent immigrants who had fled Europe during and after the 1848 liberal revolutions and brought their own anti-Catholic prejudices. These prejudices, along with the other factors mentioned, created an image problem for the Church and gave rise in popularity to nativist secret societies. Historian William Kurtz observes that the growth of the Catholic Church in the United States "contributed to widespread fears that it was a pressing threat to the United States" and "set the stage for the nativism and anti-Catholicism."[13]

The Annapolis to which Rumpler and his little band came to in 1853 was quite different from Baltimore. The old Carroll property was located in a quiet corner of the city, bordered by a creek on one side, open fields on another, and stately colonial-era residences on two other sides. It was an ideal location for the novitiate. The city's population was 3,011 in 1850, 60 percent White and 40 percent Black. Of the Black population, 45 percent were free and 55 percent were slaves. Annapolis City contributed only 9 percent of Anne Arundel County's total population. The Naval

Academy, in just eight years before the Redemptorists' arrival, brought substantial economic and social change. A Naval Academy French professor and former Catholic—Arsène Napoléon Girault—provided the impetus for the 1846 establishment of a Presbyterian church on Duke of Gloucester Street, just two blocks west of St. Mary's. The Naval Academy also provided employment opportunities for many Annapolitans while merchants, hotel keepers, saloon owners, tradesmen, and retail suppliers all benefitted from the Navy's presence.[14]

St. Mary's parishioners were among those who benefitted from the Naval Academy. Even before the Redemptorists arrived in Annapolis, interest had been expressed in performing apostolic work among the young men at the Naval Academy. In 1851, Father Rumpler wrote that he had met a naval officer, a relative of Emily MacTavish, and learned that there was a movement toward "Puseyism" in the Navy. Puseyism—named after English churchman Edward Bouverie Pusey—was a trend within the Anglican Church to return to early Catholic doctrines and practices. Rumpler said that if the Redemptorists established themselves in Annapolis, it "may be quite providentially the means of doing much good in those quarters." There was no Catholic Navy chaplain assigned to the academy, so when the Redemptorists arrived in 1853 they informally fulfilled that role. As early as 1853, some midshipmen attended services of their choice outside the Academy yard but it was not stated which churches. Prior to 1859, they were required to attend Sunday morning Protestant services at the academy chapel. On January 17, 1859, the Navy Department announced a change in policy that allowed attendance at services outside the yard if the midshipman's parents declared in writing that "they cannot conscientiously attend" the mandatory services. Upon receiving formal requests, two Catholic midshipmen—fourth-class member John Nurre of Evansville, Indiana, and second-class member Horace Edward Mullan of Annapolis—were permitted to attend Mass at St. Mary's.[15]

Signs of Discontent

A media and political uproar emerged in April 1853 when a committee report and proposed legislation on public education was submitted to the Maryland General Assembly. Both were prepared by Martin J. Kerney, chair of the House of Delegates' Committee on Education, and a Democratic delegate from Baltimore City. He was also a Catholic school teacher, and later the editor of *The Metropolitan*, a Catholic literary journal, and founder of the *Catholic Youth's Magazine*, both published by Baltimore's John Murphy, the largest Catholic publisher in the United States.[16] Kerney had introduced a similar bill the year before and had been accused of wanting to establish a school system that his enemies said would lead to papal supervision of Maryland's public education and which would cause citizens to "be taxed to support a Catholic School—thereby recognizing a religion by law."[17] Kerney withdrew the 1852 bill but introduced it again in 1853, the day before the Redemptorists arrived in Annapolis.

Kerney claimed that Maryland's public school system was "unequal to the task" and "seriously defective in either theory or in practice." He recommended an appointed state school superintendent, county libraries, increased school taxes, and elected or appointed county school commissioners. The big controversy came from another recommendation: authorizing the counties and Baltimore City to fund orphan asylum schools and "for the education of children taught gratuitously in any School within their jurisdiction."[18] In other words, the report proposed public funding for non-public schools. The First Plenary Council of American bishops in Baltimore in May 1852 decreed they would follow Pope Pius IX's 1851 call to provide religious education to Catholic children. As a result, the Baltimore council encouraged the establishment and financial support of parochial schools throughout the United States. Catholic Church opponents saw this as interference in politics, giving further impetus to Maryland's Know Nothings.[19] When Kerney's report was referred back to committee, four of its five members—all but Kerney—renounced all association with its content and purpose. It was now a dead issue.[20] How the Annapolis Redemptorists viewed the Kerney bill is not known but they would have read the Baltimore newspapers and been aware of the controversy. They had no parochial school in Annapolis and felt, perhaps, they had escaped a big-city issue.

But they would read two years later in the weekly *Annapolis Gazette* about the "dangerous increase" in the numbers of archbishops, bishops, priests, churches, and dioceses throughout the United States. The *Gazette* used statistics from *Sadliers' Catholic Almanac* to highlight this growth of the Catholic Church, which had become the country's largest religious denomination. And, to invoke fear among the local electorate of northern political dominance, the article noted that only 9 percent of American Catholics lived in the slave states.[21]

The Know Nothing Spirit

During the 1903 fiftieth-anniversary celebrations of the Redemptorists' arrival in Annapolis, Redemptorist historian Father Henry Borgmann observed that "the Know Nothing spirit, then rampant in the country, was in full fruitage at Annapolis, and insult, contumely and riot met the brave endeavors of the pious fathers." When they first arrived, the Redemptorists were uncertain how they and their novices would be received in public in the predominantly Protestant town. In order to gauge the local reaction, Rumpler decided to "take the town by storm" by sending out novices dressed in their long black habits, two by two, as a test. The novices, "with bold modesty marched through the enemy's camp," reported the Redemptorists' house annals—the *Chronica Domus*—and "the very boldness of the stroke silenced the tongues of the prejudiced, while the modesty of the young men compelled the admiration of many." One local denizen viewing this unprecedented sight reportedly exclaimed "Behold them men! They go straight to Heaven!" The chronicler said that from that day forth, the priests emulated the novices and also wore their habits in public. Borgmann in 1903 observed that the spirit of Know Nothingism in town "was sufficient to arouse the bitterest fanaticism against popish intruders but happily the good people of Annapolis had better sense."[22]

John Thomson Mason Jr.—an associate justice of the Court of Appeals, Maryland's highest court from 1851 to 1857 and politically opposed to the Know Nothings—had a somewhat different take. He was not a Catholic at the time but converted during the Civil War and, before and afterward, was a strong defender of the Church and the Redemptorists. A native of Hagerstown, Maryland, Mason briefly attended Mount St. Mary's College in nearby Emmitsburg, and graduated from Princeton College in New Jersey in 1836. Mason served in the Maryland House of Delegates in 1838–39 and the US House of Representatives in 1840–43. He wrote some years later that he "well remember[ed] what unfriendly feeling, if not actual hostility, was manifested towards [the Redemptorists] by a large proportion of our community, and in some instances, even violence." He told how when they "took their unobtrusive walks along our streets, the boys, and oftentimes the men, hooted at them, and even gave more demonstrative evidence of their hostile feeling." The Redemptorists, however, Mason wrote:

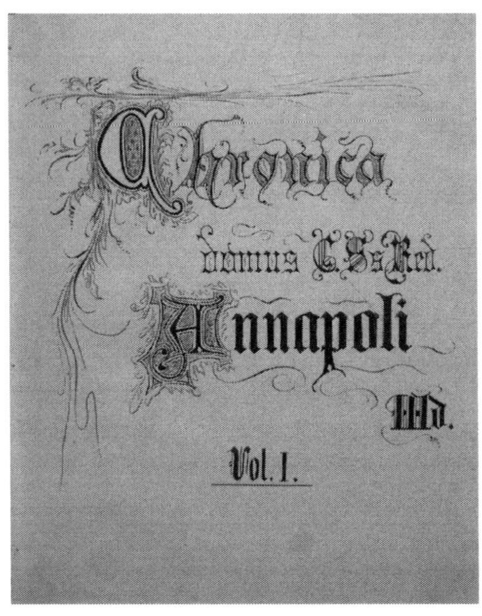

The title page of Chronica Domus C.Ss.R., Annapoli, Md., volume 1. RABP.

> pursued their onward course, unawed by fear, unmoved by ridicule and contempt, invoking blessings, and not curses, upon their persecutors,—continuing to do good and not evil,—feeding the poor and visiting the sick,—dispensing charity regardless of denomination, class, or color until, at length, the tide of public sentiment turned, and love, admiration, and respect took the place of hatred, ridicule, and contempt.[23]

But whatever acceptance they found in town was not the end of Know Nothing troubles for the Redemptorists and their parishioners. In the decades before the Civil War, and in keeping with anti-Catholic sentiments, fictional and allegedly autobiographical "convent narratives" were published to denigrate Catholic educational and religious institutions as un-American. Two widely popular books in this genre were written in the mid-1830s purportedly by young women who had "escaped" from Catholic convents. Rebecca Theresa Reed authored *Six Months in a Convent* (1835) and Maria Monk, who had been in a reformatory run by nuns, followed with *Awful Disclosures of the Hotel Dieu Nunnery* (1836). The books are replete with horror stories of unlawful confinement, maltreatment, psychological and sexual abuse, infanticide, and murder. The books were best sellers in their day, with Reed's selling 200,000 copies in the first month alone while Monk's sold 300,000 copies by 1860. Both were widely advertised in the United States and were translated into French, and other languages for distribution abroad.[24]

The convent narratives became relevant for the Redemptorists in June or July 1853. Around that time, Secretary of War Jefferson Davis allegedly received a letter from Annapolis said to have been written with the burnt end of a match by a young man "imprisoned in the cellar of the Redemptorist convent for a number of years." The writer, "through the agency of a boy who, by chance, had communicated with him through the bars of his prison," supposedly implored Davis to investigate "the iniquitous proceedings of the authorities of the house, who kept him confined with the design to murder him." Already, he declared, others had been killed and their bodies buried on the church grounds with statues placed over their graves. The letter reportedly was thrown through one of the air holes of the cellar, with a note written on the outside, asking the finder to forward it to the War Department in Washington. By one account, although Davis reportedly doubted the credibility of the letter, he directed the superintendent of the Naval Academy to conduct an investigation. Supposedly Commander Cornelius Kinchiloe Stribling, or his successor Commander Louis Malesherbes Goldsborough, accompanied by Hector Humphrey, the principal of St. John's College and an Episcopal minister, called on Rumpler to conduct the investigation. Despite their protestations that they did not believe the alleged captive's story and there really was no need to see the house, Rumpler "took them to every nook and corner." Since there was no cellar per se, only a ground floor, he could not show them the alleged place of imprisonment or the air hole through which the letter allegedly was emitted. "The gentlemen left," it was reported, "satisfied and highly pleased with the kindness with which they had been received and entertained."[25]

In an account offered by John Thomson Mason, Davis brought the matter to the attention of Henry May, a Democratic congressman from Baltimore whose wife was Catholic and who himself would convert to Catholicism in 1866. "A moment's investigation," it was written, "was sufficient to satisfy [May] of the total groundlessness of this statement, especially as the fact was, that the institution had not been in operation as many months, as this party alleged he had been years in confinement." No documentation to substantiate the investigation has been found in the Naval Academy archives, War Department or Navy Department records at the National Archives, or in the archives of St. John's College.[26]

Another incident of "a more serious disturbance of the same nature," according to the *Chronica Domus*, occurred in 1854. For some time, Matthew Walsh, a twenty-two-year old Irish-born professed student, had "given slight signs of insanity." In early May, he left St. Mary's wearing his religious habit, walked to the train station at Calvert and West streets and took "the cars"—as railroad passenger trains were called—via the Annapolis and Elk Ridge Railroad to Annapolis Junction, twenty miles to the northwest. He told people there that he had been imprisoned in the Redemptorist house in Annapolis and "had made his escape in order to save his life." A police officer brought him back to Annapolis and Edward Sparks, a physician and longtime St. Mary's parishioner, was called in. After several days of observation, Sparks declared Walsh insane. Sparks later testified that he found Walsh sometimes "calm and tranquil" but other times exhibited "maniacal excitement" and "paroxysms of wild, furious frenzy." On Sunday, May 7, Sparks took Walsh to the railroad depot. The *Annapolis Gazette, Maryland Republican,* the Baltimore *Sun*, and the *Chronica Domus* all reported on what happened next. Sparks and Walsh boarded the train and, just before it was to depart, Walsh called from the window that he was not insane and pleaded with a crowd that had assembled to rescue him. Sparks tried to reason with the growing mob but its self-assigned leaders turned on him and "began to attach to the doctor—one of our most respectable and trustworthy citizens—the vilest and most disreputable epithets." Sparks and his patient stayed on the departing train and Walsh was admitted that evening, "with undoubted mental derangement," to Mount Hope Insane Asylum, run by the Sisters of Charity just north of Baltimore City. The Annapolis mob was infuriated and on the evening of May 8 went to the novitiate with threats to destroy it. They also attempted to burn Sparks in effigy but were prevented in doing so by "respectable citizens" who quenched the "riotous spirit."[27]

A week later, an advertisement appeared in the *Maryland Republican* offering a $100 reward "for the detection and conviction of the persons who wantonly destroyed over 100 trees lately planted on the property of the late Charles Carroll of Carrollton, now occupied by the Catholic Institute." Several weeks afterward, the *Chronica Domus* noted, "the storm was dispelled" and there were no further threats. Rumpler allowed the students to go out in public in their clerical habits again and the good people of Annapolis came to St. Mary's to reassure themselves that the Carroll House was still standing.[28]

It was not the end of the episode, however. Soon after the threatened attack on St. Mary's, some of Walsh's would-be rescuers attempted a legal remedy. They appeared before the Maryland Court of Appeals in Annapolis to apply for a writ of habeas corpus, but the application was refused. Coincidently, at this time the chief judge of the Court of Appeals, John Carroll LeGrand, was Catholic. Although a resident of Baltimore, during court sessions, he likely stayed in town and attended St. Mary's Church. To his credit, in the coming years LeGrand refused to extend the United States Supreme Court's *Dred Scott v. Sandford* decision into Maryland, believing that race was not an absolute bar to civil rights in his state.[29]

Not easily dissuaded, a gang of Know Nothings went to Mount Hope and "forcibly took [Walsh] thence, and led him before a court of inquiry" in Baltimore. When interrogated by the judge of the Baltimore City Circuit Court, Walsh had nothing to say except that he had been disobedient. In a marginal note in the *Chronica Domus*, Walsh was quoted as saying: "My first fault was that I did not obey." The case was referred again to the Court of Appeals, which, in an unpublished opinion, sustained the lower court's support of the diagnosis of "lunacy." Walsh was remitted temporarily to the Maryland Hospital for the Insane in Baltimore, and, for a time, stayed with the Redemptorists at St. Alphonsus rectory, the provincial superior's house in Baltimore. But his illness persisted and he was sent back to Mount Hope, where he died in November 1855.[30]

Historian Jean Baker reports that when the Maryland General Assembly convened in January 1856, there was "a seemingly endless round of petitions involving the need to control naturalization, investigate convents, and tax exemptions on certain Catholic properties." The petitions were referred to the House of Delegates Select Committee on Convents and Nunneries, which reported back that its investigations did not sustain the allegations of "persons unlawfully confined in Convents or Nunneries." The committee advised that current laws sufficed and no further legislative action was needed to safeguard persons allegedly held against their will in religious institutions.[31] This, however, was not an end to the Know Nothing anti-Catholic spirit.

The Anti-Catholic Legacy in Maryland

Know Nothings yearned for an America where only native-born Anglo-Saxon, Protestant citizens held office and in which immigrant citizenship and voting rights were severely curtailed. Since the early 1850s when they gained a public face as the American Party, they diligently projected their nativist ideas into political action, doing all they could to forestall citizenship and voting rights for European immigrants. They also opposed what they claimed were political machinations by the Church of Rome and its supposedly blindly obedient followers. Catholics, in the Know Nothing creed, could never be true Americans as long as they believed in papal infallibility, a flaw that "proved" their disloyalty to republican America.[32]

Some slack was allowed, however, to native-born American Catholics, especially those in Maryland with its long Catholic presence. Historian William Overdyke, writing in 1950, observed that Maryland Know Nothings "did not show the same hostility toward foreign Catholics as in many other states." He also believed that "many Catholics" belonged to the American Party in Maryland but found no evidence of "open advocacy of the party by Catholic clergy as there was in Louisiana." A more recent historian of Catholic-Protestant relations in the South, Andrew Stern, takes the position that "Catholic support for slavery helped diffuse nativism in the South." Nevertheless, Maryland, with Baltimore as a major port of entry for immigrants, was a hotbed of nativism and a natural Know Nothing breeding ground. The first American Party local council was established among the Southern states in Baltimore in 1852.[33]

Upper-class Protestants and Catholics had associated easily with each other in colonial and post-colonial Maryland, and, when the nativist press emerged in the 1840s, both showed disdain for it. Old-line Catholics are said to have "deplored any action on the part of Catholic zealots in other parts [of the United States] that tended to disturb the accustomed cordiality between Catholics and Protestants in Maryland." Catholics in the antebellum period liked to remind Protestants that it was Maryland Catholics—such as Charles Carroll of Carrollton and his cousin, Daniel Carroll, a signer of the United States Constitution—who helped forge the principles of religious freedom on which the nation was founded. This "Maryland tradition"—a term used by Catholic historian Thomas Spalding and others—was a way for the Catholic minority to engage and maintain the respect of the Protestant majority. Furthermore, historian Joseph Mannard believes that Maryland enslavers who were fearful of educating both free or bound African Americans, tolerated Catholic catechizing members of the Black population "because traditional Catholic doctrine might be used to encourage blacks to accept their subordinate lot in this world." However, an *Annapolis Gazette* article trying to refute the "long-boasted [claims] of toleration" by Catholics in colonial Maryland was actually an implicit attack on native Catholics.[34]

Anti-Catholic attitudes were exacerbated when papal envoy Archbishop Gaetano Bedini visited the United States in 1853 to examine conditions of the American church. He met with President Franklin Pierce in Washington in June and on July 12, attended Georgetown College's commencement exercises, where he met Baltimore Archbishop Francis Patrick Kenrick and the Catholic governor of Maryland, Enoch Louis Lowe. The next day, Bedini visited Kenrick in Baltimore without incident. But visits to northern cities were met with "insults and mob violence." Wherever Bedini went—and even cities not visited—there were nativist protests and effigy burnings. When he suggested a return visit to Baltimore in January 1854 mobs took to the streets. He was burned in effigy just a few blocks from the Catholic cathedral. According to the *Catholic Mirror*, Baltimore's archdiocesan newspaper, Kenrick's residence, as well as St. Mary's Seminary, a Catholic orphans' asylum, and a convent were "saluted with firing of pistols and hellish yells." There was more rioting in Baltimore four days later and placards in English, French, Spanish, and German denounced Bedini's planned visit. Protesters were told "to treat him as they would a wild beast." Kenrick observed a few months later: "Times still look bad . . . . We should all be ready for martyrdom, and preparing our flocks for the trial."[35]

No notice of the anti-Bedini protests has been found in the extant Annapolis press, but seventeen months after Bedini's departure, the *Annapolis Gazette* published an anti-Catholic screed on American Party activities in Louisiana. Party leaders there had declared "a caveat against being confounded with those subjects of the Papal throne, against whose insidious influences the efforts of the American order are directed." In an interesting twist and perhaps as a veiled hint of hoped-for similar feelings among Annapolis Catholics, the article claimed that Catholics in Louisiana "belong to that division of the Church which denies the temporal supremacy of the Pope." Bedini was criticized in the article for having claimed "the right to subvert our institutions, and to demand a [Catholic] minister in the American Cabinet" just because Carroll of Carrollton had signed the Declaration of Independence.[36]

Maryland's 1851 constitution, which allowed

greater proportional representation in the state legislature for Baltimore City and the northwestern counties, led to electoral successes for the American Party, which won the office of mayor and twenty-two of the thirty city council seats in the 1854 Baltimore City elections. Nationally, the Know Nothings took control of state governments in Connecticut, Kentucky, Massachusetts, New Hampshire, and Rhode Island. In March 1855, the American Party gained control of the municipal government of Annapolis, where the Know Nothings won the offices of mayor, recorder, and all five aldermanic seats. The *Annapolis Gazette* declared the election a "Glorious Victory!" and that "Annapolis is decidedly American."[37]

Soon after the city election, the *Annapolis Gazette* informed its readers that New York State's American Party had declared that it would exhibit "[h]ostility to the assumptions of the Pope, through the bishops, priests, and prelates of the Roman Catholic church, here, in a republic sanctified by Protestant blood."[38] A follow-up article brought criticism of Catholics closer to home. It alleged that a Catholic priest in Baltimore had used his Sunday pulpit to tell people how to vote in the upcoming elections. A quote from one Valentine Heckler read:

> In the month of September last, I was in Baltimore, and went up to the German Catholic Church, where I heard the Priest preach in the German language from 11 to 1, on politics, with a newspaper in his hand, from which he would read, and then address his congregation, and he told them in my presence and in my hearing, that those who did not come the next Sunday, and pledge themselves to vote for candidates that certain parties were to nominate that week (for the Maryland election that was to come off on the following month of October), he would no longer claim Jesus as his brother, or Mary as his sister, pointing at the same time to the picture of Jesus and Mary.[39]

Although the priest was not identified in the article as a Redemptorist, the only German Catholic churches in Baltimore at the time—St. Alphonsus, St. James the Less, St. Michael the Archangel, and Holy Cross—were administered by Redemptorists. The story may have been spurious but for those inclined to believe it, it was an attack on the influence of priests and the Catholic Church. On the same page, the *Gazette* published a letter to the editor that chastised the other Annapolis weekly, the *Maryland Republican*, for "its excessive zeal to exult the Roman Catholic priesthood" and criticizing Know Nothings. Two months later, the *Gazette* published a "true copy" of a letter from Howard County, Maryland, Catholic who allegedly had been forced to resign from the Sons of Temperance by his priest-confessor. Such action by the priest, said the newspaper, "proves, most conclusively, the intolerance and tyranny practiced by the priests of that order towards their members."[40]

In the 1855 elections, the American Party succeeded in winning seventy-five seats to Congress. In Maryland the party won contests for four of the state's six seats in the House of Representatives, fifty-four of seventy-four seats in the Maryland House of Delegates, and eight of eleven contested seats in the Maryland Senate. They also won state-wide races for comptroller and lottery commissioner. As the *Baltimore Clipper* later put it, Maryland had become "the banner state of Know Nothingism."[41]

Annapolitans were kept quite aware of the American Party's political ascendancy. The *Annapolis Gazette* had a clearly pro-Know Nothing editorial policy and published numerous negative articles about foreigners and Catholics. Readers were informed there was nothing unconstitutional about Know Nothing opposition "to the political theories advocated by the Roman Catholic Church" and that they "had no objection to Catholics on account of their religious sentiments, but on account of their political sentiments" which maintained "primary allegiance both temporal and spiritual, to the Pope." Frequent advertisements appeared for a book that offered "a truthful, unadorned narrative of the plans, doings and designs of the Catholic party in the United States . . . [that] is working now, to undermine our liberties." Readers were informed that Catholics were obliged to hold to the concept of "Unceasing hostility to the Union of church and State." Know Nothings thus had a duty to counteract "the *political features*, the *worldly ambition*, the *jesuitical trickery* of the Roman Catholic Church, and all other Churches that shall dare to practice them."[42]

The *Annapolis Gazette* also claimed that the Catholic vote was controlled by the church hierarchy and was "generally cast as a unit." The pope, said the *Gazette*, had the power to release subjects from their oath of allegiance to a government. The paper even reprinted as "evidence" of this an article from Rome's *Civiltà Cattolica* that said "if the Pope should lay his ban on the government of the United States, Catholic subjects of that government would become, *ipso facto*, absolved of all fidelity thereto."[43]

Six months later, the *Annapolis Gazette* published the American Party platform adopted at its national convention in Philadelphia on July 12, 1855. Article VIII declared the party's "[r]esistence to the aggressive policy and corrupting policies of the Roman Catholic Church in our country." To make sure that *Gazette* readers understood the point, the party platform was reprinted in its entirety five more times in July and August. Democrats also were criticized because "[f]or years their party has cajoled and courted the Catholic priesthood and population of the country, until they seduced that powerful sect, or the foreign portion of it into at last their interest and service, and used them as a balance of power wherewith to control elections." Then, with fall 1855 elections for Congress and the Maryland General Assembly pending, the *Gazette* editor asked Anne Arundel County voters "only for a fair, unprejudiced, reasonable investigation" of the American Party's guiding principles. These principles, he wrote, had been "misrepresented and falsified in a thousand particulars," especially with respect the Catholic Church, and noted that a meeting had been held in Annapolis on August 25, to reaffirm those principles, including Article VIII. In keeping with their traditional secrecy, the Know Nothing participants were not identified by name.[44]

The man who did much to influence public opinion and local elections for the Know Nothings was the owner and editor of the *Annapolis Gazette*, Thomas J. Wilson. A lawyer by occupation, Wilson won the race for Anne Arundel County state's attorney in 1855. The owner and editor of the opposition press, the *Maryland Republican*, was Elihu Samuel Riley Sr., a long-time Democrat and slave owner, and printer by profession. He was identified many years later as one of five male Catholics residing in Annapolis who petitioned the Marchioness of Wellesley to donate the Carroll property to the Redemptorists.[45]

In the midst of the local newspaper support for the Know Nothings, the *Catholic Mirror* and the *New-York Freeman's Journal and Catholic Register*—both of which had Annapolis subscribers—defended immigration, especially Catholic immigration. Cleverly, their articles did not mention the Know Nothings per se but criticized the editor of *Harper's Magazine*, saying "he knows nothing of Maryland, and of Maryland Catholics . . . . He knows nothing of the Catholic, who in signing the Declaration of Independence, put at stake more of this world's goods, than any of his peers." The articles also highlighted other Catholic contributions to the United States.[46] How the parishioner of St. Mary's reacted to all this is not known, but the well-read among them surely were aware and remained cautious.

A Foreigner, a Catholic, and a Democrat

An anti-Catholic and anti-immigrant development occurred in Annapolis during the high point of Know Nothing political activism. In April 1855, the Visitors and Governors of St. John's College announced a reorganization and hiring of new faculty members set to take place in September. It appeared to be an earnest cause to benefit the college. The college was a success, according to a public notice, because of its "beautiful location" in close proximity to the Naval Academy and "freedom from Asiatic cholera." Another observed benefit was "the recent establishment here, in the venerable mansion of Chas. Carroll of Carrollton, by one of the orders of the Roman Catholic church, an Institution for the instruction of their Novices." Further, the notice boasted that "[t]here are, in Annapolis, Roman Catholic, Episcopal, Presbyterian and Methodist churches, the services of one of which the students, by the rules of the College, are required to attend on the Sabbath." The reorganization took place and new faculty members were to be hired before the fall term. Then controversy arose.[47]

One of the applicants for a faculty reappointment was Edward Sparks, an Irish immigrant, longtime St. Mary's parishioner, practicing physician, and Democratic Party member. He had taught at the college since 1820 and occasionally served as acting principal in the absence of Dr. Hector Humphreys. Now, he and the other faculty members sought reappointment under the reorganization. All faculty members whose appointments had expired, except Sparks, were reappointed. Dismayed by this treatment, he did not quietly retreat. In same edition of the *Annapolis Gazette* that published a lengthy description of the newly reorganized college, listing the faculty—sans Sparks—and curriculum, Sparks announced that he had launched his own "English and Classical Academy." He promised elementary and advanced English education, as well as "Elementary Chemistry, &c." Boarding students were to be placed with private families, "where the strictest attention will be made to their moral culture."[48]

A month later, "grave charges" were brought against St. John's College by Judge John Thomson Mason, an ex officio member of the Board of Visitors and Governors. He wrote that the college was "no longer worthy of the confidence and support of the people of Maryland" because it had come under the influence of the Know Nothing perpetrators of the reorganization. Mason said they had hired two fellow party members as professors while rejecting a third applicant because he was "a foreigner, a Catholic and a Democrat." The charges were first made in the form of a "card" dated October 8 and published in the pro-Democratic *Maryland Republican*, on October 13. The charges were responded to in the *Annapolis Gazette* on October 18 by "A Trustee" who challenged Mason to respond to eleven points regarding his own role in and knowledge of the college's hiring process. The *Gazette* reprinted Mason's "card" and offered a mocking critique of the judge. It said that "having nothing else to occupy his great mind, and fearing that his extraordinary abilities may be impaired by inactivity, [Mason] has suddenly vaulted into the political arena with the agility of a clown. . . . The ring-masters, on the occasion of his debut, are the fuglemen who do the blowing of the 'fusion' party and the audience is the people generally who may have had the misfortune to read the *Maryland Republican* of Saturday last." Not satisfied with its attack on Mason, the *Gazette* declared further that he was "no longer competent to sit on the Bench of the Court of Appeals, because he has publicly declared members of the American Party to be unworthy of any consideration whatever." A week later, the *Gazette* claimed that Mason had sought to prejudice not only the citizens of Anne Arundel County but of the entire state in an effort to gain votes for the Democratic Party. Not surprising, the controversy came on the eve of the fall elections.[49]

Besides Mason, two other men on the St. John's College Board of Visitors and Governors—Thomas Karney and Edwin Boyle—had St. Mary's connections. At age eleven, Karney had been baptized in 1820, presumably in the old Carroll House chapel, by Jesuit Father Charles Felix van Quickenbourne. Between 1829 and 1831, Karney taught at the new public grammar school on Green Street. He graduated from St. John's College in 1830 and worked in Annapolis as an attorney and later as assistant professor of ethics and English studies at the Naval Academy.[50]

Edwin Boyle, an 1835 St. John's graduate, attorney, and postmaster, was the son of Colonel James Boyle, St. Mary's trustee when the Redemptorists arrived in 1853. Although his father was a Catholic convert, his mother, Susannah, was not and some of their children either drifted away from the Church after their father's death in 1854 or had never embraced the faith., Edwin's brother, James Boyle III, had served as the godparent for a nephew when he was baptized at St. Mary's in 1852 but, in 1857, he was elected to the vestry of St. Anne's Episcopal Church.[51] Another brother, John Henry Boyle, appears to have been faithful to the Catholic Church, as were his children. Two children of a fourth brother, Llewellyn, were baptized at St. Mary's. Regardless, in 1855 Edwin may have had sympathy for members of his father's religious faith. "A Trustee" informed readers that the only person on the board who was known to be an American Party member actually had voted to reappoint Sparks, as did Democratic members Edwin Boyle and John Thomson Mason. Furthermore, it was claimed that four other members were anti-Know Nothings.[52]

In March 1856 Sparks formally asked for "a copy of *all* that is recorded of me during my connection with the college." The college obliged and, on April 4, 1856, provided a twenty-four-page transcript of his St. John's activities. The record started with Sparks' hiring as a professor of English and grammar in 1820, noting his European education, previous teaching experiences at unspecified American institutions, and that he was "eminently qualified in every respect to superintend the department which has been assigned to him." As a new professor, Sparks had not hesitated to assert his religious beliefs. Six weeks after his 1820 appointment, he and three other professors asked the college to grant free tuition to the nephew of any Roman Catholic priest, the son of any Protestant clergyman, and any youth age twelve and above who declared his intention "to devote himself to the ministry of some Christian Church." Sparks was appointed professor of ancient languages in 1822 and delegated to examine faculty candidates and to investigate the condition of the college's scientific equipment. He was granted a five-month leave of absence in 1823 to study science and medicine at the University of Maryland medical college in Baltimore. Annapolis attorney Alexander Randall temporarily assumed his teaching duties. Sparks completed his studies and was awarded a first premium medal "for the best medical Latin thesis." Thereafter, he was referred to in the record as *Dr.* Sparks. Trouble with the college emerged in 1848 when he was accused of having taken Humphreys to task "in the view & hearing of another of the professors & the students engaged with him." Sparks believed "some fancied wrong supposed to have been done to him" in not being invited to participate in the examination of another professor's teaching qualifications. The "altercation" included Sparks' use of "rude language" and having showed "insubordination & discontent" to the head of the institution. This incident was cited as "one of several instances of like sort" on Sparks' part.[53]

The college records also hinted that Sparks was not devoting "all of his time & energies to the duties of his professorship" and that he was distracted by other professional activities to the detriment of his pupils. Although his intellectual capabilities were not questioned, his moral habits came under suspicion when some of his pupils said he had attended class "under the influence of drink." Based on inquiries made of the faculty, it was the opinion of one of the two members of the investigating committee—Alexander Randall, an Episcopalian, and Dr. John Ridout, a Presbyterian—that "the answers of his fellow professors satisfactorily exculpates the accused." The board tabled the drinking charges but confirmed that all faculty members, including Sparks, were required to be punctual in their attendance at class.

In 1849 Sparks and Humphreys were both accused by the board of having "feelings so hostile to each other, as to lead frequently to unnecessary & angry altercations" concerning Sparks' "disputing & resisting the authority" of Humphreys over teaching requirements. The board concluded that if this situation persisted "it would ere long render the continuance of both in their present situations utterly incompatible with the well-being of the institution." The board, however, affirmed Humphreys' authority in any dispute over college rules with a faculty member. The issue resurfaced in 1850 and both Humphreys and Sparks were ordered to appear before the board and were handed copies of the college regulations. Trouble arose again in 1852 when Sparks intervened with "violent measures" to rescue a student being "handled . . . roughly" in class by modern languages professor Edward Josiah Stearns.

Humphreys, Sparks and Stearns, the student, and student witnesses were brought before the board for explanations. The board found that Stearns was justified in disciplining the insubordinate student but censured him for have used "improper & excessive" force, the repetition of which would be "met with serious displeasure" by the board. They found Sparks was justified in entering the room but had no cause to attack Stearns. Later the board withdrew its censure of Stearns. In 1854 Sparks was again involved in controversy when he struck an insubordinate student. Although the student was suspended, faculty and students were reminded that students were to be "punished by admonition & reproof, either public or private [at] the discretion of their Professors." No mention was made of corporal punishment and the rule was ordered to be read to the faculty, who would have known of Sparks' transgression.[54]

Among other charges against Sparks was occasional tardiness and absence from classes. From 1838 until the 1855 college reorganization, a detailed daily account was taken of professors' attendance for every day but Sunday. Sparks' absences for full or partial days were noted, usually for such reasons as indisposition or sickness, or "necessarily detained." At other times he was excused to attend a wedding or a funeral, or to travel out of town. In 1848 the board had agreed that Sparks was not required "to attend the morning devotions of the College should he entertain conscientious scruples on that subject," a veiled reference to his Catholic faith. Several times a year thereafter he was excused "as a matter of conscientious duty" so he could observe Catholic holy days and Holy Week observances. Of note was his excused absence on June 25, 1855, when he "went to Balto. with Father Rumpler" who was ailing. His absence on May 7, 1855, when he took the novice Matthew Walsh to Baltimore, however, was not recorded. Assuming the attendance record was generally thorough, between January 1, 1850 and July 13, 1855 (the last entry in the attendance book), Sparks was noted absent forty-six times, an average of nine days a year, not particularly extraordinary compared to other professors' absences. The attendance book reveals the high level of trust the college had in Sparks, such as when he was frequently called on to lead the weekly student exercises in Humphreys' place, especially in the two years leading up to his de facto dismissal.[55]

Sparks had become a controversial figure and an irritant to the college administration and governing board. He had many strikes against him and, while his being a foreign-born Catholic Democrat might not have been held against him, his altercations, absences, and alleged insobriety were problematic. In 1984 St. John's College historian Tench Francis Tilghman recounted the Sparks episode in some detail, claiming that it was Judge Mason who instigated the college reorganization in the hope of ridding it of Know Nothing influences. Tilghman says Sparks "had become a law unto himself" at the college, recounting the charges of drunkenness, being late for classes, and the "rude language" used with Humphreys. However, Tilghman seems to have misread Mason's "card," because he raised the question of whether or not Sparks himself was the Know Nothing professor whom Mason was seeking to oust.[56]

Despite his effort to establish his English and Classical Academy, nothing came of it and Sparks returned to his medical practice with an office on upper Church Street. As for Mason, he remained on the Court of Appeals until 1857 when he received a political patronage appointment from new Democratic President James Buchanan as customs collector for the Port of Baltimore. He remained in that position until 1861 when he was replaced by a Republican Party appointee.[57]

Taking Vipers to Their Bosoms

In the late 1850s, Redemptorist Father Frederick William Wayrich's "greatest troubles" giving missions was trying "to induce many Catholics who belong to secret societies to abandon their connections and renounce them publicly and forever." He had been one of the members of the first class of novices in Annapolis in 1853 and would have observed the Know Nothing prejudices in Annapolis. And, in 1853 the Catholic bishops established a rule denying the sacraments to members of secret societies. Nevertheless, some Catholics joined the Know Nothings and Maryland Know Nothings had rejected the so-called "Catholic test" which required them to renounce temporal allegiance to Rome. Horatio Tydings, a slave-owning farmer on the Broadneck Peninsula, was elected as an American Party candidate for Anne Arundel County commissioner in November 1855. Presumably he was at least a nominal Catholic since he appeared in St. Mary's marriage register as a witness to an 1862 marriage, and was likely related to the Annapolis Tydings family which included staunch St. Mary's parishioners. Thomas Spalding points out that being nativist did not necessarily mean being anti-Catholic and says that "old-stock" Catholics joined nativist clubs in Maryland. In 1856, a Know Nothing group in southern Anne Arundel County even professed to oppose threats to "the rights of our naturalized and Roman Catholic citizen."[58]

Although Catholics were unlikely to join the American Party, there were some people associated with St. Mary's Parish who were literally strange bed-fellows. Two such connections have been found. One was the marriage of Jane Goewey, a Catholic, to Walter Gantt, a local Protestant lawyer. They were married in 1856 in a Catholic ceremony in her hometown, Brownsville, Pennsylvania. Their son, William Putnam Gantt, was baptized in Annapolis by his aunt, Matilda Goewey, on April 12,

1857, because he was in danger of death following his birth. Father Francis Aloysius Baker recorded the details in the St. Mary's baptismal register on May 11, noting the conditional situation of the christening and that the father was Protestant. Walter Gantt had his law office in the county courthouse and, in 1856, was appointed clerk for the Anne Arundel County commissioners. He also was a leading member of the Anne Arundel County Committee of the American Party and gave at least one stump speech on behalf of the Annapolis Know Nothings in 1855. The family relocated in 1859 to Knox County, Missouri, where Gantt was a supporter of Republican candidate Abraham Lincoln and later served in the Union army. Know Nothings were supposed to be native born of Protestant parents and to not marry Catholics. Once again, Maryland proved to be the exception.[59]

Another person with St. Mary's connections who has been identified with the American Party was Llewellyn Boyle. He was an 1844 graduate of St. John's College and served as a first lieutenant in the US Army during the Mexican War. He was Maryland state librarian from 1857 to 1861 and was identified as "captain" and "colonel" in various publications. Llewellyn's Know Nothing connection was reported just before election day in November 1855, when Annapolis American Party members held "a large and brilliant Torchlight Procession . . . and preceded by a fine Band of Music, marched through the principle streets of the city to the Assembly Rooms," a stone's throw from St. Mary's. During the festivities, Boyle received "on behalf of the ladies of Annapolis" a "large and beautiful American flag, made of the most elegant and costly materials." After accepting the flag, Boyle made "a few appropriate and eloquent remarks."[60]

The *Annapolis Gazette* encouraged voters to support American Party candidate Millard Fillmore for president in 1856 against the new Republican Party's possible nominee, New York abolitionist William Henry Seward. The *Gazette* cast Seward as a long-time ally of Archbishop John Hughes of New York and someone who could, with the prelate's help, "obtain nearly the whole foreign Roman Catholic vote." Another such article insisted that the Germans "have gone over in a body, and the coalition between Abolition Seward and Cross-John Hughes will carry the entire foreign and native Catholic vote in the same direction." Catholics could not please the *Gazette* editor. In a contrary statement, the *Gazette* opined that the anti-slavery clamor in New England came not from the Protestant clergy but "from the church of Rome now recognized as the head quarters of the present Democratic party."[61]

The 1856 presidential election was a three-way contest involving anti-slavery Republican Senator John Charles Frémont of California, Democratic former senator and secretary of state James Buchanan of Pennsylvania, and for the American Party former president Millard Fillmore. Buchanan won by a small margin over Frémont, with Fillmore coming in a distant third. He received only eight electoral votes, all from Maryland. He received 52.9 percent of the vote in Anne Arundel County, mostly in rural areas. Voters in Annapolis favored Buchanan by a narrow 50.5 percent to Fillmore's 49.5 percent. Frémont was an electoral no show.[62]

Following Fillmore's defeat, the *Annapolis Gazette* warned its readers just how powerful Catholics and Democrats had become. Quoting from Frankfurt am Main's *Allgemeine Zeitung*, it was said that:

> The [American] Catholic Bishops have now, at least in the free States, the greatest political power. They elect Presidents and Governors, and are almost always Democratic, though they know when to change their politics.[63]

The *Annapolis Gazette* carried more of the same in 1857. The American Party, it claimed, did not practice religious intolerance, it just resisted the "aggressive policy" of the Catholic Church. The American Party was not "dead" as asserted by the Democrats—who supposedly had established their own "secret order . . . composed wholly by Roman Catholic Irishmen" and thus, had "taken vipers to their bosoms who will sting them to death." One article claimed that the American Party had not been diminished by losing the presidential race but, indeed, was becoming more popular among Southerners who saw their constitutional rights diminished in the "free soil" states and territories.[64]

State and Local Elections

After Fillmore's 1856 defeat, the American Party's national organization relinquished its formerly strong central direction over its state branches. The branches survived mostly as allies of anyone opposed to Democrats. In Maryland, however, the American Party was no temporary third-party movement. It gained control of the state legislature and sent three members to the US House of Representatives in the November 1857 elections. American Party candidate Thomas Holliday Hicks, a Dorchester County enslaver and former Whig, won the governorship. According to Hicks' official biography, the election "was marked by fraud, open intimidation of the voters, and unprecedented violence." The Redemptorist chronicler at St. Alphonsus Church in Baltimore wrote that the election was a "farce" and complained that the police protected Know Nothing rowdies instead of German and Irish voters.[65]

Many of the newly elected Know Nothing candidates in Maryland were political novices and once seated in the General Assembly they had to compromise on their party's more virulent policies. They focused instead on budgets, schools, transportation, and other practical

The Walton family pew nameplate formerly located in St. Mary's Church. Courtesy author.

issues. Despite their control of the legislature, their bills to investigate Catholic convents and remove Catholic office holders died in committee. Instead of anti-Catholic and anti-immigration issues, party members sought compromise on slavery and preserving the Union. The Know Nothings lost a crucial statewide vote in 1858 on whether or not to hold a convention to write a new state constitution. They saw this as an opportunity to reapportion the General Assembly to better represent nativist issues and possibly to even restrict religious freedom to Protestants. But their defeat further isolated the American Party. Maryland Know Nothing leaders—many of whom were slave owners, albeit in lesser numbers than their Democratic Party counterparts—avoided discussing slavery and held fast to the position that the US Constitution allowed slavery and the issue should be left alone.

Still strong locally, the American Party swept the Annapolis city elections in April 1858. They won the races for mayor, recorder, and all five aldermanic seats. Know Nothing Joshua Brown beat Democratic mayoral candidate and St. Mary's parishioner John Walton, 220 votes to 188. *Annapolis Gazette* editor Thomas Wilson was elected to the position of recorder over Democrat Edwin Boyle 218 votes to 188. Another man associated with St. Mary's, David S. Caldwell, was defeated in his bid for alderman, coming in sixth in a race in which only the top five vote recipients won. Caldwell was a sixty-five-year-old lumber dealer who, a month after the election, served as godfather at St. Mary's for the baptism of a twenty-year-old French-born convert, Adelina Fisher. In January 1859, he was godfather for ten-year-old John Airland.[66]

Following Wilson's election, he softened his newspaper's antagonism toward the Catholic Church. In doing so, he was keeping with the American Party's general retreat from its nativist stance and anti-Catholic articles mostly disappeared from the *Annapolis Gazette*. The *Gazette* even published a positive report on the veneration of a "celebrated picture of the Madonna" at a Catholic church in Hoboken, New Jersey. Quoting a *New York Times* account of the event, the *Gazette* intimated that Catholics were under no obligation to heed the criticism levied by Protestants over their religious practices. Positive news about Annapolis churches appeared in the *Gazette* in August 1858, noting that the reconstruction of St. Anne's was "progressing steadily" and the new Catholic church on Duke of Gloucester Street had "advanced rapidly." The Methodist congregation resolved to replace their Salem Church on State Circle with a larger building on the same site. Another article reported on the growth of Catholic dioceses in the United States as a result of the increasing numbers of churches, priests, and bishops. The article noted—without suggesting that this was a bad thing—that in the past fifty years the church had grown seven times as fast as the general population of the United States.[67]

The American Party's traditional proscription of Catholics gradually diminished in Maryland as the party's political stance shifted to preserving the Union from "extremism": abolitionism in the North and expansion of slavery in the South and West. As if to subtly emphasize the point, the *Annapolis Gazette* published quotes from Baltimore's *American and Commercial Advertiser* concerning Democrats opposing Catholic and Protestant nominees in upcoming Philadelphia local elections. It was usually the American Party that was criticized by Democrats "for the bringing of religion into politics." Now it was the "locofocos"—as the radical wing of the Democratic Party was called in the *Gazette*—that faced divisiveness over Catholics. "Thus," opined the report, "the Catholic and anti-Catholic question is fairly opened among the Democrats." Concurrent with this more mild approach to Catholics in the *Gazette*, the *Maryland Republican* was quick to criticize "the management of a Know Nothing Corporation." The newly elected city officials approved a new tax of 60 cents per $100, the "largest tax, we believe ever yet levied upon the people of this city."[68] Annapolis Catholics certainly had a lot of mixed messages in their newspaper reading.

Things changed after the Democrats regained control of the Maryland House of Delegates and a majority in the Senate in the 1859 elections. Although an American Party candidate was selected for state comptroller by a wide margin, the party itself soon disappeared in Maryland and its leaders and members were absorbed into the Constitutional Unionist Party, which embraced slavery within the Union as a constitutional right and opposed Federal interference with slavery in the western territories. By the end of the decade, the American Party had dissolved and many of its members morphed into the new antislavery and nativist-sympathetic Republican Party. Favoring a conservative and national party, many Catholics continued to identify with the Democratic Party, within which they avoided the slavery issue. At the same time, there was a resurgence of political influence exerted by large slave holders in southern Maryland and the Eastern Shore.[69]

Historian Thomas Spalding sums up the Catholic position amidst the political turmoil as follows. He explains that the American bishops were "[w]holly absorbed by the task at hand," that is, assimilating waves of immigrants, building churches, schools, asylums, and other institutions designed to preserve and strengthen the faith of the newcomers, recruiting mostly foreign-born religious to staff them. In general, American bishops "took little interest in national affairs," thus "such burning issues as slavery, the tariff, internal improvements, and manifest destiny found little place in their deliberations or in their correspondence." As a result, Spalding concludes, the Catholic Church "became more cohesive as other religious bodies were torn apart by political, social, and sectional discord."[70]

An Angel in Sweetness

Francis Xavier Seelos was born in 1819 in Füssen in southern Bavaria. Almost all of the inhabitants of his village were Catholic and the Seelos family lived directly across the street from St. Mang Church, where Francis' father was the sacristan. Both Mang Seelos and his wife, Francesca, were known for their piety and the entire family attended daily Mass. Two of their daughters became nuns and their second son, Francis, named after the famous Jesuit missionary, became a priest.

Young Franz Xaver—as he was known in Bavaria, or simply Xaver to his family—was sickly as a child. His mother tutored him at home and instilled in him a great piety and devotion to the Blessed Virgin. At an early age, after hearing the story of St. Francis Xavier going to Asia, Xaver decided he too would become a missionary. His family was always impressed with his prayerfulness and his unrelenting cheerfulness. Seelos began his religious studies from 1832 to 1839 at the Gymnasium bei St. Stephan, a secondary school administered by secular clergy in Augsburg, Bavaria. One of Xaver's professors was Boniface Wimmer, a Benedictine priest who would later establish his order's foundation in the United States and with whom young Seelos would renew his acquaintance a decade later. From 1839 to 1842, Xaver studied at the Benedictine-run Ludwig-Maximilians-Universität in Munich. He told his brother Adam that during this time the Virgin Mary told him in a dream to leave his homeland. Early in 1842, after reading an appeal for missionaries from Father Alexander Czvitkovicz, the Redemptorist superior in America, Xaver applied to Czvitkovicz for admission to the congregation.[71]

In the fall of 1842, Xaver transferred to Augsburg's diocesan seminary in Dillingen, Bavaria, for his second year of theological studies. The fall semester had just begun when he received a long-awaited reply to his application to join the Redemptorists in the United States. Two of his former St. Stephan classmates—Maximus Leimgruber and Thaddeus Anwander—had already answered the Redemptorists' call and gone to America to finish their studies and work among poor German immigrants. Francis decided to join them.[72]

At age twenty-four, Seelos sailed from Le Hâvre, France, on board the ship *St. Nicolas* with three Redemptorists. They arrived in New York City on April 20, 1843, and went immediately to the Redemptorists' St. Nicholas Church in Manhattan. Within days Seelos was sent to Baltimore to begin his novitiate at St. James' Church, then the Redemptorist novitiate and house of studies. There he professed his vows as a Redemptorist on May 16, 1844, and was ordained eight months later by Archbishop Samuel Eccleston. He remained at St. James until August 1845, when he was assigned to St. Philomena's Parish in Pittsburgh to work with Father John Neumann. By the time he left Pittsburgh nine years later, Seelos had become a "local legend" because of his sanctity. From March 1854 to April 1857, Seelos was assigned as rector at the German-speaking parish of St. Alphonsus in Baltimore, from which priests went daily to Redemptorist-run German churches in the city and new out-missions beyond. He also served as consultor to Father George John Ruland, the provincial superior of the Redemptorists' American Province, headquartered at St. Alphonsus. As consultor, Seelos visited Annapolis five times, plus once during his later years in Cumberland, Maryland, and became quite familiar with the property and the novitiate.[73]

Blessed Francis Xavier Seelos, C.Ss.R. (1819–67), Source: Rev. Henry Borgmann, C.Ss.R., History of the Redemptorists at Annapolis, Md., from 1835 to 1903 *(Ilchester, Maryland: College Press, 1904), 25.*

After one of his visits to Annapolis, during the waning days of Rumpler's tenure at St. Mary's, Seelos wrote to his family about his experiences:

> I often had to go to Annapolis. You have to travel there either by steamboat or by railroad. It takes about two-and-a-half hours. The novitiate is there. It is really one of the most beautiful places one can imagine: first, because of its beautiful location on the sea and the wonderful garden that reaches down to the water in terraces; and then, especially because of the fervor of the young people who are living together there in angelic innocence and are preparing themselves for their beautiful vocation. It seems as though God wants to show the virtues of these young people even exteriorly, in the great luxuriousness of the garden. The lilies especially grow in such majesty and exuberance. I have never seen the like before in my life. I counted over twenty Saint Joseph's lilies on one beautiful slender stem. How it consoled me to see the young people, who made it a point to show me their interest and love. How beautiful is a chaste person![74]

In Baltimore, however, Seelos worked himself almost to death. Besides serving as rector of St. Alphonsus, he had a myriad of administrative and sacramental duties and was also responsible for three other parishes: St. James, St. Michael's,

Father Maximus Leimgruber (1820–92). Source: Rev. Henry Borgmann, C.Ss.R., History of the Redemptorists at Annapolis, Md., from 1853 to 1903 *(Ilchester, Maryland: College Press, 1904), 23.*

Father Michael Müller, C.Ss.R. (1825–99). RABP.

and Holy Cross. In early March 1857, he suffered a hemorrhage in the throat so severe that he prepared himself for death and wrote a farewell letter to his family. But, as he began to recover, Ruland reassigned Seelos from the onerous duties in Baltimore to a more benign position in Annapolis. He traded places with his old classmate from Munich, Father Maximus Leimgruber, the superior and novice master in Annapolis. The reassignment to the quieter locale was supposed to help Seelos regain his health. He himself "very much desired" the position of novice master, "as his preference for the interior life found here the richest nourishment, and he was more fully separated from intercourse with the world," according to an early biographer. On the day after his arrival in Annapolis, Seelos wrote a letter to Father Wissel, exclaiming "I am now *Magister Novitiorum*! What luck and grace! O happy sickness that needed and obtained such a cure!"[75]

Seelos began his assignment in Annapolis on April 16, 1857. He quickly won the affection of the novices, and started a tradition at St. Mary's by instituting a May procession, crowning the Virgin Mary's statue, and other devotions in honor of the Blessed Mother. His time at St. Mary's was brief, however. One of the provincial consultors, Augustine Hewit, strongly advocated Seelos' assignment to be prefect of students in Cumberland, to resolve the restiveness of the students there, in place of Father Michael Müller. Hewit believed Seelos was the right man for the job, saying he was "a saint in spirituality, and an angel in sweetness." Seelos received his transfer order on May 18 and wrote that "I was driven out again of my terrestrial Paradise." He left Annapolis on May 21, to cheerfully assume his new duties in Cumberland. Except for a brief visit to Annapolis in 1859, did not return until June 14, 1862.[76]

Brother Jacob Engel, C.Ss.R. (1829–95). RABP.

Our Church Is Such a Barn

The novitiate at St. Mary's had received increasing numbers of candidates since its inception in 1853 and was soon pressed for space. In 1855–56, when Leimgruber was in charge, the Carroll House was enlarged with a three-story wing on its western end, providing sixteen more rooms. Although this expansion alleviated the crowded conditions in the Carroll House, it was, at best, a temporary measure to keep up with the surge of religious vocations. Parochial activities had also significantly increased since 1853. Soon after his arrival in Annapolis, Gabriel Rumpler had a small wing added to the front of the church to increase its size and to house a new 1,200-pound Meneely bell. But the wing did not add a significant amount of space, and the church was insufficient to seat all who wished to attend. Moreover, it was hoped that more conversions would take place if there was a larger and more beautiful church.[77]

Seelos was succeeded in May 1857 by Michael Müller, the prefect of students in Cumberland. Müller was born in Prussia in 1825, professed his vows as a Redemptorist in 1848, immigrated to the United States in 1851, and was ordained in 1853.[78] A forceful man who did not hesitate to speak his mind or take charge of situations when he saw the need, and now, in Annapolis, he was quick to fulfill his ambitions. On November 4, 1857, Ruland was in Annapolis for his annual canonical visitation. In a meeting with the Redemptorist community, Brother Jacob Engel blurted out his feelings about the need for a larger church. "Unser Kirch!" he blurted out, "ist wie ein Stall"—"Our church is such a barn!"[79] Although Engel may have said this on his own initiative, he must have been mindful of Müller's views on the need for a larger church. Müller was a man on a mission and, given the opening provided by Brother Jacob, he took the floor. Müller told the provincial that in order for the Lord to be praised properly, "we have to build a church in a better location." Ruland agreed with the proposal on the condition that if a certain amount of money—$2,000, two-thirds of the total needed—was collected within a certain amount of time through donations and subscriptions, construction could begin.[80]

Müller quickly began to raise money to build the new St. Mary's Church. His $3,000 budget was quite modest, considering that the Methodist congregation on State Circle believed their own proposed new church would cost $6,000 and that they would have to make appeals to the citizens of Annapolis for the funds. Moreover, the rector of St. Anne's Episcopal Church estimated he needed between $20,000 and $30,000 to rebuild his church, which had been destroyed by fire on February 14, 1858. St. Anne's vestry was encouraged at a public meeting to seek state funds, as had been set by precedent by the Catholic and Methodist churches of Annapolis in the past, and the Episcopalians assumed that the townspeople, even those "upon whom the Church had no special claim," would "rally to the rescue."[81]

US Census Office statistics on churches for 1860 report there was only one Catholic church in Anne Arundel County and that it could accommodate 1,200 persons. This is nearly three times the actual seating capacity of the new St. Mary's and appears to be more of an indication of the parish population. The value of the church property—presumably the new church and college building, the old church, the Carroll House, and the various outbuildings and land—was put at $30,000. It was the single-most valuable Catholic property outside of Baltimore, which boasted the large archdiocesan cathedral and numerous churches and convents. Müller's $3,000 thus surely was seed money, not his entire budget. But he and Ruland had available a large pool of free labor. Throughout the Redemptorist network of parishes, there were lay brothers who worked as in-house carpenters, blacksmiths, painters, and other trades. Plus, the novices in Annapolis were available for unskilled laborer. Although there was some opposition from the superiors in other Redemptorists houses, Müller was able to draft "all the province's brothers" for the project and he had to pay "not a single cent of interest."[82]

Thanks Be to God for All His Benefits

The eulogist at Müller's 1899 funeral, declared that "in spite of surprise and perhaps ridicule of others," he began to build the new church. Müller himself observed in November 1857 how wonderful it was that "all including Protestants demonstrated they were ready to help, according to their means" and concluded: "Thanks be to God for all His benefits! Thus the history of our new church had its beginning." He memorialized the saga of his fund raising and church construction in a ten-page poem that he wrote it in 1862, after leaving Annapolis. A copy—mostly in old German script with a few English-language stanzas—is included in the 1858 pages of the *Chronica Domus*.[83]

Father George John Ruland, C.Ss.R. (1817–85). RABP

After relating the roles of Brother Jacob and Father Ruland in the early stages of the project, Müller's poem continued at length about his fund-raising efforts. First he informed the parishioners of his plan to collect money. Then Müller prayed and "beseeched the novices to pray." Next he went onto the streets and door to door soliciting pledges and funds. Although he did not mention it in his poem, he was accompanied by a parishioner, Hugh McCusker, an Irish-born Naval Academy employee who would have known many townspeople. They met people on the street and in their homes and businesses and discovered the generosity of Annapolitans: "Jews, Protestants, Quakers along with poor Catholics" all gave donations for the new church. Müller may have had an inkling about potential support from the community as evidenced by a notation in the *Chronica Domus* the previous April when it was recorded that many citizens, including Protestants, had come to St. Mary's for the solemn Catholic Easter Sunday observances.[84]

Müller went on his in-town fund-raising expeditions three or four times. He also went out into the county to call on local farmers and to Washington. At least once he went by train to Baltimore where he met an unidentified "genteel man" whom he quoted in poetical manner as saying:

> The completion of her church in Annapolis is secured.
> If you, for want of money, should get into pressure,
> I will always help you with abundant measure,
> Give me only one month notice,
> And then you will have it forthwith.[85]

Müller also sent solicitation letters to people he

Excerpt of Father Michael Müller's poem, including line 3: "Unser Kirch!" sagt Bruder Jakob, "ist wie ein Stall." RAPB.

had not called on in person. He "received in this way a lot of money" and observed that begging by mail was a less mortifying than face to face. One of those to whom he wrote was former Governor Enoch Louis Lowe, who is of interest to St. Mary's history. Lowe was educated in Jesuit schools in Frederick, Maryland, and in Ireland and England before being admitted to the Maryland bar in 1842. He was elected to the Maryland House of Delegates in 1845 and from 1851 to 1854 served as the first popularly elected Catholic governor of Maryland. When Archbishop Kenrick visited Annapolis in October 1853 for Confirmation at St. Mary's, he noted in his journal that Lowe was present in church for the event. A Democrat, Lowe also was seen as "a friend of the immigrant." As governor, he was a resident of Annapolis and attended St. Mary's. His infant son, Vivian Polk Lowe, was baptized at St. Mary's on September 12, 1852, by Jesuit Father Roger Dietz. Henry May, a prominent Baltimore lawyer and soon-to-be-elected US congressman, and his wife, Henrietta DeCourcey May, served as Vivian's godparents. Müller's poem revealed that Lowe donated $100 to the construction of the new church. In 1860 Lowe would serve as a presidential elector for Southern Democrat John C. Breckinridge, advocated Maryland's secession from the Union, and even threatened "the banner of revolt" against Governor Hicks, going so far as to suggest killing Hicks if he did not lead Maryland into the Confederacy. After the war began, Lowe and his family lived in exile in Virginia and Georgia and afterward resettled in Brooklyn, New York, where he died in 1892.[86]

Edward Sparks later admitted to Müller that initially he had scoffed to himself at the idea of raising enough money to build a new church. Müller was more self-assured and not only reveled in his fund-raising skills but declared that St. Mary's "was a good 'money-house' for Father Rector." Müller also enlisted two of his confreres in the effort and one of them, Father John Cornell "[t]ried it twice despite his shyness." The other man was Prussian-born Father Joseph Maria Jacobs, a newcomer to Annapolis who had "diligently studied how it might be possible" to raise money but nothing was said about how they succeeded. Nevertheless, what is notable is that the people of Annapolis, Catholic and non-Catholic alike, provided most of the funds to build St. Mary's Church.[87]

Local church fund raising was prominently mentioned in September 1858 article in the *Annapolis Gazette*. While not mentioning any denomination by name, the openings sentence declared: "Of late the citizens of Annapolis have been much 'exercised' on the subject of subscribing to churches." It then described the attitude that "Church stock not paying any earthly dividends," many people "who haven't *time* to look eternitywards have refused thus to invest their surplus cash" in church building funds. The excuses for refusing to donate, said the *Gazette*, were "indicative of the size of the soul of the individual." But one excuse given was deemed "without a parallel in the history of 'church begging.'" A man, "better known for his wealth than his liberality," was requested to aid in the erection of an unnamed Annapolis church but when the subscription book was placed in his hands, "he looked at it anxiously and earnestly and handed it back with the astounding remark: 'No, sir! I will not give anything; not half as many people go to hell now as ought to go!'"[88] The man was not identified but the sentiment is similar to an episode in Müller's poem:

> One man of Annapolis by the name of Mr. Stocket
> Did not at all want to feel for me his pocket,
> But commenced to quarrel and to dispute,
> Which I thought will not do much good.
> When I saw I could not get from him any donation,
> I thought, this is for me a poor station.
> "Good bye, Sir," I said, and off I went,
> To find a better place for a present.

"Mr. Stocket" was Francis (Frank) Henry Stockett, a prominent lawyer and property owner, and a member of St. Anne's fund-raising committee.[89] Stockett will appear again in our story and again in a way unfavorable to the Redemptorists (see Vowed and Sworn to the Ministry of Peace, ch. 4).

Another potential donor Müller encountered in November 1857 was "a Know Nothing man," someone not likely disposed to support the Catholic Church. He was not identified but he "gave fifty dollars cash." Müller made no further comment about the Know Nothing but the generous donation and the priest's lack of commentary is interesting considering Maryland was still a hot-bed of Know Nothing fervor. As he walked the streets of Annapolis, Baltimore, and Washington and wrote letters seeking donations for the church, what was Müller to think of all these political machinations and how much did he understand? His own surviving papers are silent on the topic. He would have been conscious of the Redemptorist policy of avoiding political discussions, but he was an astute observer of human actions in general. And, he had a church to complete.

Because St. Anne's was destroyed by fire on Valentine's Day 1858, Müller thought his own fund-raising efforts would be affected. In his poem, he wrote:

> And we thought it would now be rather bad for our
> new church,
> Since the Protestants would now say to us:
> To your church we can now contribute nothing.
> But from no one was this excuse heard,
> Though their church was destroyed from the
> ground up.
> Everyone kept his word faithfully,
> And what they promised, they contributed.

As donations continued, construction on the new St. Mary's church began in earnest in the early spring of 1858. The novices and brothers excavated a trench for the foundation and the cornerstone was laid on May 11. Granite for the cornerstone, foundations, and embellishments came from Port Deposit, Maryland, and was shipped to a wharf built on Redemptorist property at the end of Duke of Gloucester Street. One of the Redemptorist brothers who undoubtedly worked on the early stages of construction was Peter Fischwenger, who had been at St. Mary's since July 1857. A native of Alsace, he was a carpenter by trade and was described in his 1867 obituary as an "architect." Brother Lawrence, as he was known in religious life, left Annapolis in May 1858 to help build another new Redemptorist church—St. Michael's—in Baltimore, construction of which had begun in August 1857.[90]

The Gothic Style of Architecture

Architect Louis L. Long reportedly completed the plans and specifications for St. Mary's new church just two weeks after the cornerstone blessing. He designed St. Michael's and St. Ignatius churches and Loyola College in Baltimore; St. Patrick's Church in Washington, DC; St. Anne's Church in Edenton, North Carolina; the Redemptorists' St. Alphonsus Church in New Orleans, and numerous other buildings between 1853 and 1860. The *Gazette* revealed that St. Mary's would "display the gothic style of architecture," with "heavy and large buttresses." A large rose window was planned as were large double windows to give light to the organ gallery from the front, with single foliated gothic windows along each side to allow light into the nave and sanctuary. A "large heavy embattlement" was to complete the top of the tower over which an octagonal spire with "trusses [that] will give a grand finish with pinnacles into crochets." It was designed to be topped with a "heavy gilded cross" 180 feet or more above ground level. A large oratory "for robing, and preparation for mass" was planned for one side of the sanctuary. Over the nave and aisles was planned a "grained ceiling," supported by columns with foliated caps. Redemptorist brothers would build "confessional boxes on each side, which will be adorned and finished with the finest kinds of gothic tracery." The pulpit, located on one angle of the sanctuary, "will finish out from the sounding board to the column of the ceiling." The organ gallery "will be of such height as to adapt the power of the instrument to the size and depth of the church." The plans called for 130 pews, "which will comfortably seat a congregation of one thousand persons, and will withal be finished in the most superior style of workmanship." The author of the article, which originally appeared on the front page of the Baltimore *American and Commercial Advertiser,* had seen a "finely traced and colored design" made by Long's partner, George T. Powell, and proclaimed that it "presents a fine external appearance." The new church was intended to be a grand edifice, unlike any other in Annapolis, and perhaps a counterpoint to the new Romanesque Revival Episcopal church rising on Church Circle.[91]

Thomas Lütte, a thirty-six-year-old Redemptorist brother, oversaw most of the construction of St. Mary's Church. He was praised in Müller's poem as "a very experienced man . . . under [whose] leadership we started the church." He came to Annapolis to prepare for his final vows as a lay brother, which he professed on June 6, 1858. A native of the Grand Duchy of Baden, he had been admitted to the Redemptorists in Baltimore in 1851 and, prior to his arrival in Annapolis, had been assigned to the Redemptorist house in New Orleans. There, between 1855 and 1857, he supervised the construction of another Louis Long-designed church, St. Alphonsus, considered at the time one of the largest and finest churches in the city. Brother Thomas arrived in Annapolis on December 7, 1857, and must have been on site at least until the fall of 1858, since Müller's poem said "He was doubtless sent by God to us, And though he did not complete God's work, We managed, under his leadership, to get under a roof." The *Annapolis Gazette* reported on August 19, that it "is expected to have it roofed and plastered before the cold weather comes." The *Chronica Domus* was silent on the departure of Brother Thomas but he was in New Orleans again in 1859 and went on to oversee construction of other Redemptorist churches and schools before dying at St. Joseph College in Windsor Springs, Missouri, in 1899.[92]

In the heat of the summer of 1858, timber was cut on John Randall's 200-acre farm—Greenfield, situated along the headwaters of Spa Creek—and used for scaffolding to build the brick walls of the church. Randall and his wife, Eliza Hodges Randall, had rented the Carroll House from around 1826 until just prior to the Redemptorists' arrival in 1853. Eliza was a stalwart parishioner of St. Mary's while John was Episcopalian by birth and would convert to Catholicism on his deathbed in 1861. Despite not being Catholic, he served as a non-canonical witness at a Catholic wedding officiated by Jesuit Father Charles Felix Van Quickenbourne in the Carroll House chapel in 1822.[93]

Bricks and lumber for construction arrived at the street-end wharf and brought to the work site hand-over-hand by the novices and brothers who prayed communally as they worked. As they labored under the hot Maryland sun, "the novices were roasted brown," said Müller. This hard work did not go unnoticed by Annapolitans. None less than "the Protestant preacher's wife" was quoted in poetic fashion by Müller. Presumably this was Mehitable Woodword Davenport, wife of St. Anne's rector, Rev. James Radcliffe Davenport. She was said to have exclaimed:

> No wonder the Catholics have with their church
> so great a luck,
> And never will, for want of money, remain
> somewhere stuck,
> Because to labor they join prayer,
> Thus God will not fail to bless their care.[94]

Several lines later, Müller wrote that as the walls "climbed up so quickly toward Heaven . . . the Protestants were all stunned, . . . [and] they started to envy us greatly, because their church was not progressing." St. Anne's reconstruction actually was well underway by July 1858 and was substantially complete in 1859.[95]

Despite the free labor, cash was needed as construction of the church continued and costs increased. This required more fund raising. During the nineteenth century, pew rents were the principle source of income for churches, including St.

The main altar at St. Anne's Church, Annapolis. Courtesy author.

Mary's. But more money was needed and soon. To help meet this need St. Mary's parishioners held a fair in March 1859 that netted $1,400.[96]

Once the church roof was in place, brothers who were carpenters made and attached laths for the vaulted ceilings. The novices learned to make laths and then nailed some 30,000 of them to the rafters. By the following spring—"in a little more than a year," wrote Müller—the church was substantially finished. The bell from the old church and three new bells hung in the tower and a new altar was in the sanctuary. The Baltimore *Sun* reported in April 1859 that the "frontispiece of an altar intended for St. Mary's church at Annapolis" was "to be seen at the stoneyard of Mr. John Whitelaw" in Baltimore. Noting that the altar would be sent to Annapolis during the present week, the frontispiece was said to be "as beautiful in design as it is novel" and that it was:

> wrought in drab stone and is four feet in length — In three circular panels are the emblems of the crucifixion. The centre panel is the cross, in the left three nails, and in the right the hammer and pincers. The panels are surrounded by clusters of grape, emblematic of the wine used in the administration of the sacraments. The frontispiece is accompanied with elegantly cut consoles, and the whole length of the altar when erected will be 7 feet 3½ inches. The artist who executed the work is Mr. Robert Thompson.[97]

The *Sun* had described a design very similar to the official emblem of the Redemptorists—the cross surrounded by three nails, a hammer, and pincers—the symbols of redemption. The reporter, however, was mistaken. The altar was not destined for St. Mary's but for St. Anne's Church where it has been since its 1859 installation.

Tradition has it that when Bishop Neumann blessed St. Mary's cornerstone on May 11, 1858, he also blessed a bell. In 1858 the only bell on site was the one Rumpler purchased in 1853 and hung inside the wing added to the front of the old church. This 1858 bell-blessing interpretation appears to be incorrect and is not mentioned in primary sources about the cornerstone blessing. Müller's poem, however, reveals that by 1859 "four bells were ringing in the tower" and that they had been blessed by Bishop Neumann. The Baltimore *Sun* reported that on Sunday, October 16, Bishop Neumann "performed the ceremony of blessing the new chime of bells for St. Mary's (Catholic) Church at Annapolis, Md." and was assisted by Fathers Michael Müller, Jacobs, and Cornell. Father John Duffy, identified as St. Mary's "new pastor," gave a discourse on the occasion.[98]

The *Chronica Domus* did not mention the bell blessing or Neumann's visit. Other than Müller's poetic mention and this single newspaper account, no other record has been found about Neumann in Annapolis in 1859 for what would have been his third and last visit. He had been in Annapolis immediately after two triennial provincial councils in Baltimore—the eighth (May 6–13, 1855) and the ninth (May 2–9, 1858). He visited Maryland twice in 1859: a brief visit to Baltimore in June and in Cumberland for ordination of minor orders in November. Neither Neumann's own diocesan newspaper, The *Catholic Herald and Visitor,* nor Baltimore's *Catholic Mirror* mentioned the 1859 bell blessing. Neumann officiated at confirmations in his own diocese on September 30 and October 23. The only hint that he might have been absent from Philadelphia in mid-October was that on October 16 Coadjutor Bishop James Frederic Wood officiated at confirmation, something Neumann would normally have done himself had he been in town.[99]

The three new bells, like the first one, were purchased from the Meneely Bell Company, of West Troy, New York. The names of the twenty-five donors of all four bells are recorded in St. Mary's first baptismal register and most have been identified as St. Mary's parishioners. The bells were given names appropriate to St. Mary's: "Gabriel" for the archangel and Rumpler; "Michael" for another archangel and Müller; "Alphonsus Teresia" for Alphonsus Liguori, the founder of the Redemptorists, and his major spiritual inspiration, Teresa of Ávila; and "Maria Joseph" for Mary, the patron of the church, and her husband St. Joseph.[100]

A New Monastery Just as Quickly

With the church progressing so well, by the fall of 1858, it occurred to Müller that he could "build a new monastery just as quickly." In a second epic poem, Müller wrote:

> The church was still not half-plastered,
> Which because of the many Gothic arches took
> much time,
> For thinking about it could work just as well
> To build a new monastery just as quickly.[101]

Thus began the new St. Mary's College building, now St. Mary's Rectory. According to Müller, the original college building—the Carroll House—was "too angly and far too desolate." The provincial superior had complained that they had "constantly to patch up something in there." Moreover, as the number of novices increased, it was no longer suitable to "maintain good breeding among them." The young men were crowded two or three to a room and some had to sleep in hallways. As Müller eloquently put it: "No corner was empty, no attic free, even the cow stall was not excluded." Unlike the new church, which was paid for with funds raised from parishioners and townspeople, the Redemptorists in other cities were "seized by compassion" and contributed money and the labor of their lay brothers "to erect a magnificent novitiate." After receiving Ruland's approval of the L-shaped building, Müller broke ground on the Feast of the Visitation (July 2, 1859). He recorded that 40,000 cubic feet of soil was excavated for the basement, with the novices and brothers working from early morning until late at night in the July and August heat. And, again, this labor of love left a deep impression on the local residents:

> Then were all Annapolitans very edified
> To see them at a task at which they would go gray.
> "Like jackapes," they said, "they work indeed,
> "Their building cannot fail, it must succeed.
> "Truly they are an industrious people,
> "This big College, the Church with the steeple,
> "Are a great improvement to our town
> "They acquire by them a great renown."

"Very soon," wrote Müller, these townspeople "were freed from their prejudices" since now they "clearly saw that we were worthy people." Some 500,000 bricks arrived at the Redemptorists' wharf, were counted, and then passed hand-over-hand up hill to the construction site. Since the bricks came by water, it is likely they were manufactured in Baltimore. According to the poem, as soon as the bricks arrived on site, the bricklayers applied them. The masonry work was completed within two months and the roof was quickly built to keep out the rain. As the cold weather arrived, the wood flooring arrived at the wharf and was carried up the hill board by board by the novices. During the winter months of 1859–60, twenty novices were each given a hatchet and set to nailing more than 100,000 laths, four nails each, to the walls and ceilings. Spring witnessed the completion of this ambitious project.

The work performed by the novices and brothers was an indication of Redemptorist devotion. All labors, whether prayer, spiritual exercises, attendance at Mass, and duties assigned were intended as devotional. Prayer and manual labor were important. When he later wrote about the excavation of the basement for the new college building, historian Father Borgmann said:

> Many a young man whose tender hands had never touched a pick or shovel, exerted all his strength to remove the hard ground. But every effort was made cheerfully and, though fingers sometimes bled from the rough work, hearts were contented and happy. Labor was consecrated by prayer.[102]

Light for the Whole Community

Around the time St. Mary's Church roof was been completed and the plaster work was underway inside in fall 1858, the advantages of natural gas in Annapolis were described in the local press. "Old fogy notions" about gas were being discarded since gas lighting and heating were introduced at the Naval Academy in 1853. John Walton's City Hotel at Church and Conduit streets, was one of the first buildings in town lighted with gas. It was expected that large supplies of gas would soon be demanded for private homes and "the public buildings, the State House, Government House, the College, and Churches." The press declared gas was more economical than sperm oil or candles, and safer than other "burning fluids." Gas lighting installed with fixed pipes also was deemed safer than movable devices, and housekeepers would appreciate not having to clean their lamps daily.[103]

The Redemptorists were among the thirty-seven share owners of the new Annapolis Gas Light Company. Other than the City of Annapolis, they were the only corporate entity to invest in the new technology. St. Mary's parishioner Eliza Randall, whose brother-in-law, Alexander Randall, was the gas company president, was one of three women investors. The Redemptorists purchased one share for $25 and Eliza Randall purchased eighteen shares for $450. Construction of the gas works, located on the Severn River, west of today's Wagner Street, was completed in January 1859 and soon the streets of Annapolis were lighted with gas for the first time.[104]

Three years later, Father Seelos attested to the use of

Redemptorist novices passing bricks from the wharf to the construction site. Original art by Constance D. Robinson.

gas lighting in Annapolis and at St. Mary's:

> In almost every larger house, they burn gas, and we, too, have it in our churches and in the corridors of the house, and everywhere that light for the whole community is needed; for example in the house chapel, in the refectory, etc. This gives so much light, without dirt and a need for cleaning, that you soon get so used to it that you nearly think you cannot live without it anymore.[105]

Keeping the church warm in the cold weather was another story. How St. Mary's new church was heated when it first opened remains open to speculation. Period documentation is silent on the subject and physical evidence of the earliest heating system has disappeared during the past 150 years. Only a single chimney appears on the church—currently and in vintage photographs—rising above the sacristy on the east side of the sanctuary. Whether that chimney was used for a coal-burning stove to heat the sacristy or was for ventilating a furnace under the sacristy is unknown. The latter seems unlikely because the space beneath the sacristy was converted into a crypt in 1864 and a new steam heating system was not installed until 1869–70.[106]

Müller must have been aware of the cause of St. Anne's fire, allegedly an improperly installed furnace. St. Anne's vestry brought suit in Superior Court in Baltimore against Collins, Heath, and Hutchinson, the Baltimore company that allegedly improperly installed four new hot air furnaces in November 1857. Forensic evidence, however, showed that the fire started not with the furnaces, located in the basement, but some eighty feet away and when the furnaces were cold. The court found in favor of the defendants. The story is instructive because of the discussion of period heating technology.[107]

There is no information on the type or source of St. Mary's furnace but, as a then-modern edifice, it must have had one. Redemptorist business records have not survived but a notebook kept in 1868 by Father Thaddeus Anwander, St. Mary's rector in 1866–68, provides a possible clue. In an undated entry between March 13 and 19, 1868, he wrote that he had paid $32.76 to "Thomas A. MaKibbin per Thomas K. Carey" for unspecified goods or services. MaKibbin, was a gas fitter and plumber and sold gas and water fixtures "of every kind, as well as every description of heating apparatus." Carey, who evidently worked as an agent for MaKibbin, and his wife Catherine O'Reilly Carey, were St. Mary's parishioners; four of their children were baptized at St. Mary's between 1856 and 1865. Carey later served as deputy register of wills for Anne Arundel County in 1863 and was elected as register in 1868.[108]

Perhaps MaKibbin maintained St. Mary's heating apparatus or was soon to be involved in the installation of a new gas-powered steam-heat system in 1869. In October 1868, he advertised that he was "prepared to introduce Gas Fittings and Fixtures into Churches, Public Buildings, and Private Residences, at the shortest notice." In 1858 there also was an Annapolis Stove Factory on West Street but it sold "parlor, plain and cooking stoves" rather than furnaces. The firm of William H. Stran and Company in Baltimore, which advertised in the Annapolis press, offered "parlor grates and stoves for parlors, dining, halls, [and] churches." Another local advertiser, Bibb and Company of Baltimore, also offered hot air furnaces. Cast iron floor grates were used in nineteenth churches for heating and very likely were used in St. Mary's before the introduction of steam heat.[109] St. Anne's has two original floor grates still in place on the side aisles but no longer in use. Made of cast iron and set in stone, they measure 26½" in diameter.

A Splendid New Organ

When mentioning the four bells in the church tower, Father Müller said: "Before one rang them for the first time: Soon there also came the magnificent organ with a Gothic frame." A Redemptorist seminarian, John Nepomucene Berger, writing home to Bohemia, described this organ as "very large and beautiful." On October 20, 1859, the *Annapolis Gazette* announced that a grand concert would be given in the new church, "for the benefit of the church, on the 27th inst., to commence at 8 o'clock." The concert was billed to include Bernard Courlaender, pianist of the king of Denmark, and the "best talent of Baltimore, including some of the members of the Baltimore Cathedral Choir, [who] had kindly volunteered their services for the occasion." Tickets cost fifty cents each and were available at the City Hotel. Since this was a piano concert, presumably the ringing of the bells had to wait, but not for long. On December 9, 1859, another "grand concert" was held at St. Mary's, "on the occasion of the opening of the splendid new organ erected in the church by Messrs. Simmons & Wilcox of Boston." It again featured the cathedral choir, and company cofounder John Henry Wilcox presided at the new organ. As in October, tickets cost fifty cents and were available from four sources, all parishioners: John Walton at the City Hotel, Adolph Robeck at his confectionary store on Church Street, Andrew Edward Denver, a Mexican War veteran and captain of the watch at the Naval Academy; and Mary Effine Lake at her fancy shop on Church Circle. Tickets also were on sale at the church door on the evening of the concert, which featured selections from Handel, Mendelssohn, Mozart, and Rossini.[110]

Although the pipes for the 1859 organ are still in place, they are no longer in use. The details of the capabilities of the organ are lost in time and missing documentation. However, another Redemptorist parish, St. Mary of the Assumption in New Orleans, purchased a Simmons and Wilcox pipe organ in 1861 and had it rebuilt around 1900. Closer to home, St. Ignatius Church in Baltimore has a Simmons organ built in 1860, rebuilt in the 1930s, and rebuilt again in 2010. These two vintage organs make an interesting potential comparison with St. Mary's long-ago-replaced 1859 organ. The capabilities of both the New

Orleans and Baltimore organs are described on their parish websites. In August 1862, after only three years use, Wilcox returned to St. Mary's to adjust and repair the organ pipes.[111]

An Earthly Paradise

Construction of the three new Annapolis churches continued throughout 1859. Newspaper reports in July claimed that work on the new Methodist and Catholic churches had progressed enough that they would probably be ready for services in the fall, despite the fact that the Methodists had laid their cornerstone only a month earlier.[112] St. Anne's was completed to the point that services were held in July and awaited only the proposed construction of two towers and "some other embellishments."[113] Duke of Gloucester Street was now anchored by a Romanesque Revival church at one end and a Gothic-style church at the other. With the African Methodist Episcopal Church on West Street, completed in 1838; the Presbyterian church on Duke of Gloucester Street, completed in 1847; the Naval Academy chapel, built in 1850; and the new Salem Methodist Church on State Circle, under construction, Annapolis now had—or would soon have—six attractive and imposing places of worship.

St. Mary's had a special visitor at year's end. Father Seelos was invited to preach at the consecration of the new St. Michael's Church in Baltimore on December 26. He left Cumberland on the train on Christmas Eve and spent several days in Baltimore. While there the new provincial, John De Dycker, urged Seelos "to visit Annapolis and the dear novices." The *Chronica Domus* had only two entries for December 1859 and made no mention of Seelos. But the visit was mentioned in the Cumberland chronicle as well as in a letter he wrote to his sister Romualda, two months later. He told her about the "genuine simplicity" of the novices, who displayed "such unaffected warmth, such joyful piety, and such visible cheerfulness!" He said there were "about thirty promising young men and although they still have their chapel right under the roof on the top floor, yet everything is arranged so devoutly and beautifully that I could have stayed there my whole life." He was referring to the novice chapel located on the third story of the Carroll House. Seelos also reported that "a big new house next to the very graceful church" was almost completed. He had a great affection for Annapolis, adding that "the location on the bay makes it an earthly paradise." He stayed only one day in Annapolis before returning to Cumberland on New Year's Eve. It would be two and half years before he would return.[114]

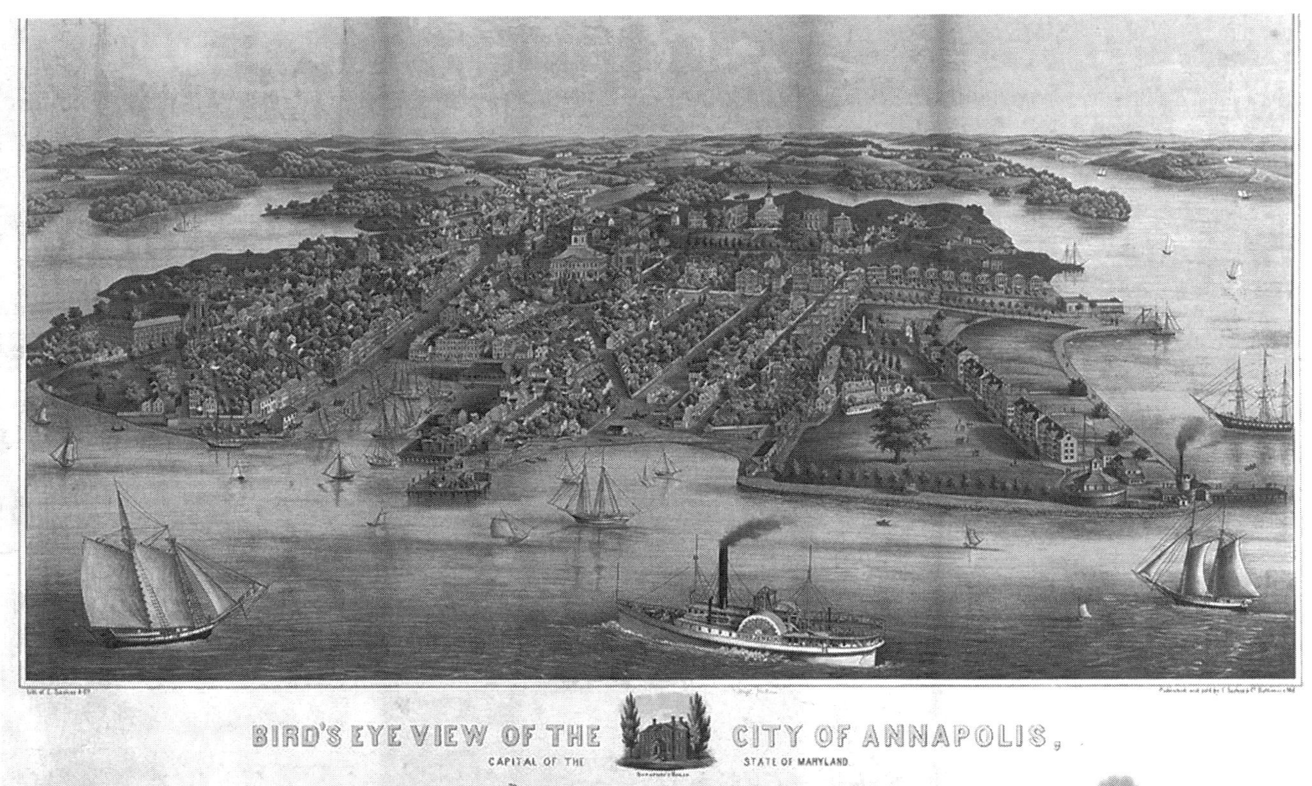

"Bird's Eye View of the City of Annapolis, Capital of the State of Maryland" Edward Sachse, Baltimore, 1860. Hambleton Print Collection, Maryland Center for History and Culture, https://www.mdhistory.org/digital-resource/2359/.

Chapter 2: 1860 — A Vast Building Has Been Erected

Annapolis on the Eve of War

The Democratic Party resumed control of the Maryland General Assembly in the 1859 state elections. When the legislature convened in Annapolis in 1860, the Democrats turned quickly to set limits on the political independence of Baltimore. As a result, the southern and Eastern Shore counties now held more than half of the seats in the legislature even though Baltimore and the northern counties had more than double the White population. The sizable free and enslaved Black populations of southern Maryland and the Eastern Shore gave these regions a legally disproportionate amount of representation. Moreover, large slave owners predominated in the legislature and both they and non-slave holders believed that a civil war would upset the discipline of Maryland's slave system.[1]

Besides the political events swirling around their city, Annapolitans experienced other significant changes. They saw the installation of gas lines to light its streets, public and commercial buildings, private homes, and new churches, including St. Mary's. In the preceding decade, old Fort Severn at the Naval Academy had been enclosed with a wooden wall and cupola and new buildings were added, including a combined laboratory and armory, an observatory, a seamanship building, a three-story recitation hall, five brick dormitories, a Greek Revival chapel, a hospital, and faculty quarters. Additional city land had been acquired for this expansion.[2]

The city built a new market house in 1858 and, in 1860 the Annapolis Telegraph Company was established and began to erect poles and wire between Annapolis and Annapolis Junction, where the telegraph line connected to Washington and Baltimore. The Redemptorists and several St. Mary's parishioners were among the investors in the new enterprise. The Redemptorists purchased two shares at $5.00 per share; parishioners Thomas Karney, James Revell, and Adolph Robeck also bought shares. Alida McParlin's Episcopal father-in-law, William McParlin, also was an investor, along with the City of Annapolis and numerous leading citizens.[3]

A Washington newspaper reported that Annapolis "with its endearments of revolutionary memory, its naval school and seats of learning, is, by the magic of the locomotive, almost at our door. . . . though now jocosely called a finished town, is destined to become a favorite place for saltwater bathing."[4] Indeed, when the first edition of *A Correct Guide to Strangers Visiting the Ancient City of Annapolis* was published in 1859, the author noted that the city was in a "central position, between north and south," and close to Washington, "giving it great commercial advantage." One building, noted as "quite a modern edifice," was the county courthouse on Church Circle, which in fact was already twenty-five years old. The considerably newer Naval Academy buildings were mentioned only for their being set in "a romantic and picturesque landscape."[5]

Other observers—all northerners—expressed a more critical view. Midshipmen Oliver Ambrose Batcheller, a seventeen-year-old New Yorker, wrote that "as far as the city of Annapolis is concerned there is but little to be said. It is a small antiquated city in which if it grows any, it is downhill." Philip Henry Cooper, another New York midshipman, told his parents that Annapolis was "the dullest town in the United States" and the "buildings in town are old tumble down rookeries built in 1700." Stephen Minot Weld from Massachusetts, a captain's clerk aboard a troop transport stopping at Annapolis soon after the war began, said the city looked to him "as if all its inhabitants and buildings had been enjoying a century's rest."[6]

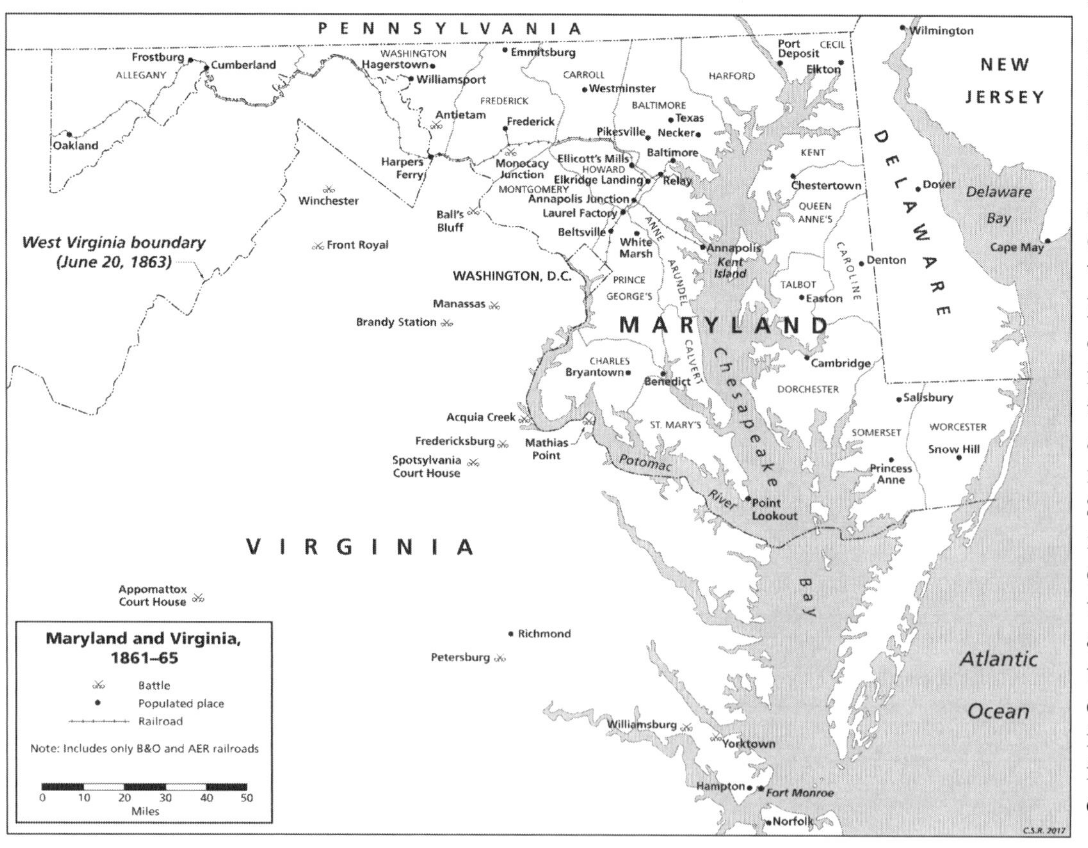

Annapolis was the state's third largest city after Baltimore and Frederick. It was compact and diverse with its Black and White populations and professional and laboring classes interspersed within the various neighborhoods. As the state capital, county seat, and home of the United States Naval Academy, Annapolis had close ties with Baltimore and the nation's capital, each nearly equidistant from Annapolis (see map "Maryland, 1861–65"). The Annapolis and Elk Ridge Railroad, a twenty-one-mile-long single-track line, connected the city to Annapolis Junction, where passengers transferred to the Baltimore and Ohio Railroad (B&O) to travel west to Washington and east to Baltimore. Anne Arundel County, including Annapolis, had Maryland's sixth largest population. It was a comparatively rich county, ranking sixth after Baltimore city and county, and Frederick, Prince George's, and Washington counties in real estate and personal wealth. Largely agricultural, Anne Arundel County ranked fifteenth in manufactured goods produced, outranking only the counties of southern Maryland and the Eastern Shore, except for Talbot County. Most of Anne Arundel's manufacturing activities were in or near Annapolis. Countywide only 176 men and 6 women were employed in 77 manufacturing establishments, annually producing $181,709 (0.004 percent of the state's total). Local manufactured goods included boots, shoes, flour and meal, sawn lumber, printing, and tin, copper, and sheet-iron ware.[7]

Anne Arundel County's numerous plantations and farms primarily grew orchard and market-garden products, wheat, Indian corn, and—above all in dollar value—tobacco. Anne Arundel ranked third in the state in tobacco production, after Prince George's and Calvert counties, producing nearly 16 percent of Maryland's total crop. Overall, Anne Arundel's total cash value of its farms was $7,512,331, giving it the seventh richest farm value among the twenty-one counties, despite having only the ninth largest amount of improved farmland. These statistics are based on the year that ended June 1, 1860.[8]

Annapolis boasted two weekly newspapers, the *Annapolis Gazette*, published on Thursdays, and the *Maryland Republican*, published on Saturdays. Much about life in town can be learned from the local press of 1860. It was still an innocent time in which the *Gazette* published on its front page poems both cheerful and melancholy, and little jokes such as:

> Father, have you got another wife besides mother?
> No, my son; what possesses you ask that question?
> Because I saw in the old family Bible that you married
> Anno Dominy 1842,
> and that is not mother, for her name is Sally Smith.[9]

Weekly news abounded with such items as the city government ordering skippers of vessel obstructing navigation in the busy harbor to move their vessel immediately. Those who declined or ignored the order were fined two dollars per hour. In a paid notice, Judge Nicholas Brewer warned the public not to "trespass with dog or gun" on his farm just outside Annapolis and warned parents "who permit the use of guns by their children" to keep them off his land or he was "resolved to enforce the penalty" for trespassing. The state's attorney for Anne Arundel County, St. Mary's parishioner James Revell, was busy prosecuting criminal cases, including murder, at the Church Circle courthouse. A three-dollar reward was offered by Richard P. Bayly for a large patch-work quilt stolen from the Gazette Printing Office at the corner of Francis Street and State Circle. In September 1860, to save money the city corporation—the mayor, recorder, and aldermen—unanimously resolved to discontinue lighting the street lamps, to suspend all improvements and repairs then in progress, and to clean the streets "only when it may be indispensably necessary to do so." They did not want to contract additional liabilities because some residents refused to pay taxes for the new gas lights. At the same time, the city government passed an ordinance requiring property owners with street frontage to keep the paved footways and gutters "free and clean from any obstruction by snow, ice, grass, sand, or anything whatsoever, at least three feet from the outside of the curb towards the centre of the street binding on such paved footways and gutters." The police were authorized to fine scofflaws between one and five dollars per offense.[10]

Numerous businesses lined the commercial streets of Annapolis—Church (as Main Street was officially known), lower Prince George, Conduit, and West. These included several "family" grocery stores in which patrons could purchase foodstuffs. Fresh oysters and meat could be ordered and preserved on ice, which also was on sale. Other shops sold cooking and dining utensils, as well as tools for the house and farm. Alcohol, cigars, chewing tobacco, and "bronchial cigarettes" for "instant relief and permanent cure" were available for those in need. Several shops sold patent remedies for such conditions as eruptive diseases, tumors, "scald head" and "toad stomach." One shop sold a toothache remedy that promised "instantaneous relief for several days duration." Shoppers who could afford it could buy ready-made dress clothes and imported accessories. For the laboring class, there was an assortment of apparel suitable for farm hands, as well as hats, caps, boots, and shoes of every description. Jewelry, watches, and clocks were offered for sale, as was a newly published bird's-eye view lithograph of the City of Annapolis for ten dollars per copy, "handsomely framed," and "worthy of place in any Annapolitan's parlor." Simon J. Martenet, a Baltimore surveyor and civil engineer, offered to publish, "if a sufficient number of subscribers is obtained," a large new map of Anne Arundel County, a specimen of which was on display at the sheriff's office in the courthouse.[11]

All manner of building materials could be obtained locally, both for new constructions and renovations. Furnaces and stoves, and many varieties of fuel for heating the house, office, shop, or church were available on West Street. One man advertised that "he is prepared to clean sinks, and other places, at the shortest notice and on the most reasonable terms." (A "sink" was not a kitchen appliance but the outhouse located in a dwelling's backyard.)[12]

Annapolitans were informed of unusual visitors to town, such as a delegation from the Japanese embassy that toured the Naval Academy in May 1860. In August the *Great Eastern,* a nearly 700-foot-long, 4,000-passenger British steamship, arrived in Annapolis Roads from New York City with *Annapolis Gazette* editor Thomas Wilson onboard. Thousands of visitors reportedly shuttled out to tour the massive ship, the largest in the world.[13]

Annapolis was the principal trading center for the county, with its more than 1,200 plantations and farms. At the top of city and county society were old-line planters, merchants, lawyers, and physicians, followed by a sizable middle class of younger lawyers, doctors, teachers, dentists, shopkeepers, hotel keepers, restaurant and saloon owners, and bakers, some of local origins but many of them newcomers from Europe and the North. At the bottom of society were the White laboring class and free and enslaved people of color.[14]

The grim reality of the times is seen in advertisements for human beings for sale. Local attorney Frank Stockett offered for sale at the county courthouse on January 27, 1860, "five young negro men and boys" belonging to a client. One West River owner offered a $25 reward for "a negro man calling himself John Atwood, or Urquhart" who ran away during the Easter holidays and "doubtless is lurking" in Annapolis or across the Severn River where he had relatives. He had been hired "by the year and left without provocation."[15]

Horse-drawn carriages were routinely advertised for sale but Annapolis was more quickly connected to the world at large via the Annapolis and Elk Ridge Railroad. The "passenger train of cars" departed from the depot at Calvert and West streets at 7:10 AM and 2:20 PM via Annapolis Junction to Baltimore ($1.00 one way, $1.50 round trip) or Washington ($1.60 one way, $2.00 round trip). Merchants and farmers also shipped their goods or produce by two packet schooners that departed Annapolis for Baltimore every Monday, Wednesday, and Friday at 10:00 AM. For end-of-life considerations, Charles R. Sullivan offered to make mahogany, walnut, poplar, and pine coffins, as well as metallic cases for the more affluent.

Amidst this rich mix of goods and services were businesses run by St. Mary's parishioners and their families. Reference was made earlier to parishioners Thomas Carey, who was an intermediary for Thomas MaKibbin, the West Street gas fitter and plumber, and David Caldwell, a Calvert Street lumber dealer. Colonel John Walton, with the assistance of his son Edward, ran the City Hotel at the corner of Church and Conduit. Two other Walton sons, physician Henry Roland and dentist John Randolph, had their offices in the hotel. The elder Walton was born in Rochdale, Lancashire, England, and immigrated to the United States in 1818, settling first in St. Mary's County, where he operated the Washington Hotel in Leonardtown, and then in Annapolis where he worked for a time as editor of the *Maryland Republican,* and acquired the hotel in 1848.[16] The City Hotel included a barbershop, which was run by Moses Lake, a Catholic "free colored" hairdresser, and sometimes barber at the Naval Academy. His wife, Mary Effine Lake, ran a fancy shop on Church Circle.

Annapolitans with a sweet tooth could go down Church Street from the City Hotel to St. Mary's parishioner Adolph Robeck's confectionary shop. Another parishioner, Henry Holmes Treadway, who, with his wife Emma Duvall and children, lived on Duke of Gloucester Street, was a master carpenter. Two other parishioners who lived on Duke of Gloucester Street, across from the city Assembly Rooms, were free Blacks David Maynard and Martha Jacobs Maynard. They worked in service trades, he as a laborer and she as a washerwoman, an important part of an African American family's income.[17]

Another St. Mary's parishioner was Francis Nicholas Daley. He was well known in town, having served as Anne Arundel County tax collector, printer, and publisher of the *Democratic Star*, a now-defunct Annapolis weekly. He had been baptized as a four-year old in 1820 by Father Van Quickenbourne in the days when the Catholic chapel was in the Carroll House. His mother was Priscilla Darnall, which gave him distant kinship to a number of illustrious Catholic Marylanders: Charles Carroll of Carrollton, the signer of the Declaration of Independence; Daniel Carroll, signer of the US Constitution, and his brother John Carroll, the first American bishop. Daley's children were baptized by Jesuits and Redemptorists in the first St. Mary's Church, and his wife, Julia Ann Wells, would serve as godparent and confirmation sponsor three times during the Civil War.[18]

John Wesley Brady, who would become a Catholic in 1868, ran a bakery with his father on Cornhill Street. His wife, Anna Maria, was a member of the prominent Catholic Revell family and sister of Anne Arundel County State's Attorney James Revell, a Democrat. Other parishioners included shoemaker John Cassidy, printer Edward Speed DuBois, ship carpenter William Henry Popham, physician Edward Sparks, and shopkeeper Ellen Elizabeth Walsh. Many St. Mary's men toiled as laborers or watermen and women as "domestics."

Henry Dunker ran a restaurant and hotel on Church Street, serving liquors, wines, ales, cigars of various superior brands as well as oysters, and crabs. Although he was not Catholic, his widow, Mary Francis (Fanny) Campbell Dunker, an Annapolis native, and their four of their six children would convert to Catholicism soon after his 1864 death.[19]

John Randall, who would convert on his deathbed in 1861, owned numerous lots of real estate. In 1860 he advertised vacant lots and frame homes for sale on Randall Street, Prince George Street, Carroll's Alley (now Pinkney Street), Bloomsbury Square, and Crocus Point on Dorsey Creek (now College Creek).

Familia Domus

At the start of each year, and occasionally twice a year, the *Chronica Domus* provided an annual listing of the Annapolis Redemptorist community's "Familia Domus" (household family). The listing for January 1860 comprised twenty-eight men, starting with Father Michael Müller, the superior of the

Redemptorist community and novice master of St. Mary's College. Following Müller and listed in order of their dates of ordination were three other priests. The first was thirty-three-year-old Irish-born John Baptist Duffy, ordained in 1849 and, after having served at St. Alphonsus in New Orleans since 1851, arrived in Annapolis in 1859. He remained only fifteen months before returning to New Orleans. Duffy held the title of *praefectus ecclesiae* (church prefect or administrator), making him the de facto pastor of St. Mary's and, when not teaching algebra, arithmetic, or English, devoted his efforts to the laity. He was said to have worked "zealously" with the parishioners but also was frequently sent to preach missions, which were multi-day courses of sermons and instructions and hearing confessions in Catholic parishes for the purpose of making the attendees "true and practical Catholics." Duffy is said to have preached missions "with the greatest energy." How much influence he may have had on St. Mary's parishioners, or vice versa, during his short tenure is unknown. His necrology says that before he was assigned to New Orleans in 1851 he had been "a staunch abolitionist" but after living there he "modified his ideas so as to make him a strong Southerner in principles as if he had been born in the South." Those ideas would have stood him well in Annapolis, although he would not have used the pulpit "as a place for politics," according to his biographer.[20]

Next in line was musically talented John Henry Cornell. He was born in New York City in 1828, the descendant of seventeenth-century English immigrants, and raised in the Episcopal faith. At age twenty, Cornell was appointed organist in St. John's Chapel (Trinity Parish) in New York. The next year he embarked on a tour of cathedrals in England and ended up converting to Roman Catholicism while in York. He returned home in 1850 and, in July 1852, professed his vows as a Redemptorist in Baltimore. Cornell was among the pioneers in Annapolis when the novitiate was established in 1853. Following his theological studies in Cumberland, he was ordained there in 1857 and, after his second novitiate (a period of post-ordination preparation for active ministry), he was assigned to Annapolis in 1858. He served as socius—an adviser and confidant—to Müller. Cornell was allowed to draw on his patrimony deposited with the Redemptorists in 1852 to purchase the organ for the new church in 1859. He also used his patrimony to publish three books of Gregorian chant and psalmody, all printed by Kelly, Hedian, and Piet in Baltimore in 1860–61. A fourth book, published in Boston in 1865, was original music and hymns written for Catholic children, a work he presumably started in Annapolis. He had no teaching duties listed in the "Familia Domus" but would have interacted with the novices and the parishioners as musician and organist as well as church prefect in Duffy's absence.[21]

The fourth priest listed was George Roesch, who was listed first among the novices. Born in Austria in 1822, he had been ordained as a secular (diocesan) priest in New York in 1847 but wanted to join a religious order. He arrived in Annapolis in 1859 to begin his novitiate.[22] In addition to Roesch, there were seventeen other novices. Normally after their novitiate and profession of vows in Annapolis, the young men went to Cumberland, where they studied rhetoric, philosophy, theology, and typical college-level courses under the direction of Father Seelos. Rounding out the 1860 roster were three seminarians who were sent from Cumberland to Annapolis for health reasons, and four lay brothers, men who entered religious life in service to the Redemptorist community and parishioners. The Annapolis complement in 1860 included Brother Louis Sterkendries, a forty-six-year-old Belgian wood carver and carpenter. It was he who built the soaring gothic altar soon to grace the sanctuary in the new church. There were two tailors, Bernard Pollmann, born in Kingdom of Hannover in 1810, and Jacob Engel, born in Bavaria in 1829, and a gardener, Rudolph Wallenhorst, born Hannover in 1821. The tailors were responsible for making and repairing the vestments, altar linens, and other cloth liturgical items and outfitting the priests, seminarians, novices, and themselves with habits and other clothing. Sometimes brother cobblers also were assigned to Annapolis to make sure all were well shod. As a gardener, Brother Rudolph would have not only tended the gardens surrounding the church and novitiate but also vegetable plots across the street from the church, and he may have tended the grounds of the new parish cemetery on West Street. Besides their assigned duties, the brothers did much more. For example, Brother Jacob was noted for his "cleverness in transacting every kind of business." A tailor by profession, Rumpler also appointed Jacob "to such offices as required special discretion," such as the dismissal of failed novices.[23]

The diversity of the Redemptorist community was observed by Frater John Berger, a student of rhetoric assigned to Annapolis for health reasons, shortly after he arrived in October 1860. He wrote:

> How manifest is the virtue of our gracious God in this one large community. Notwithstanding the dissimilarity of the countries from which they come and the manner of their language and character, the differences are so great, because here we have English, Germans, Americans and Irish. So distinguishing one nationality from the other is not easy, [but] the same land of brotherly love makes for one family with always the same goal. That goal we reach for is our love of the Mother of our Congregation.[24]

Familia Parochia

Membership or association with St. Mary's was just one of the connections existing among Annapolis and Anne Arundel County residents. They also had the bonds of workplace and neighborhood, school (if they were White), and social and familial relationships. They shopped at stores in Annapolis and perhaps occasionally rode the train or steamer together. And they mingled with their Protestant schoolmates, friends, neighbors, co-workers, shopkeepers, bankers, and many others. This did not mean parishioners voted the same way or held to all local traditions. But in the mid-nineteenth century, as Randall Miller, a historian of Southern religion, put it, churches provided "a moral compass to guide both public and private life" and they offered a different sense of belonging and bound individuals together "with common values for common purposes." Some St. Mary's parishioners were slave owners, most were not. Longtime residents were the product of Southern culture and inclination and St. Mary's White parishioners at large likely accepted the status quo of slavery. But some parishioners were enslaved, others were "free colored" but lived a world prejudiced against Black people. Catholic immigrants, who usually were not received with open arms in America, at least found a familiar home at St. Mary's and would have looked to Rome, or at least to the See of Baltimore for guidance on the American issues of slavery and abolition. These diverse peoples achieved a unity through the priests who served them and the worship they joined in together and the parish construction and maintenance in which they may have participated. All these activities, says Miller, "gave Catholics shared beliefs and experiences that formed the marrow of a distinctive religious culture." Miller also points out, however, that the Catholic Church did not have the resources to set up separate Black and White churches, "and congregational autonomy was not a recognized church practice."[25]

The Holy Catholic Religion Shone Forth

St. Mary's new church was dedicated on January 15, 1860, with the Redemptorist provincial, Father John De Dycker, presiding. Tradition has it that Bishop Neumann planned to return to Annapolis for the dedication, but he died suddenly in Philadelphia on January 5, 1860. No documentary evidence has been found to support or contradict this tradition which endures at St. Mary's.

The dedication ceremony was simply described in the *Chronica Domus*:

> January 15 — which was Sunday and the feast day of the Most Holy Name of Jesus, our new church was dedicated under the title of the Blessed Virgin Mary of the Immaculate Conception by the Very Rev. Father Provincial John De Dycker.[26]

The *Annales Congregationis Ss. Redemptoris Provinciae Americanae* (Annals of the American Province of the Congregation of the Most Holy Redeemer) recorded that most of the functional parts of the new church had been completed by the time of its dedication and that "only a few required items were still desired." The four bells of St. Mary's had been hoisted into the belfry during construction and, after the dedication, they rang "from that time on, [as] the holy Catholic religion in the city shined forth in a kind of beauty in every part of greater Annapolis."[27]

Much can be learned about the diversity of age, native place, and career by looking at the activities in the college. De Dycker remained in Annapolis after the church dedication for another important ceremony on January 16 when he presided over the profession of vows by three novices. They were Irish-born nineteen-year-old Thomas John Kenny, who spent the rest of his short life in Annapolis; eighteen-year-old John O'Brien, who grew up in a Redemptorist parish in Monroe, Michigan, and died in Cumberland six years later; and thirty-year-old Frederick Friedinger, who was born in the Kingdom of Württemberg, but was dismissed from the congregation ten months later. At the same time, Adam Dietz, a native of the Duchy of Hesse-Darmstadt, was invested to begin his novice year. He completed his studies and was ordained in 1866 but would die in 1870. John Baptist Haas, a twenty-nine-year-old Bavarian, professed his vows as Brother Bonaventure and lived a long and useful life of service to the order until his death in Baltimore in 1912.[28]

As a demonstration of the fluidity of the college population, during January 1860 the *Chronica Domus* reported the arrivals from Cumberland of six professed students. Two of them, Prussia-born twenty-three-year-old Anthony Kesseler and Swiss-born twenty-four-year-old Joseph Brandstätter, were sent to Annapolis to receive the minor order of lector. (These men were called *frater clericus* or *frater studens,* meaning brother cleric or brother student, a title used to distinguish a seminarian from a lay brother—*frater laicus.*) Kesseler, one of the 1853 pioneers at St. Mary's, was dispensed of his vows in 1863 and became a diocesan priest in New York City in 1865 and was later known as "the Saint of Harlem." He died when his ship en route to Europe sank off Newfoundland in 1898. It was said that he was one of three Catholic priests who "did their utmost to quell the panic" and was granting absolution to others as the ship went down. Another arrival was Prussian-born Redemptorist Father Frederick William Wayrich, who departed for Philadelphia after a few days. He was not part of the assigned staff, but rather a short-term visitor, a pattern that he repeated in 1864, 1865, and 1866. Among other men who arrived during this time was Timothy W. Enright, a twenty-two-year-old Irish seminarian who was sent from Cumberland to Annapolis for health reasons. He is notable because of the several parts he will play in the St. Mary's Civil War story.[29]

Two weeks after the dedication, Archbishop Francis Patrick Kenrick arrived in Annapolis to confer the sacrament of Confirmation. It was the first time for the sacrament in the new church. The thirty-seven parishioners confirmed included ten males and twenty-seven females. Of these thirty-seven individuals, twenty were converts, a sign of the fruits of the labor of the Redemptorists in the local community. They included eight African Americans (one male, seven females), all of whom were converts. The family names of the confirmands continued to resonate in St. Mary's parish life in the nineteenth century: Denver, DuBois, Sparks, and Treadway among the White parishioners and Cuper, Harris, and Jacobs among the Black parishioners.[30]

Work continued on the new college building throughout the winter. It took the novices two months to mount more than 100,000 laths and another two months to apply the plaster. Then the doors and window frames were installed and painted. Father Müller observed that "[d]uring all the construction not one of them harmed a limb" and many Annapolitans were astounded by the speed with which the building was completed.[31]

The *Catholic Mirror* reported that by February 1860 a "vast building, intended for a Novitiate and house of studies, has also been erected contiguous to the church. It contains above seventy rooms." According to one source, the new building accommodated 100 novices. It had modern fixtures, such as gaslights throughout and a potato-peeling machine in the kitchen. Father Seelos mentioned "a really tiny machine in my room . . . to sharpen pencils." These devices were seen by Seelos as signs of American industrial progress but also of their being out of touch with God. The college also had numerous large and small rooms and long corridors connecting the various parts of the building. St. Mary's College or Convent—as it was often called—was an imposing edifice, standing next to the new Gothic church, both of which could be seen with unobstructed views from the Annapolis harbor and beyond. Martenet's map of Annapolis produced in 1860 shows, inaccurately, the outlines of both the old and new churches and the new "convent." A more accurate representation of the church-college complex, also published in 1860, was Edward Sachse's "Bird's-Eye View of Annapolis."[32]

St. Mary's College and the new and old churches, detail from "Bird's Eye View of the City of Annapolis, Capital of the State of Maryland" Edward Sachse, Baltimore, 1860. Hambleton Print Collection, Maryland Center for History and Culture, https://www.mdhistory.org/digital-resource/2359/.

The old Jesuit rectory, located next to the first St. Mary's Church on Duke of Gloucester Street. Source: Rev. Henry Borgmann, C.Ss.R., History of the Redemptorists at Annapolis, Md., from 1853 to 1903 *(Ilchester, Maryland: College Press, 1904), 8.*

May 17—the Feast of the Ascension—was fair, nearly cloudless day in Annapolis. On this beautiful spring day, most of the forty-six men living in the overcrowded Carroll House marched ceremoniously into the new college building. The Blessed Sacrament was transferred in a solemn procession from the third-story chapel in the old novitiate to the new third-story chapel in the new building. The processing priests, students, novices, and brothers, led by a cross-bearing acolyte, might have sung or recited *Adorna* ("Adorn thy bridal chamber, Sion, and receive Christ the King") as an appropriate hymn for the occasion. The Redemptorists congratulated themselves that their new home truly deserved the title of "monastery."[33]

Besides the chapel, the new building had offices, classrooms, bed chambers, an infirmary, and other utilitarian spaces. The college library may have been moved to the new building or possibly remained in the Carroll House. The unfinished attic was used for storage. The basement included the kitchen, refectory, store rooms, and other functional areas, such as probably a room for the Redemptorists' printing press (Typis C.Ss.R., Annapoli). Renovations in 2011, when several layers of modern floor and wall coverings were removed, indicated a slightly different arrangement of some of the first-story rooms. The public area was smaller in 1860 and included a reception area and office near the entrance on Duke of Gloucester Street. A partition and door just beyond the public office barred further passage into the private, cloistered area. Inside the private area, there were six doors with transoms above them, many of which were still in place in 2011. Although there is no documentary or physical evidence of where the rector's bedroom and personal office was located, the rector's room at St. Alphonsus rectory in Baltimore was the room nearest the front entrance and has been restored to its appearance when St. John Neumann, Blessed Francis Xavier Seelos, and other nineteenth-century rectors used it. It is possible that one of these first-story rooms at St. Mary's was the rector's office and, therefore, the room used by Seelos.

Around this time—when the new college was under construction—the original seventeenth-century frame Carroll House was razed to its brick and sandstone foundations, some of which survive, some above ground, others below. Charles Carroll the Settler purchased the 1680s two-story, twenty-four-foot-long frame house and an acre of land at the end of Duke of Gloucester Street in 1706. Carroll used this house as his principle urban residence, and the site of the family chapel, until his death in 1720. Thereafter his widow, Mary Darnall Carroll, had a life estate on the house until she died in 1742.[34] In the meantime her son, Charles Carroll of Annapolis, in the early 1720s, commenced construction of an adjoining brick house, which survives today with several additions. When the Redemptorists arrived in 1853, the frame house was said to be "in a decayed condition." Sachse's 1860 "Bird's-Eye View of Annapolis" shows the old frame house but an 1864 photograph of the Redemptorists' sailboat fleet on Spa Creek shows it was gone. When Borgmann published his history of the Redemptorists in Annapolis in 1904, he said only that the "ancient structure was taken down some years ago." The Redemptorists, always pressed for space, presumably used the old house as an annex to the novitiate in the brick Carroll House, but with the new college building underway, it had no more useful purpose. Another credible source says that there was "a large wooden annex" on the end of the brick house and that "[o]wing to the unsafe condition, this annex was torn down in 1860." The Redemptorists were adept at using salvaged materials in their building projects; three doors and an architrave, dating to the eighteenth century and perhaps earlier, were still in place in the basement of St. Mary's Rectory in 2020. Technical analysis of the paint on one of the doors and the architrave provide clues that they did not come from the brick Carroll House but rather from the old frame Carroll House.[35]

Fulfilling the Needs of the Community

Use of the former Carroll property was both functional and communal since the beginning of the Redemptorist occupation. Archaeological investigations conducted between 1987 and 1991 provide new definition to the religious community's transformation of the property, as described as follows:

> Unlike Carroll's design for pleasure and public display, the space was organized to fulfill the needs of the community: there was a vineyard and wine cellar to the west, an arbor to the east, and a farmyard and boating facilities to the south. The area that had been Carroll's private, formal, terraced garden was used no differently by the Redemptorists than the rest of the area around the house.[36]

Archaeology uncovered remnants of a working farm that included a spring house, a chicken coop and evidence of viticulture, flower beds, and vegetable plots. In contrast to Carroll's formal waterfront garden, "the Redemptorists' property was a jumble of barns, outbuildings, religious statuary, and fields." During the last half of the nineteenth century, the Redemptorists used the property as a place where young men performed physical labor while preparing their spiritual selves for future priesthood. Communal labor, whether it was growing flowers for the altar or vegetables for the table, raising chickens or tending to the cows, was part of the daily routine for the novices and lay brothers. It was observed that "a prominent historical landmark was made invisible to the town. . . . The symbol of Carroll's patriotism, prosperity, and prominence had been hidden, and in its place stood a productive farmyard and a building of institutional scale and proportion unlike any then in Annapolis . . . . [and] whereas Carroll's garden legitimated his wealth, the Redemptorists' landscape was a consecration of their poverty and vows."[37]

Redemptorist historian Borgmann struck a similar theme in 1903:

> Many of these young men, nay, boys of sixteen to eighteen, had left homes which every comfort rendered sweet. They left loving parents and affectionate sisters and brothers, to consecrate themselves heart and soul to their Divine Master. They knew that the service of God demands sacrifice, and they were ready to make it. With manly courage they embraced the austerities of the religious life, remembering that, only by suffering and self-denial, could they become true disciples of their Redeemer, and true apostles.[38]

Borgmann also described the uncomfortable sleeping conditions, sometimes in intensely cold rooms, being at prayer in the chapel by 5:00 AM, a scanty breakfast, an hour of manual labor in strict silence, religious instructions, dinner at noon followed by an hour's recreation, then spiritual exercises until the 7:00 PM supper, and then an hour of "fraternal conversation" before retiring for the night. Seelos wrote in 1862 that during recreation periods he sat in a "simple, wooden armchair," that was once owned by Charles Carroll of Carrollton, to oversee the activities of the novices and students. He observed too, that Carroll's stately old home was highly valued by Americans and who "look upon this house with a certain reverence and would not tolerate it if we wanted to tear it down."[39]

A Matter of Curiosity

A controversy at St. Anne's Episcopal Church involving St. Mary's had its origins in 1860. A native Annapolitan and Episcopal priest, Reverend Jonathan Pinkney Hammond, was visiting his hometown and was invited by his aunt's husband to visit the new St. Mary's Church. The husband was Dr. Edward Sparks, whose first wife, whom he married in 1826, was Rosetta Pinkney, who died in 1829. Three years later, Sparks married Rosetta's sister Sophia, the aunt described in this episode. A third sister, Sarah, married John Wesley Hammond, the father of Jonathan Pinkney Hammond. An individual who remains unidentified later told Episcopal Bishop of Maryland William Rollinson Whittingham that Hammond been unfaithful to the Episcopal Church because he visited St. Mary's. In a letter of self-defense to Bishop Whittingham, Hammond referred to Sparks as "a Romanist" and said his aunt was "firm in her allegiance to our own Ch[urch]." On his first visit to St. Mary's, Hammond and Sparks went to "the Institution of the Redemptorists simply as a matter of curiosity." Hammond claimed he had "no communication whatever with any of the priests, except to exchange the courtesies of life, with one or two of them to whom I was introduced." On a second visit, Hammond went with his aunt, his wife Ann "Nannie" Page Hammond, and "several friends to hear a remarkably fine organ, which had recently been put up in the Church." The group spent twenty or twenty-five minutes there, during which time they listened "as one of the priests performed on the organ in the gallery; he being concealed from view by a curtain." The organist would have been John Cornell. As unusual as it must have been for a Protestant clergyman to visit St. Mary's and be introduced to some of the priests, no mention was made of the visit in the *Chronica Domus*.[40]

Nothing came of Hammond's visits to St. Mary's until 1866. After the war started, Reverend Hammond returned to Annapolis as chaplain to Army General Hospital Division No. 2, located at St. John's College, and served as editor of its weekly newspaper, *The Haversack*. During this time, he made a singular contribution with his 286-page *Army Chaplain's Manual*, completed in March 1863 for Protestant chaplains. It covered Federal laws concerning chaplains; army regulations; the pay, rank, and uniforms; how to obtain an appointment as a hospital chaplain; the trials and difficulties of chaplains; the comforts and encouragements of army chaplains; qualifications; temporal duties; soldiers' recreations; pastoral work (public and private); prayers and scripture reading for the sick; private devotions; and the texts of fifty-seven devotional hymns. The manual also quoted at length from *A Treatise on Hygiene, with Special Reference to the Military Service* published the same year by Surgeon General of the Army William Alexander Hammond, Jonathan's brother.[41] General Hammond notably wrote a letter to Lincoln in 1862 praising the exemplary work of the Catholic Sisters of Charity as "a corps of faithful, devoted and trained nurses . . . trained to obedience, are of irreprochable [*sic*] moral character and most valuable are their ministrations." He said this in comparison to the Protestant nurses who "cannot compare in efficiency and faithfulness with the Sisters of Charity."[42]

From 1865 to 1869, Hammond served as the rector of St. Anne's. He was elected to the position because he "profess[ed] a conversion to Secession views," according to one diarist. It was during this time that the communication to Bishop Whittingham accused Hammond of unfaithfulness to the Episcopal Church. Whether Whittingham heard the accusation in person or in writing cannot be determined as no additional relevant documents have been found. However, Hammond's tenure at St. Anne's became tenuous as he was criticized by the vestry about how he conducted communion services, having introduced "many novel and unauthorized practices," conducted services as done "in the Romish Mass," and demonstrating "Romanizing tendencies." The vestry member who prepared the "specifications" against Hammond was John Randall's younger brother, Alexander, who also criticized Hammond's brother, William, for alleged attacks on Bible history. Moreover, Randall had opposed Hammond's 1865 selection as rector, but later wrote mostly positive things in his diary about the new rector and only became thoroughly disenchanted with his "novel practices" by 1868.[43] Although the Hammond-at-St.-Mary's episode was not played out in public, it attests to periodic tension between the two churches and their members.

About 200 Catholics

The Federal Census of 1860 reported an aggregate of 687,049 individuals living in Maryland. Of these, 171,131 (25 percent of the total) were recorded as Black or "mulatto"—mixed race—of whom 83,942 (12 percent) were "free colored" and 87,189 (13 percent) were slaves. Anne Arundel County (including the city of Annapolis) had an aggregate population of 23,900 White and Black persons. Of these, 12,196 (51 percent) were Black or mixed race, and of this population, 4,864 (20 percent) were free and 7,332 (31 percent) were slaves. Anne Arundel County, including Annapolis, was the seventh largest county in terms of overall population, third in terms of free Black population (only Baltimore—city and county—and Frederick County had more), and third in terms of slave population (only Prince George's and Charles counties had more).[44] Annapolis had an aggregate population of 4,529 White, free Black persons, and Black and mixed race slaves. The total Black population of Annapolis was 1,301 persons (28 percent of the aggregate), of whom 826 (18 percent) were free and 475 (10 percent) were slaves.[45]

Between June 1 and 23, 1860, William H. Bryan, a former and future Anne Arundel County sheriff and Annapolis merchant, served as assistant marshal for the Census Office to enumerate the city's population. Official instructions from Washington directed Bryan to go dwelling to dwelling, carrying a portable inkstand, good ink, suitable pens, and blotting paper, and to make a personal inquiry at each household.[46]

Bryan arrived at St. Mary's College on June 11 to record "in a plain neat hand" the name, age, gender, occupation, and place of birth of each inhabitant. The census data was probably provided by Michael Müller. There were fifty-two men present, including four priests (Müller, Duffy, Cornell, and Roesch); thirty-two "students of divinity"; and sixteen lay brothers. Their places of birth were diverse: thirty-one were born in German states (which were not individually enumerated but other sources reveal them to have been the Baden, Bavaria, Hannover, Hesse-Darmstadt, Prussia, Saxony, Westphalia (then a province of Prussia), and Württemberg. Most were from Bavaria, Hannover, and Prussia. Four were from Ireland; and one man each came from Austria, Belgium, England, France, Netherlands, and Switzerland. Of those born in the United States, four were from Pennsylvania, three from Maryland, two from New York, and one each from Alabama and Michigan. The average age of the priests was thirty-four. Students (not counting Father Roesch, a novice, who was thirty-eight) who were at various stages of formation, ranged from sixteen to twenty-eight years with an average age of twenty. The brothers ranged from age sixteen to fifty-six, with an average age of thirty-two years. At age forty-six, Brother Louis Sterkendries was one of the oldest members of the Redemptorist community. The 1860 census gives an excellent snapshot of the composition of the Redemptorist

Father (earlier Frater) John Nepumucene Berger, C.Ss.R. (1839–84). RABP

community and shows the growth in size since the "Familia Domus" was recorded on January 1, when thirty-eight men were listed. Although it was a required category of each place visited, Bryan did not record the value of the real estate under Müller's supervision.[47]

The 1860 census also provides information about St. Mary's parishioners. Finding individuals in the census is difficult because of illegible handwriting, misspelled names, erroneous information, and persons missed in the canvas. Of the 4,529 individuals enumerated in Annapolis in 1860, 247 individuals have been identified with a high degree of confidence as St. Mary's parishioners or having family ties to St. Mary's parishioners. This number may not be too far off as observed by Frater John Berger in 1861 when he wrote that the "number of Catholics here is about 200 out of 5,000 inhabitants."[48]

Among the 19,371 Anne Arundel County residents living outside the Annapolis city limits, only fifty were have been identified as connected to St. Mary's. Additional individuals connected to St. Mary's before and during the war period, not included in the above counts, were found in the 1860 census living in Baltimore City and in Allegany, Baltimore, Frederick, Howard, Prince George's, Queen Anne's, St. Mary's, Talbot, and Worcester counties in Maryland. Others were identified in the District of Columbia, Virginia, Pennsylvania, New York (both state and city), Massachusetts, Missouri, and Washington Territory. Details on selected parishioners and associates are given throughout this book.

Most of the persons connected with St. Mary's who were identified in the 1860 census were White. In the city and county combined, they included 153 White males (including 50 children under age eighteen), 158 White females (including 66 children), 8 free Black males, and 11 Black females (neither count of which includes children). Enslaved Blacks were not enumerated in the general population schedule, but were counted in the "Slave Schedule" under the owner's name and only by gender, color (Black or mixed race), and age. The slaves were mostly farm laborers and domestic servants. Among the White and free Black Catholic population there was a diversity of occupations, including barber, cabinet maker, carpenter, cart driver, clerk, confectioner, cooper, ditcher, domestic, fancy store keeper, farmer, farm hand, gardener, hotel keeper, journeyman, laborer, lawyer, lumber merchant, merchant, oysterman, physician, sailor, seamstress, servant, ship carpenter, shoemaker, stone mason, store keeper, and washerwoman. At the Naval Academy, Catholics served as engineer, gunner, marine, midshipman, musician, porter, professor, and watchman. The majority (66 percent of the total) were born in Maryland with a few born in the District of Columbia, Pennsylvania, New York, Massachusetts, and Louisiana. The foreign-born (34 percent) came from Ireland, England, Scotland, Netherlands, France, and various German states.

An Old Rip Van Winkle Sort of a Place

Concurrent with the Federal census, the City of Annapolis made an accounting of its taxable base. The work was completed on June 11, 1860, resulting in a list of 524 individuals whose collective worth was $857,400. The categories enumerated were real estate, stock in trade, private and public securities, bank and other stock, livestock, household furniture, plate (dishes and other household silver objects), gold and silver watches, and "other property" of value.[49]

The totals of such property ranged from a low of $50 (typically a person who did not own a house but did have taxable household furniture) to a high of $23,650 for the wealthiest man in town. That man was John Walton, St. Mary's parishioner and City Hotel proprietor. The main source of his wealth was the hotel, which he contracted to purchase in 1845 and accommodated one hundred guests in sixty-three rooms and parlors and comprised three connected buildings: the main building (formerly the eighteenth-century Mann's Tavern) facing Church Street, a two-story wing, and a three-story annex (now Masonic Lodge 89, the only part that survives) facing Conduit Street. A rowhouse annex, still surviving, was added in 1857 on Conduit Street and continued around the

Brother Hilary Fröhlich, C.Ss.R. (1818–98). RABP.

corner onto Duke of Gloucester Street. The hotel featured a bar, wine cellar, billiard and pastry rooms, a barbershop, and professional offices. In 1860 the hotel complex was valued at $13,000, the single most valuable property in the city, exceeding the next-most-valuable single properties, owned by St. Anne's parishioners Alexander Randall, whose private home on State Circle was valued at $11,000, and Hester Ann Chase, whose private home and garden on Northeast Street (later renamed Maryland Avenue) was valued at $6,500.50

Locals may have considered the City Hotel as Annapolis' finest lodging but outsiders had different ideas. An English visitor in 1861 said it was "an old Rip Van Winkle sort of a place" with "Quaint-looking boarders" who "came down to the tea table and talked Secession." A Union army officer, who also lodged there in 1861, said the hotel was "old and dirty" and complained that the "table is very full but very extravagant at two dollars a day." He had a comfortable feather bed but had to buy his own spermaceti candles at ten cents a piece to light his room at night, and was expected to give a ten-cent tip each time to the slave who took care of his room or gave his coat an unwanted or unneeded brushing. Another army officer who arrived in February 1863 wrote to his wife that he was "stopping at a very dirty hotel, unkept, City Hotel, the best in the place, at $2 pr day." Heat for his room was an extra charge. A saving feature for this guest was that the proprietor was "a Union man."[51]

Walton also owned four other houses and lots on Church Street that had a total value of $2,950, as well as the family home on Francis Street valued at $3,500. He also was taxed $1,000 for his liquor stock, $3,000 for household furniture, $50 for plate, and $50 for gold and silver watches. Walton also owned stock in the Farmers Bank of Maryland and public and private securities, for which he was allowed to decline to provide a value. The same declining was done by many other wealthy Annapolitans.[52] All of Walton's real estate in the city combined was valued at $19,450 and his total assessment was $23,650. The next-highest total assessment was for property owned by the Annapolis Gas Light Company ($18,000), followed by total assessments for grocer and dry goods merchant James Iglehart ($14,760) and lawyer Alexander Randall ($13,665). There were other well-to-do men in Annapolis, such as these three, but the assessed values for a majority of taxable properties in the city was less than $1,000 each.

In addition to his Annapolis properties, Walton owned three farms outside of Annapolis. Those and even some of his Annapolis properties do not appear to have been included in the Federal census, which listed the value of Walton's real estate at $12,000 and his personal estate at $22,000. The census also listed several other individuals with greater real and personal wealth than Walton, suggesting that they owned properties and valuables in other locales. Another sign of Walton's wealth was the family burial vault he erected behind the original St. Mary's Church on Duke of Gloucester Street.[53]

Other St. Mary's parishioners were also included in the 1860 Annapolis tax assessment. Of interest is that among St. Mary's immigrant population the Irish-born stand out as having accumulated notable if modest amounts of taxable wealth, while the German-born had much less. The assessment also listed the "Catholic parsonage" with a value of only $550. This must have been the old wooden Jesuit rectory rather than the new tax-exempt brick college building next to the new church. The old rectory stood adjacent to the first St. Mary's Church and was not used by the Redemptorists other than as an annex to the original church.

The Catholic Approach to Slavery

Historian George Rable says that during the antebellum period "Christianity proved both appealing and ambivalent enough to accommodate slaves, slave holders, abolitionists, and those who cared little about slavery one way or another." Indeed, he writes, "Religious faith offered no solution to these issues, or at least no solution that could win support across racial and sectional lines." In regard to the Catholic Church in the South, historian Randall Miller writes: "with its loyalties and structure reaching beyond the South, [it] drew suspicious glances." But, he adds, the Church "won social and political acceptance in the South by sanctifying the secular order of slavery and states' rights." The Church, says Miller, "preached conciliation and consensus . . . promoted temperance and demanded obedience to Scripture and episcopal authority; and it urged good citizenship upon its members, it did not venture into the social and political arena, except to approve Southern positions." Similarly, historian Raymond Schmandt observes that Catholics "always took pride in the universality and uniformity of their religion, and even on socio-political issues such as the abolitionist movement they tended not to differ much in North and South."[54]

This hands-off attitude contrasted sharply with that of New England abolitionist Protestant clergy. Unlike their activist Protestant counterparts, Catholic clergy—North and South—did not petition Congress for or against slavery and avoided giving sermons dealing with divisive political issues. This stance led to some Northern criticism of the Catholic Church as an implicit ally of the Southern slavocracy. But Catholics were not alone viewing abolition as atheistic and unconstitutional, and saw emancipation as a radical and utopian idea. Conservative Presbyterians, Episcopalians, Unitarians, Lutherans, and others North and South saw slavery as an evil but tacitly agreed with the Catholic position. More specifically, the Catholic Church did not condemn slavery nor consider it a sin to own slaves. Catholic theologians saw the equality of all persons before God as moral or spiritual equality, which was not the same as social equality. Unlike some Protestant sects that split between North and South in the antebellum period, the Catholic hierarchy avoided divisiveness, striving instead to keep the Church strong, unified, and apolitical in both sections of the nation. This posture made Catholics appear even more suspect. But in the South, the Catholic position on slavery and the Church's acceptance of Southern life somewhat ameliorated the anti-Catholic thrust of Southern nativists.[55] Judging from reports circulating in Annapolis, the educated local population was aware of these developments. To the extent these reports influenced attitudes in Annapolis and throughout Maryland is difficult to measure.

Pope Gregory XVI's 1839 apostolic letter, *In Supremo Apostolatus*, explicitly condemned the slave trade. He called attention to the moral dangers of slavery, declaring that Catholics, "under any pretext or . . . excuse," could not morally defend slave trading. This declaration did not bode well for Catholics in the American South and was seized upon by the defenders of slavery as a new device to attack the Church. Charleston Bishop John England publicly insisted that Gregory had condemned only the slave trade and inhumane treatment of slaves, not domestic slavery in the United States. If he had condemned American slavery, England argued, the Southern bishops would not have formally accepted the letter as a Church teaching. Conversely, in the North, where abolitionists accused the Church of supporting the institution of slavery, the letter was seen as an encouragement to Catholics to now embrace emancipation.[56]

One of the leading American Catholic theologians of the period was Irish-born Bishop Francis Patrick Kenrick. His three-volume *Theologiae Moralis*, completed in 1841 when he was coadjutor bishop of Philadelphia, sought to clarify the Church's position on slavery. In the chapter entitled "De Servitute," Kenrick said that all men are created equal according to natural law and that "no one is by nature master of another." He added that "slavery does not abolish the natural equality of men." In a statement viewed by some as supportive of the Southern position on slavery, Kenrick declared that "the master has perpetual right to all those services which one man may justly perform for another" as long as the master took good care of his slaves and treated them humanely. Although this viewpoint considered all humans equal, property rights were "conceded to man over man" and a master had the lawful right both to the labor of his slaves and to sell them if he chose to do so. Kenrick said slavery should not be quickly abolished but, at the same time, certain rights of slaves should be secured. Since a master retained the right to a slave's life and body, he would be gravely unjust if he treated slaves cruelly, forced them to excessive work, or did not provide adequate clothing. The slave himself retained "the right to his good name" and, with regard to harm to his life or body, he was to be considered a free man (women were included in this formulation). Kenrick regretted that there were so many slaves in the United States and that laws existed that prevented their education and thus hindered their practice of religion. Since this was the domain of law, it was up to lawmakers to resolve the law's deficiencies, and that "nothing is to be done against the laws." To further clarify his position, he wrote, "Nor should we do or say anything illegally by which slaves may be liberated, or on account of which they may be discontented with their state." He put on notice enslavers—and the priests who counseled them—that since slaves depended solely on the will of the master, the master must provide proper food, clothing, shelter, and other necessities. "It would seem," wrote a twentieth-century theologian, that Kenrick "placed the sin in the danger to life—an obligation to charity—rather than in justice owed to the slave by contract."[57]

Furthermore, Kenrick believed that abolition was "injurious instead of beneficial to the slave" and that "Christian charity alone will effect the liberation and . . . the elevation of the negroe slave." Catholics were reminded that they "must ever stand aloof from the abolition movement" but "in their own way" they should "labor to effect the great end." He recognized the oppressive nature of slavery and the neglect the goal of the spiritual salvation of slaves. Kenrick saw slavery as a social evil but, like others in the South, he feared the ramifications of immediate emancipation.

In 1851 Kenrick was elevated to be archbishop of Baltimore and, as head of the See of Baltimore, and by the prerogative assigned by Rome, he was considered the leading theological authority in the United States. With his approval, "De Servitute" was reprinted in *The Metropolitan* in 1855 and Catholic Marylanders could read anew Kenrick's position on the enslavement. Some historians believe that *Theologiae Moralis* contributed to the Southern pro-slavery arguments." Although Archbishop John Hughes of New York, the liberal Catholic theologian of the period, criticized slavery as an "evil" he did not believe it was "an absolute or unmitigated evil."[58] Such was the guidance of the Church available to the laity, including Annapolis slave owners and those who might favor abolition.

But what of saving the souls of slaves? Baptism is required both for the remission of original sin and membership in the Catholic Church. Normally parents or godparents make the decision to have newborns and infants baptized while older children and adults received formal instruction to gain an understanding of the meaning and obligations of membership. So it was in the mid-nineteenth century with free and enslaved Blacks. Even if they could not receive full instruction in the faith, they could be conditionally baptized if they expressed belief in God and detestation for their sins. If their faith was sincere, they thus could be admitted to the Church through baptism and later, perhaps, receive the sacrament of confirmation following fuller instruction.

Kenrick had declared in 1841 that "persons of color and other ignorant persons" converting from a previously professed religion to Catholicism were not required to recite the formal act of abjuration. Slaves could be admitted to the Church without their masters' permission but care had to be taken in case an unsympathetic enslaver might inflict vengeance on his slave and thus inflict criticism on the Church. In such cases, Kenrick counseled secret slave baptisms. Catholic masters were expected to have the children of their slaves baptized if one of the slave parents was Catholic. But, if neither parent was Catholic, the Catholic master's rights over his slaves required him only to have those infants baptized if their lives were in danger, a common situation in an era of high infant mortality.

Kenrick was more explicit in other writings on baptism, saying that even if the non-Catholic parent opposed Catholic baptism, the power the master had over his slaves was such that he could overrule such opposition and have slave children baptized, thus showing concern for their eternal salvation. Priests were advised to grant penitential absolution when slaves themselves were in "a necessary occasion of sin," namely, when enslavers abused their slaves sexually. Outside the danger of death, however, Kenrick advised that confessional absolution for slaves could be deferred as a way to encourage better behavior in the future and to approach receiving Holy Communion "with better morals." This approach also was applied to harsh enslavers. Moreover, there was a strict obligation to ensure that slaves received Holy Communion when in danger of death.[59]

Randall Miller writes that "Catholic slaves lived in greater social isolation than did Protestant slaves." He estimates that there were around 100,000 Black Catholics in the South in 1860, living in a variety of regional, cultural, and geographic circumstances. There were older Black populations in Maryland and Virginia, dating back many generations of White ownership. In western Kentucky, Catholic slaves were often owned by French and German immigrants. In South Carolina and Florida there were enclaves of émigré West Indian Catholic slaves, and larger concentrations of Blacks in former Spanish and French colonial holdings along the Gulf Coast and in Louisiana. In the latter region, Miller also observed caste barriers between non-Creole slaves and free persons of color and Creole free persons of color.[60]

Bound To Service

Maryland was one of sixteen slave-owning states and, although partially Southern in outlook, it was not a "cotton state," a term more appropriate in designating the Lower South.[61] Maryland's cultural and economic makeup was an amalgam of Southern culture with a gradual inclusion of Northern outlooks brought by settlers who crossed the Mason-Dixon Line. This was especially true for those moving into the northern-tier and western Maryland counties where the slave economy was less useful for seasonal agricultural pursuits. Landowners in southern Maryland and Eastern Shore counties, however, had long been and continued to be committed to the use of slaves on large plantations and small farms alike.

Article I, Section 1, of the United States Constitution declared that, for the purposes of taxation and representation in Congress, "those bound to Service" were counted as three-fifths equivalent of a free person. Article II, Section 2, protected the legal right of slave holders to maintain ownership of their slaves, the laws of other states notwithstanding. These two sections of the Constitution were abrogated by the Fourteenth Amendment in 1868 and Thirteenth Amendment in 1865, respectively.[62]

But, in 1860, the three-fifths protections were still in force and were the cause of the national political turmoil. Beginning with the first census in 1790, only the numbers of free White males and females over the age of sixteen, "other free persons," and slaves were enumerated. As time went on, the Federal censuses sought more specific information, enumerations by sex, age group, and race, with only the head of the household listed by name through 1840. In 1850, for the first time, the Census Office required a more detailed enumeration that included name, age, sex, occupation, and place of birth of all White and free Black persons. The "Slave Schedule" provided the names of enslavers, followed by the numbers of slaves identified only by age, gender, and color. The same scheme was followed for the 1860 schedule.

Many Maryland Catholics, like Catholics in other border slave states, generally did not identify with abolitionist views, nor with any other kind of perceived radicalism. Catholics in Annapolis and Anne Arundel County were no different, and there were a number of enslavers among them. Although the Annapolis Redemptorists owned land where slave labor had once been used, there is no evidence that they ever owned or employed enslaved people there or elsewhere. The land in question was a farm on the north side of the Severn River called Mulberry Hill that had been purchased by Father Gabriel Rumpler in 1855 (see Father Rumpler's Farm and New Assignments, ch. 6).

Although the Redemptorists did not own slaves, this was not true of other religious orders. Jesuits had owned slaves since the early days of colonial Maryland. Three orders of Maryland nuns—Carmelites, Sisters of Charity, and Visitation—as well as Archbishop John Carroll of Baltimore, also owned slaves. But Carroll manumitted slaves who had been bequeathed to him. Elsewhere in the South, Capuchin priests, Ursuline nuns, and Bishop Benedict J. Flaget of Bardstown, Kentucky, were slave owners. A former Redemptorist, Mathias Alig, pastor of St. Mary's Church in Washington, DC, is listed in the 1850 Slave Schedule as owning a thirty-year-old female slave. Her name is unknown and she may have served as a rectory housekeeper or cook. Alig's name did not appear among slave holders in the 1860 Slave Schedule. The Carmelite nuns of Port Tobacco in Charles County, sold their slaves when they relocated to Baltimore in 1831. The Jesuits, who owned nearly 400 slaves in the 1820s, when faced with severe financial difficulties and increasing discomfort with owning chattel in a changing America, sold all of them in 1838. In a controversial move, three shiploads totaling 272 men, women, and children living on Jesuit plantations in Charles, Prince George's, St. Mary's, Cecil, and Talbot counties, were sold to a Louisiana Catholic planter and his business partner. The sale scandalized fellow Jesuits, non-Jesuits, and Catholic and Protestant laity alike. Father Thomas Mulledy, the American provincial at the time, was forced to resign over the matter. The controversial sale contributed to the anti-Catholicism of the era and still made national news in 2016–21 when there was renewed interest in finding the descendants to make amends and Georgetown University student demands for reparations. The Sisters of Charity in Emmittsburg sold their slaves in 1839 and the Visitation sisters of Georgetown, DC, relinquished their slaves for compensation from the government only when

Congress passed the District of Columbia Emancipation Act on April 16, 1862. The Jesuit community at St. Inigoes in St. Mary's County evidently held slaves right up to the eve of Maryland's emancipation on November 1, 1864.[63]

The 1860 Slave Schedule for Annapolis enumerated 225 male and 250 female slaves, who together represented 10 percent of the city's population. Within this enumeration there were thirty males and forty-three females listed as "Fugitives from the State" and fourteen others were noted as manumitted and may have been enumerated by name in the population schedule as free Blacks. Five of the seventy-three fugitives were also noted as manumitted, leaving some question as to their "fugitive" status. It appears then that the actual count of enslaved persons living in the city in June 1860 thus was 388. The oldest slave recorded in the Slave Schedule was a man, age ninety, owned by parishioner John Walton. There were 124 slaves ages ten and younger, including seven infants (those less than one year old), the youngest of whom was only a month old.[64]

Of the 115 Annapolis slave owners in 1860, eighty-eight were men and twenty-seven were women. Census taker William Bryan himself had five slaves and Governor Hicks owned six. The owner with the largest number of slaves in the city was Frank Stockett, who held twenty-six men, women, and children in bondage. He had eighteen more slaves on his county farm outside Annapolis. Parishioner John Walton owned fifteen slaves, some of whom worked at the City Hotel and others in the family home on Francis Street. This number placed Walton among the largest holders in the city, those who owned between ten and nineteen slaves each. A City Hotel guest in 1861 reported that all the waiters were slaves "from 60 down to 8 years old" and that he had met "one bright small little fellow" who did not know his own age but that he had belonged to "Massa Walton" since he was a baby "and liked his home ever so much." The 1860 schedule lists among Walton's slaves a seven-year-old male who may have been the boy the guest had "taken quite a fancy too."[65]

Other than Stockett, Walton, and a few others, the majority of slave owners (70 percent), had between one and four slaves each. This level of ownership included three St. Mary's parishioners David Caldwell, John Mullan, and Thomas Tydings. Others associated with St. Mary's held between seven and ten slaves. Although she was not a parishioner, Susannah Boyle, the widow of Colonel James Boyle, late trustee of St. Mary's Church, owned twelve slaves in the city and twenty-four more on her county farm. What is not known is how many St. Mary's non-slave-owning parishioners may have hired persons held in bondage from time to time.[66]

When the City of Annapolis conducted its property assessment in June 1860, an assessment and valuation of slaves also was made. Although Walton was listed in the 1860 Slave Schedule as owning fifteen slaves in Annapolis and thirteen more on his farms in the county, none of his human property was listed in the city's assessment.[67] William Bryan knew of Walton's city slaves but why not the city tax assessor? Because they were taxable in the city, apparently Walton convinced the city assessor that all of his slaves lived in the county.

In Anne Arundel County's rural districts there were an additional 6,857 slaves. Several St. Mary's parishioners were enumerated among the county slave holders, including Walton, later identified as a staunch pro-Union man, and Horatio Tydings, later identified as pro-secession. The extended Steuart family was among rural slave owners. They collectively owned a total of 316 slaves in the county and one in Annapolis in 1860. Although not all members of this family were associated with St. Mary's, the biggest concentration of Steuart slaves with a connection was at Dodon, a 345-acre plantation located fifteen miles from Annapolis. Dodon was owned by Dr. Richard Sprigg Steuart, whose wife and daughters were Catholic. There were 111 slaves living in nine slave houses at Dodon according to the 1860 Slave Schedule. At a nearby plantation, owned by Richard's older brother, George Hume Steuart, there were 116 more slaves. Another relative, C. A. Steuart, had forty-three slaves living in five slave houses. George Biscoe Steuart who, with his wife, Louisa Ann Darnall, is buried at Our Lady of Sorrows Catholic Church in West River, had twenty-four slaves.[68]

St. Mary's baptismal register records the christening of slaves at Dodon and the other Steuart properties. Others may have been baptized but not recorded. The priest who officiated at the most Dodon baptisms was Father John Cornell, who baptized ten Dodon slaves, both children and adults, between 1858 and 1860. He also ministered to Maria Louisa de Bernabeu Steuart, Richard Steuart's wife, at a point when she was ill enough to receive the Eucharist as *viaticum*, normally reserved for persons in danger of death. Maria Louisa, and her daughters, Emily and Isabella, served as godparents for numerous Dodon baptisms. Another Steuart daughter, Mary, became a Sister of Mercy in New York City before her death in 1853.[69]

The Steuart family's Catholic legacy goes back even further, to Ann Digges who married Dr. George Hume Steuart of Annapolis in 1744, the grandparents of Richard Steuart. They lived in the Francis Street house later owned by John Walton, and purchased the county plantation that became Dodon (from the French, *Dieu Donne*, "Gift of God"). Ann Digges Steuart was a staunch Catholic who reputedly donated money for clothes for her relative, John Carroll, when he went to France for his seminary studies in 1748. Carroll was ordained as a Jesuit priest in 1761 and later became the first bishop (1789) and first archbishop of Baltimore (1808). As bishop and archbishop, Carroll occasionally visited Ann Digges Steuart at her Francis Street home and sent priests "to administer to her and her servants, (most of them Catholics), the rites of the church in which she had been born and educated." Carroll also "was intimate" in the house of Dr. James Steuart, Ann's son and father of Dr. Richard Steuart who wrote in 1868 that Carroll "often came uninvited to take his dinner with the family."[70]

Another Anne Arundel County slave-owing family was that of Dr. Martin Fenwick, a member of an old Maryland Catholic family and related to two deceased Catholic bishops,

Benedict Joseph Fenwick, S.J., of Boston and his brother, Edward Dominic Fenwick, O.P., of Cincinnati. Adding to these credentials was his marriage in 1815 to Ann Louisa Ghequiere at St. Peter's Pro-Cathedral in Baltimore, officiated by Archbishop John Carroll, an old friend of the bride's family. Fenwick had thirteen slaves in 1860. The Fenwicks were instrumental in establishing the Catholic mission serving the West River and other south county areas and baptisms of five White, free Black, and slave children were performed by a Jesuit from White Marsh at the Fenwick home in 1831. In 1859 the Redemptorists began making occasional visits to celebrate Mass at Evergreen, the Fenwick home. According to the *Chronica Domus*, the Fenwicks were the "only one Catholic family... with some other persons" in the West River (Owensville) area. In 1862 Father Adrian Van de Braak began routine visits to Evergreen and, as the number of Catholics in the area increased, it was decided that a chapel and formal out-mission status was needed (see Pastoral Duties at the Out-Missions, ch. 4).[71]

Free Black Marylanders lived an anomalous existence, one often not too different from persons held in bondage. Journalist Isabel Wilkerson writing about the United States in general, said: "In the days before Emancipation, as long as slavery existed, no freed black was truly free." They may have been born free or manumitted as adults but they faced numerous legal limitations. Violation of laws, such as for vagrancy or more serious crimes, could mean a return to slave status for a term of years or, after 1858, they could be sold into slavery after being convicted of a crime. Although legally free from enslavement, free Black movements were circumscribed and they had to go to court to obtain certificates verifying their free status. Families often were of mixed status, some members free, some slaves for life, and others slaves for a term of years. Such situations divided families if owners moved to another state or decided to sell some of their slaves despite their family ties. Children born to slave mothers were legally enslaved; those born to free women and a slave father were free. Free Blacks could not own dogs or firearms and were forbidden to purchase liquor or ammunition without a special license. They were limited on what they could sell in the marketplace unless they could prove to a justice of the peace that the products were raised or acquired "honestly." Some counties forbade daytime entry into taverns or shops and they might not be able to legally operate a boat or work as a pedlar. Only in Baltimore and Annapolis were they allowed to attend religious services not conducted by White ministers, but even then only when permitted by the White minister. Thus, life for the "free colored" in Maryland was not so free and racial traditions in the slave society kept them tightly restricted.[72]

In colonial and post-Revolutionary Maryland, the Catholic Carroll family of Annapolis owned the greatest number of slaves. One of Charles Carroll of Carrollton's granddaughters, Mary Ann Caton Patterson, sponsored twenty-six baptisms—primarily free Blacks and slaves—in Annapolis in 1821 and 1822. There were other early enslavers with St. Mary's connections. According to the Federal censuses from 1820 to 1850, they included Colonel James Boyle, the church trustee who died in 1854; Thomas Karney; Catherine Welch Maccubbin, who converted in 1863; Alida McParlin's father-in-law, William McParlin; and John Randall. Some others, such as John Mullan, who owned a slave later, also had a free Black boy of ten or fewer years of age living in his house in 1840. Politically, slave owners were more likely to be Democrats than Whigs or Republicans, but members of all parties owned slaves and generally had occupations as farmers, lawyers, physicians, merchants, and other business owners.[73]

Whether or not St. Mary's Parish was involved in the Uunderground Railroad—the informal path to freedom in the North for runaway slaves—is worth considering. No evidence of such involvement has been found, and despite the Underground Railroad neither being underground nor a railroad, myths about tunnels on St. Mary's property leading to Spa Creek persist but without any basis in reality.

Although there is no evidence of Catholic underground stations in Annapolis, there are unsubstantiated claims that several Baltimore Catholic institutions may have been involved in the Underground Railroad.[74] An 1872 book on the Underground Railroad reported runaway Catholic slaves and cruel Catholic slave owners but not any Catholic conductors. It did mention the escapes of numerous Maryland slaves but only three cases in Anne Arundel County and only one in Annapolis. An 1898 map showing hundreds of Underground Railroad routes, indicated only three routes through Maryland and none through Annapolis. A modern book on the Underground Railroad documents only African Methodist Episcopal, Baptist, Mennonite, Methodist, and Quaker participation in the Underground Railroad.[75]

A corollary question might be raised concerning possible slave labor at St. Mary's. Much of the Carroll family's wealth was based on the ownership of slaves who labored as house servants, in plantation fields, in manufacturing, and in construction projects. The Carroll House, built in the 1720s and expanded in the 1770s and 1790s, was built using both slave and indentured labor. And, Charles Carroll of Carrollton may have had slaves from his Doughoregan Manor and Poplar Island plantations work on the first St. Mary's Church in 1821–22.[76] The Redemptorists owned no slaves but it is possible that when the new church and college were built in 1858–60, slave-owning parishioners, such as John Walton and John Randall, may have loaned or hired out their slaves to assist with the construction. However, no documentary evidence has been found to support this supposition.

How Beautiful Is the Chaste Generation

June 21, 1860, was a day of celebration for the Redemptorists. Father Roesch completed his novitiate, professed his Redemptorist vows, and departed for his first assignment, at St. Peter the Apostle Church in Philadelphia. Two other novices, John Matthew Bohn and George Augustine Pingel, also professed their vows. Both twenty-two-year-old Baden-born Bohn and twenty-one-year-old Hannover-born Pingel spent the next two

Father John De Dycker, C.Ss.R. (1822–83). RABP.

years in Annapolis studying "grammar" before they embarked on their advanced theological studies. Their curriculum likely included secondary-school subjects such as English composition, geography, modern and classical foreign languages, algebra, geometry, and natural sciences. Two other young men were received and invested as choir candidates: nineteen-year-old John Baptiste Runge from Hannover and twenty-seven-year-old John Baptiste Blanchet from Baden.[77]

It was the practice, at least in the warm weather and presumably not in the early morning when it was banned by city ordinance, for the novices to bathe in Spa Creek. The creek borders the southeast side of St. Mary's property, its bank lined with an iron-laden sandstone wall built by slaves under the direction of Charles Carroll of Carrollton between 1770 and 1776.[78] Carroll had two summer houses extending over the water at either end of the seawall and, although they had disappeared by 1864 (based on dated photographic evidence), they may still have been in place in 1860, although by then probably in ruinous condition. Either they or their remnants may have provided a convenient entryway to the creek, or one might have simply splashed into the water anywhere along the 435-foot-long stone wall. Nevertheless, professed student George Schad, after his evening prayers, took advantage of the cool creek water. According to the *Chronica Domus*:

> June 27 — was very calamitous, for this day Frater Schad, on the preceding evening had gone to bathe in the creek. He was not skillful swimmer and fell into a deep pit. Frater [Hubert] Bove, who was not far from the place, where he himself washed, heard him cry out and, with a great effort, pulled the Frater out when he appeared on the surface of the water. Full of seawater, he was taken inside. The following day, because of all the water he swallowed, he vomited blood.[79]

Schad's condition worsened and, on July 3, a fellow student, Augustine Freitag, accompanied him to St. Alphonsus in Baltimore where he could get urgently needed treatment for the typhoid he had contracted. The *Chronica Domus* reported that at St. Alphonsus he "had a very grievous fever from day to day, [but] showing example of piety and resignation, he gave up his soul to God in the arms of the Very Rev. Father Provincial [John De Dycker]" on July 13. As was the custom, a brief tribute to the deceased was inscribed in the house annals. It begins by saying that it was "necessary to mention a few things about this beloved Frater that others may learn from his example, and continues with a quote from the Book of Wisdom:

> How beautiful is the chaste generation with glory: for the memory thereof is immortal: because it is known both with God and with men.[80]

The brief biography that follows provides an excellent example of what led a young man to the religious life in mid-nineteenth century America. Schad was born 1841 in Bavaria and entered school at age six. He was said to be "always modest, diligent, and well loved" and always tried to practice the virtue of obedience and, from his early years, wanted to join a religious order. He emigrated to America with his parents who settled in Baltimore, where young George worked as a tailor. Although his coworkers "were unbelievers who tried to pervert the pious young man to the wickedness of contempt for religion," he "constantly resisted the temptations." He also worked with his parents preparing food to sell to help pay off a $200 debt. The Schads lived near St. Alphonsus Church and, with the encouragement of the Redemptorists there, George studied Latin and further improved on his practice of piety, often by reciting the rosary. In 1859 he went to the novitiate in Annapolis and was invested in the Redemptorist habit on the feast of the Annunciation of the Blessed Virgin Mary (March 25). From that time on, George is said to have become an example for the other novices. Among the virtues for which he was praised were self-abnegation, great devotion to prayer, and always paying attention with "splendid filial sincerity" to Father Müller. These virtues, as well as Schad's sincere devotion to the will of God, the Blessed Sacrament, and the Blessed Virgin Mary, held great promise for a long life as a religious. But, as God's will dictated, according to the *Chronica Domus*, young Schad "gave back to the Lord a burnt offering of his life." He is buried in the Redemptorist section in Most Holy Redeemer Cemetery in Baltimore.[81]

Plans for a Parochial School

As interior work on the new church neared completion and construction of the college building was well underway, thought was given to establishing a parochial school. Although documentation is scant, instruction of parish children—certainly for sacramental preparation—had been going on since the days when St. Mary's was a Jesuit mission and thereafter as a formal Redemptorist parish. After John Neumann became Bishop of Philadelphia, his interest in the Annapolis parish continued beyond the blessing of the cornerstone and bells in 1858 and 1859, respectively. He had held one or more discussions, probably in 1859 or earlier, about stationing a religious order of sisters in Annapolis. And this was not just any order of sisters he had in mind but one that had Redemptorist connections. In 1843 Mother Mary Theresa Duchemin, wanted to change the name of her Baltimore-based order of African American women—the Oblates of Divine Providence—to the Sisters of St. Charles (Charlottines) to honor Charles Carroll of Carrollton. This idea was broached with the hope attracting financial assistance from Carroll's granddaughter, Emily MacTavish. When that support did not materialize and despite help given by the Baltimore Redemptorists, Mother Mary Theresa left the Oblates in 1845 and moved to Monroe, Michigan, at the urging of Redemptorist Father Louis Florent Gillet. There she changed her persona from a French-speaking light-skinned woman of color to a bilingual White woman and called herself Theresa Maxis. That same year, under Gillet's direction, Theresa and two other women established the Congregation of the Sisters, Servants of the Immaculate Heart of Mary (IHM).[82] The new congregation adapted to their own needs the rules for religious life written by St. Alphonsus Liguori and Gillet served as their spiritual director. The Redemptorists also took charge of the financing and construction of the sisters' convent, school, and annex in Monroe, Michigan.

The only extant evidence of the effort to bring the IHM sisters to Annapolis is its failure. On January 4, 1860, Neumann wrote to their superior, Mother Mary Magdalen Martin in Reading, Pennsylvania. He noted the unsettled state of the new IHM congregation that had moved from Monroe to Reading. He then added that "the new foundation in Annapolis cannot at present be undertaken; but with the consent of the Most Rev. Archbishop of Balt. [Francis Patrick Kenrick], which has as yet not been solicited, it may be commenced as the older Novices will have made their Vows." This letter was written the day before Neumann's sudden death in Philadelphia and is the only documentary evidence found of the proposed IHM foundation in Annapolis. The issue obviously had been discussed earlier between Neumann and Mother Magdalen. Neumann had seen Mother Magdalen when he visited the sisters novitiate in St. Joseph, Choconut Township, Susquehanna County, in rural northeastern Pennsylvania, on May 4 and July 24, 1859, and in Reading on September 2, 1859, when he was accompanied by an unidentified Redemptorist father from Cumberland, but presumably Father Adrian Van de Braak. Neumann and Mother Magdalen met again in Reading on December 8, 1859.[83]

Another Annapolis-IHM connection was through Father James Sheeran who joined the Redemptorists in Annapolis in 1855, was professed there in 1856, and ordained in Baltimore in 1858. He was the widowed father of Sister Mary Ignatia (Isabella) Sheeran, one of the novices who left Michigan for Pennsylvania. When Neumann wrote his letter in January 1860, Sister Ignatia had entered the order as a postulant in 1858 in Michigan, and professed her vows before Neumann on July 24, 1859, in Pennsylvania. She may have been one of "the older Novices" who might have been assigned to Annapolis.[84]

Further evidence of the Redemptorist efforts to bring the IHM sisters from Michigan emanated from Annapolis. On May 4, 1859, Father Jacobs, then in Annapolis, wrote to Sister Colette Myers in Monroe. Invoking the names of Mother Theresa, Bishop Neumann, and Father Aegidius Smulders, all of whom "want you in St. Joseph's" (in Pennsylvania), he urged Colette to leave Monroe "as soon as this letter reaches you." Fathers Smulders and Henry Giesen, who had past and future Annapolis connections, respectively, wrote letters to other sisters in Monroe with similar import. Nevertheless, Neumann's death and the immediate accession of Bishop James Frederic Wood was followed by the division of the IHM sisters into East (Reading, Pennsylvania) and West (Monroe, Michigan) provinces. With that separation and Neumann's sudden demise, the Annapolis venture disappeared. It would be another two years before a school would be established.[85]

Seminary Life During Peacetime

During the last pre-war summer, life at the Annapolis college continued in both routine and unusual ways. One of the students, Swiss-born Frater Joseph Brandstätter, who had been promoted to the lector ministry in January, was dismissed from the Redemptorists in July. "The cause of his ruin is forgiven," it was recorded and "God is well disposed." No clue as to his offense was offered either in the *Chronica Domus* or in the *Province Annals* maintained in Baltimore. Two years after leaving the Redemptorists, he went to Westmoreland County, Pennsylvania, to seek his vocation with the Benedictines but that too did not work out and he disappeared from the historical record.[86]

Father Müller presided over the profession of vows of novice Philip Rossbach on July 22. A native of Hesse-Darmstadt, Rossbach, having celebrated his seventeenth birthday just five days before, was attached to the grammar school within the college. He proceeded through the rest of seminary life in orderly fashion and would be ordained in 1869. The same day as Rossbach's profession, and in preparation for the coming academic year, three other teenagers were invested and received into the novitiate: Hannover-born Hugo Victor (age seventeen), who also was ordained in 1869 but was dispensed of his Redemptorist vows four years later; Bavarian-born Joseph Weber (age sixteen), who would be dispensed of his vows in 1865; and Pennsylvania-born Peter Morio (also sixteen), who did not last long in the austere life of St. Mary's College and was dismissed four months later.[87]

An extraordinary canonical visitation was made to Annapolis in September 1860 to review the practices and procedures of the religious community and make sure they conformed explicitly to the Redemptorist Rule (a framework of daily life) and Constitutions (seven of them, codified regulations and traditions, with an extensive index with definitions of terms and the canon law authorities). This visitation was "extraordinary" because it was made by representatives of Father Nicholas Mauron, the Redemptorist superior general in Rome. It was led by Francis Verheyen, consultor general from

Rome, and Louis Coudenhove, rector of Maria am Gestade, the Redemptorist provincial house in Vienna, as socius. The *Chronica Domus* notes rather mundanely that the "Reverend Fathers were received in a solemn manner." It was the only extraordinary visitation made to America by a representative of the Redemptorist superior general during the 1860s.

Although it might be expected that under Müller's strict regime everything was in order at St. Mary's College, such visitations always uncovered some infraction of the Rule or current policies, and new on-the-spot decrees were issued to improve the quality of religious life. For example, Verheyen ordered that henceforth the students, despite their profession of vows, were not to use "reverend" in front of their title "frater." The entire community was reminded that they must follow exactly the rule established by St. Alphonsus. Although no violations were mentioned, the community was reminded that Mauron had forbidden participation in fairs, picnics, excursions, raffles, and similar activities. One bright spot for the students was the decree extending the annual holidays from four to six weeks as a special indulgence from the visitors. The students received this news "with great joy."[88]

The remaining months of 1860 at St. Mary's College saw the resumption of studies and the addition of new members to the community. Thirty-seven-year-old Westphalian-born Father Henry Fehlings arrived in August as lector of moral theology and philosophy. In September two more priests arrived from Philadelphia where they had served as briefly assistants at St. Peter the Apostle Church following their ordinations. One was twenty-eight-year-old Virginia-born Father William V. Meredith, who had studied at St. Charles College, the Sulpician-run diocesan minor seminary near Ellicott's Mills, Howard County, Maryland. Meredith's schoolmates at St. Charles included William Hickley Gross, Nicholas Jaeckel, Eugene Grimm, and Adam Kreis, all of whom later studied at the Redemptorist college in Annapolis. Meredith, along with Eugene Grimm, Michael Dausch, and others, was among the first group of novices in Annapolis in 1853. The other new arrival was twenty-four-year-old Baltimore native Father Michael Dausch. When Father Seelos asked the archbishop for a dispensation for Dausch in 1859 because he was underage for ordination, he proclaimed the young man as "exemplary in every respect."[89]

Meredith served as a parish priest at St. Mary's and Dausch became church prefect, *zelator domus* [house disciplinarian], professor of dogmatic theology, and subprefect of students. Neither man remained long in Annapolis. Meredith departed without notice in the *Chronica Domus* sometime after mid-December 1860. He died in New Orleans in 1884. The only record he left at St. Mary's was of the baptisms he performed between October and December 1860. Dausch departed in June 1861 for a new assignment at St. Joseph's Parish in Rochester, New York. He was dispensed from his Redemptorist vows in 1863 and became a diocesan priest in the Archdiocese of Baltimore.[90]

Father Verheyen returned to Annapolis in mid-October to preside over the investitures of six novices and a new lay brother and the reception of a new candidate novice. During

The earliest known photograph of St. Mary's main altar, sometime before 1885, and closest in appearance to when it was built and painted in 1860. RABP.

his visitation to Cumberland, he had decided it was better for the younger students to live in a single community with older students already in Annapolis. Not only was the Annapolis house larger, but had what he saw as a better environment for the newly professed to spend their time in study. For these reasons, the younger students in Cumberland were sent to Annapolis. Ten of them arrived on October 18. They were students of rhetoric and ranged in age from eighteen to twenty-six and were natives of Bavaria, Bohemia, Prussia, Saxony, and Ireland, and more locally from Poughkeepsie, Rochester, and New York City in New York State and Frostburg, Maryland, where Redemptorist missionaries had labored hard to gain vocations. Coming with them was their lector, Frater John Gerdemann, twenty years old and a native of Cumberland. Of note among this group of students was John Nepumucene Berger, the nephew and future biographer of deceased Bishop John Neumann. In the midst of these changes in his community, Müller decided took a tour in November of Redemptorist houses in Philadelphia, New York, Pittsburgh, and Cumberland. The house annals are silent as to his real purpose but he returned with various unspecified items needed for the seminary and perhaps for the new church.[91]

On the Feast of the Immaculate Conception (December 8), Müller presided over the profession of vows by two novices, both of whom then began their grammar studies. He also invested and received three candidate novices. One of them was Henry Koering, a thirty-eight-year-old Westphalian-born diocesan priest from the Diocese of Vincennes, Indiana. He evidently was lacking in his determination to become a member of a religious congregation and left the novitiate the following March but remained a diocesan priest for the rest of his life, working in Ohio. Earlier in the month, Father John Duffy received orders to return to New Orleans where he eventually became rector of the Redemptorist community from 1865 to 1868. Duffy's replacement was Father Peter McGrane, who had been in Cumberland with Seelos. After ordination Duffy and McGrane served together in New Orleans.[92]

Finishing the New Church

Although the new church had been dedicated on January 15, it still had more needed work. Although it was fully functional for liturgical purposes, it was far from being the highly ornamented worship space it would become. For example, as related in Müller's poem, "in a little more than a year, one saw already an altar in the church." A temporary altar used in St. Mary's Church in 1859–60 was replaced by a soaring Gothic altar completed in 1861. The only sign of the old altar today is a masonry structure now surrounded on all sides and above by the new wooden altar.[93]

Brother Louis Sterkendries performed the carpentry work for the new altar. Each piece was cut from raw lumber, shaved, planed, and sanded and then meticulously shaped and carved into a vast assemblage. Brother Hilary Fröhlich applied the painted decorations. Brother Hilary was born in 1818 in Hesse-Darmstadt and had earned his living as a professional artist before entering religious life in 1855. Work on the altar began in earnest on the Feast of the Immaculate Conception 1860 and was completed by Christmas Day 1861. The finished altar appeared much the way that it does today, with some minor adaptations. There also were two temporary side altars, one dedicated to St. Joseph, the other to St. Alphonsus.[94]

In the months before and after the January 15 dedication and the commencement of work on the high altar on December 8, Brother Louis was gainfully employed making pews, confessionals, a communion rail, and other church fixtures, as well as overseeing carpentry work in the new college building. He also most likely built the temporary main and side altars. The architect's plan announced in 1858 called for 130 pews to seat 1,000 persons, a greatly overstated number. Initially, it seems that pews were installed only along the center aisle. The side-aisle pews were not in place until 1869, as "another step" in the completion of the church. The configuration of pews in place at least since 1885 has twenty-one rows on each side of the main aisle and can accommodate 500 adults. Twentieth-century City of Annapolis fire marshal regulations allowed 532 persons in the church, including the choir loft.[95]

Trouble Ahead

The presidential campaign and the ongoing rancorous debate about the extension of slavery into the Federal territories were paramount news in 1860. The local press included editorials defending the Compromise of 1850 against the Northern abolitionists. Among other things, the compromise admitted California as a free state and abolished slave trade—but not slavery—in the District of Columbia (see The Southern Feeling Prevailing, ch. 4). Some thought the compromise weakened rather than strengthened Southern rights and Southerners called for respecting the rights and privileges of the fifteen slave-owning states, insisting that the slavery issue was not the only one dividing the country. There also were calls for reforming the national economic system and putting an end to political corruption. Sectional political party disunity was also the subject of ongoing commentary.[96]

Maryland Governor Hicks, who had been elected as a Know Nothing candidate in 1857, declared support for anti-secession Constitutional Union candidate John Bell of Tennessee. The *Annapolis Gazette* declared that the US Constitution, the Union, and enforcement of the laws were preeminent requirements for an orderly state of government for the United States and, accordingly, also supported pro-Union Bell. It advised its readers that Northern Democrat presidential candidate Stephen Douglas of Illinois was someone who imbued a "reckless spirit of Demagogueism," while Southern Democrat candidate John C. Breckinridge of Kentucky, the current vice president of the United States, personified "irrepressible conflict." The fourth presidential candidate, the Republican Party's Abraham Lincoln—"a man unknown"—garnered little pre-election attention in Annapolis.[97]

November was a momentous month in the history of the United States. Lincoln was elected, with only 39 percent

St. Mary's College and Church, circa 1860. RABP.

of the nationwide vote but enough to win in the Electoral College, much to the dismay of those who believed his election would be disastrous for the Union. In Maryland, pro-South Breckinridge won 45.9 percent of the popular vote, while pro-Union candidates Bell, Douglas, and Lincoln received 45.1, 6.5 and 2.5 percent, respectively. Bell won narrowly in Anne Arundel County (48.2 percent to 47.1 percent for Breckinridge), with Douglas accruing only 4.5 percent. Lincoln received 0.2 percent, only three votes, which is more than he won in most other Maryland counties. Thus, a clear majority of Marylanders (54.2 percent) voted for pro-Union candidates. They believed that Unionism and slavery were not incompatible and votes for Breckinridge were not an endorsement for secession. However, in Annapolis, as historian Jane McWilliams points out, when they read that only one vote had been cast for Lincoln, it was realized that "99.8 percent of the voters . . . had backed the losers . . . [and] knew trouble was ahead."[98]

Bibliotheca C.Ss.R. Annapolis stamp found in Sacrorum BibliorumVulgatæ Editionis Concordantiae *(Insulis: L. Lefort, 1837). SMPA.*

Shortly after the election, Governor Hicks was encouraged to convene the General Assembly to discuss Maryland's position amidst the growing Southern secession crisis. Hicks resisted calls for the legislature to convene even though he found "the times are big with peril" and despite the "fearful responsibilities" he owed to the people of Maryland with the "unfortunate result of the recent election." Among local prominent men who petitioned Hicks to hold what they hoped would be a secession session was one with a St. Mary's association: Llewellyn Boyle.[99]

Toward the tumultuous year's end, President Buchanan issued a proclamation recommending a national day of prayer throughout the United States. Governor Hicks concurred and issued the same proclamation for Maryland. It was a sign of recognition that the nation needed serious reflection, with the hope for a better future. During this last year of peace, fifty-seven baptisms, thirty-eight confirmations, three marriages, and at least seven funerals were held at St. Mary's. So ended the year 1860.[100]

Part Two — Bellum Civile

Chapter 3: 1861 — Neither Taking the Part of *Septentrionalibus* or *Meridianis*

To Save the Union and Avert Civil War

Days of thanksgiving and prayer had been proclaimed by civil authorities in America since the early colonial period. They were an opportunity to express gratitude for good harvests or, in times of tribulation, days of supplication to divine authority. They were observed on weekdays rather than Sundays and were a sign of the emergence of civil religion among the American people.[1] In response to the "present danger and calamity" facing the nation after Lincoln's election and the secession of several southern states, President James Buchanan designated Friday, January 4, 1861, as a national day of "humiliation, fasting, and prayer." American Catholics widely supported the president's call and Governor Hicks endorsed it for the people of Maryland. But given the dire political situation, the *Annapolis Gazette* was pessimistic about the outcome of such an observance:

> We hope the good people of Maryland will duly observe the recommendation; it can do no harm and may do some good. But we are heathenish enough to fear that it is too late to hope for much benefit from sackcloth and ashes . . . God has frowned upon us as a nation, and will assuredly punish us for abusing the blessings of liberty and independence with which He has so abundantly blessed us. But let the prayers be offered. If they cannot avert present evils, they may prevent worse evils in the future.[2]

And so Annapolitans offered prayers. The *Gazette* reported that there had been an "unusual solemnity in our city," with all the churches "open, and appropriate ceremonies performed, in the presence of much larger congregations than usually attend divine worship." The attendees included the "Old and young, matron and maiden, rich and poor, bathed in tears, united in solemn invocations to God for His interposition to save the union and avert civil war." The *Gazette* article gave most its attention to the observances held at St. Anne's where Reverend James Radcliffe Davenport "exhorted his hearers to yield their political passions and prejudices, by submitting to the will of those who rule us by their own election, and whose authority over us has the divine sanction taught in the Bible." Passing mention was made of the Methodist, Presbyterian, and Catholic churches in which "the day was duly and impressively observed." At St. Mary's, it was reported that:

> there was no sermon delivered, the Archbishop having so directed; fearing "that the tranquility of the house of prayer should be disturbed by reflections on exciting topics," and saying that "it will be sufficient simply to invite the faithful to pray earnestly for peace, harmony and prosperity of the United States, the maintenance and perpetuity of our civil institutions, and the increase of true religion."[3]

The *Gazette* concluded its coverage, saying that if the day "was everywhere as appropriately and solemnly observed as it was here, the occasion must have accomplished a vast deal towards inclining the hearts of men towards a speedy and bloodless end to the difficulties that overshadow us." But, the *Gazette* thought, it was "too late to hope for much benefit." This dark premonition soon became reality.

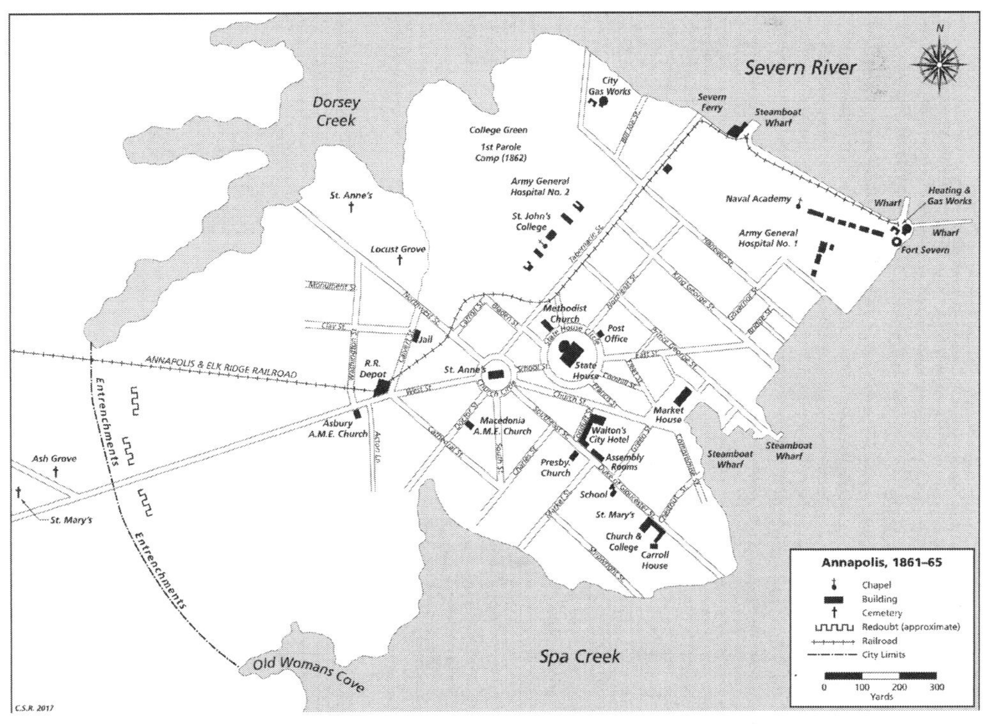

Annapolis 1861-1865

REFERENCES.—1. Catholic College.—2. City Hotel.—3. Battery.—4. Capitol.—5. Midshipmen's Quarters.—6. *Constitution*.—7. Recitation Hall.—8. Chapel.—9. Observatory.—10. Officers' Quarters.—11. St. John's (Episcopal) College.—12. Hospital.—13. Monument—the same that was in front of the Capitol at Washington.—14. Naval Monument.

GENERAL VIEW OF ANNAPOLIS, WITH THE "CONSTITUTION" IN THE FOREGROUND.

"General View of Annapolis," *Harper's Weekly, 5, no. 228 (May 11, 1861):294. Author's collection.*

Soon after New Years, two St. Mary's parishioners took political action. John Walton was elected vice president of a meeting held on January 17, 1861. The attendees passed a resolution saying that although they regretted Lincoln's election, the state had no authority to secede. On January 31, Walton was elected vice president of another meeting, this one held in the city's Assembly Rooms. It was billed as a "workingman's meeting" and passed a resolution that said Maryland had an "unalterable attachment to the Union." The other St. Mary's parishioner who took action was Naval Academy employee Andrew Edward Denver. He and two other pro-Union men convened their own meeting on January 31 and invited Clerk of the Court of Appeals of Maryland William A. Spencer to address the gathering. Denver would later be recognized as having "stood by" to protect the Naval Academy when it threatened by secessionists. At a public meeting held on May 4, Mayor John Read Magruder was elected president and Colonel Walton and Dr. Dennis Claude were elected vice presidents. This meeting's attendees rejected a proposal made by state legislators to form a committee of public safety, saying it "was an act of lawless despotism." Later in the year, Walton was elected to the House of Delegates for a special session of the General Assembly. He was widely recognized as a "Union man."[4]

Detail of artist's rendering of "Catholic College" *from "General View of Annapolis,"* Harper's Weekly, 5, no. 228 *(May 11, 1861):294. Author's collection.*

Changes in the Redemptorist Community

Amidst the national turmoil, St. Mary's Redemptorist community was experiencing substantial change. Michael Müller continued as superior and novice master, John Cornell was associate pastor and socius to Müller, Henry Fehlings was lector of moral theology and philosophy, Peter McGrane as church administrator and thus de facto pastor, and Michael Dausch was church prefect, zelator, lector of dogmatic theology, and subprefect of students. Father John Duffy had departed in December for a new assignment in New Orleans. The college had seven upper-level seminarians studying dogmatic theology, three studying philosophy, and one studying moral theology. Among these eleven, two had been elevated from among their peers to the position of lector and were teaching courses to the younger students of grammar and rhetoric, respectively. They were Anthony Kesseler, born in Prussia in 1836, and John Gerdemann, a native of Cumberland, Maryland, born in 1840 of Prussian parents.[5] These two men had been recognized early in religious life for their abilities as teachers. Sadly, they would share another common fate; both would become drowning victims in the future. There were eleven grammar students and thirteen studying rhetoric. Below the student level were nine novices and two candidate novices.[6]

Rounding out the New Year "Familia Domus" were the four professed lay brothers who had been in Annapolis the year before: carpenter Louis Sterkendries, tailors Jacob Engel and Bernard Pollmann, and gardener Rudolph Wallenhorst. On January 10, they were joined by another professed lay brother, Adam Parr, a thirty-six-year-old Bavarian who worked as a cobbler. Adam came to Annapolis from Cumberland, where he had been assigned since the Redemptorist house there had been established in 1851. Not listed among the brothers in January 1861 was Hilary Fröhlich, the artist, who, although he was engaged to paint the high altar, was not recorded in house annals until July. All of the brothers were European born, one from Belgium, the others from Bavaria and Hannover, and ranged in age from thirty-one to fifty years.[7]

Altogether the Redemptorist roster included fifty-six men at the beginning of 1861. As was the case in the prior year, they were a diverse group. The priests ranged in age from twenty-four to forty-five and hailed from Baltimore, New York City, Ireland, Prussia, and Westphalia. The advanced students were the ages from twenty to twenty-eight and came from Bavaria, Hannover, Prussia, and Württemberg; only one—John Gerdemann—was American born. The twenty-two lower-level students showed the American outreach of the Redemptorists with twelve born in the United States. Of the others, eight were born in German states, one in England, and one in Ireland. Of the American-born, however, many had German parents. They came from Baltimore City, Baltimore County; Cumberland and Frostburg, Maryland; Philadelphia, New York City, Poughkeepsie, and Rochester, New York; Monroe, Michigan; and Mobile, Alabama. They ranged in age from sixteen to twenty-four, but most fell into the seventeen- and eighteen-year-old age group. However, none of the new novices were born in the United States, all but one had been born in German states and the one non-German was from Ireland.[8]

Father Peter McGrane had arrived at St. Mary's from New Orleans in December 1860 and had been assigned as church administrator. Born in Dublin, Ireland, in 1815, McGrane was the first Irish Redemptorist, professed on September 24, 1848, and ordained in 1849. During his brief time in Annapolis, McGrane performed three baptisms. Rather than a permanent transfer, McGrane was in Annapolis awaiting a final decision from his superiors in Baltimore and Rome as to his future. Although he did not receive the written notice until early March, he was officially dispensed from his Redemptorist vows retroactive to February 4, 1861. The only clue as to why he was dismissed is a sentence in the *Chronica Domus* recording his departure on March 3: "This holy Father worked hard in the vineyard of the Lord, but for many years he was a cross to his superiors and had grown weary of the duties of religious life." McGrane headed north to Philadelphia where he was accepted as a diocesan priest assigned to St. Patrick's Church. Although Philadelphia was far from the war front, it would become an important rear-support area and McGrane was soon busy ministering to troops there. He was appointed as an army hospital chaplain and assigned to the US Army's Satterlee Military Hospital, a 2,500-bed facility administered by the Daughters of Charity in West Philadelphia. He went to the hospital daily to minister to wounded and dying soldiers, heard confessions, offered Mass, instructed and baptized, and often arranged burials of Catholic soldiers. But he must have missed the life as a religious because in 1881 he joined the Trappists in Gethsemani, Kentucky, and remained there until he died in 1891.[9]

By May 1861, the Redemptorist community increased from fifty-six to seventy, a figure that at the time was said to comprise the largest Redemptorist community in the world. However, by the end of the year, it would grow further, to eighty-three men.[10]

The Southern Feeling Prevailing

Southern secession from the Union over the slavery issue was not a new idea. It had been avoided by Congressional actions in 1820 with the Missouri Compromise, which had prohibited slavery in former Louisiana Territory except in Missouri. The second time was with the Compromise of 1850, which enshrined the concept of "popular sovereignty," admitted California as a free state; prohibited slave trade in the District of Columbia; and amended the Fugitive Slave Act, giving slave holders the legal right to reclaim runaway slaves who had fled to free states (a serious threat to Maryland slaves who had sought freedom in neighboring Pennsylvania). In 1854 the Kansas-Nebraska Act repealed the Missouri Compromise and allowed politically contentious popular sovereignty to determine the slavery issue in the two new territories. Violence then erupted in Kansas between pro-slavery and anti-slavery settlers. Then, on March 6, 1857, the United States Supreme Court released its majority opinion in the *Dred Scott v. Sandford* case that Congress did not have the authority to prohibit slavery in the territories and Black persons—whether free or enslaved—were citizens and could not expect protection from the Federal Government or the courts.[11]

Lincoln's election led South Carolina to secede from the Union on December 20, 1860. It was followed in January and early February 1861 by Mississippi, Florida, Alabama, Georgia, Louisiana, and Texas. Some staunch abolitionists in the North favored such disunity as a way to weaken slavery by eliminating the Federal government's support of it through the Constitution and to hasten the inevitable civil war that would cleanse the nation of the taint of human bondage. On their side, the Southern states made clear their reasons for secession. Four issued formal declarations of secession that gave the perpetuation of slavery as their principle reason, with leaders in four other states declaring similar sentiments. The main states' right they wanted to protect was the right to own slaves. The constitution of the Confederate States of America, adopted March 11, 1861, invoked "the favor and guidance of Almighty God" and included ten references ensuring the continuance of enslavement.[12]

Secession was a serious topic in Maryland as well. Democrats demanded that Governor Hicks call a special session of the legislature—which they controlled—to discuss Maryland's position on secession. Strongly pro-Union Hicks resisted the calls for the legislature to meet and insisted instead that the border states ally themselves against the extremism of both North and South.[13]

The editor of the pro-Union *Annapolis Gazette* agreed with Hicks:

> The Maryland Secessionists desire to see our State joined to the Southern Confederacy. The Southern feeling prevailing in the hearts of all Marylanders has given great advantage to the proposition; and this will make itself seen and felt in the event of the secession of our State. We do not propose to discuss the impracticality of the proposition, as matters now stand [Maryland not being a cotton state] . . . . But we desire to see the pride of Marylanders sufficiently aroused to make them take a properly independent position for the honor as well as the interests of the State.[14]

To bolster its point, the editorial quoted Confederate President Jefferson Davis on the lack of homogeneity between Maryland and the lower South cotton states. Maryland's homogeneity, said the *Gazette*, "is with the Border States." As tensions were increasing, the *Gazette* declared: "He who is not for the union is against it.—There is no half place—no middle ground."[15]

After months of tension, failed reconciliation efforts, and the formation of the Southern Confederacy, the Civil War began with the first cannon shots fired at Fort Sumter on April 12, 1861, and the US Army garrison surrendered two days later. On April 15, President Lincoln declared an insurrection and called for 75,000 volunteers to enlist for ninety days and, on April 19, he ordered a naval blockade of rebellious Southern ports. In the meantime, as a consequence of Lincoln's call for volunteers, four more states—Virginia, Arkansas, Tennessee, and North Carolina—seceded between April 17 and May 20. Four border slave states—Delaware, Maryland, Kentucky, and Missouri—remained in the Union, a situation that was a setback for the Confederacy.

On April 19, Baltimore experienced the first belligerent casualties of the Civil War. Pennsylvania and Massachusetts militia regiments arrived in Baltimore by train on their way to Washington. As they moved on foot from one railroad terminal to another, they were attacked by Southern sympathizers. Twelve rioter civilians and seven Union soldiers died; numerous others were injured. That night city officials ordered railroad bridges north of the city burnt and telegraph lines cut. This was done not so much in sympathy with the South as it was to avoid more bloodshed by preventing more Federal troops from entering Baltimore. Shortly, this action had a direct implication on Annapolis.[16]

Immediately after the Baltimore riot, an anti-Union poem was written with the opening line "The despot's heel is on thy shore." The poem—"Maryland, My Maryland"—quickly put to music, mentioned several Catholics with Annapolis connections. Charles Carroll of Carrollton's "sacred trust" is invoked in the third stanza. Pro-South former governor Enoch Louis Lowe, Maryland's first elected Catholic governor, was hailed as "fearless" in the fourth stanza. And "dashing May"—a reference to Congressman Henry May, a future Catholic convert seen as sympathetic to the Confederacy, also appears in the fourth stanza. The writer, Baltimorean James Ryder Randall, a Catholic, was living in New Orleans and one of his friends had been killed in the riot. Years later Katherine Kent Walton, granddaughter of John Walton and lifelong St. Mary's parishioner, painted a portrait of Randall that was installed in the House of Delegate in the Maryland State House in 1909. "Maryland, My Maryland" became the official state song in 1939 and was abolished as such in 2021.[17]

Anne Arundel County secessionists tore up Annapolis and Elk Ridge Railroad tracks connecting the state capital to the Washington Branch of the B&O Railroad at Annapolis Junction. To avoid this now disrupted route and further possible conflict with Baltimoreans, on April 22 steamers carrying troops from New York and Massachusetts landed at the Naval Academy wharf. The landings occurred despite protests made by Governor Hicks both to Brigadier General Benjamin Franklin Butler, the commander of the Eighth Massachusetts Regiment, and to President Lincoln.[18]

The landing of troops brought renewed pressure on Hicks to convene the General Assembly. This time he reluctantly acquiesced. Baltimore newspaper publisher William Wilkins Glenn wrote in his diary on April 21 that Dr. Richard Sprigg Steuart, the owner of Dodon, had "forced" Hicks to call the legislature into session and asserted that Steuart "would have shot [Hicks] if he had refused." Hicks and other Unionists perceived considerable Southern sympathy in Annapolis and felt western Maryland was safer location in which to meet, so, on April 24, the legislature met in Frederick. The presence of Federal troops in and around the state capital and fear of a possible slave uprising in southern Maryland contributed to the decision to meet in Frederick. But by this time, even the Democratic majority in the legislature opposed any effort to discuss secession and were strongly pro-Union. This did not mean, however, that they supported Lincoln's war policies.[19]

Both Annapolis weekly newspapers manifested a distinctly pro-Union attitude. The *Annapolis Gazette* was characterized in later years as "a paper of unquenchable Union sympathy" whose former Know Nothing editor "was violent in his denunciation of secessionists." Its pro-Democratic Party competitor, the *Maryland Republican*, carried patriotic slogans weekly under its second page banner. "The Union of Democrats and Whigs, for the sake of the Union," cried one slogan. Another was "The Union: One and Inseparable: Now and Forever!!" And, as a sign that patriotism was more important than party politics, editor Elihu S. Riley Sr. proclaimed: "We join ourselves to no party that does not carry the flag and keep step to the music of the union." However, an editorial in the *Annapolis Gazette* criticized the *Maryland Republican* for calling for a "Sovereign Convention of the people to declare the position of the State of Maryland in the present crisis," an action seen as tantamount to being "secesh." The Baltimore *Sun*, also read in Annapolis, was a traditionally pro-South and pro-Democratic Party paper. It viewed Lincoln's election, as one scholar put it, as "causing an inevitable collision course between North and South."[20]

The level of crisis in Annapolis is seen in an *Annapolis Gazette* editorial published on April 25:

> the people of Annapolis are highly indignant at the occupation of our city. But we are powerless to oppose them. Yielding to the advice of the more prudent, our people have refrained from any open demonstration against the troops . . . . The excitement here is terrible. No man seems to know what is to be done to avert the evil that has come upon us; and all admit that we are utterly powerless of offer any resistance.[21]

Instead of demonstrations and resistence, ever-practical Annapolitans chose a different route. The editorial reported that "Horses and wagons and provisions have been sold to the strangers, at high prices, for cash." But the *Gazette* editor also said it was his impression that the legislature meeting in Frederick would pass an ordinance of secession and that "[t]he feeling hereabouts is almost unanimous on the subject."

Annapolis was now occupied by Union troops. The harbor was filled with steamships and light craft of all sorts. Carts, wagons, and foot traffic crowded the streets. Two farms across the Severn River from the Naval Academy were seized, one to protect the academy and the other to harvest timber for building temporary quarters on the Yard. On the first Sunday after the arrival of troops from the North, there was:

> presented a spectacle in the ancient city which has not been witnessed for years. Some two hundred soldiers attended worship at St. Mary's (Catholic) Church, while others were busily engaged in carting supplies from the Naval Academy to the depot for transportation to Washington.[22]

The impact of the war suddenly was being felt at St. Mary's. It was not a bad thing to have hundreds of soldiers crowding into the church, but it must have upset the usual daily routines of both laity and clergy.

Dark Clouds of Adversity

Historian Randall Miller says the Catholic Church policy during the war was to allow Catholics "to follow their section." Political disunity was accepted as long as Catholics remained faithful to the institutional church. It was an opportunity for Catholics to show their sectional patriotism. Thus northern Catholics, with some reservations, supported the Union cause while most southern Catholics supported the Confederate cause. Annapolis Catholics were split several ways in their political leanings. They might be pro-Union or pro-South while remaining faithful to their universal church.[23]

St. Mary's Redemptorist chronicler (presumably Michael Müller) did not note the large influx of Mass attendees mentioned above, but he did observe the beginnings of the war. He summed up the recent events as follows:

> At this time, political unrest began and troops were conscripted. Many were justly afraid of great troubles in our state and especially for our students. But God disposed matters in a way that the fear was in vain. For civil war, which so easily could assault our state (Maryland), began without bringing harm to us. At God's disposal, Maryland remained in the "union," as it is called, and the battles took place mainly in Virginia.

It continued:

> In the following days, Father Superior ordered that all the more-valuable things in the church and house—books, religious articles, etc.—be hidden underground. He consulted Father Provincial about sending the students in groups to different houses in the province if great danger should come; this the Provincial ordered. But God disposed things differently. The danger of the first stage of the war passed by, and gradually our fears lessened, and the students regained hope of staying here. Even though there were close to Annapolis many camps of soldiers from the most diverse parts of the "Union," and at other times large groups gathered, no trouble came to us either from their leaders or from the rank-and-file. Actually there was a friendly spirit among all. Many who were coming to Annapolis for the first time wanted to see our house and this was easily granted.[24]

This account was entered under an April 1861 heading but the reference to battles in Virginia indicates it may have been written some months later, perhaps after First Manassas (or Bull Run), the first major battle of the war, on July 21. Moreover, no civilians were enrolled for the draft in Maryland until August 1862. The chronicler used incorrect terminology when he said "troops were conscripted," a compulsory action. He probably meant that tens of thousands of men had voluntarily enlisted in northern state militia units in response to the Lincoln's call for 75,000 troops. Nevertheless, the arrival of Union troops at the Naval Academy and securing Annapolis under Federal control—"the first stage of the war"—is surely what increased Müller's fears for his students.[25]

What would become a devastating four-year-long war had direct effects on Maryland and its civilian population. Thirty-one major and minor military engagements and hundreds of raids and skirmishes occurred in Maryland. The state was a crossroads for spies, dealers in contraband goods, blockade runners, men heading south to join the Confederacy, and escaped slaves heading north to freedom. The Federal military occupation and economic

Martin Fannen Revell Jr. (1839–1901). Courtesy Ann Jensen.

hardship affected the entire state, as did the deaths of local men in service. Although Annapolis escaped any direct military action, the presence of tens of thousands of troops in and around the city had profound implications.

The *Chronica Domus* account thus gives a sense of the fears held by the Redemptorists and their parishioners as their quiet city was now awakened by war. The Redemptorists soon felt threatened by the possibility of being drafted by the Maryland authorities. Colleges elsewhere, both secular and religious, "emptied out at an alarming rate," according to one historian, as young men left to serve either the Union or the Confederacy.[26]

A related chronicle entry in May was simultaneously pessimistic and hopeful:

> Political troubles continue to grow, but relying on God, our spirits were not agitated. " If God be for us, who is against us?" This truth seems especially clear in these times of trouble.[27]

As good a record keeper as he was, the chronicler concentrated on the affairs of the college rather than on the war. "I decided to omit many items," he wrote in May, "especially those referring to the nation rather than to us. Perhaps some day they can be part of American history." Frater John Berger, writing to his family in Bohemia, was more blunt. He said he hoped that none of the novices would be "taken away" but he did not make clear if he meant to a safer location or to be conscripted.[28]

Edward Sparks had his say about the Federal occupation of Annapolis in a way that indicated his pro-Union position. He told a patient, sixteen-year-old Ella Holland, who later repeated Sparks' words to her cousin, that despite the thousands of troops passing through town, "there is no call for the women to be frightened." But Ella was not fearful, judging from what she added to her account: "I almost died with the blues," she wrote, and hoped that her regular physician would soon return to Annapolis. Her spirits were later raised, she reported, because she had seen "such a handsome [Union soldier]" that "I almost lost my heart."[29]

A different view was expressed by nineteen-year-old Martin Fannen Revell Jr., a lumber yard clerk and St. Mary's parishioner. He was outspoken about the early days of the war as seen in letters he wrote to his "dear friend"—his Episcopalian future wife and Ella's cousin—eighteen-year-old Susannah (Susie) Sands. When the war began, Susie's father, steamboat captain James H. Sands, sent his wife (Jane Catherine Holland) and children to a safe location in Centreville, Queen Anne's County, on Maryland's Eastern Shore. Martin wrote "in great haste" to "My absent friend" on April 29, that "I would to Heaven . . . I could write something that is cheering and pleasing but that is impossible now; we are still surrounded by the enemy and the cry is 'still they come.'" He relayed the ominous news that Union soldiers were seen everywhere in town and that when he and others encountered them "we can say nothing, we can do nothing; will Maryland always permit this! will she forget her former glory! will she be conquered without striking a blow!" He answered his own rhetorical questions in the next lines:

> no never, she will be free, she will soon burst the chains that now bind her; and her sons will have freedom stamped upon their brow, and the song of liberty upon their lips, we must hope this, we must not judge the future by the present, because the dark clouds of adversity hang over us now we must not give up.[30]

He went on to declare for "the 'cause' that I am for." Brave words from a young man who had not yet "gone South." He continued to lament that many families had left Annapolis and how badly he felt when Susie departed for Centreville.

In a letter on May 1, Martin informed Susie that "we are very busy now selling lumber, for or to the Garrison (no longer the Naval Academy here), they are building warehouses, stables, and quarters down there." He reported that "Annapolis is no longer the quiet little place of former days, vehicles of every kind and description rattle through our streets, our sidewalks are crowded with persons from all parts (of the North)." He said that ships were continually unloading at the Naval Academy and that it looked like "business camp" with campfires burning all over the Yard, and soldiers, about 3,000 of them, "eating here and there" and that 5,000 more were expected. Although the soldiers were "still civil," he observed that "military despotism reigns here." Nearby farms had been taken over by the army and "they have planted cannons on all of them." He lamented that this situation might last upward of four years, the period of Lincoln's term in office, "or may be for ever."[31]

Martin wrote again to Susie a week later, saying that "it is, you might say, suicide to speak for the South here." He revealed that he could not remain much longer in his "oppressed" native city and would leave for "some clime more congenial to my feelings" even though his ties to his native town, family, and friends "must be severed" if he left. As for local news, he reported that "it is very noisy down this way as nearly all the boats land at this wharf." He said the authorities operated five omnibuses between the wharf at the end of Prince George Street, close to the Sands family home, and the railroad depot. He complained that passengers used his lumber yard office as a waiting room. Without further comment, he also told Susie that "Mrs. Lincoln and Major Anderson have just passed through."[32]

Perhaps he feared making impolitic comments in correspondence that might be interdicted by Union authorities. Other sources reveal that on May 10, Mary Lincoln took an afternoon train to Annapolis with her cousin, Elizabeth Todd Grimsley, and Interim Commissioner of Public Buildings William S. Wood. Major Anderson, who accompanied the party, was none other than Major Robert Anderson, the former commander of the US Army Garrison at Fort Sumter. The party was bound for New York City as part of Mrs. Lincoln's project to purchase new and extravagant furnishings for the White House. Perhaps while resting in Martin's office, they changed their travel plan and returned to the Calvert Street depot and took a late train back to Annapolis Junction and on to Baltimore and Philadelphia for the night.[33]

Martin Revell left home, family, and friends on May 21 (or May 22, accounts vary) and made his way to Baltimore with plans to travel by train to Virginia where he intended to join the Confederate army and "perhaps some day come back crowned with laurels." When he reached Baltimore, however, he heard that Union troops were arresting suspicious passengers at Relay House, a transfer point for western- and southern-bound trains west of Baltimore City.[34]

His way thus blocked, Martin returned to Annapolis the next day. He was determined to leave again, but on June 1, he was arrested by Federal troops. Susie Sands, writing to Ella Holland, told of Martin's arrest "for what we know not," adding that "they have been arresting the secessionists ever since we got back" (from Centreville on May 17). Martin was released the same evening and, according to Susie, "a short time after he left for the country." He presumably went to stay with his older half-brother, Dr. William Theodore Revell, in northern Anne Arundel County, near Stony Creek. He later returned to town, was enrolled for the draft, and would run afoul with the authorities again in 1863 (see Election of the Disloyal, ch. 5). Not at all a coincidence in this pro-rebel family, William Revell's son born on April 23, 1861, was named Frank Southern Revell. Long after the war, Frank became sheriff and county clerk of Anne Arundel County.[35]

Martin's sister—Mary Teresa—is another story. "Mollie," as she was known to family and friends, had a number of St. Mary's activities to her credit. She served as godmother to her niece, Mary Elizabeth Brady in 1859 and nephew John Roland Brady in 1861. They were children of Mollie's elder sister, Anna Maria Revell Brady (Mrs. John Wesley Brady). Mollie was confirmed by Archbishop Kenrick in 1860 when she was about sixteen.[36]

Soon after the war started, Mollie demonstrated her pro-Southern feelings. A family story passed on by Mildred Revell Brady Chadeayne, a granddaughter of Anna Maria Revell Brady, has it that a Confederate flag was flown from the front porch of the Revell's home across from the Maryland State House. While this defiance has not been corroborated from other sources, a contemporary observer reported that several days before General Butler landed in Annapolis, Southern sympathizers hoisted a Confederate flag on a pole on nearby West Street, but he did not associate the Revell family with the incident.[37] Regardless, the Brady family tale continues:

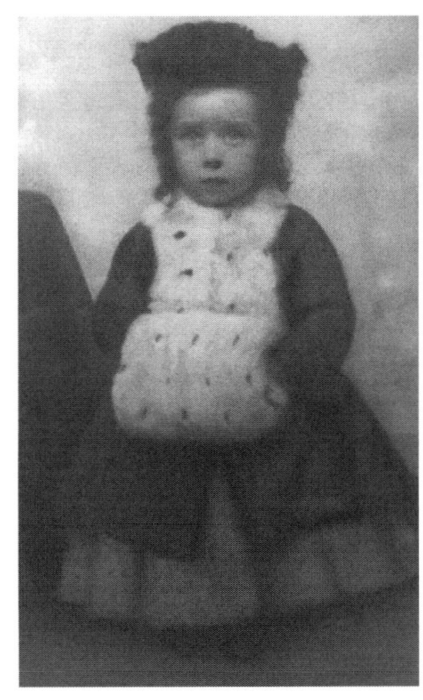

Mary Elizabeth ("Be Be") Brady (1859–1940). Courtesy Deborah Chadeayne Oliver.

> Although it is not recorded, tradition in the family and from the memories of living Annapolitans who recall the incident, it was Molly [*sic*] Revell who had made and hung out the flag. Afterwards, sitting in a swing in front of the house with her cousin, Kitty Hutton, [they] sang "Hang John Brown's Body" much to the anxiety of neighbors who . . . . expected Union soldiers to appear any moment to arrest them.

When exactly this rebellious event occurred was not stated. But a contemporary observer writing a quarter of a century later said that:

John Roland Brady (1861–1922) with his nurse Rosa. Courtesy Stephen Noonan.

> a young company of secession youths boldly dressed in red, with wooden guns, paraded the town without fear or molestation, and on the night of July 21, 1861, when the news of the Battle of Bull Run reached Annapolis, a crowd of young Southern sympathizers marched down town singing and rejoicing over the

defeat of the Federal troops. But that was the last of it.[38]

It was, perhaps, at this time that Mollie and Kitty sang their protest song. The song's full title was "We'll Hang John Brown's Body from A Sour Apple Tree," a reference to abolitionist John Brown who was executed for his insurrection at Harpers Ferry in 1859. The melody came from an old southern camp meeting song, "Grace Reviving in the Soul," and the words were a parody of "John Brown's Body," a marching song popular with Union troops since early in the war and which included the line "they will hang Jeff Davis from a tree." Julia Ward Howe, the wife of one of John Brown's secret financial backers, used the same melody for her "Battle Hymn of the Republic," first published in February 1862.[39]

Another act of resistance was made by Mollie's brother-in-law John Wesley Brady, a later convert to Catholicism. In 1861 he was a charter member of the local Masonic organization, Annapolis Lodge No. 89. According to Brady family lore, at the time of the occupation of Annapolis, Federal troops went door to door looking for pro-Southern paraphernalia. Perhaps fearing what might be found in his home, Brady "hung his Masonic apron across the front door and [the soldiers] passed him by." While this display would not have won the favor of his Catholic wife, it would have impressed his fellow Freemasons.[40]

When Mildred Chadeayne applied for admission to the United Daughters of the Confederacy in 1934, she offered as historical proof, her grandmother Anna Maria Brady and Anna Maria's siblings, James, Martin, William Theodore, Elizabeth, and Mollie Revell as "Confederate Patriots" who "rendered financial aid and physical comfort to the Confederacy."[41] The application, which was accepted, concentrated on the political activism of the three brothers, especially James Revell, but did not mention Mollie's flag raising or singing. Mollie's song partner, Catherine "Kitty" Hutton, was a cousin on her mother's side of the family.[42]

The Secession Feeling Prevails

There was a clear contrast between how Federal troops were received in Annapolis as compared to the deadly riots in Baltimore. In fact, General Butler, a pro-War Democrat, reported to his civilian superior, Massachusetts Governor John Albion Andrew, that he had no fear of mob action in Annapolis, and had promised Governor Hicks and the people of Annapolis "that he would protect them and himself from any such uprising." When Butler landed his troops at the Naval Academy, he received a report that slaves on the north side of the Severn River "were in a state of insurrection." Since he had promised "to put down a white mob," he said he also "was bound, in good faith, to protect the citizens against a black one." There were no mob riots or slave uprisings, but because of his promises, claimed Butler, "there is now no city in the Union more loyal than Annapolis."[43]

The resentments against the Yankee occupation, however, remained largely beneath the surface. When Lieutenant William Henry Sterling of Philadelphia arrived in town two years later, he observed that "[w]ith a few exceptions this place is 'very secesh' but people do not seem to be very violent, at least in public, but they are said to be very violent at home."[44] He obviously must have meant violent in opinion about the occupation of Annapolis and the ongoing war. When his wife Matilda arrived in Annapolis a few weeks later, she wrote to her mother in Philadelphia saying:

> The Secession feeling prevails here, there being but a small number of Unionists. I hear that the Secessionists are very bitter in their feelings, but they keep quiet because they are obliged to. They hate all Federal officers and soldiers, especially as their presence here obliges them to behave themselves. Still I hear that the women of Annapolis (although so bitter) have never acted in the unladylike and outrageous manner that the women of Baltimore and other Southern cities have done.[45]

The situation appeared quite differently depending on the source of information. The *New York Daily Tribune* reported that a "large and enthusiastic Union meeting" was held in Annapolis on May 5. The "[p]rominent citizens" who participated in the meeting—only former American Party member Dennis Claude was mentioned by name—passed resolutions "to sustain the government" while "[s]ecession resolutions" made by John Thomson Mason, "were received with groans and hisses."[46]

Another issue that upset Annapolitans and involved at least one St. Mary's parishioner was the construction in May 1861 of a military railroad spur between the railroad depot at Calvert and West streets to the steamship wharf at the Naval Academy. The purpose of the spur was to provide direct access to and from the Severn River for shipping and receiving military supplies and the movement of troops. "As soon as his troops landed in the city," writes historian Rockford Toews, "General Butler saw the need for the railroad spur." He had a survey made of the mile-long route and construction was completed in less than a month. Martin Revell, writing on April 29, said "I hear they intend to carry it through the Episcopal church yard, but I can not believe that." Two days later he wrote that work had commenced and that soldiers were posted as guards about ten yards apart along the route. Another of Susie Sands' correspondents wrote that soldiers were "keeping guard on our streets for fear that somebody will pull the stakes up." She also reported that the Annapolis Telegraph Company office had been seized and the local operator replaced by men from Philadelphia. The railroad spur was enclosed with a fence, and, when it was completed, troops from the Eighth Massachusetts and the Thirteenth New York infantry regiments, both under Butler's command, paraded through the city in celebration.[47]

The original survey for the railroad spur has not been found and the precise route "is open to conjecture," according to Toews. What is known is that seven claims were made against the Federal government for compensation for the use of land to build the spur. The first claimant was the City of Annapolis, made within weeks of construction, for the obstruction of public right of ways and the removal of a public well and pump on Northwest Street. Following the war and after the tracks had been removed, six other claims were made for back rent and reimbursement for replacing privies and fences removed to build the spur. The claims help define the route of the spur from the north side of the railroad depot on Calvert Street, crossing through public streets and private properties on Calvert, Northwest, Carroll, Bladen, and Tabernacle streets.[48]

One of the claimants for compensation for the railroad spur was David S. Caldwell. He was a lumber merchant doing business on Calvert Street near the county jail; a stock holder in the Annapolis and Elk Ridge Railroad; a slave holder; owner of property on West, Northwest, Prince George, and Green streets, and Market Space; a widower living in a large brick house on Northwest Street; a member of the Democratic Party; and a member of the local Masonic lodge. He also was associated with St. Mary's. He served twice as a godparent in the 1850s and his name is listed among those who donated money for St. Mary's new bells in 1859.[49] Nearly seven years later, in January 1868, the Depot Quartermaster's Office in Washington recommended that the government pay claims made by Caldwell and three of his neighbors for "injury sustained in the removal of fences &c. . . . and in doing so occupied the property" of the claimants. Caldwell's compensation was to be $192, representing $48 per year for ground rent and $151 for replacing his fence.[50]

A Dangerous Place

Beginning in December 1860, numerous officers and midshipmen resigned from the Naval Academy and joined the Confederacy. Approximately one-third of the midshipmen were from slave states and one of them, a pro-Union southerner, had felt earlier that "the tone of the institution itself was distinctly southern and pro-slavery as distinguished from northern and anti-slavery."[51]

Whatever happened to the Naval Academy also affected its civilian employees, many of whom were St. Mary's parishioners. After the April 12 bombardment of Fort Sumter, concern for the academy's safety increased and one observer believed it was "rather a dangerous place for a government institution." Academy superintendent Captain George Smith Blake wrote on April 15 to Secretary of the Navy Gideon Welles describing defensive measures he had taken. Howitzers were placed at the gates into town and a practice battery was moved from Fort Severn to the frigate USS *Constitution*—"Old Ironsides"—then attached to the academy as a training ship. Sailors and midshipmen boarded the *Constitution* as a defense force. The next day, Blake sent Lieutenant Stephen B. Luce to report directly to Captain George A. Magruder, chief of the Bureau of Ordnance and Hydrography, concerning "the extremely threatening condition of public affairs & the comparatively helpless situation" of the *Constitution*—warning that it might fall into enemy hands—and pointing out "the indefensible condition of the academy generally." Luce, on his own accord, told Magruder that "the ship, in the event of an attack, would be defended to the last extremity and destroyed rather than suffered to fall into the hands of parties inimical to the Government." Blake suggested that first class midshipmen be graduated and the lower classes—since they were young and some were sympathetic to the "disaffected States"—be given leaves of absence. Luce's sense of his "interview" with Magruder was that there was a lack of a sense of urgency in Washington. However, when the question of Maryland's possible secession arose, Magruder surprisingly advised Luce that Blake "would have to act according to his own discretion in the matter" of whether or not to turn over the academy property to the governor should he demand it.[52]

Welles replied to Blake on April 18, approving the measures he had taken but counseling that he should not "add to the excitement, or create unnecessary alarm by a premature movement." Like Magruder, Welles allowed Blake to act on his "own convictions in that emergency" should the telegraph lines be cut. Despite these ominous developments, day-to-day life at the academy continued. The "usual routine of studies" was observed, midshipmen attended Sunday services, boat exercises took place, and upper classmen practiced fencing and pivot gun drills. In the meantime, guns and ammunition were loaded onto the *Constitution* and battalion infantry drills were held. On Saturday, April 20, liberty was granted to those whose turn it was to go into town, and a "hop" was held in the evening.[53]

The *Constitution* was towed out into Annapolis Roads the same day Butler's troops landed. The situation ashore remained tense enough that Sunday services were cancelled and extra guards were mounted throughout the Yard. When a suspicious boat approached the academy wharf and failed to respond to the sentinel's three hails, a warning musket shot was fired and the boat departed. It was a wise move on the sentinel's part since the boat reportedly was "filled with armed men."[54]

The commandant of midshipmen at the Naval Academy, Lieutenant Edward Simpson, wrote in July 1862 to the United States Senate's Committee on Naval Affairs about "the outrage committed by a mob in Baltimore, on a regiment from Massachusetts" and how it had "excited interest" at the academy. He described in detail the measures taken to secure the academy, noting that there was concern that the agitation in Baltimore might lead to an attack on the *Constitution* and the academy armory. Simpson said every precaution was taken to protect the academy. Of the inhabitants of Annapolis, he wrote, "I never had any suspicion." There had been rumors, however, that "it was the intention of a band of lawless men to plant a battery on the bank of the Severn" across from the *Constitution*, so the ship was moved out to Annapolis Roads for its protection.[55]

On April 24, some first class members were ordered to report to Washington, and Blake wrote again to Welles, this time seeking permission to move the academy to Fort Adams, an army post near Newport, Rhode Island. Blake cited rumors of a possible attack on the academy by local Southern sympathizers and was still concerned that they might seize the *Consti-*

tution. In response, he ordered the remaining 150 midshipmen to board the ship, which then departed under tow for Newport on April 26. Officers and faculty members boarded the steamer *Baltic* on May 5 and 6 and, along with the library and scientific instruments, also departed for Newport. Classes resumed at the new location less than a week later.[56]

Throughout this time, a number of civilian employees of the Naval Academy "stood by" Commodore Blake as he prepared to defend Federal property against the feared secessionist attack. These local men declared their loyalty to the Union and pledged assistance to Blake. An extensive list of loyal civilian employees prepared in 1870 included St. Mary's men: Andrew Denver (watchman), Thomas Denver (fireman in the gas and steam works), John Joseph Geoghan (laborer), Michael Gesner (master laborer), Hugh McCusker (superintendent of the gas and steam works), Michael Naughton (fireman in the gas and steam works), and August Schwallenberg (gas and steam fitter) were noted as having "stood by" or "remained at the Academy" when Blake anticipated an attack on the academy. Richard M. Chase, secretary of the Naval Academy, later testified that "Confidential persons were sent to Baltimore to be on the look out, & to advise [Blake] of any threatenings from that City. . . ." This episode may refer to Hugh McCusker, who was cited in the 1870 report as having "rendered valuable service, in watching the enemies of the Gov't." McCusker and most of the above-named St. Mary's parishioners went to Newport for the duration of the war.[57]

Another parishioner associated with the Naval Academy who relocated to Newport was Thomas Karney, an assistant professor of ethics and English studies since 1852. His sister, Arabella, served as godmother at St. Mary's baptisms four times in the early 1850s, twice on the same day for two fourteen year olds: a Black boy named Samuel George Carder and a White girl identified only as Theresia Christiana.[58] Karney's loyalty came under suspicion in August 1861 when Welles wrote to Blake that the "Department has information that . . . Prof. Kearny [*sic*] . . . [is] disloyal." Karney responded to Welles' allegation in a letter to Blake that "I lose no time in denying most emphatically, but respectfully, that I am or have been, in any manner disloyal to the Constitution or the Government of the United States" and noted he had a "sworn obligation as a servant of the Government." The matter did not die quietly, however. In June 1862, the Senate adopted a resolution directing the Committee on Naval Affairs to investigate presumed disloyalty to the government by Blake and others at the Academy. Blake, who continued to serve as superintendent until 1865, firmly denied any disloyalty on his own part and by any person still connected to the academy. Karney also responded, in a letter sent directly to Senator John Parker Hale, the naval affairs committee chairman. He supported Blake's claims of loyalty and maintained that neither he himself nor "any other person now connected with this institution, manifested or exhibited any feelings or sentiments hostile to the Government of the United States." He was one of twenty-two faculty and staff members who replied and all, except one, declined to answer the Senate inquiries. In the end they all were deemed by the Senate committee as truthful and loyal to the United States. In regard to the charges of disloyalty, Commandant Lieutenant Edward Simpson said they had come from a "foul source" and were a "calumny."[59]

Another person associated with St. Mary's who went to Newport was an accomplished landscape artist, illustrator, and printmaker. Edward R. Seager was born in England in 1809, migrated to Canada around 1832, and became the academy's first professor of drawing and drafting in 1850. His wife, Mary De LaRaintre—the Baltimore-born daughter of immigrants from Saint-Domingue and Ireland—and their teenage daughter Mary were listed among the donors of the St. Mary's new bells in 1859. After departing for Newport, Seager was required to respond to the 1862 Senate inquiry about disloyalty. He, like his colleague, Karney, supported Blake, avowed his own integrity and loyalty, and said he believed "in the perfect loyalty of every member of the academic staff who remained after April 1861." It is not known whether Mary and their five children remained in Annapolis or went to live in Baltimore during the war because only Edward was listed in a Rhode Island state census taken on June 1, 1865. A year after Seager relocated to Newport, his oldest son, Edward R. Seager Jr., was admitted to the Naval Academy. Edward Jr. and his brothers, Henry and John Louis, were confirmed at St. Mary's by Archbishop Kenrick in January 1860. Although Edward Jr.'s "order of merit" in drawing ranked eighth in his class of twenty-eight acting midshipmen, he failed algebra, geometry, and history and composition, was "found deficient," and discharged from the academy in 1864.[60]

The Naval Academy Band also relocated to Newport, taking with it four St. Mary's parishioners. Peter Klippen was born in Hesse-Darmstadt in 1834 and immigrated to the United States in the late 1840s. He had served with the academy band since 1853 as a second-class musician playing the cornet and was promoted to first-class musician in 1856. Soon after arriving in Annapolis, Klippen became active at St. Mary's, where he was baptized in 1854, confirmed in 1857, and married Rebecca Grant, a non-Catholic from Philadelphia, in 1858. Father Joseph Maria Jacobs officiated at the Klippen-Grant wedding. One of the witnesses, Redemptorist Brother Jacob Engel, is of interest. Although he was a witness at a marriage not a baptism, priests, monks, lay brothers, and nuns were excluded by canon law from serving as godparents because their secluded lives kept them from assuming the duties of sponsors to instruct god children and exhort them to lead a Christian life, especially if the parents should die or neglect their obligations. Such sponsorship, however, had precedents at St. Mary's. Between 1858 and 1865 fifteen baptisms and marriages are recorded as witnessed by priests or brothers. Klippen himself is listed seven more times in the baptismal register as the father of newborn daughters—Mary Elizabeth and Anna Agnes—in 1859 and 1860, respectively, and as a godparent five times for children in the local German-Catholic community between 1856 and 1860. The German connections are not to suggest that Klippen interacted socially only with his native countrymen. The other witness at Peter and Rebecca's marriage was Ellen Fee Walsh, a native of County Longford, Ireland. Their daughters' godparents were Bridget Farrell (whose husband Simon was a laborer at the academy) and John Thomas Walsh (Ellen Fee Walsh's husband), also a native of Ireland.[61] These choices suggest that the commonality among these people was not their national origin but their Catholic religion.

The Kilppen's next door neighbors on the academy grounds were band member Peter Hilgert and his wife, Meta Strohmeyer. Hilgert, a native of Bavaria, had been with the band at least since 1853 and was rated in 1861 as a first-class musician playing the baritone horn. He and Meta, a native of the Duchy of Saxe-Weimar-Eisenach, were married at St. Mary's in 1858 by Father Müller. Theirs was another mixed marriage, he a Catholic and she a Lutheran. In the eyes of the church such a marriage had impediments that had to be resolved before the ceremony could be held. Meta's brother, Gustavus Strohmeyer, a band member, served as one of the witnesses. But a practicing Catholic was needed, and a fortuitous choice was made. Müller asked his young assistant and an accomplished musician himself, Father John Cornell, to serve as the canonical witness. Peter and Meta's infant daughter, Mary Louise, was baptized at St. Mary's in 1859. National diversity again came into play: Mary Louise's godmother was Ann Powers, a native of Ireland.[62]

Christian Wirth (or Würth) is listed in various census records as born in the Netherlands and Germany; the latter is more likely. He was rated as a second-class musician and played the clarinet and cornet for the academy band. Born about 1819, he was older than his fellow band members and, in fact, had served as godfather to Peter Klippen when he converted to Catholicism in 1854. Wirth also served as godfather for three sons of a local German-American couple, George and Anna Margaret Salzmann Meyer.[63]

Another band member who went to Newport also was a convert. Charles Garlieb Wilhelm Zimmermann was a native of either the Electorate of Hesse-Cassel or the Kingdom of Prussia and was twenty-eight years old when he joined the band in 1859. He played alto horn in the band and French horn in the orchestra, holding a first-class rating. In 1860 he married Baltimore-born Catholic Elizabeth Gesner in a ceremony at St. Mary's presided over by Father John Duffy. Two of Elizabeth's brothers (Francis Joseph in 1865 and John Michael in 1870) later became band members. One of the Zimmermann-Gesner marriage witnesses was Michael Kraus, also a band member. Two months after the wedding, Charles was baptized by Father Henry Fehlings. Elizabeth's father, Simon Gesner, did double duty, serving as canonical witness at the marriage and as godparent at his son-in-law's baptism. When Charles and Elizabeth departed for Newport in 1861, Elizabeth was in the latter stages of pregnancy with Charles Adams Zimmermann. He was the first of their four sons and later became St. Mary's organist and the academy's band master.[64]

A Navy officer who most probably attended St. Mary's Church years earlier was killed in action on June 27, 1861. He was Commander James Harmon Ward, one of the founding faculty members of the Naval Academy in 1845. He died aboard the USS *Freeborn* at the Battle of Mathias Point, in King George County, Virginia, and was the first US Navy officer killed in battle during the Civil War and his death attracted nationwide attention, even in the South. He had served as an instructor of gunnery and steam engineering at the Naval Academy in 1845 and later wrote naval ordnance, gunnery, tactics, and steam engineering manuals. One of the numerous news reports of his career and death mentioned that he was a devout Catholic. Although his demise attracted little attention in the local press, old timers in Annapolis would have remembered him from his Naval Academy days.[65]

Preparing for Death

By mid-summer 1861, military authorities issued strict orders for the conduct of soldiers in Annapolis. General Orders No. 3, issued on July 28, 1861, by Colonel A. Biddle Roberts, commander of the First Pennsylvania Reserve Corps, "directed and required" the troops garrisoned at the Naval Academy "to guard with special care and attention the public property of every description . . . and every portion of the same is to be left in the position in which it was received from the former commandant and in no event is it be either removed or destroyed." The troops were to "deport themselves with the greatest propriety and in such manner as to leave the Naval School uninjured and the shrubbery, trees and yard in as neat a condition as possible." Buildings, gas fixtures, water works, and boats also were to be maintained in the same way. No mention was made of private property or the deportment of the troops outside of "the garrison," as the Naval Academy was now called. Roberts issued General Orders No. 4 the same day. It directed Army companies stationed at Annapolis Junction to post guards along the rail line and its bridges and "to conduct themselves with the utmost decorum and propriety." Pickets were to be positioned "at any points" that the local commander "may deem advisable."[66] Presumably, these soldiers also checked passes issued to civilian travelers by the provost marshal in Annapolis (see Forced to Take an Oath of Loyalty, ch. 4).

Around this time, the Redemptorists in Cumberland, under the direction of Father Seelos, were confronted with situations that soon had implications for the Annapolis community. Cumberland was close to the war front and, like Annapolis, was occupied by Union troops. The Eleventh Indiana Regiment of Zouaves commanded by Colonel (later Brigadier and Major General) Lewis (Lew) Wallace, of subsequent *Ben-Hur* fame, was encamped in Cumberland from mid-June to early July 1861. The Hoosiers soon caused problems for the Redemptorists. Father Peter Zimmer wrote of an instance in which seminarians out on a recreational walk were mistaken for Confederate soldiers. At a distance, perhaps because of their clerical garb, they looked suspicious. Union guards took aim "but the error was discovered only the moment before the command was to be given to fire."[67]

Father Thomas Mooney (1824–77), chaplain of the Sixty-Ninth New York Infantry. Prints and Photographs Division, Library of Congress https://www.loc.gov/pictures/item/2017896821/.

On June 19, a false report that Confederate troops were advancing on Cumberland caused great anxiety in the city and among Sts. Peter and Paul's parishioners and the Redemptorists. The house chronicler reported that, upon entering the church, "we saw the confessionals surrounded by anxious women, who as it seemed were preparing for death." Fearing they might have to flee, Seelos told the seminarians to be ready to depart on short notice. Father Van de Braak, lector of moral theology and church minister for Sts. Peter and Paul, divided the house money and "kept portions in readiness" to distribute to fleeing Redemptorists. The same day, local rowdies accused the Redemptorists of concealing firearms and wanted to storm the seminary. Captain John Fahnestock, a company commander in the Eleventh Indiana, volunteered to search the building with several armed men, including two parishioners. When they arrived, Van de Braak readily agreed to allow them to search the premises, but they demurred and several days later, Colonel Wallace sent a written apology to the Redemptorists.[68]

A more serious, incident occurred in August. Redemptorist seminarians were playing baseball outside the city, on a hill near the north branch of the Potomac River, which formed the border with Virginia. Because of their long black garb, their running around, and being across from Virginia, the students were taken by a distant Union picket to be enemy soldiers. Three soldiers were dispatched to reconnoiter and when they found the students playing ball, the soldiers berated them for raising a false alarm. One angry soldier leveled his musket at Frater Charles Wensierski and pulled the trigger. Three times the musket misfired, leaving the thirty-four-year-old Prussian a very lucky man. In the meantime, several companies of troops arrived but the incident ended with no harm to the students.[69] Such a close call was sobering for the Cumberland Redemptorists and the situation was not improving. Cumberland had become a potentially dangerous place for the Redemptorists and plans were revived to transfer the students to Annapolis.

One of the Most Devoted Priests

Shortly after the war began, Father Thomas J. Mooney was deployed to Annapolis with the Sixty-Ninth New York Infantry Regiment. The Sixty-Ninth was made up mostly of New York City Irish Catholic immigrants and was part of the famous "Irish Brigade." Mooney immigrated from Ireland to United States in 1848 during the potato famine. He was ordained in New York City in 1852 and by 1860 was pastor of St. Bridget's Church, an "Irish famine" parish on Manhattan's East Side. When the war began, Archbishop John Hughes allowed Mooney to enlist with the Sixty-Ninth New York on April 20, 1861, and he was commissioned as its chaplain. Before the regiment's departure from New York on April 23, Mooney addressed his new comrades, telling them that "the best soldier was he that respected his God while he fought for his country." This was a variation of a noble sentiment repeated by other clergy, politicians, and newspaper editors—North and South—throughout the war: "God is on *our* side." Hughes blessed the troops of the Sixty-Ninth as they marched past him on the way to their ships. The regiment traveled to Annapolis on the steamships *Harriet Lane* and *James Adger,* arriving in the Severn River on evening of April 25.[70]

The regiment's Irish nationalist Catholic commander, Colonel Michael Corcoran, wrote home on the day of their arrival reporting on the trip south to Annapolis. He extolled Mooney's work among the troops during the voyage. His letter was published in the New York Times on May 1, and read in part:

> Poor Father Mooney did infinite service, and was never ceasing in his labors. I earnestly hope the Most Reverend Archbishop will allow him to remain.[71]

Mooney's "infinite service" included keeping the men's spirits up during the two-day voyage with words of encouragement, hearing "innumerable confessions," and offering Mass aboard the *James Adger* on the morning of April 25.[72]

Subsequent events reveal that tension existed between Mooney and his prelate. Although the archbishop called Mooney "a virtuous, zealous & efficient priest," he was not Hughes' first choice for the chaplaincy. Hughes advised Mooney before his departure from New York on how to deal with the Fenian Brotherhood, radical expatriates who supported Irish independence by violent means if necessary. The Sixty-Ninth had Fenians within its ranks—including Colonel Corcoran—and Hughes told Mooney that these men should not be allowed to receive the sacraments of the Catholic Church nor be given a Christian burial, unless they renounced their Fenian associations. He warned Mooney further "to exercise all the discretion and all the charity that religion affords" and to tell each Fenian individually that "he is jeopardizing his soul if he perseveres in this uncatholic species of combination."[73]

The Sixty-Ninth disembarked at Annapolis on April 26 and was quartered overnight at the Naval Academy. The next day, the regiment was moved to guard Annapolis and Elk Ridge Railroad tracks near Crownsville, eight miles northwest of Annapolis, Mooney celebrated Mass in a farm field near Crownsville, on Sunday, April 28. The event was reported as follows:

> The solemn scene will ever be remembered. There on a rising hillside beside the road under a tent made of blankets resting on bayonets was an altar erected on which the holy sacrifice was offered and around in supplicating attitudes were the kneeling forms of some seven or eight hundred men who had left their homes and the bosoms of their families to serve their adopted country even unto death. It was a scene worthy of a painter's pencil and was such as drew tears from many of those brave fellows present in whose behalf the Divine sacrifice was being offered. During the service a heavy shower drenched us through but all were too much interested to think of bodily discomfort.[74]

While encamped near Crownsville, the Sixty-Ninth's soldiers were ordered to not give local residents any cause to complain or incite further depredations against the train tracks, some of which had been torn up or were missing spikes, as well as the telegraph lines having been cut. Despite the presence of southern sympathizers, the daughter of a pro-Union family in nearby Millersville displayed the US flag from their house. In return, the regiment saluted the flag and the daughter as they marched by with their band as it played the Irish drinking song "Garryowen."[75]

Mooney made a good impression on a group of Baltimoreans who visited the Sixty-Ninth's encampment on the day it was set to depart for Washington. Reporting on the visit, the *Sun* said Mooney was "extremely popular with the men, and pays constant attention to their spiritual welfare." During the visit, Mooney gave "an eloquent and very feeling address to the men." He spoke of Maryland's "devotion to civil and religious liberty" and expressed gratitude for the provisions Marylanders had sent to Ireland during the famine years. At the end of his speech, Mooney recited the text of a song he had written during his voyage to the United States in 1848. It expressed gratitude for the American people's assistance to the suffering Irish during the famine. As he recited his song, the soldiers and the band joined in with the chorus. Later in the evening, the men of the Sixty-Ninth held "cotillions and jig dancing around blazing bonfires."[76]

On the night of May 2, the Sixty-Ninth moved west to Annapolis Junction and then into the District of Columbia for guard duty at Georgetown College. The college, located on the western periphery of the District of Columbia, had become part of Washington's defense even as classes continued. The Sixty-Ninth soon set to work building a wood-and-earthwork redoubt called Fort Corcoran—named for their commander—in Arlington Heights, across the Potomac River from Georgetown. Fort Corcoran guarded the approaches to the Aqueduct Bridge that connected Georgetown and Arlington Heights. On May 30, the day the flag was first raised over Fort Corcoran, Mooney "by song and sentiment contributed to the enjoyment of the occasion."[77]

The following Sunday (June 2), Mooney celebrated "the grandest Mass" at Fort Corcoran, accompanied by the regimental band and chorus. The altar, which probably was the same one used in Crownsville, consisted of:

"Sunday morning mass in camp of 69th N.Y.S.M." This view was taken at Fort Corcoran, Virginia, on June 2, 1861, but a similar setting might have been seen in Crownsvile, Maryland, on April 28, 1861. Prints and Photographs Division, Library of Congress https://www.loc.gov/pictures/item/00652518/.

a rude table, placed on a slightly elevated platform and situate[d] in an ordinary sized camp tent, the canvas of which was raised in front so that the worshipers could witness the ceremonies. The altar was tastefully decorated with flowers... two candles were lighted and placed respectively on the Gospel and Epistle side of the tabernacle, the candlesticks also being adorned with flowers.[78]

At the end of Mass, the same account continues, Mooney gave "a very excellent and eloquent discourse." Then, "before the reverend prelate unrobed, his portrait was taken, in the act of reading, by an employee of Mr. [Matthew] Brady, the New York photographist."

Two weeks later, when the first large cannon, a rifled sixty-four pound Columbiad, was emplaced at the fort, Mooney was asked to bless it, which, as he said, he did "with more than ordinary pleasure." Not only did he bless the cannon, he christened it with holy water, saying that "this noble son of a great father" was "anxious to speak . . . in a thundering voice, to the joy of his friends and the terror of his enemies."[79]

News of the affair was printed on the front pages of newspapers in Washington and Baltimore. Archbishop Kenrick sent a clipping of the Baltimore article to Archbishop Hughes and a letter informing him of Mooney's actions. Kenrick said Mooney had been "extremely imprudent" and that the "blessing of a cannon is a ceremony unknown to me." He added that Mooney's remarks were "shocking to Christian feeling, and may render the speaker irregular *defectu lenitatis*." Hughes responded to Kenrick on July 3 with praise for Mooney as priest and saying he did "not attach much importance to the printed report of his remarks." But he hinted that Mooney was a bit of a renegade: "one of the most devoted priests of my diocese – when under proper restraint" and "more or less given to levity which, however, is his natural temperament." He informed Kenrick that he had censured Mooney for the "unauthorized process of blessing a gun" but also criticized priests in New Orleans and Charleston, respectively, for having blessed flags and sung a "solemn *Te Deum* . . . for a fatal victory." This non-canonical, seemingly sacrilegious act upset Hughes, who wrote to Mooney, also on July 3: "Your inauguration of a ceremony unknown to the Church, *viz.*, the blessing of a cannon, was sufficiently bad, but your remarks on that occasion are infinitely worse. Under the circumstances, and for other reasons, I wish you to return, within three days from the receipt of this letter, to your pastoral duties at St. Brigid's."[80]

There is no record of Mooney's having visited St. Mary's during his few days in Anne Arundel County. The Sixty-Ninth was quartered for only one day at the Naval Academy and seven days on a Crownsville farm. Mooney was popular with the officers and men of the regiment, for which he established a temperance society, celebrated daily Mass, heard confessions, and repeatedly reminded fallen-away members that, as they headed for battle, it was "a great opportunity for them to return to the Faith."[81] While he must have been busy ministering to the men of his regiment, it is possible that Mooney was among those, as the Redemptorist chronicler put it, who "wanted to see our house." The Sixty-Ninth was later involved in the First Battle of Manassas on July 21, 1861, and numerous subsequent battles as part of the "Irish Brigade," but all without Father Mooney.

You Have My Permission

In his *Theologiae Moralis* Archbishop Kenrick said that slaves had a right to marry as long as the marriage did not deprive the master of their just labor. If a master unjustly refused to allow slaves to marry, natural law permitted the couple to "make a contract for life," even without the assistance of a priest. But the assistance of a priest and permission by the master were the order of the day at St. Mary's in May 1861. Although there were numerous proscriptions levied by Maryland law against both free and enslaved Blacks, the Maryland Code in force in 1861 did not prohibit the marriage of a slave to a free Black person. The only requirement was that "No persons within this State shall marry without a license" and that aspect of the law appears to have applied only to White persons.[82] Father James Francis Bradley, St. Mary's new thirty-two-year old, Irish-born church minister, was well within his prerogatives in officiating at such a marriage.

On May 18, William H. Turton wrote to Bradley as follows:

> My Rev. Sir, This is to certify That you have my permission to Marry my Woman Clarisa Addison to Annanias Diggs Esq. (free col'd) on This day.[83]

Turton was an eighty-three-year-old wealthy Crownsville major slave holder. In 1850 he was listed as owning forty-five slaves, including two females ages five and six, either of whom could have been "his woman," Clarissa Ann Addison. In 1860 he had twenty-eight slaves, including three females ages fifteen, sixteen, and seventeen, one of whom also could have been Clarissa. Turton's daughter, Mary Robinson, who lived with him, also was a slave owner in 1860, holding five persons in bondage, but none of Clarissa's age. Clarissa appeared in St. Mary's records in 1857 when she was baptized at age fifteen. Her parents were listed as Isaac Jennings and Mary Addison, both

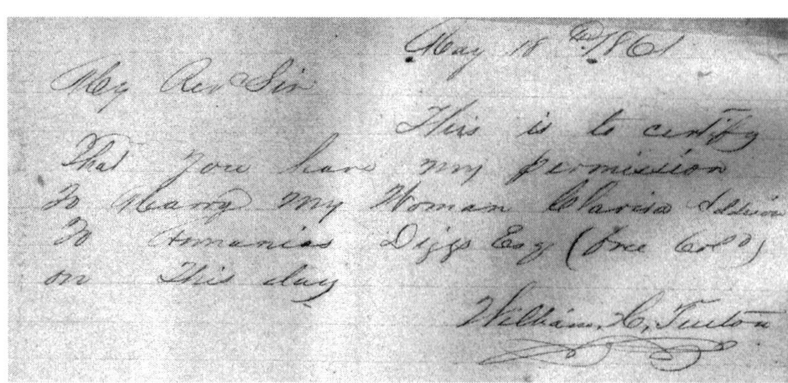
May 18th 1861
My Rev Sir
This is to certify
That you have my permission
To Marry my Woman Clarisa Addison
To Annanias Diggs Esq (free col'd)
on This day
William H. Turton

William Turton's permission for Clarissa Addison to marry Ananias Diggs. Inserted in St. Mary's Marriage Register B#1 (May 18, 1861).

of Anne Arundel County. Father Francis A. Baker officiated and Rachel Smothers, also a slave, served as the godparent. Other than his marriage to Clarissa, there is no record at St. Mary's of Ananias Diggs. Turton's note attests that he was "free colored" and of some substance since Turton added the honorific "Esq." after his name, or was being facetious. In 1846 an Annanias Diggs, no age given, was apprenticed to Benjamin A. Welch, a farmer in the First Election District, "to learn the art, trade or mystery of farming" until age twenty-one. He may have come from one of two farms, both near Dodon. A free Black named Azaria Diggs, age eighteen, was enumerated in the 1860 census living in Election District 2, with a Davidsonville, Anne Arundel County, post office address. A free Black Annania Diggs appeared in Election District 1, with an Owensville post office address, but his age was given as nine years. It is more likely this Annania was nineteen, an age that corresponds with that given for Annanias in the 1870 census for Annapolis, when he was twenty-eight years, living with Clarissa at an unspecified address, and in the 1880 census, when they were living on Market Street in Annapolis and he was thirty-eight years old. Clarissa Addison's was the only slave marriage recorded at St. Mary's during the Civil War.[84]

Great Consolation to the Camps

An example of the hard life in a religious order comes to light in the house annals around this time. Father Henry Fehlings was reported on June 3 as having "said 'farewell' to the Congregation with a relief of someone freed from jail." Fehlings was born in Westphalia in 1823, immigrated to the United States sometime before 1850, and was ordained in 1854. But, as the chronicler put it, "[f]or many years, this father seemed to seek human approval rather than the love of God and self-abnegation. Religious life brought boredom and trouble, and for a long time, he wanted to be free of this burden." He arrived in Annapolis around August 1860 and applied for and had received permission from Father De Dycker, pending approval from Rome, to be dispensed from his vows. His dispensation was dated October 10, 1860, but upon its receipt, to continue the chronicle account, "Father Michael Müller . . . intervened, asking him to spend a year in the Novitiate, away from all the worldly business, trying to recapture his religious spirit. This opportunity did not appeal to him and he told the professed students that he was sent away from Annapolis as a punishment." Fehlings went on to a more successful life as a diocesan priest, first in Ohio, where he had responsibility for Catholic churches in three counties; followed by ministries in Jersey City; New York City (where he lived in a rectory with the aforementioned Anthony Kesseler); and finally in Utica, New York, where he died in 1888. He was credited with having established fifteen churches during his career.[85]

During June Father De Dycker left militarily occupied Baltimore for a visit to the relatively quieter but also occupied Annapolis. The *Chronica Domus* relates that "This month everything was calm in the city. The soldiers stayed in nearby camps." De Dycker was accompanied by Father Joseph Wuest (Wüst in the original German) and Frater James Henry Harvey. Wuest was born in Prussia in 1834, had immigrated to the United States in August 1854, and professed his vows four months later. After ordination in 1859, he was stationed in St. Peter's in Philadelphia. Now he was assigned to the Annapolis college where he taught Greek and exegesis (the interpretation of sacred scripture). The next year, he also taught philosophy, scripture, and algebra. In following years, Wuest was a frequent visitor to Annapolis and other Redemptorist houses throughout the American Province. After the war, from 1868 to 1919, he distinguished himself as the second and longest-serving archivist of the Redemptorists' Baltimore Province and it was he who documented many of the careers of Redemptorists discussed in this book. He died in Ilchester, Maryland, in 1924.[86] Frater Harvey's career was much briefer, as will be related below.

Father Michael Dausch left Annapolis in June 1861 for a new assignment in Rochester, New York. He was replaced as church prefect and lector of dogmatic theology by Father Joseph Maria Jacobs. Although Jacobs' name did not appear in the *Chronica Domus* until June 1861, he had been present at the blessing of the cornerstone for the new church in May 1858 and officiated at a marriage in December that year. He was in Annapolis in January 1859, when he made his declaration of intent at the Anne Arundel County Circuit Court to become an American citizen, and again (or still) in May 1859, when he encouraged the Immaculate Heart of Mary sisters to leave Michigan. A guidebook for Annapolis published in 1859 listed Jacobs as the pastor of St. Mary's. During these years, the priest who had charge of the parish church and was the main interlocutor with the laity held the position of church administrator, prefect, or minister, and thus considered by outsiders as pastor. The highest ranking member of the Redemptorist community, however, was the superior, who at this time doubled as novice master. The term rector was not at St. Mary's used until June 1862, when Seelos replaced Müller. In October 1860, Jacobs officiated at the baptism of Joanna Maria Brady, a twenty-two-year-old convert from Methodism. Throughout this period, he was not listed in the "Familia Domus", suggesting that he was officially assigned elsewhere. Just before appearing in Annapolis in 1861, he and

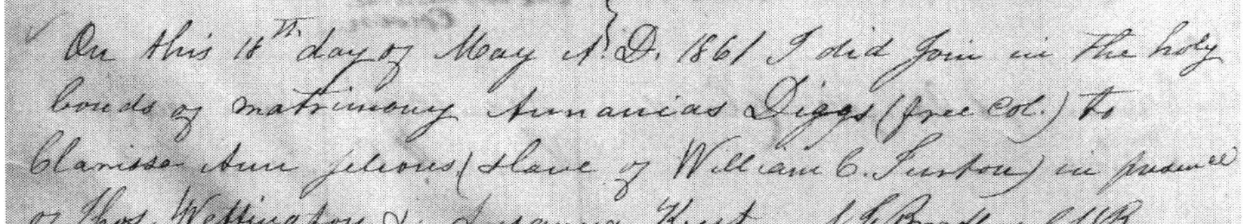
On this 18th day of May A.D. 1861 I did join in the holy bonds of matrimony Annanias Diggs (free Col.) to Clarissa Ann Jelious (slave of William C. Turton) in presence of Thos. Wellington & Susanna Kent. J. J. Bradley C.SS.R. priest.

Father James Bradley's record of having married Clarissa Addison and Ananias Diggs, May 18, 1861. Inserted in St. Mary's Marriage Register B#1 (May 18, 1861).

Father Joseph Wissel had given missions in Cumberland and in Parkersburg and Mason City, both in Virginia. Returning to Annapolis, he was busy with pastoral duties. He baptized an African American infant, Jacob Bishop, on May 30, 1861, and two newborns, Marcellus Matthew Jacob Coulter and William Curran, respectively, on June 8 and 9, and officiated at a marriage on June 15.[87]

At this point, the war was not expected to last long. There had been some Union victories on the western front but the disastrous Union defeat at Manassas had not yet occurred and enthusiasm still ran high in the North for an early conclusion to the rebellion. The thousands of troops in and around Annapolis were being trained to ensure the assumed victory. At the onset of the war, Union troops had come through Annapolis on their way Washington, DC, and, as the year progressed, others came to "camps of instruction" around Annapolis where they were trained for expeditions to the south. When soldiers became ill from the often unhealthy sanitary conditions in camp, the more serious cases became patients at Army General Hospital Division No. 1 at the Naval Academy. For the Catholics among them, the benefit of clergy was welcome. Father Müller recognized the need to minister to these soldiers, many of whom had neglected their faith, in some cases, for many years. Joseph Jacobs was first of the St. Mary's Redemptorists to regularly visit the camps, and by means of his benevolent but firm approach, he convinced many to confess their sins. He also would have provided spiritual counseling and distributed religious articles, such as rosaries and scapulars. Thus, the *Chronica Domus* reported during June that Father Jacobs "worked hard for the welfare of the soldiers." He celebrated Mass in the camps, sometimes in the open air, and is reported to have given "instructions and exhortations [that] softened even the hardest of hearts with sincere repentance . . . . so many souls were saved for God."[88]

Father Jacobs delivers his oration at the State House, July 4, 1861, Original art by Constance D. Robinson.

Although there were Union regiments that were predominantly Catholic with Catholic chaplains, priest-chaplains were exceedingly scarce in the Union army, especially at the early stages of the war. By war's end, only 2 percent of Union chaplains were Catholic priests, the same percentage as in the Confederate forces. Catholics in mixed or largely Protestant regiments with Protestant chaplains had little access to clergy of their choice. So Jacobs was surely welcomed by Catholic soldiers in the camps. As Jacob's workload increased, other priests assisted him in ministering to the soldiers.[89] The *Province Annals* put it thus:

> Military camps are visited. War is very evil, but in many ways it leads to good things. Military camps encircled the city. There soldiers coming from all parts of the North were stationed and trained for various forays. It is clear that many of them had neglected their religious duties. But, an opportunity to get ready for their death arose—many were certain to die. Therefore, Father Jacobs often visited the camps, heard the confessions of many hardened sinners and celebrated many Masses. He brought great consolation to the camps. Father Jacobs could not do all this salutary work, so Father Wissel helped him until transferred to Baltimore. Other fathers continued to go out to the other soldiers passing through our area.[90]

Jacobs' reputation quickly resonated with people, especially among some of the local "leading citizens" of Annapolis. These leading citizens, whose names were not recorded in the *Chronica Domus*, were said to have included "in particular the civil authorities" who invited Jacobs to deliver an oration at the Maryland State House on the Fourth of July. Considering the divergence of pro-Union and pro-Southern viewpoints among the people of Annapolis regarding secession and the war, he was wisely chosen. Maybe these leading citizens were aware that Catholic priests had been ordered by their superiors to "prudently" avoid political discussion and, thus, Jacobs was thus a safe choice to speak at an Independence Day celebration.[91]

Although the text of Jacobs' State House oration went unrecorded, it did not go unnoticed. In its July 4 morning edition, the *Annapolis Gazette* noted under the heading "Celebrations," that "Rev. Mr. Jacobs will deliver an Oration to-day, at the State House, and the Declaration of Independence will be read by Prof. W. H. Thompson. Celebration to commence at 11 o'clock A.M." The *Sun*, reporting via its "Annapolis Correspondent" two days after the event, said that the Fourth of July "was publicly celebrated at Annapolis" and that Jacobs delivered the oration at the State House and the Declaration of Independence was read by St. John's College Professor William H. Thompson.[92]

The most revealing but succinct account of Father Jacobs' oration is in the *Chronica Domus*, which concluded:

> His talk did not cause offense, neither taking the part of septentrionalibus or meridianis (or if you wish to invoke the vulgate "Northerners and Southerners"). He was praised by all.[93]

The terms *septentrionalibus* and *meridianis* are archaic references—even in 1861—referring to northern and southern tribes or geographical locations. They must have sounded quite erudite to the assemblage of local citizens on the State House lawn.[94] The rest of the entry provides insight into attitudes in Annapolis concerning the Redemptorists and, perhaps, toward Catholics in general.

> Thus the fathers more and more gained the goodwill of the people, especially among those who previously had been full of prejudice toward us. Then and subsequently, our house was frequently visited by all that the civil war has brought to Annapolis — by soldiers as well as by officers of every rank. We gained the goodwill of all those whom we graciously received.[95]

Further afield, the *New York Daily Tribune* carried a three-column description of the army's Fourth of July observances at the Naval Academy but only a brief paragraph about the State House event. It said: "The citizens of Annapolis extemporized a celebration in the morning, but it was a tame affair. A short oration was delivered by a Catholic priest, and several national airs performed by the band."[96]

The army celebrations were hardly a "tame affair." A thirty-four-gun salute was fired at sunrise, one shot for each state, "no allowance being made for the hallucinations of Jeff. Davis." This was followed by "Hail Columbia" and enthusiastic cheering. At 9:00 AM, a full-dress parade was held. Troops of the Sixth New York Infantry Regiment, joined by Revenue Service and Navy officers and one hundred marines, left "the garrison" and marched through Annapolis. "As troops filed through the streets, the citizens came out en mass, crowding the sidewalks, windows, and doorsteps." After an hour, the marchers returned to the academy for patriotic exercises. These included prayers, playing "Hail Columbia" again, reading the Declaration of Independence, playing the "Star Spangled Banner," and an oration (quoted at length) by regimental adjutant Joel W. Mason. He condemned the "breeze of disunion" that was "fanned . . . into a hurricane" by the southern secessionists and ended with a call to put down the rebellion. The program was attended by "a large number of ladies and gentlemen of the city" and concluded with "Columbia, Gem of the Ocean" and benediction by the regimental chaplain. Afterward, "to the gratification of a large number of spectators from the city," the soldiers put on gymnastic and other sports demonstrations. Officers of the Sixth New York were cordially received by Governor Hicks and, at sunset, a salute was fired by land- and ship-mounted cannons. At eight o'clock, a large circle was formed on the garrison grounds and illuminated by one hundred red, white, and blue paper lanterns suspended from "great bunches of evergreens planted around the circle." Specially invited local citizens attended a *fête champêtre*, which included dancing "on the greensward" and fireworks "greeted with cheers." At 10:30 "Taps" was played, lanterns extinguished, and guests bade farewell. Surely a full day, with everyone "pleased and delighted," far outshining the "tame affair" addressed by Father Jacobs.

During the following month, the contrast between the non-political Redemptorists and more strident individuals was seen at St. John's College, with at least one Catholic involved. In August, it was reported, the trustees "voted to destroy the College" by declaring all but one of the faculty positions vacant "for no other reason than that they were union men." Tensions had been rising since the previous year when enrollments had declined; there was no graduating class in 1861 because older students had left to join either the Union or Confederate forces and younger students had returned to the safety of home. The *Annapolis Gazette* called the trustees' action "a piece of Secession vandalism."[97]

The "secessionists" identified among the trustees who voted to close the college were James Lawrence Bartol and the aforementioned Edwin Boyle. Bartol, a Democrat and a Catholic, was appointed in May 1857 to fill the vacancy resulting when John Thomson Mason resigned from the Maryland Court of Appeals to become collector of the Port of Baltimore. The judgeship had been subject to popular election in the fall 1857 and, after initially declining the nomination, Bartol was elected to a full ten-year term and later became the chief justice of the court. But now, thanks to secessionists such as Bartol and Boyle, according to the *Gazette*, St. John's College "was completely broken up and its venerable associations utterly destroyed." The reality was different. The college was badly in debt with only the principal receiving his pay. Economics and civil war conspired to force the closure of the college.[98]

Political controversy enveloped Judge Bartol the next year when he was arrested by the provost marshal in Baltimore and incarcerated for ten days at Fort McHenry. Bartol reportedly was detained because he criticized the arrest of Judge Richard Bennett Carmichael, a States' Rights Democrat and presiding circuit court judge for Kent, Queen Anne's, Caroline, and Talbot counties. While presiding in his Easton courtroom in May 1862 Carmichael was arrested for "treason" by a Federal provost marshal backed by 125 soldiers from the Second Delaware Infantry Regiment. His offense was to instruct the local grand jury to indict Federal officers for arresting men who had heckled Unionists at a political rally.

Bartol had objected to his fellow judge's arrest and was himself arrested but not charged.[99]

Southerners thanked God for their victory following the Union defeat at the First Battle of Manassas. Divine intervention was called for in the north as Lincoln proclaimed "a day of public humiliation, prayer and fasting. It was to be observed by the people of the United States with religious solemnities and offerings of fervent supplications to Almighty God for the safety and welfare of these States, His blessings on their arms, and a speedy restoration to peace." He designated Thursday, September 26, as the day and recommended religious observances, "in order to obtain Divine aid and the return of peace and prosperity." In Maryland Governor Hicks urged the "strict observance" of September 26, and on the appointed day, public and private business was suspended and banks and government offices were closed. Martin Revell's pro-Confederate friend, Susie Sands, saw this as nothing more than "a day of fasting and prayer for success to the armies of the Federals," and added that "a most unholy prayer it is." She also said that none of her family went to church that day.[100]

In compliance with the president's request, Archbishop Kenrick ordered the pastors of all the Catholic churches in the Province of Baltimore—which then extended over much of the mid-Atlantic and the South—to offer the prayer *Pro quacumque tribulatione* (For Whatever Tribulation), to recite the Litany of the Saints, and to read Bishop John Carroll's 1791 prayer for civil authorities. He also directed each parish, henceforth, to continue to read Carroll's prayer at all Sunday Masses "irrespective of all political and personal considerations." The prayer included supplications for the president of the United States and the preservation of the Union. Father (later Cardinal) James Gibbons, who just had been ordained on June 30, remarked years later that some clergy had "begged [the archbishop] to omit the prayer" and that all of the priests in cathedral had "begged to be excused" from reading Carroll's prayer. In the face of this protest, the archbishop himself read the prayer and, as he did, some congregants left in protest when he reached that part where he prayed for the president and the preservation of the Union. Others in the congregation were said to have expressed their disapproval with "a great rustling of papers and silk."[101]

Earlier in the year, Kenrick had cautioned priests and religious in the archdiocese to "Be cautious not to take sides in the politics which divide the country, but pray for peace and respect the constituted authorities." In a letter to Bishop Martin John Spalding in Louisville, however, Kenrick said that Marylanders were being "treated as a conquered people," and he is said to have "increasingly resented the Lincoln administration's heavy-handed policies." It is notable, however, that Kenrick's name was on a list of Baltimore's loyal Union men kept by the next governor of Maryland, Augustus Williamson Bradford.[102] The prayer for civil authorities was not mentioned in the *Chronica Domus* and there are no extant issues of the *Annapolis Gazette* or *Maryland Republican* reporting the day's activities.

Around this time, the Redemptorists sold the first parcel of land of their "legacy" property given to them in 1852 by the Caton granddaughters. It was part of a lot at the end of Chestnut Street, bounded on one side by the water of City Dock, and later divided when Compromise Street was extended by the city across this property.[103]

Content With Mere Praise

Two unusual visitors arrived in Annapolis on Friday, July 12, 1861. Their visit was the first documented presence of Roman Catholic nuns in the city. They were members of the Oblate Sisters of Providence, the first religious congregation of African American nuns established in the United States. The visit was even more extraordinary in that one of sisters was the superior general of the Oblates and had been invited to stay in a private home in Annapolis to recuperate from an illness.

The nuns were Mother Gertrude Thomas, O.S.P., and her companion, Sister Gabriel Addison, O.S.P. The Oblate Sisters' annals reveal that Mary Effine Lake—"a friend of the house" —had issued the invitation "thinking that a trip to Annapolis might be of some benefit." Mother Gertrude stayed for three weeks at the Lake's Church Circle home, but instead of getting better and despite "the kindness of the family and every one else to make her comfortable," her health declined. Mother Gertrude returned to Baltimore on August 2 and died there on October 6. Her companion, Sister Gabriel, had a circumstantial connection to Annapolis. As Georgianna Addison, she had been manumitted from slavery in 1832 by Richard Caton, the son-in-law of Charles Carroll of Carrollton. The manumission occurred in Baltimore where Caton, his wife, Mary Carroll Caton, and the elder Carroll were then living. Georgianna was received into the Oblates in 1843 as Sister Mary Louise Gabriel. There were Catholic Addisons in Annapolis before and during the Civil War and Sister Gabriel may have been related to them or taken from Annapolis to Baltimore before her manumission.[104]

The Oblate Sisters were founded in 1828 by Elizabeth Lange, who, as Mother (now Venerable) Mary Lange, became the first superior. The Oblate School for Colored Girls (later St. Frances School) was also founded in 1828 and was the first formal day school for Black pupils, with a curriculum similar to schools for wealthy White girls. St. Frances Chapel, built next to the school in 1836, is said to be the first church in the United States specifically for Black Catholics. There was a strong Redemptorist connection to the Oblates. In 1847 Father John Neumann, the Redemptorist superior in America, appointed Father Thaddeus Anwander, a future rector of St. Mary's in Annapolis, to serve as the sisters' spiritual director. According to historian Diane Batts Morrow, "Redemptorist lack of familiarity with United States culture from a racial perspective benefitted the Oblate Sisters; not yet acculturated to racist influences, the newly immigrant priests perceived people of color as human beings fully deserving of pastoral care." Anwander assisted the Oblate Sisters until 1855, bringing about a revival of both the order and the school, which increased from ten or twenty students in 1847 to 140 by 1852–55.[105]

The Lake family had a long-standing relationship with the Oblates. Moses and Mary Lake's daughter, Mary Augusta, attended the Oblate School for Colored Girls. School financial records include payments for Mary Augusta's room, board, and tuition, as well as entries for money for books, piano and music lessons, sewing supplies, clothing, bonnets, a veil, shoes, boots, gaiters, winter fuel, doctors' fees, medicine, postage, and other expenses such as a loan of fifty cents for a picnic. The entries appeared routinely (monthly, quarterly, and sometimes semi-annually) between November 1846, when Mary Augusta was just five years old, to January 1860.[106]

Among Mary Augusta Lake's expenses is an 1852 entry for worsted (needlework yarn). The nuns considered needle work "to be one of the most basic subjects in preparation for motherhood and the sisterhood" and Mary Augusta became a skilled practitioner.[107] Her achievements were first publicized in 1856 in the *Annapolis Gazette*:

> Lovers of the beautiful in art will be much gratified by a visit to Mrs. Moses Lake's Fancy Store, on Church Circle; where they will find a most magnificent specimen of Worsted Wear. It presents George Washington resigning his commission; is about four feet by three in size; and in its grouping, shading, and auxiliaries would do no discredit to a superior artist. It is the production of Mrs. L.'s daughter, a colored girl, about fifteen years of age; and certainly exhibits proofs of a high order of taste and artistic skill.[108]

The Oblate Sisters' ledger has notations "to cash for needle work" and "to cash for framing" in July 1856. Those entries were made just prior to the needle-work specimen being displayed in Annapolis.[109]

On what Mary Augusta based her Washington art is open to speculation. The painting of Washington resigning his commission by artist Edwin White, displayed in the Maryland State House, was commissioned in 1856 and not completed until 1859, three years after Mary Augusta's version was publicized. Instead she may have seen the original of John Trumbull's earlier work which was hung in the rotunda of the United States Capitol in 1826, or perhaps a reproduction of it published in a book or as a lithograph. As far as can be determined, Mary Augusta's Washington needlework has either not survived or is in private hands.[110]

The praise Mary Augusta received in the *Annapolis Gazette* was high indeed for a teenage "colored girl." But praise was all she later received when her needlework was displayed at the National Fair. Although an August 1859 report in New York's *Weekly Anglo-African* was not specific, it probably was the National Fair held in Richmond in October 1858. This annual event, sponsored by United States Agricultural Society, was often referred to in the press as "the National Fair."[111] Mary Augusta's needlework was displayed again in June 1859 at the end-of-year convocation at St. Frances School. The report, emanating from Baltimore, said:

> The "Sisters of Providence" (Catholic) gave a grand demonstration at the close of their school. . . . I witnessed their exhibition of needle-work; wife and other lady judges better qualified than myself in such matters, say that their efforts have been climaxed. Miss Lake, of Annapolis, worked "The Father of his Country" in full size. The judges at the National Fair pronounced it the best they had ever seen; but as there was no premium for colored girls, Miss L. had to content herself with mere praise. Well, it is some satisfaction to be praised, for we so seldom get even that.

Besides paying for her daughter's attendance at St. Frances School, Mary Lake also was a benefactor of and provider of services to the school. For example, when paying her daughter's board and tuition in June 1847, Mary made a $3.00 donation for unspecified purposes. On two occasions in 1852, she sent a total $3.25 to be given to Father Anwander. In January 1854, Mary Lake gave $10.00 for flowers, while an entry in July 1861 notes a $1.00 "Donation Mr Lake and Mrs Deaver." In other cases, Mary Lake appears to have been paid for services to the sisters. In March 1856 an entry reads "making a Dress $1.50 making 2 baskets $1 each." And, in October the next year, the account page for Mrs. E. M. Lake carries an entry for $2.18½ "for trimming a bonnet & finding materials" and in December $1.50 for "Making a plaid Dress." An expense noted in March 1857 was for making a calico dress at a cost of $1.81½. After all, Mary Lake's Annapolis dress shop would have sold such items.[112]

Mary Lake also paid tuition and board at St. Frances School for another student with an Annapolis connection. Her unusual name was given in the Oblate's records invariably as John Ann Price. In September 1856, the sisters received payment in advance from Mary Lake for three months of John Ann's tuition and board ($20.00), winter fuel ($1.00), and books ($1.50).

Sister Mary Lucy (Mary Augusta) Lake O.S.P. Original art by Constance D. Robinson.

In 1857 Mary Lake paid a total of $51.49½ for John Ann's tuition, board, boots, stockings, cash for needlework and framing, and winter fuel and, in 1858 a total of $103.12½. After that, no more payments for John Ann by Mary Lake appear in the ledger. But the record shows that Mary Lake was not the only one supporting John Ann at St. Frances School. In 1857 and 1858, her grandfather, Henry Price, paid the school costs. Price was a well-to-do free Black property owner and a minister at the Asbury African Methodist Episcopal Church on West Street from around 1818 until his death in 1863. In August 1856, just before she entered the Oblate school, and after her mother had become "deranged," John Ann was formally apprenticed to her grandfather until age eighteen. As one of the elite Blacks of Annapolis in the antebellum period, Price would have been well known to Moses and Mary Lake. He also was their near neighbor, with his home and confectionary store on upper Church Street and theirs on the corner of Church Circle and South Street. It was not unusual for children of other religious denominations to attend St. Frances School, and John Ann Price undoubtedly benefitted educationally from her two years with the Oblate Sisters.[113]

Study at St. Frances School was aimed at developing "one of two acceptable careers." One career was that of the religious life, the other that "of a dutiful wife and mother."[114] Mary Augusta Lake chose the former. On January 9, 1860, she and two other pupils at St. Frances, "who for some time wished to become sisters," were received as postulants. Five weeks later, Mary received the habit of a novice and took the name Sister Mary Lucy.[115] There is no evidence, however, that Sister Lucy professed her final vows and she apparently left the Oblate Sisters, possibly for health reasons and returned to Annapolis. She died from tuberculosis, or phthisis—a "wasting" disease then known as consumption—in 1869 and is buried in an unmarked grave in St. Mary's Cemetery. She and her parents were so well regarded that her death was briefly noted in the *Annapolis Gazette*:

> In this city, December 1st, of consumption, Mary A. Lake, only daughter of Moses and the late Effie Lake.[116]

Mary Effine Lake was the second wife of Moses Lake. He married his first wife, Mary Anne Folks Norris of Annapolis, in 1830. Mary Anne died in 1837 and Moses married Effine Peterson in Baltimore in 1838. She was born in New York around 1809 and nothing has been discovered about her early life. But she was very well known in antebellum Annapolis and at St. Mary's Church. Between 1851 and 1867, she was godmother to four infants, two minor children, four teenagers, nine adults, and two persons of unspecified ages but probably adult converts. Most were Black, some were slaves, some were White. For Mary Lake and other church women with large numbers of god children, serving as godparent was the culmination of motherly assistance to families, educational preparation for older persons being baptized, and ongoing coordination with clergy. In one case, Mary herself baptized a four-year-old Black boy who was *in periculo mortis* (in danger of death), according to the 1859 baptismal register. Rachel Smothers, a slave possibly acting as a midwife or nurse—having skills that would have given her greater mobility in antebellum Annapolis—may have brought Mary Lake to the ill or injured William Joseph Contee, son of Charlotte Contee. Charlotte, a free Black, had two other children baptized at St. Mary's but had neglected to attend to William's christening. Father Cornell later performed a supplementary baptism in church with Rachel as godmother. Whatever William's problem was in 1859, he survived and later served in the US Navy, which earned burial for himself and his wife in the Naval Academy Cemetery. He died in 1933 and his wife, Mary, died in 1938.[117]

Proximity and a family relationship brought about Mary's action in another situation. Jacob Bishop was born in April 1861 to Nicholas Bishop and his wife Mary Nichols. They were not Catholic but the newborn must have been in danger of death in the house next door to the Lake residence. Mary took Jacob to Father Jacobs for baptism when he was less than a month old. Little Jacob did not survive long; he died in September and was buried in St. Mary's Cemetery.[118]

The last of Mary Lake's god children—baptized in 1867—was twenty-year-old John Ann Price. The baptismal register gave her Latinized name as Joanna A. and recorded her place of birth in Baltimore in 1847, the daughter of John Price and Elisa Brown. John Ann Price died from consumption in 1874 and was buried in St. Mary's Cemetery.[119]

Mary Lake made her living running a "fancy store" on Church Circle. The shop operated out of the side door of a two-story frame house at the corner of Church Circle and South Street. The Lake's next-door neighbors to the east were William Bishop and Charity Folks Bishop, both well-to-do property-owning former slaves. William was superintendent of the city's chimney sweeps and Charity was the younger sister of Mary Anne Folks, Moses Lake's first wife, and thus Moses' former sister-in-law.[120]

Mary Lake's shop had a prominent location. It faced St. Anne's Church in the middle of Church Circle and was across street from the county courthouse. Farmer's National Bank and various law offices were nearby, also on the circle. The top of Church Street, with its shops, hotels, boarding houses, and residences was just yards away. Lodging, offices, and eating establishments filled the block from Church Circle to the Annapolis and Elk Ridge Railroad depot on Calvert Street. The State House was only a block away from Mary's shop. The homes of prominent and not-so-prominent Annapolitans all were within close proximity. An invoice from her shop in 1852 listed purchases by a prominent Annapolis lady, including a small patent leather bag, a small plain cap, a fancy bottle, three silk tassels, a plain glass, a small candle, cotton fabric, three-quarter-inch white ribbon, cologne, a fancy ball, and seventy-five cents worth of cords and tassels.[121]

Mary may also have sold cosmetics, pins, needles, thread, buttons, pin cushions, toys, and more. Before the Civil War, she advertised in the *Maryland Republican* for her fancy goods and once had the newspaper's press print one hundred hand bills advertising her jewelry. She also appealed to Baltimoreans by advertizing in the *Sun*. In one advertisement, she expressed her thanks for "past favors" and "respectfully announce[d] to the Ladies of Annapolis, and those who visit the Metropolis this Winter to attend Assemblies," that she had, at considerable expense, supplied herself "with the most splendid assortment in her line ever before introduced in this city." These wares included the "latest and most fashionable French style, consisting in part of Head-Dresses; Artificial Flowers; Sashes; Handkerchiefs; Ribbons; Laces, &c." all of which were "of the VERY BEST quality" and, as an assurance to her customers, "her stock [was] unsurpassed." Besides these fancy goods, Mary Lake also sold tickets at fifty cents a piece for St. Mary's "Grand Concert" that was held in the new church before Christmas 1859.[122]

John Randall's niece Kate used to visit Mary Lake's shop and on one occasion bought a nail brush there. Two days after Christmas in 1854, when Kate was eleven years old, she and her little sister, Fanny, visited the shop and were given marbles by Mrs. Lake as Christmas presents.[123]

During the Civil War, the Federal tax authority assessed Mary Lake as a "retail dealer" at $10 per annum. Advertisements in 1861 and 1862 reveal that she sold Minnehaha hair gloss for gentlemen and ladies, Hiawatha hair restorative to return one's hair to its original color, and Excelsior toilet powder, "an unsurpassed article for improving the complexion and making the skin smooth and white."[124]

According to the two Federal Census reports in which she appears, Mary Lake was born in New York. She was listed as age forty-five in both the 1850 and 1860 censuses, making her born between 1805 and 1815. Her St. Mary's interment record put her age at death as sixty, giving her a birth year of 1809.[125]

Many years later, Esther Winder Polk Lowe, widow of former Governor Enoch Louis Lowe, wrote about people she knew in Annapolis in the late antebellum period. In her 1913 autobiography, she revealed some first-hand details about Mary Lake, who was:

> as near in color to white as he [Moses Lake] was to the coal black, and quite as elegant, claiming right to highest regard having been brought up in the aristocratic family of Commodore Porter. She was indeed a most dignified woman and by general consent of every one, white and colored, was called Mrs. Lake.[126]

It may have been true in Mrs. Lowe's high-brow circle about everyone calling her "Mrs. Lake." But St. Mary's Church records referred to her as Maria Elena, Mary E., Effey, Effin, Effieme, and other variants. In her daughter's newspaper death notice, she was referred to "Effie Lake." The Porter connection is another matter. Esther Lowe was alluding to David Porter who served in the US Navy during the Barbary War of 1801, the War of 1812, and several postwar commands until 1825, including the suppression of piracy in the Caribbean. He then served in the Mexican navy in 1826–29 and later held American diplomatic posts in Algiers and Constantinople.[127] Where Mary Effine Lake fit into the Porter family's life has not been determined, but she evidently lived in the home of David Porter and his wife, Evalina Anderson Porter, in Chester, Pennsylvania, before her marriage to Moses Lake in Baltimore in 1841.[128]

It can be inferred from Esther Lowe's statement that Moses Lake was "quite as elegant" as his wife. Although no artistic or photographic image of him survives, he was surely that and more in character. He was both gracious and aware of opportunities as attested by a notice he paid to have published in the *Annapolis Gazette* several days after St. Anne's Church burned on February 14, 1858:

> Moses Lake respectfully tenders his sincere thanks to the citizens of Annapolis, and the young men of the Naval Academy, by whose strenuous and united efforts his dwelling was saved from destruction on Sunday night last, when St. Anne's Church was consumed by fire.[129]

The paid notice was a nice touch by someone Mrs. Lowe characterized as "an aristocratic black 'gentleman' who enjoyed the distinction of professional barber." She was also intrigued by a trip Moses Lake made to England and Ireland in 1837. He served on the six-month journey as a valet for John Buchanan, chief judge of the Maryland Court of Appeals. Buchanan and two other men had been appointed by Governor James Thomas as commissioners to negotiate the sale in London of $8 million of state securities to help finance the Chesapeake and Ohio Canal, the B&O Railroad, the Eastern Shore Railroad, the Annapolis and Potomac Canal, and the Maryland Canal.[130] Mrs. Lowe reminisced that:

> It was in London, at a great function, where guests were announced in loud voice that Moses, unused to that custom, imagined that the Marquis of Wellesley, or some other grand dignitary was receiving more honor than the Chief Justice, who was just approaching. Moses cried out in a stentorian voice: "The Lord Chief of Justice of America."[131]

While showing the outgoing side of Moses Lake's character, Mrs. Lowe's story connects with other parts of his life. Moses was born in Washington County, Maryland, in 1802, and his family lived in Clear Spring, twelve miles west of Hagerstown. His employer, Judge Buchanan, studied law under John Thomson Mason Sr. in Hagerstown, and resided near Williamsport, about seven miles southeast of Clear Spring. Mason Sr. was the father of the aforementioned John Thomson Mason Jr., who also served on the Maryland Court of Appeals.[132] The Mason family seat was in Clear Spring. These Washington County intersections may be coincidental or are the reason Moses Lake ended up in Annapolis through his connections to such important White patrons as Judge Buchanan and the Masons.

Esther Lowe was not the only memorist to provide character information on Moses Lake. Shortly before the Naval Academy opened for its first classes in 1845, three professors who had been transferred from the US Naval School in Philadelphia came to Annapolis to meet the new superintendent, Commander Franklin Buchanan. In the words of one of the professors, Henry H. Lockwood, we have another indication of Moses Lake's garrulous nature:

> I remember very well our arrival in the old delapidated [*sic*] city and our reception by the city functionaries and outsiders. Among the latter I must name the exquisite colored barber Moses Lake, as most conspicuous. Moses took us in tow, guided us to his shop at the hotel to wash and brush, and he conducted us most gallantly while cramming us with the merits of the city, to the residence of Commander [*sic*, he was Lieutenant, Edward G.] Tilton, where we found Commander Buchanan awaiting us.[133]

Moses Lake's 1870 obituary placed him in Annapolis as early as 1824, when he was about twenty-two years old. He was said to have been "the bugler of Col. Contee's troop of horse, when General Lafayette was received with military honors at Annapolis." The events surrounding Lafayette's visit occurred on December 17–21, 1824. It may have just been a mythical story about Moses or the details were muddled over time. The only horse troop mentioned in a contemporary local report was that of Captain Sellman of South River.[134]

The obituary also said that subsequent to the Lafayette event, Moses Lake went to sea "for several years" aboard the USS *North Carolina*, the flagship of the Navy's Mediterranean Squadron, supposedly in the company of Lieutenant Isaac Mayo, an Anne Arundel County man. Although no record of formal naval service has been discovered for Moses Lake, the *North Carolina* did serve in the Mediterranean between April 29, 1825 and May 18, 1827, and Mayo was aboard. The *North Carolina* made port calls in Greece, Turkey, and Spain. If Moses accompanied Mayo when he was on shore leave from October 1826 to February 1827, he would have visited Spain, France, Switzerland, Italy, and Monaco. One reliable source places him in Annapolis again by the late 1820s and he was recorded by name in the 1830 Federal Census as a free Black resident of the city, living with his wife and another female, age between ten and twenty-four years.[135]

Moses Lake was certainly well established by 1833 when he started advertising in the *Maryland Gazette* as a "professor" who "cuts hair Phisiognomically and shaves Delectably!" He boasted of having "unrivalled [*sic*] talents" with his "magic razor" and was superior to barbers in Philadelphia and New York City. He also sold "the best" razors, combs, stocks, collars, soap, and other items and superintended "a scouring establishment" and offered to "cleanse clothes of every description at reasonable terms." His hair dressing parlor was next to the bar in the City Hotel.[136]

Barbering had been a path since colonial times to upward mobility for both slaves and free Blacks. It gave these men a relatively rare and rather intimate connection with elite White society when few such opportunities were available to them and hair dressing was not considered a dignified trade for a White man. It has not been discovered how or when Moses Lake acquired the skills he bragged about but he had them by the time of his grand journey to the British Isles. In operating what must have been a first-class establishment in the City Hotel, Moses could blend his deference to his White-only clientele with his sense of self-esteem and well-being as he became one of the leading African Americans of Annapolis.[137]

When the 1860 Federal Census was taken in Annapolis, there were only six men whose occupations were classified as barber and all were Black. Moses Lake was by far the most affluent with $1,200 in real estate and a $500 personal estate. He had three apprentice barbers, one of whom was presumably Moses' nephew, Samuel W. Lake, and all of whom lived in the Lake residence. None of the other barbers in town owned real estate and all or some of them may have worked for Moses Lake.[138]

Also in 1833, Moses Lake and William Bishop jointly purchased a house and lot on Cornhill Street. This was likely an investment property since Moses' mother-in-law, Charity Folks, had already given her daughter, Mary Anne, the frame house on the corner of Church Circle and South Street. In 1838 Moses Lake purchased another property, on Southeast (Duke of Gloucester) Street, between the home of Martha Maynard and the Presbyterian church. He did this just after his first wife died and perhaps it was to be a future home or an investment property. He sold the other property (now the site 167 and 169 Duke of Gloucester Street) in 1855.[139]

By 1841 Moses Lake was selling "a splendid assortment of cutlery, such as razors, (superior to anything of the kind previously imported,) pen knives, bird scissors, &c.," all acquired from London, which he had visited just four years earlier and contracted to import items for his shop. His offerings were so notable that they appeared in a news report on the proceedings of the Maryland Senate in 1842. That report gives evidence that Lake's business was not just about grooming hair and selling imported razors but he also offered "a handsome lot of gentlemen's robes or cravats, stocks, gloves, suspenders, perfumery, and all the *et ceteras* essential to the toilet of the man of fashion or of taste." His products were so well received that in the same year Moses sold four penknives and two head brushes for $13 for use in the Senate's committee room. So while Mary Effine was selling fancy goods to ladies on Church Circle, Moses was a purveyor of a wide range of gentlemen's accouterments on Church Street. A few years later he was selling Liverpool knives that were so "handsomely finished" that a *Sun* article "recommend[ed] them particularly to the editorial fraternity." He also sold one tonic that could turn "Red, grey or white hair . . . instantaneously to a beautiful brown or black" and another that could cure ring worm, herpes, and other skin conditions.[140]

Moses had favorable credit ratings during the antebellum years. He was reported to a New York City credit monitoring agency as "a respectable Negro" and was "considered good for small amounts" of credit up to $1,500. Despite having "Lost some money by California Speculations" in the early 1850s, his credit level increased to $5,500 by the time the Civil War began. As a property owner and having two successful shops—his own and Mary's—he was "honest and good for purchases" on credit. His creditworthiness was bolstered by having never been sued as he continued over the years to be "hon[est] & of good char[acter]." The credit report noted in the early 1850s that Moses Lake owned two slaves. Whether these were family or friends he had purchased with the hope of manumitting them or the notation was a mistake is not known. There is a barely legible entry in the 1850 Federal Slave Schedule for Annapolis—a smudgy name that might be "M. Lake"—as owner of one Black female slave, age ten. However, no slaves were enumerated for Moses Lake in the 1830 and 1840 Federal censuses, nor in the 1860 Federal Slave Schedule, the 1860 inventory of slaves made by the City of Annapolis, or in the index of slave-owner names for Anne Arundel County.[141]

Moses Lake is most often remembered as a barber at the City Hotel and at the Naval Academy, the latter position given to him by Superintendent Buchanan, in 1845 and continued, except for brief periods, until he died in 1870, when Commodore John Lorimer Worden was superintendent. Moses Lake's Naval Academy shop was located near the main gate on Northeast Street and had four barber chairs, a wash stand, shears, sharpening hones, shaving mugs, puff boxes, hair dusters, a large supply of towels, and other hair dressing needs. On the walls hung pictures of places he had visited in England and Ireland in 1837. One visitor to his shop exclaimed that Moses Lake's "scientific hands" were "a luxury fit for a eastern king."[142]

The Civil War years were not easy for Moses Lake. His major source of income—the Naval Academy—moved to Rhode Island and his hair-dressing business was restricted to the City Hotel shop, for which advertisements in the local newspapers continued. Hair still needed to be cut and there was a new influx of customers from the North. But it is likely that sales of imported razors and other luxury goods diminished in wartime. The war also presumably took a toll on Mary Lake's fancy good sales. Both Moses and Mary paid Federal excise taxes during the war. Taxes were imposed on Moses' gold watch (valued at $100) and piano (valued at $200) in the family home. Mary Effine paid $10 a year for a license for her retail business.[143]

Before the war, Moses and Mary had been considered "very honest and respectable" in their business dealings and were very good credit risks. But as wartime inflation drove up their credit levels, which remained "good," it diminished their overall financial worth. In the immediate post-war years, Moses' credit worthiness remained sound but he was warned to pay cash for his purchases rather than buy on credit. Although not mentioned in his credit reports, at some point Moses Lake also owned a half interest in what has been described variously as a bottling establishment or a soda fountain in Baltimore.[144]

Also during the war, Moses and Mary Lake went about their business activities outside of Annapolis. Using passes issued by the provost marshal, they each left the city on a number of occasions, traveling by rail to Baltimore and Washington.[145]

Unlike his wife, Moses Lake did not play an extraordinary role at St. Mary's Church. The sole notice in the church records appeared when he died in 1870. The interment register says he "Received last sacts," indicating that his confession had been heard, he had received communion, and received Extreme Unction, the rite in which blessed oil was used anoint a sick person in danger of death and providing spiritual strength and comfort to the dying person. Father Augustine Freitag officiated.[146]

As the paterfamilias, Moses contributed financial and moral support to his wife, who was heavily involved at St. Mary's, and to his daughter, who attended Catholic school and, for a time, entered religious life. Sadly, the family met a rather abrupt end. "They were each of them sick for a long time and required a great deal of nursing and attention," according to one of the caretakers. Mary Effine died from cancer on November 20, 1869, Mary Augusta died from consumption on December 1, 1869, and Moses died from dropsy on March 20, 1870. Moses Spriggs of Annapolis served as their "regular nurse and attendant" during their final illnesses, which were attended to by Dr. William Govane Ridout. Spriggs himself was not Catholic but two of his daughters and a granddaughter were baptized as converts at St. Mary's in the mid-1850s. Mary Effine Lake was godmother for all three.[147]

It was a difficult end for an illustrious family. As the last to go and "being sick and weak in body," Moses left monetary bequests to Moses Spriggs and John Ann Price for their "kind attention and services to me and my family during our sickness and affliction." When the estate went to probate, Spriggs submitted a bill for $135 for having worked as a "Nurse, day & Night" for three months. Moses also left bequests to his niece Catherine Caution, "who is now living with me" and who cared for Moses during his final illness. He also left a bequest to Mary Hemsley "who has been so attentive and faithful all the time that she lived with my family." One of the claims against the estate of Moses Lake was from Rachel Smothers, for unspecified goods or services owed her between July 1860 and January 1869.[148] The Lake family lies in unmarked graves at St. Mary's Cemetery.

Permission to Move About

As part of the establishment of Federal authority over Annapolis, the army provost marshal assigned to the area set up a system to control the movement of the population. Individuals were required to swear an oath of allegiance to the United States Government and to carry passes issued by the provost marshal. The earliest extant record of passes dates to June 27, 1861, a day when 104 men (including soldiers), women, boys, and whole families were given permission to move about in the city, on local waterways, and in the countryside as they engaged in their occupations and travels. Civilians were required to have passes to work at nearby army camps of instruction and the military hospital; to deliver food, beverages, and telegrams; and to pilot boats in the harbor. Passes also were issued to boat captains to visit vessels that had been seized by the army. Because the Federal authorities kept a close eye on Maryland politicians, the governor, his staff, and family; members of the General Assembly, and Annapolis Mayor John Read Magruder, a Unionist, all were required to swear an oath and carry a pass.[149]

Each pass included a person's name, purpose of travel, and status or occupation. The occupations of slaves and free Blacks often were not specifically noted, just that they were "servants" or "colored." If the work they did was noted, it usually was "washerwoman."

St. Mary's parishioners were among the pass recipients. Martin Gill, a teamster, needed one to go to work at the army quartermaster at the Naval Academy. Edward Denver, his brother Thomas, and James Farrell, all former Naval Academy employees kept on by the army, needed passes to go to work at the gas works. Edward Denver was granted passes three times in June and July to cross the Severn River to Fort Madison. John Hughes' pass allowed him to deliver milk and vegetables and Thomas Tydings, who had been employed as a Naval Academy watchman before the war, evidently retained a similar function as he was granted a pass to the army hospital. Other parishioners, such as Maria Weinberger, Harriet Johnson, Moses Lake, Edward Sparks, Colonel John Walton—and his sons, Dr. Henry Roland Walton and Edward Walton—and Ferdinand Mullan also were issued passes. Mullan's father, retired army sergeant John Mullan, and "Denver" (presumably Edward) were later issued passes by the US surgeon rather than by the provost marshal. Apparently Sergeant Mullan had the authority to recommend the issuance of a pass, as happened for his son, Dennis, on September 5. Two parishioners received passes on the recommendation of Mayor Magruder, a fairly common occurrence that summer: Martha Coulter was granted a pass to sell "Cakes &c." and John Cavanaugh to deliver or sell milk.[150]

The first Redemptorist's name to appear in the pass records was "Jacobs Rev. & Friend" for July 31. He and a "companion" also were given a pass on September 3. A fortnight later, a pass was issued to a "messenger from Father Jacobs," presumably one of the lay brothers or a student, although the *Chronica Domus* does not record any travel out of Annapolis during this time.[151]

Throughout the war, those who arrived in Annapolis from elsewhere and had round-trip passes did not need return passes from the local provost marshal. For example, Father De Dycker came from Baltimore, where Federal authorities administered their own passes, to Annapolis for the annual examinations on August 10 and departed on August 14. He was accompanied by two other visiting priests and two professed students, none of whom were issued passes in Annapolis. During the summer of 1861, lay brothers Leo Zwerger, George Meyer, and Edward Zwickert were assigned to other Redemptorist houses and Father John Cornell left for out-of-state mission work and none were issued passes; either different rules applied or were waived, or the records are missing. The name of a candidate novice, one "P. Schmitt," who arrived in Annapolis on September 6, and was dismissed before the investiture ceremony on October 15, also does not appear in the record book during a period when the pass records appear to be complete with daily entries. It is also possible that they had obtained round-trip passes in Baltimore for which pass records are not extant for this period.[152]

Weddings and Baptisms

In June Joseph Jacobs officiated at an unusual wedding, that of a non-Catholic free African American couple. It is surmised that this couple had been receiving instructions in the faith from Jacobs but wanted to be married before they were baptized. The facts revealed in the parish records are that the wedding took place on June 15 and the baptisms on July 14 for the bride and September 8 for the groom, a highly unusual situation. The groom, twenty-four-year-old Richard Joseph Alphonsus Smith, was noted in the marriage record as "a Methodist in *via conversionis*" while the status of the bride, twenty-three-year-old Sarah Elizabeth Lee, was not noted. However, when the new Mrs. Richard Smith was baptized by Jacobs on July 14 as Elizabeth Sarah, she was noted as a convert from Methodism. Her husband's baptism followed on September 18, again with Jacobs officiating.[153]

The witnesses at the Smith-Lee wedding ceremony are also of interest. One was Maria Anna Lee, the bride's sister and also a convert from Methodism. Maria Anna and her sister were baptized the same day, so she could not have been a canonical witness at the June wedding since she was not yet Catholic. Rachel Smothers was the other witness at the wedding and also served as Sarah's godmother a month later. Maria Anna Lee's godmother was Elizabeth (Eliza) Anne Harris, also a convert from Methodism and goddaughter of Rachel Smothers. Eliza also was Richard Smith's baptismal sponsor. This demonstrates a tight circle of fellow Black Catholics who were well known to each other, as sponsors and witnesses should be. But there is a larger story here of service to the Catholic Church among women members of the African American community in Annapolis.

A Highly Respected Colored Woman

Rachel Teresa Smothers was a phenomenal woman whose name appears numerous times in St. Mary's sacramental registers as a sponsor for baptisms and confirmations and witness to one marriage. During the Civil War period alone, she was godmother for sixteen African Americans, some newborns and young children, others young and older adult converts. Fathers Jacobs and William Gross were the priests with whom Rachel appears to have coordinated her evangelization work during the war years. Rachel also had been active before the war, serving as godparent for fourteen children and adults baptized between 1856 and 1860. Rachel's own baptism predates extant sacramental registers. Soon after the war ended, she was godparent for four more African American children and sponsor for five children and adult converts—all females—when they were confirmed by the new archbishop, Martin John Spalding. Her service as godmother continued in subsequent years—forty-three more times between 1867 and 1899.[154]

Although Rachel Smothers was not alone in this church work—there were other Black and White parishioners who served numerous times as godparents and witnesses—she was by far the most active. It is clear that she was well known within the Black community and to the priests at St. Mary's. She often brought Black newborns and infants of non-Catholic parents to the priests for baptism and she probably instructed or at least encouraged many others to convert.

Other than her evangelization work at St. Mary's, Rachel Smothers has largely escaped notice in the historical record. But enough information exists to describe her origins and give her a place in the social history of Annapolis. She was born a slave in 1821 at Oakland, a plantation in Anne Arundel County's Eighth Election District. Oakland was owned by Thomas Franklin, cashier, and later president, of the Farmers National Bank of Maryland in Annapolis and a member of the House of Delegates and the Maryland Senate in the 1850s. Rachel probably moved as a child to Franklin's Annapolis home on State Circle, in the house once owned by John Shaw, the well-known Annapolis cabinet maker. When Shaw's daughter Elizabeth married 1833, she devised the house to her husband, widower Thomas Franklin. Since Oakland was owned by an Episcopalian family, it is likely that Rachel's first encounter with Catholicism was with the Jesuits who served St. Mary's in Annapolis. No record of her baptism exists because there is a gap in the Jesuit records for Annapolis between November 1832 and September 1851. The earliest governmental record concerning Rachel appeared in an 1860 city tax assessment of Annapolis slaves. A slave named Rachel, age forty, with a value of $300, appears under the heading for Thomas Franklin. In the 1820, 1830, and 1840 censuses, Franklin always had a female slave whose age correlates with a birth date of about 1820 for Rachel. Franklin's listing in the 1850 Slave Schedule has no female slaves who match Rachel's age but the 1860 Slave Schedule has one whose age is close to hers.[155]

Rachel must have been manumitted before Maryland's slaves were freed by the 1864 Constitution because her name does not appear in Anne Arundel County Slave Statistics, a county-wide listing of former slaves as of November 1, 1864—Emancipation Day in Maryland. The only Federal Census in which Rachel's name has been found is for 1880 when she was enumerated as a servant in the household of James Shaw Franklin and his half-sister Ann, the children of Thomas Franklin. James served for three years as a first lieutenant in the Confederate Second Maryland Infantry Battalion. He later owned a large undeveloped block of property on Doctor (renamed Franklin) Street between Cathedral and Shaw streets.[156]

Rachel Smothers worked most, if not all of her life—both as a slave and a freed person—for the Franklin family in the figurative shadow of the Maryland State House. She was well known locally in both the Black and White communities for her evangelization work at St. Mary's and, perhaps, as a midwife. When she died in 1899, the *Evening Capital* called her "a highly respected colored woman."[157]

One of Rachel's many goddaughters was the aforementioned Eliza Harris. Eliza had converted from Methodism at age twenty-one in 1859. She, in turn, became godmother for a teenager and three adults, all converts from Methodism, between 1859 and 1861, and was herself confirmed by Archbishop Kenrick in 1860. A housekeeper by profession, it is not clear whether or not she was free or enslaved before 1864. As far as can be determined Eliza remained single and died at age seventy-seven in 1913, with burial in an unmarked grave at St. Mary's Cemetery.[158]

Another African American woman of note was Martha Jacobs Maynard, born in 1833. She was godmother for three children, one adult, and one female of unspecified age. Additionally, Martha was confirmation sponsor for five teenagers in 1866. Unlike Rachel and Eliza, Martha Maynard was married and the mother of at least two children: Maria Cecilia (born 1860) and Joseph David (born 1862), who were christened together just two weeks before Martha herself was baptized in 1864. Her husband, David Maynard, received a certificate of freedom in 1858 at age twenty-five and he and Martha are listed together in the 1860 Federal Census, respectively, as a laborer with a personal estate of $40 and washerwoman. They lived either in part of or next to what is known today as the Maynard-Burgess House on Duke of Gloucester Street. The owner of this frame, two-story house was John Maynard, probably David's brother. Whether John and David were Catholic is not known but St. Mary's records show that John's wife, Maria Spencer Maynard, had two St. Mary's connections. Her daughter Phebe Ann Spencer was baptized at St. Mary's in 1855 and her mother, Maria Phebe Spencer, was confirmed in 1857. Also unlike Eliza Harris, Martha's godmother was a White woman, Catherine Bright, herself a convert from the Episcopal Church at age forty in 1859.[159]

As noted earlier in this chapter, a third Black woman of prominence in St. Mary's community—Mary Effine Lake—was godmother to twenty newborns, infants, children, teenagers, and adults between 1851 and 1867. Some of her god children were slaves and some were free. One of them was Phebe Ann Spencer.

Martha Maynard died from consumption but was "well prepared" sacramentally in 1866; Mary Lake died "a saintly death" from cancer in 1867; and Eliza Harris died of heart disease in 1913. Like Rachel, all are buried in St. Mary's Cemetery. Perhaps as a sign of their economic position at the times of their deaths, they rest in unmarked graves.[160]

Vows Professed and Assignments Made

On the Feast of St. Mary Magdalene (July 22), a diverse group of nine professed their Redemptorist vows before Father De Dycker. Some of the newly professed men came to America specifically to join the Redemptorists, others found their vocations in Redemptorist parishes after their arrival. They were students John Baptiste Blanchet, John Runge, and Joseph Weber, and lay brothers Leo Zwerger, George Meier, Gabriel Kirchner, Edward Zwickert, Charles Stabel, and Hilary Fröhlich. As usual they were a diverse lot. Twenty-seven-year-old Blanchet was from Baden, eighteen-year-old Runge from Hannover, and seventeen-year-old Weber from Bavaria. Of the brothers, thirty-one-year-old Leo Zwerger was born in Baden and worked as a gardener; twenty-eight-year-old George Meier was from German-speaking Lorraine in eastern France and worked as a tailor; twenty-seven-year-old Gabriel Kirchner, who worked as a clothes washer and later as a sacristan, was from Bavaria; thirty-year-old Edward Zwickert was born in Westphalia, and served as a cobbler; and thirty-six-year-old Charles Stabel, a Prussian, was a nurse and carpenter. Of special interest to the history of St. Mary's was the final professee, Hilary Fröhlich, who, with Brother Louis Sterkendries, built and decorated the Gothic high altar in St. Mary's Church. After completing their work in Annapolis, Hilary and Louis performed similar duties in other Redemptorist parishes, but Hilary returned to Annapolis in his later years and died there in 1898. Of the other newly professed brothers, Leo, George, and Edward were soon assigned to other Redemptorist houses.[161]

Angry Frogs and Union Shriekers

In May, according to the *Maryland Republican*, General Benjamin Butler declared that "Maryland is not in a state of rebellion" and that "there is now no city in the union more loyal than Annapolis."[162] The large presence of Union army units made sure of that. However, in the same issue and on the same page as the Butler statement—under the title "Men of Maryland: Read This!!,"—the *Republican* issued a warning. Editor and friend of St. Mary's Elihu S. Riley Sr. decided it was time to publish the text of the Fourth Amendment to the US Constitution:

> "The RIGHT of the PEOPLE to be SECURE in their Persons, Houses, Papers and Effects against unreasonable searches and seizures shall not be violated, but upon probable cause, supported by oath or affirmation, and particularly describing the place to be searched and the persons or things to be seized.[163]

Whether by omission or intent, one phrase was omitted from Riley's published text: "and no Warrant shall be issued,. . . ." It appears in the Fourth Amendment after the words "shall not be violated." He clearly was objecting to searches of Annapolis homes by Union soldiers.

In September Riley hinted that citizens' First Amendment rights also were threatened. He reprinted an article from the *Syracuse Courier*, entitled "Freedom of the Press," that criticized the Federal government for suppressing various Northern newspapers, including religious newspapers. "Now it assails Democratic journals," warned Riley, "a few years or months hence a like usurpation may with equal right annihilate the Republican."[164] He probably referred to his own newspaper—the *Maryland Republican*—rather than the pro-Republican Party press, the *Annapolis Gazette*. Whichever meaning was implied, the Federal government was perceived as a threat to freedom of the press and other constitutional rights.

The "climax of despotism" on the part of the Lincoln administration, according to Riley, was the arrest of numerous public officials in Baltimore on September 11, 1861. By this action, he wrote, the Lincoln administration "wields the sceptre of absolutism, grasps a power hitherto unprecedented, and crushes every vestige of right with an unsparing and resistless arth [*sic*]" in its attack on Maryland, "the cradle of liberty of conscience."[165]

According to Riley, the *Maryland Republican* represented the "peace movement" in Annapolis and he did not flinch in his criticism of the "war press." The war press, he said, was "cringing and kneeling and bowing to those in authority" while those who favored war were "lauding their own degradation and humbly begging for more, while they swell themselves almost to bursting—like angry frogs—in the hope of attracting the attention of their superiors and frightening those who differ with them by a grandiloquent display of their bogus importance." So that no mistake was made by Annapolis readers, the *Maryland Republican* cited an *Annapolis Gazette* article published the previous April 25 that had given "vent to . . . treasonable language." The *Gazette* said that the Maryland General Assembly was about to approve an ordinance of secession, which local people felt "*almost unanimous on the subject*," that the people of Annapolis were "highly indignant at the occupation of our city," and that "WE ARE POWERLESS TO OPPOSE THEM" [emphasis as in the original]. But soon, the Republican insisted, the *Gazette* editor "hailed [the Union army] with hosannas" and "found out what to do to turn the 'evil' to advantage, by using it to help build up a party, which might secure both patronage and power."[166] After all, the Democrats strongly supported the Constitution and its Bill of Rights, and the sentiment "the Constitution as it is, the nation as it was." This idea supported the constitutional right to own slaves and to reunite the country as it was before.

By September, according to the *Maryland Republican*, *Annapolis Gazette* editor Thomas Wilson had been commissioned a lieutenant colonel in the Thirty-Ninth Regiment. This appears to have been a facetious reference confirming Wilson's pro-war stance. The Thirty-Ninth Maryland was a militia regiment during the War for Independence and the War of 1812. Another Maryland regiment, the Thirty-Ninth US Colored Troops (USCT) was raised in 1864. Wilson would also be referred to at the rank of "major" several years later.[167]

Regardless, Wilson represented the pro-war element in Annapolis and he saw his newspaper and the readers who favored it as pro-Union and excoriated those who claimed to seek peace. "'Peace movements,'" wrote Wilson, are "subordinate to or in conflict with the loyalty of the State." The conflict he saw was economic. As one of only two loyal tobacco-growing states, Maryland, along with Kentucky, was in a perfect situation to corner the tobacco market among the northern states but only if the "Rebel element in the Chesapeake" did not prevail. But the danger that they might prevail was real, according to Wilson, who wrote, that the "greater part of the Maryland Secessionists" resided in Anne Arundel, Calvert, Prince George's, Charles, and St. Mary's counties, where "the madness of the hour has demented them, and drags them on slowly but surely to their ruin."[168] Thus spoke the two media organs of Annapolis as their editors sought to influence the town's citizens.

The *Annapolis Gazette* announced that on September 12 a "large and beautiful American flag" would be presented "to the Union men of Annapolis this (Thursday) afternoon, on Market Space, at 5 o'clock." The new flag was be raised on a pole near the city market house. Reporting on the event several days later, the *Maryland Republican* gleefully reported that after playing band music and parading through the streets, the marchers reached Market Space and, "to the astonishment and disappointment of the assemblage, no 'Union' orators could be found." The report continued that "after an interval of awful silence the flag was produced by a bystander, who unceremoniously hung it up, and with three cheers the disappointed crowd dispersed." The *Republican* said it was "discreditable to this community, that the flag which we all so justly love and venerate could not find one, of all the Union shriekers, to do it with reverence." The *Republican* also took a critical swipe at troops from the Twenty-First Massachusetts Infantry Regiment who marched with the local militia in the parade to Market Space. Editor Riley reminded his readers that September 12 was Defenders Day in Maryland, a day to commemorate the successful defense of Baltimore against the British in 1814. The Massachusetts troops, Riley pointed out, were from a state "which opposed the war of 1812, and cared very little if Baltimore burned or not, as she refused to assist in protecting it."[169] Annapolitans had a long memory of such Yankee slights.

It is not known if St. Mary's parishioner Colonel John Walton was present or not at the Market Space event. As it turned out, there was no oration that day but he would have been a likely speaker at the event had he been there. In August Walton had been elected president of the Anne Arundel County Union Convention, which then nominated him to run for the House of Delegates in the upcoming election. A week before the Defenders Day event, the formerly staunch Democrat was praised twice in one issue in the *Annapolis Gazette*. One letter to the editor said Walton was "a strong Union man" and "that a more competent person for this position could not be selected from this county." Another writer said there were "few men more interested in the prosperity of this country and State" than Walton. He was noted in positive terms as a "large holder of real estate as well as owner of negroes" and had a "strong inducement to exert his utmost ability and extensive influence for whatever may conduce to the interests of the slaveholder and the agriculturalist." He was lauded as the friend of "the working and laboring class" who had "himself commenced the world a poor man, and by his own industry and untiring exertions accumulated a handsome fortune. . . ." Walton was said to be "[s]till more deserving . . . of the confidence and respect of our Union loving people for the noble stand he has taken in the present unfortunate disruption of our country." He had long been "an uncompromising Democrat" but when his party's leaders "raised the banner of rebellion," Walton, "at all hazards cut himself loose from his old party associates, and unhesitatingly and uncompromisingly stepped forth the firm and steadfast supporter of the Union." The unidentified letter writer declared of Walton that "Rebellion finds no favor in his sight" and that he was a most worthy candidate for the House of Delegates.[170] The praise for Walton concentrated on preservation of the Union while ignoring the slavery issue that had caused such divisiveness.

Several weeks later, the *Annapolis Gazette* reminded voters that "every man in Maryland who votes the 'Peace Ticket' is aiding the rebels, and is a traitor to the Government." The "Peace Ticket" was the slate nominated by the States' Rights Party—as Maryland Democrats were then temporarily known—for governor, comptroller, judges for the court of appeals and circuit court, Senate and House of Delegates, county commissioners, and county surveyor. When the election came, the Union Party was the overall winner. Augustus Bradford, of Harford County, won the governorship over Benjamin Chew Howard, a Baltimore Catholic and, ironically, a nativist. John Walton was the top vote getter for one of the three seats for Anne Arundel County's representatives to the House of Delegates. All three seats were claimed by the Union Party over the States' Rights Party. It was a close election though, with a margin of only thirty-one votes between Walton and the sixth- and bottom-ranked candidate, William Tell Claude. Although the Union Party won the majority of votes in Annapolis and in the Third and Eighth electoral districts, the States' Rights candidates out-polled the Unionists everywhere else in the county. The Eighth District was an unlikely place for Union Party candidates to succeed. But on election day, the States' Rights candidate for the Maryland Senate, Dr. Thomas Jacobs Franklin, was arrested "on a charge of treason," an act that evidently intimated some one hundred voters from casting their Eighth District ballots. Franklin was the older half brother of the aforementioned James Shaw Franklin.[171]

Amidst this political divisiveness, the Walton family was in mourning, having lost infant John Walton—Colonel Walton's grandson—just a few weeks before the election. John was son of Edward and Joanna Brady Walton and had been baptized at St. Mary's by Father Jacobs on July 14. The godfather was the baby's uncle, Henry Roland Walton, a local physician. Baby John's godmother is of special interest. She was Corine Mary Cherbonnier Bartol, wife of Maryland Court of Appeals Judge James Bartol. Although not permanent residents of Annapolis—they lived in Pikesville in Baltimore County—the Bartols would have stayed in town during court sessions. They became acquainted with the Walton family, perhaps from lodging at the City Hotel and attending Mass at St. Mary's Church. Their once-common political affiliation as Democrats, and as fellow Catholics, led Mrs. Bartol to become godparent for infant John Walton.[172]

Examinations, Holidays, and a New Academic Year

As St. Mary's parishioners became involved in the throes of war-inflamed politics, Father De Dycker returned to Annapolis in mid-August to conduct the annual examinations. For three days, he examined the students and, although there is no record of the specific results, the students as a group were praised for their academic progress.[173]

The academic year 1860–61 was over and the students enjoyed a brief respite. The *Chronica Domus* gives a tantalizing but incomplete glimpse at what they did during these hot, late summer days:

> August 16 – Student holidays begin. The students enjoyed many trips, especially by boat as is the custom in Annapolis. During this time, they encountered some dangers, but we will mention them only in passing here. They would be less interesting to readers. The reader will find them at the end of this year's annals.[174]

The record provides two more cryptic entries: "August 28—Everyone planned to go on an excursion, but the weather was not in our favor." Whether the weather was too hot and humid or it rained, the disfavor is not known. And, on September 2, it was promised again that "You can read about a most dangerous excursion [*excursio periculosissima*] at the end of this year's record."[175] Unfortunately, the chronicler failed to fulfill his promise to provide the details of any of these exploits at the end of the year.

New novice candidates began to arrive just prior to the start of the new academic year. On either August 25 or 26, the annals reported:

> a candidate showed up from the city of Washington named 'Mr. Ladde.' He was a most eager candidate but lacked the ability to bear such rigors. He was a convert from Protestantism and both his parents were still Protestant.

Mr. Ladde was not mentioned again in the *Chronica Domus* and has not been clearly identified but might have been sent to Annapolis by Mathias Alig, pastor of St. Mary's Church in Washington, DC.[176]

Swiss-born Mathias Alig had been a member of the Redemptorist congregation from 1837 to 1849. In 1838 at the request of Archbishop of Baltimore Samuel Eccleston, the Redemptorists provided a German-speaking priest to work among German immigrants in Washington. Father Peter Czackert, C.Ss.R., first ministered to a small German congregation in a basement chapel at St. Matthew the Apostle Church, a largely Irish parish locate at Fifteenth and H streets Northwest. By 1845 Czackert had acquired land through gift and purchase on Fifth Street Northwest, between G and H streets, and promised to build a German-congregation church there. He was succeeded later that year by Alig, who saw the project to completion and the Church of the Mother of God (popularly known as St. Mary's) was opened in October 1846. He warmed to this apostolate but when his Redemptorist superior insisted he commute from Baltimore for weekend services in Washington, Alig argued that he was needed there during the week as well and asked to be dispensed from his vows. His request was approved and he became a diocesan priest. But his links with the Redemptorists continued as witnessed by a number of trips made by Annapolis Redemptorists recorded in the *Chronica Domus* during the Civil War. Although some entries did not mention Alig by name, it is likely that all the visitors lodged with their former confrere. When he died in Washington in 1882, one of Father Alig's honorary pallbearers was Redemptorist Father Bernard Beck, who was ordained in Annapolis in 1863.[177]

Between September 6 and 14, six candidates arrived, Joseph Michael Dreisch, P. Schmidt, and John Henry Schagemann from Baltimore; John Baptist Bausch and Charles Kern from Philadelphia; and Charles Kearful from Cumberland. Of the six, only Baltimore native John Schagemann and Charles Kern, a Hessian, remained in the seminary and both were ordained in 1872. The life of a Redemptorist novice and student was challenging. Some worked hard at it and remained, others were unsuited for the cloistered environment and departed. The Germanic discipline and European austerity made the life particularly hard for the American-born men. However, although they were dismissed, men such as Bausch and Kearful had strong vocations and both were ordained later as diocesan priests and went on to long and fruitful careers. Bausch worked among the German-speaking population in west-central Pennsylvania and Kearful was an itinerant missionary in the frontier state of Kansas.[178]

Academic year 1861–62 started on September 17. In preparation for a year of study and contemplation, Father Müller led the students in a five-day retreat. During the first three days, Forty Hours devotions were held for the entire community but, as the *Chronica Domus* noted, it was "especially for the benefit of the students." On the final retreat day, the new program of studies was announced. Father Jacobs was in charge of the Department of Dogmatic Theology, with six students assigned. The Department of Philosophy, which included the study of ethics, historical philosophy, geometry, and physics, was led by Father Joseph Wuest, with four students.[179] Wuest had injured his right leg in August, perhaps during one of the holiday boating excursions, and had been laid up to the extent that he experienced many sleepless nights because of the pain and could not even celebrate Mass for more than three weeks. But when the school year began, he resumed his role in the classroom. One of the advanced students, Frater John Gerdemann, was the lector for the Department of Rhetoric and had charge of fourteen students. There were two grammar departments, an upper-level with Frater Anthony Kesseler serving as lector for ten students, and a lower level with Frater James Keitz as lector for five students. Second-level studies were arranged as follows. Wuest taught exegesis for students of dogmatics, while Jacobs taught Church history and Müller taught French. The hard-working Wuest also taught

Greek and algebra. Presumably all of the advanced students took all of these second-level subjects as their names were not mentioned under the subject listings. In a final cryptic note on the curriculum, the *Chronica Domus* noted simply that other courses were "all delivered by appropriate teachers." Thus, on September 23, "the studies for the new year [began] again with restored vigor of mind and body."[180]

Journey into the Kingdom of Ideas

Although one might expect that faculty at St. Mary's College were the most erudite members of the Redemptorist community, on occasion it was a student whose accomplishments were worthy of note. One such occasion materialized on the Feast of St. Michael the Archangel (September 29). It was Father Müller's name day and cause for celebration. One of the new students, Joseph James Kammer had arrived in Annapolis two weeks earlier. But the *Chronica Domus* reported that this mere twenty-year-old student "gave a complicated oration full of innuendos for all the listeners." His oration "dealt with 'the journey of a certain over-educated man into the realm of ideas'—which he rendered as *"Reise in's Idearreich"* (German for "journey into the kingdom of ideas"). The chronicler, who may have been Müller himself, only humbly noted that the speech was directed at "a certain over-educated man." But the meaning is clear that a very well-educated man of considerable learning was the object of praise on his name day and subtle humor by one of the students, and a newcomer at that.[181]

October 15, 1861, was another day of celebration and "journey" at St. Mary's. It was the Feast of St. Teresa de Jesús, the renowned Discalced Carmelite nun better known as St. Teresa of Ávila. The writings of St. Teresa significantly influenced the thinking of St. Alphonsus Liguori, the founder the Redemptorists in the Kingdom of Naples in 1732, and thus are of importance to those who follow the Redemptorist Rule. She also is the patroness of the Redemptorist community in Annapolis and her statue, which once had its own side altar, now resides on the high altar of the St. Mary's Church in counterpoise to a statue of St. Alphonsus. This particular feast day was the one chosen for the profession of vows by Hugo Victor, a lower-level grammar student, and the investiture of eight new novices, all but one of whom were teenagers.[182]

Because permission had not been received from Baltimore in time for the October 15 ceremony, it was not until nine days later that two more men—Joseph Colonel and John Blanchet—professed their vows. Of the three newly professed students, nineteen-year-old Hugo Victor, from Hannover, was ordained in 1869 but dispensed of his vows in 1873. Joseph Colonel, whose younger brother, Philip, had been invested at Annapolis in 1860, had been born in Bavaria in 1834. He and eighteen-year-old John Blanchet would be ordained in St. Mary's Church in 1867 and went on to fruitful careers as Redemptorist priests: Colonel in New Orleans until his death in 1885, and Blanchet in Buffalo, New York, and then in Baltimore until his death in 1898. Many of the others fell away from the religious life.[183]

A journey of a different sort took some the novices and students underground. This occurred during a period of several weeks, beginning at the end of October. Father Müller put them to work excavating a new cellar to store beer ("in the vernacular . . . 'Lagerbier'"). Those involved in this hard labor "expended a lot of sweat on this project, although," wrote the chronicler, "it is not expedient to give their names for posterity. Far better to have their praises and their names found in the Book of Life." The stone used for the beer cellar had been used previously as the foundation for an old cow barn. What was left of the cow barn was converted into a carpenter shop.[184] The chronicler for the Redemptorists' *Province Annals* took special interest in the beer-brewing enterprise at St. Mary's. He wrote that beer making was started there because of the shortage of local wine and for that reason, Brother Vincent Kieninger, who had the necessary skills, was assigned to Annapolis. He built an "apparatus" to make beer and oversaw the construction of the "bierbrouerey." The importance of the effort expended by the students and novices in building the underground storage for the beer was noted: "The work they have done will show the inhabitants of Annapolis their devotion and benefit that their work brings to the institution." Although the annals do not indicate where this beer cellar was, it is probably the one still extant and adjacent to today's rectory kitchen, on the northeast corner of the old college building. The precise historic location of the cow barn that became a carpenter shop also is subject

Frater Joseph James Kammer, C.Ss.R. (1840–63). RABP.

to speculation but possibly it was adjacent to the south side of the west wing of the Carroll House. Brother Vincent, known as Michael before entering religious life, was born in Württemberg in 1819 and immigrated to America where he joined the Redemptorists in Annapolis in 1861. He professed his final vows as a lay brother in 1866 and spent many years in Annapolis as the beer brewer. He was described as a simple, hardworking soul. Toward the end of his life, "Though feeble and worn out, he dragged himself to the exercises of the Community," according to a biographer. He died at St. Mary's in 1888 and is buried in the Redemptorist cemetery.[185]

The final journey of one of the Redemptorist students was the only note in the *Chronica Domus* for November 1861. The chronicler wrote: "November is most memorable because of the final illness and holy death of our dear confrere, 'James Henry Harvey.'" Although ample space was left in the chronicle for "a few details of his life" none were recorded there. Fortunately, other resources survive to reveal his story. He arrived in Annapolis on June 21, 1861, the same day as Father Wuest, who later wrote about Harvey's exemplary life. Wuest said Harvey seemed to have a sense of piety from childhood and early in his life decided to devote himself wholly to God. Those who recalled him in later years said Harvey was an inspiration to others and, because of his encouragement to another young man, he helped set in place a series of events that had historic implications for St. Mary's Parish.[186]

Harvey was born in Washington, DC, in 1834 and had an early vocation to religious life. He enrolled at St. Charles College and briefly considered entering the Jesuit novitiate in Frederick, Maryland. But rather than embark on the long preparation in an order devoted to teaching, he decided to join the Redemptorists with their singular devotion to the Blessed Sacrament. He entered the Annapolis novitiate, where he was invested on December 8, 1853. He professed his vows exactly a year later and entered the Redemptorist seminary in Cumberland in 1855. His studies there were interrupted when he became ill and in 1856 he was sent to St. Joseph's, the Redemptorist house in Rochester, New York, where "the air was better," for treatment.[187]

While recuperating in Rochester, Harvey met a local young man, two years his junior, Charles Constantine Pise O'Donoughue. Their acquaintance grew into a close friendship and Harvey encouraged O'Donoughue to make a spiritual retreat in Cumberland under the direction of Father Seelos. O'Donoughue followed his friend's advice and with Seelos' encouragement, he applied for admission to the Redemptorists. He arrived in Annapolis in July 1858, was formally admitted to the novitiate as a candidate the following month, and professed his vows there in August 1859.[188] After Seelos was reassigned to Annapolis in June 1862 and the determination was made to establish a parochial grammar school, Charles O'Donoughue's sister, Josephine, was selected as the first teacher. Without this chain of causation that began with the illness of James Henry Harvey, subsequent developments in Annapolis surely would have occurred differently.

After nearly five years in Rochester, then in New York City and Baltimore, Harvey returned to Annapolis on June 21, 1861. The new college building was thought to be better suited for his care but, during the following months, his illness worsened and, on November 24, he told Father Müller that he hoped "the day of our Lord will come as quickly as possible, for I want to be with him." Nevertheless, the manner in which he endured his prolonged suffering continued to inspire his fellow students. He died on November 26. The exact nature of illness was never disclosed but, as will be seen, consumption was a major problem in St. Mary's College and it is possible that Harvey died from it. Even though several other Redemptorist students who died in Annapolis in the 1850s were buried at the new St. Mary's Cemetery on West Street, it appears that Harvey may have been buried on the parish property, possibly next to two other students who died in 1863 and were buried next to each other "in the garden near the church." He and other Redemptorists buried there were disinterred in 1864 and their remains placed in a new vault under the sacristy of the church (see Many Useful Improvements, ch. 6).[189]

Visitationis Canonicae

Father De Dycker made his annual canonical visitation in Annapolis between November 24 and December 2. At the end of the visitation, he laid out seventeen requirements for the Redemptorist community. Some were routine, while others were gentle prodding where he thought corrections were needed. No group under Müller's supervision would have been lax. However, De Dycker noted that silence was required "most religiously and diligently" and to be kept according to the Redemptorist Rule. Perhaps there had been some infractions because he added that this applied to "the entire community." Unless necessary, no classes were to be held in private rooms. Lectors were told to hold regular classes and to begin and end them precisely "according to the Rule and the Constitution." He also reminded the lectors that "all things concerning prayer to methods of teaching, shall be religiously observed." Strict regulations also were to be followed in regard to the study of rubrics, music, and foreign languages. Everyone was warned that "the orders of the superior and their officials must be obeyed. No one may ever presume to take a superior's place or make a superior repeat their observations or corrections."[190]

When at public worship in the church, students and brothers were reminded that they must remain in their pews until the celebrating priest leaves the sanctuary and enters the sacristy. In a nod to behavior among the lay brothers, they were told to be courteous to each other when carrying out their assigned duties and that "works of obedience and charity always come before private devotions, but especially Sundays when they are helping in the kitchen." Everyone in the community was expected to be punctual and present for all meals and, "unless obliged by need, should not be absent from table." Those who came late for a meal were to be seated at a second table and, in such circumstances, a bell was to be rung as the signal to a brother in the kitchen that food was needed at the second table. In what was probably in response to a plea from the brother in charge of the kitchen, the provincial ordered that henceforth "the bucket for drinking water is not to be used for any other purpose" and that no one, other than those who were required by official duty, was allowed to enter the kitchen. In order to maintain their vows of poverty, all members were directed to "use the same kinds of clothes and linen [underwear]." Everyone, especially the students, were directed to always show great respect for each other.

Another directive said that the priests were permitted to subscribe to "three or, at most four newspapers or magazines and they should not spend too much time reading them." What these newspapers were is not known but presumably, the Redemptorists would have subscribed to the two Annapolis weeklies, the *Annapolis Gazette* and the *Maryland Republican*, (clippings from both have been found glued into the *Chronica Domus*). They probably subscribed to the weekly *Catholic Mirror* and the daily Baltimore *Sun*. With the significant German-speaking population in the community, they may also have had a subscription to the *Katholische Volkszeitung*, the leading German-Catholic newspaper in the United States, also published in Baltimore. It is possible that newspapers from Washington, Philadelphia, New York, and other cities also found their way to the Duke of Gloucester Street college. One title that has been verified as subscribed to by the Redemptorists in Annapolis was the weekly *New-York Freeman's Journal and Catholic Register*. Several people associated with St. Mary's also were subscribers. They included James Alexis Iglehart, Mary Effine Lake, Edward Sparks, and Edward DuBois, who also was the local agent for the Catholic weekly.[191]

Based on a much later eye-witness account, some of these Civil War-era newspapers survived in the Carroll House until the mid-1950s. At that time, the master of novices for the post-ordination second novitiate, Father Leo St. Lawrence, ordered an overall clean up of the Carroll House, then used for classrooms. While working in the library, one of the newly ordained priests found a large stack of Civil War-era newspapers and asked the novice master if they could be saved because of their historical value. Permission was denied, the vow of obedience was strictly followed, and the newspapers were discarded along with other historically valuable publications.[192]

Another directive from 1861 brings to mind the one Father Jacob received before he gave his Fourth of July oration at the State House in July. Now, in December, De Dycker reminded the community that:

> Debates about political topics are to be earnestly avoided. Everyone must be careful in conversation at home, to in no way harm fraternal charity, or when outside to put himself or the Congregation into a dispute.[193]

Political talk and taking sides in discussions concerning the ongoing war were forbidden both among the Redemptorists and when they might meet parishioners or others on the street. The fear of anti-Catholic backlash, always a possibility, was preeminent among the Redemptorist community.

Another concern raised addressed contact with the opposite sex. To avoid any sign of impropriety, the priests were exhorted to always have someone else present when meeting with women. De Dycker put it this way:

> When certain women come for instruction, as far as possible, it will always be given in the most public place. If it be possible, make sure that women are always accompanied, lest the dialogue be one-on-one.[194]

Concurrent with De Dycker's visitation, the Twenty-Seventh Massachusetts Infantry Regiment was bivouacked outside Annapolis. After the weekly Sunday inspection of arms, one of the soldiers and a fellow sergeant ventured into town during their free time. "We went all over the city," wrote Chauncey Holcomb, and "[s]aw the largest church that I ever saw—Catholic—in all my travels here." The Twenty-Seventh had left its mustering place—Springfield, Massachusetts— on November 2 and had traveled by railroad and steamer to Annapolis, where they remained for two months for military training. Holcomb's previous travel experiences must not have been all that extensive, but St. Mary's new Gothic church was a highlight for him.[195]

The Burnside Expedition

Some events that took place early in 1862 began with the arrival in Annapolis of Brigadier General Ambrose Everett Burnside on December 18, 1861. He was commander of a newly formed expeditionary force, the Coast Division, a planned amphibious invasion to establish a foothold on the North Carolina coast. The participating regiments were mostly composed of men from New England who were used to working in boats. They assembled in Annapolis, where they set up camp in "beautiful grounds just outside of the town." Because it was Christmas time, "the camps [were] beautifully decorated and made very comfortable, by large log huts &c." Burnside set up his headquarters at the City Hotel, by then under the proprietorship of John Walton's sons, Henry Roland and Edward. It was later stated later that throughout the war "hundreds of Union officers" stayed at the City Hotel.[196]

Burnside and his wife, Mary ("Molly") Richmond Bishop Burnside, rented room No. 52 at the City Hotel. Members of his personal staff also lodged together at the hotel and sometimes Burnside used their room as an office and other times he used his adjutant's office at the Naval Academy. One of the lodgers was Burnside's private secretary, Daniel Read Larned, an avid writer who had much to say about Annapolis in letters to his family. Soon after he arrived, Larned wrote that he was "terribly disappointed in the place and more so with the people." He said "all is as dull as can be" in Annapolis and he had never seen a city "so far behind the age" and "compared unfavorably with bright New England." The main thing that bothered him was that the town itself was a "secesh hole!" He also complained that although the City Hotel was "the best in the place," it was "worse than 'Old Stiles' Tavern' in Thompson," a reference to an antiquated stagecoach stop in

Camp Burnside, Christmas Day, 1861, Edward Sachse, Baltimore, 1862.
Mrs Harry R. Slack Collection, SC 626-1, Maryland State Archives

his hometown in Connecticut. Larned complained that Annapolis had only one public carriage "that can never be found" and that the post office—which on at least one occasion did not have any stamps to sell—was open only two hours a day. He also found that when he needed them, many of the shops were locked "while the proprietor has gone off." He appreciated the "small but very pleasant" St. Anne's Church, which he attended his first Sunday in town. He served as an escort to Molly Burnside and other staff officers' wives, but he seems to have gone to St. Anne's mostly to see "the aristocracy" of Annapolis, whom he discovered were "nearly all Secesh, while the plain common people are Unionists." After exiting St. Anne's that morning, Larned and the women "passed four ladies talking on the street" and overheard one of them say "Oh, did you see in the paper last evening that England says she will raise the blockade and blockade all the Northern ports within 3 days." One of her interlocutors replied, "I hope my soul they will . . . & clear out these Yankees." This, Larned believed, was said for the "benefit" of the army wives and himself. He felt even more unwelcome when he perceived that the local women had "sneered" at his uniform. Another day he climbed up to the State House copula and observed the radiating streets of the city, which he illustrated with a tiny drawing in one of this letters. After leaving the State House, he saw a local woman walking her pet greyhound. He heard her call the dog's name, "Dixie," another indication of pro-South leanings. He told his sister in New Haven that he refused to have his photograph taken in Annapolis because he "would not patronize a Secesh establishment." But Larned also declared that the Annapolis harbor, in the moonlight and filled with the expedition's fleet, was "beautiful beyond description." On December 20, in anticipation of an imminent departure for the south, Burnsides hosted a Christmas party at the City Hotel for his staff and their wives. During this time, Burnside went several times to Washington to confer with President Lincoln and his immediate boss, Major General George Brinton McClellan, commander of the Army of the Potomac.[197]

Larned looked forward to leaving Annapolis, exclaiming, "I am heartily sick of this place." He complained again about the local secessionists, who were "quite thick and seem to delight in making their speeches for our benefit." Some, he told his sister, are "all very rude."[198] Despite Larned's disdain for Annapolis and its accommodations, the hotel run by a St. Mary's parish family played an important role as the headquarters for the Burnside expedition.

Christmas 1861

Daniel Larned also observed how Christmas was celebrated in Annapolis. On the Sunday before Christmas, he visited some local churches, accompanied by his roommate, Burnside's staff clerk, William Harrison French, from Providence, Rhode Island. First they listened to the singing at the Methodist church. Then they went to the Presbyterian church, where they heard what French called "a d__d good sermon." On Christmas Eve, Larned visited St. Anne's again and afterward saw local people "out in gala dress." African Americans "from the country [had] come in town, and it is a sort of 4th of July" for them as they were "firing of crackers [and] torpedoes."[199]

Larned did not get as far as St. Mary's Church, but had he done so, he might have seen the same thing another person had observed about St. Mary's at Christmastime. In a letter to his family in Bohemia, seminarian John Berger noted that at 11:30 PM on Christmas Eve, the Redemptorist community assembled in the house chapel to sing Matins. Afterward, Father Müller sang a High Mass and then, according to the tradition of the time that allowed a priest to say three Masses on Christmas Day, he also celebrated two Low Masses without singing. Then Müller offered a meditation on the wonder of the newborn Baby Jesus and led the priests, students, and brothers in a renewal of their religious vows. These solemn activities ended by 4:00 AM and preparations then were made for High Mass in the church for the parishioners at 5:00. This Mass was followed by two Low Masses at 8:00 and 9:00. At 10:00 AM another High Mass was sung and the Christmas sermon was preached. Vespers were sung at 3:00 in the afternoon, and at 7:00 in the evening there was exposition of the Blessed Sacrament. Thus ended St. Mary's observances for Christmas Day.[200]

The *Province Annals* noted St. Mary's parish statistics for 1861. It reported five marriages, seven funerals, eleven converts, forty-four baptisms, and 4,100 communions distributed. The *Annals* noted that "Nothing of importance happened with the school." Since the statement was made in context with parish statistics, it presumably meant there had been no further developments toward establishing St. Mary's grammar school.[201]

Toward the end of 1861, several letters were received by Susie Sands, the woman to whom Martin Revell had proposed marriage several times but who had put him off. They reveal her reaction to the Federal occupation of the city. A cousin replied to earlier letters using Susie's own words that there "was great confusion in Annapolis owing to the war" and that she was "much disturbed by [the soldiers'] depredations."[202] The first seven and a half months of the Civil War were past and Annapolitans struggled to maintain their way of life as they recalled much happier times.

Chapter 4: 1862 — Sworn to the Ministry of Peace

The Evils of War

Despite expectations in both North and South that the war would end quickly, the armed conflict proved complicated. The Confederate army achieved notable victories on the eastern-front battlefields in 1861 and the initial enthusiasm for volunteering for military service and the North's hope for an easy victory over the southern insurrectionists had waned. Some northerners would have been happy to let the South go, while others wished for a status quo ante—"the Union as it was—the Constitution as it is!" Marylanders were caught in the middle. Some were sympathetic to the South and Southern culture and were not opposed to Confederate independence. Others were loyal to the Union but resentful of the Federal occupation of their state and concerned about the threat of war spilling over from neighboring Virginia.[1]

When the war moved close to Cumberland, the Redemptorist provincial and his consultors had important decisions to make concerning the safety of their students there. They also were apprehensive about the possibility of the priests, brothers, and seminarians being drafted into military service. Lincoln, confronted with the never-ending need for more troops, called on governors to enlist and—as needed to meet quotas set for each state—to draft men into state militias. Both of these issues would lead to momentous events for St. Mary's, its religious students, and its parishioners.

Frater John Berger wrote home to his family early in the new year. Wanting to calm their fears for his safety in the face of war, he revealed the Redemptorists' plans should the war come close to Annapolis:

> So far we have not experienced the least of the evils of civil war. I'm not saying that our superiors do not notice anything. Since outbreak of war, we have seen the fatherly care of our superiors as to the safety of our people. Everyone, even the novices keep civilian clothes in their cells in case a quick escape should be necessary; and the different [Redemptorist] houses in the northern states have already prepared for the increase. But we have not been deprived of the protection of Jesus and Mary and the joys of community life.[2]

Berger then described the general situation in Annapolis:

> At present there are 17–18000 men in camps around the city and many warships to carry them to the battlefield. One of our priests goes to the various camps to give lessons to the few Catholics and to celebrate Mass. Some of these men have been away from God for as long as 5–10 years or even their entire lives. On Sundays there are more soldiers in our church than civilians. One of our fathers from New Orleans is serving as an army chaplain.

The chaplain to whom Berger referred was James Sheeran, chaplain of the Confederate Fourteenth Louisiana Infantry Regiment. Another Redemptorist served with the Confederacy: Aegidius Smulders, chaplain of the Eighth Louisiana Infantry Regiment. Both regiments fought in numerous battles throughout the war as part of the Army of Northern Virginia.[3]

Burnside's amphibious expedition was set to depart Annapolis for North Carolina in early January. Army units had arrived daily in December by ship and by train, overwhelming Annapolis and the surrounding countryside. Despite the troops' enthusiasm about finally boarding their transports and heading south, as Burnside passed through snow-covered streets, he noted that "the inhabitants . . . were not remarkable for their loyalty." A modern-day Burnside biographer added to this characterization, writing that "Annapolis citizens contributed to the chill, either ignoring the spectacle or affording it unenthusiastic eyes." The transport ships were loaded January 6–8 and departed on the ninth for Fort Monroe. Daniel Larned wrote home that nearly all the regimental bands played "Dixie" as the soldiers embarked. More than 15,000 troops and fifty-eight ships of all descriptions left Annapolis and rendezvoused with twenty-one navy ships at Hampton Roads and Hatteras Inlet. It was the largest combined-forces operation in American history to date.[4]

Soldiers around this time complained about Annapolis. One said it was "the dirtiest and mudiest place you ever saw, you can't go without getting into the mud up to your nees [*sic*] and such a thing as a nice house you can't find." Another called the city "a low dirty place." Although such criticisms were common among northern soldiers passing through Annapolis, these were not conditions that locals, whose town had been severely disrupted by war, were accustomed (see fig. 3, Annapolis, 1861–65). Rather it was the army's horses and wagons that had torn up the streets. Another soldier observed that he had seen "no one in the street but blacks and soldiers." Many of the soldiers were now gone, but a large numbers of "contrabands"—runaway slaves—had flooded into the city and county. The provost marshal ordered a 10:00 PM curfew for contrabands, a move that reportedly "caused considerable excitement among the colored population." Historian Jane McWilliams succinctly summarized the impact of the war on Annapolis up to this point: "no matter what side the locals favored, disease, noise, mud, confusion, and the ever-present strangers overwhelmed them all."[5]

Physician of the Soul

As 1862 began, Father Michael Müller had eighty-three men assigned to his charge. They included four priest-professors, forty-four students, sixteen novices, and eighteen brothers.[6] The students began the new year with a day of recollection on January 3. Despite the not-so-distant war and the presence of thousands of Federal troops in town, it was a good start for the coming term of study and introspection. The next day, the first snow of the year fell on Annapolis.[7]

As in earlier years, change was the constant in the college. One of the brothers, Jacob Engel, departed on January 7 for a new assignment. He was one of the original Redemptorists who had come to Annapolis with Gabriel Rumpler in March 1853. At Brother Jacob's funeral in New York City in 1895, the eulogist, Father Joseph Wissel—another of the 1853 Annapolis pioneers—said that "Brother Jacob [was] another ornament amongst the lay-brothers of the American Province." With such a tribute, his story is worth relating here for the work he did in Annapolis and elsewhere. Jacob was born in Bavaria in 1829, arrived in the United States in 1851, and was admitted to the Redemptorists in New York City in 1852. A year later, he arrived in Annapolis where he was invested in the Redemptorist habit. A tailor by trade, Jacob—or James as he was sometimes called—was in charge of the tailor shop and served concurrently as porter and attendant reading brother of the novitiate. Jacob completed his second novitiate in 1856 and professed his final vows in 1857. After leaving Annapolis, he served at St. Joseph's Church in Rochester, New York, for nine years and then at St. Alphonsus Church in New York City for twenty-four years as sacristan, tailor, janitor, and porter. He died in Boston in September 1895.[8]

During his time in Annapolis, Jacob endeared himself to the novices and students with acts of kindness. An example of this emerges from a humble source, a small prayer card found in his personnel file at the Redemptorist Archives of the Baltimore Province. He obviously cherished the card since it survived among his meager belongings for some thirty-three years. The front of the card features an image of Jesus holding a communion host and embracing an angel, with the inscription *Ecce Panis Angelorum* (Behold the Bread of Angels). It was inscribed on the back in old German script by one of the students. The poem, which rhymes in the original German, translates as follows:

> Where the bond of sweet love is beautifully joined
> in the Sacrament;
> Where God reveals the love of the heart and gives
> it until the end,
> There our two hearts will be joined in prayer.
> When cross and pain press upon us,
> There may be our resting place.
>
> To beloved Brother Jacob
> from his unworthy confrere,
> Jos. Jas A. Kammer, C.S.S.R.

This was the same Joseph Kammer who had given the "complicated oration" on the occasion of Father Müller's feast day in September 1861 (see Journey into the Kingdom of Ideas, ch. 3). His poem indicates both a fondness for Brother Jacob and deep insight into the value of prayer, Holy Communion, and eternity, which he seems to have learned from the pious brother. Perhaps the card had special meaning for Jacob, not only because it was written by an erudite young man, but because Kammer became seriously ill several weeks after Jacob departed, and died in Annapolis in January 1863. Jacob's successor at St. Mary's was Brother Christopher Fröhlich, the younger brother of Hilary who was busy decorating the new altar. Christopher remained in Annapolis for twenty-two months and then was assigned to Pittsburgh. In later years, he worked at the new Redemptorist college in Windsor Springs, Missouri, where he died in 1899.[9]

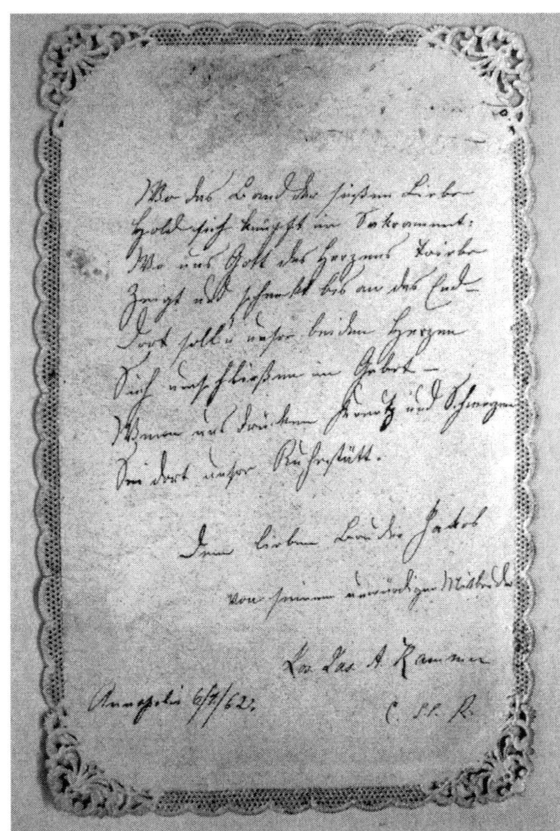

Reverse side of Frater Kammer's Ecce Panis Angelorum holy card. RABP.

Thirty-one-year-old Father Peter Zimmer arrived in Annapolis just before New Years 1862. He would leave his mark on St. Mary's and on the Redemptorist congregation for years to come. A native of Luxembourg, he had arrived in the United States in 1854 and proceeded directly to the novitiate in Annapolis where he professed his vows later that year. He went to study in Cumberland and was ordained to the subdiaconate on April 30 and diaconate on May 1, 1857, at Sts. Peter and Paul Church there by Bishop John Neumann. On June 6, Zimmer was ordained to the priesthood by Archbishop Kenrick at St. Alphonsus Church in Baltimore. His first assignments were to St. Philomena's in Pittsburgh and St. Alphonsus and St. Michael's in Baltimore. He became the subprefect of students and prefect of brothers in Annapolis on December 20, 1861. He gave his first sermon to St. Mary's parishioners—in English—on January 19, 1862. Father Seelos later noted that all the preaching and teaching at St. Mary's was "given only in English." The following June, Father Zimmer began to work closely with Seelos, the new head of the Redemptorist college.[10]

On January 8, Father Joseph Jacobs was reassigned to

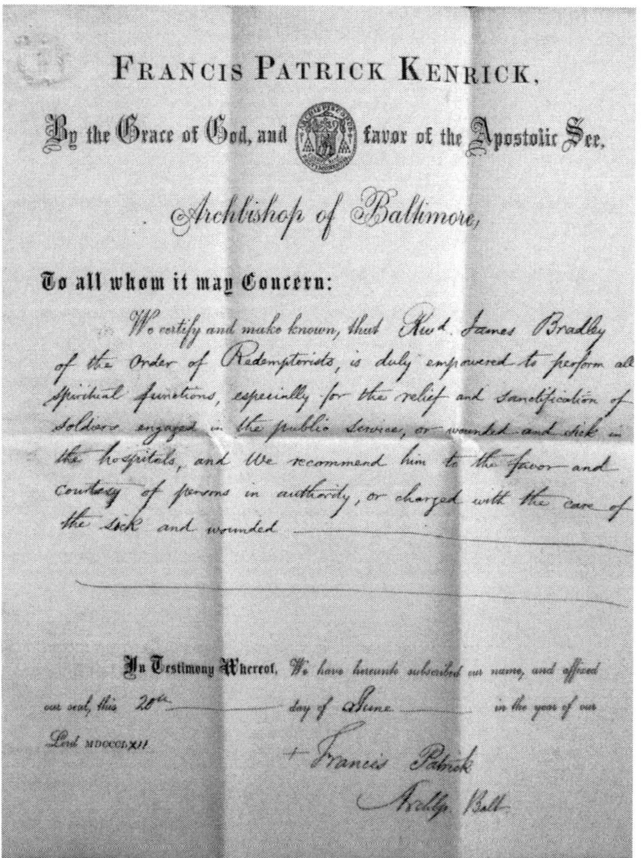

FRANCIS PATRICK KENRICK,

By the Grace of God, and favor of the Apostolic See,

Archbishop of Baltimore,

To all whom it may Concern:

We certify and make known, that Revd. James Bradley of the Order of Redemptorists, is duly empowered to perform all Spiritual functions, especially for the relief and sanctification of soldiers engaged in the public service, or wounded and sick in the hospitals, and We recommend him to the favor and courtesy of persons in authority, or charged with the care of the sick and wounded

In Testimony Whereof, We have hereunto subscribed our name, and affixed our seal, this 20th day of June in the year of our Lord MDCCCLXII

+ Francis Patrick
Archbp. Balt.

Father James Bradley's authorization to minister to "soldiers engaged in the public service." RABP.

English-language mission work. The *Chronica Domus* noted that Jacobs "was ready to depart the same day."[11] His time in Annapolis had been notable for his having attended the church cornerstone ceremony in 1858, the oration he gave at the Maryland State House on July 4, 1861, his work as professor of dogmatic theology and church minister, and as an unofficial chaplain to troops in and around Annapolis. As a parish priest, Jacobs officiated at thirty-one baptisms and three marriages between December 1858 and December 1861. Although he was assigned to give missions elsewhere, he continued to be carried on the Annapolis roster until January 1863. After leaving Annapolis, he traveled widely as a mission priest and, in New Orleans in 1867, became ill with yellow fever, during the same epidemic that would claim Father Seelos. But Jacobs recovered and returned to Annapolis in 1868 when he officiated at the baptisms of two converts, a former Lutheran, Henry Smith, and former Methodist and Revell in-law John Wesley Brady. Around 1873 Jacobs was dispensed from his Redemptorist vows and continued his ministry as a secular priest until he died in Rio de Janeiro in 1892.[12]

Jacobs' successor was Father James Bradley. He arrived in Annapolis on January 8 and quickly became involved in parish life as church minister and de facto pastor. As a native English speaker, Bradley was welcomed among the parishioners. During his first week at St. Mary's, he gave the Sunday sermon. He also preached on the Passion of Christ on Good Friday and delivered the main sermon on Easter. Bradley also taught moral theology in the college.[13]

Like Jacobs, Bradley ministered to the troops, but he wanted official status. As early as February 6, 1862, he petitioned Secretary of War Edwin McMasters Stanton for an official army chaplaincy for the pastor of St. Mary's. He explained that since April 20, 1861—the day the first Federal troops arrived in Annapolis—the pastor of St. Mary's had been "continually engaged in attending to the spiritual wants of the Catholic soldiers who formed part of nearly every regiment which came here." He said the services of the priest "have been called for by U.S. soldiers at all hours, and in all seasons" and that those services "have never been refused." He went on to note that in the performance of what he considered "an imperative duty," the priest:

> has been subjected to many inconveniences, arising, not from any disposition of men or officers but from the strict enforcement of the rules of army discipline, so that it was frequently, with great difficulty, he could procure admittance to a soldier who had called for his spiritual assistance, even at the hour of death.

The cause of this situation, he said, was that the pastor of St. Mary's was not an army chaplain and "consequently, cannot enjoy the privileges possessed by a regularly appointed chaplain." He said that as long as his services were confined to the former Naval Academy,

> there was not so much difficulty, but now, camps are scattered in different directions, and at different distances around the city, and, in consequence of bad roads, it is, sometimes almost impossible to reach them. I have walked for a distance of six or seven miles, through mud and rain, to visit a sick soldier; no horse would be granted going or returning. The Catholic Congregation here is small and poor, and of ourselves we have not the means of keeping a horse.

Pressing on with his request, Bradley said "it is a duty, imposed on us by charity, to respond to the call of any soldier who should need our assistance, and we intend, under any circumstances, to fulfill, as far as possible, this duty." He then asked: "Could not the pastor of this church receive the appointment of chaplain to the U.S. troops, so long as they should be stationed here?" Reaching for the height of reasonableness, Bradley said he would forgo "the salary arising from such an office . . . if it should not be considered perfectly just to grant it."

He offered to provide references from the "most respected citizens of this place," but suggested it was sufficient, at this point, to provide the recommendations of his religious superiors, Archbishop Kenrick and Father De Dycker.[14]

The War Department received Father Bradley's request and forwarded it to the Adjutant General's Office for a recommendation. The adjutant general, Brigadier General Lorenzo Thomas, replied to the War Department on March 7. He ignored the chaplaincy application, focusing instead on the request for a horse. He recommended that "the writer and his colleagues" be furnished by the quartermaster "with transportation in kind to and from the different camps around Annapolis whenever the services are called for by the soldiers." He suggested "that no obstacle be thrown in the way of their lending all spiritual assistance in their power to the Catholic soldiers in the neighboring camps." Such assistance, Thomas wrote, was "due to our soldiers, who have no Chaplains of their own faith with them, and due to the Gentlemen who are doing all the good they can gratuitously." Rather than accept Thomas' recommendation, the War Department returned the matter to him asking "what law or regulation would authorize the Secretary of War to grant the transportation asked for in this case." Thomas replied on March 17 that providing transportation to Bradley was a case of "unforeseen necessity . . . not provided for in any specific law or regulations." He stated that he was not recommending expenditure of funds to procure transportation in this case but that any large quartermaster depot always has "a considerable amount of the means of transportation allotted and which occasionally is lying idle." He closed with the analogy that if there was no medical officer available, "no officer would hesitate to employ the means of transportation in procuring for a sick soldier the services of a physician." He repeated his recommendation that "facilities should be extended where the sick soldier called for the services of a physician of the soul." No further evidence has been found of how or if, the War Department concluded this matter.

The issue of Catholic chaplains had come up early in the war. President Lincoln asked Archbishop Hughes in October 1861 for nominees for hospital chaplains and told one of them that he would seek authority from Congress to pay them at the same rate as regular army chaplains. He did this in his first annual message to Congress on December 3, 1861. Lincoln believed hospitalized soldiers had greater need for the services of a chaplain in their respective faiths than "the healthy soldiers in the field." Thereafter, Lincoln "strove for a nonsectarian policy in Congress regarding chaplain appointments." But the government appointed relatively few chaplains during the war. Instead it depended largely on regiments to provide their own chaplains from among their ranks. The United States Christian Commission, an interdenominational Protestant organization, was established in June 1861 to provide volunteer civilian chaplains and distribute Bibles and other Christian literature. The commission was largely evangelical in nature and eager to foster revivalism in the army ranks.[15]

Although Bradley did not receive an official US Army chaplaincy, on June 20, 1862, he was empowered by Archbishop Kenrick "to perform all spiritual functions, especially for the relief and sanctification of soldiers engaged in the public service, or wounded or sick in the hospitals." He now had an official church document to support his ongoing work among the soldiers in Annapolis.[16]

Quite a Few Showed Little Religious Spirit

Illness was a frequent visitor at St. Mary's College in 1862. On January 12, student of rhetoric Frater Andrew Ziegler was reported "sick and intensively so at times." Two days later, novice Brother Raphael Hartmann was "at the point of death, he lives, but suffers somewhat with serious convulsions." Raphael's illness was so grave that Mass was celebrated in his sick room on January 30. On April 14, Raphael (known as Valentine in civilian life) "was dismissed, to go away at the end of this month" because he had "spent much time in bed and gave up his vocation because of an incurable disease." He had been invested at Cumberland in 1858 but, as with most men who were dismissed from the congregation before profession, there is scant information about him. Further research turned up numerous men named Valentine Hartmann of his estimated age, both married and single, some in the Union army, but nothing conclusive has been found to match him with the brother once "at the point of death."[17]

"Now Frater Kammer is ill," the *Chronica Domus* reported in late January. Several months later, he was sent to Rochester to recover his health but the consumption was so advanced that he returned to Annapolis in September (see Devout Since Childhood, ch. 5). During the war, consumption was the leading cause of death in Maryland and throughout the United States.[18]

Illnesses continued to affect the Redemptorist students. Because of his health condition—unexplained in the house annals—Frater John Berger departed for Baltimore in June and did not return until September. Berger, however, had a relapse because two days before Christmas he returned to Baltimore for recuperation and stayed there until mid-April 1863. Andrew Ziegler was sent to Baltimore for health reasons on August 11. What his ailment was also was left unstated and it must have been a short stay in Baltimore because he was listed among the students when classes began again on September. Throughout this time, Father Peter Zimmer was assigned collateral duties as prefect of the sick. Surely he and the brother nurses were kept busy.[19]

February 1862 began with a day of recollection for the students. The same month a communication arrived from Father Nicholas Mauron—the superior general in Rome—with copies of the 1861 edition of the revised and updated Redemptorist Rule and Constitutions. Each member of the Redemptorist community was given their own copy. The community reportedly "responded with joy" at the receipt of letters from Mauron, because "they gave us encouragement in our vocations." Perhaps not all the students were joyful though and some found the new rules too difficult and even an impediment to their vocation.[20]

On February 8, "somewhat unexpectedly," John De Dycker arrived from Baltimore and stayed three days. Father Müller was absent in Baltimore but returned the same day that De Dycker departed, so perhaps the provincial was merely covering for the novice master during a brief absence. But soon after Müller's return, seventeen-year-old Joseph Dreisch's dismissal from the novitiate was announced. He later married Mary Elisabeth Schagemann, the sister of John Henry Schagemann who would be ordained as a Redemptorist priest in 1872. Dreisch settled into civilian life as a clerk in Baltimore and died in 1907.[21]

After Dreisch's departure, the remaining novices attended a one-day retreat. The house annals said that "the story of the Infant Jesus is too good an opportunity right now for us to not consider," and because St. Alphonsus encouraged it, they began to meditate on the birth of Christ on the twenty-fifth of each month. Thus, it became the custom in the novitiate to celebrate "Little Christmas" monthly on that date. However, three of the novices, unidentified in the *Chronica Domus*, did not participate in the retreat and two of them "were forced in obedience to withdraw for a full month in punishment" for unspecified errors.[22]

Perhaps like Dreisch, who was said to be lacking in vocation, the unidentified novices needed some serious contemplation of the new Rule if they were to remain. In March, the day before Ash Wednesday, novice Theodore Hentrich left the novitiate since he no longer felt a calling to the Congregation. He had been invested the previous year and, perhaps, was one of the two who had been forced to withdraw from community activities for a month. A few days later, two more novices were dismissed. One was Matthew McEnerny, who was allowed to remain at St. Mary's, wearing civilian clothes, until he could find a place to live and resume life as a layman.[23]

The other dismissed novice was Henry Jacobs. He had arrived at St. Mary's on the evening of July 27, 1861, and was greeted by his brother, Father Joseph Jacobs. Henry had been invested on December 25, 1860, at the Benedictine cloister of Maria-Hamicolt, in Dülman, Westphalia and had come to America to join the Redemptorists. Although Father Jacobs was happy to see his younger brother he was not pleased with Henry's lifestyle because "he did not show enough humility and self-abnegation—which are most necessary for Redemptorists." The elder Jacobs was correct and after only eight months, Henry was sent away. Coincidently or not, three days before his dismissal, letters were received from Maria-Hamicolt. What the letters contained was not recorded, but that fact that their receipt was noted in the *Chronica Domus* suggests they had negative information about the younger Jacobs. Now, he was dismissed and left "immediately" for Baltimore.[24]

The cycle of departures was still not complete. On March 15, a candidate lay brother, Joseph Kraemer, left the novitiate having "found our life too hard." He and his brother, Matthias, also a candidate brother, had arrived at the doors of St. Mary's only on January 6, 1862. Mathias returned home—"displeased with our life"—the following July.[25] On March 21, three more candidate novices were dismissed: Charles Mattingly, Peter Joseph Centner, and Charles Kenning. Many of these young men were those who had been invested and received into the novitiate on October 15, 1861. Their names, origins, and ages were all dutifully inscribed in the *Chronica Domus* on that date. But a later scribe, reviewing the deeds of the past, quoted Isaiah 9:3 about this novice class: "Thou hast multiplied the nation, and hast not increased the joy" (Isaiah 9:3). To this was later added a mournful note: "Out of this group, quite a few showed little religious spirit, as the future would show."[26]

Several of the men that the Redemptorist chronicler said "had given no indication of a vocation," went on to faithfully serve the Church for the rest of their lives as diocesan priests. Henry Jacobs was ordained in 1865 in the Archdiocese of Milwaukee, and was pastor of several parishes, where he reduced debts, founded a school and a hospital, and ended his days as pastor of St. Boniface Church in Manitowoc, Wisconsin. When he died there in 1881, the local press said he had "worked for the public good and the public, without regard to creed, mourn for his untimely death." Charles Mattingly went on to study at the Franciscan St. Bonaventure College in Allegany, New York, and was ordained in 1871 in the Diocese of Scranton, Pennsylvania. He founded St. Francis of Assisi church and school in Nanticoke, Pennsylvania, and served as its pastor until he died in 1882. Peter Centner and Charles Kenning found their vocations in married life, Centner in Pittsburgh as a carpenter and Kenning in Chicago as a building contractor.[27]

The timing of these dismissals may also have been keyed to the upcoming annual examinations overseen by the provincial in early April. Exams were held for students of dogmatics, ethics, rhetoric, and grammar. Several weeks later the results were revealed as the provincial sent word concerning which students would take which courses in the coming semester. Some needed private lessons.[28]

But all was not dismissals and examinations. Pre-Lenten observances were held with appropriate solemnity, including the celebration of Forty Hours devotion. On the Feast of St. Joseph (March 19), Father Wuest celebrated a special solemn Mass "for the spiritual and temporal welfare of our house." The same day, Father De Dycker arrived from Baltimore for an overnight visit accompanied by Father George William Wingerter, from St. Michael's Parish in Baltimore. Wingerter, visiting his old novitiate, expressed great pleasure in seeing so many young men studying for the priesthood. On the evening of the Feast of St. Joseph, Father Peter Zimmer returned home on the train from Washington, DC. He had gone there on March 15 to assist Father Alig with weekend Masses and may have conducted spiritual exercises for the parishioners.[29]

A glimpse of wartime parish life of the Annapolis laity was provided around this same time. The annals recorded that:

> Twice per week during the Lenten season the people say the "Stations of the Cross" followed by Benediction with opening of the tabernacle door of the Blessed Sacrament, at 7 P.M. Also on Sunday evening at the same hours there is a sermon on the passion of Our Lord Jesus Christ.[30]

Holy Week was marked with great solemnity that year. The annals noted that:

> All the rubrics of the Sacred Triduum were completed; in very powerful fashion. Part of the service was sung; part was recited; the office for Good Friday was used for

part of the sermon by Rev. Father Bradley on Christ's Passion; the Holy Saturday service was very transfixing with the "Exultet" [hymn of praise sung at the blessing of the Paschal candle] recited for lack of cantors.[31]

On Easter itself, "Solemn Mass was sung and Rev. Father Bradley preached. Nothing unusual happened." Despite the routine observances on Easter, the following week something out of the ordinary did occur. Father Zimmer had gone to St. Mary's Redemptorist "sister parish" in Baltimore, St. Michael's, to help with weekend confessions and masses. When he returned to Annapolis, he brought with him a new lay brother candidate who had been converted to Catholicism during a mission given by the Redemptorists. Martin Burke had been a baker in the army but now joined the Redemptorists taking the name Brother Ambrose. It is unclear whether he served in the army before or after the war began. Civil War soldier registries have entries for seven men named Martin Burke (from Pennsylvania, New York, Massachusetts, and Connecticut) who enlisted in the army prior to April 28, 1862, the date Brother Ambrose arrived in Annapolis, as well as two men by that name who enlisted in the army before the Civil War, one of whom had been rejected during basic training. In this time of war, however, it must have been of great interest to the other brothers at St. Mary's to have a former soldier in their midst. Ambrose remained in Annapolis until mid-June, when he was reassigned to Cumberland with a group of other candidate brothers. He later left the Redemptorists and was supposed to have sought his vocation with the Trappists in Canada but they have no record of him.[32]

Another unusual arrival was Father William O'Connor, a thirty-five-year old diocesan priest from Ohio. His interest in joining a religious order was the result of the "fruits of the missions" of itinerant Redemptorists. O'Connor immigrated from Ireland in 1848 and studied at the diocesan seminary in Cleveland. He was ordained in 1851 and assigned to parishes in Toledo from 1851 to 1860 and was pastor of St. Mary's in Youngstown, Ohio, from 1859 to 1862. After being released by the bishop of Cleveland, he was invested in Annapolis by Father Müller on June 9, 1862, and then departed for Cumberland for his novice year with Father Seelos. Unlike the above-mentioned unsuccessful vocations, Father O'Connor professed his Redemptorist vows in 1863 and worked on the missions from his home base in Cumberland until the Redemptorists left there 1866. Afterward he went to St. Alphonsus in Baltimore followed by mission work in New York City, Québec, and Boston where he was "the idol of the poor and afflicted" until he died there in 1899. But it was in Annapolis that O'Connor began his long career as a Redemptorist missionary and where his investiture was noted as "*Postero die*" (a day for posterity).[33]

A letter O'Connor wrote during the Civil War survives. On September 30, 1862, after he had been in Cumberland for three months, he wrote to an old friend in Ohio, a "Mr. Geratty," to whom he had promised to send a copy of "The Purcell & Campbell" debates. He had not done so because of "these war troubles which still continue and which prevent me as yet from sending it, as it may not go safe." He asked for the Geratty family's prayers and offered spiritual advice to pass on to various mutual acquaintances, including one Michael Coony, who had joined a secret society, which, O'Connor advised, he would have to renounce if he hoped to "die a Catholic."[34]

Another diocesan priest spent part of his novitiate in Annapolis and part in Cumberland. Andrew Andolshek was born in 1827 in Slovenia (then part of the Austro-Hungarian Empire). After immigrating to the United States, he served several years in frontier missions in Wisconsin and Michigan before being invested with the Redemptorists in Annapolis on November 13, 1861. In June 1862 he moved to Cumberland but left before his profession of vows. By 1863 he was pastor of a church in Knox Township, Clarion County, Pennsylvania, and in the ensuing years ministered in the dioceses of San Francisco, Green Bay, and Sault Sainte Marie and Marquette, the latter of which included parts of Ontario, Michigan, and Wisconsin. Although he did not become a Redemptorist, Andolshek fittingly ended his long secular career as pastor of Holy Redeemer Church in Eagle Harbor, Michigan, on an isolated peninsula on the shore of Lake Superior, where he died in 1882.[35]

Soldiers at Every Corner

Despite not being near the battlefront, Annapolis had its share of wartime problems. The huge influx of Union troops inevitably resulted in illegal and bad behavior. Many soldiers were young and away from home for the first time, far from the guiding hands of parents, community, and clergy. Public intoxication, thefts, brawls, trespassing, destruction of property, and other such disturbances were prevalent. When the legal sale of intoxicating beverages became problematic, the provost marshal banned their sale to soldiers and citizens alike.[36]

There also were houses of prostitution and gambling in town. An army hospital patient claimed he saw "wenches in every window" in Annapolis, an obvious invitation to vice. Soldiers causing disturbances could also have dangerous results for innocent passers by. In one instance, a provost guard on West Street fired his weapon at a soldier who had resisted arrest and fled. The shot came close to passers by and was a sign of "recklessness on the part of the Guard," according to the *Maryland Republican*.[37]

A New York infantry officer passing through Annapolis in June was disgusted with what and who he saw:

> The military have full possession of the city, and armed bands of soldiers meet you at every corner; while one person here, and another there, with an arm or a leg off, are seen in every street. . . . There are a few ladies, who turn up their noses in a very unladylike manner at the sight of a Union soldier, and who delight to spit on the American flag. . . . You may see a few men who put on airs, and declare themselves southern born; a sprinkling of mean whites, plenty of hungry, thieving sutlers, who would sell their country for gold . . . .[38]

The provost marshal's troops served as a military police force and did what they could to control the behavior of soldiers in and around Annapolis. Nevertheless, crime and unruly behavior continued. The priests at St. Mary's, like their peers at other churches, surely had concerns about the security of their property and parishioners. Father Seelos wrote later in the year that the soldiers "steal everything that they can get their hands on in the fields or in the houses." Obviously immediate security measures were needed and John Himmelheber was the man to take charge of them. He arrived with the first Redemptorists in 1853 and was thereafter always involved in parish affairs. Father Henry Borgmann wrote in 1904 that Himmelheber "was most of the time employed in the house and about the premises. In time of need he was always at hand to render assistance," which included digging graves at the parish cemetery. At one point, he and his family lived in the former Jesuit rectory on Duke of Gloucester Street before buying their own home on Prince George Street in 1857. In 1867 the family purchased a property close to St. Mary's, a Greek Revival house on Green Street. Now, in wartime, St. Mary's needed security and John Himmelheber provided it. According to family legend, Himmelheber, armed with a musket, guarded the property "against the troops."[39] Whether he was so employed before or as the result of the crime described next, is not known.

Edward Rice enlisted in New York City as a private, for three years, on August 29, 1861. He was assigned to Company F, Fifty-First New York Infantry Regiment, one of the regiments assigned to Burnside's Coast Division. Rice was no callow youth, fresh off the farm looking for adventure, but an Irish immigrant, unmarried, a tailor by trade, variously described as between thirty-five and forty years of age but obviously not willing to go into battle. He deserted from his regiment before it embarked on January 6 for the trip south.[40]

Rice did not flee the area, however, and instead committed a heinous crime against a St. Mary's parishioner. The *Sun* reported on January 14:

> The person of Alina Wineberg, a little child from six to seven years of age, was outraged a few evenings since by a private of the 51st New York regiment, named Rice. It is alleged he caught her on her way to the Catholic Institution, in the rear of the city, and took her in his arms, placed her in a small batteaux [*sic*], and crossed Spaw [*sic*] creek, where he detained her all night endeavoring to accomplish his designs. She is now lying dangerously ill, and he is confined in jail.[41]

Alina Wineberg actually was Alena Weinberger, daughter of Michael Weinberger and Maria Seidenberger, Bavarian immigrants and parishioners of St. Mary's. Known as "Lena" to her family, she was born in Baltimore in June 1855, shortly before the family moved to Annapolis. Three younger siblings (Maria, Anna, and John) were born in Annapolis and baptized at St. Mary's between 1858 and 1860. Alena's parents quickly made friends in the local German community and served as godparents for three newborns of German-born parents. Michael Weinberger was a carpenter by trade and had immigrated unaccompanied, arriving at Baltimore in 1853. When he tried to register to vote in the Annapolis city election in 1860 he was denied by the election judges as "non naturalized."[42]

The "few evenings since" in the *Sun*'s dateline (January 13) might have placed Alena's abduction near St. Mary's sometime between January 6 when Rice deserted and January 9 when his regiment finally departed for Hampton Roads, or a day or two later. Once his crime was discovered, he was quickly caught and put in jail. One might expect the army to have subject Rice to court martial. The laws of war governing the conduct of Union soldiers gave army judge advocates the authority to charge soldiers for depredations against civilian property, threatening civilians, attempted rape, and other such crimes. "But such charges were rare," writes military law code expert John Fabian Witt, who found only thirteen trials for such crimes between 1861 and 1865. However, other sources claim that Union military courts prosecuted at least 450 cases involving sexual crimes during the war.[43]

Rice was tried in the Anne Arundel Circuit Court on a charge of assault with intent to rape. Nicholas Brewer was the presiding judge, the prosecutor was Anne Arundel County state's attorney James Revell, and attorney for the defense was Edward Chandler Gantt. The grand jury met on April 15 and subpoenaed Michael Weinberger, John Wolf, and John Frank, each of whom later testified at Rice's trial. John Himmelheber also was subpoenaed by the state but did not testify. On April 22, the grand jury subpoenaed Alena Weinberger, who appeared with her father, as well as John Frank and John Wolf. The next day, a bench warrant was issued for Rice on a charge of "an assault upon Alena Weinberger with intent to commit a rape." Jurors were sworn in and heard the testimony on April 28 and 30. The witnesses included Alena herself; her father and mother; Adolphus M. Guinzburg, a Market Space clothing merchant from Bohemia who served as a German-language interpreter; Anne Arundel County sheriff William Bryan; John Wolf, a St. Mary's parishioner; John Frank and his wife, Ann, who were not parishioners but probably family friends (Anna Beller, godmother of two of the Weinberger children, served as godmother for John Frank Jr. in 1866); Henry Medford Sr., whose granddaughter, Mary Elizabeth Jones, was baptized at St. Mary's later in 1862; and Lydia Mason, a person of uncertain connection to the case. A guilty verdict was quickly reached and on May 9 Rice was sentenced to eight years in the state penitentiary in Baltimore.[44]

As sensational as the trial must have been, the press accounts were subdued. Rice was identified as the culprit but, other than the initial *Sun* article, Alena was identified as only "a German child six years of age" in other reports. Rice's indictment, trial, and sentencing were reported without embellishment. His prisoner record noted that he was illiterate, had been orphaned at age three, and had been bound in service until age twenty-one. It also revealed that Rice had been "occasionally intemperate" but had "attended church." He was released from prison in 1870 at the expiration of his term and no more is known about him.[45]

Alena's father, Michael, was enrolled for the draft later in 1862 but the medical examining board declared him "diseased" and exempted him from service. In 1862 he, his wife, and "two small children" were given a pass to travel by railroad to Baltimore. That is the last evidence of the family in Annapolis. Alena and her family eventually relocated to Dayton, Ohio. She married around 1872, had a son and a daughter, was widowed after 1900, remarried in 1905, died in 1926, and is buried in Dayton's Catholic cemetery.[46]

There were other less-serious court cases involving St. Mary's parishioners around this time. Thomas Denver was found guilty of assault and battery against Michael Jones and fined one dollar. Jones, as a sailor, was the son-in-law of the aforementioned Henry Medford and, although he was not Catholic, Jones' infant daughter, Mary Elizabeth, was baptized at St. Mary's on Christmas Day 1862. Denver was defended by James Shaw Franklin, whose father owned Rachel Smothers.[47]

In another case, Emma Sophia Murdoch, a Catholic child of six years, was old enough to have known that her Protestant father, William, was arrested for assault and battery against Nancy Frazier, a washerwoman. Despite testimony from the victim and four witnesses, Murdoch was found not guilty. The only defense witness was lawyer Alexander Randall, the brother of John Randall. Murdoch's attorney was Alexander Burton Hagner, the Randall brothers' nephew.[48]

St. Mary's parishioner Edward Walton had William Cook, a Black man, arrested on charges of drunkenness and disorderly conduct. Cook was fined one dollar and court costs. In July parishioner John Gunning had Samuel Bryan, a former slave, arrested for stealing his corduroy jacket. Sometimes the charges did not stick, such as in December when Gunning's hog was stolen. Upon examination of the case in court, however, the charges were promptly dropped. Edward's brother, Dr. Henry Roland Walton, made a grisly discovery on his father's farm just outside the city. There he found the body of an unidentified dead soldier with two bullets in his head.[49]

Doing the Union Party Injury

Colonel John Walton owned three farms in Anne Arundel County. One, purchased in 1856, was sixty-six-acres on the south side of the South River, next to the county alms house and the lower ferry and known as London Town Farm (see fig. 1). The other two were adjacent to each other, a quarter mile from the Annapolis city limits. He purchased the first one, a one-hundred-acre tract called Sandgate, in 1845. In 1858 Walton sold a half acre of Sandgate to the Redemptorists for "Five dollars and divers good causes and other valuable considerations" to use as a parish cemetery.[50] In 1860 Walton bought Part of Brushy Neck, a ninety-two-acre tract immediately south of Sandgate. The two farms were bounded on the north by today's West Street, on the east by Spa Road, and on the south and west by Forest Drive and Chinquapin Round Road. Several small streams flowing into Spa Creek divided the two tracts. Together the two tracts comprised the Walton's "garden farm," the produce from which supplied the City Hotel, with the rest sold at market. About half of the acreage was divided into five- and ten-acre lots for growing crops. These lots included twenty-five to thirty acres planted with corn, some for feed and some for the hotel and market. Two acres were used to raise potatoes and three acres for cabbage, celery, and turnips. Two to three acres were devoted to strawberries and seven acres to watermelons and cantaloupes raised from seeds originally given to Walton by a US Navy officer who brought them from Smyrna, Greece. Apple and peach orchards comprised about forty acres, with a total of 600 to 700 trees. Some ten to twenty acres of fields were used for growing oats. Clover and timothy grass were both planted in eight acres of low meadows near the creek branches and twenty-five acres in dryer, well-fertilized upland parcels. They produced hay and silage for farm livestock and the City Hotel's livery stable. A pond on Part of Brushy Neck provided ice harvested in the winter and stored in an on-site ice house for use by hotel guests during the summer. There also was a forty-acre strip of dense woods—about twenty adjoining acres on each farm—where chestnut, hickory, oak, and pine trees were preserved for timber and as protection from wind. Walton also kept cattle and presumably hogs and fowl there, as well as sheep for the hotel's daily "ram, lamb, sheep & mutton" dinner board.[51]

Substantial post-and-rail fences, both functional and ornamental, surrounded the farms on the exterior and divided individual garden plots on the interior. They were constructed from timber raised on the farm and consisted of series of eleven-foot-long panels. The exterior fence panels had five chestnut rails and two cedar or locust eight-foot-long posts to support them. The interior fencing had hemlock boards instead of rails and, as an expensive touch, was white washed on both sides. Walton's son Dr. John Randolph Walton managed and lived on the farm from 1862 to 1864, and later reported that his father "spared no expense in keeping this farm in first class condition." The farm reputedly was "brought to high fertility by years of judicious care and labor" and "on account of its fertility and its propinquity to market" and had "for many years been productive of great profit." A fellow county farmer familiar with Walton's property later testified that the soil was "a sandy loam and specially adapted to the raising of fruits and vegetables." The northern section was mostly level while the southern section comprised a more rolling landscape cut deeper where creek branches flowed through in declivities. There were two farm houses, two corn houses, a twenty-foot-long shed for storing wagons, carts, and farm implements, a sixty-foot-long cow shed with a hay loft, two horse stables, a large barn, the ice house, a mill shed, and small outbuildings. Walton's overseer was a St. Mary's parishioner, John Basnett. He lived in a farmhouse on Brushy Neck with his wife Catherine and three small children. Walton owned twenty-eight slaves, fifteen lived in the city and thirteen in the county. The farm hands lived in a slave house on the farm property. Walton's

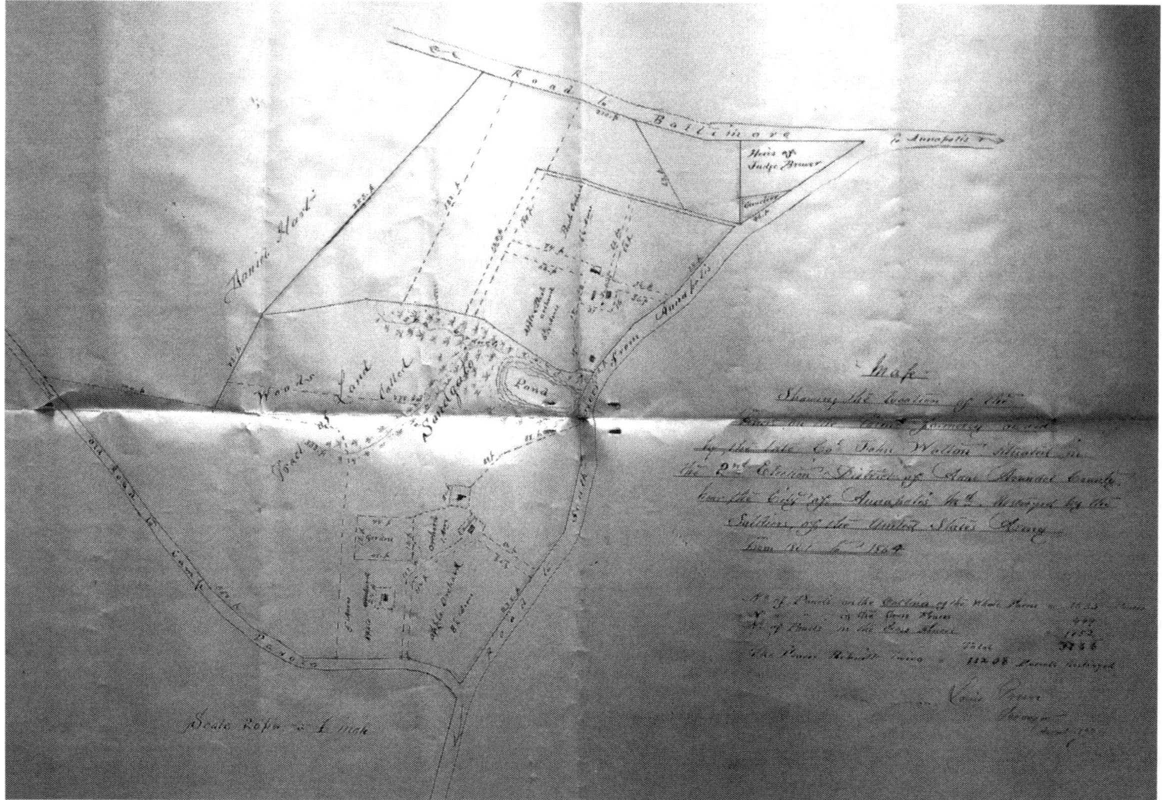

Survey map of Walton's farm, 1892. Entry 22, Box 995, CD 9419, Records of the U.S. Court of Claims, RG 123, National Archives, Washington, DC.

son Edward later testified that his father "prided himself on these farms and spent much time and money on them for the purpose of enhancing their value and making them productive."[52] All was well on this valuable and prosperous farm until the war began.

The first soldiers to occupy Walton's farm were among those assembled in Annapolis for Brigadier General Thomas West Sherman's amphibious expedition to Port Royal, South Carolina. Between 16,000 and 30,000 men reportedly were camped in and around Annapolis by mid-October 1861. Sherman himself boarded at the City Hotel. His Third Brigade, commanded by Brigadier General Horatio Gouverneur Wright, established Camp Walton on Sandgate and Brushy Neck on October 5–9. Wright's brigade comprised the Fourth New Hampshire, Sixth and Seventh Connecticut, Ninth Maine, and Fiftieth Pennsylvania infantry regiments, some 6,600 officers and men. About 7,000 more soldiers in Sherman's two other brigades were camped elsewhere.[53]

A member of the band of the Ninth Maine, Private John W. Warren, observed while at Camp Walton that:

> We are encamped in a rabid secession neighborhood and we hear a good many curses – but no one dare make any overt demonstrations. We have to keep a guard on the wells we draw water from, and exercise the greatest care to keep from being poisoned. The people are absolutely crazy with the din of secession.[54]

Another Ninth Maine private wrote home from Camp Walton about a "funeral" held for a hog slaughtered by the company cooks. Unfortunately, it was found to be "almost covered with magits." Whether or not it was one of Walton's hogs is not known. Sergeant Benjamin Franklin Whitten of Company B, Ninth Maine, reported to his family that while at Annapolis they lived in tents at Camp Walton. When time came for departure on October 18–19, they marched a mile and a half to the Naval Academy where they embarked on a steam tug that carried them out to the Bay to board ships bound for Fort Monroe. By the time the Third Brigade departed, the Walton farms had become a source of fuel from fences torn down by soldiers; an encampment, wagon-train park, and parade ground; and for learning military maneuvers and target practice. Further devastation was soon to come.[55]

After Sherman's division left for South Carolina, Brigadier General John Porter Hatch established his cavalry brigade headquarters in the Brushy Neck farm house. Camp Walton was occupied by Hatch's troops from December 1861 to March 1862 and, from early February to March 28. Hatch also commanded the Annapolis post. His brigade comprised at least three cavalry regiments: the First Massachusetts, First Vermont, and Fifth New York. Members of all three regiments called their encampment Camp Harris after one of their commanders. While there is evidence that part of this camp was located on farms located south of Brushy Neck, some of Camp Harris was on Walton's property. A private of the First Vermont said his regiment camped near the Fifth New York in a corn field, which may have been at Camp Walton, but moved to a tobacco plantation, which was not a crop mentioned in reference to Walton's farm. The fact is, the three regiments were temporarily brigaded together when camped near Annapolis and Camp Walton and Camp Harris were adjacent to or overlapped each other. Once the fences were gone, the only observable boundaries were rough country roads. The soldiers cut new thoroughfares through the farm which may have led to confusion about which camp they were in at any given time. On Sunday, January 5, 1862, services were held at Camp Harris by a Vermont Protestant chaplain. When a board of inquiry was appointed to investigate Walton's claims against the government in February 1862, it met at Camp Harris.[56]

One of Walton's principal complaints was the destruction of his fences. A Vermont trooper claimed "we were very saving of the fences of citizens" and obtained their firewood from the woods. However, most of Walton's fences were taken down and used for fuel during the winter of 1861–62. Some of the fences were kept for use in cavalry jumping practice. The Vermont troopers also performed both mounted and dismounted saber drills. The brigade's horses trampled across Walton's land and watered at the ice pond, not only causing damage to the land but tainting the water. Around-the-clock mounted guards patrolled the perimeters of the camps, further trampling the outer reaches of the farmland. Edward Walton later claimed he had seen 1,200 to 1,500 army wagons hauling supplies to the troops occupying his father's farm in the early months of the war.[57]

At the same time that Hatch's occupation, some of General Ambrose Burnside's troops also used Camp Walton until they departed for North Carolina in January 1862. One of Burnside's regiments identified with Camp Harris was the Fifth Rhode Island Heavy Artillery. Walton claimed that their mules and wagons daily crossed from one part of his farm to the other "completely destroy[ing] every particle of grass." After Sherman's Third Brigade departed in October 1861, Walton erected new fences, but they were again torn down. Although Spa Road, Chinquapin Round Road, and the Baltimore Road (West Street extended) surrounded most of Walton's property, the soldiers "took away the fences, drove in all directions to suit their convenience which made a public thoroughfare through both places, making roads, digging ditches, holes & wells where they encamped – they cut out timber wood for stables, cabbins [*sic*] & kitchens &c – burnt & destroyed all my vegetable garden." One of the farm houses was used as a hospital for the sick. Soldiers took sixty barrels of corn and the entire turnip crop and three tons of hay for human and horse consumption. They destroyed a pump, and took weather boarding from outbuildings and stole numerous farming implements "too tedious to mention" but later revealed to include four plows, four harrows, and two cultivators.[58]

General Hatch ordered a board of inquiry to investigate Walton's claim for damages. The board determined that he should be paid $1,200. Dissatisfied with this amount and anxious to recoup his losses and begin spring planting, Walton complained to Colonel Augustus Gardner Morse, Twenty-First Massachusetts Infantry Regiment, commander of the Annapolis army post, and a resident of the City Hotel. He wrote to Morse with the expectation that he would "obtain the rights and dues which the government properly owes me." He employed his status as a member of the Maryland House of Delegates by using its official letterhead for his complaint. Walton's main issue was that one of his "most valuable Servant men" had contracted small pox from the soldiers. The unnamed slave was under a local physician's care at Walton's farm house when he was forcibly removed by one of Sherman's officers. Although the thirty-two-year-old patient was then being treated by an army surgeon, he contracted a "violent cold" that resulted in an inflammation of the eyes and loss of sight. Walton lamented that "he is no longer of service to me, but on the contrary a dead expense," so he demanded compensation. Walton also reported that a "valuable young woman" belonging to him had been enticed by one of Sherman's Black servants to run away. In this case, Walton did not demand compensation. Burnside appointed a board of inquiry which in turn ordered a survey of the damages but not a valuation of what compensation might be offered. After Burnside's expedition departed, a second board was appointed by Hatch. It recommended that Walton be compensated for 1,351 fence panels (posts and rails) but at a rate much lower than Walton considered fair. The loss of ice alone had cost him $500 and, altogether, Walton lamented, $4,000 compensation "would even be a great sacrifice and loss to me."[59]

Walton had to resume farm production quickly to support his hotel. Morse told Walton to proceed with repairs to his farm since "there would be no more troops to disturb them." Walton had his fences repaired "at heavy expense," using timber he brought from his South River farm or that he purchased from neighbors. He planted new crops which flourished until there was a new setback. In late July, a hail storm destroyed much of his corn crop. Plus new troops had arrived in Annapolis and, by August 1862, Camp Walton was occupied again.[60]

July 1862 also brought the first paroled Union prisoners to Annapolis. They were soldiers who had been captured by Confederates and released after taking an oath not to bear arms again until they had been officially exchanged for similarly paroled Confederate troops. Initially, some 500 parolees camped at St. John's College, but by late August the number increased to 2,000. In September more paroled prisoners who had been incarcerated in Southern prisons began to arrive. To accommodate their growing numbers, a new parole camp was established, mainly on the 319-acre farm of Jacob Howard and his wife Araminta—bounded by Chinquapin Round Road (today's Forest Drive), a neighboring farm to the northwest (around today's Bywater Road), Church Creek, South River, Crab Creek, and another farm to the southeast—and partly on Brushy Neck.[61]

The *Maryland Republican* reported that on one day alone 5,000 parolees arrived in the Annapolis harbor on three ships from Belle Isle, a rocky island prison camp in the James River at Richmond. Three thousand more arrived the next day. By mid-September, 12,000 former prisoners reportedly were in the new Camp Parole. The ill and wounded were admitted to the army hospitals at the Naval Academy and St. John's College; others, after they were bathed and had received new clothes and gear at St. John's, were sent to the new parole camp where they lived in tents without adequate heat or sanitary facilities. Now free from prison, they wanted to be either mustered out of service and go home or returned to their units. When neither choice was possible (they first had to be officially exchanged for Confederate prisoners of comparable rank), the parolees became unruly. Lieutenant Colonel George Sangster, the parole camp commander, testified in reference to Walton's farms that "without sufficient assistance to keep them in proper control . . . they strolled from the camp, wandering over the neighborhood, causing great destruction." Sangster and another officer associated with Camp Parole noted that the camp was partially situated on Walton's farm, an assertion repeated in a later court case. Moreover, the second board of inquiry, appointed in February 1863, found that 628 panels of Walton's fence "was situated around the camp of Paroled Prisoners." Fences in adjoining fields of Walton's farm also were taken down by the soldiers and used for cooking fuel and building shanties that usually were burned down by the soldiers as they departed. Also, thirty-five bushels of seed potatoes were destroyed; had they been allowed to be planted and ripen, Walton estimated they would have produced between 400 and 500 bushels.

The *Maryland Republican* reported that the parolees did "not pay much attention to whose property from which they help themselves, as the farms around their camp can show." Walton's heirs later claimed that overall some ninety tons of hay were taken from Walton's farm and used as bedding for the soldiers and fodder for horses. They also claimed that soldiers built fires in the orchards, thus damaging the fruit trees. And, after all the apples and peaches had been taken, the soldiers cut down the trees for fuel. Some trees survived but bore blighted fruit in 1863 and 1864. Joshua Sevoy, a former slave testified years later that he passed the Walton farm daily during the war and heard the soldiers say "they were not going to stay there and freeze, and would burn up every damn fence rail on the place but they would make themselves comfortable." These soldiers either did not know or did not care that Walton was staunchly pro-Union and would suffer financially from these losses. Sevoy also observed that the soldiers built a bridge over the marsh leading to Walton's woods. They cut down Walton's best trees both for the bridge and a plank road they constructed to haul wagon loads of timber to adjoining camps. By the time the last soldiers left the farm in 1864, these woods were almost totally destroyed. As if this was not enough, caterpillars ravaged the fall vegetable crop.[62]

The impact on Walton's farm was immediate and he quickly raised the level of discourse by writing to Secretary of War Stanton. He informed Stanton that his "yield was prolific of all kinds of fruits ready, vegetables and farming crops generally" but when the paroled soldiers arrived they "destroyed nearly everything on the two farms, in spite, of my own attentions and the Guard of the 67th Pa. Regiment." He explained that his farms were "adjacent to the City and in a line to the Camp by the two Roads leading there – and these prisoners pass through the farms in going to & from the Camp & City – and have not only destroyed my property – But have threatened my Life as well as the overseers." John Basnett, "in open day was set upon by 5 of these men, who held him, robbed his house & trunk not only of provisions but took his clothes, put them on and wore them away leaving theirs." Making matters worse, the soldiers "threatened violence to [Basnett's] wife who fortunately escaped to the attic secretly and thereby saved her honor & Life." Walton exclaimed that "this kind of conduct is doing the Union party injury for miles around." The letter to Stanton ended saying the soldiers destroyed a large apple orchard "in full bearing" and a large peach orchard and that his watermelon and cantaloup crops "and all other kinds of gardening [were] totally destroyed." He demanded compensation of at least $2,500 for the crops. To support his claim, Walton asked Annapolis Mayor J. Wesley White to add his endorsement. White said the soldiers' "depredations and wanton destruction of property has been the cause of general complaint both in the City and surrounding County since they have been here & I am sure if the proper authority could apply a corrective it would be a source of satisfaction to all."[63]

By early 1863, Walton's farms "were again surrendered, with assurance from the commanding officers that their future use would not be required by the Government." Accepting that, Walton had new fences built a third time and crops planted. When Burnside's army returned to Annapolis in spring 1864 to prepare for another campaign, the farms "were necessarily reoccupied as camping grounds etc." With this occupation and others, which lasted until nearly the end of the war, the United States Senate Committee on Claims many years later concluded that "the farms were virtually destroyed . . . and were greatly deteriorated in value," the fences again gone, the orchards and cultivated fields devastated, and the ground "torn up by trenches and cesspools, and its use for former purposes was practically abandoned." In addition to the trenches dug for sanitary purposes, testimony was given that "in some places intrenchments [*sic*] [were] made for military purposes." These presumably were part of an advance line of rifle pits and breastworks constructed in July 1864 to ward off a threatened Confederate invasion (see Compelled to Shoulder a Musket, ch. 6).[64]

Three boards of army officers had been appointed between 1862 and 1865 to assess damages done by the soldiers to crops, buildings, and fences, and for rent of the land. In 1867 a detailed report of the findings was submitted by one of the army's Quartermaster General's Office bureaus to the Quartermaster General. It stated that the two Walton farms had been "taken possession of" from October 15, 1861, until December 1, 1864, "with a few intervals which cannot be definitely stated." It said that Walton "was thrice put to great expense in these particulars" during the war and again after his property "was finally delivered to him" in December 1864. It was revealed in addition to the damages detailed above that two acres of white oak and three acres of pine (a total of 100 cords of timber) had been cut down and fruit from the claimed 670 apple trees and 600 peach trees had been taken and the trees damaged.

Post commander Colonel Morse, in supporting Walton's claims, called Walton "a firm and decided Union Man." The 1863 board of inquiry noted "the loyalty and uncomplaining submission of Mr. Walton regarding the losses sustained by him from the Govt. occupation of his property." The parole camp commander, whose men had so heavily damaged Walton's property, urged his superiors to pay for the damages done to the farm of a man who "so earnestly & faithfully sustain[ed]" the Federal government. Before he departed from Annapolis in April, at the start of the Overland Campaign, a hard-fought series of eleven major battles between May 5 and June 24, 1864, Burnside wrote that the money already paid to Walton—"one of the great Sufferers"—did not compensate him "for anything like the necessary loss he was subjected to." These and other supporting documents were submitted by Walton's attorney in December 1866 to the quartermaster general. A Senate committee later reported that Walton had been "in constant and intimate intercourse with officers of the Union Army; was admitted to their counsels in regard to the movements of army. . . . and gave valuable information and advice." A friend of Walton's and a colleague when they served together in the House of Delegates, Daniel Randall Magruder, said Walton had an "uncompromising boldness and firmness" in legislatively supporting the Union cause.[65]

A number of army officers who had been stationed in Annapolis wrote letters supporting Walton's war claims. All of them, including Burnside, indicated Walton's unswerving and devoted loyalty to the United States and thanked him for his assistance to them during their time in Annapolis. Two prominent local civilians, Maryland attorney general Alexander Randall and Annapolis postmaster Thomas Ireland, swore to Walton's loyalty to the United States Government. Despite such support, his war claim was never fully paid. In October 1865, Walton was informed by Assistant Adjutant General Edward Davis Townsend that claims for damage to "fences, farms &c. by the U.S. Troops, cannot be paid from any appropriation yet made." He was advised to "resort to whatever appropriation, and whatever tribunal Congress may hereafter provide, for the settlement of claims for damages."[66]

By then governor of Rhode Island, Burnside wrote again in 1866 in support Walton's "just claim"and testified that Walton had given gave him "all the aid in his power" during his two sojourns in Annapolis. But no action was taken until early 1867 when the Office of the Chief Quartermaster sent an officer to personally investigate and gather "evidence elicited from citizens of Annapolis" concerning Walton's claim. The statements of the officers noted above also were taken into consideration. A nine-page report reviewed the entire case and declared Walton's claim "a just one" and that he was "entitled to a speedy settlement." The claim amounted to $17,084.66 (between $2 million and $4 million in 2019 dollars, depending on how and for what the losses are calculated). It was an amount that others testified "[would] not cover his losses." However, the report concluded that the "Q.M. or any other particular Bureau cannot be charged with all [the damages and deprivation of use]; as but [only] part of the area of the farms was actually occupied and then not continually, but occasionally as circumstances demanded." An initial assessment by the Quartermaster General argued that the fencing taken and other destruction was done not "by authority . . . [but] by the unauthorized acts of troops" and therefore was not covered by appropriations. Also not covered and considered "a total loss" by Walton was that throughout the occupation of his farm he had employed ten workers "at wages and subsistence" on the "almost daily hope" of regaining his farm, but he acknowledged he would not obtain compensation for this expense. A subsequent thirteen-page report said the best the Quartermaster General could pay was three years rent—$1,620—less than 10 percent of what Walton expected. When the Treasury Department reviewed the case, a payment of $3,055 was initially recommended and then, taking "a more just view of the obligation," the amount—based on the market value of the land but excluding damages—was increased to $4,860. The War Department objected to the increase but it was sustained by Treasury. The "rent" was finally paid but the claim for damages was disallowed.[67]

John Walton died in 1871 and his eldest living son, Dr. Henry Roland Walton, was appointed administrator of the estate. The younger Walton reopened the case in 1873 with a claim for "stores and supplies." It was rejected by both the War Department's Commissary General for Subsistence and the Quartermaster General, which were satisfied for having paid rent for the property. He appealed through his Fifth District congressman, Eli Jones Henkle, who introduced a bill in January 1876 "for the relief of the heirs of John Walton, late of Annapolis. It authorizes the payment of $12,224.66 to said heirs for damages to property, destruction of fruit, crops, &c. by United States troops while quartered ons aid Walton's premises." The bill did not progress and another eight years passed before Walton renewed his effort with a new petition to House of Representatives in 1884. The claim was reviewed by the House Committee on War Claims, which noted that the War Department had already declined to consider the full amount as "beyond its jurisdiction" and reported that the claim was "a stale one and ought not to be allowed." The committee thus returned an adverse report.[68]

Despite this rebuff by Congress, it was not the end of the Walton claim. In 1886 Walton's lawyer again petitioned the House of Representatives and a bill for compensation of $12,224 was introduced by Fifth District Congressman Barnes Compton. The bill was read twice and referred to the Committee on War Claims, which duly forwarded the matter to the United States Court of Claims in Washington, DC, early in 1887. The Court of Claims had been established in 1855 to settle private claims against the Federal government and its jurisdiction had been expanded in 1883 via the Bowman Act to relieve Congress of having to address the large influx of war claims. Walton's claim was added to the court docket. Five years passed with no action and Walton's attorney filed several new motions. One of them listed, among other losses, a total of

11,208 fence panels destroyed and asked for a total compensation of $28,609. Another petition was submitted to the court in July 1894, claiming $20,379. In October depositions were taken in Annapolis before notary public John Randall Magruder on the part of the claimant. Attorneys for both the complainant and the US Government questioned witnesses, who included a surveyor, two local farmers, two Walton sons, a carpenter, and Magruder's uncle, Judge Daniel Randall Magruder, formerly of the Maryland Court of Appeals. One of the farmers was Joshua Sevoy who passed the Walton farm daily during the war until April 1864 when he enlisted in the Thirtieth USCT and went off to war with Burnside's Ninth Army Corps (see African American Enlistments, ch. 6). Among evidence submitted this time was a detailed survey map showing the exterior lines and subdivisions of the Walton farm and the locations of buildings, orchards, and timber land between 1861 and 1864. Testimony by the surveyor indicated there were 3,736 exterior and interior fence panels. One of the October deponents, Judge Magruder, had served with Walton in the House of Delegates in 1861–62. He testified that Walton was "an avowed, pronounced and decided Union man, zealous and active in behalf of measures for the suppression of the rebellion." Magruder's cousin, Alexander Burton Hagner, by then an associate justice of the Supreme Court of the District of Columbia, gave an effusive deposition on November 2. He noted his long friendship with Colonel Walton, saying he "was a very decided character and his straightforward and downright English manner made him very attractive to me." Hagner said Walton was never afraid to tell his honest opinion, free from deceit, and "an inveterate Democrat" whose political opinions "seemed to be intensified by the Know Nothing excitement." When the Civil War came, "he heartedly disapproved of secession," from the start was "an out-and-out Union man" who "deserted his old party affiliations," and at every Union meeting or procession "he was one of the most prominent participants. . . with his hat off and hurrahing for the Union." Nevertheless, the court found that the Bowman Act did not provide an "adequate remedy" to Walton's claim.[69]

No further court proceedings took place until after another bill for the relief of the Walton heirs was submitted in January 1895 by Maryland Senator Arthur Pue Gorman authorizing the Treasury Department to pay Walton's heirs $20,379. It was referred to the Committee on Claims in February but died there. Gorman renewed the bill in January 1896 and this time the Committee on Claims took action. It invoked the provisions of the Tucker Act (enacted in 1887) which gave the Court of Claims additional jurisdiction and Congress again referred the Walton claim to the court. The complainant's lawyers filed briefs with detailed descriptions of the claim, copies of depositions, and transcripts of letters assuring the court of Colonel Walton's loyalty. The government lawyers responded a year later with a motion to dismiss *res judicata,* because the case already had been adjudicated and was not subject to be pursued further by the same parties and that, even though the original petition had been submitted under the Bowman Act and the new petition under the Tucker Act, they actually were the same case. Walton's lawyers protested and the court overruled the government's motion to dismiss, giving the claimant's lawyer thirty days to proceed. He did so and asked that the evidence in the two cases, being the same, be considered by the court.[70]

There were arguments back and forth about the merit of the claim. The government gave the court a lengthy point-by-point rebuttal, saying some of the evidence was "very defective," that the property had been occupied by proper military authority; that Walton had already been properly compensated in 1868 and that the rent paid included use of "the fruits of the land"; and that the award made had been done "in the most sympathetic and generous spirit." The government lawyers also pointed out discrepancies between statements made in the original 1860s claim documents and the statements in the 1890s petitions. The government's findings of fact declared that an additional $5,083 was adequate compensation for the diminished value of the land, given that $4,860 had been paid thirty years earlier. Walton's lawyers accepted some factual points but insisted the government made "errors in law and fact" and that the testimony of their witnesses was "unimpeached and unimpeachable." The Court of Claims, however, sustained the government's proposed payment of $5,083. Walton's lawyers requested and were allowed a new trial but the court again found for the government. At that point Walton's lawyers submitted a motion, agreed to by the Justice Department, to transmit the findings of fact to the Senate.[71]

It was another four years before Congress appropriated the funds to pay the Walton estate's award of $5,083. It did so as part of an omnibus bill to settle claims under the Bowman and Tucker acts for some 280 individuals and estates in twenty states and territories. The Walton family, however, was busy in the meantime, not waiting for what they perceived was partial payment. In 1899 Senator Gorman introduced a new bill for the relief of Henry R. Walton and again it was referred to the Committee on Claims. The next year Maryland Senator Lewis Emory McComas introduced a similar bill, for $10,786 compensation, and again it was referred to committee. As before, nothing happened and McComas introduced it again in 1901. Although the Court of Claims decision on Walton's claim had been received in the House of Representatives in 1898, no action was taken so Maryland's Fifth District Congressman Sydney Emanuel Mudd submitted a similar bill in the House of Representatives in 1900. The omnibus bill was finally approved in 1902 but still the Waltons were not satisfied. McComas sought an appropriation in 1903 for $10,786 but it never made it out of committee. In 1906 the Court of Claims reported to Congress that the Walton claim had a "date of dismissal" of June 10, 1901. No further action was taken and the effort to be fully compensated for the war claim was at an end more than forty years after the first damages were done by soldiers at Sandgate and Brushy Neck. Walton received $4,860 in 1868 and his heirs received an additional $5,083 in 1902, an amount less than half of the $20,379 claimed in 1894. In the meantime, Edward Walton, the new owner of the two farms, sold two small parcels of it in 1873 and 1876 to the Redemptorists to enlarge their cemetery, and most of the rest of the farm in 1875 and 1876 to individuals who developed the property.[72]

Unstated in the voluminous US Court of Claims documentation is whether or not any damage was also done to St. Mary's Cemetery. That was not the case, however, with land adjacent to the cemetery that was later purchased by the Redemptorists to further enlarge the burial ground. That parcel was part of Judge Nicholas Brewer's vegetable and flower garden and had on it a two-story dwelling house. According to the Brewer family's US Court of Claims case, Union troops "occupied the dwelling for hospital purposes," which means they also used the surrounding land and its produce. The Brewer heirs sought payment of rent for the house along with other parts of the family's "first class market and truck garden." In 1901 the Redemptorists purchased a 1.9-acre piece of the Brewer garden on which the old house was located. Ten years later, they razed the old house to expand the cemetery. Other parts of the cemetery expansion, acquired in 1875 and 1878 had been parts of John Walton's farm, which was heavily used by Union troops throughout the war. Although the troops may have respected the original cemetery land purchased in 1858, they likely made extensive use of the parcels acquired later by the Redemptorists.[73]

The Thunder of Cannons

The initial fears that the Confederate army might attack Cumberland dissipated when Federal troops occupied the strategically located city the previous June. By January 1862, the situation was worrisome for another reason: the city was "crambed [*sic*] full of soldiers." Sometimes "the thunder of cannons could be distinctly heard" by the Redemptorists who also saw wounded soldiers carried into the city. Then Father Seelos shared ominous news with his confreres in Annapolis when he warned that the Union army was threatening to occupy the Redemptorist house of studies. An army surgeon and quartermaster officer had arrived without notice to examine the Cumberland studentate with plans to turn it into a hospital. But after speaking with Father Van de Braak, they decided the rooms were too small and the whole place poorly ventilated. The immediate pressure was off, but the fear that the authorities might still seize their property lingered among the Redemptorists as did fear of wartime depredation against the seminary. In March Van de Braak bought a watch dog to help secure the property.[74]

A major realignment of the Annapolis and Cumberland houses had been under discussion since Verheyen's canonical visitations to both cities in 1860. Now, "for mighty reasons"—the anxieties caused by the war—confronting the Redemptorists, the realignment idea was renewed. Verheyen thought Annapolis offered a more modern facility and better climate than Cumberland. Some of the advanced students of philosophy and theology and those suffering from pulmonary problems already had been transferred there. But nothing formal was done until January 1862 when De Dycker wrote to Mauron in Rome asking him to revisit the idea of uniting all the upper- and lower-level students in Annapolis and sending the novices to Cumberland. It was reasoned that the young men in the novitiate could survive a short stay in the colder climate of Cumberland and then move back to Annapolis for their advanced studies. Although nothing was said about the dangers of war being less in Annapolis and greater in Cumberland, this factor must have played a role in the decision. The students, in whom the Redemptorists had a much greater financial and emotional investment, would be further from the war front. De Dycker received Mauron's approval of the realignment in early April. He did not act immediately because he hoped to be relieved as provincial and had suggested as his successor, in order of preference, Michael Müller, Maximus Leimgruber, or Francis Seelos. Instead, Mauron general reappointed De Dycker who then carried out on the realignment.[75]

News of the imminent changes was received by Seelos in Cumberland on May 18 and, on May 20, Müller was summoned to Baltimore to be similarly informed. Müller was aware that if De Dycker was reappointed the realignment would occur. But he also learned that Seelos was to be appointed rector (a promotion from superior, the title Müller held) in Annapolis and prefect of the senior students (those studying theology). Peter Zimmer, who was already in Annapolis, was appointed prefect of the younger students (those studying humanities and philosophy). Müller was to become superior and novice master in Cumberland. He had a large stake in Annapolis and was unhappy with the changes. Moreover, he learned that had he stayed in Annapolis, he would have been promoted to the new position of rector of St. Mary's. He told De Dycker that Seelos was not a good prefect for the students and the realignment was not a good idea. He argued for a delay in the transfer at least until the end of the current term in August. De Dycker held firm, and on May 21, he and Müller took the B&O train to Cumberland so Müller could start making preparations for his relocation. Müller returned to Annapolis "deep in gloom" on May 23 to reveal to his confreres the change that was about to take place. He also wrote to Mauron to state his objections.[76]

The realignment was supposed to take effect immediately but the war caused delays. Father Wuest, who also was to be reassigned from Annapolis to Cumberland, set out in advance on May 26, but when he reached Relay House by train to transfer to the Cumberland line, he learned that westbound trains were not running "because a battle closed the road." Union forces had been defeated at the First Battle of Winchester on May 25 and had retreated first to Martinsburg, Virginia (now West Virginia) and then to Williamsport, Maryland. When the Union troops abandoned Martinsburg, B&O employees also fled, leaving the line to Cumberland inaccessible. On May 28, Confederate forces led by General Thomas Jonathan "Stonewall" Jackson burned the B&O bridge at Martinsburg, thus closing the rail line that Wuest would have used. According to a modern-day historian, the recalcitrant Müller "began to think God was intervening."[77]

With no way to reach Cumberland, Wuest went into

Baltimore City instead to seek De Dycker's advice. On May 30, Wuest returned to Annapolis, accompanied by De Dycker, to decide upon "a more opportune time to depart." The final novice investiture ceremony was held on June 9 and, between June 10 and June 16, Wuest, the novices, and both professed and candidate lay brothers, with the rail line reopened, departed for Cumberland. Müller left on June 12, sad to leave his beloved St. Mary's and foreseeing "the ruin of the American Redemptorist foundations" with Seelos in charge of the seminary.[78]

Before the departures for Cumberland took place, three more novices were dismissed, with no reasons stated. They included Henry Singer, from New York, and Francis Theodore Heidenis, from the Netherlands, both sixteen years old. Although Singer's later days have not been discovered, Heidenis appears to have settled into married life and died in Patterson, New Jersey in 1886. The third dismissed novice was twenty-year-old John Bausch from the Duchy of Nassau, who found his religious vocation elsewhere. Unlike the other two who were dismissed, Bausch returned to the Redemptorist congregation. After a renewed novitiate in Cumberland, he professed his vows in 1863, returned to Annapolis in 1864, and received tonsure and minor orders in 1865. Although he was dispensed from his Redemptorist vows in 1868, his religious vocation was not lost. He joined the Carmelite fathers and was ordained in 1869 as Father Norbert Bausch, O.C.C. He served at Sts. Peter and Paul in Cumberland after the Carmelites took it over from the Redemptorists in 1866. He had left the Carmelites by 1887 and became a priest (as John N. Bausch) in the Diocese of Pittsburgh and later served as pastor of St. Alphonsus Church (named for the Redemptorists' founder) in Wexford, Pennsylvania. Bausch died in 1917 in Johnstown, Pennsylvania, where he had served for nineteen years as pastor of Immaculate Conception Church. His connection to the Redemptorists did not end in 1868. His brother Peter was ordained a Redemptorist priest in 1875.

Father Seelos was assigned to St. Mary's, Annapolis from June 1862 to September 1863. RABP.

Several days after Bausch's departure, Brother Louis Sterkendries left Annapolis for New York City. His carpentry work on the high altar was complete and other embellishments in the new church were advanced enough that Brother Louis was sent off on a temporary assignment. He returned to Annapolis in August and stayed, except for brief trips to perform carpentry elsewhere, until 1864 when he was reassigned to St. Joseph's Church in Rochester, New York.[80]

The Great Evacuation

Faculty and students from Cumberland began to arrive in Annapolis on June 12, the same day Father Müller departed. The Cumberland chronicle called the move the "great evacuation of Cumberland." The vanguard was led by Father Van de Braak and included five students and Brother Paul Steinfeldt, who was no stranger to Annapolis. He had been part of Rumpler's first contingent in 1853, and served as a cook until 1855 when he was transferred to Cumberland where he worked as a gardener. Back at St. Mary's, Brother Paul resumed his cooking duties. For Van de Braak, however, St. Mary's was a new experience, having been there only once before, while on vacation in 1857. He was born in the Netherlands in 1820, ordained there in 1848, and, after teaching theology at the Redemptorist college in Wittem in the Dutch province of Limburg, migrated to the United States in 1852. In Annapolis, as in Cumberland, he was a busy man: consultor to the rector, admonitor (responsible for keeping the rector informed of lapses in observance of the Redemptorist Rule), lector of moral theology, and prefect of visitors (responsible for the accommodations and comfort of house guests).[81]

Seelos and the final group of six students and two brothers set out on June 13 on a frightening trip. First their train crossed the bridge at Martinsburg that had been burned by Jackson's troops just two weeks before but had been quickly rebuilt. They proceeded to Harpers Ferry where they saw utter destruction. In April 1861, withdrawing Federal troops had burned the arsenal and destroyed weapons and munitions rather than let them fall into rebel hands. Then in June, the Confederates entered Harpers Ferry and burned more buildings and destroyed the railroad bridge crossing the Potomac River from Virginia into Maryland. The B&O workers rebuilt the bridge but in September it was carried away in a flood. By late March 1862 they had rebuilt the bridge, but it was "carried out by high water" from massive spring floods and again out of service between April 22 and June 15. Thus the train passengers had to brave the crossing the river in open boats.[82]

After they arrived in Annapolis, Seelos related what they had seen:

> On my trip from Cumberland to Annapolis, I was able to see with my own eyes the devastation that this war has caused right near us. At Harpers Ferry, a very beautiful and romantically situated town, the finest buildings, the big arsenal, and large factories, as well as the magnificent railroad bridge, were totally destroyed. We

and all the passengers could only be brought over the Potomac, a very rapidly-flowing river, on a flat-bottomed boat. The Potomac forms the boundary between Virginia, which has declared for the South, and Maryland, which in sentiment is also for the South but is in the possession of Northern troops.[83]

On June 14, De Dycker arrived in Annapolis, accompanying three students who had stopped over in Baltimore to see their parents before they went on their new home on Spa Creek. The *Chronica Domus* notes that "at 3 P.M. Very Rev. Father Seelos arrived to take up the post of rector of this house and was received, according to the Rule, in the presence of the whole community and the Very Rev. Father Provincial."[84]

The Annapolis to which Seelos returned was a much different place then when he had last seen it in 1859. The new church and college building had been completed and the old church was being used as a parish hall. The city was the scene of great wartime activity, with the outskirts filled with troop encampments, the once quiet harbor bustled with military transports, and the railroad line connecting Annapolis to Baltimore and Washington had become a strategic military route. The Naval Academy was gone and its buildings and those of St. John's College had been turned into army hospitals filled with battlefield casualties and sick troops. A new burial ground, across from St. Mary's Cemetery was filling up with the war dead.

A Most Loving Father

As related earlier, Father Seelos had been in poor health in 1857 and, as a result, was reassigned briefly as novice master in Annapolis. Now, after more than five years as prefect of students in Cumberland, he was reassigned to Annapolis. His tenure at St. Mary's reveals much about the man and the times. When he took charge on June 14, he was rector of a community of ninety-three men. These included nine priests, sixty-five professed students of all academic levels, and nineteen lay brothers with numerous skills.[85]

One of the students—Frater John Berger—wrote to his sister in Bohemia about a month after Seelos arrived. He called his new superior "a most loving father" and said that although the large community was a "lovely burden" for Seelos, he (Seelos) found "the sweetest consolation for his heart, that he sees how they are zealous with the most intimate love in and for God."[86]

To better manage such a large community, Seelos established three divisions. The first was composed of thirty-one advanced theology students with himself as prefect. He also served as lector of church history, exegesis, and hermeneutics. The second division included the other thirty-four students, with Father Zimmer as prefect. Zimmer also taught dogmatic theology and served as prefect of brothers and of the sick. The third division was the priests and brothers. Each division functioned separately from each other except for morning meditation, conferences, meals, and night prayers. Students were required to make their confession to their respective prefects once a month but they were advised also to confess occasionally to one of the other priests and three or four times a year to the rector. Students attended Mass in the third-story seminary chapel while the brothers attended Mass in the choir loft of the church. Both groups received communion in the chapel out of public sight.[87]

Father Ferreol Girardey, C.Ss. R. (1839–1930). Denver Province Archive at RABP.

With Father Seelos in charge of St. Mary's College, classes were held only in the morning and for the rest of the day the students participated in physical recreation, put on plays, worked among the military forces in town, and performed manual labor. The students also had free access to the college library and engaged in debates. Seelos had the students clean the church and the college building, care for the sacristy, and serve as infirmarians. In cold weather, they also shoveled coal for the fireplaces, sometimes as much as three hours a day, with the rector helping them. They were rewarded for their labor by Father Seelos with coffee and cream tarts.[88]

Besides Fathers Seelos, Van de Braak, and Zimmer, six other priests were assigned to St. Mary's as of June 14. They were James Bradley, the number two man on the roster who continued to serve as church minister and de facto pastor. John Cornell was absent in New York from June 2 to around mid-July. Joseph Jacobs also was absent having been assigned to mission duty. Adam Conrad Kreis, the church prefect, had come from Cumberland in April 1862 but, in late June, was reassigned to St. Michael's in Baltimore and was succeeded as church prefect by Zimmer. Rounding out the priestly assignments were two newly ordained men: Joseph Theodore Henning, lector of rhetoric and mathematics, and Ferreol Girardey, lector of philosophy and subminister of the church. Their ordinations at St. Alphonsus Church in Baltimore, had just occurred on June 11, with Archbishop Kenrick presiding. According to one of his confreres, Girardey "often boasted that he was going to give it to the people, that he would pepper them" in his sermons. Seelos knew this energetic new priest well since he had been one of his students in Cumberland, and sometime after he arrived in Annapolis, he thought Girardey needed a bit of gentle tempering. So "not once but several times," Seelos told him '*Ganz gefehlt, ganz gefehlt lieber Pater*' (All wrong, completely all wrong, dear Father)." This tempering advice must have resonated because Girardey continued on to a long and devoted service with the Redemptorists.[89]

Zimmer related another episode that illustrated the humility in Father Seelos' acceptance of small sacrifices and the state of poverty. He told how "on account of poverty, there were no suitable side altars in the church, but only altar tables, crucifixes and rough wooden ornaments and candle-sticks, for which reason none of the Fathers liked to read mass at them." Seelos had appointed "a certain Father" to make the assignments for times and particular altars for priests to offer daily Mass. Thinking that if he routinely assigned Seelos to one of the undesirable side altars, he and the other priests would benefit from the changes that the rector would certainly require. Surely he would order better candlesticks. Making such assignments normally would be the responsibility of the church prefect, who happened to be Zimmer himself. Zimmer had known Seelos since they were friends in Munich but he did not yet know his man as well as he would later. Seelos, "without a word of opposition,. . . was entirely content" with saying Mass at the lowly, poorly lit side altars.[90]

Father Seelos also took his personal pastoral ministry into the neighborhoods of Annapolis. In one documented instance, he was brought "by a lady in Annapolis" to visit a poor, sick Black woman. As he climbed a ladder to reach the woman's upper chamber, a swarm of bees buzzed around his head, but "he heeded them not." When he reached the sickroom, he was so moved by the woman's condition that he exclaimed, "O sweet poverty!" The sick woman was consoled by Seelos' spontaneous reaction and became more accepting of her own poor situation. Seelos is said to have thus strengthened his own "deep love for holy poverty." He wrote around this same time that to be poor in spirit meant "not to be so much taken up with this world . . . to be content with the various demands made on you . . . . All this and still more is part of this poverty of spirit. It is the greatest treasure to have this kind of poverty."[91]

Seelos also discovered several German families in the city who "were no longer Catholic but in name." Although, according to Zimmer, Seelos "was overwhelmed with labor," he "considered it his duty to make every sacrifice" to help bring them back to the faith. He and one of the German-speaking students visited "these lukewarm families" and invited them to attend German-language catechetical instructions at the parish school house on Saturday afternoons. As promised, he gave instructions several times, but those invited failed to appear.[92] It was another lesson in humility for the saintly rector.

Father Seelos counseled others in need from a distance. He wrote many letters, both in German and English, while living in Annapolis, and signed them "your poor Father Seelos." In a series of letters to "Miss Mary," a young American woman—whose surname remains unknown to historians—who was seeking a religious vocation despite family opposition. Seelos advised Miss Mary to "to make of Your devotion and Your duty but *one thing,* and you will increase in devotion as well as in real perfection." Another time, he encouraged her to act like a "child of Providence" and to "win the affection of the children" in her charge. When Mary complained about cold and indifferent treatment by her relatives, he sagely advised: "When we please everybody, watch out. It is then that we are in danger" and told her to "make good use of these heart-rending and at the same time, heart-changing circumstances, so that you really learn to be meek and humble of heart." In his encouragement to obtaining these spiritual improvements, Seelos told Mary

Father Seelos entering a poor woman's sick room. Original art by Constance D. Robinson.

that if she were to accept his advice and "apply it practically to your soul by making it a rule of your life, you would, as a matter of fact, be led to holiness." And again, he suggested "practice heroic patience, and give yourself completely into the hands of Providence." Always, he urged her to pray.[93]

Seelos' message to others, both during his lifetime and since, is paraphrased by his preeminent biographer, Father Carl Hoegerl, C.Ss.R.:

> If you want to be happy, try to be holy; if you want to be very happy, try to be very holy. . . . All you have to do is live your life, as God ordained it for you, in the best way you know how and every day. Everyone can do that: married or single; homemaker, office worker, carpenter, salesman—everyone. The heroics consist in doing it all the time and to please God.[94]

Despite the holy demeanor and good will Seelos brought to his work, others failed to find virtue in the way he operated. Through the efforts of other Redemptorists—primarily Michael Müller and Joseph Wuest—he was relieved as prefect of students on November 21, 1862. Müller had written two long letters—one in May when he was still in Annapolis and the other in July after he moved to Cumberland—to Father Mauron in Rome. He accused Seelos of lacking "the judgment, wisdom and reflection, the manner and method to direct students in the spirit of the Congregation." He also claimed that Seelos "does not and cannot understand" that spirit. Accepting these accusations on face value and without due diligence by his consultors, Mauron replaced both Seelos and Zimmer with an old-school Dutch Redemptorist, Gerard Dielemans. The two divisions of students were abolished, when Dielemans arrived from Europe and he became prefect for all of the students.[95]

Although Seelos must have been disappointed with this perfidy of his confreres, he cheerfully accepted it, even said he was grateful for it. In a letter to a former student, he said he was "happy of having been freed of the overwhelming burden." He continued as rector, which left him in charge of studies and of the general direction of the college. Each week he still taught two hours of scripture, two hours of church history, and an hour of Greek. Under Dielemans, both morning and afternoon classes were held, manual labor was reduced, and open access to the library and participation in debates and theatrical presentations—which Müller saw as abuses perpetrated by Seelos—were ended. Mauron agreed that many of the manual tasks in which the students were employed had been "entirely incompatible with true spiritual and academic progress." One wonders what he would have thought about Müller's use of the novices to haul bricks and to hammer lath nails when the church and college were being built in 1858 and 1859. In fact, Dielemans later complained to Mauron that the current students, when they were novices under Müller, had been employed in too much manual labor building the church and college and that more lay brothers were needed for manual tasks. For his part, according to James Keitz, one of the advanced theology students at the time, Seelos "stood firmly and affectionately at [Dieleman's] side."[96]

Later on Dielemans wanted even more changes, such as regulating how the students served at table, washed dishes, and even had their hair cut. Sweeping the church and corridors of the house was not objectionable. Although he recognized Seelos' goodness, humility, and trust in everybody, Dielemans complained that the rector "never saw a studentate or well-regulated community." Seelos was always ready to agree with anyone who insisted on having things their way and did not object to the changes made by Dielemans. Mauron reminded Dielemans that "You do not have to reform the studentate in one day." But Dielemans was all for reform of those aspects of the American house of studies that were different from Wittem. James Keitz complained that "Father Dielemans came to America full of preconceived ideas, and saw the studendate as needing reform . . . . [and had] complete ignorance of our conditions in America." But Dielemans' reforms were suffered in silence and "so it happened that he never won the confidence of the older students." Moreover, Keitz observed another unsettling trait in Dielemans: he "displayed openly his aversion toward Father Seelos, his rector; and toward De Dycker the provincial."[97]

Forced to Take an Oath of Loyalty

Anne Arundel County was within the territory included in the Federal naval blockade of the Southern states proclaimed in April 1861. A March 31, 1863, US Treasury Department regulation governing internal and coastal commerce, specified "the north side of the Potomac, and south of the Washington and Annapolis railroad" as areas in which "no goods, wares, or merchandise whatever may be the ostensible destination thereof" for transportation to areas "under the control of insurgents."[98]

Although the Annapolis area was not under insurgent control, the Federal authorities saw sufficient reason to control the movement of its people. This was effected by the issuance of provost marshal passes beginning in June 1861. Although a few passes had been issued to the Annapolis Redemptorists it seems not to have been done routinely. However, when Father Van de Braak took Frater Andrew Ziegler for medical care to Baltimore using the steamboat on August 11, 1862, they "both were forced to take an oath of loyalty to the government and the Constitution."[99] This was the first and only time such action was mentioned in the *Chronica Domus* and, although not a new requirement, it was newsworthy and a matter of concern to the Redemptorists. With priests, students, novices, and lay brothers used to traveling freely among the Redemptorist houses in other cities, any restraint was problematic.

Only one day's worth of 1862 Annapolis pass records survives—February 10—and no records are extant for oaths. A loyalty oath signed in Baltimore by John Thomson Mason on August 23, 1862, however, is of interest. He had been arrested as a suspected Confederate spy in Chambersburg, Pennsylvania, in 1861. Mason insisted that he was on a charitable mission to see if he could find someone in Chambersburg who would buy the freedom of three children of a slave whom Mason had manumitted in 1857. He was detained briefly and "dismissed on his parole of honor, to await instructions from Washington." The War Department finally agreed it had no authority to hold him and in August 1862, after he was arrested a second time, for refusing to take an oath of allegiance, Mason swore on his "sacred honor" that he would "not take up arms against the United States or give aid or comfort to the enemies thereof."[100] Thereafter, he remained mostly behind the scenes for the duration of the war, during which time he converted to the Catholic faith.

Rigors and Joys of Religious Life

In the midst of developments in 1862, the rigors of religious life resulted in some departures among the brothers. In July three candidate brothers returned to Annapolis from Cumberland and then left the congregation. The first was Matthias Kraemer who departed on July 11. He was followed on July 14 by Martin Burke who left "for a variety of reasons," according to the house annals, "most of all because he believed he could not come together with the other lay brothers, who are Germans while he is Irish." Then, on August 1, Adalbert Wehner returned home where, according to what he told some other brothers, he could enjoy "the favor of elegance and charm." In September Prussian-born novice brother Adam (Brother Boniface) Franz, who had been with the Redemptorists since 1858, departed. The chronicler noted that "for some time he has not been content, and eagerly sought the joys of this world.[101]

Summer holidays began on August 15, the Feast of the Assumption. But the academic year had ended on an unusual note, with examinations held at Easter because of "the great changes that took place" with exchange of novices and students between Cumberland and Annapolis. About three days after the summer recess commenced, Michael Müller arrived from Cumberland and remained for two weeks, temporarily taking vacationing Peter Zimmer's place among the junior students. The house annals revealed that "[t]he holidays were of great delight to all."[102]

During the hot weather, Father Seelos had the students go daily for thirty minutes to two bath houses on St. Mary's Spa Creek waterfront. He believed that the "salty sea air strengthens the body and refreshes the whole person." And, in spite of the austere life and hardship, there was time for recreation for the seminarians. Like many Annapolitans of future generations, the Redemptorist students took to the water. Shortly after a visit to Annapolis as consultor in 1856, Seelos told his family that the novices had "a couple of boats in which, when the weather is calm, they make excursions on the water during times of recreation and relaxation. And they sing beautiful hymns."[103]

During Müller's tenure in Annapolis, there had been a near boating accident on the Severn River. Müller and some novices barely avoided disaster when a working sailboat heavily loaded with sand tacked suddenly in front of their boat putting them in "eminent [*sic*] danger of death." Müller cried out, "Jesus and Mary help us!" and the collision was avoided at the last second. The sand boat captain, said Müller, "exclaimed that it was "a miraculous escape."[104]

By 1862 the Redemptorist fleet had increased. For their "main diversion during vacation," wrote Seelos, "we have a little fleet of four boats, of which, three are sailboats, but the fourth is a small one, mostly for the use of the sick and the convalescent, and similar purposes." He explained that the largest boat was thirty-eight feet long, had two masts and square sails, and a third "pointed sail . . . called a 'chipsail.'" He was describing a two-masted gaff-rigged boat that carried a jib. Also, this boat could be rowed with its sixteen oars. Another sailboat—the fastest—was thirty feet in length and had two sloop-rigged sails and a jib and could be manually propelled by twelve oars. "I usually go in this one," wrote Seelos. The third boat was a twenty-footer that evidently had been found abandoned on Kent Island that summer and taken back by the Redemptorists. It had one mast with a gaff-rigged sail, a jib, and six oars. It "goes very fast." The fourth boat was a rowboat.[105] In a letter describing the fleet, he drew sketches of the two larger boats. All four of the boats are seen in photographs taken by Ferreol Girardey in 1864.

Soon after arriving in June, Seelos laid down rules for use of the fleet of boats. He directed: "The most experienced and prudent students shall be appointed as captains of the boats; if the sails are used then a Father ought always to be present, who is to be punctually obeyed as he shall be responsible for the carelessness and imprudence." During his year-end visitation, Father De Dycker declared further: "If the sailboats are to be used, all rashness and disturbance of order is to be avoided with utmost diligence; moreover, all those things connected to the operation of the boats must be strictly observed." Proper seamanship was essential for the safety of the students when out on Chesapeake Bay. Although Frater Hubert Bove handled one of the sailboats "like a veteran seaman," Frater Charles Rathke was not allowed to steer a boat "because he is too rash." One creative student, Charles Hahn, "wanted to build his own boat with paddle wheels" but his "lofty ideas" did not materialize.[106]

During the summer of 1862, Seelos and the students made six all-day sailing excursions

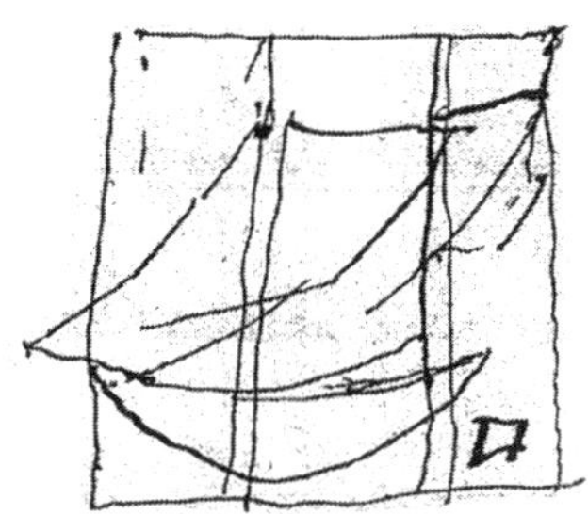

Second-hand copy of Father Seelos' drawing of boats, October–December 1862. Seelos Papers, RABP.

across Chesapeake Bay to Kent Island. The fifteen-mile trip took them one to two hours depending on the wind. Seelos noted that sometimes "the waves here get pretty high" and some of the seminarians became seasick. William Gross, writing six years later, compared what he recalled as calm sailing on the Chesapeake to the bad weather he encountered along the Atlantic coast on his way from New York City to Savannah in 1868.[107] But in 1862, after the sailors arrived on Kent Island, "everything was fine again," according to Seelos. On one occasion, he and the students:

> made a big fire in a wooded area and set up a kitchen and the food was cooked, boiled, and roasted; but the chief cook has to be [of] a hearty appetite, which everyone brings for himself. Then we wandered about the island a little, which looks very beautiful. It's full of big farms, owned by very rich Americans. The work is done by blacks, mostly slaves, who are very content with their lot, since they have it better than servants with us. We make these excursions in our religious habit, and this arouses the wonderment of these good, quiet people.[108]

On one Kent Island excursion, some field hands from a distance saw the Redemptorists in their black cassocks. They thought they were soldiers and "retreated back into their houses." Seelos approached and found a Black woman inside one of the houses. Noticing her fear, he explained that the Redemptorists were "peaceful people" and only wanted to buy some fruit. She took them inside and brought them "a big bushel basket full of the nicest peaches and apples," which they purchased.[109]

Sometimes the Redemptorist sailors needed navigation aids for their return trip in the evening from Kent Island. As with other American technologies, Seelos was fascinated by the lighthouses near Annapolis and even visited one of them. He wrote:

> When you come out from Annapolis into the bay, it is as stormy as on the high seas, and so they have set up four lighthouses, where I have put the marks [on the sketch in the letter]. I was inside one of them to see how it was fitted out. It is an ordinary oil lamp, but gives such a bright light because it is all surrounded by crystal prisms, that is, bundles of three-sided pieces of glass, inside of which the light burns. The state pays the cost.[110]

At the end of summer recess, Müller returned to Cumberland. On September 15, the students began a five-day retreat before classes began again. The advanced students studied moral theology under Van de Braak while the dogmatic theology students studied with Zimmer. Girardey taught philosophy, using the writings of an Italian Jesuit, Father Matteo Liberatore, a "new authority" whose works had been "praised and commended" by the Redemptorist superior general, Father Mauron. Henning taught rhetoric and Seelos taught exegesis and Church history to students of dogmatic theology. But on November 17, Gerard Dielemans arrived from

Second-hand copy of Father Seelos' map of Chesapeake Bay and Kent Island, October-December 1862. The four Xs at the mouth of the Severn River denote lighthouses. Seelos Papers, RABP.

Europe, with letters of appointment from Mauron making him prefect of students in place of Seelos.[111]

Pastoral Duties at the Out-Missions

In addition to their academic duties and parochial work in Annapolis, the Redemptorists performed two kinds of outside mission work. One type of mission work was conducting multi-day spiritual retreats or renewals in Catholic parishes throughout the northern United States and eastern Canada. The second kind of mission work was providing pastoral services to Catholic chapels in Anne Arundel and nearby counties. Many nineteenth-century parishes, especially in the South and Midwest, had outlying mission stations. These kept priests occupied with itinerant duties away from their home church. When priests were not available, which was the norm, lay persons might conduct Sunday prayer services in their homes for family and neighbors and sometimes prayers at burials. Mothers or older sisters might teach catechism lessons to children and lead home devotions. These lay activities provided a sense of unity for small rural Catholic communities as they waited in expectation of the monthly arrival of a priest.[112]

Before the Civil War, the Annapolis-based Redemptorists heard confessions, baptized babies, and said Mass on an occasional basis in private homes outside Annapolis, such as at the plantations of Dodon and Evergreen in southern Anne Arundel County. They also crossed Chesapeake Bay to Kent Island, in Queen Anne's County, to administer the sacraments. Throughout the war years, their horizons expanded considerably as the Annapolis Redemptorists had an increased presence in northern Anne Arundel and Howard counties, areas where the Baltimore Redemptorists provided pastoral services before the war. The war kept them busy in Baltimore city and county and, even then, the Annapolis Redemptorists occasionally were called upon to help out on weekends in Baltimore parishes.

The wartime out-mission work began in earnest for the Annapolis Redemptorists in 1862. In May Father John

Cornell made the first monthly visit to St. Augustine's Church in Elkridge Landing, in Howard County. He heard confessions and celebrated Sunday Mass and was joined on that one occasion by some of the Baltimore Redemptorists who turned over their responsibilities to him. They had been in charge of St. Augustine's since it became a Redemptorist mission station in 1846. From 1849 to 1851, it was attended by Father John Neumann, then assigned to St. Alphonsus in Baltimore. In October the St. Mary's Redemptorists told the Elkridge Landing congregation that they would send a priest every week for the next year except for Easter. It is not clear how and when these weekly visits occurred because only once-a-month visitations from Annapolis were recorded in the *Chronica Domus* during the next three years. The trip to Elkridge Landing took two train rides, first on the Annapolis and Elk Ridge Railroad to Annapolis Junction and then the B&O to Elkridge Landing.[113]

The Redemptorists also occasionally visited Ellicott's Mills in Howard County. The Christian Brothers ran a boys' boarding school, located just outside the village, called Rock Hill Academy. In late June 1862, John Cornell was welcomed at Rock Hill by the superior and spent eight days leading the brothers in a spiritual retreat. The next year this same duty was performed by Ferreol Girardey in August, also for eight days. The last Annapolis Redemptorist to give a retreat at Rock Hill was Augustine Freitag who arrived there on July 26, 1864, and again led an eight-day retreat.[114]

The Consequences of War

Leaving their Duke of Gloucester Street home, the Redemptorists went throughout the city and nearby countryside to minister to the Federal army. In the spring of 1862, some 50,000 infantry, artillery, and cavalry troops were slated to undergo training in and around Annapolis under the command of Major General John Ellis Wool. A huge camp extending from Spa Creek to South River was envisioned and, it was reported, "there may be a considerable increase in the business of the 'ancient city' and their advent is eagerly looked for by the pie-hucksters and venders of small wares throughout the city." Ominous for local merchants, it was reported that "numbers of shop-keepers from Baltimore city are about to start temporary places of business in our midst."[115] Because recruits were urgently needed at the front for the Virginia Peninsula Campaign of March–August 1862, it was deemed impractical to hold so many back for instruction, and the proposed huge training camp did not materialize.

Hospitalized and paroled Union troops, as well as officers and men assigned to provost and administrative duties, remained in and around Annapolis. The hospitals to which the Redemptorists walked, one at the Naval Academy (US Army General Hospital, Division No. 1) and another at St. John's College (US Army General Hospital, Division No. 2), were described by a contemporary medical doctor as having a "modern and agreeable appearance." Division No. 1 had an "amplitude of room ventilation, cleanliness, and general management" and the rooms were "large, well lighted, and aired, perfectly clean, and contain but three patients each, and their clean, neat-looking, comfortable mattrass [*sic*] beds." When the same doctor visited the parole camp, initially located at St. John's College, he found it "orderly and comfortable as most camps" but saw that "all descriptions of filth were accumulating in great and alarming quantities all around and in the immediate vicinity of the camp." By September 1862, the newspapers reported that there were 10,000 to 12,000 soldiers at the new parole camp established just outside the city, beyond St. Mary's Cemetery and John Walton's farm on Spa Road.[116]

No account has been found of precisely how the Annapolis Redemptorists went about these duties but they would have performed many of the same functions as a regimental chaplain, in the field or an officially appointed hospital chaplain in rear areas. On November 15, 1862, President Lincoln issued a statement that he "desire[d] and enjoin[ed] the orderly observance of the Sabbath by the officers and men of the military and naval services." Even earlier, on September 6, 1861, General McClellan, as commander of the Army of the Potomac, had issued a general order to the effect that, unless attacked by the enemy or in case of extreme military necessity, all work should be suspended on the Sabbath, no unnecessary movements be made, and the men should be permitted rest from their labors and time to attend divine service.[117] That was on the war front, but in Annapolis much the same would have been expected. Those soldiers who were able could attend week-day and Sunday Mass at St. Mary's Church, have their confessions heard, and receive spiritual counseling. Officers and men restricted to hospitals or the parole camp had the advantage of both formal and temporary chapels on site. There they could meet Redemptorist priests who performed duties similar to chaplains in the field.

"Guarding and guiding the spiritual well-being of the soldiers was the primary responsibility of army chaplains," writes historian John W. Brinsfield. Catholic chaplains in the field heard confessions and celebrated Mass for the soldiers of their own and other nearby regiments. They held money for troops and kept lists of soldiers with notes about their illnesses and religious preference and information about their families should a priest have to contact them. Priests wrote letters for the illiterate or semiliterate to send to their loved ones, adding to the envelop that it contained a "soldier's letter" to be delivered free of charge. Like their Protestant counterparts, priests served as friends to the lonely and troubled. Jesuit Father Peter Tissot, chaplain of the Thirty-Seventh New York Infantry, had a wooden altar in a small tent and always kept the Blessed Sacrament in a little wooden tabernacle with a vigil light burning.[118]

While conscious of the troops' spiritual needs, chaplains also helped with temporal requirements, such as obtaining clothing, food, and medicine beyond what the government provided. They might also provide guidance to the men on army regulations in the hope of making them better soldiers. Chaplains prayed with the soldiers before battle and kept letters the men had written home in case they were killed. Catholic soldiers might go to confession, attend Mass, and receive communion and general absolution before going into battle. George Rable points out that during battles some soldiers reported they would "load, fire, and pray at the same time." During and after battle, chaplains ministered to the wounded and dying on the battlefield itself. In hospitals they performed many of the same tasks but more in the way of helping sick and wounded troops maintain their morale, avoid idleness, participate in recreation when they were able, and occupy their minds not with idleness but music and songs, games (chess, checkers, or backgammon rather than card playing), literary society activities (including publishing newspapers), lectures, and reading classes.[119]

Union soldiers gathered at the depot at Relay House, Maryland. Courtesy https://www.pinterest.com/pin/192810427784341023/.

Chaplains also provided both spiritual and "profitable" reading materials to the troops and, when at a hospital, to establish a library. Protestant tract societies and the United States Christian Commission worked diligently during the war to distribute pocket-size Bibles, hymnals, and inspirational pamphlets to Union troops. The American Bible Society alone published more than 5 million Bibles, most of which were distributed by the Christian Commission. Some Bibles even reached Confederate soldiers under flags of truce. Evening revival meetings were a good time to proselytize the troops and distribute tracts. Although Catholic parishes both North and South supplied prayer books and other devotional materials to troops in the field, the effort did not match the Protestant chaplains' accomplishments and Catholic troops instead received inspirational literature provided by the Christian Commission. Rable and Kurtz point out religious hostility between Catholics and Protestants decreased as the war went on and soldiers of both persuasions saw themselves as comrades and friends and attended each other's services. The only local mention found of Catholic Church-approved Douay Bibles was not until February 1865 and they were sponsored by the United States Sanitary Commission. This was a Protestant-based support organization founded in 1861 to provide medical and material aid to Union volunteer forces and was sometimes a rival of the United States Christian Commission. The commission's Annapolis branch reportedly "sent a lot of Douay Testaments to the Catholic clergy residing at Saint Mary's Church, in this city, to be distributed by them among the Catholic soldiers in the hospitals and Camp Parole." Earlier in the war, the St. Vincent de Paul Society in New York City published *Manual of the Christian Soldier,* a book of prayers, devotional exercises, meditation, instructions, and brief explanations of church teaching. It was disseminated to Catholic soldiers and families but it is not known if copies were available in Annapolis.[120]

Father Seelos reported to his family in Bavaria in December 1862 that:

> Here in Annapolis, the whole hospital is filled with the wounded who are being sent here from the battlefield. And then, close by, there are 6,000 parolees, that is, those who were captured by the Southerners but were given their freedom on their word of honor not to bear arms against the South anymore. Until a short time ago, there were 20,000, but all except 6,000 were sent to the West. All of them looked more like brigands than regular soldiers, and a regiment from New York had to be expressly commandeered to keep them in check and to hold them in some kind of order. They can only bear arms against the South when they can be exchanged for an equal number of soldiers from the South. For this reason they don't carry any weapons now, but steal everything they can get their hands on in the fields or in the houses. All this does not cause me to wonder, because I know that the consequences of war bring such things about, otherwise, war would not be a scourge.[121]

Although there is no documented evidence that Father Seelos personally went to the hospitals and camps to minister to soldiers, it is likely that he did. Other Redemptorists did so routinely. Sometimes seminarians accompanied the priests on their rounds, gaining first-hand experience in ministering to wounded, ill, and paroled troops. Priests often were called several times a day to attend to troops in and around the city. Hundreds of dying soldiers were given the last rites and hundreds if not thousands more availed themselves of the sacrament of penance. Mass was often offered in the military hospitals, soldiers' camps, and parole camps.[122] The Naval Academy chapel, built in 1854, was in operation throughout the war and may have been used by the Redemptorists. The St. John's College hospital also had a chapel that also may had a Redemptorist presence.[123]

The *Chronica Domus* reported that Fathers Bradley and Girardey took the train to Relay House in October 1862. This critical railroad junction, where connections were made to Frederick, Harpers Ferry, and Cumberland, had been occupied by Union troops since May 3, 1861, as part of the effort to stop supplies and recruits heading from Baltimore to the Confed-

Railroad depot, passengers, and troops at Annapolis Junction. Edward Sachse lithograph, circa 1863, Prints and Photographs Division, Library of Congress https://www.loc.gov/pictures/item/96516953/.

eracy and to block a possible Southern advance from Harpers Ferry. Just days before Bradley and Girardey arrived in Relay, Lincoln himself had taken a special train through there on his way to and from a meeting with General McClellan near Antietam battlefield at Sharpsburg, Maryland. Relay was not one of the usual out-missions but the Union soldiers in camp there were found to be "in need of spiritual assistance." The priests remained two days "and many soldiers benefitted."[124] Although this was the only instance in *Chronica Domus* about ministering at Relay, it is probable that other visits there from Annapolis went unrecorded.

On their way north to Elkridge Landing and Relay, the Redemptorists had to connect to B&O trains at Annapolis Junction. An army hospital known as US General Hospital at Annapolis Junction was also located at this rail hub and it is possible that while waiting for connecting trains, they ministered to Catholic troops there.[125]

The Ministry of Peace

A critical issue faced Redemptorists and other religious orders during the Civil War was the threat of conscription into military service. It threatened to deplete the ranks of the clergy and seriously disrupt seminary training. Many Redemptorists were of European birth and, as non-US citizens, they were not liable to the draft early in the war. But their American-born confreres and the foreign-born who had become US citizens were subject to mandatory draft enrollment. As draft laws evolved, those who had expressed their intention to become citizens became eligible for enrollment. The sense of unease concerning the draft of the Annapolis Redemptorists was heightened by their living near the war front in a border-state capital under martial law. Father Seelos had declared his intent to become a US citizen in 1848 and was sworn in as a citizen in 1852. Thus, at age forty-three, he was enrolled for the draft.[126]

Defeats in battle and heavy casualties during the first year of the Civil War contributed to a substantial decline in voluntary enlistments in the North. In December 1861, the Federal government transferred the responsibility for recruiting military volunteers from individual states to the War Department. There were positive results and, by late March 1862, the Federal army had 23,308 regular troops and 613,818 state volunteers, not including militia units still under state control. By early summer 1862, however, the war was at a turning point and, with enlistments declining, President Lincoln issued an order on July 2 calling for an additional 300,000 three-year volunteers. Despite a declining enthusiasm for going to war and unpopular quotas assigned to each state, the states responded by raising 421,465 men for three-year voluntary enlistments. At that point, Congress amended a 1795 act authorizing the use of state militias by the Federal government to suppress a rebellion. In effect, the amendment was the United States' first draft law, although the conscription process still was administered by state adjutants general. The Baltimore *Sun* reported that the Militia Act passed in the Senate on July 15 and was signed into law on July 17. The Redemptorist provincial most certainly read this ominous news and the Annapolis Redemptorists also would have learned about the new law in the *Sun* or local newspapers.[127]

The Militia Act authorized Lincoln to call forth state militias "to be employed in the service of the United States." (The Confederate congress passed its own draft law on April 16, 1862, but it exempted clergy.) If the states did not provide sufficient men, the president was authorized "to make all necessary rules and regulations" for the enrollment of militia to "in all cases include all able-bodied male citizens between the ages of eighteen and forty-five, and . . . apportioned among the States according to representative population." The new law also extended the previous three-month's call-up to nine months. The Federal government also sought a volunteer force of 100,000 men, as infantry, for nine months. Upon enlistment, they would receive their first month's pay and a bounty of $25. Those who volunteered for twelve months were given a $50 bounty. It also authorized the president "to receive into service . . . any man or boy of African descent." Nowhere did law mention exemptions, except for those physically unfit for service and non-US citizens. Other exemptions, such as for justices of the peace, sheriffs, constables, and ministers of churches were later allowed by special orders of Secretary of War Stanton but were not included in the new statute.[128]

Annapolitans could read about the draft in the *Annapolis Gazette* and the *Maryland Republican* as well as the daily (except Sunday) Baltimore *Sun*. The *Sun* carried frequent news about the progress of the war and the forthcoming draft. One report from Annapolis said that 2,000 cavalry had been despatched to block the "exodus . . . of so many for Dixie" to avoid the draft. Once Congress passed the Militia Act, news about the new law, how enrollments were proceeding in other states, and who was exempt appeared frequently in the press. The full text of the Militia Act was published by the *Sun* on July 17, the same day it was signed by Lincoln and, since it would "doubtless possess some interest at this time," it was published again on August 5.[129]

Reference also was made to Maryland's own militia law on the *Sun*'s August 5 front page. Maryland's law differed in important ways from the Federal statute: it allowed extensive exemptions. Section 1, Article 63 of the Maryland Code, enacted in January 1860, said the militia included:

> all able bodied white male citizens between eighteen and forty-five years of age . . . except officers of the Government of the United States and their clerks, postmasters, ferrymen employed at any ferry on a post road, stage drivers employed to carry the United States' mail, the Secretary of State, Comptroller, Treasurer, the Commissioner of the Land Office, and their respective clerks, the judge of the several courts in the State, and the clerks of said courts, the registers of Wills, the members of the General Assembly and their clerks while in session, the professors and tutors of colleges and public schools, school masters, practicing physicians, ministers of the Gospel, ordained, licensed or recognized by any religious society, pilots and their apprentices, marines actually engaged in trade or sea-service, and all persons conscientiously scrupulous of bearing arms, who shall produce

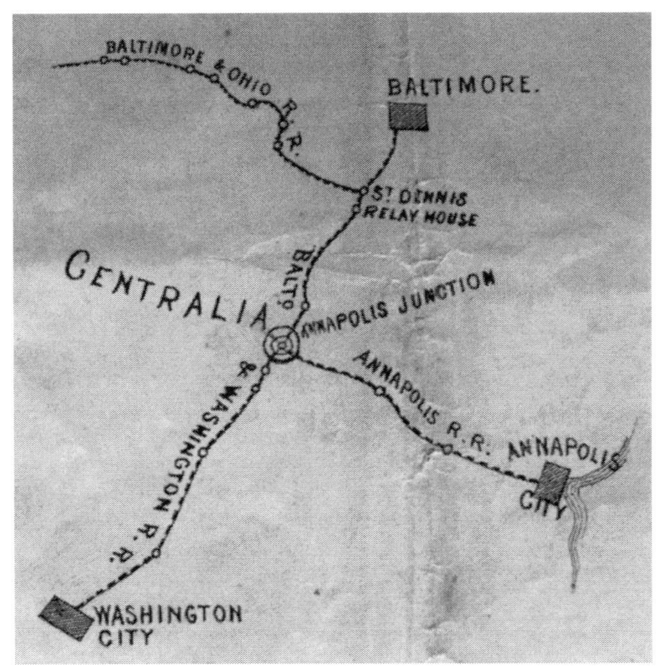

Routes converging on Annapolis Junction (later called Centralia) from an 1866 map. SMPA.

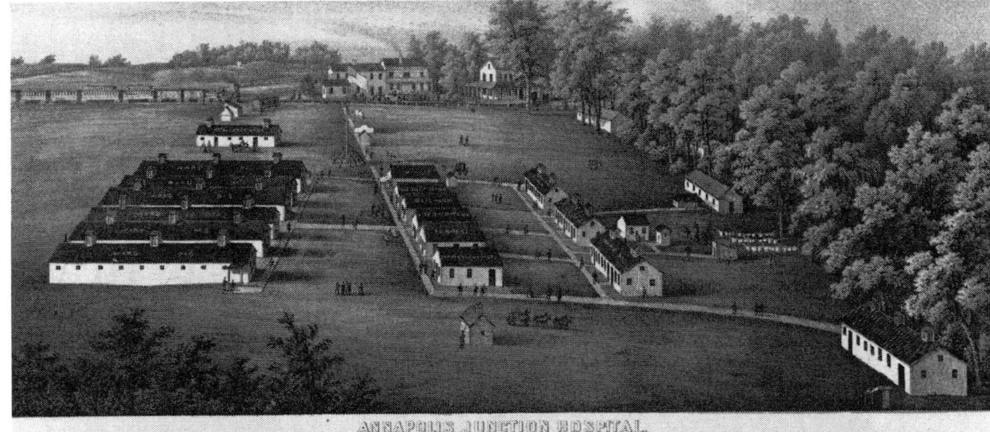

Annapolis Junction Hospital and street-level view, 1863. Prints and Photographs Division, Library of Congress https://www.loc.gov/pictures/item/2003655795/.

to the captain or commanding officer of the district proof that he is so conscientious.[130]

The Maryland General Assembly amended Article 63 of the 1860 Maryland militia act in June 1861 but left the exemptions intact. When the General Assembly met in 1862, it repealed parts of the 1861 act and added new provisions for relief to families of militia members but again kept the exemptions. The new Federal law, however, caused considerable concern in the Redemptorist seminary because it superseded the Maryland law with its generous exemptions. Accordingly, in early August, the *Sun* reported that new Federal law referred to "defects in existing laws, or in the execution of them in the several States." That news plus the president's call for 300,000 troops and the assignment of state quotas must have given pause to the Redemptorist administration.[131]

Legal notices regarding draft enrollment appeared in the *Sun* starting August 13 and continued thereafter. Presumably, no-longer-extant issues of Annapolis newspapers carried the same or similar notices. The *Sun* reported the schedule for holding sessions "for the purpose of revising and perfecting the enrollment of the Militia" and inviting persons knowing of omissions from the enrollment lists or other errors, to come forth. It also provided dates and locations for individuals claiming exemptions to present their claims.[132]

On July 17, the same day Lincoln signed the Militia Act, Governor Bradford, issued an executive call for four volunteer infantry regiments. He declared that Maryland was "still menaced with invasion" and he needed to act quickly. Bradford appointed a committee of fifty prominent citizens to adopt measures to ensure the success of call for the four regiments. The call was published on the front page of the *Sun* on July 21 and continued to attract news reports in subsequent days. In the hope that volunteers would satisfy Maryland's quotas, Bradford did not mention the politically charged issue of a draft. But the *Sun* clearly explained the implications of there not being enough volunteers by publishing an article in the same edition entitled "Drafting—How They Do It."[133]

Bradford declared at a mass rally in Baltimore on July 28 that only the Federal authorities could call for a draft but that he was authorized to carry out the necessary step of an enrollment throughout Maryland of all men capable of bearing arms. At the same time, the issue of alien residents' allegiance to the United States government was raised by the diplomatic corps in Washington. In some states, military authorities required alien residents to take oaths of allegiance to the United States, but a July 21 presidential executive order said that while aliens had a duty to submit to and obey the laws and respect the authority of the government, they were not required to take an oath of allegiance to the Federal government.[134] This may have provided some small assurance to non-citizen members of religious communities.

On August 1, Stanton wrote to Bradford, informing him that he should proceed "with all convenient diligence" to enroll Maryland men for militia service and report the results to the War Department. Bradford wrote immediately to John Angel James Creswell of Elkton, Cecil County—who would shortly be appointed assistant adjutant general and superintendent of enrollment with the rank of colonel—discussing how best to nominate men to represent the various enrollment districts. On August 4, Stanton's General Orders No. 94 ordered the draft of 300,000 militia from the various states. Those not filling the War Department quotas were directed by August 15 to hold a special draft from among militia members into the service of the United States to fulfill the quota. States with deficient or no conscription laws were subject to direct Federal intervention.[135]

To identify those eligible for the draft, all able-bodied men were first subject to enrollment. Enrollment did not guarantee being drafted. Moreover, various categories of Marylanders were still exempt from enrollment. An August 5 letter from Bradford to Creswell revealed that enrolling officers, appointed by the governor, were compensated by the state at a rate not exceeding ten cents for every person enrolled, giving them a monetary incentive to enroll as many men as possible. On August 9, the War Department published a list that excluded from the draft men who held such critical jobs as telegraph operators, constructors, workers in armories and arsenals, locomotive engineers, members of Congress, the vice president of the United States, customs officials and their clerks, postal office clerks, stage coach drivers employed in carrying US mail, men employed on ferries or post roads, ship pilots and engineers, the merchant marine, and all those exempted by state law "who belong to any of the aforesaid classes." Exemption for disability was allowed only if the condition was permanent and rendered the person unfit for service for more than thirty days as certified by a state-appointed surgeon. Stanton informed Bradford on August 12, that the instructions for the draft of the militia "were given rather as a guide than a positive direction if found inconvenient or inapplicable to the circumstances and conditions of your state." Furthermore, Stanton told Bradford that he was authorized "to modify and depart from [the instructions] in any particular where their operation would embarrass you in making a draft and you may adopt any other roles and regulations that will better contribute to the main object" That same day, Bradford issued a proclamation announcing that preliminaries to the enrollment of the Maryland militia were underway and that Maryland's quota was 8,532 men.[136]

Against this legal and discretionary framework, all able-bodied male citizens between eighteen and forty-five years of age, including students of religious orders, had to make themselves known to the local enrollment board. Each county had a enrollment commissioner, who maintained records, and a surgeon, who examined enrollees for medical fitness. The preliminary work was conducted in subdistricts of the county, each headed by an enrolling officer who recorded the names, post office address, age, and occupation of each eligible man. When there was doubt about a man's eligibility, he was enrolled anyway and his case referred to the enrollment board for adjudication. The normal method was for the enrollment officer, or his assistants, to walk or ride throughout the subdistrict to record names. The officer left at each enrollee's residence formal notification of enrollment and a warning "to hold yourself in readiness for such military duty as under the laws and constitution of the United States may be required of you." Once the names were accumulated, they were recorded in alphabetical order in lists certified by the enrolling officer and presented to the county commissioner. The final enrollment books were sent to Creswell in Baltimore and he, in turn, forwarded state consolidation reports to the War Department. In the meantime, once enrollment lists had been sent to Creswell, county commissioners announced the date and place of the forthcoming draft and when exemptions would be determined. They posted handbills "in at least five of the most visible places of each Election District" or in at least three daily newspapers in cities.[137]

Anne Arundel County's enrollment commissioner was Frank Stockett, a prominent Annapolis lawyer. Stockett was well known to the Redemptorists and had been memorialized in Father Müller's poem about building St. Mary's new church (see Thanks Be to God for All His Benefits, ch. 1). The enrollment board's surgeon was Dr. William Brewer, of Annapolis, and the enrolling officer for Annapolis was Andrew W. Chaney, a local building contractor.[138]

Once the process was underway, Chaney, or an assistant, canvassed the Redemptorist college and enrolled twenty-five men for the draft, all listed as twenty years of age and having the occupation of "student." Of these twenty-five, according to the *Chronica Domus*, twenty-two were professed students and three were lay brothers.[139]

A Redemptorist source said that in 1862 "all the citizens in the [Annapolis] house were enrolled" whereas the commissioner declared that only the students were "liable to be drafted." Seminarians were not among the approved exemptions. In fact, names of the nine priests, forty-three other students, or sixteen other lay brothers did not appear in the final 1862 Annapolis enrollment book. Among those not listed were the non-citizens while others were not in the vulnerable age range, but presumably Chaney made some exemptions on his own and omitted them in the enrollment book. Or, after an initial visit to St. Mary's, he may have enrolled everyone but after further deliberation, included only twenty-five in the final list. Although Father Seelos later wrote that he would go to prison rather than bear arms, none of those enrolled were listed as conscientious objectors. Exemptions to the draft, however, were fairly common, both throughout the North and in Maryland. Of 29,319 Maryland residents enrolled for the draft during the four years of war, 11,011 (38 percent) were exempted (the national exemption rate was 40 percent). Because of the system of substitutes and commutation fees, only 1,426 Marylanders were eventually drafted (others served as volunteers). However, this eventuality was not known to the Redemptorist superiors in 1862 and their concern was focused on the fate of the students.[140]

In an action presumably taken to help gain exemptions for the students, on September 1 minor orders were conferred on twenty students, five of whom were on the draft commissioner's enrollment list. The Redemptorists also protested the enrollment of their twenty-five men. Father James Bradley, minister of St. Mary's and the number two man in the Annapolis community, took the lead. As a result of his protest, Chaney asked Stockett how to proceed. Stockett recommended they seek an answer from higher authority. On September 3, Chaney wrote to Creswell in Baltimore, saying:

> I wish to inquire whether I shall enroll the Students in the College of the Redemptorists at this place (A Catholic institution) who are citizens and of the proper age. I called Mr. Stocketts attention to the matter and he directed me to inquire of you. I shall await an answer before closing my books.[141]

The Maryland adjutant general letter-books from 1862 that might have recorded Creswell's response to Chaney have not survived. However, Creswell's response must have come quickly and was clear as to what action was directed. On September 19, Chaney certified the Annapolis enrollment book as complete and the names of the twenty-five Redemptorist students were included. Although Creswell's response to Chaney's September 3 letter has not been found, it was noted in a letter written to Creswell by Stockett on September 19—the same day that Stockett received applications for exemption at the county courthouse. Stockett wrote that he was in the process of examining the enrolling books and hearing claims for exemptions. "Among those who have applied," wrote Stockett, "are the students of Divinity at the Roman Catholic College here." He said that his impression was that "they are exempt but the enrolling officer here tells me you instructed him to enroll them." Stockett also made a case for granting exemptions to masters of private schools and asked Creswell to "please inform me if you recognize both of the above classes as exempt."[142]

Bradley wrote a polite letter to Creswell on September 19, making a persuasive case on behalf of the students. Bradley, rather than Seelos, wrote the letter because of his native English fluency and knowledge of the law and also because, as minister of the church, he was equivalent to a pastor and had signed himself as such in the past. He also was well known for his preaching, which "was not fiery, but persuasive; his logic was irresistible," according to a later source. Bradley's style of delivery carried over into his writing. He told Creswell that he had spoken with Stockett "concerning our liability to draft, & as he could give me no positive information I determined to explain the circumstances of our case to yourself." Using language taken directly from the Maryland Code, he told Creswell that the Redemptorists belonged "to a 'Religious Order', the members of which are bound by *vow* & *oath* to the Service of God & the ministry in the Church." He informed Creswell that the enrollment commissioners in Baltimore "made not the least difficulty in exempting those members of the order residing there." Bradley also explained that the Redemptorist students "are 'ordained &

recognized' by our church as ministers of the Gospel, & may at any time be sent by our Superiors to preach the Word of God." This was an oblique reference to the minor orders conferred on them on September 1. Bradley then observed that Creswell "may perceive" from what he had written:

> that as persons *vowed* & *sworn* to the ministry of *'peace'* we must have conscientious scruples against bearing arms; & in the words of the law, we are 'persons conscientiously scrupulous of bearing arms,' and we are prepared to produce any proof of this that may be required.

Bradley admitted to Creswell that when he posed the "conscientiously scrupulous" circumstance to Stockett "he seemed to consider it a 'Construction' which would not be received." Nevertheless, Bradley persevered, saying that "the law, plainly, is *general*; it does not specify any manner or class of persons, and if we give the proof which the law requires, I cannot understand how or why we should be debarred the benefit of that law more than any other citizen of the State."[143]

At this point, a remarkable development occurred. Brigadier General Lorenzo Thomas, the adjutant general of the US Army, accompanied by an assistant adjutant general, Colonel William Augustus Nichols, visited Annapolis September 20–23. The purpose was to observe first-hand the problems associated with the increasing numbers of paroled prisoners of war arriving in Annapolis. But on September 22, they also visited the Redemptorist seminary, or, as Father Ferreol Girardey, the keeper of the house chronicle, put it, they "came to see our house." Thomas and Nichols were told about the difficulties the Redemptorists were having with the enrollment commissioner, whom Girardey called "a bitter Protestant." Whether he meant Creswell, Stockett, or Chaney is not clear; only Stockett was a commissioner but Creswell seems to have been an obstacle as evidenced by Chaney's and Stockett's letters to him. After hearing about the situation, Thomas told the Redemptorists that "we had nothing to fear; and that if the commissioner attempted to force us, we could write to the Secretary of War or to the Adj. Gen. himself, and all would be settled as we desired." The account in the *Chronica Domus* is a bit confusing at this point. Either Girardey had the wrong date of the Thomas visit or he was not clear about when Bradley's letter was written or sent to Creswell. In his note in the chronicle, Girardey said that it was "a few days" after the Thomas visit that "we wrote to the commissioner of the draft in Baltimore asking him to exempt us." Bradley's letter was dated September 19 but perhaps he did not mail it until after the Thomas visit. Girardey's note concludes that Bradley's request "was favorably heard, and the commissioner here received the order for our exemption." Father Joseph Wuest, writing fifty years later, had another interpretation. "After his return to Washington, Adj. Gen. Thomas sent orders exempting all in the house from the draft." A search was made of official communications sent by the adjutant general's office for three months after his return to Washington, but no such orders were found.[144]

Brigadier General Lorenzo Thomas (1804–75).
Prints and Photographs Division, Library of Congress
https://www.loc.gov/pictures/item/2018666502/.

Creswell's responses to the letters of September 19 from Stockett and Bradley also have not been found. However, when Stockett wrote to Creswell again on October 23, he said he had been in Baltimore the previous Friday to see Creswell concerning the enrollments in Anne Arundel County "and the exemptions granted." Although Stockett complained about the large number of men who had obtained disability certificates, no mention was made of the Redemptorists and their plea of conscientious scruples. Nor were the Redemptorists mentioned when Stockett wrote to Creswell on November 11, reporting that the enrollment in Anne Arundel County had been completed on October 29 and that he was "most exceedingly tired of the business" of bringing closure to exemption claims throughout the county. Annapolis was not mentioned among the recalcitrant districts.[145]

On October 23, the same day Stockett wrote to Creswell, the *Sun*'s Annapolis correspondent reported good news for the Annapolis Redemptorists:

> Among the enrolled and exempted in this city were seventy of the Fathers, Brothers and students in the Redemptorist College. Mr. Stockett, the commissioner, received orders to erase their names from the roll, on the ground of "religious society."[146]

Evidence of these exemptions is found in the Annapolis enrollment book. Although not all seventy of the Redemptorist priests, brothers, and students were included in the enrollment list certified on September 19, the twenty-five who had their occupation listed as "student" had the phrase "of Divinity Exempt" written in red ink in the remarks column, and their names were crossed out, also in red ink. Creswell had finally used his discretion to rule favorably on the request for exemption. The Redemptorist students no longer eligible for the draft. It was a good thing because as of October 1, 1862, the aggregate number of men needed to fulfill Anne Arundel County's militia quota was 595 and only 70 volunteers had appeared., leaving a deficit of 525 and a net residue to be drafted of 491.[147]

Draft exemption hearings were held in Annapolis from late September and to mid-November. The *Sun* reported that 58 percent of those enrolled were exempted from the draft, which was originally set for October 15 but postponed several times. It was finally held at the county courthouse on December 3 and, of those still eligible, 491 were drafted. Elihu Samuel Riley Jr., son of the *Maryland Republican* editor—"known as a rebel" and later arrested—said that many of the conscripts were southern sympathizers, which "made miserable men and women" in Annapolis. Some, he wrote, suddenly found they experienced "unsuspected sources of pain and impediment" when their "unlucky number" was drawn, while others paid for substitutes. A citizen committee was formed to monitor the progress of the draft so that Annapolis did not furnish more than its quota of soldiers. Of the 110 men drafted from Annapolis, eleven were long absent from the city and "supposed to be in the South." In the meantime, the Redemptorists were saved from the perils of military service. Or, as Father Girardey put it when learning of the Redemptorists' exemptions, "the storm passed over thanks to God and the intercession of Mary."[148]

The draft also was of concern to St. Mary's laity. Sixty-nine men identified as connected to St. Mary's were enrolled for the 1862 draft. Other male parishioners not identified through sacramental registers or other means also would have been enrolled for the draft and would have increased the St. Mary's enrollment number substantially. Of the sixty-nine enrolled, only ten were subject to military duty and fifty-nine were granted exemptions. Forty-four met the criteria that Frank Stockett complained about: "diseased," which meant they had been exempted by the surgeon for real or imagined medical conditions. They were not alone: 157 other Annapolis men were examined and found to be "diseased," amounting to 37 percent of the total city enrollment (525). Five other St. Mary's men were above the age of forty-five and deemed too old to serve. Seven were listed as "foreigner, never naturalized." Two were already in the army and two were in Newport with the Naval Academy. The rest—one in each category—were exempted for the following reasons: "practicing physician," "discharged from Marine Corps for honorable service and by reason of family application," and "gone South." Fifteen of the sixty-nine men enrolled were non-Catholic male relatives of St. Mary's parishioners.[149]

One of the St. Mary's men appearing in the 1862 draft enrollment was Orrin Judson Brombley. He appears only twice in parish records—both times in 1859—as "John Bapt. Brumbley, alias Orin." In the first instance, his own baptism, it was noted that he had never before been baptized and had converted to Catholicism from "nihilism" at age twenty-seven. Three weeks later, Brombley served as godfather to four-year-old Thomas William Airland, whose three older brothers had been baptized a week earlier. Although his name never appears again in the church records, he did receive notice in public records. He tried to register to vote in the 1860 city elections but was overruled by the Annapolis election judges because he was a "non-resident." In documentation he provided later, Brombley claimed he was born in Annapolis in 1832, the son of Jesse and Roby Brombley, natives of Rhode Island, and that before the war worked as a seaman and sailor. None of these claims have been substantiated. After he was enrolled for the draft in 1862, he was found "diseased" and exempted. But the enrollment record also said he had been discharged from previous volunteer service in the US army. Brombley had enlisted in Baltimore on October 8, 1861, then sent to Camp Hoffman and assigned to Company B, Fifth Maryland Infantry, also known as the Public Guard Regiment. As a result of serving a double shift of guard duty in the cold November rain without a proper uniform overcoat, Brombley contracted pneumonia and was admitted to the regimental hospital in Baltimore. He was released from the hospital in January 1862 and in March went with his regiment to Fort Monroe. His health further deteriorated and on May 10 he was given a medical discharge for pulmonary tuberculosis. After the war he settled in Fair Haven, Connecticut, and later in nearby Meriden. He was married and widowed twice and had at least one child who died "from pure want." He never fully recovered his health and held only odd jobs with the Town of Fair Haven and at the Grand Army of the Republic post in Meriden. He applied for a Federal invalid pension in 1877 that was finally granted in 1888. After a series of illnesses, he died in the Meriden hospital 1915. He is buried in Meriden's Walnut Grove Cemetery, where his cemetery headstone has his name spelled as Bromley and notes his Civil War service with the Fifth Maryland.[151]

Two St. Mary's men who were not exempted enlisted in the Union army: John Jackson, Company D, Fifth Maryland Infantry, and William Young, Company A, First Maryland Infantry. Two others—Joseph Daley, Company D, Fifth Maryland Infantry, and William C. Lee, possibly with Company C, Forty-Seventh New York Infantry—were exempted because they already were in the army. Louis James DuBois, a former Redemptorist seminarian dispensed from his vows in 1861, and his brothers Edward Speed DuBois and William R. DuBois, were among those exempted as "diseased." James Revell sought an official exemption from the War Department because of his elective position as state's attorney. Instead, both he and his brother Martin were certified as "diseased" by the examining surgeon. John Himmelheber was one of the men exempted because of age (forty-eight at the time, three years old than the maximum age liable to military duty).[151]

Confirmation and Tonsure

Archbishop Kenrick visited Annapolis for confirmation of fourteen persons on August 30. They represent an interesting cross section of the parish and an indication of the small-town intimacy of Annapolis. Twelve were White, two were Black, six were male, eight female. They ranged in age from teenagers to middle-age adults. Two were converts. All were Annapolis residents. They and their families are discussed here in the order in which they are listed in the confirmation register, males first, females next, and "colored" last.[152]

First on the list is the most prominent confirmand, thirty-four-year-old Henry Roland Walton. He was the second of Colonel John Walton's four sons and was usually known as H. Roland Walton. He graduated from St. John's College in 1847 and the University of Maryland School of Medicine in Baltimore in 1850. His medical office initially was located in or adjacent to his father's City Hotel complex but, by 1862, it had moved to the family home on Francis Street. He was one of the donors of the new church bells in 1859 and, in addition to his 1862 confirmation, his name appears in the parish baptismal registers five times during the Civil War as the father and godfather of children. Four months before H. Roland's confirmation, he married twenty-three-year-old Julia Ballard Kent of a slave-owning family of Anne Arundel and Prince George's counties. Her father, DeWitt Kent, was a gentleman farmer and her grandfather, Joseph Kent, had been governor of Maryland (1826–29) and a US Senator (1833–37). The family was Episcopalian but two years after her marriage, Julia converted and was herself confirmed. Julia had a double influence on her conversion. Not only was her husband Catholic, but her younger sister, Ella Lee Kent, had converted a month before Julia. Ella then served as godparent, along with H. Roland, at Julia's baptism. Their brother, Etheridge Kent, served as a landsman in the US Navy on the blockade of the Texas coast and during the joint Army-Navy attacks on Fort Fisher, which guarded the port of Wilmington, North Carolina, in December 1864 and January 1865.[153]

The second confirmand, John Clark, was not well known. He presumably was the same as parishioner John H. Clark, who, with his wife Bridget O'Brien Clark, immigrated from Ireland via England in 1858 or 1859. He was thirty-eight years old in 1862 and worked as a laborer at the Naval Academy and as a waterman. He and his wife were parents of five daughters and one son. One of the daughters—Anne Theresa, who like two of her sisters was born in England—married into the musical Gesner family. Another—Bridget, known as "Bessie"—joined the School Sisters of Notre Dame in Baltimore in 1885, taking the name of Sister Mary Imelda.[154]

Luke Burns, listed as Lucas Bairne in the confirmation register, was a twenty-six-year-old Irish immigrant. He worked as a laborer during the Civil War and, because he was not a US citizen at the time, was exempted from the 1862 draft. After the war, he worked as a wagon driver. He and his wife, Mary Quinn Burns, were parents of five children baptized at St. Mary's. Luke, who died in 1912, and Mary, who died in 1883, are buried at St. Mary's Cemetery.[155]

John Mahan was born in Ireland and appears only twice in the St. Mary's Civil War-era records. The first time was his confirmation. The second was at the baptism of his newborn son, Marcus, later in 1862. His Irish-born wife, Elizabeth Hassler Mahan, appears only in the baptismal record. Anna Mahan Curley, the mother of another infant baptized the same day, was the godmother for Marcus, presumably her nephew. Anna, her husband Timothy Curley, a Union soldier, and their daughter later lived in Baltimore.[156]

Another Irish immigrant was Edward Powers who, at age thirty-eight, was one of the two oldest men confirmed. He immigrated to the United States around 1849, was working as a watchman at the Naval Academy by 1852, and became a naturalized citizen in 1856. By 1860 or earlier he ran a grocery business. Powers served on a committee appointed in September 1860 to support the Northern Democratic presidential candidate Stephen A. Douglas. During the war, he served on a county board of coroners and jurors of inquest. He became an Annapolis police officer in 1868 and city tax collector in 1870, a position he apparently retained for many years. Edward and his wife, Ann Ellen Dunn Powers, were godparents for nine local men, women, and children between 1858 and 1868. They had one child of their own, an adopted daughter, Eugenie, who was born in 1876. She and her parents are buried at St. Mary's Cemetery. When Powers died in 1904, the Redemptorist chronicler noted that he was "one of the oldest, most respected, and most reliable members of the parish" and it was thought that he "was the last survivor of those who attended the old church far back in the '50s."[157]

Somewhat rare in Annapolis for the period was an Italian immigrant, thirty-eight-year-old John Baptiste Parodi. He had married a Dorchester County woman, Susan B. Carroll, sometime before 1845 and confirmed in 1862. Parodi was not enrolled for the 1862 or 1863 drafts, thus avoiding the opportunity for military service. In 1865 and 1866 he was indicted for selling liquor to minors but found not guilty. Parodi died from consumption in 1875. Susan Parodi lived to age ninety-four before joining her husband in St. Mary's Cemetery in 1903.[158]

Julia Ann Wells Daley was the widow of Francis Nicholas Daley, newspaper editor and Annapolis tax collector. She was confirmed two years after her husband's death. She also served as godparent to three of the ten children in the family of Thomas Denver, a city constable and an "indifferent Catholic," and his Protestant wife, Maria Stansbury. Five years after Julia's death from jaundice at age fifty-two in 1877, one of her daughters, Harriet Ann, married into another St. Mary's Parish family, that of Charles Henry Treadway, son of Henry Holmes Treadway and Emma Duvall Treadway, who are discussed elsewhere in this book.[159]

Another confirmand was Maria Carroll, who was godparent in 1856 for newborn twins Maria and John Gunning, children of John J. Gunning, an Anne Arundel County farmer, and Catherine Carroll Gunning, both from Ireland. In 1864 Maria Carroll served as godmother for a namesake, Maria or Mary

Carroll, daughter of John Carroll and Brigitta Kelly Carroll, both from County Roscommon, where Catherine Carroll was born. Two young women, Bridget Carroll (age twenty) and presumably her sister, Margaret (age eighteen), lived with the Gunning family on a farm outside Annapolis, according to the 1860 census. Margaret Carroll married Matthew McLoughlin, from County Westmeath, Ireland, in July 1863 (with Bridget as a witness), and Matthew McLoughlin served as godparent, along with Maria Carroll at the baptism of the baby Maria Carroll in 1864. The relationships indicate close interfamily ties for a family about which little else was found.[160]

Confirmand Joanna Mary Brady Walton was the daughter of John and Sarah Brady and sister of John Wesley Brady, all of Cornhill Street in Annapolis. She married Edward Walton, younger brother of H. Roland Walton, in 1857. Like her brother-in-law's wife, Julia Ballard Kent, Joanna Brady was a convert, in this case from Methodism. She was baptized by Father Jacobs three years after her marriage to Edward. Her sponsor was Alida McParlin, wife of Colonel Thomas Andrew McParlin, the army surgeon in charge of US General Hospital, Division No. 2. Edward worked with his father managing the City Hotel. During the 1860 election campaign, Edward was appointed to the Northern Democrats' Annapolis committee supporting Stephen A. Douglas for president. Edward was exempted in the 1862 Maryland draft as "diseased" but when the Federal enrollment was carried out in 1863, he was declared "subject to do military duty." He was not drafted, however, and continued managing the hotel and the hotel's supply farm, plus operating another farm he owned near Round Bay on the Severn River. Between 1858 and 1883, Joanna gave birth to fifteen children, all of whom were baptized at St. Mary's. After 1900 Edward and Joanna moved to Contra Costa County, California. Although they both have grave markers at St. Mary's Cemetery, they died and were buried in California in 1906 and 1922, respectively.[161]

Mary McBride was born in Ireland around 1845. Four years after her confirmation, she married Henry Esmond, identified in the 1870 census as an Irish immigrant and bartender in Annapolis. Mary appears several times in St. Mary's records: in 1863 as a witness (with Darby Mullan) to the marriage of soldier Sylvester McCabe to Margaret McBride, and as godparent to James Marius Casey; in 1866 for her own wedding; and in 1918 for her burial at St. Mary's Cemetery. She and her husband, Henry Esmond, had two children (Elizabeth, born in 1868, and Bartholomew, born in 1870). Henry died in 1880 and she and the two children went to live with her sister, Catherine McCabe Riordan on Prince George Street. Mary's brother-in-law was Bartholomew John Esmond. Before the war he lived in Brooklyn and less than two weeks after the war started enlisted as a private in Company D, Fifth New York Infantry. His regiment was involved in the Virginia Peninsula Campaign (March–August 1862) but in May 1862 he was in an army at Annapolis and was noted in October as a deserter by in his New York State service record. If he deserted from the army in Annapolis, it is unlikely he would have remained in town. It was not uncommon for state adjutants general to list men as deserters when their names were not found on updated rosters. Instead Bartholomew stayed in Annapolis where he worked as a barkeeper and, after the war, as a police officer. The 1870 Federal Census listed him as a thermometer maker. He died from consumption in 1888. Bartholomew's wife, Mary Benson Esmond, was born in Dublin, Ireland, in 1840 and died from consumption in Annapolis in 1877. Bartholomew's son, John Henry Esmond was born in 1865 and died in 1872 from croup; another son, born in 1872, was given the same name. All of the Esmonds are buried in St. Mary's Cemetery. Mary McBride Esmond's role as a godmother was brief. Her godson, James Marius Casey, was born, baptized, and died all on the same day, August 14, 1863, and buried the next day.[162]

Catherine Wells Blackburn, born in Annapolis in 1833, was a convert from Methodism, baptized at St. Mary's in August 1859 and married to Francis Blackburn (a non-Catholic who later converted), in November 1859. Catherine also was the granddaughter of Christopher Hohne, a Revolutionary War veteran from Annapolis, and thus related to the Brady, DuBois, and Revell families, all of which had members who were St. Mary's parishioners.[163]

A member of the aforementioned DuBois family was among the August 1862 confirmands. She was Sarah Ann DuBois, seventeen-year-old daughter of Edward Francis DuBois, a French immigrant, Annapolis attorney, and clerk of the Maryland Court of Appeals, and Rosetta Jane Holland, a native Annapolitan. Sarah Ann's parents were married at St. Mary's in 1835. She later married Robert Wiley Milligan, who had entered the Naval Academy in 1863 and retired as a rear admiral in 1905.[164]

Sarah Elizabeth Lee, a free Black woman, was introduced earlier (see Marriages and Baptisms, ch. 3). Now, in August 1862, she was confirmed. Sarah was found two other times in St. Mary's records. In 1865 she was a witness to the marriage of teamster Edmund Payne to Anna Lee, who may have been her sister. The next year, as further evidence of a familial relationship, Sarah served as godmother to Anna's infant daughter, Maria Elizabeth Payne. Although Anna and Edmund Payne appeared in the 1870 census, no clear evidence has been found in public records of Sarah Elizabeth Lee Smith. A Richard Smith, a Black laborer married to Lizzie, a thirty-two-year old "mulatto" servant, appeared, without children, in the 1880 census for Annapolis. This couple lived in the home of George W. Moss, a White merchant, and Mary J. Moss, on Main Street. Perhaps "Lizzie" was the same as the 1862 confirmand Sarah Elizabeth.[165]

The last name on the confirmation list is Mary Ann Lee Campbell. She was a young Black woman of Annapolis whose son, James Robert Campbell, had been baptized at age two at St. Mary's in 1857. Mary Ann and the baby's father, Robert Campbell, an Annapolis slave, were married at St. Mary's in 1860. Shortly before her confirmation day, Mary Ann served as godmother for an infant, Sarah Jane Lee, daughter of James Henry Lee, a non-Catholic from Baltimore, and Henrietta

Anna Peake, a free Black woman born in Annapolis. Henrietta Peake had converted from Methodism the previous year with her baptism at St. Mary's at age eighteen. She was a free Black woman, the daughter of Grandison Peake, a former slave who, in 1850, lived with his family in the First Election District. There is insufficient information to determine if Mary Ann Lee Campbell was related to little Sarah Jane Lee, who died at age nine months. Soon after her goddaughter's burial at St. Mary's Cemetery in January 1863, Mary Ann served as godmother for John Urias Brown, infant son of Stephan Brown from the Eastern Shore, and Delphine Stepney, a native of Anne Arundel County; and then for Charles Nathanael Balden, infant son of John Balden and Maria Stepney, both born in Anne Arundel County. In both cases, the parents were Protestants and the baptisms were conducted in private homes by Father Girardey (for John Urias) and Father Henning (for Charles Nathanael). It was noted in the case of John Urias that he was *"in articulo mortis"* (at the moment of death) at the time of his baptism. Although Mary Ann Lee Campbell does not appear again in the St. Mary's records during the Civil War, these latter two baptisms reveal her collaboration with the Redemptorists to "save souls" in the Black community of Annapolis.[166]

John Runge, a seminarian who had professed his vows in July 1862, was reported in the *Chronica Domus* as having been among eighteen persons confirmed on August 31. The parish confirmation register lists only fourteen confirmands and did not include Runge, and gives the date as August 30. It is unlikely that Runge's name was left off the confirmation register if he had been confirmed but equally unlikely that the Redemptorist chronicler would say he had been confirmed if he had not been. It is possible that Kenrick confirmed Runge in a separate, private ceremony before he conferred tonsure and minor orders on Runge and nineteen other students on September 1.[167]

After attending to the parishioners who had prepared for confirmation, Archbishop Kenrick conferred tonsure on twenty students of rhetoric. This rite involved the shearing of hair, investment with a surplice, and initiation into the four minor orders or ministries of the Catholic Church: porter, lector, exorcist, and acolyte. This is the stage preliminary to the major orders of subdeacon, deacon, and priest. The rite of tonsure gave the young men clerical status in the eyes of the Church, allowing them certain ecclesiastical privileges, including precedence over the laity in religious assemblies and processions. In this case, the conferral of minor orders is presumed to have had a hoped-for bearing on the men's draft status.[168]

The Pope's Bull

A major change took place in the District of Columbia earlier in 1862 that had an immediate impact on Maryland. On April 16, President Lincoln signed into law the District of Columbia Emancipation Act. It provided for the immediate emancipation of slaves in the District and provided compensation of up to $300 per slave to former owners who declared allegiance to the Union. It also provided payments for up to $100 to freed people who were willing to migrate to Haiti, Liberia, "or such other country beyond the limits of the United States." Maryland would not emancipate its enslaved people for another two and a half years. In the interim, numerous individuals, small clusters of families and friends, and even large groups of Maryland fugitive slaves, including many from Anne Arundel County, escaped into the District of Columbia. They were often followed by owners seeking to reclaim their property under the 1850 Fugitive Slave Act.[169]

The reaction in the local news media to the District of Columbia Emancipation Act was negative and cautionary. The *Maryland Republican* called the act a "most heinous outrage" and a "wicked and disgusting work." The *Annapolis Gazette* cautioned its readers to "gracefully accept an evil we cannot avoid" and called for a plan "for the protection of slave owners."[170]

The following July, Lincoln drafted his Preliminary Emancipation Proclamation and held it in abeyance for an opportune moment to make it public, ideally after a major Union battlefield victory. The opportunity came after the September 16–17 Battle of Antietam and Lincoln released the preliminary proclamation on September 22. It reiterated that the purpose of the war was to restore the constitutional relation between the United States and each of the states. But furthermore, Lincoln declared that all persons held as slaves in any state, or part of a state, in rebellion against the United States, as of January 1, 1863, "shall be then, thenceforward, and forever free." The proclamation applied only to states in rebellion against the Federal government, but not to parts of southern states that had come back under Federal control nor to loyal slave states, such as Maryland. The document also proposed to seek financial compensation from Congress to those states that accepted voluntary, immediate or gradual abolition of slavery and the colonization of persons of African descent "with their consent, on this continent, or elsewhere." Lincoln also invoked an act of Congress of March 13, 1862, that forbade the Federal army and navy to return fugitive slaves to their owner unless— according to a July 17, 1862 law— the owner swore an oath of allegiance to the Federal government.[171]

In the opinion of the *Maryland Republican,* Lincoln's proclamation was "unconstitutional and violates the solemn pledge of Congress in 1861, endorsed by the president, that war is waged not to interfere with slavery in the states but to restore the Constitution and the Union and enforce the laws." The *Annapolis Gazette,* reporting on other Maryland newspapers, wrote that "very few have condemned it but one, *Cambridge Intelligencer,* has endorsed it."[172]

A week previous to signing the proclamation, Lincoln made a joking reference to the pope in a letter to Chicago clergymen who petitioned him to free the slaves. Lincoln replied:

> What good would a proclamation from me do, especially as we are now situated? I do not want to use a document that the whole world will see must necessarily be inoperative, like the pope's bull against the comet! Would my word free the slaves, when I cannot

even enforce the Constitution in the rebel States?[173]

He had his proclamation already for release and yet he seemed to tease the Chicago clergy with this statement. But the American Catholic hierarchy—both North and South—and the Catholic press, even those newspapers that were pro-war, were unhappy with the Preliminary Emancipation Proclamation. They saw it as radical and unconstitutional. Two days after the proclamation, Lincoln imposed martial law nationwide, causing fear of a still-stricter wartime regime.[174]

William Paca House, Annapolis, before 1890. Historic American Building Survey, Library of Congress https://www.loc.gov/pictures/item/md0052.photos.084102p/.

Morals of the Pupils

Catholic education had been offered in Annapolis on an informal basis, by itinerant Jesuits and an occasional lay instructor, at least since the early eighteenth century. In colonial times, women played an important educational role in what was basically a home ministry and this continued into the nineteenth century. In 1812 Charles Carroll of Carrollton's granddaughter, Emily Caton, provided Catholic religious instructions to twenty or thirty persons. In 1819 Archbishop Ambrose Maréchal sent her a package of catechisms that she and her friend Mary Theresa Murdoch used to teach Sunday school, mostly to non-Catholic boys whose parents evidently allowed them to attend. Such instructions also took place at Doughoregan Manor, the Carroll family country estate in Howard County, where in 1861 enslaved persons attended Sunday Mass followed by a catechism lessons for the children.[175]

In the 1820s, when public schools were being widely established in the United States, the American bishops urged the establishment of Catholic parochial schools. This initial call was renewed at the First Plenary Council of Baltimore in 1852 and while progress was made in larger cities, nothing happened in Annapolis. Things began to change, however, with the arrival of the Redemptorists in 1853. First there was Bishop Neumann's 1859 attempt to bring the Immaculate Heart of Mary sisters to Annapolis (see Plans for a Parochial School, ch. 2). That effort did not materialize, but in October 1861 a public notice advertised the opening of a new day school on twenty-fifth of that month. The school was to provide "the rudiments of an English education" for boys and girls. Although no tie was made directly to St. Mary's or to Catholics, those seeking further information were directed to contact the principal, Miss M. Hayne, or the Rev. J. M. Jacobs. Who Miss M. Hayne was has not be determined, but there was a parishioner in 1864, eighteen-year-old Barbara Hayne who may have been Miss M. Hayne's sister. The clergyman must have been Father Joseph Maria Jacobs, since no other priest or minister named Jacobs with the initials J. M. was in Annapolis at the time. The same advertisement also noted that a "University for Young Ladies" would be inaugurated the following March, and, again, with no connection made to St. Mary's. The young ladies' school was to be located "on Prince George street, at the house formerly occupied by Col. William A. Spencer" and the day school was in "a building attached to the Academy." This was the same wing of the house that in an early rental advertisement offered "a fine Office and Library Room." Spencer rented the William Paca House on Prince George Street during part of his tenure as clerk of the Court of Appeals of Maryland from 1852 to 1863.[176] Whether or not either of these academic institutions actually opened is not known, but the impetus existed to start a parochial school and Father Jacobs, who had played a role in the 1859 attempt, was involved.

After liturgical services were shifted to St. Mary's new church when it opened in late 1859, the old church was converted into a parish hall. Plans soon were made to start a parochial school in the hall. One of the enduring contributions Father Seelos left to St. Mary's was the establishment of this school. To make space for classrooms, a second story was added internally by extending the upper gallery for the full length and width of the building. The second story was used as the parish hall and the ground story was divided into two classrooms. The school opened on September 29, 1862. By the next year, the attached old Jesuit rectory was renovated and

ST. MARY'S CATHOLIC SCHOOL.

SOUTH EAST STREET, FORMERLY DUKE OF GLOUCESTER.

THIS School will commence on Monday, 29th Sept. at 9 o'clock, A. M.

Particular attention will be paid to the morals of the pupils.

Children of other denominations attending the School will not be interfered with as regards their religion.

All will be required to render prompt obedience to the rules of the school.

For the terms apply at the school house, on South East street, to

MISS J. O'DONOUGHUE

Sept. 27, 1862--2m*

Advertisement for the opening of St. Mary's School, Maryland Republican, *November 29, 1862. Dr. Robert L. Worden Collection, SC 5725-3, Maryland State Archives.*

used as a residence and office space for the lay teachers.[177]

A notice for the new school appeared for the first time in the *Maryland Republican* on September 27. It informed the public that the school would open and that:

> Particular attention will be paid to the morals of the pupils. Children of other denominations attending the School will not be interfered with as regards their religion. All will be required to render prompt obedience to the rules of the school.[178]

Redemptorist historian Henry Borgmann wrote forty years later: "Besides secular training, the children received regular instruction in our holy religion, and its effects were gradually perceived in their good behavior." Soon after the school was established, Father Seelos reported that "not a Sunday goes by but there are several Protestants present, of whom several have already come over to the Church, and probably still more will come over, for these Protestants are, by nature and from the liberal education of this country, not very bitter and even send their children to the Catholic school that we have opened near the church."[179]

Secular education would have involved typical elementary school subjects. An 1868 report on St. Mary's School, just a year after the School Sisters of Notre Dame took charge, said that the students were awarded for their achievements in deportment, Christian doctrine, general application, geography, grammar, self improvement, penmanship, and regular attendance. Girls were recognized for their excellence in plain sewing, knitting, crochet, tapestry, and fancy and needle work.[180]

Issues of *The Catholic Youth's Magazine*, published in Baltimore by Martin Kerney, might have been read by young Catholics in Annapolis before and during the Civil War. The stated purpose of the magazine was "to supply useful and pleasant reading, to cultivate the affections and to chasten the fancy" and as an antidote to "the strenuous efforts which are made to pervert the minds of Catholic youth and to draw them from the Church." Catholic youth learned about such historical figures as George Washington and Charles Carroll of Carrollton, who was cast as an example of a public servant devoted to his religion. They also read descriptions of the American states as well as articles about national monuments, the ancient world, arithmetic, astronomy, and nature. On the behavioral side, the magazine published brief morality tales touching on obedience, honesty, brotherly affection, meddling, lying, swearing, the dangers of drunkenness, and more. There also were words of advice, such as "wicked children have no resting place either in this world or the next"; "they are happiest who even in their sports remember the golden rule"; and "if you keep your thoughts pure, your life will be guiltless." On the more domestic side, there were useful hints for young house keepers: "it is a sacrifice of money to buy poor cheese" and "old rice sometimes has little black insects inside the kernels." For spiritual reading there were stories about the Infant Jesus, Christmas, guardian angels, Mary and the saints, poems, the origin of the rosary, and prayers. Also included were stories about lions, bears, fish, whimsical horses, unicorns, and ghosts. When the war began, more martial themes and illustrations appeared. The April 1861 issue featured a picture of a cannon and declared "every boy knows what cannons are, and the terrible use they are put to in war."[181] All these readings were suitable for forming young Catholic minds in parochial and Sunday schools, such as in Annapolis.

The first teacher at St. Mary's parish school was Josephine O'Donoughue, the sister of Frater Charles O'Donoughue, a Redemptorist seminarian who would be ordained at St. Mary's in 1867. Josephine was born in Rochester, New York, on October 7, 1834, the daughter of John O'Donoughue and Rose Ann Clary. Her father was in the retail furniture business and ran an auction house in downtown Rochester and performed public service as a member of the board of directors of the New York State Western House of Refuge, a reformatory for juvenile delinquents. After Josephine completed her own education, she became a public school teacher in Rochester, by which time her brother Charles had entered the

Father (earlier Frater) Charles Constantine Pise O'Donoughue, C.Ss.R. (1836–71). RABP.

Redemptorist novitiate in Annapolis. He professed his vows in 1859 and went to Cumberland to study under Father Seelos and returned to Annapolis with Father Seelos in June 1862 as a student of philosophy.[182]

Although it is not recorded, it is possible that Charles and other seminarians joined Josephine in teaching at the school. Josephine's younger sister Catherine also apparently was helping out with religious instruction. In April 1864, Kate, as she was known, served as godparent for fifteen-year-old Ella Lee Kent, a convert from the Episcopal church.[183]

Although Josephine may have left temporarily in 1864, she was in Annapolis at least through 1866 and was active in extracurricular affairs. She was godmother for twelve-year-old John Denver in 1863; a witness at the marriage of waterman Henry P. Moore to Amanda Daley in 1864; godmother for seven-year-old Henry H. Dunker, Jr., a convert from Methodism along with the rest of his family, in 1865; and confirmation sponsor for Elizabeth McCabe, of unknown age, in 1866. Josephine's good works may have been manifested still further. When Archbishop Martin Spalding came to Annapolis for confirmation in December 1864, sixteen-year-old Black convert Elizabeth Hodges took the name Josephine. And in January 1866, two adults took Josephine as their confirmation names. One was Frances Campbell Dunker, the mother of Henry; the other was Catherine O'Rourke, of unspecified age.[184]

By 1866 about fifty children were in attendance at St. Mary's School. And, by this time, classes also were being offered for Black children, of any faith.[185] As for Josephine, she found a calling to the religious life. She tried two other religious orders before she entered the Sisters of Mercy in Brooklyn, New York, on December 7, 1869, taking a name that harkened back to her Redemptorist connections: Sister Mary Liguori. She professed her vows on July 16, 1872, and resided at St. Francis of AssisiConvent in Brooklyn. The Sisters of Mercy ran St. Patrick's parochial school as well as an industrial school for orphans. Unfortunately, like her brother Charles, she did not enjoy good health, and she died on June 18, 1879, and is buried in the Mercy plot at Holy Cross Cemetery in Brooklyn. The Sisters of Mercy records say that Josephine (Mary Liguori) O'Donoughue "was a most exemplary religious."[186]

Cover of The Catholic Youth's Magazine, *IV (September 1860–August 1861). Rare Books and Special Collections Division, Library of Congress.*

St. Mary's School (1862), the former first St. Mary's Church (1823–60). Original art by Nathaniel R. Worden.

As a final note on Josephine O'Donoughue: it is possible that she was the same person as Mother Mary Liguori who arrived in Annapolis with an undetermined number of Sisters of Mercy in 1872 to take charge of the parish school after the temporary departure of the School Sisters of Notre Dame. The *Chronica Domus* stated simply that on September 26, 1872, administration of the school had been entrusted to the "Sisters of Our Lady of Mercy" and on January 23, 1873, that one their members, Sister Maria Scholastica Liguori, was professed in the church.[187]

On June 16, 1873, the Sisters of Mercy, "now located and established in the City of Annapolis," purchased the Upton Scott House on Shipwright Street. Although they did not have full use of the house—the late owner's widow, Mrs. Dennis (Elizabeth) Claude, had a life estate on certain parts of the house—the sisters presumably used it as a convent. In the meantime, they probably used the former convent of the School Sisters of Notre Dame, the old Jesuit rectory on Duke of Gloucester Street. The Sisters of Mercy remained at St. Mary's only one year. After their departure from Annapolis, Mother Mary Liguori and her trustee, James Revell, signed a deed on February 6, 1874, for the sale of the Scott House to John Kelly of Philadelphia.[188] A extensive effort was made, with no concrete results, in the early 2000s to determine who this Mother Mary Liguori was and whence she came. The records of the Sisters of

Mercy in Josephine O'Donoughue's home convent in Brooklyn are scant and silent on her activities during the 1872–73 period. Given her prior connections with Annapolis and its parish school and the similarity of names and religious order, it seems likely that it was she who returned to Annapolis in 1872.

A Dutiful and Exemplary Son

Joseph Daley, according to a life-long acquaintance, was "a most dutiful and exemplary son." By age eighteen, he had gone to work as a printer's apprentice to support his widowed mother, four younger brothers, and three younger sisters. By age twenty, he was dead, killed in action at the Battle of Antietam.

Joseph was born in Annapolis in 1842, the eldest son of Francis Nicholas Daley and Julia Ann Wells. The elder Daley had been editor of two local newspapers, the *Maryland Republican* and the *Democratic Star,* and then served as the state and county tax collector in Annapolis from 1849 to 1855. These credentials fixed Francis well within the Democratic Party orb. Julia's father, Elijah Wells, was a veteran of the War of 1812 and, in 1840, was the locomotive engineer on the first Annapolis and Elk Ridge Railroad train run into Annapolis. Although Francis and Julia were married at the Methodist Church on State Circle in 1839, Francis had earlier Catholic connections in Annapolis. He and two younger sisters were baptized by Jesuit Father Van Quickenbourne, presumably in the Carroll House chapel, in 1820. Extant parish records list baptisms for the younger four of the seven Daley children, Julia's confirmation and her service as godmother, and a daughter's marriage during the Civil War. In 1866 Julia again served as a confirmation sponsor.[189]

Francis Daley died in 1860 leaving Julia a thirty-nine-year-old widow with Joseph and seven minor children. Joseph, the eldest, supported the family with the wages received as an apprentice printer. In October 1861, just six months after the Civil War began, he went to Baltimore to enlist in the Fifth Maryland Infantry Regiment. The regiment—known as the Public Guard Regiment—was formed in September to guard railroads and government property. Joseph was mustered in as a private in Company D for three years on December 3. The regiment trained for four months at Camp Hoffman in Baltimore and then was assigned to Fort Monroe in March 1862. When the Confederates invaded Maryland in September 1862, the Fifth Maryland was reassigned to the Army of the Potomac and quickly marched north, reaching their rendezvous point northeast of the village of Sharpsburg, on September 16. They camped overnight in the rain near Samuel Pry's mill.[190]

The fighting started after dawn on September 17, on farmland north of Sharpsburg. Joseph's regiment was held in reserve as Union and Confederate forces clashed first in a cornfield northwest of the Fifth Maryland's position and then in woods on the Hagerstown Pike. After nearly two hours of fierce fighting, Union forces pushed the Confederates south toward Sharpsburg and a brief lull occurred. The Union advance halted as the rebels dug in along a narrow, rutted farm road—known locally as Hog Trough Road—that had been worn down two to three feet below the surface by erosion and years of heavy farm wagon travel. The Confederates piled up fence rails on the northern embankment of the Sunken Road, as it was also known, to improve their defensive position and waited the Union onslaught. The Sunken Road was soon being called "Bloody Lane."[191]

A new battle sector opened around 9:00 AM. Joseph's regiment, along with nine other infantry regiments, waded across waist-deep Antietam Creek and, supported by three artillery batteries, they marched in parade formation through an apple orchard and across William and Margaret Roulette's farm. Most of Joseph's division are said to have been "green, their banners clean and whole, and their advance was glorious." The Fifth Maryland, First Delaware, and Fourth New York were in the vanguard of the Union attack along the Sunken Road. As they moved forward, the Fifth Maryland was the middle of the three regiments, an extremely vulnerable position aimed at the center of the well-entrenched Southern line. The Marylanders went into action with nearly 600 officers and men. Because the quartermaster wagon with additional ammunition had not caught up with the regiment, each man carried only ten cartridges—forty was typical—for their 54-caliber Austrian-made rifles. When they came face-to-face with the Southerners, they were met with "sudden and terrible fire" from Alabama and North Carolina troops. Col. John B. Gordon, the commander of Alabama troops directly facing the Fifth Maryland, later said that with the opening volley the "entire front line [of Union troops], with few exceptions, went down in the consuming blast." The commander of an adjacent Confederate regiment reported that their first volley "brought down the enemy as grain falls before the reaper." As fresh Union regiments moved forward, the vanguard fell back but not before thirty-nine Fifth Maryland soldiers had been killed and 109, including all of the officers, were wounded. Some of the wounded later died from their injuries. An army surgeon documented that Joseph Daley had been "shot through the heart" and killed.[192]

Nearly 5,600 men were killed or wounded on both sides during the three-and-a-half hour carnage at Bloody Lane. An eyewitness saw the dead soldiers laid in piles three and four deep and told how "one could not step foot upon the ground without stepping on some of the effects of the mighty struggle." After four hours, the Confederate line finally collapsed and fighting continued south of Sharpsburg. Antietam produced an estimated 22,270 casualties, the highest singe-day total of the Civil War and in American history. Joseph Daley was one of 2,100 Union and 1,550 Confederate soldiers killed that day. The fourteen-hour-long Battle of Antietam is said to have changed the course of the Civil War, a turning point that gave Lincoln the opportunity to announce his Preliminary Emancipation Proclamation.[193]

News of war deaths traveled quickly, with anxious family members checking at the local news agencies for lists of the dead, wounded, and captured. It is not known when Julia learned of her son's death. Possibly the news was carried to her by Corporal William McCrea, a comrade from Company D, Fifth Maryland, who had been wounded and sent home. The *Maryland Republican* reported McCrea's presence in the city on October 4, noting also that "Private Joseph Daley, of this city, was killed in the battle of Sharpsburg."[194]

A report written three days after the battle appeared on the front page of the *Sun*. It said: "some of the most desperate fighting ever recorded in history took place . . . . the dead lying thick and in rows, where they had fallen on the enemy's centre" at Antietam and noted that an estimated 13,000 Union men had been killed or wounded. It also revealed that some of the dead had been "torn to pieces" by artillery shells. Churches and other buildings in the vicinity were filled with wounded soldiers and the "scenes at the hospitals and elsewhere in the vicinity of the battlefields were terrible." Ominously, it noted that Joseph's brigade commander's arm had been shot off during the battle.[195]

During his eight months in the army, Joseph regularly sent his mother an average of nine dollars a month out of his thirteen-dollars-a-month pay. When she applied for a widow's pension in 1865, witnesses testified that Julia had been wholly dependent on Joseph before the war and remained so after he enlisted in the army. She did not own property, had a large family of young children, and, with Joseph gone, "depended upon her own exertions for support." On July 27, 1865, Julia was granted a pension of eight dollars a month, retroactive to September 17, 1862, the day Joseph died. Julia herself died of jaundice in 1877 and rests in peace at St. Mary's Cemetery, along with three of her children and a great-grandson.[196]

Joseph Daley's final resting place is uncertain. Immediately after the battle, some soldiers were buried in single graves while hundreds of others were placed in long, shallow trenches near where they fell. Other burials were in more organized space, such as the 700 men buried on the Roulette farm. Grave markings "were somewhat haphazard, from stone piles to rough-hewn crosses and wooden headboards," according to the National Park Service, and many men were buried by farmers who did not record the identities. In 1864 the Maryland General Assembly appropriated money to purchase land for a formal cemetery and the next year many remains were disinterred and, to the extent possible, were identified and reburied in the new national cemetery in Sharpsburg, which was dedicated two years later by President Andrew Johnson. Of the 4,776 Union burials there, 1,836 are unknown. Joseph Daley is likely among these unknowns in this or another nearby cemetery, or his remains were not recovered from their now unidentified place on the battlefield. Remains have been found buried on the Antietam battlefield as recently as 1988. They were of men of the Sixty-Third New York, an infantry regiment that attacked the adjacent sector of the Sunken Road from Joseph Daley's regiment.[197]

Joseph's death was a bittersweet memory for his sister, Amanda Julia Daley Moore. When she gave birth to a son in 1865 she named the infant after her brother, calling him Joseph Washington Moore.[198]

Spiritual Help to the Unfortunate Soldiers

At the request of Archbishop Kenrick, the Annapolis Redemptorists' missionary work sent them far afield. Late in 1862, they went south to visit Catholic troops at Fort Monroe. The first St. Mary's visitor to Fort Monroe was Father James Bradley who was there from around November 9 to November 13. He was followed about a week later by Father Joseph Henning. He recorded in St. Mary's baptismal register in Annapolis the names of three children he baptized at Fort Monroe on November 23. They were Robert Henry Bright, an African American infant whose parents were natives of the James River area; Agnes Kelly, unidentified age and of Irish-born parents; and Mary Elizabeth Heppel, infant daughter of Sergeant John Heppel, Second US Artillery Regiment assigned to the fort, and his wife, Catherine McShane, who also served as godmother for Robert Henry Bright. Whether Catherine McShane Heppel stepped in at a moment's notice or played some role in bringing infant Robert and her own infant daughter for baptism is open to speculation. Henning returned to Annapolis sometime before December 7.[199]

In December Father Seelos went to Fort Monroe where, in his own words, he was "to give spiritual help to the unfortunate soldiers in the hospital there." Since there was no direct steamboat service from Annapolis, he had to go to Baltimore to obtain a pass and other documents. He was joined there by Frater Anthony Kesseler, who had been in Annapolis earlier but at this time was teaching Latin in Baltimore. They traveled at government expense on the steamboat *Adelaide*, leaving Baltimore on the evening of December 6 and arrived at Fort Monroe at 7:00 the next morning, the second Sunday of Advent. Seelos remarked in his account of the trip "how terribly cold it was" and that although there was no snow, "there was a cutting wind, fresh from the north." The two Redemptorists went directly to the church at Fort Monroe, St. Mary Star of the Sea Church, a small wooden building erected in 1860 to accommodate army personnel. They set up living quarters in the sacristy and lighted a fire. Mass was offered at 11:00 AM, and Seelos preached in English. After a simple meal of bread, butter, and wine, he spent the entire afternoon hearing confessions of soldiers quartered in and around the fort. Afterward, Kesseler, who apparently had visited Fort Monroe at least once before, escorted Seelos "to some Irish Catholics to get warmed up a bit." They were so friendly, according to Seelos, "that they actually constrained us to share with them at their table" and enjoy a warm meal. Early the next morning, he wrote, "divine Providence arranged it that a soldier brought us to his house for supper." This unidentified soldier, possibly an officer, was from the German Rhineland and had an Irish wife. He "hosted us with the greatest joy and loaded us with woolen blankets," wrote Seelos. Returning to the church afterward, Seelos heard confessions until midnight and then to bed down in the chilly sacristy, where even the blankets given to them were not enough to ward off the bitter cold. Seelos wrote, "I woke up several times during the night from the cold."[200]

On December 8, Seelos and Kesseler traveled about two

U.S. Military Hospital and chapel at Hampton, Virginia. Courtesy Casemate Museum, Fort Monroe, Virginia.

miles by carriage to an army hospital, probably the Hampton Military Hospital for enlisted men.[201] Seelos said:

> This hospital consists of twenty-one large barracks in which there are about fifty beds. The officers were most obliging and polite. Most of the sick were not so sick that they had to stay in bed but could walk around, and almost all of them could come to the room that was separated from the big sick ward, and there I heard their confession.
>
> On the first day, I hardly finished half the barracks. Afterwards I went to a heated room that was given me and where the apothecaries had set up their equipment. I was now eating and drinking with the soldiers and slept in a room with soldiers, but they conducted themselves in such a way that in the evening I could still pray my breviary in peace. The next morning, I was brought back to the church, and took with me Holy Communion for those soldiers who had been to confession the day before, and then I continued the confessions and the next morning I brought them Communion, for which the mess hall of the officers was given me.[202]

He described the communion service as follows:

> I had the table covered with white, set on it a crucifix and two candles, said a few words to the soldiers, made with them the acts of faith, hope, and charity, made with them a short thanksgiving, and dismissed them then with a short admonition to be real faithful in the service of God for the great grace that they had now received. All were moved to tears, and often the words were repeated that the appreciative soldiers addressed to me in gratitude: "God bless you!" This was necessary because I couldn't expect any money, because for many months now they had not received any pay. I was richly repaid by the fine attitude of the soldiers, most of whom had not been to confession for three or four years. For many it was even longer, and with several, twenty years. Some did not even know the principle truths of our holy faith and so you see, dear brother [Ambrose Seelos], that my stay there was very much needed.

The same service was repeated on December 9 and 10.

On their last day at Fort Monroe, Seelos and Kesseler were taken by the "head doctor and supervisor of the whole place" in his own carriage to the house of a Catholic officer. This presumably was the assistant surgeon, First Lieutenant Ely McClellan. He was not Catholic but Seelos found him "very well disposed to our faith that he will one day become a Catholic." The doctor asked many questions "and was unusually satisfied with the explanations I gave him." The unidentified Catholic officer and his Austrian wife hosted "a glorious dinner." Seelos was quite pleased to find that the Viennese wife had engaged a governess, "a real good, well educated German girl," to teach German to the couple's children.[203]

On the evening of December 10, the two Redemptorists departed aboard the steamboat *Georgiana*, arriving in Baltimore at 7:00 the next morning. They went directly to St. Alphonsus Church, where Seelos celebrated Mass, and then took the evening train to Annapolis. Returning home, he found the weather in Annapolis "was like summer" and advised that the "weather changes so quickly here in America and makes it highly dangerous and unhealthy for foreigners."[204]

Year-End Visitation

St. Mary's College ended 1862 with the annual canonical visitation. Father De Dycker, with Father Van de Braak as socius, spent nine days reorganizing the college and inspecting the parish registers. As a result of his findings, De Dycker issued seventeen corrective guidelines. Six of them applied solely to the students, two to the Redemptorist community in general, three to the priests, two to the lay brothers, and four to the parish.[205]

De Dycker's guidelines indicate some of the daily practices in the seminary and the Redemptorist community. The students were required to be in church when feast-day solemnities were observed rather than in the house chapel. Until further word was received from the superior general in Rome, Benediction of the Blessed Sacrament for the students was to be held in the chapel, in place of vespers, only during the octave of the Feast of the Immaculate Conception (December 8), all first- and second-class feasts of the Blessed Virgin Mary, the feast of St. Alphonsus, and on Tuesdays after Easter and Pentecost. At least twice a week, the students were permitted to go outdoors for walks, and, unless there was a valid necessity, the prefect was not to dispense them from this exercise. If they did not go for a walk, the students were free from manual work but could spend the time instead in the garden. After returning home from walking, the students were required to pray in the house chapel. In regard to recreation using the sailboats, "all rashness and disturbance of order is to be avoided with utmost diligence; moreover, all those things connected to the operation of the boats must be strictly observed." The final student rule required them, if able, to go to the church at 10:00 AM each day or, otherwise to the chapel or stay in their rooms to pray or meditate. They also were informed that the church was "intended for use only for worship or singing."

In an addendum to the guidelines dated December 31, 1862, a new schedule of classes and new rules were outlined. Classes were to be held every day, except for Thursdays but including Saturdays. Moral theology, dogmatic theology, church history, philosophy, and rhetoric were taught to respective student sections, beginning at 8:00 AM. In the afternoon, starting at 3:00, classes were held for exegesis, dogmatic theology, philosophy, and rhetoric. Mission studies were held on Wednesdays at 10:00 AM. On an occasional Sunday after vespers, for one hour and no more, theological case studies were to be presented to the students. Also, rhetoric class, oddly enough, was held on *Dominica* (Sunday) at 9:45 AM. Otherwise, classes were to begin "at not more than five minutes before the hour; in the afternoon, when the signal is given, class shall end at once, so that the fourth hour can be free for spiritual reading." Afternoon classes were suspended the day before solemn feast days, when students were required instead to read together from their breviaries. Wednesdays classes sometimes began at 9:00 instead of 8:00 AM, at which time a "chapter of faults" (*capitulam culparam*) was scheduled. This was a time of introspection, during which the students would accuse themselves, either privately or publicly, of ordinary faults and minor infractions of the Redemptorist Rule. This was not the same as sacramental confession but nevertheless an important part of preparation for the sacerdotal life.

A second addendum laid out seven guidelines involving student behavior as directed by the prefect and socius in dealing with ordinary and extraordinary matters. They included but were not limited to giving the prefect (that is, Dielemans) decision-making authority over the students during recreation. The socius had authority in matters of minor significance, such as "the corporal and temporal needs of food and drink."[206]

There also were guidelines for the Redemptorist community at large. The students were to receive regular conferences on the Redemptorist Rule and the priests were directed to regularly discuss moral issues with the them. Daily prayers as a community were required, "especially particular examination and evening prayers."[207]

The priests also received guidelines as a result of the visitation. The first decreed that "the time for preaching is to be rigorously defined," and "[d]uring meals or at any other time it is not proper to discuss indiscriminately what has been learned in sermons in Church." Moreover, De Dycker stipulated that "it is never allowed . . . to inquire about the opinions of outsiders" concerning their sermons, and the younger fathers were forbidden to give a sermon until the rector had first reviewed it. It was expected, "according to the Rule," that sometimes the priests were to help in the kitchen, serving food and washing dishes. The father zelator was charged with investigating accusations made against members of the religious community "but not, indeed, to tell the faults to the whole house." The final internal guideline directed that one of the lay brothers be appointed to make sure "that at any time the doors and windows of the chapel and of the whole house are closed as is appropriate at the time." The brothers who were tailors were reminded to ensure that the length of clothing they made was as prescribed by the Rule.[208]

The guidelines of more external nature directed that the rector "accurately preserve things according to the Rule and the Constitutions when reconciling the books of the house and the church." This was to be done monthly and he was to note his consultors' names as well as his own. (The author's inspection of the original house annals and parish registers reveals that this practice was not carried out although, when the provincial came for his annual visitation, his signature and sometimes that of his socius appears in these books. Other records, such as financial accounts, are no longer extant.) The maintenance of parish registers was not always done in a standard fashion. To help reconcile this, De Dycker directed that "in the baptismal register and in all the registers, the fathers must note the name of the person as well as the name of their native place." Parishioners were required to pay pew rent in the church and parents had to pay tuition or fees for the parochial school, "at set times, as far as possible, as provided by the Rule." Finally, it was stated that if a library was started for lay people, it had to be "vigorously maintained" and managed by the laity who, at set times, were to "make the books available in the parish school, but not in other places used by the laity."[209]

Christmas 1862 was celebrated in Annapolis, as one correspondent put it, as "a season of great festivity and social reunion," recognizing "the ability of Annapolitans to have a 'good time of it' upon all such occasions." A "grand dinner" was prepared for the wounded soldiers at General Hospital No. 1, as well as for the troops camped on College Green at St. John's College. Religious services were held at all the Annapolis churches, and St. Mary's and St. Anne's were noted as having been "tastefully decorated and festooned for the occasion."[210]

Chapter 5: 1863 — I Go to See Father Abraham

Not the Least Idea of Religious Life

On January 3, 1863, Martin Burke—the one-time soldier who yearned for religious life—reappeared at St. Mary's. He last was seen the previous July when he had "gone home" but had actually sought to join the Jesuits. But after living with them for a time, according to the *Chronica Domus*, "he was far less pleased there, than he had been here." Now he "endeavored to be readmitted among us, promising that he would no more leave us." The chronicler noted that once-again Brother Ambrose "had a good will but did not seem to have any real vocation." When he heard that Congress had enacted a new draft law in March 1863, Ambrose feared the government might recall him because of his earlier army service. "Therefore," it is recorded in the *Chronica Domus*, "he thought it well to leave the country." When last heard of, Martin Burke said he was going to try to become a Trappist in Nova Scotia. There was such a community, Our Lady of Grace Monastery in Antigonish County, Nova Scotia. However, Trappist archives have no record of Martin or Ambrose Burke.[1]

Soon after Burke's reappearance, another former soldier arrived on St. Mary's doorstep on February 25. He was twenty-four-year-old Irish-born Luke Cavanaugh and he wanted to embark on the religious life. Father De Dycker, visiting the college at the time, agreed to Luke's request to be admitted as a candidate lay brother. According to the *Chronica Domus*, he had been granted an honorable discharge from the Union army "because of his weak health." And Cavanaugh already was a known entity at St. Mary's. His name had been entered in the parish baptismal register the previous November 30, as godfather to James Monroe Hall, the infant son of John Hall and Adelina Kent, a free Black couple of Anne Arundel County.[2]

There were numerous men named Luke Cavanaugh (or close variants) who served in the Union army but the one whose military service record matches closest with the dates of Luke's first and second appearances at St. Mary's was a thirty-year-old native of County Galway, Ireland, and private in Company I, Sixty-Third New York Infantry. His service record reveals that he was wounded while on picket duty on June 26, 1862, at Fair Oaks, Virginia, and taken prisoner on June 30. He was confined at Richmond, hospitalized, and paroled in mid-September 1862. His name appears on the rolls of the US General Hospital in Annapolis from September 16 to October 11, 1862. It was noted in his military record that Luke returned to duty with his regiment on February 6, 1863, and that he received a medical discharge because of chronic rheumatism and the effects his bullet wound on February 18, at a camp near Falmouth, Virginia. After his discharge he appears to have made his way to Annapolis.[3]

Cavanaugh prospered only briefly with the Redemptorists. The chronicler reported that he had "a great desire to stay with us, so that he assigns as much time to work as to prayer." But soon it became clear that Luke "had no notion of religious life." Nevertheless, he persisted for two more months. On May 1, 1863, he served as godfather at the baptism of Patrick Coolahan, infant son of Michael Coolahan and Bridget Brady, both from County Galway. What connection, if any, Luke had with the Coolahans is not known and perhaps he was drafted to serve as godfather by Father Nicholas Jaeckel, who officiated at the baptism. But at this point, Luke's days with the Redemptorists were numbered. He had not been at St. Mary's long enough to be formally invested in the Redemptorist habit and thus there is no official record of his presence other than two entries in the *Chronica Domus* and two in the baptismal register. His departure from St. Mary's was a good thing as far as the Redemptorists were concerned. On May 11, the chronicle reports that Luke was dismissed from the Redemptorist community: "he had no vocation, and in addition he was full of lice."[4] What became of ex-army private and former candidate brother Luke Cavanaugh remains unknown.

Another person with a failed vocation also appeared in Annapolis around the same time as Luke Cavanaugh. John Regan arrived in the company of Father James Bradley, who had been on the road for five months giving out-of-town missions in Ohio, Connecticut, and New York, between November 1862 and March 1863. His mission work was interrupted by brief returns to Annapolis and a second stint to Fort Monroe in late February and early March 1863.[5] Somewhere in his travels, he met John Regan. The chronicler wrote about his situation:

> When Father Minister returned from Baltimore on the 9th Inst., he took along with him a certain man named John Regan, who came from a place where Father Bradley had given a mission a short time before, and who desired to become a brother in our Congregation. But he had not the least idea of religious life, he thought he could lead a most delicate and comfortable life in the Cong. But when he saw how things were going on, he was quite surprised, and said that his parish priest had cheated him. Moreover he behaved most ridiculously here, and returned home next day.[6]

Exactly who this John Regan was has not been determined. Except this mention in the *Chronica Domus*, he left no mark in the Redemptorist records. And, the "short time before" Father Bradley had met him is imprecise. Numerous young men named John Regan (and variant spellings) of an approximate age of twenty appeared in the 1860 census, including in cities visited by Bradley during his missions. If they met in Baltimore, there was a John Reagan listed there in the 1860 census and attending school. He would have been sixteen in 1863, an appropriate age to begin a novitiate.

Another member of the Redemptorist community departed on May 19. The *Chronica Domus* succinctly states that "[e]arly in the morning candidate lay brother Gustavus

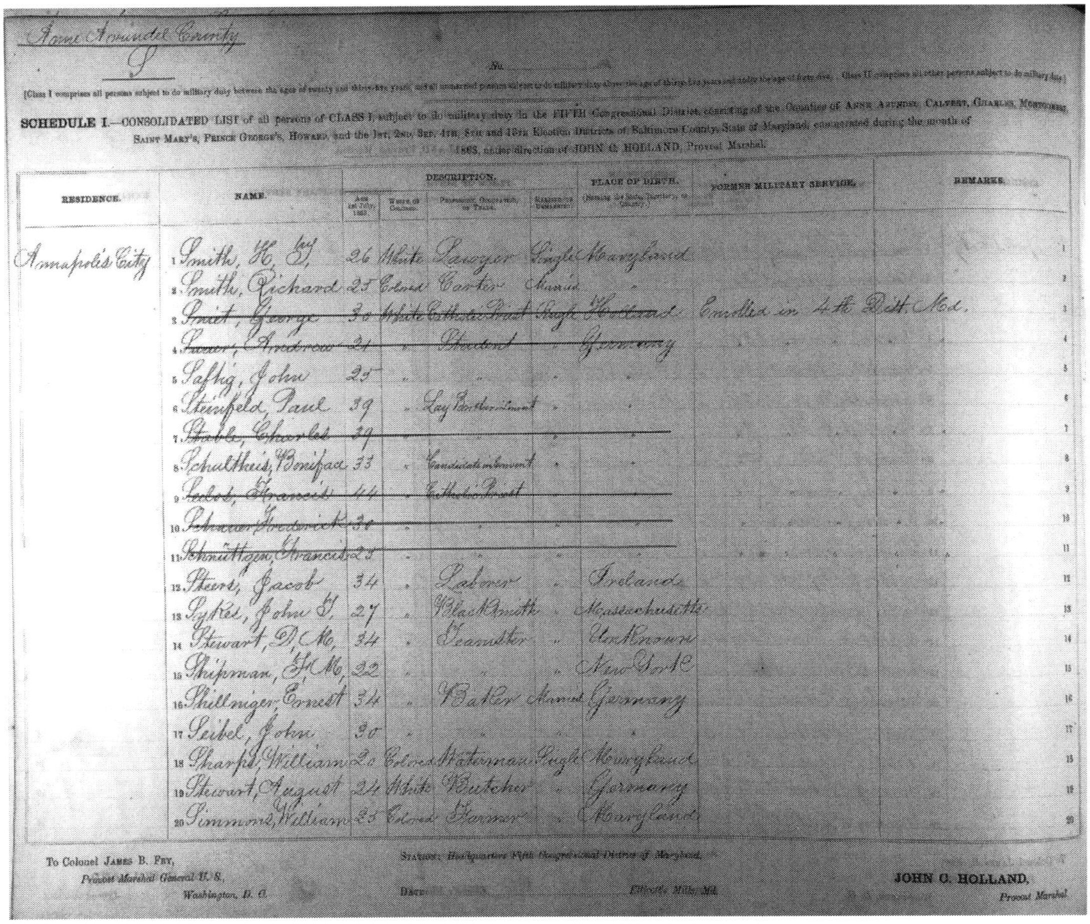
Anne Arundel County

SCHEDULE I.—CONSOLIDATED LIST of all persons of CLASS I, subject to do military duty in the FIFTH Congressional District, consisting of the Counties of Anne Arundel, Calvert, Charles, Montgomery, Saint Mary's, Prince George's, Howard, and the 1st, 2nd, 3rd, 4th, 5th and 13th Election Districts of Baltimore County, State of Maryland, enumerated during the month of 1863, under direction of JOHN C. HOLLAND, Provost Marshal.

Residence	Name	Age	White or Colored	Profession, Occupation, or Trade	Married or Unmarried	Place of Birth	Former Military Service	Remarks
Annapolis City	1 Smith, H. G.	26	White	Lawyer	Single	Maryland		
	2 Smith, Richard	25	Colored	Carter	Married			
	3 Smit, George	30	White	Catholic Priest	Single	Holland	Enrolled in 4th Distr. Md.	
	4 Sauer, Andrew	31		Student		Germany		
	5 Safting, John	25						
	6 Steinfeld, Paul	39		Lay Brother in convent				
	7 Stoble, Charles	39						
	8 Schultheis, Boniface	33		Candidate in convent				
	9 Seelos, Francis	44		Catholic Priest				
	10 Schwarz, Frederick	30						
	11 Schnuttgen, Francis	25						
	12 Sheens, Jacob	34		Laborer		Ireland		
	13 Sykes, John G.	27		Blacksmith		Massachusetts		
	14 Stewart, D. M.	34		Teamster		Unknown		
	15 Shipman, G. M.	22				New York		
	16 Shillinger, Ernest	34		Baker	Married	Germany		
	17 Seibel, John	30						
	18 Sharps, William	20	Colored	Waterman	Single	Maryland		
	19 Stewart, August	24	White	Butcher		Germany		
	20 Simmons, William	25	Colored	Farmer		Maryland		

To Colonel James B. Fry, Provost Marshal General U.S., Washington, D. C.

Station: Headquarters Fifth Congressional District of Maryland. Date: Ellicott's Mills, Md.

JOHN C. HOLLAND, Provost Marshal.

The names of Father Seelos (line 9) and other Redemptorists appeared in the 1863 Federal draft register for Annapolis. Consolidated Lists of Civil War Draft Registrations, 1863–1865. Entry 172, Records of the Provost Marshal General's Bureau (Civil War), Record Group 110. National Archives, Washington DC.

fled in secret, stealing some shoes and garments." As with the other departees, he had not been long enough at St. Mary's to be formally invested and admitted or otherwise recorded. Gustavus, whose surname went unrecorded, had arrived from Philadelphia on March 24, in hope of entering the congregation as a candidate brother. Now he was gone into the night of springtime Annapolis, never to be heard from again.[7]

Life in the religious community was also difficult for other reasons. The Redemptorists had animals on the property and in this case a high-strung horse may have given his keeper second thoughts about remaining at St. Mary's. The following event was recorded in the *Chronica Domus*:

> June 30 — A candidate brother almost lost his life trying to hitch our horse to a wagon. Note that our horse was not use to the harness and was always hot-tempered and restless.

A footnote to this account explained that the reason the Redemptorists had acquired the horse "is that on account of the great want of brothers, we could not get through the work, without ruining the health of all the brothers." Following this incident, in August, novice Brother Anselm Knecht fabricated a machine to be worked by the horse to grind malt grain and wash clothes. In October Brother Anselm devised another machine to pump water into a tank, and in November "or thereabouts" the same machine was used to saw wood. The writer explained that "the whole machine is moved by the horse: this is of the greatest assistance to us." Brother Anselm was born on a farm near Cumberland, in 1840, the son of Lorenz and Elizabeth Knecht, natives of Bavaria and the Electorate of Hesse-Cassel, respectively. He was invested in the Redemptorist habit by Father Seelos in Cumberland in 1861 and arrived in Annapolis in January 1863. Anselm was enrolled for the draft in Annapolis but his name was crossed out and it was noted that he was enrolled instead in Cumberland. The Cumberland enrollment book also had him crossed out with the note that his records had been transferred to Twenty-eighth District of New York, which included Buffalo and Rochester. He was not transferred there but stayed in Annapolis where he professed his final vows on October 15, 1866, and remained until June 1867. He was a multi-talented brother, working variously as "baker etc., etc., etc.," blacksmith, factotum (in his case, probably a handyman), and machinist. In November 1866 he was credited for having improved the condition of the private latrines of St. Mary's College. Unlike Martin Burke, Luke Cavanaugh, John Regan, and Gustavus, and perhaps the hot-tempered horse, Anselm remained in the Redemptorist Congregation the rest his life, working in Ilchester, Québec City, and Baltimore, where he died at Most Sacred Heart of Jesus Parish in 1916.[8]

Consecrate to God the Four Seasons

Catholics in the United States above the age of twenty-one at this time were required to fast (eat only one full meal) and abstain (from meat) every Friday in Advent; every day in Lent, except

Sundays; and on the vigils of Pentecost, Assumption, Sts. Peter and Paul, All Saints, and Christmas. Fasting also was required on ember days, which occurred in winter, spring, summer, and autumn in sets of three days (Wednesdays, Fridays, and Saturdays of the same prescribed week). Ember days were a penance "to consecrate to God the four seasons" (the term is derived from the Middle English word *ymber*, meaning cycle). Catholics also had to abstain from meat all other Fridays throughout the year except when Christmas fell on Friday. This meant Catholics were supposed to fast and abstain at least 110 days each year, "unless exempted for some legitimate cause." During the Civil War, Pope Pius IX dispensed soldiers and sailors in the service of the United States from the abstinence rule except for Ash Wednesday, Thursday, Friday and Saturday of Holy Week, and the vigils of Assumption and Christmas.[9]

Church attendance on Sundays was mandatory and Catholics were obliged "under pain of mortal sin" to attend Mass every Sunday as well as on eight holy days (Circumcision, Epiphany, Annunciation, Ascension, Corpus Christi, Assumption, All Saints, and Christmas). They also were to avoid servile work on Sundays and holy days, "unless sickness or some other important reason dispense us from this obligation." Confession of sins and reception of the Holy Eucharist were required at least once a year.[10]

Catholics in the Archdiocese of Baltimore must have read with interest the regulations prescribed for Lent in 1863. Ash Wednesday that year fell on February 18 and Archbishop Kenrick's eleven orders for the season appeared on the front page of the *Sun* the day before. His orders defined some fine points of procedure, such as, by dispensation, individuals were allowed to eat meat on Sundays and once a week on Mondays, Tuesdays, Thursdays (except Holy Thursday), and Saturdays (except the second and last Saturdays of Lent). Meals on fast days were not to be eaten before noon and when fasting was dispensed with later in the day, the faithful were not to consume both meat and fish at the same time nor were they allowed to use seasoning. In the morning, it was lawful to drink a warm liquid, such as tea, coffee, or thin chocolate made with water, and in the evening a small collation of bread, butter, cheese, fruit, salad, vegetables, and fish—but no milk or eggs—was allowed, but altogether never to exceed one-quarter the size of the full meal. Regulation number eight read: "Necessity and custom have authorized the use of hog's lard instead of butter, in preparing fish, vegetables, &c." Exemptions were allowed for those under twenty-one, the sick, the weak who could not fast "without great prejudice to their health," those of "tender or advanced age," nursing women, and those obliged to do hard labor. While this must sound onerous to modern-day Catholics, it was part of routine parish life for the faithful before, during, and after the Civil War.

Opposite Our Garden

The impact of the Federal occupation of Annapolis came physically closer to St. Mary's in 1863. The following brief entry appeared in the *Chronica Domus* in February:

> At this time, Federal cavalry soldiers built a stable on our property opposite our garden."[12]

The entry is cryptic and the matter was never mentioned again. Union troops had been using the city's Assembly Rooms (now Annapolis City Hall) on Duke of Gloucester Street since the summer of 1861. At the onset of the war, the building was used for drill two nights a week by the Governor's Guard, a local volunteer militia unit. Subsequently, Federal troops took over the building for the provost marshal's office, a guard house, and quarters.[13]

In January 1863, a new provost marshal and troops were assigned to Annapolis replacing the departing Sixty-Seventh Pennsylvania Infantry Regiment. The new provost marshal was Captain Francis J. Keffer who, like may army officers, boarded at Walton's City Hotel and, on occasion, used his room there for official business. The new guard detail included thirty troopers from Maryland's Purnell Legion Cavalry Regiment commanded by Captain Thomas Hodges Watkins, a local Anne Arundel County man. Watkins' cavalry policed the city and county with a degree of unpopularity (see The Mills of the Gods Grind Slowly, ch. 7).[14]

The Assembly Rooms were located just 200 feet from the northwest corner of St. Mary's property. It meant there was a daily presence of troops (and miscreants bound for the lockup) close to the parish school, church, and college. Although Keffer was explicitly ordered to use stables for the Purnell Legion "on the ground in the rear of St. John's College," he evidently wanted something closer to his office. It is not clear from the *Chronica Domus* statement "built a stable on our property opposite our garden" where exactly the stable was located. But a surmise can be made. "Our garden" may have meant the cloistered area behind the college building and the enclosing brick wall running parallel to the southeast side of Duke of Gloucester Street. An alternative site would have been the area near the old church (and by 1862 the school) that formerly was used as a burial ground. It was referenced once before in the chronicle as "the garden near the church." In 1863 this garden had become the school yard on the northwest end of the property and diagonally across the street from the Assembly Rooms. Although this location is closer to Keffer's headquarters, it is more likely that the stable "on our property" and "across from our garden," was on the open field across the street from St. Mary's College (the area between today's Newman Street and the waterfront end of Duke of Gloucester Street). Father Seelos described this "piece of farmland," across the street from the formal garden, "which in part we cultivate and in part use for a pasture of grass and clover for five cows." This field was used by the Redemptorists at various times for grazing animals and as a kitchen garden and would have been ideal for a stable and paddock for cavalry horses. Charles Carroll of Carrollton's carriage house once was on the same location. Later in 1863, the City of Annapolis applied for back rent for the provost marshal's use of the Assembly Rooms, which had "sustained much injury from such occupation" since 1861.[15] No evidence has been found, however, of a similar Redemptorist claim for rent or damage to their property.

Another reference to a cavalry unit at St. Mary's College appeared in the post-war unit history of the Fifth New York Cavalry Regiment. It said: "During their stay here most of the men were quartered in St. Mary's College and yard. On the 28th [of November 1861] they left this capital and pitched their tents about three miles from the city, and named the place Camp Harris." The reference is erroneous and confused St. John's College with St. Mary's College.[16]

Other new residents on the parish property may have been microbes dwelling in a new cistern that was constructed in February 1863 to "collect river water." At the same time, new pumps were acquired to bring brackish Spa Creek water to a receptacle that supplied water to the kitchen and the privy.[17]

Devout Since Childhood

Death came to the Redemptorist community early in 1863 when two students died from consumption. Joseph Kammer died on January 17 and Herman Krastel on February 27. Both men had great prospects as religious but were lost to the earthly service of God.

Joseph Kammer was born in 1840 in Hesse-Darmstadt and immigrated to the United States with his parents. He converted to Catholicism and first joined the Jesuits in Baltimore as a lay candidate. But Borgmann related in 1904 that Kammer "became acquainted with the Redemptorist Fathers in Baltimore and conceived the desire of entering the Congregation." He arrived in Annapolis in 1856 and was invested in the Redemptorist habit and spent his novice year first with Father Leimgruber and briefly with Father Seelos. In 1857 he and fellow novice Hubert Bove transferred to Cumberland where they professed their vows and began their seminary education with Seelos. Kammer fell ill sometime after his profession on March 19, 1858, and but did not return to Annapolis for better health care until September 1861. As mentioned earlier, upon his return to Annapolis, he gave a sophisticated oration in honor of Father Müller. Six months later, he was sent to Rochester, New York, to recover his failing health but his physician there said there was little that could be done for him. At Kammer's own request, he returned to Annapolis because "he desired to have the comfort of dying among his confreres." He arrived at St. Mary's on September 12, 1862, and was so ill that he was given the last rites the next day and "for many nights it was necessary for one, two or three students to stand vigil." His health continued to fail, took a "grave turn" in December, and "notwithstanding the Superiors' paternal care the career of this promising young man was cut short," wrote Borgmann. On the day of his death (January 17, 1863), the house chronicler wrote that "[t]his good frater's vocation was much admired, he was a model in his studies, open, sincere, candid toward his superiors; when admitting to be at fault against either the rules or charity, he always did everything to make good." He influenced his confreres with his innate happiness with them and by always distinguishing himself "by his toil and labor done with joy and gladness." In his final months, Kammer "was often at the point of death, and he surrendered his spirit . . . in the end he was fortified with all the sacraments, and acquiesced to the Divine will, placing himself in the hands of Mary and Jesus Christ, he was most faithful to his vocation right to the end." His father and mother came for his funeral on January 18 and he was interred "in the garden near the church."[18]

Herman Krastel was born in rural Baltimore County in 1839, the son of immigrant farmer parents from Hesse-Darmstadt. According to the *Chronica Domus*, Herman had practiced "a devout life since childhood." After he received his First Communion, he asked his parents—Joseph and Mary Krastel—for their permission to join the Redemptorists. He is said to have been attracted to the Redemptorists "by the piety and zeal of the Fathers in Baltimore." The Redemptorists had established a mission church—St. Joseph's in Necker, a farming community also called Perry Hall and now known as Fullerton—in 1850 with the tireless assistance of Joseph Krastel. His parents refused their permission for him to enter religious life but, because of the intercession of Father Henry Giesen, they later agreed to allow him to pursue studies and obtain a proficiency in Latin, a necessary first step to enter the novitiate.

"From that time on," reads the *Chronica Domus* "he made progress in love and devotion toward God and toward Mary and Joseph." Daily he recited the rosary, prayed the Five Psalms to the Blessed Virgin, and read the Stations of the Cross. He went to confession and received Holy Communion weekly. Despite "a mediocre background in school, he strove with all his heart to make progress in his studies." But shortly after he entered the novitiate in 1858, he contracted smallpox (*variola*). During this illness, he was said to have been "a great example to all" and the novitiate "was like paradise for him." He was a source of edification for the other novices "with his zeal for regular observance, and his simple charity to all." After he professed his vows in 1859, he was sent to Cumberland to study with Father Seelos but after a few months was forced to return to Annapolis because of illness, now diagnosed as consumption, which "was gradually destroying him." He partially recovered and continued his preliminary studies and then advanced to philosophy courses in April 1862. But consumption made him too weak to study, which saddened him, "but he accepted God's will." On February 25, 1863, Krastel took a turn for the worse and the next day made his last confession. He begged Father Seelos to not tell his parents of his grave illness "lest they be saddened, and also, lest they come to Annapolis and he should be distracted from God." He was given the last rites on the February 27 and, at 11:15 AM, "he gave back his pure and innocent spirit to God, holding a crucifix in his hands and with a rosary wrapped around his arm." The Redemptorist Rule was by his side and the entire community watched as he passed away. His funeral was held the next day with his parents and brother in attendance, and he was buried next to Kammer.[19]

From Merriment to Military Duty

In early March, Father Seelos traveled to Philadelphia, an absence not noted in the *Chronica Domus* and an indication that many other such trips and events must have gone unrecorded. But the trip was noted in annals of St. Peter's in Philadelphia. On March 1, 1863, the chronicler revealed that "Father Seelos, rector of Annapolis, came to help the fathers of this house."[20]

In May a most welcome visitor appeared at St. Mary's. He was "Seniore" Father Francis Xavier Tschenhens, C.Ss.R. He was a native of the Kingdom of Württemberg, where he was born in 1801. He had been ordained in Alsace, France, in 1827 and was among the first group of Redemptorists—three priests and three brothers—who came to the United States in 1832, making him one of the founders of the Redemptorist Congregation in North America. Tschenhens initially worked in frontier mission churches in Ohio and it was he who admitted St. John Neumann into the Redemptorist novitiate in Pittsburgh in 1840. By 1863 he was legendary within the congregation and revered wherever he went. Accompanied by Father De Dycker, he arrived in Annapolis in mid-May and remained for ten days. During this time, he reviewed the work of the students and congratulated them on their accomplishments. In return the students "gave many testimonies of honor and respect, for which the Senior Father was affected with the greatest delight and showed the greatest joy and merriment." Many of the students were already acquainted with Father Tschenhens from the years he was assigned to the Cumberland studentate.[21]

The Redemptorists' freedom from the draft in 1862 was short lived. The summer and autumn of 1862 witnessed particularly bloody battles and eventually led to the replacement of the dilatory General McClellan as commander of the Army of the Potomac. By December 6, 1862, the War Department reported that some 100,000 men were absent without leave from the army and that much of this absenteeism was a result of fraud in the bounty system. A week later, the Union army suffered a major defeat at Fredericksburg, Virginia, where, on December 13 alone, more than 10,000 were killed or wounded. As one historian later said, Fredericksburg "symbolized the end of any remaining ardor for war in the North." Or, as it was rather simply put after the war ended, "the strength of the Army was deemed inadequate for offensive operations .... [and the] insufficiency of the system of recruitment previously pursued had been demonstrated."[22]

The two-year enlistments of the men who joined in April 1861 were coming to an end, volunteerism was waning, and a severe personnel shortage was obvious. Despite the disaster at Fredericksburg, Lincoln issued his historic Emancipation Proclamation on January 1, 1863. Whereas the preliminary proclamation had referred to the idea of colonizing freed slaves "upon this continent, or elsewhere," the final document did not mention it, indicating that Lincoln had changed his mind and that the freed people deserved citizenship in the country of their birth and the opportunity to serve in the military.[23]

At the same time, Secretary of War Stanton informed Congress that there were "serious defects" in the 1862 militia law and called for new legislation. The Thirty-seventh Congress reconvened on January 5, 1863, and by early February a new bill had been introduced in the Senate for enrolling and drafting troops. The 1862 militia law was based on a state-controlled recruiting system and had produced only about 25 percent of the anticipated conscripts. Now Congress, amidst "hot discussion," debated what would become the first truly national draft law.[24]

During the Congressional debate on the bill, an amendment was proposed that would allow exemptions for those who had "religious scruples against bearing arms." Potential draftees would be required to affirm their objections by oath before a draft board official or by "any judge of any court of the United States for relief from military services." Consequently, the objector would be "duty bound" to contribute a "peace offering in accordance with his means" to a public hospital or through charitable service. The amendment was requested by the Society of Friends (Quakers) who refused to fight or pay for exemptions or substitutes. The clause "and ministers of the gospel regularly licensed" was added to the proposed amendment in the House. The House disagreed with the "religious scruples" amendment on February 25 and the amendment failed in the Senate on February 28. After further debate, the bill was approved on March 3 by both houses of Congress and the Enrollment Act of 1863 was signed by an anxious Lincoln the same day.[25]

The Redemptorists did not have the financial means to avoid military conscription by paying the $300 commutation fee or pay for a substitute as provided by the new law. A new "bounty" system—an enlistment bonus—also was authorized by the 1863 act but was subject to abuse and fraud and soon became a national disgrace. Federally mandated state recruitment quotas—based on the numbers of men enrolled by local draft boards—also were unpopular and often subject of protests by governors and state delegations sent to Washington.[26]

While the minimum draft age was increased from eighteen to twenty (the upper limit of thirty-five was retained), the 1863 law broadened eligibility to include persons of foreign birth "who shall have declared on oath their intention to become citizens." Unlike the 1862 law, which depended on administration by the states, the 1863 act established a Federal conscription system. Also, unlike the 1862 act, section 2 of the 1863 law listed specific exemptions for the physically or mentally unfit, the vice president of the United States, Federal judges, heads of Federal executive departments, state governors, and men upon whom their widowed mothers, aged or infirm parents, or siblings or motherless children under the age of twelve depended. Up to two eligible male members of the same family and household in which the father and son (or two sons) were already in military service also could claim exemption. Convicted felons were not allowed to be enrolled or serve in the armed forces. And, exemptions could not be claimed until a man had been officially drafted. And the law included a stipulation of extreme concern to religious orders: "And no persons but such as are herein excepted shall be exempt."[27]

The commutation and substitution clauses were evidently seen as sufficient by Congress to make up for the lack of occupational exemptions and exemptions for religious scruples, unless those so conscientiously scrupulous wanted to pay the commutation fee. It was not until the law was amended on July 4, 1864, that those who "were conscientiously opposed to the bearing of arms"—and they alone—who were allowed to pay a commutation fee.[28]

News of the impending enrollment bill and finally the enacted law frequently appeared in the press in the early months of 1863 and would have been read by the Redemptorists in Baltimore and Annapolis. The *Sun* reported that in accordance with the Enrollment Act and in hope of filling the ranks with seasoned troops, Lincoln issued a proclamation on March 10 recalling soldiers absent without leave. He promised there would be no penalty if they returned to their regiments by April 1. Although this would not have affected the Redemptorists, it brought scant relief to them and several days after the *Sun* article De Dycker hastened to Annapolis to meet with Seelos concerning the new draft crisis.[29]

Archbishop Francis Patrick Kenrick (1796–1863). Catholic Historical Research Center, Archdiocese of Philadelphia.

With Greatest Joy

The *Chronica Domus* entry for March 13, 1863, noted that Father De Dycker had arrived "unexpectedly" in Annapolis. After a long consultation with Seelos and his consultors, De Dycker decided to ordain twenty of the students "as soon possible." They quickly arranged the ordinations of the advanced students. As one of the students, Elias Frederick Schauer, put it, "Father Provincial informed us quite on a sudden that he wishes twenty of us to be ordained."[30]

The *Chronica Domus* provided this rational:

> It had already before been determined to ordain the Moralists, or at least most of them about Pentecost [May 7]: but it was determined to get them ordained before Easter, on account of the great "Draft" ordered by Congress this year, The conscription bill did not exempt clergymen or religious: but the Superiors thought that it would be easier to get the Fathers exempted than the students; and, as it was believed that they would proceed immediately on with the draft, it was thought better to get as many of the moralists ordained as possible.[31]

Of the twenty men to be ordained five were born in the United States, twelve in German states, and one each in Belgium, Netherlands, and Ireland. One of the five born in the United States was a native of Baltimore, two were from Cumberland, one from Sag Harbor, New York, and one from St. James, Louisiana. Of the twenty, only one—William Hickley Gross of Baltimore—had long roots in America; his New World lineage dated to his late eighteenth-century Alsatian immigrant ancestors. The parents of the other four American-born were natives of Ireland, France, and German states (see table 1, Redemptorist Ordinations, 1860–67, Appendix). Twelve of the students—the five American-born and seven foreign-born—had been recorded and then exempted in the 1862 draft enrollment.

Following De Dycker's decision, the twenty men held a retreat, an intense period of reflection, in anticipation of their ordination. Prior to the appointed day, Father Van de Braak went to Baltimore to accompany Archbishop Kenrick back to Annapolis on the evening of March 18. On March 19, in St. Mary's Church, the archbishop ordained the twenty men as subdeacons, the first of three orders. The following day, the group was elevated to the rank of deacon. Then, on Saturday, March 21, the twenty deacons were ordained as priests. It was an unusual and colorful ceremony for Annapolis, the first ever to occur there. The *Sun* reported that Kenrick was assisted at the "very solemn" ceremonies by Father Seelos "and several reverend gentlemen (professors at the college) and of a number of students." These reverend gentlemen were Fathers Gerard Dielemans, prefect of students; Adrian Van de Braak, professor of moral theology; Nicholas Jaeckel, professor of dogmatic theology; Joseph Henning, professor of rhetoric and mathematics; and Ferreol Girardey, professor of philosophy. The *Sun* also reported that the ordinations were attended "by a large number of both Catholics and Protestants, most of whom had never before witnessed such a ceremony." One of the ordinands, Elias Schauer, agreed, reporting that besides faithful Catholics, there were "protestants and infidels" present and that "all were exceedingly pleased." At the end of the ceremony, Kenrick declared "with the greatest joy, that never before had a larger number of priests been ordained on one occasion, in one place in America."[32]

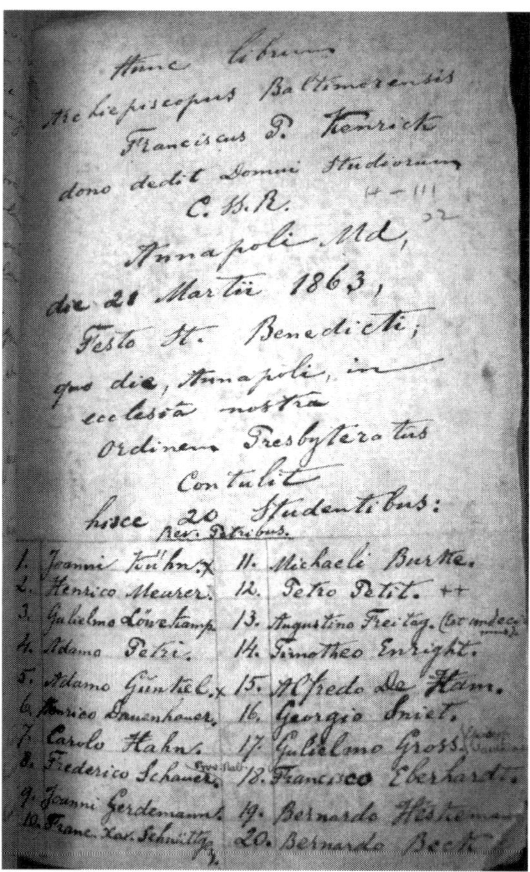

Hunc librum
Archiepiscopus Baltimorensis
Franciscus P. Kenrick
dono dedit Domui Studiorum
C.SS.R.
Annapoli, Md,
die 21 Martii 1863,
Festo St. Benedicti;
quo die, Annapoli, in
ecclesia nostra
Ordinem Presbyteratus
Contulit
hisce 20 Studentibus:
Rev. Patribus.

1. Joanni Kühn — 11. Michaeli Burke.
2. Henrico Meurer. — 12. Petro Petit.
3. Gulielmo Löwekamp — 13. Augustino Freitag.
4. Adamo Petri. — 14. Timotheo Enright.
5. Adamo Güntzel — 15. Alfredo De Ham.
6. Henrico Dauenhauer — 16. Georgio Sniet.
7. Carolo Hahn. — 17. Gulielmo Gross.
8. Frederico Schauer — 18. Francisco Eberhardt.
9. Joanni Gerdemann — 19. Bernardo [illegible]
10. Franc. Xav. Schnüttgen — 20. Bernardo Beck.

Flyleaf of Pontificale Romanum *with the names of the twenty men ordained on March 21, 1863. RAPB.*

Newly ordained Father Schauer wrote a letter to his sister in April. In an earlier letter, he had told her that he was among a group to be ordained and that she "should pray for them." Now he added:

> I have no doubt that you corresponded well to this pious request, for I felt the grace of God operating most extraordinarily on my poor soul during the days of my holy ordination. These days were days of the purest pleasure, of the most heavenly consolation, and of the most awful and tremendous significance and reality. I will never forget them in my whole life.[33]

In researching the events surrounding the March 1863 ordinations, a marvelous discovery was made. The author asked Dr. Patrick J. Hayes, archivist at the Redemptorist Archives of the Baltimore Province, if there were any period books in the archives that might describe a mid-nineteenth-century ordination ceremony. He found a volume entitled *Pontificale Romanum Clementis VIII et Urbani PP. VIII* published in Brussels in 1735. Part one of the book provides descriptions and illustrations of ordinations and thus served my initial purpose. But this particular copy is special because not only was it inscribed on the flyleaf as having been part of Kenrick's personal library but also that it was presented to the Annapolis Redemptorists on the occasion of the ordinations on "Festo St. Benedicti" (March 21) and it included the names of the twenty men ordained. So presumably Kenrick gave the book to Seelos and it was accessioned into the St. Mary's College library (the title page is stamped "Dom. Stud. C.SS.R. F.A.S."). Later it probably traveled to Ilchester, Maryland, when the college moved there in 1868, and eventually was deposited in the Redemptorist Archives. The volume appears to have had earlier travels based on a set of anonymous inscriptions and doodles inside the front cover. The handwriting is suspected to be that of St. John Neumann and it is theorized that the volume may have been given to him by Kenrick when Neumann himself was consecrated as bishop of Philadelphia in 1852, and was returned to Kenrick after Neumann's death in 1860. Kenrick, perceiving the intimate Redemptorist connection to the volume, gave it to Seelos on the momentous occasion in 1863. The *Chronica Domus* notes that Seelos accompanied Kenrick back to Baltimore on March 21 and that "Baltimore as requested has given Rev. Father Rector works of ancient ecclesiastical writers written in Latin and Greek."[34] If Kenrick had not brought the volume with him to Annapolis, then he probably gave it to Seelos when he went to Baltimore after the ordination.

Following the ordinations and to accommodate the large number of new priests wanting to celebrate their first Mass, two temporary altars were set up. One was near the organ in the church choir loft and the other was in the infirmary on the third story of the college building. After "a long deliberation," rules of precedence were established for scheduling Masses for the twenty-seven priests then in residence. Life was not simple, especially for the students, with so many priests on hand. In this regard, a footnote in English was later added to the *Chronica Domus* notes about the ordinations:

> The students were appointed to serve all the masses said by the older Fathers, and of those of the younger fathers who said mass immediately after one of the older fathers. But as to the masses of the younger fathers who said mass after another young father at the same altar, the young father who had said mass was appointed to serve the mass of the father who followed him, and to do so as his thanksgiving. Further the students who had to serve mass at 6 or 6½ o'clock were not to assist at 5½ o'clock mass, nor were they to receive communion on communion days if they did not assist at the first mass, but they were to go next day instead to communion. This rule admitted no exception except on recreation days and days of retreat. This arrangement lasted as long as the younger fathers remained here.[35]

With these rules established, William Gross, Augustine Freitag, and Bernard Beck celebrated their first masses on the Feast of the Annunciation (March 25), "some in the church, some in the chapel." On the Feast of the Seven Sorrows (March 27), Adam Anthony Petri, John Gerdemann, Francis Xavier Schnüttgen, Alfred De Ham, George Anthony John Sniet, and Francis Aloysius Christian Eberhardt celebrated their first Masses, "some in the chapel, some in the church."

Others did not celebrate their first mass until Palm Sunday (March 29) or Easter (April 5). But surely they did so with the greatest joy and, in accordance with the prescribed rituals of the Church, wearing violet vestments on Palm Sunday and white on Easter. Their joy continued as they offered mass on a daily basis thereafter.[36]

Not long after the ordinations, Father Van De Braak gave a Palm Sunday afternoon lecture at St. Mary's on the "Creation of the Angels." He cited Bible verses and early Church writers to support Catholic beliefs about angels as "pure spirits . . . of a most sublime understanding and endowed with great Knowledge." He noted too the fallen angels, who had rebelled against the future humanity of the Son of God, claiming they had divine superiority over humanity, and, as a result, were condemned to Hell because of their sin of pride and wanting to be like God. The *Maryland Republican* said it was "indeed a highly interesting lecture and was listened to with marked attention." While Van de Braak certainly had no political motive in his lecture, the prominent notice given it in the local press suggests perhaps that Editor Riley wanted to draw a subtle parallel to the pro-war devils in local society.[37]

Around this same time, perhaps on Sunday, April 12, or so thereafter, an Episcopalian couple, Lieutenant William Sterling and his wife, Matilda, visited St. Mary's Church. Tillie, as she was known, made a brief mention of it in a letter to her mother in Philadelphia: "Will and I went into the Catholic Church one afternoon last week to hear the music which was very grand."[38]

Something of a Tiger Trait

News appeared in the March 14 edition of the *Catholic Mirror* that surely tempered the enthusiasm of the then-soon-to-be ordained priests. The requirements of the new enrollment law and a list of exemptions were laid out for all to read.[39] The Annapolis Redemptorists and St. Mary's parishioners who subscribed thus could follow news of the new law as well read weekly state-by-state war reports from a Catholic but pessimistic perspective. For example, a *Catholic Mirror* editorial published on March 21 said:

> We are fearful that war is going to become an established institution in this country. . . . It is easier to make a ploughman a soldier, than to bring the soldiers back to trudge in the new made furrow behind the plough again. . . . Man has something of a tiger trait about him naturally; a single taste of blood gives him a perpetual relish for it.[40]

The publishers of Baltimore's *Catholic Mirror*, Michael J. Kelly, P. J. Hedian, and John B. Piet, were unabashedly anti-Lincoln, anti-abolition, and pro-Southern states' rights. They made a name for themselves not only in the Catholic and secular publishing worlds, but for a controversial book they published in March 1863 entitled *Fourteen Months in American Bastiles.* It was written by Frank Key Howard, a grandson of Francis Scott Key and one of the Baltimoreans arrested and incarcerated, sequentially, at Fort McHenry, Fort Monroe, and Fort Lafayette in New York City, in September 1861. Kelly and Piet were briefly arrested by military authorities in October 1863 for publishing Howard's incendiary book. It was extremely critical of the Lincoln administration for its suppression of states' rights and free speech since the onset of the war. These critical sentiments continued on the pages of the *Catholic Mirror* after the publishers were freed from prison but the *Mirror* would be one of the Baltimore newspapers that was suppressed in the summer of 1864 for having sold photographs of Confederate generals at its premises.[41]

The *Sun* and, most likely the Annapolis newspapers, few of which are extant for 1863, also frequently reported progress in implementing the Enrollment Act throughout the North. War Department regulations regarding exemptions from the conscription law were published in May as front-page news in the *Sun*. Fifty-one categories of physical and mental disability were listed but no mention was made of membership in a religious society or having conscientious scruples against bearing arms.[42]

Appointments for provost marshals, enrolling officers, and surgeons were reported in May as were War Department instructions to the provost marshals that emphasized that "all persons subject to military duty, whether white or black" were to be enrolled. Additionally, "all able-bodied males between the ages of twenty and forty-five, not exempt by law; and . . . all persons of foreign birth who shall have declared their intention to become citizens" were eligible for enrollment. Of great concern for the Redemptorists must have been Regulation 80, which stated that "a discharge from one draft furnishes no exemption from any subsequent draft, except that when the person drafted has furnished an acceptable substitute, and has received a certificate of discharge from a preceding draft."[43] In other words, the 1862 draft exemptions were superceded by the new act.

The *Sun* reported on June 10 that "all persons coming within the provisions of the act for enrolling and calling out the national forces are to be enrolled." The only exception was for men already in military service. More chilling was the mid-June War Department order that, in accordance with the Enrollment Act, "that if any person shall resist any draft of men enrolled under this act . . . or shall counsel or aid any person to resist any such draft, . . . or willfully dissuade them from the performance of military duty, as required by law, such person shall be subject to summary arrest by the provost marshal" and be subject to fines and imprisonment. The March ordinations could easily have been construed by an unsympathetic enrolling official as an avoidance of the draft. However, widespread discontent with the draft and its provisions throughout the North also was newsworthy. As one historian put it, "Rather than greeting it with anticipation . . . citizens that spring and summer dreaded the prospect of federal conscription." The top official of the draft process stated it more bluntly. Provost Marshal General Colonel (after April 21, 1864, Brigadier General) James Barnet Fry wrote in 1866 that "military service was no longer popularly regarded as a privilege, but exacted as a duty . . . . and hence [the people] beheld the prospect of compulsory service in the Army with an unreasonable dread."[44]

There were three classes of men subject to enrollment. Class I included "all persons subject to do military duty between the ages of twenty and thirty-five and all unmarried persons subject to do military duty above the age of thirty-five years and under the age of forty-five." Class II included married men above age thirty-five and under forty-five. Class III was for those already drafted but still had to be enrolled. Most of the Annapolis Redemptorists were subject to Class I enrollment.[45]

Enrollment board jurisdictions coincided with congressional election districts. Anne Arundel County was in the Fifth Congressional District, which also included parts of Baltimore County as well as Howard, Montgomery, Prince George's, Calvert, Charles, and St. Mary's counties. The enrollment headquarters for the Fifth Congressional District was in the town hall in Ellicott's Mills in Howard County, with Captain John C. Holland serving as provost marshal. As was done in 1862, local enrollment officers went to "the doorstep of every home" to complete the registration lists. Each enrollment board had a provost marshal, commissioner, and surgeon.[46]

As in the year before, the 1863 draft enrollment had impacts on St. Mary's parishioners and their non-Catholic male relatives, but this time in a radically different manner. Of the sixty-nine men associated with St. Mary's enrolled in 1862, only ten (14 percent) had been subject to military duty. In 1863, with Federal law in force, ninety-nine (98 percent) of 101 enrolled men associated with St. Mary's were subject to the draft. Of the St. Mary's parishioners and men associated with parishioners, seventy-five were listed in Class I and twenty-six in Class II. James Revell was granted one of the two exemptions, and it was not because of his position as state's attorney but "by election of [his] widowed mother," Mary Anne Hohne Revell. The other exemption, granted for the same reason, was for Richard Wells, the non-Catholic brother of converts Catherine Maria Wells Blackburn and Henry C. Wells.[47]

Some of the enrolled men were already serving or had served in the military but were still listed as "subject to do military duty." They included three men currently in the army: John Jackson, Company D, Fifth Maryland Infantry; and George A. Morgan and William Young, both of Company A, First Maryland Infantry. There were three former St. Mary's servicemen: barkeeper Sylvester Ambrose McCabe, formerly with Company A, Sixty-Seventh Pennsylvania Infantry; Charles J. Murphy, who had served in the Navy and was working in Annapolis as an army sutler; and John B. Nichols, a waterman who had served as a gunner with the Navy. Three Mullan brothers were enrolled in Annapolis for the 1863 draft: Charles Nevitt, who was working with the army as a "pioneer" in Washington Territory; James Augustus, who was employed as a civilian military surgeon, also in Washington Territory; and John Jr., who had resigned his captain's commission in the army in May 1863 (see Characterized by Urbanity, Justice, and Charity, this ch.). Nineteen of the enrolled men were non-Catholic fathers, brothers, or husbands of St. Mary's parishioners. Edward Sparks Jr., the son of Dr. Sparks who was listed as "diseased" in 1862, was included with the Class I enrollees in 1863. Of anyone on this list, he should have been exempted because of his health. He died at age twenty-four on December 4, 1863 and was buried in St. Mary's Cemetery.[48]

African Americans, both slaves and free, were enrolled for the draft for the first time in 1863. Twenty Black men associated with St. Mary's were listed. One of them was thirty-four-year-old Perry Primrose, a married, "free colored" farm hand from the St. Margaret's area. In addition to the 1863 Federal draft enrollment, he appears only briefly in the historical record: in the 1850, 1860, and 1870 Federal censuses, and in the St. Mary's baptismal register as the father of nine-month-old Emma Theresa Primrose, who was baptized at St. Mary's in 1859. Emma Treadway was the godmother, indicating a possible work relationship between her carpenter husband Henry Holmes Treadway and Perry Primrose. Primrose was not drafted and continued working on a farm at Greenbury Point until August 1870 when he suffered a seizure while sailing a small boat across the Annapolis harbor and fell overboard and drowned. The *Annapolis Gazette* reported that it had learned "from good authority the deceased was an honest, sober, industrious and highly respectable member of the community." Even the *Sun* reported the untimely death of this humble Black man.[49]

When the draft finally came in Maryland in 1864, eight laymen associated with St. Mary's had their names drawn. Although officially drafted, six ultimately avoided military service. Two other men drafted, John Jackson, Fifth Maryland Infantry, and William Smothers, Twenty-Eighth US Colored Troops, were already in the army. In addition, two other men, whose names were not found in the 1863 enrollment, were drafted in 1864 but were not enlisted.[50]

Personal Friend of the President

The ordination scheme did not relieve the anxieties in the Redemptorist community. Father Seelos must have been greatly alarmed when news arrived in Annapolis of Lincoln's June 15 call for 10,000 Maryland militia (along with 90,000 others from Pennsylvania, West Virginia, and Ohio) "to be mustered in the service of the United States forthwith."[51] Immediate action was needed. Father De Dycker returned to Annapolis on June 20 and he and Seelos spent several days discussing options. They talked about sending the students to Canada but rejected the idea. The cost of paying for substitutes was financially untenable. De Dycker instead directed the students to recite the Psalms of St. Bonaventure every day in order to place themselves under the protection of the Blessed Virgin Mary in hope of gaining draft exemptions.

Following these consultations, Seelos sent Fathers Adrian Van de Braak and Joseph Henning to Washington on June 24 to intercede with the civil authorities. They met with and received assurances from Postmaster General Montgomery Blair that the Annapolis Redemptorists would not be drafted but that if such a danger arose, all they had to do was inform him.[52]

Seeking help from the postmaster general seems like on odd choice. But Montgomery Blair was an important Maryland politician and, as postmaster general, was a member of the president's cabinet, and Blair and his family were of considerable influence. Blair had served in 1856 as legal counsel for Dred Scott in his unsuccessful Supreme Court fugitive slave case. In 1860, he had served as president of the Republican Party's state convention in Baltimore. He was a powerful political figure who had Lincoln's ear and many other important connections. His brother, Francis Preston Blair Jr., was a former member of Congress and a major general in the Union army. A brother-in-law was the assistant secretary of the navy while another brother-in-law, Samuel Philips Lee (a third cousin of Robert E. Lee), was an acting rear admiral in the US Navy. Blair's father, Francis Preston Blair Sr., had served in Democratic President Andrew Jackson's "kitchen cabinet" in the 1830s. The senior Blair also was the influential editor of the *Washington Globe* and one of the founders of the Republican Party. And, it was Francis Blair Sr. to whom Lincoln entrusted the offer of commanding the Union army to Robert E. Lee, just before Virginia seceded. Lincoln is said to have "often played with the grandchildren of Francis P. Blair, Sr." and Montgomery Blair "was a personal friend of the President, who had the warmest possible feeling for him and a conviction of his ability and integrity."[53]

The Blairs also were important to Lincoln because they were natives and power brokers of Maryland, a loyal border slave state. Plus the Blairs offered Lincoln an important counterpoise to the radical wing of the Republican Party, which favored full abolition of slavery and all-out war against the South. Blair was clearly the most important Marylander in the Lincoln administration and the go-to man for local favor seekers such as Van de Braak and Henning. Once described as "the meanest man in the whole government," Montgomery Blair was an influential figure and Seelos might have been satisfied with the reassurances he had received had not the next development occurred.[54]

In early July, all eligible members of the Annapolis Redemptorist community—sixty-eight men—were formally enrolled for the draft. Draft enrollment records for Anne Arundel County also indicate that other local clergy were not exempted. Among men enrolled between July 15 and September 16, 1863, for example, were William S. Edwards, a Methodist clergyman of Crownsville; Claudius R. Haines, a Episcopal minister from West River; and two Annapolis ministers of uncertain affiliations: Richard Lane and Isaac Peterson. Of these four local clergymen, only one—Edwards—was later drafted but apparently never served.[55]

Lincoln Was Very Friendly to Me

Earlier in the year, on March 14, John Walton accompanied former Governor Hicks and Annapolis postmaster Thomas Ireland in a meeting with President Lincoln at the White House. They sought a promotion for Lieutenant Colonel George Sangster, commandant of Camp Parole; a promotion that did not materialize. But Walton may have suggested to Father Seelos the idea of appealing directly to Lincoln for help. Faced with the renewed draft threat, the normally optimistic but now skeptical Seelos decided to take a bold step. He decided, as he wrote later to his sister, "with the permission of the provincial, to go to Washington with another father and to present personally to the President and other officials our situation."[56]

Father Seelos wrote to his spiritual advisee Miss Mary on July 17 that:

> Next Monday [July 20], I go to Washington-city to see, if possible, Father Abraham and to have a talk with him about the draft. If I do not succeed in obtaining a release from that injust injunction, we will rather go to prison than to take up arms, and to pay for so many we are not able.[57]

There may have been a delay in departing. The *Chronica Domus* entry for July 22 says Seelos and Van de Braak "went to Washington to seek exemption from the military for all of us." All the details on the Washington visit were entered under July 22; there was no July 23 entry. The entry for July 24 simply reads: "the Reverend Fathers returned to Annapolis" without making clear which day they met Lincoln.[58]

What the chronicle does report (under July 22) was that the two priests met Lincoln and three other high-level officials but it seems unlikely—although possible—that they achieved all of these visits on July 22. And, if they did hold four meetings in one day, there was no reason, except the lateness of the hour, to stay an the extra day on July 23, at least none was given. It also is possible that they did depart on July 20, as Seelos said he would, and used that day and July 21 to make their preliminary inquiries or schedule appointments at the various offices. There are no chronicle entries for July 20 and 21.

There is no mention of their having taken the train but railroad travel between Annapolis and Baltimore was the usual mode of travel. They would have departed on the Annapolis and Elk Ridge Railroad at 5:30 or 6:00 AM, traveling to Annapolis Junction where they transferred to the B&O's Washington Branch line. In the summer of 1863, the B&O train that picked up Washington-bound transfer passengers at Annapolis Junction left Baltimore at 8:00 AM and 5:00 PM every day except Sunday and arrived in Washington in less than two hours.[59]

As Seelos and Van de Braak approached their destination they would have seen the District of Columbia guarded by earthen forts and artillery batteries. Exiting the B&O terminal, they might have looked to the southeast and seen the Capitol's unfinished dome. Beyond that imposing high point, the city below was one of government buildings, the Smithsonian Castle, the partially finished Washington Monument, and markets, retail shops, banks, theaters, restaurants, hotels, churches, boarding houses, private homes, stables, and, in the distance, the port of Georgetown. Being wartime, there were numerous sutler stores selling supplies to soldiers and

Union troops on east front of the U.S. Capitol. Note the unfinished dome. Prints and Photographs Division, Library of Congress https://www.loc.gov/pictures/item/2009631455/.

Numerous individuals sought audiences with Lincoln. They included cabinet secretaries, members of Congress, military officers, foreign dignitaries, state governors, office seekers, old and new friends, distant in-laws, and numerous other members of the general public. Most petitioners sought jobs, government contracts, or personal favors. Others came with unsolicited advice on how fight the war. There was nobody to bar a visitor's passage into the White House itself, according to Noah Brooks, "and the multitude, washed or unwashed, always has free egress and ingress." Or, as John Milton Hay put it many years later: "There was little order or system about it; those around [Lincoln] strove from beginning to end to erect barriers to defend him against constant interruption, but the President himself was always the first to break them down." Hay said that some days around noon, the president would "order the doors to be opened and all who were waiting to be admitted. The crowd would rush in, thronging the narrow room, and one by one would make their wants known."[63]

sailors. There also were eighteen military hospitals. The Sisters of Mercy provided sixty beds for transient paupers under contract with the surgeon general of the army. Members of St. Aloysius Parish built St. Aloysius Hospital on North Capitol Street according to army specifications to avoid their Jesuit-run church being requisitioned for use as a hospital.[60]

Rather than stay in a hotel, Seelos an Van de Braak most likely went to one of the six Catholic parishes in Washington within walking distance of the train station and the White House and other government offices. Father Michael Müller was acquainted with Father Charles Ignatius White, the diocesan pastor of St. Matthew's, at 15th and H streets Northwest, and he might have offered lodging. However, Seelos and Van de Braak probably stayed with their former Redemptorist confrere, Father Mathias Alig, at St. Mary's Church on Fifth Street Northwest.[61]

What the two priests observed in Washington was not pretty. The wartime population had soared from 60,000 to around 100,000. The unpaved streets were crowded with horse-drawn artillery, supply wagons, and vehicles of all kinds and were described in mid-July 1863 as being "very filthy, filled with dirt and slush most offensive to the smell." Despite the poor street conditions, residents complained that carriages drove through their neighborhoods "at a furious and dangerous rate." Thoroughfares were crowded day and night with troops heading south to battle and the wounded and paroled coming north. Drunken gamblers, prostitutes, poor wartime refugees, and hot humid weather added to the unpleasant mix. Seelos himself said "Washington is a miserable and destestible [*sic*] city and Baltimore is a thousand times nicer."[62]

Lincoln received petitioners in his second-story office, which was also used for cabinet meetings and is now called the Lincoln Bedroom. Visitors lined up at the main entrance on Pennsylvania Avenue, wended their way through corridors, and up the stairs to Lincoln's office. One colorful description reports a "dense crowd that swarmed in the staircases and corridors . . . . the numbers were so great, the competition was so keen that they ceased for the moment to be regarded as individuals, drowned as they were in the general sea of solicitation." Lincoln himself could avoid the hallway crowds by using a private passageway connecting his office through an adjacent library and a reception room to the family quarters. The two Redemptorists were faced with this unwelcoming situation.[64]

There is no record of who received Seelos and Van de Braak. Lincoln had three private secretaries, who, along with an usher, served as guardians of the presidential office. The principal secretary, or chief of staff, was Bavarian-born John George Nicolay, who had been with Lincoln since the 1860 election campaign. But he was in Illinois at the time. So, they might have encountered one of Nicolay's assistant secretaries: John Milton Hay and William Osborn Stoddard; or one of three clerks: Nathaniel S. Howe, Gustav Matile, and Edward Duffield Neill, an ordained Presbyterian minister.[65]

Had they met Hay, they might have found a bemused receptionist. The previous Sunday, he attended at St. Aloysius Church where he listened to "a dry priest" who "declaimed against science & human reason & after demolishing both, glorified the dogma of the Immaculate Conception." On July 21, Hay had been in another Catholic church—St. Matthew's—with the president's son, Robert Todd Lincoln, the secretaries of state and war, the families of the secretary of the navy and the attorney general, and other dignitaries to attend a noon society wedding. What impression Seelos and Van de Braak made on Hay following these two very recent visits to Catholic churches—if he met them at all—was left unrecorded in his diary. Or, perhaps they were met by a doorkeeper or some other minor functionary. In any event, no record of their visit to the White House has been discovered. There are no extant White House records from this period at the National Archives and evidently no record was kept of the large flow of daily visitors.[66]

Noah Brooks, writing just three and a half months later, described the situation in which Seelos and Van de Braak likely found themselves on or about Wednesday, July 22:

> Breakfast over, by nine o'clock [the President] has directed that the gate which lets in the people shall be opened upon him, and then the multitude of cards, notes and messages which are in the hands of his usher come in upon him. Of course, there can be no precedence, except so far as the President makes it; and, as a majority of the names sent in are new to him, it is very much of a lottery as to who shall get in first. The name being given to the usher by the President, that functionary shows in the gratified applicant, who may have been cooling his heels outside for five minutes or five days, but is now ushered into a large square room, furnished with green stuff, hung around with maps and plans, with a bad portrait of Jackson over the chimney piece, a writing table piled up with documents and papers, and two large, draperied windows looking out upon the broad Potomac, and commanding the Virginia Heights opposite, on which numberless military camps are whitening in the sun.[67]

Early in his administration, Lincoln held day-long receptions of visitors throughout the week, but later visiting days were reduced to twice weekly, from 10:00 AM to 3:00 PM and still later until only 1:00 PM when the "doors were shut promptly at the appointed time, forcing countless visitors to leave disappointed." A first-hand observer writing about events in 1863, however, said by then Lincoln typically received visitors daily, including Saturdays, between 9:00 AM and 3:00 PM and, if Congress was in session, several hours in the evening as well. Some office-seekers even pursued the president on Sundays.[68]

Lincoln's day on Wednesday, July 22, was not as busy as most. After a "frugal breakfast," he rode by carriage from his summer residence at the Soldiers' Home, four miles northeast of the White House, in time to start work at 8:00 AM. But he was not feeling well that morning and scarcely took food all day. He had at least one official meeting, to receive the credentials of Colombia's new ambassador. Lincoln missed an appointment with Major General Robert C. Schenck, commander of the Army's Middle Department, headquartered in Baltimore, who came to the White House but departed before Lincoln had time to receive him. Among Lincoln's published letters, only two were written on July 22. The next day also was not one of Lincoln's busier days. He had an interview with the chairman of the Republican Party Central Committee of New Hampshire regarding military draft issues and wrote three letters.[69] As with the day before, he had ample time to receive the Fathers Seelos and Van de Braak.

That Lincoln found the time to meet two priests, out of all of his daily visitors, is perhaps indicative of his outgoing nature rather than any regard for institutional religion. Lincoln was a religious skeptic who, at best, believed in some unpredictable Divine Providence and, according to one analysis, he adhered to "the predestinarianism of Old School Presbyterianism" when dealing with moral questions. Another view says he "was sympathetic to and detached from religion beliefs." Or still yet, according to William Henry Herdon, his old law partner in Springfield, Illinois, "Mr. Lincoln belonged to no church and believed in none." However, Elizabeth Keckley, a former slave who was Mary Lincoln's modiste and confidant from 1861 to 1865, wrote that on occasion in 1863 she observed the president reading his Bible "with Christian

President Lincoln meets with Fathers Seelos and Van de Braak. Original art by Constance D. Robinson.

eagerness." Historians debate whether or not Lincoln was a formal member of or attended church in Springfield or in Washington, and much has been said about his wary attitude toward organized religion.[70]

Despite having met clergy who tested Lincoln's patience with seeking favors and trying to preach to him about his moral duties, Stoddard wrote that "the President invariably treats with marked respect all clergymen of all denominations, with an exceptional increase on behalf of Quakers." Nicolay and Hay observed that "Himself of Quaker ancestry, he felt a peculiar sympathy with their scruples, and yet he could not legally relieve them from their liabilities, and he clearly perceived the impolicy of recommending to Congress any specific measure of relief."[71]

With such an amenable but cautious demeanor, Lincoln received the two Redemptorists. Noah Brooks said he would have acted:

> With admirable patience and kindness, Lincoln hears his applicant's requests, and at once says what he will do, though he usually asks several questions, generally losing more time than most businessmen will by trying to completely understand each case, however unimportant, which comes before him. He is not good at dispatching business, but lets every person use more time than he might if the interview were strictly limited to the real necessities of the case.[72]

Seelos himself gave several accounts of his visit with Lincoln. One was recorded in the *Chronica Domus*, others in various letters. He offered the president reasons why the Redemptorists should be exempt from military service. He found the session with Lincoln cordial and he wrote soon after the meeting that:

> The President, Abraham Lincoln, was very friendly, and promised to do everything in his power; and when the drawing [for the draft] was over, we should come again and he would give us a private audience.[73]

Seelos' biographer Father Peter Zimmer, who was present when Seelos returned from Washington, wrote that Lincoln "was friendly and received the request of the Fathers with consideration." Even though the Confederacy was far from a state of collapse, Lincoln's popularity was increasing after the early July victories and it would have been easy for him to be magnanimous toward the two priests. John Hay observed that during this particular time he had "rarely seen [Lincoln] more serene," although Robert Todd Lincoln said his father "grieved silently but deeply about the escape of Lee" after Gettysburg.[74]

The *Chronica Domus* gives a somewhat different account of the Seelos-Lincoln meeting. The writer must have heard the report first hand from Seelos and Van de Braak. Nevertheless, he wrote that "the Reverend Fathers went to Washington: there they went to see President Abraham Lincoln himself who received them most kindly and spoke as a father, but said he did not know what could be done." But Seelos' own words—that Lincoln "promised to do everything in his power"—leave quite a different impression.[75]

However reassuring Lincoln may have sounded to the priests, in reality Lincoln himself would have known that there was actually little he could do "in his power" to circumvent the draft law. Seelos himself was somewhat realistic about the prospect of avoiding the draft when he wrote from New York City on April 11, 1865, that:

> it appeared that we too would be pulled into this business of the war, but our loving God has averted this misfortune from us. For this reason, I was in Washington and spoke with President Lincoln, who was very friendly to me and my companion, but he did not settle anything.[76]

Three days after Seelos wrote that letter, Lincoln was assassinated. Writing again from New York City on April 17–18, Seelos reminisced again about his 1863 meeting. He told his sister Antonia that "[h]is personality did not strike me unfavorably. He spoke with us very openly and freely and was very friendly, and if we returned, promised us a private audience."[77]

During the weeks after meeting the two priests, none of Lincoln's correspondence touched on any request made by Father Seelos. Nor has any trace of the meeting been found in government records or the press.[78]

Another religious order's appeal to Lincoln may have influenced the positive tenor of the Lincoln-Seelos meeting. Just a month before Seelos and Van de Braak visited Lincoln, the president received a long letter from Seelos' old professor in Augsburg, Abbot Boniface Wimmer, head of the Benedictine Abbey of St. Vincent in Westmoreland County, Pennsylvania. Six of his priests and eight brothers had been drafted. Wimmer reminded the president that earlier, through his "very kind favor," he had received an order from the secretary of war relieving from military duty four Benedictine monks who had been drafted. As a reference, he enclosed a copy of the order, dated November 28, 1862. However, Wimmer was newly concerned that the Enrollment Act had made the order void and he asked Lincoln to prevent taking clergy of any denomination "away from the pulpit and the altar."[79]

Lincoln forwarded Wimmer's letter to Stanton on June 11. Wimmer, who was then in Washington, sent a similar letter to Stanton himself on June 11, saying "the new law presses harder on the Catholic clergy in general than on clergymen of other denominations because Catholic clergymen are not married, and the other ones very generally are married. But the law presses heavier yet on religious orders." He explained at length the organization and role of the Benedictines, the benefits they provided gratis to the United States, and the need to exempt their professors and students from the draft. He said, as Father Seelos must have, that they could not afford to pay the commutation fee. At least, he argued, the War Department could grant furloughs to the students until they finished their religious studies, at which time, he hoped the law would be changed to allow exemptions. In the end, two Benedictine priests and two brothers had their commutation fees paid, four others were exempted as "unfit" by the examining surgeons, and five brothers were enlisted. But the abbot's appeals to Lincoln and Stanton succeeded in part. Although the War Department refused to release the monks from military service, they were assigned instead to the hospital corps. They did not have to bear arms and, for two years, they cared for the wounded on the battlefield. The drafted Benedictines, however, were never far from danger. One was wounded at Antietam and released from the army, another was seriously wounded during the siege of Petersburg.[80]

Promises to Intercede

Seelos and Van de Braak visited three other Federal government offices in Washington. Whether they occurred the same day as the Lincoln visit or before or after is not clear. They are discussed here in the order mentioned in the *Chronica Domus*.

The first visit was to the General Post Office, a nine-block walk east from the White House. There they met Postmaster General Montgomery Blair, from whom Van de Braak and Henning had already received assurances on June 22. According to the *Chronica Domus*, Blair "received them kindly and promised to intercede for them," much the same as he had done a month earlier. No official or personal record of the Redemptorists' visit with Blair has been found.[81]

The second call was made, as the *Chronica Domus* put it, on *"Seward filium Secretary of State"* (Seward son of the Secretary of State). Various secondary sources have confused whether Seelos and Van de Braak met with Secretary of State William Henry Seward himself or his son. From the word *filium* and the position Frederick William Seward held, it is clear that it was he who received Seelos and Van de Braak. The younger Seward was assistant secretary of state in charge of the consular service and among his official duties was the adjudication of draft exemptions based on alienage. Resident aliens who had been drafted could appeal to Seward for release from military service on the basis of their foreign citizenship. Seward regularly communicated about these matters with Union army commanders, foreign consuls in Washington, and American consuls overseas. Thus, during the meeting at the White House it is very likely that Lincoln told the two priests to "go see Fred Seward," who might help assist with their foreign-born confreres. At the time, the Department of State building was on the east side of the White House, in front of the Treasury building on Pennsylvania Avenue. The *Chronica Domus* reported that Seward received the two priests "kindly and promised to intercede for them." Nothing in official State Department records has been found concerning the meeting or any formal intercession acted upon.[82]

Keep Your People from Rioting!

Kind greetings did not occur during the next visit. Seelos and Van de Braak proceeded to the War Department, located on the west side of the White House. As secretary of war, Stanton concentrated on military affairs and reportedly restricted public petitioners to Mondays and congressional access on Saturdays. Monday was July 20 but the *Chronica Domus* recorded the Stanton visit—and the other three visits—under a heading for July 22. No government documentation has been found to prove the date.[83]

Stanton was a diligent, hard working man dedicated to the Union and prosecution of the war. Lincoln is said to have "loved" and "trusted" Stanton and affectionately called him "old Mars." Over time, the two men developed close working and friendly social relationships. But most people approached him with trepidation. Nicolay and Hay said Stanton was "genial and kind" but exhibited "occasional exhibitions of temper and brusqueness of manner." On public access days they reported, he stood at behind a tall desk "where he compelled each applicant or interviewer, high or low, to state his request publicly and audibly in presence of the assembled throng, so that the stenographer at his elbow could record it as well as the Secretary's answer." Any "verbal solicitations and personal interviews diminished suddenly under this staring publicity." Noah Brooks also noted the standing desk and said that "From that awful tribunal . . . the great War Secretary . . . issued many orders of supreme moment." Stanton's confidential secretary, Albert E. H. Johnson, said his boss "did not cultivate sweetness of temper, nor amiability of character, but rather a character of stern activity." Frederick Seward said Stanton was "stern and

Secretary of War "greets" Fathers Seelos and Van de Braak. Original art by Constance D. Robinson.

inflexible in discharge of his duty" and was "impatient of visitors who [came] to seek personal ends." Despite all this, historian George Rable believes Stanton "took a surprisingly tolerant attitude toward conscientious objectors," something that might have instilled some sympathy for the two priests.[84]

As Seelos and Van de Braak approached Stanton's desk at the War Department, they might have encountered Colonel James Allen Hardie. He was an assistant adjutant general who "presided in [Stanton's reception] room, ascertaining each caller's business and dispatching it if he could, or sending in the names of those individuals whom he thought the Secretary would wish to interview personally." He was on duty at the War Department on July 21–23, as evidenced by telegrams he sent on Stanton's orders. Hardie was Catholic and likely to have been sympathetic to the two priests, if not to for their precise mission. One of Hardie's fellow classmates at the US Military Academy (Class of 1843) was George Deshon, who later became a Redemptorist priest and subsequently joined the Paulists. Hardie converted to Catholicism in 1847 and in 1848 raised funds to build the first post-colonial Catholic church in San Francisco when he was commandant of The Presidio.[85]

Stanton treated many people rudely so it is no wonder then that gentle Father Seelos, who ordinarily said nothing ill of others, said Stanton was a "rough character." Seelos and Van de Braak probably had heard of Stanton's reputation but they had other reasons to fear him. On August 8, 1862, he issued orders to arrest and imprison anyone liable to the draft who left the country, as well as anyone who "by act, speech, or writing discourag[ed] volunteer enlistments." Although these orders were in abeyance, the priests may have had reason for concern that asking for relief from the draft for their confreres could be seen as treasonable.[86]

But it was not Stanton's infamous demeanor or the fear their request was treasonable that made Seelos and Van de Braak's timing bad. Just days before, widespread anti-draft rioting had occurred in New York City. The names for the draft were published in city newspapers on Sunday, July 12, just as news of the carnage at Gettysburg and warnings of more battles to come also made headlines. Mobs formed on July 13 and during four days of violence thousands of rioters, including Irish Catholic immigrants, attacked and burned draft offices and an armory, besieged abolitionist newspaper offices, looted stores, assaulted presumed pro-war members of the Republican Party and sacked their homes, and attacked and murdered Black residents throughout lower and upper east side Manhattan. The riots inspired similar disturbances in nearby Brooklyn, Jamaica, Staten Island, Yonkers, and in towns north along the Hudson River to Albany, east to Boston, south to Newark and Jersey City, and as far west as Detroit. A furious Stanton deployed army units from Gettysburg to New York City to control further rioting.[87]

Now the two priests faced Stanton, who was still seething from the riots. And he received them "very coldly," according Zimmer. He reportedly exclaimed:

> Keep your people from rioting! Keep your people from rioting! That's your duty, that's all you have to do![88]

Seelos wrote to his sister a few weeks later, noting the impression Stanton had made on him. He wrote: "the Secretary of war was very rough, and so it went back and forth, now harsh, now friendly." To another correspondent, he said that "Father Abraham . . . . treated me kindly but Stanton ——! If the feast of rough characters should ever be celebrated in the Church, Stanton will get an octave added to it." Even Stanton's defenders, Nicolay and Hay, admitted that there was "a certain roughness of Stanton's manner under strong irritation."[89]

Nothing relevant to the Seelos visit has been discovered in War Department documents or in Stanton's personal papers. The National Archives has a register of individuals who entered the War Department building but it covers only from December 1863 to August 1865. The corresponding volume for the prior period did not survive. Military records specialists at the National Archives and Stanton biographer Walter Stahr believe the stenographic records mentioned by Nicolay and Hay also did not survive. At the more local level, the Annapolis correspondent of the *Sun*, who was usually well attuned to town gossip, did not report the visit of an Annapolis clergyman to the president of the United States.[90] Had it not been for the *Chronica Domus* and Father Seelos' letters, a record of this historic meeting would have been lost.

The two priests, weary from their days in Washington and shaken by their reception by Stanton, returned to Annapolis. In a letter to Miss Mary written two weeks later, Seelos said that "thirty-six of our students, besides myself, are in danger of being selected for military service." He wrote to his sister in mid-August that "whether we have settled anything, or will yet settle anything, remains God's secret and that of the Blessed Mother." Seelos was convinced that it was prejudice against Catholics and hatred of Catholic priests that motivated some Northern officials to demand that priests be drafted. Two Redemptorist priests and two brothers were drafted in Baltimore but exempted for reasons of poor health (the priests) or non-US citizenship (the brothers). In Pittsburgh, three Redemptorist priests and one brother were drafted but had their commutation fees paid. Seelos knew these payments could not continue since the Redemptorists could not afford the $300 fee for all who were enrolled. He told his sister that "we have so many young members, that would have amounted for us to the gigantic sum of $25,000 or more" and that he continued to have his confreres daily pray the Psalms of St. Bonaventure in hope of a good outcome. Zimmer wrote twenty years later: "Thus the man of God did not neglect to have recourse to human means, although in his confidence in God, he awaited help especially from Heaven."[91]

On the Sunday before Seelos' visit to Washington, Governor Bradford recommended that Marylanders assemble in their usual places of worship to give thanks following Lee's retreat from Gettysburg through Maryland. At the same time, Lincoln issued a proclamation for a national day of "thanksgiving, praise, and prayer" to be held on August 6 in recognition of "the recent successes of the Federal arms." But on October 17, Lincoln issued a call for more troops. The terms of service of many army volunteers were going to expire during 1864 and the president needed 300,000 more volunteers to serve for three years or until the end of the war but not exceeding three years. The sheer volume of troops who had been and were now being called since the war began had reached a total of 1,775,000 men.[92] The threat of clerical military service had not gone away but had grown ominously.

The Salvation of Many Souls

Father James Bradley continued Father Seelos' ministry at Fort Monroe. He went there twice in 1863. In January he baptized newborn William Walsh, son of Sergeant John Walsh, Fourth US Light Artillery, and Jane Fullerton Walsh, both from Ireland. The baptism was recorded in the parish register in Annapolis. After a second and final trip in February, Bradley returned to Annapolis and was sent in early March to preach parish missions in Connecticut and New York.[93]

The Annapolis Redemptorists had first visited Easton, in Talbot County on the Eastern Shore, in 1858. They conducted services in a private home, which has not yet been identified. Then, in 1863, they were invited to say Mass for local Catholics at the recently acquired property of Henry May and his Catholic wife, Henrietta. The Mays had purchased the 189-acre Locust Grove plantation and moved from Baltimore to Talbot County in 1862. The river-front plantation was about four miles northwest of Easton. It included a recently built Italianate-style mansion called The Villa, a working farm, and an estate of "abounding hospitality and luxury." The Villa is important to the story because the Redemptorists celebrated Mass there. The Mays had an earlier St. Mary's connection, in 1852 when they served as godparents for Vivian Lowe, the son of Governor Enoch Lowe, when he was baptized in Annapolis.[94]

May was a Baltimore attorney and served in the US House of Representatives as a Democrat in 1853–55 and as a Unionist in 1861–63. Shortly after his election in June 1861, May took it upon himself to travel to Richmond, as the *New York Times* put it, "to arrange terms of conciliation or peace with the bogus Confederacy." Despite his good intentions, May's action was seen as sympathetic to the enemy and he was rebuked by Speaker of the House Schuyler Colfax. May was exonerated by the House Judiciary Committee but later in the year he was arrested, along with Baltimore Mayor George William Brown, a number of members of the Maryland General Assembly, several newspaper editors, and other suspected Southern sympathizers. The men, seventeen in all, were arrested on unspecified charges by order of the secretary of war, incarcerated at Fort McHenry, and later released.[95]

In spring 1863, at the request of Henrietta May and with the approval of Archbishop Kenrick, the Annapolis Redemptorists agreed to start an Easton mission, on a six-month trial basis. Previously, Jesuits from St. Joseph's in Cordova, nine miles north of Easton, ministered to one hundred or so local Catholics. In 1840 Father James F. M. Lucas, S.J., rented a hall in Easton and furnished it for Mass, and in 1842 he started a Catholic Total Temperance Society. In spring 1863, the first Redemptorist in Easton, Father John Cornell, held a public meeting to announce the decision to build a Catholic church there.[96]

The *Chronica Domus* reported that Cornell "was favorably received, and a tolerably large sum was subscribed." He arranged to rent the town hall on Washington Street as a place of worship until further arrangements could be made. Cornell returned to Annapolis with an enthusiastic report on prospects for Easton. Easton was important as an economic center, with a population of 2,000 inhabitants, and the seat of Talbot County. It was described in the *Chronica Domus* as:

> quite a thriving business place, and owing to the railroad now in course of construction in that part of the State, and its own favorable position, it will probably increase greatly. The loss of so many hundreds of blacks, free and slaves, has made the farmers and citizens desirous of obtaining German and Irish laborers. And, knowing that this cannot be effected, so long as no Catholic Church is established among them, they are very desirous to see one and willing to aid in its erection. The number of Catholics in the town and its environs is probably about one hundred. This number will be greatly increased by the measures which the farmers have taken to procure laborers from Ireland.[97]

Cornell promised that he or another Redemptorist would visit Easton on the third Sunday each month to perform pastoral duties. His impending return was announced in the *Easton Gazette* on July 11 and July 18:

> Religious services will be held by Rev. Father Cornell, a Catholic Clergyman, in the town hall, in Easton, Sunday, 19th of July, at 10 o'clock A.M. All who feel disposed are invited to attend.[98]

Father (later Bishop and Archbishop) William Hickley Gross, C.Ss.R. (1837–98). RABP.

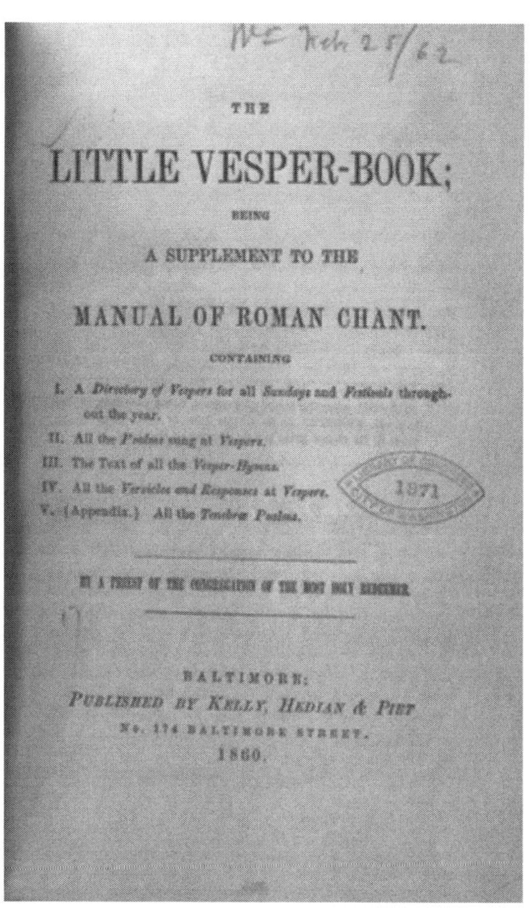

THE

LITTLE VESPER-BOOK;

BEING

A SUPPLEMENT TO THE

MANUAL OF ROMAN CHANT.

CONTAINING

I. A *Directory of Vespers for all Sundays and Festivals throughout the year.*
II. *All the Psalms sung at Vespers.*
III. *The Text of all the Vesper-Hymns.*
IV. *All the Versicles and Responses at Vespers.*
V. (Appendix.) *All the Tenebræ Psalms.*

BY A PRIEST OF THE CONGREGATION OF THE MOST HOLY REDEEMER.

BALTIMORE:
PUBLISHED BY KELLY, HEDIAN & PIET
No. 174 BALTIMORE STREET.
1860.

Title page of Father John Cornell's 1860 Little Vesper Book. *General Collections, Library of Congress.*

No. 66
Copyrt Recd Nov 25 1862

Hand-written copyright deposit notice in the 1863 Mission-Book. *General Collections, Library of Congress.*

Below: Part of the Editor's Advertisement in the 1863 Mission-Book. *General Collections, Library of Congress.*

6 EDITOR'S ADVERTISEMENT.

Finally, we commend the success of this little work to the mercy of God, trusting that it may promote his greater glory, by spreading the knowledge of religion, and preserving the fruits of the holy Mission; and we beg the occasional prayers of those to whom the book may be of any benefit.

ANNAPOLIS, MD., Sept. 1862.

Cornell placed the advertisements during his previous visit to Easton, but, as it turned out, the Mass was one of his last acts as a Redemptorist. He wrote to Father De Dycker reminding him that Mrs. May expected "some one to give them church on the 19th" and "to take along everything for Mass." So in place of Cornell, Father Bradley made the trip across Chesapeake Bay for the July 19 services and performed two baptisms. The next month, Bradley was joined by recently ordained Father Michael Stanislaus Burke, who may have been under consideration to head the mission. However, Burke's classmate, Father William Gross, was selected instead and faithfully braved the bay voyage each month starting in September.[99]

By this time, another Easton-area couple, Howes and Catherine Goldsborough, had become involved in the mission's development. Howes Goldsborough was not Catholic but had a long and warm relationship with the Talbot County Jesuits. His first wife, Hester Ann Pascault, was probably Catholic. His second wife, Catherine Jarboe, was Catholic and she took a leading role in the new mission, inviting the Redemptorists to stay at Galloway, the Goldsborough's country home two miles northeast of Easton. Acknowledging her leadership, Father Gross wrote to Catherine Goldsborough in October 1863, saying "I have no fear that you will refuse to do your part in the good enterprise started at Easton and which — I hope and pray will be the source of salvation of many souls."[100]

Meanwhile, in Anne Arundel County, the West River mission was visited at least three times in 1863. Adrian Van De Braak was there in mid-March. John Cornell went to West River in July after visiting Easton for several days. He would have taken the steamboat from near Easton to West River but because he did not have to be in Baltimore until July 6, he took a carriage from West River to Annapolis to spend Independence Day at his home parish. The last recorded visit of the year to West River occurred in November when Father Joseph Helmprächt, the new vice rector of St. Mary's in place of Father Seelos, made an overnight visit to check on the status of his new charges.[101]

St. Augustine's in Elkridge Landing in Howard County continued to receive nearly monthly visits from the Annapolis Redemptorists. Joseph Henning attended most frequently but, toward the end of the year, he was assigned to preach missions elsewhere and responsibility for Elkridge Landing was passed to Ferreol Girardey. According to tradition, St. Augustine's feast day (August 28) was specially commemorated by the Annapolis Redemptorists. Henning was joined in celebrating Solemn High Mass by Father Augustine Freitag and a group of seminarians. Although it was not recorded, it is likely that the seminarians sang as a choir and served at the altar.[102]

Our Life and Rule Being Too Hard for Him

It is a sad day when the Redemptorist congregation loses one of its members, especially one with considerable talent. In the preceding years, several priests, students, and brothers left Annapolis, some willingly dispensed of their vows, others expelled for lack of a vocation. The departure of Father Henry

Fehlings in 1860 had long been pending at his own request and he went on to serve as a diocesan priest. This was not so in the case of John Cornell. When he left Annapolis for Baltimore on July 6, the house chronicler observed that "none of us thought he had it in mind to leave the Congregation" and that "this father left the Congregation was beyond all of our expectations."[103]

The chronicler observed that Cornell had "always considered himself kind and therefore always displayed cheerfulness, but this time he behaved in another way" in which he seemed sad and was "very sparing of words." In violation of the Redemptorist Rule, Cornell left Baltimore for New York City without permission from the provincial, an act that was grounds for automatic expulsion from the congregation. De Dycker informed the Annapolis community that Cornell had left because "our life and living according to our Rule being too hard for him." He concluded that Cornell came to this reasoning "after consulting with the others, that we have not known, but which can be found in the Provincial Chronicles." The "others" turned out to be members of the Missionary Society of St. Paul the Apostle (Paulists), the founders of which were five former Redemptorists, all America-born, English-speaking converts who established their new order in 1858. Father Isaac Thomas Hecker, the Paulist superior, was confident that Cornell would join them. One of the co-founders, Francis Baker, had earlier "endeavored to induce" Cornell to join him in leaving the Redemptorists. But, at the time, Cornell told Baker that "he was firmly resolved to live and die in the [Redemptorist] Congregation."[104]

This resolve did not endure. Cornell's 1863 departure and the issues that led to it were well known to De Dycker and presumably by Cornell's immediate superior, Father Seelos. Problems began in 1862 when Cornell was assigned to update and republish the *Mission-Book of the Congregation of the Most Holy Redeemer.* According to the "Editor's Advertisement" in the front of the new *Mission-Book,* dated Annapolis, September 1862, the completed work was a "new and improved edition" using "a considerable amount of matter" from the 1858 Dublin edition of the same book. The new *Mission-Book* was published by Kelly, Hedian, and Piet in Baltimore and a copyright registration copy was deposited at the Federal court in Baltimore on November 25, 1862. Shortly after that Cornell went on a four-month mission trip in the North.[105]

While Cornell was on the road, the new edition came to the attention of Isaac Hecker, whose Paulist congregation had published its own version of the *Mission-Book.* Hecker accused the Redemptorists and their printer of plagiarizing his copyrighted translations, made during the time when he was still a Redemptorist and based on the Redemptorists' German-language original. Worried about being sued, Kelly, Hedian, and Piet wrote to Cornell asking him to explain the situation to Hecker. He did so and Hecker launched a lengthy rebuttal and threats of litigation. But, Hecker also suggested a solution: Cornell should produce a new edition that did not infringe on Hecker's copyright.[106]

This dispute was not easy for the meticulous Cornell. He was caught between orders from De Dycker and the harsh reaction from Hecker. He also had been preaching missions on the road and found the work increasingly stressful. In March 1863, he wrote to De Dycker saying he was "completely broken down, and am looking forward with joy to the prospect of a spell of quiet life." He said he would await De Dycker's further orders in regard to resolving the dispute with Hecker. De Dycker replied that a new edition would be discussed when Cornell returned to Maryland. Whether discussion was held or not is not known.[107]

John Cornell's pastoral activities in Annapolis and at the various out missions are an indication of his dedicated work as a musician, parish priest, preacher of missions and retreats, and co-founder of new missions in Easton and West River. During his time in Annapolis, besides the *Mission-Book,* he wrote and published *A Manual of Roman Chant* and a supplement to the manual entitled *The Little Vesper Book,* both in 1860, and *The Vesper-Psalter: or, Psalmody Made Easy* in 1861. He was away from Annapolis for eight months in 1862–63, during which time the Redemptorist mission band to which

Father Joseph Helmprächt (1820–84). Source: Rev. Henry Borgmann, C.Ss.R., History of the Redemptorists at Annapolis, Md., from 1853 to 1903 *(Ilchester, Maryland: College Press, 1904), 45.*

he was assigned preached a total of twenty-seven missions in Michigan, Ohio, Pennsylvania, New York, and Connecticut. The *Province Mission Book* kept during this period did not record the missionaries' names but the *Chronica Domus* verifies Cornell's absences on missions between August 20, 1861, and April 24, 1862. After his return to Annapolis, he was engaged in out-mission work in Elkridge Landing, made a trip to New York City, gave an eight-day retreat to the Christian Brothers in Ellicott's Mills, and then, from New Year's Day 1863 to late April was on the mission band again. During this time, the *Province Mission Book* recorded eleven missions in Ohio, Pennsylvania, Rhode Island, Connecticut, and New York. Again, no priest names were associated with the missions, but letters in the Provincial File note that Cornell preached missions in Norwalk, Connecticut, and Hudson, New York, with Father Henry Giesen, in March 1863. He had only a brief respite in Annapolis before going to Baltimore to deal with the *Mission-Book* plagiarism charges. It is not clear how the *Mission-Book* affair concluded but the publisher continued to advertise it weekly for the rest of the year.[108]

In early July 1863, Cornell made his last visits to Easton and West River. By then he had come to a difficult decision, writing to De Dycker in mid-July that "[w]ithout having anything against any member of the Congregation, I yet found myself unhappy in it." He said he could not possibly perform the annual renewal of vows in good conscience and that the "almost exclusively German character of the Congregation, and the great severity of the Rule, were the two chief causes" of his decision to leave. He further complained that although he was a parish priest, he was "not allowed to mingle among the people as other priests do." During his time in Annapolis, he performed fifty-one baptisms but officiated at only one wedding and no funerals. He was so anxious to be dispensed from his vows that he said he would go to Rome to request a release directly from the superior general. Upon his return, he hoped to become a secular parish priest. He also reminded De Dycker that he had "given nearly all my property to the Congregation" but now found himself "with but very little left." "Considering what I have done for the Congregation," he continued, he asked if the provincial would "remit to me such debts that you may have against me," namely some items that Father Rector (Father Leopold Petsch at St. Alphonsus in New York City) permitted him to take: "a coat, some few pieces of wash, my Breviary, shaving materials, and two or three books." Father Rector also gave him eight dollars and Father William Lürhman loaned him ten dollars. He finished the letter saying that at another time he would write about purchasing from De Dycker the copyright and printing plates for his book *Vesper-Psalter* published in 1861. Cornell wrote to Archbishop Kenrick concerning his priestly credentials and was sent a reply in mid-July 1863. Although neither letter is extant, the archbishop's letter register records that a response was made.[109]

While in New York City, Cornell booked passage to Europe to make his request for dispensation and sent a telegram to De Dycker seeking his permission to go. Cornell received the answer—"a[n] uncertain one"—by telegram but which was clear enough that Cornell cancelled his passage on a ship that was to leave the next day and waited for the dispensation to arrive without his personal appearance in Rome. He then proceeded to Perth Amboy, New Jersey, to stay with his mother, Amelia Cornell, again without De Dycker's permission. Cornell wrote to De Dycker in August that it "would be very painful for me to remain in one of the [Redemptorist] houses" and that Petsch had allowed him to stay with his mother until a dispensation was received. He repeated his desire to become a parish priest and now sought permission to say Mass at St. Mary's Church in Perth Amboy. He told De Dycker, "I have already received permission from the Bishop [James Roosevelt Bayley] & the Parish Priest."[110]

Cornell's dispensation was granted, effective September 9, 1863, and, around that time, he took charge of the church in Perth Amboy. He was immediately active, having a small bell hung in the steeple and starting the custom of ringing it when the Angelus was prayed each day. He bought an organ for the church, held a church fair, and hosted Bishop Bayley for Confirmation. He was said to have been "very zealous in the performance of his parish duties, teaching the children many pretty hymns, some of his own composition." In 1864 he became one of the incorporators of St. Mary's Church and also started to minister to Catholics in nearby Woodbridge. But, in the spring of 1865, he resigned his position and left for Europe.[111]

Cornell's connection to the Catholic Church after the European trip was short-lived. In February 1868 he married thirty-four-year-old Mary Emma Windsor. By then he had become the organist of St. Paul's Chapel of Trinity Episcopal Parish in New York City, a position he retained until 1877. He worked as a music teacher and a prolific writer of technical books on liturgical and secular music. He also was a composer of music, opera, and poetry and, in 1885, was recognized "as one of the most learned and accomplished musicians of our day." But he also was called an agnostic. In 1888 a short sketch of his achievements as a layman was published in *Appleton's Cyclopaedia of American Biography.* John Cornell died in 1894 "in Apostasia," according to a Redemptorist source, but supposedly on his deathbed he embraced again the Episcopal faith of his birth.[112]

Only God Knows What May Still Happen

Father Seelos' replacement as prefect of students by Father Gerard Dielemans in 1862 was followed by new round of complaints about him. Dielemans, like Müller before him, sent letters to the provincial in Baltimore and the superior general in Rome complaining about Seelos' easy-going manner with the students. Dielemans felt this undermined his own authority and he demanded a stricter regimen for the students. He did away with "incompatible" manual activities, such as serving at table, washing dishes, and cutting hair, and criticized the precedent set by Müller when novices under his supervision had helped build the new church and college building. Finally, "in the interest of harmony," de Dycker decided that Seelos should give up his post as rector and become the superior of the traveling mission band.[113]

On September 22, 1863, Father Seelos left Annapolis for the last time. Although he retained the title of rector of St. Mary's Redemptorist community—normally a three-year term—there is no evidence he ever returned to Annapolis. The closest he probably came was Cumberland, where the missionaries spent their vacations. The day after Seelos departed, Father James Bradley joined him on the mission band. In their place, the provincial appointed Father Joseph Helmprächt to serve as acting or vice rector and Father Van de Braak became church minister and pastor of St. Mary's, respectively. Helmprächt had arrived in Annapolis from St. Philomena's in Pittsburgh a month earlier to serve as prefect for the twenty new priests in their second novitiate. A forty-three-year-old Bavarian, Helmprächt had been in the United States since 1843 and was ordained in Baltimore in 1845. He then served in Redemptorist parishes in Baltimore, Buffalo, New York City, and Pittsburgh. With Seelos gone, the less-experienced Helmprächt gave Dielemans full rein in running the studentate. Dielemans' direction of the seminarians was tempered only by De Dycker's overruling hand. This led to Dielemans' gradual dissatisfaction and eventual return to Europe in 1865.[114]

During his time in Annapolis, Father Seelos wrote to his family about the causes of the war. He believed that many Americans had a disdain for church and religion and "at home, they pray little or not at all." This led children to "become thorough creatures of nature" and the young "who are thus so corrupted have a very peculiar hatred for the Catholic religion and its ministers." He concluded that this was:

> the reason for this terrible war, in which thousands and thousands have already been purged by God's avenging hand; and still more will probably be purged, since there is not the slightest sign that peace will be restored and the former tranquillity be attained.[115]

In the same letter, he also observed some of the causes of social problems in United States:

> The Americans were too proud of their free system of government and looked down on all other countries with a certain sense of pity. They loved their country too much, and in doing so, forgot about God and their true home. They loved a materially comfortable life, where everything is judged by the greatest comfort.

Several weeks after visiting Lincoln, Seelos wrote a letter to Frater John Berger's mother Katherine in Bohemia. He reported that her son was "not actually sick" but "very feeble" and in need of "constant prayer." He then related more about the situation facing the Redemptorists:

> We are living in very sad times. Everywhere war, revolt, and rebellion; only God knows what may still happen and yet, up until now, his Providence has protected us wonderfully. We do not let ourselves get sidetracked but continue our missions everywhere; and actually, with a special blessing from God. O my dear good people, if you only knew how many difficulties and dangers we find ourselves in at all times in this country, you would then certainly pray real fervently for us.[116]

Shortly after leaving Annapolis in September 1863, Seelos wrote about the forthcoming 1864 presidential election and his hope for change. He said that:

> With regards to the war, everything is still going the same way, and only through a change of administration, if the coming elections turn out well, or through, etc. etc., is there room for hope. It is a punishment for this proud and profligate country. The Americans have to become impoverished and humbled. May God direct everything to our well-being.[117]

Besides the draft problems that Seelos had encountered, his personal beliefs about the war must have made living in Annapolis difficult. Several of his charges had voluntarily departed for military service and others had fled to avoid conscription. He and his confreres perceived the terrible waste of war as they were confronted daily with the suffering and deaths of sick and wounded troops. His thoughts about the war and slavery, however, evolved over time. Writing from Cumberland in January 1862, he told his sister that Maryland "until now is counted with the North but will probably soon be joined to the South."[118] He was wrong, of course, but later in the year, he wrote from Annapolis to his family, expressing a similar opinion about Maryland and a hope for foreign intervention:

> The Potomac forms the boundary between Virginia, which has declared for the South, and Maryland, which in sentiment is also for the South but is in the possession of Northern troops. All business is at a standstill and the misery is daily getting the upper hand; and also, up to this moment, there is little prospect that the conflict will be settled soon, unless either England or France get involved, which hopefully will soon happen. Daily the enormous sum of three million dollars is being spent for the Northern army, and there are countless frauds, so that much of this great sum does not get where the government intends it to.[119]

In the same letter, Seelos mentioned with some hyperbole about a visit to Kent Island, noting that on the island "all are thoroughly for the South, just like most of the people in Annapolis and in particular in Baltimore, and mostly in the whole State of Maryland." An additional glimpse of his views on slavery also is revealed in this letter. In a section addressed to his brother Ambrose, he noted how Kent Island was "full of big farms, owned by very rich Americans" and that the "work is done by blacks, mostly slaves, who are very content with their lot, since they have it better than servants with us." The statement "servants with us" apparently referred to hired servants back in Bavaria.[120]

He further revealed his political sentiments in a July 17, 1863, letter to Miss Mary:

> I cannot help feeling great sympathy with the so called Rebels. I would find no reasons, on the basis on which every nation in our times is entitled to create their own

government, to call the Southern people Rebels. In the Declaration of Independence this principle is called "self-evident." Again I hate the principles of the black Republicans, as I hate the devil and I believe that if they succeed now in suppressing the South, they will begin to suppress our holy Religion; at least they will make us go through an ordeal as the Roman tyrants did.[121]

As early as 1845—two years after he arrived in America—Seelos observed the plight of both immigrants and African Americans. He was living in Baltimore at the time and had become aware of the evolving culture of Maryland and the struggles of free Blacks and slaves as well as numerous refugees from Ireland and the German states. He perceived the great need for priestly work among them. He told his family that:

The poverty and neglect of the greatest portion of the Germans, instruction of their children, and with time, even more, that of the blacks, since they are here, provide superabundant material to lay claim to all the activity of a priest who wants to dedicate himself fully to the well-being of his neighbor.[122]

Writing from Annapolis in the July 17, 1863, letter, he again expressed his views on slavery:

I never could see how the poor Irishmen rushed with such an eagerness into that bloody war, which was for nothing else than these same Abolitionists, who will reward them by persecuting their religion and faith, if they succeed to crush a whole nation out of existence. But you must well understand, I do not favor just slavery, but I think this is not the proper way to root it out; particularly not by such hypocrites, who hate the Negro more than any slaveholder could do.

Toward the end of this letter, Seelos said he had spoken with the bishop of Wheeling and that they both had the "same opinion and the same sentiments" on these subjects. "I leave all to the wise Providence of God. He only knows how to bring good out of evil." The bishop of Wheeling was Richard Vincent Whelan, a native-born Marylander who privately sympathized with the Confederacy and frequently denounced the war. The views of Seelos and Whelan were similar to those expressed by many mainstream Catholics who saw immediate abolition as a threat to the social order and to the Constitution and the feared a resurgence of anti-Catholic actions when the war was over.[123]

Father Seelos not only was sympathetic to the South but he also seemed to fear a resurgence of the Know Nothings, and with good reason. When he was in Pittsburgh there were virulent threats not only against Catholics but specifically against at the Redemptorists and St. Philomena's, the German congregation church of which Seelos was pastor from 1851 to 1854. Because of these threats, he had a wall constructed around the church as protection against Know Nothing rowdies. He also had been in Baltimore during Know Nothing-inspired riots in 1856. St. Alphonsus Church, of which he was rector, was close to the scenes of deadly street fighting during the election of a Know Nothing mayor and Millard Fillmore's garnering all of Maryland electoral votes.[124]

Father Seelos' fullest explanation about the war was expressed in an August 21, 1863, letter to his sister, Sister Romualda. This time, his "few words about the war" exhibited a more nuanced analysis:

The chief reason were the slaves, the "Negroes," the blacks. The evil of slavery came into the Southern states with their founding. The present slave owners received them from their forebears, and the Constitution of the United States approved their right to have slaves and sanctioned this by law. But now the Northern Abolitionists, that is, those people in the North who want to root out slavery – contrary to the Constitution – are trying, in every possible way, to restrict and oppose the Southern States. The Southerners did not tolerate this, and declared themselves independent of the North, and so the war began. Who, then, has right on his side? According to the law and the Constitution, which the North has broken, the Southerners are in the right; more especially so because they have declared themselves prepared to do away with slavery gradually; and because the blacks are really not capable of governing themselves.[125]

He then expressed a typical southern view of Blacks and slavery, tempered by northerners' view of slave owners, then condemned both northern and southern behavior:

The blacks are happiest when they have a strict and virtuous master; when they are left to their own devices, they rot in vice and in mischief. Unfortunately, however, the Southern slave holders were not virtuous and lived a very immoral life, and often sinned against the slaves by not giving them any education, etc. As far as material things are concerned, the slaves were well taken care of; they had plenty to eat and drink, and servants in Europe have it harder than slaves over here. It is entirely false if one conjures up the gruesome treatment that, for example, the ancient Romans abused their slaves with. Here the Southerners are to be blamed mostly for the immorality and the lack of education; otherwise they are entirely in the right. On the other hand, the Northerners want to abolish slavery not out of love for the blacks, whom they actually hate, so much so that the blacks in every way are separated from the whites; they want to get rid of them or send them to a distant colony. There should only be whites in the North as well as in the South; then, they think, they could establish a heaven upon this earth. All the men who are prominent in the North, especially these Abolitionists, are inveterate Freemasons, lacking in any supernatural faith; and want to establish a heaven upon this earth.

For a Redemptorist who was not supposed to discuss politics, his views were quite well developed. He continued in the same letter that the abolitionists were "determined to continue the war as long as they can and until the South is entirely destroyed and annihilated." He never mentioned Lincoln or the Emancipation Proclamation in his explanation of slavery. He seems to have confused those who were anti-slavery but also anti-Black with those abolitionists who had the best of intentions toward future liberated African Americans. Or, perhaps, amidst the violence of war, he saw no differentiation between the two. He did warn that when the abolitionists were:

> finished with the South. . . . I am thoroughly convinced, they will go after the Catholic Church, which they hate with all their soul, with all their spirit, and with all their energy. For this reason, most Catholics who have an insight into these things, are completely for the South.

This view was close to that expressed by some Northern Catholic newspaper editors. Others thought, however, that Catholic loyalty to the Union and their contributions to the war effort would be celebrated in the postwar period.[126]

After making his postwar prediction, Father Seelos returned to the theme that Maryland "wanted to declare itself completely for the South, and I see it as the clearest disposition of God that this did not happen." Otherwise, he wrote that Maryland "would have become the center of the war and so many churches and religious houses would have been destroyed and only God knows if we had then escaped with our lives." Seelos told Sister Romualda that only the many prayers and God in his mercy had kept Maryland safe.

We do not know to what extent Seelos knew about either the Preliminary Emancipation Proclamation of September 22, 1862, and its final version of January 1, 1863, or Lincoln's General Orders No. 100 (*Instructions for the Government of Armies of the United States in the Field*, issued April 24, 1863). General Orders No. 100 was a code of military conduct written by the Prussian-born American political philosopher and international law expert Franz (Francis) Lieber. Seelos' sentiments, judging from what he told his family in Bavaria, might have been similar to what historian Harry Stout wrote nearly 140 years later. While freeing the slaves in the rebellious states (but not in Maryland or the other Union border states), the Emancipation Proclamation "put to final rest any thoughts of a negotiated peace by which the South would be permitted to leave the Union or, conversely, to return with slaves and existing leaders intact." Stout characterizes General Orders No. 100 as having rationalized total warfare that morally justified civilian suffering and that "Americans in the North and the South would not look back to restrained codes or charity." Father Seelos surely would have disapproved.[127]

This Illness Went on for Weeks

Frater Joseph Martin Weber, a nineteen-year-old Bavarian-born rhetorician, contracted smallpox in August 1863. It happened during the students' summer holidays, when they remained in Annapolis. Other illnesses were frequent in the college in the autumn of 1863. In late September, Father Van de Braak had "already had been sick for many weeks with serious health problems (Dysentery etc.)" and had been "unable to celebrate Mass, leave his room or even get out of bed." He recovered enough by November to celebrate Mass but then retreated in pain to his sickbed. He was back on his feet three days later and able to perform his duties unimpeded. Others also were sick beginning in early September and into the subsequent months. The most serious cases were the newly ordained Fathers Adam Petri, Henry Dauenhauer, and Francis Schnüttgen and Fraters Charles Anselm Rosenbauer, Andrew Henry Lindenfeld, John Joseph O'Brien, and Michael Oates. Others were sick but were not identified in the *Chronica Domus* other than to indicate additional illnesses with "etc. etc." and that "all this illness went on for more weeks." On September 26, Frater Charles O'Donoughue, for an unspecified reason, underwent the medical practice of bleeding, "but not dangerously so: this was forbidden him in the future."[128]

The overall situation became so acute that a new infirmary was set up in October in "the old house" (the Carroll House). The infirmarian was newly arrived professed Brother Stephan Lindenfelser. He was a forty-year-old a native of Baden and since the 1850s had been in Pittsburgh, where he completed his novitiate under Father Seelos. Brother Matthias (Charles) Stabel, a thirty-nine-year-old Prussian, also was available for nursing duties. In the middle of October, two of the patients—Father Petri and Frater O'Brien—were sent to Baltimore for more advanced health care. Petri returned to Annapolis "in robust health" at the end of November. O'Brien returned on a date that was not recorded but the following January left Annapolis and went to Cumberland with Father Müller "because of his health," and died there on April 1, 1864. On November 28, Frater Michael Dunn, who had not been named among the sick but presumably was included in the "etc. etc.," was sent to Baltimore for recuperation from an unspecified condition that was revealed later as a hernia and perhaps another illness. Father Schnüttgen was sent to St. Peter's in Philadelphia for recuperation from illness and permanent new assignment.[129]

Still another illness was noted in the year-end *observanda*:

> Rev. Father [Peter] Petit was very ill this year, but not so much more so it seems he will live. But with God's favor, and the help of Mary, his strength will be recovered, for which we offer Mass every day.[130]

Although much was written in the *Chronica Domus* about the long bouts of sickness in the autumn of 1863, it provided no specifics as to the nature of the illnesses and whether or not they contributed to or were the result of the smallpox epidemic that hit Annapolis in January 1864. Perhaps the crisis ended before then as Brother Stephan, the infirmarian, was reassigned to Pittsburgh in late December.[131]

During this season of sickness, between March and September, the twenty new priests continued their moral theology studies. Three other men who had not advanced to the priesthood in March also were studying moral theology. They were Fraters Andrew Henry Lindenfeld, Benedict A. Neithart, and Charles William Rathke. In May two of the new priests—William Gross and William Löwekamp—went to Baltimore with Fathers Seelos and Jaeckel to help with spiritual retreats. The academic year ended on July 31 and during the month-long holiday, newly ordained Michael Burke received practical experience by accompanying James Bradley to Easton for weekend Mass, while Augustine Freitag became prefect of the sick in place of Joseph Henning who joined Seelos' mission band. On September 7, nineteen of the twenty men ordained by Archbishop Kenrick in March began their second novitiate under the direction of Father Helmprächt. The twentieth man, Francis Eberhardt, had been sent to Cumberland on August 28 or 29 to work as a lector for the novices. Besides the newly ordained priests, the three moral theology students also participated in the second novitiate even though they would not be ordained until March 12, 1864.[132]

Election of the Disloyal

Men who came to the polls in Annapolis and refused to take the oath of allegiance to the United States were considered disloyal by the Federal authorities and denied the right to vote. A week before the November 4 elections, the Middle Department issued General Order No. 53 directing local provost marshals to arrest any "evil-disposed persons . . . who have been engaged in the rebellion against the lawful government, or who have given aid or comfort, or encouragement to others so engaged, or who did not recognize their allegiance to the United States . . . found at or hanging about or approaching any poll or place of election." Governor Bradford protested the order to Lincoln as "without justification" and Lincoln countermanded it in part as "wrong in principle" but allowed the rest of it to stand. As was required by the order, the provost marshal reported the names of thirteen such "evil-disposed" men in Annapolis who refused to take an oath of allegiance to the United States and were thus denied the right to vote on November 4. They were arrested "on the ground of Disloyalty" on November 21 and sent on parole to Fort McHenry. Two of the men were St. Mary's parishioners: James Revell, the Democratic candidate for Anne Arundel County state's attorney, and his brother Martin. They and nine others were released after taking an oath of allegiance; the two recalcitrants were taken to City Point, Virginia, for banishment to the South.[133]

Despite the onerous treatment of voters, the "Secession Ticket," so-called by the provost marshal, did quite well in the Anne Arundel County elections. Democrats won a seat in Congress, three seats in the House of Delegates, and the positions of clerk of the county Circuit Court, register of wills, state's attorney, sheriff, three judges on the county Orphans' Court, all seven county commissioner seats, and county surveyor. (No Annapolis city positions were at stake in this election.) They thus made a sweep of all contested positions, except three state-wide races for which the Democrats had no candidates: comptroller and commissioners of public works and the land office. State's attorney incumbent James Revell was substantially out-voted (302 to 147) in Annapolis, but he trounced his Union Party opponent, Henry M. Murray, in the six rural districts of Anne Arundel County (972 to 333, for a total of 1,119 votes—64 percent—to 635).[134]

In the county commissioner race, a St. Mary's associate won a position. Democratic Party nominee wealthy farmer Horatio Tydings tied for third among seven winning candidates. The year before he had been noted as a member of a "secession" family. Clearly, the county-wide electorate favored the pre-war status quo with all its racial disparities and conservative ways.[135]

Annual Visitation

Father De Dycker arrived in Annapolis on November 14 for his annual canonical visitation, which took place from November 16 to 24. As in 1862, Father Van de Braak served as his socius. De Dycker's observations concerned student health, the need for a "time of relaxation, to relieve the minds of the students," that they not to be overworked in their studies, be given proper meals and medication, dress properly when going out in the rain, and to not assume too arduous labor. Their superior was directed to "not neglect to tell the students to take care of themselves" and "to consider their health with all sincerity." For their part, the students were told that when they were appointed to read at table (that is, to read from Scripture or other religious works during meals), they "always should review first what they are to read, and if this is done there will be fewer errors." The rector was held responsible for making corrections and "to see to it that if a father or a student is going to make a blunder while reading, to make suitable corrections." Silence in the refectory was "to be religiously observed according to the Rule." The brothers henceforth were given days off from work, to the extent possible, on the feasts of the Immaculate Conception (December 8) and St. Stephen (December 26), and the second Sundays after Easter and Pentecost. Whether it was the brother in charge of the kitchen or someone else who complained to De Dycker, an order was issued that "great care [was] to be taken in the refectory" and that the "tables themselves and all the dishes belonging to the refectory [were] to be kept clean."

Was there a problem in the front office? Perhaps so since De Dycker found it necessary to remind his Annapolis confreres that the baptismal register was "to be kept under lock and key," and the brother porter was reminded to keep closed the curtains that covered the windows of the parlor. Presumably this referred to the public area of the college building, where the laity had access to the parish office which, as it is today, had windows facing the hallway. Finally, the provincial gently reminded that, as was expected in all Redemptorist houses, "after lunch and dinner that the community shall come to the church, together to adore the Blessed Sacrament by kneeling on the *floor* rather than the bottom step of the altar." As in other years, the provincial sought to make minor adjustments in how the seminary and the parish was run but there appeared to be no major issues in 1863.[136]

Although Van de Braak was socius to De Dycker, he accompanied Father Dielemans to Baltimore for six days during the visitation. When he returned, Van de Braak learned that he was to be reassigned to St. Mary's Church in Buffalo to replace the superior there, Father Louis H. Claessens, who was to succeed Van De Braak in Annapolis. Claessens, a Dutchman, was professed as a Redemptorist in 1849 and had arrived in the United States in 1851. He and Joseph Wissel were ordained in Philadelphia by Bishop John Neumann on March 26, 1853. Claessens then served in Cumberland, New York City, Philadelphia, Detroit, and Buffalo. He was well thought of, as witnessed by this statement after his death in 1866: "Every one, Protestant as well as Catholic, who was brought within the power of his influence, acknowledged, by respect and affection, the purity of his character, the amiability of his temper, and the gentleness of his manners." Now, in 1863, he assumed the jobs Van de Braak held as church minister and pastor, as well as lector of moral theology.[137]

Urbanity, Justice, and Charity

On Christmas Eve 1863, the *Annapolis Gazette* reported the death of Sergeant John Mullan, a parishioner, who had died "at an advanced age" two days earlier. Mullan, the newspaper reported:

> was connected with the Naval School in this city for many years before the war broke out, since which time he has been in the employ of the Government here. He was ever faithful to his duties and much respected by his superior officers.[138]

The Annapolis correspondent for the *Sun* wrote that Mullan's name was "quite familiar both to the army and the navy" and that he "was a soldier of the old school." Because of "his meritorious conduct, faithfulness and fidelity, [he] was detached from the army" and given the position of postmaster and other light duties—such as tolling the bell, delivering messages, and keeping time records for civilian employees—when the Naval Academy was established in 1845. In 1850 the superintendent of the Naval Academy asked that Mullan "remain here in performance of such light duties as might be assigned him as a reward for long and faithful service in the Army." He retained his non-commissioned army status until 1855, and when the war began, he was given a post office position in General Hospital Division No. 1 and held it until his death after a brief illness. The *Sun* ended its report saying Mullan "was much respected in this community, and died lamented." The *Maryland Republican* initially published a one-line notice of Mullan's passing but followed with a more detailed report two weeks later. It acknowledged his many positive attributes ("a worthy high-toned gentleman," among others), and concluded with a remark about his religion: "He was a member of the Roman Catholic Church, and received all the consolations given by it to departing souls, and we feel assured that he has secured for himself a blissful immortality." The funeral was held at St. Mary's, with Father Girardey officiating, and Sergeant Mullan's remains were "followed [to the cemetery] by a large concourse of relatives and friends" and "buried with honors of war." A book published nearly a half century after his death still recalled that John Mullan "was a man characterized by urbanity, justice, and charity."[139]

In modern terms, John Mullan was not so "advanced" in age, he was only sixty-three years old, but he did have a long association with Annapolis. A native of County Armagh, Ireland, Mullan immigrated to the United States in 1824 with the intention of joining relatives on a farm in Kentucky. Instead he enlisted in the army in New York City, signing on for three-years' service with the Third US Artillery. He subsequently reenlisted five times, serving at Fort Monroe, Virginia; Fort Moultrie, Charleston, South Carolina; Washington, DC; and finally at Fort Severn in Annapolis. He retired from the army in 1855 as an ordnance sergeant. His longest service was at Fort Severn, where he had been posted since 1832. In 1837 he was sworn in for a new term of service by the fort's commandant, Colonel John DeBarth Walbach, whose surname would be used as the middle name of Mullan's eighth child, Dennis Walbach Mullan, when he was born in 1843.[140]

John Mullan's connection to St. Mary's Parish was longstanding. He was married in Annapolis in September 1829 to Mary Ann Bright and they were the parents of eleven children. One notice of his death noted that Mullan "was the father of a large and interesting family, and lived to see his children occupying honorable and prominent positions in life, with bright prospects for their future career." The eldest son, John Jr., was born at Fort Monroe in 1830 and baptized at St. Mary's in Annapolis in 1832. St. Mary's extant baptismal registers include a record of only one other Mullan baptism—that of their youngest child, Virginia Isabel, in 1854. It is likely, however, that the nine other children also were baptized at St. Mary's between 1833 and 1849, years for which records no longer exist.[141]

John Mullan's wife, Mary Ann Bright, was a convert to Catholicism and is said to have had an influence that "was quite strong for good on every phase" of one of her sons' life, so it is assumed she performed equally well for her other children. Mary Ann is mentioned three times in the St. Mary's records: as the mother of newborn Virginia in 1854; when she was confirmed in 1860 (as Maria Joseph); and when she died after having received Extreme Unction in 1888. Her burial at St. Mary's Cemetery, along with her husband, eight of their eleven children, one grandchild, a daughter-in-law, and her sister, stands as a silent testimony to her as a good and patient mother who raised her children in the enduring tenets of the Catholic Church.[142]

Mary Ann Mullan had links to two other parish families. She was born in Anne Arundel County, possibly in Annapolis, in 1805 to James Bright and Mary Ann Tydings. The Tydings were members of All Hallows Episcopal Parish near Birdsville (now in Edgewater), in southern Anne Arundel County, so in all likelihood Mary Ann was baptized there in the Episcopal tradition. When Mary Ann's younger sister,

Catherine "Kitty" Bright, was conditionally baptized by Father Jacobs at St. Mary's at age forty in 1859, it was noted that she had been christened earlier as an Episcopalian. Father Seelos wrote that "in this country all Protestants are rebaptized conditionally, since one can no longer be sure that their preachers have administered this sacrament properly." When Catherine Bright was confirmed the same day as her sister (and both taking the same name—Maria Joseph) in 1860, they both were noted as converts.[143]

Catherine Bright is identified as only "Aunt Kitty" on her

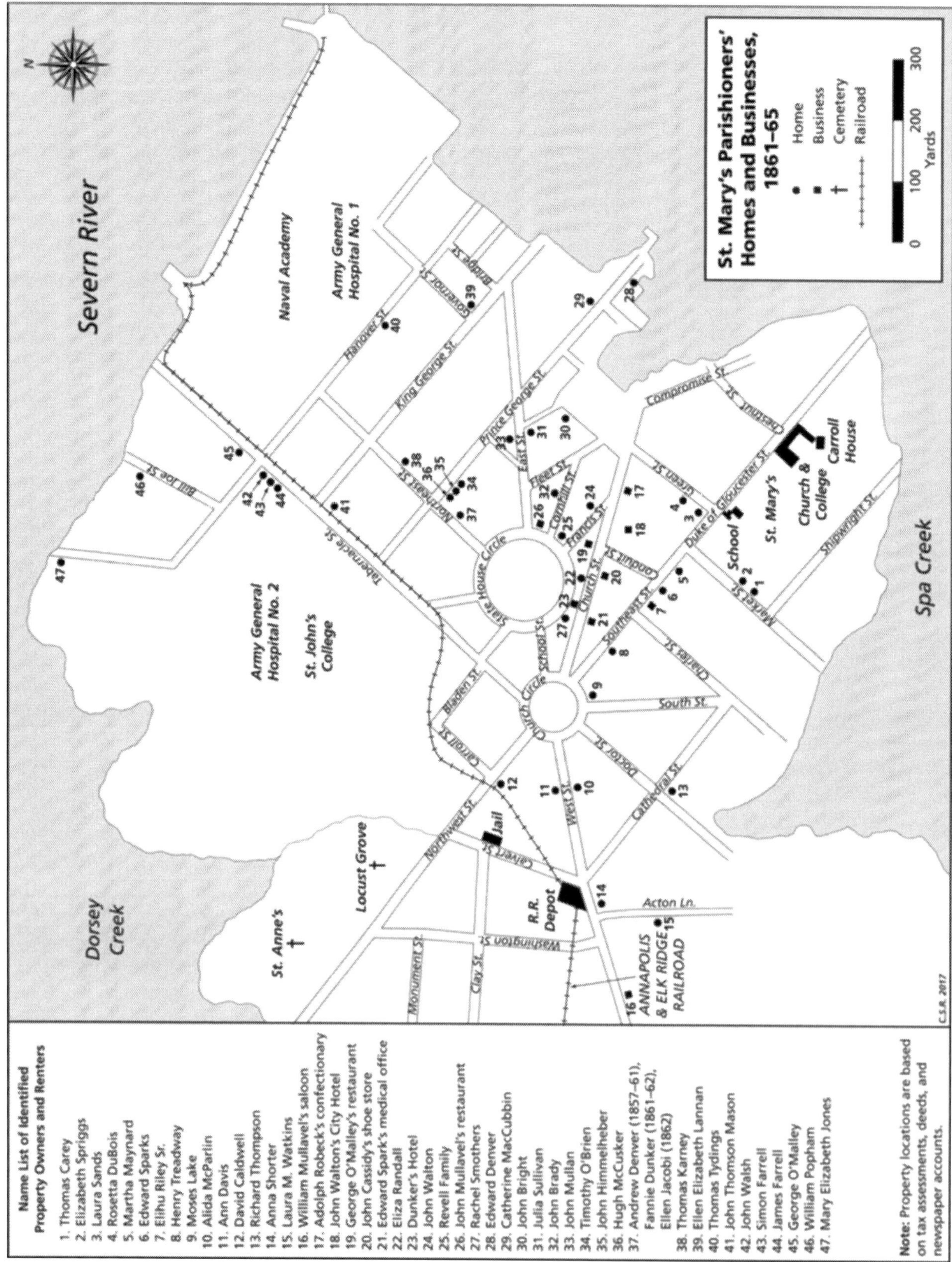

headstone in the Mullan lot at St. Mary's Cemetery. As a favored aunt, she presumably helped out in the Mullan household over the years and continued to live with the family until her death in 1902. She was also aunt to three other converts, the children of her brother, John Henry Bright, an Annapolis carpenter, and his wife, Catherine V. Hubbard. John and Catherine were married in 1843 and were parents to eleven children, seven of whom survived into adulthood. One who did not survive was Kate Amelia Virginia. She was born in Annapolis on August 28, 1859; baptized at St. Mary's on December 18, 1859; and died May 3, 1862. Although the religion of little Kate's parents was not mentioned in her baptismal information recorded by Father John Cornell, when Kate's brother John Henry Bright Jr. and sister Katherine Cavay Virginia Stewart Bright were baptized at St. Mary's, it was duly noted that the parents were not Catholics. None of the other Bright children were baptized at St. Mary's. John Henry Jr. was eleven years old when he was baptized in 1863 and Katherine was five months old when she was received into the church in 1866. Surely Catherine Bright and Mary Ann Mullan had some influence on these children being baptized but neither served as godparents. Instead Ann Elizabeth Davis was godmother to the girls and Edward Powers was godfather to young John Henry. These sponsors reveal more parish networking. Irish-born Edward Powers had been appointed in 1852 as a watchman at the Naval Academy, John Mullan's place of employment.[144]

Life had been good for the Mullan family as evidenced by the considerable amount of property they owned in the city. The family home on East Street (today the location of 8 Martin Street) was purchased by Mary Ann Tydings Bright in 1820 and signed over to her daughter, Mary Ann Bright Mullan, in 1835. Together, the Mullans wisely invested in another property on East Street as well as properties on Bridge, Governor, Scott, King George, and Prince George streets (see map "St. Mary's Parishioners' Homes and Businesses, 1861–65"). When the Naval Academy expanded its acreage in 1853, the Mullans were among the thirteen property owners who sold land to the government.[145]

Another sign of Mullan prosperity was ownership of slaves. Although the 1850 Federal Slave Schedule did not enumerate any slaves owned by John Mullan, the 1860 schedule listed him as the owner of four slaves: a twenty-year-old female, who was a "fugitive from [the] state"; two other females, one five years old, the other eight; and a ten-year-old male. This latter slave probably was William H. Brown, who was born in 1848 and baptized at St. Mary's by Father Jacobs in 1861 with Mullan family friend Ann Elizabeth Davis as godmother. William was issued a travel pass, as "Sergt. Mullens Col'd Boy William," for an unspecified destination in September 1861. He was manumitted by Mary Ann Mullan three months after John's death so that he could join the US Colored Troops.[146] There is no record concerning the other three slaves who, if not manumitted or having escaped earlier, would have been freed by the new Maryland constitution on November 1, 1864.

John Mullan was a naturalized citizen and politically active as a Democratic voter. Toward the end of his life, he was elected alderman for the City of Annapolis. He was sworn in on April 14, 1863, but did not serve out his term, having died in December that year.[147]

Three of John Mullan's seven sons held commissions in the armed forces during the Civil War and a fourth served before the war as a military surgeon in the Pacific Northwest. The eldest, John Mullan Jr., earned a bachelor's degree from St. John's College in 1847 and then, on the recommendation of his father's old commander, Colonel Walbach, attended the US Military Academy at West Point, graduating in 1852. He served as a lieutenant in the US Second Artillery but spent much of his pre-Civil War career in the Pacific Northwest as a topographic engineer laying out military roads between army posts in Washington and Oregon territories. In 1858 the *Annapolis Gazette* reported his "near being killed" during an Indian uprising while laying out a road from Fort Benton to Fort Walla Walla, both in Washington Territory. He survived the ordeal and was cited for his "gallant conduct."[148]

John Mullan Jr. is most well known for supervising the construction of the 624-mile-long military road that connected the headwaters of the Missouri River in Montana with the headwaters of the Columbia River in Oregon between 1859 and 1862. The route, which became known as the Mullan Road, bridged numerous rivers and traversed rugged Rocky Mountain territory to open the interior Pacific Northwest to commerce and development. Western sections of Interstate 90 today follow much of the same route as the old Mullan Road. Both Mullan Pass on the Continental Divide near Helena, Montana, and the city of Mullan, Shoshone County, Idaho, are named for John Mullan Jr., and several monuments and statues celebrate him and the Mullan Road. The Catholic boy who came of age in Annapolis made a good name for himself.[149]

Mullan was promoted to the rank of captain on August 11, 1862, as he completed his road in the Northwest. He then traveled to Washington to write an after-action report. Although his Second Artillery Regiment fought at the battles of First Manassas, Antietam, Fredericksburg, and others, John Mullan Jr. did not see any military action during the war. He viewed the Southern "revolution" as a "fraud . . . which will sink its perpetrators and abettors into eternal infamy," but he did not participate in the fight. Instead he sought appointment as Idaho's territorial governor and when this was denied, he resigned his army commission on May 23, 1863. After leaving the army, he moved to San Francisco where he passed the law bar exam before the end of 1863. Thereafter, he worked as a commissioner for the Walla Walla Pacific Railroad Company in Washington Territory, a freight and stage coach operator in Idaho Territory, and a public land dealer in San Francisco. After the war, he relocated to Washington, DC (see Parish Legacies, ch. 9).[150]

John Mullan Sr.'s fourth son, Horace Edward Mullan, served in the Navy during the Civil War. He entered the Naval Academy in 1857 and, because of the urgent need for naval officers at the onset of the war, he and nineteen other first class members were detached from the academy on May 9, 1861, and ordered to active duty as warranted midshipmen. Horace served aboard the USS *Anacostia* of the Potomac Flotilla in 1861, saw action at Aquia Creek, Virginia; then in 1861–62, with the South Atlantic Blockading Squadron, he was involved in the Army-Navy amphibious assault on Port Royal, South Carolina, on November 7, 1861. After that he served on board the USS *Iroquois* of the North Atlantic Blockading Squadron, and was promoted to lieutenant on July 16, 1862. After an assignment at the Naval Academy in Newport, Rhode Island, he served aboard the USS *Nereus*, first with the West Indies Squadron then with the North Atlantic Blockading Squadron. The *Nereus* was involved in the attacks on Fort Fisher, North Carolina, in December 1864 and January 1865. Horace's service continued after the war until 1883 when he was dismissed from the Navy at the rank of commander because of "drunkenness on duty; hazarding the vessel under his command, in consequence of which it was run upon a rock and lost; and neglect of duty." He had been in command of the USS *Ashuelot* (of the Asiatic Squadron) which, while under way in heavy fog on February 18, 1883, between Xiamen and Shantou on China's south-eastern coast, struck a rock off Zhongpeng Dao (East Lamock Island) and suffered such severe damage that the ship had to be abandoned and eleven crew members died. He recovered from this disaster and graduated from Georgetown University Law School in 1886. He appealed his dismissal from the Navy but it was affirmed by the US Supreme Court in 1890. Horace Mullan and lived and practiced law in Washington, DC, until he died from illness while visiting Annapolis in 1903.[151]

John Mullan's sixth son, Dennis Walbach Mullan, also served in the Navy during the Civil War. He took courses at St. John's College in Annapolis and graduated from St. Mary's College near Bardstown, Kentucky, in 1860. In September 1860, he was appointed to the Naval Academy, and left with the academy when it relocated to Newport in April 1861. Dennis was considered a southerner and thus was under suspicion as to his loyalty to the government. He was among thirteen other southern acting midshipmen at Newport whose names were listed in a May 1861 letter that was intercepted by academy authorities and forwarded to the Navy Department. Suspicion about Dennis was overcome and he and thirty other second classmen were detached early from the academy, on September 30, 1863, and ordered to active duty. From 1863 to 1864, he served on the USS *Monongahela*, assigned to the West Gulf Blockading Squadron and saw action at the Battle of Mobile Bay on August 5, 1864. He then served aboard the USS *Malvern*, Rear Admiral David Dixon Porter's flagship in the North Atlantic Blockading Squadron, which was involved in the attacks on Fort Fisher in December 1864 and January 1865. After the Civil War, Dennis had a distinguished naval career and received an honorary master of arts degree from St. John College in 1872. He retired at the rank of commander in 1901 after which he and his wife, Ada, returned to Annapolis and lived with his sisters, Ann Catherine and Virginia Isabella Mullan, and his aunt, Catherine Bright, on College Avenue. He was the last of the eleven Mullan children to die, in 1928. Military veterans John Jr., Horace, and Dennis Mullan are all buried in the family plot at St. Mary's Cemetery in Annapolis.[152]

Two other sons also had military connections. James Augustus Mullan, the second eldest son, attended and was expelled from St. John's College in Annapolis but later graduated from the University of Maryland's medical school in Baltimore in 1857. He worked at Bellevue Hospital in Baltimore before joining his brother John in Idaho and Montana where he worked under contract with the army as a surgeon. When the Civil War began he was working in the Flathead Agency in Washington Territory. He visited Annapolis in May 1863 and then returned to Washington Territory where he made his permanent home and practiced medicine. By the end of the war, James was employed as a physician for the US Army at Fort Walla Walla, Washington. James died in Baltimore in 1882 but his place of interment has not been determined.[153]

Another son, Ferdinand Tydings Mullan, had a more fleeting association with the military. He was appointed to the US Military Academy in 1865 but did not matriculate. Instead, after appropriate study, Ferdinand was admitted to the Maryland bar in Annapolis in 1866. He practiced law in Annapolis in the late 1860s and early 1870s and then worked as a real estate agent in Annapolis and Washington until his death, which occurred at his sisters' house on College Avenue in 1892. Ferdinand, the seventh son, is buried at St. Mary's Cemetery.[154]

Two others sons had no military service but did have notable but relatively short lives. Charles Nevitt Mullan, the third son, attended St. John's College and then went west where, like his brothers, he worked for the army in Washington Territory. Later he worked as a farmer and a miller but his health failed and he returned to Annapolis in 1867. He served as a clerk in the United States House of Representatives in 1875–76 and "was noted for his charitable and good work in the Annapolis area." He died in 1876 and is buried at St. Mary's Cemetery in Annapolis.[155]

The fifth son, Louis Augustus Mullan, received an appointment to the US Military Academy in 1856 on the recommendation of twenty-four members of the Maryland General Assembly. But he did not matriculate and instead joined his brothers in Washington Territory, where he studied law at Walla Walla. In 1869 he was conferred with a master of arts degree from St. John's College, at which he had previously studied. Louis practiced law in Washington and California and then became a newspaper editor and judge in Yuma, Arizona, where he died in 1884 and is buried in the Catholic section of Yuma Pioneer Cemetery.[156]

John and Mary Ann Mullan had four daughters. The oldest, Mary Elizabeth, as discussed below, became a source of grief for her staunch Catholic family. The third daughter, Maria Teresa, died in 1856 at the age of six or seven. The other two daughters were Ann (Annie) Catherine and Virginia (Jennie) Isabella. Annie, the second daughter, served with her mother as a godparent for a Baptist convert, twenty-four-year old Maria Cecilia Hail, during the Civil War. It is probable that

Annie and her mother had a role in the instruction and conversion of Miss Hail, who was baptized by Father Claessens in 1864. Annie Mullan lived with her mother, her sister Virginia, several brothers, and her Aunt Kitty in the house bought by her brother Dennis in 1875 on Tabernacle Street (now College Avenue). Annie died in 1923 and Jennie died four years later; both are buried at St. Mary's Cemetery with their parents, five of their brothers, and one sister.[157]

In 1855 at the age of twenty-four, and against her parents' wishes, Mary Elizabeth Mullan went to St. Anne's parsonage where she married James Campbell, an Episcopalian. So severe was the break between Mary and her family that, when John Sr. wrote his will two years later, he disowned his daughter, bequeathing her "one shilling." After both of her parents were deceased, her siblings paid Mary $500 to give up any rights she might claim on her mother's estate, real or personal.[158]

Mary Elizabeth's husband, James Campbell, was a bricklayer and later a waterman. In August 1862, he enlisted in Baltimore for three years service in the Sixth Maryland Infantry Regiment, for which he received a twenty-five-dollar bounty. His regiment fought at the Second Battle of Winchester on June 13–15, 1863, during which James was listed as missing in action. He returned to his regiment which then participated in battles at the Wilderness, Spotsylvania, Cold Harbor, and Petersburg in 1864. Private Campbell was injured during the siege of Petersburg and admitted to the Eighth Army Corps Hospital in Baltimore. In July 1864, he requested permission to be near his family and was allowed to transfer to General Hospital Division No. 1 in Annapolis. He was formally discharged from the service in June 1865 but met a sad end seven years later. He died after accidently drinking a vial of laudanum at a fellow waterman's home on Horn Point in 1872. He was buried the next day in St. Anne's Cemetery.[159]

Mary Elizabeth, now a widow with three children, lived on King George Street, in close proximity to but still estranged from her birth family. In 1890 she applied for and received an eight-dollars-per-month pension based on her husband's Civil War service. Relations with her family never healed and at the time of her death in 1901, her siblings, then living on College Avenue, reportedly "watched the funeral procession as it wound around St. Anne's Church on the way to . . . a Protestant Cemetary [*sic*]. None of them left the security of the front room curtain draped windows, none turned up at the funeral." Mary Elizabeth Mullan Campbell lies next to James Campbell at St. Anne's Cemetery.[160]

Before leaving the Mullan family, one more Mullan needs mention. Despite much searching, how and if Darby Mullan was related to John Mullan has not been determined. They could have been brothers or cousins or just had the same surname. The 1860 Federal Census for Annapolis lists Darby Mullan as a forty-year-old gardener, born in Ireland, living with Bridget Mullen [*sic*], age twenty, also born in Ireland, no occupation listed. Marital status was not tabulated in the 1860 census and Bridget could have been Darby's young wife, a niece, or even a daughter if he was a widower. Bridget does not appear in St. Mary's parish records during the antebellum and Civil War periods. Darby was not found in any later censuses, at least not in a way that matches him clearly with the 1860 Annapolis gardener. However, he appears seven times in St. Mary's sacramental registers: in 1860 as godfather of James Hughes; in 1862 as godfather of Michael Burns; in 1863 as a witness to the marriage of Margaret McBride to Sylvester McCabe and as godparent of Jacob Gill; in 1864 as godparent of Thomas Patrick Gunning; and in 1869 as godparent for Michael Burns' brother John and as the father of his newborn daughter Jane Mullan (the mother is listed as "Margaret Byrne").[161] All of these reveal Irish connections but none of these families had been employed by the Naval Academy nor were they related to the John Mullan, Bright, or Tydings families. The four boys for whom Darby served as godfather all were newborns and perhaps he was the Irish community's favorite honorary uncle.

Celebrated With Great Solemnity

Christmas fell on a Friday in 1863. The year's end brought a report from the Annapolis correspondent of the Baltimore *Sun* that "[t]he coming holidays will be extensively observed in the ancient city" and that "great preparations are being made to celebrate the occasion by both civilians and military." The correspondent revealed that the "principal business thoroughfares are crowded to excess, the merchants, confectionary and toy stores are doing a 'tip-top' business."[162]

Christmas at St. Mary's in this tumultuous year of war was celebrated by the clergy, religious, and laity in "the usual way" according to the Redemptorist annals:

> December 25 — Feast of Our Lord's Nativity was celebrated with great solemnity. The first Mass was solemnly celebrated in the chapel by Reverend Father Rector at midnight. After this Mass renewal of vows according to our Rule also took place in the chapel. At the hour of 2 o'clock, private masses began; at 4:15 solemn Mass was celebrated in the church; and the other Mass was solemnly celebrated at 10 o'clock during which Rev. Father Claessens preached, and a collection to pay the debt on the church was taken up. Not many people were present for the solemnities of this day. The rest of the ecclesiastical functions were completed in the usual way.[163]

At year's end, the basic facts of life at St. Mary's College and in the parish were recorded in the Provincial Annals at St. Alphonsus in Baltimore. It was noted that there had been twenty-six baptisms, five conversions, ten deaths, four marriages, and 2,500 communions distributed. The success of the new parish school also was noted: thirty-four students were enrolled.[164]

An ominous public notice came from the provost marshal was published on December 26. All persons claiming exemption from the draft were ordered to present themselves in person to Thomas N. Pindle, the deputy provost marshal for Anne Arundel County.[165]

Chapter 6: 1864 — It Would Move the Heart of a Tiger

Ice and Illness in Annapolis

> January 1864: This month has been cold and the Chesapeake Bay has been frozen in and around Annapolis in such a way as to hinder navigation, and our students were able to walk on the ice on several occasions![1]

So reads one of the first *Chronica Domus* entries for 1864. Rarely did temporal events merit such note. But starting in December 1863 and continuing until July 1866, the affable Father Ferreol Girardey was the "Chronista." This was just one of his many duties. He was lector of dogmatic theology, church history, geometry, and physical science; admonitor for the seminary; and consultor to the rector. He also worked in the out-missions, and preached missions in and out of state. The record does not credit him with another activity, photographer, but it was Girardey who took the two photographs of the Redemptorist sailboat fleet that appear in this book. The history of St. Mary's was thus greatly enriched by the pen and photography of this talented man.[2]

Smallpox broke out in Annapolis in early January, first in one part of town and then spread to other neighborhoods. This contagious disease was well known in Annapolis, where breakouts occurred almost yearly in the late eighteenth century and, along with scarlet fever, was a leading cause of death at mid-nineteenth century. This new outbreak brought widespread fear and calls for vaccinations in town. By mid-January, the mayor of Annapolis and local physicians reported a total of twenty-four smallpox cases. The city authorities established a smallpox hospital on Judge Brewer's property adjacent to the new soldier's cemetery. It had "every comfort and convenience necessary for patients, and to which, should any new cases occur, they will be immediately removed." By the end of January, the *Annapolis Gazette* reported, the "dreadful malady. . . has nearly or entirely abated."[3]

The Redemptorists had their own infirmary at St. Mary's and were quite familiar with smallpox in the past. Most of the community apparently escaped the 1864 epidemic. Herman Krastel, who died of consumption in 1863, had contracted the disease soon after he entered the Annapolis novitiate in 1858. Although he recovered from smallpox, contemporary medical literature—as well as some modern medical researchers—indicate a correlation between smallpox vaccinations and consumption (tuberculosis).[4]

Frater Joseph Weber had contracted smallpox in August 1863 and in March 1864 "began again to get sick and vomit." Although he had been full of "fervor and piety" as a novice, his enthusiasm waned when he became ill. As the months went by, Weber's commitment to religious life declined and, in January 1865, after it was clear that "he had lost all his faith," he left the community and was dispensed of his vows a month later. The Redemptorist record reveals that Weber's brother, a medical doctor who himself had lost his faith, was the cause of Weber's demise as a seminarian, not smallpox.[5]

Although smallpox was not mentioned in the case of twenty-three-year-old dogmatic theology student Frater William Bernard Hanley, he was sick enough to be sent to Baltimore on January 5, 1864. Hanley remained there for nearly ten weeks recuperating, but his problems may have been more spiritual than physical. Even before he was sent to Baltimore, Hanley had been observed to have neglected his duties, his fervor had diminished, and he wanted out. After returning to Annapolis, Hanley, according to the *Chronica Domus,* "imagined" that he was afflicted with bronchitis and "was not able to recover health" unless New York City doctors were consulted. He was dispensed of his vows in July and dismissed from Annapolis on August 1. Hanley had left the congregation once before. He originally had been admitted and invested in Annapolis in 1857 and then left but was readmitted in 1858 and continued on until his 1864 dismissal. Now he was gone for good.[6]

Fire and Gunfire

Fires struck the properties of several parishioners in early 1864. In January, the home of Henry and Emma Treadway was saved "through the exertions of a number, the fire was stopped after doing $150.00 damage." The Treadway's frame house stands today at 203 Duke of Gloucester Street, with a later brick addition on the front. In February, fire exacerbated by a violent wind mostly destroyed "Noah's Ark," a three-story brick building at the foot of Church Street near the wharf (now the site of 87 Main Street). It was owned by Dr. John Henry Boyle Sr. and his wife Ellen Slemaker, the Catholic pro-South son and daughter-in-law of Colonel James Boyle. It was home to twelve families "of all colors and complexions" and when it caught fire numerous residents, soldiers, General Assembly members, and Russian sailors then in port helped put out the fire. But it spread to a neighboring building owned by Ellen's brother John and three Confederate flags were found among rescued items. This discovery caused fury among the loyal Unionists and, it was supposed by the *Annapolis Gazette* that the flags were "intended to wave conspicuously when Jeff. Davis moves his headquarters from Richmond to Annapolis."[7]

Another tragic event in early 1864 brought an Eastern Orthodox priest to Annapolis. He presided at the February 6 funeral of Nikolai Demidoff, a seaman from the Russian Imperial Navy Ship *Almaz.* Demidoff had been shot to death on February 4 in a saloon near the Naval Academy, the result of the "too free use" of liquor. Russia's Atlantic Squadron had been deployed in 1863 as a deterrent against possible British and French involvement in unrest in Russian-controlled Poland and was visiting various ports in the United States. Two of the squadron's five ships spent part of the winter anchored in the Severn River and the sailors enjoyed shore leave in town with the unfortunate result of their comrade's death. Demidoff's nearly two-hour funeral service at the Naval Academy chapel involved a High Mass in the Eastern Orthodox rite. Russian

"Bird's Eye View of the City of Annapolis, Md." Charles Magnus, New York, 1864. Miriam and Ira D. Wallach Division of Art, Prints and Photographs: Print Collection, New York Public Library. "Bird's eye view of the city of Annapolis, Md." New York Public Library Digital Collections. https://digitalcollections.nypl.org/items/510d47d9-7dce-a3d9-e040-e00a18064a99.

sailors sang as a choir and others served as acolytes. After Mass Russian sailors carried the open coffin on their shoulders, while another sailor carrying the lid in his arms, and led the procession to Ash Grove Cemetery (now the Annapolis National Cemetery). The cortege included the chanting priest, a dirge-playing Russian naval band, an honor guard of US Marines and Invalid Corps troops, members of the Maryland General Assembly, and local citizens. The rites resumed at the cemetery with chanting of Psalms, the sprinkling of earth on the body, and burial of the cross that had stood at the head of the coffin during Mass. This religious event, unprecedented in Annapolis, went unnoted in the Redemptorist chronicle, despite press coverage.[8]

An Instrument in the Hands of God

On February 24, 1864, Congress passed, and President Lincoln signed, an amendment to the Enrolling Act of March 3, 1863. The new Amendatory Act gave the president broader authority to call up unlimited numbers of men for military service and established procedures for determining quotas and providing for drafts in states where quotas were not met by volunteers. It also provided for the enrollment of "able-bodied male colored persons" and compensation to slave masters loyal to the Union if their men were mustered into military service. Provisions for substitutes, commutation fees, bounties, eligibility for enrollment, disallowance of foreign birth as an exemption from military service, exemptions for men physically or mentally unfit for military service, and other requirements also were covered. Section 17 allowed members of religious denominations to declare under oath or affirmation—supported by "satisfactory evidence"—that they were "conscientiously opposed to bearing arms, and who [were] prohibited from doing so by the rules and articles of faith and practice of said denomination." Conscientious objectors who were drafted were to be considered noncombatants and assigned to hospital duty or the care of freed slaves. Otherwise, conscientious objectors could pay a $300 commutation fee which was "to be applied to the benefit of the sick and wounded soldiers." Members of the clergy, however, were not mentioned as part of the conscientious objector category. For the Redemptorists, this still meant either a loss of personnel if they were drafted or having to pay the $300 fee.[9]

The Amendatory Act had been approved by Congress only after extensive debate over the controversial commutation fee, which was criticized by some as the basis for a "rich man's war, poor man's fight." During the debate, Colonel James Fry, the War Department's provost marshal general—the man in charge of administering the Federal draft—had urged Congress to repeal the commutation fee, except for certain religious groups and to allow them to claim conscientious objector status. The commutation fee clause was included in the February 24 act but was repealed on July 4, 1864. Other Section 17 provisions that provided for conscientious objectors were left unaltered.[10]

During the run-up to the passage of the Amendatory Act, Father Müller decided to take action. He developed a scheme to register the novices and students with enrollment boards in congressional districts where there was less chance they would be drafted. Müller made an unexpected visit to Annapolis on December 31, 1863, and left the next day for

Frederick with twenty-two-year-old moral theology student Joseph Firle. He believed that the authorities in the Fourth Congressional District, which included Frederick, were more likely to not draft the Redemptorists. According to the *Chronica Domus*, he did this "to preserve [Firle's] exemption from military conscription." In mid-January 1864, Müller returned to Annapolis to continue his efforts to free the students from military conscription.[11]

Having succeeded in getting Firle enrolled at Frederick, Müller exploited his success by dealing directly with military authorities in Washington in February 1864. He had an acquaintance there who proved to be very helpful: Father Charles Ignatius White, pastor of St. Matthew's Church. White introduced Müller to Major Thomas McCurdy Vincent at the War Department's Adjutant General's Office. Vincent was responsible for organizing and administering Union volunteer regiments and apparently also dealt with chaplain commissions. But he was not the right one to deal with Redemptorist draft problems, so Vincent introduced Müller to Colonel Fry, the provost marshal general, who was in charge of the draft. Fry assured Müller that his problems could be resolved. Müller wrote later that he found Fry "a very kind gentleman and not begotted [*sic*, bigoted] at all," and very willing to help.[12]

Still not content that he had solved the enrollment problem, Müller wrote to Fry on February 24, thanking him "for [his] kindness of having settled the enrollment affair of our people." He then asked Fry "for another small favor" and went on to explain that "six or eight of our young priests are to be sent to different houses of our Society in the North and West of the United States and one to New Orleans" and asked Fry to direct the enrollment board at Frederick, to examine them before the draft occurred. He argued that if they went off to their new assignments without having been examined—and presumably granted exemptions—"much time and heavy expenses" would be incurred to return later to Frederick. The young priests were among those who had been ordained in March 1863 and soon would complete their second novitiate in Annapolis. Fry approved Muller's request and on February 25, an order was sent to Captain James Smith, provost marshal at Frederick, to examine the new priests prior to the draft so they could be sent on to their new assignments. On the same day, a letter was sent to Müller informing him of the action.[13]

Father Müller wrote to Major Vincent in mid-March thanking him for his kindness and taking him up on an offer of "further services." Müller asked Vincent to "settle with Gen. Fry, if it be in your power, the following little affair." The "little affair" involved Fraters Louis Koch and Francis Xavier Müller and the February 24 Amendatory Act. Section six of the act required the enrollment of minors who would reach the age twenty years between the time of the last enrollment and that of the coming draft. Müller pleaded that their original enrollment was erroneous because they had been under age at the time and because they "were enrolled in the wrong place, as they belong to this college." Although he did not say so, the "wrong place" was Annapolis, in the Fifth Congressional District. Müller posed the dilemma he was in. For Captain John Holland at Ellicott's Mills to strike Koch and Müller from the Fifth Congressional District rolls, he needed a certificate from Captain Smith at Frederick, and the enrolling officer at Frederick could not register Koch and Müller without orders from Washington. Müller feared that the impending April 1 draft date would arrive before the two students could be stricken from Annapolis and enrolled in Frederick. On March 18, Fry's office referred the request to Holland in Ellicott's Mills, asking "if any reason exists why the names of the Rev. L. Koch & Rev. F. Müller should not be erased from the enrollment lists in the 5th Dist Md." Five days later, Holland forwarded Müller's request and the Provost Marshal General's Office referral to Captain Smith in Frederick, asking him to enroll Koch and Müller in the Fifth Congressional District and to forward to certificates of enrollment to Ellicott's Mills. Smith complied and reported back to Fry's office on March 24 that the two men were enrolled in Frederick and that he had forwarded their certificates of enrollment to Holland in Ellicott's Mills. Müller was duly informed on March 28. His scheme was working.[14]

With this success in hand, Müller persisted in his correspondence with Major Vincent. In a five-page letter in April, he thanked him for past favors, saying he was "sorry to trouble you again." He described the Redemptorists as an "exclusively Missionary Society," which, like "a political government, frequent changes of officers and exchanges of soldiers become necessary." He noted that four priests in the previous week had been reassigned to other Redemptorist houses and two more were likely to leave in the next week or two. He pointed out that if any of them should be drafted, "the expenses and loss of time would be too great to go back to their respective places of enrolment [*sic*] to present themselves for examination." Or, he argued, they might not be able to leave for their new post at all. In such cases, they would be forced to pay the $300 commutation fee to the government unless they could return to the enrollment site to plead their case. But it was not possible to be examined (and possibly be found unfit for service) before being drafted, unless—Müller suggested—the draft board was empowered to do so by Colonel Fry. Plus, some of the priests had been enrolled in more than one state. This posed another bureaucratic problem that Müller, who claimed to be their superior, and the officers of the various enrollment boards were unable to resolve. Having shown how "many troubles, inconveniences and expenses" were caused by the draft, Müller returned to the issue of cost. He said the Redemptorists had already paid $1,500 to the government in commutation fees for five drafted members and that he himself had spent not less than $100 since January 1, 1864, "travelling for myself and others for this same affair of the draft." He pointed out that the Redemptorists were "poor and that our Churches are in great debts, and each time when a Missionary is drafted the money must be begged from the Poor." The prospect of future drafts and an extended war thus posed a serious burden on the congregation. Finally, he made his request "to do business in a shorter way, with less trouble, inconvenience and annoyance both to myself as Superior of the Society and especially to the Respected Gentlemen of the War-Department at Washington." The suggestion was that Fry should issue a certificate:

> . . . in which he says that, if the Rev. Mich. Miller [*sic*], Superior of the Missionary Society of the Redemptorists, presents either in person or by letter a member of the Society who was obliged for the greater good of the Society and Religion to leave his station, to a Provost-Marshal of the U.S. for enrolment, such Provost-Marshal shall enroll such Missionary member and give or send to the Rev. M. Miller a certificate of the enrolment, upon the production of which certificate the Provost-Marshal of the place which the missionary left shall strike his name from the list of Enrolment, that moreover the Board of Enrolment is empowered to examine, for good reasons, such a Missionary even before the draft.[15]

Müller allowed that if Major Vincent knew of "a better expedient, I will thank you for it most sincerely in the name of our whole society." He must have known he had overstepped the his bounds because, in closing, he suggested that Vincent take the proposal to Fry "when he is at leisure," providing it was a time when he (Vincent) knew that Fry "will not be displeased, if he is again troubled on our account, as he might have reasons to feel annoyed, since this is the fourth time that I plague him." Good priest that he was, Müller promised "fervently praying [to] the Lord every day to reward you for [the favor to the Redemptorists] in this life as well as in the next." Since this was only the third letter found in the Provost Marshal General's Bureau files, the statement that this was the fourth time that Müller had plagued Fry, indicates that some correspondence is missing or misfiled or that the first "plague" was the office visit in February. Also enclosed with Müller's April 4 letter is a note dated April 6, 1864, from Father Charles White to Major Vincent. Müller had said in his March 12 letter to Vincent, that White had made introductions back in February. But now White wrote, "I beg leave to introduce V. Rev. Father Miller, Superior of the Redemptorists in the U. States, & to convey to your favorable attention the business which he has in hand."[16] Müller, of course, was not the superior of the Redemptorists in the United States, and either White assumed he was or made the claim regardless.

On April 11, Müller received a response to the request sent to Major Vincent. It was not what he asked for but it surely sufficed. The response came from Colonel George David Ruggles, an assistant adjutant general, saying Fry would "not feel displeased" if Müller applied to Fry with individual cases. Not wasting any time, Müller, then in Baltimore, addressed a cover letter the same day to Fry summarizing the Ruggles letter and enclosing eleven or more separate petitions. Petitions for eleven priests, all dated April 11, are on file at the National Archives but others whose names were listed in a letters-received index are missing. Unfortunately, if Müller wrote on behalf of Father Seelos, that letter is among the missing or misfiled documents. Seelos, and some of the young priests named in correspondence, did not appear in the index of Provost Marshal General's Bureau correspondence for the year 1864. The endorsement on the file states simply: "Copies made to Pro. Mars. to effect desired transfer, April 15, 1864."[17] Success was nearly at hand.

The process of transferring from one enrollment board to another was complex, occurred rather quickly, but was not without protest. For example, one of Müller's April 11 petitions was on behalf of Adrian Van de Braak. The petition said Van de Braak was to be transferred from Annapolis to St. Mary's in Buffalo, New York. The petition was received at the Provost Marshal General's Bureau on April 13 and, on April 15, a copy of the letter was referred by Colonel Ruggles to Captain Smith of the Fourth Congressional District in Frederick via Colonel N. L. Jeffries, Acting Assistant Provost Marshal for Maryland and Delaware, headquartered in Baltimore. Smith was asked if "any reason exists why the name of the Rev. Adrian Van de Braak should not be erased" from the Fourth District and transferred to the Thirtieth Congressional District of New York, and if not, to send the name on to the New York board. The request was received on April 22 and on April 27, Smith returned the file with his endorsement to Fry through Jeffries, but he had his suspicions. His enrollment book indicated that Van de Braak had originally been enrolled in the Fifth Congressional District (Annapolis) and had been transferred to the Fourth District (Frederick), "claiming their [*sic*] residence to be in the 13th sub-dist." (Cumberland) and "that the Board has had reason to believe that such transfers proposed in many cases have had as their object the evading of the draft." Smith added that Van de Braak's name "may form part of the number of names from which the quota for this Dist. was seduced; which the Board thinks likely to be the case." The assignment of state enlistment quotas was controversial and there was a reluctance on the part of enrollment officers to interfere with them once they were set. Moreover, Smith's response said that the Board "does not feel authorized therefore to make the transfer requested without instruction." Smith's endorsement was received in Baltimore on April 29, reviewed without comment, and returned to Washington. On May 3, Ruggles replied to Smith with the instruction: "erase the name & forward this paper to Major [A. T.] Dixon [acting assistant provost marshal general] at Elmira N.Y. to have it enrolled in the 30th Dist." On May 23, Captain W. Y. Rogers of the Thirtieth District stated simply that "this man has been enrolled in the 5th Sub District [Buffalo] of this District." On May 24, Dixon in Elmira forwarded the report back to Fry in Washington. Van de Braak was enrolled in Buffalo and safely so since at that time it was more likely that western New York laborers rather than professional men would be conscripted.[18]

A similar routing process took place in the case of Father Joseph Helmprächt, then officially assigned to St. Philomena's in Pittsburgh. Except in this case, Captain J. Heron Foster, chairman of the enrollment board in Pittsburgh said they "had no evidence of change of residence, or of improper enrolment" and that neither he nor the Board of Enrollment had authority "to make such change, in case of removal from the District after July 1st 1863." After this response made its way back through Harrisburg to Washington, Ruggles ordered Smith in Frederick "to enrol the name of the Rev. J. Helmprächt" and to forward the documents to Foster, who was directed to "drop the name of Mr. Helmprächt. . . ." What is odd, however—and the kind of thing that would have given draft boards pause had they known—is that at this time Helmprächt was actually living at St. Mary's in Annapolis, where, in Father Seelos' absence, he served as vice rector, from September 1, 1863 to April 17, 1865.[19]

When the case of Father Nicholas Jaeckel, who was being reassigned from Annapolis to St. Joseph's in Rochester, New York, was sent to Pittsburgh, the enrollment officer reported back that he was not enrolled there. Since Müller had stated that Jaeckel was from both Pittsburgh and Annapolis, the action was shifted to Ellicott's Mills. Unlike the Van de Braak and Helmprächt cases, there was no protest and Jaeckel was reenrolled in Rochester.[20]

The same actions were taken for Fathers Michael Burke, Joseph Henning, John Blanchet, and William Löwekamp, Frater Charles Dammer, and Brothers Adam (Anselm) Knecht, Michael (Polycarp) Haas and Mathias (Charles) Stabel, plus others whose petitions are misfiled or missing. What is interesting in the cases of Burke, Henning, Knecht, Blanchet, and Stabel, all of whom had been reassigned to Rochester, is that the enrollment board in Frederick reported that their names had previously transferred "at their own request" from Annapolis to Cumberland. As with Van de Braak, the board suspected draft evasion and that these men may have been included in the enlistment quota for the Fourth District, which did not have the authority to reassign them. And, as with Van de Braak, the Provost Marshal General's Bureau directed that their names be deleted and forwarded to Elmira. The board at Elmira and the subdistrict board at Rochester complied with Washington's orders. The case of Brother Michael Haas, who also was reassigned to Rochester, was handled by the enrollment board at Ellicott's Mills. There, Captain John Holland found no irregularities and simply removed Haas' name from the list and forwarded it to Elmira for enrollment in Rochester.[21]

There were other Annapolis Redemptorists who Müller could not get shifted to enrollment boards in districts that had plentiful local volunteers. They had to undergo examination by the enrollment board in Ellicott's Mills, which Müller said was "begotted" [*sic*, bigoted]. Normally, a medical examination was given only to a man who had been drafted. Then, if he passed the medical examination, he could appeal to the draft board for an exemption. According to Müller, all the Redemptorists examined by the Ellicott's Mills board were eventually exempted. One claimed "he could not keep the water" while another pleaded "mental disability." They both were exempted as were "others for other reasons." Father Seelos told a friend in Germany that "we were always excused [from the draft] with the exception that both in Annapolis and in other camps, we visited the soldiers and gave them spiritual assistance."[22] As will be seen, this was not strictly true (see Again the Draft, this ch).

At end of the year 1864, the Redemptorist chronicler summarized the main events and achievements of the year. The primary item related to Müller's efforts:

> In the first place, the studentate & Congregation must be very thankful to Divine Province & our dear Mother Mary for having so fortunately escaped the various "Drafts." We prayed much, and others prayed much for us; and these prayers were not fruitless. Rev. F. Michael Müller, Rector of Cumberland & Master of Novices, was the instrument in the hands of God to free us from the misfortunes of being drafted. May Jesus & His holy Mother continue to protect us.[23]

Lay members of the parish also were subject to the draft. Henry (or Harry) Coulter, was

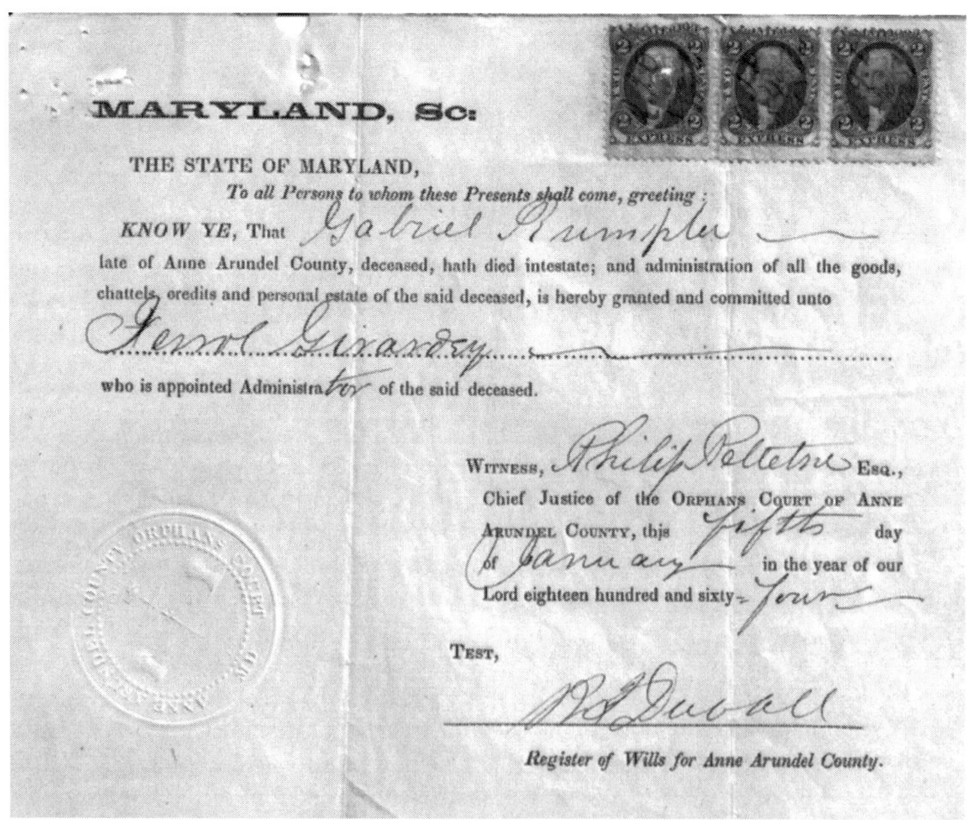

MARYLAND, Sc:

THE STATE OF MARYLAND,

To all Persons to whom these Presents shall come, greeting:

KNOW YE, That Gabriel Rumpler

late of Anne Arundel County, deceased, hath died intestate; and administration of all the goods, chattels, credits and personal estate of the said deceased, is hereby granted and committed unto

Ferrol Girardey

who is appointed Administrator of the said deceased.

Witness, Philip [illegible] Esq., Chief Justice of the Orphans Court of Anne Arundel County, this fifth day of January in the year of our Lord eighteen hundred and sixty-four

Test,

R L Duvall

Register of Wills for Anne Arundel County.

Anne Arundel County Register of Wills certificate appointing Father Ferreol Girardey administrator of Father Rumpler's estate. SMPA.

enrolled for the draft in 1862 and again in 1863. When the Annapolis names were drawn in the draft in late May 1864, his was among them. A news report said he had "been drafted both times the draft has taken place here, and is not now a resident of this city." The deputy provost marshal for Anne Arundel County later reported that Harry Coulter had "Deserted before [the] Draft." There is no evidence that the twenty-year-old carpenter, son of Leonidas and Martha Ellen Boone Coulter, ever enlisted in either the Union or Confederate armies. Henry's father was a purveyor of oysters and his mother was a convert; they had four children baptized at St. Mary's. Henry himself had been confirmed in 1857 and in 1860 was living in the household of master carpenter Henry Treadway. Another man drafted was Thomas Old, a non-Catholic laborer whose wife Cecelia Clifford Old and daughter Margaret Ann were Catholics. Old's name was drawn in the 1864 draft but there is no record he was enlisted. Richard Thompson, Jr., a twenty-seven-year-old painter by profession, also was drafted but also seems not to have served. His association with St. Mary's is unclear but his sister Susanna Thompson Rawlings had four children baptized at St. Mary's between 1863 and 1866 and she herself converted to Catholicism in 1866. Their father, Richard Thompson, Sr., a master painter, was buried in St. Mary's Cemetery when he died in 1871.[24]

Father Rumpler's Farm

On January 6, 1864, Father Girardey conveyed title to Mulberry Hill, a 120-acre tract at the head of Martin's Cove on the Broadneck Peninsula, across the Severn River from Annapolis. He acted in the capacity of administrator of the estate of Father Gabriel Rumpler, the founding Redemptorist superior of St. Mary's, who died in 1856. Girardey was represented in the Anne Arundel Orphans' Court proceedings by parishioner James Revell. Rumpler purchased Mulberry Hill for $1,200 in April 1855 to use as a source of crops, firewood, and other farm supplies needed by St. Mary's College. But before the farm could be put into use, Rumpler changed his mind and sold the farm to Joshua and Harriet Brown. Rumpler suffered a mental breakdown the next month and in early June was taken by Father Seelos to Mount Hope, a mental institution run by the Sisters of Charity in Baltimore. Rumpler's legal representative at the time was Matthias Benzinger of Baltimore. But Benzinger did not know about the sale to Brown and transferred the property title to the Redemptorist corporation. Although Brown had paid part of the sale price, he failed to record a deed with the Anne Arundel Circuit Court. When Brown attempted to sell the land in 1863, he found a cloud on the title and a balance due of $505.08. When this situation became known, Girardey was appointed to act on behalf of Rumpler's estate and complete the transfer to the Browns who sold the land the next day to pay off their debts to Farmer's National Bank.[25]

Baltimore, Buffalo, and Beyond

The Redemptorists ordained in March 1863 completed their second novitiate at St. Mary's on February 7, 1864. They then participated in a spiritual retreat from February 14 to 18, received their assignments, and prepared to depart. Michael Burke was assigned to the mission band while Alfred De Ham was sent to St. Mary of the Assumption in New Orleans, George Sniet to St. Mary's in Detroit, Charles Hahn to St. Michael's in Chicago, William Löwekamp to St. Philomena's in Pittsburgh, John Kühn to St. Peter's in Philadelphia, Bernard Beck to St. Joseph's in Rochester, Henry Meurer and John Bernard Heskemann to St. Mary's in Buffalo, Elias Schauer and Timothy Enright to Most Holy Redeemer in New York City, and Adam Gunkel and Henry Dauenhauer to St. Michael's in Baltimore. Five others were assigned to Annapolis: John Gerdemann as lector of dogmatic theology and German literature, and socius to the prefect of students; Augustine Freitag as lector of Greek and prefect of the sick; William Gross as lector of algebra and English literature; Peter Petit as lector of syntax; and Adam Petri as lector of syntax, German, and English. Francis Eberhardt did not participate in the second novitiate in Annapolis. Instead, he had been sent to Cumberland in late August 1863 to serve as lector for the novices. Francis Schnüttgen took ill and was sent to St. Peter's in Philadelphia on December 11, 1863, to recover his health and to complete his second novitiate there.[26]

Between March 6 and 8, 1864, Fraters Lindenfeld, Neithart, and Rathke held a preordination retreat in Annapolis before going to Baltimore for their elevation to the priesthood. They were ordained at St. Alphonsus Church on March 12, 1864, by the Most Reverend Richard Vincent Whelan, Bishop of Wheeling, the capital of the Union's newest state, West Virginia.[27]

Often I Was Stirred to Tears

Officially appointed Catholic chaplains assigned to army regiments or hospitals were a rarity during the Civil War. Historian William Kurtz provides a list of fifty-three Catholic clergymen who held such commissions, a ratio of only one priest for every 3,773 Catholic soldiers. Historian Father Robert Miller of Chicago has compiled a working list of 104 full- and part-time chaplains, not counting the Annapolis Redemptorists, for a future publication. Those few who served as chaplains had a variety of duties. They ministered to Catholic soldiers before, during, and after battle, and celebrated outdoor Masses, often preceded or followed by endless hours in makeshift confessionals. They preached on Sundays and holy days, encouraged sobriety, provided religious instructions, wrote letters for incapable soldiers or read letters received or newspapers that were available. They administered baptism and extreme unction to the dying. At times they gave general or conditional absolution to troops about to engage in battle, and to some on the battlefield itself, often under fire. They also provided spiritual and nursing relief to the wounded and dying. Sometimes priests offered blessings to Catholic and non-Catholic soldiers alike as they marched toward an uncertain death. Catholic chaplains held evening services in hospitals and ministered to the spiritual needs of the dying "irrespective of denomination or creed."[28] There were no official Redemptorist Union chaplains

"Parole Camp Annapolis, Md," Edward Sachse, Baltimore, 1864. Geography and Map Division, Library of Congress http://hdl.loc.gov/loc.gmd/g3844p.cw0245390.

during the war, but except for the absence of mortal danger, arduous camp life, and government pay—the work of the Annapolis Redemptorists was similar to that of the Catholic chaplains in official government capacities.

The *Chronica Domus* noted that "a great amount of good was done to the soldiers" in and around Annapolis during 1864. Despite not having official appointments, the Redemptorists received high-ranking support. Now-Major General Ambrose Burnside just completed a recruiting trip in the East and arrived in Annapolis on April 8 to join the troops of his reorganized Ninth Army Corps. These troops had rendezvoused at Annapolis to prepare for what became known as the Overland Campaign. It was aimed at relentlessly confronting Lee's forces in the field between the Rapidan and James rivers. At the same time, other Union armies pressed on in the Shenandoah Valley in the northwest and against Richmond from the southeast.[29]

By the time Burnside arrived in Annapolis, some 21,000 troops in four divisions plus artillery and cavalry brigades were bivouacked outside Annapolis. Most of the troops were battle-hardened veterans transferred from Tennessee or returning from reenlistment furloughs. They were joined by about 9,000 new recruits, including six recently formed USCT regiments plus an African American militia regiment from Connecticut, swelling the numbers to around 30,000 troops.[30]

The main encampments were located on the north side of the Annapolis and Elk Ridge Railroad, across from Camp Parole, on farms owned by Elisha Taylor and Daniel Hart. Other encampments lay west of Camp Parole and still others were east of the camp, strung out along the rail line leading into Annapolis. In modern terms, this places Ninth Army Corps camps straddling both sides of West Street from Spa Road to Riva Road and along Chinquapin Round Road.[31]

Burnside lodged again at the City Hotel, as he had done in December 1861 to January 1862. He arrived on the evening of April 8 and stayed through April 23. His wife, Molly, arrived by train on April 13 with Daniel Larned—now Captain Larned—who was still Burnside's private secretary and again offered his observations about Annapolis. He said that Mrs. Burnside had to ride in the train engine itself while the rest of the party and the baggage were in the tender. Upon arrival Larned found nothing had changed at the City Hotel, and there were the "same old rooms, same old table and everything in the same style as when we left." He reported that the proprietor (either Colonel Walton or his son Edward) was "cross as fury" and "cross & crazy." Walton, said Larned, feared that "his old shanty [of a hotel] will be seized and taken for military headquarters." Larned was pleased though that an old bootblack and waiter greeted him upon his arrival "with a scrape of the foot & touching his old gray wool" and recognized him from his earlier stay. Larned complained that the hotel was still "old & dirty," four men had to share a room, and meals consisted of "'ram, lamb, sheep & mutton,' every day potatoes & hominy are the only entrées."[32]

On the day Larned and Molly Burnside arrived, they found the Union army's new general in chief, Lieutenant General Ulysses Simpson Grant, and his staff having breakfast at the City Hotel. Grant had come for a hasty inspection of the Ninth Army Corps. After breakfast and a two- to three-hour private meeting, Grant and Burnside left to review the troops. Instead of the soldiers passing in review before the two generals as was normal, the regiments lined up in ranks and, to save time, Grant and Burnside stayed on their horses and galloped past the assembled regiments.[33]

Because of the huge numbers of troops in and around Annapolis and the perceived need to minister to them, Fathers Gross and Freitag met several times with Burnside. An account of this meeting was published the next year, quoting a letter written by Freitag:

> In April of the previous year the Reverend Father Gross and I decided to perform pastoral work for the Army. . . . General Burnside, who arrived here the previous spring with his army, appeared to be especially friendly toward us. Although many distinguished persons were waiting in the entrance hall, when Father Gross and I made our first visit, he allowed us to come in at once. In our favor, he wanted to provide the opportunity for Catholic soldiers to receive the Holy Sacrament. He immediately issued an order, according to which we were to be always allowed the freedom to go unhindered into the different encampments.[34]

So the Redemptorists went freely about their work. The Ninth Army Corps departed at noon on April 23, this time not by ship as Burnside's troops had done in 1862 but by foot on a three-day, forty-mile-plus march to Alexandria.[35]

After the army's departure and the beginning of the deadly Overland Campaign, Girardey wrote that "the hospitals began to be filled with sick & wounded soldiers, and later with paroled prisoners." He added that:

> Hundred [*sic*] of dying received the last sacraments, and hundreds of others were able to have their numerous sins washed away in the sacred tribunal of penance. Some of the fathers often had to spend whole days among the soldiers.[36]

The same account said the priests were called "several times a day" to minister to the troops and emphasized that Fathers Freitag, Gross, Petri, and Jaeckel were the priests who did the most spiritual work among the soldiers. In June, July, and August, these four were joined by Fathers Claessens, Gerdemann, and Girardey. Gross wrote to a correspondent on the Eastern Shore in mid-April and, without revealing exactly what he was doing, said "I have an immense amount of business on hand just now."[37] A Redemptorist letter writer in July said that "The young fathers here are saintly indeed. They give proves [*sic*] of every priestly virtue, especially of zeal of souls, going daily either to Camp Parole or the Hospitals, to assist the dying soldiers."[38]

Only one record has been found in which a seminarian, Frater Francis Joseph Oberle, an advanced theology student, accompanied Father Girardey on his hospital visits. In this instance, Oberle was noted as a witness to a marriage performed by Girardey at an army hospital. It can be inferred from this that other seminarians also accompanied the priests on their rounds. Hospital regulations required passes for all visitors except officers and they were allowed in only between noon and 6:00 PM. No mention was made of visiting clergy and what rules applied to them. Religious services of unspecified denomination were held at General Hospital Division No. 1 on Sundays at 2:00 and 7:00 PM and Wednesdays at 7:00 PM.[39]

Freitag's 1865 letter provides further details about Redemptorist ministries to the soldiers. He claimed there were "approximately 46,000 men from all nations and of all colors; and a large number of them were Catholics." Since Burnside's Ninth Army Corps had upward of 30,000 troops, Freitag may have included in his estimate soldiers at Camp Parole, patients in the army hospitals, and provost marshal troops stationed in Annapolis. Regardless the exact number, the Redemptorists were busy. Freitag wrote that "[a]lmost constantly, especially at the beginning, we had much work to do side by side with the Protestant preachers, which the Army had provided in large quantity." The general wariness between Catholic and Protestant clergy was overcome, as Freitag observed, since "the dear God always gives us victory, thus as He has ordained, our greatest enemies became our closest friends."

Freitag's description continues:

> In the middle of the main [parole] camp there was a large chapel, in which on Sundays and feast days and also often during the week, we could celebrate Mass, preach, and distribute Holy Communion. The chapel was almost always completely full. And not just with Catholics, but also many of whom were of several other beliefs who were instructed and became Catholics.

Freitag admired one of the "higher-ranking officers" in Camp Parole who was "marked by an especially ardent piety." The unnamed officer "reckoned for himself that it was

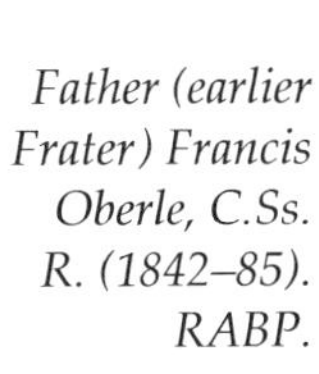

Father (earlier Frater) Francis Oberle, C.Ss. R. (1842–85). RABP.

Father Augustine Freitag, C.Ss.R. (1836–82). RABP.

the highest honor to be allowed to serve at Mass, and when a dying soldier was brought in for the Last Rites, he accompanied him each time to our dear Savior with a burning candle in his hand." Freitag told how he often secretly watched the officer sweep the chapel, decorate the altar, and adorn the pictures of the Blessed Virgin and St. Joseph. "His example made a very good impression on the other Catholic officers as well as on the common soldiers," wrote Freitag.

Freitag and other priests also were busy handing out religious articles to the soldiers. "It was almost impossible," wrote Freitag, "to have enough scapulars, rosaries, *Agnus Dei,* and other religious articles." A period prayer book has an invocation for those who wore or carried an *Agnus Dei,* a traditional sacramental using fragments of wax discs impressed with the figure of a lamb, blessed by the pope, and sewn into a small cloth pouches worn by the faithful to protect them from malign influences and protection in combat and other life-threatening situations. The invocation probably used by the Redemptorists asked Jesus, as the Lamb of God, to "pardon my iniquities . . . preserve me this day from all sin and evil," an appeal certainly appropriate for a soldier in wartime.[40] So taken was Freitag with what he observed that he said "[o]ften I was stirred to tears when I saw how the brave bearded men squabbled like children over the scapulars."

An Agnus Dei of the type carried by soldiers. Author's collection.

May—a month Catholics devote to Mary—was "especially solemn" for the soldiers, according to Freitag, and the camp chapel was decorated "at its prettiest." Each morning the soldiers said a collective prayer and twice daily recited the rosary together. In the evening, the chapel was illuminated and, if a priest was not there, one of the officers "would choose a half-hour meditation appropriate for 'Mary's Month.'" As a result of these devotional activities, "the miracle of conversion among the poor soldiers was forthcoming."

Little is known about the Camp Parole chapel. An 1864 panoramic view of Camp Parole shows more than a hundred wooden buildings, including those labeled headquarters, commissary, hospital, and sutler shop among others, but none is labeled chapel. A solitary structure off to one side of the camp headquarters, which was in the middle of the overall encampment area, may have been the chapel. The Camp Parole chapel was mentioned briefly in a report published in 1869 by the United States Christian Commission. It said that an Irish soldier at Camp Parole found great solace in "a certain corner of the chapel in which he had been wont to sit about the time when the Saviour was seeking him." Another Christian Commission report provided an exterior sketch and interior description of a Ninth Army Corps chapel erected at Meade Station, near the Petersburg battlefront in Virginia. It serves as an indication of what the Camp Parole chapel may have looked like inside and out.[41]

Not everything Father Freitag observed at Camp Parole was edifying. One day, while he was sharing a noontime meal with officers in the camp, a captain introduced him to an Italian army officer. This officer "was unusually friendly and obliging." However, when the Italian discovered that Freitag was a Catholic priest and a member of a religious order, "you should have seen his face fall." An officer sitting next to Freitag whispered an ominous message: "He is a follower of Garibaldi."

Giuseppe Garibaldi was a sensitive issue for Catholics worldwide. The pope had been the temporal ruler of States of the Church—also known as Papal States—since the mid-eighth century. The states were scattered throughout Italy and eventually made the pope the peninsula's largest landowner. With the onset of the liberal revolutions in Europe and desire of nationalists to unify Italy, the Papal States came under attack by Garibaldi. In 1848 his army captured Rome, forcing Pope Pius IX into exile in Naples. After the collapse of the Roman Republic in 1850, the Holy Father returned to Rome under the protection of French soldiers. However, a papal volunteer army was defeated in 1861 and Rome was declared the capital of the new Kingdom of Italy. Garibaldi threatened Rome again in August 1863 and, in 1864, the Italian kingdom reached agreement with France to withdraw its soldiers. The final collapse of the Papal States did not occur until 1870, but when Freitag met the Garibaldi man at Camp Parole, the pope, the papal states, and the Church in Italy were under siege and Catholics worldwide were concerned.[42]

Throughout 1864, and earlier, both the *Annapolis Gazette* and the *Sun* frequently published articles about the pope, his health, his political problems with Garibaldi, his interest in the American Civil War, and even that he had contributed $500 for "gallant wounded soldiers" from Buffalo, New York. In February 1864, the *Annapolis Gazette* ran a story about an American priest who had joined the Papal Zouaves and personally pledged to the pope that "he was willing to give his life to defend the States of the church." This was the kind of talk that made non-Catholics suspicious of Catholic loyalties to the American form of government, especially in a time of civil war. But, according to Freitag, Garibaldi's man at Camp Parole "had nothing more to say."[43]

Father Gross also wrote about this ministry to the troops. He said "it would move the heart of a tiger to witness the hideous scenes which our hospitals present." He wrote in July 1864 about the "immense number of sick and wounded [who] have been filling the hospitals in our environs to repletion." He lamented that "many of these unfortunate victims of a cruel war are in a frightful condition." Camp Parole had been converted "into one immense receptacle for the wounded" and an attending physician told him that "a thousand of them arrived in one night." Gross was touched by the "spectacle . . . presented when these poor cripples hobble up as well as they can in long lines to receive their daily rations." He also marveled at the diversity of the soldiers he met: "I have myself spoken to French, Norwegian, Belgian, Indians, Swiss, Italians, Germans and, of course, to any number of Irish." Although he found the work quite hard, "and disgusting too," and he foresaw that he would have to forsake his summer vacation time to work in the hospitals. He assured his correspondent that it all was "very consoling to a priest." He prayed that "a merciful God [may] soon stop this frightful carnage and sacrifice of human life."[44]

The chapel at Meade Station, Virginia, from Lemuel Moss, Annals of the United States Christian Commission *(Philadelphia: J. B. Lippincott, 1868), following pp. 182 (exterior) and 184 (interior), Library of Congress.*

Received All the Sacraments

Kurtz estimates that more than 200,000 Catholics served in the Union army during the Civil War. They included native-born Catholics as well as numerous Irish-born men, who made up 72 percent of Catholic soldiers, and a smaller number of Germans.[45] Enlistment and service records during the war did not include a man's religious preference but pension records often contain marriage certificates or sworn affidavits to prove a widow's relationship to a deceased veteran, making it possible to determine religious affiliation for some men. However, there is no reliable way to estimate the number of Catholic soldiers who were present in Annapolis during the war. However, seventy-seven military men have been identified as connected to St. Mary's (see table 2, Military Associated with St. Mary's, 1860–1868, Appendix).

Father Freitag wrote in his 1865 letter that in "one of the local hospitals, of some 5,000 patients, more than 100 died daily." In a typical week, he asserted, "I alone had more than 400 men to prepare for death." Preparing a man for death was an important obligation for chaplains. Freitag and his confreres likely prayed with the dying man, assuring him—according to

The grave at Ash Grove Cemetery (now Annapolis National Cemetery) of James Higgins who was ministered to on his deathbed by a St. Mary's priest. Original art by Constance D. Robinson.

the Redemptorist *Mission-Book*—that he deserved "to quit this world in the peace of a good conscience, and in the embrace of [Christ's] love."[46]

The Redemptorists encountered thousands of men in the parole camps, the army hospitals, the training camps, and on the streets of Annapolis as well as those who came to St. Mary's Church during the war. Historian Drew Gilpin Faust reports that "attendants of the dying may not have simply waited to report a Good Death but worked instead to compel it by demanding courage and calmness from the moribund or even as Catholic nurses and chaplains frequently reported, winning consent for last-minute baptisms."[47]

Perhaps the Redemptorists kept pocket notebooks of their work among the Union troops, but none have been discovered. How many deathbed conversions, baptisms, confessions, communions, and last rites were conferred will never be known. Good record keeping was overtaken by the exigencies of bringing spiritual comfort to the sick, wounded, and dying. Also incalculable is the impact that Redemptorist spiritual ministering had on the men who survived the war and returned home or went back to the war front.

Of all the deathbed ministering the Redemptorists accomplished, only three cases were entered in St. Mary's records. In the first case, an unidentified priest returned home after ministering to a dying man in General Hospital Division No. 1. The following entry appears in the parish interment register:

> [1864] — 15. *Namen Defuncti: James Higgins* | *Patria*: Ireland County Carlow | *Dies mortalis sive Ætas*: 41 *annos* | *Dies Sepulturae:* 15 Jan. 1864 | *Notae*: Soldier died in the Hospital of the Navy rec'd all the sacraments.[48]

The Crutch, the four-page weekly newspaper published at General Hospital Division No. 1, reported that "James Higgins, Private Co A 173d N Y Vols" died on January 13. It is not clear why only Higgins' name was entered in the parish register. Perhaps Higgins was to be buried at St. Mary's Cemetery but official records list Higgins as buried at Annapolis National Cemetery on January 15, in grave 507. Today, a modern marble headstone marks his grave in section K, site 905.[49]

Higgins' widow's pension file reveals he was born in Ireland, married Irish-born Mary McCabe in 1847, and worked as a laborer. They attended St. James Church in Brooklyn, New York, where their four children were baptized. The youngest, Sarah Ann, was born just three months before James enlisted in Company A, 173rd New York Infantry on September 3, 1862. The regiment departed in December for Louisiana, where it was assigned to the Department of the Gulf, Nineteenth Army Corps. Although the 173rd fought several battles, Higgins' service record states "[t]his soldier was never in any engagement." Perhaps because of his age (forty) he was assigned to quartermaster or other camp duty. He was a patient in army hospitals in New Orleans and Baton Rouge between March and June 1863. Then, while marching from Port Hudson back to Baton Rouge on August 23, Higgins was taken prisoner and incarcerated in Richmond, where he suffered from dysentery and was confined in General Hospital No. 21, a former tobacco factory.

Higgins was paroled at City Point, Virginia, on October 28, and sent by boat to Annapolis, where he was admitted the next day to General Hospital Division No. 1. He was treated for dysentery and debility with morphine and other medicaments and, at one point, was fed gin and raw eggs for nutriment but was unable to keep it or other food down. To ease his condition, Higgins was bathed frequently with warm vinegar. He slowly improved but in early January was declared "in a very weak and reduced condition." It was during this time that he would have received the ministrations of one of the Redemptorists. He died of chronic diarrhea on January 13, and was buried two days later. Because the Archdiocese of Baltimore had a rule that Catholic burial rites could be performed only in Catholic cemeteries, it is unlikely that a Redemptorist accompanied Higgins' remains to Ash Grove Cemetery. Instead, he and others who were to be buried that day would have had a secular service on the hospital grounds. Higgins' widow remarried in 1865 and lost her $8.00 per month pension but the four children received survivor's pensions until they reached age eighteen.[50]

The second case of a soldier death noted at St. Mary's concerned Private William Ford. He was a native of Ireland, and before the war worked in New York City as a boiler maker. He joined the army at age twenty-nine as a volunteer with the Sixty-Ninth New York Infantry (part of the Irish Brigade) in New York City on April 15, 1864. His regiment was engaged in bloody battles during the Overland Campaign and the subsequent siege of Petersburg. The luck of the Irish and other units ran out on August 25 at the Reams' Station, a railroad depot near Petersburg. The Union side suffered 140 killed, 529 wounded, and 2,073, including Ford, were taken prisoner.[51]

Ford and his comrades were sent to Belle Isle at Richmond. Although some had tents, many of the prisoners were forced to live outdoors where exposure led to a high death rate. He was treated for remittent fever and, not wanting to deal with sick prisoners, the Confederates released him and others on September 12. They were taken by the ship *New York* to Annapolis and admitted to General Hospital Division No. 2 on September 14. Unlike James Higgins' service records, Ford's do not include his medical treatment, only that he died of chronic diarrhea on October 3, 1864, and was reputedly buried in grave No. 158 at Ash Grove Cemetery, although the St. Mary's interment register indicates burial at St. Mary's Cemetery.[52]

Ford's record at St. Mary's notes he was a soldier, born in Ireland, age unknown, that he had been "fortified with the sacraments," and was buried on October 5. But that is not the only St. Mary's notice for Ford. On September 29, 1864, Father Ferreol Girardey officiated at Ford's marriage at the army hospital. His bride was Alice "Aety" Fisher. Her maiden name, or at least the surname of her father, was Parkinson and her mother was Anna Lawson. Fisher was a name from a previous marriage from which she was a widow. According to Girardey's notes in the marriage register, Ford was a soldier suffering from a serious illness at the St. John's army hospital and that he and Aety "had been living in sin for a long time" but considered themselves a married couple. In view of these circumstances, Girardey married them in accordance with the rites of the Catholic Church, with Frater Francis Oberle as the witness. Two days after William's burial, Aety appeared at the Anne Arundel County Circuit Court to submit her widow's pension declaration. She swore an oath before the county clerk and signed with her X mark that she and William had been lawfully married by a magistrate in Meriden, Connecticut, and had just remarried in the Catholic Church. Aety also said they had a daughter—Alice—who was three years old and resided near Meriden. Furthermore, she said that her maiden name was Alice Eaty [*sic*] Lawson, an indication that her mother and father were not married to each other.

Girardey and Oberle accompanied Aety Ford to the courthouse and served as her witnesses on the pension declaration. In a separate affidavit, dated October 6, Girardey certified that on September 30 [*sic*], 1864, he had joined the couple "in holy bonds of Matrimony according to the rites of the Catholic Church." That was necessary, he wrote, because he "could not minister to the said William Ford the consolations of our holy religion without first blessing the marriage as prescribed by the Catholic Church." In an addendum signed on October 7, Girardey further explained that Ford told him that the former Mrs. Fisher was already his wife before he married them in the Catholic rite. The Widow Ford went to live to Washington, DC, for a few months then, in March 1866, she returned to Meriden, Connecticut. She was awarded an $8.00 per month widow's pension but no further mention was made of her daughter Alice.[53]

The third soldier death case, that of Thomas F. Gosson, first came to notice in St. Mary's records when he had died on November 3, 1864. He was listed as a fifty-year-old native of Ireland whose remains were sent to New York for burial. He was not a known Annapolis "regular," so it was surmised that he was a soldier, which proved correct. Gosson enlisted at the relatively advanced age of forty-four in Alexandria, Virginia, on October 7, 1861, for two years as a private in Company H, Thirty-Eighth New York Infantry Regiment. He served as a laborer in the regimental quartermaster department and was wounded by buckshot in the left groin and fell during his regiment's June 1, 1862, retreat at the Battle of Fair Oaks (also known as Seven Pines) on the outskirts of Richmond. As a result of his injuries, he suffered an inguinal hernia that was severe enough that he was admitted to the division hospital near Savage's Station. Then more misfortune struck. The hospital was overrun by Confederates during the Battle of Savage's Station on June 28 and the patients were taken prisoner. Gosson and others were incarcerated at Prison No. 4 in Richmond until July 22, when he was paroled at City Point. He was sent first to Mill Creek US Army General Hospital near Fort Monroe where he was treated for rheumatism. He then went by steamer to Annapolis and was admitted to the General Hospital Division No. 2 on August 7. "The man is old," declared examining surgeon Dr. Thomas McParlin. He was bled as part of the treatment for rheumatism and released from the hospital on August 17 and sent to Camp Parole. Still suffering from rheumatism, he was admitted to the camp hospital in early December and, after a two-month period of being unfit for duty, he was granted a medical discharge on February 11, 1863.[54]

Although free to return home, Gosson remained in Annapolis. Perhaps his physical condition prohibited travel or he found some light employment. Maybe he was taken in by a St. Mary's parishioner or some other Annapolis family. In May 1863, he applied for and received an invalid pension of $4.00 a month, retroactive to his date of discharge. On November 4, 1863, he applied for US citizenship at Anne Arundel County Court. That was the last public notice of Thomas Gosson until his name appeared in the St. Mary's interment register on November 3, 1864.[55]

Other Redemptorist soldier conversions went unrecorded but they may have numbered in the hundreds or even thousands. Randall Miller points out that "[s]ome non-Catholics even tried to cheat the devil with deathbed conversions," something that likely was perceived by the ministering Redemptorists.[56]

Although kept busy with the troops, parish work was not neglected. In addition to his other duties, Father Girardey prepared eleven White children for their First Holy Communion. The event took place on Sunday, April 17 (the Feast of St. Joseph). Familiar family names appear in the First Communion register, including Elijah Daley, Philomena Himmelheber, Ella Kent, Maria Robeck, and Maria Treadway. Girardey "made some very touching remarks on the occasion," according to the *Catholic Mirror*. At Sunday evening vespers, the new communicants renewed their baptismal vows.[57]

Soldier Weddings

Thirty-seven marriages were recorded at St. Mary's Church between January 1861 and December 1865. While most of the couples were Catholic, nine of the marriages were mixed, between Catholics and non-Catholics. Three of the spouses were converts to Catholicism. Fourteen of the grooms during this period were active or former military men. Seven, including Private Ford, were married in 1864. Prior to 1864 there were four identifiable soldier wartime marriages at St. Mary's. Although some of the fourteen brides were local, most were not. The war brought tens of thousands of soldiers to Annapolis; it also brought many women. Some worked as nurses, cooks, laundresses, and charwomen in the army hospitals. Some military officers stationed in the city brought their families—and possibly eligible daughters—to Annapolis. Other women may have been associated with one of the benevolent organizations active in town, such as the United States Sanitary Commission or the United States Christian Commission. Soldier-patients were visited by wives, mothers, and sisters. Fiancées and girl friends likely also came to Annapolis to help nurse their man and once in town were married.[58]

One of the pre-1864 grooms was Captain George M. Mittnacht, a thirty-two-year-old native of Hesse-Darmstadt. Prior to the war, he worked as a safe manufacturer in New York City and held a captaincy in Company E, Sixth Regiment, New York State Militia. His regiment was called up for ninety days in April 1861 and was among the units that landed at Annapolis later that month. Mittnacht's time in Annapolis and service with the Sixth was brief because his wife, Rosa Nemartini Mittnacht, took ill. He hurried back to New York City, where she died on May 16. He returned to his regiment a week later, serving in Washington until July 31, when the regiment was mustered out of service. He returned home a widower with four minor children.

Mittnacht soon joined the 103d New York Infantry Regiment and commissioned captain of Company H. He was mustered in on February 18, 1862, and the regiment departed for Washington in early March. Just before that, Mittnacht was back in Annapolis to marry seventeen-year-old Mary Rebecca Brady at St. Mary's Church on January 20, 1862. Mary was a native of Anne Arundel County and a Protestant. One of the witnesses at the marriage was Horatio Tydings, a pro-secession Democrat. Mittnacht did not stay long in the army, resigning his commission in August 1862, as "disabled at present to do any further duty." The nature of his disability was not noted and ten months later he rejoined the Sixth Regiment but was mustered out after only one month. Mittnacht's name appeared one more time in St. Mary's records, in 1869 when his daughter, six-month-old Maria Rebecca Georgianna Mittnacht, was baptized. Although the parents resided in New York, the infant was baptized in Annapolis. Perhaps Mary had returned to her parents' home for the birth. Mary died in New York in 1877 and daughter Rebecca, as she was known, died in 1882. George succumbed in 1889.[59]

Another pre-1864 marriage was between Sylvester Ambrose McCabe and Margaret McBride of Harrisburg, Pennsylvania, on January 14, 1863. He was a second lieutenant, Company A, Sixty-Seventh Pennsylvania Infantry, a regiment that performed provost marshal duties in Annapolis. He had joined the Sixty-Seventh in Philadelphia as a wagoner in September 1861 and was promoted first to sergeant and then to second lieutenant. He was honorably discharged from the army on account of disability on March 17, 1863, and stayed in Annapolis, working as a bar keeper. Before the war was over, the McCabes moved to Neosho County, Kansas, where Sylvester died on December 3, 1865, from lung disease contracted while he was in the army. He left Margaret a childless widow. She remarried in a Catholic ceremony in St. Paul, Kansas, in 1868, and had four children, and died in New Mexico in 1929. In 1862, before Sylvester and Margaret were married, they served as godparents for newborn John B. Hughes, who became a Redemptorist professed student in 1883. This hints that Margaret was in Annapolis prior to her marriage to Sylvester. Whether she followed him to Annapolis from Harrisburg or met him there is not known. After her marriage, Margaret also served as godparent for Thomas Oscar Quinn, the newborn son of Edward Quinn, a former soldier and then-current navy employee working in Annapolis, and Mary Callen Quinn, of Cambria County, Pennsylvania. As an adult, Thomas became professional baseball player in Pittsburgh and Baltimore.[60]

On June 7, 1863, Father Seelos joined two fellow Bavarians in Holy Matrimony. Although Seelos was not from the same region of Bavaria as Michael Liebel and Anna Elizabeth Diemer, he must have felt an affinity with the young couple and decided to officiate. It was one of only four marriages he performed in Annapolis. (Of the other three ceremonies, one was for a German-Irish couple, another for a German-German couple, and the third for an African American couple.) A painter by trade, Liebel was a private in Company A, Fifty-Fourth New York Infantry and was assigned as a hospital nurse. The regiment's first engagement after he joined was the Battle of Chancellorsville (April 30–May 6, 1863), a Union defeat in which Liebel was first reported as a straggler and then as deserter. The truth, however, was that he had been captured on May 3 and was confined at Richmond from May 9–14 before being released on parole and sent to Annapolis. He was admitted to the Camp Parole convalescent hospital for five days followed by a few days in Washington for unspecified treatment or recuperation. Liebel returned to Annapolis and was married on June 7. He was readmitted to the Camp Parole hospital on June 16 for treatment of diplopia (double vision). Then he disappeared. The record states that he "deserted from Camp Parole Aug. 14, 1863." Or, maybe it was on August 28, both dates appear in his official record. Regardless, he and Anna were gone. Given this apparent desertion, it is not surprising that Michael did not apply for a Civil War pension. After leaving Annapolis, they eventually settled in Buffalo, New York, and raised a family there.[61]

Private Harvey Lee Rose, Company F, First Michigan Infantry, married Eliza Jane Lloyd on June 16, 1863. He enlisted in Ann Arbor, Michigan, on September 9, 1861, but was admitted to the camp hospital while still in Michigan and remained there after his regiment was deployed to Washington. He rejoined his regiment by January 1862, at which time it was guarding railroad bridges between Bladensburg in Prince George's County, and Annapolis Junction in Anne Arundel County. In March 1862, the regiment was assigned to the Army of the Potomac and deployed in numerous battles in Virginia during the summer of 1862. Rose survived the engagements unscathed but by mid-August had contracted a fever and was hospitalized near Fort Monroe. He was transferred to the US Army General Hospital at Annapolis Junction in late August, where he was treated for debility and later sent to Soldiers' Rest, a United States Sanitary Commission facility in Washington. Rose's service record notation for December 1862 says he was still (or again) at the **hospital** in Annapolis Junction. It was presumably there that he met Eliza Jane Lloyd.[62]

Eliza Jane was the daughter of a wealthy Maryland farmer, Joseph Manning Lloyd, and Calista Stuart Lloyd. Harvey and Eliza Jane were issued an Anne Arundel County marriage license on June 12, 1863, and married at her parents' home four days later. Father Van de Braak officiated at the marriage but just before the ceremony he baptized Harvey. There is no record in the *Chronica Domus* of Van de Braak being away from Annapolis at that time, further proving that not all absences were noted. There is no record of Harvey's baptism in St. Mary's baptismal records, only the note in the marriage record that he was baptized before the marriage ceremony. The marriage record also mentions the names of the couple's fathers, where they were born, and that Harvey was a soldier. The witnesses were "Miss Lloid," probably Eliza's sister Maryland ("Landa") Lloyd, and "Mr. Sharer," who might have been a fellow patient at Annapolis Junction. When Harvey applied for a Civil War pension in 1887, he said they were married at Laurel Factory (now simply Laurel, the Annapolis Redemptorists occasionally served St. Mary's Church there).

According to his service record, Harvey Rose had been dropped from the First Michigan rolls on February 9, 1863, and later "restored" when he reenlisted in the same company on February 17, 1864. There is no clue as to his whereabouts during the interim, perhaps he and Eliza were at the Lloyd family farm in Anne Arundel County or in Laurel Factory. On May 15, 1864, Harvey's regiment fought in the Battle of Spotsylvania Court House, but that same day Eliza Jane died at her father's farm. Harvey returned to Michigan when the war ended and later in the year remarried, this time before a Methodist minister. Despite his wartime injuries (he was hurt while building breastworks in front of Petersburg), he lived until 1918, dying at age eighty-three.[63]

In addition to the aforementioned marriage of William Ford and Aety Fisher, there were five other weddings for soldiers and one for a navy man at St. Mary's in 1864. The first was that performed by Father Girardey for Irish-born Thomas Gaffney and English-born Mary Jane Amilia Jarvis on February 12. The marriage record reported that "the groom is a soldier" but an extensive search of newspaper, military service, pension, and census records failed to confirm which of the numerous men named Thomas Gaffney who served in the army and navy during the Civil War was the man married at St. Mary's. The most likely candidates are privates in either the Independent Battery, Thirty-Fourth New York Light Artillery, or Company K, Seventy-Ninth New York Infantry, or the captain of Company G, First Regiment Michigan Sharpshooters. All of these regiments were part of the Ninth Army Corps, which rendezvoused at Annapolis in March and April 1864. It is possible that Gaffney, knowing he was being sent to Annapolis, met his bride there to marry her before going into battle. Another aspect of the marriage is unusual. The St. Mary's record says Gaffney had "entered into marriage in Utah with a bride who had not yet been baptized." Since canon law does not recognize such marriages, Gaffney evidently was free to remarry Mary Jane Amilia Jarvis, a convert from Mormonism who was baptized at St. Mary's on her wedding day. Her sponsors were Charles J. Murphy, an army sutler, and Catherine Murphy.[64]

Another soldier, George Charles White, apparently was also married twice but under very different circumstances. Father Girardey again was the officiating priest when, on March 31, he joined Private White, a native of Dublin, and Mary Kirby, from County Limerick, in the bonds of matrimony. White was identified as a soldier—*Sponsus miles*—in the marriage record but there were more than 700 men named George White in the Union army, including ten with the middle initial C. However, only one George C. White has been identified in Annapolis around the time of the wedding. *The Crutch* reported that Private George C. White, Company K, Twenty-Eighth Massachusetts Infantry, had been a patient at General Hospital Division No. 1 until February 20, 1864, when he was released and sent to Camp Parole. White, a bootmaker, had enlisted at Milford, Massachusetts, on November 11, 1861. He was wounded at the Battle of Secessionville, South Carolina, on June 16, 1862, and again at Gettysburg on July 2, 1863. In the latter battle, his regiment—part of the Irish Brigade— was initially held in reserve near the center of the Union line on Cemetery Ridge. The brigade chaplain, Father William Corby, gave general absolution to the troops before they went into battle. White was wounded and taken prisoner, paroled at Richmond, sent north to Camp Parole, and admitted to the hospital, having suffered a gunshot wound to the right foot. After his release from the hospital "perfectly healed"—and his marriage to Mary Kirby—he was assigned to Camp Parole until May 14, 1864, when he was formally exchanged and returned to his regiment. He was honorably discharged in September 1864 and returned to home in Massachusetts.

All seems routine until White's pension file is considered. Unless it was another George C. White who was married at St. Mary's in 1864 to Mary Kirby, the George C. White of the pension file was a bigamist. The file has ample evidence that he was married to Mary Greeley in St. Mary's Church in Milford, Massachusetts, on July 7, 1850, by Father George A. Hamilton and that it was with Mary that he lived until he died of dropsy in 1881. Mary Greeley White survived George, received a pension based on his Civil War service, and died in 1904. Of Mary Kirby nothing more has been discovered and the circumstances of her involvement with George C. White remain suspicious. Perhaps it was just a coincidence of names, but another Mary Kirby—or the same—also of County Limerick, married a supposed soldier, James Smith of County Cavan, on May 8, 1865, with Father Gerdemann officiating and Simon Farrell and Bridget Farrell as witnesses. Minimal information on this couple was provided in the St. Mary's record. More than 3,000 men named James Smith served in the Union army and identifying him without knowing his regiment is unlikely.[65]

Laurence Murray from Ireland married Ellen Lucy from England at St. Mary's on April 10, 1864. Father Louis Claessens officiated. The witnesses were Private Charles Francis O'Malley of Company I, Eighty-Eighth New York Infantry and a former patient at General Hospital Division No. 1, and Fanny Speliman. Murray's military affiliation is uncertain and his name was not found among the rosters of units organized in Elmira, New York, the city where lived before and after the war. Even though only eleven men in the Union army had this name, none could be connected to Annapolis in 1864. He was not listed among patients at the army hospitals but could have been assigned to Camp Parole at the time. Although no service or pension records have been found for Laurence Murray, more is known about his later life in Elmira, New York, where he was active in Democratic Party politics, labor union activities, alcoholic beverage sales, the Ancient Order of Hibernians, and the Catholic Mutual Benefit Association, of which he was the local president. At the time of his death in 1906, he was remembered as "the best constable in the history of the [Elmira] city court and occasional spectator in police court." Ellen Lucy Murray did not fare as well. She died in 1868 and Murray remarried about 1871 and raised a family of five children in Elmira.[66]

Father William Gross performed the marriage ceremony for an African American couple, Benjamin Cornell and Anne Ella Maynard, on June 15, 1864. The bride's birthplace information was omitted in the marriage register and Benjamin's place of birth was noted only as "U.S." No witnesses were listed. The groom may have been the same Benjamin Cornell identified as a twenty-year-old former slave and native of Anne Arundel County, who enlisted in the USCT in March 1864 (see African American Enlistments, this chapter). An African American named Benjamin Cornell was on the roster of sailors at the US Naval Academy in 1870 but nothing else has been found about him or his bride.[67]

"NB. Married in the Navy" was the marriage register notation for Irishman John O'Neil, who married Eliza Dunn at St. Mary's on December 2, 1864. Father Adam Petri officiated and Emma Treadway served as the witness. Eliza may have been the same as Elizabeth Dunn, age thirty, who was listed with her mother Rachel (widow of George Dunn) in the 1860 census for Annapolis. The marriage record identified O'Neil as "captain" but Navy lists for the period do not include anyone with that name and rank. Instead, the only officer named John O'Neil was an acting third assistant engineer who served aboard the blockade ship USS *Vanderbilt* from October 21, 1862, until he was honorably discharged on December 2, 1866. The *Vanderbilt* was deployed to search for the commerce raider CSS *Alabama* and interdict blockade runners in 1863 and 1864, and was involved in the attacks against Fort Fisher in December 1864 and January 1865. The O'Neils may have settled in Baltimore, Philadelphia, or Fall River, Massachusetts, after the war, at least there were couples in those places named John and Eliza O'Neil (or O'Neill). He evidently never applied for a government pension.[68]

Patrick H. Connaughton married Margaret Ellen Lamb at St. Mary's on December 15, 1864. Connaughton was a twenty-three-year-old former Union soldier who met Annapolis native twenty-one-year-old Margaret Lamb. He was an Irish Catholic immigrant who enlisted on July 20, 1863, as a draftee in Company B, 118th Pennsylvania Infantry at Lancaster, Pennsylvania. He just missed the 118th's engagement at Gettysburg and caught up with his regiment at Beverly Ford, near Culpeper, Virginia, in mid-September. He was with the 118th throughout the autumn but by the time the 118th Pennsylvania went into winter camp, it was discovered that Patrick, as an alien and British subject, had been wrongly drafted. The War Department issued an order on December 18, 1863, directing that he be discharged and paid for his term of service. That apparently did not occur until March or April 1864, when he was reported on leave in Philadelphia. It is not clear how Connaughton ended up in Annapolis, where he was first noted as a bowling alley and saloon keeper by May 1864 when he was issued a pass to take the train to Baltimore and July to go to Camp Parole.[69]

Margaret Lamb was baptized on the day of her wedding by Father Claessens. Her baptismal sponsor was Mary Eva Bettendorf (Mrs. John) Himmelheber. Mrs. Himmelheber, along with John Mullan's daughter Annie, then served as a witness to the Margaret's marriage to Patrick Connaughton, which was officiated by Claessens.[70] There must have been considerable tension surrounding these nuptials. Not only had their Protestant daughter converted to Catholicism, but Margaret's parents, Andrew Lamb, an Annapolis carter and slave owner, and his wife, Mary Atwell Lamb, were Southern sympathizers.

Andrew Lamb owned at least four properties on West and Washington streets, inside the city, and more property outside the city. When Annapolis was occupied by Union forces in April 1861, their home on West Street was allegedly selected as General Butler's headquarters. Another source claimed his headquarters was in "City Tavern," by which it probably meant City Hotel. A more reliable source, Thomas Karney, identified his own former office in the Ethics Department, in Room Number 5 in the Naval Academy Recitation Hall, as Butler's headquarters. By early May, Butler's "representative" was stationed at the railroad depot to monitor the loading of troops bound for Washington. It is possible that Butler and other officers met at the Lamb residence because it was conveniently located near the depot. As the story goes, Margaret's six-year-old sister, Annie, was playing outside the door of the Lamb house and overheard Butler and his officers' discussion during a staff meeting. Annie allegedly was accused of being a spy, arrested, taken to the guard house, and "only released after being subjected to a grueling examination."[71]

Margaret's brother, John P. Lamb, was a private in the Confederate army, Company D, Second Maryland Battalion. He was captured during the Gettysburg Campaign in 1863 and was at the Union prisoner-of-war camp at Point Lookout, in St. Mary's County, Maryland, before being exchanged in February 1865, hospitalized briefly in Richmond, returned to duty, and killed in action at Hatcher's Run, near Petersburg, Virginia, the same month. He was buried at City Cemetery (now part of St. Anne's Cemetery). With such a family history, the Lambs could not have been happy about the marriage of their daughter not only to a Yankee but an immigrant Catholic to boot. Margaret Lamb's affection for her betrothed, which led to her conversion and marriage, trumped the political and cultural inclinations in which she had been raised, and the marriage endured. By 1870 they had moved to the West Roxbury section of Boston, where they eventually had nine children. Patrick worked as a laborer and coach driver and died in 1925. Margaret died in 1941.[72]

Not all St. Mary's parishioners who married in 1864 did so locally. At least one case comes to the fore, that of Julia Ann Sullivan who, along with her older sister Mary Rebecca Sullivan, converted to Catholicism at St. Mary's as teenagers in 1857. Julia married Englishman George Alfred Watkins, evidently at St. John's Catholic Church, in Indianapolis, on April 10, 1864, and news of the nuptials was published in the *Maryland Republican*. George may or may not have served in the military. Several men named George A. Watkins did serve: one in the Twenty-Seventh Massachusetts Infantry and another in the Twelfth Missouri Cavalry. The couple later settled in New York City, where Julia was "keeping house" and George worked as a paint salesman. They had five children. He died in 1882 and she in 1912. Julia's niece, Ida Mary Sullivan, was baptized at age nineteen at St. Mary's in 1881 by William Gross, by then bishop of Savannah, Georgia. Earlier that same year, Ida married the future famous Naval Academy Band master, Charles Adams Zimmermann.[73]

African American Enlistments

The enlistment in the Union Army of freed slaves and free Black men was mentioned in the Emancipation Proclamation on January 1, 1863, and approved by Congress in the Enrolling Act on March 3. Recruitment started after the Preliminary Emancipation Proclamation was issued following the Battle of Antietam, on September 22, 1862, and the first Black regiments were formed and engaged Confederate forces the following month. Before this time, army recruiters had turned away free Black men wanting to fight because of a 1792 Federal law prohibiting Black men from bearing arms for the US Army. But now that changed. On May 22, 1863, the War Department issued General Orders No. 143, which established the United State Colored Troops. All Black men—former slaves and born-free—could now join the fight, and join they did. Some 180,000 men enlisted in the army. Another 20,000 served in the navy, which had always allowed Black enlistments. Nearly 40,000 of these men gave their lives for the Union cause.[74]

Several men with St. Mary's connections joined USCT regiments. One was the aforementioned William H. Brown, who had been enslaved by John and Mary Ann Mullan. According to county records, he was freed by Mary Ann Mullan and "enlisted in service of U.S." He enlisted for three years in Company E, Thirtieth USCT, on March 3, 1864, the date he received his freedom. His enlistment papers indicate he was age sixteen (born circa 1848), born in Anne Arundel County, and was a waiter by occupation. If this was true, then the Mullans must have hired him out to work in an Annapolis hotel or restaurant. Remarks on his service record named Mary Mullan as his former owner. St. Mary's Church records have a William Joseph Brown, *nigri col. conv ex Method.*, born March 1, 1848, and baptized on July 28, 1861. No mention is made of his being a slave or any connection with the Mullan family but his baptism is something the Mullans likely would have encouraged and it is possible, despite the different middle names, that this is the same person.[75]

Brown's regiment trained at Camp Stanton, a stockade facility built by the recruits near Benedict in Charles County. He was issued a drum, drum sling, and drum sticks. The regiment was assigned to Burnside's Ninth Army Corps, which meant it was among the units bivouacked at Annapolis and preparing for the Overland Campaign. After leaving Annapolis, the Thirtieth USCT guarded the corps' supply trains in Virginia. During the siege of Petersburg, Brown's regiment built fortifications and rifle pits. Then, on July 30, 1864, the Thirtieth was involved in the infamous Battle of the Crater. During the preceding weeks, Union miners had excavated a 500-foot-long tunnel under the Confederate entrenchments and placed 8,000 pounds of gunpowder that was detonated at the start of the battle. The blast was literally earth shattering, killing some 350 Confederate soldiers and creating a massive crater through which Union troops attacked the rebels. An initial but unsuccessful assault was made by Ninth Corps White troops who charged into the huge crater. They were followed by seven regiments of Black troops that "went forward with undaunted bravery," according to one soldier. The Thirtieth was in the vanguard of the USCT troops and suffered 200 casualties, including 18 killed, 104 wounded, and 78 missing in action. There were more than 5,000 casualties that day on both sides and the Confederates were victorious. William Brown survived.

The Thirtieth USCT was later involved in attacks against Fort Fisher, North Carolina, in December 1864 and

January 1865. After Fort Fisher, Brown was detached from the Thirtieth to work as a hospital attendant. After the fall of Wilmington, North Carolina, the last Confederate seaport receiving blockade runners, on February 22, he worked in the Union army hospital there until April 1865 when the regiment went into action further south in North Carolina. After the Thirtieth moved on to New Bern on September 24, 1865, Brown incurred an infraction (not specified in his service record), was court martialed, and fined six months of his $8.00 per month pay. He was mustered out of service with the rest of his regiment at Roanoke Island, North Carolina, on December 10, 1865.[76]

Another Thirtieth USCT soldier with a possible St. Mary's connection was Benjamin Cornell, who married Anne Ella Maynard in mid-June 1864 (see Soldier Weddings, this ch.). He enlisted as a twenty-year-old former slave and native of Anne Arundel County in Company I on March 18, 1864, and was a patient in McKim US Army General Hospital in Baltimore from June 15 to July or August 1864. He missed the Thirtieth's guard-duty assignment during the Battle of the Wilderness (May 5–7, 1864) and the initiation of the siege of Petersburg (starting June 15, 1864), but may have been involved in the Battle of the Crater in July and the first attack on Fort Fisher in December 1864. Cornell missed the second attack on Fort Fisher, because he had been admitted to the hospital on January 8 for an unspecified reason. He rejoined his regiment by May 1865 and was with the occupying army in North Carolina until when he was mustered out of service at Roanoke Island in December 1865. After the war it appears he enlisted in the Navy. He or another African American Benjamin Cornell was on the roster of sailors at the Naval Academy in 1870.[77]

Infant John Henry Sevoy was baptized at St. Mary's on August 24, 1865. His father, Charles Sevoy, was a private in Company D, Thirtieth USCT. Both Charles and his brother Joshua had been manumitted by Annapolitan George Wells, who received $300 compensation for each manumission. Both men enlisted in Company D at Annapolis on February 25, 1864, and were mustered into service three days later. Charles experienced many of the same duties and battles as Brown and Cornell, and was discharged in December 1865. His brother spent much of the war in army hospitals in Baltimore and North Carolina, and was discharged in June 1865. Both men later received Civil War pensions. Neither Charles nor John Henry's mother, Elizabeth Ann Robinson, were Catholics. Little John Henry was brought to St. Mary's for baptism by Mary Ann Hopkins, a White parishioner from southern Anne Arundel County.[78]

Dennis Larkins served in Company C, Forty-Third USCT. His daughter Priscilla was baptized at Dodon in 1860 by Father Cornell. Her parents were noted as Protestants and both were slaves. Priscilla and her mother, Adeline Sparrow, were born at Dodon. Dennis Larkins' military record says he was age thirty-three in 1864—so he was born about 1831—and a native of West River, Anne Arundel County. At the time of his enlistment his occupation was noted as "sailor." He enlisted as a private in the Forty-Third in Philadelphia on March 17, 1864. He signed his enlistment paper with an X and his muster-out record has a remark that he was "Free." In April the Forty-Third was assigned to the Ninth Army Corps and sent to Annapolis to rendezvous with Burnside's troops.

Like the Thirtieth USCT, the Forty-Third was first involved in guarding supply trains during the Overland Campaign and during the siege of Petersburg its troops frequently came under fire while building fortifications. Larkins' regiment fought in the Battle of the Crater and sustained 41 killed (including the regiment's commander), 104 wounded, and 2 White officers taken prisoner. Larkins survived the battle and his regiment went on to fight at Hatcher's Run (October 27–28, 1864), where they served as skirmishers and repulsed repeated enemy charges, suffering twenty-one casualties. The Forty-Third was present at Appomattox Court House when Lee surrendered on April 9, 1865. After the surrender, the Forty-Third was assigned to the Twenty-Fifth Army Corps and briefly performed duties in Virginia before being sent to the Rio Grande border with Mexico. During this time, Private Larkins was twice confined to the army hospital in Brownsville, Texas, for rheumatism and diarrhea, respectively. When he was mustered out with the rest of his company at Brownsville on October 20, 1865, he was due $100 in bounty money for enlisting. However, his service record reveals he owed the government $138 for clothing, arms, equipment, and unspecified other gear. What became of Dennis Larkins and his daughter Priscilla is unknown. Priscilla's mother, Adeline Sparrow, appears in various records. She was baptized at All Hallows Parish at age four in 1846 and was freed according to the new Maryland constitution on November 1, 1864; her owner was Maria Louisa Steuart of Dodon, who had served as Priscilla's godmother in 1860. According to the 1880 census, Adeline was living on Bridge Street in Annapolis, married, but not living in a household with her husband. Priscilla was not listed.[79]

John Robert Smothers' father may also have been a USCT soldier. John Robert was born in October 1865 and baptized by Father James Keitz in June 1866. His parents were listed as William "Smoters" and Julia Eglin (presumably Eaglin). St. Mary's custom was to note when the parents were not Catholic but there was no such note for John Robert's parents. The godmother, Jane Eaglin Baden, perhaps Julia's sister, appears several times in the St. Mary's registers as godmother, marriage witness, and mother of a christened child. William was born free around 1837 and in 1860 received an Anne Arundel County freedom certificate to prove his status. That same year, William Smothers ("colored") was recorded in the Annapolis tax assessment as owning a house and lot on Prince George Street worth $150. A married Black laborer named William Smothers was enrolled for the draft in Annapolis in 1863 and was reported in the *Annapolis Gazette* in July 1864 as eligible for the draft. Three men named William Smothers served in the USCT: one enlisted in Baltimore in August 1863 in the Fourth USCT, but was from Frederick County. Another enlisted in July 1864 in the Twenty-Eighth USCT. The third was in the Sixty-Third USCT, which was organized in Louisiana. The most likely candidate was the man who served in the Twenty-Eighth USCT: William Smothers, laborer, age twenty, born in Bath, Virginia, resident of Baltimore, enlisted as a substitute at Ellicott's Mills on July 24, 1864. But a lack of further information or a pension file make it difficult to prove he was the same man as the father of John Robert Smothers.[80]

Another Smothers who enlisted in the Union army was Henry Smothers, the younger brother of Rachel Smothers. He was one of twenty-one slaves freed by Dr. Thomas J. Franklin in the Eighth Election District in 1864, when he joined Company H, Thirty-Ninth USCT. The regiment's military actions were mostly the same as the Thirtieth USCT, including the Battle of the Crater, the attacks on Fort Fisher, and ending their service in North Carolina.[81]

Again the Draft

The *Annapolis Gazette* reported "good news" in mid-May 1864: Annapolis had met its quota for volunteer soldiers and a new draft was not required. Two weeks later, however, the same newspaper reported that the War Department had ordered another draft to take place in July. Despite these conflicting announcements, on May 27 sixty-five new names were drawn in Annapolis, with no Redemptorists among them. The name of another Catholic religious and friend of the Annapolis Redemptorists—"Rev. Swithin"—was drawn in Howard County on July 7, 1862. He was Brother Swithin (Francis) Brenken, F.S.C., of the Christian Brothers' Rock Hill Academy, outside Ellicott's Mills. Between July 11 and July 18, ninety-one more names were drawn to help fill Anne Arundel County's deficiency in the quota for three-year men. This time the list included two Redemptorists: John Becker, a student, and Titus Wissel, a lay brother.[82]

Although Becker's and Wissel's names were drawn in the July draft neither was inducted into the army. Becker had been in poor health for a number of years. He was sent to Baltimore in 1861 to recover from an unspecified illness and was back in Annapolis two weeks later. No further mention was made of his condition during the next three years but in March 1865 he went again to Baltimore, returned to Annapolis at the end of the same month, and died from consumption in late May. According to an October 1864 report on delinquent draftees, it was his alienage that kept him from serving.[83]

Brother Titus's case is less clear. There was an opportunity in August 1864 for he and Becker to make their cases for exemption before the Fifth District's provost marshal in Ellicott's Mills. Their exemption claims could have been based on alienage (non-citizenship), age, non-residence, or health. At thirty-eight, Brother Titus was within the eligible age range but he might have claimed alienage or that he was going to be reassigned elsewhere by his religious superiors (he was sent to Buffalo in 1866). But he was not named in the October 1864 delinquent draftees report. Another mitigating factor for Becker and Wissel was that both Annapolis and Anne Arundel County had filled their assigned quotas with volunteers and substitutes in response to a nationwide July 18 call for volunteers, allowing these two men and others to avoid army enlistment. However, the Redemptorist administration in Baltimore gave Father Müller credit for having saved them from military service.

Although John Becker and Titus Wissel did not serve, there were others among the Redemptorists and would-be Redemptorists who had military experience. They included Ambrose Burke and Luke Cavanaugh who were mentioned earlier (see Not the Least Idea of Religious Life, ch. 5). Jacob Habermeier (known as Brother Anthony in religious life) had served in the Bavarian army before immigrating to the United States and was assigned as a tailor at St. Mary's in 1866. Brother Chrysostom Zimmer, who was at St. Mary's from 1857 to 1874, also had military service before immigrating to the United States. Pennsylvania-born George Reuss was listed as a lay brother, age sixteen, among the Redemptorists at Annapolis in the 1860 census but does not appear in any official Redemptorist ledgers and may be the same George Reuss who, in 1863 at age nineteen, enlisted as a substitute for another man in Company B, 111th Pennsylvania Infantry, and died in 1864 as a prisoner of war at Florence, South Carolina.[84]

A curious entry is found in the Redemptorist *Catalogus Novitiorum* for Brother Theobald Schreiner. He was born in Baden in 1828 and admitted to the novitiate in Cumberland in December 1864 as John Schreiner. But when he professed his vows at Annapolis in 1868, he gave his name as John Zimmermann. An explanation was added anonymously later in the *Catalogus Novitiorum* where it says "Brother Theobald, as far as I can remember, had been drafted to serve during the Civil War; he therefore escaped and assuming the name 'Schreiner' entered the Congregation." Numerous men named John Zimmermann appear in draft registration records but without additional information it is impossible to tell which may have been the future Brother Theobald.[85]

The People Show a Good Liberal Spirit

By January 1864, it had been almost a year since a Redemptorist had been visiting the Fenwick home in West River. But then Father Joseph Helmprächt made three visits within seven weeks. At the end of 1864, St. Mary's chronicler reported that "collections & preparations are being made to get a church" at West River. Rather than neglecting West River, it might be inferred from this entry that the Redemptorists had been busy there and it was the recording of the visits in the *Chronica Domus* that was neglected. During this time, Anna Louisa Fenwick died at her West River home. Shortly after her death, her husband, Dr. Martin Fenwick, conveyed part of his property to his son Henry Aloysius Fenwick, who maintained a home on the property known as The Cottage. When Dr. Fenwick died in 1865 he left his home Evergreen, the Mass site since 1859, and the rest of his property to his daughters, Harriet Emily Fenwick Donaldson and Chloe T. Fenwick. Further developments of the West River mission would occur in 1865.[86]

Monthly visitations to St. Augustine's in Elkridge

St. Augustine's Church, built in 1844–45. Courtesy Rev. Gerard J. Bowen, St. Augustine's Parish, Elkridge.

Landing in 1864 usually took place on the first weekend of the month. Father Girardey was the most frequent visitor but Fathers Helmprächt and Jaeckel also journeyed there. The feast day of St. Augustine (August 28) was celebrated by Fathers Girardey and Freitag, assisted by Frater Augustine John Stuhl, a Hessian-born student of rhetoric. The highlight of the year at St. Augustine's was a mission held from September 18 to 25 by Fathers Bradley, Gerdemann, and Girardey.[87]

A year-end summary for 1864 said:

> With regard to our station at Elkridge Landing every thing goes on prosperously, especially since the mission. This year the Church was repaired and rendered more beautiful. The people show a good liberal spirit.[88]

"Very thick ice" on Chesapeake Bay prevented the Redemptorists from visiting Easton during the winter of 1863–64. Father Gross finally crossed the bay on February 21 for the first time since December 20. He visited again on the second or third weekends each month thereafter through November, except for August when he and Father Girardey made a two-day "recreation" trip to Washington. In May Gross was accompanied by Father Jaeckel and in September by Father Helmprächt, who made the rounds of all the Annapolis missions. On the Western Shore, from October 20 to November 8, Gross and Father Henry Giesen also presented a mission at St. Charles Borromeo Church, in Pikesville, Maryland, gaining nine converts.[89]

During the time he had charge of the Easton mission, Gross and other Annapolis Redemptorists maintained a steady correspondence with Howes and Catherine Goldsborough, the main supporters of the mission. A collection of letters has been preserved and adds many details about the mission, the Goldsborough family (including their slaves), and problems with transportation from Annapolis. The Redemptorist letters sent to the Goldsboroughs during the Civil War provide insights into their pastoral work in Easton and other out-missions.

Gross worked with the Goldsboroughs to establish the best transportation route from Annapolis. Depending on which day he traveled (Friday or Saturday, and this was subject to occasional change), the steamboat from Annapolis stopped either at Clora's Point, about twelve miles south of Easton on the Choptank River, or at Easton Point, on the east side of the village on the Tred Avon River. The problem encountered at Clora's Point was that the stagecoach went only to Easton and not all the way to Galloway, the Goldsborough's plantation northeast of the town. He asked Catherine Goldsborough, "[i]f it would not be trespassing too much on your kindness," to send a carriage to Clora's Point to take him directly to Galloway.[90]

The alternating schedule presented another problem. A certain "very good" but unnamed Irishman, reported Gross, frequently took the Annapolis–Easton route on Fridays. When he did not see a priest on board he would tell his Catholic friends in Easton that Mass would not be offered that weekend. Sometimes Gross took the Saturday steamboat with the result that not as many people attended Mass that Sunday. He imposed again on Catherine Goldsborough to inform the people of his Saturday arrivals. A later change in schedule brought the steamboat closer to the Goldsborough residence, landing near the Dover Bridge on the Miles River. Weather also was a factor. In early March 1864, the steamboat trip back to Annapolis proved to be a "tough time," but Gross "arrived all safe" at home. Howes Goldsborough provided the Redemptorists with "a free or 'complimentary' ticket for the boat, *i.e.*, one in which nothing is charged either for the passage or for the meals." One of the steamboats by which the Redemptorists traveled was identified as the *Kent*.[91]

Catherine Goldsborough ran a plantation Sunday school and was commended by Gross for her "zealous efforts towards instructing the poor little ones." But, he advised, "you must arm yourself with considerable patience for the work which is incalculably precious to children." As an encouragement, and a sign of the pastoral zeal that would one day see Gross promoted to bishop and archbishop, he told Catherine Goldsborough, "I have often thought of you all and have not failed to recommend to Almighty God in the holy mass our undertaking for his glory."[92] He also urged Catherine at one point, as a woman of "good Catholic piety," to try to convince her "highly esteemed and most deserving husband"—who was then in poor health—to convert to Catholicism. The letter encouraging Howe's conversion was the last letter he addressed to Catherine, or at least the last that survives. Thereafter, all of the letters from Gross—and they are all most cordial—were addressed to Howes Goldsborough. Whether or not Howes was ready to convert, judging from comments made in the correspondence, he was clearly committed to building a Catholic church in Easton. Gross's advice was successful and Howes Goldsborough converted in 1865.[93]

The Goldsboroughs owned twenty-two slaves and encouraged their religious upbringing and it was most likely these slaves and young members of the extended family who attended Catherine's Sunday school. In a letter written on New Year's Eve 1863, Gross addressed himself, through Catherine, to the slaves:

> You must tell your good servants that I have two hymns for them so fine that I believe that they will have to admire *my taste* for music. The melodies are really very devotional and the words full of piety. I will tell them when I see them next, the fine celebration, we had on Christmas for our colored folks of Annapolis.[94]

At one point, Mrs. Goldsborough was preparing Rebecca, presumably one of the slaves, for her First Holy Communion. Gross told her to "make her pray much" and to "instruct well" another person, unnamed, for the reception of baptism. Gross also provided guidance on making wax tapers for lighting altar candles and gathering "cedar or pine branches" to be blessed on Palm Sunday. Gross did not forget his "dear little 'parish' in your family" later in the spring when he brought them "a couple of charming little hymns."[95]

The Gross-Goldsborough correspondence also reveals progress toward building a church. Early on Gross approved of Goldsborough's efforts "towards procuring in a manner so generous, a permanent place of worship for our holy religion." He advised Catherine on financing the church through loans to be repaid with pew rents from a hoped-for "flourishing congregation . . . in the once neglected Easton." In the meantime, the Easton town hall was used for services, but the "subscriptions [received were] too precarious" to keep up with the "heavy" rent. Thus building a church was high priority, the sooner the better since otherwise Gross "greatly fear[ed] that the whole enterprise may fail." He asked Catherine to approach both her husband and Henry May, who, along with his wife Henrietta, were the other major benefactors of the Easton congregation, about the urgency of the building program. Following Müller's precedent in Annapolis in 1857–58, Gross recommended an appeal made to Catholics and Protestants alike and promised "I will instantly start every means towards obtaining this end." As 1864 progressed, Gross congratulated Howes Goldsborough on his determination to purchase land and build a church. He recommended the "immense advantage" of having a cemetery adjacent to the church but to seek the approval of the county commissioners to ward off any possible opponents. He also had advice on the wording in the property title so that the Catholic Church would be given ownership once the money Goldsborough used to purchase the land was repaid to him and to avoid any misunderstanding in the future.[96]

By March 1864, Gross had been assured by Henry and Henrietta May that he "could depend upon them for their portion of the expense of the church." Moreover, Henrietta May said she would start a subscription drive in Baltimore and by April had already provided subscription books to "several ladies whose influence will no doubt raise a considerable amount for us." But, after four weeks, Gross found that the May's collections "have been anything but thriving." As the year progressed, Gross himself went to Baltimore on fund-raising expeditions, which he confessed "[were] not according to my opinion very successful," but he admitted that he had "met with only two or three refusals." The individual sums contributed, however, were small. He received $7 from "a lady friend of mine," $46 collected by Henrietta May, and a total of $318.75 from his other efforts. "What the promises made me will realise [*sic*]," he wrote, "is hard to say." Later on, after "begging for Easton day & night," he collected another $100.[97]

Gross also was closely involved in designing the Easton church. He wrote to Goldsborough on March 10, 1864, telling him that upon his return to the Western Shore from Easton, he had "called on an old friend of mine who is a first class merchant and has passed his life in working upon church buildings." Subsequent correspondence identified the church builder as "Mr. Roach." This actually was Michael Roche, a Baltimore master carpenter and builder of both Catholic and secular buildings in Baltimore city and county, some of them in cooperation with Louis L. Long, the architect of St. Mary's Church in Annapolis. Roche was a native of Ireland and a member of the Ancient Order of Hibernians in Baltimore. According to Gross, Roche prepared "a plan for a neat church according to our wishes and furnished me with some valuable hints as to *cheap* buildings." He also suggested to Goldsborough that they use the free labor of local Easton Irishmen who had "offered [him] their services in building the church."[98]

A problem arose, however, when Gross showed Roche's church plans to Henry and Henrietta May in mid-April. They told him that they preferred to use the same design as the new Catholic church in Cape May, New Jersey, and would ask the priest there to send them a copy of his plan. When the Cape May plans had not arrived by late April, Gross reported to Howes Goldsborough that Henrietta May "sketched for me its plan roughly and I will get my old friend to draw up a regular artistic plan of this which I will bring to you on my next visit." Roche used the rough sketch to complete the drawings, which Gross found awaiting him when he returned to Annapolis after the weekend of May 14–15. Father Helmprächt, however, found a problem with the measurements and believed that "the height of the sides . . . are not in proper proportion with the length of the church, but this fault can be easily remedied." Gross feared that the cost of the new plan might be prohibitive and suggested that both plans—Roche's adaptation of Henrietta May's sketch of the Cape May church and Roche's original drawings—should be presented to "the persons who are to undertake the erection of the church" for reconciliation. Gross exhibited a conscientiousness that would serve him well in later years as a prelate. He told Goldsborough that "Our

Father Joseph Wissel, C.Ss.R. (1830–1912). Source: Rev. Henry Borgmann, C.Ss.R., History of the Redemptorists at Annapolis, Md., from 1853 to 1903 *(Ilchester, Maryland: College Press, 1904), 45.*

means are so limited I think that we must be very careful about adopting plans for a building which may be indeed very pretty but will only result in laying heavy expenses upon us." In late November 1864, Gross sent the plan for the church to Baltimore. "One of our lay brothers there," he told Goldsborough, "is a most excellent builder and quite an architect; I have desired him to send me all the information we need in regard to the lumber, etc." Although he did not name the brother, it must have been Thomas Lütte, who supervised the construction of St. Mary's Church in 1858. To help lower the costs, Henry May apparently provided timber from his Easton-area estate to be used in constructing the church.[99]

Land was purchased for the church in downtown Easton and Gross took out a paid notice in the *Easton Gazette*, announcing that he wished "to commence the building at the earliest practicable moment." He asked all those who had subscribed to the project, to pay the amount of their pledge. Eastern Shore donors were asked to send their contributions to Goldsborough and those on the Western Shore to the banking house of John S. Gittings in Baltimore.[100]

In November 1864, Gross was reassigned to the Redemptorist mission band with Father Seelos. His last visit to Easton was on November 19–21 to say farewell. He was succeeded in Easton by Father Louis Claessens, who made his first trip there on Christmas Day 1864.[101]

The success of the Redemptorists' work in Easton for 1864 was concluded as follows:

> As to our station at Easton, every thing is progressing favorably: the number of Catholics is steadily increasing. Collections & preparation have been made to build a church: many protestants have been exceedingly liberal. The church will be commenced in the spring of 1865 – perhaps 1866.[102]

Terrify the Sinner

In early 1864, eight priests stationed at St. Mary's were assigned to preach missions throughout the North. They, along with priests from other Redemptorist houses, were members of four- and five-man teams working under the direction of Father Seelos as superior of the mission band. Missions in the nineteenth century were the Catholic version of revival meetings. Father Joseph Wissel, a member of Seelos' mission team and later called "the foremost Redemptorist revivalist," described missions as follows:

> A mission consists of a regular course of sermons and instructions to the members of Catholic congregations, in connection with the administration of the sacraments for the purpose of making them true and practical Catholics. The discourses of a mission form a compendium of the entire Christian doctrine. They comprise the Word of God, brought from heaven by Jesus Christ, through the operation of the Holy Ghost.[103]

Missions not only had the purpose of renewing and strengthening the spiritual life of the faithful but also sought the conversion of lapsed Catholics. Wissel told priests that before the mission started to personally seek out the community's

> well-known Catholics who never go to church, and are not disposed to go to church even during a mission. A visit that is made to them at their houses and a special invitation that is given to them, have often been blessed with the happiest results.[104]

Jay Dolan uses the terms "parish mission" and "Catholic revival" interchangeably when describing mid-to-late-nineteenth-century religious-order preaching. He emphasizes that the Redemptorist, Paulist, Jesuit, and other religious orders of preachers "were following centuries-old European tradition" that emerged from the sixteenth-century counter-reformation period. The first Redemptorists in the United States did not establish parishes but mostly preached missions and thus played a seminal role in American Catholic revivalism soon after their 1832 arrival.[105]

Missions were aimed at strengthening and rekindling the commitment of Catholics to their faith. Gaining converts was a bonus for the missionaries. During the Civil War, missions took on an additional urgency of consoling the survivors and preparing the faithful for life in the hereafter. Father Robert Miller notes "a remarkable wave of religious revival" among army troops, both North and South, during the war, a situation capitalized on mostly by Protestant ministers. Although Protestant ministers often held revival meetings in army camps, Catholic clergy was less available for such work. And, there is no evidence that Redemptorists preached missions for army audiences per se. Their missions typically were held in large cities and attended by members of local parishes and the general public. However, soldiers on furlough and men who had completed their war service and had returned home could have attended Redemptorist missions. Family members of veterans, as well as men and women who had lost fathers, husbands, brothers, and sons during the war, would have been among the attendees. They were in need of the Redemptorists' message of consolation, acceptance of their fate, and preparation for their own eventual deaths and life eternal.[106]

Key to Redemptorist mission work, according to the 1863 *Mission-Book* edited by Father John Cornell in Annapolis, was to preach to the faithful

> on the most terrible truths of religion, show them the importance and dangers of salvation, and the occasions and sad consequences of sin, animate them to the love of God, to new zeal for Christian perfection, to prayer and the frequent reception of the Sacraments . . . and point out to them, in general, the means of persevering in good to the end.[107]

Between twice-daily preaching sessions, the missionaries heard confessions, celebrated Mass, officiated at the renewal of baptismal vows, and led prayers to the Virgin Mary, all in sight of a special mission cross that was left with the parish as a reminder of what had transpired. The exercises were said to be "admirably adapted to move the hearts of all, to terrify the sinner, to awaken the tepid out of their sleep, and to maintain the good in their fervor."

The Annapolis Redemptorists involved in mission work included Fathers James Bradley, Michael Burke, Henry Giesen, and Joseph Henning. Their preached primarily in Pennsylvania, New York, Connecticut, Rhode Island, Ohio, and Illinois, plus at a few missions in Maryland. Other Annapolis priests worked closer to home. Fathers Joseph Helmprächt, Louis Claessens, Henry Dauenhauer, and Adam Gunkel gave Lenten missions at German-speaking St. Alphonsus and St. James parishes in Baltimore.[108]

Redemptorist records provide statistical information on the level of participation and success of missions. One given at St. Paul's Cathedral in Pittsburgh was attended by 6,800 persons and resulted in twenty-five converts. St. Patrick's Church in Cleveland saw 2,400 persons in attendance, with thirteen converts. Some 2,200 went to a mission at St. Mary's Cathedral in Chicago, with six converts. Smaller towns and parishes had lesser numbers of attendees.

The Annapolis team that went to St. Alphonsus and St. James parishes in Baltimore addressed some 2,600 individuals and gained eighteen converts. Father Bradley, a veteran of at least twenty-eight missions between November 1862 and November 1864, was joined by Father John Gerdemann for a week-long mission at St. Augustine's Church in Elkridge Landing in September 1864. The *Chronica Domus* reported that "Great was the number of people present, great was the fervor, great was the liberality." About 220 confessions were heard, more than 200 communions distributed, and seven were converted. Mostly men attended this particular mission and many of them received scapulars and rosaries from the priests. A notable accomplishment occurred on the day after the mission closed: a public reconciliation between two men who for two years had been engaged in "hostility and disputes." At the start of the mission, one of the men had refused reconciliation but by the end of the Redemptorists' exhortations he had come around to do the right thing. "Many were the fruits of this mission," it was recorded.[109]

St. Mary's itself was the site of Redemptorist missions. Notice of one such mission was published in April 1864 in the *Annapolis Gazette*, which reported that "A mission for the colored people of our city will be held in St. Mary's Church, Annapolis, commencing on Sunday May 1st, at 4 o'clock in the afternoon." The mission lasted a week and included morning and afternoon sessions with talks given by Fathers Helmprächt, Claessens, Gross, Gerdemann, and Freitag. The *Chronica Domus* noted that on the first day "many Negroes attended the mission; the rest of the days, especially in the early morning, fewer of them were present." This is not surprising since whether enslaved or free, Black people did not have the leisure time during the week to attend church. But, the chronicler continued, "if the fruits of the mission are not immediately apparent, it cannot be said that it was unproductive, for of the Protestant Negroes who attended the mission, about twelve of them turned to the true faith." About thirty confessions were heard during the mission.[110]

Father Gross referred to "my negroes" when writing to Howes Goldsborough in July. He said he had been preparing a number of them for their First Communion and St. Mary's planned "quite a solemnity for the occasion." The reception of First Communion was held at St. Mary's on July 10 and noted in the *Chronica Domus* with the overly succinct statement: "First communion is solemnly held for Negroes." Although the names of eleven White children who received First Communion on April 17 are listed in the parish records, no such list was made of the names of the Black recipients on July 10.[111]

Sixteen African Americans turned to the Catholic faith in 1864 and fourteen more in 1865. Some of these were children and probably did not attend the mission. The twelve Gross mentioned as having converted as a result of the mission may have included seven he baptized plus three baptized by Gerdemann in the months after the mission. The next year, Gerdemann baptized nine more Black converts, some adults from Dodon and others were Annapolis children. Ten Black converts, all women, ranging in age from sixteen to thirty-two, were confirmed at St. Mary's December 8, 1864. Five of the confirmands had been baptized by Gross during the previous thirteen months.

A mission was held for St. Mary's White parishioners on September 18–25, 1864. Fathers Henry Giesen, Joseph Wissel, and Michael Burke led the exercises at which a "large number of people attended every day, both Catholics and non-

Catholics, especially in the evening." Redemptorist seminarians also attended the mission. The talks were held daily at 8:00 AM and 7:00 PM. "Many and great were the fruits of this mission," according to the *Chronica Domus*, and resulted in 220 confessions heard and some 200 communions distributed.[112]

St. Mary's Ladies Hold a Fair

St. Mary's women staged a two-week-long fair in 1864 to help reduce the church debt. The fair began on Monday, May 16, in the parish hall. It was advertised in the Baltimore *Sun*, which said "the ladies [of St. Mary's] would invite their friends and the public generally" and that "useful and fancy articles" were to be sold. The *Catholic Mirror* later reported that the fair was well-attended and raised $1,230 (nearly $16,000 in modern currency) "to be applied to the improvement of the splendid edifice on Gloucester Street." Although the fair was a significant achievement for the parish women, the Redemptorist chronicler noted dryly that "none of the Fathers took any active part in it." This noninvolvement was to be expected. The Annapolis Redemptorists had been reminded several years before by their superior in Baltimore that "it is best to remember that Father Rector Major [in Rome] has forbidden Nundinas (commonly known as Fairs), Pic-Nics, Excursions, raffles or similar things."[113]

Passes Still Required

The occupying Federal authorities continued to require travel passes for Annapolitans wanting to travel for a day or period of days, either for short excursions nearby or longer trips, such as to Baltimore and beyond. Numerous passes were issued to St. Mary's parishioners, both Black and White, and to Catholic clergy in 1864. Pre-printed pass forms were issued at the provost marshal's office in the Assembly Rooms on Duke of Gloucester Street and required applicants to state where they wanted to travel, for how long, and by what sort of conveyance. Longer periods of validity were allowed and the signed oath of allegiance to the United States Government was still required. In the extant May–August 1864 records, only one man was noted as having refused to sign and the filled-out but unsigned pass is still in the record book, with the note "would not take the oath." He was not a St. Mary's parishioner.[114]

The army's Middle Department, headquartered in Baltimore under Major General Lewis Wallace, issued Special Orders No. 107, on April 26, 1864, requiring "all persons embarking at Annapolis by steamer or sailing vessel . . . to present passes from the commanding officer of the post." This officer was Colonel Adrian Rowe Root, commander of the Ninety-Fourth New York Infantry Regiment. Boat captains were put on notice that their vessels were liable to seizure and their passengers detained if they allowed anyone to board at Annapolis without a pass from Root. The provost marshal complained to Root that there was "a leakage in the pass system." Some persons traveling by steamboat from Baltimore to the Eastern Shore via Annapolis no longer had possession of their passes issued at Baltimore because they "were taken up by the Guard at Baltimore." The solution was for the Baltimore guards to return the passes to passengers en route to the Eastern Shore. This had implications for Redemptorists who had passes issued in Baltimore.[115]

The issuance of passes provides insight into daily life of St. Mary's parishioners. For example, a pass was issued on April 27 to "Miss Revell and children" to cross the Severn River and was valid a year and three days. Which Miss Revell this was is unknown; she might have been Mollie Revell or her sister Elizabeth, perhaps in charge of the older children of their sister, Annie Revell Brady, or another family's children or even parish school students. Another pass, issued to Martin Revell's future father-in-law, James Sands, on June 20, allowing him to go to Baltimore on business. Interestingly, neither of these passes were signed on the back. The absence of a signature implies either inattention by issuing officer or refusal to sign the oath by the pro-South Revells and Sands who were issued passes anyway.[116]

Other St. Mary's parishioners and clergy were granted passes, some valid for one day, others for longer periods. John Walton's pass was "good until further orders" and allowed him to travel to Baltimore by rail or steamer. His son Edward, noted as a farmer, was permitted to go by carriage or small boat to the mouth of Round Bay during a three-week period ending May 20. The "Misses Sparks"—daughters of Edward Sparks—were issued a pass to travel to Washington by rail with no expiration date. "A. Larkins," a "colored servant" was granted a pass to take a small boat across the Severn accompanied by a child and an unnamed woman and her child. She may have been Anne Frances Larkins, an African American parishioner and mother of several children baptized at St. Mary's. Their father, Solomon Larkins, a free Black and lifelong Protestant converted to Catholicism on his deathbed in 1865. African American parishioner Henrietta Cooper was given a two-day pass to take the train to Baltimore, while another Black parishioner, Harriet Johnson, was given a three-day pass to go "across the Severn" by small boat.[117]

A pass issued on May 13 to John Thomas Denver, "Boy of Annapolis," destination "Up Spar [*sic*] Creek" by small boat, provides an opportunity to discuss the family's religious inclinations. A year earlier, John had been baptized conditionally at age twelve by Father Bradley and St. Mary's School teacher Josephine O'Donoughue was his sponsor. His father was Thomas Denver, a former city watchman and currently a waterman, who is noted in the parish registers as a "nominal Catholic." His mother, Mary Stansbury Denver, was Protestant, probably Episcopalian. Nevertheless, between 1858 and 1865, eight of this couple's children were presented for baptism at St. Mary's at ages ranging from five days to fourteen years. One wonders if the pressures of war led the Denvers to baptize their older children after so many years since their births, with the younger children christened more quickly.[118]

Catherine Bright, John Cassidy, Moses Lake, and Sophia Sparks were among other St. Mary's parishioners whose names appear in the pass book for May 1864. Three women obtained a joint pass on June 24, to take junket to

Baltimore on the train. They were listed as "Misses Dubois, Davis and Mullen" and were probably nineteen-year-old Sarah Anna DuBois, daughter of Edward and Rosetta DuBois, and twenty-two-year old Ann Catherine Mullan, daughter of Sergeant John and Mary Ann Mullan, both having been found in St. Mary's parish records. The identity of Miss Davis has not been determined.[119]

A group of parish adults and children were issued passes for a steamer trip to West River in late July. Instead of an expiration date, these passes were valid "until used." The group included Catherine Bright and her eleven-year-old niece, Virginia Mullan; Emma Treadway and her eleven-year-old daughter, Mary Cecilia; and Harriet Tydings and her eleven-year-old son, George. Mary Treadway and Jennie Mullan received a joint pass, while George received his own pass. The two mothers were listed with "& child," which may or may not have been the two girls mentioned or were unnamed younger siblings since both women had younger children. The three children were probably St. Mary's parochial schoolmates enjoying a summer outing with their adult chaperons. Moreover, Emma Treadway was George Tydings' godmother and Catherine Bright was kin to Harriet's husband, Thomas Tydings Sr. They would have taken the steamer from Annapolis to West River and returned the same day. The boat traveled daily from Baltimore in the morning, picked up passengers at Annapolis, and proceeded to West River. On the return trip, it left West River at 2:00 PM, stopping at Annapolis, where it departed at 3:30 to return to Baltimore.[120]

Redemptorists were among the 1864 pass recipients. The first found was "Rev. Mr. Miller" who was granted a rail pass to Annapolis Junction on May 7, 1864. This pass coincides with a visit he made to Annapolis from April 27 to May 7, to deal with draft problems. Since he was a veteran instigator, Father Müller may have encouraged his confreres to do something about the requirement to obtain passes in order to go freely about their pastoral and missionary duties. Starting on May 6, when a new pass book was opened and pass no. 1 was issued, through December 31, the provost marshal gave out nearly 7,800 passes for travel from and around Annapolis. Of this number, sixty-five passes were issued to twenty-seven different Redemptorist priests and five brothers. When comparing the issuance of passes to entries in the *Chronica Domus* concerning travel, it is apparent that either not all of the passes were used or the chronicler failed to record the absences. Some pass dates coincide with known travel, others do not. Although all of the passes claimed Annapolis as the place of residence of the pass holder, some of them were issued to Redemptorists stationed in Baltimore, such as John De Dycker, who came for the annual examinations in July and the annual canonical visitation in November. Most of the passes issued in 1864 were to groups of Redemptorists, once as many as fifteen on one day, and a mix of Annapolis and Baltimore priests. This suggests the possibility that individual sworn oaths were not always required at the time of issuance and perhaps not ever in some cases. Some of the Redemptorists may have traveled without any pass at all. This was the case when Jaeckel and Gross went across the bay to Easton, a trip verified by the *Chronica Domus*. Only Gross had been issued a ten-day pass on May 10 to take the steamer to Baltimore, yet he ended up in Easton on May 13 with Jaeckel, who must have had a Baltimore-issued pass.[121]

As time went on, passes issued to the Redemptorists for up to thirty days were replaced with passes that read "good until further orders." The cumulative effect of the passes granted was that almost all of the Annapolis priests—except those working long term on the mission band, but including some of the brothers, as well as priests stationed in Baltimore—had secured the freedom to travel between the two cities by railroad or steamer. From there, or from Annapolis Junction, they could travel onward to other points, such as Elkridge Landing, Ellicott's Mills, and Cumberland by rail or via the Baltimore steamer to Easton or West River.[122]

Gone South

A young man associated with St. Mary's, surely with no pass in hand, was arrested on April 23, 1864. Provost Marshal Captain Francis J. Keffer reported to Colonel Root that one of his men, "acting as a guard or detective," at the Annapolis steamboat landing had learned from a local informant that "two young men . . . citizens of this place" had taken passage that morning "on their way to the South" on the steamboat to West River. The informant also told the detective that a third man, identified as sixteen-year-old Francis C. White, had hoped to join them but remained behind. Francis C. White, also known as Frank, was the son of George Francis White, a wealthy Millersville farmer, and Elizabeth Louisa Brewer White. No other Francis or Frank Whites have been identified in the area at the time, and it is believed he is probably the same as Frank White whose name appears in the St. Mary's confirmation register in December 1864, where he is noted as age thirteen and having taken Augustus as his confirmation name.[123]

Keffer detained White, who said he had been approached by two men who encouraged him to go South and he agreed to go because he, like them, "did not like the Government of the United States." But when pressed by the two to depart with them on April 23, White said he had to work as a clerk in his uncle's shop and could not leave. His uncle was former Annapolis mayor John Wesley White, a dry goods merchant. When White refused to take an oath of allegiance Keffer placed him under arrest. White still refused to take the oath so Keffer sent him under guard to his uncle's shop. There the elder White must have spoken quite adamantly to his nephew because the young man returned to Keffer's office in twenty minutes and signed the oath of allegiance. White was released after he promised to "discourage, discountenance, and forever oppose Secession, Rebellion, and disintegration of the Union" and "pledged my property and my life to the sacred performance" of his oath. White's erstwhile companions who had started for the South were apprehended two days later. They refused to take the oath so Keffer "placed them in irons" and kept them in custody.[124]

Barricades at the Naval Academy gate, July 1864. Courtesy William Smith Ely Collection, AN 111, Edward G. Miner Library, University of Rochester Medical Center, Rochester, NY.

Frank White was among several individuals associated with St. Mary's who had proven Southern sympathies. There were the Revell and Steuart families with publicly known sympathies for the Confederacy, and John Henry Boyle Jr. who served as a Confederate agent throughout the war (see The Mills of the Gods Grind Slowly, ch. 7). Some parishioners subscribed to the *Maryland Republican*, which was sympathetic to the South. Otherwise, St. Mary's had few identifiable connections to the Southern cause.

William Hogarty was a parishioner with a Southern connection. He was born around 1822, probably in Ireland. He appeared twice, in 1855 and 1856, in the St. Mary's marriage register as a witness for Irish-born friends and a possible relative. He also was listed five times as a godparent in the parish baptismal register between 1857 and 1861. Some of those baptized were of Irish descent but one of his god children stands out as unusual. Hogarty was the godparent for Sophia Williams, a forty-two-year-old free Black washerwoman who was baptized by Father Cornell in *periculo mortis* (in danger of death) in 1860. When the war began, Hogarty was working as a gardener but when the draft enrollment took place the next year his name was crossed out in red, meaning he was exempt. The reason given was that he had "gone south."[125]

Hogarty went south to Richmond where he enlisted in Company D, First Battalion, Maryland Infantry, on September 7, 1862. The battalion deployed to the Shenandoah Valley during the winter of 1862–63 and saw its first action in April 1863 when taking part in a raid that destroyed B&O Railroad bridges, track, rolling stock, machine shops, and other facilities in western Virginia and western Maryland. Hogarty's battalion was assigned to General George Hume Steuart's brigade when Robert E. Lee launched his invasion of Maryland and Pennsylvania in June and July 1863. The First Maryland Battalion suffered severe losses at Gettysburg: 48 percent of its men were killed or wounded. Hogarty, however, never saw this action, having been taken prisoner in Greencastle, about thirty miles west of Gettysburg, on July 1.

The circumstances are not known but Union prisoner of war records indicate that Hogarty "gave himself up." He was sent first to Fort McHenry in Baltimore, then to Fort Delaware, an island prison in the Delaware River near Delaware City, then to Fort Columbus in New York Harbor. His final destination, in September 1863, was the prisoner-of-war camp at Point Lookout, Maryland. Paroled on December 24, 1863, Hogarty used an X mark to sign his name, and was exchanged on December 25. He returned to his unit, renamed the Second Maryland Battalion during his absence. The Second Battalion saw action in southern Virginia between summer 1864 and spring 1865, but between September 1864 and February 1865, Hogarty was listed as absent and sick in a field hospital. On April 4, 1865, as the defenses of Petersburg collapsed, he was captured again. He was transported to Hart Island in New York Harbor, where he remained until June 21, when all enlisted rebel prisoners were discharged after signing oaths of allegiance to the United States. Hogarty, whose home of residence was listed as Anne Arundel, Maryland, again signed with an X mark. He returned to Annapolis and was last noted in a published list of registered voters in the Sixth Election District (City of Annapolis) in 1868 and as a gardener in the 1870 Federal Census.[126]

Compelled to Shoulder a Musket

On July 5–6, 1864, Confederate Lieutenant General Jubal Early's Army of the Valley crossed the Potomac River into western Maryland. The invasion was aimed at Washington, a tactical move the Confederates hoped would draw Union troops away from Petersburg and Richmond. Besides attacking Washington, Early planned a thrust against Baltimore and to liberate Confederate prisoners at Point Lookout, in St. Mary's County. A battle fought on the west side of Frederick on July 7 pushed a small Union force south of the city, to Monocacy Junction, where the B&O Railroad crossed the Monocacy River. Wounded Union troops from the Frederick battle were evacuated to hospitals in Annapolis and, in turn, Ohio soldiers assigned to guard Camp Parole at Annapolis, as well as troops from Baltimore and Washington, were rushed to Monocacy Junction under the command of Major General Lewis Wallace. On the morning of July 9, Early's 15,000 troops engaged Wallace's force of 6,600 mostly inexperienced soldiers. After eight and a half hours of fighting the Union troops were overwhelmed and retreated toward Washington and Baltimore. Although the Battle of Monocacy Junction was a Union defeat, it delayed Early's attack on Washington, giving time for battle-hardened Union units to arrive in Washington.[127]

Monocacy was just seventy miles from Annapolis and the threat to central Maryland was paramount. Sunday, July 10, was quiet in Annapolis, according to the *Maryland Republican*, and "remarkably free from rumors and scares" until about 9:00 PM when the city's fire bell began ringing. It called residents together "for the purpose of devising plans for the defence of the city against the Confederates." Henry Hollyday Goldsborough, president of Maryland's Constitutional Convention then meeting in Annapolis, chaired the late-night gathering. He "warmly urged citizens and others to take measures to defend the capital of the State." Goldsborough assumed the position of captain of a company of volunteers that eventually grew to 130 members. The *Annapolis Gazette* later complimented Goldsborough and his convention colleagues for "not only bearing arms but [being] among the first and most constant workers with pick and shovel in throwing up defences." The meeting attendees also appointed a committee of citizens to confer with the local military authorities and to impress Black men to entrench the city. They also posted volunteer guards in and around town.[128]

The "excitement began to manifest itself" on July 11 as Dr. Bernard A. Vanderkieft—the army surgeon in charge of General Hospital Division No. 1—ordered "an embankment to be thrown up" in front of the Naval Academy main gate. Supposedly this order was countermanded by Colonel Root, who asked Vanderkieft instead to provide a thirty-six-man convalescent detail to serve as an extra provost guards in the city. However, one of Vanderkieft's nurses later wrote that outside the two entrances to the hospital grounds "were dug two moats, protected by ramparts of earth and a very ludicrous structure of barrels."[129]

The same day, Goldsborough and Dr. Washington Tuck, representing the citizen committee, advised the mayor and aldermen of Annapolis "with regard to the apprehended danger of a rebel raid into the city." The city council authorized Mayor Magruder to telegraph the military authorities requesting "that measures be immediately taken to erect suitable defences for this city" and asking that Annapolis be placed under martial law. The same day, the "city fathers" issued a call for 500 volunteers to fortify the land approaches to the city. Colonel Root marked out a line of breastworks and rifle pits and, over the course of "three days of alarm," entrenchments were built. A newspaper report said: "The fortifications extend from 'Grave-yard creek [College Creek],' an arm of the Severn, to Spa, another branch of the same river, thus completely environing Annapolis with water and redoubts." In the meantime, similar precautions were being taken in Baltimore.[130]

The entrenchments, according to several modern analyses, are believed to have followed the 1860 city limit boundary line, beginning on the north at the upper end of College Creek. Then, following the rolling terrain, they continued along the west side of today's Presidents Hill (then Miller's Hill) and intersected with West Street around today's Jefferson Place and Monticello Avenue. Then it continued south, probably along the high ground, through James Murray's plantation (now Murray Hill) to Old Womans Cove on Spa Creek. The distance from College Creek to Old Womans Cove is about a mile. The high point, on Miller's Hill, gave the guards a commanding view of both the railroad right-of-way and the county road running between Camp Parole and the city. Some of the entrenchments were built using posts and rails taken from fences on the property of Judge Nicholas Brewer, across whose property the battlements north of West Street were constructed. Live peach and locust trees were cut down on Brewer's property to make clear fields of fire and to reinforce the earthen fortifications. It is probable that fences from John Walton's farm and other nearby properties also were used for the same purpose along the section south of West Street.[131]

Governor Bradford's private secretary, John Merriken Carter, arrived in Annapolis on July 11 to offer "any assistance in the power of the State towards repelling the expected raid." As the day progressed, the War Department ordered a 337-man battalion of convalescent soldiers at Camp Parole to go to the District of Columbia to assist in its defense. Other convalescent soldiers and local citizens worked throughout the night on the excavations. Because only seventy-five men responded to the initial call for 500, the impressment of Black laborers began. By late morning of July 12, it was obvious that work still proceeded too slowly and Root declared martial law and ordered all able-bodied men to report to the provost marshal for duty. Boys age fourteen and older and men up to "advanced age" were put to work digging, carrying water, and other tasks. Some were prepared to bear arms. Under the provost marshal's supervision streets were cleared, houses searched, and "the stores were almost all closed, and the streets had the appearance of Sabbath." Annapolis was "[f]or a time . . . completely isolated 'from all the world and from the rest of mankind;' all exits from the city were interdicted."[132]

Daily impressment by the provost guard, according to an eyewitness, was "obnoxious to many who were strongly southern in their sentiments, and who did not relish the idea of fighting against people they thought were in the right." The impressed men were marched out daily in double files to work on the "grand fortifications." Word was received on July 12 that the Confederate force had cut the railroad line between Annapolis Junction and Washington. This forced the conva-

Artillery and entrenchments near city limits, July 1864. Courtesy William Smith Ely Collection, AN 110, Edward G. Miner Library, University of Rochester Medical Center, Rochester, NY.

lescent battalion to begin constructing an advance line of rifle pits and breastworks about one mile out from the newly built entrenchments. A twelve-pounder gun was emplaced on the advance line. If the distance provided in 1864 is accurate, it would place these rifle pits approximately along Chinquapin Round Road, just east of the third Camp Parole. The pits may have been part of the entrenchments that John Randolph Walton said he saw erected on his father's farm (see Doing the Union Party Injury, ch. 4).[133]

Also on July 12, John Carter, who had responsibility for state property in the city, turned over three state-owned six-pounder brass field pieces to Colonel Root and 300 muskets to Colonel Charles William Le Gendre, a patient at the army hospital who was helping organize the defense. Root had a force of 500 convalescent troops that he said could defend the city against a cavalry attack but would be "entirely inadequate" against a "determined attack" by infantry with artillery, so he asked Eighth Army Corps headquarters in Baltimore to send two gunboats and 10,000 percussion caps for Enfield rifles.[134]

On July 13, the USS *Vicksburg*, a seven-gun Navy gunboat arrived from Hampton Roads and anchored up the Severn River to "give the rebels a warm reception" in case they chose a water route to Annapolis. The four-gun USS *Daylight* was placed on "the other side of town" so the entrenchments protecting the city were covered from the water. The steam tug *Grace Titus*, armed with a ten-man crew and a twelve-pounder howitzer, was placed as a picket "up the creek on the line of the rifle pits." It is not clear whether this meant Spa or College Creek. Earlier in the day, the same tug had gone up the South River where it "scoured the shores of the river on both sides" looking for "scows and other craft which might be used by the enemy in transporting troops." Among the seizures was a boat owned by John Walton and kept at his South River farm near the Lower Ferry. A schooner and ten small boats were towed back to Annapolis "to prevent the rebels crossing in the rear of our rifle pits."[135]

By July 13, three redoubts had been built and volunteer artillerists mounted the three six-pounder guns and two twelve-pounder guns. Work continued apace as it was rumored that Confederate cavalry had come within ten miles of Camp Parole and threatened to burn the camp. But the rebels "retired upon being informed of the preparations which had been made to receive them," according to an official source. A news account claimed that the hastily thrown up defenses "were capable of resisting a cavalry attack of five thousand men" and opined that "the ruffians who were doubtlessly apprised of the condition of things, by sympathizing friends in our midst, concluded on the whole, to by pass Annapolis, and seek plunder elsewhere." Perhaps feeling satisfied with this result, and with the entrenchments completed, the citizens were relieved from duty on July 14. At sundown that day, the troops were withdrawn from both the advance and inner defense lines and marched back to Camp Parole and to the in-town hospitals, accompanied by a hospital band. Martial law was discontinued on July 15 and troops relieved of their Annapolis duties were sent "fully armed and equipped" to assist in the defense of Washington, where the Battle of Fort Stevens had been fought on July 11–12, resulting in the withdrawal of Early's army.[136]

Some individuals felt personally threatened should the Confederates be successful in capturing Annapolis. The deputy provost marshal for Anne Arundel County later reported that some of his enrollment officers, whom he called "Rebels" merely because they were residents of a southern state, were fearful that they would be hung by the Confederates for having served as Yankee government officials. They requested military escorts.[137]

Southern sympathizers, shopkeepers losing business, and slave holders were dismayed by the impressment of men to build the defense works. But they were not alone. The *Chronica Domus* includes a brief narrative entitled "Great fear and trembling invaded our city of Annapolis." It reported on the events of July 12 and 13 and reflected the fear of a Confederate attack on Annapolis which, wrote the chronicler, "caused a good deal of panic in the country generally." The Redemptorists responded to the citywide urgent call for laborers by sending some hired workers and candidate brothers to work on the fortifications. At this time, there were four candidate brothers assigned at St. Mary's and would have been the men sent. They were Nicholas (Brother Joseph) Knapp, a cobbler; Isidor (Brother Boniface) Schultheiss, a clothes washer; and Bernard (Brother Anthony) Pitz and Louis (Brother Hieronymus) Weingärtner, both of whom were cooks. The Redemptorists' provincial annals, noted that these brothers were treated courteously by the civil and military authorities.[138]

After the brothers and hired hands went to work on the entrenchments, an order was issued, according to the Redemptorist account, that "every man met in Annapolis was compelled to shoulder a musket." When "two of the fathers were met in the streets and accordingly ordered to do the same: they refused, and with difficulty were let go unmolested." Father Gross wrote letters on July 15 and 21 providing additional details on this episode. He said that "Annapolis was in the wildest state of unnecessary alarm" and that the authorities "even called upon us to take up arms – which was of course refused." He told how one of the priests "was twice stopped on the streets by an officer and his squad of armed soldiers, and the choice offered him was to appear with a musket or take quarters in the prison." But "the Rev. Gentleman unhesitatingly accepted the latter alternative – he was – doubtless from prudential motives – allowed to go in peace." After things calmed down, Gross reported that "we have lived for the last ten days amid 'wars and rumors of war.'" He added that the Confederate raid "has so disturbed our community as to almost paralyze public business." He noted—as of July 15—that the steamboat had not been running for several days, "and there is no telling when it will commence again its usual trips."[139]

Still more was written about the threatened invasion. An unidentified Redemptorist priest writing from Annapolis on July 23, facetiously said "the Rebels! o dear, the Rebels! how much did they frighten us; 6 of them, on horseback were in the very midst of the Capital." He scoffed at the threat, as did the house chronicler, who ended his narrative with the words "All ended in a Big Scare."[140]

But the invasion threat was real if the final results were not. Confederate Brigadier General Bradley T. Johnson had planned to attack Baltimore City and then move south through Maryland to the Union prison-of-war camp at Point Lookout. Once there he planned to release and arm 10,000 to 12,000 Confederate prisoners. A small cavalry force commanded by Colonel Harry Gilmore reached villages north of Baltimore on July 10, so the threat to Annapolis seemed imminent. The raiders captured a railroad train, entered the northern part of Baltimore City, burned the home of Governor Bradford, and attacked a B&O construction crew and work train. Meanwhile, on July 13, Johnson's troops skirmished with a Union cavalry force at Beltsville in Prince George's County, about thirty miles from Annapolis, forcing the Union counterattackers to retreat back into the District of Columbia. But, by the time that the Confederate detachment was prepared to head south to Point Lookout, Early's attack on Fort Stevens had failed. The action at Monocacy had delayed the attackers long enough for Union troops to rush north to heavily defend the District of Columbia's forts and repel the invaders. Plus, Early's army was diminished in size and the troops were fatigued. The Point Lookout operation was abandoned and Early's army retreated into Virginia. But the Confederates continued their depredations as they passed through western Maryland and were close enough to Cumberland on July 31 to cause the population there to panic. The Cumberland Redemptorists were aware of this near threat but blandly noted only that the "public tranquility was disturbed."[141]

The Confederate attack on Annapolis never materialized, and the Redemptorists avoided another crisis. If Early's attack on Fort Stevens had succeeded and Johnson proceeded South, he likely would have skirted Annapolis to avoid a confrontation there. Although the July attack on the District of Columbia failed, Early's Maryland campaign caused significant disruption with its battles at Frederick and Monocacy Junction, extraction of ransoms, burning of bridges and homes, skirmishes, and other depredations. But life in Annapolis went on and, as the *Maryland Republican* noted, by July 14 "the citizens and Negroes were discharged" and "Business began to assume its old channel" the next day.[142]

Some days later, the provost marshal strengthened its routine day- and night-time patrols and despatched soldiers to visit every public house, store, and private dwelling in the city to notify occupants to return "all arms and ammunition belonging to the United States in the hands of citizens." If all such items were not deposited with the provost marshal by July 23, every public and private house in the city would be searched. No mention of such notification was recorded at St. Mary's.[143]

Father Friday and a Dying Girl

One of Father Augustine Freitag's Civil War activities became the subject of a children's story published in 1890 in *Ave Maria*, a family-oriented weekly religious magazine. The story relates how "Tom," an eighteen-year-old Union army private was detailed by his unit's commander to serve as a guard for "Father Friday," an obvious reference to Father Freitag, whose name in German means Friday. His pastoral duties sometimes took him to out-of-the-way locales at odd hours.

One October morning, so the story goes, the two set out in silence, Father Friday wore his black cassock and a black felt hat and carried the Blessed Sacrament to an invalid living five miles from Annapolis. Once out in the countryside and into the deep woods, they became disoriented and could find neither the invalid's house nor the way back home. As darkness descended, Father Friday stopped to recite the daily prayers of his priestly office and Tom climbed a tree from which he spied a light through the woods. They followed the light and reached the cabin of a poor White couple, "Josh" and his wife, "Mirandy." The couple fed them and made provisions for the night. Because he was still carrying the Blessed Sacrament, Freitag decided to stay up all night praying by an outdoor fire while Tom planned to sleep nearby on a bed of pine needles.

Before they retired, Josh told them about a stranger who had recently stumbled onto their isolated cabin, a bedraggled and seriously ill girl of about twelve years. Josh and Mirandy had been nursing the girl, who prayed that she would not die without something she badly needed. The two rustics did not comprehend what she wanted but Father Friday immediately understood the situation. Upon seeing the priest, the girl said "I knew you would come, Father." She had been praying to the Virgin Mary for a priest to bring her Holy Viaticum before she died. After hearing her confession, Father Friday gave her communion using a hastily set up altar with bowls of burning tallow for candles. Afterward, Father Friday told Tom it was now clear why they had been "providentially led from the path and guided to the bedside of this poor girl." He then spent the rest of the night in prayer with the dying girl. By morning she had passed away. Tom and Father Friday returned to the cabin two days later to attend to her burial in the forest, beneath a rough cross made by Josh. They added the inscription "A Child of Mary" because they had never learned her name. A true story? There are enough elements to the story to make it plausible but the Redemptorist records provide no confirmation of this unusual event.[144]

A Grand Excursion

The 1864 annual holidays for the Redemptorist community were a welcome respite. The year had begun with the smallpox scare, the war news was always discouraging, as was the ongoing presence of thousands of Union troops in and about Annapolis, and then there had been the threat of a Confederate invasion. The annual examinations in late July themselves were a small bit of normality amidst the travails of wartime life. Four of the priests, two by two, as was the custom—first Girardey and Gross, and then Jaeckel and Petri—for two days each, went off to Washington "for recreation." Around this time, the house chronicler—Father Girardey—entered an uncharacteristically

The St. Mary's fleet with its sails raised and an inscription by the "eminent Artist, Ferréol Girardey, C.Ss.R." RABP.

humorous and detailed account of a student excursion up the Severn River. It provides an interesting account of how a group of religious order priests and students spent a summer's day, despite the earlier proscription of such activities from higher headquarters. Other such outings are mentioned briefly in Redemptorist literature, but none with such detail.[145]

The account of the late August outing is entitled "Grand Excursion" and took up the better part of five hand-written pages in the *Chronica Domus*. It was written in English instead of Latin, a rarity for the period, and was lighthearted throughout. It begins:

> The vacations this year passed off splendidly: the students enjoyed themselves very much, and very little happened to disturb the joy and delights of the season. On the last day of this month, the most remarkable of all the excursions that had ever been made in the studen-tate, took place.

Several times the chronicler noted that the excursion was "a most mysterious and remarkable one" and was so "for many reasons." As way of background, the chronicler explained that changes were rumored soon to take place in the studentate and that one of the lectors was to be transferred from Annapolis. Father John Gerdemann, lector of dogmatic theology and German and English literature, was scheduled to give a mission in Elkridge Landing in September. Some of the students believed that it was Gerdemann who was to be transferred, "for, said they, he looks very pale and thin and Father Provincial thinks he will lose his health if he remains here any longer shut up in the house to teach." One of these students asked Father Helmprächt whether Gerdemann was departing and the vice rector "answered that he was going soon" but his "meaning [was] that he was soon going to give the mission in Elkridge Landing." Believing they had found out a secret and so sure that they were not being deceived, the students—described as "the former Rhetoricians"—decided to prepare a speech to express their gratitude to Gerdemann upon the occasion of his permanently leaving Annapolis. They asked Helm-prächt's permission and, "after some deliberation he allowed it, under condition that they should take leave of him publicly on the last and grandest excursion of the whole vacations."

The long-anticipated excursion day arrived on Wednesday, August 31. The priests and students embarked on the sailboats and rowboats moored along the St. Mary's Spa Creek waterfront. At the time, there were eight priests and as many as thirty-four students who may have made the trip. Only Helm-prächt knew the destination and he kept it secret even from the helmsmen. After having set sail for several minutes, the steersmen inquired about their course but Helmprächt continued to keep them in suspense "by causing the boat in which he was to tack about in some many different directions that all the other boats were at a loss as to what they should do." The "suspense and anxiety" lasted until numerous maneuvers in sailing and rowing brought them to "one of the branches of the Severn River" to which the students had never before taken an excursion. The location "was indeed fine and beautiful" but the river bank was "so steep that it was almost impossible to ascend it." It was announced that the "most mysterious part of the day" would occur after their picnic meal. What happened before then was "not of such a mysterious character as to deserve mention."

The account, replete with military terminology, continued:

> After dinner all were called together and a mysterious procession was formed; no one knew the end of it: a generalissimo (R.P. Rector) was appointed, a marshal was chosen, and the students formed in line of battle array, class by class, and the mysterious march was begun towards the top of the hill: the procession was headed by the former Rhetoricians, and closed by the Fathers. Having arrived at the top of the hill, about a dozen cows were frightened by our approach and began to flee; but seeing us take a stand, they also stopped and watched us and our movements closely. All the prelimi-naries being arranged, one of the most mysterious acts of the day took place: none of the students knew its mysteriousness at the time but that only made it still more mysterious and marvelous.

After "the usual preliminaries had been settled," a student "orator of the day. . . took a supereminent position at some distance from the line of battle." Words "cannot express with what pathetic strains of eloquence the orator addressed" Father Gerdemann, "thanking him for his labor, lauding him to the skies for his abilities, expressing sorrow and regret at his leaving &c." Here the chronicler waxed eloquent about the eloquence of the orator, describing how with his words, you:

> would have fancied yourself transferred back to the days of ancient Greece and Rome, when Demosthenes and Cicero, those masters of human eloquence, held the hearts and wills of their hearers in their hands.
>
> Indeed, the orator, seemed to have become a second Cicero and equal of Demosthenes, nay, it is not saying too little, when I say that never had such tremendous peals of eloquence come forth from the mouth of those two until then unsurpassed orators.

The writer could not resist poking more fun at the unsuspecting and unidentified orator who, with "each new burst of eloquence, streams of tears flowed, and the cows took anew to flight." When the speech was over, Gerdemann reportedly "was so overcome by the emotion that he could scarcely respond a few words to the most eloquent harangue he had ever heard." After the farewell speech, the assembly sang Beethoven's "Das Lebewohl" (The Farewell) as a parting hymn. It was rendered "with a degree of sadness never before seen on that mysterious spot."[146]

Afterward, the Redemptorist regiment marched to a new destination, an enclosure which was not described. At that point, "the generalissimo mysteriously announced that the great mystery was about to be solved in the following manner." A single file was formed outside the enclosure and the generalissimo passed around a box filled with tickets, as many as there were students present. All the tickets, except one, were blank and the "mysterious one contained the mysteriously sought for mystery." Each student drew a ticket and the one who drew the mysterious ticket, read it to himself with "an expression of awe, admiration, amazement, consternation and stupefaction." Each of the students who wanted to know the secret was "obliged to go to the lucky student, who would then charge him a high price for telling him the mysterious secret." The account related that "the excitement was intense!" and all rushed over in order to hear the secret, for which they "had to pay dearly for it, v.g. a rosary &c." When all had found out the secret, "the orator of the day. . . fainted. . . ." The ticket revealed that the students all had been greatly fooled and that Gerdemann, except for the Elkridge Landing mission, was not leaving Annapolis. "The effect of the proclamation had on the assembly," wrote the chronicler, "was vivid & intense; it can be better imagined than depicted."[147]

But Redemptorists, then and now, enjoy a good joke, and the affair was not over. According to a "secretly preconcerted arrangement," one of the students publicly accused Helmprächt "of having cheated and deceived the students." The accusation:

> was made in such a seemingly earnest manner that many of the students got frightened and kept at a distance: some even begged one of the other students to keep back the accusing student, saying that that was not the place suitable for scolding R.F. Rector: others did not know what to make of it.

But since the accusation had been made, a court was assembled "to try the accusations." A judge was appointed, the accuser chose an attorney, as did also the accused, but no one wanted to serve on a jury since "all were seized with fear." When the court was called to order, the prosecuting attorney "set forth in the most glorious and eloquent harangue until then unsurpassed in the American or African bar, the enormity & heinousness of the deception and crime in general, leaving the hearers to make the application to the present case." One witness called spoke incoherently and was altogether unintelligible, while another "ran out of the court frightened, thinking the whole affair was a serious one." The defense attorney was logical and cool, so much so that the judge "was easily convinced of the innocence of the accused." The preappointed accuser was "condemned" and had to "pay damages & the costs" which were unfortunately omitted from the otherwise detailed transcript. "Thus ended the famous trial, which at first frightened many of the students but which caused them much enjoyment when they had found out it was only a mock trial." The excursion ended and the group sailed and rowed back down the Severn River, turned into Spa Creek, and returned to St. Mary's College, prepared to embark on the next semester.

Research into the Federal pass system imposed on Annapolis provides still another surprise about this grand

The St. Mary's fleet its sails furled. More of the waterfront shows in this view. RABP.

expedition. Despite the availability in the National Archives of the pass books for this period and for the very day of the trip up the Severn, no passes were issued for this intrepid group of perhaps forty Redemptorists. They had flaunted the military orders from the post commander in Annapolis and the Middle Department in Baltimore, enjoying instead, implicit permission from a much higher authority. And where the spot is that the group enjoyed their picnic and faced Father Rector's test remains open to speculation. But the best guess is on Salt Pan Creek (now called Saltworks Creek, in the Epping Forest community), a narrow body of water, on the south side of the Severn, with steep banks on both sides. Coincidently—or not—Judge Mason owned a nearby 228-acre farm called Sherwood Forest and it was perhaps his squad of cows that were encountered by the Redemptorist invaders.[148]

Have Mercy on His People

Father De Dycker arrived for his annual canonical visitation to St. Mary's on the morning of November 7. He began his work that evening and was joined two days later by his socius, Father George Ruland, the former provincial, now one of the consultors stationed at St. Alphonsus in Baltimore. Meetings were held with the Redemptorist community until November 14, when the "visitation came to a happy close."[149]

The year 1864 was the last of the *triennium,* the three-year period after which new clergy assignments were made. De Dycker observed that when someone was transferred to another Redemptorist house, his current community was required to provide all the necessities: summer and winter clothing, for both secular and religious use, and "linen goods" (four shirts, four pairs of breeches, six pairs of stockings, and six handkerchiefs). If these were not available when the confrere departed, the house of destination should be financially compensated for them. Nothing more was observed about reassignments. Instead, there were apparently some unstated frictions among the seventeen brothers then in residence. De Dycker alluded to the situation by telling the brothers to "develop mutual charity" and to "work hard at this effort." They were told that "by all means they should avoid hurtful speech, never speaking badly about one another or of their superiors or other confreres."[150]

An admonition from the superior general in Rome, originally issued in a letter dated Good Friday (April 6), 1860, was reiterated in the observations. It is one that later-day historians find most regretful:

> I must admonish those Fathers who have skills with photography, or who have other talents in depicting life-like scenes. This does not seem fitting for religious, much less for sons of St. Alphonsus. We claim to imitate the life and virtues of Our Lord Jesus Christ. Work hard to oppose this abuse with all your efforts and skills and never give it any concession.

This order of 1860 was implicitly directed at Ferreol Girardey, for it was he who has been identified as the "eminent Artist" who took the photographs of the Redemptorists' fleet of sailboats on Spa Creek in the summer of 1864. They are rare photographs of Redemptorists at recreation and of the Annapolis waterfront and skyline. Unusual too are *carte-de-visite* images of Redemptorists during this period, a scarcity attributable to the 1860 admonition. And, although De Dycker did not prohibit the Redemptorists from writing, he invoked the rector major's prohibition against using gold pens "that are so common everywhere."

However, the main thrust of De Dycker's observations was not contentious brothers or shutterbug priests, it was the avoidance of politics. He ordered that the brothers "must never read secular news accounts of the web of politics." Nor should they talk about political matters among themselves. The entire community was reminded that the rector major "has forbidden us from taking sides in this civil war, neither of the Federal or the Confederate cause." Rather, the rector major advised "all to pray that the good God have mercy on his people and that the Lord promotes His glory and the salvation of souls." Moreover, in order to "prevent imprudent conversations and activities, at recreation and meals," all were advised to "refrain from talking about current issues in the Congregation." They also were told they "should not discuss, publicly nor in small groups, the faults of members of other religious communities nor of diocesan priests." This sentiment was clearly in accord with policy of the Archdiocese of Baltimore. Archbishop Spalding wrote in July 1864:

> Non-intervention in political things always was a law to be followed by our priests and Bishops, to which even during our Civil War almost all have strongly adhered: it is a prudent and wise law, and most fitting for our sacred duties and in accord with the most holy canons.[151]

Even more specifically, De Dycker revealed that the rector major "has quietly informed us that confreres are no longer allowed to read the ideas of Brownson." However, he allowed that permission to read Brownson could be given "to some of the more prudent fathers, lest matters treated in these writings be completely unfamiliar in our communities." Special permission could be obtained only from the provincial himself. The reference was to Orestes Augustus Brownson, a prominent convert and outspoken apologist for the Catholic Church during the mid-nineteenth century. Brownson was described by historian George Rable as "a one-time Presbyterian, Universalist, socialist, freethinker, Unitarian, and transcendentalist" who had converted to Catholicism in 1844 and became a conservative defender of law and order and orthodoxy, but remained a reformer within the Catholic tradition. With such attributes working for or against him, Brownson was a thorn in the sides of some of the American bishops and most of the American Catholic press. Even so, Archbishop Kenrick had once attempted to shield Brownson from the wrath of the American hierarchy. But when Kenrick wrote his *Vindication of the Catholic Church* in 1855, he too was critical of Brownson. He pointedly reiterated his opposition and that of the other bishops to "views [Brownson] might afterwards entertain" that might cast doubt on the loyalty of American citizens to their government. Kenrick was convinced, or at least said he was, that Brownson did not mean what he said about the suspected political alliance of American Catholics to the pope during the height of Know Nothing hysteria. Then, during the 1860 presidential campaign, Brownson warned Catholics in his *Brownson's Quarterly Review* to avoid party politics, which weakened their influence in a democracy where voters were expected to make up their own minds on public issues. After the war began in 1861, Brownson declared that both the Union and slavery could not be preserved and he criticized Catholic newspaper editors for their lukewarm patriotism even as young Catholic men were joining the army. "The South," he wrote, "is more infidel or pagan, and far less Christian than the north, and is and always has been . . . far more anti-Catholic."[152]

In 1862 Brownson endorsed emancipation—a radical concept among conservative Catholics—even though by then some of the Northern hierarchy (but not pro-South Martin Spalding) were also beginning to accept the proposition.153 It is no wonder De Dycker counseled his Annapolis confreres about Brownson. Perhaps they needed no such counsel. Father Van de Braak had complained several years earlier to Archbishop Kenrick, that:

> I have just finished the reading of Brownson's last number, Dear Archbishop I cannot help asking you: shall the ecclesiastical authorities remain silent in regard to Brownson's theological opinions or rather heresies???[154]

In his reply, Kenrick agreed with Van de Braak about Brownson's errors and regretted that others had not rebutted them.[155]

Unfortunate Incidents

Carrying a sidearm may have saved parishioner the life of Dr. John Randolph Walton. He and his wife, Margaret, lived on his father's Spa Road farm. On October 4, 1864, he discovered soldiers from nearby Camp Parole in the barn. When he ordered them to leave, one of the soldiers, who was drunk, attacked Walton with a knife, stabbing him in the breast. Margaret Walton suffered a severe slash on her hand during the sudden attack. Walton then drew his revolver and shot the miscreant, who was taken away by his comrades and placed under arrest at Camp Parole. The soldier died, however, and Walton was charged with manslaughter and tried in 1865 (see Other St. Mary's Parishioners in Court, ch. 7).[156]

Another parishioner who ran afoul of the law was Irishman William Mullavel, a West Street bowling and oyster saloon proprietor. His saloon was shut down by the provost marshal for selling liquor to enlisted soldiers and his liquor stock, worth $200, was emptied in the street, 200 cigars were confiscated, and he was fined fifty dollars. He was allowed to reopen only "with the understanding that he is not to sell intoxicating liquor of any kind without permission from the Provost Marshal." Next he appeared in Circuit Court during the October 1864 term for running a bawdy house. State's Attorney James Revell prosecuted Mullavel and another man and they would have been fined $150 each but both men were discharged, evidently for lack of evidence. Mullavel was confirmed at St. Mary's two months later by Archbishop Spalding. He sold his business the next year and left Annapolis. He may have been the older brother of John Mullavel, a parishioner who owned a restaurant on State Circle. Like William, John found himself in court (in 1866) on a charge of selling liquor to a minor but was found not guilty. He and his wife Bridget appear several times in St. Mary's records as godparents for infants.[157]

Another parish family also had legal issues in 1864. Parishioner Patrick Connaughton acted as the "next friend"—a legal term for someone representing a minor or incompetent person—in proceedings in Anne Arundel Circuit Court on behalf of eight-year-old Mary Elizabeth Walsh and her six-year-old sister, Anne Teresa, to secure their share of their deceased father's estate. They were the daughters of Irish-born parents: John Thomas Walsh, an Annapolis grocer who died intestate in 1861, and Ellen Elizabeth Fee. The suit was brought against Elizabeth, and her new husband, Martin J. Lannan, on behalf of the two sisters. James Revell was appointed the girls' trustee and given the task of auctioning a lot of ground and frame dwelling house, "now used as a store," located on the northwest side of Tabernacle Street (today the northwest corner of College Avenue and King George Street). A newspaper notice said the property was in "a rapidly improving part of the town, [and] makes a very desirable business stand." The property had been purchased in 1856 by the girls' father and run as a grocery store by their parents. In June 1860, Walsh was assessed $600 for the building, $150 for grocery stocks, and $30 for the family's household furniture. But he must have become ill by then because Ellen alone was noted as the store keeper in the 1860 Federal Census, also conducted in June. A court settlement was made and an auction to sell the Walsh property was held on the premises on September 10, 1864. Ferdinand Freytag brought the property for $1,430. After this settlement, Lannan opened the United States House, a hotel and "first class oyster and dining saloon" on Northeast Street. Ellen's daughters attended St. Mary's School and both were married at St. Mary's, Mary Elizabeth in 1874 and Anne Teresa in 1877.[158]

A highly unusual situation arose sometime before October 11. That was the day Archbishop Spalding responded to a letter from Father Girardey. Girardey's letter has not survived but the gist of the situation emerges from Spalding's letter register, which includes brief synopses of letters sent. Girardey had met a soldier who was under arrest for desertion and threatened with execution. What was unusual is that the soldier claimed he was a priest. If that was true, it was an extraordinary situation since he could have served as a chaplain instead of a soldier. Several authorities on Civil War chaplains say they had never heard of a priest who served as a soldier, nor one who was threatened with execution. Without Girardey's original letter and having no name of the soldier, there is no way to verify the validity of the story and where he might have met the man, in Annapolis or elsewhere. Spalding's response was curt: "[Father Girardey] asked me to intervene but I refused."[159]

Supreme Court Chief Justice Roger Brooke Taney died on October 12, 1864. He was the highest-profile Catholic in the United States, a Marylander, and a divisive figure before and long after his death because his authorship of the Dred Scott decision. Taney was a slave owner who had freed his slaves and treated Black people as equals in church matters. But the Supreme Court ruling declared that Black people, whether slave or free, had "no rights which the White man was found to respect," meaning had they had no claim to US citizenship nor the ability to sue in Federal courts. Taney's court also ruled that the Missouri Compromise was unconstitutional and that Congress had no right to prohibit slavery in the western Federal territories; citizens there could prohibit slavery only at the moment of admission to statehood and not before, a finding by which "in effect, the court had sanctioned the free spread of slavery." Because he wrote the majority opinion in the seven-to-two Dred Scott decision, Taney was a saint to some and a devil to others. He was a hero to former Maryland Court of Appeals Judge John Thomson Mason, who appeared before the court in Annapolis on October 20 and gave a lengthy tribute to Taney, "a great and good man." No mention was made of Dred Scott amidst Mason's extensive praise of Taney; he noted instead that Taney was the "last of that noble band of Maryland lawyers," and with his burial came the end of an era. In one of the ironies of history, Taney died the same day that Marylanders went to the polls to vote on the new state constitution that would abolish slavery.[160] Taney's demise was a fitting prelude to what happened next in Maryland.

New Constitution, Old Laws, Celebrations

On October 12 and 13, Marylanders went to the polls to vote on whether to adopt or reject the new state constitution, the key provisions of which were the emancipation of slaves and a new public education system. The *Maryland Republican* railed against "the abominable Constitution . . . presented by the late bogus State convention" and encouraged "All who love liberty and freeman's rights" to vote against it. As it turned out Anne Arundel County voters rejected the proposed constitution with 281 in favor and 1,360 against. Most of those in favor lived in Annapolis but even there it was rejected with 161 in favor and 218 opposed. The constitution also was rejected throughout the state with 27,541 in favor and 29,536 against. Only Baltimore city and county and the northern and western counties had clear majorities in favor. However, when absentee soldier ballots were counted, the constitution passed 30,174 to 29,799 and became effective on November 1, 1864. To the joy of those held in bondage, Article 24 of the Declaration of Rights in the new constitution declared that "all persons held to service or labor as slaves are hereby declared free."[161]

Despite emancipation, former enslavers quickly took advantage of an 1860 state law permitting the involuntary apprenticeship of White and free Black males under twenty-one years of age and females under eighteen whose parents allegedly could not care for them or who had failed to appear in court on the day of their children's seizure. Annapolis Provost Marshal Captain George W. Curry protested the illegality of such indentures to the judges of the Anne Arundel Orphans' Court on November 18. But his protest was rejected. Curry forwarded the court's letter of explanation to Colonel Root with his own cover letter stating that the judges "have been binding out colored children to whoever might apply for them (but giving their former owners the preference) against the express wish of their parents and in many cases said parents were entirely ignorant of the fact that their children were apprenticed until they went to get them from their former owners." Curry asked for authority to seek to annul any apprenticeships that had been made since November 1. Root forwarded both letters to General Wallace, commander of the Middle Department. Wallace instructed Curry to "inform the Judge of the Court that it will be for the interest of all parties, court, Masters, and apprentices, if the indenturing is delayed until further notification." The court ignored Wallace's request. Antebellum apprenticeship laws violated the spirit of emancipation but remained in force until they were proscribed retroactively by the Federal Civil Rights Act of April 9, 1866, which provided for the "full and equal benefits of all laws and proceedings for the security persons and property as is enjoyed by white citizens" in accordance with the Thirteenth Amendment of the US Constitution. The 1860 Maryland apprenticeship law itself was declared unconstitutional by Supreme Court Chief Justice Salmon Chase sitting as circuit justice for the District of Maryland on October 13, 1867. But two years before that, the issue would bring two parish families into court as adversaries (see From Conscientious Christian to Convict, ch. 7).[162]

The Baltimore Catholic press read by St. Mary's parishioners had little to say about emancipation but its negative attitude was clear. In a lengthy editorial that appeared four days after emancipation took place, the *Catholic Mirror* hailed past times when the best government was that which allowed "the widest latitude of opinion." It also asserted "that a high degree of virtue can alone prevent the pernicious effects engendered by the spread of unsound doctrines" such as abolition. While not specifically criticizing Maryland's emancipation, the editorial foresaw as a result the rise of future "fanaticism and moral antagonisms" and the "indefinite continuance" of the war. The editors ended by "commending our country to the benignant mercy of heaven."[163]

The 1864 presidential election pitted Abraham Lincoln and Andrew Johnson, a pro-war Democrat, running on the Union Party ticket against the Democrats' George B. McClellan and George Hunt Pendleton. By the time the war began, former American Party members—the Know Nothings—had substituted their animosity toward Catholics and foreigners with fervent devotion to the Union and Lincoln. Main-line Republicans and pro-war Democrats joined together as the Union Party. They had their national convention in Baltimore in June and nominated Lincoln for a second term. Lincoln was pessimistic about his reelection given the numerous battlefront setbacks. However, when Major General William Tecumseh Sherman captured Atlanta in early September, Union Party fortunes improved considerably. When the returns came in on the night of November 8, Lincoln received 55 percent of the popular vote and 91 percent of the electoral votes.[164]

Lincoln won 55 percent of the popular vote in Maryland. Anne Arundel County, however, favored McClellan, giving him 1,574 votes to Lincoln's 416. Statewide, fourteen of Maryland's twenty-two counties—Southern Maryland and the Eastern Shore predominating—supported McClellan but Lincoln carried the state and won its seven electoral votes. Many Maryland Democrats stayed away from the polls because the new state constitution required voters to swear an oath that they had never desired the victory of or gave support to the Confederacy. Locally, "unswerving Unionist" Alexander Randall, brother-in-law of St. Mary's parishioner Eliza Hodges Randall, won the statewide election for attorney general on the Union Party ticket.[165]

Annapolis resident Michael C. Stevens must have been gratified with the local election result but devastated by the state and national totals. When his son was born on September 9, 1864, Michael and his wife, Louisa Chaney Stevens, named him George Brinton McClellan Stevens. Catholic Michael and Methodist Louisa were issued an Anne Arundel County marriage license on April 27, 1864, but, instead their of St. Mary's, their marriage was solemnized by Rev. Elisha D. Owen at the Salem Methodist Church on State Circle. Their son, however, was baptized at St. Mary's on July 30, 1865. Michael had enlisted as a private in Company E, Fortieth New York Infantry, but before his regiment went into its first battle Michael took sick with debilitas. On March 9, 1862, he was transferred to an army hospital in Annapolis, where he was treated for haemoptysis, coughing up blood, a possible indication of consumption. He was well enough to work as a nurse at the hospital and was discharged on August 31. Soon after rejoining his regiment, the Fortieth New York was assigned to guard the Monocacy River bridge near Poolesville, Maryland, and from there it made raids into Virginia while the main army was engaged at the Battle of Antietam. He was with the Fortieth at the battles of Fredericksburg (December 13, 1862), Chancellorsville (April 30–May 6, 1863), and the second day at Gettysburg (July 1–3, 1863). The regiment was involved in "very hot" fighting at Gettysburg Devil's Den and helped secure the strategic Little Round Top. Stevens suffered a gunshot wound to the left arm and was sent to an army hospital in Newark, New Jersey. In March 1864, he was reassigned to the 119th Company, Second Battalion, Veterans Reserve Corps, in Annapolis. He served in this company until he was discharged on June 15, 1864. He remained in Annapolis with his young family after the war.[166]

Michael Stevens died in 1868, at age of thirty, from dropsy according to the St. Mary's interment record. His medical records, however, suggest he suffered from consumption during the war and his widow's pension application gave consumption as his cause of death. The burial interment record indicates he received extreme unction and was buried at St. Mary's Cemetery. He rests there in an unmarked grave. Two months after Michael's death, Louisa applied for a pension, testifying that Michael had been "strong and hearty and in good health" before he joined the army but had contracted consumption while in the service and continued to suffer from it until he died. Louisa's application reveals that he had a previous marriage and two children, John S., born about 1856 and then living in Michigan, and Kate, born about 1858 and then living in Annapolis. Louisa and Michael had a second son together, Charles E., born in 1867. Unlike his brother George, Charles was not baptized at St. Mary's. In 1870 a twelve-year-old Kate Stevens was living with parishioners Henry and Emma Treadway on Duke of Gloucester Street. That same year Kate received her First Holy Communion at St. Mary's. What became of Louisa and Charles has not been discovered. Her pension claim was not approved and, in 1880, her lawyer wrote to the Bureau of Pensions asking them to "please state condition of case and indicate what is necessary to affect settlement." No action was taken and, in 1887, in an attempt to clear the law firm's file, a second inquiry led the bureau to ask the law firm for Louisa's address. The response was "not in U.S." George Brinton McClellan Stevens died in Baltimore in 1928.[167]

On November 11, one hundred cannon shots were fired at Camp Parole in celebration of Lincoln's reelection and the recent battlefield victories. But the local festivities were marred that evening when a teenager was shot to death in Annapolis. City coroner William R. Thompson held an inquest the next day at George Charles O'Malley's Continental Shades public house on Church (Main) Street, "over the body of a youth, aged about fifteen years, named Patrick McHaney of Western Virginia." He was killed accidently by William Fee, of Columbia House, a West Street lodging. The coroner's jury rendered a verdict "that deceased came to his death from the carelessness and accidental discharge of a revolver in the hands of said Wm. Fee, who was subsequently discharged." Patrick McHaney's name has been found in available records only three times. The first time was in the November 14 Baltimore *Sun*, which reported his untimely death. Patrick's body evidently went unclaimed for nearly a month because he was not buried until December 13 in St. Mary's Cemetery. And, when the burial was recorded, only his personal name—Patrick—was entered. It was noted that he was from Virginia, fourteen years old, and had been "shot by accident." His was the last entry in the old interment register. A new register was started and the burial records from 1856 to 1864 were transcribed into a new book. By the time the transcriber reached December 13, 1864, he added Patrick's surname: McHaney. Additional information revealed that Father Freitag conducted the funeral and that Patrick had "Recd the Sacraments." If this notation is accurate, then Patrick may not have died immediately after being shot or his dead body was anointed with the oil used in the rite of extreme unction. There were McHaney families in Virginia during this period but no record of Patrick. He rests today, far from home, in an unmarked grave on West Street.[168]

Another shooting associated with O'Malley's establishment occurred in December 1864. The provost marshal guard found five soldiers from Camp Parole there around midnight, three with expired passes, two without any passes. Instead of proceeding to the guard house as ordered, two ran away. Although warned to stop, they kept running and one was shot in the back by the guard. The wounded man was taken by ambulance to the army hospital where he was expected to recover.[169]

George O'Malley, in whose Continental Shades public house these shootings took place, was a St. Mary's parishioner. He enlisted for two years as a private in Company E, Seventeenth New York Infantry in May 1861. He had health problems, however, and was hospitalized first in Georgetown, DC, in June 1861 and a month later in Annapolis. He was treated for acute rheumatism at General Hospital Division No. 1 until November 1861, when his health improved enough that he was attached to the hospital as a nurse. O'Malley was ordered to return to his regiment in August 1862 but in November 1862 was dropped from the regimental roll, six months before his term of service expired. He thus avoided such horrendous battles as Second Manassas, Fredericksburg, and Chancellorsville. He evidently liked Annapolis and remained, becoming a bar keeper. He married Mary Anne Riordan at St. Vincent de Paul Church in Baltimore on March 31, 1864. In 1865 he served as godparent at St. Mary's for newborn Nicholas Gill, and in 1866 he and Mary Anne had their daughter, Mary Agnes, baptized at St. Mary's.[170]

George O'Malley was engaged in a number of business ventures in Annapolis, first the Continental Shades restaurant until 1866, then he ran another saloon on lower Prince George Street, near the steamboat landing. By 1870 the family had moved to Washington and later to Baltimore. He died in 1894 and Mary Anne died in 1933; both received pensions based on his Civil War service. Their daughter Mary Agnes remained single and worked as a school teacher in Baltimore and died in 1938. All three are buried in New Cathedral Cemetery in Baltimore.[171] The perpetrator of the shooting accident, William Fee, also had Catholic connections. His daughter, Anna Veronica, born in 1871, entered the School Sisters of Notre Dame in 1891 as Sister Mary Theonilla.[172]

Post-election celebrations in Annapolis continued on the evening of November 14. There was a grand illumination and torchlight procession of troops and citizens from the outer end of West Street through the major streets of Annapolis to Market Space. "The ancient capital of Maryland was all life and enthusiasm," wrote the Sun's correspondent. Colonel Root led several hundred officers, attendants, and paroled prisoners into the city "bearing torches and handsome transparencies, and insignias, and the music of the band belonging to Camp Parole." They were joined by officers, hospital patients, a band, and a fire engine decorated with flags and mottoes of its company. The parade also included a boat on wheels drawn by six horses and decorated with flags and torches. The military procession was followed by a "long line" of pro-Union Party citizens and visitors who carried torches and transparencies. Many houses along the route were illuminated and decked with flags. John Walton's City Hotel and other commercial establishments were also well lighted. According to the Redemptorist chronicler, "Great was the rejoicing among the soldiers and Republicans, and many of the houses here also were illuminated; we were invited by the military authorities to do the same." By order of the provincial, St. Mary's College was illuminated.[173]

Many Useful Improvements

At the end of 1864, the *Chronica Domus* reported that "many improvements were made this year in our house & garden." They included painting the house chapel, for which a new altar also was built. The altar was probably constructed by Brother Matthias (Charles) Stabel, the infirmarian and house carpenter, and painted by Brother Hilary, who was noted as having arrived from Cumberland on October 3. A quick worker, Hilary remained in Annapolis only until December 15 when he set out for Baltimore.[174]

Other improvements "were made in the garden &c." These included digging a new well and building a new cistern "for the purpose of doing away with the multitude of barrels in the Wash house." It was noted that "in making this cistern, cement alone was used." This cistern presumably is the one partially excavated by archaeologists in 1990. That cistern is made of brick, parged with Portland cement, and located a few feet north of the former frame Carroll House. The location of the cistern makes it likely that water entering it was collected from gutters and downspouts on the brick Carroll House and the college building and that it supplemented the cistern constructed in 1863.[175]

Another project was building a burial vault under the church sacristy, to which "the corpses of our deceased confratres were removed thither." An 1855 ordinance forbade burials within the city limits except at the Public Burial Ground (also known as Locust Grove Cemetery and City Cemetery, adjacent to St. Anne's Cemetery). Because Father Müller wanted to bury his deceased confreres according to Redemptorist practice, he petitioned the City Council in 1861, asking that he be allowed to build a vault on St. Mary's premises. To do this, the council repealed the 1855 ordinance and reenacted it with a special provision allowing the Redemptorists to build and use a burial vault beneath the church. It took three more years before construction started.[176]

The need for bricks, evidently for the new vault, was raised in a letter written in April 1864 by Father Gross to Howes Goldsborough. He noted "the exorbitant height of $20. pr thousand" for bricks in Annapolis and "$14. in Balto. independent of transportation," and inquired about the cost of 12,000 bricks manufactured in Easton and shipped by schooner to be "discharge[d] at the wharf on our own grounds and thus save cartage."[177] It is not known if the bricks were acquired from Easton, but the vault was built. The space, no longer used for interments, measures eight feet by seventeen feet and has a barrel-vaulted ceiling.

Six seminarians had died at St. Mary's since the Redemptorists arrived in 1853. The first to die, in October 1854, was candidate novice Patrick Kean, who was buried "near the house." This is taken to mean he was interred in the parish burial ground behind the old church on Duke of Gloucester Street.[178]

The second death was that of a recently professed student, George Reichert in December 1855. The *Chronica Domus* says his "body was taken to a location outside the city for burial, since it was no longer allowed to bury inside the city." His childhood friend, Father Ferreol Girardey, writing in 1891, said Reichert was "buried in the Catholic Cemetery at Annapolis." St. Mary's interment records are extant only from 1856 onward but a letter written in Annapolis in June 1856 by Father George Deshon to Father Ruland, states that Reichert was interred in the Carroll family burial ground four miles outside of Annapolis. St. Mary's Cemetery on West Street was not formally established until 1858 so the Carroll burial ground was the only Catholic option.[179]

The third man to die, in January 1858, was candidate novice Peter Damian Straub. The records note only that he was buried but not where.[180]

The remains of Kean, Reichert, and Straub were "were dug up from the cemetery" on November 26, 1864. On December 1, three more bodies were exhumed: James Harvey, who died in November 1861, Joseph Kammer, who died in January 1863, and Herman Krastel, who died in February 1863. No mention was made of where Harvey was buried but the fact that his body was exhumed the same day as Kammer and Krastel, argues for a site in common with the other two. According to the *Chronica Domus*, Kammer was buried "in the garden near the church" and Krastel "was buried next to Frater Kammer." The "garden near the church" could have been the former burial ground on Duke of Gloucester Street or another location on the parish property. With Harvey's burial, the Redemptorists either ignored the city ordinance prohibiting in-town burials or received permission to do so pending construction of the planned vault. The six sets of remains were placed in the new vault on December 1, 1864. Four of the men (Kean, Reichert, Straub, and Krastel) died from consumption; the other two (Harvey and Kammer) passed away from unspecified but lingering illnesses that also may have been consumption.[181]

Kindness and Charity

Feeding the large Redemptorist family was an ongoing concern for the rector. Although some crops were grown on the parish property, they were insufficient. Having just received fifty barrels of potatoes at high cost from Baltimore, Father Helmprächt called upon the "kindness & charity" of Howes Goldsborough in Easton. As autumn set in, he asked Goldsborough to provide "thirty barrels of Winter-apples, which keep long, & of three barrels of sweet potatoes." Another time Helmprächt wrote to Goldsborough advising him that there were "12 barrels on the wharf for the apples" and "the barrels must be sent several times" filled with apples for St. Mary's. Moreover, Helmprächt instructed Tommy, a man who served as a messenger between the Redemptorists and Goldsborough, to be on the lookout on the Eastern Shore for 400 head of cabbage (for sauerkraut?), three or four barrels of sweet potatoes, three barrels of sweet turnips, fifty barrels of "Main" potatoes, and other staples. He also wanted the apples shipped in bags instead of barrels and sent a barrel from Annapolis containing twenty-six bags. Helmprächt also revealed what appears to have been a sideline industry at the college, presumably carried on by one or more of the lay brothers. He wrote to Goldsborough that the barrels he had sent "don't cost me any thing; I even sell barrels." As winter approached, Helmprächt received a shipment of apples from Easton, not in bags but in bushels, thirty of them. He thanked Goldsborough but said he wanted fifty to sixty more bushels, "for I like to have apples for my young people up to May & June." He also asked for one or two more bags of sweet potatoes and two or three barrels of kohlrabi, a term he said Goldsborough's farmer, Frank Dietz—a German Catholic immigrant known for his "honesty and good morals"—would understand. The next year, Goldsborough provided the Redemptorist community with a very welcomed gift of shad.[182]

A Second Confederate Invasion

The Annapolis Redemptorists welcomed an unusual visitor to their midst on December 6, 1864: Father James B. Sheeran, C.Ss.R. He was born in County Longford, Ireland, in 1817 and had been married with children. His wife Margaret died in 1849 and Sheeran gradually discovered his late-in-life vocation as a teacher at and school master of the Redemptorist-run St. Mary of the Immaculate Conception parish in Monroe, Michigan. He also became a staunch defender of Catholic education during the Know Nothing era. His son Sylvester had died in infancy in 1846. In time two other children were old enough to live apart from their widowed father. Sheeran provided for daughter Isabella to join the Immaculate Heart of Mary sisters in Monroe and son John to live with a teacher at the parish school. Both later entered religious life, Isabella as an Immaculate Heart of Mary novice and John in an unknown capacity with the Benedictines at St. Vincent Abbey in Pennsylvania. Their father rejected suggestions of remarriage as he increasingly developed an attraction to the religious life, mainly through the influence of his spiritual advisor, Aegidius Smulders, the Redemptorist rector in Monroe. Sheeran sold his property to provide for the financial support and education of his children and began "living in the happiness of poverty." He became a Redemptorist novice in 1855 in Annapolis, where he professed his vows in 1856. He studied under Michael Müller in Cumberland, was ordained in Baltimore in 1858, and was ministering at St. Mary of the Assumption Parish in New Orleans when the Civil War began.[183]

When Sheeran returned to Annapolis in December 1864, it was as chaplain of the Confederates' Fourteenth Louisiana Infantry Regiment. His work with the troops had placed him at or near most of the major battles and many minor skirmishes in Virginia, Maryland, and Pennsylvania between 1861 and 1864, including the invasions of Maryland in 1862, 1863, and 1864. In the fall of 1864, he witnessed the Confederate defeat in the Shenandoah Valley and became a prisoner of war. Sheeran kept a detailed journal of his wartime experiences that reveals his strong Southern sympathies and frank assessments of "Lincoln's bandits," the "Abolition Robbers" who made up the Union army, and the New England "religious fanatics and political demagogues" who had "shattered forever" the Union he had loved.[184]

Sheeran's spiritual advisor, Father Smulders, also served as a Confederate chaplain, with the Eighteenth Louisiana Infantry Regiment. Father Seelos alluded to Sheeran and Smulders in a letter he wrote in 1862 to his family in Bavaria:

> Two of our fathers are field chaplains in the Southern army. They were stationed in New Orleans and accompany the Catholic soldiers. These too, up until now, have had nothing to suffer and are esteemed and respected by all, and have helped many a dying soldier get into heaven. One of them blessed all the flags of the Southern army and probably at his suggestion the generals put the cross in the flag. Only our loving God knows how he can use this temporal evil for the genuine good of the country.[185]

After the Confederate defeat at the Third Battle of Winchester (September 19, 1864), Sheeran requested permission to cross enemy lines to render aid to wounded Confederates who had been taken prisoner during the battle. He was granted passes for himself and his horse on September 25 by Union Sixth Army Corps Commander Major General Horatio Gouverneur Wright, and spent the next four weeks among the wounded, sick, and dying, hearing confessions, celebrating Mass, and performing last rites, for both Confederate and Union soldiers. During this time, Sheeran wrote to Father De Dycker in Baltimore asking him for "some Greenbacks." Because Father Müller at the Cumberland novitiate was the closest Redemptorist to Winchester, De Dycker asked him to deliver $100 to Sheeran for traveling expenses. Müller found his confrere on October 22 at the home of an Episcopal minister in Winchester. Müller was the first Redemptorist, other than Smulders, he had seen in three years. Returning together to Sheeran's lodging, Müller passed on the provincial's advice "to take the Yankee Oath," a proposition that Sheeran "rejected with much warmth." He was willing to obey De Dycker's "wish" that he return to New Orleans but said that he "must first in an honorable manner, relieve [him]self of the obligation to the Confederate Army or Government." Müller apparently accepted this approach, although Sheeran believed that Müller did not really expect him to follow the provincial's advice nor immediately return to New Orleans.

The next day, after celebrating Sunday Mass together, Müller proposed that Sheeran go with him to Cumberland for a few days. When they went to the Union headquarters to request a pass the post adjutant, Captain James William Latta, refused to issue one on a Sunday. He also rejected Sheeran's service to wounded Union soldiers as reason to be allowed to move about freely and said Sheeran, as a Confederate officer, had no right to travel where he wished. Müller asked the officer, as a favor, to grant the pass but was rebuffed by the "Yankee upstart." When Sheeran showed him Wright's pass he was told it was "insufficient" and that only the commander of the Army of the Shenandoah, Major General Philip Henry Sheridan, could issue him a pass. When Müller "again begged" for a pass, Sheeran angrily interrupted, declaring he wanted no favor from Latta. Müller departed for Cumberland and Sheeran returned to his boarding house, "reflecting on the impertinent ingratitude of a Yankee in officer's uniform."[186]

More friendly Union officers advised Sheeran to obtain a pass from Sheridan to return South. On October 29, he presented himself at Sheridan's Winchester headquarters. presumably with expectation of success. He had been ministering to both Union and Confederate Catholic troops, as well as to the local civilian population. Morever, Sheridan was Catholic, although deemed by historians as "religiously lax." Thinking he would meet with a lower ranking officer, Sheeran unexpectedly was received by Sheridan himself. The general "answered me very roughly," telling him to go see Captain Latta, "at the same time closing the door in my face." It is no wonder Sheeran decided to wait until the following Monday. When he returned on October 31, he met with Latta who, after conferring briefly with "the Brute Sheridan," returned with an armed guard who took Sheeran to the provost marshal's office. Whether through Sheridan's willful act or the prejudice of his staff Latta called Sheeran "a d – – d old Catholic Priest"—not only was the pass denied but Sheeran was arrested and jailed without specific charges. On November 1, Sheeran wrote a lengthy letter to Sheridan with the hope that a direct appeal would help. It did not.[187]

After four days of imprisonment in Winchester, Sheeran and numerous local civilians who had been arrested were taken by train to Martinsburg for another four days, and then on to Baltimore, arriving there on November 8. Sheeran reminisced in his journal about his days in Martinsburg, observing the contrast of the war-ravaged town with the "scenes of peaceful industry" he had seen on his way from Annapolis to Cumberland in 1856. He noted his own changed circumstances: from being a religious order member who had "quit the world" to becoming a chaplain "in obedience to [his] superiors" and now was a prisoner. Once in Baltimore, he hoped he would be paroled and allowed to go to St. Alphonsus Church overnight. Instead he and some eighty others were incarcerated in an old slave pen near the Baltimore inner harbor before being moved on November 11 to a former cavalry stable at Fort McHenry.[188]

When he had arrived in Winchester in September, Sheeran sent the first of three letters to an old correspondent, James Alphonsus McMaster, former Redemptorist novice and editor of the anti-Republican and anti-war weekly, the *New-York Freeman's Journal and Catholic Register.* McMaster referred to the first letter, written before Sheeran's imprisonment, in an article published on November 19. McMaster praised Sheeran's work in Michigan and noted that after crossing the Union lines at Winchester he had been "diligently engaged in affording spiritual consolations, and administering the Sacraments, to the sick and wounded of both the Confederate and Federal Armies." Sheeran's second letter from Winchester and a third letter from Fort McHenry were discussed at length in the same article. McMaster wrote that he was "shocked and grieved" to learn that Sheeran had been arrested and "treated with gross indignity." The article addressed the details of his arrest and provided the text of the Sheeran's November 1 correspondence with Sheridan. McMaster condemned Sheridan's treatment of Sheeran as "an outrage on the laws of war" and "an outrage on common decency" and demanded that the general "make reparation to God and man" for the treatment of "the devoted Redemptorist chaplain [who] gladly perilled [*sic*] his life, to speak faith, and hope, and love of God, to the dying—on either side." The Annapolis Redemptorists and several parish families subscribed to the *Freeman's Journal* and would have read about Sheeran's situation. McMaster's article also quickly drew the attention of the War Department.[189]

In the meantime, the ever-resourceful Father Müller sought to free Sheeran. Because not all letters from prison made it to their intended recipients, Müller sent word to Sheeran to use an "underground railroad" for correspondence. During his incarceration at Fort McHenry, Sheeran wrote his third letter to McMaster as well as letters to Father De Dycker and Secretary of War Stanton, protesting his arrest as illegal and unjust. On November 17, he was informed that he could be released if he took an oath of allegiance to the United States. He refused and after more two weeks of horrendous jail conditions, Sheeran became ill and more cantankerous. In the meantime, Müller was shuttling between Washington, Baltimore, and Annapolis seeking Sheeran's release. But, he informed Sheeran via an underground railroad letter on November 22, that the letters to the *Freeman's Journal* had "spoiled everything" and angered Stanton who continued to deny his release. Unknown to Sheeran and perhaps to Stanton, was that as of November 20, Sheridan had ordered Sheeran's release and even said he "was sorry that he should have received bad treatment, it was not intended by me."[190]

Sheeran wrote again to Stanton on November 28 to plead his case and to De Dycker hoping that if he could be released for just one day on parole he could "arrange my spiritual matters, and then submit with patience to my lingering martyrdom, or I should say, my slow murder." Sheridan's release order was received at Fort McHenry on December 4. Sheeran again refused to take an oath of allegiance but agreed to "not to give any military information to the enemy." This was not a problem for Sheeran since his enemy was the Union army and he was not about to divulge anything to them. Parole was granted and the next morning he was released. He went to St. Michael's, the nearest Redemptorist church, where he was effusively greeted by Father Henry Giesen and others. After rest and refreshment, he and Giesen walked to the provincial house at St. Alphonsus. De Dycker greeted Sheeran kindly but rather too quickly admonished him to "be prudent be cautious etc." and not to go out visiting. This "ruffled my feelings some," wrote Sheeran, for he intended to visit Archbishop Spalding and a few others, which he did the same day, to thank them for their efforts to help him while in prison.[191]

Sheeran returned to St. Michael's that evening to find Müller there. The latter was passing through on his way to Washington, still seeking Sheeran's release. "Of course he was agreeably disappointed, in seeing me at liberty" remarked the former prisoner. The two stayed overnight at St. Michael's and the next afternoon, December 6, with De Dycker's permission and a new set of clothes, Sheeran and Müller set out by train for Annapolis. His reception there, wrote Sheeran:

> . . . was a warm one, and my mind wandered rapidly back to the days of my novitiate and studies; for I found here many of my fellow novices and students. I was sorry I could not answer at length all the questions about battles etc. I found myself both sick and tired, and consequently made an early bed time.[192]

The *Chronica Domus* noted Sheeran's arrival on December 6, saying he had just been released from prison and "has filled all with great joy: he told us many things he experienced in his service to the Confederate soldiers." The next day Sheeran celebrated Mass for the first time in six weeks. He spent the rest of the day with the students who were preparing for the arrival that evening of Archbishop Spalding on his first visit to Annapolis and for the patronal day of St. Mary's—the feast of the Immaculate Conception—on December 8. Spalding, accompanied by De Dycker, arrived the evening of December 7 and gave a lecture in the church on "The True Church" to a large audience, "especially Protestants." A banquet with the Redemptorist community followed. As a friendly gesture of welcome, Dr. Vanderkieft sent the hospital band to St. Mary's to "serenade" Spalding. The archbishop thanked the band members in a short speech and "told them to save their souls."[193]

The next morning, Spalding administered confirmation to thirty-seven persons. Among the confirmands were three soldiers. One was thirty-six-year-old Private Patrick Gavin, Company K, Second Massachusetts Cavalry, who had been wounded at Charlestown, Virginia, on August 27, 1864, taken prisoner, and then paroled and sent to Annapolis for medical treatment. Another was eighteen-year-old Private Terence Keenan, Company F, Seventy-Fifth New York Infantry, who had been wounded and taken prisoner at the Third Battle of Winchester, paroled, and sent to Annapolis where he was admitted to General Hospital Division No. 1. The third was Patrick Dougherty, about whom more will be said later (see More Military Marriages, ch. 7).[194]

After the Confirmation Mass, Spalding delivered a sermon on devotion to the Blessed Virgin Mary. A dinner honoring the archbishop was held at noon. The seminarians had festooned the refectory and, when the guest of honor arrived, they offered him greetings in eight languages to which he responded in all but two.[195]

Among the guests at the noon dinner were Colonel Adrian Root and his adjutant, First Lieutenant John S. Wharton.

According to Sheeran's account, Spalding and De Dycker sat at the head of the table. "Next came Col. Root, the Yankee commander of the post." Sheeran was furious.

> I deem it my duty to make some remarks about this Yankee scoundrel, who I considered disgraced our refectory on this solemn and otherwise happy occasion. He was a Col. commanding a large regiment at the battle of Gettysburg. He and his whole regiment were captured by our boys in that memorable battle . . . . Every officer and many of the five thousand [captured] pledged their word and sacred honor (but it was Yankee honor) that in case Lincoln would not acknowledge their parole they would return to our lines and give themselves up . . . . Col. Root was one of the officers who made this solemn promise. But the unprincipled creature never fulfilled his promise, for he soon accepted active service under the Yankee government as a commander of Annapolis.[196]

Here Sheeran wandered into a controversial area. Root ostensibly had not honored his parole agreement. The Lincoln administration early on held that since secession was illegal there could be no negotiations with those in rebellion, even when it meant men who had been captured could be paroled on their honor to return to their side and not bear arms again until formally exchanged for prisoners of like rank. Public opinion both North and South favored the parole system so sons, brothers, and husbands could return home. Both sides eventually agreed on a prisoner exchange system that worked well until 1863 when the Confederates threatened to treat captured US Colored Troops as slaves and to execute their White officers. The Federal government retaliated by temporarily halting the exchange system.[197]

But Sheeran had another problem with Root. "This contemptible creature," he wrote, "affected to have great regard for the Catholic religion; and even was under instructions to become a Catholic." He went on to explain that he asked the priest who had been instructing Root:

> . . . how he could receive such a creature into the church; whilst he was daily violating his pledged faith and honor; and in the eyes of the military men and gentlemen, committing an act more disgraceful than even perjury. I could get no satisfactory answer to this question. As a matter of policy it was thought prudent to invite him to dinner to day.[198]

Sheeran devoted three handwritten pages of his diary complaining about Root, including his chastisement of the unidentified Redemptorist who was instructing Root. Sheeran compared Root with the men who had treated him in prison "in a most sacrilegious and barbarous manner, indeed almost murdered [me], and here now I see this specimen of perjured faith sitting at our festive board, I must confess I felt indignant, and shared very little in the festive rejoicing." When the nearly two-hour dinner ended, "the Yankee scamp and the thing in uniform called his Adjutant, retired, relieving me, somewhat, of his objectionable presence, and leaving me at liberty to spend a few pleasant hours with the students."[199]

Sheeran should not have worried about the Yankee scamp becoming a co-religionist. If Root was indeed being instructed in the Catholic faith in Annapolis the effort failed. After the war, Root returned to his native Buffalo, New York, where he was an active parishioner, trustee, and choir director of the First Presbyterian Church. When he died in 1899, his funeral service was conducted by the pastor of the same church, of which the newspaper reported Root "was a lifelong member."[200]

Spalding, De Dycker, Müller, and Sheeran left for Baltimore late on the afternoon of December 8. Spalding said he was delighted with his visit to Annapolis. His journal entry reads:

> I have visited the church and the College of the Redemptorist Fathers at Annapolis, where I had a very splendid reception, with allocutions directed to me in nine [*sic*] tongues. There were 46 students there, who gave a good hope that they would become fine priests, God willing. Many among the people here are found who have been already come to the Holy Faith, and many others who are diligently inquiring. I gave a lecture to the people on the Church of Christ at Vespers on the 7th, and a sermon after Solemn Mass and Confirmation on the day of the Feast. Musicians from the Navy Yard were present, of their own accord, and serenaded me.[201]

Sheeran and Müller returned to St. Michael's on the evening of December 8. Sheeran departed the next day for Cumberland, where he stayed as Müller's guest until December 19, and then proceeded to Winchester, where he had two more contentious meetings with Sheridan. The general finally relented and allowed Sheeran to pass through his lines to Confederate-controlled territory, which he did on January 3, 1865, reaching Richmond on the tenth. He wrote to McMaster that Sheridan was "neither a Christian nor a gentleman" and had only let him return south because Sheeran "threatened to expose him again." Sheeran stayed in Richmond with the Sisters of Charity until April 1865, during which time he witnessed the fall of the capital and the demise of the Confederacy. Anxious to return to New Orleans, he went by railroad to Philadelphia, where he stayed two days with the Redemptorists of St. Peter's Church. They noted in their house annals that Sheeran was "almost broken down." He started for New Orleans on May 7 by steamship from New York City. The next year, he was reassigned to St. Alphonsus Parish in New York City but he soon requested to be released from his Redemptorist vows and, in 1871, he became a diocesan priest and pastor of St. Mary's Church in Morristown, New Jersey. He died there in 1881.[202]

The Sad Case of Rosa Morsell

Anna Rosa Ford Morsell experienced joy and great sadness during the Civil War. She moved to Annapolis with her young family in 1861, had a new baby born and two sons baptized at St. Mary's, and saw her husband promoted in military rank.

But she was crushed by the death of a son and then of her husband. Rosa, as she was known, was born in Carlisle, Pennsylvania, about 1835, and grew up in the District of Columbia, where her father, Stephen Calvert Ford, was a clerk in the War Department and later in the Interior Department. She attended the Academy of the Visitation of the Blessed Virgin Mary in Georgetown, where she had a very commendable academic record, having received premiums in orthography, reading, history, geography, Christian doctrine, grammar, rhetoric, prose competition, arithmetic, plain and ornamental writing, and plain sewing, all in her first year (1844–45). At the end of that academic year, President James Knox Polk was present at the ceremony at which Archbishop Samuel Eccleston distributed awards to Rosa and other outstanding students. In her final year (1851) at Visitation Academy, Rosa received the highest award, the academic crown and gold medal.[203]

Rosa Ford married Richard Albert Morsell at St. Matthew's Catholic Church in Washington on April 29, 1854. He was a native of Prince George's County, Maryland, and grew up in the District of Columbia where his father, Benjamin, was a police magistrate. Morsell entered the Revenue Marine Service, the predecessor of the US Coast Guard, in 1852 as an acting third lieutenant. By 1854 he was a third lieutenant assigned to revenue cutters patrolling Chesapeake Bay and its tributaries. In the early years of their marriage, the couple lived on a farm near Hyattsville in Prince George's County, where their sons Albert and Thomas Kent were born in 1857 and 1861, respectively. Thomas was baptized by Father Francis Xavier Boyle of St. Peter's Church in Washington in January 1861, probably in urgency at the family home because of danger of death at birth. He was baptized a second time at St. Mary's in Annapolis in September by Father Joseph Jacobs. The ceremonial christening marks the family's move to Annapolis. The godmother at Thomas' Annapolis baptism was Alida McParlin, who served as the proxy in place of the canonical godmother, Sarah Cantatora, a District of Columbia resident and possibly one of Rosa's Visitation schoolmates.[204]

Rosa's first sadness came in 1862. The following note appears in an affidavit provided in 1898 by Harriet R. Johnson, an African American parishioner of St. Mary's:

> Albert L. H. Morsell, eldest child of Captain Richard A. and Rosa F. Morsell died in my house in Annapolis Md. near midnight August 19th 1862. I was by his bedside and closed his eyes, he was 5 years of age.[205]

Albert's death went unrecorded, as had many others at St. Mary's in 1862. When Father De Dycker inspected St. Mary's interment register in December that year, he discovered that only two names of parishioners who had died during 1862 had been recorded. His signed notation in the register reads: "*Defuncti omnes non fuerunt inscripti, qui desunt ad huc inscribendi sunt. Annapoli, die 29 Dec. 1862* (All the deceased who have not been listed need to be inscribed here. Dec. 29, 1862). Despite the directness of this order, it was not carried out. Although there may have been a funeral at St. Mary's that went unrecorded, little Albert was buried in Mount Olivet Cemetery in Washington.[206]

At the time of Albert's death, Rosa was pregnant with her third child and Richard had been assigned to the Revenue Marine Schooner *Philip Allen*, stationed at Baltimore. The *Philip Allen* patrolled the upper Chesapeake Bay under the command of Captain Thomas Sands, an Annapolis native and veteran Revenue Marine Service member since 1833. Sands provides another St. Mary's connection. His three-story brick home still stands on the corner of Duke of Gloucester and Green streets, diagonally across from the first St. Mary's Church. His daughter, Laura Virginia Sands, had been a member of St. Anne's Episcopal Church until she converted to Catholicism at age twenty-nine in 1858. She donated money toward the new church bells in 1859 and served several times as godmother at St. Mary's. One of those times was for Rosa's third son Raymond Percy Morsell. He was born on July 9, 1863, and baptized at St. Mary's seven days later by Father Van de Braak. The baptismal register entry noted correctly that the baby's father was not a Catholic but stated erroneously that he was "an officer in the U.S. Navy," perhaps an easy mistake for the Dutch priest to make.[207]

Lieutenant Morsell was promoted to captain in July 1864 and given command of the Revenue Marine Cutter *Bronx*, assigned to patrol New York Harbor. He was transferred in November to a newly commissioned steam-powered cutter, the seven-gun *Kankakee*, berthed at Hoboken, New Jersey. Although the Revenue Marine Service was organizationally part of the Department of the Treasury, it was considered to be part of the national military force. Established to monitor United States export/import revenues, the service could, "at the pleasure of the President, be accounted as part of the navy." During the Civil War, Lincoln ordered the Revenue Marine Service to cooperate with naval operations.[208]

Rosa received a letter from Richard on December 22, saying he was under Navy orders to take the *Kankakee* to a destination he was not at liberty to divulge. On the evening of December 23, Morsell and his second in command, First Lieutenant William Briggs, reported to the Brooklyn Navy Yard to receive orders to sail immediately in support of a convoy of ships carrying cotton from recently captured Savannah, Georgia, back to the North. After receiving his orders and returning to the wharf at Hoboken, Morsell signaled a boat to take himself and Briggs back to the *Kankakee*. The boat pulled up to a tarpaulin-covered lighter that was moored to the wharf. Unfortunately, when Morsell jumped from the wharf to the lighter, it tipped and he slipped on the icy tarpaulin and fell into the frigid water. One account reported that he drowned; another said he was rescued after twenty minutes but died from hypothermia. Rosa, still in Annapolis, was informed of his death by "a letter of condolence" the next day from Briggs, who had pulled her husband from the water. The *New York Herald* reported that Morsell had been "a pride and ornament to the service." His funeral was held three days after Christmas in Washington, with burial at Congressional Cemetery.[209]

Rosa returned to Washington after the war but her tribulations continued. In 1873 a special act of Congress was introduced to provide her a pension based on her husband's service and untimely death. A bill passed in the House of Representatives but, because of the unwillingness of the Senate Committee on Pensions to grant pensions to Revenue Marine Service personnel, it was "reported adversely" and indefinitely postponed.[210]

Rosa tried again in 1897 but her application to the Bureau of Pensions was denied because "the records of the Navy and Treasury Departments do not show whether the United States Revenue Cutter '*Kankakee*' was cooperating with the United States Navy at the time the Officer, Richard A. Morsell, lost his life." This was despite an 1897 letter from the Treasury Department to the Interior Department (the parent organization of the Bureau of Pensions) that stated that Lincoln had ordered the Revenue Service vessels on which Morsell served to "co-operate with the Navy from June 14, 1863, to the close of the war." The tragedy of war was followed those many years later by this unjust decision by the bureaucracy.[211]

Rosa's sons attended Georgetown College. Thomas became a printer and died of consumption in Washington in 1886. Raymond joined the Navy for three years in 1880 and later became a contractor in New York City. His first child was born in 1892 and named Rosa Ford Morsell, after her grandmother. Rosa Morsell died in Washington in 1907. A Requiem Mass was celebrated at St. Paul's Catholic Church followed by a private interment at Mount Olivet Cemetery, where her sons Albert and Thomas also are buried.[212]

Year-End Illnesses and Great Preparations

Despite the illnesses described above, notes on the last page of the *Chronica Domus* for 1864 declared that "there were very few sick this year in the house, thanks to divine Protection." However, it was revealed that Father Peter Petit "was several times very sick during the year & not able to say mass." It also noted that Frater Henry Wüller, a dogmatic theology student, had become sick in the latter months of the year, adding ominously that he "was obliged to remain in the infirmary: his lungs are probably affected." Among the notes for Christmas Day, the house annals revealed that Father Dielemans "was a very sick person for the last two weeks of this year; but his health has improved: the greatest thanks to the Infant Jesus and his mother Mary."[213]

The *Sun* reported that "great preparations" were being made "to spend Christmas day in a becoming manner" at St. Mary's Church. Both it and St. Anne's were "handsomely festooned and decorated for the occasion." All secular business generally was suspended for the day, which was Sunday, and divine services were held at all of the Annapolis churches. St. Mary's chronicler reported that the Feast of the Nativity was celebrated "with great solemnity." After the Midnight Mass, the members of the Redemptorist community renewed their religious vows. Sometime before Christmas, the chronicler reported, that "a beautiful wax figure of the Infant Jesus was bought for the church."[214]

In the fall of 1864, parishioner Martin Revell went into business for himself, forming a partnership to run a general store. Martin's friend and future wife, Susanna Sands, wrote to a cousin toward the end of the year about local conditions. She lamented that "you would scarcely know the 'Ancient City' now, it has changed so, even the people have changed."[215]

As 1864 drew to a close, the Federal government needed to augment the army. The president issued a call on December 10 for 300,000 volunteers, threatening another draft if the quota was not met. Eight days later, a new draft was ordered and was unwelcome news for the Annapolis Redemptorists. During 1864 St. Mary's recorded fifty baptisms, married nine couples, achieved twenty converts, had twenty-three deaths, distributed 2,650 communions, and had thirty-five students in the parish school.[216]

Chapter 7: 1865 — He Was in a Theater on Good Friday Evening

Her Child Since Deceased

Thursday, January 5, 1865, was a big day in the very short life of Maria Willetta Young. It was the day Father Ferreol Girardey christened her at St. Mary's. The baptism might not have happened at all but for a decision made by her mother or godmother. According to a note in the baptismal register, Maria Willetta's mother had fallen away from the Catholic faith. But now, for the sake of the newborn child, she decided to have the newborn baptized as a Catholic. Born on December 17, 1864, Maria Willetta was the daughter of William Young, an Annapolis shoemaker, and Elizabeth Ann (Eliza) Cornea. They were married in Annapolis by Reverend John H. Ryland, the pastor of Salem Methodist Church, on July 27, 1862, when William was twenty-two and Eliza about eighteen. In mid-July 1862, Governor Bradford announced that Maryland was "still menaced with invasion" and needed four more volunteer infantry regiments. Perhaps assuming he would be conscripted anyway, William enlisted for three years as a private in Company A, First Maryland Infantry Regiment, two weeks after the wedding and just before the Anne Arundel County draft enrollment began. Bradford's announcement likely hastened William and Eliza's wedding.[1]

William Young answered the call and went off to Baltimore to join the war effort. When he enlisted in the First Maryland Infantry, part of the Eighth Army Corps, was responsible for the defense of Baltimore. However, the day after the Battle of Antietam on September 17, the regiment was rushed to Sharpsburg and remained there to defend the upper Potomac River. During this time, William was detached to work as a teamster at First Division headquarters. In July 1863, the regiment was reassigned from the Middle Department to the Army of the Potomac, and became part of the First Army Corps, then on the front lines. On October 19, 1863, Private Young's Company A skirmished with rebel forces at Haymarket, Virginia. In March 1864, William was on detached service and must have had an opportunity for a home visit resulting in Maria Willetta's conception. During the same month, the First Maryland was reassigned to the Fifth Army Corps then engaged in the Overland Campaign. More than 86,000 casualties were incurred on both sides during this campaign and William Young was among them. He was wounded by enemy gunfire during a Union victory at an engagement at Harris Farm (May 19) during the Battle of Spotsylvania Court House (May 8–21, 1864) and died later the same day in the regimental hospital. His place of burial remains unknown and he lies, perhaps, in one of the thousands of Union graves in Virginia marked "Unknown."[2]

News of battlefield casualties moved quickly and on June 4, Eliza, with two witnesses, presented herself before Annapolis Justice of the Peace Owen M. Taylor to sign a Declaration for Widow's Army Pension. Although pregnant, Eliza stated that she had no children. The declaration was forwarded two days later to the United States Sanitary Commission Claim Agency in Washington. Having heard nothing back, Eliza filled out a second declaration on September 26, 1865. It was approved three months later, granting her an $8.00 monthly pension, retroactive to William's date of death. The second declaration restated the basic facts of Eliza's marriage and William's enlistment and cause of death. It also included a baptismal certificate certified by Father Joseph A. Firle, C.Ss.R., "of her child since deceased."[3]

There is no record at St. Mary's of Maria Willetta's death or burial. Her widowed mother remarried in 1866, to John Henry Jacobs, an Annapolitan who also served in the First Maryland Infantry but had not joined until a year after William's death. Eliza's marriage to Jacobs did not take place at St. Mary's. In her second marriage, Eliza gave birth to thirteen children between 1867 and 1887. She died of consumption in 1890, "received all the sacraments," had a funeral at St. Mary's, and was buried in City Cemetery (now part of St. Anne's Cemetery). John Jacobs and his second wife, Anna Rebecca Boone, are buried in the Annapolis National Cemetery.[4]

A Plea from North Carolina

Three Redemptorists associated with Annapolis—Fathers Henry Giesen, Timothy Enright, and Thaddeus Anwander—went to North Carolina in 1865. Giesen had been assigned to Annapolis since 1862 but was frequently on the road preaching

Father Henry Giesen, C.Ss.R. (1826–93). RABP.

Father Timothy Enright, C.Ss.R. (1837–1911). Denver Province Archive at RABP.

missions. Enright was one of the 1863 ordinands and, after his six-month second novitiate in Annapolis in 1863–64, had been assigned to Most Holy Redeemer, a Redemptorist parish New York City. Anwander was minister and prefect of St. James Church in Baltimore and an occasional visitor to Annapolis and would become St. Mary's rector in 1866.[5]

The mission to the south was in response to a request from Archbishop Spalding to the Redemptorists to send a priest or two to New Bern, North Carolina. New Bern was a strategic transportation hub located near Pamlico Sound and the Atlantic Ocean and had been occupied by Union troops since 1862 and served as staging ground for military operations in the state throughout the war. Not only were there thousands of Catholic soldiers, sailors, and Federal civilian employees in and around New Bern, there had been no resident priest there since 1863 and services at the parish church—St. Paul—were held by lay leaders. Seven Sisters of Mercy arrived shortly after the Union occupation began to care for wounded and sick soldiers but stayed only a short time. A yellow fever epidemic broke out in 1864 and many families had fled New Bern and most troops had withdrawn to safer areas. One of the surviving lay leaders, John Prime, appealed for assistance to Spalding in October 1864.[6]

St. Paul's Church, New Bern, North Carolina. Courtesy author.

Father De Dycker appointed Henry Giesen and Timothy Enright to go south. Assistance with transportation was provided by Inspector General of the Army Colonel (soon to be promoted to Brevet Brigadier General) James Allen Hardie, a Catholic, and they arrived in New Bern in January 1865. Giesen ministered to the Union troops and local congregation until March. Enright did the same until August and also served other local communities near New Bern, such as Bachelor Creek, Goldsboro, Kinston, and Edenton. Thaddeus Anwander arrived in April or May and stayed only briefly. While no sacramental record was left of their service to the Union forces, they did leave evidence of their work among the laity of New Bern and the other towns. Between January and August 1865, they recorded the baptisms of thirteen children and adults and officiated at five marriages. Enright returned in Edenton in September 1866 and performed seven baptisms during a nearly one-month stay.

Around the same time that Giesen and Enright were first in New Bern, their confrere Aegidius Smulders, chaplain of the Eighth Louisiana Infantry, was preaching 250 miles to the west. The previous October Smulders had asked Jefferson Davis to allow him to carry out an experiment with the Irish Catholic prisoners of war "with the view of bringing them over to the Confederate cause." Davis approved Smulders' scheme and, after some delay, a special temporary prisoner-of-war camp for foreign-born Catholic Union soldiers was established near Salisbury, North Carolina. Smulders preached an eight-day retreat, heard confessions, celebrated Mass, distributed Holy Communion, and encouraged some 700 to 900 prisoners (both Irish and German) to join the Confederate army. According to Smulders' own account "few availed themselves of the opportunity" and later they were paroled and sent north.[7]

Correspondence from Archbishop Spalding in May 1865 indicates that Father Anwander was expected to also go to Charleston, South Carolina. However, Father John Moore, the vicar general in Charleston wrote to Spalding in June that he had "heard nothing of Father Anwander." Anwander also appears to have visited the Union the prisoner-of-war camp for Confederate soldiers at Point Lookout in St. Mary's County, Maryland. He was granted a pass and traveled there on the steamer *Louisiana*, which had a regular route running between Baltimore and Fort Monroe. No additional information has been found about Anwander's proposed visit to Charleston or about the visit to Point Lookout. Fathers James Sheeran and Smulders both visited Charleston when the city was still under Confederate control.[8]

With the war suddenly over in April, there was a greater need than ever for priests in the South and the Redemptorists again were asked to help. In late April 1865, Spalding wrote to the Redemptorist provincial asking him to send priests to Charleston, South Carolina. Father De Dycker had left for Rome and Father George Ruland, one of his consultors, responded in his stead. He reported that he had written to New Orleans asking that either Sheeran or Smulders, or both, be selected to go to Charleston. This did not happen and instead two French Jesuits of their New Orleans Province were to be sent: Father Darius Hubert—before the war a faculty member of the Jesuits' College of the Immaculate Conception in New Orleans and later the chaplain of the First Louisiana Infantry—and Louis-Hippolyte Gaché—before the war vice president of St. Charles College, Grand Coteau, Louisiana, and later chaplain of the Tenth Louisiana Infantry. Both of these men were mentioned frequently in Sheeran's Civil War diary. When the war ended, Father Hubert, who was paroled in Richmond, became ill and remained there, never making it to Charleston. Father Gaché, also was paroled at Richmond, eventually made it to Charleston but only stayed a few months.[9]

Inspector General of the Army Brevet Brigadier General James Allen Hardie (1823–76). Prints and Photographs Division, Library of Congress https://www.loc.gov/pictures/item/2018668593/.

Still Not Exempt

In January 1865, Congress received numerous petitions from Protestant denominations calling for exemptions for "all ministers of the gospel in actual pastoral duty." While Catholics and Quakers were not among the petitioners, they stood to benefit from any exemptions that might be added to the Federal Enrolling Act. Besides the cases of Redemptorists and Benedictines described above, the Congregation of the Holy Cross, the order administering the University of Notre Dame in Indiana, also sought exemption from the draft. In 1863 Notre Dame president Father Edward Sorin, C.S.C, made his case based on the service of six Holy Cross fathers serving as army chaplains and nearly forty Holy Cross sisters serving as nurses in army and navy hospitals. Endorsements supporting Sorin's request were made by then-Major General Ulysses Grant, commander of the Army of the Tennessee, and Major General William Tecumseh Sherman, commander of the Fifteenth Army Corps. In the autumn of 1863, the Lincoln administration decided to grant paroles to Holy Cross members who had been drafted. When the dispensation was later withdrawn in December 1864 because of alleged anti-Unionist votes by some Holy Cross members, Ellen Sherman, General Sherman's Catholic wife, and his brother, Republican Senator John Sherman of Ohio, interceded on behalf of the Holy Cross congregation. On March 3, 1865, Congress further amended the 1863 and 1864 enrollment acts but still failed to provide exemptions for members of religious orders or ministers of the gospel. The 1864 Amendatory Act exemption for individuals having religious scruples against bearing arms remained in force and draftees still were required to serve as noncombatants or pay a $300 commutation fee. The Jesuits, confronted with draft problems in Maryland, Kentucky, and Missouri, also sought exemptions from the draft. Only the war's end would bring relief for the Redemptorists and other religious orders.[10]

Archbishop Martin John Spalding (1810–72). Rev. John Lancaster Spalding, The Life of the Most Rev. M. J. Spalding, D. D., Archbishop of Baltimore *(New York: Catholic Publication Society, 1873), ii; Library of Congress Digital ID http://hdl.loc.gov/loc.gdc/scd0001.00135161044.*

A small victory for Catholic soldiers wanting Bibles occurred in February 1865. The headquarters of the Annapolis branch of the United States Sanitary Commission announced that it had "sent a lot of Douay Testaments to the Catholic clergy residing at Saint Mary's Church, in this city, to be distributed by them among the Catholic soldiers in the hospitals and Camp Parole." The United States Christian Commission also distributed publisher-donated Douay Bibles. Lucas Brothers of Baltimore testified after the war that they had provided at least 8,480 Douay Bibles to the Christian Commission. An additional 400 Douay Bibles were sent to the army through other distributors. But this was a minuscule percentage of the more than 3 million Bibles reportedly distributed during the war.[11]

Extinguishment of Liability

The *Chronica Domus* reported on February 13, 1865, that "the women of our Annapolis church congregation held what in English is called a 'Fair,' that lasted two and a half weeks." The *Sun* reported a week before that the fair was to begin on February 13, "on the second floor of the house in the occupancy of Mr. George O'Malley, on Main street." This location was presumably above O'Malley's Continental Shades restaurant. It seems likely that the fair lasted two and a half weeks as the Redemptorist chronicler stated, not the one day implied by the *Sun's* Annapolis correspondent. A parishioner, O'Malley likely offered the rooms above his restaurant for the event, perhaps for several days or weeks. The *Chronica Domus* also reported that Dr. Vanderkieft sent a military chorus from General Hospital Division No. 1 to sing at the fair. After expenses were paid the parish women raised $2,500 "to be applied to the extinguishment of an existing liability on their splendid edifice."[12]

Another sign of normality during wartime was the establishment of a new parish organization, St. Mary's chapter of the Holy Childhood Association. In July the *Catholic Mirror* carried a report from the association's chief director in the Archdiocese of Baltimore, Father Bernard Sylvester Piot: "We hear good news from Hancock. Two hundred members are enrolled. Elkridge Landing and Annapolis also doing well." The association was founded in France in 1843 "to encourage all children to be aware of the needs of children living in mission dioceses through the world."[13]

Later in the year, the *Catholic Mirror* reported charitable contributions made by parishioners. St. Mary's was credited with donations totaling $64.44 when the annual Peter's Pence Collection was taken up in the Archdiocese of Baltimore to benefit the pope's personal ministries.[14]

All Navigation Was Impeded

Chesapeake Bay and its tributaries were ice covered as 1865 began, so much so that those "fond of skating, have an opportunity to enjoy the luxury in and about Annapolis," according to *The Crutch*. It added a week later that "all kinds of craft pass freely from and to the Bay" although "lively skaters" were still "making the Severn a crystal track between the two shores." *The Crutch* also noted that there was an "ice-embargo" on the Potomac River, Baltimore harbor, and other points. Because the Potomac was ice bound and boat travel on it was temporarily impossible, a special visitor passed instead through Annapolis. President Abraham Lincoln, accompanied only by a valet and a body guard, walked unobserved by the public from the railroad depot at Calvert and West streets to the Naval Academy wharf on February 2. He boarded a ship that carried him to Hampton Roads for what turned out to be a failed peace conference with senior Confederate officials. He returned to Annapolis on February 4, took a special train waiting for him at the Academy wharf and returned to Washington. It was Lincoln's only visit to Annapolis.[15]

In keeping with the cold-weather reports, the *Chronica Domus* noted in January that Father Louis Claessens was unable to go to Easton to perform pastoral work because the bay had frozen and "all navigation was impeded." He finally made it to Easton in mid-March and for three successive days held jubilee exercises prescribed by Pope Pius IX in his encyclical *Quanta Cura* (Condemning Current Errors) issued on December 8, 1864. The encyclical was a reaction to the withdrawal of the protection given to the Papal States by French troops and reiterated an 1846 encyclical and warnings given to the College of Cardinals in 1854 and 1862 that refuted liberal and humanistic ideas that "society be conducted and governed without regard being had to religion any more than if it did not exist." To counteract this removal of religion from civil society, Pius prescribed a jubilee in which Catholics were asked to visit designated churches, fast, say devotional prayers, go to confession, receive Communion, and give alms to the poor. Anyone following this regimen was granted a plenary indulgence with the remission of all their sins. Some American newspaper editors viewed *Quanta Cura* as "a covert declaration of war against the American Republic," while even some Catholic newspapers thought it appeared at odds with American democratic principles and asked the Catholic hierarchy for clarification. The Vatican's explanation was that there was "a difference between state principles and their application in specific cases."[16]

To prepare for the jubilee in Easton, Claessens sent the Howes Goldsborough copies of the encyclical and a pastoral letter from Archbishop Spalding that described in detail the reasons and rubrics for the jubilee. Claessens' letter gives a clue that Easton's Catholics held prayer services on Sundays when there was no priest. He wrote that the archbishop's pastoral letter was to be read on the Sunday proceeding the start of the jubilee, and told Goldsborough that he had requested Mr. Lerowe [*sic*, illegible handwriting], "the gentleman living at the house of Hon. Mr. H. May," to read the pastoral on Sunday, March 12, "before the Catholics assembled in their usual place worship." He also asked Goldsborough, with the assistance of Lerowe and others not named, to "get up a small choir of chanters, who would be able to sing a Mass, or at least some of the religious canticles, with accompaniment of the piano or melodeon, as this would contribute a great deal to the solemnity of the Jubilee."[17]

The jubilee observances, which occurred during

Lent, were followed by the celebration of Easter in mid-April. Claessens wrote again to Goldsborough to explain that he had to go off to preach a mission but that he would "send . . . a good substitute in the person of Rev. Father Henning whom you saw in Annapolis." This letter also noted the fulfilment of the Redemptorists' hope for Goldsborough's conversion. Claessens said, "[w]ith regard to your first communion, you can either make it with Father Henning or wait until May when I hope to pay you again a visit." Henning arrived either by steamboat from Baltimore or, as he himself suggested, a more circuitous route by train from Baltimore to Wilmington, Delaware, and then south via the Eastern Shore Railroad to Princess Anne, the seat of Somerset County. From there he would have had to take horse-drawn transportation sixty-five miles northwest to Easton. Henning celebrated Easter Sunday Mass in Easton and gave a lecture on Catholic doctrine in the evening.[18]

The trip to Easton was only the first part of Henning's itinerary. Spalding had asked him to make a tour of the "Lower Parishes" on the Eastern Shore and sent fifty dollars (contributed by a Mr. Banks in Princess Anne) to help cover expenses. After tending to the Redemptorists' flock in Easton, Henning went on a "reconnoitering expedition" to assess the state of Catholicism on the lower Eastern Shore. The record is not clear exactly when Henning made this expedition. He was in Easton for Easter (April 16) and told Spalding, when he wrote to him before his departure from Annapolis, that on Monday or Tuesday after Easter he would go to Princess Anne and "make all the necessary arrangements." He did not say what those arrangements were but he planned to "write to the parties in Princess Ann immediately & to notify them of my coming." The arrangements must have been successful because, when he returned to Princess Anne in June, he officiated at several baptisms and a marriage. Since there is no record of his having returned in the interim to Annapolis, it is possible he traveled further south or returned to Easton to enjoy the hospitality of the Goldsboroughs and others before setting off on two months of travel on the Eastern Shore.[19]

Henning's first documented stop was on June 9, when he arrived in Salisbury, then part of Somerset County. A week later, Henning wrote to Spalding, telling him he would soon return to Baltimore "as my supplies are run out," and that he had hoped to find about a hundred Catholics in Salisbury, a town of 3,000 persons. A later source reported that in 1865 "only two or three Catholic families were known to live in the Salisbury area." Upon investigation, however, Henning had found only one family, that of John Tracy—the Scottish-born proprietor of a hotel, the Peninsula House—his Irish wife Anne, and their four children, plus two laborers. With Tracy's assistance, the Odd Fellows Hall was rented and Henning gave "a course of public lectures" on the Catholic religion. The lectures were "very well attended and helped to dispel a great amount of prejudice," he reported. The *Province Mission Book* records a mission on the Eastern Shore on June 9, 1865, but without any details. At some point, Henning gave Tracy's daughter Katie her First Communion. During his stay in Salisbury, Henning met with a number of influential Protestant gentlemen to discuss building a Catholic church. He said they "promised to do all in their power" to advance the Catholic cause in town and one of them intimated to Henning that he thought $8,000 to $10,000 could be collected. Two years later, John Tracy conveyed a parcel of land on West Church Street, across from his hotel, to the Archdiocese of Baltimore and erected, at his own expense, an "unpretentious frame building." It was known as St. Mary's and became a mission of Holy Cross Parish in Dover, Delaware, and remained so until 1890.[20]

After leaving Salisbury, Henning traveled to Snow Hill in Worcester County. There, on June 18, he baptized nine-year-old Edward Duffield Martin, son of a widowed farm owner, Sarah "Sallie" L. Richardson Martin, a former slave owner and employer of slaves, and the late Edward Duffield Martin, former clerk of the Worcester County Circuit Court, who died in 1856. No note on the parents' religious affiliation was entered in the record so presumably they were Catholic. Since there was no church or chapel in Snow Hill to maintain such records, when Henning returned home he entered this and other baptisms in the St. Mary's register.[21]

By June 20, Henning was back in Princess Anne, where he baptized four-year-old Margaret Fitzgerald and her one-year-old brother John. They were the children of Michael Fitzgerald, a day laborer, and his wife Margaret, both Irish immigrants. The godmother was Catherine Mulchinock in whose Princess Anne home the baptisms may have taken place. A second baptism took place the same day. This time—with Catherine and Francis Mulchinock as godparents—Julia Anne Bright, an eighteen-year-old from Milford, Delaware, and a convert from Methodism, was baptized. It was a special day for Julia because it also was her wedding day. She married thirty-five-year-old Irish-born Timothy Spillane. Information on this couple is sparse but they probably were the same as Timothy and July [*sic*] Anne Spalane [*sic*] recorded in the 1870 census for Princess Anne. By that time, Timothy was listed as a railroad worker and they had three children.[22]

The two-month expedition in 1865 may have been Henning's second trip to the Eastern Shore. He evidently was there in summer 1864 and had lost the reusable steamboat ticket, given gratis to the Redemptorists by Howes Goldsborough. Shortly after his return to the Western Shore in June 1865, Henning departed for a two-year sojourn in England to perform mission work by order of Father Nicholas Mauron in Rome.[23]

Father Timothy Enright was in Easton in September, October, and November 1865, performing the mid-month pastoral duties. He had additional work to do in November when he stayed a week to prepare those who were to receive the sacrament of Confirmation. On November 20, Archbishop Spalding began an extensive episcopal visitation to parishes and missions in Baltimore and Harford counties and then moved on to the upper Eastern Shore, visiting churches in Cecil, Kent, and Queen Anne's counties, confirming and lecturing as he went. He was accompanied by Father Bernard J. McManus, a diocesan priest and pastor of St. John's Church in Baltimore. By December 3 they were at St. Joseph's Church in Cordova, Talbot County, before heading east to St. Elizabeth Church in Denton, Caroline County. Joined by Enright in Easton, Spalding completed his Eastern Shore tour there. In the town hall on the morning of December 5, he confirmed twenty-six persons, eight of whom were converts. In the evening, he gave a lecture at the Talbot County courthouse. During his tour, Spalding initiated the first steps in erecting churches, with hopes for "their early completion," at Reese's Corner (near Rock Hall) in Kent County; Centreville and an unspecified location "near the bridge to Kent Island" in Queen Anne's County; and in Easton. Enright returned to Easton in mid-December and was there again during the Christmas holidays.[24]

Pour Down His Blessing

The Annapolis Redemptorists continued to provide monthly services at St. Augustine's in Elkridge Landing. In April Fathers Henning and Gerdemann gave a mission of renewal there to the congregants. Although priests from St. Alphonsus Church in Baltimore were available to serve St. Augustine's, on August 6 Father Girardey announced that a diocesan priest would be assigned to take charge of St. Augustine's.[25]

The year 1865 was also one of progress in West River. Father Helmprächt visited on New Year's Day and Father Gerdemann in June to officiate at the first recorded West River baptism, that of infant George Hume Steuart, the son of George Biscoe Steuart and Louisa Ann Darnall. The baby was named for his father's kinsman, Brigadier General George Hume Steuart of the Confederate cavalry of the Army of Northern Virginia. Between then and December, Gerdemann baptized twenty-nine infants, children, and adults, mostly African Americans. During the same period, Father Enright baptized a child and an adult, and newly ordained Father James Gleeson baptized an infant. Chloe Fenwick, daughter of Dr. Martin Fenwick, was godmother once in 1865. Otherwise the godparents were usually family members of the individual being baptized, suggesting their own Catholicity. At nearby Dodon, Dr. Richard Sprigg Steuart's daughter Isabella served as godmother for twelve baptisms and his other daughter, Emily, for two.[26]

St. Alphonsus Church, Baltimore. RABP.

The *Catholic Mirror* reported that on September 17, the little congregation at West River had collected $4.00 for the archdiocesan collection for the suffering poor of the South. In early December, Gerdemann gave instructions at Henry Aloysius Fenwick's home to those preparing for confirmation. On December 6, Archbishop Spalding, accompanied by Fathers McManus and Enright, traveled from Easton on the steamboat to Galesville and then by carriage to the Fenwick home in West River to administer confirmation that day to fourteen persons (seven Black adults, six Black teenagers, and one White teenager). The next day, they went to Dodon where nine individuals (four Black adults—one of whom was a convert—four Black teenagers and one White teenager) were confirmed. After the confirmations, Spalding, McManus, and Enright, plus Gerdemann took the steamer from Galesville to Annapolis. There they enjoyed the Redemptorists' hospitality and, according to the *Chronica Domus* "the Most Rev. Archbishop and Very Rev. McManus returned to Baltimore after dinner." During the last week of December 1865, Gerdemann traveled throughout western Anne Arundel and eastern Prince George's counties to collect money for building a church in West River.[27]

Some of the Redemptorists went further afield in their mission work during the fall of 1865. Girardey served as socius to the provincial on a canonical visitation to Cumberland and then participated in a mission with Father Bradley in Massillon, Ohio. Afterward, he participated in another canonical visitation with the provincial, this time to Philadelphia. Gerdemann was sent to "set up a Jubilee" at St. Peter's Church in Oakland, in Allegany (now Garrett) County in western Maryland. He was joined there by Father Joseph Wuest. The Cumberland Redemptorists had an earlier involvement with St. Peter's when Father John Neumann was given charge of the Oakland mission in 1847 and supervised the construction of the first church there in 1848. The church was consecrated in 1858 when Father Seelos had charge and in 1859 Father Van de Braak oversaw improvements inside the church. There was a hiatus until Redemptorists returned in 1863. During this interim, Father Michael O'Reilly, the Irish diocesan pastor of St. Michael's in Frostburg, made occasional visits to Oakland. But when the war made travel there difficult and the number of church goers dwindled, O'Reilly's visits ceased. Given the largely Germanic origin of many of the Redemptorists, it is not surprising that when they were about to take charge of St. Peter's again, O'Reilly's parting shot was that he was being succeeded by the "sauerkraut Redemptorists." The Redemptorists had charge of the mission until 1866 when the Cumberland novitiate was transferred to Annapolis and the Carmelite fathers took charge of both Cumberland and Oakland.[28]

In late March, Father Claessens led jubilee exercises at

St. Mary's as prescribed in Pope Pius IX's encyclical, the same as he had in Easton. He was assisted by Father Gerdemann.[29]

Archbishop Spalding returned to Annapolis in the waning days of the Civil War. From March 30 through April 1, 1865, he ordained ten new priests. Nine of the men were of European birth and only one, Joseph Aloysius Firle from Frostburg, Maryland, was American born. On the evening of March 30, Spalding gave a well-attended lecture to the general public in St. Mary's Church. The *Catholic Mirror*, reporting on the ordinations, said "We are sure that all will pray for the young ordinands, that God may pour down His most abundant blessing on their heads." During the following days, nine of the ten new priests celebrated their first Masses at St. Mary's. Newly ordained John Nepumucene Berger left for Baltimore to start his first assignment, at St. Alphonsus Church, and presumably offered his first Mass there.[30]

The Mills of the Gods Grind Slowly

While camped with the Confederate army's Louisiana Brigade in Culpeper County, Virginia, in October 1863, Father James Sheeran received a visit from "Mr. Boyle of the Md. cavalry and [made] him stay for dinner." Sheeran's diary says he had met Boyle the previous July in Pennsylvania, after the Battle of Gettysburg, and "found him a high-toned gentleman and truly a devout Catholic." There was only one "Mr. Boyle" associated with the Maryland cavalry—John Henry Boyle Jr.—and he indeed had good Catholic connections. He was the grandson of Colonel James Boyle, former mayor of Annapolis, former deputy attorney general of Maryland for Anne Arundel County, a convert Catholicism, and trustee of St. Mary's Church in Annapolis when ownership was conveyed to the Redemptorists in 1853.[31]

Boyle Jr. was born in Annapolis in 1843, the second son of John Henry Boyle Sr., M.D., and his wife, Ellen Slemaker. By 1850 the Boyles had moved to Upper Marlborough, the seat of Prince George's County, but maintained their local familial ties and owned Annapolis property that Ellen had inherited. In 1852 John and Ellen's youngest child, Edwin Llewellyn, was baptized at St. Mary's, with his uncle James Boyle III serving as godfather. St. Mary's records for 1840s are not extant but it is likely that John Henry Jr. and his three other siblings also were baptized there.[32]

John Henry Boyle Jr.'s uncle, state librarian Llewellyn Boyle, was father of two sons, Alphonsus Albert, born in 1863, and Samuel Joseph, born in 1865. They were baptized at St. Mary's by Father Ferreol Girardey on July 18, 1866, with Rachel Smothers as godmother. The parents both were noted in the baptismal records as Protestants and the children as illegitimate. Their mother was identified in the baptismal register as "Celestina Müller" of Annapolis, and in the 1880 Federal Census as "Cilest Boyle," a thirty-five-year-old Black servant living with Llewellyn Boyle in Baltimore. No further trace of these children has been found in genealogical records.[33]

Boyle Jr. had a promising life ahead of him. He attended Georgetown College for one year in 1858, but in 1859 and 1860 problems arose concerning nonpayment of his tuition. In 1860 he also got into a fight with a free Black man in Upper Marlborough. Boyle received stab wounds but recovered. Soon after the Civil War began, he went to Richmond to enlist as a private in Company C, First Virginia Artillery. By this time, Boyle's father was in Richmond practicing medicine.[34]

After serving briefly as a private in the artillery, Boyle became a spy, with the rank of captain, for Major General James Ewell Brown (J. E. B.) Stuart, the flamboyant Confederate cavalry commander. He was arrested by Federal agents in January 1863 at the family home in Upper Marlborough, where he supposedly was found with "more than a hundred letters to Jefferson Davis, and other Southerners." He was incarcerated at the Old Capitol Prison in Washington to await trial as a spy, usually a capital offense. Although news reports referred to him as a captain on Stuart's staff, his official prison record listed his rank as "gentleman," indicating civilian status. Despite the serious charge against him, after four months he was paroled and exchanged for a Union army captain. Boyle was serving as a civilian aide (with the title of "Mr.") to Brigadier General George Hume Steuart at Gettysburg in July 1863 when he first met Father Sheeran. Steuart singled out Boyle and three other staff officers to whom he was "greatly indebted for valuable assistance rendered, and of whose gallant bearing I cannot too highly make mention" for their actions at Gettysburg. General Steuart—known as "Maryland Steuart" to differentiate him from J. E. B. Stuart—was the nephew of Dr. Richard Sprigg Steuart of Dodon and after the war retired to his country estate in southern Anne Arundel County.[35]

Boyle was in southern Maryland by 1864 conducting guerrilla activities against pro-Union citizens. These included, according to an account from Annapolis in 1865, "many lawless acts, especially in horse stealing." His most serious offense, however, was the murder of Captain Thomas Hodges Watkins, the former provost marshal of Annapolis. Watkins had arrested Boyle in September 1864 for horse stealing but on the way to Fort McHenry, Boyle broke loose, seriously wounded his captor, and escaped with threats to kill Watkins the next time they met. Historian James O. Hall says that Boyle then "disappeared in the extensive Confederate underground apparatus" and "continued to be active in running the blockade and other clandestine operations." He also made frequent death threats to Watkins through the grapevine.[36]

Watkins was the son of slave owner Benjamin Watkins, a retired physician turned gentlemen farmer in Davidsonville in western Anne Arundel County. Unlike many of his pro-South relatives, friends, and neighbors, Thomas was a hard-line "unconditional unionist" who supported the war against the Confederacy. He joined the Union army in Baltimore in December 1861 as captain of Company B, a cavalry component of the Purnell Legion, a Maryland home-guard regiment. Because of his knowledge of local people and county roads, Watkins' company was detached from the Purnell Legion in 1862 and assigned to assist the provost marshal in Annapolis. Their duties included arresting Confederate soldiers on home leave in Anne Arundel County, which outraged pro-South county residents. One of the Confederate soldiers apprehended by Watkins and accused of spying was Daniel Martin Kent, a private in Company B, Thirty-Ninth Battalion Virginia Cavalry. Kent, a near neighbor of the Watkins family, was home on furlough in Davidsonville in April 1863 when he was arrested. After a brief confinement at Fort McHenry, he was exchanged in May and returned South. Coincidently, the mission of the Thirty-Ninth Battalion was to provide scouts, guides, and couriers, not unlike some of John Boyle's duties. Kent's family was on both sides of the war: while Daniel served in the Confederate army, his cousin Etheridge Kent was a US Navy landsman. Etheridge's sister, Juliana Ballard Kent, a Catholic convert at St. Mary's, married into the Unionist Walton family. Another sister, Ella Lee Kent, also was a Catholic convert at St. Mary's. The sisters are buried in St. Mary's Cemetery.[37]

On the night of March 25, 1865, Boyle and two accomplices arrived on foot at Velmeade, Watkins' farm near Davidsonville. He allegedly shot Watkins, fatally wounding him in the chest. One of the men responding to the murder scene was a kinsman of Watkins, James Alexis Iglehart, a Catholic benefactor of St. Mary's who lived on a nearby farm. Boyle and his accomplices escaped into southern Maryland with the governor's bounty on their heads. Union cavalry pursued Boyle but failed to find him. He was finally apprehended on April 15 in Woodsboro, Frederick County, Maryland, and brought to the county jail in Annapolis.[38]

Federal authorities and the news media briefly and erroneously believed that Boyle was responsible for the attempted assassination of Secretary of State William Henry Seward on the evening of April 14. Boyle's supposed connection to John Wilkes Booth was apparently based on his activities in southern Maryland. Following the November 1864 presidential election, Boyle had issued death threats to Dr. George Dyer Mudd, a pro-Union man and cousin of Dr. Samuel Alexander Mudd, both of Bryantown in Charles County. When Union cavalry descended on Bryantown on April 15, they were actively searching for Booth and Boyle as the assassins of Lincoln and Seward, respectively. Samuel Mudd's wife Frances told detectives that when she heard a knock on their door on the night of April 14–15, she thought it was Boyle who had come to her home—possibly because of the threat to George Mudd—to harm her husband or herself. She later testified that it was fear of Boyle that had kept her husband from immediately reporting to the authorities that it was Booth and co-conspirator David Herold who came seeking medical attention for the injured Booth. *The Crutch* reported that there were "many rumors afloat relative to the arrest of the murderers, Booth and Boyle. None of them quite satisfactory." Even Samuel Mudd initially believed that Boyle, whom he feared, was Booth's accomplice. It also is possible that Mudd was acquainted with Boyle since he, like Boyle, reportedly had been involved in handling Confederate underground correspondence. George Atzerodt, another man charged in the Lincoln assassination, also implicated Boyle as one of the co-conspirators. Atzerodt knew that Boyle killed Watkins but it is unclear why he felt Boyle was part of the Lincoln conspiracy. Boyle's name came up twice during the Lincoln conspiracy trial but nothing more came of it. As an indication of Boyle's "blood-thirsty stock," the action of his sister, Susan Boyle Pearson also came up in the trial evidence. Then living near Philadelphia, she and her children reputedly were "in the habit of giving utterance to disloyal sentiments and to even go so far as to wish for the President's death." She supposedly was the "first one in the neighborhood to hear the intelligence [of Lincoln's assassination] and circulated it with joy."[39]

Boyle went on trial in Annapolis in May 1865 for the September 1864 horse theft and attempted murder of Watkins. Boyle's uncles, James Boyle III, Edwin Boyle, and Llewelyn Boyle, arranged for his legal defense. One of three lawyers they hired was John Thomson Mason Jr., who had represented the Boyle brothers in other cases. James Revell was the state's prosecutor. It was a case of associates of St. Mary's opposing each other in court. Because of the high profile of the case, and possibly because of the prosecutor's known Southern sympathies, Revell was assisted by Alexander Randall, Maryland's newly elected attorney general. Boyle was found guilty of both charges at a bench trial and was sentenced to four years for horse stealing and an additional five years for the attempted murder of Watkins. He was incarcerated the same day at the Maryland Penitentiary in Baltimore.[40]

Mason successfully argued for a change of venue to Howard County for the murder of Watkins and a second horse theft. The trial was set to begin on September 26 in Ellicott's Mills, with Alexander Randall as the chief prosecutor. But Mason's change-of-venue strategy was successful. He pointed out to the court that Boyle was in prison and cited a Maryland statute that someone already in prison had to serve the full sentence before he could be tried for another crime. Boyle's luck was with him as the judge, in effect, ordered a nine-year continuance. Watkins' father, who was present at the hearing, wrote in his journal, "What mockery I say of public justice! . . . . Who shall be living at the end of 9 years the Lord only knows."[41]

The resolution came sooner than nine years and not at all what Benjamin Watkins would have hoped for. Still attempting to get Boyle into the Howard County courtroom for trial, the prosecution asked the county court clerk to request a writ of error from the Maryland Court of Appeals on October 20, 1865. The prosecution hoped that the appellate court would find an error in Mason's request for a change of venue and require Boyle's presence in Howard County court. The higher court, however, dismissed the writ on the grounds it was defective and the lower court clerk had exceeded his authority in requesting it. The opinion, coincidently, was written by Associate Justice James Lawrence Bartol, an occasional attendee of St. Mary's Church. Thus Boyle continued to avoid prosecution for murder.[42]

Boyle and another convict escaped from the Maryland Penitentiary in mid-February 1866, but were captured in Virginia three weeks later and returned to the penitentiary. Six years later, as the result of an appeal evidently engineered by

John Thomson Mason, the newly appointed secretary of state, Boyle was pardoned by Governor William Pinkney Whyte for the crimes for which he had been convicted (horse theft and attempted murder). Whyte also directed that a *nolle prosequi* be entered with the Howard County Circuit Court, formally abandoning the Watkins murder indictment. The pardon docket reveals that "Numerous citizens & Physicians, Judges of the Court of Appeals, Legislative Committees &c." had written in support of the Boyle pardon and included seven medical certificates, all favoring Boyle's immediate release because of an alleged terminal case of consumption; eighteen letters supporting a pardon; and six pardon petitions with a total of 318 signatures. Twenty men (mostly Watkins' relatives and kin) protested the pardon in person to the governor. There also was an anti-pardon petition with forty-eight signatures, including those of jurors from the 1865 proceedings. Despite these pleas, Boyle's pardon and *nolle prosequi* were made official by Whyte on April 30, 1872. The only condition was that he was banned from Anne Arundel County for two years from the date of his release from the penitentiary. At least two St. Mary's parishioners—Thomas K. Carey and Ferdinand Mullan—signed petitions on behalf of Boyle. No identifiable St. Mary's parishioners petitioned against Boyle's release.[43]

After regaining his freedom, Boyle moved to Mississippi, worked as a railroad detective, gained media attention for tracking down two murderers in Louisiana, and was arrested for passing counterfeit money in Vicksburg in October 1879. He went on trial in US District Court in Jackson, Mississippi, in December but the case ended in a mistrial. News of his arrest and trial brought Boyle unwanted publicity. On June 20, 1880, after a Sunday evening stroll with his wife Susan and infant son John Llewellyn, Boyle—the same "high-toned" and "devout Catholic" met by Father Sheeran in 1863—was sitting in the yard behind his house in Liberty Grove in Tougaloo, Hinds County, Mississippi. His wife and son were on a porch nearby. According to Susan's account, "some cruel coward crept up within 30 feet of him, and shot him in the back." He suffered two blasts of buckshot to the head and shoulder and died on Wednesday, having never regained consciousness. Susan Boyle hoped the governor would offer a reward for solving the crime but the Hinds County sheriff informed the local press that there were "reasons why an active investigation was not gone into" but gave no further details. Perhaps Boyle was disliked in the area and his death was not worthy of investigation. Some believe Boyle's violent end was an act of revenge by one of Watkins' old cavalry troopers. "Truly," read a southern Maryland report of John Henry Boyle Jr.'s death, "the mills of the gods grind slowly, but they grind exceedingly small." Slowly indeed, because rumors persist to the present day that it was not Boyle who killed Watkins, but another local man whom Watkins arrested during the war.[44]

Joyous Hilarity . . . Then Wrapped in Gloom

The Confederate Army of Northern Virginia surrendered at Appomattox Court House on Palm Sunday, April 9, 1865. When news reached Annapolis, the army camps began firing artillery salutes and the city government ordered a parade and illumination of buildings, which occurred on the evening of April 12:

> the streets were thronged with soldiers, as jubilant as boys on the 4th of July. The public buildings were illuminated, and many private dwellings were transfigured into fairy temples of light . . . . Stirring speeches were made . . . . The bands of [Hospital] Division 1 and 2 played alternately, while rockets were flying in all directions from the steps and balcony of the State House. For several hours the air was vocal with huzzas, and the scene one of joyous hilarity.[45]

Unlike the details provided in the *Chronica Domus* when Lincoln was reelected in November 1864, the end-of-war celebrations were not mentioned at St. Mary's.

Holy Saturday, April 15, 1865, should have been a day of several departures from St. Mary's College. Father Thaddeus Anwander, of St. James' Church in Baltimore, was in town and had planned to return home after leading a Holy Week retreat for the seminarians. Fathers Claessens and Giesen were supposed to leave the same day for a French-language mission in Detroit. Pastoral work in Easton required Father Henning's presence across the Bay. Suddenly everything changed. The news of President Lincoln's assassination the evening before brought all travel to a halt. The *Chronica Domus* reported that "because of the great commotion that [took] place on account of the assassination of the president . . . the fathers could not travel." It went on to say that Lincoln "was in a theater on Good Friday evening and by [blank space] and was killed by Booth, who once had been an actor. Until he would be caught, all had to remain indoors."[46]

After receiving news of the assassination, flags were lowered to half staff at the State House, army headquarters, and the hospitals. The local *Sun* correspondent reported that the city was "wrapped in gloom," with the State House, churches, post office, express office, telegraph office, city hall, and many private residences "draped in mourning."[47]

Several parishioners had been issued passes on April 15 and, if they departed before news of the travel ban was received in Annapolis, they may have completed their journeys or had been turned back. Matthew Eaglin, an African American parishioner, or his son of the same name, was given a pass to "go up the Severn River," and Henrietta Johnson was one of fourteen Black women and men who were granted passes to cross the Severn River. Colonel John Walton, his son Edward, and Edward's family had permission go by boat up the Severn to a family farm near Round Bay. John Bright and John Thomas Denver, two St. Mary's thirteen-year-olds, had been given a joint pass to go "3 miles out of Annapolis Md." by unspecified conveyance.[48]

The three traveling priests were finally allowed to leave Annapolis on April 17. The same day, Father Helmprächt left with Father de Dycker for Rome. Father Dielemans

Conjectural view of St. Mary's Church front door hung in black mourning. Original art by Constance D. Robinson.

assumed the office of vice rector in Helmprächt's absence, with Father Girardey as his consultor. It was an eventful trip for Helmprächt because, as a result, he was appointed superior of the American Province, succeeding De Dycker, who then became rector of St. Peter's in Philadelphia. A Federal government message was received in Annapolis on April 17 suspending the draft. A new draft call had been issued on December 19, 1864, but now the Redemptorists, for the first time in three years, could rest easy in regard to the threat of military conscription.[49]

Father Seelos was in New York City when Lincoln was assassinated. He wrote to his sister Antonia in Bavaria four days later, telling her that "Everything is deep in mourning because President Lincoln, who I personally saw and spoke with in Washington, was murdered by an assassin at the theater. Everything is closed and almost everyone, women as well as men, are wearing cockades or something similar to show their sympathy." His next comments were quite telling of his opinion of American society:

> At the beginning, everyone complained and mocked and swore about this president, but he has become the idol of the people, and this tragic end has increased the shared feelings for his tragic death. Ah, God! These people do everything only for this world, and it certainly was not proper to go to the theater on Good Friday where he was shot.[50]

No event, even one of such consequence as the observances for the assassinated president was without controversy. On the day of Lincoln's death, Archbishop Spalding issued a circular letter to "fellow citizens" throughout his archdiocese. He called the assassination "a deed of blood" which "has caused every heart to shudder." He did not refer to Lincoln by name, but mentioned him as "the President of these United States [who] was foully assassinated" on Good Friday. He was circumspect, saying he was "quite sure that we need not remind our Catholic brethren of this Archdiocese of their duty . . . of being united with their fellow-citizens in whatever may be deemed most suitable for indicating their horror of the crime, and their feelings of sympathy for the bereaved." He invited Catholics "to join together in humble and earnest supplication to God for our beloved but afflicted country" and to toll the bells of their churches on the day of his funeral. What upset Federal authorities was a statement in the middle of Spalding's circular: "Silence is, perhaps, the best and most appropriate for a sorrow too great for utterance."[51] That was clearly an insufficient response to the great national tragedy.

Spalding's Catholic friend General James Hardie wrote to the archbishop on April 16, telling him in no uncertain terms to join with other denominations in proper mourning:

> I *earnestly advise*, as a measure of prudence that you authorize immediately the display of crape or mourning on all Catholic edifices, for religious or benevolent or for educational purposes. If not done we are in danger of disorder, destruction of property, riot and perhaps bloodshed. It will lead to a bitter feeling against the Catholic faith & its professors which we will all feel the consequences of.[52]

Without criticizing Spalding's call for silence, Hardie used Father Charles White, pastor of St. Matthew's Church in Washington, as his foil. Hardie had gone to see White, but White told him he could not drape his church in mourning without orders from Spalding. Hardie complained to Spalding "nothing can be done with [White]" and was shocked to hear White say "he is not responsible for the consequences." As a postscript, Hardie suggested that Spalding telegraph his instructions to White. By the time the archbishop replied to Hardie it was 10:00 PM on April 16 and the telegraph office was closed. Instead he wrote a note to Hardie, enclosing a letter to White with the instructions Hardie requested. Spalding asked Hardie to make copies of his letter to White and give them "to all the Pastors & heads of asylums & schools." The letter instructed White "to have crepe or other insignia of mourning placed in Catholic churches & other religious buildings." In his own cover memorandum to the Catholic clergy, Hardie urged compliance with Spalding's directive and added that even the private residences of clergy should be draped in mourning. Although this exchange was about Catholic institutions in the District of Columbia, its intent covered the entire archdiocese.[53]

Hardie wrote to Spalding again on April 19, thanking

him for the measures he had taken, which he said "no doubt avert difficulty." But he warned again that special care needed to be taken by the clergy "to avoid popular disturbances, however, for some time to come." Hardie was a practical man, not a rumor monger, and must have had field intelligence that led him to so sternly advise Spalding. He noted that "the clerical body here are all sufficiently cautious and prudent" and hoped that Spalding's actions "will have had the effect to properly dispose the less prudent."[54]

Several days earlier, St. Mary's in Annapolis had started to carry out the mourning observances for Lincoln differently from what Spalding had initially prescribed. The Redemptorist chronicler noted, "Through a misunderstanding of what was being done in the Churches in Baltimore, we draped the whole church in black, had a black flag hanging out of the steeple &c." Now, with Spalding's new directive, St. Mary's was already in compliance.[55]

The back story to the Spalding-Hardie exchange involves Spalding's political attitude. He was the descendant of an "old stock" Maryland Catholic family that had migrated to Kentucky in the late eighteenth century, bringing with them their religious and Southern social beliefs. He was ordained in Rome in 1834, returned to Kentucky, and within ten years had become vicar general of the Diocese of Louisville. In 1848 he was consecrated as coadjutor bishop of St. Louis with right of succession, which occurred in 1850. He gained a national reputation as a writer and speaker in defense of the Catholic Church in the era of emerging nativism. Although he distanced himself from politics and politicians, he used his position when necessary to defend Church interests and to influence public policy. As civil war drew closer, he denounced abolitionists and northern Protestant preachers and urged Catholics to respect the Federal Constitution, which allowed slavery. He himself had inherited two or three slaves from his father and as bishop owned twenty or more slaves who worked on diocesan properties. When Spalding learned of Lincoln's Preliminary Emancipation Proclamation in September 1862, he exclaimed "Alas! for our country! God alone can help us." To him the war was one of "confiscation, violent emancipation, destruction and desolation, and ultimately, if need be, the extermination of the entire South," and an unscrupulous violation of the Constitution. In a lengthy letter to Rome in early 1863, he protested the pro-abolition position of Cincinnati Archbishop John Baptist Purcell and defended the South's constitutional right of secession. Spalding admitted that slavery was a "great social evil" but pointed out the plight faced by free Blacks in the segregated North where some states had refused to resettle emancipated slaves. He castigated the Lincoln administration and believed that total abolition could lead to future repercussions against Catholics who were neutral on the subject. So it is not surprising then that two years later Spalding declared that silence was "the best and most appropriate expression" to Lincoln's assassination.[56]

April 19, the day of Lincoln's state funeral in Washington, was a national day of mourning. An immense funeral procession from the White House to the Capitol included members of various religious denominations, among them the pastors of all the Catholic churches in the District, which meant former Redemptorist Mathias Alig would have participated.[57]

Simultaneously, funeral observances were held in other cities. The *Sun* correspondent reported that the day in Annapolis "was solemnly and appropriately observed by all classes of our citizens in honor of the late President Lincoln." Public and private business activities were suspended and religious services were held in all the churches, "the pulpits of the respective charges [*sic*] draped in black," and the "sermons selected were suitable to the melancholly [*sic*] occasion." Soldiers fired minute guns and church bells tolled throughout the day. Members of the Veterans Reserve Corps, convalescent patients, officers, and hospital stewards and attendants at General Hospital Division No. 2 marched with the hospital band up Northeast Street to a service at St. Anne's. Another service was held at General Hospital Division No. 1. The Naval Academy chapel was draped in mourning, the windows darkened, and the gas lights turned on. Singing and instrumental music was provided by the hospital band and choir. At St. Mary's "a discourse was held appropriate to the national calamity, without bringing in politics." According to the *Chronica Domus*, St. Mary's was "well crowded by persons belonging to all kinds of religions & conditions of life."[58]

Lincoln's funeral cortege left Washington by train on the morning of April 21 for Baltimore, stopping briefly at Annapolis Junction where Governor Bradford and other state officials joined the mourners. Spurred on by Hardie's messages, Spalding made sure there was an adequate show of mourning. The *Sun* reported that "about sixty" Catholic clergy and Christian Brothers marched in the funeral cortege, led by Father Henry B. Coskery, the vicar general of the Archdiocese of Baltimore. A modern source says there were some 150 priests and seminarians in the procession. The annals of the Redemptorist parishes in Baltimore, however, made no note of these observances. Because of prior arrangements to visit parishes in the western part of the archdiocese, Spalding had left town and did not return until May 8.[59]

Incidental Connections

There was an incidental tie-in between the Annapolis Redemptorists and the Lincoln assassination. In March 1859, Father John Cornell was changing trains at Annapolis Junction when he was asked to go to the farm of John Cratin Thompson, less than a mile west of the railroad station. Thompson's wife, Mary Ellen, had given birth three days earlier and the parents wanted the child baptized. Cornell baptized the new-born Francis Xavier Thompson and, after he returned to Annapolis, he dutifully registered this out-of-parish christening. The godparents were the maternal grandparents, William Queen and his wife Henrietta. Dr. Queen, once a Jesuit novice and a graduate of Georgetown College and the Baltimore School of Medicine, was a wealthy farmer and slave owner living near Bryantown, Charles County. One of his daughters joined the Order of Visitation in Baltimore. John Cratin Thompson was a native of Telfair County, Georgia, and also a graduate of Georgetown. He and his wife, Mary Ellen Queen, were second cousins and had to obtain an ecclesiastical dispensation before they were married in 1851 at St. Mary's Church in Mattawoman in Charles County. They were faithful Catholics and all their children were baptized in the Catholic Church. By 1864 John Cratin Thompson and family had moved to Charles County. He met John Wilkes Booth at his father-in-law's farm in November 1864. Booth purportedly sought business investments in Charles County and also wanted to purchase horses. Thompson discussed land values with Booth but, not being an expert, he referred the actor to tobacco plantation owner Henry Lowe Mudd, who might have had land to sell. The following day, before Sunday Mass at St. Mary's Church in Bryantown, Thompson introduced Booth to Mudd's son, Dr. Samuel Alexander Mudd. Booth sat in the Queen family's pew and it was through this acquaintanceship with Mudd that Booth purchased a horse that was later ridden by Lewis Payne, one of the Lincoln conspirators. As with accused conspirator Mary Surratt, Catholics were seen as playing a contributing role in the plot. Although Thompson was not implicated, during the Lincoln conspirators' trial, his name came up four times as the one who introduced Booth to Mudd.[60]

Another distant connection occurred between the Annapolis Redemptorists and people involved in the Lincoln assassination investigation. In this case it was Eliza Jane Lloyd who was married by Father Van de Braak to Private Harvey Rose in 1864. Eliza Jane's first cousin was John Minchin Lloyd who leased Mary Surratt's tavern in Surrattsville after she departed for the District of Columbia in 1864. Mary Surratt came to the tavern three days before Lincoln's assassination to warn Lloyd that two carbines, stashed there by her son John the previous autumn, would soon be needed. And, she came again to the tavern on the day of the assassination to say the carbines would be needed that night. Or so Lloyd testified as state's witness at the Lincoln conspirators' trial. Booth waited outside the tavern after shooting Lincoln, as David Herold retrieved the carbines, ammunition, and binoculars. Then they fled further south to Dr. Mudd's home. When Federal authorities arrived in Surrattsville the next morning, Lloyd initially denied that he had seen Booth but later recanted. He was arrested and imprisoned in the same jail with Mary Surratt. When the case came to trial, he testified against Mrs. Surratt and was later exonerated. Eliza Jane died eleven months before her cousin became involved in the search for the Lincoln conspirators.[61]

Father Michael Stanislaus Burke (1837–91). Source: Rev. Henry Borgmann, C.Ss.R., History of the Redemptorists at Annapolis, Md., from 1853 to 1903 *(Ilchester, Maryland: College Press, 1904), 65.*

Coincidently, both Father Seelos and President Lincoln had premonitions about their untimely deaths. Sometime prior to April 14, 1865, Lincoln told his wife and bodyguard Ward Hill Lamon that he had dreamed of his own wake, after his assassination, being held in the White House East Room on a catafalque surrounded by a guard of soldiers. In case of Father Seelos, he and Brother Lawrence Fischwenger, who had been in Annapolis between 1857 and 1860, were traveling south by train from Detroit to New Orleans in late September 1866. While on one leg of the trip, Father Seelos met two School Sisters of Notre Dame who asked him about his destination and how long he would stay there. He told the sisters he was heading to New Orleans, would remain there a year, and then would die of yellow fever. He did exactly that, succumbing to the disease on October 4, 1867. Brother Lawrence also died in the epidemic, on September 27, in a room across the hall from Father Seelos.[62]

Into the Hands of God

During the summer of 1865, Archbishop Spalding learned from southern bishops and priests of the great sufferings that war had inflicted, the damage done to Catholic properties, and the staggering debts incurred. On August 28, he issued a circular calling for a collection to respond to "the cry of distress which comes to us from all parts of the South." He directed that the circular be read at all Masses in the archdiocese on Sunday, September 10, and that a collection be taken up the following Sunday. The *Annapolis Gazette* published the full text of the circular on the Thursday before it was read at St. Mary's. Spalding called on all Christians to aid "the suffering poor of the South" and he reported the following month that the collection had been "popular with Protestants as well as Catholics." St. Mary's parishioners donated $53 and the Easton and West River missions donated $27 and $4, respectively. The total amount collected in the archdiocese was $12,263, which was sent to bishops and priests in the South for distribution to needy families and individuals, "irrespective of creed." The *Annapolis Gazette* reprinted the *Catholic Mirror* report on the results of the collection and its distribution.[63]

Consumption continued to deplete the ranks of the Annapolis Redemptorists in an era when there was no effective cure. A communicable disease, consumption was easily spread, especially in the close quarters of a nineteenth-century seminary. Four, and possibly six, novices and seminarians had died from consumption at St. Mary's between 1854 and 1863. Three more died from it in the course of five weeks in 1865. This loss of nine men also speaks significantly for the care the Redemptorists provided to their own. Rather than sending seriously ill men home to their families, they stayed with their Redemptorist family and were lovingly cared for until their dying moments.[64]

On the evening of the day that mourning services were held for President Lincoln at St. Mary's, the office for the dead was partly sung and partly recited for Father Peter Petit, who had died four days earlier. He had suffered silently from consumption for two years but religiously adhered to the Redemptorist Rule. He always kept an image of the Holy Cross in view and strictly followed his doctor's orders without complaint. He died at 2:30 AM on Holy Saturday, April 15, 1865. Petit was interred in the church vault on Easter Sunday afternoon, in the presence of the entire Redemptorist community.[65]

On May 22, twenty-two-year-old theology student Henry Wüller died from consumption. A New York City native and son of German immigrants, Wüller entered the novitiate at Annapolis in 1858, professed his vows a year later, and left for Cumberland to study under Father Seelos. Because of his lingering illness he returned to Annapolis in 1860 and spent the rest of his life at St. Mary's. He was exempted from the 1862 draft and, even though he remained in Annapolis, he was one of the Redemptorist seminarians whose enrollment Müller asked the government to change from Annapolis to Cumberland. Three weeks after his death the *Catholic Mirror* published a glowing tribute to Frater Wüller undoubtedly written by an Annapolis Redemptorist. The article referred to his "amiable disposition and fervid piety" which "caused him to be beloved by all." His exacting observance of the Redemptorist Rule and punctual obedience "caused him to be a bright example of edification to the entire community," wrote his anonymous eulogist. Wüller also was a talented musician and for several years had played the organ at Masses at St. Mary's "until his declining health obliged him to retire to the infirmary." He had long had "a great and tender devotion to the Blessed Virgin" and as a child had taken delight in erecting little altars in her honor. It also was revealed that Wüller, when he was about two years old, had become deathly ill. His father, "full of confidence in the powerful intercession of the Queen of Heaven," went to church and prayed before an altar dedicated to Mary for the recovery of his son. "On his return," Mr. Wüller "found the child cured entirely." Shortly before he died, Wüller rejected the suggestion that he pray for his recovery "as he wished to be certain of dying as a Redemptorist." He recited the Rosary daily and, about an hour before his death, he renewed his vows, and then continued to pray the Rosary as "the last act of his life." The last words he was heard to say were "Sancta Maria, Mater Dei," the mid-point of the Hail Mary prayer. His funeral was held in the church and, after the office of the dead was recited and "Libera" sung, his remains were carried in a procession, chanting the "Miserere," to the burial vault "where the last ceremonies were performed."[66]

The *Catholic Mirror* also memorialized Frater John Becker, a theology student who died from consumption on May 29. He was born in Bodenheim, Hesse-Darmstadt, in 1841 and immigrated to the United States in 1852 or 1856. He entered the Annapolis novitiate in 1859 and professed his vows in 1860. He is mentioned above as having had his name drawn in the draft in 1864 despite his poor state of health. The *Mirror* published a detailed account of Becker's young life and the way he "went to receive the reward of his virtuous and holy life." It described how he had suffered from consumption for several years and more than once was thought to be at the point of death. During those years of "his long and painful disease, he was never heard to utter a word of complaint." He went to the chapel each day for community prayers even though barely able to walk. Moreover, he was often unable to study. The eulogist said Becker "possessed a noble and generous soul, and the courage and resignation which he manifested in his illness were truly heroic." Despite the painful disease, his prayers to Jesus, Mary, and Joseph continued as "not once did he complain of the great sufferings which he was obliged to undergo." As a professed student he "retained the fervor of his novitiate, though he was careful to avoid anything like a display of devotion. His life was truly hidden in God." Toward the end, when confined to bed and no longer able to recite the Rosary alone, he invited other students to recite it with him. Despite his sufferings "he always remained calm, cheerfully conversing with all who came to visit him," and it seemed "that all fear of death had been banished from him." He kept two small pictures close to his bed, one of the Virgin Mary and the other of Redemptorist founder St. Alphonsus Liguori. His last act was to devoutly kiss the picture of the Blessed Virgin as he "sweetly breathed forth his pure soul into the hands of God." The funeral arrangements were the same as for Frater Wüller. The *Mirror* article ended with the following:

> These two children of St. Alphonsus have taken their flight to Heaven. In them we see verified those words of the Apocalypse: "Blessed are the dead, who die in the Lord."—Requiescat in pace.[67]

A Day of Genuine Joy

Although Father Seelos was officially still the rector of St. Mary's, he never returned to Annapolis after leaving in September 1863. In a review of key events of June 1865, the *Chronica Domus* noted that the "Rev. Fathers Missionaries Seelos, Bradley, Gross etc. returned to Cumberland with Rev.

Father Burke." Bradley, Burke, and Gross were assigned to the mission band and, like Seelos, were still officially part of the Annapolis community. The house at Cumberland had been designated as a place of relaxation for the traveling missionaries since 1864 and Seelos and his band spent the summers of 1864 and 1865 there. June 1865 was the last time Seelos would be in Maryland. It also was the end of his assignment as superior of the mission band. Afterward, he led retreats for priests in Chicago and Buffalo and assisted at missions in St. Louis, Cincinnati, Dayton, and Toledo. In November 1865, he was assigned to parish work at St. Mary's in Detroit and continued to conduct missions and retreats. He was in Detroit only ten months before being reassigned to New Orleans.[68]

Father Helmprächt departed for Europe on April 17, 1865, and Father Dielemans was promoted to vice rector. But in early July, discouraged with his work in Annapolis and in poor health, Dielemans was permitted to return to the Netherlands. Ironically, this stern, old-school European task master was succeeded as prefect by American-born Father Michael Burke, then serving as lector of English. Father James Keitz later reminisced about the time of his advanced studies and 1865 ordination. He wrote that "the Fourth of July, 1865, the day of [Dielemans'] departure after two-and-a half years of misguided activity, was for many in Annapolis a day of genuine joy." In the meantime, the superior general appointed Helmprächt to head the American Province, so it was necessary to have a new rector in Annapolis. On July 28, 1865, Father Leopold Petsch arrived to fill the position; he appointed Fathers Claessens and Burke as his consultors and Father Girardey as admonitor. Forty-three-year-old Petsch was a native of Moravia, then part of the Austro-Hungarian Empire (now part of the Czech Republic). He was ordained in 1846, immigrated to the United States two years later, and served in Redemptorist parishes in Baltimore, Buffalo, Rochester, New York City, Baltimore again, and back to New York City where he was pastor of St. Alphonsus Church from 1862 to 1865. The former vice rector, Father Helmprächt, just back from Rome and now the provincial superior, visited Annapolis for two days in August.[69]

From Conscientious Christian to Convict

A situation involving three St. Mary's parishioners—the defendant, the plaintiff, and the prosecutor—and several other parishioners as witnesses, had to be resolved at the Anne Arundel County courthouse in 1865. The case involved the binding of African American children into apprenticeships with or without their parents' consent, an action viewed then and now as a form of slavery. Two criminal cases were presented by the State of Maryland against Julia Prout Handy, former slave, mother of five minor children, widow, and Catholic convert. She was accused of having "enticed" three of her children to "run away" from Colonel John Walton, the master to whom the children had been bound as apprentices. The prosecutor was James Revell.

The situation began the previous November 1, as soon as the new Maryland Constitution took effect, abolishing slavery in the state. The three judges of the Anne Arundel County Orphans Court devoted numerous sessions to approving apprenticeships for Black children in apparent contravention of the new state constitution. John Walton was among those who hastened to the Church Circle courthouse, appearing there on November 3 to seek approval of five indentures from a single family: fourteen-year-old Sophia Handy and her brothers, eleven-year-old Thomas, ten-year-old George, eight-year-old James Philip, and six-year-old Vincent. Sophia was bound until she reached age eighteen and her brothers until they were twenty-one. The children were ordered to live with Walton and each to serve as a "good and faithful apprentice ought to do." In return Walton promised to provide "good and sufficient food, clothing, washing, lodging, and all other necessaries fit and convenient for such an appren-

Anne Arundel County Courthouse on Church Circle, Annapolis, ca. 1892. The former home of Moses and Mary Lake can be seen on the corner immediately to the left of the courthouse. SC 985-1-264, Maryland State Archives.

tice" and "to teach . . . the art of a house servant" for the boys and "house girl" for Sophia. At the expiration of each term of service, Walton agreed to give two suits of clothes to the apprentices. Their mother, Julia Handy, was present at the court hearing and it was formally noted that "objecting to the binding, [she] preferred Col. Walton to any other master if bound at all." Although not stated in the indenture record, she herself had been Walton's slave in the 1850s and it is possible that some of her older children also had been his slaves. Each of the five indenture documents was witnessed by Thomas K. Carey, deputy register of wills and St. Mary's parishioner.[70]

St. Mary's parishioners had apprentices bound to them for training before the war. John Wesley Brady, Thomas Denver, John Randall, and James Revell had free Black apprentices under their direction between 1855 and 1859 learning to be farmers, a house servant, a mariner, and a waiter. Parishioners Henry Treadway had a nineteen-year-old White apprentice carpenter. Robert Ackwood (sometimes referred to Aquar), an elderly free Black parishioner, on his deathbed, petitioned the Orphans Court to bind his twelve-year-old son Nathan to Dr. H. Roland Walton in 1860 to be trained as a waiter. These apprenticeships, however, lacked the insidious nature of those approved after November 1, 1864.[71]

It is not clear exactly when Julia "enticed" her children to leave Walton's service. It could have occurred anytime, or at various times, between November 3, 1864, and early May 1865. The Circuit Court criminal proceedings against her began on May 18, 1865, following Walton's complaints presumably made some days or weeks earlier. One case brought against Julia Handy was for enticing her sons George and Thomas to run away, another for enticing daughter Sophia to run away. Evidently, Julia either did not encourage the two youngest boys, Philip and Vincent, to run away or, if she did, Walton chose not to press charges. Walton, his son John Randolph Walton, Dr. Bernard A. Vanderkieft, surgeon in charge of General Hospital Division No. 1, and county sheriff designee John E. Stalker were called as state witnesses. Defense witnesses were St. Mary's parishioner Sarah Woodland and two friends, Adeen Samuel and Elizabeth Wells. Sarah Woodland was the godmother of three of Julia's children and for Julia herself when she converted to Catholicism in 1857. Julia and her late husband, George Handy, were the parents of these four sons baptized at St. Mary's between 1853 and 1858. Because the sons were all baptized at St. Mary's, it is assumed that their eldest child, Sophia, also had been baptized there sometime before September 1851, the date from which the extant sacramental records begin. George Handy was confirmed at St. Mary's in 1857 and died in 1861, with burial at St. Mary's Cemetery. Julia and a man identified only as Ignatius had another child—August Francis Handy, who was born thirteen months after George's death and was baptized at St. Mary's with Rachel Smothers as godmother. August died in 1863 and was buried in the parish cemetery. Julia served in 1860 as a godparent at the baptism of a forty-two-year-old Black convert, John Woodland, possibly a brother or nephew of Sarah Woodland.[72]

Julia Handy's attorney was William Tell Claude, a local lawyer and former States' Rights Party politician. "Elaborate and very eloquent arguments were made by Messrs. James Revell for the State and William Tell Claude for the traverser," according to the *Maryland Republican*, and "involv[ed] many questions of constitutional law and State policy." Claude objected to the charges, pointing out that the 1864 Maryland Constitution abrogated the 1860 statute under which Walton had indentured the children. Article 6 of the 1860 statute provided for binding into indentured service, both White children and Black children of free Black parents, until age twenty-one for males and eighteen for females. It also allowed masters of runaway apprentices "to recover possession of such apprentice . . . as the owner of a personal chattel may recover possession thereof." The statute further declared that no children could be bound if the parent or parents had the means and were willing to support such a child and kept the child employed "so as to teach habits of industry." Anyone who enticed apprentices to run away or abscond was subject to prosecution and, if convicted, to a fine and imprisonment of up to four years but not less than eighteen months. Article 24 of the 1864 Constitution abolished slavery and involuntary servitude (except for convicted criminals) but did not address apprenticeships. Claude's position was supported by a June 1865 Baltimore City Criminal Court decision by Judge Hugh Lennox Bond that sustained the 1864 Constitution and allowed Black apprentices to be remanded to their parents. In Annapolis, however, presiding Judge William Tuck overruled Claude's demurrer, thereby sustaining the 1860 law. Julia was indicted and pleaded not guilty. The jury, however, failed to reach consensus on the charges and was discharged. As a result, Judge Tuck remanded the case to the October 1865 term for a new trial.[73]

The second trial began on November 10. This time Julia Handy was represented by Annapolis attorney James R. Howison. Sarah Woodland, Adeen Samuel, and Elizabeth Wells were again called to testify. Her children, Sophia and Thomas, also testified but to no avail. The jury found Julia guilty and she was fined one cent plus $55.56 court costs and sentenced to four months in jail for each case, a total $111.14—about $1,600 in modern prices)—and eight months imprisonment.[74]

Despite the conviction, jail sentence, and financial distress caused by the case, it was a pyrrhic victory for Walton and the State of Maryland. Sensing the injustice of the case, five individuals petitioned Governor Bradford to pardon Julia Handy. One petition requesting executive clemency was signed by two of the jurors at Julia's first trial: former Annapolis mayor John Wesley White and future mayor James Munroe. They revealed "that after a full and impartial hearing . . . the jury were divided in their opinion, and could not agree upon the verdict and were finally discharged by the Court after having been confined to the jury room for more than twenty four hours." White and Munroe now said they "could not conscientiously find her guilty" because it was not proven to their satisfaction that Julia actually had persuaded her children to leave Walton's service. They also stated that not only were the children bound without their mother's consent but that she was "fully capable of taking care of her children." Sophia was about sixteen years old and capable of hiring herself out; George and Thomas already had been hiring themselves out at twelve dollars per month to help support the family. Once her sons became Walton's apprentices, Julia lost this income. In conclusion, White and Munroe said they had known Julia for many years and that she was "one of the most respected colored persons of our city. . . . honest, industrious and well behaved."[75]

A second petition was signed by the wives of two prominent Annapolis politicians: Emily Irving Nicholson Magruder, the wife of former mayor John Read Magruder, and her mother, Eliza Ann Hagner Nicholson, the wife of Colonel Joseph Hopper Nicholson, former clerk of the county court and former acting Maryland secretary of state, among other political positions, and a former enslaver. The women said they had known Julia Handy "for a number of years" and that she was "late a slave of Col. John Walton of Annapolis, now confined in the jail of Anne Arundel County." They declared Julia "a most excellent character in every respect" and that she had "no intention of violating the law, being a poor ignorant woman." The letter closed with a plea for clemency based on their statement of facts and "in consideration of her previous good character."[76]

The third petition came from Father John Gerdemann, assistant pastor of St. Mary's. He wrote "in favor of Julia Handy, a colored person now imprisoned, with whom I warmly sympathize." He noted that Julia was well known to the Redemptorists at St. Mary's and that he had "never heard anything but what showed her to be a very respectable & thoroughly conscientious Christian woman." Because of his personal acquaintance with Julia, Gerdemann wrote that he did not believe she was "wilfully guilty" of breaking the law of which she was accused and convicted. He closed with the request that the governor "do for this poor person whatsoever the law permits and your kind heart dictates."[77]

Legal notices were published in the local press for two weeks, advising the public that petitions had been submitted on Julia Handy's behalf and offered to consider any protests. There were none and on January 9, 1866, based primarily on the petition of White and Munroe, Julia Handy was pardoned by Governor Bradford. He ordered her immediate release from jail. The pardon itself focused on the constitutional issue as the most convincing basis for freeing her, that, in effect, the 1864 Maryland Constitution had abrogated state laws that allowed the apprenticeship of Black children. Black apprenticeships were struck down nationwide by the US Supreme Court in another Maryland case in 1867, which saw them as essentially involuntary servitude.[78]

Selling Whisky on Sunday

Julia Handy was not the only St. Mary's parishioner in court in 1865. The Anne Arundel Circuit Court docket for the April and October 1865 terms carries many familiar names. One was Dr. John Randolph Walton who was charged with manslaughter in the killing of a soldier who attacked him and his wife Margaret on his father's farm in October 1864. His trial was held in June 1865 and he was found not guilty, despite the testimony of four soldiers for the state. This was offset by testimony by four witnesses, including two army officers and Margaret Walton. One of the state's soldier witnesses, Thomas Carpenter, did not get off so easy. He was charged in a second case with assaulting Margaret Walton with intent to kill her. His trial was remanded to the October term. The October 1865 court docket lists Carpenter's as the second trial to be held, but inexplicably has no annotations other than repeating the charges and that Margaret Walton was called as the witness, but there was no indication of guilt or not. The vagaries of war, this time, may have been on the side of the soldier who had probably long gone home.[79]

Parishioner and bar keeper Bartholomew Esmond was found guilty of running a disorderly house and fined $50 plus court costs. Ten witnesses testified against him, none of them St. Mary's parishioners. But three Irish-born parishioners came to his defense: Timothy O'Brien (a former US Marine sergeant who saw action early in the war and had become an Annapolis butcher), Mary O'Brien (Timothy's wife), and Martin Gill (a laborer). Hoping to get on the right side of the law, Esmond later became one of the first police officers when the Annapolis Police Department was formally established in 1867.[80]

Grocery shopkeeper Jane Elizabeth Flood pleaded guilty to "selling whiskey to sailors & negroes on Sunday" and was fined $20 plus court costs. John Cavanaugh was found guilty of assault and battery on a constable "whilst in the discharge of his duties" and sentenced to ten days in the county jail. This time Timothy O'Brien testified for the state. Other parishioner names, such as John and Anne Geoghan, John Himmelheber, Moses Lake, John Mullavel, George O'Malley, John Baptiste Parodi, and Thomas Tydings appear in the court docket for a variety of cases, appeals, posting bonds for others, and as defendants and witnesses.[81]

The Navy Returns

After more than four years at Newport, Rhode Island, the Naval Academy returned to Annapolis in August 1865. A number of St. Mary's parishioners who had gone north with the academy in 1861 came back to Annapolis. Michael Naughton, a laborer, and his wife, Mary Ann Drury Naughton, had three children born in Newport: Margaret (who later became a School Sister of Notre Dame) in October 1861 and Joseph Francis in June 1863, and Mary, reportedly born in Newport in July 1866, after her father's return to Annapolis. Hugh McCusker's son, James F., was born in Newport in 1862. In July 1865, the Navy's Bureau of Navigation in Washington specifically requested McCusker's early return to Annapolis so he could "superintend the heating management" at the academy. Andrew Denver's son, Cornelius Joseph, was born in Newport in 1864. Denver himself returned to Annapolis in 1865 as captain of the watch and later became better known as "Old Denver," the academy band's imposing drum major. Simon Farrell, a laborer who went to Newport in 1861, did not stay the whole time there because he appeared as godfather at a baptism in Annapolis in May 1863 and as witness to a marriage in May 1865. Laborers John Joseph Geoghan and Michael Gesner and gas fitter August Schwallenberg also returned to Annapolis on unspecified dates. Another man who became a St. Mary's parishioner, Patrick Hoban, a fireman in the gas and steam works, had joined the academy's civilian staff in 1864 in Newport. His daughter, Mary, was born there in 1865, indicating that Patrick's wife, Catherine Connors Hoban, was with him during the war and in Annapolis soon after the war's end. All of these men and members of their families are buried at St. Mary's Cemetery.[82]

Drawing professor Edward Seager and his family also returned to Annapolis. During his stint in Newport, he visited the White Mountains of New Hampshire to improve his portfolio of American landscape art. In May 1864, President Lincoln gave him a commission in the Navy. He retired from the Naval Academy in 1867 and by 1870 Seager, his wife, and five adult children had left Annapolis for Baltimore, where he taught art. Sometime after 1880, the elder Seagers moved to Washington, DC, where they died, she in 1882 and he in 1886, and are buried at the Holy Rood Cemetery, the old burial ground for the Jesuits' Most Holy Trinity Church in Georgetown. Thomas Karney, assistant professor of ethics and English, also returned to Annapolis and became Naval Academy librarian from 1872 to his death in 1885. He is buried at St. Mary's Cemetery. The academy's sword master, Justin Bonnafous, came with the other new faculty members to Annapolis in 1865. The then-forty-eight-year-old Frenchman appears only once in St. Mary's records: in 1866 when he was a witness at the marriage of Charles Gerard of Versailles, France, to Victoria Villamier of St. Liège, France.[83]

Band member Christian Wirth returned to Annapolis and continued as a musician. His date of death is unknown but occurred sometime after the 1870 Federal Census, when he was last noted in Annapolis. His wife, Catherine, died at age seventy-five in 1877 and is buried at St. Mary's Cemetery. When Charles Garlieb Zimmermann and his wife Elizabeth Gesner returned to Annapolis, they brought with them their son, Charles Adams Zimmermann, who was born in Newport on July 22, 1861. Charles Garlieb continued to play in the band and led St. Mary's choir until he died in 1885. Charles and Elizabeth had four other sons, three of whom died in childhood. The two survivors became well-known band masters (see Parish Legacies, ch. 9). Two of Elizabeth's brothers became academy band members: Francis (Frank) J. Gesner in 1865 and violin in the orchestra; and John Michael Gesner in 1870.[84]

Three men with St. Mary's connections joined the band while it was at Newport and came with it to Annapolis in 1865. Early in the war, Peter Francis Schoff had been a cavalry bandmaster and, on June 12, 1865, was appointed as the fifth bandmaster of the Naval Academy, a role he continued until 1887. He was not Catholic but his Irish-born wife, Cecilia Manahan, was. They had eight children, four of whom were born in Annapolis and baptized at St. Mary's, and two of whom (Edward T. and Peter Francis) joined the band in the 1880s.[85]

Alfred C. Woolley joined the band in 1863 as a clarinetist. An Englishman by birth, he was not Catholic but his Irish-born wife Elizabeth Corcoran was. Two of their sons, Alfred Jr. and David Edward, joined the band in 1880 and 1886, respectively. Alfred Sr. converted to Catholicism on his deathbed in 1887. He, his wife, most of their children, and some their grandchildren are buried in St. Mary's Cemetery.[86]

William Nayden enlisted in 1863 and played the bass tuba in the band and the French horn in the orchestra. He came with the band to Annapolis, where he settled with his wife, Elizabeth. She died in 1873 and William remarried, this time to a Catholic woman, Margaret Lafferty, who was born in Philadelphia of Irish parents. Although William and his first wife are buried in St. Anne's Cemetery in Annapolis, his second wife, Margaret, two children, a daughter-in-law, and two grandchildren are buried at St. Mary's Cemetery and a grandson, Father William Alphonsus Nayden, C.Ss.R., is buried in the Redemptorist Cemetery behind St. Mary's Church.[87]

One of the parishioner band members who did not return to Annapolis after the war was first-class musician Peter Klippen. After playing cornet at Newport for two years, he enlisted in the Fifth US Artillery Band at Fort Hamilton, New York. He evidently had not been officially released from the

Francis Augustus Schwallenberg (1833–1908), Naval Academy gas fitter and St. Mary's parishioner. Courtesy James Schwallenberg.

Naval Academy because he was reported as a "deserter," apprehended and placed under arrest, and taken back to Newport. Once his status was resolved, he rejoined the Fifth Artillery Band and was stationed, sequentially, at Fort Monroe, Virginia, and Atlanta, Georgia, where he was honorably discharged in 1868. Peter and his wife, Rebecca, died within a month of each other in 1910 are buried together in Greenmount, a public cemetery in Philadelphia.[88]

Peter Hilgert, a parishioner who was in Annapolis with the band before the war, apparently left the band by 1864, and by 1870 was working in Philadelphia, as a sugar refiner. Peter died in 1881 and is buried in St. Peter's Cemetery in Philadelphia. This cemetery, coincidently, is operated by the Redemptorists and appertains to St. Peter's Church, now the National Shrine of St. John Neumann. His wife, Meta Strohmeyer Hilgert, died in 1896 and is buried in Philadelphia's Mount Moriah Cemetery.[89]

Forty-four-year-old Sergeant Thomas Gately was a Marine Corps veteran of the Mexican War who went to Newport with the Naval Academy, returned to Annapolis in 1865. He had served at the academy since the early 1850s aboard the USS *Constitution*. He died in 1867 and his funeral was held at St. Mary's "where religious services were performed, and from thence to the cemetery, where they were deposited with the honors of war." His comrades later erected an elaborate stone over his grave in St. Mary's Cemetery. It reads in part: "Strict and impartial in the execution of the duties devolving upon him as a noncommissioned officer, he was kind, obedient and honest, he exercised a moral influence through the entire command of which he was a member . . . [and] was highly esteemed and respected by all who knew him."[90]

More Military Weddings

Three soldier weddings celebrated at St. Mary's occurred soon after the war ended and were officiated by Father Louis Claessens. The first was Patrick John Dougherty, a native of County Cork, Ireland, and Jane Dunworth Strohmeyer, a native of County Roscommon, on October 15. Jane was a twenty-five-year-old widow with a two-year-old daughter, Mary Louise. Her first marriage was at St. Mary's in 1862 to Charles Strohmeyer, a Lutheran and a baker by profession who had died in 1864. Charles' father, Franz, had been a member of the Naval Academy Band and his sister, Meta, was married to Catholic band member Peter Hilgert. At the time of Jane's first marriage she was employed as a "servant" (probably a chamber maid) at Walton's City Hotel. The witnesses at Patrick and Jane's wedding were two Irish-born Catholic friends of Jane's: Margaret Regan, a coworker at the City Hotel, and Bridget Curtin, a servant in the home of Colonel Joseph Hopper Nicholson. Their daughter Mary Louise was baptized at St. Mary's in September 1863.[91]

Patrick Dougherty's Annapolis connection began when he was admitted to General Hospital Division No. 1 on June 15, 1863, suffering from a head wound. He enlisted in Philadelphia in April 1861 for three months in Company A, Twenty-First Pennsylvania Infantry, and was involved in minor skirmishing around Martinsburg, Virginia (later West Virginia). He reenlisted in October 1861 in Troop A, Sixth US Cavalry. The regiment had an unexpected "baptism of fire" on May 4, 1862, in a prelude to the Battle of Williamsburg on May 5, and again on May 11, when Troop A clashed with Confederate cavalry. The regiment was deployed in September 1862 to Antietam but Dougherty was reported "absent on parole at Governors Island" in New York Harbor between September and December 1862.[92]

Dougherty returned to his regiment in time for two historical actions. The first was known as Stoneman's Raid, in which a 10,000-strong cavalry operation led by Brigadier General George Stoneman deployed south of the Rappahannock River as a diversion prior to and during the Battle of Chancellorsville (April 30–May 6, 1863). Between April 13 and 30, the Sixth and four other cavalry regiments under the command of Brigadier General John Buford secured river crossings and supply points. Although the raid saw little fighting, it provided valuable experience to Dougherty and his fellow troopers and forced Confederate units further south to reinforce Richmond. Although the Sixth had no troops killed during the raid, the men and horses suffered considerably from incessant riding in inclement weather.[93]

The second significant action in which Private Dougherty participated was at the Battle of Brandy Station, near Beverly Ford in Culpeper County, on June 9, 1863. The day-long battle is famous for having been the largest cavalry engagement in American history, involving 21,456 troops on both sides, of which 18,456 were cavalry. The Sixth's troopers and other mounted units, again under Buford's command, repeatedly charged and clashed with J.E.B. Stuart's Confederate cavalry during a running twelve-hour battle, all while coming under heavy artillery, musket, and pistol fire and deadly saber slashing. The Sixth US Cavalry and the Sixth Pennsylvania Cavalry "fiercely contested" the battleground as they made "a brilliant charge across the open field." A Confederate captain who fought at Brandy Station that day, wrote years later that:

> Never rode troopers more gallantly than did those Regulars, as under a fire of shell and shrapnel, and finally of canister, they dashed up to the very muzzles, then through and beyond our guns.[94]

The battle was a Union defeat in which the Sixth Cavalry saw more than 25 percent of its combatants killed, wounded, or taken prisoner. Company A was heavily involved in the action, with two killed in action, including the company commander, eight wounded, and one who died later from his wounds. Dougherty was among the wounded with a saber cut to the forehead and was taken prisoner. He was quickly paroled and sent to Annapolis for hospitalization.[95]

Dougherty's medical care at Annapolis continued until October 14, when he was furloughed and then discharged from the army when his term of service expired on October 8, 1864. He remained in Annapolis, attended St. Mary's Church, was confirmed there by Archbishop Spalding on December 8, 1864, and married there in October 1865. From 1865 to 1877, Dougherty claimed in his pension application that he enlisted in the Navy and served on the USS *Santee* and other Naval Academy practice ships There is no evidence of a Navy enlistment but other records indicate he worked at the academy as a civilian laborer. By 1877 Patrick and Jane had four children, all baptized at St. Mary's: Elizabeth Jane (known as Lisette), Joseph Patrick, Catherine (Kate) Agnes, and Mary Theresa, in addition to Jane's daughter Mary Louise Strohmeyer.[96]

The Irish-Catholic network appears to have been at work for Patrick and the Widow Strohmeyer to meet, perhaps at St. Mary's after Sunday Mass through a mutual Irish acquaintances. Ann Reilly, who was one of the witnesses at Patrick and Jane's wedding, married Thomas Hickey, a Navy coal heaver during the war and afterward was a watchman at the Naval Academy. After Hickey died in 1874, Ann married an Irish bar keeper, Bartholomew Esmond (see Domestic Concerns, ch. 8).[97]

Troubled times came to the Dougherty family, perhaps from residual effects of Patrick's old head wound or some other health problem. The 1880 Federal Census for Annapolis reported in the occupation column that Patrick was "Away" and there was a check mark in the column headed "Insane." He next turns up in the records in 1897 when he first applied for a Civil War pension. He was residing in Catasauqua, an industrial borough in Lehigh County, Pennsylvania, and said he was unable to earn a living "because of rheumatism, injury to left knee, general debility, heart trouble, cramps, blind in left eye." Later the same year, he submitted an affidavit listing his residence at Centre Valley, a nearby village. Dougherty said he had had rheumatism ever since he left the army. A medical exam confirmed some but not all of his claimed ailments and his pension application was rejected. Two years later, Dougherty was scheduled for another medical exam but he "objected to having his eyes examined & left before exam was concluded." Among the Bureau of Pensions' medical board findings was that Dougherty had "no special evidence of vicious habits" (the bureau's term for heavy tobacco or alcohol use), that he was "living a sort of tramp life," and that the loss of sight in the left eye was the "result of a blow, probably of a fist." Nevertheless, he was granted a $6.00 a month pension in 1899. He died on January 1, 1909, still living in Lehigh County. Several months after his death, Jane Dougherty, who remained in Annapolis, applied for and received a widow's pension of $12.00 per month which continued until she died in 1919. She is buried at St. Mary's Cemetery next to her daughter Kate.[98]

The second 1865 soldier wedding occurred on October 16, when Captain Henry C. Williams married Barbara Hayne. It was a mixed marriage, with Barbara the Catholic half of the couple. The witnesses were unusual. They were Father Andrew Ziegler, one of the April 1865 ordinands, and Brother Eustachius Reinhardt, a tailor at the college since the previous January. Why these two religious men were chosen as witnesses is a mystery. Williams had many military comrades in the city and Barbara, who had been confirmed at St. Mary's in December 1864, was a native of Anne Arundel County. A Philadelphia native, Williams had been in the army for four years and was about to be released. He served as a sergeant in the Nineteenth Pennsylvania Infantry and then with the Eighth Pennsylvania Cavalry. After several brief hospitalizations, he was promoted to second lieutenant in March 1862 and first lieutenant in July 1862. The regiment was involved in the defense of Washington and participated in major battles at Yorktown, Fair Oaks, Antietam, Fredericksburg, Chancellorsville, and Gettysburg.[99]

In recognition of Williams' participation at Gettysburg, his name is cast in bronze on the Pennsylvania State Memorial installed in 1913 at the Gettysburg National Military Park. After Gettysburg, the Eighth provided reconnaissance for the Army of the Potomac but Williams was afflicted with neuralgia in November and admitted to the Seminary Army General Hospital in Georgetown. After his release from the hospital, Williams was promoted to captain in January 1864 and detached for recruiting duty in Philadelphia until the end of his term of service. He was mustered out in November 1864 as "unfit for duty." Despite this, Williams joined Company E, 213th Pennsylvania Infantry in March 1865 and the regiment was immediately ordered to Annapolis to guard Camp Parole. The next month, Williams was appointed provost marshal for the city. He served in this position until he was mustered out in November, shortly after the wedding. Barbara Hayne was mentioned in an Annapolis newspaper notice of her marriage as being "of this city" and Henry Williams as "of Philadelphia." Little else is known about this couple. There are no other mentions of them in St. Mary's records but a Henry C. Williams of comparable age and nativity died from consumption in Portland, Connecticut, and was buried in Philadelphia in 1876.[100]

In November 1865, Father Claessens officiated at the wedding of John Felix Gilfeather and Cecelia Bridget Conlon. Little is known about Cecelia (or Bridget, the names were used interchangeably). Census and pension records indicate she was born in Exeter, New Hampshire, around 1843 and in 1860 was living in Roxbury, Massachusetts, where she met her future husband. Felix Gilfeather was born in County Donegal, Ireland, around 1829. After immigrating to the United States, he worked as a laborer in Boston. Perhaps seeking more steady employment, in January 1861 he enlisted for five years as a private in Battery D, Second US Artillery Regiment. When the war began, Gilfeather's regiment was assigned to the defenses of the District of Columbia and later fought at the First Battle of Manassas (July 21, 1861). Whether Felix fought in the battle is not clear because his service record indicates he was absent and sick from July to October 1861. His illness continued and he was found "unfit for duty, incapable of performing duties as soldier because of Chronic Rheumatism," and discharged on December 29. Not dissuaded by the rigors of military life, Gilfeather enlisted in the Navy for three years at Boston on May 27, 1862, as a coal heaver. This was strenuous, hot, dirty, and dangerous work that involved hauling 140-pound buckets of coal from the ship's bunker to the boiler. But it paid more than

Brother Peter Recktenwald, C.Ss.R. (1824–1906). RABP

an ordinary seaman received. He served aboard the USS *Tioga* in the North Atlantic Blockading Squadron and later on the USS *Massasoit*, which patrolled the New England coast. During the latter assignment, Gilfeather took ill again and was discharged at the Navy hospital in Boston on October 31, 1864. But the new illness was still not enough to keep him from enlisting a third time. On November 28, 1864, he presented himself at the Marine Corps recruiting station in Boston and enlisted as a private. On completion of training, he was assigned on July 9, 1865, to serve onboard the USS *Winnipec*, a Naval Academy practice ship. Once he was in Annapolis, Felix Gilfeather arranged for Bridget to join him and they were married on November 16. She returned to Massachusetts after the wedding and at some point became ill. Gilfeather's days in Annapolis were numbered. He deserted his post in November 1866 and returned to Massachusetts to care for his ailing wife.[101]

Felix and Bridget Gilfeather had three children and lived in the Boston area where Felix worked as a gardener. He was denied a pension because of the desertion from the Marines in 1866 but received state aid. He died in 1890 from pneumonia and general debility. Bridget applied for a Massachusetts pension seven months after Felix's death and received it until 1892 when state officials learned of the 1866 desertion. At that point, she appealed to the Bureau of Pensions, explaining why her husband "run away from the Naval Academy[,] he run away from there on my account" and saying "I am a poor woman and need a pension." After two years of bureaucratic inaction, she hired a District of Columbia lawyer who obtained the needed evidence that Felix had served honorably in both the army and the navy during the Civil War. But a new problem arose when it was discovered Felix had been married before to Sarah Jane Duffey and had a daughter by her. The Bureau of Pensions rejected Bridget's claim but after she wrote to President Theodore Roosevelt to plead her case, they investigated the first marriage and verified that Sarah Jane had died in 1857 and that the 1865 Gilfeather-Conlon wedding at St. Mary's was legitimate. Finally, in 1903, Bridget Gilfeather received an $8.00 per month pension. She died in Weymouth, Massachusetts, in 1908.[102]

Base Ball Fever

A notable new development occurred in Annapolis in the autumn 1865. Parishioner John Floyd Maley was one of the seven "young men of this city" who founded the Annapolis Base Ball Club. They did this "for the purpose of enjoying themselves in the exciting and healthful amusements afforded by this game." Locals had seen Union soldiers play the game in Annapolis during the war and now, as journalist Elihu Riley Jr. put it, "Annapolis caught the base ball fever prevalent in the country." Maley, an Irish-born printer by trade, had been a private in Company I, Fifteenth Massachusetts Infantry, when he was captured at the Battle of Ball's Bluff (October 21, 1861) in Loudoun County, Virginia. He was paroled in February 1862 and sent to Camp Parole where he worked as a clerk in the camp quartermaster's department from October 1862 to June 1864. He was discharged in July 1864 and went home to Worcester, Massachusetts. During his time at Camp Parole, Maley met Josephine Legg, the daughter of an Annapolis butcher. He returned to Annapolis in 1866 and they were married at the Salem Methodist Church. Although John was Catholic, Josephine was not, and eight of their eleven children—the ones born in Annapolis—were baptized at St. Mary's between 1867 and 1880. He worked as a paymaster's steward on the USS *Constitution* at the Naval Academy in 1866–67. The family later moved to the District of Columbia where John was a compositor at the US Government Printing Office. He suffered the rest of his life from wartime injuries and illnesses. John died in 1916 and Josephine in 1919; both are buried in Mount Olivet Cemetery in the District of Columbia.[103]

New Assignments and Newcomers

August saw the departure of two of the ten priests ordained in April. Charles Rosenbauer and George Lawrence Werner both were assigned to parishes in Baltimore. Four more left St. Mary's in September: James Gleeson to Cumberland, Hubert Bove to Philadelphia, Francis Oberle to Detroit, and Rhabanus Preis to New York City. John Berger had gone to St. Alphonsus in Baltimore right after his ordination on April 1 and remained there for several years. Joseph Firle and Andrew Ziegler stayed in Annapolis until January 1866 and then went to Cumberland to complete their second novitiate. James Keitz stayed in Annapolis to teach sacred scripture and hermeneutics (the science of the interpretation of scripture).[104]

Father Timothy Enright returned to St. Mary's College after an eighteen-month absence. He had left Annapolis in

March 1864 for assignment to Most Holy Redeemer Church in New York City. Following a short assignment in North Carolina between January and August 1865, he returned to New York City and was back in North Carolina in September 1866 before starting his permanent new assignment in Annapolis, teaching algebra, English, geography, and secular history. He also had charge of the Easton mission as described above.[105]

Another new man was assigned to St. Mary's in December 1865. Thirty-one-year-old Peter Recktenwald was a professed lay brother who was assigned to Pittsburgh (1849–60) and Cumberland (1860–65). In Annapolis he worked as a tailor and was in charge of the college laundry. His first assignment at St. Mary's lasted only eight months (he was assigned there again in 1874) but he left his mark wherever he went. Peter was born in Prussia in 1824 on the day after the Feast of Our Lady of Sorrows (April 9), to whom he became devoted. He left Prussia in 1846 to seek his fortune in the United States. While on the transatlantic ship, he befriended a Bavarian family, the Weingärtners, who also sought a better life in America. Peter helped the younger children learn their prayers and, so the story goes, kept them from falling overboard. One little fellow, six-year-old Ludwig (known in America as Louis), became a particular favorite of Peter's and Peter saved him from harm on several occasions. After the ship landed in New York City, Peter and the Weingärtner family went their separate ways, Peter to find a Catholic church to offer thanks for a safe voyage and the Bavarian family to western New York. Peter found his vocation with the Redemptorists, was invested by Father Seelos in Pittsburgh in 1849, and professed his vows in 1851. But his humble and holy approach to life had left an impression on little Louis who later joined the Redemptorists as Brother Jerome (sometimes called by his Latin name, Hieronymus). Jerome arrived in Annapolis in November 1863 and worked as a cook and in the laundry, where he was joined by Brother Peter in 1865–66. Brother Peter kept busy making and repairing habits and other clothing for the seminarians. In later years, some of the priests who had been students during Peter's reign in the tailor shop at Annapolis recalled how his virtue of poverty carried over into making "sixty-cent habits" of inferior fabric he himself bought in town. He also attached black cuffs to the worn ends of trousers and made work overalls from different colored scraps of cloth. "No article of clothing was so old that he ever refused to patch it," reads an entry in his personnel file. The results of Peter's work were said to resemble the Biblical Joseph's coat of many colors (Genesis 37:3). He insisted on maintaining silence in the tailor shop and spoke only when necessary but was always moving his lips in quiet prayer. In later years he was renowned for making thousands of Seven Dolors rosaries.[106]

The Almighty Has His Own Purposes

Most historians acknowledge there were at least 620,000 military deaths during the Civil War. When civilian war-caused fatalities are included, the number may have reached as high as 750,000. Drew Gilpin Faust agrees with the 620,000 figure, noting that some 2.1 million Northerners and 880,000 Southerners took up arms. She also points out there were 50,000 civilian deaths; the consequences of war, such as civilian casualties on or near battlefields and during the sieges at Vicksburg, Petersburg, and Atlanta. Thomas Fleming, however, estimates that up to 850,000, or nearly 3 percent of the nation's population, both military and civilian, may have died, about 550,000 from the North and 300,000 from the South. These numbers included wartime tragedies such as the seventy-four mainly Irish-Catholic women and children who were killed in 1862 when black powder detonated at Allegheny Arsenal, where they worked filling small-arms cartridges. It was not far from Father Seelos' old St. Philomena's Parish in Pittsburgh and may have included some of his former parishioners. Among other cases were the forty-five women and children who died in explosion at an ordnance factory in Richmond in 1863.[107]

Measles, mumps, small pox, diarrhea, dysentery, typhoid, malaria, and other diseases resulted in twice as many deaths among soldiers than from battle wounds. Diseases that might have been avoided in peacetime and led to high mortality rates among military men also killed many civilians. An estimated 9 percent of Civil War dead lost their lives in prison camps. About 40 percent of deceased Yankee soldiers and sailors who died were identified only as "unknown." Many of the soldiers' bodies simply went missing and wartime records accounted for only 101,736 registered burials, which is less than one-third of the estimated Union fatalities. Still more veterans later died as the direct result of their wounds or chronic diseases.[108]

Despite the tragedies of war, Americans—North and South—endured. They lived in an era in which many were inclined toward religion and could seek solace in their faith during this time of national devastation and its aftermath. Father Robert Miller points out that "it was a deeply religious country that went to war in 1861" and that it was religious institutions that brought people together—North and South—more than other cultural or voluntary organizations.[109]

During the war, governments both North and South proclaimed national and state-wide days of humiliation, fasting, and prayer. In Lincoln's second inaugural address, delivered as the war still raged, he wondered aloud what it all meant when he noted that the people North and South:

> Both read the same Bible and pray to the same God, and each invokes His aid against the other. It may seem strange that any men should dare to ask a just God's assistance in wringing their bread from the sweat of other men's faces, but let us judge not, that we be not judged. The prayers of both could not be answered. That of neither has been answered fully. The Almighty has His own purposes.[110]

But, Lincoln went on, if God wills that the war continued "so still it must be said 'the judgments of the Lord are true and righteous altogether.'"

Lincoln's post-war plan included forgiveness and social and economic reconstruction. But he died tragically and those who succeeded were more inclined to retribution and punishment. As alluded to earlier, Father Seelos believed the post-war times would be hard, especially on Catholics.[111]

What then must St. Mary's parishioners have thought when they read a lengthy article in the *Annapolis Gazette* about the ultimate retribution taken against one particular Catholic? It might have appeared to be a return to the earlier years when the *Gazette* took a hardline against Catholics. Heinrich (Henry) Wirz, a native of Switzerland and commander of the infamous Andersonville prisoner-of-war camp in Georgia, was the only Confederate soldier executed by the Federal government for war crimes. The *Gazette* could not have been more emphatic about his Catholic faith at the time of the November 10 execution in Washington:

> Yesterday and last night, Wirz . . . received the ministrations of his spiritual advisors Fathers Boyle and Whelan. . . . This morning at an early hour he received the consolation of religion at the hands of Fathers Boyle and Weichert; accompanied to the scaffold by Fathers Boyle and Wiget . . . Father Boyle stooped over the criminal, reciting to him the Catholic death service . . . . [after the reading of his death sentence] the clergy took leave of the criminal, he previously passing the crucifix to his lips.[112]

Press accounts in other cities either only mentioned the Catholic priests in passing or not at all. Annapolitans got a full dose when reading about this war criminal.[113]

Another *Annapolis Gazette* article gave a more cheerful outlook on life. Christmas 1865 was celebrated in Annapolis "by a general cessation of all business pursuits, and by religious rejoicings appropriate to the occasions." Christmas Day, a Monday, was "wet and rather disagreeable" but the churches "were all well attended—more so than has been usual on former occasions." It was reported that "although everyone seemed to enjoy the day to the utmost, it was also to be noticed that few if any, could be seen who were intoxicated or noisy, save in the harmless way of gunpowder, fire-crackers, drums, tin horns, &c., with which our young gentry tried to out-do each other."[114]

So ended the fateful year of 1865.

Part Three — Mors Lamentabilis

Chapter 8: Hunger for the Supernatural

Most fighting between Union and Confederate forces ceased when Robert E. Lee surrendered at Appomattox Court House on April 9, 1865. His troops were released and allowed to return home. The army of General Joseph Eggleston Johnston surrendered near Durham, North Carolina, on April 26. The last battle of the war, a Union loss, was on the Mexican border, at Palmito Ranch, Texas, on May 12–13. Other Confederate regiments and naval ships surrendered in the following months and by autumn most Union volunteers were mustered out of service. President Andrew Johnson proclaimed the war officially over on April 2, 1866.[1] Normalcy slowly descended on the broken and greatly changed nation as "reconstruction" brought the South slowly back into the fold but without resolving the racial inequalities faced by freed people.

This uncivil war had come unbidden to Annapolis and, despite its impact on the town and surrounding county, the people endured. Babies were born, marriages were celebrated, old people—and young—died. Just as they had in peacetime, conscientious Catholics observed 110 fast days a year, attended Mass on the eight obligatory holy days and fifty-two Sundays, and observed their religious duty to confess their sins at least once a year. Some local businesses thrived with the influx of Federal troops on their way to war and those returning from the battlefront suffering wounds and illness. Soldiers arrived in large numbers and various conditions of health after having been captured in battle and returned North on parole. While most soldiers and sailors temporarily in Annapolis returned home to reclaim their delayed domestic lives, others stayed after the war, settled in town and married local women. The Naval Academy returned to Annapolis and the damage caused by four years of occupation as a major army hospital complex was repaired and classes resumed. St. John's College also had been appropriated for hospital use and as a transit camp for paroled soldiers, but wartime reparations actually saved the college from extinction. The sentiments that brought about the war did not disappear but they slowly adjusted to the new post-war realities. At St. Mary's Parish and elsewhere there were Unionists who rejoiced that their nation had been reunited but saw their slaves go free and lost a source of wealth. Some pro-South Democrats at St. Mary's had mixed feelings about how the war was resolved but had no slaves to lose. Families had sons who died in battle for the Confederacy and for the Union. During and after the war, Protestant men married Catholic women and vice versa, Irish married Germans, and pro-South families had seen daughters marry Union soldiers. Black Catholics and non-Catholics alike who had been held in bondage and then freed in 1864 still faced prejudice, segregation, and second-class citizenship, while free Blacks before the war now found themselves in situations similar to the former slaves. But the people endured and life went on, if not quite the same as before.

Annapolis entered the post-war years with six well established churches: St. Mary's Catholic, St. Anne's Episcopal, and two Methodist churches—the new Salem Church on State Circle and, in 1863, a small frame church—Macedonian African Methodist Episcopal Church—on Doctor (now Franklin) Street. The older Presbyterian Church on Duke of Gloucester Street and Asbury African Methodist Episcopal on West Street also were quite active. In addition, there was a small group of Jewish merchants drawn to Annapolis by the increased wartime trade. For a brief time, there were enough of them to form a small congregation, as is evidenced by an itinerant religious functionary who traveled from Baltimore to perform the Jewish rite of circumcision on some of their sons, and who referred to the "holy congregation" of Annapolis in his record book. This small group of worshipers likely met in a member's home or storeroom.[2]

Religious belief, while not universal, was an important part of life in Annapolis and throughout Anne Arundel County. The war and all its dangers, as well as personal loss, had brought much soul searching and conversion. Post-war population growth brought the need for more country chapels and mission stations, both Catholic and Protestant. Over the next half century, St. Mary's would become the "mother" and "grandmother" of the Catholic parishes of Anne Arundel County.

The Passage Between the New and Old Houses

As the year 1866 began, St. Mary's College had nine priests teaching in the seminary and administering the parish. Father Leopold Petsch was rector, with Father Louis Claessens in charge of parish affairs. Father Ferreol Girardey served as church prefect and keeper of the house chronicle. There were thirty-one seminarians studying rhetoric, philosophy, or moral theology, depending on their class level. Sixteen lay brothers provided support as steward, sacristan, cook, tailor, cobbler, carpenter, washer, gardener, beer brewer, handyman, or various unspecified duties. The new provincial, Father Joseph Helmpracht, visited St. Mary's in January for an overdue canonical visitation.[3]

Archbishop Spalding arrived in Annapolis on January 29 for confirmation. He was accompanied by Father Jacob Walter, confessor to convicted Lincoln assassination conspirator Mary Surratt. He confirmed thirty-four persons, of whom half were African Americans. Thirteen were males, twenty-one females, seven adults, twelve children, and fifteen of unspecified ages. Fifteen of the confirmands were converts. In the evening, the archbishop gave a discourse entitled "The Church:

The Civilizer of Nations." The lecture was open to the general public and among those specially invited were officers from the Naval Academy. In response superintendent Rear Admiral David Dixon Porter assured the Redemptorists that "as many as can make it convenient [will] attend with pleasure."[4]

The month of March brought an innovation to St. Mary's. Around this time, Frater Colonel [whether Philip or his brother Joseph was not stated] was St. Mary's organist. But now, evidently for the first time, a layman, "A. Koch" was hired to play the organ. "From then on," recorded the *Chronica Domus*, "lay people sang in our parish choir until Koch died in June." He has not been further identified and his death was not recorded in the parish interment register. Frater Colonel resumed his duties as organist. In keeping with their nearly annual tradition, in April the women of St. Mary's held a twelve-day fair in the school to help offset the debt on the church. They raised $860 toward this goal.[5]

Father Anwander's January 2, 1868, notations for paying for a barrel of flour and subscribing to the Messenger of the Sacred Heart. *SMPA.*

The Redemptorists' beer cellar, constructed in 1866; as it appeared in 2020. Courtesy author.

A local chapter of the Apostleship of Prayer was established at St. Mary's in April under Father Claessens' direction. Its purpose was to foster the "union of Christian hearts with the Heart of Jesus, and in the identification of our interests with those of this Divine Master."[6] The organization was established by a French Jesuit in 1844 and subsequently spread throughout the world. The Jesuits also began publication of *The Messenger of the Sacred Heart* in 1866 as part of the Apostleship of Prayer program. An account book kept by Father Anwander when he was vice rector in Annapolis (1866–68) reveals that he paid for five subscriptions to *The Messenger of the Sacred Heart*. This monthly publication might have been used by the more advanced parochial school students as well as by the novices and seminarians and possibly by Naval Academy midshipmen who visited St. Mary's. Evidence of Anwander's interaction with Naval Academy personnel is observed when he forwarded $15 collected by Marines stationed at the academy to the *New-York Freeman's Journal*, which was raising money on behalf of Pope Pius IX.[7]

An ongoing occupation of the Redemptorist brothers was beer and wine making. A beer cellar, probably the one adjacent to the kitchen in the new college building, had been excavated in 1861 during Father Müller's time. In October 1866, the *Chronica Domus* reported, "a new brewery is built by our lay brothers; a cellar to store the beer is finished; also the wine cellar is improved." The two-story frame brewery building and the underground brick and granite beer cellar were attached to the west end of the Carroll House, with only the cellar remaining today. The chronicle continued: ". . . and the passage between the new and old houses is completed." The passage connected the main college building (today's rectory) and the old novitiate (the Carroll House). It connected the first and second stories of the new and old houses, allowing the Redemptorists to move between them without going outside. It was an enclosed two-story frame bridge-like affair, with windows facing east and west and wood-grained finishes on the interior woodwork. At some point a bell was installed on top of the roof to call the novices to prayer. In 1928 the open ground level was enclosed with a brick structure and furnaces were installed under the passage. New furnaces were installed in the rectory basement in 1989–90 and the historic passage and later furnace room were demolished in 2006.[8]

Military men who had come to Annapolis because of the war and stayed continued to marry at St. Mary's. But the post-war ratio of soldier and sailor marriages was indicative of the return to normalcy. Of the three military marriages in 1866, one was of a former soldier and two were sailors attached to the Naval Academy. Charles Gerard, a Frenchman and formerly a private with the Thirty-Ninth New York Infantry, had been hospitalized at Annapolis for an unspecified illness in July 1863 and then transferred to the invalid corps in March 1864 until mustered out in June 1864. He married Victoria Villamier, also a native of France, on January 4, 1866, with Father Claessens officiating. Their witnesses were Justin Bonnafous and Theodore Maurice, sword master and assistant sword master, respectively, at the Naval Academy. Charles worked in Annapolis as a butcher and he and Victoria had four children, all of whom were baptized at St. Mary's. By 1880, however, the family had moved to Minnesota, where Charles returned to his pre-war occupation of gardener.[9]

Thomas Hickey, an Irish-born Navy coal heaver who served during the war on the USS *Pensacola, Ossipee,* and *Savannah*, married Ann Reilly, born in Ireland, on April 24, with Father Claessens presiding. They had a daughter, Mary, born in Annapolis in 1867. Thomas left the Navy and became a Naval Academy watchman. He died in 1874 of consumption, apparently contracted during the war. He is buried at St. Mary's Cemetery next to his daughter Mary, who died in 1918, and sister-in-law Margaret Reilly, who died in 1881, also of consumption. Ann married a second time, in 1879, to Irish bar keeper and widower Bartholomew Esmond. She died in 1931 and is buried near both husbands.[10]

Father James Keitz officiated at the marriage of John E. N. Nelson and Jane Kelly on October 11. Non-Catholic Nelson was born in Sweden and served as a seaman onboard the USS *Marion*, and later on the USS *Santee*, Naval Academy practice ships. He may have served earlier in Company B, Eleventh New Hampshire Infantry from December 1863 until he was given a disability discharge in October 1864, after having been severely wounded at the Battle of Spotsylvania Court House (May 16, 1864). Jane was born in County Cork, Ireland, but nothing else is known about her and no children have been found in baptismal or census records. Nelson was discharged from the Navy in 1870, converted to Catholicism in 1882, and died eleven months later of "brain softing," with burial at the parish cemetery.[11]

One of Its Best Citizens

In August 1866, Colonel John Walton, worn out from the exertions of the war, sold the City Hotel. The previous September he had advertised in the *Annapolis Gazette* that he was "desirous to retire from business" and was ready to lease the City Hotel for a term of years. But, instead of leasing, John and his wife, Mary Eggerton Duke Walton, sold the hotel for $35,000 to two Civil War veterans from Leominster, Massachusetts: Augustus Gardner Morse and his nephew, George Franklin Morse. Augustus Morse had been commander of the Annapolis army post in 1861 and 1862, lodged at the hotel, and in 1863 wrote a letter supporting Walton's claims for war damages to his farms. Morse returned to Annapolis in 1864 and renewed his acquaintance with Walton. In 1866 the two Morses and their wives signed two mortgages with Walton covering the sale price. But, after a year, George Morse sold his share to his uncle and by 1870 Augustus Morse defaulted on the loans and filed for bankruptcy.[12]

In "consequence of embittered feelings superinduced by business transactions between them," Edward Walton

The City Hotel as seen from Conduit Street, late nineteenth century. Courtesy Annapolis Lodge No. 98, Ancient, Free and Accepted Masons.

assaulted Augustus Morse in 1870. Edward had helped his father run the City Hotel for many years and was resentful of Morse. He admitted his guilt in court and was fined $50. Edward wrote to Governor Oden Bowie asking that his fine be remitted because he had many expenses, a large family, and needed the money. His petition stated that his father's health was already failing and that "the extraordinary excitement of his mind was still further heightened by the late 'War' [when] he was thrown in with Col. Morse." His encounter with Morse, wrote Edward, had been "brought on by the sting of injustice and fraud which I considered [Morse] had inflicted on our family and particularly my helpless father." The fine was remitted. In the meantime, the hotel was closed for renovations and reopened later in the year under the management of "Edward Walton and Brothers." This arrangement did not last, and in 1871, Edward transferred his share to his older brother, Dr. John Randolph Walton.[13]

Colonel John Walton died at age seventy-eight in 1871. Both Annapolis weeklies paid warm tribute to Walton, noting that the city had "lost one of its best and most estimable citizens" and that he was "respected and loved by all who knew him." The *Maryland Republican* said it well,

Inscription of a tree above the date 1866 in St. Mary's beer cellar. Courtesy of the author.

that "In speaking of him . . . we are paying but slight tribute to departed worth." Colonel Walton's funeral at St. Mary's was "largely attended" and his remains were interred in the Walton family vault on the church property. Mary Walton had died four years earlier at age sixty-four and also was interred in the Walton vault. Their remains and those of other family members were moved to the parish cemetery on West Street in 1901 and the vault removed from the old Duke of Gloucester Street burial ground.[14]

A New Rector

In October 1866, Father Thaddeus Anwander was assigned to St. Mary's as vice rector, completing the term of Father Leopold Petsch that normally would have run until July 1868 had it not been for a temporary mental breakdown (see My God, Have Mercy on Me, ch. 9). Bavarian-born Anwander was known for his extraordinary energy in the service of his parishioners (especially African Americans), his devotion to the Redemptorists, and his love of God. One of the first things that Anwander recognized was that St. Mary's School was outmoded. To suit the needs of the growing Catholic community, he made arrangements in early 1867 with Mother (now Blessed) Theresa of Jesus (Caroline Gerhardinger), S.S.N.D., to assign the School Sisters of Notre Dame to Annapolis and to build a new school for them. Two sisters arrived the following August but the new school was not built until 1880. The School Sisters had been founded in Bavaria in 1833 by Mother Theresa, who led the first group of her order to the United States in 1847 in response to the educational needs of German immigrant children. At that time, Father John Neumann helped find them a suitable place for a motherhouse in Baltimore. Thus the ties between the School Sisters and the Redemptorists became well forged.[15]

Father Thaddeus Anwander, C.Ss.R. (1823–93). RABP.

There were other momentous changes afoot during Anwander's rectorship. The Redemptorists turned over their house of studies in Cumberland to the Carmelite fathers in August 1866 and the novices were transferred to Annapolis. This was part of a major transition for the Redemptorists. On July 21, they purchased 110 acres of land, with a large stone house and several farm buildings, in Ilchester, about twelve miles west of Baltimore, near Ellicott's Mills. There was discussion as to whether it would be used for the novices or the students. It was reasoned that because the Annapolis climate was the cause of "fever and ague," and because the students would be studying for a number of years and the novices for only one, the decision was made that Ilchester would become new studentate. The new college building was named Mount St. Clement College and the first superior was Father Adrian Van de Braak. The students left Annapolis in September 1868 while the novices remained in Annapolis. The novitiate continued at St. Mary's in Annapolis until 1907, by which time the students at Ilchester had moved to a new house of studies in Esopus, New York. The novices took over Ilchester which had been renamed St. Mary's College. After 1907 novice lay brothers continued their formation in Annapolis.[16]

Wartime Conversions

The Annapolis Redemptorists were quite successful in gaining converts before and during the Civil War. Prior to the Redemptorists' 1853 arrival, only two conversions were recorded during the two years (1851–52) for which Jesuit records are extant. Between 1853 and 1860—during the height of the Know Nothing era—St. Mary's registered ninety-three conversions, an average of 11.6 per year. During the war years, there were seventy-seven conversions, an average of 15.4 per year. The fruits of the Redemptorists' wartime labor also continued in record fashion in 1866 when there were eighteen more conversions. And, although some soldiers were recorded among the converts, many deathbed conversions in the army hospitals went unrecorded. Only adults, teenagers, and children who had reached the age of reason (around the age of seven) or who were specifically recorded as converts, have been included in these counts. Converts of unspecified ages, however, are included. Numerous baptisms of newborns and infants, some in danger of death, who had Protestant parents, were recorded at St. Mary's but are not included in the tabulation (see table 3, Converts to Catholicism at St. Mary's, 1851–66, Appendix).

The St. Mary's converts came from various denominations or from no faith at all. Unfortunately, the St. Mary's record keepers often neglected to note the original affiliations of the majority of converts (114 or 53 percent) who joined the Catholic Church during the period under consideration. Of the affiliations that were recorded, most were noted as Methodists, Episcopalians, or noted simply as Protestants. There were small numbers of Lutherans, Presbyterians, and Baptists, and one former member each of the Mormon and United Brethren faiths. Some people were noted as converts from heresy, nihilism, infidelity, or paganism.[17]

A twenty-first-century Redemptorist, Father Philip Dabney, wrote that there is "hunger in the world for the supernatural." Historian Randall Miller perceived the same thought when he wrote about the nineteenth-century devotional revolution that provided "access to the supernatural." That desire, perhaps, was what brought at least some of the many converts to the Catholic Church in Annapolis and elsewhere during the dark days of the Civil War.[18]

Nineteenth-century Protestant critics of Catholicism cited an "endless array of superstition" as evidenced by ornate churches and cathedrals, elaborate ceremonies, use of incense, bowing and genuflecting, adoration of images, celibate clergy, colorful and ornate liturgical garments, special holy days, exorcisms, processions, and the use of Latin, an archaic language. But ironically what disgusted American puritan sensibilities were the very things that likely attracted potential converts to Catholicism. The Church's age-old traditions in a time of civil disunity and war, the hierarchy of priests, bishops, archbishops, and the pope as universal father figure had to have been appealing. Moreover, liturgies were celebrated daily, which meant the church doors were open and welcoming to White and Black people who found something special, even comforting, going on inside, including the Catholic belief in the real presence of God in the form of consecrated communion hosts kept in tabernacles.[19]

St. Clement's College in Ilchester, late nineteenth century. RABP.

The expanding Catholic institutional structure during a period of severe divisiveness in the United States—at least in large cities such as Baltimore—included elaborate Catholic social networks, which also attracted converts. The distinctiveness and fullness of Catholic tradition also may have been features that attracted members of secular society and the divided religious denominations. This book has demonstrated that St. Mary's parishioners of the same national origin aided each other while those of different national backgrounds frequently intermarried. The Catholic press and parochial schools, which were suspect to those opposed to the Catholicism, attracted others who sought something special for their own spiritual lives and those of their children. An aspect that may have drawn some converts to Catholicism was what historian George C. Rable notes as "lukewarmness" and "coldness" that prevailed when the "war spirit" among Protestant preachers took over in some congregations. A historian of St. Anne's Episcopal Church in Annapolis, for example, noted that pro-Union preaching and policies enforced by the Diocese of Maryland caused the parish rolls to dwindle during the Civil War. These factors, perhaps, pushed some individuals to the stable atmosphere of the unified Catholic Church with its generally apolitical clergy. Family stability may also have been a factor in conversion of Protestant men and woman whose spouses were practicing Catholics or who sought a religious affiliation in common with their Catholic children.[20]

Historian Anne Rose summarized it well when she wrote that mid-19th century:

> converts were impelled by longings for the authority of a historical church, the orderliness of religious hierarchy and a spirituality evoked by rituals woven into daily routines. Behind every conversion was a history of spiritual turmoil and resolution.[21]

Catholics put special emphasis on Mary as the Mother of God. Most Protestant sects looked askance at Marian devotional practices by Catholics that brought maternal comfort to those seeking succor during the misery of war. The profile of Mary's special status had increased when Pope Pius IX decreed Mary's Immaculate Conception, the dogma that she was conceived without the stain of Original Sin, making her and her alone suitable to become the mother of Jesus. The Redemptorists have a special devotion to the Immaculate Conception, and it was a book written by their founder, St. Alphonsus Liguori—*The Glories of Mary*, which includes his "Discourse on the Immaculate Conception of Mary"—that was placed next to the Bible on the altar of St. Peter's Basilica when Pius IX proclaimed the dogma on December 8, 1854. Present for the occasion was Bishop John Neumann who, as the Redemptorist provincial, once held title to St. Mary's Church in Annapolis. And, indeed, the official name of St. Mary's, given to it by the Redemptorists, is the Church of the Immaculate Conception.[22]

The example of the Redemptorists' work as chaplains in the military camps and hospitals and in the community at large in Annapolis and Anne Arundel County must have impressed non-Catholics and served as an inspiration for conversion. Although civilians and soldiers would have had little opportunity to interact with the novices and seminarians, they may have been impressed with the diversity of their national origins unified under St. Mary's roof. There would have been more community interaction with the lay brothers, similarly diverse, whose domestic functions took them to local businesses, trade shops, professional offices, and farm markets. Indeed, as stated in 1861, "the fathers more and more gained the goodwill of the people, especially among those who previously had been full of prejudice toward us. . . . We gained the goodwill of all those whom we graciously received."[23]

Another factor comes into play in regard to African American conversions. When writing about slaves in colonial-period Maryland, historian Robert Emmett Curran says that they "might well have found in Catholicism several features that closely resembled those in the traditional religious practices of West Africa, such as devotions to saints and the use of relics and holy water." In the first half of the nineteenth century, this was likely also true both for bonded and free Blacks, with their substantial oral traditions. Similarly, although historian Albert Raboteau was referring to Cuba, Haiti, and Brazil when he wrote the following statement, the same conditions might relate to Maryland as well:

> The use of sacramentals (blessed objects), such as statues, pictures, candles, incense, holy water, rosaries, vestments, and relics, in Catholic ritual is more akin to the spirit of African piety than the sparseness of Puritan America, which held such objects as idolatrous. Holy days, processions, saints' feasts, days of fast and abstinence were all recognizable to the African who had observed the sacred days, festivals, and food taboos of his gods. . . . The nature, then, of Catholic piety with its veneration of saints, use of sacramentals, and organization of religious fraternities among the slaves offered a supportive context for the continuity of African religious elements in recognizable form.[24]

For some African American converts, whose forebears had been enslaved in Maryland for generations, there may have been another connection. The Catholic Carroll family owned hundreds of slaves, many of whom worked on the family farm on the outskirts of Annapolis and at the Carrolls' house in town. In the 1810s and 1820s, Charles Carroll of Carrollton's granddaughters were active in bringing African Americans into the Church. Although further evidence is lacking, instructing and baptizing slaves may have been a Carroll family tradition since the late seventeenth century. Antebellum and Civil War-era Black converts with local ties may well have had a grandparent, an aunt or uncle, or some other relative who was Catholic and now sought to reclaim a familial religious tradition. Another possibility is that some individuals, if they had Angolan Catholic ancestors, may have had a yearning to embrace the religion of their ancestors.[25]

There was another religious practice connected to the Carroll House that may have related to conversions. During archaeological excavations on the ground story of the Carroll House in 1991, a cache of a dozen smokey quartz crystals and other associated artifacts were found buried in the northeast corner of a room used by Carroll's domestic slaves. These included two coins, dating 1773 and 1803; numerous white pierced disks, buttons, pins and a smooth black pebble, all collectively covered with a broken, upside-down ceramic bowl with a symbolic asterisk-like design. Some anthropologists believe this assemblage has spiritual significance and is associated with the West African practice of communicating with deceased ancestors and that it was buried there by house slaves for their own purposes. Subsequently, similar bundles were found in other elite Annapolis homes. Such a practice was particularly important to an enslaved population that was prevented from using traditional language, names, clothing, and customs. The spirit bundle was a secret tie to their African origins. That the cache was hidden beneath floor boards on the ground story, directly below the study where Catholic Charles Carroll of Carrollton penned his defense of freedom of conscience against his Protestant opponents in 1773 has its own intrigue. There may have been oral tradition and a sense of commonality among Black Annapolitans, passed down from the time the cache was hidden in the early nineteenth century to the antebellum and Civil War generation, that led African Americans to conversion at St. Mary's.[26]

A review of the parish sacramental records provides insight into conversions that took place during the Civil War. A convert baptized on July 7, 1861, was Mary Margaret, a slave belonging to Colonel Joseph Hopper Nicholson, a prominent Annapolis lawyer and slave owner. Mary Margaret, for whom no surname or parentage was given in the baptismal register, had been a Methodist and was thirteen years old at the time of her conversion. Her godparent was free Black Mary Effine Lake. Mary Margaret lived only three more years and is buried at St. Mary's Cemetery. The interment register's only additional information was that she had been enslaved by Colonel Nicholson. Another Black teenager baptized the same day as Mary Margaret was Margaret Alicia Jackson, also formerly Methodist and a slave held for life in bondage by Annapolis postmaster Thomas Ireland. Her godparent was a fellow slave, Rachel Teresa Smothers. Perhaps Mary Margaret and Margaret Alicia, both baptized by Father Joseph Jacobs, were friends since their owners lived nearby to each other, Nicholson on Duke of Gloucester Street and Ireland on Green Street, both close to St. Mary's Church.[27]

Some other African American conversions were unusual. Thirty-two-year-old Ann Jeanette Shorter Maynard converted at St. Mary's in 1857. She was the daughter of Charles Shorter, the master carpenter who built the original Asbury African Methodist Episcopal Church on West Street in 1838. Ann Jeanette later served as godparent at the christenings of two infants and a teenager at St. Mary's between 1865 and 1868 and is buried at St. Mary's Cemetery. Another such convert, in 1863, was Laura Maria Watkins, the teenage daughter of Noble Watkins, a lay minister at Asbury. Daniel Boston, an 1866 convert at age sixty-one, had been a "free colored" exhorter—an unordained lay preacher—for fifteen years at Chew's Chapel (now Chew Memorial Church) in West River. Although not included in the 1851–66 analysis, John Ann Price, a granddaughter of Reverend Henry Price, a minister at Asbury, converted to Catholicism in 1867.[28]

Daniel Boston was not the only convert of advanced years. At age seventy and in danger of death, Benjamin Keene, a White farmer from Dorchester County, converted from Methodism in 1860. John Randall, an Episcopalian who once rented the Carroll House and was a member of the Masons and served as their treasurer in 1848, attended Mass at St. Mary's with his Catholic wife Eliza. He converted to Catholicism on his deathbed in 1861 at age seventy-three. Another seventy-three-year-old convert was White waterman William Johnson in 1863. Catherine Welch Maccubbin converted at age seventy-nine the same year but when she died in 1864 she was buried at St. Anne's Cemetery next to her husband, Nicholas Z. Maccubbin. She owned seven slaves and lived at 110 Prince George Street (now known as Gibson's Lodging). Father John Gerdemann baptized the two oldest converts at Dodon in 1865. They were Mary Grace Parker (age eighty-five) and Charley Parker (age eighty-seven), both former Methodists and presumably former slaves. Isabella Steuart served as their godparent. They both were also confirmed on December 7, 1865, by Archbishop Spalding.[29]

When slavery ended with emancipation elsewhere—and with the 1864 constitution in force in Maryland—there were an estimated 100,000 Black Catholics, both free and former slaves. Most were concentrated in Louisiana and Maryland. After emancipation African Americans were free to choose what church to belong to and this often resulted in separate Black and White congregations. St. Mary's did not have a separate Black congregation in Annapolis until 1949 when St. Augustine's Church was built at the request of Black Catholics who had endured segregated seating and treatment in the majority White parish. Before emancipation enslaved people might have been raised in or converted to the religion of their owner, something that was true at Dodon. In the urban setting of Annapolis, where free Blacks frequently associated with slaves, those held in bondage might have been persuaded to join the church of their free colored brethren or by the example of lay leaders such as by Rachel Smothers, a slave, or Mary Effine Lake, a free person. Between these two, they were godmothers to 107 souls at St. Mary's. Whatever the situation, 50 percent of the converts in 1865 were Black and chose to join St. Mary's or its missions at West River and Dodon.[30]

A notable case of a family conversion was that of John Robert Hunt Sr., his wife Catherine Foote Hunt, and their two sons. Within the course of four days in May 1865, they all were baptized at St. Mary's by Father Adam Petri. John was an Englishman, an Episcopalian, and a private in Company B, First Delaware Infantry. He was wounded at Antietam in 1862 and wounded again and taken prisoner at Gettysburg in 1863, after which he was paroled and sent to Annapolis. Hunt was admitted to General Hospital Division No. 1 in August 1863 and returned to his regiment in September. He was wounded a third time at the Battle of Bristoe Station (near Manassas, October 14, 1863) and taken prisoner and confined for a month at Belle Isle. He was paroled and was a patient in several army hospitals until transferred to General Hospital Division No. 1 in Annapolis in August 1864. At the expiration of his three-years service, Hunt was discharged in September at Petersburg, Virginia, in poor health. He returned to Annapolis where he was joined by his wife, Catherine, who was born in New Jersey

Sts. Peter and Paul Church, Easton, built 1866–68, after the Redemptorists departed. Courtesy author

and was a member of the United Brethren Church, and their sons, seven-year-old John Robert Jr. and three-year-old Jacob Kimball, both born in Delaware. The family returned to Delaware where John worked on a farm and died from consumption in 1879. Catherine moved to Illinois and then to California, where she died in 1907.[31]

Labors in the Out-Missions

Although the Redemptorists at St. Alphonsus Church in Baltimore had agreed to resume their visits to St. Augustine's in Elkridge Landing, the Annapolis Redemptorists continued to minister there. But transition was underway. The assignment of priests to St. Augustine's was taken over by Archdiocese of Baltimore and in January 1866, Father Ferreol Girardey went to Elkridge Landing to introduce the first resident pastor, diocesan Father Desiderius C. DeWulf, who also had charge of St. Mary's in Laurel Factory. Girardey's last visit to St. Augustine's was April 6–9, 1866, when he went there to help DeWulf prepare parishioners for confirmation.[32]

In August 1865, Archbishop Spalding acquired an acre of land in Owensville (two more acres were added ten months later). Father John Gerdemann, who was in charge of the mission, made a series of four- and five-day visits to West River between January and April 1866. On Saturday, May 26, Fathers Louis Claessens and Gerdemann, with "impressive ceremonies," oversaw the cornerstone laying proceedings for a one-hundred-seat "neat little Church." They were assisted by Redemptorist philosophy students Francis Xavier Müller and John Runge and members of the West River congregation on hand to celebrate this special accomplishment.[33]

Also in May 1866, care of the Easton mission was transferred from the Annapolis Redemptorists to their Baltimore confreres and Father William Lürhmann, rector of St.

Michael's, succeeded Father Timothy Enright. The cornerstone for the new Catholic church, to be called Sts. Peter and Paul, was laid on June 18, 1866, with Lürhmann presiding and Fathers Claessens and Frederick William Wayrich assisting. Mass in Easton continued to be celebrated in the town hall and the Odd Fellows Hall until the church was completed in 1868. When the Diocese of Wilmington was established in March 1868 and took charge of Maryland's Eastern Shore parishes, the Redemptorists withdrew from Easton and the mission was attached to the Jesuits at St. Joseph's in Cordova, Maryland. Sts. Peter and Paul became an independent parish in 1878.[34]

During the Civil War, the Redemptorists changed trains at Annapolis Junction and, while waiting for a connecting train, they ministered to the Catholic troops. In 1886 the Redemptorists purchased lots six and seven on Broadway (now Brock Ridge Road) in Centralia, a planned town laid out in 1866 immediately south of the Annapolis Junction railroad connections. Their purchase may have been in response to the modest success of the Episcopalians who started "cottage services" in Centralia around 1867 and in 1890 built All Saints' Chapel which operated until 2005. The Catholic chapel was never built and the land was sold in 1921.[35]

St. Mary's Colored School

Article 8, sections 4–6 of Maryland's 1864 constitution provided for a uniform system of free public schools throughout the state. They were to be funded with property taxes disbursed proportionately to the various counties and Baltimore City. While this was good news to the White population and ostensibly to the Black population, issues of racial disparity quickly emerged. School funding was based on a percentage of property taxes paid and since comparatively few Blacks owned property, it automatically meant Black schools would receive fewer resources, leaving the Black community to support its own schools.[36]

The Maryland General Assembly made tentative provisions in the January 1865 Public Instruction Act for educating Black pupils by providing part of general school tax revenue for the construction of separate schools. However, the law left it up to county school commissioners to decide how to spend the money, if at all. On June 12, 1865, Asbury African Methodist Episcopal Church asked the Annapolis city government for permission to establish a free school for Black children. The City Council approved the request two weeks later and, by October 1, the Baltimore Association for the Moral and Educational Improvement of the Colored People had established a school in Annapolis with ninety-eight Black pupils, one of twenty-four such schools the association founded in Maryland. At Edwin Stanton's direction, the War Department turned over to the Baltimore Association empty Army barracks at Camp Parole to be dismantled and the lumber reused for school buildings. For this reason, the Annapolis school was named in Stanton's honor. The National Freedman's Relief Association of New York sent numerous White teachers to Maryland and was criticized for its reluctance to hire Black teachers. But in 1866 Black teachers hired by the American Missionary Association outnumbered White teachers eighty-six to thirty-six throughout the state. By this time, the Stanton School had two "departments," one for males, the other for females, and 130 students. It was claimed to be the "finest schoolhouse in the State owned by colored people."[37]

In January 1869, a group of Annapolis men purchased the land on Washington Street on which the Stanton School had been built. Among the men who contributed the money to purchase the property were Moses Lake, a Catholic, and the fathers of two Catholic converts Charles Shorter (father of Ann Jeanette Shorter Maynard, baptized in 1857) and Noble Watkins (father of Laura Maria Watkins, baptized in 1863).[38]

It is not known exactly when Black children began to receive formal education at St. Mary's but, by late 1865 or early 1866, a free school had been established for Catholic and non-Catholic Black pupils. Catholic education for African Americans in Maryland dated to the colonial period, primarily through religious devotions. Itinerant Jesuits visiting Catholic-owned plantations and urban dwellings instructed the White adult women of the family who, in turn, instilled basic Catholic principles in their slaves. Catholic slaves and owners attended Mass and received the sacraments together. Because Protestants and government authorities were suspicious of such practices, priests in Maryland usually confined their teaching of African Americans to oral instruction and spiritual counseling. In the minds of slave owners, learning to read and write threatened to subvert the master-slave relationship, so slaves learned those abilities in

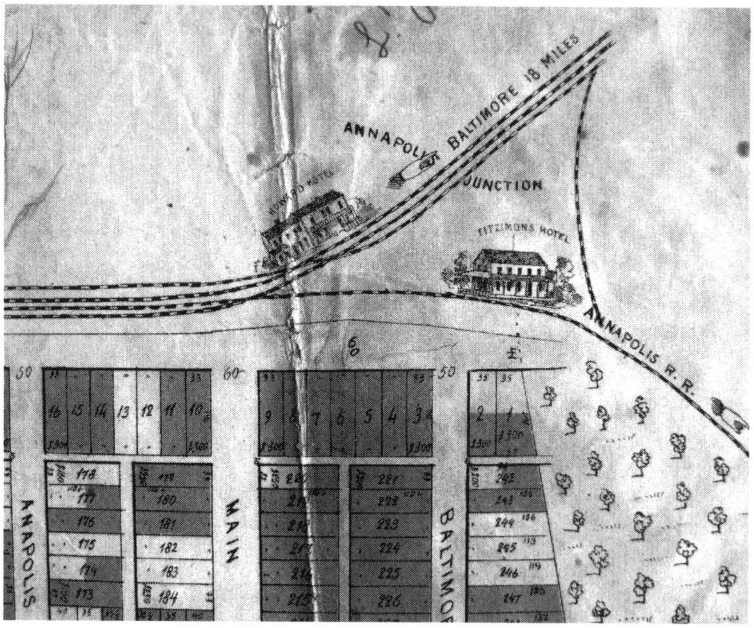

Annapolis Junction, later known as Centralia. Detail from an 1866 map. In 1886 the Redemptorists purchased lots 6 and 7 near the railroad depot in hopes of establishing a mission there. SMPA.

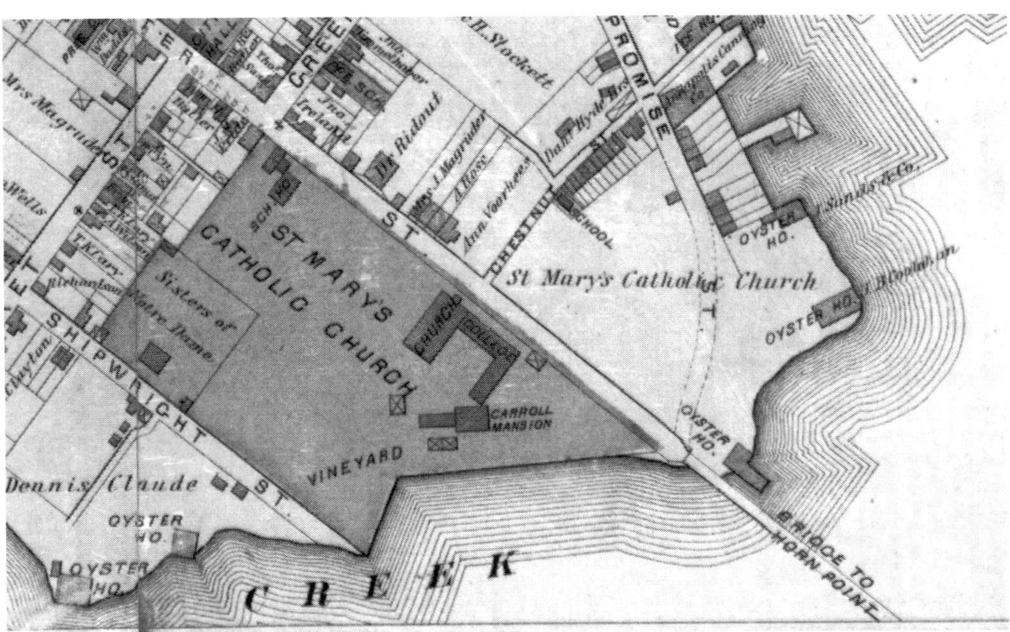

St. Mary's Colored School (shown here as "School"), on Chestnut (now Newman) Street, detail from pages 12–13, Griffith Morgan Hopkins Jr., compiler, Atlas of Fifteen Miles around Baltimore, including Anne Arundel County, Maryland *(Philadelphia, 1878). Geography and Map Division, Library of Congress http://hdl.loc.gov/loc.gmd/g3843am.gct00071.*

secrecy. Interest in improved education for Black Catholics increased after 1822 when Liberia became a destination for freed slaves and free-born Black Americans and again in 1833 when the American bishops provided support for missionaries to be sent to the new African colony. Prior to his 1832 death, Charles Carroll of Carrollton was a leading supporter of the African colonization concept.[39]

African Americans in Annapolis are said to have "received the careful attention" of the Redemptorists ever since their arrival in 1853. Father Seelos was reportedly in awe of the poverty of the African Americans to whom he personally ministered in Annapolis and used it as an example of how he could deepen his own love for "holy poverty." Fathers Claessens, Gross, and Gerdemann were noted in 1864 as having taken a special interest in the spiritual well-being of the Black people and were involved in evangelization among African Americans in the Annapolis area. In May that year, they received twelve African Americans into the Catholic faith and in July "a special solemnity was inaugurated" at the First Communion of African American children. Father Adam Petri's devotion to the Black population was noted in 1865. It was recorded in the annals of St. Michael's in Baltimore that the few priests there "had to struggle as the best they could until Father Petri could tear himself away from his dear darkies in Annapolis."[40]

The earliest mention of a Catholic-run "colored school" in Annapolis dates to July 1866. It was founded sometime before then with classes held in a one-story wooden building on Chestnut Street (now Newman Street), just down the hill from the front doors of St. Mary's Church. Father John Gerdemann was noted as the "conductor of the Colored Catholic School here." The July 1866 reference predates a pastoral letter that emerged from the Second Plenary Council of Baltimore, which met from October 7–20, 1866, to discuss important matters facing the postwar church, including giving "greater attention to the freedmen and the welfare of their souls." The bishops' letter called for the clergy and people of the various dioceses to extend Christian education to emancipated slaves.[41]

The issue of a teacher or teachers for St. Mary's Colored School raises an interesting speculation. Gerdemann was in charge of the school but the Redemptorists generally did not engage in teaching laity so it is possible that he did not conduct day-to-day classes for the pupils.

Even with their respect for the White priests, a Black teacher might have been best. A likely candidate for this job is Mary Augusta Lake, at least for the female classes. She had been well trained at St. Frances School in Baltimore and, as Sister Mary Lucy, had started but did not finish her novitiate with the Oblate Sisters of Providence. Her experience with the Oblate Sisters gave her the potential educational background and spiritual bearing to teach at the St. Mary's school. She lived just three blocks away on Church Circle and her parents, Moses and Mary Effine Lake, were well known in the community and at St. Mary's. It is conceivable that the former Sister Lucy was a teacher at St. Mary's Colored School.

Father Anwander presumably directed his attention to St. Mary's Colored School after he became vice rector in October 1866. He was well known for his apostolate to Baltimore's African Americans and for his work with the Oblate Sisters of Providence, whose order had fallen on difficult times after the death of their founder, Sulpician Father James Mary Hector Nicholas Joubert de la Muraille in 1843. With Father Anwander's energetic assistance and spiritual directorship, the Oblate Sisters prospered and ever since they have considered him one of their greatest benefactors. In 1853 he helped establish the first Catholic school for boys of color in the United States—St. Francis School, administered by the Oblate Sisters in Baltimore. After he was assigned to Annapolis, he took the steps necessary to incorporate the Oblate Sisters as a legal entity in 1867.[42]

Chapter 9: Soldiers of the Cross

My God, Have Mercy on Me!

Tragedy struck St. Mary's in 1866. Around four o'clock on the hot afternoon of Monday, July 9, four priests and three seminarians set out on a recreational sailing expedition. They were wearing their long black religious habits—as required—and proceeded "with the special dispensation of Providence," according to one of the participants. The group included thirty-eight-year-old Father Louis Claessens, the Redemptorist community's number two man and minister of St. Mary's Church, consultor to the rector, and professor of moral theology and French in the college. Father James Bradley, thirty-seven years old and one of the original novices at St. Mary's in 1853, had been assigned to St. Mary's since 1861 and had been working for four years as a traveling missionary and was currently on home convalescent leave. Father Timothy Enright, twenty-eight years old and one of the 1863 ordinands, was professor of secular history, geography, algebra, English, and French. Father John Gerdemann, twenty-six years old and also one of the 1863 ordinands, was professor of rhetoric, English, and German literature, prefect of the brothers, director of St. Mary's Colored School, and in charge of the Catholic congregation at West River. The seminarians were twenty-four-year-old John Thomas Bernard Kenny, a student of moral theology; and twenty-four year-old John Baptist Runge, a student of philosophy; and twenty-three-year-old Wendelin Guhl, a student of rhetoric.[1]

Around 5:00 PM they anchored their sailboat—the *St. Alphonsus*—in Cat Hole Creek (a secluded place now known as Lake Ogleton), near Tolly Point, about four miles southeast of St. Mary's, where the Severn River joins Chesapeake Bay. The sailors disembarked and all but Father Enright changed into their swim suits and went to bathe in the cool water. Father Gerdemann and Frater Kenny waded in chest-deep water some 300 to 400 feet from shore. Suddenly Kenny sank into a hole and swallowed a large amount of salt water. Gerdemann, who was closest, and Guhl a bit further away went to Kenny's aid. Guhl reached Kenny first and brought him back to shore but Gerdemann "noiselessly disappeared under the water and was seen no more." It was now around 6:00 PM.[2]

Guhl swam back to the spot where Gerdemann was last seen but failed to find him. After he returned to land, the others searched the shoreline without success. Finally they boarded the boat to continue the search and then went out into the mouth of the Severn River and onto Chesapeake Bay looking for the missing priest. They searched until it became too dark to look further. Around 10:00 PM, they sorrowfully decided to hoist sail and return home. Then fate struck again.

A torrential thunderstorm hit. The boaters navigated with difficulty through the storm and when the wind finally subsided, they lowered the sail and started to row to a nearby lighthouse. When the wind increased again, they decided to hoist the sail, but just as they did so, the round-bottom *St. Alphonsus* was struck by a large wave and capsized. Kenny and Runge were lost almost immediately and it was later reported that "their last words were prayers." Kenny exclaimed "Jesus, Mary, Joseph assist me!" and Runge cried "Oh my God, have mercy on me!" Enright fell clear of the boat as it turned over and rescued Claessens. They quickly heard each other's confessions and then righted the boat, rescuing Guhl who had been trapped in an air pocket underneath for about fifteen minutes. But as they did so the boat turned over again and Claessens lost his grip and "immediately sank to rise no more." With the boat finally upright, the three survivors—Bradley, Enright, and Guhl—tried to take in the sail but and the boat overturned again. This time the anchor broke loose and fastened to the bottom of the bay, "and the waves dashing against the boat and the anchor reacting, kept the boat constantly rolling, which made it more difficult to cling to than otherwise."[3]

Father Enright and Frater Guhl cling to the capsized boat. Original art by Constance D. Robinson.

After a long night in rough seas and praying and encouraging each other, the three still hung on even though the boat rolled over several times. At one point Guhl's legs became entangled in the sail but he was able to free himself in time to pull Enright free from the foresail to the relative safety of the boat. Enright and Guhl clasped hands across the bottom of the overturned boat while Bradley clung to the rudder. About an hour before dawn, heavy waves caused the boat to roll again and Bradley lost his grip and slid beneath the waves as the other two struggled to hold on. When daylight arrived, the two exhausted survivors found that the storm had pushed them around Tolly Point south to an area now known as Highland Beach. They were within a few hundred feet of land and the boat was no longer moving because the mast or anchor had become stuck in the underwater mud. They discovered that the water was shallow enough to slowly wade ashore.

Enright and Guhl reached dry land near the farm of Charity Brashears, "a colored woman, well-known and respected in this community," according to a press report.[4] She gave the men a "restorative" of bread and milk and offered to take them into Annapolis, but, to wear off their chill, they refused Mrs. Brashears' kind offer and instead walked more than four miles in the rain to John Barber's farm on the bank of Spa Creek across from St. Mary's. There, at about 7:30 AM on July 10, they signaled their confreres. Several students quickly crossed the creek in a boat to bring them home.

During the next three days, local watermen formed recovery parties—Guhl reported that the area "was crowded with rescue ships." Guided by Enright and Guhl, the bodies of Bradley, Claessens, Gerdemann, Kenny, and Runge, still wearing their black habits, were recovered over a period of three days. As they were returned to St. Mary's, the sorrowful funeral bell tolled. Services were held in church for Bradley and Gerdemann. But "because of the condition of the bodies [Claessens and Kenny] were immediately entombed with ordinary ceremonies." Runge's body reposed in the burial vault underneath the sacristy.[5]

When the sailing party had not returned by early evening of July 9 and the Redemptorists observed the stormy weather, the tragic consequences began to unfold. The rector, Father Leopold Petsch, kept a night-long vigil on the third story of the college building, looking out toward the bay for his long-overdue confreres. "Again and again he approached the window of the corridor, scanning the horizon for the sail of the '*St. Alphonsus*,'" according to an account of Petsch's life, and "[a]ll night the Community remained in prayer." When Enright and Guhl finally returned the next morning and confirmed that the others had drowned, Petsch fell into a state of collapse; six weeks later he resigned his post. He recovered eventually and went on to serve as rector of St. Alphonsus in Baltimore and Our Lady of Perpetual Help in Boston. But he was haunted until his dying day by the loss of his confreres. On his deathbed in Boston in 1882, in a state of delirium, he reputedly cried out "The bay, look to the bay!" A myth began that on the night of July 9–10 thereafter; Petsch keeps his vigil on the third story of St. Mary's Rectory, watching for the missing sailors.[6]

News of the drownings was widespread and swift thanks to telegraphic services. A report from Annapolis appeared as early as July 10 in Philadelphia's *Evening Telegraph*. Newspapers from Baltimore to Boston, and Wilmington, Delaware, to Wilmington, North Carolina, and farther south to Augusta and Macon, Georgia, and New Orleans, and as far west as Sacramento, California, carried stories about the "disaster at Annapolis" during the next several weeks. Most stories repeated the basic facts with varying degrees of detail and accuracy. As St. Mary's public affairs person, Father Ferreol Girardey provided "the particulars of the sad calamity" to the local press. The *Annapolis Gazette* said the "sad and afflicting occurrence has cast a gloom over this community," noting that a "large reward" was offered for the recovery of the bodies, and that the "lamentable fate of this [*sic*] reverend gentlemen elicited feelings of the deepest sympathy from the entire community." Seminarian Augustine John Stuhl wrote later that "All of us has witnessed the heartrending spectacle of seeing their confraters brought home, dragged along in the water at the stern of some boat . . . the entire Congregation was thrown into the greatest affliction by the sad and doleful incident."[7]

Father Leopold Petsch, C.Ss.R. (1821-82). RABP

Upon hearing the tragic news, Archbishop Martin Spalding went to St. Alphonsus Church to offer a Requiem Mass for the deceased Redemptorists. James McMaster, who had met Claessens and Bradley just a few weeks before in New York City, published two lengthy reports on the drownings in the *New-York Freeman's Journal*.[8]

Another lengthy article, published in the *Catholic Mirror* six weeks after the drownings, was less an account of the event and more a tribute to the deceased. It began as follows:

> Although considerable time has elapsed since the dreadful calamity happened which resulted in the death of our good priests and brothers, and although the brotherhood to which they belonged, as well as our community generally, have become reconciled in a measure, to their great loss, still a deep, heartfelt and settled sorrow continues to pervade every circle, and but one sentiment of sympathy and grief has been manifested at this appalling occurrence.[9]

The writer waxed theological as he noted the resiliency of Annapolis Catholics in dealing with the tragic loss of five men in their prime and the acceptance of the "striking illustration" of the "the shortness and uncertainty of life." He observed that unlike those of us who are "rarely ever prepared to meet [our] last solemn end," the men who died were different. After Gerdemann drowned, "no fewer

Our Lady of Sorrows Church, Owensville, Maryland, dedicated in 1867 to the memory of Father John Gerdemann. Photo from Francis X. Welch, A Centenary for Our Lady of Sorrows, Owensville, Maryland, 1866–1966 *(Owensville, Maryland: 1966).*

than four perished in noble, but fruitless, efforts to rescue a companion from the perils of the situation." And, when faced with their own perilous situation, they were men "for whom death had no terrors, and to whom to die was no sacrifice." To the writer, they were truly heroic:

> Regardless of self, they struggled for one another's safety, not only by physical effort, but by prayers, confessions, and absolutions. They clung to one another, offering mutual aid and spiritual consolation, until one by one, failing in strength, they sunk to rise no more. Soldiers of the Cross! they died not for worldly glory and honor, like a warrior upon the field of battle, but they perished heroes and martyrs, to vindicate their faith in their Lord and Saviour Jesus Christ!

The survivors—Enright and Guhl—were praised too, for "after exhausting every means that human and spiritual power could employ to rescue [their confreres], they were in the end saved, that they might bear the glad tidings of the triumphant death of their brothers, and that they might, by their testimony, bear witness to their heroic conduct, piety, and self-sacrificing spirit, in the cause of God and charity." The article was signed only by the initial "M." It was revealed some years later that the author was John Thomson Mason who, even long before his conversion to Catholicism, had been a staunch defender of the Catholic Church and friend to the Redemptorists.[10]

When the new church was completed in Owensville in 1867, it was dedicated to Our Lady of Sorrows as a memorial to John Gerdemann, who had labored long and hard to get the mission established. In 1894 Cornelius David Kenny, a successful Baltimore coffee and tea merchant, donated the money to build a new St. Augustine's Church in Elkridge Landing. It was dedicated on November 23, 1902, as a memorial to his "beloved brother," John Kenny.[11]

Father Seelos—who had encouraged boating at Annapolis—was giving a retreat to nuns in Alton, Illinois, when he learned the tragic news. He wrote to Enright in the wake of the accident, saying that he:

> . . . was thunderstruck and could hardly realize it. It was too much at once, but the ways of divine Providence are hidden to men, and he only knows that there was a great deal of mercy and love for those of our Confreres who were so suddenly taken from us.[12]

Seelos counseled Enright regarding his having survived:

> . . . it was something more than natural that You escaped, and the only reason is because God has reserved You to suffer a great deal more for his glory and the salvation of others. Therefore, keep to the true principles in order to suffer in the right line and to walk on the right way. Remain the docile Child of obedience; in Cumberland you have so well continued this martyrdum [*sic*] of obedience, which you had begun in the Noviciate [*sic*] of Annapolis.

The drowning accident had another impact on Seelos that would have a life-ending repercussion. The Redemptorists had to replace Enright, who was transferred to Baltimore, and the three faculty members who drowned. One of the priests sent to Annapolis was Father Fridolin Lütte from New Orleans. Lütte's replacement in New Orleans was Seelos who was assigned there in September 1866 and would die from yellow fever twelve months later.[13]

The drowning was the worst tragedy the Redemptorists had experienced since their founding in 1732. The sad testimony of this event can be seen today in the Redemptorist Cemetery behind St. Mary's Church. Five headstones bear the dates July 9 or July 10, 1866. The tragedy also was an impetus to relocate the more robust students away from the now-feared water during the rest of the summer vacation. Some were sent to Cumberland and some to the house recently purchased in Ilchester.[14]

Parish Legacies

This book has offered numerous accounts of achievements and failures, agreements and disagreements, pro-war or anti-war sentiments, pro-emancipation or pro-slavery beliefs, and pro-Confederate versus pro-Union allegiances or something in between. There were priests who fostered a joyful approach to seminarian studies and others who favored old-school methods. There were young men who had to decide whether to profess perpetual vows or to forsake religious life. Soldiers renewed their lax faith or converted to a new one; some married local women and remained in Annapolis, others took their brides back north to raise families in the hard-fought-for peace. Some slaves and free Blacks left Protestant denominations for the Catholic Church in their search for the path to God and freedom. Much like today with its divisive political and social issues, the Civil War emphasized many differences among people and often routine ups and down of daily life were exacerbated. But there was something that joined these disparate and seemingly antagonistic people. Religion is defined as a sense of right, a moral obligation or duty, conscientious convictions, a regard for sacred things, devoutness, piety, and reverence. The etymology of the word religion is found in its Latin origin—*religio* and its root word, *religare*—which means to bind together. Religion bound St. Mary's parishioners in a common faith that superceded hard-held social and economic beliefs and practices. Black, White, rich, poor, young, old, progressive, conservative, clergy, laity—they all were "soldiers of the cross" and bound by a common faith and ability to forgive or at least tolerate one another.

While other religious denominations throughout the United States divided into two or more parts over race, abolition, political persuasion, and other rancorous issues during the antebellum and war periods, Catholic parishes remained unified, although often racially segregated. The unity of the Church was a deeply seeded aspect of Catholicism and although there were members of the clergy and hierarchy who took personal political stances on the divisive issues of the day, religious unity prevailed. The oneness of the Church trumped divisiveness.[15]

St. Mary's Parish in Annapolis had special circumstances during the Civil War. Its historical legacy dated back to the intolerant days of late seventeenth-century colonial Maryland where, after 1692, the state religion—Anglicanism—was enforced by a distant government and its local loyal officials. The tiny Catholic congregation in Annapolis centered around the prosperous Carroll family and their private house chapel. Circuit-riding incognito Jesuits served this colonial-era community, as well as later, when religion emerged free of governmental restraint in the newly independent nation. Rarely were there resident priests in Annapolis and it was not until 1823, after Charles Carroll of Carrollton retired to Baltimore and the family chapel was closed, was there a separate, public-access church building, known from the start as St. Mary's.

Nine years before the Civil War began, Carroll's granddaughters gave the Annapolis property to the Redemptorists. The Jesuits' once-a-month appearances were replaced by the permanent presence of Redemptorist priests, brothers, novices, and seminarians. St. Mary's went overnight from being a mission station to a full-fledged parish. Despite the difficulties of the anti-Catholic, anti-immigrant Know Nothing era, Catholicism flourished with the Redemptorist presence, with improved opportunity for personal faith practices, through conversions, and from Catholic immigration from Europe. When war came, it suddenly brought tens of thousands of soldiers and civilians to Annapolis. These temporary residents included both fervent and lax Catholics, many of whom benefitted from the Redemptorist parish and ministries. Some outsiders stayed but most moved on, either to untimely graves or their post-war circumstances.

The presence of St. Mary's Colored School as an integral part of the parish at the end of the war brought further increase in the number of Black Catholics. In 1949 a separate Redemptorist-run Black mission church and school named St. Augustine's was established in the Clay Street neighborhood. The school lasted until the Archdiocese of Baltimore integrated its schools in 1957. The church survived until 1966 when it was condemned as structurally unsafe and its congregation was invited back to St. Mary's.[16]

The end of the war brought new developments for St. Mary's and the Redemptorists. The novitiate that had been transferred to Cumberland in 1862 returned to Annapolis in 1866. The college for advanced students outgrew itself and left Annapolis for new and larger quarters in Ilchester in

St. Augustine's Church, Elkridge, Maryland, dedicated as Kenny Memorial in 1902 in memory of Frater John Kenny. Courtesy of the author.

John Michael Himmelheber (1813–95) and Mary Eva Bettendorf Himmelheber (1819–97) in their home at 172 Green Street, Annapolis. Courtesy Judy Himmelheber Dohner.

Rev. Joseph Himmel (formerly Himmelheber), S.J. (1855–1924). Courtesy Georgetown University Archives, GU_archives_ presidents_ 00025 Himmel Joseph.

1868. The population of Annapolis grew from 4,500 in 1860 to 5,700 in 1870, a 22 percent increase that led to an influx of new parishioners.[17]

The Civil War generation of Annapolis Catholics left an impressive legacy. The following are some examples of that legacy, some more significant than others.

• Because of his many special contributions to the Redemptorists and St. Mary's Parish, John Himmelheber (1813–95) was conferred with the honorary status of Redemptorist oblate, a special lay affiliation. When he died, he was interred among the deceased Redemptorists. His eldest son, Joseph (1855–1924), studied one year (1867–68) at St. John's College Preparatory School on a scholarship provided by John Thomson Mason, and later at the Redemptorists' St. James School in Baltimore. He also evidently was a lay student at the Redemptorist house of studies in Ilchester but left there and became Jesuit novice in 1873. He was ordained in 1885, celebrated his first mass at St. Mary's in August that year. Later he served as superior of the Jesuit mission band (1890–98 and 1913–18) and president of Georgetown University (1908–12). His sister Agnes (1861–1926), was an honors graduate of the Institute of Notre Dame in Baltimore, taught at the Annapolis commercial and high school, and later served as librarian of Notre Dame College in Baltimore. Her brother Charles (1866–1917) became city clerk of Annapolis, assistant examiner of Anne Arundel County schools, clerk to the County Commissioners, and secretary to the Maryland Commissioner of Motor Vehicles. Charles' daughter, Eva (1901–96) became a School Sister of Notre Dame (Sister Mary Carola) in 1921.

• John Randall (1788–1861) was raised as an Episcopalian and once established a Masonic lodge in the Carroll House, where he lived with his Catholic spouse, Eliza Hodges Randall (ca. 1798–1881), from around 1826 to 1852. In 1858–59, he provided lumber from his farm to help build St. Mary's Church and College. John converted to Catholicism on his deathbed. When Eliza died, it was noted that she "had always been a pious and devoted Catholic" and that after the Redemptorists arrived in 1853, she "was ever ready to render them any service within her power."[18] John and Eliza rest in peace in St. Mary's Cemetery on West Street.

• Edward Sparks (1791–1871) valiantly battled the Know Nothings and was defender of and physician to the Redemptorists before, during, and after the Civil War. But his fortunes declined in the post-war years and he died of apoplexy in 1871. Several years before his wife Sophia Pinkney Sparks (1807–70) died, her Episcopalian nephew, Reverend Jonathan Pinkney Hammond, said she was "firm in her allegiance" to the Episcopal faith.[19] Nevertheless, she was received into the Catholic Church on her deathbed. Edward, Sophia, and four of their children lie buried in the family lot at St. Mary's Cemetery.

• The family home of Colonel John Walton (1794–1871) before, during, and after the Civil War was at 10 Francis Street. Since 2006 the former Walton home has been owned by the Archdiocese of Baltimore and serves as headquarters for the Maryland Catholic Conference, which "advocates for the Church's public policy positions before the Maryland General Assembly and other civil officials" on behalf of the Archdiocese of Baltimore, the Archdiocese of Washington, and the Diocese of Wilmington. How Colonel Walton came by his title has not been discovered; some believe it may have come from British army or St. Mary's County militia service, or was honorary. A reminiscence published many years after his death recounted how, when he and his family all mounted on horseback to ride out to their farm, young Annapolis boys greeted this spectacle with "Here comes Walton's cavalry!" From around 1890 to 2015 there was a Walton Street in West

Annapolis honoring the Walton family.[20]

• Elizabeth (Lizzie) Hohne Revell (1836–1906), a lifelong St. Mary's parishioner, wrote in her diary that April 21, 1897, was the anniversary of when Northern troops landed in Annapolis: "How times flies & what troubles all have had since, individually & collectively, country troubles & family made troubles, thirty six years!" She continued, "how I remember the miseries of the war, after the war & now." When war was declared against Spain in 1898, she again saw Northern morality applied to the enemy which suffered "great loss . . . & forts demolished . . . just like it was during the Southern War [when] the Revell family [were] Southern sympathizers." But now, whereas "the Southerners were rebels, traitors &c., the Cuban insurgents are patriots, brave, honorable gentleman, Spaniards demons, uncivilized, no christians." Recalling the Civil War, she said "Soon we will see 'carpet baggers' and the 'Christian' ministers, with stackes [*sic*] of bibles (counterfeit editions) & numerous tracts telling of the old man of sin of the seven hills of Rome &c. &c. converting the superstitious to the ways of the God of peace."[21] She, her sister Mary Teresa (Mollie, 1846–1904), and brother James (1831–1908) lived out their lives together in their home on the first block of West Street. They now rest at St. Mary's Cemetery.

• James Revell served as the elected state's attorney for Anne Arundel County from 1858 to 1876. In 1892 he was elected associate judge of the Fifth Judicial Circuit of Maryland (comprising Anne Arundel, Howard, and Carroll counties), a position he held until his death in 1908. His brother Martin Fannen Revell Jr. (1839–1901) received a canonical dispensation to marry his long-sought-after Episcopalian love, Susanna Sands, in a ceremony held at St. Mary's in 1877. All three of their children were baptized at St. Mary's. Martin is buried at St. Mary's Cemetery but separated in death from Susanna, who was interred at St. Anne's Cemetery in 1917. From around 1894 to 1908, there was a Revell Street in West Annapolis but it was renamed Ridgely Avenue when a new Revell Street was opened between Shipwright Street and Spa Creek, behind St. Mary's.[22]

• James Revell's nephew, William Martin Brady (1866–1936), son of Anna Maria Revell Brady (1833–1900) and John Wesley Brady (1828–93), served as deputy clerk (1896), chief deputy clerk (1920–25 and 1927–33), and clerk (1925–27 and 1933) of the Anne Arundel County Circuit Court. William's brother, Albert Theodore (A. Theodore) Brady (1868–1935) represented Anne Arundel County in the Maryland Senate (1910, 1920, and 1922) and then served as the county state's attorney (1924–35). Both William and A. Theodore are buried at St. Mary's Cemetery.

• Four St. Mary's parishioners were among the fourteen incorporators of the Mutual Building Association of Annapolis when it was chartered in 1868 to develop the first suburb of Annapolis—Eastport—on the eastern side of the Annapolis harbor. They were John Wesley Brady, Andrew Edward Denver, William Brewer Gardiner, and James Revell. Among the St. Mary's parishioners who purchased the first Eastport properties were Luke Burns, Simon Farrell, John Gunning, Ellen Hughes Jacobi's husband George Jacobi, Hugh McCusker, James Revell, Cecelia Manahan Schoff's husband Peter Schoff, and Alfred Woolley.

• John Thomson Mason Jr. (1815–73) converted to Catholicism and was baptized at the Cathedral of the Assumption of the Blessed Virgin Mary in Baltimore on August 7, 1863. When the war ended, he returned to Annapolis with a home on King George Street ((now called Ogle Hall) and a law office on West Street in the former home of Colonel James Boyle. He served as a special judge for Anne Arundel County (1866), Democratic presidential elector (1868), director of the Annapolis and Elk Ridge Rail Road (1870), and as Maryland secretary of state (1872–73). He died suddenly on March 28, 1873, in Elkton, Maryland, after having argued a civil case before the Cecil County Circuit Court. His funeral was held

The former Walton Family home at 10 Francis Street, Annapolis, owned since 2006 by the Archdiocese of Baltimore and headquarters for the Maryland Catholic Conference. Courtesy author.

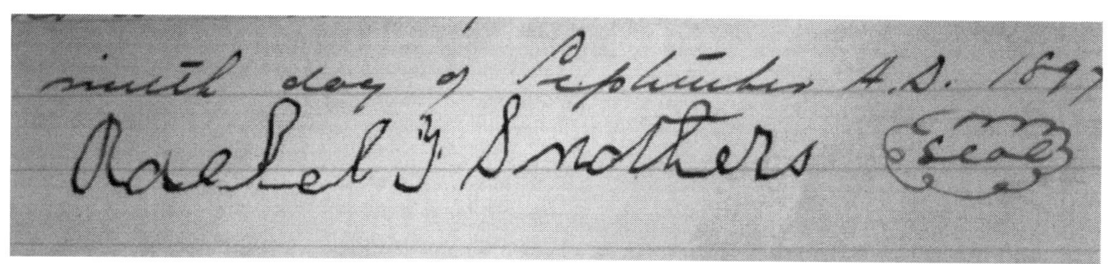
ninth day of September A.D. 1897
Rachel T. Smothers (Seal)

The signature of Rachel Teresa Smother (1821–98) on her 1897 will. Anne Arundel County Register of Wills, C155-57. Maryland State Archives.

two days later at the cathedral in Baltimore. Among his pall bearers were men mentioned in this book: Governor William Pinkney Whyte, Judge James Lawrence Bartol, and Dr. Richard Sprigg Steuart. Mason was buried in Hagerstown, in his native Washington County. On April 28, 1873, a special Requiem Mass was celebrated at St. Mary's "for the repose of the soul of our late lamented distinguished townsman, John Thomson Mason." Father Francis Joseph Oberle (1842–85), one of the 1865 ordinands, delivered a eulogy "in a touching and most appreciative manner, relating especially to the two great cardinal virtues—faith and humility." When the Annapolis Bar Association met several days later, they praised Mason's long public service and referred to his as an "example of an unsullied Christian life."[23]

• The death of Rachel Teresa Smothers on June 2, 1899, at age seventy-eight, was reported in the Baltimore *Sun* and the Annapolis *Evening Capital*. It was highly unusual to give such notice to an African American woman. The *Sun* noted her longevity while the *Evening Capital* called her "a highly respected colored woman." Annapolis diarist Elizabeth Hohne Revell wrote that Rachel had been "an old family servant of the Franklins upwards of eighty years, some say near ninety" and that she had "lived through all the fortunes & misfortunes of the family & although she alone a Catholic has faithfully lived up to her faith." That faith is exemplified by the incredible legacy of service to the Catholic Church recorded in St. Mary's sacramental registers. Between June 4, 1856—the earliest entry associated with Rachel—and April 2, 1899 (two months before she died), she was a witness to one marriage, five times a confirmation sponsor, and eighty-three times a godmother. Although there is no evidence that she was ever married or had children of her own, Rachel was a mother figure for a significant number of Annapolitans and undoubtedly an inspiration to countless others. She also a co-founder of St. Teresa's Catholic Beneficial Society, established at St. Mary's in 1870 or 1872 (there are conflicting dates) to provide members financial assistance in time of sickness and death. Although she reportedly lived all of her life in the Shaw House, Rachel had personal funds sufficient to buy property in Annapolis. The first was bought jointly with her brother, Henry Smothers, on Monument Street in 1878. The next year, she purchased two adjacent lots on Shipwright Street behind St. Mary's. She had a one-story frame house built there and in 1898 rented it out to the builder. She willed the Shipwright property jointly as a life estate to a family group—all god children of hers—and then to the Oblate Sisters of Providence. The St. Mary's interment record noted that she died of "heart failure (suddenly)." In her will, Rachel asked that she "be plainly and decently buried." She is interred at St. Mary's Cemetery in a unmarked grave. The memory of her name and her good works in Annapolis were still recalled, albeit vaguely, in 2015.[24]

• After the Civil War ended and having spent time in the West, John Mullan Jr. (1830–1909), the famous Mullan Road builder, relocated with his wife and three children to Washington, DC. He worked as a lobbyist for the state or territorial governments of California, Nevada, Oregon, and Washington and, for a time, was president of the Bureau of Catholic Indian Missions. Although he did not return to live in Annapolis, after his death in Washington in 1909, his funeral was held at St. Mary's Church with burial—per his will—"in a suitable lot in the Catholic Cemetery at Annapolis." His wife, Rebecca Williamson Mullan, whom he married in Baltimore 1863, died in 1898, with burial in Bonnie Brae (now New Cathedral) Cemetery in Baltimore City. She was a cousin of Mother (later St.) Katharine Drexel, a benefactor of St. Mary's Catholic Colored School in Annapolis. Rebecca and John named their son Frank Drexel Mullan after this special family connection. Their daughter, Mary Rebecca (Mrs. Henry Hepburn Flather) owned Tulip Hill, a large Georgian mansion in southern Anne Arundel County, from 1918 to 1945.[25]

• Charles Adams Zimmermann (1861–1916), who moved from Newport to Annapolis with his parents as a four-year-old, became internationally known as the Naval Academy's bandmaster from 1887 to 1916, and composer of "Anchors Aweigh" in 1906 and many other melodies. He also was St. Mary's choir director from 1885 until his death. His brother, John Sylvester Michael Zimmermann (1873–1949) also was musically talented. He was bandmaster of the US Soldiers Home in Washington from 1900 to 1943 and, like his brother, a composer.[26]

The Redemptorists inspired numerous of religious vocations among St. Mary's parishioners.

• Louis James DuBois (1836–1921) was the first native Annapolitan to join the Redemptorists. He entered the novitiate in Annapolis in 1858 and professed his vows in Cumberland in 1860. That vocation did not materialize and Louis left in 1861. Twelve years later he joined the Brothers of the Holy Cross in Notre Dame, Indiana, as Brother Sulpicius. He spent the rest of his life at Notre Dame. His brother Charles Aloysius DuBois (1847–1911) for many years ran an oyster packing business and was elected Republican mayor of Annapolis (1901–3) and was one of the founders of the Annapolis Emergency Hospital on Franklin Street (1902). Another brother, Edward (Ned) Speed Dubois (1838–1905) worked as a printer and assistant agent of the Adams Express Company during the Civil War, and, after the war operated a stationery store on Main (formerly Church) Street.

• The second religious vocation from St. Mary's was Mary Augusta Lake (ca. 1841–69). She joined the Oblate Sisters of Providence in Baltimore as a postulant in 1860 taking the name Sister Mary Lucy. Unfortunately, ill health kept her from realizing the fulfilment of her vocation and she returned to Annapolis, where she may have taught in the Catholic school for Black children. She died from consumption and lies in an unmarked grave at St. Mary's Cemetery near her parents, Moses Lake (1802–70) and Mary Effine Peterson Lake (ca. 1809–69).

• John J. Gunning (ca. 1827–1910) and his wife, Catherine Carroll (ca. 1834–1895), both natives of County Roscommon, Ireland, must have been gratified when their youngest child, Andrew J. Gunning (1867–1939), graduated from St. Mary's School in 1881 and then went on to bigger things. With encouragement from the School Sisters of Notre Dame and the Redemptorists, he entered the Redemptorists' new minor seminary in North East, Pennsylvania, graduating in 1888, completed his novitiate year in Annapolis (1888–89), and became the first native Annapolitan to become a Redemptorist priest when he was ordained in 1894. He spent the next thirty-five years on the Redemptorist mission band.

• The Civil War-era St. Mary's family with the greatest number of vocations was that of Ferdinand Hogan, a Naval Academy employee, and Mary Cummings Hogan. Two granddaughters and two great-great-granddaughters became School Sisters of Notre Dame and one great-grandson became a Redemptorist priest. All of these except one Hogan granddaughter were descendants of Ferdinand's daughter, Bridget, wife of Patrick Lamb, a Navy sailor during the war (see table 4, Religious Vocations from the St. Mary's Civil War Generation, 1860–1950, Appendix).

During the Civil War, thirty men were ordained in Annapolis and eight others in Baltimore. Several of them later held important positions in the Redemptorist Congregation:

• Four became rectors of St. Mary's: Nicholas Jaeckel (1868–71), Augustine Freitag (1871–73), Henry Dauenhauer (1873–77 and 1887–90), and Joseph Henning (1890–93). Father Henning's service to St. Mary's was memorialized in one of the new stained glass windows installed in the church in 1918, a gift from his young brother, Dr. Francis X. Henning and his wife Caroline.

• Five of the ordinands became Redemptorist provincial superiors: Nicholas Jaeckel (St. Louis Province, 1875–84); Elias Schauer (Baltimore Province, 1877–90), William Löwekamp (St. Louis Province, 1884–93), Ferreol Girardey (St. Louis Province, 1894–98); and Joseph Firle (St. Louis Province, 1904–7).

• One of the 1863 ordinands, William Hickley Gross became bishop of Savannah in 1873 and archbishop of Oregon City (later renamed Portland) in 1885. He was a frequent visitor to Annapolis and made his last visit there in 1898, shortly before he died in Baltimore.

• Father Peter Petit lived only two years after his 1863 ordination and died of illness in Annapolis. Almost all of the other Civil War-era ordinands—the thirty-eight ordained in Annapolis and in Baltimore—had long and fruitful lives as priests. The last survivor of the Civil War ordinands was the versatile Father Ferreol Girardey. He served at St. Mary's in Annapolis until August 1866 when he was assigned to the Redemptorists' new Western Province headquartered in St. Louis. Between 1870 and 1891, he ministered in New York City, St. Louis, New Orleans, St. Louis again, then back to New Orleans, and as superior of the Western Province seminary at Kirkwood and later at Kansas City, Missouri. He then served as vice provincial and temporary provincial in St. Louis before he was appointed provincial in 1894. After serving his term, he went on to other Redemptorist parishes and continued to hold important Redemptorist provincial positions into his last years, including being called to testify in the official investigation into the virtues of the deceased Father Seelos. He died in St. Louis in 1930, sixty-eight years after his ordination in Baltimore.

• Cumulatively, this group of thirty-eight served a total of 1,385 years of sacerdotal life, an average of thirty-six years as priests. Twenty-nine remained Redemptorists until death, nine were later dispensed of their Redemptorist vows and became diocesan priests. All but one remained priests for life. The one was John Bernard Heskemann whose end story is complicated and conflicting, with evidence that he married, had a daughter, absconded with his wife's money, may have reinvented himself as John Heskemann Bernard, a diocesan priest, and later allegedly became Alexius Bernard, a Franciscan.[27]

• Following his time in Annapolis in 1861–63, Father Peter Zimmer served in Redemptorist parishes in Baltimore, Buffalo, Chicago, and Rochester. He returned to Annapolis in 1883 to serve as novice master and to complete the first official biography of Father Seelos, *Leben und Wirken des hochwürdigen P. Franz Xaver Seelos aus der Congregation des Allerheiligsten Erlösers* (Life and Labors of the Rev. Father Francis Xavier Seelos of the Congregation of the Most Holy Redeemer), published in 1887. He then ministered in Pittsburgh from 1890 to 1901 and returned to Annapolis in August 1901 and died at St. Mary's on October 26 that year, in the care of his younger brother, Brother Chrysostom Zimmer. He is buried in the Redemptorist Cemetery behind St. Mary's Church.[28]

• The two survivors of the 1866 boating accident had full lives as priests. Shortly after the accident, Father Timothy Enright (1837–1911) left Annapolis for St. Michael's in Baltimore and in September spent a month in Edenton, North Carolina. In 1867 he preached missions in New York and Connecticut and

(continues on page 234)

Father Nicholas Jaeckel, C.Ss.R. (1834–99).

Father Henry Dauenhauer, C.Ss.R. (1833–91).

Father Augustine Freitag, C.Ss.R. (1836–82).

Father Joseph Henning (1838–1912).

Father Elias Schauer, C.Ss.R. (1832–1920).

Father Nicholas Father William Löwekamp, C.Ss.R. (1837–99).

Father Ferreol Girardey, C.Ss.R. (1839–1930).

Very Rev. William Hickley Gross, C.Ss.R. (1837–98), as Bishop of Savannah (1873–85).

Father Wendelin Guhl (1842–1917).

Father Joseph Firle (1841–1919)..

Father Peter Zimmer, C.Ss.R. (1830–1901)

Father Michael Müller, C.Ss.R., in later years (1825–99), Source: Rev. Henry Borgmann, C.Ss.R., History of the Redemptorists at Annapolis, Md., from 1853 to 1903 *(Ilchester, Maryland: College Press, 1904), 28*

then was assigned to parishes in New York City and St. Louis, Missouri. He was back in Maryland, at Ilchester, in 1870 and in 1874 was ministering at Our Lady of Perpetual Help Parish in Boston. He later served parishes in Chicago and St. Louis and by 1891 was a professor at the Redemptorists' seminary in Kansas City, Missouri. He remained there for the rest of his life. Wendelin Guhl (1842–1917) continued his theological studies at Annapolis and Ilchester but suffered from the effects of the boating accident. Despite his desire to remain a Redemptorist for life, he was dispensed of his vows in 1872 and ordained as a priest in the Diocese of Brooklyn the same year. Guhl quickly showed his mettle in 1873 by organizing a new German Catholic parish in the Greenpoint section of Brooklyn. He remained at this parish—St. Alphonsus—until he died in 1917. Over the years, he sent many young men to study at the Redemptorist minor seminary in North East, Pennsylvania. In 1877, the Redemptorist superior general in Rome conferred the honor of Redemptorist oblate on Guhl, giving him permission that upon his retirement, with agreement of the local and provincial superiors, he could live in any Redemptorist community until his death. Having never retired, he did not enjoy this honor.

• After the war, Father Michael Müller (1825–99) served in parishes in Baltimore, St. Louis, Chicago, and Pittsburgh. He became a prolific writer of books for laity and religious alike. An advertisement for one of his books said he had "already won his place in the front rank of the graver Catholic writers of the day," while a modern-day journalist called him "the Bishop [Fulton John] Sheen of his day." Müller returned to Annapolis in 1898 to celebrate his fiftieth anniversary of profession of vows. The parishioners and his confreres thanked him for having built St. Mary's Church and College. An outdoor procession of thirty-four priests, numerous novices, lay brothers, altar servers, and fifty school children preceded a special High Mass on December 8. He was praised at Mass for his "eminent virtues" and, in the evening, a group of parish men, led by his old fund-raising companion, Hugh McCusker (ca. 1832–1907), presented Müller with an illuminated manuscript that expressed the love and greetings of the parishioners, and a purse containing $112.25 "as a token of the lasting gratitude of the Annapolis Catholics." Charles Adams Zimmermann (1861–1916), St. Mary's organist and Naval Academy bandmaster, and ten band members then serenaded the jubilarian. Many of his Civil War-era confreres were present at the jubilee Mass: George J. Dusold, Nicholas Firle, John Baptist Hespelein, Ferdinand Aloys Litz, Benedict

Xavier Seelos, C.Ss.R. (1819–67), Original art by Giuseppe Antonio Lomuscio, National Shrine of Blessed Francis Xavier Seelos, New Orleans

A. Neithart, Joseph Wissel, and Andrew Wynn. Already in declining health, Müller spent his last months at St. Mary's and died there of apoplexy and paralysis on August 28, 1899. He was eulogized as having "accomplished great things for God," after which his remains were carried to the mortuary chapel by veteran parishioners Hugh McCusker, Louis Mullan, Horace Mullan, Edward Powers, Henry Roland Walton, and Bernard Wiegard. On May 14, 1900, a grateful parish placed a memorial tablet in the church vestibule.[29]

• According to his biographer, Brother Hilary Fröhlich, the self-taught artist who painted St. Mary's gothic altars, was "devoted to the profuse decoration of the churches, chapels and oratories of the Congregation," both before and after his days in Annapolis. He returned to Annapolis in retirement in 1893, died there in 1898, and is buried in the Redemptorist Cemetery. His altar-building partner, Brother Louis Sterkendries, traveled to other Redemptorist parishes to build altars, decorative church furnishings, and cabinetry and was in Annapolis again in 1870 to build permanent side altars. In 1871, two large reproduction paintings by Swiss artist Melchoir Paul von Deschwanden were installed above them. One showed Mary with the Infant Jesus and three angels representing the Nativity, the Passion, and the Resurrection. The other, still in place, shows St. Joseph with Jesus and John the Baptist as children. After completing his work, Brother Louis was transferred to St. Peter's in Philadelphia, where he died in 1873.[30]

• After leaving Annapolis in September 1863, Father Francis Xavier Seelos (1819–67) became head of the Redemptorist mission band, giving retreats and missions in Missouri, Illinois, Ohio, Pennsylvania, New Jersey, New York, Connecticut, and Rhode Island. He was relieved as mission band superior in August 1865, perhaps because of his delicate health, but continued to conduct retreats in Buffalo, Chicago, St. Louis, and Toledo before being assigned to St. Mary's Parish in Detroit. He worked there as a simple parish priest until September 1866 when he was ordered to New Orleans where he became prefect of St. Mary of the Assumption Church. He also served as needed in two other Redemptorist parishes in New Orleans: St. Alphonsus and Notre Dame. He ministered to the sick and dying during the yellow fever epidemic of 1867 and died of the viral disease on October 4, 1867. After his death there were reports of miraculous cures and one of them, in 1966, led to Francis Xavier Seelos' beatification by Pope John Paul II in Rome in 2000.[31]

We end St. Mary's Civil War saga with an epitaph for Elizabeth Ann, daughter of Michael Gesner, a Naval Academy laborer, and his wife, Bridget Mangin Gesner. Annie, as she was known, was born on Friday, December 28, 1866—the Feast of the Holy Innocents—and was baptized by Father Fridolin Lütte two days later. Her godparents were her uncle, Francis Gesner, a Naval Academy Band member, and family friend Susanna Farley. She did not know war nor would have been much aware of the ensuing peace into which she was born. She died from croup on Christmas Day 1868. The epitaph on her headstone in St. Mary's Cemetery speaks for all the deceased—young and young of heart—of the Civil War generation:

May she rest in peace.
I take this little lamb, said He,
And lay it on my breast;
Protection it shall find in me
And be for ever blest.[32]

Annie Gesner's headstone at St. Mary's Cemetery, Annapolis. Courtesy author.

Abbreviations and Acronyms Used in Text, Tables, and Notes

A.B. Archives of the Archdiocese of Baltimore, Associated Archives at St. Mary=s Seminary and University, 5400 Roland Parkway, Baltimore, MD

AACLR Anne Arundel County Land Records

ACWRDB American Civil War Research Database (http://as6new.alexanderstreet.com)

AnnalesAnnales *Congregationis Ss. Redemptoris Provinciae Americanae* (Ilchester, Maryland: Typis Congregationis Sanctissimi Redemptoris)

Balt. priest of Archdiocese of Baltimore

B&O Baltimore and Ohio Railroad

C.S.C. Congregatio a Sancta Cruce (Congregation of the Holy Cross)

C.Ss.R. Congregatio Sanctissimi Redemptoris (sometimes given as Congregationis Sanctissimi Redemptoris, Congregation of the Most Holy Redeemer, also known as Redemptorists)

F.S.C. Fratres Scholarum Christianarum (Brothers of the Christian Schools)

GU-CSC Booth Family Center for Special Collections, Georgetown University

I.H.M. Sisters, Servants of the Immaculate Heart of Mary

LoC Library of Congress, Washington, DC

MIHP Maryland Inventory of Historic Places

MSA Maryland State Archives, 350 Rowe Boulevard, Annapolis, Maryland

NARA National Archives and Records Administration. Unless noted that a document is the National Archives at College Park, Maryland, or Philadelphia, Pennsylvania, all records are at the National Archives in Washington, DC

NPS National Park Service

O.F.M. Order of Friars Minor (Franciscans)

O.S.P. Oblate Sisters of Providence

O.S.U. Order of St. Ursula (Ursulines)

RABP Redemptorist Archives of the Baltimore Province, 1019 North Fifth Street, Philadelphia, PA (formerly in Brooklyn, NY)

RG Record Group

R.G.S. Religious of the Good Shepherd

R.S.M. Religious Sisters of Mercy

S.J. Society of Jesus (Jesuits)

SMPA St. Mary's Parish Archives, Annapolis, MD

S.S.N.D. School Sisters of Notre Dame

USCC United States Christian Commission

USNA United States Naval Academy

USSC United States Sanitary Commission

V.H.M. Ordo Visitationis Beatissimae Mariae Virginis (Order of the Visitation of Holy Mary, or Visitation Order)

Appendix

Table 1. Redemptorist Ordinations, 1860–67

Name	Born	Invested	Professed	Died	Notes
1860 – June 2 – St. Alphonsus Church, Baltimore (3)					
Bernard Arant	1832 Heiligenstadt, Saxony	1856	1857	1897 Annapolis, MD	C.Ss.R. (1857–97)
Louis Ewald	1822 Westphalia, Prussia	1858	1859	1886 Philadelphia, PA	C.Ss.R. (1859–86)
John Nicholas Jaeckel	1834 Utrichshausen, Hesse-Darmstadt	1853	1854	1899 St. Louis, MO	C.Ss.R. (1854–99); Rector, St. Mary's (1868–71); St. Louis Provincial (1875–84)
1861 – August 28 (Klaphake) and September 21 (Kreis and Wensierski) – St. Alphonsus Church, Baltimore (3)					
Bernard Klaphake	1835 Ankum, Hannover	1853	1854	1910 New Orleans, LA	C.Ss.R. (1854–1910)
Adam Conrad Kreis	1837 Baltimore, MD	1853	1854	1899 Melrose, Bronx, NY	C.Ss.R. (1854–99)
Charles William August Wensierski	1827 Berentii, Prussia	1858	1859	1894 St. Louis, OR	C.Ss.R. (1859–64); diocesan priest (New York, Illinois, Oregon, 1864–94)
1862 – June 11 –St. Alphonsus Church, Baltimore (2)					
Ferreol Girardey	1839 Rougegoutte, France	1855	1856	1930 St. Louis, MO	C.Ss.R. (1856–1930); St. Louis Provincial (1894–98)
Joseph Theodore Henning	1838 New York, NY	1854	1855	1912 Melrose, Bronx, NY	C.Ss.R. (1855–1912); Rector, St. Mary's (1890–93)
1863 – March 21 – St. Mary's Church, Annapolis (20)					
Bernard Beck	1835 Minderlachen, Bavaria	1858	1859	1891 Philadelphia, PA	C.Ss.R. (1859–91)
Michael Stanislaus Burke	1837 Sag Harbor, NY	1856	1857	1891 Saratoga Springs, NY	C.Ss.R. (1857–91)
Henry Charles Dauenhauer	1833 Dahn, Bavaria	1855	1856	1891 Saratoga Springs, NY	C.Ss.R. (1857–91); Rector, St. Mary's (1877–80, 1887–90)
Alfred De Ham	1830 Ghent, Belgium	1856	1858	1899 New Orleans, LA	C.Ss.R. (1857–99)
Francis Aloysius Christian Eberhardt	1837 Traveris, Prussia	1857	1858	1888 Philadelphia, PA	C.Ss.R. (1858–88)
Timothy W. Enright	1837 Limerick, Ireland	1856	1857	1911 Kansas City, MO	C.Ss.R. (1857–1911)

Name	Born	Invested	Professed	Died	Notes
Augustine Maria Freitag	1836 Wakke, Hannover	1856	1857	1882 New York, NY	C.Ss.R. (1857–82); Rector, St. Mary's (1871–73)
John M. Gerdemann	1840 Cumberland, MD	1856	1857	1866 Annapolis, MD	C.Ss.R. (1857–66)
William Hickley Gross	1837 Baltimore, MD	1857	1858	1898 Baltimore, MD	C.Ss.R. (1858–98); Bishop of Savannah (1873–85); Archbishop of Portland (1885–98)
Charles Adam Gunkel	1832 Heiligenstadt, Prussia	1855	1856	1897 St. Cloud, MN	C.Ss.R. (1856–67); diocesan priest (Wisconsin, Minnesota, 1867–97)
Charles Hahn	1839 Kirchhassel, Hesse-Darmstadt	1855	1856	1913 Chicago, IL	C.Ss.R. (1856–1913)
John Bernard Heskemann	1835 Westphalia, Prussia	1857	1858	possibly 1894 Indianapolis, IN	C.Ss.R. (1858–65); diocesan priest (Illinois, 1865–72, maybe Nebraska 1874–77); maybe O.F.M. (Indiana, 1877–94)
John Blasius Kühn	1839 Stelberg, Prussia	1855	1856	1892 Marietta, OH	C.Ss.R. (1856–69); diocesan priest (Pennsylvania, Ohio, 1869–92)
William Henry James Löwekamp	1837 Hunteberg, Hannover	1855	1856	1899 St. Louis, MO	C.Ss.R. (1856–99); St. Louis Provincial (1884–93)
Henry Meurer	1836 Montabaur, Nassau	1855	1856	1915 Oshkosh, WI	C.Ss.R. (1856–1915)
Peter Ludgerus Petit	1832 St. James LA	1856	1857	1865 Annapolis, MD	C.Ss.R. (1857–65)
Adam Anthony Petri	1839 Cumberland, MD	1855	1856	1889 North East, PA	C.Ss.R. (1856–99)
Elias Frederick Schauer	1832 Milhausen, Bavaria	1855	1856	1920 New York, NY	C.Ss.R. (1856–1920); Baltimore Provincial (1877–90)
Francis Xavier Schnüttgen	1839 Westphalia, Prussia	1854 and 1856	1857	1897 New York, NY	C.Ss.R. (1857–97)
George Anthony John Sniet	1832/33 Amsterdam, Netherlands	1857	1858	1887 Buffalo, NY	C.Ss.R. (1858–87)
1864 – March 12 – St. Alphonsus Church, Baltimore (3)					
Andrew Henry Lindenfeld	1837 Dieburg, Hesse-Darmstadt	1855	1856	1910 Louisville, KY	C.Ss.R. (1856–76); diocesan priest (New York, Kentucky, 1876–1910)

Name	Born	Invested	Professed	Died	Notes
Benedict A. Neithart	1840 Flieten, Hesse-Darmstadt	1856	1857	1915 Chicago, IL	C.Ss.R. (1857–1915)
Charles William Rathke	1836 Pittsburgh, PA	1855	1856	1904 Rochester, NY	C.Ss.R. (1856–1904)
1865 – April 21 – St. Mary's Church, Annapolis (10)					
John Nepumucene Berger	1839 Prachatice, Bohemia	1858	1859	1884 Baltimore, MD	C.Ss.R. (1859–84)
Hubert Bove	1836 Dollendorf, Prussia	1856	1857	1907 Annapolis. MD	C.Ss.R. (1857–1907)
Joseph Aloysius Firle	1841 Frostburg, MD	1857	1858	1919 Windsor Spring, MO)	C.Ss.R. (1858–1919); St. Louis Provincial (1904–7)
James Gleeson	1837 Tipperary, Ireland	1856	1859	1907 Grand Island, NE	C.Ss.R. (1859–75); C.S.C. (ca. 1875–90); diocesan priest (Dakota Territory, Iowa, Nebraska, 1890–1907)
James Keitz	1841 Neu-Leiningen, Bavaria	1857	1858	1900 Hoboken, NJ	C.Ss.R. (1858–99); diocesan priest (New Jersey, 1899–1900)
Francis Xavier Joseph Oberle	1842 Schweinheim, Bavaria	1858	1859	1885 Ellenville, NY	C.Ss.R. (1859–74); diocesan priest (Ohio, Illinois, North Carolina, New York, 1874–85)
Rhabanus Preis	1829 Herolzi, Hesse-Darmstadt	1859	1860	1894 New York, NY	C.Ss.R. (1860–94)
Charles Anselm Rosenbauer	1838 Ellwangen, Württemberg	1854	1855	1919 Saratoga Springs, NY	C.Ss.R. (1855–1919)
George Lawrence Werner	1838 Offenbach, Bavaria	1857	1858	1908 Ilchester, MD	C.Ss.R. (1858–1908)
Andrew Ziegler	1836 Oberwestern, Bavaria	1858	1859	1896 New York, NY	C.Ss.R. (1859–96)
1867 – April 4 – St. Mary's Church, Annapolis (7)					
Joseph P. Colonel	1834 Klosterbrach, Bavaria	1860	1861	1885 New Orleans, LA	C.Ss.R. (1861–85)
Nicholas Firle	1842 Frostburg, MD	1858	1859	1910 Philadelphia, PA	C.Ss.R. (1859–1910); Rector, St. Mary's (1877–80)
Henry Charles Bernard Kuper	1842 Oldenburg, Saxony	1858	1859	1887 Ilchester, MD	C.Ss.R. (1859–87)
John Baptiste Blanchet	1833 Brauling, Baden	1860	1861	1898 Baltimore, MD	C.Ss.R. (1861–98)
Charles Constantine Pise O'Donoughue	1836 Rochester, NY	1858	1859	1871 New York, NY	C.Ss.R. (1859–71)
John Baptist Saftig	1839 Miesenheim, Prussia	1858	1859	1901 Baltimore, MD	C.Ss.R. (1859–1901)

Name	Born	Invested	Professed	Died	Notes
Andrew Joseph Sauer	1844 Poughkeepsie, NY	1858	1859	1917 Orangetown, NY	C.Ss.R. (1859–77); diocesan priest (New York, 1877–1917)

Note: C.S.C. — Congregatio a Sancta Cruce (Congregation of the Holy Cross).
C.Ss.R. — Congregatio Sanctissimi Redemptoris (Congregation of the Most Holy Redeemer, Redemptorists)
The birth place names are as given in Wuest (see below) and may vary from modern spellings.
O.F.M. — Order of Friars Minor (Franciscan).

Sources: Rev. Joseph Wuest, *Annales Congregationis Ss. Redemptoris Provinciae Americaniae*, 4:2 (Boston: Typis Congregationis Sanctissimi Redemptoris, 1914); Personnel Files, RABP; various newspapers, Catholic directories, diocesan archives, and other sources.

Table 2. Military Associated with St. Mary's, 1861–65

Name	Military Unit (dates)	St. Mary's Event (dates)	Notes
Joseph Boucher	Sgt, Co F, 25th Pennsylvania Inf (1862)	father of child baptized (1861)	local, husband of Catholic, b. Pennsylvania, ca. 1829
Horace Edward Bright	Pvt, Co B, 3rd Maryland Inf (1864–65)	teenage brother baptized (1863)	local, brother of Catholic convert, b. Annapolis 1849
Orrin Judson Brombley	Pvt, Co B, 5th Maryland Inf (1861–62)	baptized (convert) (1859); godparent of baptized child (1859)	local, b. Rhode Island 1832 (although he claimed he was born in Annapolis)
William H. Brown	Pvt, Co E, 30th USCT (1864–65)	baptized (convert) (1861)	local, formerly enslaved by John and Mary Mullan, b. Anne Arundel Co., 1848
William Henry Carroll	unk rank, US Revenue Marine Service (1861–65)	father of child baptized (1852)	local, b. Annapolis, ca. 1829
Luke Cavanaugh	Pvt, Co I, 63rd New York Inf (1861–63)	godparent of 2 children (1862–63)	outsider, applied to be lay brother Feb 25, 1863, dismissed May 11, 1863, b. Ireland ca. 1831
Peter C. Cheeks	3rd class boy, USN (1859–61), Pvt, Co D, 13th US Inf (1861–65), Pvt, USMC, USNA (1865–69)	baptized (convert) (1866)	outsider, b. New Jersey 1844
George W. Clark	Corp, Co A, 14th New York HA (1863–64)	baptized (convert) (1864)	outsider – stayed, b. New York ca. 1841
Patrick H. Connaugton	Pvt, Co B, 118th Pennsylvania Inf (1863)	married Margaret Lamb (1864)	outsider, b. Ireland 1841
Horatio Cooper	2d Class Fireman, USN (1864–65)	father of infant baptized (1854)	local, formerly enslaved, b. Annapolis ca. 1825
Benjamin Cornell	Pvt, Co I, 30th USCT (1864–65)	married Ella Maynard (1864)	local, formerly enslaved, b. Anne Arundel County ca. 1844
Patrick Coyle	unknown	witness to marriage of soldier George C. White (1864)	outsider, b. unknown place and date
Timothy Curley	possibly Pvt, Co G, 104th Pennsylvania Inf (1861)	father of infant baptized (1862)	outsider, b. Ireland ca. 1836, lived in Baltimore after the war

Name	Military Unit (dates)	St. Mary's Event (dates)	Notes
Joseph Daley	Pvt, Co D, 5th Maryland Inf (1861–62)	baptized (ca. 1842)	local, KIA at Antietam, September 18, 1862, b. Annapolis 1842
Patrick John Dougherty	Pvt, Co A, 6th US Cav (1861–64)	confirmed (1864); married Jane Dunworth (1865)	outsider – stayed, b. Ireland ca. 1840
Bartholomew John Esmond	Pvt, Co D, 5th New York Inf (1861–62)	father of baptized child (1865)	outsider – stayed, b. Ireland ca. 1835
Henry Fisher	Seaman, USN (1860–66)	baptized (convert) (1859); godfather of adult convert (1859)	local, African American, b. Annapolis ca. 1833
William Ford	Pvt, Co K, 69th New York Inf (1864)	married Alice Aety Fisher (1864); funeral (1864)	outsider, died in Annapolis, b. Ireland ca. 1835
Thomas Gaffney	unknown	married Mary Jane Amilia Jarvis (1864)	outsider, identified as *Sponsus est miles*, b. Ireland ca. 1836/42
Thomas Gately	Pvt, Corp, & Sgt, USMC (1847–67), on USS *Constitution*, USNA (1866–67)	funeral (1867)	outsider – stayed, died in Annapolis, b. Ireland 1821
Patrick Gavin	Pvt, Co K, 2nd Massachusetts Cav (1863–65)	confirmed (1864)	outsider, b. Ireland ca. 1826
Charles Gerard	Pvt, Co E, 39th New York Inf (1862–64)	married Victoria Villamier (1866)	outsider, b. France 1822
Francis J. Gesner	Musician, USNA Band (1865–89)	godparent for newborn (1866)	local, b. Baltimore 1849
Felix Gilfeather	Pvt, Co D, 2nd US Artillery (1861), Coal heaver, USS *Tioga* & other ships (1862–64), Pvt, USMC on USS *Winnipec*, USNA (1864–67)	married Cecelia Bridget Conlon (1865)	outsider, b. Ireland ca. 1830
Thomas F. Gosson	Pvt, Co H, 38th New York Inf (1861–62)	funeral (1864)	outsider, died in Annapolis, buried in New York, b. Ireland ca. 1817
Thomas Hickey	Coal heaver, USN (1862–65)	married Anna Reilly (1866)	outsider – stayed, b. Ireland ca. 1832
James Higgins	Pvt, Co A, 173d New York Inf (1862–64)	funeral (1864)	outsider, buried at Annapolis National Cemetery, b. Ireland ca. 1822
Peter Hilgert	Musician, USNA Band (1853–63)	married Meta Strohmeyer (1858)	outsider – stayed, b. German state ca. 1835
William Hogarty	Pvt, Co D, 2d Bn, Maryland Inf (CSA) (1862–65)	witness to two marriages and godfather four times (1855–61)	local, "gone south," b. Ireland ca. 1821
Charles Hoover	Pvt, Co E, 87th Pennsylvania Inf (1861–65)	baptized (convert) (1864)	outsider – stayed, b. Pennsylvania ca. 1844
John Robert Hunt	Corp, Co B, 1st Delaware Inf (1861–64)	baptized (convert) (1865)	outsider, b. England 1825
John Jackson	Pvt & Capt, Co D, 5th Maryland Inf (1861–62)	father of infant baptized (1853)	local, b. Annapolis ca. 1834

Name	Military Unit (dates)	St. Mary's Event (dates)	Notes
Terence Keenan	Pvt, Co F, 75th New York Inf (1861–65)	confirmed (1864)	outsider, b. Ireland 1846
Michael Kelly	Gunner, USN (1858–60)	father of newborn baptized (1863)	outsider – stayed, b. Ireland ca. 1829
Peter Klippen	Musician, USNA Band (1853–63), Musician, 5th US Army Band (1863–68)	baptized (convert) (1854); married Rebecca Grant (1858)	outsider – stayed, b. German state 1834
John P. Lamb	Pvt, Co D, 2nd Bn, Maryland Inf (CSA)	sister baptized and married Catholic (1864)	local, brother of convert, KIA Hatcher's Run, Mar. 27, 1865, b. Annapolis 1841
Patrick Lamb	2d Class Fireman, USN (1864–67, at USNA)	married Bridget Hogan (1868)	outsider – stayed, b. Ireland 1835
Dennis Larkins	Pvt, Co L, 43d USCT (1864–65)	father of infant baptized (1860)	local, formerly enslaved, father of Catholic daughter, b. Anne Arundel County ca. 1831
William C. Lee	Pvt, Co E, 2nd Bn, Maryland Inf (CSA) (1862–63)	father of 3 children baptized (1860)	local, b. Anne Arundel County ca. 1838
George Leichnam	unknown	baptized (convert) (1864)	outsider, identified as *Miles vag.*, b. unknown 1843
Michael Liebel	Pvt, Co A, 54th NY Inf (1862–63)	married Anna Elizabeth Diemer (1863)	outsider, b. German state ca. 1832
John Floyd Maley	Pvt, Co I, 15th Massachusetts Inf (1861–64), Paymaster, USN, at USNA (1866–67)	father of ten children baptized (1867–81)	outsider – stayed, b. Ireland 1839
Sylvester Ambrose McCabe	2d Lt, Co A, 67th Pennsylvania Inf (1861–63)	godparent of child baptized (1862); married Margaret McBride (1863)	outsider – stayed, b. Ireland ca. 1834
Thomas Andrew McParlin	Col (Surgeon), US Army Medical Corps (1849–89)	husband of Alida McParlin who was godmother of two children at St. Mary's	local –assigned to Army General Hospital Division No. 2
Lemuel J. Mitchell	Pvt, Co A, 1st Maryland Inf (1862–63)	father of infant baptized (1862)	local, father of Catholic son, b. Anne Arundel County ca. 1834
George M. Mittnacht	Capt, Co F, New York State Militia (1859–61), Capt, Co H, 103d New York Inf (1861–63)	married Mary Rebecca Brady (1862)	outsider – stayed, b. German state 1830
George A. Morgan	Pvt, Co A, 1st Maryland Inf (1862–63)	witness to marriage of Thomas Hickey and Ann Reilly (1866)	local, b. Annapolis 1840
Richard Albert Morsell	Lt & Capt, US Revenue Marine Service (1853–64)	father of two infants baptized (1861–63)	outsider – stayed, husband of Catholic, b. District of Columbia 1829
Dennis Walbach Mullan	Acting Midshipman, USNA (1860–64); Midshipman, USN (1864–66), Ensign, USN (1866), career officer (until 1901)	baptized (ca. 1843); funeral (1928)	local, b. Annapolis 1843

Name	Military Unit (dates)	St. Mary's Event (dates)	Notes
Horace Edward Mullan	Acting Midshipman, USNA (1857–61), Lt, USN (1863), career officer (until 1883)	baptized (ca. 1837); funeral (1903)	local, b. Annapolis 1837
James Augustus Mullan	Military Surgeon, Washington Territory (1861–65)	baptized (ca. 1833)	local, b. Annapolis 1833
John Mullan, Sr.	Pvt & Sgt, US Artillery (1824-55)	married Mary Ann Bright (1829); funeral (1863)	local, b. Ireland 1800
John Mullan, Jr.	2d Lt, 1st Lt & Capt, US Artillery (1852–63)	baptized (ca. 1832); funeral (1909)	local, b. Fort Monroe, Va., 1830
Charles Joseph Murphy	unknown	father of infant baptized (1863); godparent of adult convert (1864)	outsider – stayed, b. England ca. 1831
Laurence Murray	possibly unidentified New York regiment	married Ellen Lucy (1864)	outsider, b. Ireland 1837
John E. N. Nelson	Seaman, USNA (1864–66)	married Jane Kelly (1866)	outsider – stayed, b. Sweden 1835
Michael Newman	Pvt, Co B, 19th US Inf unknown	godparent for soldier Charles Hoover (1864)	outsider, b. unknown place and date
John Baptiste Nichols	Gunner, USN, at USNA (1856-60)	father of two children baptized (1859–61)	outsider – stayed, b. France 1830
Timothy O'Brien	Pvt & Sgt, US Marines (1853–62)	father of child baptized (1860)	outsider – stayed, b. Ireland ca. 1831
Charles Francis O'Malley	Pvt, Co I & Sgt, Co B, 88th NY Inf (1862–65)	witness to marriage of Laurence Murray and Ellen Lucy (1864); godparent of child baptized (1865)	outsider – stayed, b. Ireland ca. 1832
George C. O'Malley	Pvt, Co E, 17th New York Inf (1861–63)	godparent of child baptized (1865); father of newborn baptized (1866)	outsider – stayed, b. Ireland ca. 1837
John O'Neil	Acting Asst 3d Engineer, USN (1862-66), USS *Vanderbilt*	married Eliza Dunn (1864)	outsider, b. Ireland ca. 1831
Edward P. Quinn	Corp, Co H, 10th Pennsylvania Inf (1861), 2d Class Fireman (as a civilian), USS *Macedonian* (1864)	father of newborn baptized (1864)	outsider – stayed, b. Ireland 1835
George Reuss	maybe Pvt, Co B, 111th Pennsylvania Inf (1863–64)	listed in 1860 census as lay brother at St. Mary's	outsider, b. Pennsylvania 1844
Harvey L. Rose	Pvt & Sgt, Co F, 13th Michigan Inf (1861–65)	married Eliza Jane Lloyd (1863)	outsider, b. Michigan 1835
Charles Sevoy	Pvt, Co D, 30th USCT	father of infant baptized (1865)	local, formerly enslaved, b. Anne Arundel County 1828
Edward R. Seager, Jr.	Midshipman, USNA (1862–64)	confirmed (1860)	local, b. Annapolis 1846
Thomas R. Silk	Pvt, Co A, 5th Maryland Inf (1861–63)	father of infant baptized (1864)	outsider, b. Baltimore ca. 1838

Name	Military Unit (dates)	St. Mary's Event (dates)	Notes
Edward R. Seager, Jr.	Midshipman, USNA (1862–64)	confirmed (1860)	local, b. Annapolis 1846
Thomas R. Silk	Pvt, Co A, 5th Maryland Inf (1861–63)	father of infant baptized (1864)	outsider, b. Baltimore ca. 1838
John Henry Smith	1st Class Boy, USS *Marion* (1865),	baptized (convert) (1864)	local, African American, b. Anne Arundel County 1849
Henry Smothers	Pvt, Co H, 39th USCT (1864–65)	brother of Rachel Smothers, godmother of numerous children and adults at St. Mary's	local, former slave, b. Anne Arundel County 1823
Michael C. Stevens	Pvt, Co E, 40th NY Inf (1861–64), Pvt, 119th Co, 2 Bn, VRC (1864–65)	father of infant baptized (1865), funeral (1868)	outsider – stayed, b. New York ca. 1837
George C. White	Pvt, Co K, 28th Mass Inf (1861–64)	married Mary Kirby (1864)	outsider, b. Ireland 1833
Henry C. Williams	Sgt, Co 19th Pennsylvania Inf (1861), 1st Sgt, 2d Lt, 1st Lt, Co K, 8th Pennsylvania Cav (1861–64), Capt, Co E, 213th Pennsylvania Inf (Annapolis provost marshal, 1865)	married Barbara Hayne (1865)	outsider, b. Pennsylvania ca. 1839
Christian Wirth	Musician, USNA Band (1853–70)	godparent adult, 2 infants & 1 teenager (1854–60)	local, b. German state ca. 1820
Alfred C. Woolley	Musician, USNA (1863–87)	converted on deathbed, funeral (1887)	outsider – stayed, b. England 1824
William Young	Pvt, Co A, 1st Maryland Inf (1862–64)	father of newborn baptized (1865)	local, KIA at Harris' Farm, Virginia, May 19, 1864, b. Annapolis ca. 1841
Charles Garlieb Zimmermann	Musician, USNA (1859–85)	married Elizabeth Gesner & baptized (convert) (1860)	local, b. German state 1831

Notes: Names in *italics* indicate non-Catholic father, brother, or husband of St. Mary's parishioner. Those noted as "local" were men born in or were long-term residents of Annapolis and Anne Arundel County, including USNA Band members. "Outsider" includes elsewhere in Maryland and in other states.

Abbreviations:

Bn = Battalion
Cav = cavalry
Co = company
Col = colonel
Corp = corporal

HA = heavy artillery
Inf = infantry
KIA = killed in action
Lndm = landsman
Lt = lieutenant

Pvt = private
Sgt = sergeant
USMC = US Marine Corps
USN = US Navy
USNA = US Naval Academy
VRC = Veteran Reserve Corps

Sources: St. Mary's baptismal, confirmation, and marriage records B#1; Compiled Military Services Records, RG 94, NARA; US Federal Census records.

Table 3. Converts to Catholicism at St. Mary's, 1851–66

Date	White	Black
Noted as converts at time of baptism		
1851	1	0
1852	1	0
1853	2	3
1854	1	3
1855	0	2
1856	1	9
1857	6	8
1858	6	6
1859	9	15
1860	10	12
1861	3	9
1862	0	1
1863	8	8
1864	9	16
1865	12	15
1866	13	5
Noted as converts at time of confirmation		
1857	1	0
1860	2	1
1864	3	3
1866	3	9
Noted as converts at time of death		
1860	0	1
1865	0	1

Note: There are no baptismal records for those noted as converts at time of confirmation or death.
Source: St. Mary's baptismal, confirmation, and interment registers.

Table 4. Religious Vocations from St. Mary's Civil War Generation, 1860–1950

Name (Religious Name) (Dates)	Relationship	Professed[1]	Ordained	Order
Louis James DuBois (Brother Sulpicius) (1836–1921)	son of Edward and Rosetta Jane Holland DuBois	1860[2] and 1875	—	C.Ss.R. and C.S.C.
Mary Augusta Lake (Sister Mary Lucy) (ca. 1841–69)	daughter of Moses and Mary Effine Peterson Lake	1860[3]	—	O.S.P.
Joseph J. Himmelheber (later known as Himmel) (1855–1924)	son John and Mary Bettendorf Himmelheber	1871[4] and 1875	1885	C.Ss.R. and S.J.
Johanna Hughes (Sister and Mother Mary Ursula Josephine) (1858–1942)[5]	daughter of John L. and Mary Brady Hughes	1886	—	O.S.U.
Thomas B. Hughes (1856–1932)	son of John L. and Mary Brady Hughes	ca. 1875	1880	Balt.
John B. Hughes (1862–aft. 1911)	son of John L. and Mary Brady Hughes	1883[6]	—	C.Ss.R.
Andrew J. Gunning (1867–1939)	son of John and Catherine Carroll Gunning	1889	1894	C.Ss.R.
Catherine Elizabeth Denver (Sister Maria Oktavia) (1868–94)	daughter of Andrew and Mary Ann Dunn Denver	1888	—	S.S.N.D.
Mary C. Riordan (Sister Mary of the Holy Redeemer) (1870-1964)	daughter of John J. and Catherine McCabe Riordan	1911	—	R.G.S.
Margaret Naughton (Sister Mary Dionysia) (1861–1925)	daughter of Michael and Mary Ann Drury Naughton	1895	—	S.S.N.D.
Catherine Naughton (Sister Maria Fidelis) (1860–1907)	daughter of Michael and Mary Ann Drury Naughton	1886	—	S.S.N.D.
Brigitta (Bessie) Clark (Sister Mary Imelda) (1866–1943)	daughter of John and Bridgit O'Brien Clark	1889	—	S.S.N.D
Francis Aloysius Christian Schwallenberg (1870–1947)	son of Francis Augustus and Caroline Bohn Schwallenberg	ca. 1892	1897	Balt.
Anna Veronica Fee (Sister Mary Theonilla) (1870–1904)	daughter of William and Sarah Chaney Fee	1895	—	S.S.N.D.
Alipia Lamb (Sister Mary Anina) (1885-1954)	granddaughter of Ferdinand and Mary Cummings Hogan, daughter of Patrick and Bridget Hogan Lamb	1907	n/a	S.S.N.D.
Catherine Denver (Sister Mary Clement Hofbauer) (1887–1975)	granddaughter of Edward and Catherine Kerney Denver	1908	—	R.S.M.
Anne Louise Quinn (Sister Mary Alipia) (ca. 1876–1971)	granddaughter of Alfred C. and Elizabeth Corcoran Woolley	1909	—	S.S.N.D.
Margaret Mary Naughton (Sister Mary of the Holy Child) (1887–1974)	granddaughter of Bernard and Elizabeth Jane Fee Flood	1922	—	R.G.S.

Mary Hogan (Sister Mary Clare) (1884–1910)	granddaughter of Ferdinand and Mary Cummings Hogan, daughter of Ambrose Hogan and Catherine Cusack	1909	—	S.S.N.D.
Margaret Mary Woolley (Sister Mary Renovata) (1896–1975)	granddaughter of Alfred C. and Elizabeth Corcoran Woolley	1918	—	S.S.N.D.
Leila Josephine Sanders (Sister Mary Columbanus) (1896–1959)	granddaughter or Patrick and Jane Dougherty	1919	—	I.H.M.
Eva Himmelheber (Sister Mary Carola) (1901–96)	granddaughter of John and Mary Bettendorf Himmelheber	1921	—	S.S.N.D.
Sarah Frances Kramer (Sister Mary Dulcidia) (1895–1995)	granddaughter of Edward and Catherine Kerney Denver	1924	—	S.S.N.D.
Ellen Maurine Colburn (Sister Clephia) (1910–2006)	great-granddaughter of Michael and Ellen Maloney Curran	1927[7]	—	S.S.N.D.
Giles Riordan Gardiner (1913–2014)	grandson of John J. and Catherine McCabe Riordan	1934	1939	C.Ss.R.
Paul Warren Callahan (1915–92)	great-grandson of Ferdinand and Mary Cummings Hogan, grandson of Patrick and Bridget Hogan Lamb	1936	1941	C.Ss.R.
Margaret Mary Flood (Sister Theonella) (1912–88)	granddaughter of Bernard and Elizabeth Jane Fee Flood	1938	—	S.S.N.D.
Mary Ellen Kimball (Sister Marie Perpetua) (1922–2007)	great-great-granddaughter of Ferdinand and Mary Cummings Hogan, great-granddaughter of Patrick and Bridget Hogan Lamb	1947	—	S.S.N.D.
William Alphonsus Nayden (1924–91)	grandson of William and Margaret C. Lafferty Nayden	1944	1949	C.Ss.R.
Rose Marie Kimball (Sister Mary Aurea) (1929–2011)	great-great-granddaughter of Ferdinand and Mary Cummings Hogan, great-granddaughter of Patrick and Bridget Hogan Lamb	1950	—	S.S.N.D.

Note: Listed in order of date of profession.

[1] Column indicates final profession of vows, from one to five years after entrance.
[2] Louis Dubois: Professed Redemptorist vows (1860), dispensed vows (1861), entered C.S.C. (1873), professed final vows as brother (1875).
[3] Mary Augusta Lake: Postulant (1860), left before final profession of vows.
[4] Joseph Himmelheber: Studied at Redemptorist seminary in Ilchester (1871–73), left and entered Jesuits (1873), professed vows (1875).
[5] Johanna Hughes: called "sister" when she took her first vows (1882) after entering the Ursulines (1881). Final vows professed (1886) and in accordance with Ursuline tradition, thereafter called "mother." She also served in various convents as mother superior.
[6] John Hughes: vows dispensed (1884).
[7] Ellen Colburn: novice (1927), left before profession (1930).

Essay on Sources

The key sources used in researching this book were the sacramental registers of St. Mary's Church, Annapolis, Maryland, and Redemptorist records at the Redemptorist Archives of the Baltimore Province, originally in Brooklyn, New York, and now in Philadelphia. Valuable archival and primary-source information also was obtained from the Library of Congress; National Archives branches in Washington, DC, College Park, Maryland, and Philadelphia; Archives of the Archdiocese of Baltimore and Maryland Center for History and Culture in Baltimore; and the United States Naval Academy Archives and Special Collections, Maryland State Archives, and Maryland State Law Library in Annapolis. Unique and essential documents were obtained from the Redemptorist archives in Denver, Colorado, and Rome, Italy. Other Catholic repositories providing essential research material included the University of Notre Dame Archives in Notre Dame, Indiana; Georgetown University Library Special Collections Research Center and Georgetown Visitation Academy Archives, both in Washington, DC; archives of the Oblate Sisters of Providence and the School Sisters of Notre Dame in Baltimore; and St. Vincent Archabbey Archives, Latrobe, Pennsylvania. In addition, biographic information was obtained from numerous diocesan and religious-order archives in the United States and Canada. They are noted in the acknowledgments.

Digital copies of otherwise hard-to-obtain historical articles, books, documents, photographs, and maps were found on American Civil War Research Database, America's Historical Newspapers from NewsBank/Readex, Ancestry.com, Civil War Trust/American Battlefield Trust, FamilySearch.org, Fold3.com, HathiTrust.org, Internet Archive, Library of Congress, and National Park Service Soldiers and Sailors Database. Key titles of historic newspapers available on original paper, microfilm, and digitally included: *American and Commercial Advertiser, Annapolis Gazette, Catholic Mirror, Daily National Intelligencer, Easton Gazette, Evening Star, Maryland Republican, New York Daily Tribune, New-York Freeman's Journal and Catholic Register, New York Herald, New York Times, Philadelphia Inquirer,* and *Sun* (Baltimore). Many issues of the *Annapolis Gazette* and the *Maryland Republican* cited herein are not readily available online or elsewhere. They were purchased at an estate sale in 2014 and donated to the Maryland State Archives in 2021 and can be seen in the Robert L. Worden Collection, MSA SC 5725-3.

Important published sources include books by Jean H. Baker, *Ambivalent Americans: The Know-Nothing Party in Maryland, and The Politics of Continuity: Maryland Political Parties From 1858 to 1870*; Rev. Henry Borgmann, C.Ss.R. *History of the Redemptorists at Annapolis, Md., from 1853 to 1903*; Rev. Michael J. Curley, C.Ss.R., *Cheerful Ascetic: The Life of Francis Xavier Seelos, C.Ss.R.* and *The Provincial Story: A History of the Baltimore Province of the Congregation of the Most Holy Redeemer*; Robert Emmett Curran, *Shaping American Catholicism: Maryland and New York, 1805–1915*; Jay P. Dolan, *The American Catholic Parish: A History from 1850 to Present; The Civil War Diary of Father James Sheeran, Confederate Chaplain and Redemptorist*; and three books by Rev. Carl W. Hoegerl, C.Ss.R., *Novae Aureliae Beatificationis et Canonizationis Servi Dei Francisci Xaverii Seelos Positio Super Vita, Virtutibus, et Fama Sanctitatis, Sacerdotis Professi Congregationis Ss.Mi. Redemptoris (1819–1867)* (Documentary Study of the Life, Virtues and Holiness Fame of the Servant of God, Francis Xavier Seelos, Professed Priest of the Congregation of the Most Holy Redeemer); *Sincerely, Seelos: The Collected Letters of Blessed Francis Xavier Seelos;* and *With All Gentleness: A Life of Blessed Francis Xavier Seelos, CssR.* Also used were Carl Hoegerl and Alicia von Stamwitz, A Life of Blessed Francis Xavier Seelos, Redemptorist, 1819–1867; William B. Kurtz, *Excommunicated from the Union: How the Civil War Created a Separate Catholic America*; Robert Harry McIntire, *Annapolis Maryland Families*; Jane Wilson McWilliams, *Annapolis, City on the Severn: A History*; Randall M. Miller and Jon L. Wakelyn, *Catholics in the Old South: Essays on Church and Culture*; George C. Rable, *God's Almost Chosen People: A Religious History of the American Civil War*; Rev. Joseph Wuest, C.Ss.R. *Annales Congregationis Ss. Redemptoris Provinciae Americanae* (various volumes, 1888–1914); and articles in the *Maryland Historical Magazine* (1912–2017).

Sources not mentioned here, and full bibliographic citations, can be found in Notes. The URLs for Internet sources are subject to change and those appearing in the notes may no longer be valid. Some URLs are from subscription databases that were accessed at the Library of Congress.

Notes

Introduction

1. John W. Brinsfield, William C. Davis, Benedict Maryniak, and James I. Robertson, Jr., eds., *Faith in the Fight: Civil War Chaplains* (Mechanicsburg, Pennsylvania: Stackpole Books, 2003), ix, 129–255. Rev. Robert J. Miller, St. Dorothy Church, Chicago and former president of the Chicago Civil War Roundtable, is developing a new list of Catholic chaplains to include unofficial chaplains.
2. In addition to two volumes of *Chronica Domus*, the following were used at the Redemptorist Archives of the Baltimore Province (RABP): *Catalogus Novitiorum ad Oblationem Admissorum*, vols. I and II; *Liber Vestitutiones Provinciae, 1842–1924; Liber Professionis Provinciae, 1813–1923; Album Provinciae C.Ss.R. Americanae; Minute Book 1813-1965* New York, an inventory of investiture, professions, and ordinations, and death dates for New York and the rest of the United States.
3. "Notitiae, Archdiocese of Baltimore, St. Mary's Church, Annapolis, 1874." Archives of the Archdiocese of Baltimore (AAB), Associated Archives at St. Mary's Seminary and University, Baltimore, Maryland.
4. Randall M. Miller and Jon L. Wakelyn, eds., *Catholics in the Old South: Essays on Church and Culture* (Macon, Georgia: Mercer University Press, 1999), xvii; Gary B. Mills, "Piety and Prejudice: A Colored Catholic Community in the Antebellum South," in *Catholics in the Old South*, 173; Kenneth J. Zanca, ed. and comp. *American Catholics and Slavery: 1789–1866: An Anthology of Primary Documents* (Lanham, Maryland: University Press of America, 1994), Document 68 (April 12, 1840). A particularly useful secondary source is Robert Harry McIntire, *Annapolis Maryland Families* (Baltimore: Gateway Press, 1979).
5. Wissel's April 15, 1903, fiftieth jubilee address quoted in *History of the Redemptorists at Annapolis, Md., from 1853 to 1903* (Ilchester, Maryland: College Press, 1904), 205. The author is listed as "A Redemptorist Father," but it is usually credited to Rev. Henry Borgmann, C.Ss.R., whose initials "H. B." appear at the end of the Introduction and who was assigned to St. Mary's Annapolis at the time. Annals, Annapolis, 1900–9, 318 (October 8, 1904), 321 (December 18, 1904), RABP, notes Rev. Joseph Wuest as the book editor.

Prelude

1. Officer of the Day's Journal (May 11, 1858), vol. 5, Entry 151d, Records of the United States Naval Academy (Record Group [RG] 405), 1836–1991, Special Collections and Archives, Nimitz Library, United States Naval Academy, Annapolis, Maryland (USNA); *Maryland Republican*, May 15, 1858. The eyewitness was Father Michael Müller, in his nine-page poem entitled "1858. Nova Ecclesiae aedificatio ab ipso Rev. P. Magistro descripta Cumberlandii in festo Immaculatae B.M.V. Conceptionis, 1862" (1858. Building the New Church as Described by Father Rector, Cumberland, on the Feast of Blessed Virgin Mary of the Immaculate Conception [December 8,] 1862," in *Chronica Domus* I:95–104 (end of 1858). Also, Robert L. Worden, *Saint Mary's Church in Annapolis, Maryland: A Sesquicentennial History, 1853–2003* (Annapolis: St. Mary's Parish, 2003), 48–49. Brother Thomas W. Spalding, C.F.X., *The Premier See: A History of the Archdiocese of Baltimore, 1789–1989* (Baltimore: Johns Hopkins University Press, 1989), 171, says Archbishop Francis Patrick Kenrick typically gave the task of laying cornerstones and blessing churches to religious order superiors or to his vicars general.
2. *Chronica Domus* I:89 (May 13, 1858); *Maryland Republican*, May 15, 1858; *Annapolis Gazette*, May 13, 1858.
3. The list of possible attendees is partially based on donors of the bells. Their names appear in "Sponsors of Bells," last leaf of St. Mary's Baptismal, Confirmation, and Interment Register B#1, follows (with original spellings and corrections): "Maria Joseph" (Mrs. Mary Walton, Miss Cath. Bright, Mrs. Mary Himmelheber); "Alphonsus Teresia" (Colonel Jno. Walton, Andrew Denvir [Denver], Jas. A. Iglehart [James Alexis Iglehart]); "Michael" (David S. Caldwell, Dr. Edward Sparks, Jno. Purra [not identified]), and "Gabriel" (Henry Treathway [Treadway], Dr. Roland Walton, Thos. G. Ford, Mrs. Harriet A. Tydings, Mrs. Mary McCoskey [McCusker], Mrs. Mary A. Rivel [Revell], Mrs. Emma Treathway [Treadway], Mrs. Mary Seager, Miss Mary Seager, Miss Alide McParlind [Alida McParlin], Mrs. Anna Wells, Miss Anna Sparks, Mrs. Rosetta Sparks, Mrs. [*sic*] Laura Sands, Mr. Hugh McCosky [McCusker], Mr. [John] Himmelheber). See Worden, *Saint Mary's*, 50–51, 193 n65 and n66, for details on the Meneely bells.

Chapter 1: 1853–59 — Always Consecrated to Religion

1. Jean H. Baker, *The Politics of Continuity: Maryland Political Parties From 1858 to 1870* (Baltimore: Johns Hopkins University Press, 1973), 4–6, 10–11. Free Black population statistics from Maryland State Archives, "Legacy of Slavery in Maryland," accessed May 5, 2014, http://slavery.msa.maryland.gov/html/antebellum/faastat.html.
2. Robert J. Brugger, *Maryland: A Middle Temperament, 1634–1980* (Baltimore: Johns Hopkins University Press, 1989), 258–59; Baker, Politics of Continuity, 4–5.
3. Brugger, *Middle Temperament*, 258–59.
4. The gift is detailed in Worden, *Saint Mary's*, 34–37. For Pig Point see "White Marsh/Bowie Register of Baptisms, Marriages, Burials, 1818–1895," Maryland Province Collection, Box 3, Folder 3, GTM.GAMMS53, Booth Family Center for Special Collections, Georgetown University (GU-CSC), Washington, DC. Elizabeth Kryder-Reid, "The Construction of Sanctity: Landscape and Ritual in a Religious Community," in *Landscape Archaeology: Reading and Interpreting the*

American Historical Landscape, eds. Rebecca Yamin and Karen Bescherer Metheny (Knoxville: University of Tennessee Press, 1996), 232; *Sun* (Baltimore), December 15, 1851, March 22 and July 5, 1852; *Maryland Republican*, Commercial Number, July 18, 1896; *Province Annals, Chronica Pro. Am. C.SS.R., 1832–1871*, 241, RABP; Rev. Joseph Wuest, C.Ss.R., *Annales Congregationis Ss. Redemptoris Provinciae Americanae* (Ilchester, Maryland: Typis Congregationis Sanctissimi Redemptoris, 1888, *Annales*), I:360–61.

5. Three Redemptorists listed as "joint tenants in fee simple, for the sum of six thousand dollars which hath been fully disposed of under the orders and directions of the parties of the said parties of the second part"; NHG 1:341 (March 20, 1852), Anne Arundel County Land Records (AACLR), Maryland State Archives, Annapolis (MSA). The trustee (party of the first part) was Baltimore lawyer John Eager Howard. The heirs (parties of the second part) were the four daughters of Mary Carroll Caton (1770–1846) who inherited the property from her father, Charles Carroll of Carrollton (1737–1832), in 1832, and the granddaughters in 1846. They were Mary Ann Caton Patterson Wellesley (1788–1853); Elizabeth Caton Jerningham (1789/90–1862); Louisa Catherine Caton Hervey Osborne (ca. 1792–1874)—all three residents of England—and Emily Caton MacTavish (1793–1867) of Baltimore, the latter of whom negotiated with Rumpler for the donation to the Redemptorists. The acreage is not mentioned in the deed. The figure used here is quoted from *Baltimore American*, March 23, 1903. The 40 acres includes St. Mary's church, rectory, Carroll House, and school properties plus land on the north side of Duke of Gloucester Street between Newman Street and the Spa Creek bridge and the properties on both sides of Compromise Street between the bridge and the Fleet Reserve Club.
6. "Conditiones implendae, quoad donationem Annapolitanae," in Wuest, *Annales*, II:470–71. What appears to be the handwritten original is in the Annapolis/St. Mary's file, RABP.
7. *Sun*, February 14, 1848.
8. Carroll to Patterson, WSG 9:488 (May 21, 1823), parcel recorded at 39,204 square feet, measured 148.51′ x 264′. Mary Wellesley to James Boyle, JHN 5:593 (March 29, 1851), Boyle to Hafkensheid [*sic*], Newman [*sic*], and Rumpler, NHG 2:74 (February 24, 1853). A second deed, needed to clarify the title following Boyle's death on September 30, 1854 and Mary Ann Wellesley's death in 1853, was signed by James Boyle Jr. [*sic* actually James Boyle III], to Redemptorists, NHG 9:55 (December 28, 1859), all in AACLR. By 1859 Hafkenscheid and Neumann had signed their interest in the properties to the Redemptorist congregation; Gabriel Rumpler died in 1856 and his ownership was assigned to the Redemptorists. For the church property, see Newman [*sic*] to Redemptorists, NHG 7:628 (October 28, 1858); Hafkenscheid to Redemptorists, NHG 8:222 (May 21, 1859). For Carroll House, surrounding land, and endowment properties, for Neumann see NHG 7:630 (October 28, 1858); for Hafkenscheid, NHG 8:221 (May 21, 1859). Redemptorists incorporated by Maryland General Assembly, December 1841.
9. Borgmann, *Redemptorists at Annapolis*, 18–19; Congregation of the Most Holy Redeemer, *Catalogus Congregationis Sanctissimi Redemptoris, Anno MDCCCLIX: Concinnatus et Publicatus* (Rome: Typis Propaganda Fide, 1859), 34. A *hospitium* had a small number of members led by a superior; a *domus*, with a greater number of members, was led by a rector; email from Rev. Carl Hoegerl, C.Ss.R., to author, February 28, 2014.
10. Redemptorists first visited Cumberland in 1843, established Sts. Peter and Paul in 1847. See Spalding, *Premier See*, 138; Rev. Michael J. Curley, C.Ss.R., *The Provincial Story: A History of the Baltimore Province of the Congregation of the Most Holy Redeemer* (New York: Redemptorist Fathers, Baltimore Province, 1963), 117–18; Borgmann, *Redemptorists at Annapolis*, 204, quoting Wissel's April 15, 1903, jubilee address in St. Mary's Church.
11. Jean H. Baker, *Ambivalent Americans: The Know-Nothing Party in Maryland* (Baltimore: Johns Hopkins University Press, 1977), 4–5, 15, 16–18. Although Baker notes the 51,000 Catholic population on p. 18, on p. 45 she says "Maryland had a high, if uncounted Catholic population." She attributes that 51,000 figure to the *Sun*, October 9, 1855, and says the number may be 31,000 Catholics in sixty-five parishes, citing J. D. B. DeBow, *Statistical View of the United States . . . Being a Compendium of the Seventh Census to Which Are Added the Results of Every Previous Census, Beginning with 1790* (New York: Gordon and Breach Science Publishers, 1970), 133–38. Also, Sister Mary St. Patrick McConville, *Political Nativism in the State of Maryland, 1830–1860* (Washington: Catholic University of America, 1928), 24–26, for analysis of an April 11, 1853, incendiary anti-Catholic speech by Presbyterian minister, William Swan Plumer (1802–80), pastor of the Franklin Street Presbyterian Church in Baltimore. 1850 Irish and German statistics from Spalding, *Premier See*, 132, who cites Baker, *Ambivalent Americans*, 18, that the 1850 census disclosed that Catholics constituted the third largest denomination in Maryland.
12. Eileen Mary Brewer, *Nuns and the Education of American Catholic Women, 1860–1920* (Chicago: Loyola University Press, 1987), 15. By 1860 there were 4,005 nuns, 381 convents, and 202 female academies. Also, Jay P. Dolan, *Catholic Revivalism: The American Experience, 1830–1900* (Notre Dame, Indiana: University of Notre Dame Press, 1978), 26; Jay P. Dolan, ed., *The American Catholic Parish: A History from 1850 to Present* (Mahwah, New Jersey: Paulist Press, 1987), 1:127–28; Robert Emmett Curran, *Shaping American Catholicism: Maryland and New York, 1805–1915* (Washington: Catholic University of America Press, 2012), 101.
13. McConville, *Political Nativism*, 51; Ryan K. Smith, "The Cross: Church Symbol and Contest in Nineteenth-Century America," *Church History* 70, no. 4 (December 2001): 715; Sabrina P. Ramet and Christine M. Hassentab, "The Know Nothing Party: Three Theories About Its Rise and Demise," Politics and Religion 6, no. 3 (September 2013): 576–77;

William B. Kurtz, *Excommunicated from the Union: How the Civil War Created a Separate Catholic America* (New York: Fordham University Press, 2016), 22.

14. Jane Wilson McWilliams. *Annapolis, City on the Severn: A History* (Baltimore Johns Hopkins University Press, 2011), 151–53, 382 (quotes from and references to this book are taken from the corrected, second printing); Willard R. Mumford, *The First 100 Years: The First Presbyterian Church of Annapolis, Maryland* (Annapolis: First Presbyterian Church of Annapolis, 2018), 228.
15. Rumpler to Hafkenscheid, October 27, 1851, RABP; Worden, *Saint Mary's*, 110–11. Redemptorists continued to serve Naval Academy personnel informally and voluntarily from 1853 to 1929, when the Military Ordinariate officially requested that a St. Mary's priest serve as the official Catholic spiritual director, which continued until 1947, when the Navy's first Catholic chaplain was appointed. A contractual arrangement initiated in 2015 continued in 2023. Officer of the Day's Journal (June 5, 1853 and October 9, 1853), vol. 3, Entry 151d, USNA, notes midshipmen going off campus for Sunday worship at churches of their choice but without specifying which churches. Secretary of the Navy Isaac Toucey to Captain George S. Blake, USNA, January 17, 1859; Blake to Commander Thomas T. Craven, February 1, 1859 (Nurre); and same to same, February 19, 1859 (Mullan), vol. 9, box 1, folder 2, Entry 4, Letters Sent by Superintendent George S. Blake, 1857–1865, USNA.
16. Richard R. Duncan, "Catholics and the Church in the Antebellum Upper South," in *Catholics in the Old South,* 95; James S. Burns, C.S.C., "School Life and Work in the Immigration Period," *Catholic Educational Review* 3 (January–May 1912): 35; Spalding, *Premier See*, 160–61, 172. *The Metropolitan* was published 1853–58; *Catholic Youth's Magazine* 1857–61.
17. *Sun*, April 23, April 26, and October 11, 1852.
18. *Sun*, March 25, 1853; Maryland, House of Delegates, Committee on Education, *Report of the Committee on Education to the House of Delegates* (Annapolis: Thomas E. Martin, Printer, 1853), 4–6, 8–10, 27–28. The offending part of the 1852 bill was section 27. For full text of the bill, see *Sun*, April 26, 1852.
19. McConville, *Political Nativism*, 31, 37
20. Spalding, *Premier See,* 172; *Sun*, April 19, 1853.
21. *Annapolis Gazette*, January 18, 1855, for Catholic Almanac statistics.
22. *Baltimore American,* March 23, 1903 Borgmann, *Redemptorists at Annapolis,* 22; Wuest, *Annales*, II:281; Robert L. Worden, "Parish Historical Note: Taking Annapolis By Storm," *St. Mary's Moorings* 13, no. 4 (June 1982): 4.
23. "John Thomson Mason (1815–1873)," *Archives of Maryland* (Biographical Series), MSA SC3520-2065, accessed October 17, 2013, http://msa.maryland.gov/megafile/msa/speccol/sc3500/sc3520/002000/002065/html/2065bio.html; "Mason, John Thomson, (1815–1873)," *Biographical Directory of the United States Congress from 1774 to Present*, accessed October 17, 2013, http://bioguide.congress.gov/scripts/biodisplay.pl?index=M000219; Maryland Center for History and Culture, "Biographical Note," accessed October 17, 2020, https://mdhistory.libraryhost.com/repositories/2/resources/422. Mason's Mount St. Mary's attendance was for "a preliminary course" according to John Thomas Scharf, *History of Western Maryland* (Philadelphia: L. H. Everts, 1882) II:1114. For Mason quotes, see *Catholic Mirror,* August 25, 1866. The author was listed only as "M" but identified as Mason in Borgmann, *Redemptorists at Annapolis,* 48.
24. Catherine McGowan, "Convents and Conspiracies: A Study of Convent Narratives in the United States, 1850–1870" (PhD diss., University of Edinburgh, 2009); reprints in Nancy Lusignan Schultz, ed., *Veil of Fear: Nineteenth-Century Convent Tales* (West Lafayette, Indiana: NotaBell Books, Purdue University Press, 1999), vii, xiii, xvi, and xxi; *Six Months in a Convent, or, The Narrative of Rebecca Theresa Reed, Who Was under the Influence of the Roman Catholics for About Two Years, and an Inmate of the Ursuline Convent on Mount Benedict, Charlestown, Mass., Near Six Months, in the Years 1831–32* (Boston: Russell, Odrione, and Metcalf, 1835), 6, 14, 141; *Awful Disclosures of Maria Monk, as Exhibited in a Narrative of Her Suffering During Residence of Five Years as a Novice, and Two Years as a Black Nun, in the Hotel Dieu Nunnery at Montreal* (New York: Howe and Bates, 1836), 48, 81, 88, 113, 126; Thomas T. McAvoy, *History of the Catholic Church in the United States* (Notre Dame, Indiana: University of Notre Dame Press, 1969), 135; Ramet and Hassentab, "Know Nothing Party," 583.
25. Borgmann, *Redemptorists at Annapolis*, 22–23, which provides no indication of where the story originated and it does not appear in *Chronica Domus* I:21–23 (April–December 1853).
26. Officer of the Day's Journal, USNA, searched from March 1, 1853–February 28, 1854, which reported Stribling's and Goldsborough's absences only when they left Annapolis. A search also was made of Letters Sent by the Superintendent, 1845–74, Microfilm Publication M945, RG 405, for correspondence, March 1, 1853–February 28, 1854, relevant to the St. Mary's investigation. Henry May (1816–66) represented Maryland's Fourth Congressional District (Baltimore City) as a Democrat, Thirty-third Congress, March 4, 1853–March 3, 1855, and as a Unionist, Thirty-seventh Congress (March 4, 1861–March 3, 1863). He was benefactor of the Redemptorist mission church in Easton, Maryland, and converted to Catholicism shortly before his death. See *Biographical Dictionary of the United States Congress.* For Henrietta DeCourcey May (1820–1919), see "Roberts Family History," Ancestry Plus, updated November 1, 2001, http://awt.ancestry.com. May is mentioned in *Catholic Mirror*, August 25, 1866. For May's baptism, see Basilica of the Assumption Baptisms, 1854–70, Register #12:396 (September 20, 1866), MSA SCM1513.
27. Matthew Walsh (1831–55), born Thurley, County Galway, Ireland, invested September 5, 1852 (in Baltimore), professed September 15, 1853 (in Annapolis), died November 4, 1855 (in Baltimore County), listed in *Catalogus Novitiorum ad Oblationem Admissorum* I, 8 (1853), *Catalogus Novitiorum ad*

Oblationem Admissorum II:17 (1853), *Liber Professionis Provinciae,* 7:105 (1853). His 1853 profession was made before Rumpler, with Joseph Wissel as witness. His insanity case is covered in detail in *Chronica Domus* I:28–29 (May 1854), with marginal notes added by Wissel. Also *Sun*, May 15, 1854, quotes from *Annapolis Gazette* and *Maryland Republican*, neither of which are extant for relevant dates. *Sun* quoted a letter from Dr. William H. Stokes, a physician at Mount Hope, on Walsh's mental state, May 11, 1854.

28. *Sun*, May 15, 1854; *Chronica Domus* I:28–29 (May 1854).
29. *Annapolis Gazette*, May 18, 1854; "John Carroll LeGrand (1814-1861)," *Archives of Maryland* (Biographical Series), accessed January 22, 2022, https://msa.maryland.gov/megafile/msa/speccol/sc3500/sc3520/001600/001623/html/1623bio.html; Charles W. Mitchell and Jean H. Baker, eds., *The Civil War in Maryland Reconsidered* (Baton Rouge: Louisiana State University Press, 2021), 75; *Dred Scott v. Sandford,* 60 U.S. (19 How.) 393 (1856) (enslaved party), https://tile.loc.gov/storage-services/service/ll/usrep/usrep060/usrep060393a/usrep060393a.pdf, December Term 1856, issued March 6, 1857.
30. *Sun*, July 13, 1854; Baltimore City Circuit Court, Minutes, July 6–11, 1854, MSA T473–2; *Chronica Domus* I:29 (May 1854).
31. Ray Allen Billington, *Protestant Crusade, 1800–1860* (New York: Macmillan, 1938), 416; Baker, *Ambivalent Americans,* 91–92; Maryland, House of Delegates, Select Committee on Convents and Nunneries, *Report of the Select Committee on Convents and Nunneries,* Document Q, March 4, 1866 [*sic*, 1856], 2–4, accessed October 7, 2014, http://aomol.msa.maryland.gov/megafile/msa/speccol/sc4800/sc4872/003174/html/m3174-0735.html.
32. McConville, *Political Nativism,* 39–41; Willa Young Banks, "A Contradiction in Antebellum Baltimore: A Competitive School for Girls of 'Color' within a Slave State," *Maryland Historical Magazine* 99, no. 2 (Summer 2004): 140; Lawrence M. Denton, *A Southern Star for Maryland: Maryland the Secession Crisis* (Baltimore: Publishing Concepts, 1995), 10.
33. William Darrell Overdyke, *The Know-Nothing Party in the South* (Baton Rouge: Louisiana State University Press, 1950), 57, 223; Laurence Frederick Schmeckebier, *History of the Know Nothing Party in Maryland* (Baltimore: Johns Hopkins Press, 1899), 13–15; McConville, *Political Nativism*, 64; Anna Ella Carroll, *The Great American Battle; or, The Contest Between Christianity and Political Romanism (New York: Miller, Orton, and Mulligan, 1856), 270.*
34. Spalding, *Premier See*, 131; Andrew H. M. Stern, *Southern Crucifix, Southern Cross: Catholic-Protestant Relations in the Old South* (Tuscaloosa: University of Alabama Press, 2012), 16; John D. Krugler, "An 'Ungracious Silence': Historians and the Calvert Vision," *Maryland Historical Magazine* 110, no. 1 (Spring 2015): 143–57; Joseph G. Mannard, "'We Are Determined to Be White Ladies': Race, Identity, and the Maryland Tradition in Antebellum Visitation Convents," *Maryland Historical Magazine* 109, no. 2 (Summer 2014): 137, 148; *Annapolis Gazette*, January 18, 1855.
35. *Plain Dealer* (Cleveland), January 6, 1854; James F. Connelly, *The Visit of Archbishop Gaetano Bedini to the United States of America (June, 1853–February, 1854)* (Rome: Pontificatiae Universitatis Gegorianae, 1960), 17–20, 22, 25, 131 (citing the *Catholic Mirror* of January 21 and 28, 1854); *Boston Evening Herald*, January 17, 1854; Kenrick, Baltimore, to Archbishop John Purcell, Cincinnati, August 5, 1854, Archdiocese of Cincinnati Collection, University of Notre Dame Archives, Notre Dame, Indiana, as quoted in Kurtz, *Excommunicated from the Union,* 24.
36. *Annapolis Gazette*, July 26, 1855.
37. Stern, *Southern Crucifix,* 171; Baker, *Ambivalent Americans,* 2, 27; *Annapolis Gazette*, April 5, 1855. The new mayor was Nicholas Brewer III who served one term (1855–56)
38. *Annapolis Gazette*, May 17, 1855.
39. *Annapolis Gazette*, September 13, 1855, quoting the *Richmond Post*.
40. Email Rev. Carl Hoegerl, C.Ss.R., to author, September 3, 2013. Also, John H. Foertschbeck, Sr., *German Catholic Parishes of Maryland and Pennsylvania* (Woodbine, Maryland: self published, 2013), 85–86, 87–89, 94, 96. *Annapolis Gazette*, September 13, 1855, letter to editor signed George D. Armstrong. The 1850 and 1860 Federal censuses for Eastern District, Henrico County, Virginia, identified the two Valentine Hecklers, born about 1809 and 1839, living in the same household. *Annapolis Gazette,* March 15, 1855.
41. Billington, *Protestant Crusade*, 407–9, says there were 43 American Party members in the 34th Congress, but US Congress, House of Representatives, Office of the Historian, "Congress Profiles: 34th Congress (1855–1857)," accessed May 7, 2014, http://history.house.gov/Congressional-Overview/Profiles/34th/, says there were 51. Continuously switching political affiliations explains such discrepancies; *Annapolis Gazette*, November 8, 1855; Overdyke, *Know-Nothing Party,* 59, provides the following General Assembly election results for the House of Delegates: American Party (54), Unionists (10), Democrats (9), and Whigs (1); in the Senate: Whigs (9) Americans (8), Democrats (3), Unionists (2). Also, Baker, *Ambivalent Americans,* 2, 27. The *Baltimore Clipper* quote appears in Overdyke, 129, and the dates November 4 and November 8, 1857, are given in Overdyke, 187 n3.
42. *Annapolis Gazette*, November 16, 1854, May 31, 1855. The book was *The Arch-Bishop or Romanism in the United States*, see ad, which ran weekly for many months, in *Annapolis Gazette,* November 23, 1854. Also, *Annapolis Gazette*, December 21, 1854.
43. *Annapolis Gazette*, January 11, 1855.
44. *Annapolis Gazette*, July 12, 19, 26, August 2, 9, 16, and September 6, 1855.
45. *Baltimore American*, March 23, 1903.
46. *New-York Freeman's Journal* and *Catholic Register*, May 26, 1855, 5, reprinted the "sensible article" from the *Catholic Mirror*.
47. *Annapolis Gazette*, April 19 and August 23, 1855. The same

notice appeared in the *Annapolis Gazette* on October 11, 1855, January 3 and 10, 1856.

48. St. John's College Alumni Association, *1789–1889: Commemoration of the One Hundredth Anniversary of St. John's College* (Baltimore: William K. Boyle and Son, 1890), 89–90; *Annapolis Gazette*, September 20, 1855.
49. *Annapolis Gazette*, October 18 and 25, 1855. *Chronica Domus* made no mention of this episode, remaining focused on religious activities.
50. Thomas Karney (1810–85), son of Thomas and Anna Karney, baptized in Annapolis, November 12, 1820, see "White Marsh/Bowie Register of Baptisms, Marriages, and Deaths, 1818–95," Box 3, Folder 3, Maryland Province Collection, GU-CSC. Also, "Maryland, Marriages, 1666-1970," accessed October 28, 2013, FamilySearch.org, for Thomas Karney-Anna Richardson marriage, February 11, 1812, Anne Arundel County, Maryland; Pat Melville, "A School House in Annapolis," *Archivists' Bulldog: Newsletter of the Maryland State Archives* 14, no. 17 (September 11, 2000): 2; *Annapolis Gazette*, October 25, 1855, appended list of Board of Visitors and Governors of St. John's College; *Catalogue of St. John's College, Annapolis, Maryland, for the Academic Year 1916–1917 (Annapolis, 1917), accessed September 16, 2013, https://digi*talarchives.sjc.edu/items/show/149; McIntire, 1:384.
51. Worden, *Saint Mary's*, 32, 186 n84, said James Boyle (1784–1854) and Susannah Maccubbin (1795–1864) both had converted to Catholicism but author now doubts Susanna became Catholic. Only James was interred at St. Mary's burial ground on Duke of Gloucester St. (1854) and reburied in St. Mary's Cemetery on West St. (1900). Susannah was buried in All Hallows (Episcopal) Cemetery in Edgewater, Maryland (1864). St. Mary's baptismal records include christening 1852 in B#1 (September 3, 1852) of Edwin Llewellyn Boyle (1851–1936), with his uncle, James Boyle III (1813–89), as godfather. See Find A Grave Memorial ID 45573719 for Edwin Boyle who is buried in the Odd Fellows Lawn Cemetery, Sacramento, California, indicating that he too did not remain in the Catholic Church. William K. Paynter, *St. Anne's Annapolis: History and Times* (Annapolis: St. Anne's Parish, 1980), 115, lists James Boyle as a vestry member, first elected in 1855.
52. *Annapolis Gazette*, October 18, 1855. The Democrat who voted for Sparks was James Murray Sr. Those identified as anti-Know Nothings were William George Baker, Edward Hammond, William McDaniel, and William Price.
53. James Mackubin to Sparks, May 20, 1856, responding to Sparks' March 24, 1856, request, and same to same, April 3, 1856, transmitting the 24-page transcript, approved by the Board on April 2, 1856; Papers of the Board, St. John's College Archives Collection, MSA SC–5698–2–428. See Elihu S. Riley, Jr., *"The Ancient City," A History of Annapolis in Maryland* (Annapolis: Record Printing Office, 1887), 259.
54. Mackubin to Sparks letters, St. John's College Archives.
55. Professors Attendance Book, 1838–55, St. John's College Archives Collection, MSA SC–5698–2–3. The "morning devotions" reference was found in the 24-page transcript (July 1, 1848).
56. Tench Francis Tilghman, *The Early History of St. John's College in Annapolis* (Annapolis: St John's College Press, 1984), 78–80.
57. *Annapolis Gazette*, July 2, 1857, and numerous subsequent editions.
58. Rev. George Stebbing, C.Ss.R., *The Redemptorists* (London: Burns Oates and Washbourne, 1924), 2; Spalding, *Premier See*, 134–35, 164; Tracy Matthew Melton, "The Case of Catholic Know-Nothings," *Maryland Historical Magazine* 10, no. 3 (Fall 2014): 351–71; Duncan, "Catholics and the Church in the Antebellum Upper South," in *Catholics in the Old South*, 96; Schmeckebier, *History of the Know Nothing Party in Maryland*, 167; *Annapolis Gazette*, November 8, 1855. Tydings and wife, Henrietta Rebecca Stinchcomb Tydings, witnesses to marriage of George Mittnacht and Mary R. Brady, see St. Mary's Marriage Register, Marriage Register, B#1 (January 20, 1862); *Annapolis Gazette*, October 16, 1856.
59. Jane D. (Putnam Gantt) Chauven Widow's Pension Application No. 386725, Records of the Veterans Administration, RG 15, National Archives and Records Administration, Washington (NARA), for marriage information; St. Mary's Baptismal Register (Baptismal Register) B#1 (May 11, 1857) (the godmother was Matilda Goewey of Brownsville, Pennsylvania). Francis Asbury Baker (1820–65), an Episcopalian convert to Catholicism who, with four other former Redemptorists (Isaac T. Hecker, George Deshon, Augustine Hewit, and Clarence Walworth), founded the Missionary Society of St. Paul (Paulists) in 1858. See James McVann, *The Paulists, 1858–1970* (New York: Missionary Society of St. Paul the Apostle, 1983), I:21–23, 40, 43. Also, *Annapolis Gazette*, October 18, 1855, November 1, 1855, March 6, 1856, May 1, 1856, and up to April 16, 1857; 1860 Federal Census, Center Township, Knox County, Missouri, (William must have died by 1860 because he is not listed with the family); *History of Lewis, Clark, Knox and Scotland Counties, Missouri* (St. Louis: Goodspeed Publishing Co., 1887), 42, 641–42, 709; US Secretary of War, *Official Army Register of the Volunteer Force of the United States Army for the Years 1861, '62. '63, '64, '65. Part VII: Missouri, Wisconsin, Iowa, Minnesota, California, Kansas, Oregon, Nevada* (Washington: Adjutant General's Office, 1867), 11; John E. Swager, comp., *Official Manual of the State of Missouri for the Years 1907–1908* (Jefferson City: Hugh Stephens Printing Company, 1908), 116; *Glasgow Weekly Times* (Glasgow, Howard County, Missouri), August 24, 1866. See Stern, *Southern Crucifix*, 171, for the Know-Nothing proscriptions.
60. *Register of Graduates and Alumni of St. John's College at Annapolis, Maryland* (Baltimore: Williams and Wilkins, 1908), 45; M. C. Dugan, *Outline History of Annapolis and the Naval Academy* (Baltimore: B. G. Eichelberger, 1902), 66; *Annapolis Gazette*, November 1, 1855.
61. *Annapolis Gazette*, May 29, 1856, July 31, 1856, and August 7, 1856, quoting *Knoxville Whig*; Edgar DeWitt Jones, *Lincoln*

and the Preachers (New York: Harper and Brothers, 1948), 79, for Seward-Hughes relationship. During the war, Seward often passed Hughes' letters on to Lincoln, "who read them with interest."

62. Harry S. Stout, *Upon the Altar of the Nation: A Moral History of the American Civil War* (New York: Viking, 2006), 2–3; Baker, *Ambivalent Americans*, 120, table 24, and 134–35; Baker, *Politics of Continuity*, 31; *Annapolis Gazette*, November 13, 1856, gives a district-by-district tally for Anne Arundel County.
63. *Annapolis Gazette*, December 11, 1856.
64. *Annapolis Gazette*, March 5, April 2, and October 29, 1857.
65. Stern, *Southern Crucifix*, 175; Billington, *Protestant Crusade*, 430; Frank F. White, Jr., *The Governors of Maryland 1777-1970* (Annapolis: Hall of Records Commission, 1970), 153; St. Alphonsus (Baltimore) Annals, October 12, 1857, 48, RABP.
66. *Annapolis Gazette*, April 8, 1858. The election was held April 5. For David Caldwell's role as godfather, see Baptismal Register B#1 (May 24, 1858, January 16, 1859). Three Airland children were baptized in January 1859: four-year-old Thomas William, five-year-old Richard, eight-year-old George, and ten-year-old John. According to the record, they had been baptized by a *ministero heretico*—a Protestant minister—and identified their parents as John Airland and Charlotte Weber, about whom nothing else has been discovered except for the father's Philadelphia birthplace and the mother's Hannover (German) birthplace, noted in the baptismal records.
67. Baker, *Ambivalent Americans*, 23, 49; *Annapolis Gazette*, July 1, 1858, August 19, 1858, September 9, 1858; Isabel Shipley Cunningham, *Calvary United Methodist Church, Annapolis, Maryland: Our 222–Year Heritage of Methodism in Annapolis*, 2d ed. (Annapolis: Calvary United Methodist Church, 2010), 19, 23.
68. *Annapolis Gazette*, October 14, 1858; Baker, *Politics of Continuity*, 34; *Maryland Republican*, May 15, 1858.
69. Baker, *Ambivalent Americans*, 49, 50, 80, 81, 90, 98, 104. Timothy R. Snyder, "'The Susquehanna Shall Run Red with Blood,'" *Maryland Historical Magazine* 108, no. 1 (Spring 2013): 51, for 1859 election figures (Democrats 49 seats in the House to the Americans 29 seats and 12 out of 22 seats in the Senate); John V. Mering, "The Slave-State Constitutional Unionists and the Politics of Consensus," *Journal of Southern History* 43, no. 3 (August 1977): 404, 406; Spalding, *Premier See*, 174; Kurtz, *Excommunicated from the Union*, 27–29; Barbara Jeanne Fields, *Slavery and Freedom on the Middle Ground: Maryland during the Nineteenth Century* (New Haven: Yale University Press, 1985), 61, 83.
70. Brother Thomas W. Spalding, C.F.X., *Martin John Spalding: American Churchman* (Washington: Catholic University of America Press, 1973), 122–23.
71. Rev. Carl W. Hoegerl, C.Ss.R., *With All Gentleness: A Life of Blessed Francis Xavier Seelos, CSsR* (New Orleans: Redemptorists/Seelos Center, 2018), 7–23; Rev. Michael J. Curley, C.Ss.R., *Cheerful Ascetic: The Life of Francis Xavier Seelos, C.Ss. R.* (New Orleans: Redemptorist Fathers, New Orleans Vice Province, 1969), 2–7, 10, 13, 17, 25, 28, 31, 33–36; Rev. Richard Boever, C.Ss.R., *Zealous Missionary: From the Perspective of Blessed Xavier Seelos* (Liguori, Missouri: Liguorian Publications, 2021), *23–30*.
72. Hoegerl, *With All Gentleness*, 61–68; Curley, *Cheerful Ascetic*, 34–36, 39.
73. Curley, *Cheerful Ascetic*, 49, 54, 56, 61, 94, 96; Rev. Carl W. Hoegerl, C.Ss.R., and Alicia von Stamwitz, *A Life of Blessed Francis Xavier Seelos, Redemptorist, 1819–1867* (New Orleans: Seelos Center, 2000), 37–39. For the Seelos visits to Annapolis, see (1) *Chronica Domus* I:32 (November n.d., 1854, which mentions the visitation of Ruland to Annapolis; Curley, *Cheerful Ascetic*, 112, says Seelos accompanied him as *socius*); (2) *Chronica Domus* I:45 (May n.d. 1855; Curley, 113, says May 30); (3) *Chronica Domus* I:45 (June 4, 1855); (4) *Chronica Domus* I:46–47 (June 22–24, 1855; Curley, 120, says June 21–25); (5) *Chronica Domus* I:67 (December 8–9, 1856); (6) Seelos, Cumberland, to Sister Romualda Seelos, S.S.N.D., [Bavaria], February 21, 1860, Letter 86 in Carl W. Hoegerl, C.Ss.R., ed. and trans., *Sincerely, Seelos: The Collected Letters of Blessed Francis Xavier Seelos* (New Orleans: Seelos Center, 2008), 239, mentions a one-day visit to Annapolis probably on December 29 or 30, 1859, on his way back to Cumberland after giving a sermon at the consecration of the new St. Michael's Church in Baltimore on December 26; Chronicles of the House of Studies, Cumberland, Md., RABP, 68 (December 1859), which mentions he returned home on December 31.
74. Seelos, Baltimore, to Mother and Family, Füssen, Bavaria, January 14, 1856, Letter 32, Hoegerl, *Sincerely, Seelos*, 107–9.
75. Curley, *Cheerful Ascetic*, 145–49; Rev. Carl W. Hoegerl, C.Ss.R., *Novae Aureliae Beatificationis et Canonizationis Servi Dei Francisci Xaverii Seelos Positio Super Vita, Virtutibus, et Fama Sanctitatis, Sacerdotis Professi Congregationis Ss.Mi. Redemptoris (1819–1867)* (Documentary Study of the Life, Virtues and Holiness Fame of the Servant of God, Francis Xavier, Professed Priest of the Congregation of the Most Holy Redeemer (1819–1867), *Positio*), (Rome: Tipografia Guerra, 1998), 2, Part 1, 585, RABP; *Chronica Domus* I:74 (April 16, 1857); Curley, *Cheerful Ascetic*, 145–49; Rev. Peter Zimmer, C.Ss.R., *Leben und Wirken des hochwürdigen P. Franz Xaver Seelos aus der Congregation des Allerheill. Erlösers* (Life and Labors of the Rev. Father Francis Xavier Seelos of the Congregation of the Most Holy Redeemer) (New York: Benziger Brothers, 1887), 123, as translated in typescript, 118 (quotes from this book are based on a typescript translation in Seelos File, RABP); Seelos, Annapolis, to Joseph Wissel, Rochester, New York, April 17, 1857, Letter 41, Hoegerl, *Sincerely, Seelos*, 126.
76. Borgmann, *Redemptorists at Annapolis*, 28, 216-17, 246; Curley, *Cheerful Ascetic*, 150–51; *Chronica Domus* I:76 (May 18, 1857); Seelos, Cumberland, to Sister Paulina [Millard], Visitation Convent, Georgetown, DC, June 25, 1857, Letter 44, Hoegerl, *Sincerely, Seelos*, 131. For a detailed account of Seelos' tenure in Cumberland, see Rev. Blaine Burkey,

O.F.M. Cap., *Seelos: The Cumberland Years: The Life and Labor of Blessed Francis Xavier Seelos in Maryland's Allegheny Mountains 1857–1865* (New Orleans: Seelos Center, 2010).

77. Borgmann, *Redemptorists at Annapolis,* 20. Robert L. Worden, "Historic Structures Report: Charles Carroll House of Annapolis," 3rd draft, February 23, 1997, 36, personal archive, notes "G[abriel]. Rumpler, Memorandum Book, Jan 9th 1854," RABP, which has notations, dating between January 9, 1854 and May 19, 1855, listing a variety of building materials including lath, flooring, planks for steps, shingles, and lumber. Although substantial amounts of these materials are listed in Rumpler's book, James T. Wollon, Jr., the Carroll House restoration architect, Havre de Grace, believed they were not enough to complete the West Wing; letter from Wollon to author, June 18, 1987, on file at the Carroll House. It is possible, however, that these materials were used either to construct part of the west wing or to complete the bell-tower wing on the first St. Mary's Church. *Province Annals—Chronica Pro. Am. C.SS.R.—1832–1871,* 395 (1858, Annapolis), RABP.
78. Wuest, *Annales,* IV Part 2:448.
79. *Chronica Domus* I:79–80 (November 3–4, 1857) notes visit of Ruland (provincial superior, January 30, 1854–April 24, 1859); St. Alphonsus (Baltimore) Annals, October 12, 1857, 48, says he was in Annapolis November 4–7 for visitation. Brother Jacob's quote appears in Müller's poem, "Nova Ecclesiae."
80. The $2,000 is mentioned in *Chronica Domus* I:80 (mid-November 1857) rather than in the poem.
81. *Annapolis Gazette,* February 18 and August 19, 1858, and May 26, 1859, which reprinted a *Sun* article of May 23, 1859 in full, stating cost of $30,000; Paynter, *St. Anne's,* 51, which quotes a $20,000 cost.
82. US Superintendent of the Census, *Statistics of the United States (including Mortality, Property, &c.,) in 1860; Compiled from the Original Returns of the Eighth Census, Under the Direction of the Secretary of the Interior* (Washington: Government Printing Office, 1866), 407; *Chronica Domus* I:85 (January 1, 1858) lists thirteen professed and novice brothers, I:105 (January 1, 1859) lists ten professed and novice brothers, I:125–26 (January 1, 1860) lists four professed brothers. This influx of brothers during the two years of church and college construction is, perhaps, thus partially explained, although I:17 (January 1, 1857) also listed thirteen brothers in Annapolis well before construction began.
83. Annals, Annapolis, 1889–1900, 378 (August 30, 1899), RABP (the eulogy was given by Joseph Wissel); *Chronica Domus* I:80 (November n.d., 1857).
84. Borgmann, *Redemptorists at Annapolis,* 89, identified McCusker as Müller's companion. McIntire, 1:461, identifies McCusker (ca. 1832–1907) as a USNA steam heating plant employee for 54 years and retired as superintendent. *Chronica Domus* I:74 (April 12, 1857).
85. The "genteel man" whom Müller met in Baltimore on one of his fund-raising trips possibly was Henry May but no relevant May family papers have been discovered at the Maryland Center for History and Culture, Maryland State Archives, or other repositories. May's wife was Catholic and he was congressman for the Fourth Congressional District of Maryland (representing Baltimore City; Democrat, Thirty-third Congress, March 4, 1853–March 3, 1855, and Unionist, Thirty-seventh Congress (March 4, 1861–March 3, 1863), and future benefactor of the Redemptorist mission church in Easton, Maryland. Brugger, *Middle Temperament,* 271, identifies May as a Stephen A. Douglas Democratic Party elector in the 1860 presidential election.
86. Spalding, *Premier See,* 135; Episcopal Diary, Box 32, Folder B21, Kenrick Papers, AAB; *Woods' Baltimore City Directory* (Baltimore: John W. Woods, 1860), 250; "May, Henry (1816–1866)," *Biographical Directory of the United States Congress;* Snyder, "'Susquehanna Shall Run Red,'" 39, 41; *Sun,* February 20, 1861; "Enoch Louis Lowe," *Archives of Maryland* (Biographical Series), accessed January 3, 2014, http://msa.maryland.gov/megafile/msa/speccol/sc3500/sc3520/001400/001460/html/1460extbio.html; Baptismal Register B#1 (September 12, 1852—Vivian's baptism).
87. *Chronica Domus* entries and church baptismal and marriage registers, Cornell arrived in Annapolis in March 1858 and Jacobs by December 1858. Jacobs professed vows in Europe in 1854, arrived in the United States in 1855 and, after a brief period in Annapolis for recuperation from an unspecified illness, was ordained in 1856. He is sometimes referred to as Joseph Gerard Jacobs. Wuest, *Annales,* IV:2:451; *Chronica Domus* I:65 (September 4, 1856), I:66 (October 30, 1856).
88. *Annapolis Gazette,* September 9, 1858.
89. Francis (Frank) Henry Stockett (1821–96) is buried at St Anne's Cemetery, Annapolis, with wife Mary Priscilla Hall Stockett (1827–1900) next to him; her stone carries this epitaph "In the Communion of the Catholic Church." Her name does not appear in St. Mary's Interment Register (Interment Register) B#2 for her death date nor is there any other evidence she was a member of the Roman Catholic Church. *Annapolis Gazette,* February 25, 1858, lists the members of St. Anne's appointed to the committee immediately after 1858 fire. Stockett had been elected to St. Anne's vestry for the first time in 1852. See Paynter, *St. Anne's,* 115.
90. *Liber Professionis,* 64; Benedict A. Neithart, *Short Account of the Edifying Life and Precious Death of Our Dear Confreres Who Died at New Orleans During the Epidemic of 1867* (Annapolis: Typis C.Ss.R., 1867), 5–7; St. Alphonsus (Baltimore) House Annals, May 2, 1858, 53; Foertschbeck, *German Catholic Parishes,* 94. Brother Lawrence died of yellow fever in New Orleans, September 27, 1867, a week before Seelos died of the disease.
91. *Annapolis Gazette,* May 27, 1858, quoting "A New Church Building," *American and Commercial Advertiser* (Baltimore), May 15, 1858. "Mr. Powell" was George T. Powell who worked with Long on two Catholic projects in 1858; email from James T. Wollon, Jr., Havre de Grace, Maryland, to author, December 22, 2013. The spire, completed in 1876,

reaches 160 feet. "Louis L. Long," Baltimore Architecture Foundation, accessed May 7, 2015, http://baltimorearchitecture.org/biographies/louis-l-long/; *Washington Union*, May 26, 1857; St. Anne's Catholic Church, Edenton, "Our Church's Rich History, "accessed November 3, 2017, https://edentoncatholic.weebly.com/our-history.html. Long married Anna E. Storm at St. Joseph's Catholic Chapel in Emmitsburg, Maryland, in 1854. The March 2, 1854 marriage record, stating *nullo impedimento legittimo detecto*, in Daughters of Charity Archives, Emmittsburg, Maryland.

92. Dorothy Stewart Krotzer, "St. Alphonsus Church, New Orleans, Louisiana: Documentation, Analysis and Interpretation of Interior Finishes" (M.A. thesis in historic preservation, University of Pennsylvania, 2001), 10; *Annapolis Gazette*, August 19, 1858; St. Alphonsus (New Orleans) Annals, September 1, 1857; St. Alphonsus (Baltimore) Annals December 7, 1857; *Chronica Domus* I:85; Wuest, *Annales*, IV:2:465; *Catalogus Novitiorum ad Oblationem Admissorum*, I:6, II:207, II:218; *Liber Professionis* on the date of Lütte's profession before Müller in Annapolis. Thomas Zeller, C.Ss. R., "Death of Brother Thomas Luette, C.Ss.R.," 61–62 in Peter Geiermann, C.Ss.R., *Annals of the St. Louis Province of the Congregation of the Most Holy Redeemer, 2, 1898–1912* (St. Louis: 1924).

93. John Randall's "Notice" warning trespassers, *Maryland Gazette*, June 8, 1826, 3, says he then occupied the Carroll House. Borgmann, *Redemptorists at Annapolis*, 19, says John and Eliza Randall "had taken charge of the mansion, a sublet it to others" in 1827. The farmhouse, according to Simon Martenet's 1860 *Map of Anne Arundel County*, was located on an inlet on the south shore of Spa Creek then called Long Cove (now Hawkins Cove, near the end of Boucher Avenue). An 1859 survey of adjoining property to west shows Randall's property extending around creek headwaters as far west as Spa Road and today's Silopanna neighborhood. See Equity Papers OS 95 (digitized from microfilm CR 40715, image 2), Anne Arundel County Circuit Court (Plats from Equity), 1852–1949, MSA C72–9. After Randall's death, his property, identified as Greenfield, was advertised as a 200-acre farm "well adapted to the growing of Wheat, Corn and Tobacco, and lying with a half mile of Annapolis, and adjoining the water" with a stable, tobacco and corn houses, an apple orchard, and "an abundance of good Timber and Meadow land and good water." *Annapolis Gazette*, March 28, 1861. One hundred acres of Greenfield were sold to parishioner Michael Coolahan, NHG 10:256 (April 18, 1861), AACLR.

94. Mehitable Woodworth Davenport (1812–94), wife of James Radcliffe Davenport (1812–96), rector of St. Anne's (1857–65) per email from Eric Fredland, Archivist, St. Anne's, to author, June 11, 2013. Also, Paynter, *St. Anne's*, 113.

95. Paynter, *St. Anne's*, 51.

96. *Annapolis Gazette*, March 10, 1859; Spalding, *Premier See*, 165, on pew rents as principal source of income.

97. *Sun*, April 20, 1859.

98. "Blessing of Church Bells," *Sun*, October 25, 1859, 4. No other newspaper reports of this event have been located.

99. Neumann's visits to Annapolis on May 17, 1855 and May 10–11, 1858, are documented in *Chronica Domus* I:43 (May 17, 1855), I:89 (May 13, 1858). His personal record of visitations only includes parishes in his own diocese. See "Note Book of the Venerable Bishop John Nepomucene Neumann, C.SS.R.," *Records of the American Catholic Historical Society of Philadelphia* 41, no. 1 (March 1930): 1–26, no. 2 (June 1930): 162–92. Similarly, correspondence with his patron, Archbishop Kenrick of Baltimore, revealed only that he had been in Baltimore in early August 1855: Neumann, Easton [Pennsylvania], to Kenrick, Baltimore, August 23, 1855, Box 30, Folder U17, Kenrick Papers, AAB. St. Alphonsus (Baltimore) Annals, 62 (June 22, 1859), RABP mention Neumann's visit of "some days" and "went today back to Philadelphia"; Chronicles of the House of Studies, Cumberland, 68 (November 9, 1859) notes "a sudden despatch came recalling him to Philadelphia. He therefore remained only two days." "Note Book of the Venerable Bishop John Nepomucene Neumann," 41, no. 2 (June 1930): 175, 180, notes confirmations by Neumann at St. Edward's, Shamokin, Northumberland County, on September 30, 1859; at St. Stephen's, Port Carbon, Schuylkill County, on October 23, 1859. Email from Shawn Weldon, Assistant Archivist, Philadelphia Archdiocesan Historical Research Center, to author, March 20, 2013, says he screened Philadelphia and Baltimore diocesan newspapers and checked archival files to no avail regarding a visit to Annapolis.

100. See Prelude, note 3.

101. "1859. Nova domus origo a Rev. P. Magistro descripta" (1859: Origins of Our New House Described by Father Rector), a five-page poem written in old German script in *Chronica Domus* I:116–20, following entries for the year 1859.

102. Borgmann, *Redemptorists at Annapolis*, 35.

103. *Annapolis Gazette*, October 28, 1858.

104. McWilliams, *Annapolis*, 161 and 425 n65; *Report, By-Laws, and List, &c of Stockholders of the Annapolis Gas Light Company*, July 27, 1859, 7, Annapolis Mayor and Alderman (Proceedings), 1858–1861, Box 24, Folder 14, MSA M49–7; "Reminiscences of the Late Col. John Walton," undated, unattributed article in Walton Album, Historic Annapolis Inc., probably *Evening Capital* or *Maryland Republican* between 1894 and 1912.

105. Seelos, Annapolis, to Antonia Seelos and other family members, Füssen, Bavaria, October 12, December 3 and 18, 1862, Letter 119, Hoegerl, *Sincerely, Seelos*, 315. This is one letter, 16 pages in published form, written over a period of months.

106. *Annapolis Gazette*, December 2, 1869.

107. *Annapolis Gazette*, February 25, 1858; *Sun*, May 23, 1859; *Annapolis Gazette*, May 26, 1859, reprinted the *Sun* article in full. The smoke pipes for the new furnaces were connected to chimneys that had been added to each side of the church

in 1828, before which there was no heat.

108. Thaddeus Anwander, C.Ss.R., Receipts Book, 1868, St. Mary's Parish Archives (SMPA). Also, *Annapolis Gazette*, December 24, 1868. For Carey baptisms see Baptismal Register B#1 (May 13, 1856, October 31, 1859, March 13, 1862, December 18, 1865). The Careys later relocated to Baltimore where Thomas worked as an insurance agent (1870 census) and real estate agent (1880 census, by which time Catherine had died and Thomas was listed as a widower). For Carey's December 22, 1863, and September 8, 1868, signatures see Anne Arundel County Test Book, MSA C147–1.

109. *Annapolis Gazette*, August 5, 1858, June 2, 1859, and other duplicate advertisements, also, October 11, 1866,. For Baltimore firms, see *Annapolis Gazette*, October 27, 1859. William E. Wood of Baltimore supplied the cast-iron radiators still in use at St. Mary's Rectory in 2023, was not yet in business in 1860 or at least was not listed in *Wood's Baltimore City Directory, Ending Year 1860* (Baltimore: John W. Wood, 1860), 420. The first listing for the company appears in *Wood's Baltimore City Directory, 1867–'68* (Baltimore: John W. Wood, 1867), 555. *Wood's Baltimore City Directory, 1868–'69* (Baltimore: John W. Wood, 1868), ad following 811, indicates Wood offered steam heaters and warm-air furnaces. An advertisement in George W. Howard, *The Monumental City, Its Past History and Present Resources* (Baltimore: J.D. Ehlers, 1873), 212, lists "New Forms of Cast Iron for Direct and Indirect Radiators, for steam or hot water."

110. Borgmann, *Redemptorists at Annapolis*, 31–32; John N. Berger, C.Ss.R., Annapolis, to Aunt and Sister [in Bohemia], "am Feste Himmelfahrt Ch. 1861" (on the Feast of the Ascension of Christ [May 9] 1861), John Berger Personnel File, RABP; *Annapolis Gazette*, October 20, 1859, transcribed in *Chronica Domus*, I:113 (October 20, 1859). For Bernard C. Courlaender (1818–98), a widely published composer then residing in Baltimore, see "Bernard Courlaender," in Elizabeth A. Allen, *"Gold Nails" to Hang Memories On: A Rhyming Review under their Christian Names of Old Acquaintances in History, Literature and Friendship* (New York: Thomas Y. Crowell, 1890), 20; Courlaender's obituary in *New York Dramatic Mirror*, April 23, 1898. Also, *Annapolis Gazette*, December 1, 1859, which was transcribed in *Chronica Domus* I:114 (December 1, 1859). A second announcement appeared in *Annapolis Gazette*, December 8, 1859, and included the music program list. The article only mentions J. H. Wilcox [John Henry Wilcox (1827–75)], who worked with William B. D. Simmons, see Douglas E. Bush and Richard Kassel, eds., *The Organ: An Encyclopedia* (New York: Routledge, 2006), 265.

111. "St. Mary's Assumption Catholic Church, New Orleans, LA., Pipe Organ Specification, " accessed January 20, 2011, http://www.neworleanschurches.com/stmaryasum/stmaryasum.htm; "Our Organ," accessed March 1, 2015, http://www.pjmorgans.com/HTML/projects/electric_opus/opus56_St_Ignatius_baltimore.html. Also, John H. Cornell, Ex-C.Ss.R. File, RABP; *Chronica Domus* I:200 (August 25–28, 1862).

112. *Annapolis Gazette*, July 21, 1859, a transcript of which appears in *Chronica Domus* I:110 (July 21, 1859); Cunningham, *Calvary United Methodist Church*, 23, on the June 1859 cornerstone. The location of Mary Lake's shop appeared in *Annapolis Gazette*, August 14, 1856.

113. *Annapolis Gazette*, October 6, 1859; Paynter, *St. Anne's*, 51–52. The two towers were never built, instead a single steeple was constructed, using remnants of the 1792 structure.

114. Chronicles of the House of Studies, Cumberland, 68 (December 1859); Seelos, Cumberland, to Sister Romualda Seelos, S.S.N.D., [Bavaria], February 21, 1860, Letter 86, Hoegerl, *Sincerely, Seelos*, 239.

Chapter 2: 1860 — A Vast Building Has Been Erected

1. Fields, *Slavery and Freedom*, 61, 83, 92; Harold W. Hurst, "The Northernmost Southern Town: A Sketch of Pre-Civil War Annapolis," *Maryland Historical Magazine* 7, no. 3 (September 1981): 240–41.
2. Jack Sweetman, *The U.S. Naval Academy: An Illustrated History*, 2d ed., rev. Thomas J. Cutler (Annapolis: Naval Institute Press, 1995), 43, 47.
3. McWilliams, *Annapolis*, 162; Anne Arundel Circuit Court (Land Records), NHG 10:83, December 22, 1860, recorded February 27, 1861, MSA CE59–10. There was a total of 61 shareholders.
4. *Annapolis Gazette*, October 7, 1858, quoting *National Intelligencer* of Washington, DC.
5. Citizen of Annapolis (suspected to be Owen M. Taylor), *A Correct Guide to Strangers Visiting the Ancient City of Annapolis* ([Annapolis:] 1859), 3 (digital copy provided by Jane McWilliams).
6. Batcheller to Brother, December 5, 1859, and Cooper to Dear Parents, October 14, 1860, quoted in Anne Marie Drew, ed., *Letters from Annapolis: Midshipmen Write Home, 1848–1969 (Annapolis: Naval Institute Press, 1998), 34, 54;* Stephen Minot Weld, *War Diary and Letters of Stephen Minot Weld, 1861–1865* (Cambridge: Riverside Press, 1912), 28 (entry for October 18, 1861).
7. US Superintendent of the Census, *Statistics of the United States (including Mortality, Property, &c.,) in 1860; Compiled from the Original Returns of the Eighth Census, Under the Direction of the Secretary of the Interior* (Washington: Government Printing Office, 1866), 214, 304, 327; *Manufactures of the United States in 1860; Compiled from the Original Returns of the Eighth Census, Under the Direction of the Secretary of the Interior* (Washington: Government Printing Office, 1865), 220, 228; Daniel Carroll Toomey, with Steve Hammond, *The Annapolis and Elk Ridge Railroad, 1837–1885* (Annapolis: Ann Arrundell County Historical Society, 2017), 9.
8. United States, Superintendent of the Census, *Population of the United States in 1860; Compiled from the Original Returns of the Eighth Census, Under the Direction of the Secretary of the*

Interior (Washington: Government Printing Office, 1864), iv, 213, 214; *Agriculture of the United States in 1860; Compiled from the Original Returns of the Eighth Census, Under the Direction of the Secretary of the Interior* (Washington: Government Printing Office, 1864), 72–73; *Manufactures of the United States in 1860*, 220, 228.

9. *Annapolis Gazette,* May 31, 1860.
10. *Annapolis Gazette,* May 31, August 9, and September 6, 1860.
11. *Annapolis Gazette,* May 10, 1860. This is Edward Sachse's "Bird's Eye View of the City of Annapolis."
12. *Annapolis Gazette,* October 27, 1859.
13. *Annapolis Gazette,* May 31 and August 9, 1860.
14. Hurst, "Pre-Civil War Annapolis," 240–41.
15. *Annapolis Gazette,* January 19, January 26, and May 31, 1860.
16. For Leonardtown and *Maryland Republican* references, see *Maryland Republican,* October 21, 1871. For the colonel title reference, see Deposition of Alexander B. Hagner in *Henry Roland Walton v. United States*, File 1277, Box 230, Entry 22, Congressional Jurisdiction Case Files, 1884–1943, Records of the United States Court of Claims, RG 123, NARA.
17. Mark S. Warner, *Eating in the Side Room: Food, Archaeology, and Africa American Identity* (Gainesville: University Press of Florida, 2015), 9.
18. Francis Nicholas Darnall Daley (1816–60), Julia Ann Wells Daley (1821–77). For Francis' baptism, June 11, 1820, see "White Marsh/Bowie Register of Baptisms, Marriages, Burials, 1818–1895," Maryland Province Collection, Box 3, Folder 3, GU-CSC. For the children and confirmation, see Baptismal Register B#1 (January 25, 1852, October 2, 1853, August 8, 1856, June n.d., 1858, June 18, 1861, April 16, 1862, January 27, 1863). Also, *Sun*, March 26, 1860. For the Carroll connections, see Pat Melville, "Daley/Darnall Connection," October 2016, in author's file; Ronald Hoffman, ed., *Dear Papa, Dear Charley: The Peregrinations of a Revolutionary Aristocrat, as Told by Charles Carroll of Carrollton and His Father, Charles Carroll of Annapolis, with Sundry Observations on Bastardy, Child-Rearing, Romance, Matrimony, Commerce, Tobacco, Slavery, and the Politics of Revolutionary America* (Chapel Hill: University of North Carolina Press, 2001), 3:1540–41 (Chart F); "The Blurred Racial Lines of Famous Families: The Brothers Darnall," PBS Frontline, accessed November 30, 2016, http://www.pbs.org/wgbh/pages/frontline/shows/secret/famous/darnall.html.
19. Henry Herman Dunker (1831–64), Mary Frances (Fanny) Dunker (1836–1912); both are buried in lot number 13 Locust Grove Cemetery, also known as City Cemetery or the Public Burying Ground, later incorporated into St. Anne's Cemetery, purchased from Nicholas Brewer Jr. and Frank H. Stockett by Henry Dunker, NHG 12:103 (February 10, 1864), AACLR. Also, *Maryland Republican,* January 27, 1855; *Annapolis Gazette,* July 28, 1864 and August 18, 1864, which reveals Henry a member of Odd Fellows, a group proscribed by the Catholic Church. Baptismal Register B#1 (October 14, 1865, December 8, 1865, February 4, 1866). Fanny's funeral was held at St. Mary's; Interment Register D#1 (February 15, 1912).
20. John Baptist Duffy (1826–74). *Chronica Domus* I:125 (January 1, 1860); *Sketch of the Life of Rev. Jno. B. Duffy, C.SS.R* (New Orleans: T. Fitzwilliam and Company, 1881), 34–36, Personnel Files, RABP (this sketch was serialized three years after Duffy's death, in *The Morning Star and Catholic Messenger* (New Orleans), March 25, April 1, April 8, April 15, April 22, 1877); Wuest, *Annales*, IV:2:448. *Sun*, October 25, 1859, referred to Duffy as "the new pastor" of St. Mary's. For mission definition, see Joseph Wissel, C.Ss. R., *The Redemptorist on the American Missions* (West Chester, New York: Catholic Protectory, 1886), I:1. The first edition was published in New York in 1875.
21. John Henry Cornell (1828–94). John Cornell, *Genealogy of the Cornell Family: Being an Account of the Descendants of Thomas Cornell of Portsmouth, R.I.* (New York: T. A. Wright, 1902), 223–24. He arrived in New York aboard the ship *Victoria*, see "New York Passenger Lists, 1820–1891," accessed March 4, 2016, FamilySearch.org. Professed vows July 16, 1852, ordained June 6, 1857, Wuest, *Annales*, IV:2:449. Cornell, Ex-C.Ss.R. File, RABP. His early published works include *A Manual of Roman Chant: Compiled from Authentic Roman Sources, for the Use of Ecclesiastical Seminaries, Religious Communities, and Churches* (Baltimore: Kelly, Hedian, and Piet, 1860); *The Little Vesper-Book: Being a Supplement to the Manual of Roman Chant* (Baltimore: Kelly, Hedian, and Piet, 1860); *The Vesper-Psalter: Or, Psalmody Made Easy; All the Vesper-Psalms, with the Canticle, Magnificat, Set in Modern Notation, to the Roman Psalm-Tones, with Easy Organ-Accompaniments* (Baltimore: Kelly, Hedian, and Piet, 1861); *Cantica Sacra; Or, Hymns for the Children of the Catholic Church, Set to Original Music* (Boston: P. Donahoe, 1865).
22. George Roesch (Rösch, 1822–77). *Chronica Domus* I:125 (January 1, 1860); Wuest, *Annales*, IV:2:449, 458; *Liber Vestitutiones Provinciae,* June 21, 1859, which lists Roesch's investiture. *Metropolitan Catholic Almanac and Laity's Directory, 1859*, 134, lists Roesch at St. Peter's Church in Poughkeepsie, New York.
23. Wuest, *Annales*, IV:2:462–64; Jacob Engel Personnel File, RABP.
24. Berger, Annapolis, to Aunt and Sister [in Bohemia], May 9, 1861.
25. Miller and Wakelyn, *Catholics in the Old South,* 5, 167, 235 (which says that in Louisiana, Maryland, Kentucky, and Missouri, ethnically diverse Catholics divided the religious vote). Curran, *Shaping American Catholicism,* 95: "Catholics, like most other Americans, proved loyal to their respective sections" even though the Church itself did not split over the issue.
26. *Chronica Domus* I:126 (January 15, 1860).
27. Wuest, *Annales*, IV:2:181–82.
28. *Chronica Domus* I:127 (January 16, 1860); Wuest, *Annales*, IV:2:457, 459, and 465.

29. Frederick William Wayrich (1834–1907). *Chronica Domus* I:127 (January 16, 1860), I:251 (March 18, 1864), II:9 (March 29, 1865), I:35 (June 13, 1866); Wuest, *Annales*, IV:2:449. For Kesseler's death, see "Father Kesseler," *Kentucky Irish American* (Louisville), July 28, 1898, 1; "Tributes of Protestant Writers: Heroic Father Kesseler," *Sacred Heart Review* 20, no. 6 (August 6, 1898): 114. *Chronica Domus* I:127 (February 23, 1860), and Wuest, *Annales*, IV:2:454 for Enright.

30. *Chronica Domus* I:127 (January 29, 1860); St. Mary's Confirmation Register (Confirmation Register) B#1 (January 29, 1860).

31. "1859. Nova domus origo a Rev. P. Magistro descripta" (1859: Origins of Our New House Described by Father Rector), a five-page poem written *alte deutsche Schrift* (old German script) in *Chronica Domus* I:116–20, following entries for the year 1859.

32. *Catholic Mirror*, February 4, 1860; Kenrick, Baltimore, to Messrs. Directors of the Society [Society for the Propagation of the Faith—Propaganda Fide], Lyon, France, April 4, 1860, typescript in George Ruland, Provincial Papers, RABP; no record of this request or response was found in Finbar Kenneally, O.F.M., ed., *United States Documents in the Propaganda Fide Archives: A Calendar*, 1st ser., II (1845–1862), (Washington: Academy of Franciscan History, 1966) or in Kenneally, *United States Documents in the Propaganda Fide Archives: Index to Calendar*, I–VII (Washington: Academy of Franciscan History, 1981). Also, Borgmann, *Redemptorists at Annapolis*, 35; Seelos to Antonia Seelos and family members, October 12, December 3 and 18, 1862, mentions machine to peel potatoes and a pencil sharpener.

33. Officer of the Day's Journal (May 17, 1860), USNA; First Council of Baltimore, *Manual of Ceremonies for the Use of the Catholic Churches in the United States of America*, 2nd ed. rev. (Baltimore: John Murphy and Company, 1852), 15; *Chronica Domus* I:129 (May 17, 1860); Wuest, *Annales*, IV:2:180.

34. Indenture between Col. Henry Ridgely and Charles Carroll, April 20, 1706, WT 2:372, MSA C97–8; James Stoddert, "A Ground Plot of the City of Annapolis" (1718), St. Mary's Church Collection, MSA SC430–1–1, B5/01/01 (item transferred to MSA Map Collection and accessioned as MSA SC1427–1–3), a survey commissioned by Charles Carroll the Settler; Indenture between Samuel Howard and Henry Ridgely, May 21, 1687; Liber B, MSA SC922, http://speccol.mdarchives.state.md.us/pages/speccol/collection.aspx?speccol=922; Charles Carroll the Settler's Last Will and Testament, December 1, 1718, recorded in Liber CG No. 3, folio 293, February 12, 1721, Prerogative Court (Wills, Original Record), 1635–1766, MSA S1276–9.

35. Borgmann, *Redemptorists at Annapolis*, 9. *Maryland Republican*, Commercial Number, July 18, 1896. James T. Wollon, Havre de Grace, Maryland, to Frank S. Welsh, Historic Paint Color Consultant, Bryn Mawr, Pennsylvania, July 19, 1989; Welsh to Wollon, September 29, 1989, attaching "Microscopic Analysis to Determine and Evaluate the Nature and Colors of the Original Surface Coatings: Charles Carroll House," September 29, 1989, 14–15 (Salvage 22–23 and Salvage 26). Copy on file at the Charles Carroll House, 107 Duke of Gloucester Street, Annapolis.

36. Kryder-Reid, "Construction of Sanctity," 234. Also, Kryder-Reid, "Landscape as Myth: The Contextual Archaeology of an Annapolis Landscape" (PhD diss., Department of Anthropology, Brown University, 1991); Matthew M. Paulus and Kryder-Reid, "Report on Archaeological Investigations Conducted at the St. Mary's Site (18AP45), 107 Duke of Gloucester Street, Annapolis, Maryland, 1987–1990," 1: Site History, Results and Recommendations; 2: Artifact Catalogue and Codes, Archaeology in Annapolis, University of Maryland at College Park, 2002; copy on file, SMPA; Kryder-Reid, "The Archaeology of Vision in Eighteenth-Century Chesapeake Gardens," *Journal of Garden History* (London) 14, no. 1 (Spring 1994): 42–54.

37. Kryder-Reid, "Construction of Sanctity," 235, 239, 240.

38. Borgmann, *Redemptorists at Annapolis*, 24–25. For an analysis of the lives of novices and lay brothers, see Elizabeth B. Kryder-Reid, "'With Manly Courage': Reading the Construction of Gender in a Nineteenth-Century Religious Community," in *Those of Little Note: Gender, Race, and Class in Historical Archaeology*, ed. Elizabeth M. Scott (Tucson: University of Arizona Press, 1994), 97–114.

39. Borgmann, *Redemptorists at Annapolis*, 25. Seelos to family, October 12, December 3 and 18, 1862, Letter 119, Hoegerl, *Sincerely, Seelos*, 312.

40. McIntire, 1:557, 658; Jonathan Pinkney Hammond, Annapolis, to Bishop William Rollinson Whittingham, Baltimore, November 5, 1866, Archives of the Episcopal Diocese of Maryland, Episcopal Diocesan Center, Baltimore. The archives catalog dates the letter 1860 but the context and further documentation, as well as close inspection of the hand-written year itself, establish 1866 as the more likely date.

41. Jonathan Pinkney Hammond, *The Army Chaplain's Manual, Designed as a Help to Chaplains in the Discharge of Their Various Duties, Both Temporal and Spiritual* (Philadelphia: J. B. Lippincott, 1863). The Preface, vii–viii, is dated "St. John's College U.S. Army Hospital, Annapolis, Md., March 10, 1863." Also, Paynter, *St. Anne's*, 57–58; William Alexander Hammond, M.D., *A Treatise on Hygiene, with Special Reference to the Military Service* (Philadelphia: J. B. Lippincott, 1863), v. Hammond's newspaper editorship is noted in *Haversack*, July 20, 1864, the weekly newspaper of General Hospital Division No. 2.

42. Hammond, Washington, to Lincoln, Washington, July 16, 1862, Series 1, General Correspondence, 1833–1916, Abraham Lincoln Papers, Manuscript Division, LoC, Washington, DC (LoC), accessed July 17, 2016, http://memory.loc.gov/ammem/alhtml/malhome.html.

43. Elizabeth Blanchard Randall, Family History Journal, February 13, 1869, Randall-Brune-Philpot Family Papers 1760–1983, Subseries I: Elizabeth Blanchard Randall Books and Papers, 1830–1882, MS 2824, Maryland Center for History and Culture (transcripts provided to the author

by Catherine Randall). Loose sheets, drafts of the "specifications," inserted between August 29 and September 26, and after November 21, 1868, and diary entries for January 30, 1869, and Easter Monday [March 29] 1869. Alexander Randall Diaries, vol. 10, MS 652, Maryland Center for History and Culture. Another loose sheet inserted after February 10, 1876, appears to be the draft of a letter to the editor of a newspaper criticizing William Hammond. Also, Paynter, *St. Anne's Annapolis,* 63; Miles Smith, "The Thousand Ridiculous and Romantic Representations: Severn Teackle Wallis' Anglo-Catholicism in Nineteenth-Century Spain," *Maryland Historical Magazine* 110, no. 3 (Fall 2015): 403.

44. *Population of the United States in 1860,* iv, 213, 214; Agriculture of the United States in 1860, 72–73; *Manufactures of the United States in 1860,* 220, 228. William L. Calderhead, "Anne Arundel Blacks: Three Centuries of Change" in *Anne Arundel County, Maryland: A Bicentennial History, 1649–1977,* ed. James C. Bradford (Annapolis: Anne Arundel County and Annapolis Bicentennial Committee, 1977), 10–25, provides an economic and social analysis of African American life in Anne Arundel County during the antebellum period.

45. *Statistics of the United States (including Mortality, Property, &c.,) in 1860,* 214 (table 2, Population by Color and Condition, and table 3, Population of Cities, Towns, &c.).

46. Census Office, US Department of the Interior, *Instructions to U.S. Marshals; Instructions to Assistants,* (Washington: George W. Bowman, Public Printer, 1860), 7 and 11, accessed June 17, 2014, http://www.census.gov/history/pdf/1860instructions.pdf. Bryan was former Anne Arundel County sheriff (1848–51, elected to second three-year term in 1861), also sold ready-made apparel on Main Street and had a carpentry and undertaking partnership with John W. Davis on State Circle. In the 1860 census, Bryan enumerated his own household first, reporting himself as a merchant with wife and seven children, with one White and four Black servants in his home, all of whom were born in Maryland. His real estate was valued $2,500 and personal estate $800. Bryan also was an enslaver. The 1860 Federal Slave Schedule for Annapolis, which Bryan also recorded and listed himself first, reports that he owned three male and two female slaves, ranging in age from 1 to 62 years of age. For information on Bryan as sheriff, see Maryland State Archives, "Anne Arundel County Sheriffs, 1658–present," accessed June 4, 2012, http://www.msa.md.gov/msa/speccol/sc2600/sc2685/county/html/aasheriffs2.html.

47. 1860 Federal Census, Annapolis; *Chronica Domus* I:125 (January 1, 1860).

48. 1860 Federal Census, Annapolis; Berger to Aunt and Sister, May 9, 1861.

49. Annapolis Mayor and Aldermen, Assessment of Property in the City of Annapolis, June 11, 1860, MSA M72–3.

50. "Inventory of personal property of [Richard] Swann and [James H.] Iglehart in the City Hotel, taken 24th March 1845, and sold at public auction on 11th June 1845 by James Iglehart Trustee under a decree of the Chancellor [Chancery Court of Maryland] to John Walton," copy in Shirley Baltz Collection, MSA SC2692. The sale was in 1848, see Thomas H. Alexander, trustee, to John Walton, JHN 3:374 (July 22, 1848), AACLR. Also, Maryland Historical Trust, State Historic Sites Inventory Form, Survey No. AA–437 (George Mann's Tavern, City Tavern, City Hotel), March 28, 1996, accessed February 11, 2016, http://msa.maryland.gov/megafile/msa/stagsere/se1/se5/001000/001500/001563/pdf/msa_se5_1563.pdf.

51. William Howard Russell, *My Diary North and South* (Boston: Burnham, 1863), 421–22. Russell (1820–1907) was a correspondent for *The Times* (London) and visited City Hotel, July 15, 1861. Daniel Read Larned (1828–1911), City Hotel, Annapolis to Dear Sister, December 27, 1861; Larned, Coast Division Headquarters, Annapolis, to Dear Sister, December 29, 1861; Box 2, Daniel Read Larned Papers, MSS 29470, Manuscript Division, LoC; Lt. William Henry Sterling, Annapolis, to Matilda Sterling, Philadelphia, February 26, 1863, Sterling Family Papers, Box 1, Folder 1: Correspondence, Special Collections and University Archives, University of Maryland, accessed September 2, 2012, http://hdl.handle.net/1903.1/9017.

52. Dividend Book, 1854–72, Farmers Bank of Maryland, various semiannual entries, MSA SC55–1–4.

53. 1860 Federal Census, Annapolis. Hurst, "Pre-Civil War Annapolis," 243, depended solely on the 1860 Federal Census and thus gives a different perspective on the relative wealth of Annapolis residents. The Walton vault remained on the Duke of Gloucester Street property until the remains were reinterred in St. Mary's West Street cemetery in 1901. See Borgmann, *Redemptorists at Annapolis,* 131; Worden, *Saint Mary's,* 69. Annals, Annapolis, 1900–1909, 317 (October 28, 1904), says the vault was "just in the rear of the school" and was exchanged by the family for the construction of a wall around the new family plot in the West Street cemetery.

54. George C. Rable, *God's Almost Chosen People: A Religious History of the American Civil War* (Chapel Hill: University of North Carolina Press, 2010), 13, 21; Miller, "Introduction," in *Catholics in the Old South,* 13–14, 70; Raymond H. Schmandt, "An Overview of Institutional Establishments in the Antebellum Southern Church," in *Catholics in the Old South,* 70.

55. Rable, God's *Almost Chosen People,* 27–29; Miller, "Introduction," 17; Duncan, "Catholics and the Church in the Antebellum Upper South," in *Catholics in the Old South,* 87.

56. Curran, *Shaping American Catholicism,* 92–83; Stern, *Southern Crucifix,* 159, 167. For partial text of the pope's letter, see Zanca, American Catholics and Slavery, Document 17 (December 3, 1839), 27–29; Bishop England's article in the *Catholic Miscellany,* Document 46 (March 14, 1840), 128–29. Pope Gregory XIV reigned 1831–46.

57. Francis Patrick Kenrick, *Theologiae Moralis* (Philadelphia: Eugenium Cummiskey, 1841), I: 255–58, as quoted in McConville, *Political Nativism,* 84–84, fn 20; Joseph Delfmann Brokhage, *Francis Patrick Kenrick's Opinion on Slavery* (Washington: Catholic University of America Press, 1955),

55, 57–58, 64–65, 100–1, 110.

58. Kenrick, "The Catholic Church and the Question of Slavery," *The Metropolitan, or Catholic Monthly* (Baltimore), 3, June 1855, 265–73; McConville, *Political Nativism,* 85–86, quoting from *The Metropolitan,* June 1855, 273; Duncan, "Catholics and the Church in the Antebellum Upper South," in *Catholics in the Old South,* 88. Spalding, *Premier See,* 175, agrees with Duncan's premise, saying that, while opposed to disunion, Maryland Catholics viewed abolitionists as subversives. Also, Rable, *God's Almost Chosen People,* 28.
59. Brokhage, *Kenrick's Opinion on Slavery,* 182–85, 186–87.
60. Randall M. Miller, "The Failed Mission: The Catholic Church and Black Catholics in the Old South," in *Catholics in the Old South,* 151, 152.
61. This count includes New Jersey, which did not abolish slavery until 1865.
62. Commission on the Bicentennial of the United States Constitution, *The Constitution of the United States,* 18th ed. (Washington: The Commission, 1992), 1, 14.
63. Curran, *Shaping American Catholicism,* 43, 47–49, 95, 97, 100; 1850 Federal Slave Schedule, Ward 4, Washington City, July 18, 1850 for Mathias Alig (1805–82); Duncan, "Catholics and the Church in the Antebellum Upper South," in *Catholics in the Old South,* 89–90; Mannard, "We Are Determined to Be White Ladies," 145, 150; Kurtz, *Excommunicated from the Union,* 106, citing Basil Pacciarini, S.J., St. Inigoes, to Charles C. Lancaster, [Baltimore], October 14, 1864, Folder 3, Box 15, Jesuit Maryland Province Archives, GTM.GAMMS119, GU-CSC; Robert Emmett Curran, *Papist Devils: Catholics in British America, 1574–1783* (Washington: Catholic University of America Press, 2014), 284; Rachel L. Swarns, "Georgetown Confronts Its Role in Nation's Slave Trade," *New York Times,* April 17, 2016, 1 and 16.
64. *Statistics of the United States (including Mortality, Property, &c.,) in 1860,* 214 (table 2, Population by Color and Condition, and table 3, Population of Cities, Towns, &c.). There were 826 free and 475 enslaved African Americans; 1860 Federal Slave Schedules for Annapolis and 2nd District, Anne Arundel County.
65. 1860 Federal Slave Schedules for Annapolis and 2nd District, Anne Arundel County. Daniel Read Larned, City Hotel, Annapolis, to My Dear Sister, December 24, 1861, Larned Papers. Magruder (1829–1916) was mayor of Annapolis (1860–62, 1863–64), and St. Anne's Church vestry member. Stockett's farm was in the area of modern Tyler Avenue and Forest Drive, within Annapolis today.
66. 1860 Federal Slave Schedules for Annapolis and 2nd District, Anne Arundel County.
67. Assessment of Negro Slaves in the City of Annapolis, June 11, 1860, MSA M72–4.
68. *Population of the United States in 1860,* 211, 213; 1860 Federal Slave Schedule for 1st District, Anne Arundel County (Steuart); Find A Grave Memorial IDs 6199371 and 61993723.
69. Richard Sprigg Steuart (1797–1876), Maria Louisa de Bernabeu Steuart (1800–83). Kenrick to John H. Cornell [Annapolis], August 20, 1861, in John De Dycker, Provincial Papers, RABP (concerning *viaticum*). Also, Richard Sprigg Steuart, "Another Paper by Dr. Richard S. Steuart, Written 1868," in Gladys P. K. Nelker, "The Clan Steuart–Stewart–Stuart, 800 to 1970 A.D.," (unpublished manuscript, 1970), 70, 131, 132, used with permission of Roberta Pittman, Dodon, September 2, 2014; McIntire 1:669.
70. Steuart, "Another Paper," in Nelker, 123, 131–32; Maryland Historical Trust "Donaldson-Steuart House, 10 Francis Street," Inventory No. AA–948, Section 8, page 4, accessed May 11, 2015, http://msa.maryland.gov/megafile/msa/stagsere/se1/se5/001000/001600/001627/pdf/msa_se5_1627.pdf; Archdiocese of Baltimore, "Most Rev. John Carroll," accessed May 14, 2017, https://www.archbalt.org/most-rev-john-carroll/.
71. Martin Fenwick (1786–1865), Ann Louisa Ghequiere (ca. 1791–1864). For the Fenwick baptisms, see October 10, 1831, "White Marsh/Bowie Register of Baptisms, Marriages, and Deaths, 1818–1895," Box 3, Folder 3, Maryland Province Collection, GU-CSC. Also, *Chronica Domus* I:206 (November 23, 1862); John F. Byrne, C.Ss.R., "Redemptorists in America, Baltimore (Continued) and in Rochester, N.Y.," *Records of the American Catholic Historical Society of Philadelphia* 41, no. 4 (December 1930): 368; Francis X. Welch, *A Centenary for Our Lady of Sorrows, Owensville, Maryland, 1866–1966* (n.p., ca. 1966), 16–17; Borgmann, *Redemptorists at Annapolis,* 64; Donna M. Ware, *Anne Arundel's Legacy: The Historical Properties of Anne Arundel County* (Annapolis: Anne Arundel County, 1990), 33. Benedict Joseph Fenwick (1782–1846), second bishop of Boston (1825–46), Edward Dominic Fenwick (1768–1832), first bishop of Cincinnati (1822–32). For the baptism, see Lady of Sorrows (Owensville) Register of Baptisms, 1865–1908, 2 (June 4, 1865), Microfilm SCM2625, MSA SC1172.
72. Isabel Wilkerson, *The Warmth of Other Suns: The Epic Story of America's Great Migration* (New York: Random House, Books, 2010), 290; Fields, *Slavery and Freedom,* 24, 28, 35, 7; Constance M. McGovern, "Constructing Lives: Free People of Color in Antebellum Cumberland, Maryland," *Maryland Historical Magazine* 110, no. 3 (Fall 2015): 343. Jeffrey R. Brackett, *The Negro in Maryland: A Study of the Institution of Slavery* (Baltimore: Johns Hopkins University, 1889) refers to Maryland colonial and state laws restricting movements and activities of slaves and free Blacks. Also, Thomas W. Henry, *Autobiography of Rev. Thomas W. Henry, of the A. M. E. Church* (Baltimore: The Author, 1872), 27, for reference to 1832 Maryland law prohibiting free Blacks or "mulattos" from holding a "religious or tumultuous gathering" without the presence of an ordained White man.
73. See Annapolis records for 1821 and 1822 in "White Marsh/Bowie Register of Baptisms, Marriages, and Deaths, 1818–1895," Box 3, Folder 3, Maryland Province Collection, GU-CSC; Baker, *Politics of Continuity,* 214, tables D–9 and D–10.
74. For unsubstantiated claim for St. Frances Academy and

Oblate Sisters of Providence, see "Facts about Black Catholic History in the Archdiocese of Baltimore," http://www.archbalt.org/wp-content/uploads/2017/05/Facts-about-Black-Catholic-History-in-the-Archdiocese-of-Baltimor1.pdf; for Institute of Notre Dame and School Sisters of Notre Dame, see "The IND Story: Witness to History," https://www.indofmd.org/page/list-detail?pk=100214&fromId=230880; for St. Ignatius Church in Port Tobacco, Charles County, see Mark Sullivan, "B.C. Geologists Chart Mystery Tunnel at Maryland Church," *Boston College Chronicle* 7, no. 3 (April 29, 1999): 8, https://newspapers.bc.edu/?a=d&d=bcchronicle19990429-01.2.23&e=-------en-20--1--txt-txIN-------; and for St. Mary's Church in Rockville, Montgomery County, see Maryland Public Television, "Pathways to Freedom: Maryland and the Underground Railroad" (2018) http://pathways.thinkport.org/library/sites4.cfm, all accessed January 7, 2018.

75. William Still, *The Underground Railroad: A Record of Facts, Authentic Narratives, Letters, &c.* (Philadelphia: Porter and Coates, 1872), 71, 392, 461, 465, 467, 524, 661, 759 (for Catholics), 206, 411, 444 (for Anne Arundel County), and 314 (for Annapolis); Wilbur H. Siebert, *The Underground Railroad From Slavery to Freedom* (New York: Macmillan, 1898), 113 ("'Underground': Routes to Canada Showing the Routes of Travel of Fugitive Slaves"); William J. Switala, *Underground Railroad in Delaware, Maryland, and West Virginia* (Mechanicsburg, Pennsylvania, Stackpole Books, 2004), various pages for mentions of church-sponsored escape efforts. But Switala's claim of an underground railroad route (page 81) "suddenly beginning in Annapolis" misinterprets the actual route shown in Siebert's 1898 map; and his claim of a Catholic conductor in Wilmington, Delaware (page 56), citing Still, is incorrect. Still (page 636) used the term "broadly catholic" (lower case c) to describe the character of a Wilmington Quaker abolitionist.

76. "Charles Carroll of Carroll Family" in 1820 Federal Census, Fifth Election District [now Howard County], Anne Arundel County, lists 238 persons engaged in agriculture and 19 in manufacturing, all were slaves except 43 free colored and several White overseers. No slaves were found in census enumerations for men named James Dunn, the church builder.

77. Roesch made it to his new assignment in Philadelphia and was enumerated a second time there in the 1860 Federal Census, in 18-member Redemptorist community at St. Peter's, June 30, 1860. Also, *Chronica Domus* I:129 (June 21, 1860); Wuest, *Annales*, IV:2:458. St. Aloysius Gonzaga (1568–91).

78. McWilliams, *Annapolis*, 144, for reference to the 1830s ordinance. The earliest mention of the stone wall appears in a letter from Charles Carroll of Annapolis, Doughoregan Manor, to Charles Carroll of Carrollton, Annapolis, August 12, 1770; and the latest in Charles Carroll of Carrollton, Philadelphia, to Charles Carroll of Annapolis, Doughoregan Manor, March 15, 1776, transcribed in Ronald Hoffman, *Dear Papa, Dear Charley*, 2:521, 2:873–74. The length of the wall is from field investigations by the author in the mid-1980s.

79. *Chronica Domus* I:130 (June 27, 1860).

80. *Chronica Domus* I:130 (July 3, 1860); and Wisdom 4:1. Scriptural translations in this book are based on the *Douay-Rheims Translation Challoner Revision, 1749–1752,* accessed various dates, https://www.ccel.org/c/challoner/douayrheims/dr.html.

81. *Chronica Domus* I:129–31 (June 27, July 3, 1860); Wuest, *Annales*, IV:2:181 and 457; Borgmann, *Redemptorists at Annapolis*, 36; Brother Barnabas Hipkins, C.Ss.R., "Annapolis Aquatic Tragedies," *The Province Story: A Redemptorist Historical Review—Baltimore Province* 1, no. 1 (November 1, 1974): 9. Schad originally was buried in St. Alphonsus Cemetery, which closed in 1917; his remains were reinterred at Most Holy Redeemer Cemetery.

82. Mary Theresa Maxis Duchemin (1810–92), daughter of a Haitian mother and British father. Maria Alma Ryan, I.H.M., *Sisters, Servants of the Immaculate Heart of Mary, 1845–1967* (Lancaster, Pennsylvania: Dolphin Press, 1967), 80; Marita-Constance Suphan, I.H.M., "Dangerous Memory: Mother M. Theresa Maxis Duchemin and the Michigan Congregation of Sisters, IHM," in Sisters, Servants of the Immaculate Heart of Mary, Monroe, Michigan, comp., *Building Sisterhood: A Feminist History of the Sisters, Servants of the Immaculate Heart of Mary* (Syracuse: Syracuse University Press, 1997), 37–38, 40.

83. Neumann, Philadelphia, to Sister Magdalen [Martin, I.H.M.], Reading, January 4, 1860, St. John Neumann Collection, Letters 1860, RABP. Neumann revealed in this letter, one of his last, that "I am not well these last few days." Ryan, *Sisters, Servants* (1967) 76–77, 86; Maria Alma Ryan, *Sisters, Servants of the Immaculate Heart of Mary, With Life and Letters of Our Founder Reverend Louis Florent Gillet* (Philadelphia: Dolphin Press, 1934), 87; Member of the Scranton Community, Sisters, Servants of the Immaculate Heart of Mary, *The Sisters of the I.H.M.: The Story of the Foundation of the Congregation of the Sisters Servants of the Immaculate Heart of Mary and Their Work in the Scranton Diocese* (New York: P.J. Kenedy and Sons, 1921), 65. The assumption that it was Van de Braak is based on an entry in Chronicles of the House of Studies, Cumberland, 65 (n.d. 1859): "A few days after [vacation days, which occurred in August] F. Van de Braak left for Baltimore to assist as *socius* in the visitation, and after his return set out again for Pittsburgh to make his retreat, after which he visited Philadelphia and Annapolis, and returned to Cumberland about the 15th October." The only other Redemptorist noted absent from Cumberland at this time was Frederick William Wayrich, who went to New York "for the improvement of his health" during August.

84. 1850 Federal Census for Monroe enumerates Issabella [*sic*] Sheeran, age 7, born in Pennsylvania, living in a "nunnery" with 25 other students (ages 4 to 18). James B. Sheeran, C.Ss. R. (1819–81) had been a lay teacher in the Redemptorist-administered school at Monroe and, after the his wife's death in 1849, placed his daughter, Isabella, in the care of

the I.H.M. sisters in Monroe and joined the Redemptorists. Fifteen-year-old Isabella was invested as an I.H.M. postulate, taking the name Mary Ignatia, July 2, 1858. When Neumann invited the I.H.M. sisters to establish a foundation in Pennsylvania, an angry Detroit Bishop Levere ordered the I.H.M. sisters, including Theresa Maxis, Mary Ignatia Sheeran, and others to leave Monroe in April 1859 for Pennsylvania. Mary Ignatia professed her vows in St. Joseph's, Susquehanna County, Pennsylvania, on July 24, 1859. Smulder's sister also was an I.H.M. sister, Mary Aegidius Smulders. In January 1861, Ignatia Sheeran, then living in Reading, Pennsylvania, became "so low, that her death was looked for at any moment." Plans were made for her funeral but she rallied and lived until February 26, 1861; buried in Reading. See Ryan, *Sisters, Servants* (1934), 54, 56–57, 80, 89–90; Ryan, *Sisters, Servants* (1967), 47, 49, 74, 77; Sisters, Servants of the Immaculate Heart of Mary, *Building Sisterhood*, 53. Scranton Community, Sisters of the I.H.M. (1921), 69, says Ignatia died on February 20, 1861.

85. Jacobs, Annapolis, to Sister Colette [Myers], Monroe, May 4, 1859; Smulders, Philadelphia, May 15, 1859, to Sister Xavier, and May 25, 1859, to Sister Aegidius Smulders; Giesen, n.p., December 1859, to Mother Mary Joseph Shaughnessey, copies on file in Neumann Collection, Letters 1859, RABP. Also, *St. Mary College and Academy, Monroe, Michigan* (Monroe: The Sisters, 1932), *36; Building Sisterhood, 47;* Ryan, *Sisters, Servants of the Immaculate Heart of Mary*, 60–79.
86. *Chronica Domus* I:132 (July 17, 1860) and *Province Annals*, 1832–71, 433–35 (1860, Annapolis), do not mention Brandstätter among the novices dismissed in 1860.
87. *Chronica Domus* I:132 (July 22, 1860) and I:134 (November n.d. ["this month"], 1860); Wuest, *Annales*, IV:2:456, 458, 459.
88. *Chronica Domus* I:133 (September n.d. ["this month"], 1860); Visitation Recess Recommendations for Annapolis and Cumberland, September 28, 1860, RABP.
89. Seelos, Cumberland, to Kenrick, Baltimore, June 20, 1859, Box 28, Folder F18, Kenrick Papers, AAB.
90. *Chronica Domus* I:133 (September 28, 1860), I:157 (June n.d. ["this month"], 1861); Wuest, *Annales*, IV:2:450; Borgmann, *Redemptorists at Annapolis*, 19; Andrew H. Skeabeck, C.Ss.R., "Most Rev. William H. Gross, C.SS.R.: Missionary Bishop of the South," *Records of the American Catholic Historical Society of Philadelphia* 65, no. 1 (March 1954), 20.
91. *Chronica Domus* I:112 (October 15, 1859), I:133–34 (October 15–18, 1860); Wuest, *Annales*, IV:2:456–57. Berger professed his vows at Annapolis, October 15, 1859. For Müller's tour, see *Chronica Domus* I:134 (November n.d. ["this month"], 1860).
92. *Chronica Domus* I:135 (December 8, 1860), I:154 (March 4, 1861). Information on Koering's pre- and post-Annapolis service from Hermann Alerding, *History of the Catholic Church in the Diocese of Vincennes* (Indianapolis: Carlon and Hollenbeck, 1883), 383, 384, 391; *Souvenir Album of American Cities: Catholic Churches of Cincinnati and Hamilton County Edition,* (Cincinnati: United States Church Publishing Company, 1896), on unnumbered page describing the of Good Shepherd Convent. Koering died 1896, Find A Grave Memorial ID 5347000. *Sketch of the Life of Rev. Jno. B. Duffy*, 40–41; *Chronica Domus* I:135 (December 4, 1860) for Duffy's departure, and Baptismal Register B#1 (December 23, 1860—McGrane's first baptism). Also, Hoegerl, *With All Gentleness*, 180 and 183, for Duffy and McGrane as novices under Seelos.
93. The base of the original altar apparently survives beneath the newer altar. Inside the wooden superstructure of the 1860–61 altar is a stucco-coated masonry structure that is possibly the base for the 1859 altar. Resting on top of this base is a slab of what appears to be sandstone, possibly the top of the 1859 altar but not enough of the upper surface can be seen to determine if there is a cavity for an altar stone. Robert L. Worden, "Investigation of Probable Remnants of the Original Altar in St. Mary's Church, February 18–19, 2013," copy on file in SMPA.
94. Wuest, *Annales*, IV:2:465. *Chronica Domus* I:135 (December 8,1860). This entry, as with others, was added later since it referred to the completion of the altar "the next year." Berger, to Aunt and Sister, May 9, 1861.
95. *Annapolis Gazette*, February 11, 1869.
96. "Compromise of 1850," accessed December 7, 2016, https://guides.loc.gov/compromise-1850; *Annapolis Gazette*, August 16, 1860; Baker, Politics of Continuity, 40, for statement about Know-Nothing support—"almost without exception"—of the Constitutional Union Party; John V. Mering, "The Slave-State Constitutional Unionists and the Politics of Consensus," *Journal of Southern History* 43, no. 3 (August 1977): 409.
97. *Annapolis Gazette*, May 31, 1860, June 28, 1860, July 5, 1860, August 16, 1860, September 6, 1860. Douglas' second wife (whom he married in a Catholic ceremony in 1856) was Rose Adèle Cutts, a Catholic who attended Georgetown Visitation Academy. With his permission, she raised and educated Douglas' two sons by his first wife (Martha Martin) as Catholics, a fact that might have swayed some Catholic voters. See "Adele Douglas," https://www.womenhistoryblog.com/2010/07/adele-douglas.html and "Adele Cutts Douglas," http://hd.housedivided.dickinson.edu/node/16443, both accessed May 17, 2016.
98. Debra Reddin van Tuyll, "Lincoln and the Southern Press: The Election of 1860," in *A Press Divided: Newspaper Coverage of the Civil War*, ed. David B. Sachsman (New Brunswick, New Jersey: Transaction Publishers, 2014), 28; Charles W. Mitchell, "Maryland's Presidential Election of 1860," Maryland Historical Magazine 109, no. 3 (Fall 2014): 320, 323; Mitchell and Baker, *Civil War in Maryland Reconsidered*, 86–87; *Annapolis Gazette*, November 8, 1860; McWilliams, Annapolis, 166.
99. *Annapolis Gazette*, November 29, 1861, for Hicks' November 27, 1861, response to a petition from former governor Thomas G. Pratt, Maryland treasurer Sprigg Harwood, former states attorney James Shaw Franklin, Anne Arundel

County Clerk Nicholas Harwood Green, former state librarian Llewellyn Boyle, and former clerk of the Senate Jonathan Pinkney. Also, Mitchell and Baker, *Civil War in Maryland Reconsidered,* 90.

100. *Annapolis Gazette*, December 20, 1860 and December 27, 1860.

Chapter 3: 1861 — Neither Taking the Part of Septentrionalibus or Meridianis

1. Kurtz, *Excommunicated from the Union*, 32.
2. *Annapolis Gazette*, December 20, 1860.
3. *Annapolis Gazette*, January 10, 1861.
4. *Sun*, February 6, 1861; *Annapolis Gazette*, February 7, 1861; Riley, *Ancient City*, 284 and 297; McWilliams, *Annapolis*, 166.
5. Gerdemann's mother, Anna Maria Gerdemann, a widow, age 70, is listed in the 1870 Federal Census, District 13, Allegany County, Maryland, as born in Prussia. It has not been proven, but is likely that his father, John Bernard Anthony Gerdemann, born ca. 1800, also was Prussian. The 1850 census lists them both as born in Germany and they were not found in the 1860 census.
6. *Chronica Domus* I:151–52.
7. *Chronica Domus* I:151–52 (ostensibly January 1, 1861, but Adam Parr did not arrive until January 10,1861, see *Chronica Domus* I:153).
8. The analysis of age and birthplace is drawn primarily from Wuest, *Annales*, IV:2:458; *Catalogus Novitiorum ad Oblationem Admissorum* I and II; *Liber Vestitutiones Provinciae; Liber Professionis,* RABP. Müller recorded in *Chronica Domus* I:152 (January 1, 1861) as Philipp and I:154 (March 4, 1861) as John.
9. John B. Duffy Personnel File, RABP, mentioning McGrane; *Chronica Domus* I:151 (January 1, 1861) and I:154 (March 4, 1861); Baptismal Register B#1 records McGrane officiating on December 23 and 26, 1860, and March 3, 1861, the day before he left Annapolis. Aiden Henry Germain, *Catholic Military and Naval Chaplains, 1776–1917* (Washington: The Author, 1929), 56; Christine McCullough-Friend, "Daughters of Charity Nursed Wounded Civil War Soldiers at West Philadelphia Hospital," Philadelphia Archdiocesan Historical Research Center, accessed March 24, 2011, http://www.pahrc.net/index.php/sisters-of-charity-nursed-wounded-civil-war-soldiers-at-west-philadelphia-hospital/. Also, Rev. Thomas J. Peterman, *Catholic Priests of the Diocese of Wilmington: A Jubilee Year 2000 Commemoration* (Devon, Pennsylvania: William T. Cooke Publishing, 2000), 17; email from Carl Hoegerl, C.Ss.R., to author, March 20, 2013.
10. *Chronica Domus* I:151 (January 1, 1861) records names of 56 members by category; Berger to Aunt and Sister, May 9, 1861, RABP, notes 70 members and says that community "is largest in our Congregation." *Chronica Domus* I:181 (January 1, 1862) records the names of 83 members.
11. Allen C. Guelzo, *Abraham Lincoln: Redeemer President* (Grand Rapids, Michigan: William B. Erdmans, 1999), 144–45. Also, LoC, Digital Reference Section, "Missouri Compromise," "Compromise of 1850," "Kansas-Nebraska Act," and Dred Scott v. Sandford," http://www.loc.gov/rr/program/bib/ourdocs/nationalexpanhome.html, all accessed June 11, 2010; Mitchell and Baker, *Maryland in the Civil War Reconsidered,* 62ff.
12. Albert Marrin, *A Volcano Beneath the Snow: John Brown's War Against Slavery* (New York: Knopf, 2014), 83, 108; "Declarations of Secession" and "Constitution of the Confederate States," accessed February 17, 2022, https://avalon.law.yale.edu/subject_menus/csapage.asp; Clint Smith, *How the Word is Passed: A Reckoning with the History of Slavery Across America* (New York: Little, Brown, 2021), 151–54.
13. Baker, *Politics of Continuity*, 48–50.
14. *Annapolis Gazette*, February 28, 1861.
15. *Annapolis Gazette,* April 4, 1861.
16. Daniel Carroll Toomey, *The War Came by Train: The Baltimore and Ohio Railroad During the Civil War* (Baltimore: Baltimore and Ohio Railroad Museum, 2013), 23; Mitchell and Baker, *Civil War in Maryland Reconsidered,* 111–12, 133 n16; "Straddling Secession: Thomas Holliday Hicks and the Beginning of the Civil War in Maryland," accessed September 28, 2015, http://msa.maryland.gov/msa/educ/exhibits/hicks/html/case4.html; Kathleen Waters Sander, *John W. Garrett and the Baltimore and Ohio Railroad* (Baltimore: Johns Hopkins University Press, 2017), 126.
17. James Ryder Randall (1839–1908), "Maryland, My Maryland" (Maryland state song enacted by Chapter 451, Acts of 1939; Maryland Code General Provisions Article, sec. 7–318), accessed July 31, 2016, http://msa.maryland.gov/msa/mdmanual/01glance/html/symbols/lyricsco.html; James Ryder Randall, *Maryland, My Maryland, and Other Poems* (Baltimore and New York: John Murphy Company, 1908), 17–20; Samuel May, *A Genealogy of the Descendants of John May Who Came from England to Roxbury in America, 1640* (Boston: Franklin Press, Rand, Avery and Company, 1878), accessed July 14, 2017, http://www.orrinstevens.com/MaryFrances/family_history/A_Genealogy_of_the_Descendants_of_John_May.pdf. For the portrait, see *Sun*, January 24, 1909; for Gibbons' stay at St. Mary's for the event, see Annals, Annapolis, 1900–1909, 451–53 (January 23–24, 1909). The 31"x25" oil-on-canvas portrait is part of the Maryland Commission on Artistic Property's Maryland State Art Collection, MSA SC1545–1072. It originally was displayed near the speaker's rostrum in the House of Delegates chamber; it now hangs in a non-public State House location, per email of Christopher J. Kintzel, Associate Curator and Collections Manager, Maryland Commission on Artistic Property, to author, December 13, 2017. Katherine Kent Walton (1865–1928) is buried in St. Mary's Cemetery.
18. McWilliams, *Annapolis*, 167.
19. Ellen Marks Bayly and Mark Norton Schatz, eds., *Between*

North and South: A Maryland Journalist Views the Civil War: The Narrative of William Wilkins Glenn, 1861–1869 (Rutherford, New Jersey: Fairleigh Dickinson University Press, 1976), 10–11, 31. Glenn was owner of the pro-Southern *Daily Exchange* and, because of his anti-administration editorials, was arrested, September 14, 1861, and incarcerated at Fort McHenry until December 2. Baker, *Politics of Continuity*, 55–56.

20. Harry Wright Newman, "Anne Arundel During the War of Secession," in *Anne Arundel County, Maryland: A Bicentennial History, 1649–1977*, 269; *Maryland Republican*, March 30, 1861 (repeated weekly in extant issues in 1861); *Annapolis Gazette*, February 7, 1861; David W. Bulla, "Newspaper Coverage of the Rise of Lincoln in 1860: Cooper Union, the Republican Convention, and the Election," in *A Press Divided*, 8; Bulla, "The Suppression of the Mid-Atlantic Copperhead Press," also in *A Press Divided*, 233.
21. *Annapolis Gazette*, April 25, 1861.
22. *Philadelphia Inquirer*, May 1, 1861.
23. Randall M. Miller, "Catholic Religion, Irish Ethnicity, and the American Civil War," in *Religion and the American Civil War*, eds. Randall M. Miller, Harry S. Stout, and Charles Reagan Wilson (New York: Oxford University Press, 1998). 263.
24. *Chronica Domus* I:155 (April n.d., 1861).
25. Curley, *Cheerful Ascetic*, 202.
26. Kurtz, *Excommunicated from the Union*, 44.
27. *Chronica Domus* I:156 (May n.d., 1861). Romans 8:31.
28. Berger, Annapolis, May 9, 1861, to Aunt and Sister, RABP.
29. Ella S. Holland, Annapolis, to Susie Sands, Centreville, May 9, 1861, Dowsett Collection of Sands Family Papers, MSA SC2095–2–169.
30. Revell, Annapolis, to My absent friend [Susie Sands], Centreville, April 29, 1861, Dowsett Collection.
31. Revell, Annapolis, to My friends [*sic*, it is clearly intended for Susie], Centreville, May 1, 1861, Dowsett Collection.
32. Revell, Annapolis, to Dear friend, Centreville, May 10, 1861, Dowsett Collection.
33. Wayne C. Temple, "Mary Todd Lincoln's Travels," *Journal of the Illinois State Historical Society* 52, no. 1 (Spring, 1959): 182.
34. Draft letter Susie Sands, Annapolis, to Ella S. Holland, Anna, Illinois, May 28–June 2, 1861, in Susie Sands Notebook of Poetry and Letters 1860–97, Moss Collection of Sands Family Papers, MSA SC732–1–4, accessed May 26, 2015, http://mdhistory.net/msa_sc732/msa_sc732_1/html/msa_sc732_1-0287.html. She said Martin departed May 21, but Susie Sands Journal, May 22, 1861, Dowsett Collection, says he left on the evening of May 22. Trains through Relay House went to Harpers Ferry, where passengers could transfer to points south, or continue west to Cumberland and the terminus at Wheeling, Virginia (now West Virginia). Ray Chism, "A Brief History of Relay," accessed February 23, 2013, http://www.relaymaryland.com/Welcome_files/HistoryofRelay.pdf; Toomey, *War Came by Train*, frontispiece map.
35. Frank Southern Revell (1861–1930). "Frank S. Revell," *Archives of Maryland* (Biographical Series), MSA SC3520–13111, accessed March 10, 2016, http://msa.maryland.gov/megafile/msa/speccol/sc3500/sc3520/013100/013111/html/13111bio.html. He was sheriff in 1897–99 and 1909–11, county clerk in 1927–33, and many other positions.
36. Baptismal Register B#1 (June 4, 1859—Mary Elizabeth Brady, and September 30, 1861—John Roland Brady) and Confirmation Register B#1 (January 29, 1860). There is a two-year discrepancy concerning Mollie's birth date. Interment Register B#2 (September 23, 1904), says she was 60 years of age at the time of her death (born ca. 1844). Her gravestone inscription agrees with this age. However, the 1900 census gives March 1846 as her birth month and year. It appears that some grave markers in the Brady-Revell plot, St. Mary's Cemetery, were installed concurrently, sometime after the original burials, and the family may have depended on Interment Register information for her age.
37. Email of Ann Jensen to author, September 11, 2012, quoting letter from her cousin, Mildred Revell Brady Chadeayne. The original story appears to be credited to William Martin Brady (1866–1936) who is listed in Baptismal Register B#1 (March 23, 1866) and First Communion Register F#1 (May 29, 1879), and served as Anne Arundel County deputy clerk (1896, 1927), chief deputy clerk (1920), and clerk (1925, 1933). Also, "William Martin Brady," *Archives of Maryland* (Biographical Series), MSA SC3520–13112, accessed March 10, 2016, http://msa.maryland.gov/megafile/msa/speccol/sc3500/sc3520/013100/013112/html/13112bio.html. The property is located on the southwest corner of State Circle and Cornhill Street, JHN 4:545 (April 13, 1850), AACLR. Also, Maryland Historical Trust, "42–44 State Circle, Annapolis," MIHP AA–1594, accessed October 5, 2016, https://mht.maryland.gov/secure/medusa/PDF/AnneArundel/AA-1594.pdf; Elihu S. Riley, *A History of Anne Arundel County, in Maryland* (Annapolis: Charles G. Feldmeyer, 1905), 96.
38. Riley, *Ancient City*, 297.
39. Charles Bruckner Hudgins, *The Convert* (New York: Neale Publishing Company, 1908), 75, a novel recounting the song sung by a post-war hunting party in Georgia; "Mrs. Matilda Rogers Dies at Age of 113," The *News-Record* (Marshall, North Carolina), September 19, 1963, 1 and 8, for her obituary which says she remembered Confederate volunteers singing: 'We'll hang John Brown's body to a sour apple tree.'" Also, John Stauffer and Benjamin Soskis, *The Battle Hymn of the Republic: A Biography of the Song That Marches On* (New York: Oxford University Press, 2013), 18, 47, 82–83, 92; Ray B. Browne and Lawrence A. Kreiser, Jr., *The Civil War and Reconstruction* (Westport, Connecticut: Greenwood Press, 2003), 126, which mentions two other parodies:"We'll Hang Abe Lincoln's Body from A Sour Apple Tree" and "We'll Hang Jeff Davis' Body from A Sour Apple Tree." Also, *Daily Exchange* (Baltimore), August 19, 1861, which published text of the "dreary composition" honoring John Brown's memory, including the hanging Jeff Davis line; Thomas Fleming, *A Disease in the Public Mind: A New Understanding of Why We Fought the Civil War* (New York: Da Capo

Press, 2013), 277.

40. Deborah Chadeayne Oliver (great-granddaughter of John Wesley Brady), Rolla, Missouri, to author, April 12, 2014. Also, Edward T. Schultz, *History of Freemasonry in Maryland of All the Rites Introduced into Maryland from the Earliest Time to the Present* (Baltimore: J. H. Mediary, 1887), 3:257–58. Participation by Catholics in Free and Accepted Masons (Freemasonry) was proscribed because of principles "irreconcilable with the Church's doctrine" and said membership was a "grave sin" (1983 statement of the Congregation of the Doctrine of the Faith, headed by Cardinal Joseph Ratzinger), and has been prohibited since the eighteenth century. See Peter M. J. Stravinskas, ed. *Our Sunday Visitor's Catholic Encyclopedia* (Huntington Indiana: Our Sunday Visitor, 1991), 417–18; Matthew Bunson, *Our Sunday Visitor's Encyclopedia of Catholic History* (Huntington Indiana: Our Sunday Visitor, 1995), 341; Frank K. Flynn ed., *Encyclopedia of Catholicism* (New York: Facts on File, 2007), 294–95.
41. "Application for Membership: United Daughters of the Confederacy," accepted by St. Louis chapter, October 1, 1934; entered Missouri Roll Book, January 18, 1935; registered Registrar General, UDC, August 31, 1935; and certificate issued December 20, 1935; copy provided by Archives, United Daughters of the Confederacy, Richmond, Virginia, to author, March 18, 2016.
42. Catherine "Kitty" or "Kate" Hutton (1846–1928), a lifelong resident of Annapolis was not associated with St. Mary's. Her mother was Mary Hohne Hutton (1821–after 1880), a cousin of Mollie's mother Mary Anne Hohne Revell (1802–79).
43. *Maryland Republican*, May 18, 1861; *Annapolis Gazette*, April 25, 1861. For full text of Butler's correspondence, see draft letter, Butler, Annapolis, to John Albion Andrew, Boston, May 9, 1861, Generals Papers (Butler), Box 1, Entry 159G, RG 94, NARA.
44. William Henry Sterling, Annapolis, to Matilda Farquhar Sterling, Philadelphia, February 26, 1863, Box 1, Folder 1, Sterling Family Papers.
45. Matilda Farquhar Sterling, Annapolis, to Anna Virginia Farquhar, Philadelphia, March 18, 1863, Box 1, Folder 1, Sterling Family Papers.
46. *New York Daily Tribune*, May 7, 1861.
47. Rockford E. Toews, *Lincoln in Annapolis, February 1865* (Annapolis: Maryland State Archives, 2009), 5; Rebecca Wilson, "In Annapolis: Lincoln's Walk," *The College* [St. John's College, Annapolis and Sante Fe] 42, no. 1 (Spring 2017): 6–7; Revell to My absent friend, April 29, 1861; Revell to My friends, May 1, 1861; Lizzie J. Davis, "of the Southern Confederacy," Annapolis, to Susie Sands, Centreville, May 9, 1861, Dowsett Collection; *Maryland Republican*, May 18, 1861.
48. Toews, *Lincoln in Annapolis*, 5–6.
49. 1820 Federal censuses for Anne Arundel County and 1830–60 for Annapolis; ad in *Maryland Republican*, November 5, 1862; Maryland, Senate, *Report of the President and Directors of the Annapolis and Elk Ridge Railroad Company in Compliance with the Senate, February 25th 1870* (Annapolis: William Thompson, State Printer), Document Z, 5; Annapolis Mayor and Aldermen Property Assessment, June 11, 1860, MSA M72–3; *Annapolis Gazette*, November 23, 1854; *Annapolis Gazette*, April 8, 1858, (Caldwell, a Democrat, received 192 votes, sixth of ten candidates, top five won seats); Annapolis Lodge No. 89 Ancient Free and Accepted Masons, "History of Annapolis Freemasonry," accessed October 12, 2013, http://www.annapolislodge.com/no_javascript/index.aspx?target=annapolis.php. Also, Baptismal Register B#1 (May 24, 1858—20-year-old convert Adelina Fisher, and January 16, 1859—10-year-old John Airland); "Sponsors of Bells," [circa 1859], last leaf of B#1.
50. Report of E. S. Allen, agent, and William H. Salter, clerk, Depot Quartermaster's Office, to Brevet Brigadier General John C. McFerran, Deputy Quartermaster, Washington, DC, January 25, 1868; McFerran to General Daniel Henry Rucker, Quartermaster General, Washington, DC, January 27, 1868, Entry 225, Box 38, Consolidated Correspondence File, 1794–1915, Records of the Office of the Quartermaster General, RG 92, NARA.
51. John C. Pegram, *Recollections of the United States Naval Academy,* Personal Narratives of Events in the War of the Rebellion, Being Papers Read before the Rhode Island Soldiers and Sailors Historical Society, Fourth Series, No. 14 (Providence: The Society, 1891), 20.
52. Pegram, *Recollections*, 25; Luce to Blake, Naval Academy, Annapolis, April 17 and 19, 1861, Office of the Superintendent, Letters Received by the Superintendent, 1845–1887, Folder 8, Box 5, Entry 25, RG 405, USNA.
53. Gideon Welles, Washington, to Blake, Annapolis, May 18, 1861, Office of the Superintendent, Letters Received by the Superintendent, 1845–1887, Folder 9, Box 5, Entry 25; Officer of the Day's Journal (April 14–20, 1861), USNA.
54. Office of Day's Journal, April 21, 1861; letter of Commander Christopher Raymond Perry Rodgers, Commandant, Naval Academy, Annapolis, April 22, 1861, Office of the Superintendent, Letters Received by the Superintendent, 1845–1887, Folder 8, Box 5, Entry 25, RG 405, USNA.
55. Edward Simpson, on board U.S. Practice Ship *John Adams,* Newport, Rhode Island, to Hale, July 16, 1862, Entry 25, Box 8, Folder 8, RG 405, USNA.
56. McWilliams, *Annapolis*, 170–71; Sweetman, *Naval Academy*, 59–63; Edward Chauncey Marshall, ed., *History of the United States Naval Academy* (New York: Van Nostrand, 1862), 46–47; Officer of the Day's Journal (April 21, 1861), USNA (this was the last entry in the journal before the transfer to Newport).
57. Eight-page list of 45 current civilian employees (of whom 17 have known St. Mary's connections), included with "Papers Related to the Removal of Democrats and Appointment of Republicans, at the Naval Academy, 1870, Based on a Resolution Passed by the Republican Central Committee on March 7, 1870, and referred by the President to Commodore John L. Worden, Superintendent, USNA," Office of the Superin-

tendent, Letters Received by the Superintendent, 1845–1887, Folder 9, Box 9, Entry 25, RG 405, USNA. Richard M. Chase, Newport, to John P. Hale, Chairman, Committee on Naval Affairs, US Senate, Washington, Hale, July 20, 1862, Entry 25, Box 8, Folder 8, RG 405, USNA.

58. Letters Sent by the Superintendent, 1845–74, Microfilm Publication M945, Box 1, vol. 4, RG 405, USNA, for a copy of a letter from Captain Cornelius K. Stribling, Superintendent, to Assistant Professor Thomas Karney and others, June 30, 1852 (earlier letters may be available). Also, McIntire, 1:384. For Arabella Karney as godmother, see Baptismal Register B#1 (February 22, 1852, September 25, 1853 [twice], and October 21, 1853). After the Civil War, Karney served as the Naval Academy librarian and is buried in St. Mary's Cemetery. "Nimitz Library History Timeline, 1845–2017," accessed August 13, 2018, https://www.usna.edu/Library/about/timeline.php; Interment Register B#2 (April 2, 1885); Find A Grave Memorial ID 213129510.

59. Welles to Blake, August 21, 1861; Karney to Blake, August 24, 1861; Hale to Blake, July 1, 1862; Blake to Hale, July 7, 1862; Karney to Hale, July 7, 1862; Edward Simpson, Newport, Rhode Island, to Hale, July 16, 1862, Entry 25, Box 8, Folder 8, RG 405, USNA. The published letters can be seen in Committee Report No. 68, Committee on Naval Affairs, July 12, 1862, 19 pp., in US Congress, 37th, 2nd Session, Senate, *Reports of the Committees of the United States, 1861–'62* (Washington: Government Printing Office, 1862).

60. Edward Seager (1809–86) and Mary De LaRaintre Seager (1812–82). "Sponsors of Bells" [1859], last leaf of B#1; Seager to Hale, July 7, 1862, Entry 25, Box 8, Folder 8, RG 405, USNA; Senate Committee Report No. 68, 13–14; Confirmation Register B#1 (January 29, 1860); United States Naval Academy, *Official Registers of the Officers and Midshipmen of the United States Naval Academy, Newport, Rhode Island, November 1, 1864* (Newport: Frederick A. Pratt, 1864) 5, 17. Also, Edward Seager, *No. 1 of Progressive Studies of Landscape Drawing; Adapted to the Practice of Sketching from American Scenery* (Boston: J. H. Bufford, 1849); Navy Department, Bureau of Ordnance, *Exercises in Small-arms and Field Artillery: Arranged for the Naval Service, Under an Order of the Bureau of Ordnance And Hydrography of the Navy Department* (Philadelphia: T. K. and P. G. Collins, 1852), includes small and broadsword exercises by Seager, 151–68; US Naval Academy Museum, "Edward Seager, Professor of Drawing," USNA Museum, Annapolis, October-November 1986.

61. Peter Klippen (1834–1910). Pension File Certificate No. 617257, RG 15, NARA; "New York Passenger Lists, 1820–1957," accessed May 1, 2013, Ancestry.com (arrived August 9, 1848 on *Clothilda* from Antwerp, Peter Klippen, age 22, along with possibly an uncle and aunt (Christoph and Juliana Klippen; his parents were listed on his baptismal record as Conrad and Ursula). St. Mary's registers in B#1 (January 8, 1854—baptism; March 29, 1857—confirmation; and December 26, 1858—the marriage; and July 27, 1856 [twice], January 17, 1858, November 10, 1860, and December 16, 1860—as godparent; and November 20, 1859, and January 27, 1861—as father). Also, information on Klippen was generously provided by the late R. Bruce Horner to author, March 10, 2014 (Horner Notes, March 10, 2014), quoting USNA bandsman David G. Pfeiffer in Elihu S. Riley, "Annapolis at the Advent of the Naval Academy," Article 23, *The Evening Capital* and *Maryland Gazette*, December 31, 1921. Also, Kenrick, *Theologiae Moralis*, 3:55, section 56; P. Charles Augustine, O.S.B., *The New Code of Canon Law* (St. Louis: B. Herder, 1920), Book III, vol. 4:75.

62. 1860 Federal Census, Annapolis; St. Mary's registers B#1 (April 19, 1858 marriage and December 26, 1859 baptism of daughter); Horner Notes, March 10, 2014; "Mixed Marriage," Donald Attawater, ed., *A Catholic Dictionary* (New York: Macmillan, 1958), 327–28, for implications of Catholic/baptized non-Catholic and Catholic/non-baptized person marriages.

63. Baptismal Register B#1 (January 8, 1854, May 31, 1857, June 12, 1859, November 10, 1860); 1860 Federal Census, Annapolis; Horner Notes, March 10, 2014 on Wirth.

64. Horner Notes, March 10, 2014 on Zimmermann; Marriage Register B#1 (June 28, 1860) gives Hesse-Cassel as the birthplace while Baptismal Register B#1 (August 7, 1860) gives Prussia as his parents' birthplace. McIntire, 1:792, gives Hesse-Cassel as the birthplace. Michael Kraus does not appear again in the sacramental registers and probably was not Catholic.

65. *Daily Evening Bulletin* (San Francisco), July 16, 1861; Naval History and Heritage Command, *Dictionary of American Naval Fighting Ships*, accessed November 23, 2015, http://www.history.navy.mil/research/histories/ship-histories/danfs/w/ward.html; Find A Grave Memorial ID 19082.

66. General Orders Nos. 3 and 4, July 28, 1861, Part 4, Entry 1535, Records of United States Army Continental Commands, 1821–1920, RG 393, NARA.

67. Will H. Lowdermilk, *History of Cumberland, (Maryland)* (Washington: James Anglim, 1878), 397–98, places arrival of Eleventh Indiana in Cumberland on June 8, 1861. Wuest, *Annales*, IV:1:433 says it "was about May." Burkey, Seelos: *The Cumberland Years*, 44–56, covers these early war period in detail. Also, Zimmer, *Leben und Wirken*, 216 in original, 211 in translation.

68. Chronicles of the House of Studies, Cumberland, 86 (June 19, 1861).

69. This episode is well covered in Edward Day, "The Studentates Weather the Storm: Cumberland and Annapolis During the Civil War," *Speciligium historicum Congregationis Ssmi Redemptoris*, 10 (1962): 225, accessed March 14, 2013, http://www.santalfonsoedintorni.it/Spicilegium/10/SH-10-1962(I)218-237.pdf. Also, Chronicles of the House of Studies, Cumberland, 87 (June 19, 1861), 88–89 (August 19, 1861); Wuest, *Annales*, IV:1:433–35. It is not clear which troops were involved but it was not the Eleventh Indiana, which had been deployed to western Virginia in July and was mustered out of service August 2, 1861. See "Regiment

Data: 11th Indiana Infantry Regiment (Union)," Historical Data Systems, American Civil War Research Database (ACWRDB), accessed August 21, 2012, https://asp6new.alexanderstreet.com/cwdb/.

70. Thomas S. Townsend, *The Honors of the Empire State in the War of the Rebellion* (New York: A. Lovell, 1889), 246; Harry S. Stout, *Upon the Altar of the Nation,* xvii, 53–59, 249, 253; Drew Gilpin Faust, *This Republic of Suffering: Death and the American Civil War* (New York: Alfred A. Knopf, 2008), 33, for analysis of the God-is-on-our-side sentiments. Also, Patrick Daniel O'Flaherty, "The History of the Sixty-Ninth Regiment of New York State Militia, 1852–1861," (PhD diss., Fordham University, 1963), 230; Sixty-Ninth Historical Roundtable, "History of the Sixty-Ninth Regiment, New York: 'Fighting Sixty-Ninth'" 53, 55, accessed June 3, 2014, https://dokument.pub/history-of-the-sixty-ninth-regiment-new-york-fighting-flipbook-pdf.html; *Sun,* May 4, 1861, quotes Mooney on coming to the United States from Ireland in 1848.
71. *New York Times,* May 1, 1861. The letter was written from Annapolis, April 27, 1861. Kurtz, *Excommunicated from the Union,* 59, identifies Corcoran as Catholic, regardless his level of personal piety, and says he was a source of pride for many Catholics during and after the war. Miller, "Catholic Religion, Irish Ethnicity, and the American Civil War," 274–75, notes Corcoran as a "rabidly Irish nationalist commander."
72. O'Flaherty, "History of the Sixty-Ninth," 234.
73. Hughes to Kenrick, July 3, 1861, Box 29, Folder J11, Kenrick Papers, AAB. The first choice, who declined the appointment, was George Deshon, 1843 graduate of the US Military Academy, former army lieutenant, and former Redemptorist who had joined the Missionary Society of St. Paul (Paulists) in 1858. He later became the Paulists' superior general (1897–1903). See "George Deshon, No. 1168. Class of 1843," Association of Graduates, United States Military Academy, *Thirty-Fifth Annual Reunion of the Association of the Graduates of the United States Military Academy, June 14th, 1904* (Saginaw, Michigan: Seemann and Peters, 1904), 189–90; O'Flaherty, "History of the Sixty-Ninth," 59, 231; *Dunigan's American Catholic Almanac and List of the Clergy, 1858* (New York: Edward Dunigan and Brothers, 1858), 38; Germain, *Catholic Military and Naval Chaplains,* 85–86.
74. *Irish American,* May 18, 1861.
75. O'Flaherty, "History of the Sixty-Ninth," 236–37.
76. *Sun,* May 4, 1861; *New York Daily Tribune,* May 7, 1861; *Irish American,* May 18, 1861.
77. Margaret Leech, *Reveille in Washington, 1860–1865* (New York: Harper, 1941), 71; *Daily National Intelligencer,* May 6, 1861 and June 1, 1861; David V. Miller, *The Defenses of Washington During the Civil War* (Buffalo, New York: The Author, 1976), 21, map 171–96; Benjamin Franklin Cooling III and Warren H. Owen II, *Mr. Lincoln's Forts: A Guide to the Civil War Defenses of Washington* (Lanham, Maryland: Scarecrow Press, 2010), 110–14.
78. *Irish American,* June 22, 1861.
79. *American and Commercial Advertiser,* June 18, 1861; Frank Moore, *The Civil War in Song and Story, 1860–1865* (New York: P. F. Collier, 1889), 217–18, which recounts the story; O'Flaherty, "History of the Sixty-Ninth," 258.
80. Kenrick to Hughes, June 24, 1861, Box 1, Folder 9: Correspondence–K, Henry Joseph Browne Papers, MS 0158, Rare Book and Manuscript Library, Columbia University, New York City. The term *defectu lenitatis* (defect of mildness) refers to a canonical impediment brought about by those who "voluntarily, actively, and proximately take part with sanction of public authority in the lawful killing or mutilating of another," the consequence of which "a person becomes unworthy of the reception of orders or their exercise or have been imposed on account of certain defects which would be indecorous in a sacred minister." See "Irregularity," Attwater, *Catholic Dictionary,* 262; Hughes to Kenrick, July 3, 1861, Box 29, Folder J11, Kenrick Papers, AAB; Miller, "Catholic Religion, Irish Ethnicity, and the American Civil War," 269, which says Mooney "acted too much like a warrior for Archbishop Hughes." Also, Cooling and Owen, *Mr. Lincoln's Forts,* 111–12; Gus Person, "Answering the Call: The New York State Militia Responds to the Crisis of 1861," 5, accessed October 1, 2011 http://dmna.ny.gov/historic/reghist/civil/AnsweringTheCall_Person.pdf; Phillip Thomas Tucker, *History of the Irish Brigade: A Collection of Historical Essays* (Fredericksburg, Virginia; Sergeant Kirkland's Museum and History Society, 1995), 57–58; Phillip Thomas Tucker, *"God Help the Irish": The History of the Irish Brigade* (Abilene, Texas: McWhiney Foundation Press, McMurray University, 2007), 32; Donald R. McClarey, "Matthew Brady, Father Thomas H. Mooney, Dagger John and the Fighting 69th," *American Catholic,* July 19, 2011, accessed October 11, 2011 http://the-american-catholic.com/2011/07/19/matthew-brady-father-thomas-h-mooney-dagger-john-and-the-fighting-69th/#sthash.lhfNjL9W.dpuf, which quotes the July 3, 1861, letter from Hughes; "Endurance and Pluck," *Irish Times,* July 23, 2011, accessed October 1, 2011, https://www.irishtimes.com/life-and-style/endurance-and-pluck-1.608291.
81. McClarey, "Brady, Mooney, Dagger John and the Fighting 69th."
82. Brokhage, Kenrick's *Opinion on Slavery, 187–88;* Maryland, General Assembly, January Session 1860, *The Maryland Code: Public General Laws and Public Local Laws, 1860* (Baltimore: John Murphy, 1860), Article 30, Section 129, 236, and Article 60, Section 5, 404, accessed May 18, 2015, http://aomol.msa.maryland.gov/000001/000145/html/am145--404.html.
83. Inserted in Marriage Register B#1 (May 18, 1861).
84. Baptismal Register B#1 (March 22, 1857); Indentures, 1846–58, Register of Wills, Anne Arundel County, March 20, 1846, BEG 1:50–51 (Diggs), MSA C82–3; 1860 Federal Census, District 1 (Owensville), Anne Arundel County, for Annania, and District 2 (Davidsonville) for Azaria. Turton is listed in the 1850 and 1860 Federal population and Slave Schedules,

Anne Arundel County, District 2.

85. *Chronica Domus* I:151 (January 1, 1861), I:156 (June 3, 1861); Baptismal Register B#1 records baptisms at which Fehlings officiated August 7 and 30, 1860, and April 22, 1861; Wuest, Annales, IV:2:449. On Fehlings' later career see "Saint Joseph's, Cardington, Morrow County's First Catholic Church, 1868–1972," *Catholic Record Society Bulletin* 8, no. 9 (September 1982): 161, and "Saint Aloysius, Lewis Center, Delaware County, Ohio, 1864–ca. 1920," *Catholic Record Society Bulletin* 8, no. 12 (December 1982): 185, both accessed May 10, 2015, https://columbuscatholic.org/catholic-record-society/issues-listing#volumes-vii-ix-1981-1983; James R. Lytle, *20th Century History of Delaware County, Ohio, and Representative Citizens* (Chicago: Biographic Publishing Company, 1908), 253; Joseph M. Flynn, *The Catholic Church in New Jersey* (Morristown, New Jersey: 1904); 1870 Federal Census, New York City; *Utica Morning Herald*, June 12, 1879; *Daily Times* (Troy, New York), December 31, 1888, which reported Fehlings, who "died Sunday" (December 30, 1888), had been pastor of St. Mary's German Catholic Church in Utica for sixteen years, and was "instrumental in building fifteen churches"; "Obituary," *Sadliers' Catholic Directory, Almanac, and Ordo, 1890* (New York: D. and J. Sadlier, 1890), 34; up to 1866 it was called *Sadliers' Catholic Almanac and Ordo.*
86. *Chronica Domus* I:157 (June n.d., 1861, June 21, 1861); Wuest, *Annales*, IV:2:451. Joseph Wuest Personnel File, RABP. Wuest archivist (1867–1919). He succeeded Joseph Wissel, who served 1861–67.
87. *Correct Guide to Strangers*, 16, says: "Churches . . . Catholic.—On the Duke of Gloucester street.—Rev'd. Father Jacobs." Also, Anne Arundel County Test Book, Declaration of Citizenship: Joseph Jacobs, January 7, 1859, MSA C147–1; *Catalogus Congregationis Sanctissimi Redemptoris, Anno MDCCLIX, Concinnatus et Publicatus* (Rome: Typis S. C. de Propaganda Fide, 1859), 34, RABP, which does not list Jacobs in Annapolis. See *Chronica Domus* I:193 (June 14, 1862) for first use of "rector." Baptismal Register B#1 (October 24, 1860); Chronicles of the House of Studies, Cumberland, 82 (April 14 and 27, 1861); Wuest, *Annales*, IV:2:179 (Jacobs arrived in October 1860); *Province Annals, 1832–1871*, 434 (1860, Annapolis), RABP (Jacobs arrived in October) and 1861:471 ("May – in this same month came R.P. Jacobs, he is given charge of the church."). *Chronica Domus* I:157 notes Jacob's arrival as follows: *"Hoc mense (Junio) ineunte Rev. P. Jacobs Annapolim venit."* This asserts he arrived at the beginning of June. Baptismal Register B#1 (May 30, 1861) reveals the slightly earlier arrival. This is one of the cases revealing the occasional imprecision of the house annals. Also, Baptismal Register B#1 (June 8 and June 9, 1861). The June 15 marriage as that of Richard Smith and Sarah Lee (*see also below*).
88. *Chronica Domus* I:157 (June n.d., 1861, following June 21); Wuest, *Annales*, IV:2:286.
89. Wuest, *Annales*, IV:2:286; *Province Annals, 1832–1871*, 472–73 (1861, Annapolis), RABP. Brinsfield, *Faith in the Fight*, 45, gives a figure of 3 percent but their "Roster of Union Chaplains," 129–209, lists 53 Catholic chaplains which, out of 2,398 total, produces 2 percent.
90. *Province Annals, 1832–1871*, 472–73 (1861, Annapolis), RABP.
91. *Chronica Domus* I:157 (July 4, 1861). Kurtz, *Excommunicated from the Union*, 30, says the bishops "implored their priests to refrain 'prudently' from commenting on political issues" at the 1858 Ninth Provincial Council in Baltimore.
92. *Annapolis Gazette*, July 4, 1861; *Sun*, July 6, 1861.
93. *Chronica Domus* I:157 (July 4, 1861).
94. E. A. Andrews, *A Copious and Critical Latin-English Lexicon* (New York: Harper and Brothers, 1860), 944, 1397.
95. *Chronica Domus* I:157 (July 4, 1861).
96. *New York Daily Tribune*, July 9, 1861.
97. *Kent News* (Chestertown), August 19, 1861, quoted in Tilghman, *History of St. John's College*, 94–97; *Annapolis Gazette*, October 12, 1861.
98. "James Lawrence Bartol (1813–1887)," *Archives of Maryland* (Biographical Series) MSA SC3520–1625, accessed February 3, 2015, http://msa.maryland.gov/megafile/msa/speccol/sc3500/sc3520/001600/001625/html/1625bio.html; *Sun*, May 2, 1857; *Annapolis Gazette*, November 19, 1857; *Sun*, June 25, 1887, which reported Bartol's funeral held at St. Ann's Catholic Church in Baltimore. Also, *Archives of Maryland* (Biographical Series) James Lawrence Bartol (1813-1887) MSA SC3520-1625, accessed January 8, 2015, http://msa.maryland.gov/megafile/msa/speccol/sc3500/sc3520/001600/001625/html/1625bio.html; Find A Grave Memorial IDs 109094254 and 109094255. Emily H. Murphy, *"A Complete and Generous Education," 300 Years of Liberal Arts, St. John's College, Annapolis* (Annapolis: St. John's College Press, 1996), 27–28.
99. *Sun*, July 1, 1862; Hall Hammond, "Commemoration of the Two Hundredth Anniversary of the Maryland Court of Appeals: A Short History," *Maryland Law Review* 38, no. 2 (1978): 235, 238, 229–41; "Excitement in Maryland," *New York Times*, May 29, 1862. Diarist William Wilkins Glenn wrote in detail about Carmichael's arrest on May 27, 1862. Also, Bayly and Schatz, *Between North and South*, 308–12; Frederick Emory, *Queen Anne's County, Maryland: Its Early History and Development* (Baltimore: Maryland Historical Society, 1950), 504–6; and Mitchell and Baker, *Civil War in Maryland Reconsidered*, 147.
100. *Sun*, August 14, 1861 and September 7, 1861; *Annapolis Gazette*, August 15, 1861; Stout, *Upon the Altar of the Nation*, xviii. Lucas E. Morel, *Lincoln's Sacred Effort: Defining Religion's Role in American Self-Government* (Lanham, Maryland: Lexington Books, 2000), 112–13, which lists the following days, but not September 26, 1861: August 12, 1861 (National Fast Day), November 28, 1861 (Day of Thanksgiving), April 10, 1862 (Thanksgiving Day for Victories), March 30, 1863 (National Fast Day), July 15, 1863 (Day of Thanksgiving), October 3, 1863 (fixed annual Thanksgiving Day on last

Thursday of November), July 7, 1864 (National Day of Prayer), September 3, 1864 (Day of Thanksgiving and Prayer), and October 20, 1864 (Day of Thanksgiving). *Sun,* September 18, 1861, and September 26, 1861; diary entry for September 27, 1861, Susie Sands Notebook of Poetry and Letters, 1860–1897, Moss Collection, MSA.

101. Spalding, *Premier See,* 176. The quote is from Gibbons, seen in John Tracy Ellis, *The Life of James Cardinal Gibbons, Archbishop of Baltimore, 1834–1921* (Milwaukee: Bruce Publishing Company, 1952), I:46–47, and citing Gibbons' article "My Memories," *Dublin Review,* 160, nos. 320–21 (January–April 1917): 165–66. The text of the prayer can be seen in Peter Guilday, *The Life and Times of John Carroll, Archbishop of Baltimore (1735–1815)* (New York: Encyclopedia Press, 1922), II:432 n21, which ascribes it to around the time of the first national synod of bishops (November 7–11, 1791). *Sun,* September 7, 1861, says it was "prescribed" during the 1791 synod, but the introduction to the United States Conference of Catholic Bishops' "Liturgical Resources For A Presidential Inauguration," http://www.usccb.org/prayer-and-worship/liturgical-resources/liturgical-resources-for-a-presidential-inauguration.cfm, says it was written for George Washington's 1789 inauguration. The ecclesiastical Province of Baltimore during the Civil War comprised dioceses of Baltimore, Charleston, Erie, Philadelphia, Pittsburgh, Richmond, Savannah, and Wheeling, the Vicariate Apostolic of East Florida, and extended over the District of Columbia, and the states of Maryland, Pennsylvania, Delaware, Virginia, North Carolina, South Carolina, Georgia, and the eastern part of Florida. See *Sadliers' Catholic Almanac,* 1864, 53.

102. Eleanor C. Sullivan, *Georgetown Visitation since 1799* (Washington: 1975), 102–3, citing letter of Kenrick to Sisters of the Visitation Convent in Georgetown, DC, April 22, 1861, in regard to the threat to house Federal troops at the convent. The sisters were given discretionary power during the crisis," but were under no circumstances to do anything that would incur expense. Kurtz, *Excommunicated from the Union,* 34–35, citing Kenrick, Baltimore, to Spalding, Louisville, December 2, 1862, Archdiocese of Baltimore Collection, University of Notre Dame Archives, Notre Dame, Indiana. William Starr Meyers, "Governor Bradford's Private List of Union Men in 1861," *Maryland Historical Magazine* 7, no. 1 (March 1912): 84. Archbishop John Hughes called Kenrick "a friend of peace and union." See Hughes to Kenrick, July 3, 1861.

103. The Redemptorists sold part of lot 31 to George M. Taylor for $200, NHG 10:229 (July 3, 1861), AACLR. After Compromise Street was extended across Taylor's property, a confirmatory deed, SH 4:194 (November 3, 1872), was executed but a dispute continued between city government and the Redemptorists, see Worden, *Saint Mary's,* 117–18.

104. Mother Gertrude Thomas, O.S.P. (ca. 1794–1861, superior general 1851–61). Annals, 81 (June 21), 82 (August 2), and 83 (October 6, 1861), Box 32, Folder 3, Oblate Sisters of Providence Archives, Baltimore (OSP Archives). Sister Gabriel Addison, O.S.P. (ca. 1800–66). Congregation Sisters, Deceased, Gabriel Addison, Box 36, Folder 10, OSP Archives. Manumission (May 4, 1832), says Georgianna was "being of the age of twenty years" and cost of manumission $200 paid to Caton. The document was recorded in Baltimore County Court, Liber A.I. 48, Folio 5, May 17, 1832. See Motherhouse Papers, Box 17, Folder 11, OSP Archives. 1860 Federal Census, Baltimore, gives Sister Gabriel's age as sixty and born in Maryland.

105. Elizabeth (Mother Mary) Lange (ca. 1794–1882). Sharon C. Knecht, *Oblate Sisters of Providence: A Pictorial History* (Baltimore: Oblate Sisters of Providence, 2007), 18, 19, 97, 138; Willa Young Banks, "A Contradiction in Antebellum Baltimore: A Competitive School for Girls of 'Color' within a Slave State," *Maryland Historical Magazine* 99, no. 2 (Summer 2004): 133–34, 153, 158; "The Oblate School for Colored Girls: Historical Background–Maryland Historical Society," accessed August 24, 2014, https://slidelegend.com/the-oblate-school-for-colored-girls-maryland-historical-society_5b14bf9c7f8b9a6e448b4596.html. The school was located on Richmond (now Read) Street; name changed to St. Frances School for Colored Girls in 1853 and to St. Frances Academy and School for Colored Girls by 1866. The O.S.P. co-founder with Mother Mary Lange was James Hector Nicholas Joubert de la Muraille, S.S. (1777–1843), a French-born refugee from Saint-Domingue (Haiti) who, after his arrival in Baltimore in 1804, joined the Society of St. Sulpice (Sulpicians), ordained 1810, and worked among French-speaking Haitian immigrants. See "Father Joubert," Oblate Sisters of Providence, accessed December 15, 2015, https://www.oblatesisters.com/our-history. Also, Diane Batts Morrow, "The Difficulty in Our Situation: The Oblate Sisters of Providence in Antebellum Society," in, *Uncommon Faithfulness: The Black Catholic Experience,* ed. M. Shawn Copeland (Maryknoll, New York: Orbis Books, 2009), 37, 41.

106. Motherhouse RG, Box 3, folders 1, 2, and 4 (1846–60), OSP Archives.

107. Motherhouse RG, Box 3, Folder 1, (September 27, 1852), OSP Archives; Banks, "Contradiction in Antebellum Baltimore," 142.

108. *Annapolis Gazette,* August 14, 1856.

109. Ledger, Box 3, Folder 2 (July 28, 1856), OSP Archives.

110. Edwin White (1817–77). *Washington Resigning His Commission,* dated 1858, oil on canvas, dimensions: 92" x 168", MSA SC1545–1112, http://msa.maryland.gov/msa/speccol/sc1500/sc1545/apc_website/apcpaintings_washingtonresigning.html. John Trumbull (1756–1843). *General George Washington Resigning His Commission,* dated 1824, oil on canvas, dimensions: 144"x216", http://www.aoc.gov/capitol-hill/historic-rotunda-paintings/general-george-washington-resigning-his-commission, both accessed December 15, 2015. Moses Lake's estate inventory lists "1 worked picture of Gen. Washington [$]10.00." See Account of Sales and Inventory, Register of Wills, Anne Arundel County, no. 1, 317–22, MSA C88–28. A "full length likeness of Genl of George Washington

worked by my daughter Mary A Lake" was bequeathed by Moses Lake to William Bishop, Last Will and Testament of Moses Lake, Register of Wills, Anne Arundel County, signed January 3, 1871, MSA C155–46. There is no mention of the needlework picture in Bishop's will because he died before Lake's will went through probate. See MSA C155–46, original will of William Bishop, filed January 3, 1871, which left all his belongings to his wife, Charity Folks Bishop.

111. *Weekly Anglo-African*, August 13, 1859. For the National Fair, see *DeBrow's Review and Industrial Resources, Statistics, Etc.* New Series, 1, no. 6 (December 1858): 465–66 (premiums were offered in "General Utility and Art"); "Addresses at the Late Agricultural Fair in Richmond, (Va.)," *Daily National Intelligencer* (Washington), November 2, 1858, 2 (fair started on October 26 and continued during the last week of October); *New York Daily Tribune*, August 24, 1859, (seventh annual United States Agricultural Fair to be held in Chicago September 12–17, 1859); *Dispatch* (Richmond), October 30, 1858 (lists premiums awarded in "Class 71.—Paintings, Maps, Designs &c.").

112. Box 3, folders 1 and 2, OSP Archives.

113. Box 3, Folder 2 (September 4, 1856; March 4–December 24, 1857; March 7–July 31, 1858), Box 3 Folder 4 (September 9, 1856; February 19, 1857, January 1, 1858, December 14, 1858), OSP Archives; Register of Wills, Anne Arundel County, August 26, 1856, Indentures, 1846–58, BEG 1:328 (Johanna Price), MSA C82–2; *Sun*, February 21, 1863; *Sun*, February 24, 1863; *Annapolis Gazette* not extant for these dates. Email from Lenora Calvin, historian of Asbury United Methodist Church, Annapolis, to author, February 4, 2014; Jerry M. Hynson, "Maryland Freedom Papers," vol. 1, Anne Arundel County, 13 "Henry Price. Certificate issued 14 Nov. 1815, "Born free and raised in AA Co."; "Price House, 230-232 Main Street" [earlier 118 Main Street], Annapolis, MHT Inventory of Historical Properties AA-588, 1994, accessed December 20, 2015, http://msa.maryland.gov/megafile/msa/stagsere/se1/se5/001000/001700/001725/pdf/msa_se5_1725.pdf.

114. Banks, "Contradiction in Antebellum Baltimore," 142.

115. Annals, 74 (January 9, 1860), Box 32, Folder 3, OSP Archives; email from Sharon Knecht, OSP Archivist, to author, March 25, 2014, citing an entry for Mary A. Lake/Sister Lucy in the "large sister roster."

116. Interment Register B#2 (December 2, 1869); *Annapolis Gazette*, December 9, 1869; Box 3, Folder 1 (September 1, 1855), OSP Archives, notes "To [cash] One qr in adv up Oct. 15th, taking of the time she was sick," an indication that Mary Augusta was absent for reasons of health; Box 3, Folder 2 (November 26, 1855) "Doctors fees &c." amounting to $3.30.

117. Marriage of Moses Lake and Mary Anne Norris, March 28, 1830, Anne Arundel County, and to Effine Peterson, November 7, 1838, Baltimore, "Maryland, Marriages, 1666–1970," accessed January 28, 2014, FamilySearch.org. Mary Anne Folks (1788–1837), daughter of Thomas and Charity Folks, was married first to Philip Norris (1819) and then to Moses Lake (1830). She is buried in an unmarked grave at St. Anne's Cemetery. See Joan C. Scurlock, "The Bishops of Annapolis," 17, unpublished manuscript, revised February 2000, copy loaned to author by Jean Russo. Baptismal Register B#1 (July 24, 1859—William Joseph, July 25, 1852—John Francis, and December 26, 1858—Mary Teresa). Charlotte Contee (1815–96) is listed in the 1850 Federal Census living in Annapolis with four Karney siblings. Charlotte Contee is buried at St. Mary's Cemetery, see Interment Register B#2 July 26, 1896. Also, 1910 Federal Census, Washington, DC, lists William J. Contee as a Navy fireman living with his wife Mary E. Contee; Find A Grave Memorial ID 75029204 for burial information on William J. Contee (1855–1933) and Mary Contee (1856–1938). Also, Rahsida L. Harrison, "Midwives," in Daina Ramey Berry and Deleso A. Alford, eds. *Enslaved Women in America: An Encyclopedia* (Santa Barbara, California: Greenwood, 2012), 205–6.

118. Baptismal Register B#1 (May 30, 1861); Interment Register B#2 (September 5, 1861). 1860 Federal Census, Annapolis, lists Nicholas Bishop as 20-year-old mulatto carter, living in William and Charity Bishop household. Mary Nichols Bishop is not listed among ten members of the household. Also, Jessica Millward, "Charity Folks, Sr. (ca. 1757–1828) and Charity Folks Bishop (1795–1875)," in *Enslaved Women in America*, 188–89.

119. Baptismal Register B#2 (May 30, 1867); "Maryland, Marriages, 1666–1970," accessed September 15, 2014, FamilySearch.org. 1850 Federal Census, Baltimore, Ward 6, lists Johanna Price living with Ann E. Price and nine members of the Brown family (presumably Ann's birth family). It is probable that Ann E. Price is the same person as Elisa Brown, John Ann's mother. The head of the household was William H. G. Brown, a mulatto engineer, age 44, born in Pennsylvania, but all other members of the household, including William's presumed wife, Charlotte, age 43, born Maryland, as well as Ann E., age 23, born in Ohio, and Johanna, age 3, born Maryland, are listed as "colored." Interment Register B#2 (May 28, 1874); the grave is unmarked.

120. The Lakes and Bishops settled "in a friendly manner the divisional line" between their properties in 1847; see JHN 2:380 and JHN 2:382 (both dated May 17, 1847), AACLR. There also was an August 6, 1835, law suit between Moses' first wife, Mary Anne, and her sister Charity, over the erection of a gate and fence that blocked access to the Lake residence. The case was decided in favor of the Lakes. See Scurlock, "The Bishops of Annapolis," 22–25, which does not give a citation, but the case is found in Maryland Chancery Court Papers, 1713–1853, MSA S512–9231.

121. Receipt signed by E. M. Lake for payment by "Mrs. Dr. Ridout," August 2, 1852, Ridout Papers Collection, Box 24, MSA SC910–24–19. This was Prudence [Mrs. John] Ridout.

122. Maryland Republican Advertising and Printing Ledger, Elizabeth V. Davis Collection, MSA SC414–1–6, p. 53, entries for Moses Lake, 1843–57; *Sun*, December 29, 1849; *Annapolis*

Gazette, December 1, 1859 and December 8, 1859.

123. Catherine [Kate] Wirt Randall diary entries December 27, 1854, April 23, 1855, March 27, 1856, Alexander Randall Diaries, vols. 3, 4, and 5, MS 652, Maryland Center for History and Culture.

124. "U.S. Tax Assessment Lists, Annapolis," 1864, p. 97, 1865, p. 142, accessed January 8, 2013, Ancestry.com; *Maryland Republican*, May 10, 1862 and October 4, 1862 (which note that the ad had been paid to run since August 1861).

125. 1850 and 1860 Federal censuses, Annapolis; Interment Register B#2 (November 20, 1869).

126. Esther Winder Polk Lowe (1824–1918). Esther Lowe, "Autobiography of Mrs. Enoch Louis Lowe, March 14, 1913 (copied April, 1925 from the original)," Enoch Louis Lowe Papers, MS 1949, Maryland Center for History and Culture; can be viewed at MSA, accessed August 1, 2016, http://msa.maryland.gov/megafile/msa/speccol/sc3500/sc3520/002200/002263/pdf/m1616.pdf.

127. David Porter (1780–1843). "Finding Aid for David Porter and David Dixon Porter Papers, 1803–1889," William L. Clements Library, University of Michigan, accessed January 5, 2016, https://quod.lib.umich.edu/c/clementsead/umich-wcl-M-495por?rgn=Entire+Finding+Aid;view=text;q1=david+porter.

128. "David Porter & Evalina Anderson," accessed January 5, 2016, http://sallysfamilyplace.com/new/david-porter-evalina-anderson/. Numerous Porter biographical and genealogical sources were consulted with no results for Mary Effine Peterson Lake. David Porter's listing in 1820 Federal Census, Washington, DC, does not enumerate any free Black females in his household but there were two White females age 10 and under, if Mary Lake passed as White. Porter in 1830 Federal Census, Chester, Pennsylvania, does not enumerate any free Black persons in his household but there was one White female age 20 to 30. The Porter Papers are not cataloged at item level and reference to Mary Lake would require on-site research to determine if she is mentioned. Most of the 231 items deal with Porter's naval career. See "Finding Aid for David Porter and David Dixon Porter Papers, 1803–1889."

129. *Annapolis Gazette*, February 25, 1858.

130. "Autobiography of Mrs. Enoch Louis Lowe." John Buchanan, associate judge (1806–24) and chief judge (1824–44) of the Maryland Court of Appeals. See "John Buchanan (1772–1844)," *Archives of Maryland* (Biographical Series), MSA SC3520–1622, accessed December 21, 2015, http://msa.maryland.gov/megafile/msa/speccol/sc3500/sc3520/001600/001622/html/1622bio.html. The other men were George Peabody (1795–1869) and Thomas Emory (1782–1842). Along with Buchanan, they were appointed December 1836 under Act of 1835, Chapter 395. See James McSherry, "The Former Chief Judges of the Court of Appeals of Maryland," *Report of the Tenth Annual Meeting of the Maryland State Bar Association (1905)*: 106–34, *Archives of Maryland Online*, accessed December 21, 2015, http://aomol.msa.maryland.gov/html/appeals.html; Alan M. Wilner, "The Maryland Board of Public Works: A History," *Archives of Maryland Online*, 216:19, accessed February 19, 2016, http://msa.maryland.gov/megafile/msa/speccol/sc2900/sc2908/000001/000216/html/am216--19.html.

131. "Autobiography of Mrs. Enoch Louis Lowe."

132. "John Thomson Mason (1765–1824)," *Archives of Maryland* (Biographical Series), MSA SC3520–1495, accessed February 19, 2016, http://msa.maryland.gov/megafile/msa/speccol/sc3500/sc3520/001400/001495/html/01495bio.html.

133. "The Eighth Annual Dinner," [June 1, 1893] United States Naval Academy Graduates Association, *8th, 9th, 10th, and 11th Annual Reunions and Registers f Graduates* (Baltimore: Deutsch Lithographing and Printing, 1897), 25.

134. *Sun*, March 23, 1870, 1; McWilliams, *Annapolis*, 135, 137. *Maryland Republican*, December 21, 1824. Text of this article is largely repeated in Riley, *Ancient City*, 239–43. Captain Sellman was presumably later-Colonel Richard Sellman (1799–1861) of Birdsville, Anne Arundel County.

135. Isaac Mayo (1894–1861). "North Carolina I," *Dictionary of American Naval Fighting Ships*, accessed February 22, 2016, http://www.history.navy.mil/research/histories/ship-histories/danfs/n/north-carolina-i.html; Ship Log, USS *North Carolina*, vols. 1 and 2, Entry 118, RG 24, US Navy Ship Logs, NARA; *Sun*, March 23, 1870; Byron A. Lee, *Naval Warrior: The Life of Commodore Isaac Mayo* (Linthicum, Maryland: Anne Arundel County Historical Society, 2002), 49–67; William L. Calderhead, "Experiment in Freedom: Maryland's Answer to Lincoln's Dilemma," 101, unpublished manuscript, © 1966, copy loaned to author by Jane McWilliams; 1830 Federal Census, Annapolis, which only names of head of household and gender and age range for others.

136. *Maryland Gazette*, January 31, 1833, repeated frequently through December 27, 1833.

137. Douglas Walter Bristol Jr., *Knights of the Razor: Black Barbers in Slavery and Freedom* (Baltimore: Johns Hopkins University Press, 2009), 6–7, 31, 41, 51–53, 91.

138. 1860 Federal Census, Annapolis. The other barbers were R. A. and George F. Richardson, presumably brothers and a father-and-sons group of Judson, Judson Jr., and James Steuart. The apprentices listed with Moses Lake were George Adams (age 14), Samuel W. Lake (age 19), and William Matthews (age 20). Draft Enrollment Records, Annapolis, 1863, listed Wesley Lake, age 30, colored, barber, single.

139. Alexander Randall, trustee, to William Bishop and Moses Lake, WSG 18:553 (April 19, 1834), AACLR; Indenture between Charity Folk and Mary Lake, wife of Moses Lake, "in consideration of love and affection which the said Charity hath and beareth towards her daughter" plus $1.00, WSG 19:34 (June 12, 1834), AACLR. Robert and Adelia Ramsey, Baltimore County, to Moses Lake, WSG 23:93 (July 6, 1838), AACLR, for $1,200; mortgage granted by Farmer's Bank of Maryland to Moses Lake for $500, WSG 23:97 (July 1, 1838); NHG 1:92 (March 4, 1852) releasing the bank's hold on the property; Moses and Mary E. Lake to

Matilda B. Harrison, for $1,200, NHG 5:19 (September 20, 1855). Also, Maryland Historical Trust, "Capsule Summary of 167 Duke of Gloucester Street," MIHP AA-1338, accessed October 2, 2016, https://mht.maryland.gov/secure/medusa/PDF/AnneArundel/AA-1338.pdf.

140. *Sun*, November 30, 1841; the introduction to "Annapolis Darkies," a "promiscuous" poem in B. T. Pindle, *Miscellaneous Poems, Intended for the Amusement If Not for the Instruction* (Baltimore: 1851), 150–51; *Sun*, January 24, 1842. The remarks were made by Senator Alexander Donoho of Somerset County, who had seen "the dressing room of Moses Lake" when passing through the City Hotel. Also, *Sun*, February 18, 1842 (reports Committee on Claims rejected Lake's bill for $13); *Sun*, December 20, 1842 and November 6, 1845 and advertisement repeated many times over the years, sometimes, for example, under the title "Wonderful Discovery," *Sun*, July 15, 1846; "Read This Wonderful Cures! Lake's Solution," *Maryland Republican*, January 27, 1855, and other dates through November 5, 1862.

141. R. G. Dun and Company Credit Report Volumes, 2:9 (Moses Lake), Microfilm no. 84–1014, Reel 10, Baker Library Historical Collections, Harvard Business School, Boston, Massachusetts; 1850 Federal Slave Schedule, Annapolis, 3 (right-hand column); Assessment of Negro Slaves in the City of Annapolis, June 11, 1860, MSA M72–4. Lake's name does not appear in Owner Index, Card Index 35, Search Room, MSA.

142. *Sun*, March 23, 1870; Account of Sales and Inventory (Moses Lake), vol. 1 (1868–72), 320–21, Register of Wills, Anne Arundel County, MSA C88–28; Esther Lowe, "Autobiography of Mrs. Enoch Louis Lowe." The brief periods were when Lake was not a barber at the Naval Academy in 1850 and during the Civil War when the Naval Academy relocated to Rhode Island. The location of the shop was noted in *Sun*, February 14, 1848. The writer—F—exclaimed "and who should I find as master of ceremonies but worthy Moses Lake, with his inimitable jampooning [*sic*] brightening up the ideas of embryo heroes—and I speak from practical experience when I say that jampooning, under such scientific hands, is a luxury fit for a eastern king."

143. "U.S. Tax Assessment Lists, 1862–1918", Annapolis, 1864, 97 (Effin Lake), and 1865, 142 (Effie Lake and Moses Lake), accessed various dates, Ancestry.com.

144. Dun credit report. Account of Sales and Inventory (Moses Lake), vol. 1 (1868–72), 321; Register of Wills, Anne Arundel County, MSA C88–28; William Bishop Answers, Folder 2, Case 167 (Moses Lake), Equity Papers, Register of Wills, Anne Arundel County, MSA C70–84.

145. Annapolis Passes, Old Book 294, Part 4, Entry 1535 (July 3, 1861); Old Book 309, Part 4, Entry 1536 (May 16, 1864), War Department, Provost Marshal General Office, Middle Department [Annapolis]; Old Book 288, Middle Department [Annapolis], Part 4, Entry 1537 (June 14, 1864 and June 27, 1864), and Old Book 309, Middle Department [Annapolis], Part 4, Entry 1538 (March 3, 1865), all in RG 393, NARA.

146. Interment Register B#2 (March 21, 1870). Augustine Freitag was officiating priest. Definition of Extreme Unction from Redemptorist Fathers, *The Mission-Book of the Congregation of the Most Holy Redeemer: A Manual of Instructions and Prayers Adapted to Preserve the Fruits of the Mission*, New, Revised, and Enlarged Edition (Baltimore: Kelly, Hedian, and Piet, 1863), 243.

147. Interrogatory of Moses Spriggs, filed December 5, 1870; claims paid, among many others, January 3, 1871, $150.29 to Drs. John and William Govane Ridout, and $22.60 to Rachel Smothers for an unspecified debt, filed May 9, 1871, Moses Lake Equity Papers. *Sun*, December 4, 1869; *Annapolis Gazette*, December 9, 1869; *Sun*, March 23, 1870; *Annapolis Gazette*, March 24, 1870. Also, Interment Register B#2 (November 20, 1869 for Mary Effine; December 2, 1869 for Mary Augusta; March 21, 1870 for Moses). Baptismal Register B#1 (August 3, 1856—Margaret, September 7, 1856—Charlotte [the granddaughter], and May 17, 1857—Elizabeth).

148. Moses Spriggs' bill, at rate of $45.00 per month for total $135.00 plus additional twenty-five-cent charge for "passing & probate"; Moses Lake Equity Papers; Last Will and Testament of Moses Lake, Wills (1866–71), Register of Wills, Anne Arundel County, MSA C155-46; Elisha Caution bill (in behalf of daughter Catherine), Lake Equity Papers, at the rate of $2.50 per week for a total of $35.00 (fourteen weeks). Mary Helmsly [*sic*] listed in 1860 census as Black female, age 10, born Maryland, attending school within the year, as occupant of Lake's dwelling. Rachel Smothers bill, May 3, 1870, Moses Lake Equity Papers. Her total account $61.60½, of which $27.60 still owed. The only charge that listed a good was $1.00 for lard on unspecified date.

149. Hurst, "Pre-Civil War Annapolis," 244, identifies Magruder as pro-Union. He was a nephew of John and Alexander Randall, McIntire 1:445.

150. Annapolis Passes (June 27–September 27, 1861), NARA.

151 Annapolis Passes (July 31, 1861, September 3, September 13, 1861), NARA.

152. *Chronica Domus* I:158 (July 22, 1861) for the three lay brothers; I:159 (August 10-14, 1861) for the annual exams; I:160 (September 6, 1861) for dismissed candidate P. Schmitt. The only name in the pass book that is similar to P. Schmitt is Phillip Smith who was granted a pass on September 6 on the recommendation of Governor Hicks, but unlikely the same man since P. Schmitt arrived at St. Mary's that same day.

153. *Chronica Domus* I:157 (June 1861) says: "At the beginning of this month Father Jacobs came to Annapolis." Marriage Register B#1 (June 15, 1861); Baptismal Register B#1 (July 14, 1861, September 8, 1861).

154. Baptismal Register B#1 (various dates between August 17, 1856 and October 26, 1865); B#2 (July 1, 1866 baptisms). The Confirmation Register is included in B#2 (January 29, 1866).

155. Rachel, born June 10, 1821, daughter of Susanna and sister of Henry Smithers [sic]. born June 21, 1823, in Jacob Franklin Accounts, 1702–1818, Anne Arundel County, Maryland, MS 282, Maryland History Society, partially transcribed and

analyzed in Douglass F. Hayman Jr., "Franklin Account Book—Part II: The Slaves of the Franklin Family of Oakland, A Plantation of West River: A Genealogy," *Anne Arundel Readings* 4, no. 1 (January 2001): 12–17; Assessment of Negro Slaves in the City of Annapolis, June 11, 1860, MSA M72–4; Maryland Historical Trust, "History of the State House and Its Dome" (2007), accessed September 29, 2015, http://msa.maryland.gov/msa/mdstatehouse/html/story.html; "John Shaw House," MIHP AA–689, accessed April 15, 2015, https://mht.maryland.gov/secure/medusa/PDF/AnneArundel/AA-689.pdf; McIntire, 1:250; Federal censuses 1820–50 for Annapolis.

156. Anne Arundel County Slave Statistics, District 6 (Annapolis), MSA C142. Rachel Smothers' name (and variants) also does not appear Anne Arundel County slave indexes 33, 34, and 35 in the MSA search room, nor in "Anne Arundel County, Manumission Record, 1848–66," *Archives of Maryland Online,* vol. 832, accessed February 27, 2018, http://aomol.msa.maryland.gov/megafile/msa/speccol/sc2900/sc2908/000001/000832/html/index.html. Also, 1880 Federal Census, Annapolis. See Thomas Franklin (1786–1865), Genealogy at Pitard.net, accessed April 27, 2015 https://ancestors.pitard.net/getperson.php?personID=I3331&tree=1sttree; Maryland Historical Trust, "John Shaw House," Section 8:5 and unnumbered "Chain of Title 21 State Circle" pages; "James S. Franklin," *Archives of Maryland* (Biographical Series), accessed January 17, 2015, https://msa.maryland.gov/msa/speccol/sc3500/sc3520/013800/013843/html/msa13843.html; "City of Annapolis," map 3, in Griffith Morgan Hopkins Jr., *Atlas of Fifteen Miles Around Baltimore, Including Anne Arundel County, Maryland* (Philadelphia: G. M. Hopkins, 1878).

157. *Evening Capital,* June 5, 1899,

158. Baptismal Register B#1 (February 12, 1859, May 8, 1859, June 26, 1859, July 14, 1861, September 8, 1861). Eliza Harris was confirmed January 29, 1860, Confirmation Record B#1. Interment Register D#1 (May 28, 1913) reports that Eliza died of "Valvular Heart Disease."

159. Baptismal Register B#1 (July 3, 1864, February 27, 1865, July 6, 1865, September 12, 1865, November 28, 1865); Confirmation Register B#2 (January 29, 1866). Martha's own confirmation, December 8, 1864. Baptismal Register B#1 (December 9, 1855, May 28, 1864, June 12, 1864; Confirmation Register B#1 (March 29, 1857). No ostensibly religious artifacts were found in archaeological testing and excavations at the house in 1990–92, Mark P. Leone and Mark S. Warner, "Final Archaeological Investigations at the Maynard-Burgess House (18AP64): An 1850–1980 African-American Household in Annapolis, Maryland," AP64 Artifact Catalog, Digital Repository at University of Maryland, 1995, accessed May 20, 2015, https://drum.lib.umd.edu/handle/1903/11023. Also, Warner, *Eating in the Side Room,* 4–9. Warner's book addresses Maynard-Burgess families at 167 Duke of Gloucester Street. Although he does not mention David and Martha Maynard, he does mention Maria Phebe Spencer and granddaughter, Phebe Ann Spencer, both Catholic converts who lived in house owned by John and Maria Maynard. Maria Maynard was the mother of Phebe Ann Spencer. Baptismal Register B#1 (August 7, 1859).

160. Interment Register B#2 (June 13, 1866–Martha Maynard who died "Without Sacr'ts, but well prepared"), (November 20, 1869–Mary Lake who received "Last Sacraments [and] died a saintly death"); D#1 (May 28, 1913–Eliza Harris).

161. *Chronica Domus* I:158 (July 22, 1861); Wuest, *Annales,* IV:2:465.

162. *Maryland Republican,* May 18, 1861.

163. *Maryland Republican,* May 18, 1861.

164. *Maryland Republican,* September 14, 1861.

165. *Maryland Republican,* September 14, 1861.

166. *Maryland Republican,* October 26, 1861.

167. *Maryland Republican* May 18, 1861; US Army Center of Military History, "Baltimore 1814," *CMH News and Features,* September 2014, accessed May 25, 2015, http://history.army.mil/news/2014/140900a_baltimore1814.html. For later references, see *Annapolis Gazette,* May 12, 1864; *Sun,* May 3, 1864, which report Major Thomas J. Wilson, paymaster, US Army, detached from Army of the Cumberland, arrived in Annapolis for new assignment as paymaster for general hospitals and Camp Parole.

168. *Annapolis Gazette,* September 5, 1861.

169. *Maryland Republican,* May 18, 1861 and September 14, 1861; *Annapolis Gazette,* September 12, 1861.

170. *Annapolis Gazette,* August 8, 1861, September 5, 1861, October 10, 1861.

171. *Annapolis Gazette,* October 10, 1861. Augustus Williamson Bradford (1806–81) took office, January 1862. Baker, *Politics of Continuity,* 69; *Maryland Republican,* October 26, 1861; *Annapolis Gazette,* November 7, 1861.

172. Baptismal Register B#1 (July 14, 1861). Infant John Walton died three months later, see "Died," *Annapolis Gazette,* October 10, 1861, 2. See 1860 Federal Census, Baltimore County, Third Electoral District, Pikesville, Post Office for Bartol's residence.

173. *Chronica Domus* I:159 (August 10–14, 1861).

174. *Chronica Domus* I:159 (August 16, 1861).

175. *Chronica Domus* I:159 (August 28, 1861), I:160 (September 2, 1861).

176. Ancestry.com search on January 4, 2011, revealed two possibilities. One was a Nicholas E. Ladde who was assessed a $1.00 excise tax in District Columbia for 1865. The other was Easton Ladd, age 21, born Virginia, lived with (presumably his mother) Harriet Ladd (Harriet Ladde in the 1865 tax assessment), in 4th Ward of District of Columbia, according to Federal Census taken on August 4, 1860. Coincidently, Mathias Alig's parish church, St. Mary's, was located at 372 Fifth Street Northwest, in the 4th Ward.

177. *History of St. Mary's Church of the Mother of God, Washington, DC, 1845–1945,* 2d ed. (Washington: St. Mary's Church, 1946), 13–14, 32. Page 18 says the construction cost for the

church was "between $45,000 and $50,000, most of which was paid by Father Alig." The current St. Mary's Church is located at 372 Fifth Street Northwest. Also, Spalding, *Premier See*, 138; Michael J. Curley, C.Ss.R., *Venerable John Neumann, C.Ss.R.: Fourth Bishop of Philadelphia* (New York: Redemptorist Fathers, Baltimore Province, 1952), 116, 123-24, and 136; Curley, *Provincial Story*, 91–92, 110; Wuest, *Annales*, IV:2:496; *Album Prov. C.Ss.R. Americanae*, page 1 of priests. For examples of overnight visits by the Annapolis Redemptorists, see *Chronica Domus* I:186 (March 19, 1862), I:228 (June 24, 1863), I:229 (July 22, 1863), I:257 (August 3, August 16 and 26, 1864), I:268 (November 1, 1864).

178. Wuest, *Annales*, IV:2:459. Bausch ordained June 29, 1869, pastor of Immaculate Conception Church, Johnstown, Pennsylvania, for nineteen years, died in Johnstown, May 17, 1917, and buried in Immaculate Conception Cemetery. Kearful ordained 1872 in cathedral in St. Joseph, Missouri, spent five years in St. Joseph diocese then served as itinerant missionary in Kansas, 1878–95, returned to Diocese of St. Joseph 1896, worked in several parishes until retirement 1923, died of pneumonia, St. Joseph, January 4, 1924, is buried Mount Olivet Cemetery, St. Joseph. Necrology: Father Charles Kearful, Diocese of Dodge City, Kansas, accessed February 18, 2013, https://www.dcdiocese.org/images/necrology/KearfulCharles1-4-24.pdf.

179. *Chronica Domus* I:160 (September 17–20, September 21, 1861); Wuest, *Annales*, IV:1:277.

180. *Chronica Domus* I:159–60 (August 15, September 10, 1861), I:160 (September 17–20, 1861), I:160 (September 21, 1861), I:161 (September 23, 1861); Wuest, *Annales*, IV:1:277 and IV:2:285.

181. *Chronica Domus* I:161 (September 29, 1861). In the original text, *Reise in's Idearreich* [Journey into the Kingdom of Ideas] was written in old German script. Email Carl Hoegerl, C.Ss.R., to author, December 2, 2010, discussing this passage, said: "This fits in with the immediate previous [sentence]. Frater Kammer gave a speech for the name day of Father Michael Müller, the superior, which was very full of ideas about a journey of a certain very learned man into the realm of ideas, which he called Journey into the Kingdom of Ideas."

182. Teresa De Jesús (1515–82, Teresa Sánchez de Cepeda y Ahumada), discalced (shoeless) Carmelite nun whose feast day of October 15; also known as St. Teresa of Ávila, Doctor of the Church, an honor conferred by Pope Paul VI in 1970. *Metropolitan Catholic Almanac*, 1855–59, various pages; *Statuta Visitationis Canonicae for House of Studies Cumberland (1851–1862) and Annapolis (1862–1868)*, also titled *Statuta et Decreta, Cumberland–Annapolis (Statuta et Decreta)*, RABP, canonical visitations for 1861, 1862, and 1869 refer to St. Teresa. This volume was transferred from SMPA to RABP on March 26, 2018. Also, *Chronica Domus* I:161 (October 15, 1861).

183. *Chronica Domus* I:162 (October 24, 1861); Wuest, *Annales*, IV:2:458–59.

184. *Chronica Domus* I:162 (no date, after October 24, 1861).

185. *Chronica Domus* I:162 (no date, after October 24, 1861); *Province Annals, 1832–1871*, 472 (1861, Annapolis), RABP; *Catalogus Novitiorum* I:46 and II:238 (which includes Vincent's signature); annual "Familia Domus" entries in *Chronica Domus* 1862–72; Borgmann, *Redemptorists at Annapolis*, 242.

186. *Chronica Domus* I:162 (November n.d., 1861); Wuest, *Annales*, IV:1:278–86.

187. Chronicles of the House of Studies, Cumberland, 35 (n.d. 1856); Wuest, *Annales*, IV:1:281–82.

188. "O'Donoughue, Rev. Charles C.Ss.R.," in Joseph Wuest, C.Ss.R., and Antoninus Wilmer. O.M. Cap., "Register of the Clergy Laboring in the Archdiocese of New York From Early Missionary Times," 102, in *United States Catholic Historical Society: Historical Records and Studies*, eds. Joseph F. Delany, Stephen Farrelly, and Thomas F. Meehan, 11 (December 1917) (New York: The Society, 1917), 98–112; *Chronica Domus* I:90 (July 7, 1858), I:91 (August 15, 1858), I:111 (August 18,1859); Wuest, *Annales*, IV:2:452.

189. Wuest, *Annales*, IV:1:283, says Harvey arrived in May 24, 1861. *Chronica Domus* I:157 (June 21, 1861) reports the date used here.

190. "Recessus: Visitationis Canonicae habitae in domo nostra ad Sta. Teresia Annapolis a die 24 Novis ad diem 2um Decis 1861", in *Statuta et Decreta*, 190–91, RABP. At the end visitation entry: "Note Well. This book of Regulations was in Cumberland before, but was brought to Annapolis with the transfer of the students." It is not clear if *Statuta et Decreta* was in Cumberland when De Dycker wrote the 1861 guidelines for Annapolis. The November 24–December 2, 1861, visitation is another indication of omission from the *Chronica Domus* which failed to record it or any events for December 1861, instead leaving seventeen blank pages (163–80).

191. Spalding, *Premier See*, 161, for comment about *Katholische Volkszeitung*, which began publication in 1860. Also, *New-York Freeman's Journal and Catholic Register* (*New-York Freeman's Journal*, April 24, 1858, (states Redemptorist Convent Annapolis paid $2.50 for subscription until February 11, 1859), and November 11, 1865 (lists Father Claessens of Annapolis, subscriber paid $3.00 through August 23, 1866); also July 3, 1847 (Sparks, Iglehart, Lake, DuBois), June 15, 1850, (DuBois as agent).

192. Conversation between Rev. Joseph Oppitz, C.Ss.R., and author, Esopus, New York, October 21, 1987. Father Oppitz was a member of the second novitiate class of 1955–56.

193. Recessus, November 24–December 2, 1861, *Statuta et Decreta*, 191, RABP.

194. Recessus, November 24–December 2, 1861, 191.

195. Sergeant Chauncey Holcomb, Camp Springfield, Maryland, to Dear Friends at Home, November 23–25, 1861, "Soldier Studies: Civil War Voices," accessed July 1, 2015, http://www.soldierstudies.org/index.php?action=view_letter&Letter=1184; Massachusetts 150 Sesquicentennial Commission, "The 27th Massachusetts Regiment Leaves Springfield," accessed July 1, 2015, https://www.ma150.org/day-by-day/1861-11-02/27th-massachusetts-regiment-leaves-springfield.

196. Ambrose E. Burnside, *The Burnside Expedition* (Providence: N. Bangs Williams, 1882), 7–8; David E. Long, "Burnside When He was Brilliant: Ambrose Burnside and the Union Combined Operations in Pamlico Sound," in *Union Combined Operations in the Civil War*, ed. Craig L. Symonds (New York: Fordham University Press, 2010), 20–21; Daniel Read Larned, City Hotel, Annapolis, to Dear Henry, December 27, 1861 (two letters of the same date), Larned Papers; City Hotel, H. R. & E. Walton, proprietors, receipt for Room No. 17, December 18, 1861–January 8, 1862 (Gen. A. E. Burnside for Mr. Larned, for "21 days & ½ fire @ $2.25, Tea lodging & Bft $1.50" for a total of $48.75, Generals Papers (Burnside), Box 5, Entry 159F, RG 94, NARA. The file also contains receipts for seven other staff officers. File 1277, Box 230, Entry 22, Congressional Jurisdiction Case Files, 1884–1943, Records of the United States Court of Claims, RG 123, NARA.

197. Receipt for City Hotel room no. 52, January 9, 1862, $397.28, included room and board, and a $2.00 cash loan, for Burnside and wife, Larned, and ten staff; a second receipt for November 17, 1861–January 8, 1862, for $226.49, covering the Burnside's board (at $4.50 a day), food, beverages, washing, and his orderly sergeant's room and board, Generals Papers (Burnside), NARA. Also, William Marvel, *Burnside* (Chapel Hill: University of North Carolina Press, 1991), 39–41; Larned, City Hotel, Annapolis, to Henry, December 18 and 21, 1861; Larned to Amelia R. Larned, New Haven, December 19, 1861; Larned to Dear Sister, December 22 and 27, 1861, Larned Papers. See "History of the Village of Thompson, Connecticut," accessed May 21, 2016, http://www.connecticutgenealogy.com/windham/history_village_thompson.htm, for Stiles Tavern. Larned to Dear Sister, January 4, 1863, says that Burnside's office was then in a front room on the second floor of a brick building at the Naval Academy.

198. Larned, Coast Division Headquarters, Annapolis, to Dear Sister, December 29, 1861, Larned Papers.

199. Larned, City Hotel, Annapolis, to Dear Sister, December 24, 1861, Larned Papers; Augustus Woodbury, *Major General Ambrose E. Burnside and the Ninth Army Corps* (Providence: Sidney S. Rider and Brother, 1867), 263.

200. Berger, Annapolis, to Aunt and Sister, Prachatitz, Bohemia, undated but probably January 2, 1862, RABP. Berger referred to the visit to Annapolis of De Dycker, who "today" was to return to Baltimore. *Chronica Domus* I:183 (January 1, 1862) notes De Dycker arrived December 31, 1861, and was to leave for Baltimore January 2, 1862.

201. *Province Annals*, 1832–1871, 473 (1861, Annapolis), RABP.

202. Margaret M. Smith, to Susie Sands, October 31, 1861, Dowsett Collection, quoting Susie's Annapolis "great confusion" statement, and undated letter of Smith to Sands, enclosed in same to Jane Holland Sands, December 29, 1861, quoting Susie's "depredation" comment. Margaret Smith addressed Jane Sands as "Aunt."

Chapter 4: 1862 — Sworn to the Ministry of Peace

1. *Maryland Republican*, June 15, 1862; Mitchell and Baker, *Civil War in Maryland Reconsidered*, 2, 86–87.
2. Berger, Annapolis, to Aunt and Sister, Prachatitz, Bohemia, no date, probably January 2, 1862.
3. Curley, *Provincial Story*, 145.
4. McWilliams, *Annapolis*, 174–75; John S. Carbone, *The Civil War in Coastal North Carolina* (Raleigh: Office of Archives and History, North Carolina Department of Cultural Resources, 2001), 28–30; Long, "Burnside When He was Brilliant," 11, 13–14; Daniel R. Ballou, *The Military Services of Maj.-Gen. Ambrose Everett Burnside in the Civil War, And their Value as an Asset of His Country and Its History*, Seventh Series, No. 8 (Providence: Rhode Island Soldiers and Sailors Historical Society, 1914), 15–17; Marvel, *Burnside*, 41; James M. McPherson, *War on the Water: The Union and Confederate Navies, 1861–1865* (Chapel Hill: University of North Carolina Press, 2012), 50–56; David C. Skaggs, "A Thorn, Not a Dagger: Strategic Implications of Ambrose Burnside's North Carolina Campaign," in Symonds, *Union Combined Operations*, 27. For the "Dixie" reference see Larned, Coast Division Headquarters, Annapolis, to Dear Sister, January 4–6, 1863, Larned Papers.
5. Private Joseph B. Farnam, Co. I, Eighth Connecticut Infantry Regiment, US Army Hospital, Annapolis, to Dear Seth, February 8, 1862, letter seen for sale at Back Creek Books, 45 West Street, Annapolis, June 14, 2011; Sergeant Chauncey Holcomb, Co. F, Twenty-Seventh Massachusetts Infantry Regiment, Camp Springfield, Maryland, to Dear Friends at Home, November 23, 1861, Civil War Soldiers Letters and Diaries Archive, accessed December 2, 2015 http://www.soldierstudies.org/; August 19, 1862; McWilliams, *Annapolis*, 177.
6. "Familia Domus", *Chronica Domus* I:182 (January 1, 1862).
7. *Chronica Domus* I:183 (January 3 and 4, 1862).
8. *Chronica Domus* I:183 (January 7, 1862). Jacob Engel Personnel File, RABP; Wuest, , IV:2:464. For the date of Engel's arrival, see "New York Passenger Lists, 1820–1957," accessed August 2, 2012, Ancestry.com, which lists Jacob Engel age 21, born Bavaria and arrived New York City from Le Havre on *La Duchesse d'Orleans* September 17, 1851. Another Jacob Engel, born in Bavaria, arrived in New York in 1852 but his age (24) and being accompanied by family members do not as closely match Brother Jacobs' circumstances. For his Annapolis investiture, see *Liber Vestitutiones Provinciae*, May 15, 1853.
9. *Album Provinciae C.Ss.R. Americanae*, 18; *Catalogus Novitiorum* II:61; Wuest, *Annales*, IV:2:455 and 464; *Chronica Domus* I:169 (September 29, 1861); Borgmann, *Redemptorists at Annapolis*, 235–36; *Chronica Domus* I:182 (January 3, 1862), I:234 (November 30, 1863).
10. Seelos to Antonia Seelos and family members, October

12, December 3 and 18, 1862, Letter 119, Hoegerl, *Sincerely, Seelos,* 313; Wuest, *Annales,* IV:2:451 (Peter Zimmer); *Chronica Domus* I:184 (January 19, 1862); Peter Zimmer Personnel File, RABP.

11. *Chronica Domus* I:182 (January 8, 1862).
12. Joseph Jacobs, Ex-C.Ss.R. File, RAPD; Baptismal Register B#2 (July 7, 1868 and July 12, 1868); Wuest, *Annales,* IV:2:451. The 1873 supposition is based on Jacob's May 24, 1873, application as a US naturalized citizen for a passport to go abroad. See "U.S. Passport Applications, 1795–1925," accessed August 2, 2012, Ancestry.com; Curley, *Cheerful Ascetic,* 163–64, 295, 302 (notes that a dying Seelos warned Jacobs he might loose his vocation as a Redemptorist unless he mended his social-minded ways).
13. *Chronica Domus* I:183 (January 12, 1862), I:187 (April 14 and 20, 1862), I:188 (April 26, 1862).
14. File 2878, AGO 1862, filed with B78, AGO 1862, Letters Received by the Office of the Adjutant General, 1861–1870, Roll 75, Microfilm Publication M619, NARA, includes endorsements between Lorenzo Thomas and Assistant Secretary of War Peter H. Watson.
15. Lincoln to Hughes, October 21, 1861, in Roy O. Basler, ed., *The Collected Works of Abraham Lincoln* (New Brunswick, New Jersey: Rutgers University Press, 1953), 4:560; Lincoln to F. M. Magrath, October 30, 1861, *Collected Works,* 5:8–9; United State Christian Commission, *Second Annual Report, 1863* (Philadelphia: The Commission, 1864), 14–15; Brinsfield, *Faith in the Fight,* 21–22.
16. Certificate (June 20, 1862), signed Francis Patrick, Archbishop of Baltimore, James Bradley Personnel File, RABP.
17. *Chronica Domus* I:183 (January 12, 1862–Ziegler); *Liber Vestitutiones Provinciae, 1858* (Annapolis–Hartmann); *Chronica Domus* I:182 (January 1, 1862), I:183 (January 14, 1862), I:184 (January 30, 1862), I:187 (April 14, 1862).
18. *Chronica Domus* I:184 (January 31,1862), I:192 (May 19, 1862), I:202 (September 12, 1862); United States, Superintendent of the Census, *Statistics of the United States (Including Mortality, Property &c.) in 1860; Compiled from the Original Returns of the Eighth Census, Under the Direction of the Secretary of the Interior* (Washington: Government Printing Office, 1866), 24.
19. *Chronica Domus* I:182 (January 1, 1862), I:195 (June 14, 1862), I:196 (June 30, 1862), I:203 (September 23, 1862), I:207 (December 23, 1862).
20. *Constitutiones et Regulae Congregationis Sacerdotum sub Titulo Sanctimissimi Redemptoris* (Rome: Typis S. Congreg. de Prop. Fide, 1861), RABP. St. Alphonsus wrote original Rule and Constitutions, for which he sought papal recognition in 1748. See *The Apostolic Life of Redemptorists: Constitutions of the Congregation of the Most Holy Redeemer, Letters of Approbation* (Rome: 1982–2002), accessed January 20, 2016, https://www.cssr.news/redemptorists-2/rule-of-life-2/constitutions/. Nicolas Mauron was superior general, also called rector major (1855–93). *Chronica Domus* I:184 (February 1, 3, 7, and 8, 1862); Stebbing, *The Redemptorists,* 11, 44.
21. *Chronica Domus* I:185 (February 11 and 21, 1862); *Catalogus Novitiorum* I:44; "Joseph Michael Dreisch," accessed March 15, 2013, http://www.geni.com/people/Joseph-Dreisch/5049456590560038107; Wuest, *Annales,* IV:2:459; Federal Census 1880 and 1900, Baltimore; *Polk's City Directory for Baltimore, 1907,* 564.
22. *Chronica Domus* I:185 (February 21–25, 1862). Information on "Little Christmas" tradition was imparted in email from John Harrison, C.Ss.R., St. Mary's, Annapolis, to author, February 4, 2011.
23. *Chronica Domus* I:185 (March 4, 1862) and I:186 (March 10, 1862).
24. *Chronica Domus* I:158 (July 27, 1861) and I:186 (March 10, 1862).
25. *Chronica Domus* I:183 (January 6, 1862), I:186 (March 15, 1862), I:197 (July 11, 1862).
26. *Chronica Domus* I:161 (October 15, 1861).
27. Henry Jacobs' name appears twice in *Liber Vestitutiones Provinciae,* in 1860 and October 15, 1861; *Chronica Domus* I:158 (July 27, 1861) and I:186 (March 10, 1862); "Death of Father Jacobs" *Manitowoc Pilot,* April 21, 1881, accessed March 17, 2013, http://www.2manitowoc.com/43Hrobit.html#jacobsrevhenry. Information on Mattingly at St. Bonaventure College in 1869–71 provided in email of Dennis Frank, St. Bonaventure University Archives, to author, April 1, 2013; Diocese of Scranton: *Sadliers' Catholic Directory, 1883, 66; Records of the American Catholic Historical Society of Philadelphia, 17 (1906): 248.* For Centner, see 1880 Federal Census, Pittsburgh, and Find A Grave Memorial ID 43096362 for his death (1913). For Kenning, see "Ontario, Canada Marriages 1801–1928" for 1889 marriage to Mary Walker Dunn; "Cook County Illinois Death Index 1878–1922" for Kenning's 1917 death, both accessed March 8, 2013, Ancestry.com.
28. *Chronica Domus* I:187 (April 7–8, 1862).
29. *Chronica Domus* I:185 (March 2, 1862), I:186 (March 19,1862).
30. *Chronica Domus* I:185 (March 21, 1862).
31. *Chronica Domus* I:187 (note following April 14, 1862).
32. *Chronica Domus* I:187 (April 20, 1862), I:188 (April 26 and 28, 1862), I:196 (June 16, 1862), I:197 (July 14, 1862), I:221 (January 2, 1863), I:224 (March 2, 1863). For soldiers named Martin Burke, see "American Civil War Soldiers" and "U.S. Army, Register of Enlistments, 1798–1914," accessed March 8, 2011, Ancestry.com. Emails to author from Trappist archivists in Rogersville, New Brunswick (February 23, 2014), Spencer, Massachusetts (March 14, 2014), Gethsemani, Kentucky (August 18, 2015) confirmed no record of Martin Burke.
33. *Chronica Domus* I:188 (April 28, 1862). For description of O'Connor's career, see his personnel file, RABP. Wuest and Wilmer, "Register of the Clergy Laboring in the Archdiocese of New York From Early Missionary Times," in *United States Catholic Historical Society: Historical Records and Studies,* 11 (December 1917): 101; *Sadliers' Catholic Almanac,* 1866, 59; John F. Byrne C.Ss.R., *The Glories of Mary in Boston: A Memorial History of the Church of Our Lady of Perpetual Help* (Mission Church), Roxbury, Mass., 1871–1921 (Boston:

Mission Church Press, 1921), 518–22.

34. O'Connor, Cumberland, to Mr. Geratty, September 30, 1862, O'Connor Personnel File, RABP. The debates, which drew national attention at the time, were held January 13–21, 1837, between Bishop of Cincinnati John B. Purcell and Church of Christ minister Alexander Campbell. See Carroll Brook Ellis. "Background to the Campbell-Purcell Religious Debates of 1837," *Southern Speech Journal* 11, no. 2 (1945): 32.
35. *Liber Vestitutiones Provinciae,* November 13, 1861; *Chronica Domus* I:192 (June 10, 1862); Chronicles of the House of Studies, Cumberland, 104 (June 14, 1862); *Metropolitan Catholic Almanac,* 1860, 115; A. J. Davis, *History of Clarion County Pennsylvania* (Syracuse: D. Mason, 1887), 523; *Sadliers' Catholic Almanac, 1864,* 188, and 1865, 195; *Pacific Coast Business Directory for 1867,* accessed August 21, 2012, Ancestry.com; 1870 Federal Census, Chilton, Calumet County, Wisconsin; Sadliers' Catholic Directory, 1875, 204; 1880 Federal Census, Eagle Harbor Township, Keweenaw County, Michigan; Antoine Ivan Resek, *History of the Diocese of Sault Ste. Marie and Marquette* (Houghton, Michigan, 1906), I:341; History of the Upper Peninsula of Michigan (Chicago: *Historical Company,* 1883).
36. *Maryland Republican,* September 20, 1862.
37. Farnam to Dear Seth, February 8, 1862; *Maryland Republican,* May 10, 1862.
38. James H. Clark, *The Iron Hearted Regiment: Being An Account of the Battles, Marches and Gallant Deeds Performed by the 115th Regiment* (Albany, New York: J. Munsell, 1865), 32.
39. Seelos to family, October 12, December 3 and 18, 1862, Letter 119, Hoegerl, *Sincerely, Seelos,* 314; Borgmann, *Redemptorists at Annapolis,* 117; John Himmelheber's bill, Moses Lake Equity Papers, MSA, "for the digging of the three graves, Mr. & Mrs. Lake & Daughter $15.00." For Himmelheber residency in the old Jesuit rectory, see Jacob Engel Personnel File, RABP, which says to "reach the sacristy [of the old church] he [Rumpler] had to pass through the house (of the family) of Mr. John Himmelheber, who was employed by the community." For Prince George Street see NHG 6:385 (July 3, 1857), AACLR; Annapolis Mayor and Aldermen, Property Assessment, June 11, 1860, MSA M72–3, lists John Himelheber [*sic*] House & Lot P. Geo. St. 500 Total 500; and GEG 3:93 (May 20, 1867), AACLR; Maryland Historical Trust, "Brice B. Brewer House, 172 Green Street, Annapolis," MHIP AA–515, accessed February 16, 2015, https://mht.maryland.gov/secure/medusa/PDF/AnneArundel/AA-515.pdf. Email of Judy Himmelheber Dohner to author, August 5, 2011, about Himmelheber's guard service.
40. *Philadelphia Inquirer,* January 18, 1862; "51st New York Infantry Regiment (Union)," and "Edward Rice (Union)," ACWRDB, accessed September 13, 2011 (gives Rice's age as 35); Prisoner Record No. 5687, Maryland Penitentiary Prisoner Records, MSA S275–2, which gives his age as 40 and his birthplace, workplace, and trade.
41. *Sun,* January 14, 1862.
42. Baptismal Register B#1 (March 30, 1858, June 1, 1859, and December 9, 1860). The infants for whom Michael and Maria Weinberger were godparents were baptized February 10, 1858 (Clara Eisenreda), June 14, 1858 (George Beller), and March 25, 1860 (Michael Beller). Xavier and Anna Beller served as godparents for the Weinberger children. 1900 Federal Census, Dayton, Ohio, lists Mrs. Weinberger, widow, gave birth to seven children but failed to record how many were living. Besides the four who lived in Annapolis, two others are listed in the 1880 census: Anne (age 12) and Michael (age 14), both born in Ohio. Helene [*sic*] was the only child listed with her parents in 1860 Federal Census, Annapolis. John was not born yet and Maria and Anna may have died. However, there are no St. Mary's burial records for them. "Baltimore Passenger and Immigration Lists, 1820–72," accessed August 20, 2015, Ancestry.com, lists Passenger No. 233 Michael Weinberger, age 34, male carpenter, native of Bavaria and destination Missouri, having departed Bremen on *Bremerhaven,* arrived Baltimore May 3, 1853. There are no other Weinbergers listed with him and no Michael Weinberger has been found in Missouri. Michael Weinberger, a native of Bavaria, living in Anne Arundel County, was naturalized in Baltimore in 1852 or 1853 (FamilySearch metadata says October 26, 1852, but an index card has October 26, 1853, see Index to Naturalization Petitions to the US Circuit and District Courts for Maryland, 1797–1951, NARA Publication M1168, Roll 17, RG 21, NARA. Michael Weinberger was recorded as "non naturalized (overruled)" by the city election judges in Judges' Poll Book for Election of Mayor and 5 Aldermen, April 2, 1860, page 4, no. 77, accessed February 19, 2012, http://www.msa.md.gov/megafile/msa/muagser/m1/m32/000000/000049/pdf/m32-000049.pdf.
43. John Fabian Witt, *Lincoln's Code: The Laws of War in American History* (New York: Free Press, 2012), 269 and 450 n269, lists three of the thirteen cases. Rice's name does not appear in Court Martial Index, II-OO Series, 1859–68 (Raab–Szink), Entry 15, Records of the Judge Advocate General's Office (Army), RG 153, NARA. Crystal N. Feimster, "Rape and Justice in the Civil War," *New York Times Opinion Pages,* accessed April 25, 2013, https://opinionator.blogs.nytimes.com/2013/04/25/rape-and-justice-in-the-civil-war/, offers the 450 figure.
44. Baptismal Registers B#1 (December 25, 1862) and B#2 (August 20, 1866). The Rice trial is recorded under Presentments, Anne Arundel County Court Docket, April Term 1862, Case No. 4, MSA C625–21. Henry Medford Sr. is also listed among petit jurors called for the April term but did not serve, as indicated by the absence of calendar entries for him. Guinzburg is listed in the 1860 Federal Census, Annapolis, as age 34, merchant with a personal estate of $2,000, born in Bohemia. *Haversack,* April 6, 1864, advertised A. M. Guinzburg's Clothing House at the corner of Main Street and Market Space, selling "gentlemen's furnishing goods, military equipments, city made boots, felt caps and hats—with ornaments, &c."

45. *Maryland Republican*, May 3, 1862; *Sun*, May 5 and 17, 1862, which repeated the May 5 *Maryland Republic* article; Prisoner Record No. 5687, MSA.
46. Anne Arundel County, Enrollment District No. 7 (Annapolis), September 19, 1862, Adjutant General (Enrollment Record), 1862–64, MSA S352–27; Old Book 309, Part 4, Entry 1536, May 6, 1864, No. 173 (Wineburgh), War Department, Provost Marshal General Office, Middle Department [Annapolis], RG 393, NARA; 1880 and 1900 Federal censuses, Dayton, Ohio. Alena (Lena) married Christopher Reindel, an immigrant from Baden, in 1872, and George Krebs, from Germany, in 1905.
47. Anne Arundel County Court Docket, April Term 1862, Case No. 26, MSA C625–21, the trial was held on April 26; *Maryland Republican*, May 3, 1862; Baptismal Register B#1 (December 25, 1862).
48. Anne Arundel County Court Docket, April Term 1862, Case No. 23, MSA C625–21. The trial held April 23 and 30. *Maryland Republican*, May 3, 1862; 1880 Federal Census, Annapolis, identifies Frazier as 45-year old Naval Academy laundry worker and wife of waterman Levin Frazier; McIntire 1:252, reports that two of Frazier's children served prison sentences. Baptismal Register B#1 (February 22, 1857—Emma Sophia Murdoch).
49. *Maryland Republican*, August 2 and December 20, 1862; *Sun*, July 24, 1862.
50. NHG 6:294 (April 9, 1856—London Town Farm), AACLR; Sandgate on the north extended just under four-tenths of a mile along today's West Street, from St. Mary's Cemetery to halfway between today's South Cherry Grove and South Southwood avenues; bounded on the east for about six-tenths of a mile from the cemetery to Spa Road and along the west side of Spa Road to about Silopanna Road; on the south below a small branch of Spa Creek, and on the west by land owned by Daniel Hart. See JHN 1:264 (August 24, 1845). The oldest section of the cemetery was recorded in NHG 7:393 (October 13, 1858).
51. Part of Brushy Neck on the north bordered Sandgate; on east by Spa Road; on south and west it followed the original route of Chinquapin Round Road (now a section of Forest Drive); north on Chinquapin to southern boundary of Hart's land, see NHG 9:168 (April 17, 1860), AACLR. Daniel Larned, Annapolis, to Dear Sister, April 18, 1864, Larned Papers, for mention of the dinner board. Depositions, October 29–30, 1894, and November 3, 1894; US Court of Claims File 9419, Box 995, Entry 22, RG 123, NARA. The total acreage given in court testimony varies between 123 and 138 acres.
52. John Walton to Col. [Augustus] Morse, April 22, 1862, Microfilm Publication M345, Roll 278, Union Provost Marshals' File of Papers Relating to Individual Civilians, 1861–1867, War Department Collection of Confederate Records, RG 109, NARA; Walton to Secretary of War Edwin M. Stanton, September 10, 1862, endorsed by Annapolis mayor J. Wesley White, September 10, 1862, Letters Received by the Adjutant General's Office, 1860–1870, Roll 153, Microfilm Publication M619, RG 94, NARA; 1860 Slave Schedules for Annapolis and Second Election District of Anne Arundel County; United States Senate, Fifty-Fourth Congress, First Session, Committee on Claims, Report No. 1066 (To Accompany S.1421), May 26, 1896, accessed December 6, 2017, https://congressional.proquest.com/congressional/docview/t47.d48.3366_s.rp.1066; US Court of Claims File 9419. No response was noted on the endorsements to Walton's letter to Stanton nor was any found in Letters Sent by the Adjutant General's Office, January 23, 1862–October 31, 1863, Rolls 21 and 22, Microfilm Publication M565, NARA.
53. For Third Brigade troop strengths, see ACWRDB, accessed December 18, 2017; for entire expedition force of 13,000, see Robert M. Browning Jr., *Success is All that Was Expected: The South Atlantic Blockading Squadron During the Civil War* (Washington: Brassey's. 2002), 24. Sherman's stay at the City Hotel is mentioned in US Court of Claims File 9419.
54. Private John W. Warren, Field and Staff Company, Ninth Maine Infantry, Camp Walton, Annapolis, to Friend McDaniel, October 18, 1861, original loaned to author by Willard R. Mumford, Annapolis, now in Willard Mumford Collection, MSA SC 6244; *Waterbury American* (Waterbury, Connecticut), October 25, 1861, notes Connecticut men at Camp Walton who slept in unsatisfactory tents while others used more-substantial Sibley tents.
55. Ira Bisbee, Company F, Ninth Maine Infantry, Camp Walton, October 19, 1861, transcription in Mumford collection; Walton to Morse, April 22, 1862; Benjamin Franklin Whitten, off Fort Monroe, to Dear Sister, October 22–23, 1861, and Whitten. onboard Steamer *Coatracoales*, to unstated recipient, October 23, 1861, Box 1, Folder 1, Benjamin F. Whitten Papers, MSS 85476, Manuscript Division, LoC; US Court of Claims File 1277.
56. George W. Callum, *Biographical Register of Officers and Graduates of the U.S. Military Academy at West Point, N.Y.* (Boston: Houghton Mifflin, 1891), II:226; George Grenville Benedict, *Vermont in the Civil War: A History of the Part Taken by the Vermont Soldiers and Sailors in the War for the Union, 1861–5* (Burlington: Free Press Association, 1886), I:540–42; Horace Knights Ide and Elliott W. Hoffman, *History of the First Vermont Cavalry Volunteers in the War of the Great Rebellion* (Baltimore: Blue and Butternut, 2000), 20–22; Jeffrey D. Marshall, ed., *A War of the People: Vermont Civil War Letters* (Hanover, New Hampshire: University Press of New England, 1999), 63–64 quoting letter of Private William H. Daniels, Company I, 1st Vermont Cavalry, Camp Harris, to Friend Blake, February 16, 1862; George Grenville Benedict, *Vermont in the Civil War: A History of the Part Taken by the Vermont Soldiers and Sailors in the War for the Union, 1861–5* (Burlington: Free Press Association, 1886), I:540–42; Louis Napoleon Beaudry, *Historic Records of the Fifth New York Cavalry, First Ira Harris Guard*, 3d ed., enlarged (Albany: J. Mussel, 1868), 22; Vincent L. Burns, *The Fifth New Cavalry in the Civil War* (Jefferson, NC: McFarland, 2014), 20; Benjamin William Crowninshield, *A History of the First Regiment of*

Massachusetts Cavalry Volunteers (Boston: Houghton, Mifflin, 1891), 59, quoting Hatch to Lieutenant Colonel Horace Binney Sargent, commander, First Battalion, First Massachusetts Cavalry, Camp Harris, January 18,1862. The adjacent farm reference is from David Haight, "Parole Camp 2," with contributions by George Hughes, Jean Russo, and Jane McWilliams, e-file dated April 22, 2014, in author's file. For the board of inquiry, see US Court of Claims File 9419. For the Sunday service, see *Vermont Journal* (Windsor), January 18, 1862 (a letter from "Vermont Boy," Camp Harris, Annapolis, January 5, 1862).

57. Ide, *History of the First Vermont*, 22; *Vermont Journal* (Windsor), January 18, 1862; *Christian Messenger* (Montpelier, Vermont), February 6, 1862 (a letter from "O.P.Q.," Camp Harris, Annapolis, January 24, 1862). For ice pond location, see Louis Green, Anne Arundel County Surveyor, August 1892, map showing farm conditions between 1861 and 1864, in US Court of Claims File 9419; less clearly on US Coast Survey, "Chesapeake Bay from its Head to Potomac River" (Coast Chart No. 31) (Washington, US Coast Survey, 1861–62, LoC, accessed August 22, 2014, https://www.loc.gov/item/99447098/.
58. Corporal Frank J. Willis, Company A, Fifty-First New York Infantry, Camp Walton, October 19, 1861, transcription in Mumford collection; Walton to Morse, April 22, 1862; John K. Burlingame, comp., *History of the Fifth Regiment of Rhode Island Heavy Artillery: During Three Years and a Half Service in North Carolina, January 1862–June 1865* (Providence: Snow and Farnham, 1892), 9. For farm implements, see US Court of Claims File 9419.
59. US Court of Claims File 9419; *Mirror and Farmer* (Manchester, New Hampshire), October 26, 1861; *Portsmouth Journal of Literature and Politics* (Portsmouth, New Hampshire), October 26, 1861; Walton to Morse, April 22, 1862. Walton wrote, "I understand, [the government] paid $1.25 [to] $1.50 per panel, & I have only asked for $1 per panel, which Genl. Wright allowed one for the fence destroyed when he was here." Hatch wrote at least five letters to his father, Moses Porter Hatch in Oswego, New York, during his stay in Annapolis between December 27, 1861, and March 19, 1862, but said nothing about Annapolis or his camp grounds other than to say he was "sorry to leave here" but duty in the field called. See Hatch, Annapolis, to Dear Father, [Oswego, New York], March 19, 1862, John Porter Hatch Papers, MSS 25262, Manuscript Division, LoC.
60. Walton to Stanton, September 10, 1862; *Maryland Republican*, August 2, 1862.
61. US Court of Claims File 9419; McWilliams, *Annapolis*, 179; NHG 13:16 (December 30, 1864), AACLR.
62. *Maryland Republican*, September 20, 1862; Haight, "Parole Camp 2"; US Court of Claims Files 1277 and 9419.
63. Walton to Stanton, September 10, 1862.
64. Report of Brevet Brigadier General James Jackson Dana, to Brevet Major General Daniel Henry Rucker, Acting Quartermaster General, Washington, May 9,1867, which appears in two NARA files: Letters and Reports Sent by General Dana to the Quartermaster General, Entry 1037, Box 2, Volume 3, 782, RG 92; US Court of Claims Files 1277 and 9419; US Senate, Report No. 1066, May 26, 1896.
65. US Court of Claims Files 1277 and 9419; Special Order 20, Part XVIII, February 19, 1863, General Orders, War Department, 8th Army Corps, Part 4, Entry 2000, vol. 159:337, RG 393, NARA.
66. US Court of Claims File 1277. Walton's two farm tracts were assessed in 1867 at $9,000, about one-third of the market value.
67. US Court of Claims Files 1277 and 9419. Also, relative value of $17,085 calculated by MeasuringWorth Foundation, accessed July 22, 2020, https://www.measuringworth.com/.
68. US Court of Claims File 1277; *Sun*, February 1, 1876; US House of Representatives, Forty-Eighth Congress, First Session, Committee on War Claims, Report No. 661 (Heirs of John Walton), March 4, 1884, accessed December 6, 2017, https://congressional.proquest.com/congressional/docview/t47.d48.2255_h.rp.661.
69. The attorney was Thomas J. Wilson of Baltimore; it is not clear whether or not he was the same as *Annapolis Gazette* editor Thomas J. Wilson. For H.R. 8699, see Docket, Committee on War Claims, Nos. 1977–3231, entry 3076, May 10, 1886; Original House Bills Nos. 8663–8881, 49th Congress, Records of the United States House of Representatives, 1786–1990, RG 233, NARA; US Court of Claims Files 1277 and 9419 (for $28,609 claim). For background on the court, see United States Court of Federal Claims, "The People's Court" (2014 Court History Brochure), accessed January 2, 2018, https://www.uscfc.uscourts.gov/history-of-the-court. A NARA Consultation Room finding aid provides a case file number (1227) for John Walton in Entry 45, Records of the Court of Claims Section (Justice), RG 205, but no file was found, presumably its contents are filed instead with Court of Claims File 1277. Bowman Act (March 3, 1883, Statutes At Large: ch. 116, 22 Stat 485), accessed January 31, 2018, https://www.loc.gov/law/help/statutes-at-large/47th-congress/session-2/c47s2ch116.pdf, which was passed to strengthen the Court of Claims to relieve Congress from examining large numbers of private bills, see Center for Legislative Archives, NARA, ch. 6, accessed December 5, 2017, https://www.archives.gov/legislative/guide/house. The "no adequate remedy" statement appears in US Senate, Committee on Claims, Report No. 1066, May 26, 1896.
70. US Senate, Fifty-Third Congress, Third Session, S. 2005 (A Bill for the Relief of Henry R. Walton, Administrator of John Walton, Deceased), January 4, 1895; US Senate, Fifty-Fourth Congress, 1st Session, S. 1421 (A Bill for the relief of Henry R. Walton, Administrator of John Walton, deceased), January 8, 1896; Senate Committee on Claims, Report No. 1066, May 26, 1896; Senate Resolution 1421, May 26, 1896. Also, various abstracts, petitions, and motions, 1896–97, see US Court of Claims File 9419. The Tucker Act (March 3, 1887, Statutes At Large, ch. 359, 24 Stat 505), accessed January 31,

2018, https://www.loc.gov/law/help/statutes-at-large/49th-congress/session-2/c49s2ch359.pdf. The lawyers were Charles C. Lancaster and Francis Percival Dewees.

71. US Court of Claims File 9419; US Senate, Fifty-fifth Congress, Second Session, Document No. 310 (Henry R. Walton, Administrator), June 22, 1898.

72. Claims Allowed Under the Bowman and Tucker Acts (May 27, 1902, Statutes At Large, ch. 887 Stat. 207, Pub. L. 57–124), accessed January 31, 2018, https://www.loc.gov/law/help/statutes-at-large/57th-congress/session-1/c57s1ch887.pdf; *Sun*, March 19 and 20, 1900, January 7, 1901. December 5, 1901, November 13, 1903; Letter of Assistant Clerk of the Court of Claims to Speaker of the House of Representatives Joseph G. Cannon, December 8, 1906, transmitting a list of cases dismissed by the court for want of prosecution, including Case 1277 (John Walton, dismissed June 10, 1901), referred to the Committee on War Claims and ordered to be printed, Fifty-Ninth Congress, Second Session, Serial Set vol. 5152, Session vol. 49, H.Doc. 240, accessed January 10, 2018, http://docs.newsbank.com/s/Digital/sset2doc/SERIAL/1174CEDC19985A58/0D52805756D8EA80; *Congressional Record Containing the Proceedings and Debates of the Fifty-Seventh Congress, First Session* (Washington: Government Printing Office, 1902), Index to the Proceedings – House Bills, 35:338); *Congressional Record*, Senate, November 12, 1903, 217. For land sales, see SH 7:24 (January 3, 1873) and SH10:240 (March 3, 1876), to the Redemptorists, SH 9:328 (May 22, 1875), to John L. Benjamin, and SH 10:250 (March 8, 1875), AACLR, to John Henry Diefel. The amount of rent received by Walton stated in court documents varies from $4,691 to $4,860. The $20,379 claim was made July 17, 1894, US Court of Claims File 9419.

73. E. C. Taylor affidavit, April 27, 1878, in *George Brewer v. United States*, File 5008, Box 613, Entry 22, Congressional Jurisdiction Case Files, 1884–1943, Records of the United States Court of Claims, RG 123, NARA; deed GW 19:464 (January 10, 1901), AACLR; *Evening Capital*, June 23, 1911; for cemetery history, see Worden, *Saint Mary's*, 73–75.

74. John M. Buchanon to Horace Buchanon, from Ellerslie, near Cumberland, January 29, 1862, John M. Buchanon Collection, MS 2053, Maryland Center for History and Culture, quoted in Charles W. Mitchell, ed. *Maryland Voices of the Civil War* (Baltimore: Johns Hopkins University Press, 2007), 165; Zimmer, *Leben und Wirken*, 214 in original, 209 in translation; Curley, *Cheerful Ascetic*, 202; *Chronica Domus* I:185 (February 13,1862) in regard to the Seelos letter; Chronicles of the House of Studies, Cumberland, 99 (February 8, 1862), and 100 (March 28, 1862).

75. Annals, Ilchester, 1868–1902, 3, RABP; Curley, *Cheerful Ascetic*, 208–9; Day, "Studentates Weather the Storm," 228–29.

76. *Chronica Domus* I:191 (May 20 and 23, 1862); Chronicles of the House of Studies, Cumberland, 102 (May 18 and 21, 1862); Curley, *Cheerful Ascetic*, 209–10; Müller, Annapolis, to Mauron, Rome, May 31, 1862, cited in Curley, *Cheerful Ascetic*, 380 n33; Hoegerl, *Positio*, 2, Part 2, 1025–28.

77. *Chronica Domus* I:191 (May 26, 1862); Toomey, *War Came by Train*, 111; *Thirty-Sixth Annual Report of the President and Directors to the Stockholders of the Baltimore and Ohio Railroad Company for the Year Ending September 30, 1862* (Baltimore: J. B. Rose, 1864), 54, Archives, B&O Railroad Museum, Baltimore; Curley, *Cheerful Ascetic*, 210.

78. *Chronica Domus* I:191 (May 26, 1862), I:192 (June 9 and 12, 1862), and I:193 (June 16, 1862); Chronicles of the House of Studies, Cumberland, 103 (June 10, 1862); Hoegerl, *Positio*, 2, part 2, 1030.

79. Francis Arnold Theodore Heidenis (1845–86) appears in 1860, 1870, 1880 (married with a wife and daughter) Federal censuses for New York City, and in "New Jersey Deaths and Burial Index, 1798–1971" for Patterson, New Jersey, accessed July 27, 2012, Ancestry.com; *Chronica Domus* I:160 (September 10, 1861), I:161 (October 15, 1861), I:191 (May 26, 1862), I:250 (March 16, 1864), II:9 (March 30, 1865), II:71 (April 17,1868); Wuest, *Annales*, IV:2:460; *Fifty Years of SS. Peter and Paul's Church at Cumberland, Md. 1848-1898* (Cumberland: Cumberland Freie Press, 1898), 65; *History of Bedford, Somerset and Fulton Counties, Pennsylvania* (Chicago: Waterman, Watkins and Company, 1884), 589; Rev. John N. Bausch, Find A Grave Memorial ID 98682021. O.C.C. is the Order of Calced Carmelites.

80. *Chronica Domus* I:191 (May 31, 1862), I:200 (August 14 and August 18, 1862), I:205 (ca. October 15,1862), I:220 (January 1,1863), I:247 (January 1, 1864), I:254 (June 20, 1864).

81. *Chronica Domus* I:192 (June 12, 1862); Chronicles of the House of Studies, Cumberland, 103 (June 12, 1862); *Catalogus Novitiorum* I:5, June 9, 1851 (Steinfeldt's investiture) and October 15, 1859 (and profession). Also, *Chronica Domus* I:52 (December 6, 1855); 1860 Federal Census, Cumberland, Maryland; 1880 Federal Census, St. Clement's College, Ilchester, Howard County, Maryland; Borgmann, *Redemptorists at Annapolis*, 19; Wuest, *Annales*, IV:2:464. Brother Paul died at Ilchester, 1916. For Van de Braak, see Curley, *Provincial Story*, 118; *Chronica Domus* I:79 (September 1857) I:193 (June 14, 1862); Wuest, *Annales*, IV:2:446.

82. Dennis Frye, "Stonewall Stopped May 30, 1862 at Harpers Ferry," https://www.youtube.com/watch?v=5-_EvbXYSj0&t=31s; "Ten Facts About Harpers Ferry, 1859–1865," https://www.battlefields.org/learn/articles/10-facts-harpers-ferry, both accessed August 31, 2015; *Thirty-Fifth Annual Report of the President and Directors to the Stockholders of the Baltimore and Ohio Railroad Company for the Year Ending September 30, 1861* (Baltimore: William M. Innes, 1862), 47–48, Archives, B&O Railroad Museum, Baltimore.

83. Seelos to family, October 12, December and 18, 1862, Letter 119, Hoegerl, *Sincerely, Seelos*, 314. Sander, John W. Garrett, 142, says the railroad bridge at Harpers Ferry had been repaired by the end of March 1862; Toomey, *War Came By Train*, 110, says "the main line [between Harpers Ferry and Martinsburg was] put into service" during March 1862. However, the actual status of the bridge on June 13, 1862

is clarified in *Thirty-Sixth Annual Report . . . of Baltimore and Ohio Railroad*, 54–55.

84. *Chronica Domus* I:193 (June 14, 1862); *Maryland Republican*, July 4, 1862, reported Seelos' arrival.

85. Borgmann, *Redemptorists at Annapolis*, 42; *Chronica Domus* I:194 (June 14, 1862), I:196 (June 16, 1862).

86. Berger, Annapolis, to Aunt and Sister, before July 28, 1862, and to Aunt and Sister, June 29, 1862, RABP; reported the relocation of the communities between Cumberland and Annapolis and lists the number of community members under Seelos.

87. "Division of the Community at Annapolis made on 14th June 1862," in *Statuta et Decreta*, 164, RABP.

88. Curley, *Cheerful Ascetic*, 235; Hoegerl, *Positio*, 2, Part 2, 1041–42.

89. *Chronica Domus* I:187 (April 23,1862), I:193 (June 14, 1862), I:196 (June 26, 1862), I:197 (July 14, 1862). The quote is from Hoegerl, *With All Gentleness*, 401–2 and 551 n5, which cites Berger/Beck Correspondence, Text 1 (A collection of 67 texts containing information about Seelos, consisting of correspondence between John Berger, and Bernard Beck, who were working on the biography of Seelos). Henry Giesen was credited with the original Girardey and Seelos quotes.

90. Zimmer, *Leben und Wirken*, 222–23 (217 in translation); Hoegerl, *Positio*, 2, Part 2, 1124.

91. Zimmer, *Leben und Wirken*, 223 (217–18 in translation); Seelos, Annapolis, to Miss Mary, October 31, 1862, Letter 122, Hoegerl, *Sincerely, Seelos*, 331.

92. Zimmer, *Leben und Wirken*, 223 (218 in translation).

93. Seelos, Annapolis, to Miss Mary, [Pittsburgh?], listed in order of the quotations given: August 17, 1862 (Letter 114), August 28–September 7, 1862 (Letter 115), November 21, 1862 (Letter 124), May 23, 1863 (Letter 133), August 28–September 7, 1862 (Letter 115), May 23, 1863 (Letter 133), Hoegerl, *Sincerely, Seelos*, various pages.

94. Hoegerl and von Stamwitz, *Blessed Francis Xavier Seelos*, 91–92.

95. *Chronica Domus* I:206 (November 17 and 21, 1862); Müller, Annapolis, to Mauron, Rome, May 31, 1862, cited in Curley, *Cheerful Ascetic*, 382 n3, and Müller, Cumberland, to Mauron, July 25, 1862, 383 n1.

96. Seelos, Annapolis, to Hermann Hauschel, May 7, 1863, Letter 132, Hoegerl, *Sincerely, Seelos*, 350–51. Curley, *Cheerful Ascetic*, 235, which cites Dielemans, Annapolis, to Mauron, Rome, December 31, 1862, Redemptorist General Archives, Rome, also see 231–44; Hoegerl, *Positio*, 2, Part 2, 1031–37, 1040, 1044, 1046–47, and 1048, quoting Mauron, Rome, to Dielemans, Annapolis, May 2, 1863. James Keitz, C.Ss.R., "Our Studendate, 1862–1865" (circa 1887), quoted in full in Carl W. Hoegerl, C.Ss.R., "Blessed Francis Xavier Seelos: A New Biography" (2016 electronic manuscript in author's file), 28:11–18, but omitted from the published edition, Hoegerl, *With All Gentleness*, 408–10. Keitz (1841–1900) was ordained in 1865.

97. Hoegerl, *Positio*, 2, Part 2, 1048, quoting Mauron to Dielemans, May 2, 1863, and 1050, quoting Dielemans to Mauron, August 15, 1863; Keitz, "Our Studendate."

98. Lord, *They Fought for the Union*, 291.

99. *Chronica Domus* I:200 (August 11, 1862).

100. *Sun*, May 20, 1861; Thomas J. C. Williams, *History of Washington County, Maryland* (Chambersburg: J. M. Runk and L. R. Titsworth, 1906, reprinted Baltimore: Regional Publishing Company, 1968), 325; Parole of Judge John T. Mason, Baltimore, August 23, 1862, 8th Army and Middle Department, Provost Marshal Oaths of Allegiance, Box 10, RG 393, NARA.

101. *Chronica Domus* I:197 (July 11, 1862, July 14,1862, and July 29, 1862), I:202 (September 22, 1862); *Liber Vestitutiones Provinciae*, 1858 (Annapolis); *Province Annals*, 1832–1871, 505 (1862, Annapolis), RABP.

102. *Chronica Domus* I:200 (August 15, 1862) and I:200 (August 18, 1862).

103. Seelos to family, October 12, December 3 and 18, 1862, Letter 119, Hoegerl, *Sincerely, Seelos*, 312; Seelos, Baltimore, to Mother and Antonia [his sister], January 14, 1856, Letter 32, Hoegerl, *Sincerely, Seelos*, 108.

104. "About Guardian Angel, etc.," undated handwritten notes in Müller's Personnel File, RABP, 6.

105. Seelos to family, October 12, December 3 and 18, 1862, Letter 119, Hoegerl, *Sincerely, Seelos*, 322–23. This portion of the letter was specifically address to his brother Ambrose. Also, Seelos to Hauschel, November 12, 1862, Letter 123, Hoegerl, *Sincerely, Seelos*, 332–33. Hoegerl, *Positio*, 2, Part 2, 1049, identifies Hauschel as a former student. *Chronica Domus* I:61 (March 3, 1856) records the arrival at the Annapolis novitiate of Germanus Hauschel.

106. "Division of the Community" (June 14, 1862), *Statuta et Decreta*, 164, and "Canonical Visitation" (December 31, 1862), *Statuta et Decreta*, 193, RABP; Seelos, Annapolis, to Hauschel, November 12, 1862, Letter 123, Hoegerl, *Sincerely, Seelos*, 332–33.

107. Seelos to family, October 12, December 3 and 18, 1862; Seelos, Annapolis, to Hauschel, November 12, 1862; Gross, Jacksonville, Florida, to William Wayrich, [Rochester, New York?], February 16, 1868, RABP, as quoted in "William Gross, CSSR on Missions in the Deep South 1868," *Redemptorist North American Historical Bulletin*, December 2003, 4, accessed September 10, 2016, https://d2y1pz2y630308.cloudfront.net/29153/documents/2021/6/issue_20_-_2003_december.pdf.

108. Seelos to family, October 12, December 3 and 18, 1862.

109. Seelos to family, October 12, December 3 and 18, 1862.

110. Seelos to Antonia Seelos and family, October 12, December 3 and 18, 1862.

111. *Chronica Domus* I:202 (September 15 and September 22, 1862), I:202–3 (September n.d., 1862), I:206 (November 17, 1862).

112. Dolan, *American Catholic Parish*, 1:129, gives this description of lay activity for the South in general.

113. *Chronica Domus* I:191 (May 3, 1862), I:192 (May 31, 1862),

I:197 (July 6, 1862), I:200 (August 3, 1862); I:200 (August 28, 1862), I:202 (September 7, 1862), I:205 (October 5, 1862), I:206 (November 2, 1862), I:206 (December 7, 1862); Curley, *Venerable John Neumann,* 156; St. Alphonsus Annals, 1840–1903, 83, entry for 1862, RAPB; Toomey, *Annapolis and Elk Ridge Railroad,* 9.

114. *Chronica Domus* I:197 (June n.d., at end of month, 1862), I:230 (August 10, 1863), I:256 (July 26, 1864).

115. Francis A. Lord, *They Fought for the Union* (Harrisburg: Stackpole, 1960), 32; *Maryland Republican,* June 15, 1862.

116. Douglas, "A Visit to Camp Parole"; *Maryland Republican,* September 20, 1862, reported 12,000, and November 5, 1862, reported 10,000.

117. Hammond, *Army Chaplain's Manual,* 33–35.

118. Brinsfield, *Faith in the Fight,* viii; Rable, *God's Almost Chosen People,* 113, 120; Robert J. Miller, *Both Prayed to the Same God: Religion and Faith in the American Civil War* (Lanham, Maryland: Lexington Books, 2007), Miller, *Both Prayed to the Same God,* 98, 111.

119. Rable, *God's Almost Chosen People,* 160–61; Hammond, *Army Chaplain's Manual,* 87–102.

120. Hammond, *Army Chaplain's Manual,* 76–77; Rable, *God's Almost Chosen People,* 135–36; Miller, *Both Prayed to the Same God,* 42 and 87; Kurtz, *Excommunicated from the Union,* 78–79. *Sun,* February 15, 1865; Brinsfield, *Faith in the Fight,* 20–21. For *Manual of the Christian Soldier* (New York: Society of St. Vincent de Paul, 1861–62), see Miller, *Both Prayed to the Same God,* 271, which presumably is the same as *Manual of the Christian Soldier, Mostly Translated from the French [from "Manuel du soldat chrétien" by A.P.E. Guidée], and Borrowed Partly from Challoner's Garden of the Soul—Partly from Rev. Wm. Gahan's Manual of Catholic Piety* (Paris: Bailly, Divry, and Company, 1856), which itself was derived from *Enchiridion milites christiani, saluberrimis praeceptis refertum* written by Desiderius Erasmus of Rotterdam in 1503.

121. Seelos to Antonia Seelos and family, October 12, December 3 and 18, 1862.

122. Curley, *Cheerful Ascetic,* 235; Borgmann, *Redemptorists at Annapolis,* 39.

123. Sweetman, *Naval Academy,* 47. A reference to the chapel appears in *Crutch,* January 9, 1864, the weekly newspaper of General Hospital Division No. 1. An untitled notice in the same edition on page 4 indicates that religious services (presumably Protestant) were held Sundays at 3:00 and 7:00 PM and Wednesdays at 7:00 PM. Bible classes were held Fridays at 7:00 PM. *Haversack,* April 6, 1864, reported that religious services were held in St. John's Hospital College Hospital chapel on Sundays at 2:30 and 6:30 PM, prayers daily at 9:30 AM, and prayer meetings every Wednesday at 7:30 PM, page 4 notes that the USSC held religious services in the House of Delegates chamber in the State House every Sunday at 3:00 PM.

124. Toomey, *War Came by Train,* 125; Daniel Carroll Toomey, *The Civil War in Maryland,* 10th ed. (Baltimore: Toomey Press, 2000), 17, 65. The Battle of Antietam (or Sharpsburg) was fought September 16–17, 1862. Lincoln's trip occurred October 1–4. *Chronica Domus* I:205 (October 9, 1862).

125. Annapolis Index, Indexes to Field Records of Hospitals, 1821–1912, Entry 544, Box 3, RG 94, NARA.

126. Certificate of Declaration of Intent, Court of Common Pleas, Allegheny County, Pennsylvania, June 15, 1848; Naturalization Petition, US Circuit Court, Western District of Pennsylvania, October 6, 1852, Naturalization Petitions of the US District Court, 1820–1930, and Circuit Court, 1820–1911, for the Western District of Pennsylvania, Microfilm Publication M1537, NARA.

127. Lord, *They Fought for the Union,* 2–3; James W. Geary, *We Need Men: The Union Draft in the Civil War* (Dekalb: Northern Illinois University Press, 1991), 3, 7, 8; Walter Stahr, *Stanton: Lincoln's War Secretary* (New York: Simon and Schuster, 2017), 188; *Sun,* July 17 and July 18, 1862. There are no extant issues of the *Annapolis Gazette* or the *Maryland Republican* for the dates on which the draft law would have been reported.

128. US Congress, *Statutes at Large, Treaties, and Proclamations of the United States of America from December 5, 1859, to March 3, 1863,* ed. George P. Sanger (Boston: Little, Brown, 1863), vol. 12, 1862, chap. 201: 597–600, accessed September 10, 2016, http://www.loc.gov/law/help/statutes-at-large/36th-congress/c36.pdf; US Congress, 37th, Second Session, *Journal of the Senate of the United States of America (Washington: Government Printing Office, 1861* [*sic*]), 824, 836, 843–45, 862, 869–70. Also, Geary, We Need Men, xv, 3–4, 12, 22, 27; Barnet Schecter, *The Devil's Own Work: The Civil War Riots and the Fight to Reconstruct America* (New York: Walker and Company, 2005), 103, 272; *Sun,* August 29 and September 16, 1862, 4; Rable, *God's Almost Chosen People,* 149.

129. *Sun,* July 17, 1862, August 5, 8, 19, and 20, 1862.

130. Article 63, Militia, Sec. 1, *The Maryland Code: Public General Laws, Adopted by the Legislature of Maryland, January Session, 1860* (Baltimore: John Murphy, 1860), I:415–16. Geary, *We Need Men,* 36–37, discusses religious exemptions allowed to various states he studied: Michigan refused any religious exemptions and New York excused Quakers and clergy, as did Ohio but for a $200 fee.

131. Chapter 79, passed June 24, 1861, *Laws of the State of Maryland, Made and Passed At a Special Session of the General Assembly, Held at Frederick, April 26, 1861* (Annapolis: Elihu S. Riley, 1861), n.p.; "Exemptions from Draft," undated news clipping in file labeled 1862, Enrollment of 1862, Adjutant General (Civil War Papers), 1860–67, MSA S935–1. For 1862 see Chapter 276, Militia, *Supplement to the Maryland Code, Containing the Acts of the General Assembly Passed at the Extra Session of 1861, and the Regular Session of 1862* (Baltimore: John Murphy, 1862), I:55; *Laws of the State of Maryland, Made and Passed at a Session of the General Assembly Begun or Held at the City of Annapolis on the Third Day of December, 1861, and Ended on the Tenth Day of March, 1862* (Annapolis: Thomas J. Wilson, 1862), does not include any new militia acts. *Sun,* August 5, 1862, two articles, one

on the militia law, the other for text of Secretary of War Edwin M. Stanton's August 4, 1862 order.

132. *Sun*, August 13, 25, 26, and 27, and September 3, 1862.

133. *Sun*, July 21, 1862.

134. *Sun*, July 23 and 29, 1862.

135. Stanton to Bradford, August 1, 1862, Enrollment of 1862, Adjutant General (Civil War Papers), 1860–67, MSA S935–33; Bradford to Creswell, August 5, 1862, Enrollment of 1862, Adjutant General (Civil Wars Papers), 1860–67, MSA S935–31; War Department, Adjutant General's Office, Washington, DC, August 4, 1862, General Orders No. 94, Enrollment of 1862, Adjutant General (Civil War Papers), 1860–67, MSA S935–33; Geary, *We Need Men*, 27, 34.

136. "Regulations for the Enrollment and Draft of 300,000 Militia," General Orders No. 99, Adjutant General's Office, War Department, August 9, 1862, *Official Records of the Union and Confederate Armies*, series III, vol. 2 (Washington: Government Printing Office, 1899), 334. Stanton to Bradford, Annapolis, August 12, 1862, Enrollment of 1862, Adjutant General (Civil War Papers), 1862, MSA S935–33. *Sun*, August 13 and 18, 1862; Day, "Studentates Weather the Storm," 231–32, which implies that after the September visit by Thomas the Redemptorists were exempted based on Thomas' Order No. 99 issued in August.

137. *Sun*, August 14, 1862; Murdock, One Million Men, 8–10, 27; "Instructions to Commissioners of Enrollment & Draft," undated, file labeled Enrollment of 1862, Adjutant General (Civil War Papers), 1860–67, MSA S935–33.

138. Bradford to Lincoln, June 23, 1863, Abraham Lincoln Papers, Series 1, https://www.loc.gov/item/mal2434300/, Manuscript Division, LoC; Office of the Assistant Adjutant General and Superintendent of Enrollment, "A List of the Commissioners, Examining Surgeons, and Enrolling Officers of the State of Maryland," Adjutant General Papers (Civil War Enrollment and Draft of 1862 Papers), MSA S935–35; *Sun*, August 18, 19, 23, and 28, 1862; A.W. Chaney, Enrolling Officer, Annapolis, to John A. J. Cresswell [*sic*], Assistant Adjutant General, [Baltimore], August 28, 1862, Enrollment of 1862, Adjutant General (Civil War Papers), 1860–67, MSA S935–31.

139. Anne Arundel County, Enrollment District No. 7 (Annapolis), September 19, 1862, Adjutant General (Enrollment Record), 1862–64, MSA S352–27; *Chronica Domus* I:193–94 (1861), I:197 (1862), and I:219 (1863).

140. Wuest, *Annales*, IV:2:90; Murdock, *One Million Men*, Tables, 356. Of the 292,441 names drawn nationwide in the 1862 draft, only 9,881 men (3 percent) became conscripts, while 65 percent of those examined were released because of physical disability or hardship. Of the 88,171 men held to service, 52,288 paid the $300 commutation fee and another 26,002 provided substitutes. Between 1863 and 1865, only 13 percent (46,347) of those who entered the Union army did so as Federal conscripts. See Geary, *We Need Men*, 67, 84, 168.

141. *Chronica Domus* I:202 (September 1, 1862); Chaney to Cresswell [*sic*], September 3, 1862; *Sun*, August 14, 1862.

142. Stockett to Creswell, September 19, 1862, Adjutant General (Civil War Papers), 1860–67, MSA S935–3; *Maryland Republican*, September 20, 1862.

143. Borgmann, *Redemptorists at Annapolis*, 57; Bradley to Creswell, September 19, 1862, Adjutant General (Civil War Papers), 1860–67, MSA S935-3. A review of the John A. J. Creswell Papers, MSS 17236, Manuscript Division, LoC, did not uncover any information about the Bradley, Chaney, or Stockett correspondence.

144. Letters Sent by the Office of the Adjutant General, Main Series, 1800–1890, Roll 21 (January 23, 1862–January 31, 1863), Microfilm Publication M565, RG 94, NARA; *Chronica Domus* I:204 (September 1862); Wuest, *Annales*, IV:2:90, both identify Girardey as the chronicler. During the four days he was in Annapolis, Thomas sent 25 letters and telegrams which are transcribed in Letters Sent by the Office of the Adjutant General, Main Series, 1800–1890, roll 21 (January 23, 1862–January 31, 1863), Microfilm Publication M565, RG 94, NARA. A search for the orders allegedly sent after September 23 concerning the Redemptorist seminarians was made in the same series through December 31, 1862, with no result.

145. Stockett to Creswell, October 23, 1862 and November 11, 1862, Enrollment of 1862, Adjutant General (Civil War Papers), 1860–67, MSA S935–32.

146. *Sun*, October 24, 1862.

147. Distribution of Draft of 1862, October 1st 1862. Enrollment of 1862, Adjutant General (Civil War Papers), 1860–67, MSA S935–35; *Sun*, October 11, 1862.

148. *Sun*, October 1, 4, 8, 18, November 12, December 4 and 5, 1862, 2; *Chronica Domus* I:204 (September 1862); Riley, *Ancient City*, 314; Second Lieutenant George R. Verron, Assistant Provost Marshal, Annapolis, to Col. Adrian R. Root, Commanding, Annapolis, August 2, 1864, Records of the Provost Marshal General, Part 4, Entry 1530, Old Book 305, RG 393, NARA.

149. Adjutant General, Enrollment Record, 1862–64, Enrollment District 7 (Annapolis), MSA S352–27. Records for other Anne Arundel County Enrollment Districts are included in this tabulation, see MSA S362–21 through 25.

150. Brombley's name has many variations: Oram, Orem, Oren, and Orin and Brombly, Brumbley, Brumley, and Brummele. General Orders No. 26, Adjutant General's Office, Annapolis, July 8, 1864, unidentified newspaper clipping [not found in the *Sun*], Civil War Papers, Maryland Adjutant General, MSA S935–38; Baptismal Register B#1 (January 2, 1859—John Bapt. Brumbley, and January 30, 1859—Thomas William Airland); Annapolis, Election Judges (Poll Book) 1799–1885, MSA M32–49 (April 2, 1860), which lists no. 39, O. J. Brummele. Also, Enrollment District 7 (Annapolis), Adjutant General (Enrollment Record), 1862–64, MSA S352–27; National Park Service (NPS) Soldiers and Sailors Database, "5th Regiment, Maryland Infantry," accessed December 30, 2016, https://www.nps.gov/civilwar/search-battle-units-detail.htm; Compiled Military Service Record (Orem J. Brombly,

Co. B, 5th Maryland Infantry), RG 94, NARA; Pension File No. 409245 (Orinn J. Brombley), RG 15, NARA; 1900 and 1910 Federal Census, Meriden, Connecticut; hospital card, Department of Veteran's Affairs, State Archives RG 073, Connecticut State Library, Hartford; Find A Grave Memorial ID 12917564. His pension file notes he was married a second time, in 1894, in Meriden, by Rev. Vincent Burnell. A search of Meriden City directories between 1894 and 1898 failed to turn up a clergyman of any religious denomination with this or a similar name. A man named Oram J. Brumley, born about 1844, served in the Confederate First Maryland Infantry (1861) and Third (Lillard's) Tennessee Mounted Infantry (1864), and was captured, paroled, and assigned to the western frontier with the Second Regiment, US Volunteer Infantry (1864–65). Compiled Military Service Records (Confederate) (Oram J. Brumley, Co. B, 1st Maryland Infantry, and Co. D, 3rd Tennessee Mounted Infantry), RG 109, NARA; Compiled Military Service Record (US) Oram J. Brumley Co. H, 2nd US Volunteer Infantry), RG 94, NARA.

151. Revell to Creswell, October 9, 1862, Adjutant General (Civil War Papers), MSA S935–33; Enrollment District 7 (Annapolis), Adjutant General (Enrollment Record), 1862–64, MSA S352–27.

152. Confirmation Register B#1 (August 30, 1862).

153. McIntire 1:390, 734; "Sponsors of Bells," [circa 1859], last leaf of B#1; *Maryland Republican*, May 4, 1861 and May 3, 1862; 1860 Federal Slave Schedule, District 3, Anne Arundel County; "Joseph Kent (1779–1837)," *Archives of Maryland* (Biographical Series), MSA SC3520–1450, accessed September 13, 2015, http://msa.maryland.gov/megafile/msa/speccol/sc3500/sc3520/001400/001450/html/1450extbio.html; Baptismal Register B#1 (April 7, 1862, May 28, 1864) and Confirmation Register B#2 (December 8, 1864); "Maryland Soldiers in the Civil War," 2, accessed May 1, 2013, Ancestry.com.

154. 1860 and 1870 Federal censuses, Annapolis; Enrollment District 7 (Annapolis), Adjutant General (Enrollment Record), 1862–64, MSA S352–27 (John H. Clark of Annapolis, 38, waterman exempted for medical reasons); 1860 Judges' Poll Book 6 #155, Jno H Clark, accessed February 19, 2012, http://www.msa.md.gov/megafile/msa/muagser/m1/m32/000000/000049/pdf/m32-000049.pdf; *Annapolis Gazette*, October 12, 1865. Also, McIntire, 1:135, lists seven children but mistakenly considered Bessie who became Sister Mary Imelda, with no birth date, as different from Bridget, born December 23, 1866. Also, communication of Sister Dorothy Daiger, S.S.N.D., School Sisters of Notre Dame Archives, Baltimore, January 27, 2012, to author. Bridget/Bessie entered 1885, professed: July 31, 1897, died October 15, 1943.

155. Maryland Draft Enrollment, District 7, Annapolis, 1862, MSA S352–27; 1870 Federal Census, Annapolis; Interment Registers B#2 (January 31, 1883), D#1 (December 19, 1912).

156. Confirmation Register B#1 (August 30, 1862); Baptismal Register B#1 (October 12, 1862). The Curley family, with Mary Agnes, identified in Baltimore 1870 and 1880 Federal censuses. "Timothy Corley," listed as a veteran but no unit in the 1890 US Special Schedule Surviving Soldiers, Sailors, and Marines, and Widows in Baltimore. The 1910 census also identified him as a veteran. A Timothy Curley appears as a private in the rosters of Co. I, Third New Jersey Infantry, a three-month unit, and companies G and D, 104th Pennsylvania Infantry. There are numerous military pension records for men named John Mahan, but the St. Mary's John Mahan family was not found among them.

157. For Powers' November 2, 1852 watchman appointment, see undated typescript list of watchmen appointments, Office of the Superintendent, Letters Received by the Superintendent, 1845–1887, Folder 7, Box 6, Entry 25, RG 405, USNA. Also, Anne Arundel County Test Book, Oath of An Alien to Become a Citizen: April 5, 1854, and Declaration of Citizenship, April 5, 1856, MSA C147–1; Judges' Poll Book for Election of Mayor and Five Aldermen, April 2, 1860, 4:86, accessed February 19, 2012, http://www.msa.md.gov/megafile/msa/muagser/m1/m32/000000/000049/pdf/m32-000049.pdf; Annapolis Mayor and Aldermen, Property Assessment, June 11, 1860, MSA M72–3; *Annapolis Gazette*, September 20, 1860 and March 26, 1868; *Maryland Republican*, November 5, 1862; 1870 and 1900 Federal censuses, Annapolis; Interment Registers B#2 (September 9, 1904) and D#1 (April 18, 1915); McIntire 1:561. For Edward Powers' sponsorships, see Baptismal Register B#1 (May 24, 1863 and December 18, 1865). For Ann Ellen Dunn Powers' sponsorships, see Baptismal Register B#1 (April 24, 1859, January 29, 1860, June 7, 1860, April 13, 1863, December 13, 1863, and December 18, 1865); Baptismal Register B#2 (January 29, 1866). See Annals, Annapolis, 1900–1909, 314 (September 12, 1904), RABP, for the survivor comment.

158. Confirmation Register B#1 (August 30, 1863); Interment Register B#2 (October 30, 1875—John Parodi, and April 19, 1903—Susan Parodi); Presentments, Case No. 46, April 25, 1865, Docket, April Term 1865, Anne Arundel County Circuit Court, MSA C65–27; *Annapolis Gazette*, December 6, 1866; McIntire 1:542.

159. Baptismal Register B#1 (June 18, 1861, April 16,1862, and January 27, 1863). Other Denver children were baptized at St. Mary's with different godparents. One, fourteen-year-old Ann Elizabeth Denver was noted as *conversa ex Episcopalianismo Pater est catholicus nominalis; mater est Protestans* (convert from Episcopalianism; Father is nominal Catholic; mother is Protestant); see B#1 (June 16, 1859). For Julia's death information, see Interment Register B#2 (February 14, 1877); McIntire, 1:175.

160. Confirmation Register B#1 (August 30, 1862) and Baptismal Register B#1 (April 20, 1856—Gunning, and November 27, 1864—Carroll). Also, McIntire, 1:291, for the Gunning family; 1860 Federal Census, Anne Arundel County, District 2, Annapolis Post Office.

161. McIntire 1:75, 734; Marriage Register B#1 (July 29, 1857); Baptismal Register B#1 (October 24, 1860); *Annapolis Gazette*, September 20, 1860 and June 30, 1864; Maryland

Draft Enrollment, 1862; Draft Enrollment Records, Provost Marshal General Files, 1863; Old Book 256, Middle Department [Baltimore], Entry 1536, pass no. 199 issued May 6, 1864, to go to Round Bay; Old Book 309, Middle Department [Annapolis], Entry 1538, pass no. 8091 issued April 16, 1865, to go and return to his farm by boat, Part 4, RG 393, NARA; *Sun*, March 19, 1906.

162. Confirmation Register B#1 (August 30, 1863); Marriage Register B#1 (January 14, 1863 and June 2, 1866); Baptismal Register B#1 (August 14, 1863, July 11, 1865); Interment Register B#1 (August 15, 1863) and B#2 (March 7,1872, September 2, 1877, January 21, 1880, July 11, 1888); Baptismal Register B#4 (December 1, 1872); Anne Arundel Genealogical Society List 607, St. Mary's Cemetery, for Mary McCabe burial in 1918 near Henry Esmond. Also, for Bartholomew see 1860 Federal Census, Brooklyn, New York; "New York Civil War Muster Roll Abstracts 1861–1900," accessed August 21, 2013, Ancestry.com; *Documents of the Assembly of the State of New York One Hundred and Twenty-third Session, 1900, 9*, no. 58, part 2 (Albany: James B. Lyon, State Printer, 1900), 840; 1863 Draft Enrollment, Annapolis City, lists Esmond as a barkeeper; 1870 Federal Census, Annapolis; "History of the Police Department," accessed June 2, 2019, https://www.annapolis.gov/436/History-of-the-Police-Department; 1880 Federal Census, Annapolis, for Mary Esmond's children and domicile with John J. and Kate Riordan.

163. Baptismal Register B#1 (August 7, 1859); Marriage Register B#1 (November 18, 1859); Confirmation Register B#1 (August 30, 1862); Interment Register B#2 (March 31, 1885) says Francis Blackburn was "very neglectful but died with sacraments." Also, *Annapolis Gazette*, November 10, 1859; McIntire, 1:59, 331, 749.

164. Confirmation Register B#1 (August 30, 1862); McIntire, 1:206, 484; *Maryland Gazette*, August 27, 1835; 1850, 1860, 1870 Federal censuses for Annapolis.

165. Marriage Register B#1 (June 15, 1861, February 21, 1865); Draft Enrollment Records, 1863, Provost Marshal General Files; Baptismal Register B#1 (July 14, 1861), B#2 (May 13, 1866); 1870 and 1880 Federal censuses for Annapolis.

166. Baptismal Register B#1 (June 26, 1857, July 15, 1862, February 9, 1863, and April 11, 1863); Marriage Register (April 3, 1860—Mary Ann Lee's name was left blank in the record for Robert Campbell, who was identified James Robert Campbell's father in 1857); Confirmation Register (August 30, 1862). For Henrietta Anna Peake's baptism, see B#1 (August 25, 1861). 1850 Federal Census, Anne Arundel County District 1 (Owensville, West River, South River, Birdsville, Davidsonville); Interment Register B#2 (January 20, 1863—Sarah Jane Lee).

167. *Chronica Domus* I:200 (August 30–31, 1862), I:202 (September 1, 1862).

168. *Chronica Domus* I:201–2 (August 30, September 1, 1862) and I:202 (September 1, 1862); Wuest, *Annales*, IV:2:91. For information on minor orders, see "Minor Orders," Attwater, *Catholic Dictionary*, 323, "Tonsure," 497. The ecclesiastical privileges are: personal inviolability, a special court, immunity from certain burdens, and the right to a proper maintenance (*privilegium canonis, fori, immunitatis, competentiæ*). See Johannes Baptist Sägmüller, "Ecclesiastical Privileges," Catholic Encyclopedia, (New York: Robert Appleton Company, 1911–12), 12, accessed August 15, 2013, http://www.newadvent.org/cathen/12437a.htm.

169. "An Act for the Release of Certain Persons held to Service or Labor in the District of Columbia." See "Featured Documents: The D.C. Emancipation Act," accessed September 10, 2015 https://www.archives.gov/exhibits/featured-documents/dc-emancipation-act; Kate Masur, *An Example for All the Land: Emancipation and the Struggle over Equality in Washington, DC* (Chapel Hill: University of North Carolina Press, 2010), 25.

170. *Maryland Republican*, May 3, 1862, which reprinted April 24, 1862 *Annapolis Gazette* editorial and an article from *New York Caucasian*.

171. "Preliminary Emancipation Proclamation, September 22, 1862," accessed September 10, 2015, https://www.archives.gov/exhibits/american_originals_iv/sections/preliminary_emancipation_proclamation.html; March 13, 1862 law: Act Prohibiting the Return of Slaves" (12 Stat. 354); July 17, 1862 law: "An Act to Suppress Insurrection, to Punish Treason and Rebellion, to Seize and Confiscate Property of Rebels, and for Other Purposes" (12 Stat, 589).

172. *Maryland Republican*, October 4, 1862, quotes *Annapolis Gazette*, for which no issues are extant for the date.

173. "Reply to Emancipation Memorial Presented by Chicago Churches of All Denominations," September 13,1862, in Basler, *Collected Works*, 5:420.

174. Kurtz, *Excommunicated from the Union*, 99–100; Stahr, *Stanton*, 247.

175. Worden, *Saint Mary's*, 18; Curran, *Papist Devils*, 180; Russell, *My Diary North and South*, 491–93.

176. McConville, *Political Nativism*, 37–38; *Maryland Republican*, May 10, 1862; *Annapolis Gazette*, April 1, 1858. Email of Glenn Campbell, Historic Annapolis, to author, November 5, 2015, provided information from Howard Crise of Newton, Kansas, a descendant of William A. Spencer who rented Paca House. Crise's great-grandfather, Julian Murray Spencer, coincidently, lived at 104 Duke of Gloucester, a house rented in 1888 from the Redemptorists. For Spencer's tenure, see *Archives of Maryland* (Biographical Series): "William A. Spencer," MSA SC3520-13841, accessed November 30, 2015, http://msa.maryland.gov/megafile/msa/speccol/sc3500/sc3520/013800/013841/html/13841bio.html.

177. *Chronica Domus* I:203 (September 29, 1862) and I:222 (February [n.d.], 1863); Borgmann, *Redemptorists at Annapolis*, 57–58, 124–25.

178. *Maryland Republican* November 5, 1862.

179. Borgmann, *Redemptorists at Annapolis*, 58; Seelos to family, October 12, December 3 and 18, 1862, Letter 119, Hoegerl, *Sincerely, Seelos*, 313.

180. *Annapolis Gazette*, April 30, 1868.

181. Spalding, *Premier See*, 161; quotes from *Catholic Youth's Magazine* articles: "Preface to Volume I," 1, (1858), 3; "Introduction," 1, no. 1 (September 1857) 1; "Wicked Children," 1, no. 3 (November 1857): 110; "Gentle Words" and "Take Care of Your Thoughts," 114; "Useful Hints to House-Keepers," 4, no. 5 (January 1861): 279; "The Cannon," 4, no. 8 (April 1861): 248.

182. *Geneva Gazette*, August 28, 1833; email from Sister Virginia Baeder, RSM, Archivist, Mid-Atlantic Community, Sisters of Mercy of the Americas, Merion, Pennsylvania, to author, October 24, 2011; Blake McKelvey, "Canaltown: A Focus of Historical Tradition," *Rochester History* 37, no. 2 (April 1975): 1–24 (quote on page 9), accessed October 20, 2011, https://www.libraryweb.org/~rochhist/v37_1975/v37i2.pdf; W. H. McIntosh, *History of Monroe County, New York; with Illustrations Descriptive of its Scenery, Palatial Residences, Public Buildings, Fine Blocks and Important Manufactories.* (Philadelphia: Everts, Ensign and Everts, 1877), 47–48; 1860 Federal Census, Ward 6, Rochester, NY; Wuest, *Annales*, IV:2:456.

183. Baptismal Register B#1 (April 7, 1864).

184. Baptismal Register B#1 (February 1, 1863 and December 8, 1865); Marriage Register B#1 (September 29, 1864); Confirmation Register B#2 (December 8, 1864 and January 29, 1866); Joseph Wissel, C.Ss.R., Letter Book, 1864, RABP, notes a letter he wrote from Cumberland, August [n.d.], 1864, to Josephine O'Donoughue, Rochester, providing "encouragement for her to return to Annapolis."

185. Michael S. Burke, C.Ss.R., Annapolis, to Peter Frischbier, January 22, 1866, RABP. Frischbier was lector of philosophy at Cumberland and was transferred October 15, 1866, "*ad tempus*" to Annapolis until July 1867.

186. Email from Sister Virginia Baeder, RSM, to author, October 24, 2011; New York State 1875 Census, Kings County, Brooklyn, Convent of the Sisters of Mercy, accessed October 19, 2011, FamilySearch.org; *Sadliers' Catholic Directory, 1875*, 373; *New York Herald*, June 22, 1879; *Union and Advertiser* (Rochester), June 24, 1879; "Sisters," Donohoe's Magazine (Boston) 2, no. 3 (September 1, 1879): 286; "Obituaries," *Sadliers' Catholic Directory, 1880*, 38.

187. *Chronica Domus* II:84 (September 26, 1872), II:90 (January 23, 1873). Searches of *Catholic Mirror* and *Maryland Republican* did not reveal news reports about Sisters of Mercy in Annapolis in 1872–73.

188. For a full account of the Sisters of Mercy in Annapolis and the property transactions, see Worden, *St. Mary's*, 64– 65.

189. *American and Commercial Daily Advertiser* (Baltimore), March 10, 1851; *Maryland Republican*, January 27, 1855; *Sun*, March 26, 1860. For Francis' baptism, see Annapolis, June 11, 1820, "White March/Bowie Register of Baptisms, Marriages, Burials, 1818–1895," Box 3 Folder 3, Maryland Province Collection, GU-CSC; Widow's Pension Certificate No. 52157 provides May 17, 1839 marriage date by Rev. Job Guest, pastor of Methodist Church 1831–32 and 1839–40, per Cunningham, *Calvary United Methodist Church*, 86. For children's baptisms, see Baptismal Register B#1 (January 25, 1852, October 2, 1853, August 31, 1856, and June n.d., 1858). For Julia as godmother, see B#1 (June 18, 1861, April 16, 1862, and January 27, 1863), all children of Thomas Denver and Maria Sandsbury. Also, Confirmation Register B#1 (August 30, 1862) and B#2 (January 29, 1866); Marriage Register B#1 (September 29, 1864); *Maryland Republican*, October 8, 1864; 1860 Federal Census, Baltimore, lists Julia Daley and eight children, including Joseph, a printer's apprentice living with her relative Harriet Royston, a dressmaker; 1860 census, Annapolis, lists Joseph, an apprentice printer, living with his cousin, Elijah Button, Naval Academy pharmacist.

190. Joseph Daley Military Service Record, RG 94, NARA. The Fifth Maryland was assigned to Colonel Max Weber's Third Brigade, Brigadier General William Henry French's Third Division, Second Army Corps. Brian Downey, et al., "Antietam on the Web," accessed September 21, 2015, http://antietam.aotw.org/tablet.php?tablet_id=430; Scharf, *History of Western Maryland*, 309–10; Kathleen A. Ernst, *Too Afraid to Cry: Maryland Civilians in the Antietam Campaign* (Mechanicsburg, Pennsylvania: Stackpole Books, 1999), 6, 129; John W. Schildt, *Roads to Antietam*, 2d rev. printing (Shippensburg, Pennsylvania: Burd Street Press, 1997), 149; *The Union Army: A History of Military Affairs in the Loyal States 1861–65*, New York, Maryland, West Virginia and Ohio (Madison, Wisconsin: Federal Publishing Company, 1908), II:273.

191. Cynthia Parzych, *Antietam: A Guided Tour Through History* (Guilford, Connecticut: GPP Travel, 2009), 53; Schildt, *Roads to Antietam*, 149; D. Scott Hartwig, *To Antietam Creek: The Maryland Campaign of September 1862* (Baltimore: Johns Hopkins University Press, 2012), 605; Daniel A. Masters, "A Sharpsburg Resident's View of the Battle of Antietam, Maryland, September 17, 1862," *Maryland Historical Magazine* 10, no. 4 (Winter 2015): 490; "French's Division, Second Army Corps, 8 AM 17 September to 2 PM 17 September" (Historical Tablet), accessed September 21, 2015, http://antietam.aotw.org/tablet.php?tablet_id=400; Ernst, *Too Afraid to Cry*, 130.

192. Robert K. Krick, "It Appeared As Though Mutual Extermination Would Put a Stop to the Awful Carnage: Confederates in Sharpsburg's Bloody Lane," 223–24, 230, 231, 236, in Gary W. Gallagher, ed., *The Antietam Campaign* (Chapel Hill: University of North Carolina Press, 1999); Schildt, *Roads to Antietam*, 165; Ernst, *Too Afraid to Cry*, 143; Jeffrey D. Wert, *A Glorious Army: Robert E. Lee's Triumph, 1862–1863* (New York: Simon and Schuster, 2012), 138; David Cole, *Survey of U.S. Army Uniforms, Weapons, and Accoutrements* (Carlisle, Pennsylvania: US Army Center of Military History, 2007), 38; Widow's Pension Certificate No. 52157.

193. Masters, "A Sharpsburg Resident's View," 491, quoting Augustin A. Biggs, Sharpsburg, to Elijah Kalb, Rushville, Ohio, September 29, 1862; NPS, "Battle of Antietam," accessed September 22, 2015, http://www.nps.gov/anti/learn/historyculture/casualties.htm; Schildt, *Roads to Antietam*, 150; Ernst, *Too Afraid to Cry*, 144.

194. *Maryland Republican*, October 4, 1862.

195. *Sun*, September 22, 1862.

196. "Soldier's Pay in the American Civil War," quoting Mark M. Boatner's *Civil War Dictionary*, accessed September 23, 2015, http://www.civilwarhome.com/Pay.html; Widow's Pension Certificate No. 52157; McIntire 1:108, 577. One of the witness was St. Mary's parishioner Thomas Tydings. For burials see Interment Register B#2 (February 14, 1877—Julia Daley, April 14, 1885—Henry Royston Daley, August 3, 1897—Joseph Henry Moore, great-grandson, born and died 1897, and November 29, 1900—Harriet Ann Daley Treadway, 1855–1900); Interment Register D#1 (January 9, 1906—Amanda Daley Moore).

197. NPS, "Antietam National Cemetery, "accessed September 23, 2015, http://www.nps.gov/anti/learn/historyculture/antietam-national-cemetery-part-2.htm; Ernst, *Too Afraid to Cry*, 163, 165, 235. For known burials of Maryland soldiers, see Ralph E. Eshelman and A. Douglas Rawlinson, *Graven in Stone and Buried under the Shield: A Guide to Gravestones of Maryland's Civil War Veterans* (Annapolis: Maryland State Archives, 2019), accessed January 8, 2019, https://msa.maryland.gov/megafile/msa/speccol/sc6100/sc6197/000000/000001/000000/000003/pdf/mdsa_sc6197_1_3.pdf. An 1864 map depicts numerous temporary burial locations but none for the Fifth Maryland, H. H. Lloyd, "Map of the Battlefield of Antietam," New York Public Library Digital Collections, accessed July 21, 2020, http://digitalcollections.nypl.org/items/185f8270-0834-0136-3daa-6d29ad33124f; Miller, "Catholic Religion, Irish Ethnicity, and the American Civil War," 261.

198. Baptismal Register B#1 (July 18, 1865— Joseph Washington Moore, 1865–1948). Amanda Julia Daley Moore (1844–1906) married non-Catholic Henry P. Moore (1840–66), an Annapolis waterman, see Marriage Register B#1 (September 29, 1864); *Maryland Republican*, October 8, 1864.

199. *Chronica Domus* I:206 (November 9, 13, 23 and December 7, 1862). The Kenrick Papers, AAB, reveal that relatively few Civil War-era letters to Kenrick survive and no reference to the request or the presence of the Redemptorists at Fort Monroe was found. Baptismal Register B#1 (November 23, 1862) lists Henning's three Fort Monroe baptisms. For Heppel's military record, see NPS Soldiers and Sailors Database, http://www.nps.gov/civilwar/search-soldiers.htm; US Army Register of Enlistments, 1798–1914, Ancestry.com, ACWRDB, all accessed November 8, 2012. Mary Elizabeth Heppel later married John E. Wales in 1885, and lived in Norfolk, Virginia, and died there in 1933. See "Virginia, Select Marriages, 1785–1940," Ancestry.com; 1900, 1910, and 1920 Federal censuses for Norfolk; Find A Grave Memorial ID 63231368.

200. Curley, *Cheerful Ascetic*, 236, writes about Seelos' trip to Fort Monroe but is in error that he was accompanied by Henning. See Seelos to family, October 12, December 3 and 18, 1862, Letter 119, Hoegerl, *Sincerely, Seelos*, 324. A search of finding aids at NARA for RG 393, Part 4, Baltimore passes, revealed pass records issued in Baltimore are extant only for 1861 and 1866. Seelos to Hauschel, May 7, 1863, Letter 132, Hoegerl, Sincerely, Seelos, 350, identifies Anton [Anthony] Kesseler as his companion at Fort Monroe, adding "he anticipated all my needs with every mark of love and kindness." *Chronica Domus* I:206 (December 7, 1862) notes, without details, that Seelos was at Fort Monroe performing pastoral duties. Also, Shannon McCall, "St. Mary Star of the Sea Church History," accessed September 15, 2015, http://www.smsschurch.com/1600-1899.html.

201. There were at least four army hospitals: a four-ward clinic serving the Fort Monroe garrison; the commandeered Hygeia Hotel with 1,800 beds at Fort Monroe; dozens of buildings and tents at the Hampton Military Hospital—for enlisted men—on the site of the historically Black Hampton Normal and Agricultural Institute, now Hampton University); and at the abandoned four-story Chesapeake Female Seminary (Chesapeake Military Hospital, for officers), also in Hampton. See Mark St. John Erickson, "Civil War Spawns Huge Hampton Hospital," *Daily Press* (Newport News), August 17, 2012, http://www.dailypress.com/features/history/civilwar/dp-nws-civil-war-hospitals-20120817-story.html; "Hampton National Cemetery, Hampton, Virginia," http://www.nps.gov/nr/travel/national_cemeteries/virginia/Hampton_National_Cemetery.html, both accessed September 15, 2015.

202. Seelos to family, October 12, December 3 and 18, 1862, Letter 119, Hoegerl, *Sincerely, Seelos*, 325.

203. "McClellan, Ely," in John Rossiter, editor in chief, *The Biographical Dictionary of America* (Boston: American Biographical Society, 1906), VII:111.

204. Seelos to family, October 12, December 3 and 18, 1862, Letter 119, Hoegerl, *Sincerely, Seelos*, 326.

205. "Recessus: Canonical Visitation to our House at St. Teresia in Annapolis from the 21st day of December to the 31st of this month 1862," *Statuta et Decreta*, 192–93.

206. *Statuta et Decreta*, 195.

207. *Statuta et Decreta*, 192–94.

208. *Statuta et Decreta*, 192–93.

209. *Statuta et Decreta*, 192–93.

210. "From Annapolis, Md.," *Philadelphia Inquirer*, December 29, 1862, 3.

Chapter 5: 1863 — I Go to See Father Abraham

1. *Chronica Domus* I:221 (January 2, 1863), I:224 (March 2, 1863). Email from Brother Bernard Matthews, O.S.C., St. Joseph's Abbey, Spencer, Massachusetts, to author, March 14, 2014, said his abbey has the archive of Our Lady of Grace Abbey, Monastery, Nova Scotia, but the records do not include a Martin Burke/Brother Ambrose, entering the community at that time or later and speculated that he "may have arrived there, but left soon after." Also, "A Brief History of Our Lady of Grace Monastery," accessed August 18, 2015, https://

ourladyofgracemonastery.ca/about/.

2. *Chronica Domus* I:222 (February 25, 1863); Baptismal Register B#1 (November 30, 1862—James Monroe Hall). John and Adelina Hall also are listed in St. Mary's records for the baptisms of three other children: B#1 (June 21, 1857—Lucas, and July 20, 1865—Cecilia); B#2 (November 20, 1866—Henrietta).
3. Battle of Fair Oaks (May 31–June 1, 1862). Military Service Record (Luke Cavanaugh, Co. I, 63rd New York Infantry), RG 94, NARA; Carded Medical Records, (Luke Cavanaugh, Co. I, 63rd New York Infantry), Box 2154, Entry 534, RG 94, NARA. Another Luke Cavanaugh whose dates almost coincide with the Annapolis appearances at St. Mary's was a private with Company K, 2nd Michigan Infantry. See Widow's Pension File Application No. 225036, Certificate No. 911894, RG 15 (which indicates this Luke was Catholic); Carded Medical Records, (Luke Cavanaugh, Co. K, 2nd Michigan Infantry), Box 1409, Entry 534, RG 94, NARA.
4. Baptismal Register B#1 (May 1, 1863—Patrick Coolahan); 1860 Federal Census, Second Election District of Anne Arundel County; *Chronica Domus* I:227 (May 11, 1863).
5. *Chronica Domus* I:206 (November 13, 1862), I:221 (January 15, 1863), I:222 (February 27, 1863), I:223 (March n.d., listed before March 2), I:224 (March 23,1863), I:225 (April 6, 1863), I:226 (April 9, 1863); *Province Mission Book*, 1862–63, various pages, RABP.
6. *Chronica Domus* I:226 (April 9–10, 1863, footnote mentions Regan's arrival and departure).
7. *Chronica Domus* I:224 (March 24, 1863) and I:227 (May 18, 1863). Gustavus was not listed among the lay brothers in the *Province Annals*, 1832–1871, 534–35 (1863, Annapolis), RABP; Wuest, *Annales*, IV:2:461–65 has no one named Gustavus.
8. *Chronica Domus* I:228 (June 30, 1863), I:222 (January 28, 1863), I:247 (January 1, 1864), II:6 (January 1, 1865), II:32 (January 1, 1866), II:34 (April 13, 1866), II:44 (October 15, 1866), II:45 (November 9, 1866), II:66 (June n.d., 1867); *Liber Vestitutiones Provinciae* (December 23, 1861); *Liber Professionis*, 73 (brothers); *Album Provinciae C.Ss.R. Americanae*, 8 (brothers); 1850 Federal Census, Second Election District, Allegany County, Maryland; 1860 census; 1870 Federal Census, Ellicott City, Howard County, Maryland; 1881 Canada Census, Québec City; 1900 and 1910 Federal censuses for Baltimore City. For enrollment information, see Maryland Adjutant General, Enrollment Record, Enrollment District 6, Allegany County, Cumberland, MSA S352–7.
9. *Metropolitan Catholic Almanac, 1861*, 29–32; *Sadliers' Catholic Almanac, 1864*, 11.
10. *Metropolitan Catholic Almanac, 1861*, 29–32.
11. *Sun*, February 17, 1863.
12. *Chronica Domus* I:222 (February n.d., 1863).
13. Riley, *Ancient City*, 300; Annapolis Mayor and Aldermen (Proceedings) 1858–1861, MSA M49–7, entry for September 9, 1861, as cited in McWilliams, *Annapolis*, 174, 427 n142; letter of John R. Magruder, Mayor of Annapolis, to Col. C[arlos]. A. Waite, Commander, Department of Annapolis, December 31, 1863, with December 3, 1863 enclosures, Entry 225, Box 38, RG 92, NARA; William James McKnight, *Jefferson County, Pennsylvania: Her Pioneers and People, 1800–1915* (Chicago: J.H. Beers, 1917), 1:180.
14. General Orders No. 2, January 31, 1863, Lieutenant Colonel George Sangster, Commanding Post, Annapolis, General Orders, War Department, 8th Army Corps, Part 4, Entry 2000, vol. 159, RG 393, NARA; Brief on Loyalty for Claimant, Walton vs. U.S., November 8, 1894, US Court of Claims File 9419; *History and Roster of Maryland Volunteers, War of 1861–5* (Baltimore: Press of Guggenheimer, Weil and Company, 1898), I:460 and I:785 in *Archives of Maryland*, 367:460, accessed February 16, 2015, http://aomol.msa.maryland.gov/000001/000367/html/am367--460.html. For Keffer's City Hotel residency, US Court of Claims File 1277.
15. General Orders No. 2, January 31, 1863; *Chronica Domus* I:222 (January 17, 1863); Magruder, to Waite, December 31, 1863, and Magruder to Captain Gardner S. Blodgett, Quartermaster, Annapolis, January 22, 1864, Entry 225, Box 38, RG 92, NARA, suggesting $500 as a "moderate rent" per year since September 1861. Seelos to family, October 12, December 3 and 18, 1862, Letter 119, Hoegerl, *Sincerely, Seelos*, 326.
16. Louis N. Boudrye, *Historic Records of the Fifth New York Cavalry, First Ira Harris Guard: Its Organization, Marches, Raids, Scouts Engagements and General Services, During the Rebellion of 1861–1865*, 2nd edition (Albany, New York: S. R. Gray, 1865), 22.
17. *Chronica Domus* I:222 (February n.d., 1863).
18. *Liber Vestitutiones Provinciae* (October 15, 1856); *Catalogus Novitiorum* I:24 (October 15, 1856); *Catalogus Novitiorum* II:61 (March 19, 1858); *Album Provinciae C.Ss.R. Americanae*, which notes Kammer's birth on October 21, 1840, in Grosskarben and his parents' immigration; *Chronica Domus* I:192 (May 19, 1862), I:202 (September 12, 1863), I:222 (January 17, 1863).
19. Borgmann, *Redemptorists at Annapolis*, 236; *Chronica Domus* I:223 (February 27, 1863). Additional insights on the family were derived from a conversation between Father Joseph Francis Krastel, C.Ss.R., Herman's great-grand-nephew, and author, St. Mary's Rectory, October 14, 2011; St. Joseph's, Fullerton, Maryland. *Rejoice and Remember: The Community of St. Joseph's* (Hackensack, New Jersey: Custombook, 1972), 7; St. Joseph Fullerton, "Parish History," accessed October 11, 2011, https://www.stjoefullerton.org/connect/our-story. Spalding, *Premier See*, 138, puts the beginning of Redemptorist activity at Fullerton, for migrants from Hesse-Darmstadt, in 1850.
20. St. Peter's (Philadelphia) Annals I:50 (March 1, 1863), RABP.
21. Francis Xavier Tschenhens, C.Ss.R. (1801–77). The group arrived in New York City June 30, 1832, having traveled from Vienna to Trieste where they boarded the brig *Potomac*. For Annapolis information, see *Chronica Domus* I:227 (May 18 or 19, 1863). For Tschenhens, see *Minute Book 1813-1965* New York, item 5; Wuest, Annales, IV:2:445; Curley, *Provincial*

Story, 6–7; Curley, *Venerable John Neumann*, 84. He is buried at Most Holy Redeemer Cemetery, Baltimore, Find A Grave Memorial ID 148755215.

22. Geary, *We Need Men*, 17–18, 46, 52. Many of those AWOL had received advanced bounty payments and then deserted, reenlisted, and deserted several times. James B. Fry, Provost Marshal General, to Edwin M. Stanton, March 17, 1866, in *Official Records of the Union and Confederate Armies*, series III, vol. 5 (Washington: Government Printing Office, 1900), 599.
23. Michael Burlingame, ed. *Abraham Lincoln: The Observations of John G. Nicolay and John Hay*. Carbondale: Southern Illinois University Press, 2007), 119, 128ff; George A. Russell, "Leadership in Factious Times: Leading by Teaching," *The College* [St. John's College, Annapolis and Sante Fe] 42, no. 1 (Spring 2017): 17.
24. Schecter, *Devil's Own Work*, 102–3; *Sun*, February 5 and 10, 1863; John G. Nicolay and John Hay, *Abraham Lincoln: A History* (New York: Century Co., 1886, reprinted 1896 and 1914), VII:4; Matthew Pinsker, *Lincoln's Sanctuary: Abraham Lincoln and the Soldiers' Home* (New York: Oxford University Press, 2003), 97–98.
25. US Congress, 37th, 3rd Session, *Journal of the House of Representatives of the United States of America* (Washington: Government Printing Office, 1863), 478; "Conscription Bill Again," *Congressional Globe*, February 26, 1863, 1291–92; *Sun*, February 27 and March 3, 1863; Brooks, *Washington, D.C. in Lincoln's Time*, 288–91; Geary, *We Need Men*, 62–64; Noah Brooks, "Letter from Washington," February 25, 1863, published in the *Sacramento Daily Union*, March 28, 1863, quoted in Brooks, *Washington, D.C. in Lincoln's Time*, 286–87; US Congress, *Statutes at Large*, vol. 12, 1863, chap. 75: 731–37, accessed April 2, 2015, http://www.loc.gov/law/help/statutes-at-large/37th-congress/c37.pdf; US Congress, 37th, 3rd Session, *Journal of the Senate of the United States of America* (Washington: Government Printing Office, 1863), 220, 259, 264–68, 346, 371–74, 392, 393, 400, 402; Michael Burlingame, *The Inner World of Abraham Lincoln* (Urbana and Chicago: University of Illinois Press, 1994), 164–65.
26. Eugene C. Murdock, *One Million Men: The Civil War Draft in the North* (Madison: State Historical Society of Wisconsin, 1971), 6–7, 9; Michael Burlingame, *Abraham Lincoln: A Life* (Baltimore: Johns Hopkins University Press, 2008), II:526.
27. Geary, *We Need Men*, 50; US Congress, *Statutes at Large*, vol. 12, 1863 chap. 75:731–37.
28. Geary, *We Need Men*, 109, 138.
29. *Sun*, March 2, 3, and 11, 1863. There are no extant issues of the *Annapolis Gazette* from January to August 1863. Although five issues of the *Maryland Republican* between January 31 and April 25, 1863, are available, none mention the enrollment act. Also, *Chronica Domus* I:224 (March 13, 1863).
30. *Chronica Domus* I:224 (March 13, 1863); Elias Schauer, Annapolis, to Sister [probably in Allegheny, Pennsylvania], April n.d., 1863, Provincial File, RABP. The letter is a partial document, missing its first and last pages and erroneously labeled "April 1865." The 1850 Federal Census lists the Schauer family in Allegheny City, across the Allegheny and Ohio rivers from Pittsburgh.
31. *Chronica Domus* I:224 (March 13, 1863).
32. *Chronica Domus* I:224 (March 16–21, 1863); *Sun*, March 23, 1863. No issues of *Annapolis Gazette* or *Maryland Republican* are extant that would have reported this event. *Catholic Mirror*, March 28, 1863, copied an undated *Baltimore Daily Gazette* article on the event from its Annapolis correspondent. Schauer to Sister, April n.d., 1863, repeats the largest-number assertion; Curley, *Cheerful Ascetic*, 213, gives a short description of the ordinations.
33. Schauer to Sister, April n.d, 1863.
34. Full title: *Pontificale Romanum Clementis VIII et Urbani PP. VIII; Auctoritate Recognitum Nunc Denuo Cura Annibalis S. Clementus, Presb. Card. Albanus; Sanctae Romanae Ecclesiae Camerarii, & Vaticanae Basilicae Archipresbyteri editum, pro faciliori Pontificum, & et dictae Basiliae usu. In Tres Partes Divisum. Cum Figuris aeri incisis Rich. van Horly Pictore celebri. There have been many editions; this particular copy was* published in Brussels: Typis Georgii Fricx in 1735. *Chronica Domus* I:224 (March 21, 1863), refers to the ecclesiastical works. It is not clear from the context if "Baltimore" meant the Redemptorist provincial house in Baltimore (St. Alphonsus) or the Archdiocese of Baltimore. Borgmann, *Redemptorists at Annapolis*, 43, says, "As a remembrance of the joyful occasion," Kenrick gave Seelos "a number of old volumes of the Latin and Greek Fathers."
35. *Chronica Domus* I:226 (footnote at end of entries for April 1863).
36. *Chronica Domus* I:225 (March 25, March 27, March 29, April 5, 1863); First Council of Baltimore, *Manual of Ceremonies for the Use of the Catholic Churches in the United States of America*, 2nd ed. rev. (Baltimore: John Murphy and Company, 1852), 23, 60; Schauer to Sister, April n.d., 1863. Details on Gross' novitiate, seminary training, and early priesthood appear in Andrew H. Skeabeck, C.Ss.R., "Most Rev. William H. Gross, C.SS.R.: Missionary Bishop of the South," *Records of the American Catholic Historical Society of Philadelphia* 65:2 (June 1954), 102–15.
37. *Maryland Republican*, April 4, 1863.
38. Matilda Farquhar Sterling, Annapolis, to Anna Virginia Farquhar, Philadelphia, April 20, 1863, Box 1, Folder 2, Sterling Family Papers, https://hdl.handle.net/1903.1/9018.
39. *Catholic Mirror*, March 14, 1863
40. A column entitled "The War" appeared weekly in *Catholic Mirror*. See, for example, March 14, 1863, 3; and March 21, 1863, 3.
41. Kenneth J. Zanca, *The Catholics and Mrs. Mary Surratt* (Lanham, Maryland: University Press of America, 2008), 90; Frank Key Howard, *Fourteen Months in American Bastiles* (Baltimore: Kelly, Hedian, and Piet, 1863), 89 pp.; *New York Times*, September 30, 1863; *Sun*, October 5, 1863; *Catholic Mirror*, October 3, 1863; Bulla, "The Suppression of the Mid-Atlantic Copperhead Press," in Sachsman, *A Press Divided*, 243.

42. *Sun*, May 9, 1863.
43. *Sun*, May 20 and 21, 1863.
44. *Sun*, June 10 and 12, July 14, 1863; Geary, *We Need Men*, 103. Fry to Stanton, March 17, 1866, *Official Records of the Union and Confederate Armies*, series III, vol. 5, 599, 607, 611.
45. Names of Provost Marshals, Surgeons, and Commissioners, Provost Marshal General's Bureau, 1863–66, Part 1, Entry 80, various pages, RG 110, NARA. The office of Provost Marshal General was established by the act of Congress of March 3, 1863, and Fry was appointed to the position on March 17, 1863.
46. The representative in Congress in the Fifth District was former Maryland governor Francis Thomas (1799–1876), of the Unionist Party during the 37th Congress. He was succeeded in the 38th Congress by Benjamin G. Harris (1805–95), a Democrat from St. Mary's County, *Biographical Dictionary of the United States Congress.* Names of Provost Marshals, Surgeons, and Commissioners, Part 1, Entry 80, 43 (Fourth District) and 45 (Fifth District), Records of the Provost Marshal General's Bureau, 1863–66, RG 110, NARA; *Sun*, May 20, 1863; Geary, *We Need Men*, 73, 103.
47. Consolidated Lists, Class I and Class II, Fifth Congressional District (Anne Arundel, Charles, Prince George's, Howard, Montgomery, and St. Mary's counties), Entry 172, RG 110, NARA.
48. In 1862 James Revell requested that Maryland's twenty-two state's attorneys be exempted from the draft to attend to court business and serve as counsel to sheriffs, and constables who were exempted from the draft according to Maryland law. See Revell to Creswell, September 22, 1862, Adjutant General (Civil War Papers), 1860–67, MSA S935–3. Also, Consolidated Lists, Entry 172, RG 110, NARA; Interment Register B#1 (December n.d., 1863—Sparks).
49. 1850, 1860, and 1870 Federal Censuses, Annapolis; Draft Enrollment Records (Annapolis), Class I, Provost Marshal General Files, NARA; Baptismal Register B#1 (November 20, 1859); *Annapolis Gazette*, August 30, 1870; *Sun*, September 1, 1870. Emma's mother was Frances (Fanny) Bryan, a washerwoman and non-Catholic of Anne Arundel County. In 1870 Perry Primrose was employed by Theodore Corner of Greenbury Point Farm, now the former site of the Navy's radio transmitter facility (1918–96). Also, G. M. Hopkins, "Third District, Anne Arundel Co." (1878); Maryland Historical Trust, "Naval Radio Transmitter Facility Annapolis," MIHP AA-2127, accessed June 20, 2017, https://mht.maryland.gov/secure/medusa/PDF/AnneArundel/AA-2127.pdf.
50. *Annapolis Gazette*, July 21, 1864; *Sun*, May 26 and 28, 1864.
51. US Congress, *Statutes at Large, Treaties, and Proclamations of the United States of America from December 1863, to December 1865*, George P. Sanger, ed. (Boston: Little, Brown, 1866), 13, Appendix No. 5 (Proclamation of June 15, 1863): 733, accessed September 10, 2016, http://www.loc.gov/law/help/statutes-at-large/38th-congress/c38.pdf; Geary, *We Need Men*, 55, for analysis of the call.
52. *Chronica Domus* I:228 (June 20–24, 1863). Borgmann, *Redemptorists at Annapolis*, 57, provides additional information on Van de Braak's lectures. Day, "Studentates Weather the Storm," 234, recounts this consultation but has the wrong date of De Dycker's arrival in Annapolis.
53. Postmasters general were cabinet members from 1829 to 1971. Paul D. Ledvina and Margaret McAleer, "The Blair Family: A Register of Its Papers in the Library of Congress" (Washington: Library of Congress, 2003), 3, 6. Also, Guelzo, *Redeemer President*, 256, 270; Craig L. Symonds, *Lincoln and His Admirals: Abraham Lincoln, the U.S. Navy, and the Civil War* (New York: Oxford University Press, 2008), 10–11, 307, 308; Symonds, "Grant Moves South: Combined Operations on the James River, 1864," in Symonds, ed., *Union Combined Operations in the Civil War* (New York: Fordham University Press, 2010), 87–88; Burlingame, *Inner World*, 59; William H. Crook, *Through Five Administrations: Reminiscences of Colonel William H. Crook, Body-Guard to President Lincoln*, Margarita Spalding Gerry, comp. and ed. (New York: Harper, 1910), 32–33.
54. Noah Brooks, Washington, to George Witherle, December 23, 1863, quoted in Noah Brooks, *Lincoln Observed: Civil War Dispatches of Noah Brooks*, ed. Michael Burlingame (Baltimore: Johns Hopkins University Press, 1998), 97–98; Baker, *Politics of Continuity*, 92–93.
55. *Chronica Domus* I: 229 (July 22, 1863) says "the names of all of us were enrolled." *Province Annals*, 1832–71, 536 (1863, Annapolis), RABP, says "All the students are enrolled for military service." Class I, Drafted, Maryland Fifth Congressional District, vol. 6, Ann [*sic*] Arundel County, Part 1, Entry 172, RG 110, NARA, individuals found in alphabetical order, no pagination. No service record has been found for William S. Edwards in a Maryland regiment, although seven men with that name served in other states. See NPS, "The Civil War," accessed March 2, 2016, http://www.nps.gov/civilwar/.
56. Basler, *Collected Works*, VI:136 (for Walton visit). Neither Seelos, Annapolis, to Sister Romualda (Maria Anna) Seelos, S.S.N.D., August 21, 1863, Letter 140, Hoegerl, *Sincerely, Seelos*, 366–67, or *Province Annals*, 1832–71, 535–36 (1863, Annapolis), RABP, mention visits to Washington.
57. Seelos, Annapolis, to Miss Mary, July 17, 1863, Letter 136, Hoegerl, *Sincerely, Seelos*, 358–59. Miss Mary's surname, despite intensive research by several scholars, has not yet been discovered.
58. *Chronica Domus* I:229 (July 22–24, 1863).
59. John E. Merriken, *Every Hour on the Hour: A Chronicle of the Washington Baltimore & Annapolis Electric Railroad* (Dallas: Taylor Publishing Company, 1993), 65; *Daily National Republican* (Washington), July 20, 1863, 1; *Evening Star*, July 20, 1863; *Daily National Intelligencer*, July 30, 1863.
59. They may have seen Forts Lincoln, Saratoga, Thayer, near the Washington Branch line. See two maps from Geography and Map Division, LoC, accessed June 22, 2009: "Surveys of the Military Defences, Vicinity of Washington, D.C., Compiled at Division Hd. Qrs. Of Gen. Irvin

M'dowell, U.S.A., Arlington, Jan. 1st, 1862," https://www.loc.gov/resource/g3851s.cwh00110/, and E. G. Arnold, "Topographical Map of the Original District of Columbia and Environs Showing the Fortifications Around the City of Washington" New York: G. Woolworth Colton, 1862, https://www.loc.gov/resource/g3851s.cw0674000. David V. Miller, *The Defenses of Washington During the Civil War* (Buffalo, New York: The Author, 1976), Map 171–102.

60. Constance McLaughlin Green, *Washington: Village and Capital, 1800–1878* (Princeton: Princeton University Press, 1962), 254; Michael F. Fitzpatrick, "The Mercy Brigade: Roman Catholic Nuns in the Civil War," *Civil War Times Illustrated* 36, no. 5 (October 1997): 34–40; *Daily Constitutional Union*, July 23, 1863; *Diamond Jubilee of St. Aloysius Church, Washington, D.C., 1859–1934* (Washington: St. Aloysius Church, 1934?), 18; Mary Judd, "A History of St. Aloysius Church," *America*, December 2000, accessed August 8, 2009, https://web.archive.org/web/20100122084948/http://www.stalschurchdc.org/history.htm; Masur, *Example for All the Land*, 113.

61. *Daily Constitutional Union*, July 22, 1863, this afternoon newspaper published "Arrivals at the Hotels This Morning" almost daily and Seelos and Van de Braak's names do not appear in reports on registrants at five Washington hotels on July 22 and July 23, 1863. This does not mean they did not stay at a hotel, there were other hotels whose guests were of lesser news media interest and not reported. There also were boarding houses and private homes in which they might have stayed.

62. Thomas Goodrich, *The Darkest Dawn: Lincoln, Booth, and the Great American Tragedy* (Bloomington: Indiana University Press, 2005), 23; *Daily Constitutional Union*, July 21, 22, 23, 1863; *Daily National Republican*, July 22, 1863; John Hay Diaries and Journal, July 25, 1863, Microfilm 11,599-1P (0135–1), Manuscript Division, LoC (original at Brown University Library, Providence, Rhode Island); Noah Brooks, *Washington, D.C. in Lincoln's Time*, ed. Herbert Mitgang (Chicago: Quadrangle Books, 1971), 20–21 294–95; Green, *Washington: Village and Capital*, 250; Seelos to Sister Romualda, August 21, 1863, Letter 140, Hoegerl, *Sincerely, Seelos*, 367.

63. Brooks, *Lincoln Observed*, 80; Hay, "Life in the White House in the Time of Lincoln," 34.

64. "Residents and Visitors" and "The White House," accessed April 16, 2009, https://www.mrlincolnswhitehouse.org; John M. Hay, "Abraham Lincoln: Life in the White House in the Time of Lincoln," *Century Magazine* 41, no. 1 (November 1890): 33–37; Crook, *Through Five Administrations*, 12, 30. A contemporary floor plan showing this private passageway, built at Lincoln's request, in Harold Holzer, comp. and ed., *Dear Mr. Lincoln: Letters to the President* (Reading, Massachusetts: Addison-Wesley, 1993), 15.

65. Burlingame, *Observations*, 35, which refers to the "sober, dignified [John G.] Nicolay"; Brooks, *Lincoln Observed*, 85. Brooks, *Lincoln Observed*, 247 n116 and n117; William O. Stoddard, *Inside the White House in War Times* (New York: Charles L. Webster, 1890), 14. In Stoddard's earlier work, *Abraham Lincoln: The True Story of a Great Life*, 216, he said "These three young men, with occasional help from department clerks detailed, were all the force with which Mr. Lincoln performed the ceaseless labors of the executive office during the earlier and stormier days of his administration." Also, "Mr. Lincoln's White House," accessed March 31, 2016, https://www.mrlincolnswhitehouse.org/residents-visitors/employees-and-staff/, for information on Howe, Matile, and Neill. Sources differ on Nicolay's place of birth. Stoddard, *Inside the White House*, 151, says he was from Baden. Clarence King, "The Biographers of Lincoln," *Century Illustrated Monthly Magazine* 32 (New Series 10), no. 6 (October 1886): 862, and Frank Tusa and Thomas Bigley, "John G. Nicolay Papers: A Finding Aid to the Collection in the Library of Congress" Manuscript Division, LoC, 2010, 3, accessed January 18, 2017, http://rs5.loc.gov/service/mss/eadxmlmss/eadpdfmss/2011/ms011009.pdf, both say he was from Essingen, Bavaria. Most sources agree on Bavaria.

66. Letters July 19–22, 1863, Box 3, General Correspondence, 1863 July–1866, John G. Nicolay Papers, MSS 34736, Manuscript Division, LoC. Hay's diary does not mention Seelos, John Hay Papers, LoC, Box 1, Diaries and Notebooks, 1861–1908, and John Hay Diaries and Journal, John Hay Diary, July 19–23, 1863, LoC; diary has no July 22 entry, July 23 diary entry reveals nothing relevant to Seelos' visit. The "dry priest" may have been Bernard A. Maguire, S.J. (1818–86), a Georgetown College professor and "the popular, eloquent and pious priest" who had served at St. Aloysius 1859–64 and "edified all by the lucid and logical explanations and defense of the texts and doctrines of the Catholic Church." Also, *Daily Constitutional Union*, July 22 and August 19, 1864; Bernard A. Maguire, S.J. Papers, Georgetown University, accessed July 5, 2009, https://repository.library.georgetown.edu/handle/10822/558937. Also, Burlingame, *Inner World*, 77; Dennett, John Hay, 17–18, 26–27, 65–66; *Daily National Intelligencer* (Washington), July 23, 1863; *Daily National Republican* (Washington), July 23, 1863; William H. Seward to wife, Frances Adeline Miller Seward (1805–65), July 21, 1863, says "I have stolen an hour from the office to attend the wedding of Baron [Friedrich von] Gerolt's daughter, and I return to find your letter," quoted in Seward, *Seward at Washington*, 176. It was the wedding of Carlota Wilhemina Mariane von Gerolt, eldest daughter of the Prussian minister, and John Ward of the British East India service.

67. Brooks, *Lincoln Observed*, 84–85.

68. Brooks, *Washington, D.C. in Lincoln's Time*, 248. Burlingame, *Observations*, 39, says Nicolay persuaded Lincoln to eliminate Saturday visits in April 1861. Brooks, however, was writing later and it appears Saturday visits again were allowed. Also, Holzer, *Dear Mr. Lincoln*, 4; Brooks, *Lincoln Observed*, 86.

69. Pinsker, *Lincoln's Sanctuary*, 5; Wilson, *Intimate Memories of Lincoln*, 398; "Reception of Ministers," *Daily Constitutional Union*, July 23, 1863, 1; *Daily Morning Chronicle*, July 23, 1863;

Lincoln to Schenck, July 23, 1863, and day-to-day activities in Basler, *Collected Works*, 6:343–46; Lincoln Sesquicentennial Commission, "The Lincoln Log: A Daily Chronology of the Life of Abraham Lincoln," accessed November 17, 2015, http://www.thelincolnlog.org; Michael Burlingame and John R. Turner Ettlinger, *Inside Lincoln's White House: The Complete Civil War Diary of John Hay* (Carbondale and Edwardsville: Southern Illinois University Press, 1997), 66–67; Powell, *Lincoln Day by Day*, 3:198 (July 23, 1863).

70. Guelzo, *Redeemer President*, 115, 141, 261, 318, 336–37, 418–19, 460; Rable, *God's Almost Chosen People*, 185; William Henry Herndon, *Hidden Lincoln, From Letters and Papers of William H. Herndon*, ed. Emanuel Hertz (New York: Blue Ribbon Books, 1938), 45, quoting Herndon, Springfield, to Mr. Cronyer, December 3, 1866; Elizabeth Keckley, *Behind the Scenes or, Thirty Years a Slave and Four Years in the White House* (New York: G. W. Carleton, 1868), 119. Keckley worked briefly in 1860 as a modiste for Varina Howell Davis, the wife of then Democratic Senator Jefferson Davis of Mississippi. Also, Mark A. Noll, *A History of Christianity in the United States and Canada* (Grand Rapids: Eerdmans, 2019), 322; *Evening Star*, April 18, 1865, refers to "Dr. Gurley, pastor the church attended by the late Mr. Lincoln"; James Lander, Lincoln and Darwin: *Shared Visions of Race, Science, and Religion* (Carbondale and Edwardsville: Southern Illinois University Press, 2010), 67; Stephen Mansfield, *Lincoln's Battle with God: A President's Struggle with Faith and What it Meant for America* (Nashville: Thomas Nelson, 2012), 126; Wayne C. Temple, *Abraham Lincoln: Skeptic to Prophet* (Mahomet, Illinois: Mayhaven Publishing, 1995), 37–43; "New York Avenue Presbyterian Church," accessed March 2, 2016, http://www.abrahamlincolnonline.org/lincoln/sites/nyave.htm; Byron Miller, C.Ss.R., "Destiny and Destination," *Liguorian* 104, no. 7 (September 2016): 5.

71. Guelzo, *Redeemer President*, 314, 321; Stoddard, *Inside the White House*, 27, 56, 57–58; Burlingame, *Inner World*, 178, citing Ward Hill Lamon, *Recollections of Abraham Lincoln, 1847–1865*, 2d. ed., Dorothy Lamon Teillard, ed. (Washington: 1911), 92–93n, 196; Burlingame, *Inner World*, 177–78; Stoddard, *Inside the White House*, 56; Nicolay and Hay, *Abraham Lincoln: A History*, VI:327.

72. Brooks, *Lincoln Observed*, 83.

73. Seelos, Annapolis, to Sister Romualda Seelos, August 21, 1863, Letter 140, Hoegerl, *Sincerely, Seelos*, 367.

74. Zimmer, *Leben und Wirken*, 215 (210 in translation); Hay quoted in Burlingame, *Abraham Lincoln: A Life*, II:526. In contrast, Burlingame, *Inner World*, 188, quoting Brooks, *Washington in Lincoln's Time*, 94, said that when Lee escaped with the Army of Northern Virginia across the Potomac River, Lincoln's "grief and anger were something sorrowful to behold." Also, Burlingame, 188, citing Robert Todd Lincoln.

75. *Chronica Domus* I:229 (July 22, 1863); Seelos, Annapolis, to Romualda Seelos, August 21, 1863, Letter 140, Hoegerl, *Sincerely, Seelos*, 367.

76. Seelos, New York, to unidentified friend in Germany, April 11, 1865, Letter 172, Hoegerl, *Sincerely, Seelos*, 427.

77. Seelos, New York, to Antonia Seelos, April 17–18, 1865, Letter 173, Hoegerl, *Sincerely, Seelos*, 430.

78. Basler, *Collected Works*, 6:344ff. Issues of various Washington newspapers published between July 20 and July 27, 1863, were searched for possible mentions.

79. Boniface Wimmer, Washington, to Abraham Lincoln, June 10, 1863, with Lincoln's June 11, 1863, endorsement and the November 28, 1862 order, in *Official Records of the Union and Confederate Armies*, series III, vol. 3 (Washington: Government Printing Office, 1899), 333–36.

80. Wimmer, Washington, to Stanton, June 11, 1863, *Official Records of the Union and Confederate Armies*, series 3, vol. 3, 341–45; Jerome Oetgen, *An American Abbot: Boniface Wimmer, O.S.B., 1809–1887*, rev. ed. (Washington: Catholic University of America Press, 1997), 253–55.

81. *Chronica Domus* I:229 (July 22, 1863). A search of Office of the Postmaster General, Orders, 1835–1953, vol. 52, January 9, 1863–September 19, 1863, Records of the Post Office Department, Entry 1, RG 28, NARA College Park, failed to uncover anything relevant to the Henning, Van de Braak, and Seelos visits. Similarly, nothing relevant was found for the period June 20–August 26, 1863, Office of the Postmaster General, Letters Sent, 1789–1910, vol. 77, March 7, 1861–September 27, 1864, Entry 2, RG 28, nor in the Montgomery Blair Papers, MSS 12930 and Microfilm 19713 (reels 22, 39, and 43), Manuscript Division, LoC.

82. *Chronica Domus* I:229 (July 22, 1863). Curley, *Provincial Story*, 145, incorrectly says they called on Secretary of State Seward, and Curley, *Cheerful Ascetic*, 214, inaccurately says "they went to . . . William H. Seward, the son of the Secretary of State." Documents searched in Drafts of Letters Sent Relating to Military Service, 1861–63, Entry 975, General Records of the Department of State, RG 59, NARA College Park, was made, again to no avail even though they included correspondence of both official and personal matters. Alphabetical List of Draft Cases, n.d., Entry 974, RG 59, includes four alienage cases for Anne Arundel County and one for Annapolis, none associated with St. Mary's. Similarly none of the following revealed evidence of the Seelos visit: Domestic Letters of the Department of State, Roll 55 (March 16–September 21, 1863), Microfilm Publication 40, RG59, which includes correspondence ambassadors, foreign consuls, the Office of the Adjutant General, army and navy officers, drafted aliens, and private citizens concerning alienage and draft issues; Miscellaneous Letters of the Department of State, Roll 202 (July 1–31, 1863), Microfilm Publication 179, including letters received by the department from other departments, US consuls abroad, and private citizens; Case Files on Drafted Aliens, 1862–64, Box 7 (Miscellaneous), Entry 970, RG 59, including Seward's drafts of alienage letters; Index to Letters Sent Regarding Drafted Aliens, 1862–1864, 1 vol., Entry 971; Letters Sent Regarding Drafted Aliens, 1862–1864, vol. 3 (October 22,

1862–April 13, 1864), Entry 972.

83. Crook, *Through Five Administrations,* 9; Lord, *They Fought for the Union,* 53; Benjamin P. Thomas and Harold M. Hyman, *Stanton: The Life and Times of Lincoln's Secretary of War* (New York: Alfred A. Knopf, 1962, reprinted Westport, Connecticut: Greenwood, 1980), 165, says Stanton arranged the War Department schedule "so that congressmen had Saturdays reserved for their patronage business. From Tuesday through Thursday only matters directly relating to active military operations were permitted; the public could call only on Mondays, and Stanton would see no one at his home on business."

84. Walter Stahr, *Stanton,* 188, quoting Hay to Stanton soon after Lincoln's death; Pinsker, *Lincoln's Sanctuary,* 122; Nicolay and Hay, *Abraham Lincoln: A History,* V:140–41; Noah Brooks, "Washington in Lincoln's Time," *Century Monthly Illustrated Magazine* 59, no. 1 (November 1894): 146; Brooks, *Washington, D.C. in Lincoln's Time,* 36. Leech, *Reveille in Washington,* 157, 160, for descriptions of Stanton's public audiences; Albert E. H. Johnson, "Reminiscences of the Hon. Edwin M. Stanton, Secretary of War," *Records of the Columbia Historical Society,* 13 (1910): 72. Frederick William Seward, *Reminiscences of a War-Time Statesman and Diplomat, 1830–1915* (New York: G. P. Putnam's Sons, 1916), 243; Rable, *God's Almost Chosen People,* 229.

85. Thomas and Hyman, *Stanton,* 163; letters of Col. James A. Hardie, Assistant Adjutant General, War Department, Washington, to Brigadier General Nathaniel Collins McLean, [Provost Marshal], Cincinnati, July 21, 1863, and to General Ambrose Everett Burnside, [Commander, Department of Ohio], Cincinnati, July 23, 1863, Telegrams Sent by the Secretary of War, Roll 83, July 3–October 21, 1863, Microfilm Publication M473, NARA. No telegrams sent on behalf of Father Seelos were found. A search of James Allen Hardie Papers, MSS 24877, Manuscript Division, LoC, for July 1863 and thereafter did not uncover any relevant documents. Charles Frederick Benjamin, *Memoir of James Allen Hardie, Inspector-General, United States Army* (Washington: [privately published], 1877), 7, 15–16, 71; Erwin N. Thompson and Sally B. Woodbridge, *Presidio of San Francisco, An Outline of Its Evolution as a U.S. Army Post, 1847–1990* (Presidio of San Francisco: Golden Gate National Recreation Area, 1992), 185; "George Deshon, No. 1168. Class of 1843," Association of Graduates, United States Military Academy, *Thirty-Fifth Annual Reunion of the Association of the Graduates of the United States Military Academy, June 14th, 1904* (Saginaw, Michigan: Seemann and Peters, 1904), 189–90.

86. Seelos, Annapolis, to Miss Mary, August 2, 1863, Letter 139, Hoegerl, *Sincerely, Seelos,* 362; John Wood, Philadelphia, to Major General James A. Hardie, Washington, August 28, 1876, Hardie Papers, MSS 24877, LoC. Stahr, *Stanton,* 231–34 notes that some 354 men and women were arrested between August 8 to September 8, 1862, under these orders.

87. Schecter, *Devil's Own Work,* 3–4, 48, 78, 86, 116, 123, 133, 186, 202, 211–12, 233–35, 251–52; *New York Herald,* July 12, 1863; Tyler Anbinder, "Which Poor Man's Fight? Immigrants and the Federal Conscription of 1863," *Civil War History* no. 4 (December 2006): 346, 354, 368; Geary, *We Need Men,* 108; Zanca, *American Catholics and Slavery,* Document 74 (July 20 and 27, 1863), 177; Iver Bernstein, *The New York City Draft Riots* (New York: Oxford University Press, 1990), 33, 36, 51, 62, 113; *Burlingame, Abraham Lincoln: A Life,* II:528–29.

88. Zimmer, *Leben und Wirken,* 215 (210 in translation); *Chronica Domus* I:229 (July 22, 1863).

89. Seelos, Annapolis, to Romualda Seelos, August 21, 1863, Letter 140, Hoegerl, *Sincerely, Seelos,* 367; Seelos, Annapolis, to Miss Mary, August 2, 1863, Letter 139, Hoegerl, *Sincerely, Seelos,* 362; Nicolay and Hay, *Abraham Lincoln: A History,* V:142.

90. Register of Persons Entering the War Department Building, Entry 70, Records of the Office of the Secretary of War, RG 107, NARA. Searches were made of Letters Sent by the Secretary of War to the President and Executive Departments, 1863–1870, Records of the Office of the Secretary of War, Microfilm Publication M421; Registers of Letters Received by the Secretary of War From the President, Executive Departments, and War Department Bureaus, 1862–1870, Microfilm Publication M493; Letters Received by the Secretary of War From the President, Executive Departments, and War Department Bureaus, 1862–1870, Microfilm Publication M494, all part of RG 107, NARA. Also, three boxes of general correspondence (Reel 5: June 16–August 6, 1863, Reel 6: August 7–September 19, 1863, September 20–25, 1863) and two letterbooks (Reel 14: June 4–September 9, 1863, and 1862–65), Stanton Papers, LoC (these papers are mostly of official nature, dealing with battle reports, White House letters, New York draft riots, and general military matters, none of a personal nature, such as dealing with individual draft cases). Emails from Walter Stahr to author, February 16–17, 2015, concerning the probably-no-longer extant stenographer notes. The *Sun* was screened for July 24–August 8, 1863, for Annapolis correspondent reports but nothing was found about Seelos' trip to Washington. The same correspondent occasionally reported other Redemptorist activities but not around the time of the Seelos-Lincoln meeting.

91. *Evening Star,* July 20, 1863, under "For Annapolis," it noted that trains departed Washington at 8 AM and 5 PM and that there was no trains to Annapolis on Sunday. There are no extant Annapolis and Elk Ridge Railroad advertisements for summer 1863. Seelos to Miss Mary, August 2, 1863, Letter 139, Hoegerl, *Sincerely, Seelos,* 362, and Seelos, Annapolis, to Romualda Seelos, August 21, 1863, Letter 140, 367; Zimmer, *Leben und Wirken,* 215 (210 in translation); Curley, *Cheerful Ascetic,* 215, concerning Redemptorist draftees Baltimore priests Robert Kleineidam and Michael Rosenbauer. The brothers are not identified. The Pittsburgh priests were William Wayrich and Joseph Wirth, and the brother identified only as Simon, presumably Simon Ernst.

92. *Catholic Mirror,* July 18, 1863; *Maryland Republican,* October 24, 1863; US Congress, *Statutes at Large,* 13, Appendix No. 10

(Proclamation of October 17, 1863): 736–37 (Boston: Little, Brown, 1864), accessed September 10, 2016, http://www.loc.gov/law/help/statutes-at-large/38th-congress/c38.pdf.

93. *Chronica Domus* I:221 (January 16, 1863), I:222 (February 27, 1863), I:224 (March 1863); Baptismal Register B#1 (January 18, 1863); *Province Mission Book*, March–April 1863, RABP.

94. *Dunigan's American Catholic Almanac and List of Clergy for 1859* (New York: Edward Dunigan and Brother, 1858), 58, which says: "Easton, Private Home, attended from Annapolis." "The Villa" acquired for $30,500, see STH 69:497 (June 18, 1862), Talbot County Land Records, MSA. Because of an apparent cloud on the title, May executed a second deed, with Richard France, builder of "The Villa," for $5.00, STH 69:514 (June 20, 1862). Prentiss Ingraham, *Land of Legendary Lore: Sketches of Romance and Reality on the Eastern Shore of the Chesapeake* (Easton, Maryland: Gazette Publishing House, 1898), 183; Hulbert Footner, *Rivers of the Eastern Shore: Seventeen Maryland Rivers* (New York: Farrar and Rinehart, 1944), 256–58; William H. Dilworth and Rae Smith, "Map of Talbot County; with Farm Limits," Geography and Map Division, LoC, accessed March 15, 2016, https://www.loc.gov/item/2002624021. See Baptismal Register B#1 (September 12, 1852) for Lowe baptism.

95. *New York Times*, July 20, 1861; *Sun*, September 14, 1861; Clement A. Evans, ed., *Confederate Military History* (Adams, Georgia: Confederate Publishing Company, 1899), 2:61; Jno. A. Bingham, acting chairman, Judiciary Committee, United States House of Representatives, Washington, to May, July 16, 1861, in *Official Records of the Union and Confederate Armies*, series II, vol. 2 (Washington: Government Printing Office, 1897), 791.

96. "Saints Peter and Paul, Easton," accessed April 1, 2016, https://catholic-diocese-of-wilmington.fandom.com/wiki/Saints_Peter_and_Paul,_Easton; Byrne, "Redemptorists in America, III," 369.

97. *Chronica Domus* I:236 (*Observanda*, 1863, item 2).

98. *Chronica Domus* I:229 (July 4, 1863); *Easton Gazette*, July 11 and 18, 1863. Similar ads appeared, under same title, on August 8 and September 9, 1863.

99. Cornell, [Annapolis?], to De Dycker, Baltimore, no date [circa July 4, 1863], John De Dycker Provincial File, RABP. *Chronica Domus* I:229 (July 4, 1863) reported Cornell's return to Annapolis from Easton. Baptismal Register B#1 (July 19, 1863) has entries for baptisms by James Bradley of two-year-old Catherine Dwyer ("in Easton, Talbot County, Md. Mother resides in Oxford, Md.") and five-month-old Samuel Marvel ("resides near Easton"). For the visits, see *Chronica Domus* I:231 (July 19, August 16, 1863), I:232 (September 20, 1863), I:233 (October 18, 1863), I:234 (November 15, 1863), I:235 (December 20, 1863). Also, Michael S. Burke, C.Ss.R., Annapolis, to Howes Goldsborough, [Easton], September 14, 1863, Folder 1, Howes Goldsborough Papers (ZCC), University of Notre Dame Archives, Notre Dame, Indiana, introducing Gross as the attending priest.

100. See, for example, Charles C. Lancaster, S.J., to Howes Goldsborough, Georgetown College, April 7, 1851, and St. Thomas Manor, [Port Tobacco, Charles County, Maryland], May 5, 1858, Folder 1, Goldsborough Papers. William H. Gross, C.Ss.R., Annapolis, to Mrs. [Catherine] Goldsborough, Easton, October 1, 1863, Folder 1, Goldsborough Papers. For the "Galloway" location labeled "H. Goldsborough" see William H. Dilworth and Rae Smith, "Map of Talbot County; with Farm Limits," Geography and Map Division, LoC, https://www.loc.gov/item/2002624021; Maryland Historical Trust, "Galloway," MIHP T–104, http://msa.maryland.gov/megafile/msa/stagsere/se1/se5/016000/016300/016309/pdf/msa_se5_16309.pdf, both accessed June 15, 2016; Christopher Weeks and Michael O. Bourne, *Where Land and Water Intertwine* (Baltimore: Johns Hopkins University Press, 1984), 36, 173.

101. *Chronica Domus* I:224 (March 24, 1863), I:229 (July 4, 1863), I:234 (November 11, 1863).

102. *Chronica Domus* I:221 (January 4, 1863), I:225 (April 5, 1863), I:227 (May 3, 1863), I: 229 (July 5, 1863), I:230 (August 1, 1863), I:231 (August 28, 1863), I:233 (October 4, 1863), I:234 (November 1, 1863), I:235 (December 6, 1863).

103. *Chronica Domus* I:229 (July 4, 1863), which includes observations learned about the Cornell case as it developed.

104. Curley, *Provincial Story*, 130–35; David J. O'Brien, *Isaac Hecker: An American Catholic* (New York: Paulist Press, 1992), 137 (which says Cornell was an Irish immigrant); James McVann, *The Paulists, 1858–1970* (New York: Missionary Society of St. Paul the Apostle, 1983), 1:21–23, 40, 43. For Cornell quotes, see Chronicles of the House of Studies, Cumberland, 45 ("about this time [Easter]," 1858). Also, *Province Annals*, 1832–71, 535 (1863, Annapolis), RABP, which says Cornell left after being in Baltimore for a long time.

105. Redemptorist Fathers, *The Mission-Book of the Congregation of the Most Holy Redeemer: A Manual of Instructions and Prayers Adapted to Preserve the Fruits of the Mission*, New, Revised, and Enlarged Edition (Baltimore: Kelly, Hedian, and Piet, 1863), with copyright of V. Rev. J. De Dycker, C.Ss.R., in District Court of the United States, Maryland District, and accessioned by the court's copyright library in January 1864. The original copyright copy, now in the Library of Congress, contains the handwritten copy deposit information on the flyleaf: "No. 66. Copyright secured Nov. 25, 1862 Publication Deposited same day." The author has been unable to locate a copy of the Dublin edition.

106. Hecker, New York, to Kelly and Piet, Baltimore, March 5, 1863; Kelly et al., Baltimore, to Cornell, Norwalk Connecticut, March 16, 1863; Hecker to Cornell, March 24, 1863; Kelly et al., to Cornell, March 25, 1863, John De Dycker Provincial File, RABP. Also, I. T. Hecker, *The Mission Book: A Manual of Instructions and Prayers Adapted to Preserve the Fruits of the Mission* (New York: Sadlier, 1853); Fathers of the Congregation of the Most Holy Redeemer, *The Mission Book: A Manual of Instructions and Prayers* (New York: E. Dunigan and Brother, 1854), both of which have copyright notices

by I. T. Hecker (1853) and I. Thomas Hecker (1854), District Court of the United States Southern District of New York; Fathers of the Congregation of the Most Holy Redeemer, *The Mission Book: A Manual of Instructions and Prayers Adapted to Preserve the Fruits of the Mission* (New York: Edward Dunigan and Brother, 1857), and same title published in Baltimore by Sadlier, 1858, both of which have copyright notices by George Ruland, Southern District of New York. Also, Paulist Fathers, *The Mission Book: A Manual of Instructions and Prayers Adapted to Preserve the Fruits of the Mission* (New York: Edward Dunigan, 1861).

107. Cornell, Hudson, New York, to Very Rev. and dear Father [De Dycker, Baltimore], March 26, 1863; De Dycker to Cornell, March 30, 1863, Provincial File, RABP.

108. An odd occurrence and possibly something that reflected badly on Cornell was the appearance of "convincing testimony" by him that appeared in an advertisement for "Mrs. Allen's World's Hair Restorer" in the *Columbian Register* (New Haven), March 28, April 9, April 23, and June 6, 1863: "Rev. J. J. [*sic*] Cornell, N.Y. City: 'I procured it for a relative. The falling of the hair stopped, and restored it from being grey to its natural and beautiful color.'" Also, Borgmann, *Redemptorists at Annapolis*, 19; Chronicles of the House of Studies, Cumberland, 19–20 (August 24, 1853). Cornell's travels to and from Annapolis 1853–63 are well documented in the *Chronica Domus* and are too numerous to detail here. Also, *Province Mission Book*, RABP, 1861–63. For the weekly advertisement, see *Catholic Mirror*, January 10, 1863, and every week thereafter through the end of 1863.

109. Cornell, New York, to De Dycker, Baltimore, July 17, 1863. RAPB; Kenrick Literarum Registrum II, 1862–63, 31 (July 15, 1863), included as part of Spalding Literarum Registrum, Oct 17, 1862–1869, Martin J. Spalding Papers, AAB.

110. Cornell, New York, to De Dycker, Baltimore, July 20, 1863, and Cornell, Perth Amboy, to De Dycker, Baltimore, August 7, 1863, RABP; *Sadliers' Catholic Almanac, 1864*, 117, lists Rev. J. W. [*sic*] Cornell in charge of St. Mary's Church in Perth Amboy, Diocese of Newark.

111. Joseph M. Flynn, *The Catholic Church in New Jersey* (Morristown, New Jersey: Joseph M. Flynn, 1904), 130; James A. Harding, "St. Mary's Church, 1849–1949, Commemorating the One Hundredth Anniversary of Its Parochial Erection: Historical Sketch" (Perth Amboy, n.d.), no pagination, copy provided to author by Alan Delozier, University Archivist, Seton Hall University, South Orange, NJ, from the Diocese of Newark Archives and Library. *Sadliers' Catholic Almanac*, 1864, 97, lists Rev. John H. Cornell at the Cathedral Chapel in Boston; the Roman Catholic Archdiocese of Boston Archives has no record of him, email of Thomas Lester to author, January 17, 2017. *Sadliers' Catholic Directory, 1867*, 190, lists no priest at St. Mary's, Perth Amboy, but notes it was attended from Rahway by Rev. Thomas Quinn. "Angelus," Attwater, *Catholic Dictionary*, 22.

112. J. H. Cornell, "Bonum est" (New York: William A. Pond, 1882), M2.3.U6A44, Music Division, LoC; *Brooklyn Eagle*, March 25, 1877; "New York Marriages, 1686–1980, " accessed March 4, 2016, FamilySearch.org; 1870 (two entries, one in District 15, another in District 17, Ward 21), and 1880 Federal censuses for New York City; "A New Freak of Agnosticism," *The Churchman*, July 25, 1885, 99; James Grant Wilson and John Fisk, eds. *Appleton's Cyclopaedia of American Biography* (New York: Appleton, 1888), I:742; Cornell Ex-C.Ss.R. File, RAPB; *Minute Book 1813–1965 New York*, RABP; Certificate No. 7592, John H. Cornell, March 1, 1894, "New York City Deaths, 1892–1902," accessed October 19, 2011, Ancestry.com; John Cornell, *Genealogy of the Cornell Family: Being an Account of the Descendants of Thomas Cornell of Portsmouth, R.I.* (New York: T. A. Wright, 1902).

113. Curley, *Cheerful Ascetic*, 237–45.

114. Borgmann, *Redemptorists at Annapolis*, 247, lists Seelos' tenure as June 14, 1862, to September 1, 1863. Baptismal Register B#1 records a baptism and a marriage performed by Seelos on September 3, 1863. Curley, *Cheerful Ascetic*, 244, 246, and 246 n70, and Hoegerl, *Positio*, 2, Part 2, 1052–54, both say Seelos left Annapolis in August 1863 on a trial basis, but "he never returned, so that for two years he was to be a rector without a community"and that his official title was never taken away. His term was completed by Joseph Helmprächt, who served as vice rector from September 1, 1863, to April 17, 1865. *Province Annals, 1832–71*, 566 (1864, Annapolis), RABP, has *"Adm. Rev. P. Fr. Xav. Seelos, Rector, absens in missionibus"* with Helmprächt as vice rector. Seelos' himself wrote: "Already since the 22nd of the past month, I am away from Annapolis," Seelos, Loretto, Pennsylvania, to brother-in-law [Johann Scholtz] and [sister] Lisette [Scholtz-Seelos], October 4, 1863, Letter 144, Hoegerl, *Sincerely, Seelos*, 371. See *Chronica Domus* I: 231 (August 28 or 29, 1863, for Helmprächt's arrival); I:232 (September 22 and 23, 1863, for Seelos and Bradley's departures, respectively). The September entries say Helmprächt took over as rector, but I:249 (February 12, 1864) clarifies that he "until now holding the position of Vice Rector, was made Rector of this house." Also, *In Memory of Rev. Jos. Helmprächt, 1907*, 1–4, RABP.

115. Seelos to family, October 12, December 3 and 18, 1862, Letter 119, Hoegerl, *Sincerely, Seelos*, 313–15.

116. Seelos, Annapolis, to Katherine Berger and Family, Bohemia, July 30, 1863, Letter 138, Hoegerl, *Sincerely, Seelos*, 361.

117. Seelos, Loretto, Pennsylvania, to brother-in-law John Scholz, October 4, 1863, Letter 144, Hoegerl, *Sincerely, Seelos*, 372.

118. Seelos, Cumberland, to Sister Damiana Seelos, January 16, 1862, Letter 107, Hoegerl, *Sincerely, Seelos*, 291.

119. Seelos to family, October 12, December 3 and 18, 1862, Letter 119, Hoegerl, *Sincerely, Seelos*, 314.

120. Seelos, Annapolis, to Ambrose Seelos, December 3, 1862, Letter 119, Hoegerl, *Sincerely, Seelos*, 323.

121. Seelos, Annapolis, to Miss Mary, July 17, 1863, Letter 136, Hoegerl, *Sincerely, Seelos*, 358.

122. Seelos, Baltimore, to family in Füssen, August 1, 1845,

Letter 7, Hoegerl, *Sincerely, Seelos,* 48.

123. Richard Vincent Whelan (1808–74), a native of Baltimore, ordained in 1841, first bishop of Richmond, Virginia (1841–48), and first bishop of Wheeling, Virginia/West Virginia (1848–74). See Ohio County (West Virginia) Public Library, "Wheeling Hall of Fame: Richard V. Whelan," accessed April 27, 2016, http://www.ohiocountylibrary.org/wheeling-history/4163; Kurtz, *Excommunicated from the Union,* 34, 90–91; Brinsfield, *Faith in the Fight,* 53.

124. Curley, *Cheerful Ascetic,* 73–75, 132–34.

125. Seelos, Annapolis, to Sister Romualda, August 21, 1863, Letter 140, Hoegerl, *Sincerely, Seelos,* 366.

126. Kurtz, *Excommunicated from the Union,* 126–27.

127. Francis (Franz) Lieber (1798/1800–1872), Library of Congress, Federal Research Division, "The Lieber Collection," accessed April 27, 2016, *http://www.loc.gov/collections/military-legal-resources/articles-and-essas/jags-legal-center-and-school/lieber-colltion/home.html;* Stout, *Upon the Altar of the Nation,* 188; Witt, *Lincoln's Code,* 3, 279.

128. *Chronica Domus* I:231 (August 28 or 29 [*sic*], 1863), I:232 (September 24, 1863), I:234 (November 5, 1863), I:234 (November 8, 1863), I:232 (September 24, 1863).

129. *Chronica Domus* I:233 (October 15, 17, 21, 1863), I:248 (January 4, 1864); Wuest, *Annales,* IV:2:463; Hoegerl, *With All Gentleness,* 186. Wuest, *Annales,* IV:2:457 says O'Brien, a native of Monroe, Michigan, died in Cumberland April 1, 1866, but *Liber Professionis,* 194, *Album Provinciae C.Ss.R. Americanae,* 21 (students/priests), and *Minute Book, 1813-1965, New York,* 183, say he died April 1, 1864. Chronicles of the House of Studies Cumberland, 131–32 (January 1864) and 133 (April 1864) make no mention of O'Brien nor is he listed in "Familia Domus" for Cumberland in 1865, 137 (January 1865), which is the last entry in the Cumberland chronicle. *Chronica Domus* I:234 (November 28, 1863), I:256 (July 16, 1864) for Dunn; Annals, St. Peter Philadelphia, 1858–1872, 66–67 (December 11, 1863–January 14, 1864), RABP; *Chronica Domus* I:235 (December 11, 1863); *Sadliers' Catholic Directory, 1867,* 112; 1870 Federal Census, Philadelphia for Schnüttgen.

130. *Chronica Domus* I:236 (Observanda item 1).

131. *Chronica Domus* I:235 (December 22, 1863).

132. *Chronica Domus* I:227 (May 9–12, 1863), I:230 (August 1, 1863), I:231 (August 16, 1863), I:231 (August 28 or 29, 1863), I:231 (August 31, 1863), I:231 (September 7, 1863). Eberhardt not mentioned in Chronicles of the House of Studies Cumberland, 123 (August 1863) or 124 (September 1863) but is listed in the 1864 Cumberland "Familia Domus," 129 (January 1864).

133. *Sun,* November 4 and 28, 1863; *Annapolis Gazette,* November 26, 1863 (quotes correspondence from Keffer and lists names of those arrested, all "Secession Ticket" candidates or attempted voters) and December 3, 1863, (reported former Governor Thomas G. Pratt and Col. Joseph Hopper Nicholson of Annapolis refused to take an oath of allegiance).

134. *Annapolis Gazette,* November 12, 1863; *Maryland Republican,* November 14, 1863.

135. Horatio Tydings' 1862 draft enrollment record notes "family refused to tell when any other persons were there but this was always the case at secession places." See Enrollment Record (1862–1864), Third Enumeration District of Anne Arundel County, Adjutant General, MSA S352–23. Also, *Annapolis Gazette,* October 8, 1863 (lists Tydings among Democratic county commissioner nominees) and November 12, 1863 (reports Tydings tied for third place out of seven winning candidates). Tydings was witness to St. Mary's marriage of former Union soldier George Mittnacht, see Marriage Register B#1 (January 20, 1862).

136. *Chronica Domus* I:234 (November 14, 18, 26, 1863); "Observations, Facts during the Canonical Visitation, from the 16th to the 25th of November 1863," *Statuta et Decreta,* 196–97.

137. *Chronica Domus* I:235 (December 1 and 15, 1863); Louis Claessens Personnel File, RABP; Wuest, *Annales,* IV:2:448; *Catholic Mirror,* August 25, 1866.

138. *Annapolis Gazette,* December 24, 1863.

139. "U.S. Army Register of Enlistments, 1798–1914," accessed September 20, 2012, Ancestry.com. Mullan's enlistment expired June 1, 1855. See John Mullan, Fort Severn, to General [no name], August, 19, 1845, Folder 21, Box 2, Entry 146, Miscellaneous Letters, RG 405, USNA Special Collections and Archives; Commander George P. Upshur, Superintendent, USNA, to General Roger Jones, War Department, Washington, DC, April 27, 1850, Box 1, vol. 4, Letters Sent by the Superintendent, 1845–74, Microfilm Publication M945, RG 405; *Sun,* December 24, *Maryland Republican,* December 26, 1863 and January 16, 1864; Interment Register (December 22, 1863, received "all of the sacraments"); *Sun,* December 28, 1863; Bernard C. Steiner, Lynn Roby Meekins, David Henry Carroll, and Thomas G. Boggs, *Men of Mark in Maryland: Biographies of Leading Men of the State* (Washington: Johnson-Wynne Company, 1907), I:263.

140. Mullan enlisted 1824 and reenlisted 1829, 1834, 1837, 1845, 1850. See "U.S. Army Register of Enlistments, 1798–1914," accessed September 20, 2012, Ancestry.com. Walbach's full name and title was John Baptiste deBarth, Baron of Walbach (1766–1857). For additional information on Walbach, see Worden, *Saint Mary's,* 31–32.

141. *Maryland Republican,* January 16, 1864. No Anne Arundel County marriage record has been found, the September 1829 date is from "Mary A. Bright Pedigree Resource File," accessed July 7, 2013, FamilySearch.org, which does not provide documentation but correlates well with their first-born's date of birth on July 31, 1830, provided when John Mullan Jr. (1830–1909) was baptized conditionally in Annapolis, June 11, 1832. See "White March/Bowie Register of Baptisms, Marriages, and Deaths, 1818–1895," Box 3, Folder 3, Maryland Province Collection, GU-CSC. No record for the baptism of daughter Mary Elizabeth Mullan (1831–1901) has been found. See Baptismal Register B#1 (May 21, 1854—Virginia Mullan).

142. Steiner, et alia, *Men of Mark in Maryland,* I:263. Interments

for St. Mary's parishioners appear in Baptismal Register B#1 for 1856–71, and were duplicated in B#2 for the period 1856–1906. They record seven burials of Mullan children. An eighth child, Maria Teresa Mullan, died at age six or seven in 1856 is not recorded, but she might have been interred in the old St. Mary's burial ground on Duke of Gloucester Street for which no records exist. Between 1856 and 1901, these graves were exhumed and reburied at the West Street cemetery. Presumably she is buried with her family. Mary Ann Bright Mullan is recorded in Confirmation Register B#1 (January 29, 1860) and Interment Register B#2 (November 8, 1888).

143. Catherine "Kitty" Bright (1809–1902). Baptismal Register B#1 (August 7, 1859); Seelos, Annapolis, to Ambrose Seelos, December 3, 1862, Letter 119, Hoegerl, *Sincerely, Seelos*, 317; McIntire, 1:88, identifies James T. Bright (no dates) of St. Mary's County; "Mary A. Bright Pedigree Resource File," accessed July 7, 2013, Familysearch.org, identifies James Henry Bright (1754/65–bef. December 1820) of Anne Arundel County. Both agree on the Bright/Tydings marriage on May 24, 1800. See Baptismal Register B#1 (August 7, 1859), for Catherine Bright as *conversa ex Episcopis sub condit. baptiz.*, and B#1 (January 29, 1860) for confirmation.

144. McIntire, 1:561; Baptismal Register B#1 (May 24, 1863—Bright).

145. WSG 19:532 (April 4, 1835), AACLR, notes Mary Bright purchased house and lot on East Street, June 13, 1820, but gives no prior deed reference, possibly because the seller's estate was contested; a new deed signed in 1835. There are numerous instances of property purchases and sales by the Mullans in the early 1850s recorded in AACLR. For sale to Naval Academy, see NHG 2:509 (June 25, 1853). Also, James R. Howison, attorney for John A. Semple, Purser, USNA, to Charles Morris, Chief of the Bureau of Ordnance, Washington, November 3, 1853, Letters Received by the Superintendent, 1843–74, Box 2, RG 405, USNA; it requested $22,092.68 to pay for the properties, of which $600 was to go to Mullan. McWilliams, *Annapolis*, 156, discusses this Naval Academy expansion.

146. 1860 Federal Slave Schedule, Annapolis; Annapolis Passes, Old Book 294, Part 4, Entry 1535, September 27, 1861, RG 393, NARA; Baptismal Register B#1 (July 28, 1861); Freedom Records, 1785–1867, Anne Arundel County, Owner Index 35, MSA; Compiled Military Service Record (William H. Brown, Co. E, 30th USCT), RG 94, NARA.

147. Judges' Poll Book (for April 2, 1860 election), accessed February 19, 2012, http://www.msa.md.gov/megafile/msa/muagser/m1/m32/000000/000049/pdf/m32-000049.pdf; Jane McWilliams, "Annapolis History Chronology, 1790 to 1975" (electronic file, 2010), citing Annapolis Mayor and Aldermen (Proceedings), 1862–1863, MSA M49–7.

148. *Register of Graduates and Alumni of St. John's College*, 46; "Records of the Directorate of Admissions, Records of the United States Military Academy," RG 404, NARA, accessed September 20, 2012, Ancestry.com, notes John Mullan Jr. admitted December 1847, "Son of Sergeant in the Army," recommended by Walbach, Democratic member of Maryland General Assembly. Also see *Annapolis Gazette*, November 4, 1858 and December 15, 1859 for Mullan's exploits in Oregon.

149. Keith C. Petersen, *John Mullan: The Tumultuous Life of a Western Road Builder* (Pullman: Washington State University Press, 2014), 21, 100, 150, 239, 255; Captain John Mullan Museum, (Mullan, Idaho), "Mullan: A Brief History," accessed March 14, 2016, http://www.mullanmuseum.org/history.htm (defunct).

150. "2nd Regiment, US Artillery (Regular Army)" NPS Soldiers and Sailors Database, accessed March 13, 2016, https://www.nps.gov/civilwar/search-battle-units.htm; Petersen, *Mullan*, 161–62; *Maryland Republican*, March 28, 1863. For Mullan Jr.'s military record, see ACWRDB, accessed September 20, 2012; Petersen, *Mullan*, 60, 102, 151, 161.

151. Welles, Washington, to Blake, Newport, June 4, 1861, Office of the Superintendent, Letters Received by the Superintendent, 1845–1887, Folder 1, Box 7, Entry 25, RG 405, USNA; United States Naval Academy, *Official Register of Officers and Midshipmen of the United States Naval Academy, Newport, Rhode Island, 31st December, 1861* (Newport: James Atkinson, 1862), 7. The home state of Horace (1837–1903) is listed as Kansas. For promotion to lieutenant and naval service, see Lewis R. Hammersly, comp., *The Records of Living Officers of the U.S. Navy and Marine Corps; with a History of Naval Operations During the Rebellion of 1861–5* (Philadelphia: J. B. Lippincott, 1870), 160–61. Also, "Pedigree Resource File," accessed July 9, 2013, http://familysearch.org/pal:/MM9.2.1/9CZ6-TBK, for Horace Edward Mullan, which says he "resigned" from the Navy, but *Mullan v. United States* (May 11, 1891) says he was dismissed. See "Ashuelot," *Dictionary of American Naval Fighting Ships*, accessed July 10, 2013, http://www.history.navy.mil/danfs/a12/ashuelot.htm. Horace petitioned the overturn of his court martial in 1885 to the US Court of Claims but, in reviewing the case, the Supreme Court affirmed the Court of Claims judgment. *See Supreme Court Reporter*, 11, *Cases Argued and Determined in the United States Supreme Court, October Term, 1890* (November, 1890–September, 1891) (St. Paul: West Publishing Company, 1891) 788–89. Also, *Alumni Register of Georgetown University, Washington, D.C., 1924* (Washington: Georgetown University, 1924), 286; Interment Register B#2 (April 24, 1903), lists "Grip Bronchial & heart troubles" as the causes of death.

152. Acting Midshipman John C. Pegram, USS *Constitution*, to Old Friend [O.A. Browne, forwarded to Gideon Welles], May 23, 1861, and Pegram to Welles, July 15, 1861, Office of the Superintendent, Letters Received by the Superintendent, 1845–1887, Folder 8, Box 8, Entry 25, RG 405, USNA; United States Naval Academy, *Official Register of Officers and Midshipmen of the United States Naval Academy, Newport, Rhode Island, December 31, 1863* (Newport: Frederick A. Pratt, 1864), 12. The home state of Dennis (1843–1928) in register is Kentucky. Also, Steiner, et alia, *Men of Mark in*

Maryland, I:263–65 (which mentions service on the *Malvern*); Hammersly, *Records of Living Officers of the U.S. Navy and Marine Corps*, 183 (which does not mention the *Malvern*); 1900 Federal Census, Annapolis. Dennis married Ada R. Pettit (1855–1936) on July 25, 1876. *Register of Graduates and Alumni of St. John's College*, 98, lists Dennis' honorary M.A. in 1872. Dennis' sister Ann Catherine lived at 114 College Avenue with her sister Virginia Isabella ("Jennie") and Catherine Bright (Aunt Kitty); see 1900 Federal Census. "Pedigree Resource File" for Dennis Walbach Mullan, gives the address as 132 College Avenue. The 1880 Federal Census, Annapolis. lists the location as 82 Tabernacle Street (the former name). The 1878 Hopkins map of Annapolis shows a lot and house labeled "Dennis Mullan" on Tabernacle Street across the street from Government House and the third lot from West Street, that is, now the space between the former US Post Office and the James Senate Office Building. Dennis purchased the property from Frank H. Stockett, trustee, SH 9:187 (March 23, 1875), AACLR.

153. Minutes of the Board of Visitors and Governors, February 19, 1853, St. John's College Archives Collection, MSA SC5698–1–10; Eugene Fauntelroy Cordell, *Historical Sketch of the University of Maryland School of Medicine (1807 to 1890)* (Baltimore: Press of Isaac Friedenwald, 1891), 190; "Pedigree Resource File" for James Augustus Mullan; United States Department of the Interior, *Register of Officers and Agents Civil, Military, and Naval in the Service of the United States on the Thirtieth of September, 1861* (Washington: Government Printing Office, 1862), 90 (Flathead Agency); *Sun*, November 5, 1863 (reported on letters from James Mullan about his westward travels); *Walla Walla Statesman*, August 18, 1865.

154. "Alphabetical List of Cadets Admitted July 1, 1865," United States Military Academy, *Official Register of the Officers and Cadets of the U.S. Military Academy* (West Point, New York: June 1865) 17; "Alphabetical List of Cadets Admitted July 1, 1866," United States Military Academy, *Official Register of the Officers and Cadets of the U.S. Military Academy* (West Point, New York: June 1866) 17; H. Charles Ulman, *Lawyers' Record and the Official Register of the United States*, (New York: A.S. Barnes, 1872), 864; *Annapolis Gazette*, January 2, 1870, which lists Ferdinand Mullan, attorney-at-law with an office on State Circle and offering "Collection of Claims promptly attended to." The 1880 Federal Census, District of Columbia, lists Ferdinand Mullan, age 35, real estate agent living at 736 12th St NW.

155. "Pedigree Resource File" for Charles Mullan; U.S. Congress, 47th, 2nd session House, *Journal of the House of Representatives of the United States, February 21, 1883* (Washington: Government Printing Office: 1882 [*sic*]), 458, which ordered the clerk of the House to reimburse Charles' executor, Ferdinand Mullan, "a sum not exceeding $173, for funeral expenses of said deceased, and that the same be immediately available."

156. "Pedigree Resource File" for Lewis Arthur [*sic*] Mullan, FamilySearch.org; Minutes of the Board of Visitors and Governors, July 27, 1869, St. John's College Archives Collection, MSA SC5698–1–24; Find A Grave Memorial ID 173422030.

157. Baptismal Register B#1 (September 26, 1864—Hail); Find A Grave Memorial ID 214442108 (Ann); Find A Grave Memorial ID 214442477 (Virginia).

158. *Annapolis Gazette*, March 15, 1855. The marriage license issued March 11, 1855, see "Maryland Marriages, 1666–1970," accessed August 15, 2013, FamilySearch.org. Also, McIntire, 1:502; Last Will and Testament of John Mullan, Register of Wills, Anne Arundel County, MSA C155–45. The will signed by Mullan and witnessed by William J. Bryan and Richard Swann on February 10, 1857, entered into probate February 3, 1864, with Mary Ann Mullan sole beneficiary. See SH 35:493 (September 18, 1889), AACLR, which states that for $500 Mary E. Campbell did "grant, bargain, sell and convey" to Anne Catherine Mullan and Virginia Isabella Mullan "all my individual right, title, estate and interest . . . in and to all real and personal property of the late Mrs. Mary A. Mullan of whatever the same may consist and wherever the same may be situated."

159. For Campbell's military service, Company F, Sixth Maryland Infantry, see Compiled Service Records of Volunteer Union Soldiers Who Served in Organizations from the State of Maryland 6th Infantry, Microfilm Publication M384, RG 94, NARA; "Sixth Regiment Infantry," *History and Roster of Maryland Volunteers, War of 1861–6, Volume 1, Archives of Maryland Online*, vol. 367: 222–23 and 237, accessed March 20, 2016, http://msa.maryland.gov/megafile/msa/speccol/sc2900/sc2908/000001/000367/html/am367--222.html. Also, *Annapolis Gazette*, July 9, 1872; email of Christina Simmons, Anne Arundel Genealogical Society, to author, July 11, 2013, providing St. Anne's burial information for James Campbell, buried July 4, 1872, the day after his death.

160. 1870 Federal Census, Annapolis; Widow's Pension File (Mary E. Campbell, Application No. 458973, Certificate No. 309322), RG 15, NARA; "Additional Information for Mary Elizabeth Mullan," Notes (3), "Pedigree Resource File," accessed July 8, 2013, https://familysearch.org/pal:/MM9.2.1/9CZ6-T1X, for the "cemetary" quote. Email of Simmons to author, July 11, 2013, providing St. Anne's burial information for Mary Elizabeth Mullan Campbell, buried July 18, 1901, the day after her death.

161. Baptismal Register B#1 (May 29, 1860, June 22, 1862, September 13, 1863, September 11, 1864); Baptismal Register B#2 (March 23, 1869, April 4, 1869); Marriage Register B#1 (January 14, 1863).

162. *Sun*, December 24, 1863.

163. *Chronica Domus* I:235 (December 25, 1863).

164. *Province Annals*, 1832–71, 536, (1863, Annapolis).

165. *Maryland Republican*, February 13, 1864. The notice dated December 23, 1863 and ordered published four times starting December 26, 1863.

Chapter 6: 1864 — It Would Move the Heart of a Tiger

1. *Chronica Domus* I:248 (January n.d., 1864).
2. *Chronica Domus* I:235 (December 1, 1863), II:5 (January 1, 1865), II:31 (January 1, 1866). New handwriting appears on II:38 (July 11, 1866).
3. McWilliams, *Annapolis*, 120, 140, 187, 416 n13 (the hospital was near today's Taylor Avenue police station); *Annapolis Gazette*, January 14 and 28, 1864; *Maryland Republican*, January 16, 1864.
4. "History of Smallpox," accessed July 21, 2020, https://www.cdc.gov/smallpox/history/history.html.
5. *Chronica Domus* I:231 (August 28 or 29 [*sic*], 1863), II:8–9 (March 6, 1865); *Province Annals*, 1832–71 (Annapolis, 1865), 585–86.
6. *Chronica Domus* I:248 (January 5, 1864), I:251 (March 20, 1864), I:257 (August 1, 1864); Wuest, *Annales*, IV:2:456; *Liber Vestitutiones Provinciae*, invested on March 25, 1857 and readmitted June 21, 1858. Hanley' s date of dispensation was July 6, 1864.
7. *Maryland Republican*, January 16, 1864; Annapolis Mayor and Aldermen, Property Assessment, June 11, 1860, MSA M72–3, listing "Henry Treadway House & Lot D of G st [$]800." For the "Noah's Ark" fire, see *Sun*, February 16, 1864; *Annapolis Gazette*, February 18, 1864. Also, *Sun*, November 20, 1865, which identified Dr. John Boyle as the owner; for sale of property by John H. Boyle Sr., James Boyle, Jr. [III], and others to Solomon Phillips, GEG 2:163 (September 10, 1866), AACLR. The event is summarized in McWilliams, *Annapolis*, 193.
8. *Sun*, February 8, 1864; *Crutch*, February 13, 1864; McWilliams, *Annapolis*, 182–83; Kenneth P. Czech, "The Russians Are Coming!" *America's Civil War* 9, no. 4, (September 1996): 38–45.
9. 13 Stat. 6 1864, US Congress, *The Statutes at Large, Treaties, and Proclamations of the United States of America, from December 1863, to December 1865*, ed., George P. Sanger (Boston: Little Brown and Company, 1866), 13:9, accessed September 10, 2016, http://www.loc.gov/law/help/statutes-at-large/38th-congress/c38.pdf. For analysis of the Amendatory Act of February 24, 1864, see Geary, *We Need Men*, 117–30.
10. *Statutes at Large*, chap. 237: Section 2, 379. A subsequent amendment, enacted on March 3, 1865, 1865 chap.79, pp. 487–91, did not mention conscientious objection. Geary, *We Need Men*, 132–39, concerning the Amendatory Act of July 4, 1864, which repealed the commutation clause; 167–70 for analysis of how men of a wide range of economic strata and social classes actually benefitted from the commutation clause.
11. *Chronica Domus* I:235 (December 30, 1863), I:248 (January 2, 1864), and I:248 (January n.d., 1864), which says De Dycker visited around the middle of the month and that Müller came "around the same time."
12. "Thomas McCurdy Vincent, Brigadier General, United States Army," accessed January 5, 2017, http://www.arlingtoncemetery.net/tmvincent.htm; letter of Rev. Mich. Miller [*sic*], C.Ss.R., Cumberland, to Maj. [Thomas M.] Vincent, War Department, Washington, March 12, 1864, Letters Received, Box 33, Letter M243, Part 1, Entry 18, RG 110, NARA; Brinsfield, *Faith in the Fight*, 42. Michael Müller, "The Conscription of our Fathers, Students and Brothers in Our House at Annapolis for military service," undated handwritten notes in Müller Personnel File, RABP. Müller used the term "begotted"—by which he meant bigoted—several times in his notes.
13. Miller [*sic*], Cumberland, to Fry, Washington, February 22, 1864, Letters Received, Box 33, Letter M178, Part I, Entry 18, RG 110; Assistant Adjutant General to Müller, February 25, 1864, and same to Captain James Smith, Frederick, February 25, 1864, both in Letters Sent, vol. 3:1181–83, Part 1, Entry 3, RG 110.
14. Miller [*sic*] to Vincent, March 12, 1864, and endorsements by Capt. Samuel B. Laurance, Provost Marshal General's Bureau, March 18, Capt. John C. Holland, 5th Dist., Maryland, March 23, and Capt. James Smith, 4th District, Maryland, March 24, 1864, Letters Received, Box 33, Letter M243, Part 1, Entry 18, RG 110, NARA. Endorsements on this letter refer to Enrollment District No. 4 Enrollment Books, 1:22 and 3:313–14, and Enrollment District No. 758, 3:414. Also, Assistant Adjutant General to Müller, March 28, 1864, Letters Sent, vol. 5:646–47, Part 1, Entry 3, RG 110.
15. Miller [*sic*], Superior of the Redemptorist Society, Cumberland, to Vincent, Washington, April 4, 1864, Part 1, Entry 18, Letters Received, Box 33, Letter M289, RG 110, NARA.
16. Chas. I. White, St. Matthews Church, to Maj. [Thomas M.] Vincent, April 6, 1864, Part 1, Entry 18, Letters Received, Box 33, enclosed with Letter M289, RG 110, NARA.
17. Ruggles' letter has not been found but was referred to in Miller [*sic*], Superior of the Redemptorist Society, Baltimore, to Fry, Washington, April 11, 1864, Part 1, Entry 18, Letters Received, Box 33, RG 110, NARA, enclosed with Letter M304, enclosing four petitions for eleven priests. For example, although William Löwekamp was mentioned in one of the petitions, his individual case was not located.
18. Miller [*sic*], Superior of the Redemptorist Society, Baltimore, to Very Respected Sir, April 11, 1864, Part 1, Entry 18, Letters Received, Box 33, enclosed with Letter M314, with endorsements, RG 110, NARA. Also, Acting Assistant Adjutant General to Müller, April 29, 1864, Letters Sent, vol. 5:690, Part 1, Entry 3, RG 110, NARA; Geary, *We Need Men*, 70, 99–100, 168.
19. Miller to Very Respected Sir, April 11, 1864; Assistant Adjutant General to Müller, May 3, 1864, Letters Sent, vol. 5:696, Part 1, Entry 3, RG 110, NARA. Also, Borgmann, *Redemptorists at Annapolis*, 247. After his Annapolis assignment, Helmprächt was superior of the Baltimore Province until 1877. Upon Helmprächt's departure for Rome, Dielemans became

vice rector, completing Seelos' unfinished term. He was succeeded by Leopold Petsch on July 28, 1865, see *Chronica Domus,* II:16 (April 17, 1865), II:21 (July 28, 1865).

20. Assistant Adjutant General to Müller, May 7, 1864, Letters Sent, vol. 5:699–700, Part 1, Entry 3, RG 110, NARA.
21. Acting Assistant Adjutant General to Müller, May 11, and May 28, 1864, Letters Sent, vol. 5:702 and 724, Part 1, Entry 3, RG 110, NARA.
22. Geary, *We Need Men,* 74; Müller, "Conscription of our Fathers, Students and Brothers"; Zimmer, *Leben und Wirken,* 216 (210 in translation), says when students were examined by civil authorities, all were declared unfit for military service; Seelos, New York, to unidentified friend in Germany, April 11, 1865, Letter 172, Hoegerl, *Sincerely, Seelos,* 427.
23. *Chronica Domus* I:271 (end-of-1864 *Annotationes quaedam,* item 1); Curley, *Cheerful Ascetic,* 215–16, gives brief account of the enrollment board transfers.
24. *Maryland Republican,* June 4, 1864; Provost Marshal General Files, Draft Enrollment Records, Annapolis City, 1862 and 1863; report on Annapolis draft delinquents from Thomas N. Pindle, Deputy Provost Marshal, Anne Arundel County, Annapolis, to Captain John C. Holland, Provost Marshal, Fifth Congressional District, [Ellicott's Mills], October 10, 1864, Provost Marshal General Letters Received 1864, Folder 4, Entry PH–4526, RG 110, NARA Philadelphia. For Henry Coulter's confirmation see Confirmation Register B#1 (March 29, 1857) and residence with the Treadways, 1860 Federal Census, Annapolis.
25. Anne, John G., and Eliza Jane Hanshaw to Gabriel Rumpler, NHG 4:466 (April 27, 1855); Matthias Benzinger, administrator for Rumpler, to the Redemptorists, NHG 5:546 (June 6, 1856); Farmer's Bank partial release of the debt of Joshua and Harriet Brown, NHG 8:271 (July 22, 1859); Ferreol Girardey, administrator, to Joshua and Harriet Brown, NHG 12:75 (January 6, 1864); Browns to William Anderson, NHG 12:77 (January 7, 1864), AACLR. Also, Girardey's report to the Orphans' Court, January 5 and January 12, 1864, Orphans Court Proceedings, 1784–1980, Register of Wills, Anne Arundel County, MSA CM119 (CR 262–542 and 543). The Hanshaws (and variant spellings) are not listed as enslavers in either the 1850 or 1860 Federal Slave Schedules. For further discussion of Mulberry Hill, see Worden, *Saint Mary's,* 43.
26. *Chronica Domus,* I:230 (August 28 or 29, 1863); Chronicles of the House of Studies, Cumberland, 129 (January 1, 1864) and 137 (January 1, 1864). Schnüttgen completed his second novitiate in Philadelphia, Annals, St. Peter's, Philadelphia, 1858–1972, 66 (December 11, 1863), RABP.
27. *Chronica Domus* I:235 (December 11, 1863); I:249 (February 7 and 23–24,1864); I:250 (March 1, 1864); I:250 (March 6 and 9, 1864). Whelan presided at the 1864 ordination because the See of Baltimore was vacant, Kenrick having died July 3, 1863, and Spalding appointed May 3, 1864, and enthroned July 31, 1864. See *Catholic Mirror,* March 17, 1864; *Sun,* March 18, 1864.
28. Kurtz, *Excommunicated from the Union,* 68–70, 75–77, 168–69, 191 n7; email from Rev. Robert J. Miller to author, January 25, 2018, on numbers of chaplains. Also, Miller, *Both Prayed to the Same God,* 98, 111; Randall Miller, "Catholic Religion, Irish Ethnicity, and the American Civil War," 266–67.
29. *Chronica Domus* I:271–72 (end-of-1864 *Annotationes quaedam,* item 7); Darrell L. Collins, *The Army of the Potomac: Order of Battle, 1861–1865, with Commanders, Strengths, Losses, and More* (Jefferson, North Carolina: McFarland, 2013), 160.
30. War Department Special Orders No. 16, para. 58 (January 12, 1864) in *Official Records of the Union and Confederate Armies,* series I, vol. 33 (Washington: Government Printing Office, 1891), 373, says Burnside was "assigned to recruit and fill up the Ninth Army Corps . . . to number of 50,000 men." Collins, *Army of the Potomac,* 168, says the Ninth Army Corps had 21,363 men as of April 30, 1864; Ryan T. Quint, "Ambrose Burnside, the Ninth Army Corps, and the Battle of Spotsylvania Court House," *Gettysburg College Journal of the Civil War Era,* 5, article 7 (April 20, 2015): 80, accessed April 5, 2016, http://cupola.gettysburg.edu/cgi/viewcontent.cgi?article=1052&context=gcjcwe, gives the number 21,000. *Sun,* April 14, 1864, reported Second Maryland Infantry arrived in Baltimore April 13 and had a thirty-day furlough before rejoining the Ninth Army Corps. Since his numbers date from April 30, Collins, *Army of the Potomac,* 168, does not include strength figures for the Second Maryland.
31. *Sun,* March 24, 1864; Leander W. Cogswell, *A History of the Eleventh New Hampshire Regiment Volunteer Infantry in the Rebellion War, 1861–1865* (Concord, New Hampshire: Republican Press Association, 1891), 262; George Washington Whitman, Camp near Annapolis, to Walt Whitman, [Washington, DC], April 16, 1862, Letter 46 in Jerome M. Loving, ed., *Civil War Letters of George Washington Whitman* (Durham: Duke University Press, 1975); Marvel, *Burnside,* 344; McWilliams, *Annapolis,* 188. Email from David Haight to author, April 9, 2016, confirms the locations of the farms of Hart and Taylor, both of whom made claims against the Burnside encampments for damages to land and fences, Reports to the Quartermaster General, 4:801–12 (February 9, 1869) and 5:645-67 (March 27, 1869), Entry 1037, RG 92, NARA.
32. *Sun,* April 11, 1864; Marvel, *Burnside,* 354; Daniel Larned, Annapolis, to Dear Sister, April 13 and April 18, 1864, Larned Papers, LoC; Cogswell, *Eleventh New Hampshire,* 469.
33. Larned, Annapolis, to Dear Sister, April 13, 1864, Larned Papers; Marvel, *Burnside,* 345; Quint, "Ambrose Burnside," 80; Cogswell, *Eleventh New Hampshire,* 256, 270.
34. Joseph Helmprächt, C.Ss.R., "Schreiben des P. Joseph Helmprächt, Provincials der Redemptoristen in Nordamerika, aus Rom am 10 Juni 1865 an ein Mitglied der Verwaltung der Leopoldinen-Stiftung," *Berichte der Leopoldinen-Stiftung im Kaisertume Oesterreich,* XXXV, Heft 1865 (Vienna: Verlag in der fürst-erzbischöflichen Consistorial-Kanzlei, 1865), 21–27. Although the title indicates Helmprächt's letter of of June 10, 1865, most of quotes are from Freitag's Holy Saturday [April 16], 1865 letter.

35. Marvel, *Burnside*, 345; Cogswell, *Eleventh New Hampshire*, 277–78, 469.
36. *Chronica Domus* I:272 (item 7).
37. Gross, Annapolis, to Howes Goldsborough, April 11, 1864, Folder 2, Goldsborough Papers.
38. Letter from unknown (the signature was clipped out), Annapolis, to Father Timothy Enright, [New York], July 23 [1864], RABP. The writer may have been Father Michael Müller. He is recorded in the *Chronica Domus* I:256 (July 23, 1864) as having arrived in Annapolis that day with Wuest. The handwriting is somewhat similar to specimens of Müller's handwriting and the statement referring to the "young fathers" that "I can not be their master any longer" also points to Müller. This letter was once attributed to Seelos but the hand-writing has been determined to not be his, per email from Carl Hoegerl, C.Ss.R., RABP, to author, April 16, 2009. Since the writer refers to a Confederate attack on Washington, the year—which was not included as part of the date—must be 1864, when the Confederates attacked Fort Stevens on July 11–12, 1864.
39. Marriage Register B#1 (September 29, 1864); religious services and rules and regulations for visitors covered in *Crutch*, January 16, 1864.
40. "Agnus Dei," Attwater, *Catholic Dictionary*, 13; "A Prayer to be Daily Said by those Who Carry About Them an Agnus Dei," in John Milner, *The Key of Heaven: A Manual of Prayer*, rev. ed. (Baltimore: John Murphy and Company, 1867), 299.
41. "Parole Camp Annapolis, M'd," Baltimore: E. Sachse and Company, 1864, Geography and Map Division, LoC, https://www.loc.gov/resource/g3844p.cw0245390/; Edward Parmalee Smith, *Incidents of the United States Christian Commission* (Philadelphia: J. B. Lippincott, 1869), 411; Lemuel Moss, *Annals of the United States Christian Commission* (Philadelphia: J. B. Lippincott, 1868), illustrations following pages 182 and 184, 183–85 description.
42. "States of the Church," *New Catholic Encyclopedia*, 2d edition (Washington: Catholic University of America, 2003), 13:490–97; Ron Field, *Garibaldi: Leadership, Strategy, Conflict* (Long Island City, New York: Osprey Publishing, 2011) 51–52.
43. *Annapolis Gazette*, February 11 and June 2, 1864.
44. Gross to Goldsborough, July 9, 1864, Folder 2, Goldsborough Papers. The only list of Civil War-era First Communicants at St. Mary's is April 17, 1864; the event mentioned in *Chronica Domus* I:255 (July 9, 1864): "First communion is solemnly held for Negroes" and nothing about soldiers.
45. Kurtz, *Excommunicated from the Union*, 53.
46. "Schreiben des P. Joseph Helmprächt," 21–27; Faust, *Republic of Suffering*, 16; *Mission-Book of the Congregation of the Most Holy Redeemer (1863)*, 193.
47. Faust, *Republic of Suffering*, 26–27.
48. Interment Register B#1 (January 15, 1864). At the time, the interment register lacked a column for the name of the officiating priest. Except for a few corrections and additions the handwriting is uniform throughout the page, perhaps indicating that an office brother, rather than individual officiating priests, made the entries.
49. *Crutch*, January 16, 1864; *Annapolis Gazette*, March 24, 1864; US Department of Veterans Affairs, "Annapolis National Cemetery," accessed January 20, 2012, http://www.cem.va.gov/cems/nchp/annapolis.asp.
50. Widow Claim filed January 27, 1864, Application No. 43661, Certificate No. 33678, and Minor Claim filed March 21, 1867, Application No. 144151, Certificate No. 120446, Box 32978, Case Files of Approved Pension Applications of Widows and Other Dependents of Civil War Veterans, ca. 1861–ca. 1910, RG 15, NARA; New York State Military Museum, "173rd Infantry Regiment, Civil War: History," accessed April 11, 2016, https://museum.dmna.ny.gov/unit-history/infantry-2/173rd-infantry-regiment; Lewis M. Peck, *A Brief Sketch of the 173rd Regiment, N.Y.V.* (Brooklyn: 1868), accessed April 11, 2016, https://museum.dmna.ny.gov/application/files/4715/5421/5155/Brief_Sketch_173rd_Peck.pdf; Compiled Military Service Record (James Higgins, Co. A, 173rd New York Infantry), RG 94, NARA; Michael D. Gorman, "Civil War Richmond: General Hospital #21," accessed March 8, 2018, http://www.mdgorman.com/Hospitals/general_hospital_21.htm; Spalding, *Premier See*, 164. and United States Army, Quartermaster General's Office, *Roll of Honor: Names of Soldiers Who Died in Defence of the American Union, Interred in National Cemeteries in Maine, Minnesota, Maryland, Pennsylvania, Rhode Island, Arkansas, Mississippi, Florida, Louisiana and Colorado Territory During the Rebellion* (Washington: Government Printing Office, 1866), 7:30.
51. Richmond Campaign: Reams' Station Recapitulation, *Official Records of the Union and Confederate Armies*, series I, vol. 42, part 1, (Washington: Government Printing Office, 1898), 131.
52. The "Record of Death and Interment" in Ford's service record indicates burial at Ash Grove in grave No. 158. Quartermaster General's Office, *Roll of Honor: Names of Soldiers*, 49, also lists Ford's burial at Annapolis National Cemetery but the National Cemetery Administration's nationwide gravesite locator has no entry for Ford at Annapolis or any other VA cemetery. Interment Registers B#1 (October 5, 1864), Ford's entry was re-inscribed in B#2 (October 5, 1864), and claims he was buried at St. Mary's Cemetery. Marriage Register B#1 (September 29, 1864); Compiled Military Service Record (William Ford), RG 94, NARA; Although a long list of men admitted to General Hospital Division No. 1 from the Flag-of-Truce Boat *New York* on September 14, including three other men from the Sixty-Ninth New York, appeared in *Crutch*, September 17, 1864, neither Ford's arrival at General Hospital Division No. 2 nor his death were reported in that or subsequent *Crutch* editions.
53. Widow Claim filed January 27, 1864, Application No. 43661, RG 15, NARA.
54. Peter C. Luebke, "Battle of Seven Pines–Fair Oaks," *Encyclopedia Virginia*, accessed May 25, 2016, http://www.encyclopediavirginia.org/seven_pines_battle_of#start_entry; Compiled Military Service Record (Thomas F. Gosson,

Co. H, 38th New York Infantry Regiment), RG 94, NARA; *The Union Army: A History of Military Affairs in the Loyal States, 1861-65, Records of the Regiments in the Union Army, Cyclopedia of Battles, Memoirs of Commanders and Soldiers* (Madison, Wisconsin: Federal Publishing Company, 1908), as quoted in New York State Military Museum, "38th Infantry Regiment Civil War: Second Scott's Life Guard," accessed May 25, 2016, https://dmna.ny.gov/historic/reghist/civil/infantry/38thInf/38thInfMain.htm. Carded Medical Record, Entry 534, Box 2805 RG 94, NARA; Pension File No. 15676, RG 15, NARA.

55. Test Book, 1851–1868, Anne Arundel County Circuit Court, MSA C147–1; Interment Register B#1 (November 3, 1864).
56. Miller, "Catholic Religion, Irish Ethnicity, and the American Civil War," 270.
57. First Communion Register B#1 (April 17, 1864); "Catholicity in Annapolis—Saint Mary's Church, Annapolis," *Catholic Mirror*, April 23, 1864, 2.
58. Email of Michael Fitzpatrick January 5, 2017, to author sharing knowledge of army hospital operations and employment of women there and other insights on women coming to Annapolis during the war.
59. Marriage Register B#1 (January 20, 1862); Compiled Military Service Records (George M. Mittnacht, Co. E, 6th New York State Militia, and Co. H, 103d New York Infantry Regiment), RG 94, NARA; "Green-Wood Civil War Biographies: Mittnacht, George M. (1830-1889)," accessed August 28, 2016, https://www.green-wood.com/2015/civil-war-biographies-mitchel-morrison/; "The Seward Infantry," *New York Times,* December 2, 1883, 13; Baptismal Register B#2 (June 6, 1869); "New York, New York, Death Index, 1862–1948," accessed March 18, 2014, Ancestry.com.
60. Marriage Register B#1 (January 14, 1863); Compiled Military Service Record (Sylvester McCabe, Co. A, 67th New York Infantry Regiment), RG 94, NARA; Pension Record, Application No. 139196, RG 15, NARA, for Margaret McCabe, died 1929 as Mrs. Simeon Haddan; "Smith Family Tree," accessed March 18, 2014, Ancestry.com and email exchange between Rebecca Szabo and author, March 20–24, 2014 in regard to the Smith Family Tree; 1900 Federal Census, La Junta, Las Animas County, Colorado; 1920 Federal Census, Dawson, Colfax County, New Mexico; "New Mexico, Deaths, 1889-1945," accessed March 25, 2014, FamilySearch.org. Also, Baptismal Register B#1 (November 4, 1862—John B. Hughes, who was erroneously recorded as James Hughes) and B#1 (April 26, 1864—Thomas Quinn); *Liber Professionis,* 369 (Hughes's vows dispensed June 10, 1884). Find A Grave Memorial ID 46980212 for Thomas Oscar Quinn (1864–1932).
61. Marriage Register B#1 (June 7, 1863). The other marriages, also in B#1, were Andrew Seber and Mary Hannigan (December 4, 1862); Michael Hermann and Eva Boehnlein (January 1, 1863); Louis DuFort and Louisa Jacobs (September 3, 1863). See also Compiled Military Service Record (Michael Lieble [*sic*], Co. A, 54th New York Infantry Regiment), RG 94, NARA; Carded Medical Record (M. Liebler [*sic*]), Co. I [*sic*], 54th New York Infantry, Box 2129, Entry 534, RG 94, NARA; Unit History Project, New York State Military Museum, "54th Infantry Regiment, Civil War," accessed October 30, 2016, https://dmna.ny.gov/historic/reghist/civil/infantry/54thInf/54thInfTable.htm; 1880 Federal Census, Buffalo, New York, lists Michael and Anna Liebel and four children, ages 1 to 10.
62. Marriage Register B#1 (June 16, 1863); Compiled Military Service Record (Harvey L. Rose, Co. F, 1st Michigan Infantry Regiment), RG 94, NARA; "1st Regiment, Michigan Infantry," NPS Soldiers and Sailors Database, accessed August 24, 2016, https://www.nps.gov/civilwar/search-battle-units-detail.htm; Harvey L. Rose Carded Medical Record, Entry 534, Box 1403, RG 94, NARA; Garrett Peck, *Walt Whitman in Washington, D.C.: The Civil War and America's Great Poet* (Charleston, South Carolina: History Press, 2015), 41.
63. Marriage Register B#1 (June 16, 1863) and B#2 (June 16, 1863); Harvey L. Rose Pension File, Application No. 600112, Certificate No. 479436, RG 15, NARA; Worden, *Saint Mary's*, 100. A search of land records for Anne Arundel (MSA CE 158–1 [1845–56] and CE 158–2 [1856-68], Howard (MSA CE 128–5 [1840–1993]), and Prince George's (MSA CE 22–1 [1840–84]) counties did not reveal property owned by Joseph Manning Lloyd between 1855 and his death in 1870. Charles County land record indexes (MSA CE 83–2 [1658–1832] and CE 84–1 [1832–87]) lists numerous Lloyd family holdings, especially those of Minchin Lloyd, Joseph Manning Lloyd's father, starting in 1823. Affidavit of Maryland Turner (1843–1935), Baltimore, October 21, 1918, in Harvey Rose Pension File; Compiled Military Service Record (Harvey Rose); General Orders No. 191, issued June 25, 1863 in Thomas M. O'Brien and Oliver Diefendorf, *General Orders of the War Department Embracing the Years 1861, 1862, and 1863* (New York: Derby and Miller, 1864), G.O. No. 191, June 25, 1863, 2:217–18; Daniel B. Lloyd, *The Lloyds of Southern Maryland* (Washington: The Author, 1971), 149; 1850 Federal Census, Allens Fresh District, Charles County, Maryland.
64. Marriage Register B#1 (February 12, 1864); NPS Soldiers and Sailors Database, accessed November 11, 2016, which lists thirty men in the regular and volunteer army named Thomas Gaffney. Utah Territory did not have a statute regarding the registration of civil marriages until 1887; no record has been found of the Gaffney-Jarvis marriage there. See Utah Division of Archives and Records Service, "Marriage Records," accessed November 11, 2016, https://archives.utah.gov/research/guides/marriage.htm; Brigham Young University, "Special Collections and Family History: Pre-1887 Sources for Utah Counties," accessed January 30, 2016, http://abish.byui.edu/specialcollections/westernstates/utahpre1887sources.cfm.
65. Anne Arundel County marriage license issued February 27, 1864, to George C. White and Mary Kerby, "Maryland Marriages, 1667–1899," accessed October 2, 2012, Ancestry.

com; Marriage Register B#1 (March 31, 1864), witnesses Patrick Coyle and Mary Schultz; "Division No. 1, Returned to Duty," Crutch, February 20, 1864, 3; Compiled Military Service Record (George C. White, Co. K, 28th Massachusetts Infantry Regiment), RG 94, NARA; "28th Massachusetts Regimental History: 1863," http://www.28thmass.org/history5.htm, and "28th Massachusetts Regimental Roster," http://www.28thmass.org/CompyK/CompK.htm, both accessed January 16, 2016; Pension File (Mary White, widow, Application No. 284104 Certificate No. 287669), RG 15, NARA. For the Kirby-Smith marriage see Marriage Register B#2 (May 8, 1865).

66. Marriage Register B#1 (April 10, 1864); *Crutch*, April 23, 1864; Military Service Record, RG 94, NARA, in regard to O'Malley; NPS Soldiers and Sailors Database, accessed December 31, 2016, for the 11 names; Find A Grave Memorial ID 156443709, provides Laurence Murray's dates (August 20, 1837–December 29, 1906) and two spouses: Ellen Lucy Murray (1840–1868) and Kate [Catherine] Lawlor Murray (1850–1904); Laurence and Kate are buried in St. Peter and Paul's Cemetery, Elmira, Chemung County, New York; *Watkins Express* (Watkins, New York) October 25, 1888; *Hanford's Elmira City, and Elmira Heights Directory, 1900,* 36, accessed December 31, 2016, http://www.joycetice.com/director/1900e036.htm; *Democrat Chronicle* (Rochester, New York), September 3, 1891; *Elmira Telegram,* June 17, 1894; *Elmira Daily Gazette and Free Press,* September 6, 1900; *The Telegram* (Elmira), January 6 and August 11, 1907; 1860 and 1900 Federal censuses, Elmira.

67. Marriage Register B#1 (June n.d., 1864); "Maryland Marriages, 1666–1970," accessed June 2, 2016, FamilySearch.org, lists June 15, 1864, for the Anne Arundel County marriage license. Also, NPS, "30th Regiment, United States Colored Infantry," accessed January 1, 2017, https://www.nps.gov/civilwar/; 1870 Federal Census, Annapolis, including USNA.

68. Marriage Register B#2 (December 2, 164); McIntire 1:210; WSG 25:2 (December 7, 1839), and NHG 1:643 (December 31, 1852), AACLR; 1860 Federal Census, Annapolis; Edward W. Callahan, ed., *List of Officers of the Navy of the United States and of the Marine Corps from 1775 to 1900* (New York: L. R. Hamersly, 1901), 415; "Navy Gazette: List of Volunteer Naval Officers," *Army and Navy Journal, December 15, 1866,* 272; Lewis R. Hamersly, *The Records of Living Officers of the United States Navy and Marine Corps, With a History of Naval Operations During the Rebellion of 1861–5* (Philadelphia: J. B. Lippincott, 1870), 318; Admiral David D. [Dixon] Porter, *The Naval History of the Civil War* (New York: Sherman Publishing Company, 1886), 740; "Vanderbilt," accessed January 1, 2017, https://www.history.navy.mil/research/histories/ship-histories/danfs/v/vanderbilt.html. Also, "Pennsylvania, Philadelphia City Death Certificates, 1803–1915"; "Pennsylvania, Philadelphia City Births, 1860–1906"; "[Fall River] Massachusetts Births and Christenings, 1639–1915," accessed August 28, 2016, FamilySearch.org; *Woods' Baltimore City Directory, 1886,* 1011, all of which identify couples named John and Eliza O'Neil.

69. Marriage Register B#1 (December 15, 1864); Compiled Military Service Record (Patrick Connaughton, Co. B, 118th Pennsylvania Infantry), RG 94, NARA, includes War Department Special Orders No. 560, December 18, 1863; NPS, "118th Regiment, Pennsylvania Infantry," accessed March 13, 2016, https://www.nps.gov/; Annapolis Passes, RG 393 Part 4 Entry 1536, pass no. 243 (May 9, 1864), and pass no. 5424 (July 27, 1864).

70. Marriage Register B#2 (December 15, 1864); "Maryland Marriages, 1666–1970," accessed March 14, 2016, FamilySearch.org.

71. McIntire, 1:409; 1850 Federal Slave Schedule, Annapolis, 4; Harry Wright Newman, "Anne Arundel During the War of Secession," in James C. Bradford, ed., *Anne Arundel County, Maryland: A Bicentennial History, 1649–1977* (Annapolis: Anne Arundel County and Annapolis Bicentennial Committee, 1977), 270, mentions "City Tavern." Also, Thomas Karney, US Naval Academy, to Butler, April 5 [*sic*, 25], 1861, Box 3, and To Whom It May Concern, Headquarters, Annapolis, May 1, 1861, Box 4, Benjamin F. Butler Papers, MS 12127, Manuscript Division, LoC; *Sun*, January 11, 1913, published after Annie Lamb Kimball's died in Baltimore January 10, and the story repeated in Laura Lee Davidson, "The Services of the Women of Maryland to the Confederate States," *Confederate Veteran* (Nashville) 28, no. 9 (September 1920): 333. Email from Stephanie Solt, an Andrew Lamb descendant, to author, June 9, 2017, said that the spy story "is not in the family lore."

72. "2nd Maryland Infantry CSA 'Company D,'" accessed April 3, 2016, http://www.2ndmarylandcod.com/company-d-military-files/pvt-john-b-lamb/, provides carded service record of John B. [*sic*] Lamb, notes service and place of burial. Also, *Annapolis Gazette*, December 4, 1865; Find A Grave Memorial ID 180153384; Old Book 256, Middle Department [Baltimore], Part 4, Entry 1536, pass no. 243, issued May 9, 1864, RG 393, NARA, has Connaughton's occupation as "Bowling & Saloon keeper." There are no St. Mary's baptismal records for the Connaughtons. "Massachusetts Births, 1841–1915," accessed April 12, 2013, FamilySearch.org, lists Lawrence Conocton, born 1870, West Roxbury, with parents Patrick H. Connaughton, born Ireland, and Margaret E., born Annapolis. Five other children are also listed: Richard (1874), Catherine (1877), Ann Theresa (1881), Agnes (1883), and Frances (1887). Also, 1900, 1910, 1920, and 1930 Federal censuses, Boston; "Massachusetts Death Index, 1901–1980," accessed March 21, 2016, Ancestry.com, for Boston deaths of Patrick and Margaret.

73. *Maryland Republican,* May 7, 1864. At the time, there were two Catholic churches in Indianapolis, St. John's and Immaculate Conception, the latter a German parish. See *Sadliers' Catholic Almanac, 1864,* 149. Also, 1870 Federal Census, New York City; Find A Grave Memorial IDs 34886048 (George, May 1882) and 34885946 (Julia, February 10, 1912). For Ida

Mary Sullivan, see McIntire 1:686, 792; Marriage Register B#3 (November 7, 1881). Fifty-three men named George Watkins served in the Union army, including three in Indiana regiments (see NPS Soldiers and Sailors Database), but a review of likely candidates' Compiled Military Service Records did not reveal Annapolis connections. Gross was appointed bishop of Savannah in 1873. See Rev. Andrew H. Skeabeck, C.Ss.R., "Most Rev. William H. Gross, C.SS.R.: Missionary Bishop of the South," *Records of the American Catholic Historical Society of Philadelphia* 66:1 (March 1955), 35–52, 66:2 (June 1955), 78–94, and 66:3 (September 1955), 131–53.

74. General Order No. 143, May 22, 1863, Orders and Circulars, 1797–1910; Records of the Adjutant General's Office, 1780s–1917; RG 94, NARA; Civil War Trust, "United States Colored Troops," accessed November 3, 2014, https://www.battlefields.org/learn/topics/united-states-colored-troops.

75. Compiled Military Service Record (William H. Brown, Co. E, 30th USCT), RG 94, NARA; Index of Slave or Free of Maryland Colored Troops, 74, Entry PH-4407, RG 110, NARA Philadelphia. Also, Freedom Records, 1785–1867, Anne Arundel County, Owner Index 35, MSA (William H. Brown freed by Mary Mullen [*sic*], March 3, 1864; Baptismal Register B#1 (July 28, 1861). William's parentage is uncertain but he may have been the son of Stephen and Rosa Brown, whose three daughters, Anna Maria, Henrietta, and Jane Sophia, all of them *liberae* (free), converted and were baptized at St. Mary's the same day, B#1 (February 26, 1860).

76. Compiled Service Record (William H. Brown); Freedom Records, 1785–1867, Anne Arundel County, Owner Index 35, MSA (William H. Brown freed by Mary Mullen [*sic*], March 3, 1864; Soldiers and Sailors Database, "United States Colored Troops 30th Regiment," https://www.nps.gov/civilwar/search-battle-units-detail.htm, and Civil War Trust, "The Crater," http://www.civilwar.org/battlefields/the-crater.html?tab=facts, both accessed August 21, 2016; Noah Andre Trudeau, "A Stranger in the Club: The Army of the Potomac's Black Division," in Gabor Boritt and Scott Hancock, eds., *Slavery, Resistence, Freedom* (New York: Oxford University Press, 2007), 107, quoting *Christian Recorder,* August 20, 1864, which quoted a member of the Twenty-Seventh USCT; "Thirtieth Regiment Infantry, US Colored Troops, Maryland Volunteers," in Allison Wilmer, J. H. Jarrett and George W. F. Vernon, *History and Roster of Maryland Volunteers, War of 1861–5, Archives of Maryland Online,* 366:2 (Baltimore: Guggenheimer, Weil, 1899), 245, accessed August 21, 2016, http://aomol.msa.maryland.gov/000001/000366/html/am366--245.html. For Camp Stanton, see Patricia Samford, "Camp Stanton and the U. S. Colored Troops." accessed June 5, 2021, https://jeffersonpatterson.wordpress.com/2021/02/11/camp-stanton-and-the-u-s-colored-troops/. Another William Brown from Company E, Thirtieth USCT transferred to the Navy in 1864, was discharged on September 15, 1865, and received an invalid pension in 1892. See Pension File Application No. 909363, Certificate No. 756244, William Brown, Company E, Thirtieth USCT, and US Navy, RG 15, NARA.

77. Marriage Register B#1 (June, no date, 1864); "Maryland Marriages, 1666–1970," accessed June 2, 2016, FamilySearch.org; Wilmer, *History and Roster of Maryland Volunteers,* 366:2; NPS Soldiers and Sailors Database, "30th Regiment, United States Colored Infantry" (Benjamin Carmel), accessed January 1, 2017, https://www.nps.gov/civilwar/; Compiled Military Service Record (Benjamin Cornell, Co. I, 30th USCT), RG 94, NARA; Index of Slave or Free of Maryland Colored Troops, 89, Entry PH-4407, RG 110, NARA Philadelphia; 1870 Federal Census, Annapolis.

78. Baptismal Register B#1 (August 24, 1865); Military Service Record (Charles Sevoy, Company D, Thirtieth USCT), RG 94, NARA; Index of Slave or Free of Maryland Colored Troops, 191, PH-4407, RG 110, NARA Philadelphia; Wilmer, *History and Roster of Maryland Volunteers,* 366:2; NPS Soldiers and Sailors Database, lists Joshua Sevoy in same company and regiment but not Charles; Pension File Index, RG 15, NARA, lists both Charles Sevoy (d. 1908) and Joshua Sevoy (d. 1907) in the same company and regiment. Also, Judith Cabral and Kunte Kinte-Alex Haley Foundation, "Anne Arundel County Slaves – USCT," e-file provided to author, January 20, 2014.

79. Baptismal Register B#1 (March 20, 1860); Compiled Military Service Record (Dennis Larkins, Co. C, 43rd USCT), RG 94, NARA; Carded Medical Records, Entry 534, RG 94, NARA; "Forty-Third United States Colored Regiment" in Samuel P. Bates, *History of Pennsylvania Volunteers, 1861–5,* 5 (Harrisburg: B. Singerly, State Printer, 1871) 1081–84, 1089; "43rd US Colored Troops Infantry Regiment," ACWRDB, accessed April 3, 2014; NPS Soldiers and Sailors Database, "United States Colored Troops, 43rd Regiment, United States Colored Infantry," accessed August 21, 2016; "Maryland, Births and Christenings Index, 1662–1911," accessed February 27, 2014, Ancestry.com; "Anne Arundel County Slave Statistics," District 1, MSA C142; 1880 Federal Census, Annapolis.

80. Baptismal Register B#2 (June 22, 1866); William Smothers Freedom Record, AA Index, 1805–1864, MSA S1407; Annapolis Mayor and Aldermen, Property Assessment, June 11, 1860, MSA M72-3; Annapolis Draft Enrollment Records; *Annapolis Gazette,* July 21, 1864. There is no record of property owned by William Smothers in AACLR Grantee Index, 1839–1908; his property evidently went unrecorded or was in another person's name but he paid the taxes.

81. Card Index 35 (Owners Index—Thomas J. Franklin), MSA Reading Room; Index of Slave or Free of Maryland Colored Troops, 192, PH-4407, RG 110, NARA Philadelphia; NPS Soldiers and Sailors Database, "United States Colored Troops, 43rd Regiment, United States Colored Infantry," accessed February 2, 2017, https://www.nps.gov/civilwar/search-battle-units-detail.htm; Judith Cabral, "Unsung Heroes: 122 Slaves from Anne Arundel County Became Union Soldiers and Sailors," *Anne Arundel County History Notes,* 34, no. 2 (January 2003): 3–6.

82. *Annapolis Gazette*, May 12 and 26, July 21, 1864; *Sun*, May 28, July 8 and 19, 1864. Information on Swithin provided in email of Brother Joseph Grabenstein, F.S.C., to author, June 6, 2015, and letter with enclosures, June 24, 2016.

83. *Chronica Domus* I:153 (February 4, 1861), II:9 (March 29, 1865), II:9 (March 30, 1865), II:18 (May 29, 1865); Thomas N. Pindle, Deputy Provost Marshal, Anne Arundel County, Annapolis, to Captain John C. Holland, Provost Marshal, Fifth Congressional District, [Ellicott's Mills], October 10, 1864, Provost Marshal General Letters Received 1864, Folder 4, Entry PH–4526, RG 110, NARA Philadelphia; Holland to Fry, Washington, June 12, 1865, pages 3, 4–4A, 5A, Microfilm Publication M1163, Roll 2, Historical Reports of State Acting Assistant Provost Marshals General and District Provost Marshals, 1865, RG 110, NARA. War Department orders dated April 13, 1865, *Official Records of the Union and Confederate Armies,* series III, vol. 4 (Washington: Government Printing Office, 1900), 1263. Also, *Maryland Republican,* August 20, 1864; *Province Annals,* 1832–71, 569 (1864, Annapolis), RABP. City Council appointed a committee on July 26, 1864, to discuss a revision of the city's quota with the draft authorities, given that the Annapolis enrollment was "very greatly in excess of the population made liable to do military duty." See Annapolis, Mayor and Alderman Proceedings, July 26, 1864, 41–42, MSA M49–10.

84. Jacob Habermeier Personnel File, RABP; 1860 Federal Census, Annapolis; Compiled Military Service Records (George R. Reuss Jr.), RG 94, NARA; Wuest, *Annales,* IV:2:466; Chrysostom Zimmer Personnel File, RABP; Brother Raphael Rock, C.Ss.R., "Life of Our Departed Redemptorist Brothers of the Baltimore Province, 1847–1938," ca. 2013, 40–41, RABP.

85. "Catalogus Novitiorum," I:51, RABP; "Catalogus Novitiorum." II:208:50 and 204.

86. *Chronica Domus* I:267 (October 6 and 30, 1864), I:269 (November 27, 1864), I:271 (end-of-1864 *Annotationes quaedam,* item 5). Ann Louisa Ghequiere Fenwick died at West River, February 22, 1864, accessed February 6, 2015, http://trees.ancestrylibrary.com/tree/21902123/. Also, deeds for 180 acres to Henry A. Fenwick, NHG 12:297 (May 19, 1864); 183 acres to heirs of Harriet E. Donaldson and Chloe T. Fenwick, GW 34:151 (October 2, 1903), AACLR. The "Cottage" reference is found in Our Lady of Sorrows Register of Baptisms, 1865–1908, 196–97 (confirmations), Microfilm SCM 2625, MSA SC1172.

87. *Chronica Domus* I:248–69 (twenty-four days between January 3 and December 4, 1864, including week-long mission).

88. *Chronica Domus* I:271 (end-of-1864 *Annotationes quaedam,* item 3).

89. Gross, Annapolis, to Catherine Goldsborough, Easton, January 14, 1864, Folder 1, Goldsborough Papers; *Chronica Domus* I:235–69 (fifteen dates between December 20, 1863 and November 30, 1864); for Gross' mission activities after leaving Annapolis see *Province Mission Book,* entries for October 20–November 10, 1864, December 4–11, 1864, and thereafter; Rev. Andrew H. Skeabeck, C.Ss.R., "Most Rev. William H. Gross, C.SS.R.: Missionary Bishop of the South," *Records of the American Catholic Historical Society of Philadelphia* 65:3 (September 1954), 142–57, 65:4 (December 1954), 216–29, 66:1 (March 1955), 35–52.

90. Gross to Catherine Goldsborough, October 1, 1863, Folder 1; Gross to Howes Goldsborough, April 11, 1864, Folder 2, Goldsborough Papers. Period and modern maps "improperly" refer to Chlora's Point; see Oswald Tilghman, *History of Talbot County Maryland, 1661–1861* (Baltimore: Williams and Wilkins, 1905), II:319. Gross, Annapolis, to Howes Goldsborough, Easton, May 3, 1864 and September 12, 1864, Folder 2. The Dover Bridge was opened to traffic in 1861, see "Opening of the New Bridge," *Easton Gazette,* February 23, 1861, 2.

91. Gross to Howes Goldsborough, March 10, 1864, Folder 1; Timothy Enright, C.Ss.R., Annapolis, to Howes Goldsborough, Easton, September 23, 1864, Folder 2; Helmprächt, Annapolis, to Howes Goldsborough, Easton, November 2, 1864, Folder 3.

92. Gross to Catherine Goldsborough, November 2, 1863 and December 5, 1863, Folder 1, Goldsborough Papers.

93. Gross, to Catherine Goldsborough, no date (first page missing, probably written in January or February 1864), Folder 1, Goldsborough Papers.

94. Gross to Catherine Goldsborough, December 31, 1863, Folder 1, Goldsborough Papers. The 1850 Federal Slave Schedule for Talbot County lists Howes Goldsboroughs as owner of seven male and five female slaves between ages of two and sixty years; in 1860 he was listed as owner of eight male and fourteen females slaves between ages of one and fifty years.

95. Gross to Catherine Goldsborough, December 5, 1863, and same to Howes Goldsborough, March 10, 1864, Folder 1; Gross to Howes Goldsborough, May 3, 1864, Folder 2, Goldsborough Papers.

96. Gross, to Catherine Goldsborough, December 5, 1863, and no date ; Gross to Howes Goldsborough, March 10, 1864; Gross to Howes Goldsborough, February 19, 1864, and March 10, 1864, all in Folder 1; Gross to Howes Goldsborough, March 28, 1864, Folder 2, Goldsborough Papers.

97. Gross to Howes Goldsborough, March 28, 1864, April 20, 1864, May 3, 1864, April 20, 1864, May 3, 1864, October 10, 1864, Folder 2; Helmprächt to Goldsborough, November 2, 1864, Folder 3, Goldsborough Papers.

98. Michael Roche is identified among "Architects and Engineers" and as "manager" of the Hibernian Society of Baltimore in *Woods' Baltimore City Directory, Ending Year 1860* (Baltimore: John W. Woods, 1860), 463 and 538. Email of James T. Wollon, Havre de Grace, to author, June 9, 2016, identified two Catholic projects by Roche reported in *Sun,* August 13, 1855 and October 30, 1858. Wollon's notes on Roche received June 15, 2016, also list work done on St. Agnes Church (Catonsville). Gross to Goldsborough, March 10, 1864, Folder 1, and March 28, 1864, Folder 2,Goldsborough Papers.

99. Gross to Goldsborough, April 20, 1864, Folder 2; same to same, May 3, 1864, May 18, 1864, July 15, 1864, October 10, 1864, and November 24, 1864, Folder 3, Goldsborough Papers.
100. Gross to Goldsborough, March 28, 1864, Folder 2, Goldsborough Papers (in regard to the purchase); *Easton Gazette*, weekly between August 6, 1864 and September 10, 1864. The paid notice read "J. L. Gettings," *Woods' Baltimore City Directory (1864)*, accessed March 9, 2017, https://archive.org/details/woodsbaltimoreci1864balt, has several listings for John S. Gittings and Benjamin H. Williams, bankers and stock brokers, 29 South Street, Baltimore, and none for Gettings.
101. *Chronica Domus* I:270 (December 25, 1864). After leaving Easton, Claessens went directly to Baltimore and then to Cumberland, returning to Annapolis on December 31.
102. *Chronica Domus* I:271 (*Annotationes quaedam*, 1864, item 4).
103. Joseph Wissel, C.Ss.R., *The Redemptorist on the American Missions* (West Chester, New York: Catholic Protectory, *1886*, vol. I:1 (first edition published in New York 1875); Dolan, *Catholic Revivalism*, 70.
104. Curley, *Cheerful Ascetic*, 248; Wissel, *Redemptorist on the American Missions*, I:36.
105. Jay P. Dolan, *Catholic Revivalism: The American Experience, 1830–1900* (Notre Dame, Indiana: University of Notre Dame Press, 1978), xvi, 12–13, 19; Miller, "Catholic Religion, Irish Ethnicity, and the American Civil War," 268.
106. Randall Miller, "The Failed Mission: The Catholic Church and Black Catholics in the Old South," in Miller and Wakelyn, *Catholics in the Old South*, 153; Robert Miller, *Both Prayed to the Same God*, 121–23; Faust, *Republic of Suffering*, 177; Rable, *God's Almost Chosen People*, 241; Dolan, *Catholic Revivalism*, 142.
107. *Redemptorist Fathers, The Mission-Book of the Congregation of the Most Holy Redeemer: A Manual of Instructions and Prayers Adapted to Preserve the Fruits of the Mission*, New, Revised, and Enlarged Edition (Baltimore: Kelly, Hedian, and Piet, 1863), 3–4.
108. *Province Mission Book*, 1864, RABP; *Chronica Domus* I:245 (January 1, 1864), I:249 (February 19 and 20, 1864), I:249 (February 23, 1864), and I:250 (March 3, 1864).
109. *Province Mission Book*, 1862–64, RABP; *Chronica Domus* I:265–66 (September 18, 1864).
110. *Annapolis Gazette*, April 21, 1864; *Chronica Domus* I:253 (May 1, 1864).
111. Gross to Howes Goldsborough, July 9, 1864, Folder 2, Goldsborough Papers; *Chronica Domus* I:255 (July 9, 1864).
112. *Chronica Domus* I:265 (September 18, 1864).
113. *Chronica Domus* I:253 (note following entry for May 19, 1864); "Visitation Recess Recommendations for Annapolis and Cumberland," September 28, 1860, RABP; *Maryland Republican*, May 7, 1864; *Sun*, May 17, 1864; *Catholic Mirror*, June 11, 1864.
114. Old Book 288, Middle Department [Annapolis], Part 4, Entry 1537, June 8–29, 1864, RG 393; Old Book 310, Middle Department [Annapolis], Part 4, Entry 1538, June 30, 1864–April 27, 1865, RG 393. Old Book 309, Middle Department [Annapolis], Part 4, Entry 1536, May 14, 1864, No. 1062, RG 393, includes pass refused for William Winchester, resident of Anne Arundel County, to cross Severn River by small boat.
115. *Sun*, April 28, 1864; *Maryland Republican*, March 26, 1864; *Crutch*, April 30, 1864; Captain George H. Curry, Provost Marshal, Annapolis, to Col. Adrian Root, Annapolis, December 10, 1864, Annapolis Provost Marshal Letters, 1864–65, Part 4, Entry 1538, RG 393 NARA. A search of NARA finding aids for RG 393, Part 4, revealed that pass records issued in Baltimore are extant only for 1861 and 1866.
116. Revell and Sands passes, personal collection of Ann Jensen, Annapolis.
117. Old Book 309, Middle Department [Annapolis], Part 4, Entry 1536, May 6, 1864, No. 2, Walton and No. 40, Sparks, and May 7, 1864, No. 120, A. Larkins and Julia Ann Spence, RG 393, NARA. Children baptized at St. Mary's: Joanna Rebecca Larkins (February 9, 1859); Catherine Julia Larkins (July 1, 1860); William Joseph Larkins (April 7, 1861); Alphonsus Larkins (September 14, 1862, and died and was buried at St. Mary's Cemetery on August 13, 1863). Daniel Henry Larkins, who was listed as son of Solomon Larkins and Fanny Butler was baptized September 12, 1865, and buried at St. Mary's Cemetery at age seven days September 13, 1865. Solomon Larkins buried at St. Mary's Cemetery November 11, 1865, with comment "Rec'd Baptism" (Interment Register B#2, November 11, 1865) but no record of baptism in the Baptismal Register. For Edward Walton, see May 8, 1864 pass no. 199; for Henrietta Cooper and Harriet Johnson, see May 11, 1864, no. 715 and 717. Cooper had a second pass, no. 902, issued May 14, 1864, to go to Baltimore on the steamer.
118. Old Book 309, Middle Department [Annapolis], May 13, 1864, Denver, No. 860, Part 4, Entry 1536, RG 393, NARA. The baptisms appear in B#1 on following dates: October 24, 1858 (three-month-old George Washington), June 16, 1859 (fourteen-year-old Anna Elisabeth), June 18, 1861 (eighteen-month-old William Franklin), April 16, 1862 (five-day-old Thomas), January 27, 1863 (six-month-old Sarah Rebecca), February 1, 1863 (twelve year old John Thomas), July 9, 1864 (nine-month-old Susanna Augusta), and November 11, 1865 (nineteen-day-old Joseph). Two other children were born to this couple, James Emmet in 1867 and Eliza Virginia in 1870 but neither appear in the baptismal register. "History of the [Annapolis Police] Department," http://www.annapolis.gov/government/city-departments/police/about-annapolis-police-department/history-of-the-department, August 23, 2012: says in 1856 Thomas Denver was one four men sworn in as "Constables and Watchmen."
119. "Misses Dubois, Davis and Mullen," Old Book 288, Middle Department [Annapolis], Part 4, Entry 1537, June 24, 1864, No. 3684. RG 393, NARA.
120. Old Book 310, Middle Department [Annapolis], Part 4,

Entry 1538, No. 5441, RG 393, NARA, for Mary Treadwell [*sic*] and Virginia Mullen [*sic*]; No. 5442 for George Tidings [*sic*]; No. 5459 for Mrs. Treadwell [*sic*] and child; No. 5460 for Mrs. [*sic*, she was not married] Bright; No. 5461 for Mrs. Tidings [*sic*] and child. For George Tydings' baptism, see B#1 (January 1, 1854). Catherine Bright was daughter of Mary Ann Tydings (ca. 1769–1852). Also, "Change of Route: Eastern and Western Shore Steamers." *Easton Gazette,* July 23, 1864, 4. The steamer was operated by the Individual Enterprise Steamboat Company.

121. Old Book 309, Middle Department [Annapolis], Part 4, Entry 1536, May 7, 1864, No. 171, Miller [*sic*], and May 10, 1864, No. 423, Gross, RG 393, NARA; *Chronica Domus* I:252 (April 27, 1864) and I:253 (May 13, 1864).

122. Old Book 288, Middle Department [Annapolis], passes issued May 7–December 22, 1864, Part 4, Entries 1536, 1537, 1538, RG 393, NARA.

123. Keffer to Root, Annapolis, April 23, 1864, Records of the Provost Marshal General, Old Book 305, Part 4, Entry 1530, RG 393, NARA. The other men were Charles D. Hyde and Richard R. Riley, who were later exonerated, see Keffer to Root, May 2, 1864, Old Book 306. For the White family: Federal censuses, Annapolis, 1850 and 1860; Confirmation Register B#2 (December 8, 1864). A Frank White of unspecified age, perhaps the same as the confirmand, applied for passes twice in 1864, Old Book 310, Middle Department [Annapolis], Part 4, Entry 1538, pass no. 7205, August 9, 1864 (to Millersville by railroad) and no. 6129, September 9, 1864 (Chesapeake Bay by small boat), RG 393. The numbering system is out of chronological or numerical order.

124. Keffer to Root, April 23, 1864, same to same, April 25, 1864; McIntire, 1:756; "John Wesley White (1822–1870)," *Archives of Maryland* (Biographical Series), MSA SC3520–13863, accessed September 4, 2016, http://msa.maryland.gov/megafile/msa/speccol/sc3500/sc3520/013800/013863/html/13863bio.html, for John Wesley White, a St. Anne's parishioner and mayor in 1862–63; *Boyd's Business Directory of the State of Maryland, 1875* (Washington: Wm. H. Boyd, 1875), 298, "White M. B. dry goods, 4 Francis." Presumably this is Marbury B. White (1851–85), son of John Wesley White.

125. As witness, Marriage Register B#1 (December 16, 1855, and March 23, 1856); as godfather, Baptismal Register B#1 (January 4, 1857, February 27, 1859, May 16, 1859, January 27, 1860, July 21, 1861); 1860 Federal Census, Annapolis, for Sophia Williams' age and occupation; Enrollment District 7 (Annapolis), Adjutant General (Enrollment Record), 1862–64, MSA S352–27, for Hogarty's enrollment.

126. Military Service Record (William Hogarthey [*sic*], Company D, 2nd Battalion, Maryland Infantry), War Department Collection of Confederate Records, RG 109; Toomey, *The War Came by Train,* 143–58; "2nd Maryland Infantry CSA 'Company D,'" accessed February 28, 2017, http://www.2ndmarylandcod.com/history/; Andrew Johnson, "Executive Order—General Orders: 109," June 6, 1865, The American Presidency Project, accessed February 28, 2017, https://www.presidency.ucsb.edu/documents/executive-order-general-orders-109; *Annapolis Gazette,* October 8, 1868; 1870 Federal Census, Annapolis.

127. Steven Bernstein, *The Confederacy's Last Northern Offensive: Jubal Early, the Army of the Valley and the Raid on Washington* (Jefferson, North Carolina: McFarland, 2011), 13, 22, 29–30, 69; email of Michael Fitzpatrick to author, September 3, 2014, identifying the 144th Regiment company sent from Annapolis; Brett W. Spaulding, *Last Chance for Victory: Jubal Early's 1864 Maryland Invasion* (n.p.: The Author, 2010), 35–40, 68–72, 78–129; Charles C. Osborne, *Jubal: The Life and Times of General Jubal A. Early, CSA, Defender of the Lost Cause* (Chapel Hill: Algonquin Books of Chapel Hill, 1992), 75. For troop strengths, see NPS, "The Battle of Monocacy," accessed August 18, 2020, https://www.nps.gov/mono/learn/historyculture/the-battle-of-monocacy.htm.

128. *Maryland Republican,* July 16, 1864; *Annapolis Gazette,* July 14, 1864; Baker, *Politics of Continuity,* 109; John M. Carter, Annapolis, to General John S. Berry, Baltimore, July 13, 1864, Civil War Papers, Maryland Adjutant General, MSA S935–38.

129. *Maryland Republican,* July 16, 1864; *Annapolis Gazette,* July 14, 1864, 2; Eudora Clark, "Hospital Memories," *Atlantic Monthly* 20, no. 119 (September 1867): 332; Root to Vanderkieft, Annapolis, July 11, 1864, Records of the Provost Marshal, Annapolis District, Part 2, Entry 4876, RG 393, NARA.

130. Annapolis, Mayor and Alderman Proceedings, July 11, 1864, 39–40, MSA 49–10; *Maryland Republican,* July 16, 1864; General Orders, July 11, 1864, Part 4, Entry 2000, RG 393, NARA. Riley, Ancient City, 314, recalled fortifications extended "in a line parallel with the Annapolis and Bay Ridge Railroad from the Annapolis, Washington and Baltimore railroad to the public road." Also, Richard R. Duncan, "Maryland's Reaction to Early's Raid in 1864, *Maryland Historical Magazine* 64, no. 3 (Fall 1969): 260–63.

131. McWilliams, *Annapolis,* 52, 190, 201; Jane McWilliams, "Annapolis Boundaries 1708 to 1951," December 28, 2007, electronic file provided to author; email of Michael P. Parker, Annapolis, to author, August 6, 2009; Michael P. Parker, *Presidents Hill: Building an Annapolis Neighborhood, 1664–2005* (Annapolis: Annapolis Publishing Company, 2005), 1, 15, 21; *Crutch,* November 19, 1864; General Orders, July 11, 1864, Part 4, Entry 2000, RG 393, NARA; *George Brewer v. United States,* File 5008, Box 613, Entry 22, Congressional Jurisdiction Case Files, 1884–1943, Records of the United States Court of Claims, RG 123, NARA; American Battlefield Trust, "Glossary of Civil War Terms," accessed September 4, 2018, https://www.battlefields.org/glossary-civil-war-terms; Lieutenant Colonel John M. Gates, *Evolution of Entrenchments During the American Civil War: A Vision for World War I Leaders* (Carlisle Barracks, Pennsylvania: US Army War College, 1991), 29, accessed September 4, 2018, https://apps.dtic.mil/sti/pdfs/ADA238243.pdf.

132. Carter to Berry, July 13, 1864; "John M. Carter," MSA

SC3520–13429, *Archives of Maryland* (Biographical Series), accessed September 27, 2016, http://msa.maryland.gov/megafile/msa/speccol/sc3500/sc3520/013400/013429/html/13429bio.html; *Maryland Republican*, July 16, 1864; General Orders, July 12, 1864, Part 4, Entry 2000, RG 393, NARA.

133. The eyewitness was Elihu S. Riley Jr. in *Ancient City*, 314. Also, "From Maryland, Camp Parole, Near Annapolis, Md, Tuesday, Nov. 15, 1864," *New York Times*, November 21, 1864, 2; US Court of Claims File 9419.

134. Carter to Berry, July 13, 1864; Samuel Stephenson. "Charles William Le Gendre, 26 August 1830–1 September 1899," 1, Reed Digital Collections, Reed College, Portland, Oregon, accessed September 27, 2016, https://rdc.reed.edu/c/formosa/s/r?_pp=20&query=gendre&s=98e5385dbc3797b9618ee65e9ce96ca6d1381b33&p=3&pp=1&part=1; Root, Annapolis, to Major General E. O. C. [Edward Otho Cresap] Ord, Commander, 8th Army Corps, Baltimore, July 12, 1864, and Root to Lieutenant Colonel Samuel B. Lawrence, Middle Department, Baltimore, Records of the Provost Marshal, Annapolis District, Part 2, Entry 4876, RG 393, NARA.

135. Lieutenant Commander Daniel L. Braine, USS *Vicksburg*, Annapolis Harbor, to Rear Admiral S. P. Lee, North Atlantic Blockading Squadron, Hampton Roads, July 14, 1864, enclosing Acting Ensign Francis. G. Osborne, USS *Vicksburg*, to Braine, July 14,1864, United States, Naval War Records Office, *Official Records of the Union and Confederate Navies in the War of the Rebellion*, series I, vol. 10: North Atlantic Blockading Squadron (May 6, 1864–October 27, 1864), (Washington: Government Printing Office, 1900), 270–71. Also, "Vicksburg I (ScGbt) 1863–1865," https://www.history.navy.mil/research/histories/ship-histories/danfs/v/vicksburg-i.html and "Daylight," *Dictionary of American Naval Fighting Ships*, https://www.history.navy.mil/research/histories/ship-histories/danfs/d/daylight.html, both accessed February 9, 2018.

136. General Orders, July 12–15, 1864, Part 4, Entry 2000, RG 393, NARA; Root to Ord, July 12, 1864; "The Rebel Invasion," *Haversack*, July 20, 1864, 2.

137. Thomas N. Pindle, Deputy Provost Marshal, Anne Arundel County, Annapolis, to Captain James O. P. Burnside, Acting Provost Marshal, Fifth Congressional District, July 26, 1864, Provost Marshal General Letters Received 1864, Folder 3, Entry PH–4528, RG 110, NARA Philadelphia.

138. *Chronica Domus* I:247 (January 1, 1864) and I:255 (July 12 and 13, 1864); *Province Annals, 1832–71*, 569 (1864, Annapolis), RABP.

139. *Chronica Domus* I:255 (July 12 and 13, 1864); Gross to Goldsborough, July 15, 1864, same to same, July 21, 1864, Folder 2, Goldsborough Papers.

140. Unknown sender, Annapolis, to Father Timothy Enright, [New York], July 23 [1864], RABP.

141. Toomey, *Civil War in Maryland*, 124–29; Wagner, *Library of Congress Illustrated Timeline*, 198; Bernstein, *Confederacy's Last Northern Offensive*, 68–70, 80–81, 121; Osborne, *Jubal*, 266, 287; Chronicles of the House of Studies, Cumberland, 134–35 (July 1–August 1, 1864).

142. *Maryland Republican*, July 16, 1864.

143. Captain George W. Curry, Provost Marshal, to Lieutenant H. Preston, Commanding Provost Guard, Annapolis, July 19–20, 1864, Old Book 306, Records of the Provost Marshal General, Part 4, Entry 1530, RG 393, NARA.

144. Mary Catherine Crowley, "Youth Department: Uncle Tom's Story," *Ave Maria* 31, no. 21 (November 22, 1890): 500–502, and no. 22 (November 29, 1890): 526–28. Joan Stromberg, *Willy Finds Victory: A Blessed Francis Seelos Story* (Ellettsville, Indiana: Ecce Homo Press, 2004), is a fictional story about Seelos and a boy searching for his brother-in-law at a Fort Monroe army hospital after the Battle of Fredericksburg.

145. "Visitation Recess Recommendations for Annapolis and Cumberland," September 28, 1860, RABP.

146. *Chronica Domus* I:258–63 (August n.d., 1864).

147. *Chronica Domus* I:265 (September 17, 1864). Gerdemann went to Elkridge Landing, with Bradley and Girardey, on September 17.

148. In regard to speculation about Salt Pan Creek (formerly Underwoods Creek), email of Jane McWilliams to author, October 10, 2013; Martenet, *Map of Anne Arundel County* (1860); US Geological Survey, "Round Bay, MD," map 50579, 2014. For Judge Mason reference, see SH 1:378 (March 3, 1866), AACLR, which mentions the decree of May 5, 1852, passed by Anne Arundel County Court, sitting as court of equity, ordered Catherine Steele Ray, trustee, to sell the property to John Thomson Mason, who, in turn conveyed the property to Luther Giddings on March 3, 1866. Also, John Eric Fredland, *An Interesting Career: The Life and Work of Luther Giddings (1823–1884)* (Annapolis: West Annapolis Heritage Partnership, 2015), 21–22, 45 n70.

149. *Chronica Domus* I:268 (November 7, 9, and 14, 1864).

150. "Observations on the Occasion of the Canonical Visitation and the End of the Present Triennium, Annapolis, November 14, 1864," *Statuta et Decreta*, 197–98.

151. "Acta Episcopalia a die 31 Julii 1864 Martini Joanne Spalding Archiepiscopus Sub. Baltimorensis (Baltimore Journal of Martin John Spalding from 31 July 1864)," 7, translation from the Latin by Peter E. Hogan, S.S.J., Spalding Papers, AAB.

152. Archbishop Francis Patrick Kenrick, *A Vindication of the Catholic Church in a Series of Letters Addressed to the Rt. Rev. John Henry Hopkins, Episcopal Bishop of Vermont* (Baltimore: John Murphy and Company, 1855), 225–27; Duncan, "Catholics and the Church in the Antebellum Upper South," in Miller and Wakelyn, *Catholics in the Old South*, 96; Baker, *Ambivalent Americans*, 40–47; Spalding, *Premier See*, 162; Kurtz, *Excommunicated from the Union*, 26. Rable, *God's Almost Chosen People*, 37, cites Brownson, "Politics at Home," *Brownson's Quarterly Review*, Third New York Series, 1, no. 3 (July 1860): 360–91, 85, cites Brownson's "Slavery and the War," *Brownson's Quarterly Review*, 2, no. 4, (October 1861): 510–46.

153. Rable, *God's Almost Chosen People,* 155 and 191.
154. Van de Braak, Cumberland, to Kenrick, Baltimore, July 10, 1861, Box 28, Folder F23, Kenrick Papers, RG1.6, AAB
155. Summary of reply, July 13, 1861, Literarum Registrum I (October 10, 1851–October 17, 1862), 226, Box 32B, Kenrick Papers, RG1.6, AAB.
156. *Sun,* October 7, 1864, 4.
157. Captain George W. Curry, Provost Marshal, Annapolis, to William Mullavel, September 23, 1864, Curry to Colonel Adrian Root, December 10, 1864, and undated note by Curry, Old Book 306, Records of the Provost Marshal General, Part 4, Entry 1530, RG 393, NARA. Recognizances, Case No. 25, Anne Arundel County Circuit Court Docket, October Term 1864, MSA C65–26; (the other man was John M. White); Confirmation Register B#2 (December 8, 1864); Baptismal Register B#2 (November 2, 1869). Mullavel may have been the same thirty-one-year-old William Mullavel who married Bridget Devine at St. Joseph's Church in Roxbury, Massachusetts, in October 1864, and listed his current home address as New York City. See Marriages Registered in the City of Roxbury, 1864, p. 226, in "Massachusetts Marriages, 1841–1915," accessed October 23, 2016, FamilySearch.org. For the purchase of West Street business and 99-year lease from James and Catherine Murray for $70 rent per annum, see NHG 11:429 (August 12, 1863), AACLR; for the sale see *Evening Star,* February 28, 1865. Advertisements under title "Mullavell's Bowling Saloon" appeared in the *Annapolis Gazette,* January 7, 1864; *Crutch,* February 27, 1864, (saloon located at 111 West Street). Federal documents indicate William was enrolled for draft in 1863, paid Federal taxes, and was issued a provost marshal pass to go by boat on Severn River, July 1864. For John Mullavel, see Baptismal Register B#1 (May 20, 1865) and B#2 (July 15, 1866). Grantee Index, AACLR, has numerous entries for properties bought by John Mullavel, including NHG 12:190 (April 14, 1864) for purchase of State Circle property. John also enrolled for draft in 1863; paid Federal taxes. Also, *Annapolis Gazette,* December 6, 1866.
158. Appearances, April 1864 Term, 175 Anne Arundel Circuit Court, Equity Record Index, 1852–1889, MSA CM99; *Maryland Republican,* August 20 and September 24, 1864; NHG 5:602 (July 30, 1856) and NHG 13:401 (September 16, 1865), AACLR; Annapolis Mayor and Aldermen, Property Assessment, June 11, 1860, MSA M72–3; 1860 Federal Census, Annapolis; *Boyd's Business Directory of the State of Maryland, 1875* (Washington: Wm. H. Boyd, 1875), 296, 382; "U.S. Tax Assessment Lists, Annapolis, May 1865," 142, accessed January 9, 2017, Ancestry.com; *Annapolis Gazette,* March 1 and April 30, 1868; Marriage Register M#1 (August 8, 1874 and February 8, 1877). Anne Teresa Walsh Spalding died from typhoid on February 28, 1880, buried in unmarked grave at St. Mary's Cemetery; Interment Register B#2 (February 28, 1880).
159. Spalding, Literarum Registrum, 1862–1869 (October 11, 1864), RG1.7, AAB. Historians consulted were Dr. Patrick J. Hayes, RABP; Dr. William B. Kurtz, John L. Nau III Center for the Study of the American Civil War, University of Virginia, and Father Robert Miller, St. Dorothy Church, Chicago.
160. *Catholic Mirror,* November 19, 1864; Corey M. Brooks, "Sculpting Memories of the Slavery Conflict: Commemorating Roger Taney in Washington, D.C., Annapolis, and Baltimore, 1864–1887," *Maryland Historical Magazine* 112, no. 1 (Spring/Summer 2017): 11, 15; Curran, *Shaping American Catholicism,* 109.
161. *Maryland Republican,* October 8, 1864; McWilliams, *Annapolis,* 191; William Starr Myers, *The Maryland Constitution of 1864* (Baltimore: Johns Hopkins Press, 1901), 99; Edward Otis Hinkley, *The Constitution of the State of Maryland. Reported and Adopted by the Convention of Delegates Assembled at the City of Annapolis, April 27th, 1864, and Submitted to and Ratified by the People on the 12th and 13th Days of October, 1864* (Baltimore: John Murphy and Company, 1864), 723; *Sun,* October 12, 1864.
162. Masur, *Example for All the Land,* 75; Fields, *Slavery and Freedom,* 35, 139–42, 148–49, 151–56; Baker, *Politics of Continuity,* 109 n 120; 14 Stat. 27 1866 ("An Act to Protect all Persons in the United States in the Civil Rights, and Furnish the Means of Their Vindication") in US Congress, *The Statutes at Large, Treaties, and Proclamations of the United States of America, from December, 1865, to March, 1867,* George P. Sanger, ed., 14 (Boston: Little Brown and Company, 1868), 27–30; George W. Curry to Adrian Root, Annapolis, November 23, 1864 in Freedmen and Southern Society Project, University of Maryland, "Provost Marshal at Annapolis, Maryland, to the Commander of the Post of Annapolis; Enclosing a Letter from the Judges of the Orphans Court of Anne Arundel County to the Provost Marshal," accessed February 19, 2017, http://www.freedmen.umd.edu/Curry.html, which cites *Maryland Code of Public General Laws, 1860,* Article 6, sections 31–40. Reference to this letter also is made in Orphans' Court Proceedings, 1864–68 (November 30, 1864), Register of Wills, Anne Arundel County, MSA CM119–26 (CR262–5).
163. *Catholic Mirror,* November 5, 1864.
164. Stout, *Upon the Altar of the Nation,* 389; Baker, *Politics of Continuity,* xiv.
165. "Election of 1864," American Presidency Project, accessed June 18, 2014, http://www.presidency.ucsb.edu/; *Sun,* November 11, November 14, and November 18, 1864. McClellan carried Anne Arundel, Baltimore, Calvert, Charles, Dorchester, Harford, Howard, Kent, Montgomery, Prince George's, Queen Anne's, Somerset, St. Mary's, and Worcester counties. Lincoln carried Allegany, Baltimore City, Carroll, Caroline, Cecil, Frederick, Talbot, and Washington counties. Also, Baker, *Politics of Continuity,* 80, for Unionists accepting emancipation, and 131, for Democrats staying away from the polls; Hurst, "Northernmost Southern Town," 242.
166. Baptismal Register B#1 (July 30, 1865); "Michael Stevens (Union)," ACWRDB, accessed February 23, 2012; "40th Infantry Regiment," accessed December 13, 2016, http://

www.dmna.state.ny.us/historic/reghist/civil/infantry/40thInf/40thInfHistSketch.htm; Fred C. Floyd, *History of the Fortieth (Mozart) Regiment, New York Volunteers* (Boston: Gilson, 1909), 202–3, 442; Compiled Military Service Record (Michael Stevens, sometimes Stephens, Co. E, 40th New York Infantry Regiment), RG 94, NARA; Frederick H. Dyer, *A Compendium of the War of the Rebellion Compiled and Arranged from Official Records of the Federal and Confederate Armies, Reports of he Adjutant Generals of the Several States, the Army Registers, and Other Reliable Documents and Sources* (Des Moines, Iowa: Dyer Publishing Company, 1908), 1746.

167. Baptismal Register B#1 (July 30, 1865); Interment Register B#2 (March 23, 1868); Louisa Stevens Widow's Pension Claim, Annapolis, May 26, 1868, Application No. 16474, RG 15, NARA, which said it was Rev. D. C. Owens, but see Owen M. Taylor, *Annapolis Directory or Stranger's Guide,* 3d ed (Annapolis: The Author, 1865), 15, which identifies him as Rev. E. D. Owen; 1870 census, Annapolis; Find A Grave Memorial ID 235442187; St. Mary's First Communion Register (First Communion Register) F#1 (June 12, 1870); for the death of George B. Stevens, "Maryland, Deaths and Burials, 1877–1992," accessed June 19, 2014, FamilySearch.org.

168. *Crutch,* November 19, 1864; *Sun,* November 14, 1864. McHaney's interment is listed in B#1 (December 13, 1864) and B# 2 (December 13, 1864). In B#1 the entry follows De Dycker's signature, dated November 12, 1864, noting the canonical visitation.

169. Captain George W. Curry, Provost Marshal, to Colonel Adrian R. Root, December 8, 1864, Old Book 306, Records of the Provost Marshal General, Part 4, Entry 1530, RG 393, NARA.

170. Compiled Military Service Record (George O'Malley, Co. E, 17th New York Infantry Regiment), RG 94, NARA; Carded Medical Records, Entry 534, RG 94, NARA; Widow's Pension Record (Mary A. O'Malley), Certificate No. 605336, RG 15, NARA; Draft Enrollment Records, July 15, 1863, Annapolis City, George O'Malley, bar keeper; St. Vincent de Paul Church, Baltimore, Marriage Register, 1845–72 (March 31, 1864), MSA SC2533, M1612 (SCM1613); Baptismal Registers B#1 (July 24, 1865), B#2 (December 30, 1866).

171. NHG 13:122 (September 27, 1864), AACLR. Continental Shades was located on the north side of Church Street with access in the rear to Francis Street, possibly at 158–164 Main Street; Maryland Historical Trust, MIHP AA–557, accessed March 10, 2017, https://mht.maryland.gov/secure/medusa/PDF/AnneArundel/AA-557.pdf; SH 1:418 (May 5, 1866) and SH 1:43 (May 8, 1866), AACLR, by which O'Malley divested himself of the business; *Annapolis Gazette,* February 7, 1867, for the Prince George Street business; Widow's Pension Record (Mary A. O'Malley), RG 15, NARA; 1900 Federal Census, Baltimore; "Maryland, Probate Estate and Guardianship Files, 1796–1940," (noting Mary Agnes O'Malley's death on November 27, 1938), accessed May 29, 2014, FamilySearch.org.

172. Sister Dorothy Daiger, S.S.N.D., Archivist, Baltimore, to author, January 27, 2012, reported Annie Fee, daughter of William Fee and Sarah Chaney, entered S.S.N.D. June 21, 1891, professed on deathbed November 4, 1904, died December 14, 1904; McIntire 1:232; Baptismal Register B#4 (May 27, 1882).

173. *Crutch,* November 19, 1864; Louis H. Bolander, "Civil War Annapolis," *U.S. Naval Institute Proceedings, 63,* no. 417 (November 3937): 1615–16; *Sun,* November 14 and November 17, 1864; Borgmann, *Redemptorists at Annapolis,* 59; *Chronica Domus* I:268 (November 14, 1864).

174. *Chronica Domus* I:271 (end-of-1864 *Annotationes quaedam,* item 6), I:267 (October 3, 1864), I:270 (December 15, 1864), II:6 (January 1, 1865).

175. *Chronica Domus* I:271; Mark P. Leone, Matthew M. Palus, Elizabeth B. Kryder-Reid, Janice Bailey-Goldschmidt, Paul R. Mullins, Mark Warner, and Robert L. Worden, *Report on Archaeological Excavations Conducted at the St. Mary's Site (18AP5), 107 Duke of Gloucester Street, Annapolis, Maryland, 1987–1990,* vol. 1, Site History, Results and Recommendations (College Park: University of Maryland, 2002), accessed January 26, 2016, http://drum.lib.umd.edu/handle/1903/11013.

176. *Chronica Domus* I:271; Worden, *Saint Mary's,* 73. A by-law passed December 12, 1853, forbade more burials (Folder 29, Box 20) but was repealed April 17, 1854 (Folder 38, Box 20), Mayor and Alderman, Proceedings, MSA M49–3. Two by-laws passed July 2, 1855: one established the Public Burying Ground and repealed the April 17, 1854 by-law, and the second prohibited burials within the Annapolis except in the Public Burying Ground (Folder 20, Box 21), M49–4. Letter of Rev. M. Miller [*sic*], St. Mary's College, to the Mayor, Recorder and Aldermen of the City of Annapolis, no date, presented to City Council, December 9, 1861; By-Law, Section 2, adopted December 9, 1861, Annapolis, Mayor and Aldermen, Proceedings, M49–7; 01/22/01/061.

177. Gross to Goldsborough, April 20, 1864, Folder 2, Goldsborough Papers.

178. *Chronica Domus* I:31 (September 15, 1854). Patrick Kean Personnel File, RABP, says he was about twenty-one when he died.

179. *Chronica Domus* I:52 (December 5, 1855); Rev. Ferreol Girardey, *George Reichert C.SS.R., A Model for Youth* (Kansas City, Missouri: John A. Heilman, 1891), 80; George Deshon, Annapolis, to George Ruland, Baltimore, June 10, 1856, St. Mary's (Annapolis) Parish File, RABP. Also, "The Carroll Family—Buried Beneath a Shopping Center?" in Ginger Doyel, *Annapolis Vignettes* (Centreville, Maryland: Tidewater Publishers, 2005), 134–38.

180. *Chronica Domus* I:86 (January 5, 1858). *Liber Vestitutiones, 1858,* RABP, lists Damian Straub among chorists invested by Müller in 1858. The precise date of his investiture is not given but his name follows those of two others who were invested on August 15, 1857, and adds the following comment: "died of apoplexy shortly after investing" and an insertion made above the word "died" says "Dec. 8, 1857."

The description of Straub's final days, vomiting blood, etc., sounds more like consumption than apoplexy, although the former could have contributed to the latter. It is not clear here which day Straub died; he took sick and had to leave the chapel, apparently on January 1, and his headstone gives a death date of January 4, 1858. The January 5 funeral supports the January 4 death date.

181. *Chronica Domus* I:162 (November n.d., 1862, Harvey), I:222 (January 17, 1863, Kammer), I:223 (February 27, 1863, Krastel), I:269 (December 1, 1864, interments).

182. Helmprächt to Goldsborough, October 18, 1864, Folder 2; same to same, October 28, 1864; November 2, 1864; November 10, 1864, Folder 3, latter three of which mention Tomi (also called Tommy in Gross to Goldsborough, March 28, 1864, Folder 2), Goldsborough Papers. Frank Dietz is mentioned throughout the Goldsborough letters. The Annapolis Redemptorists were instrumental in getting Goldsborough to hire Dietz; see Gross to Goldsborough, December 31, 1863, Folder 1, and subsequent letters. Dielemans, Annapolis, to Goldsborough, April 20, 1865, Folder 3, mentions the shad.

183. James B. Sheeran, *The Civil War Diary of Father James Sheeran, Confederate Chaplain and Redemptorist*, ed., Patrick J. Hayes (Washington: Catholic University of America Press, 2016), 2–3; "Vocational Autobiography of Frater James Sheeran, C.Ss. R.," based on a 24-page manuscript dated August 12, 1856, RABP, transcribed in full as appendix in Sheeran, *Diary*, 555–67, this quote from 555. The 2-volume manuscript diary at RABP totals 1,556 pages. An abridged version is by Joseph T. Durkin, S.J., ed. *Confederate Chaplain, A War Journal of Rev. James B. Sheeran, C.SS.R., 14th Louisiana, C.S.A.* (Milwaukee: Bruce, 1960). A 511-page rough-draft manuscript "Soldiers of the Cross: Heroism of the Cross, or Nuns and Priests of the Battlefield" by David Power Conyngham, David Power Conyngham Papers (CCON 1/03–08), University of Notre Dame Archives, accessed August 18, 2016, http://www.archives.nd.edu/Conyngham/index.html, devotes five chapters to Sheeran's Civil War experiences. Also, Wuest, *Annales*, IV:2:453; Pat McNamara, "Father James Sheeran, Confederate Chaplain," accessed August 9, 2016, http://www.patheos.com/blogs/mcnamarasblog/2009/04/father-james-sheeran-confederate-chaplain.html; Tom Fox, *Hidden History of the Irish in New Jersey* (Charleston: History Press, 2011), 69–74, the latter of which provides an undocumented and sometimes erroneous account of Sheeran's life. Also, Wuest and Wilmer, "Register of the Clergy Laboring in the Archdiocese of New York From Early Missionary Times," 106–7. For examples of Sheeran's defense of Catholic education in Michigan, see the following, published in *New-York Freeman's Journal:* "Catholic Settlements in Michigan," August 16, 1851, 5; "School Laws in Michigan," December 11, 1852, 5; "The School Question in Michigan," February 26, 1853, 4; "The Catholic Celebration of the Fourth of July, 1854, in Monroe, Mich.," July 29, 1854, 1 and 4; "Ordinations in Baltimore," October 2, 1858, 4, which recalled Sheeran's "his great zeal for the cause of Catholic education."

184. Sheeran, *Diary*, 3–4, 13–15 (August 1–8, 1862), 26 (August 22, 1862), 58–63 (September 6–8, 1862), 74–77 (September 15, 1862), 81–82 (September 17, 1862), 432–34 (July 9, 1864), 437 (July 12, 1864), 443 (July 19, 1864); "14th Louisiana Regiment," Antietam on the Web, http://antietam.aotw.org/officers.php?unit_id=560; NPS, "14th Regiment, Louisiana Infantry," https://www.nps.gov/civilwar/search-battle-units-detail.htm?battleUnitCode=CLA0014RI, both accessed August 12, 2016.

185. Seelos to family members, October 12, December 3 and 18, 1862, Letter 119, Hoegerl, *Sincerely, Seelos,* 315.

186. Sheeran, *Diary*, 474 (October 12, 1864), 486–88 (October 22–23, 1864). *Chronica Domus* II:268–69 (November 14, 19, and 21, 1864) mentions Müller's periodic presence in Annapolis and his coming and going to Washington and Baltimore. An undated account written by Müller is in RABP and reprinted in Rev. Carl Hoegerl, C.Ss.R., "Two Redemptorist Accounts During the American Civil War," *Redemptorist North American Historical Bulletin,* June 2003, 13, accessed August 17, 2016, https://d2y1pz2y630308.cloudfront.net/29153/documents/2021/6/issue_19_-_2003_june.pdf. A greatly compressed and partly inaccurate account of the Sheeran affair appears in Helmprächt, "Schreiben des P. Joseph Helmprächt," 21–27. Latta's 1864 diary does not mention the Sheeran episode. Latta wrote on November 13, 1864, after leaving Winchester, note that the time there was "one continued scene of business of a character entirely different from field operations & of nature not worthy of being recorded." See James William Latta Papers, MMC–0895, Manuscript Division, LoC.

187. Sheeran, Winchester, to James Alphonsus McMaster, New York, January 3. 1865, General Philip Sheridan, Notre Dame Archives Calendar, 1865, accessed August 18, 2016, http://archives.nd.edu/calendar/cal1865a.htm; Sheeran, *Diary*, 489–94 (October 29–November 1, 1864); Kurtz, *Excommunicated from the Union,* 154; Bernstein, *Confederacy's Last Northern Offensive,* 158.

188. Sheeran, *Diary*, 492–505 (October 31–November 11, 1864). James Alphonsus McMaster (1820–86), a convert to Catholicism and briefly a Redemptorist novice at St. Trond, Belgium. Paul R. Stroh, *C.Ss.R. Ilchester Memories, 1868–1957, To Commemorate the Golden Jubilee of the Redemptorist Novitiate at Ilchester, Maryland* (Ilchester, Maryland: Redemptorist Fathers, 1957), 33–34; Thomas Meehan, "James Alphonsus McMaster," *Catholic Encyclopedia,* vol. 9 (New York: Robert Appleton Company, 1910), accessed August 13, 2016, http://www.newadvent.org/cathen/09506a.htm. Receipts for Prisoners Sent to Fort McHenry, February 1864–February 1865, Part 1, Entry 2387, RG 393, NARA. Daily dated, undated, and miscellaneous receipts were searched between November 8 and December 5, 1864, but only military men, those who disobeyed orders, went AWOL, deserted, etc., are listed.

189. "A Great and Cruel Wrong," *New-York Freeman's Journal,* November 19, 1864, 4–5; original copy of which is avail-

able in 19th-Century Newspaper Collection, Vault 8963, Newspaper and Periodical Reading Room, LoC. Thomas K. Carey, Edward Dubois, James A. Iglehart, Mary Effine Lake, Edward Powers, James Revell, Edward Sparks, and other unnamed Annapolis residents, as well as the Redemptorist Convent and Father Louis Claessens, were listed among subscribers under in "Remittances," in the *New-York Freeman's Journal and Catholic Register,* between 1847 and 1865. One Annapolis subscriber who is not a known to have been associated with St. Mary's, and was noted only by his initials N.H.G. as having paid $1.00 through February 13, 1865, appeared in *New-York Freeman's Journal,* December 31, 1864. This must have been Nicholas Harwood Green (1808–65), clerk of the Anne Arundel County Circuit Court (1851–65), *Archives of Maryland* (Biographical Series) accessed January 26, 2017, http://msa.maryland.gov/megafile/msa/speccol/sc3500/sc3520/013100/013115/html/13115bio.html.

190. Sheeran, *Diary,* 505–24 (November 11–26, 1864). Philip H. Sheridan, Newtown, Virginia, to James A. Hardie, Inspector General, Washington, November 20, 1864, James Allen Hardie Papers, MNN–630, Manuscript Division, LoC. Sheridan mentions his suspicion that Sheeran was "connected with" Father Joseph Bixio, S.J. (1819–98), pastor of St. Francis of Assisi, Staunton, Virginia, and suspected by Sheridan of sharing intelligence with the enemy. Sheeran, *Diary,* 546–47 (December 30, 1864) and 548–49 (December 31, 1864), and Miller, *Both Prayed to the Same God,* 116, both discuss Bixio as a double agent. Also, Cornelius S. Buckley. S.J., ed. and trans., *A Frenchman, A Chaplain, A Rebel: The War Letters of Pere Louis-Hippoltye Gache, S.J.* (Chicago: Loyola University Press, 1981), 98, says the Italian Bixio "spent an inordinate amount of time slipping back and forth across the Federal lines"; *Sadliers' Catholic Almanac, 1864,* 80, identifies Bixio's parochial assignment.

191. Sheeran, *Diary,* 524–33 (November 27–December 5, 1864. Besides Spalding, Sheeran called on Fathers Henry B. McCoskery and Thomas Foley, both members of Spalding's immediate staff.

192. Sheeran, *Diary,* 533 (December 6, 1864).

193. *Chronica Domus* I:269 (December 6, 1864), I:270 (December 7, 1864), II:272 (item 9, 1864 end-of-year summary); Sheeran, *Diary,* 534 (December 7, 1864).

194. Confirmation Register B#2 (December 8, 1864). Spalding was supposed to visit Annapolis for Confirmation on September 29 but the trip was postponed by the "continued and severe indisposition of our beloved Archbishop." See *Catholic Mirror,* September 17 and October 1, 1864, The *Mirror* failed to report the December 8 visitation. *Maryland Republican,* September 24, 1864, reported Spalding's planned lecture and Confirmation on September 28 and 29, respectively. Military Service Record (Patrick Gavin), RG 94, NARA; Carded Medical Records, Box 1220, Entry 534, RG 94, NARA; Pension Application No. 1174369, RG 15, NARA. For Terence Keenan: *Crutch,* October 22, 1864; Military Service Record, RG 94, NARA; Pension File No. 822398, Certificate No. 809754, and Widow's Pension File, Certificate No. 710980, RG 15, NARA.

195. Sheeran, *Diary,* 534 (December 8, 1864); *Chronica Domus* I:270 (December 6–8, 1864). The languages were English, Gaellic, German, Greek, Italian, Dutch, Spanish and Flemish; Sheeran, 379 [1581], says only "Belgian and Irish" were not used by Spalding); Borgmann, *Redemptorists at Annapolis,* 59. Root's adjutant is identified as First Lieutenant John S. Wharton, 14th US Infantry, Post Adjutant, Pass No. 1062, issued May 14, 1864. See Old Book 309, Middle Department [Annapolis], Part 4, Entry 1536, May 14, 1864, No. 1062, RG 393, NARA.

196. Sheeran, *Diary,* 534 (December 8, 1864). In the published version it reads "whole regiments" but Sheeran's original manuscript says "whole regiment."

197. Roger Pickenpaugh, "Prisoner Exchange and Parole," Virginia Center for Civil War Studies, Virginia Tech, accessed May 29, 2017, http://essentialcivilwarcurriculum.com/prisoner-exchange-and-parole.html.

198. Sheeran, *Diary,* 534–35 (December 8, 1864).

199. Sheeran, *Diary,* 535 (December 8, 1864).

200. Dora Briggs North, *Manual of the First Presbyterian Church of Buffalo, N.Y., with Historical Sketch and Account of the Centennial Celebration, February 2nd to 5th, 1912* (Buffalo: First Presbyterian Society of Buffalo, N.Y., 1912), 40–41 and 68; "Taps Have Sounded, Mortal Remains of Gen. Adrian R. Root Laid to Rest Today," *Buffalo Evening News,* June 8, 1899, 11. Root's Civil War service is detailed in John H. Eicher and David J. Eicher, *Civil War High Commands* (Stanford: Stanford University Press, 2001), 461.

201. "Acta Episcopalia Martini Joanne Spalding," 15–17, Hogan translation, Spalding Papers, AAB.

202. *Chronica Domus* I:270 (December 8, 1864); Sheeran, *Diary,* 535–54 (December 9, 1864–April 24, 1865); *New-York Freeman's Journal,* January 21, 1865; Sheeran, Richmond, to James Alphonsus McMaster, New York City, January 3, 1865, Notre Dame Archives Calendar, 1865, accessed June 9, 2003, http://archives.nd.edu/calendar/cal1865a.htm; St. Peter's (Philadelphia) Annals, 86 (April 16, 1865), RABP; Wuest and Wilmer, "Register of the Clergy Laboring in the Archdiocese of New York," 106–7; Find A Grave Memorial ID 6497818.

203. The 1850 Federal Census, Washington, lists Rosa Ford, age 15, born in DC, among residents of Georgetown Visitation Monastery, Mother Cecilia Brooks superior. For Rosa's academic achievements, see *Daily Union,* July 28, 1845 and August 8, 1846; "Premium Lists for Distribution, 1823–1870," Georgetown Visitation Academy Archives, second honors, Junior Circle, 1846; second honors, Academic Crown, 1848; second honors, Senior Circle, 1849; gold medal, Academic Crown, 1851. For Stephen Calvert Ford, see *Biennial Register of the Officers and Agents in the Service of the United States* (Washington: Department of State, 1838),114; *Register of the Officers and Agents, Civil, Military, and Naval, in the Service of the United States. on the Thirtieth of September, 1849* (Washington: Department of State, 1849); 1850 Federal Census,

Washington (S.C. Ford); 1860 census, Washington (Calvert Ford); *Daily Evening Star,* May 1, 1854, identifies Rosa, as "only daughter of S. Calvert Ford, Esq."

204. St. Matthew's Marriage Register 1836–1870 (April 29, 1854), St. Matthew's Cathedral, Washington, image provided via email of Belinda Barahona to author, March 27, 2014; "Married," *Daily Evening Star,* May 1, 1854, 3; "District of Columbia Marriages, 1811–1950," accessed March 3, 2014, FamilySearch.org; Widow's Pension Application, File No. 17398, Case Files of Disproved Pension Applications of Widows and Other Dependents of US Navy Veterans Who Served Between 1861 and 1910, Microfilm Publication M1272, RG 15, NARA. The family may have been in Annapolis by July 17, 1861, when "Morsell Lieut. U.S.A." was issued a travel pass, Part 4, Entry 1535, RG 393, NARA. Alida McParlin (1834–77) was the Catholic wife of Dr. Thomas Andrew McParlin, a native Annapolitan, member of St. Anne's Church, regular army surgeon, and medical director of Army General Hospital No. 2 (St. John's College). Alida donated money for "Gabriel." one of the bells installed at St. Mary's in 1859, and served in 1860 and 1863 as a godmother at St. Mary's. infant baptisms. Baptismal Register B#1 (September 8, 1861) notes the *"cerem."* baptism, as does the letter of William H. Brick, C.Ss.R., Rector and Pastor, St. Mary's Church, Annapolis, December 7, 1897, in Widow's Pension Application, File No. 17398. Alida's other godmother duties are found in B#1 (October 24, 1860, June 27, 1863).
205. Widow's Pension Application, File No. 17398.
206. Record Proof of Marriages, Births and Deaths, October 20, 1898, signed by Harriet R. Johnson, Widow's Pension Application, File No. 17398. For De Dycker's statement see Interment Register B#1 (December 29, 1862). The next names inscribed were for the deceased of 1863. Johnson appears in Confirmation Register B#2 (December 8, 1864) as a twenty-three-year-old Black convert, and Marriage Register B#2 (August 18, 1866) notes her as witness to a marriage of a Black couple. Henrietta Johnson is listed in Baptismal Register B#1 (January 25, 1852) as a slave belonging to "Mr. Randall" and mother of a newly baptized convert, Gontia Kuper; B#1 (June 26, 1864) has a baptismal record for Henrietta Johnson. Several Black Harriet Johnsons and Henrietta Johnsons show up in Annapolis and Anne Arundel county census records. A provost marshal's pass was issued to "Herriet Johnson colored" to sell or deliver vegetables; Part 4, Entry 1535, June 28, 1861, RG 393. Albert Morsell's date of death appears in Claim for Widows' Pension, File No. 17398, dated October 21, 1898. His Mount Olivet burial is recorded in Find A Grave Memorial ID 182597523.
207. Lieutenant Worth G. Ross, U.S.R.M., "Our Coast Guard: A Brief History of the United States Revenue Marine Service," *Harper's New Monthly Magazine* 73, Issue 438 (November 1886); Florence Kern, *The United States Revenue Cutters in the Civil War* (Bethesda, Maryland: Alised Enterprises, ca. 1990), 2–6, accessed February 9, 2017, https://media.defense.gov/2017/Jul/02/2001772350/-1/-1/0/USRCSINCIVILWAR.PDF; Baptismal Register B#1 (July 19, 1863—Raymond Percy Morsell). Rosa's pension file indicates her husband also had been attached to the Hercules, a steam tug stationed in Baltimore. See Kern, 6–6 and 13–1. A Tiffany Glass and Decorating Company window depicting St. Anne and Mary in St. Anne's Church, Annapolis, was given as a memorial to Thomas and Sallie E. Sands, by Laura Sands' sister, Julia Bordley Sands Clason, in 1894. See John Eric Fredland, *The Church in the Circle: Essays on the History of St. Anne's, Annapolis* (Annapolis: St. Anne's Episcopal Church, 2017), 27.
208. Ross, "Brief History," 8; "Revenue Marine: Trial Trip of the Revenue Cutter Kankakee," *New York Times,* November 2, 1864; Kern, United States Revenue Cutters, 14–6 (Kankakee), 14–8 (Bronx).
209. Rosa Morsell to H. Clay Evans, Commissioner of Pensions, October 14, 1898, and undated summary of incident, in Pension Application, File No. 17398, that states she was living in Annapolis at the time of Richard's death; *New York Herald,* December 25, 1864; *New York Times,* December 27, 1864, which reported the death caused "by syncopia [temporary suspension of respiration and circulation], superinduced by being in the water." For funeral, see *Daily National Intelligencer* (Washington), December 28, 1864, 1. Also see Kern, *United States Revenue Cutters,* 15–5, for the Savannah River reference; Find A Grave Memorial ID 130904871.
210. Bills and Resolutions, House of Representatives, 42nd Congress, 3rd Session, Read twice and referred to the Committee on Pensions: An Act Granting a Pension to Rosa F. Morsell" (passed by the House of Representatives, February 5, 1873), accessed March 23, 2017, https://memory.loc.gov/cgi-bin/ampage?collId=llhb&fileName=042/llhb042.db&recNum=13095; "House Bills: H.R. No. 3839," *Congressional Globe: Containing the Debates and Proceedings of the Third Session Forty-Second Congress; An Appendix Embracing the Laws Passed at that Session* (Washington: Office of the Congressional Globe, 1873), lxxxii; *Daily Globe,* February 5, February 6, March 3, and March 12, 1873.
211. Rosa Morsell Pension Application File No. 17398.
212. *Catalogue of the Officers and Students of Georgetown College, District of Columbia, For the Academic Year, 1872–73* (Baltimore: John Murphy, 1873), 22; 1880 Federal Census, Washington; Rosa Morsell Pension Application File No. 17398; "District of Columbia Deaths and Burials, 1840–1964," accessed March 3, 2014, FamilySearch.org; "U.S. Naval Enlistment Rendezvous, 1855–1891," accessed March 3, 2014, FamilySearch.org; 1900 Federal Census, New York City. Raymond died in East Orange, New Jersey in 1930, see "Morsell Family Tree," March 11, 2014, Ancestry.com; Find A Grave Memorial ID 98595129. For Rosa's death, see *Evening Star,* May 8, 1907, *Washington Post* May 9, 1907, and *Washington Times,* May 10, 1907; Find A Grave Memorial ID 182597600.
213. *Chronica Domus* I:270 (December 25, 1864).
214. *Sun,* December 22, 1864; *Chronica Domus* I:270 (December

25, 1864), I:271 (end-of-1864 *Annotationes quaedam,* item 6).

215. Draft letters of Susie Sands to Josie and Albert G. Holland, both dated October 25, 1864, Dossett Collection, MSA SC2095-2-167; McIntire 1:694.

216. US Congress, *Statutes at Large,* vol. 13, Appendix, No. 24, Proclamation of December 19, 1864, 750–51, accessed September 10, 2016, http://www.loc.gov/law/help/statutes-at-large/38th-congress/c38.pdf; *Province Annals, 1832–71,* 570 (1864, Annapolis), RABP.

Chapter 7: 1865 — He Was in a Theater on Good Friday Evening

1. Baptismal Register B#1 (January 6, 1865). Eliza's surname is given in various records as Cornea, Corney, Curnie, Kernee, Kirnie. The 1862 marriage certificate signed by Rev. J. H. Ryland is in Eliza Young's Pension File (Application No. 53944, Certificate No. 61290), RG 15, NARA; "Maryland Marriages, 1666–1970," accessed July 12, 2014, FamilySearch.org. See Cunningham, *Calvary United Methodist Church,* 23, for Ryland's identification with Salem Methodist; *Sun,* July 21, 1862, for Bradford's announcement. The 1862 draft enrollment lists William Young, Annapolis, age 20 "in the service Volunteer U.S. Army."
2. Compiled Military Service Record (William Young), RG 94, NARA; "Regiment Data: 1st Maryland Infantry Regiment (Union)," ACWRDB, accessed June 30, 2014; Gordon C. Rhea, "Dodging Bullets," *Hallowed Ground* 15, no. 1 (Spring 2014):20, 24; "Stop 14: The Harris Farm," in Robert M. Dunkerly, Donald C. Pfanz, and David R. Ruth, *No Turning Back: A Guide to the 1864 Overland Campaign, From The Wilderness to Cold Harbor, May 4–June 13, 1864* (El Dorado Hills, California: Savas Beatie, 2014), 57–58; Gordon C. Rhea, *In the Footsteps of Grand and Lee: The Wilderness through Cold Harbor* (Baton Rouge: Louisiana State University Press, 2007), 60–61. Young's name does not appear in US Army, Quartermaster General's Office, *Roll of Honor: Names of Officers and Soldiers Found on the Battlefields of the Wilderness and of Spottsylvania* [sic] *Court House, Va.,* (Washington: Government Printing Office, 1865), II:20, nor in other volumes recording Virginia burials in the 27-volume series; nor in Eshelman and Rawlinson, *Graven in Stone.*
3. Eliza Young Pension File 53944. The baptismal certificate for "her child since deceased" is mentioned in the September 26, 1865 declaration and a "certificate of birth" signed by "Jos. A. Firle, Catholic priest," is mentioned in an affidavit of November 22, 1865, but the certificate itself is not in the file itself. Only "Mr. Dellinger" is referred to in the pension documents and that he had left Annapolis by the time the second application was submitted. *"Archives of Maryland,* Historical List: Constitutional Convention, 1864," accessed August 20, 2014, http://msa.maryland.gov/msa/speccol/sc2600/sc2685/html/conv1864.html.
4. McIntire, 1:360, says Eliza Corney married John Jacobs on October 31, 1866; she died July 25, 1890. Interment Register B#2 (July 25, 1890). Also, Find A Grave Memorial IDs 10353770 (for John H. Jacobs, Co. F, First Maryland Infantry, died May 5, 1921) and 827668 (for Anna Rebecca Boone Jacobs, died January 8, 1946). Jacobs and Boone were married in Anne Arundel County on October 18, 1900. See John Henry Jacobs Sr. Family Tree 32627913, accessed August 18, 2014, Ancestry.com. Jacobs served in Company B, Purnell Cavalry (Maryland), November 1, 1862–November 17, 1864; transferred to Company H, 8th Maryland Infantry, November 17, 1864–June 1, 1865; transferred to 1st Maryland Infantry, June 1, 1865, until mustered out on July 2, 1865, ACWRDB.
5. A detailed account of the Redemptorist mission to New Bern appears in Robert L. Worden, "A Plea for Help: Redemptorists in North Carolina During the Civil War," *Redemptorist North American Historical Bulletin,* nos. 42–43 (Fall 2016/Spring 2017), 17–31, https://www.redemptorists.com/documents/2021/6/issue_42_43_fall_2016_spring_2017.pdf.
6. Saint Paul Catholic Church, New Bern, "History of St. Paul," accessed September 12, 2016, http://www.spccnb.org/uploads/4/3/3/4/43348967/historybook.pdf; John Prime, New Bern, to Spalding, Baltimore, October 1 and 2, 1864, Box 35, Folder P5, Spalding Papers, AAB; Sister Mary Denis Maher, *To Bind Up the Wounds: Catholic Sister Nurses in the U.S. Civil War* (Baton Rouge: Louisiana State University Press, 1989), 73; "St. Paul's Church, New Bern, N.C.," sacramental register, 1845–1896, St. Paul Church Office, New Bern, North Carolina. Entries made by Father G. C. Brühe, S.J., October 24, 1862–February 24, 1863, and by Father Thomas Willett, S.J., April 26–July 12, 1863.
7. Buckley, *War Letters,* 222–28; summary of Aegidius Smulders, [Lynchburg, Virginia], to Jefferson Davis, [Richmond], October 15, 1864, in Lynda Lasswell Crist, ed., *The Papers of Jefferson Davis* (2) *September 1864–May 1865* (Baton Rouge: Louisiana State University Press, 2003), the original is in War Department Collection of Confederate Records, RG 109, NARA; typed copy of Smulders, Fort Jennings, [Ohio], to De Dycker, Baltimore, September 26, 1865, RABP; Smulders, Holy Redeemer Church, Detroit, to Judge Henry Brooke Kelly, [New Orleans?], March n.d., 1887, Box 55-C, Louisiana Historical Association Collection, Louisiana Research Collection, Howard-Tilton Memorial Library, Tulane University, New Orleans. Also, Hoegerl, "Two Redemptorist Accounts," for Smulders letter, September 26, 1865, and related materials. Smulders' account also appears in "A Chaplain's Story," *Camp Moore News* 9: no. 1 (March 2007): 1–3, available on request from www.campmoore.com in Tangipahoa, Louisiana.
8. Spalding to Moore, [Charleston, South Carolina], May 29, 1865, *Literarum Registrum,* Microfilm Reel 32, I–114, AAB; Moore to Spalding, June 23, 1865, Spalding Papers, RG 1.7, Box 35, Folder J7, AAB; Spalding to Bishop Patrick Neison Lynch, [Rome], June 27, 1865, Lynch Administration, Box 32, Folder Q6, Office of Archives and Records Manage-

ment, Diocese of Charleston. In latter letter, Spalding said he had "sent two Redemptorist Fathers for a time to Newbern, & a Jesuit Father to Charleston." Also, "St. Paul's Church, New Bern, N.C.," sacramental register, 1845–1896; *Annals, St. Michael's, Baltimore, 1845–1891,* 46 (1865) (St. James was an adjunct of St. Michael's), RABP; *Chronicles of Convent St. James, Baltimore, 1868–1900,* 18–19 (1865), RABP; Selected Records of the War Department Related to Confederate Prisoners of War, 1861–1865, vols. 276–278: Records Relating to Individual Prisoners or Stations, Point Lookout, Md., Military Prison, Lists of Money and Property of Prisoners, 1864–65, 126:103, M598, RG 109, NARA; Sheeran, *Diary*, 291–99, 334, and 346.

9. Gaché in Charleston June 1–October 5, 1865. Ruland to Spalding, May 1, 1865, Box 35, Folder W6, Spalding Papers, AAB, references Spalding's of April 25; *Sadliers' Catholic Directory, 1867,* 86, 232; Katherine Bentley Jeffrey, *First Chaplain of the Confederacy: Father Darius Hubert, S.J.* (Baton Rouge: Louisiana State University Press, 2020); Raymond A. Schroth, S.J., *The American Jesuits: A History* (New York: New York University Press, 2007), 83; Buckley, *War Letters*, 219–26, 231; Katherine Bentley Jeffrey, *Two Civil Wars: The Curious Shared Journal of a Baton Rouge School Girl and a Union Sailor on the USS Essex* (Baton Rouge: Louisiana State University, 2016), 207–16.

10. Geary, *We Need Men*, 162–63, 238–39 n60, 239 n63; Edward Sorin, C.S.C, Notre Dame, South Bend, Indiana, to Lincoln, Washington, September 28, 1863, with endorsements by W.T. Sherman, n.d., and U.S. Grant, September 28, 1863, *Official Records of the Union and Confederate Armies,* series III, vol. 3 (Washington: Government Printing Office, 1899), 844–45; United States Congress, *The Statutes at Large, Treaties, and Proclamations of the United States of America, from December 1863, to December 1865,* George P. Sanger, ed., (Boston: Little Brown and Company, 1866), accessed September 10, 2016, http://www.loc.gov/law/help/statutes-at-large/38th-congress/c38.pdf, Chapter 13, section 17 (February 24, 1864) addressed conscientious objection; chapter 79, 487ff did not refer to or amend the sections dealing with exemptions in the 1863 or 1864 laws. Also, Robert Emmett Curran, "'Three Cheers for Jeff Davis!': Jesuit Colleges and the American Civil War," 10, e-typescript sent to the author, June 23, 2017, and "Society of Jesus Marks 200th Anniversary of its Restoration in 2014," accessed October 18, 2017, http://image.jesuits.org/newsdetail?TN=NEWS-20140109024219.

11. *Sun*, February 15, 1865; Henry W. Bellows, *The United States Sanitary Commission* (New York: G. P. Putnam's Sons, 187?), 1, accessed January 23, 2017, http://lcweb2.loc.gov/service/gdc/scd0001/2013/20130904008un/20130904008un.pdf; Lemuel Moss, *Annals of the United States Christian Commission* (Philadelphia: J. B. Lippincott, 1868), 698.

12. *Chronica Domus* II:7 (February 13, 1865); *Sun*, February 7, 1865. Issues of *Crutch* that might have reported on a chorus singing at St. Mary's are missing from the online collection at MSA. A gap in extant copies exists in vol. 2 between no. 58 (February 11, 1865) and no. 63 (March 18, 1865).

13. *Catholic Mirror*, July 15, 1865; "Holy Childhood Association," https://www.missionsocieties.ca/holy-childhood-association-hca/history-of-holy-childhood-association/ and Liz Dellinger, transcriber, "St. Paul's Church and Parish The Shepherds of the Flock," http://genealogytrails.com/mary/howard/sotf.html, both accessed September 29, 2016; Find A Grave Memorial ID 31620042.

14. *Catholic Mirror*, September 23, 1865.

15. *Crutch*, January 28 and February 4, 1865; Toews, *Lincoln in Annapolis*, 10, 15, 23. The Confederate officials who met onboard steamer *River Queen* with Lincoln and Secretary of State Seward (who passed through Annapolis on January 31) were Vice President Alexander H. Stephens, Assistant Secretary of War John A. Campbell, and Senator Robert M. T. Hunter.

16. Claessens to Howes Goldsborough, March 3, 1865, Folder 3, Goldsborough Papers; Pius IX, *Quanta Cura, Encyclical Letter Condemning Current Errors,* December 8, 1864, accessed January 31, 2017, http://www.papalencyclicals.net/Pius09/p9quanta.htm, which invoked an 1846 letter, *Apostolic Letter of Our Holy Father Pope Pius IX Proclaiming a Universal Jubilee to Implore the Divine Assistance* (Rome: St. Mary Major, November 22, 1846); *Pastoral Letter of the Most Rev. Martin John Spalding, D.D., Archbishop of Baltimore, to the Clergy and Laity of the Archdiocese; Promulgating the Jubilee* (given February 8, 1865) (Baltimore: Kelly and Piet, 1865). For American press comment, see Zanca, *Catholics and Mrs. Mary Surratt*, 107.

17. Claessens to Goldsborough, March 3, 1865.

18. Claessens to Goldsborough, April 10, 1865, Dielemans to Goldsborough, April 20, 1865, Folder 3, Goldsborough Papers; Henning, Annapolis, to Martin Spalding, Baltimore, April 13, 1865, Box 34, Folder F9, Spalding Papers, AAB; "Johnson's Virginia, Delaware and Maryland" (New York: Johnson and Ward, 1864), Geography and Map Division, LoC Digital ID lva00119; Henry W. Poor, *History of the Railroads of the United States of America* (New York: Schultz, 1860), 590.

19. *Chronica Domus* II:6 (January 1865), II:9 (April 1, 1865), II:16 (April 17, 1865); Spalding, Baltimore, to Henning, Annapolis, April 11, 1865, *Literarum Registrum, 1862–1869,* this letter on microfilm reel 32, I–94; Henning to Spalding, April 13, 1865, Box 34, Folder F9, Spalding Papers, AAB; Borgmann, *Redemptorists at Annapolis*, 68.

20. Henning, Salisbury, to Spalding, Baltimore, June 16, 1865, Box 34, Folder F10, Spalding Papers, AAB; *Province Mission Book,* June 9, 165, RABP; 1880 Federal Census, Salisbury, Wicomico County, Maryland, lists 62-year-old John Tracy as proprietor, Atlantic Hotel; Thomas Joseph Peterman, *Catholics in Early U.S. Delmarva: A Sequel to Catholics in Colonial Delmarva* (Warminster, Pennsylvania: Cooke Publishing, 2006), 528–36.

21. Baptismal Register B#1 (June 18, 1865); 1850 and 1860

Federal Slave Schedules for Snow Hill, Maryland; 1860 Federal Census, Snow Hill; Virginia Eastern Shore Public Library, MilesFiles 16.4, Person Page 979, accessed January 27, 2017, http://espl-genealogy.org/MilesFiles/site/p979.htm; Maryland Bar Association, *Report of the Twelfth Annual Meeting of the Maryland State Bar Association, Held at Ocean City, Maryland, July 3–5, 1907* (Report of the Committee on Legal Biography) (Baltimore: Sun Job Printing Office, 1907), 91.

22. Baptismal Register B#1 (June 20, 1865); Marriage Register B#1 (June 18, 1865); Marriage Reference card for Julia Anne Bright and Timothy Spillance [*sic*], accessed January 22, 2015, http://msa.maryland.gov/megafile/msa/stagsere/se1/se27/000000/000018/pdf/se27-0018.pdf; 1870 Federal Census, Princess Anne, Somerset County, Maryland.

23. Enright to Goldsborough, September 23, 1864, Folder 2, Goldsborough Papers; *Catholic Mirror*, August 19, 1865; *Province Annals, 1832–71* (1865), 586, RABP.

24. *Chronica Domus* II:23 (September 17, 1865), II:24 (October 15, 1865), II:25 (November 18, 1865), II:26 (December 3, 17, 24, 25, 1865); *Catholic Mirror*, December 30, 1865; "Acta Episcopalia Martini Joanne Spalding," Hogan translation, December 7, 1865, Spalding Papers, AAB; Peterman, *Catholics in Early U.S. Delmarva*, 536–38.

25. *Chronica Domus* II:6 (January 1, 1865), II:7 (February 5, 1865), II:8 (March 5, 1865), II:9 (entry for April 1, 1865, mission must have been held around April 12–13), II:17 (May 7, 1865), II:21 (May 21, 1865), Burke; II:20 (June 3,1865), II:21 (July 2, 1865), II:22 (August 6, 1865).

26. *Chronica Domus* II:6 (January 1, 1865), II:24 (October 15, 1865), II:25 (November 25, 1865), II:26 (December 3, 1865), II:26 (December 7, 1865), II:26 (entry following December 23, 1865).

27. *Catholic Mirror*, October 7 and December 30, 1865; Our Lady of Sorrows Register of Baptisms, 1865–1908, 2–7 (baptisms, June 4, 1865, for George Hume Steuart) and 196–97 (confirmations), Microfilm SCM 2625, MSA SC1172. *Chronica Domus* II:30 (December 1865, following the entry for December 23).

28. *Chronica Domus* II:23 (September 18, 1865), II:24 (October 5, 1865), II:24 (October 13, 1865), II:24 (October 20 or 21, 1865), II:26 (December 23, 1865); *Province Mission Book*, September 24–October 4, 1865; concerning Oakland, see letter of Adrian Van de Braak, Cumberland, to Kenrick, Baltimore, January 19, 1859, and Van de Braak to Kenrick, June 14, 1859, Box 28, Folder F16, Box 28, Folder F19, Kenrick Papers, AAB; Thomas J. Stanton, *A Centenary of Growth: The History of the Church in Western Maryland* (Baltimore: John Murphy, 1900), I:43, 55, and 274–75.

29. *Chronica Domus* II:9 (April 1, 1865).

30. *Chronica Domus* II:9–10 (March 30–April 2, 1865); *Sun*, March 6 and April 1, 1865; *Catholic Mirror*, April 1, 1865; Neither *Chronica Domus* or *Sun* revealed the topic of the archbishop's lecture. Ordinations also discussed in *Province Annals, 1832–71* (Annapolis, 1865), 584, RABP.

31. Sheeran, *Diary*, 240–43 (September 19–October 4, 1863).

32. John Henry Boyle Sr. (1815–66) and Ellen Slemaker Boyle (1820–65). Baptismal Register B#1 (September 3, 1852—Edwin Boyle, born December 2, 1851). The 1850 Federal Census, Upper Marlborough, lists James (age 11), Susan (age 9), John (age 7), Andral (age 2), and Mary (age 1); 1860 Federal Census, Upper Marlborough, lists same five (except Margaret instead of Mary), plus Edward (age 8, instead of Edwin). "Martinet's Map of Prince George's County, Maryland" (Baltimore: Simon J. Martenet, 1860), LoC Digital ID la000302, shows "Dr. Boyle" on what today is Old Marlboro Pike; Annapolis Mayor and Aldermen, Property Assessment, June 11, 1860, MSA M72–3, for Dr. John H. Boyle's taxable house and lot on Church Street; *Annapolis Gazette*, March 1, 1866, for Dr. Boyle's laudatory death notice.

33. Baptismal Register B#2 (July 1, 1866—Alphonsus Albert Boyle, born August 26, 1853, and Samuel Joseph Boyle, born November 17, 1865). 1880 Federal Census, Baltimore, lists Cilest Boyle, 35-year-old illiterate Black "servant," living with Llewellyn Boyle, single, "Retired Army Officer," in a boarding house at 47 North Liberty Street. He was last recorded in the Annapolis excise tax records in 1866 as an attorney and noted in Baltimore city directories from 1868 to 1880.

34. Boyle enlisted June 1, 1861. Compiled Service Records Showing Military Service of Soldiers Who Fought in Confederate Organizations (John H. Boyle Jr.), M324, RG 109, NARA; Joseph E. Jeffs, Georgetown University, Washington, to James O. Hall, McLean, Virginia, May 29, 1980, and enclosures in Boyle John H Guerilla file, cabinet 10, drawer 4, James O. Hall Research Center, Surratt House Museum, Clinton, Maryland. Also, in same file, James O. Hall, "The Guerilla Boyle," a 23-page manuscript later published in the *Maryland Independent-Beacon* (La Plata), May 7, 1975, A1, A14–A15, and May 14, 1975, A2, A12; partially republished in *Surratt Society News* 10, no. 4 (April 1985): 1, 5–6, and 10, no. 5 (May 1985): 6. Further references herein are to the original manuscript version. Later authors mentioning Boyle cite Hall's article in their research. For example, see John Bakeless, Spies of the Confederacy (Mineola, New York: Dover Publications, 1970), 88–89. Also, *Sun*, February 17, 1860; *Daily Exchange* (Baltimore), February 18, 1860,; "John H. Boyle (Confederate)," ACWRDB, accessed October 16, 2014; *Richmond Dispatch*, December 24, 1861; *Richmond Inquirer*, February 28, 1862.

35. *Alexandria Gazette*, January 22, 1863; *Evening Star*, January 22, 1863; Register of Prisoners Compiled by the Office of Commissary General of Prisoners, 1863–65, O.C.G. No. 1, Old Capitol, Microfilm Publication 598, vol. 349, RG 109, NARA. He was prisoner No. 329, and released May 13, 1863; Hall, "The Guerilla Boyle," 1–3; "Report of Brigadier-General George H. Steuart," *Southern Historical Society Papers* 8, no. 3 (March 1880):136. Steuart referred to his "volunteer aide" as "Mr. John H. Boyle." Also, George H. Steuart, Headquarters, Steuart's Brigade, to Captain R. W. Hunter, Acting Assistant Adjutant General, Johnson's

Division, September 2, 1863, *Official Records of the Union and Confederate Armies,* series I, vol. 27, part II (Washington: Government Printing Office, 1889), 512.

36. Hall, "The Guerilla Boyle," 2, 4– 5. Hall's work was supplemented by Jack Kelbaugh, "A Case of Murder, Part I," *Anne Arundel County History Notes* 28, no. 2 (January 1997): 1–2 and "A Case of Murder, Part II," *Anne Arundel County History Notes* 28, no. 3 (April 1997), 4, 9–10. Also, Paul Lanham, "Terror in the Dark—The Confederate Guerilla Boyle," *News and Notes from the Prince George's County Historical Society* 3, no. 1 (January 1975), accessed February 7, 2017, http://www.pghistory.org/newsand-notes/NewsandNotes1975.pdf; John Paul Jones, ed., *Dr. Mudd and the Lincoln Assassination: The Case Reopened* (Conshohocken, Pennsylvania: Combined Books, 1995), 20, 200; Samuel Carter III, *The Riddle of Dr. Mudd* (New York: Putnam's Sons, 1974), 61; Catherine Randall, "Alexander Randall Diary Excerpts" (March 26, 1865–April 14, 1866), accessed February 2, 2017, http://cathyrandall.tumblr.com/post/80716954709/alexanders-first-assignment-as-marylands; Colonel Frederick D. Sewall, Third Regiment, Veterans Reserve Corps, Commanding Headquarters, District of Annapolis, to Lieutenant Colonel Samuel B. Lawrence, Assistant Adjutant General, Middle Department, Baltimore, March 27, 1865, photocopy in Boyle file, Hall Papers, Surratt House Museum. Also, Edward Steers Jr., *The Lincoln Assassination Encyclopedia* (New York: Harper Perennial, 2010), 90, citing James O. Hall, "The Guerilla Boyle," *Surratt Society Courier* 10, no. 4 (April 1985), and no. 5 (May 1985); Lanham, "Terror in the Dark"; Thomas H. Watkins, Davidsonville, to Assistant Adjutant General, Department of Susquehanna, Chambersburg, Pennsylvania, September 21, 1864, RG 94, NARA, photocopy in Boyle file, Hall Papers, Surratt House Museum.

37. Thomas H. Watkins (1838–65). Military Service Record (Thomas H. Watkins), RG 94, NARA; "Granting a Pension to Julia Watkins," H.R. 3111, Forty-Fifth Congress, 3rd Session, *Congressional Record* 8 (February 7, 1879), Senate 1074, accessed May 17, 2017, http://heinonline.org; *Sun,* April 21, 1863; Kelbaugh, "A Case of Murder, Part I," 1–2, 4–6, which cites Carroll Brice's research that there were more than 700 men in Anne Arundel County who joined the Confederate army. Also, *Sun,* April 21, 1863. Daniel Martin Kent (1841–1919), Etheridge Kent (1849–1932). Carded Records Showing Military Service of Soldiers Who Fought in Confederate Organizations, Compiled 1903–1927, Documenting the Period 1861–1865, Roll 198, Microfilm Publication M324, RG 109, NARA; "Soldier History: Daniel M. Kent," accessed July 6, 2017, ACWRDB; McIntire 1:389–90. Juliana Ballard Kent (1838–94) married Dr. Henry Roland Walton (1828–1912) but not at St. Mary's; *Maryland Republican,* May 3, 1862. Baptismal Register B#1 (April 7, 1864, Ella Lee Kent and May 28, 1864, Juliana Ballard Kent Walton).

38. Hall, "The Guerrilla Boyle," 7–10; Kelbaugh, "A Case of Murder, Part III," *Anne Arundel County History Notes,* 28, no. 4 (July 1997), 3–4; Sewall to Lawrence, Baltimore, March 27, 1865; George H. Hooker, Assistant Adjutant General, Middle Department, Baltimore, to Brigadier General John Reese Kenly, Wilmington, April 3, 1865, in War Department, *The War of the Rebellion: A Compilation of the Official Records of the Union and Confederate Armies,* series I, vol. 46, part 3 (Washington: Government Printing Office, 1891), 542; *Evening Star,* March 30, 1865, and subsequent editions for the rewards; Benjamin Watkins Journal, March 27, April 4 and 19, 1865; Captain George W. Curry, Captain, 4th Delaware Cavalry, Annapolis (who led the 1st Delaware detachment), to Colonel Frederick D. Sewall, Annapolis, April 5, 1865, Annapolis Provost Marshal Letters, 1864–65, Part 4, Entry 1538, RG 383, NARA; *Sun,* April 19, 1865; *Baltimore Clipper,* April 20, 1865; *Examiner* (Frederick), April 26, 1865. See Find A Grave Memorial ID 21091912 (Watkins).

39. Hall, "The Guerilla Boyle," 5–6, 12–14, 18; Michael W. Kauffman, *American Brutus: John Wilkes Booth and the Lincoln Conspirators* (New York: Random House, 2004), 233, 243–44; Steers, *Lincoln Assassination Encyclopedia,* 89–90; William C. Edwards and Edward Steers Jr., eds. *The Lincoln Assassination: The Evidence* (Urbana: University of Illinois Press, 2009), 499–501, 934–35; Lanham, "Terror in the Dark"; *Crutch,* April 22, 1865; Jones, *Dr. Mudd and the Lincoln Assassination,* 27, 66, 200; Douglas Linder, "The Trial of the Lincoln Assassination Conspirators: The Confession of George Atzerodt" (May 1, 1865), accessed February 3, 2017, http://law2.umkc.edu/faculty/projects/ftrials/lincoln-conspiracy/atzerodtconf.html; William C. Edwards, *The Lincoln Assassination —The Trial Transcript: A Transcription of NARA Microfilm File M599, Reels 8 Thru 16* (2012), 679, 900, 901, 904, 958, 962, 678–79, 1062.

40. The other attorneys were Thomas Stockett Alexander and Oliver Miller, who was later chief judge of Anne Arundel County Circuit Court. Kelbaugh, "A Case of Murder," Part III, 10; Steers, *Lincoln Assassination Encyclopedia,* 90; Colonel Frederick D. Sewall, Third Regiment, Veterans Reserve Corps, Commanding Headquarters, District of Annapolis, to Lieutenant Colonel Samuel B. Lawrence, Assistant Adjutant General, Middle Department, Baltimore, March 27, 1865, photocopy in Boyle file, Hall Papers; *Maryland Republican,* June 3, 1865; *Sun,* June 9 and , June 27, 1865; Randall, "Alexander Randall Diary Excerpts" (March 26, 1865–April 14, 1866); Benjamin Watkins Journal, May 24, May 30, September 11 and 25, 1865; *Sun,* February 23, 1866; *Annapolis Gazette,* March 1, 1866. For court details, see Presentments, Case Nos. 1 and 2 (May 18, 1865), and Case No. 31 (May 23, 1865), Docket, April Term 1865, Anne Arundel County Circuit Court, MSA C65–27. Mason represented the three Boyle brothers in Boyles vs. Joseph E. Jones, Appearances, Case No. 126 (October 21, 1865), Docket, October Term 1865, Anne Arundel County Circuit Court, MSA C65–28. Also, Criminal Docket, 1865–1891, WWW 2:35, September Term 1866 [*sic*], Howard County Circuit Court, MSA C929–2, reprises the larceny and attempted murder

cases and notes Boyle's "reception" at the penitentiary.

41. Benjamin Watkins Journal, September 11 and 25, 1865; Criminal Docket, 1865–1891, WWW 2:35–36, September Term 1866 [*sic*], Howard County Circuit Court, MSA C929–2.

42. For habeas corpus, see "State of Maryland vs. John Boyle" (*State v. Boyle*, 25 Md. Rep. 509, Decided July 17th, 1866) in Nicholas Brewer Jr., *State Reporter, Reports of Cases Argued and Adjudged in the Court of Appeals of Maryland, 25 (April 1866 Term),* revised and annotated by William H. Perkins Jr. (Baltimore: M. Curlander, 1898. Also, Docket, 1862–66, Case Nos. 154 and 221 (November 1, 1865), Maryland Court of Appeals, MSA S412–8.

43. *Sun*, February 20, March 2, and March 16, 1866. *Nolle prosequi* is a formal court notice of abandonment of all or part of a suit of action. Pardon Docket, 1869–79, Case Nos. 19 and 20 (March 13, 1872), date of hearing, April 2, 1872, Maryland Secretary of State, MSA S1110–2; *Sun*, March 12 and May 1, 1872; *Annapolis Gazette,* April 30, 1872. The Boyle letters should have been filed in Pardon Papers, 1872, Maryland Secretary of State, Box 63, MSA S1031–25, but instead are filed with Miscellaneous Papers, 1867–72, Maryland Governor, MSA S1274–145, in an unlabeled folder within a group of folders tied together with a faded red ribbon with a card reading "1872 Applications, Qualifications & other papers, State House, 37 folders."

44. *New Orleans Daily Democrat,* May 5, 1879; *Somerset Herald* (Somerset, Pennsylvania), May 14, 1879; *Crawford Avalanche* (Grayling, Michigan), May 14, 1879 (all three of which reported in varying degrees of detail a *Vicksburg Appeal* dispatch that said Boyle was a "United States Detective"); *Vicksburg Daily Commercial,* October 16, October 17, and November 17, 1879, and February 6, June 25, and July 3, 1880; *Comet* (Jackson, Mississippi), October 18, November 5, and November 22, 1879, and June 26, 1880; July 3, 1880, quoting an article from *Port Tobacco Times,* which also was published in *Evening Star* (Washington), July 6, 1880; 1880 Federal Census, Liberty Grove, Hinds County, Mississippi, taken June 3, 1880, lists with J. H. Boyle, unemployed detective, wife Susan A. age 30, born in Mississippi, and an unnamed infant son, age 4 months, also born in Mississippi; 1910 Federal Census, Jackson, identifies John L. Boyle, age 30, born in Mississippi, living with his mother Susie Hendrick, age 65, born in Mississippi, married twice (the "present marriage" of twenty-five years), mother of three children, all three living. "U.S. World War I Draft Registration Cards," accessed April 4, 2017, FamilySearch.org, identifies a self-employed John Lellyen [*sic*] Boyle born on January 18, 1880, living at 161 West Pearl St., Jackson, nearest relative, an aunt, Bettie Dulaney, New Orleans. Kelbaugh, "A Case of Murder," Part III, 10, declined to name the purported murderer. Also see Robert L. Worden, "'Guerrilla Boyle' Updated," *Surratt Courier* 46, no. 4 (July-August 2021): 10-14.

45. McWilliams, *Annapolis,* 184; *Crutch,* April 15, 1865.

46. *Evening Star,* 2nd ed., April 15, 1865; *Chronica Domus* II:16 (April 15, 17, 1865); *Province Mission Book,* April 23–May 2, 1865; Goodrich, *Darkest Dawn,* 152.

47. *Sun,* April 18, 1865.

48. Old Book 310, Middle Department [Annapolis], Part 4, Entry 1538, passes 8060, 8071, 8089, 8090, 8091 all issued April 15, 1865 RG 393, NARA.

49. *Chronica Domus* II:16 (April 17, 1865); Curley, *Provincial Story,* 152; Report of John C. Holland, Captain and Provost Marshal, Fifth Congressional District, Ellicott's Mills, Maryland, to Brigadier General James B. Fry, Provost Marshal General, Washington, June 12, 1865, pp. 3, 4–4A, 5A; Historical Reports of State Acting Assistant Provost Marshals General and District Provost Marshals, 1865, Roll 2, Microfilm Publication M1163, RG 110, NARA. The War Department orders were dated April 13, 1865, *Official Records of the Union and Confederate Armies,* series III, vol. 4 (Washington: Government Printing Office, 1900), 1263.

50. Seelos to Seelos, April 17–18, 1865, Letter 173, Hoegerl, *Sincerely, Seelos,* 430.

51. "Circular of the Most Rev. Archbishop of Baltimore on the Assassination," *Sun,* April 17, 1865, also published in Washington under the same title in *Constitutional Union,* April 18, 1865.

52. Hardie to Spalding, April 16, 1865, Box 34, Folder D10, Spalding Papers, AAB.

53. Spalding to Hardie, April 16, 1865, and Hardie's April 17, 1865, synopsis of Spalding to White letter, James Allen Hardie Papers, MMC–630, Manuscript Division, LoC.

54. Hardie to Spalding, April 19, 1865, Box 34, Folder D11, Spalding Papers, AAB.

55. *Chronica Domus* II:16 (April 19, 1865).

56. Spalding, *American Churchman,* 1, 8, 10, 25, 51, 97, 118, 121, 128, 133–38, 141, 166; Curran, *Shaping American Catholicism,* 104–5; Mitchell, *Maryland Voices,* 462–63 (quoting Spalding in the *Baltimore American,* April 17, 1865): Kurtz, *Excommunicated from the Union,* 98–99.

57. *Evening Star,* April 20, 1865; *Daily National Republican,* April 20, 1865.

58. *Sun,* April 22, 1865; *Crutch,* April 22, 1865; *Chronica Domus* II:16 (April 19, 1865); Borgmann, *Redemptorists at Annapolis,* 60.

59. Kenneth J. Zanca, "Baltimore's Catholics and the Funeral of Abraham Lincoln," *Maryland Historical Magazine* 98, no. 1 (Spring 2003): 93–95; Spalding, *Premier See,* 181; Kurtz, *Excommunicated from the Union,* 33; *Sun,* April 22, 1865; "Acta Episcopalia Martini Joanne Spalding," 15–16, Hogan translation, Spalding Papers, AAB.

60. Thompson's farm shown in First Election District, Howard County, west of Annapolis Junction in Simon J. Martenet, *Martenet's Atlas of Maryland, 1865,* Huntingfield Collection, MSA SC1399–1–75. 1860 Federal Census J. C. Thompson is enumerated in First District, Howard County, Elkridge Landing Post Office; Francis' baptism recorded in Baptismal Register B#1 (March 11, 1859). The 1850 Federal Slave Schedule, Charles County, indicates William Queen owned 22 slaves; "Dr. William Queen (1789–1869)," *Dr. Samuel*

A. Mudd Society Newsletter 4, no. 2 (June 1983)" [2–3]. His daughter was Sister Mary Xavier Queen, V.H.M. Also, Benn Pitman, comp., *The Assassination of President Lincoln and the Trial of the Conspirators* (New York: Moore, Wilstach, and Baldwin, 1865), 178, 320; Edwards and Steers, *The Lincoln Assassination: The Evidence,* 940 and 947–48, includes Mudd's testimony about Thompson introducing him to Booth. Hall argues in "Dr. Mudd—Again—Part I," The *Surratt Courier* 23, no. 7 (July 1998):4, that Mudd meeting Booth at St. Mary's Church in Bryantown on November 13 was not casual or incidental but intentional on Mudd's part. His reasoning is that Mudd normally attended Sunday Mass at St. Peter's Church in Beantown, located about 5.5 miles west of Mudd's farm, where Mudd had been married and his children were baptized, but had come to Bryantown, about 4.5 miles south, to meet Booth. However, had Hall consulted *Sadliers' Catholic Almanac, 1864,* 54–55, he would have seen that St. Peter's had Mass on the first and third Sundays of each month and that on the second and fourth Sundays, Mass was offered at St. Mary's Church in Piscataway, in Prince George's County.

61. "Mary Surratt's Story," Surratt House Museum, accessed December 7, 2016, http://www.surrattmuseum.org/mary-surratt; Daniel B. Lloyd, *The Lloyds of Southern Maryland* (Washington: The Author, 1971), 272–74.
62. Leech, *Reveille in Washington,* 386; Curley, *Cheerful Ascetic,* 263, 297; Rock, "Departed Redemptorist Brothers," 81; Hoegerl, *With All Gentleness,* 443.
63. *Annapolis Gazette*, September 7 and December 14, 1865; "Distributions of the Fund Collected in the Archdiocese of Baltimore on Sunday September 17th, 1865 for the Benefit of the Suffering Poor in the South," Box 39B, Folder G1, Spalding Papers, AAB; *Catholic Mirror,* October 7, 1865.
64. US Centers for Disease Control and Prevention,"Basic TB Facts," accessed February 9, 2017, https://www.cdc.gov/tb/topic/basics/default.htm.
65. *Chronica Domus* II:10–13, 16 (April 15–19, 1865); Borgmann, *Redemptorists at Annapolis,* 60, 213–14; *Catholic Mirror,* April 22, 1865; *New-York Freeman's Journal,* May 6, 1865.
66. *Chronica Domus* II:17 (May, 22 1865); Wuest, *Annales,* IV:2:457; 1862 and 1863 Annapolis draft enrollment records; *Catholic Mirror,* June 17, 1865 (Wüller referred to as "Henry Weiller").
67. *Chronica Domus* II:18 (May 29, 1865); Wuest, *Annales,* IV:2:458; *Catholic Mirror,* June 17, 1865; "United States Germans to America Index, 1850–1897," accessed February 8, 2017, FamilySearch.org, lists two Johann Beckers, born ca. 1841, one in Germany, another in Hesse, who immigrated to the United States, one in 1852 on ship *J.Z.,* the other in 1856 on *Havre,* both in steerage. The deaths of Petit, Wüller, and Becker are also recorded in *Province Annals,* 1832–71 (Annapolis, 1865), 584–85, 603, RABP.
68. *Chronica Domus* II:20 (undated entry [*Hoc mense*] between June 3 and June 21, 1865); Burkey, *Seelos: The Cumberland Years,* 57–62; Curley, *Cheerful Ascetic,* 260–61.
69. *Chronica Domus* II:21 (July 5, 28, August 5, 1865); Hoegerl, *Positio,* 2, part 2, 1054; James Keitz, C.Ss.R., "Our Studendate, 1862–1865" (ca. 1887), quoted in Hoegerl, "Blessed Francis Xavier Seelos: A New Biography" (manuscript 2016), 28:11–18, but omitted in the published edition, *With All Gentleness,* 408–10; Borgmann, *Redemptorists at Annapolis,* 219–21; Wuest, *Annales,* IV:2:447.
70. Indentures, 1858–99, Register of Wills, Anne Arundel County, November 3, 1864, BEG 2:240–43 (Handy children), MSA C82–3. For examples of all-day binding-out sessions, see Orphans' Court Proceedings, 1864–68 (November 2, November 4, November 5, November 16, 1864), Register of Wills, Anne Arundel County, MSA CM119–26 (CR262–5). Magruder and Nicholson to Bradford, no date, in Pardon Papers, 1865, Maryland Secretary of State, Box 61, Folder 84, MSA S1031–23. Baptismal Register B#1 notes Philip as servus (July 20, 1856) but Julia only once as *serva* (April 19, 1857). The other Handy baptisms do not mention slave status.
71. Indentures, 1846–58, Register of Wills, Anne Arundel County, October 10, 1855, BEG 1:313 (Charles Murdock) to Denver; December 28, 1855, BEG 1:317–18 (Edward West) and BEG 1:318 (William West) to Randall; September 15, 1857, BEG 1:387–88 (William Thomas) to Revell, MSA C82–2; Indentures, 1858–99, Register of Wills, Anne Arundel County, October 18, 1858, BEG 2:19–20 (Dinah Jackson) to Brady; Indentures, 1858–99, Register of Wills, Anne Arundel County, January 25, 1859, BEG 2:33 (Thomas Burroughs) to Treadway; July 10, 1860, BEG 2:69 (Nathan Ackwood) to Walton, MSA C82–3.
72. Presentments, Case Nos. 7 and 8 (May 18–June 6, 1865), Docket, April Term 1865, Anne Arundel County Circuit Court, C65–27; Baptismal Register B#1 (June 2, 1853, August 18, 1854, July 20, 1856, April 19, 1857, June 27, 1858, March 6, 1860, May 5, 1862); Confirmation Register B#1 (March 29, 1857); Interment Register B#1 (March 7, 1861, August 16, 1863).
73. *Maryland Republican,* June 3, 1865; *Sun,* June 9, 1865; *Annapolis Gazette,* November 16, 1865; Presentments, Case Nos. 7 and 8 (May 18–June 6, 1865), Docket, April Term 1865, Anne Arundel County Circuit Court, MSA C65–27; Maryland Constitution of 1864, Declaration of Rights, Article 24, in *Archives of Maryland Online,* vol. 102, 723, accessed February 18, 2017, http://aomol.msa.maryland.gov/megafile/msa/speccol/sc2900/sc2908/000001/000382/html/am382b--1.html; *The Maryland Code: Public General Laws, Adopted by the Legislature of Maryland, January Session, 1860* (Baltimore: John Murphy, 1860), I:31–39, Article 6, sections 9, 31–40. Also, *A Guide to the History of Slavery in Maryland* (Annapolis: Maryland State Archives and University of Maryland College Park, 2007), 31. For Baltimore court decision, see *Sun,* May 19, 1865, and *New York Times,* June 4, 1865.
74. Criminal Continuances, Case No. 6 and Case No. 7 (November 10–17, 1865), Docket, October Term 1865, Anne Arundel County Circuit Court, MSA C65–28. Apparently, Julia Handy also posted a $400 bond October 12, 1865 to

assure her trial appearance, see Recognizances, Case No. 35 (October 12, 1865), Docket, October Term 1865, Anne Arundel County Circuit Court, MSA C65–28. Also, *Archives of Maryland* (Biographical Series) "James R. Howison (1818 –1874)," MSA SC3520-12511, accessed May 8, 2017, http://msa.maryland.gov/megafile/msa/speccol/sc3500/sc3520/012500/012511/html/12511bio.html.

75. White and Munroe to Bradford, December 23, 1865, Pardon Papers, 1865, Maryland Secretary of State, Box 61, Folder 84, MSA S1031–23; *Annapolis Gazette,* March 1, 1866 reported the case of a young man who, when he became an apprentice, gave up his previously earned salary and his mother had "become dependent upon charity for an existence."

76. McIntire 1:445, 517; *Archives of Maryland* (Biographical Series), "Joseph H. Nicholson, Anne Arundel County Court Clerk, 1845–1851," MSA SC3520–13137, accessed May 11, 2017, http://msa.maryland.gov/megafile/msa/speccol/sc3500/sc3520/013100/013137/html/13137bio.html. Magruder and Nicholson to Bradford, no date, Pardon Papers, 1865. Coincidently, Joseph H. Nicholson's name appeared as Anne Arundel County clerk on the deed that transferred the St. Mary's Church property from Marianne Wellesley to James Boyle, see JHN 5:593 (March 29, 1851), AACLR. Eliza Nicholson's brother was Alexander Burton Hagner, a lawyer and later associate justice of the DC Supreme Court, was resident of the City Hotel from circa 1845 to 1853 when he married. He may thus have known Julia Handy. See McIntire 1:293; US Court of Claims File 1277.

77. Gerdemann to Bradford, January 2, 1866, Pardon Papers, 1865.

78. Ads appeared in *Annapolis Gazette,* December 28, 1865 and January 4, 1866. Pardon Docket, 1862–69, No. 407 (Julia Handy), Maryland Secretary of State, MSA S1110–1; Pardon Record, 1865–72, p. 8 (January 9, 1866), Maryland Secretary of State, MSA S1108–3. The bonding of Black children in apprenticeships was reversed by the US Supreme Court in *ex parte Elizabeth Turner* (*In re Turner* 24 F. Cas. 337, 1 Abb. US 81, case No. 14,247, 1 Chase, 157; 6 Int. Rev. Rec. 147; 1 Ma. Law T. Rep, US Cts. 7 Circuit Court, D. Maryland, October 13, 1867, involved eleven-year-old Elizabeth Turner of St. Michael's Talbot County, Maryland. accessed May 10, 2017, https://law.resource.org/pub/us/case/reporter/F.Cas/0024.f.cas/0024.f.cas.0337.pdf.

79. Criminal Continuances, Case No. 3 (*State v. Edward Walton*) and Case No. 4 (*State v. Thomas Carpenter* (June 8, 1865), Docket, April Term 1865, Anne Arundel County Circuit Court, MSA C65–27; Criminal Continuances, Case No. 2 (*State v. Thomas Carpenter* (no date, 1865), Docket, October Term 1865, Anne Arundel County Circuit Court, MSA C65–28. NPS Soldiers and Sailors Database lists sixty-six men named Thomas Carpenter who served in the Union army.

80. Docket, October Term 1865, Anne Arundel County Circuit Court, MSA C65–28, Presentment, Case No. 3, October 24, 1865; for Esmond's police officer appointment, see Annapolis, Mayor and Aldermen Proceedings, August 13, 1867, MSA M49–10; "History of the Police Department," accessed June 2, 2019, https://www.annapolis.gov/436/History-of-the-Police-Department.

81. Docket, October Term 1865, Anne Arundel County Circuit Court, MSA C65–28, Case No. 4, October 24 and November 11, 1865 (Flood); Docket, April Term 1865, Anne Arundel County Circuit Court, MSA C65–27, Presentment, Case No. 20, May 19, 1865 (Cavanaugh); Recognizance, Case No. 32, April 19, 1865 (Revell) and grand jury witnesses listed in docket volume, May 26, 1865 (Revell), and various other cases, MSA C65–27.

82. Percival Drayton, Chief, Bureau of Navigation, Washington, to Captain George S. Blake, Naval Academy, Newport, July 3, 1865, Entry 25, Box 8, Folder 10, RG 405, USNA. First Communion Register F#1 (May 10, 1877); Cornelius Denver is listed as born in Newport in the 1865 Rhode Island Census, and born Newport October 7, 1864, in F#1; Horner Notes, March 10, 2014 on Andrew Denver; undated typescript with a list of watchmen appointments that lists Denver's appointment as watchman on August 22, 1856, and as captain of the watch on April 4, 1859, Office of the Superintendent, Letters Received by the Superintendent, 1845–1887, Folder 7, Box 6, Entry 25, RG 405, USNA; Baptismal Register B#1 (May 3, 1863); Marriage Register B#1 (May 8, 1865). First Communion Register F#1 (June 2,1878); Interment Record B#2 (May 10, 1893). The interment register lists Mary Hoban's birthplace as Newport, Rhode Island, 37 years earlier. F#1 gives her date of birth as May 19, 1865, but says she was born in Annapolis. However, there is no record of her baptism in Annapolis.

83. John J. Henderson and Roger E. Belson, "White Mountain Art and Artists: Edward Seager," revised September 7, 2014, http://whitemountainart.com/Biographies/bio_es.htm; Edward W. Callahan, ed. *List of Officers of the Navy of the United States and of the Marine Corps from 1775 to 1900,* (New York: Hamersly, 1901), 487; 1870 Federal Census, Baltimore; Find A Grave Memorial IDs 95697268 and 95697295; Interment Register B#2 (April 2, 1885); Find A Grave Memorial ID 213129510; "The Naval Academy," *New York Herald,* May 21, 1863, 1; *Official Registers of the Officers and Acting Midshipmen of the United States Naval Academy* for 1864–66; letter of Bonnafous to Blake, Newport, May 30, 1865, Office of the Superintendent, Letters Received by the Superintendent, 1845–1887, Folder 1, Box 7, Entry 25, RG 405, USNA; Marriage Register B#2 January 4, 1866.

84. 1870 Federal Census, Annapolis; Interment Register B#1 (April 5, 1877). Horner Notes, March 10, 2014 on Frank and John Gesner; McIntire, 1:268.

85. Horner Notes, March 10, 2014 on Peter Schoff and family; Baptismal Register B#2 (May 11, 1866, November 3, 1867, July 14, 1869) and B#3 (ca. April 17, 1871). 1880 Federal Census, Annapolis, lists Schoff as USNA Band musician. Also, McIntire, 1:619.

86. Horner Notes, March 10, 2014 on Alfred C. Woolley Sr., Alfred C. Woolley Jr., and David E. Woolley; 1870 and 1880

Federal Census, Annapolis; Interment Register B#2 (October [no day], 1880) and April 26, 1887); McIntire, 1:785.

87. Horner Notes, March 10, 2014 on William Nayden; 1880 and 1900 Federal censuses, Annapolis; McIntire, 1:512; Find A Grave Memorial IDs 82853479 and 82853631; Anne Arundel County Genealogical Society, "St. Mary's Roman Catholic Cemetery," 607a, headstone inscriptions, revised January 2014, courtesy Christina Simmons.

88. "Philadelphia Naturalization Records, 1789–1880" and "Philadelphia, Pa, Death Certificates Index, 1803–1915," both accessed November 7, 2013, Ancestry.com; Pension File Certificate No. 617257 (Peter Klippen), RG 15, NARA. Peter died August 5,1910, Rebecca died September 10, 1910. Also, McIntire, 1:401.

89. 1870 Federal Census, Philadelphia, lists son Adolph, ages 5 or 6—the family was enumerated twice, at different addresses in 1870—and born in Pennsylvania; 1880 Federal Census, "Philadelphia; Pennsylvania Church and Town Records, 1708–1985," accessed November 7, 2013, Ancestry.com; Philadelphia (Peter Hilgert, buried June 20, 1881, St. Peters Roman Catholic Cemetery), Find A Grave Memorial ID 135934521; "Philadelphia, Pennsylvania, Death Certificates Index, 1803–1915," accessed November 7, 2013, Ancestry.com. Meta Hilgert died September 19, 1896, buried Mount Moriah Cemetery, Find A Grave Memorial ID 32688117.

90. Muster Rolls, United States Marine Corps, 1798–1892, rolls 28–30, 35, 70, Microfilm Publication T1118, NARA; epitaph on St. Mary's Cemetery gravestone; Interment Register B#2 (February 6, 1867); *Sun*, February 20, 1867; Find A Grave Memorial ID 64252907.

91. Marriage Register B#1 (November 18, 1862), B#2 (October 15, 1865); Baptismal Register B#1 (September 24, 1863), Mary Himmelheber was the godmother; 1860 Federal Census, Annapolis; notes on William Francis (Franz) Strohmeyer provided by Horner to author, March 10, 2014.

92. 6th US Cavalry, Carded Medical Records (Patrick Dougherty), Regular Army, 1821–1884, Box 365, Entry 534, RG 94, NARA; Pension Files (Patrick: Application No. 188452, Certificate No. 991090, Jane: Application No. 976454, Certificate No. 705597), RG 15, NARA; Bates, *History of the Pennsylvania Volunteers*, I:193–95; Donald C. Caughey and Jimmy J. Jones, *The 6th United States Cavalry in the Civil War: A History and Roster* (Jefferson, North Carolina: McFarland, 2013), 34, 37, 39, 44, 48, 62. Dougherty's date and place of capture and parole do not appear in his service or pension files.

93. Dougherty Pension File; Caughey and Jones, *6th United States Cavalry*, 77–80.

94. James Franklin Hart quoted in Henry Brainerd McClellan, *The Life and Campaigns of Major-General J. E. B. Stuart: Commander of the Cavalry of the Army of Northern Virginia* (Boston: Houghton, Mifflin and Company, 1885), 266 n1, 268. Quote originally appeared in *Philadelphia Weekly Times*, June 26, 1880.

95. Dougherty Pension File; Caughey and Jones, *6th United States Cavalry*, 91–93, 163, 265n50; "Brandy Station," accessed November 14, 2017, https://www.battlefields.org/learn/civil-war/battles/brandy-station; NPS, "6th Regiment, US Cavalry (Regular Army)," accessed February 15, 2017.

96. Confirmation Register B#1 (December 8, 1864); 1870 Federal Census, Annapolis; "Papers Related to the Removal of Democrats and Appointment of Republicans, at the Naval Academy, 1870, Based on a Resolution Passed by the Republican Central Committee on March 7, 1870, and referred by the President to Commodore John L. Worden, Superintendent, USNA, Office of the Superintendent, Letters Received by the Superintendent, 1845–1887, Folder 9, Box 9, Entry 25, RG 405, USNA; US Department of the Interior, *Register of Officers and Agents, Civil, Military and Naval, in the Service of the United States, on the Thirtieth of September, 1871* (Washington: Government Printing Office, 1872), 297; 1870 and 1880 Federal censuses, Annapolis; 1890 Special Schedule, Surviving Soldiers, Sailors, and Marines, Widows, etc., Annapolis; Pension Files (Patrick: Application No. 188452, Certificate No. 991090; Jane: Application No. 976454, Certificate No. 705597), RG 15, NARA.

97. Marriage Register B#2 (April 24, 1866); Case Files of Approved Pension Applications of Widows and Other Dependents, Widows Pension (Ann Reilly Hickey Esmond), Certificate No. 2160, RG 15, NARA; Interment Register B#2 (August 23, 1874).

98. 1880 Federal Census, Annapolis; Pension Files (Patrick: Application No. 188452, Certificate No. 991090; Jane: Application No. 976454, Certificate No. 705597), RG 15, NARA. Elizabeth Jane Dougherty married Robert Louis Thomas (1856–1932) in 1886, had eight children, and died in 1906; McIntire 1:703.

99. *Annapolis Gazette*, October 19, 1865; Marriage Register B#2 (October 16, 1865) and Confirmation Register B#1 (December 8, 1864); ACWRDB, accessed October 10, 2012; Compiled Military Service Records (Henry C. Williams, 8th Pennsylvania Cavalry and 213th Pennsylvania Infantry), RG 94, NARA; Carded Medical Records, Box 3027, Entry 534, RG 94, NARA; "The Gallant Charge of the 8th Pennsylvania Cavalry At Chancellorsville," http://schuylkillcountymilitaryhistory.blogspot.com/2009/02/gallant-charge-of-8th-pennsylvania.html, and "8th Pennsylvania Cavalry Regiment," http://civilwarintheeast.com/us-regiments-batteries/pennsylvania/8th-pennsylvania-cavalry-regiment/, both accessed February 11, 2017.

100. Compiled Military Service Records (Henry C. Williams); Norman Gasbarro, "8th Pennsylvania Cavalry: Pennsylvania Memorial at Gettysburg," http://civilwar.gratzpa.org/2011/04/8th-pennsylvania-cavalry-pennsylvania-memorial-at-gettysburg/; "8th Pennsylvania Cavalry (Pleasonton Avenue)," http://gettysburg.stonesentinels.com/union-monuments/pennsylvania/pennsylvania-cavalry/8th-pennsylvania-cavalry/, both accessed February 11, 2017; Carded Medical Records, Box 3027, Entry 534, RG 94, NARA; "New York Deaths and Burials, 1795–1952" and "Pennsylvania, Philadelphia City Death Certificates, 1803–1915,"

FamilySearch.org, both accessed February 9, 2017. Although Williams died in Connecticut, his death was registered in both New York City and Philadelphia, and he was buried in Philadelphia. No pension records were found at NARA for Henry or Barbara Williams.

101. Marriage Register B# 2 (November 16, 1865); NPS Soldiers and Sailors Database, "2nd Regiment, US Artillery (Regular Army)," accessed February 27, 2015, https://www.nps.gov/civilwar/search-battle-units-detail.htm; 1860 Federal Census, Roxbury, Massachusetts; 1880 Federal Census, Boston; Navy Widow's Pensions Application No. 7300, Certificate No. 15942, M1279, NARA; Felix Gilfeather, 2nd US Artillery, Carded Medical Records, Regular Army, 1821–1884, Box 108, Entry 534, RG 94, NARA; "A Brief List of Old, Obscure and Obsolete U.S. Navy Jobs," *USNI News*, September 25, 2016, accessed February 14, 2017, https://news.usni.org/2014/12/03/brief-list-old-obscure-obsolete-u-s-navy-jobs; "Winnipec," *Dictionary of Naval Fighting Ships*, accessed February 14, 2017, https://www.history.navy.mil/research/histories/ship-histories/danfs/w/winnipec.html; "U.S. Marine Corps Muster Rolls, 1798–1958," Muster Roll of Detachment of Officers, Non-commissioned Officers, Drummers, Fifers, and Privates of the US Marines Stationed at Boston, Mass, November 1–30, 1864, same in Boston for June 1–30, 1865, same for Marines Stationed on board the USS *Winnipec*, June 9–30 1865, Marines Stationed at US Naval Academy Belonging to the USS *Winnipec*, December 1–31 1865, and same for November 1–30, 1866, accessed February 26, 2015, Ancestry.com.

102. 1880 Federal Census, Boston; Navy Widow's Pensions Application No. 7300, Certificate No. 15942, M1279, NARA.

103. *Annapolis Gazette*, October 5, 1865; McWilliams, *Annapolis*, 196; Riley, *Ancient City*, 315; email of St. Mary's parishioner Mary Anne Maley Joyce to author, May 22, 2011. Also, Old Book 310, Middle Department [Annapolis], no. 4338, issued July 4, 1864 (lists Maley's residence as Annapolis), and no. 5297, issued July 23, 1864 (lists his residence as Baltimore), Part 4, Entry 1538, RG 393, NARA; Compiled Service Records of Volunteer Union Soldiers Who Served in Organizations from the State of Massachusetts, RG 94, NARA; Civil War Pension Files for John Maley Application No. 393669, Certificate No. 806612, and Josephine Legg Maley Application No. 1069196, Certificate No. 821131, RG 15, NARA. Also, Find A Grave Memorial IDs 107375049 (John) and 107375253 (Josephine).

104. *Chronica Domus* II:22 (August 16, 1865), II:22 (late August 1865), II:23 (September 1865), II:9 (April 1, 1865), II:33 (January 29, 1866), II:17 (April 16, 1865).

105. *Chronica Domus* II:17 (September 4, 1865), II:26 (December 17, 24, 25, 1865).

106. *Chronica Domus* I:234 (November 28, 1863), I:245 (January 1, 1864), II:6 (January 1, 1865), II:26 (December 23, 1865), II:44 (August 18, 1866); Wuest, *Annales*, IV:2:462; Hoegerl, *With All Gentleness*, 186–89; Recktenwald and Weingärtner (Weingaertner) personnel files, RABP; *Catalogus Novitiorum* II:208 (October 15, 1868); Rock, "Departed Redemptorist Brothers," 72–73, 105, which says Recktenwald and the Weingärtners came on the ship *Bengal* from Le Havre. "New York Passenger Lists, 1820–1957," accessed September 28, 2011, Ancestry.com, notes the arrival in New York of *Bengal* from Le Havre on September 14, 1846, and provides a three-page passenger list but none approximating their names. This is the only arrival of the *Bengal* for 1846.

107. Susannah J. Ural, *Don't Hurry Me Down to Hades: The Civil War in the Words of Those Who Lived It* (New York: Osprey Publishing, 2013), 201 and 229 n196 citing J. David Hacker, "A Census-Based Count of the Civil War Dead," *Civil War History* 54:4 (December 2011): 306–47; Faust, *Republic of Suffering*, xi–xii, 3, 137–38, 266; Fleming, *Disease in the Public Mind*, ix–x; Civil War Trust, "Civil War Casualties: The Cost of War: Killed, Wounded, Captured, and Missing," accessed February 20, 2017, https://www.battlefields.org/learn/articles/civil-war-casualties; National Archives at Philadelphia, "Allegheny Arsenal Explosion and the Creation of Public Memory," accessed November 3, 2017, https://www.archives.gov/philadelphia/exhibits/allegheny-arsenal/house-report.html.

108. Faust, *Republic of Suffering*, 4, 102, 213.

109. Miller, *Both Prayed to the Same God*, 7 and 34.

110. "Abraham Lincoln's Second Inaugural Address," accessed February 19, 2017, https://www.loc.gov/rr/program/bib/ourdocs/Lincoln2nd.html.

111. Seelos, Annapolis, to Miss Mary, July 17, 1863, Letter 136, Hoegerl, *Sincerely, Seelos*, 358.

112. *Annapolis Gazette*, November 16, 1865; Library of Congress, Federal Research Division, United States, 40th Congress 2d Session, House of Representatives, Committee on the Judiciary, *Trial of Henry Wirz*, Executive Document No. 23, December 7, 1867, https://www.loc.gov/rr/frd/Military_Law/Wirz_trial.html, and NPS, "Andersonville: The Trial of Henry Wirz," https://www.nps.gov/teachers/classrooms/upload/Trial-of-Henry-Wirz-LP.pdf, both accessed February 20, 2017. Francis Edward Boyle was pastor St. Peter's Church, and Washington hospital chaplain; Peter Whelan was vicar general of Cathedral of St. John the Baptist, Savannah, Georgia, a frequent visitor to Andersonville, and witness for defense at Wirz's trial; Bernardine Wiget, S.J., was president of Gonzaga College, Washington. Weichert has not been identified and the report may have meant Wiget or Whelan. Only Boyle and Wiget (misspelled Wiggot in a second article) were mentioned in *Evening Star*, November 10, 1865, *Baltimore Daily Commercial*, November 11, 1865, and *Sun*, November 11, 1865; only Boyle and "attending priests" in *Daily National Republican* (Washington), November 10, 1865; no priests mentioned in *New York Times*, November 11, 1865.

113. Boyle took charge of Wirz's remains which were interred in Mount Olivet Cemetery, District of Columbia. Find A Grave Memorial ID 1659. In 1909 the United Daughters of the Confederacy erected a twenty-four-foot stone obelisk

in Andersonville, Georgia, "to rescue his name from the stigma attached to it by embittered prejudice." See "Wirz Monument – Andersonville, Ga.," accessed June 9, 2018, https://www.waymarking.com/waymarks/WMW8CV_Wirz_Monument_Andersonville_Ga; Southern Poverty Law Center, Weekend Read, Issue 83, June 9, 2018, https://www.splcenter.org/news/2018/06/08/weekend-read-executed-committing-war-crimes-%E2%80%94-then-honored-confederate-monument.

114. *Annapolis Gazette,* December 28, 1865. *Province Annals, 1832–71* (Annapolis, 1865), 603, RABP, has spaces with headings for baptisms, marriages, communions, students, and burials but omits the data.

Chapter 8: Hunger for the Supernatural

1. Francis A. Lord, *They Fought for the Union* (Harrisburg: Stackpole, 1960), 324; Civil War Trust, "Palmito Ranch," accessed March 6, 2018, https://www.battlefields.org/learn/articles/palmito-ranch.
2. McWilliams, *Annapolis,* 196–97; email Eric Goldstein, Director, Tam Institute for Jewish Studies, Emory University, Atlanta, to author, September 26, 2017, providing local Jewish community information.
3. *Chronica Domus* II:32 (January 1, 5, and 20, 1866).
4. *Chronica Domus* II:32 (January 29, 1866); *Annapolis Gazette,* January 25, 1866; Porter to Redemptionist [*sic*] Fathers, January 27, 1866, Letters Sent by the Superintendent of the US Naval Academy (Main Series), 1865–1907, Roll 1, vol. 31, October 3, 1865–July 30, 1866, Microfilm Publication M994, RG 405, USNA.
5. *Chronica Domus* II:33 (February 14 and March 2, 1866), II:34 (April 2 and 22, 1866). Confusion over whether Joseph or Philip Colonel was the organist was still in question in *Chronica Domus* II:[72] (June 7, 1868) which has an entry for "Fr. Colonel Joseph Organistta" being absent but someone later wrote in Philip's name above Joseph's.
6. "Instruction for the Direction for the Apostleship of Prayer," *Messenger of the Sacred Heart* 1, no. 8 (November 1866): insert, Woodstock Theological Library, Lauinger Memorial Library, Georgetown University, Washington, DC.
7. *Chronica Domus* II:34 (April 22, 1866); "Apostleship of Prayer History," accessed May 25, 2017, https://web.archive.org/web/20150609023113/http://www.apostleshipofprayer.org:80/history.html. Thaddeus Anwander's Receipts Book, 1868, SMPA, Annapolis: January 2, 1868: "Rec'd from Rev'd Th Anwander Ten Dollars infull for Subscription for 5 Copies of the Messenger of the Sacred Heart for 1868 $10 — J Murphy & Co."; *New-York Freeman's Journal,* February 22, 1868.
8. *Chronica Domus* II:45 (October n.d, 1866); Annals Annapolis, 1909–1921:55 (May 9, 1911), and 1922–1932:29 (March 17, 1923), RABP.
9. Marriage Register B#1 (January 4, 1866); *Annual Report of the Adjutant-General of the State of New York For the Year 1900,* Serial No. 23 (Albany: James B. Lyon, State Printer, 1901), 95, accessed October 30, 2016, https://dmna.ny.gov/historic/reghist/civil/rosters/Infantry/39th_Infantry_CW_Roster.pdf; Compiled Military Service Record (Charles Gerard, sometime Girard, Co. E, 39th New York Infantry), RG 94, NARA; Carded Medical Records, Box 2087 Entry 534, RG 94, NARA; 1870 Federal Census, Annapolis; 1880 and 1900 Federal censuses, Winona, Minnesota; Baptismal Register B#2 (February 17, 1867, August 30, 1868, April 30, 1871, August 15, 1873); Find A Grave Memorial ID 133147281.
10. Marriage Register B#2 (April 24, 1866), Baptismal Register B#2 (November 21, 1867), Interment Register B#2 (August 23, 1874 and April 27, 1881), and Marriage Register M#1 September 16, 1879); Anne Arundel Genealogical Society Inventory, St. Mary's Cemetery; Case Files of Approved Pension Applications of Widows and Other Dependents, Widows Pension No. 2160, M1279, RG 15, NARA.
11. Marriage Register B#2 (October 11, 1866); Baptismal Register B#4 (June 18, 1882); Interment Register B#2 (July 15, 1883); ACWRDB, accessed November 15, 2013; Augustus D. Ayling, *Revised Register of the Soldiers and Sailors in New Hampshire in the War of the Rebellion, 1861–1866* (Concord: Ira C. Evans, 1895), 2:585; Index to Rendezvous Reports, Civil War, 1861–65, T1099, Records of the Bureau of Naval Personnel, RG 24, NARA.
12. *Annapolis Gazette,* September 7 and 14, 1865, July 19, 1866 (sale price of $45,000); GEG 2:155 (August 23, 1866), GEG 2:158 (August 23, 1866), GEG 2:160 (September 10, 1866), AACLR. For information on buyers, see Augustus Gardner Morse (1817–88), Find A Grave Memorial ID 48192090; George Franklin Morse (1831–1913) Find A Grave Memorial ID 27816685. For later developments, see *Annapolis Gazette,* May 19 and June 9, 1870.
13. *Annapolis Gazette,* June 16, August 19, and September 20, 1870, June 20 and July 4, 1871; *State vs. Edward Walton* Circuit Court from Anne Arundel County, March 2, 1871, and Walton to Bowie, no date, Miscellaneous Papers, 1862–72, Maryland Governor, MSA S1274–112–8.
14. *Annapolis Gazette,* May 23, 1867, October 24, 1871; *Maryland Republican,* October 21, 1871, 2; Worden, *Saint Mary's,* 69.
15. Blessed Mother Theresa of Jesus (Caroline Gerhardinger), S.S.N.D. (1797–1879). See Worden, *Saint Mary's,* 63–67, for details about the school.
16. Annals, Ilchester, 1868–1902, 3–8, RABP; Rev. Paul R. Stroh, C.Ss.R., *Ilchester Memories, 1868–1957, To Commemorate the Golden Jubilee of the Redemptorist Novitiate at Ilchester, Maryland* (Ilchester, Maryland: Redemptorist Fathers, 1957), 40, 41, 44, 51, 61; WWW 25:404 and WWW 25:409 (both dated July 21, 1866), Howard County Land Records, MSA CE 53–16; Annals, Annapolis, 1900–1909, 450 (January 1, 1909), RABP.
17. McWilliams, *Annapolis,* 128–29, 138, 196–97; Rable, *God's Almost Chosen People,* 23–24; Miller, *Both Prayed to the Same God,* 62–63 and 67; *Brinsfield, Faith in the Fight,* 30.
18. Rev. Philip Dabney, C.Ss.R., quoted in Mary C. Weaver,

"Mary: The Icon of Love," *Perpetual Help* 8, no. 1 (Winter/Spring 2016):12; Miller, "Catholic Religion, Irish Ethnicity, and the American Civil War," 271.

19. Tracy Matthew Melton, "'We Will All Unite As a Band of Brothers': The Hibernian Society and Sectarian Relations in Baltimore," *Maryland Historical Magazine* 111, no. 1 (Spring/Summer 2016):44, 60, 76, quoting Samuel Miller, D.D., *Christian Weapons, Not Carnal, But Spiritual, A Sermon Delivered in the Second Presbyterian Church, in the City of Baltimore, October 13, 1826; at the Installation of the Reverend John Breckinridge as Colleague with the Reverend John Glendy, D.D., in the Pastoral Charge of the Said Church* (Princeton, New Jersey: Princeton Press, 1826), 12–13, 45, 48–49; Samuel Miller, *A History of Popery, Including its Origin, Progress, Doctrines, Institutions, and Fruits, to the Commencement of the Nineteenth Century* (New York: John P. Haven, 1834), 9–10.
20. Rable, *God's Almost Chosen People*, 241; Fredland, *The Church in the Circle*, 88; Stanley Hauerwas, "What's the Point of Protestantism," *Washington Post*, October 29, 2017, B3.
21. Anne C. Rose, "Some Private Roads to Rome: The Role of Families in American Victorian Conversions to Catholicism," *Catholic Historical Review* 85, no. 1 (January 1999):35.
22. Worden, *Saint Mary's*, 46–47; Curley, *Venerable John Neumann*, 339.
23. *Chronica Domus* I:157 (July 4, 1861); Peter J. Meaney, O.S.B., "The Prison Ministry of Father Peter Whelan, Georgia Priest and Confederate Chaplain," *Georgia Historical Quarterly* 71, no. 1 (Spring 1987):6.
24. Curran, *Papist Devils*, 157; Albert J. Raboteau, *Slave Religion: The "Invisible Institution" in the Antebellum South* (New York: Oxford University Press, 1978), 87–88.
25. Jean B. Russo and J. Elliott Russo, *Planting an Empire: The Early Chesapeake in British North America* (Baltimore: Johns Hopkins University Press, 2012), 110
26. Mark P. Leone, *The Archaeology of Liberty in an American Capital: Excavations in Annapolis* (Berkeley: University of California Press, 2005), 200–5; George C. Logan, Thomas W. Bodor, Lynn D. Jones, and Marian C. Creveling, with Mark P. Leone, Principal Investigator, *1991 Archaeological Excavations at the Charles Carroll House in Annapolis, Maryland*, 18AP45: Report Prepared for the Charles Carroll House of Annapolis, Inc. (Annapolis: Historic Annapolis Foundation and College Park: University of Maryland, July 1992), 123, 125, 128, 136–37, 139.
27. Baptismal Register B#2 (August 7, 1861); 1860 Federal Slave Schedule, Anne Arundel County, Second and Sixth election districts; 1860 Slave Schedule, Annapolis; Annapolis Mayor and Aldermen Property Assessment, June 11, 1860, MSA M72–3; Anne Arundel County Slave Statistics, 1864 (Annapolis), MSA C142.
28. Baptismal Register B#1 (May 24, 1857, November 22, 1863, June 18, 1865, June 21, 1865, May 30, 1867, December 17, 1868); Interment Register B#2 (December 17, 1887); "William H. Butler," SC 3520–13083, *Archives of Maryland* (Biographical Series), accessed October 5, 2016, http://msa.maryland.gov/megafile/msa/speccol/sc3500/sc3520/013000/013083/html/13083bio.html; 1870 and 1880 Federal censuses, Annapolis; Hannah Jopling, *Life in a Black Community: Striving for Equal Citizenship in Annapolis, Maryland, 1902–1952* (Lanham, Maryland: Lexington Books, 2015), 37, 102; Our Lady of Sorrows Baptismal Register (March 3, 1866), MSA SC1172 (SCM 2625); "Sharing Our Histories," accessed February 25, 2015, http://sharingourhistories.weebly.com/-genealogy.html, for Daniel C. Boston; website author Elinor Thompson confirmed with author, February 25, 2015, that Boston was an exhorter.
29. Baptismal Register B#1 (February 5, 1860, April 13, 1863, November 23, 1863, June n.d., 1864); Confirmation Register (December 7, 1865); Interment Register B#2 (February 7, 1861); 1860 Federal Census, Election District 1, Dorchester County, Maryland; Borgmann, *Redemptorists at Annapolis*, 22; Annapolis Lodge No. 89 Ancient Free and Accepted Masons, accessed October 12, 2013, http://www.annapolislodge.com; Alexander Randall Diary, February 8, 1861, vol. 8, MS 652, Maryland Center for History and Culture; *Annapolis Gazette*, June 23, 1864; Maryland Historical Trust, MIHP AA–651, "Nicholas Z. Maccubbin House, 110 Prince George Street, Annapolis," accessed October 6, 2016, https://mht.maryland.gov/secure/medusa/PDF/AnneArundel/AA-651.pdf; Our Lady of Sorrows Baptismal Register (no date 1865, added at end of year 1865), MSA.
30. Raboteau, *Slave Religion*, 271; Miller and Wakelyn, *Catholics in the Old South*, 167.
31. Baptismal Register B#1 (May 10–14, 1865); Carded Medical Records, Box 114 Entry 534, RG 94, NARA; Military Service Record (John R. Hunt), RG 94; John Hunt Invalid Application No. 267744, Certificate No. 173253; Catherine Hunt, Widow Application No. 277945, Certificate No. 196110; 1870 Federal Census, Mill Creek Hundred, New Castle County, Delaware; Find A Grave Memorial ID 15575402.
32. *Chronica Domus* II:34 (April 6, 1866); "History, St. Augustine," accessed February 5, 2011, https://www.ccasta.org/history. *Sadliers' Catholic Directory, 1867*, 57, listed St. Augustine's, Elkridge Landing as "Attended from St. Alphonsus', Baltimore" on first Sunday of each month, and St. Mary's, Laurel Factory (page 58) as "Attended from Georgetown College" twice monthly by Rev. J. B. Guido, S.J.
33. *Chronica Domus* II:32 (January 5, 1866), II:33 (February 2, March 2, and March 31, 1866), II:35 (May 26, June 2; June 29, 1866); *Annapolis Gazette*, June 14, 1866; *Sun*, June 12, 1866; Francis X. Welch, *A Centenary for Our Lady of Sorrows, Owensville, Maryland, 1866–1966* (n.p., ca. 1966), 17–18; SH 1:5 (August 7, 1865), SH 1:532 (May 5, 1866), AACLR.
34. Enright, Annapolis, to Howes Goldsborough, [Easton], March 11, 1866, Folder 3, Goldsborough Papers. A typescript inscription from the cornerstone in RABP reads: *"1866 Junius. Die 15. R.P. Minister (Ludovicus Claessens) profectus est Eastonium ad ponendum prima fundamina novae ecclesiae, unde reditt die 20,"* an indication of the expected

earlier laying with Claessens from Annapolis presiding. There are discrepancies as to the actual date of laying the cornerstone, see *Easton Gazette,* December 24, 1864, June 16 and 23, 1866; John F. Byrne, C.Ss.R., "Redemptorists in America, Baltimore (Continued) and in Rochester, N.Y.," *Records of the American Catholic Historical Society of Philadelphia* 41, no. 4 (December 1930): 369.

35. SH 28:503 (July 10, 1886), WNW 40–32 (June 4, 1921), AACLR. Property sales in Centralia frequently advertised in 1866, see *Annapolis Gazette,* June 14, 21, and 28, 1866; Noah Ernest Dorsey, *All Saints' Chapel in Centralia, Anne Arundel County, Maryland, Being a Short History of the First Quarter-Century (1875 to 1901) of the Work of the Protestant Episcopal Church at Annapolis Junction, Maryland* (Washington, DC: N. E. Dorsey, 1952), 20–21, 24–25, 31, 34, 43; Episcopal Diocese of Maryland, *Convention Journal* (May 13–14, 2016), 11, accessed June 4, 2017, https://images.yourfaithstory.org/wp-content/uploads/sites/6/2019/05/27095216/Journal-2016-Part-A.pdf. Although there is no mention of Centralia in *Chronica Domus* II for 1886, a plat, deeds, tax receipts, and letters relating to the property are located in "Land Records: Centralia (Annapolis Junction)," SMPA.
36. *Constitution of the State of Maryland . . .1864,* 68.
37. Heather Andrea Williams, *Self-Taught: African American Education in Slavery and Freedom* (Chapel Hill: University of North Carolina Press, 2005), 90; Robert Charles Morris, *Reading, 'Riting, and Reconstruction: The Education of Freedmen in the South 1861–1870* (Chicago University of Chicago Press, 1981), 3; Richard E. Butchart, *Northern Schools, Southern Blacks, and Reconstruction: Freedmen's Education, 1862–1875* (Westport, Connecticut: Greenwood Press, 1980), 128; McWilliams, *Annapolis,* 198; Richard Paul Fuke, "The Baltimore Association for the Moral and Educational Improvement of the Colored People 1864–70," *Maryland Historical Magazine* 66, no. 4 (Winter 1971): 370–71, 378, 392; *The Christian Recorder* (Philadelphia), September 8, 1866, quoted in Annapolis 1864 Commission, Maryland Emancipation 2014 Sesquicentennial Celebration, "The Stanton School: Annapolis, Md." (February 1, 2015), accessed February 21, 2016, https://www.facebook.com/annapolis1864/posts/435787656579993.
38. SH 3:165 (January 20, 1869), AACLR.
39. Brokhage, *Kenrick's Opinion on Slavery,* 178–81; Williams, *Self-Taught,* 9; "The African American Mosaic: Colonization," accessed November 12, 2013, http://www.loc.gov/exhibits/african/afam002.html.
40. *Saint Mary's Church, Diamond Jubilee* (Annapolis: 1928), 90; Borgmann, *Redemptorists at Annapolis,* 58. Byrne, *Redemptorist Centenaries,* 120, notes that "From the beginning the Fathers were solicitous for the spiritual welfare of the colored Catholics of the parish." For Petri's devotion, see Annals, St. Michael's, Baltimore, 1845–1891, 47 (August 17–18, 1865), RABP.
41. *Maryland Republican,* July 14, 1866, a partial copy of which is pasted into *Chronica Domus,* II:36 (following July 7, 1866); full text found in *Daily Memphis Avalanche* (Memphis, Tennessee), July 22, 1866, which identified the *Maryland Republican* as its source; Zanca, *American Catholics and Slavery,* Document 100 (October 20, 1866), 255–57; Kurtz, *Excommunicated from the Union,* 106; Borgmann, *Redemptorists at Annapolis,* 47.
42. Borgmann, *Redemptorists at Annapolis,* 228–29; Sister Reginald Gerdes, O.S.P., "Following the Footsteps of Father Thaddeus Anwander, C.Ss.R.," *Catholic Review,* April 18, 2002, 28.

Chapter 9: Soldiers of the Cross

1. Borgmann, *Redemptorists at Annapolis,* 45–48, much of which was based on letter of Ferreol Girardey, Annapolis, to Seelos, July 11, 1866; an eyewitness account by Frater Wendelin Guhl (the "participant"), Annapolis, 1866, RABP. The documents were published as "Annapolis Drownings: Father Girardey's Letter to Father Seelos, Supplement I; Frater Wendelin Guhl, C.Ss.R. (translated from German by Frater Eugen Keyser, C.Ss.R.), "The Sad Occurrence Which Happened in Annapolis in the Year 1866," Supplement II, in Brother Barnabas Hipkins, C.Ss.R., "Annapolis Aquatic Tragedies," *Province Story: A Redemptorist Historical Review—Baltimore Province* 1, no. 1 (November 1, 1974), RABP.
2. William Luecking, C.Ss.R., *Reminiscences of the Redemptorist Fathers: Rev. John Beil, Rev. Patrick M'Givern, Rev. John O'Brien, Rev. Leopold Petsch* (Ilchester: Redemptorist College, 1891), 229; Jane Wilson McWilliams and Carol Cushard Patterson, *Bay Ridge on the Chesapeake: An Illustrated History* (Annapolis: Brighton Editions, 1986), 32–33, 35; *Maryland Republican,* July 14, 1866; Riley, *Ancient City,* 321–23.
3. Guhl said he saw two lighthouses but not which one they were trying to reach. The closest lighthouses were at Thomas Point to the south and Greenbury Point to the north. However, in Seelos' letter to Antonia Seelos and family members, October 12, December 3 and 18, 1862, he reported four lighthouses where the Severn River met the bay and his sketch map showed four x's, two along Bay Ridge and two at Greenbury Point. Presumably these x's marked both a permanent lighthouse at Greenbury Point and military beacons along the river. See *Sun,* July 13, 1866; "Heartrending Disaster" for the Kenny and Runge quotes.
4. See *Maryland Republican,* July 14, 1866 for Charity Brashears; Jack E. Nelson, Raymond L. Langston, and Margo Dean Pinson, *Highland Beach on the Chesapeake Bay: Maryland's First African American Incorporated Town* (Highland Beach: Highland Beach Historical Commission, 2008), 9.
5. Borgmann, *Redemptorists at Annapolis,* 45–48; *Chronica Domus* II:38 (July 11–16, 1866); Hipkins, "Annapolis Aquatic Tragedies," 10–13, quotes 1869 statement by Augustine Stuhl, C.Ss.R., a student at Annapolis in July 1866 who witnessed the recovered bodies being dragged along in the water behind a boat, "still clothed with the habit of the Congregation."
6. Luecking, *Reminiscences of the Redemptorist Fathers,* 234; Hipkins, "Annapolis Aquatic Tragedies," 13.
7. *Maryland Republican,* July 14, 1866. Numerous newspapers

nationwide quoted and misquoted this article. Annals St. Peter Philadelphia, 1858–1872, 180–82 (July 11, 1866), RABP, has extensive hand-written and newspaper-clipping coverage.

8. Hipkins, "Annapolis Aquatic Tragedies," 13; *New-York Freeman's Journal*, July 14 and 28, 1866.
9. M., "Early Struggle of the Redemptorists in Annapolis; Father Claessens and His Companions," *Catholic Mirror*, August 25, 1866.
10. Borgmann, *Redemptorists at Annapolis*, 48, identifies Mason as author. Annals St. Peter Philadelphia, 1858–1872, 182 (July 11, 1866), RABP, also identifies Mason. "an old resident of Annapolis," as author.
11. For Gerdemann, see Welch, *A Centenary for Our Lady of Sorrows*, 18–20, 22; Borgmann, *Redemptorists at Annapolis*, 64. For Kenny, see Borgmann, *Redemptorists at Annapolis*, 237; Margaret Gallery, "The Kenny Family of Treanmanagh From c. 1650 to the Early 1900s," http://www.clarelibrary.ie/eolas/coclare/genealogy/don_tran/fam_his/kenny_family_treanmanagh_1650_1800.htm; "Ecclesiastical Items," *Sacred Heart Review* 28, no. 4 (December 13, 1902): 2, http://newspapers.bc.edu/cgi-bin/bostonsh?a=d&d=BOSTONSH19021213-01.2.4, both accessed May 26, 2017.
12. Seelos, New Orleans, to Enright, Annapolis, December 25, 1866, Letter 187, Hoegerl, *Sincerely, Seelos*, 452.
13. Curley, *Cheerful Ascetic*, 262; *Chronica Domus* II:45 (October 24, 1866).
14. Annals, Ilchester, 1866–1902, 5–6, RABP.
15. The concept of the unity of the church in difficult times was gleaned from homily of Father Joseph Francis Krastel, C.Ss. R., at St. Mary's Church, Annapolis, August 20, 2016.
16. Worden, *Saint Mary's*, 136–40, describes St. Augustine's history. Also, Fredland, *The Church in the Circle*, 10–12, 98, which notes that in 1913 St. Anne's wanted to sell its mission chapel because of low attendance. The chapel was completed in 1886 at the intersection of Prince George and East streets to serve working-class residents in the City Dock neighborhood. The rector, Joseph P. McComas, however, "resisted [the sale], fearful that it would become a Roman Catholic colored mission, which he believed would reflect badly on St. Anne's." It was finally sold in 1918 to the Kneseth Israel Jewish congregation.
17. McWilliams, *Annapolis*, 383, table 2.
18. Borgmann, *Redemptorists at Annapolis*, 72.
19. Hammond to Whittingham, November 5, 1866, Episcopal Diocese of Maryland Archives (as cited earlier).
20. McWilliams, *Annapolis*, 225; *Sun*, January 18, 1919; "Reminiscences of the Late Col. John Walton," undated, unattributed article, probably *Evening Capital* between 1894 and 1912, in Walton Album, Historic Annapolis Inc. Constance Werner Ramirez, *Street Signs to History: The Story of West Annapolis and Wardour Street Names* (Annapolis: West Annapolis Heritage Partnership, 2016), 9, 32–33.
21. Diary of Elizabeth Hohne Revell, vol. 1 (April 18–19, 1897 and April 28, 1898), Box 3, Dowsett Collection, MSA.
22. Marriage Register M#1 (June 21, 1877); Ramirez, *Street Signs to History*, 11, 28.
23. Basilica of the Assumption Baptisms, 1854–70, Register #12:313 (August 7, 1863), MSA SCM1513; *Annapolis Gazette*, November 30, 1865, April 29, 1873; *Sun*, March 31,1873; *Maryland Republican*, May 5, 1873.
24. *Sun*, June 3, 1899; *Evening Capital*, June 2 and 5, 1899; Elizabeth Hohne Revell Diary, Box 3, vol. III: Friday [June 1, 1899] MSA SC2095–2–109; SH 13:25 (May 18, 1878, Monument Street) and SH 14:2 (March 3, 1879, Shipwright Street), GW 13:364 (May 5, 1898, rental to Henry Clark), AACLR; Register of Wills, Anne Arundel County, MSA C155–57 (September 7, 1897, for beneficiaries Alphonsa Fletcher, Lily Anna Parker, Agnes D. Parker, Mary M. Parker, and Rosa L. Parker); Interment Register B#2 (June 2–4, 1899); conversations of author with African American members of St. Mary's Parish, May 3, 2015 and September 3, 2015; Book 2138:150 and Book 2138:152 (both signed January 16, 1968, sale by Oblates), AACLR.
25. Petersen, *Mullan*, 162, 199, 207, 212, 220–23, 233; Last Will and Testament, John Mullan, Washington DC, June 12, 1907, John Mullan Papers, GTM.Gamms276, Box 7, Folder 3, GU-CSC; Interment Register D#1 (November 28, 1909). For Drexel connection, see Mullan Papers, Box 8, folder 4, Katharine Drexel to Cousin Bec [Mullan], August 19, 1888; Worden, *Saint Mary's*, 86. For Tulip Hill, see articles in Mullan Papers, Box 11, folder 11; WNW 28:205 (June 10, 1918) and JHH 335:38 (July 6, 1945), AACLR.
26. For Zimmermann's career, see Worden, *Saint Mary's*, 80, 119–21; USNA Band, "Anchors Aweigh," accessed May 23, 2018, https://www.usna.edu/USNABand/about/anchors.php; "Report of the Governor of the Soldiers' Home," in *Annual Reports of the War Department for the Fiscal Year Ended June 30, 1900* (Washington: Government Printing Office, 1900), 303 (Zimmerman appointed September 17, 1900); *Washington Post*, August 5, 1920; "The Ebbitt," march and two-step by John S.M. Zimmerman; piano, copyrighted October 11, 1911, Library of Congress, Copyright Office, *Catalogue of Copyright Entries*, Part 3, Musical Compositions, New Series, 6, no. 7 (Washington: Government Printing Office, 1911), 1398.
27. *Little Rock Daily Republican*, December 4, 1873; *Daily Inter Ocean*, February 20, 1874; Mike Korgi, "Re: [NEPLATTE] Baptism Record of Emma Schlentz from Platte County, Nebraska," https://lists.rootsweb.com/hyperkitty/list/neplatte@rootsweb.com/thread/341845/ and Rev. Eugene Hagedorn, OFM, *The Franciscans in Nebraska* (Norfolk, Nebraska, Norfolk Daily News, 1931), 323, http://www.usgennet.org/usa/ne/topic/religion/catholic/Franciscans/pages/pt2/fine0009.htm, both accessed February 28, 2019 ; Find A Grave Memorial ID 77173402.
28. *Chronica Domus* II:n.p. (January 21, 1885); Zimmer, *Leben und Wirken* (New York: Benziger Brothers, 1887); Peter Zimmer and Chrysostom Zimmer personnel files, RABP; Wuest, *Annales*, IV:2:466; Rock, "Departed Redemptorist Brothers," 40–41.

29. The advertisement was in *Public School Education* (1872). Among other titles of the twenty-five or more books written by Müller are *Prayer: The Key to Salvation* (1868); *The Blessed Eucharist, Our Greatest Treasure* (1868, still in print in 2017); *The Religious State* (1872); *The Holy Mass* (1874); *Familiar Explanation of Christian Doctrine* (1875); his nine-volume *God the Teacher of Mankind* (1884); *The Catholic Dogma: "Extra Eccelsiam nullus omino Salvatur"* (1888); and *Sinner's Return to God* (1898). He also published a well-received series of catechisms—in English, German, and bilingual editions—for three levels of parochial-school classes. His *Catechism of Catholic Doctrine, No. III for the Advanced Classes of Parochial Schools* (1888) included praise for Father Müller offered by his old confrere, Archbishop William Gross, who wrote from Portland in December 1887. See Gary Potter, *After the Boston Heresy Case* (Monrovia, California: Catholic Treasures Books, 1995), 40, for the Bishop Sheen comment. Also, Curley, *Provincial Story*, 206–08; Borgmann, *Redemptorists at Annapolis*, 87–91, 230–31; *Anne Arundel Advertiser*, December 15, 1898, Death Certificate (Anne Arundel), Maryland Board of Health, Rev. Michael Miller [*sic*], August 28, 1899, MSA SE42-339; Annals, Annapolis, 1889-1900, 376 (August 28–30, 1899), RABP.

30. Rock, "Departed Redemptorist Brothers," 40 and 95; Find A Grave Memorial IDs 142424327 (Hilary) and 124870328 (Louis); *Maryland Republican*, August 19, 1871; *Ich male für fromme Gemüter: zur religiösen Schweizer Malerei im 19. Jahrhundert* (Luzern: Das Kunstmuseum, 1985), 117 (1/54), 118 (1/58).

31. Curley, *Cheerful Ascetic*, 250–60; Hoegerl, *Positio*, 2, Part 2, 1056; Hoegerl, *With All Gentleness*, 443ff, 465ff. Seelos' beatification is attributed to a miraculous liver cancer cure of Angela Boudreaux in 1966. A second purported miracle, in the case of Mary Ellen Heible, a parishioner of St. Mary's, Annapolis, who was cured in 2005 of metastasized esophageal cancer after praying to Blessed Seelos, was formally initiated by Archbishop of Baltimore Cardinal Edwin O'Brien in May 2009. In September 2010 the findings were forwarded to Rome for review by the Congregation for the Causes of Saints, which in 2011 determined that such a cure should have been in effect for ten years after the inexplicable healing to be considered a valid miracle. Unfortunately, Mrs. Heible died from other causes in October 2009.

32. The epitaph is based on Matthew 9:14 and taken from a hymn that appears in numerous nineteenth-century song books.

Acknowledgments

Many individuals and institutions provided essential support to this book. Foremost among them were members of the Annapolis History Consortium who shared my enthusiasm for learning about Annapolis during on the Civil War. They include Jane Wilson McWilliams, who read and provided numerous critical comments on an early version of the manuscript, and David Haight, who shared many valuable research finds from the Maryland State Archives and National Archives. Catherine Randall happily shared the results of her extensive research on Civil War-era Annapolis families. Other consortium members also indulged my many inquiries. They were Judith Cabral, Michael Fitzpatrick, Eric Fredland, James Gibb, Eric Goldstein, Ann Jensen, Anthony Long, Rebecca Morris, Michael Parker, Jean Russo, and Christina Simmons. I also am indebted to two other Consortium colleagues, now deceased, who provided important documentation from their own works in progress: R. Bruce Horner and Willard R. Mumford.

A fellow Georgetown University graduate schoolmate, Robert Emmett Curran, professor emeritus of history at Georgetown University, provided valuable notes from his own research on Catholics during the Civil War and read and commented on the manuscript. Mark P. Leone, professor of anthropology at the University of Maryland, College Park, read part of the manuscript that used details from archaeology he directed at St. Mary's between 1987 and 1991.

Several Redemptorists made signal contributions to the project. Foremost was the late Fr. Carl Hoegerl, who, as head of the Redemptorist Archives of the Baltimore Province, provided encouragement and ready access to official records. He also read and and provided valuable comments on the manuscript. The late Fr. Joseph Krastel of St. Mary's, Annapolis, provided information on his Redemptorist great-granduncle Herman Krastel, patiently reviewed and corrected my Latin translations, provided insights about Redemptorist community life, and read parts of the manuscript. Fr. John Harrison, an Annapolis native, also reviewed Latin translations and responded to my many inquiries from his database of St. Mary's sacramental records. Fr. Richard Luberti, then of St. Joseph's Church, Maybee, Michigan, shared information from his research on Civil War-era Redemptorists. Patrick J. Hayes, the current head of the Redemptorist Archives of the Baltimore Province, provided patient assistance in fulfilling my endless research requests and reviewed part of the manuscript. Similarly Fr. Terry McCloskey and staff of the Office of Provincial Records and Archives, Redemptorists' Denver Province, assisted with photographs and documents. Two Redemptorists closely associated with the cause of canonization of Blessed Francis Xavier Seelos gave encouragement to the book project. They are Fr. Byron Miller, formerly Executive Director of the National Shrine of Blessed Francis Xavier Seelos in New Orleans, and Vice Postulator for the cause of canonization of Blessed Seelos, and Fr. Gilbert Enderle, formerly of the Redemptorist Historical Institute in Rome and Fr. Miller's successor as vice postulator. The research and writing of the book took place during the administrations of three St. Mary's rectors: Fr. John Kingsbury, Fr. John Tizio, and Fr. Patrick Woods. They each embraced the concept of producing this book and provided encouragement and moral support.

A number of individuals provided information about or photographs of their Annapolis ancestors. They are Jan Sharik Baker, Alice Dammeyer, Judy Himmelheber Dohner, Mary Ann Elder, Mary Anne Maley Joyce, Hazel Kinnamon, Stephen Noonan, Betsy Oliver, Deborah Chadeayne Oliver, and James Schwallenberg. Parish staff also provided important help, especially Joanne Crouse, Ann Marie Foreman, and Mark Hartzell. Of critical assistance was Jody Brooks, who found the way to bring this book into printed form.

Anthony Long of Holy Family Parish in Davidsonville, Maryland, provided information on and a tour of sites associated with an 1865 murder committed by a former St. Mary's parishioner. Thanks too to the staffs of Our Lady of Sorrows, West River, Maryland; St. Peter the Apostle, Oakland, Maryland; St. Matthew the Apostle Cathedral, Washington, DC; and St. Paul, New Bern, North Carolina, parishes whose histories intersected with the Annapolis Redemptorists during the Civil War.

A number of religious archives provided timely information on matters large and small. Assistance most critical to this book was provided by Tricia Pyne and Alison Foley of the Archives of the Archdiocese of Baltimore. Sharon Knecht of the Oblate Sisters of Providence Archives and Sister Joanne Gonter, V.H.M. Georgetown Visitation Convent Archives assisted me onsite to identify useful information. Archivists at the School Sisters of Notre Dame in Baltimore; Daughters of Charity; Episcopal Diocese of Maryland; Asbury United Methodist Church in Annapolis; Georgetown University's Booth Family Center for Special Collections; St. Vincent Archabbey; Sisters of Mercy of the Americas; Sisters of Immaculate Heart of Mary; Philadelphia Archdiocesan Historical Research Center; District of Eastern North America, Brothers of the Christian Schools; Seton Hall University; St. Bonaventure University; Ursulines of the Eastern Province; Archdiocese of Boston; Diocese of Raleigh, North Carolina; Diocese of Charleston, South Carolina; Sisters of the Good Shepherd, St. Louis, Missouri; Diocese of Jackson, Mississippi; and Society of Mary (Marianists), San Antonio, Texas, all provided requested documentation. Research support also was received from the Catholic Record Society-Diocese of Columbus, Ohio; University of Notre Dame; Congregation of Holy Cross US and Midwest Provinces; Archdiocese of Chicago; Diocese of La Crosse Archives, Wisconsin; School Sisters of Notre Dame North American Archives in Milwaukee; Diocese of St. Cloud, Minnesota; Archdiocese of Portland; and Mercy International Association, Dublin, Ireland.

Staff at the Maryland State Archives, especially Maria Day, and at the Library of Congress and the National Archives in Washington provided numerous leads to resources. Special thanks are also due to Karen Theimer Brown and Glen Campbell of Historic Annapolis; Jennifer Bryan David D'Onofrio, and Samuel Limneos, United States Naval Academy Archives and Special Collections; Catherine Dixon and Cara Sabolcik, Greenfield Library, St. John's College, Annapolis; and Colleen Walter Puterbaugh, Surratt House Museum, Clinton, Maryland. Timely assistance was provided by archives and library staffs of the Maryland Center for History and Culture; B&O Railroad Museum; Historic Congressional Cemetery, Washington, DC; United Daughters of the Confederacy; New Bern-Craven County (North Carolina) Public Library; Gilder Lehrman Institute of American History; New York State Library, Albany; Rare Book and Manuscript Library, Columbia University; Connecticut State Library; and Special Collections, Harvard Business School.

Other individuals provided valuable information. They were Fr. Blaine Burkey, O.F.M. Cap., St. Francis of Assisi Friary, Denver, Colorado; James T. Wollon Jr., A.I.A, Havre de Grace, Maryland; and Civil War biographer Walter Stahr. The contributors of Internet information also was important. I wish to thank Anne Marie Singer, a major information provider on the School Sisters of Notre Dame on Find A Grave; and Brian Downey of Antietam on the Web.

Financial support for the book was provided by St. Mary's Parish; the Redemptorist Community of St. Mary's; John Barry Division of the Ancient Order of Hibernians in Annapolis; and Anne Arundel County Trust for Preservation, Inc. The latter's grant supported production of the historical maps prepared by Christopher S. Robinson of Crusoe Graphics that appear in this book. Donors to the St. Mary's Parish Archives Fund supported the preparation of original artwork by Constance Robinson illustrating the book. A special thanks goes to Jerri Anne Hopkins who provided her editing and production expertise to bring this book to its final publication.

Finally, the mainstay in all my efforts in preparing this book was my faithful companion and loving wife, Norma Chue Worden. A professional historical document researcher herself, she spent many hours with me in various archives—near and far, pouring over documents in a variety of languages and hard-to-read handwriting—looking for information for this book. She also spent countless hours reading the completed chapters, offering critical comments, and pointing out needed corrections. The work would never have been completed without her always cheerful and endlessly patient help.

Index

Unless otherwise noted, institutional, street, road, and other place names are in or near Annapolis. Notes are selectively indexed where additional biographic information is available. Readers are encourage to consult the notes for bibliographical citations and other relevant information.

B

C

D

E

G

H

I

J

K

L

M

N

O

P

Q

T

U

V

W

Y

Z

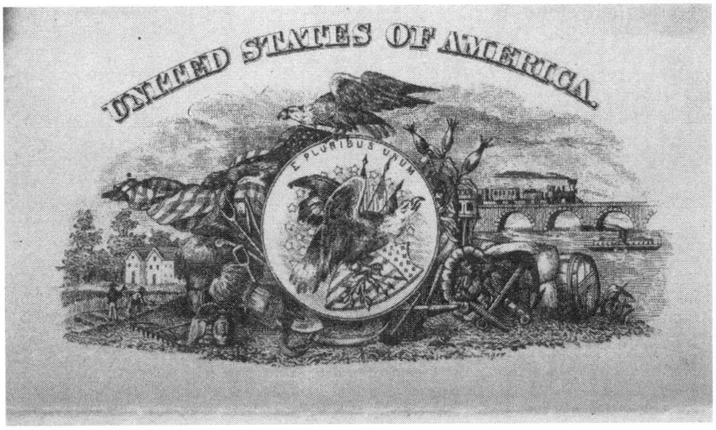
UNITED STATES OF AMERICA.
E PLURIBUS UNUM

About the Author

Robert L. Worden and his wife Norma Chue Worden have been parishioners of St. Mary's Parish since 1971. Both have served on parish commemorative committees, helped with various service projects, and worked as teachers, respectively, in the Sunday school and the elementary and high schools. Their children—Maia, Peter, and Nathaniel—are graduates of St. Mary's Elementary School and High School. Robert has been a volunteer St. Mary's archivist and historian since 1982 and published numerous historical articles in *St. Mary's Moorings* and wrote *Saint Mary's Church in Annapolis, Maryland, 1853–2003: A Sesquicentennial History*, published by the parish in 2003. He earned a B.A. from St. Bonaventure University and an M.A. and Ph.D. from Georgetown University, all three degrees in history. He had a thirty-nine-year career with the Federal government, including three years as a Peace Corps employee in Washington, two years in the U.S. Army, and thirty-four years on the research staff of the Library of Congress, from which he retired in 2007. In 2023 the superior general of the Congregation of the Most Holy Redeemer bestowed on Dr. Worden the honor of becoming an Oblate of the Redemptorist Congregation.

Robert L. Worden visits with the Blessed Francis Xavier Seelos on the grounds of St. Mary's Church in Annapolis. Courtesy author.